STUDENT'S SOLUTIONS MANUAL

VICTOR MAYMESKUL
Georgia Southern University

to accompany

FUNDAMENTALS OF DIFFERENTIAL EQUATIONS
SIXTH EDITION

and

FUNDAMENTALS OF DIFFERENTIAL EQUATIONS AND BOUNDARY VALUE PROBLEMS
FOURTH EDITION

R. Kent Nagle

Edward B. Saff
Vanderbilt Unviersity

A. David Snider
University of South Florida

Boston San Francisco New York
London Toronto Sydney Tokyo Singapore Madrid
Mexico City Munich Paris Cape Town Hong Kong Montreal

Reproduced by Pearson Addison-Wesley from electronic files supplied by the author.

Publishing as Pearson Addison-Wesley, 75 Arlington Street, Boston MA 02116

ISBN 0-321-17319-8

3 4 5 VHG 06 05

Contents

CHAPTER 1: Introduction

EXERCISES 1.1: Background, page 5

1. This equation involves only ordinary derivatives of x with respect to t, and the highest derivative has the second order. Thus it is an ordinary differential equation of the second order with independent variable t and dependent variable x. It is linear because x, dx/dt, and d^2x/dt^2 appear in additive combination (even with constant coefficients) of their first powers.

3. This equation is an ODE because it contains no partial derivatives. Since the highest order derivative is dy/dx, the equation is a first order equation. This same term also shows us that the independent variable is x and the dependent variable is y. This equation is nonlinear because of the y in the denominator of the term $[y(2-3x)]/[x(1-3y)]$.

5. This equation is an ODE because it contains only ordinary derivatives. The term dp/dt is the highest order derivative and thus shows us that this is a first order equation. This term also shows us that the independent variable is t and the dependent variable is p. This equation is nonlinear since in the term $kp(P-p) = kPp - kp^2$ the dependent variable p is squared (compare with equation (7) on page 5 of the text).

7. This equation is an ordinary first order differential equation with independent variable x and dependent variable y. It is nonlinear because it contains the square of dy/dx.

9. This equation contains only ordinary derivative of y with respect to x. Hence, it is an ordinary differential equation of the second order (the highest order derivative is d^2y/dx^2) with independent variable x and dependent variable y. This equation is of the form (7) on page 5 of the text and, therefore, is linear.

11. This equation contains partial derivatives, thus it is a PDE. Because the highest order derivative is a second order partial derivative, the equation is a second order equation. The terms $\partial N/\partial t$ and $\partial N/\partial r$ show that the independent variables are t and r and the dependent variable is N.

13. Since the rate of change of a quantity means its derivative, denoting the coefficient proportionality between dp/dt and $p(t)$ by k ($k > 0$), we get

$$\frac{dp}{dt} = kp.$$

15. In this problem, $T \geq M$ (coffee is hotter than the air), and T is a decreasing function of t, that is $dT/dt \leq 0$. Thus

$$\frac{dT}{dt} = k(M - T),$$

where $k > 0$ is the proportionality constant.

17. In classical physics, the instantaneous acceleration, a, of an object moving in a straight line is given by the second derivative of distance, x, with respect to time, t; that is

$$\frac{d^2x}{dt^2} = a.$$

Integrating both sides with respect to t and using the given fact that a is constant we obtain

$$\frac{dx}{dt} = at + C. \tag{1.1}$$

The instantaneous velocity, v, of an object is given by the first derivative of distance, x, with respect to time, t. At the beginning of the race, $t = 0$, both racers have zero velocity. Therefore we have $C = 0$. Integrating equation (1.1) with respect to t we obtain

$$x = \frac{1}{2}at^2 + C_1 .$$

For this problem we will use the starting position for both competitors to be $x = 0$ at $t = 0$. Therefore, we have $C_1 = 0$. This gives us a general equation used for both racers as

$$x = \frac{1}{2}at^2 \qquad \text{or} \qquad t = \sqrt{\frac{2x}{a}},$$

where the acceleration constant a has different values for Kevin and for Alison. Kevin covers the last $\frac{1}{4}$ of the full distance, L, in 3 seconds. This means Kevin's acceleration, a_K, is determined by:

$$t_K - t_{3/4} = 3 = \sqrt{\frac{2L}{a_K}} - \sqrt{\frac{2(3L/4)}{a_K}},$$

where t_K is the time it takes for Kevin to finish the race. Solving this equation for a_K gives,

$$a_K = \frac{\left(\sqrt{2} - \sqrt{3/2}\right)^2}{9} L.$$

Therefore the time required for Kevin to finish the race is given by:

$$t_K = \sqrt{\frac{2L}{\left(\sqrt{2} - \sqrt{3/2}\right)^2 L/9}} = \frac{3}{\sqrt{2} - \sqrt{3/2}} \sqrt{2} = 12 + 6\sqrt{3} \approx 22.39 \text{ sec.}$$

Alison covers the last 1/3 of the distance, L, in 4 seconds. This means Alison's acceleration, a_A, is found by:

$$t_A - t_{2/3} = 4 = \sqrt{\frac{2L}{a_A}} - \sqrt{\frac{2(2L/3)}{a_A}},$$

where t_A is the time required for Alison to finish the race. Solving this equation for a_A gives

$$a_A = \frac{\left(\sqrt{2} - \sqrt{4/3}\right)^2}{16} L.$$

Therefore the time required for Alison to finish the race is given by:

$$t_A = \sqrt{\frac{2L}{\left(\sqrt{2} - \sqrt{4/3}\right)^2 (L/16)}} = \frac{4}{\sqrt{2} - \sqrt{4/3}} \sqrt{2} = 12 + 4\sqrt{6} \approx 21.80 \text{ sec.}$$

The time required for Alison to finish the race is less than Kevin; therefore Alison wins the race by $6\sqrt{3} - 4\sqrt{6} \approx 0.594$ seconds.

EXERCISES 1.2: Solutions and Initial Value Problems, page 14

1. **(a)** Differentiating $\phi(x)$ yields $\phi'(x) = 6x^2$. Substitution ϕ and ϕ' for y and y' into the given equation, $xy' = 3y$, gives

$$x\left(6x^2\right) = 3\left(2x^3\right),$$

which is an identity on $(-\infty, \infty)$. Thus $\phi(x)$ is an explicit solution on $(-\infty, \infty)$.

(b) We compute

$$\frac{d\phi}{dx} = \frac{d}{dx}\left(e^x - x\right) = e^x - 1.$$

Functions $\phi(x)$ and $\phi'(x)$ are defined for all real numbers and

$$\frac{d\phi}{dx} + \phi(x)^2 = \left(e^x - 1\right) + \left(e^x - x\right)^2 = \left(e^x - 1\right) + \left(e^{2x} - 2xe^x + x^2\right) = e^{2x} + (1-2x)e^x + x^2 - 1,$$

which is identically equal to the right-hand side of the given equation. Thus $\phi(x)$ is an explicit solution on $(-\infty, \infty)$.

(c) Note that the function $\phi(x) = x^2 - x^{-1}$ is not defined at $x = 0$. Differentiating $\phi(x)$ twice yields

$$\begin{aligned} \frac{d\phi}{dx} &= \frac{d}{dx}\left(x^2 - x^{-1}\right) = 2x - (-1)x^{-2} = 2x + x^{-2}; \\ \frac{d^2\phi}{dx^2} &= \frac{d}{dx}\left(\frac{d\phi}{dx}\right) = \frac{d}{dx}\left(2x + x^{-2}\right) = 2 + (-2)x^{-3} = 2\left(1 - x^{-3}\right). \end{aligned}$$

Therefore

$$x^2 \frac{d^2\phi}{dx^2} = x^2 \cdot 2\left(1 - x^{-3}\right) = 2\left(x^2 - x^{-1}\right) = 2\phi(x),$$

and $\phi(x)$ is an explicit solution to the differential equation $x^2 y'' = 2y$ on any interval not containing the point $x = 0$, in particular, on $(0, \infty)$.

3. Since $y = \sin x + x^2$, we have $y' = \cos x + 2x$ and $y'' = -\sin x + 2$. These functions are defined on $(-\infty, \infty)$. Substituting these expressions into the differential equation $y'' + y = x^2 + 2$ gives

$$y'' + y = -\sin x + 2 + \sin x + x^2 = 2 + x^2 = x^2 + 2 \qquad \text{for all } x \text{ in } (-\infty, \infty).$$

Therefore, $y = \sin x + x^2$ is a solution to the differential equation on the interval $(-\infty, \infty)$.

5. Differentiating $x(t) = \cos 2t$, we get

$$\frac{dx}{dt} = \frac{d}{dt}(\cos 2t) = (-\sin 2t)(2) = -2\sin 2t.$$

So,

$$\frac{dx}{dt} + tx = -2\sin 2t + t\cos 2t \not\equiv \sin 2t$$

on any interval. Therefore, $x(t)$ is not a solution to the given differential equation.

7. We differentiate $y = e^{2x} - 3e^{-x}$ twice:

$$\begin{aligned}\frac{dy}{dx} &= \frac{d}{dx}\left(e^{2x} - 3e^{-x}\right) = e^{2x}(2) - 3e^{-x}(-1) = 2e^{2x} + 3e^{-x};\\ \frac{d^2y}{dx^2} &= \frac{d}{dx}\left(\frac{dy}{dx}\right) = \frac{d}{dx}\left(2e^{2x} + 3e^{-x}\right) = 2e^{2x}(2) + 3e^{-x}(-1) = 4e^{2x} - 3e^{-x}.\end{aligned}$$

Substituting y, y', and y'' into the differential equation and collecting similar terms, we get

$$\begin{aligned}\frac{d^2y}{dx^2} - \frac{dy}{dx} - 2y &= \left(4e^{2x} - 3e^{-x}\right) - \left(2e^{2x} + 3e^{-x}\right) - 2\left(e^{2x} - 3e^{-x}\right)\\ &= (4-2-2)e^{2x} + (-3-3-2(-3))e^{-x} = 0.\end{aligned}$$

Hence $y = e^{2x} - 3e^{-x}$ is an explicit solution to the given differential equation.

9. Differentiating the equation $x^2 + y^2 = 6$ implicitly, we obtain

$$2x + 2yy' = 0 \qquad \Rightarrow \qquad y' = -\frac{x}{y}\,.$$

Since there can be no function $y = f(x)$ that satisfies the differential equation $y' = x/y$ *and* the differential equation $y' = -x/y$ *on the same interval*, we see that $x^2 + y^2 = 6$ does *not* define an implicit solution to the differential equation.

11. Differentiating the equation $e^{xy} + y = x - 1$ implicitly with respect to x yields

$$\begin{aligned}&\frac{d}{dx}\left(e^{xy} + y\right) = \frac{d}{dx}(x-1)\\ \Rightarrow\quad & e^{xy}\frac{d}{dx}(xy) + \frac{dy}{dx} = 1\\ \Rightarrow\quad & e^{xy}\left(y + x\frac{dy}{dx}\right) + \frac{dy}{dx} = 1\\ \Rightarrow\quad & ye^{xy} + \frac{dy}{dx}\left(xe^{xy} + 1\right) = 1\\ \Rightarrow\quad & \frac{dy}{dx} = \frac{1 - ye^{xy}}{1 + xe^{xy}} = \frac{e^{xy}\left(e^{-xy} - y\right)}{e^{xy}\left(e^{-xy} + x\right)} = \frac{e^{-xy} - y}{e^{-xy} + x}\,.\end{aligned}$$

Therefore, the function $y(x)$ defined by $e^{xy}+y=x-1$ is an implicit solution to the given differential equation.

13. Differentiating the equation $\sin y+xy-x^3=2$ implicitly with respect to x, we obtain

$$y'\cos y+xy'+y-3x^2=0$$
$$\Rightarrow \quad (\cos y+x)y'=3x^2-y \qquad \Rightarrow \qquad y'=\frac{3x^2-y}{\cos y+x}.$$

Differentiating the second equation above again, we obtain

$$(-y'\sin y+1)y'+(\cos y+x)y''=6x-y'$$
$$\Rightarrow \quad (\cos y+x)y''=6x-y'+(y')^2\sin y-y'=6x-2y'+(y')^2\sin y$$
$$\Rightarrow \quad y''=\frac{6x-2y'+(y')^2\sin y}{\cos y+x}.$$

Multiplying the right-hand side of this last equation by $y'/y'=1$ and using the fact that

$$y'=\frac{3x^2-y}{\cos y+x},$$

we get

$$\begin{aligned} y'' &= \frac{6x-2y'+(y')^2\sin y}{\cos y+x}\cdot\frac{y'}{(3x^2-y)/(\cos y+x)} \\ &= \frac{6xy'-2(y')^2+(y')^3\sin y}{3x^2-y}. \end{aligned}$$

Thus y is an implicit solution to the differential equation.

15. We differentiate $\phi(x)$ and substitute ϕ and ϕ' into the differential equation for y and y'. This yields

$$\phi(x)=Ce^{3x}+1 \qquad \Rightarrow \qquad \frac{d\phi(x)}{dx}=\left(Ce^{3x}+1\right)'=3Ce^{3x};$$
$$\frac{d\phi}{dx}-3\phi=\left(3Ce^{3x}\right)-3\left(Ce^{3x}+1\right)=(3C-3C)e^{3x}-3=-3,$$

which holds for any constant C and any x on $(-\infty,\infty)$. Therefore, $\phi(x)=Ce^{3x}+1$ is a one-parameter family of solutions to $y'-3y=-3$ on $(-\infty,\infty)$. Graphs of these functions for $C=0$, ± 0.5, ± 1, and ± 2 are sketched in Figure 1-A.

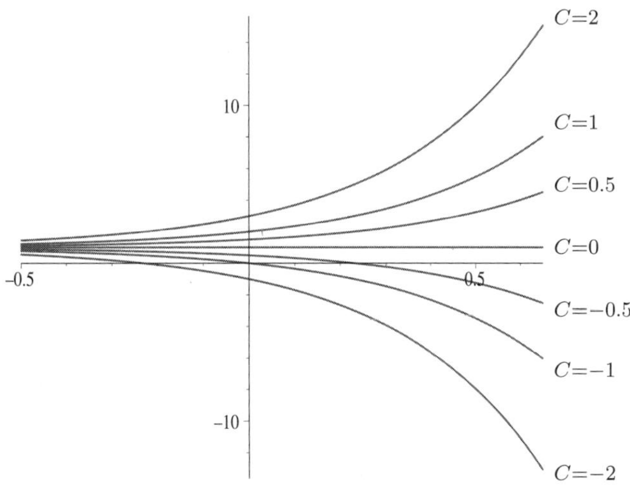

Figure 1–A: Graphs of the functions $y = Ce^{3x} + 1$ for $C = 0$, ± 0.5, ± 1, and ± 2.

17. Differentiating $\phi(x)$, we find that

$$\begin{aligned}
\phi'(x) &= \left(\frac{2}{1 - ce^x}\right)' = \left[2\left(1 - ce^x\right)^{-1}\right]' \\
&= 2(-1)\left(1 - ce^x\right)^{-2}\left(1 - ce^x\right)' = 2ce^x\left(1 - ce^x\right)^{-2}. \qquad (1.2)
\end{aligned}$$

On the other hand, substitution of $\phi(x)$ for y into the right-hand side of the given equation yields

$$\begin{aligned}
\frac{\phi(x)(\phi(x) - 2)}{2} &= \frac{1}{2}\frac{2}{1 - ce^x}\left(\frac{2}{1 - ce^x} - 2\right) \\
&= \frac{2}{1 - ce^x}\left(\frac{1}{1 - ce^x} - 1\right) = \frac{2}{1 - ce^x}\,\frac{1 - (1 - ce^x)}{1 - ce^x} = \frac{2ce^x}{(1 - ce^x)^2},
\end{aligned}$$

which is identical to $\phi'(x)$ found in (1.2).

19. Squaring and adding the terms dy/dx and y in the equation $(dy/dx)^2 + y^2 + 3 = 0$ gives a nonnegative number. Therefore when these two terms are added to 3, the left-hand side will always be greater than or equal to three and hence can never equal the right-hand side which is zero.

21. For $\phi(x) = x^m$, we have $\phi'(x) = mx^{m-1}$ and $\phi''(x) = m(m-1)x^{m-2}$.

(a) Substituting these expressions into the differential equation, $3x^2y'' + 11xy' - 3y = 0$, gives

$$
\begin{aligned}
&3x^2\left[m(m-1)x^{m-2}\right] + 11x\left[mx^{m-1}\right] - 3x^m = 0 \\
&\Rightarrow \quad 3m(m-1)x^m + 11mx^m - 3x^m = 0 \\
&\Rightarrow \quad [3m(m-1) + 11m - 3]\,x^m = 0 \\
&\Rightarrow \quad \left[3m^2 + 8m - 3\right] x^m = 0 .
\end{aligned}
$$

For the last equation to hold on an interval for x, we must have

$$3m^2 + 8m - 3 = (3m-1)(m+3) = 0 .$$

Thus either $(3m-1) = 0$ or $(m+3) = 0$, which gives $m = \dfrac{1}{3}, \, -3$.

(b) Substituting the above expressions for $\phi(x)$, $\phi'(x)$, and $\phi''(x)$ into the differential equation, $x^2y'' - xy' - 5y = 0$, gives

$$x^2\left[m(m-1)x^{m-2}\right] - x\left[mx^{m-1}\right] - 5x^m = 0 \qquad \Rightarrow \qquad \left[m^2 - 2m - 5\right] x^m = 0 .$$

For the last equation to hold on an interval for x, we must have

$$m^2 - 2m - 5 = 0 .$$

To solve for m we use the quadratic formula:

$$m = \frac{2 \pm \sqrt{4+20}}{2} = 1 \pm \sqrt{6}\,.$$

23. In this problem, $f(x,y) = x^3 - y^3$ and so

$$\frac{\partial f}{\partial y} = \frac{\partial\left(x^3 - y^3\right)}{\partial y} = -3y^2 .$$

Clearly, f and $\partial f/\partial y$ (being polynomials) are continuous on the whole xy-plane. Thus the hypotheses of Theorem 1 are satisfied, and the initial value problem has a unique solution for *any* initial data, in particular, for $y(0) = 6$.

25. Writing

$$\frac{dx}{dt} = -\frac{4t}{x} = -4tx^{-1},$$

we see that $f(t,x) = -4tx^{-1}$ and $\partial f(t,x)/\partial x = \partial(-4tx^{-1})/\partial x = 4tx^{-2}$. The functions $f(t,x)$ and $\partial f(t,x)/\partial x$ are not continuous only when $x = 0$. Therefore, they are continuous in any rectangle R that contains the point $(2, -\pi)$, but does not intersect the t-axis; for instance, $R = \{(t,x) : 1 < t < 3, -2\pi < x < 0\}$. Thus, Theorem 1 applies, and the given initial problem has a unique solution.

26. Here $f(x,y) = 3x - \sqrt[3]{y-1}$ and $\partial f(x,y)/\partial y = -\frac{1}{3}(y-1)^{-2/3}$. Unfortunately, $\partial f/\partial y$ is not continuous or defined when $y = 1$. So there is no rectangle containing $(2,1)$ in which both f and $\partial f/\partial y$ are continuous. Therefore, we are not guaranteed a unique solution to this initial value problem.

27. Rewriting the differential equation in the form $dy/dx = x/y$, we conclude that $f(x,y) = x/y$. Since f is not continuous when $y = 0$, there is no rectangle containing the point $(1,0)$ in which f is continuous. Therefore, Theorem 1 cannot be applied.

29. **(a)** Clearly, both functions $\phi_1(x) \equiv 0$ and $\phi_2(x) = (x-2)^3$ satisfy the initial condition, $y(2) = 0$. Next, we check that they also satisfy the differential equation $dy/dx = 3y^{2/3}$.

$$\begin{aligned}\frac{d\phi_1}{dx} &= \frac{d}{dx}(0) = 0 = 3\phi_1(x)^{2/3};\\ \frac{d\phi_2}{dx} &= \frac{d}{dx}\left[(x-2)^3\right] = 3(x-2)^2 = 3\left[(x-2)^3\right]^{2/3} = 3\phi_2(x)^{2/3}.\end{aligned}$$

Hence both functions, $\phi_1(x)$ and $\phi_2(x)$, are solutions to the initial value problem of Exapmle 9.

(b) In this initial value problem,

$$f(x,y) = 3y^{2/3} \qquad \Rightarrow \qquad \frac{\partial f(x,y)}{\partial y} = 3\,\frac{2}{3}\,y^{2/3-1} = \frac{2}{y^{1/3}},$$

$x_0 = 0$ and $y_0 = 10^{-7}$. The function $f(x,y)$ is continuous everywhere; $\partial f(x,y)/\partial y$ is continuous in any region which does not intersect the x-axis (where $y = 0$). In particular, both functions, $f(x,y)$ and $\partial f(x,y)/\partial y$, are continuous in the rectangle

$$R = \left\{(x,y) : -1 < x < 1,\ (1/2)10^{-7} < y < (2)10^{-7}\right\}$$

containing the initial point $(0, 10^{-7})$. Thus, it follows from Theorem 1 that the given initial value problem has a unique solution in an interval about x_0.

31. **(a)** To try to apply Theorem 1 we must first write the equation in the form $y' = f(x,y)$. Here $f(x,y) = 4xy^{-1}$ and $\partial f(x,y)/\partial y = -4xy^{-2}$. Neither f nor $\partial f/\partial y$ are continuous or defined when $y = 0$. Therefore there is no rectangle containing $(x_0, 0)$ in which both f and $\partial f/\partial y$ are continuous, so Theorem 1 cannot be applied.

(b) Suppose for the moment that there is such a solution $y(x)$ with $y(x_0) = 0$ and $x_0 \neq 0$. Substituting into the differential equation we get

$$y(x_0)y'(x_0) - 4x_0 = 0 \tag{1.3}$$

or

$$0 \cdot y'(x_0) - 4x_0 = 0 \qquad \Rightarrow \qquad 4x_0 = 0.$$

Thus $x_0 = 0$, which is a contradiction.

(c) Taking $C = 0$ in the implicit solution $4x^2 - y^2 = C$ given in Example 5 on page 9 gives $4x^2 - y^2 = 0$ or $y = \pm 2x$. Both solutions $y = 2x$ and $y = -2x$ satisfy $y(0) = 0$.

EXERCISES 1.3: Direction Fields, page 22

1. **(a)** For $y = \pm 2x$,

$$\frac{dy}{dx} = \frac{d}{dx}(\pm 2x) = \pm 2 \qquad \text{and} \qquad \frac{4x}{y} = \frac{4x}{\pm 2x} = \pm 2, \quad x \neq 0.$$

Thus $y = 2x$ and $y = -2x$ are solutions to the differential equation $dy/dx = 4x/y$ on any interval not containing the point $x = 0$.

(b) , **(c)** See Figures B.1 and B.2 in the answers of the text.

(d) As $x \to \infty$ or $x \to -\infty$, the solution in part (b) increases unboundedly and has the lines $y = 2x$ and $y = -2x$, respectively, as slant asymptotes. The solution in part (c) also increases without bound as $x \to \infty$ and approaches the line $y = 2x$, while it is not even defined for $x < 0$.

3. From Figure B.3 in the answers section of the text, we conclude that, regardless of the initial velocity, $v(0)$, the corresponding solution curve $v = v(t)$ has the line $v = 8$ as a horizontal asymptote, that is, $\lim_{t\to\infty} v(t) = 8$. This explains the name "terminal velocity" for the value $v = 8$.

5. (a) The graph of the directional field is shown in Figure B.4 in the answers section of the text.

(b), (c) The direction field indicates that all solution curves (other than $p(t) \equiv 0$) will approach the horizontal line (asymptote) $p = 1.5$ as $t \to +\infty$. Thus $\lim_{t\to+\infty} p(t) = 1.5$.

(d) No. The direction field shows that populations greater than 1500 will steadily decrease, but can never reach 1500 or any smaller value, i.e., the solution curves cannot cross the line $p = 1.5$. Indeed, the constant function $p(t) \equiv 1.5$ is a solution to the given logistic equation, and the uniqueness part of Theorem 1, page 12, prevents intersections of solution curves.

6. (a) The slope of a solution to the differential equation $dy/dx = x + \sin y$ is given by dy/dx. Therefore the slope at $(1, \pi/2)$ is equal to

$$\frac{dy}{dx} = 1 + \sin\frac{\pi}{2} = 2.$$

(b) The solution curve is increasing if the slope of the curve is greater than zero. From part (a) we know the slope to be $x + \sin y$. The function $\sin y$ has values ranging from -1 to 1; therefore if x is greater than 1 then the slope will always have a value greater than zero. This tells us that the solution curve is increasing.

(c) The second derivative of every solution can be determined by finding the derivative of the differential equation $dy/dx = x + \sin y$. Thus

$$\begin{aligned} \frac{d}{dx}\left(\frac{dy}{dx}\right) &= \frac{d}{dx}(x + \sin y); \\ \Rightarrow \quad \frac{d^2y}{dx^2} &= 1 + (\cos y)\frac{dy}{dx} \qquad \text{(chain rule)} \\ &= 1 + (\cos y)(x + \sin y) = 1 + x\cos y + \sin y \cos y; \\ \Rightarrow \quad \frac{d^2y}{dx^2} &= 1 + x\cos y + \frac{1}{2}\sin 2y. \end{aligned}$$

(d) Relative minima occur when the first derivative, dy/dx, is equal to zero and the second derivative, d^2y/dx^2, is greater than zero. The value of the first derivative at the point $(0, 0)$ is given by

$$\frac{dy}{dx} = 0 + \sin 0 = 0.$$

This tells us that the solution has a critical point at the point $(0, 0)$. Using the second derivative found in part (c) we have

$$\frac{d^2y}{dx^2} = 1 + 0 \cdot \cos 0 + \frac{1}{2}\sin 0 = 1.$$

This tells us the point $(0, 0)$ is a relative minimum.

7. (a) The graph of the directional field is shown in Figure B.5 in the answers section of the text.

(b) The direction field indicates that all solution curves with $p(0) > 1$ will approach the horizontal line (asymptote) $p = 2$ as $t \to +\infty$. Thus $\lim_{t\to+\infty} p(t) = 2$ when $p(0) = 3$.

(c) The direction field shows that a population between 1000 and 2000 (that is $1 < p(0) < 2$) will approach the horizontal line $p = 2$ as $t \to +\infty$.

(d) The direction field shows that an initial population less than 1000 (that is $0 \le p(0) < 1$) will approach zero as $t \to +\infty$.

(e) As noted in part (d), the line $p = 1$ is an asymptote. The direction field indicates that a population of 900 ($p(0) = 0.9$) steadily decreases with time and therefore cannot increase to 1100.

9. **(a)** The function $\phi(x)$, being a solution to the given initial value problem, satisfies

$$\frac{d\phi}{dx} = x - \phi(x), \qquad \phi(0) = 1. \tag{1.4}$$

Thus

$$\frac{d^2\phi}{dx^2} = \frac{d}{dx}\left(\frac{d\phi}{dx}\right) = \frac{d}{dx}\left(x - \phi(x)\right) = 1 - \frac{d\phi}{dx} = 1 - x + \phi(x),$$

where we have used (1.4) substituting (twice) $x - \phi(x)$ for $d\phi/dx$.

(b) First we note that any solution to the given differential equation on an interval I is continuously diferentiable on I. Indeed, if $y(x)$ is a solution on I, then $y'(x)$ does exist on I, and so $y(x)$ is continuous on I because it is differentiable. This immediately implies that $y'(x)$ is continuous as the difference of two continuous functions, x and $y(x)$.

From (1.4) we conclude that

$$\frac{d\phi}{dx}\Big|_{x=0} = [x - \phi(x)]\,\Big|_{x=0} = 0 - \phi(0) = -1 < 0$$

and so the continuity of $\phi'(x)$ implies that, for $|x|$ small enough, $\phi'(x) < 0$. By the Monotonicity Test, negative derivative of a function results that the function itself is decreasing.

When x increases from zero, as far as $\phi(x) > x$, one has $\phi'(x) < 0$ and so $\phi(x)$ decreases. On the other hand, the function $y = x$ increases unboundedly, as $x \to \infty$. Thus, by intermediate value theorem, there is a point, say, $x^* > 0$, where the curve $y = \phi(x)$ crosses the line $y = x$. At this point, $\phi(x^*) = x^*$ and hence $\phi'(x^*) = x^* - \phi(x^*) = 0$.

(c) From (b) we conclude that x^* is a critical point for $\phi(x)$ (its derivative vanishes at this point). Also, from part (a), we see that

$$\phi''(x^*) = 1 - \phi'(x^*) = 1 > 0.$$

Hence, by Second Derivative Test, $\phi(x)$ has a relative minimum at x^*.

(d) Remark that the arguments, used in part (c), can be applied to *any* point $\widetilde{x}$, where $\phi'(\widetilde{x}) = 0$, to conclude that $\phi(x)$ has a relative minimum at $\widetilde{x}$. Since a continuously differentiable function on an interval cannot have two relative minima on an interval without having a point of relative maximum, we conclude that x^* is the only point where $\phi'(x) = 0$. Continuity of $\phi'(x)$ implies that it has the same sign for all $x > x^*$ and, therefore, it is positive there since it is positive for $x > x^*$ and close to x^* ($\phi'(x^*) = 0$ and $\phi''(x^*) > 0$). By Monotonicity Test, $\phi(x)$ increases for $x > x^*$.

(e) For $y = x - 1$, $dy/dx = 1$ and $x - y = x - (x - 1) = 1$. Thus the given differential equation is satisfied, and $y = x - 1$ is indeed a solution.

To show that the curve $y = \phi(x)$ always stays above the line $y = x - 1$, we note that the initial value problem

$$\frac{dy}{dx} = x - y, \qquad y(x_0) = y_0 \tag{1.5}$$

has a unique solution for any x_0 and y_0. Indeed, functions $f(x, y) = x - y$ and $\partial f / \partial y \equiv -1$ are continuous on the whole xy-plane, and Theorem 1, Section 1.2, applies. This implies that the curve $y = \phi(x)$ always stays above the line $y = x - 1$:

$$\phi(0) = 1 > -1 = (x - 1)\,\big|_{x=0},$$

and the existence of a point $\widetilde{x}$ with $\phi(\widetilde{x}) \le (\widetilde{x} - 1)$ would imply, by intermediate value theorem, the existence of a point x_0, $0 < x_0 \le \widetilde{x}$, satisfying $y_0 := \phi(x_0) = x_0 - 1$ and, therefore, there would be two solutions to the initial value problem (1.5).

Since, from part (a), $\phi''(x) = 1 - \phi'(x) = 1 - x + \phi(x) = \phi(x) - (x - 1) > 0$, we also conclude that $\phi'(x)$ is an increasing function and $\phi'(x) < 1$. Thus there exists $\lim_{x\to\infty} \phi'(x) \le 1$. The strict inequality would imply that the values of the function $y = \phi(x)$, for x large enough, become smaller than those of $y = x - 1$. Therefore,

$$\lim_{x\to\infty} \phi'(x) = 1 \qquad \Leftrightarrow \qquad \lim_{x\to\infty} [x - \phi(x)] = 1,$$

and so the line $y = x - 1$ is a slant asymptote for $\phi(x)$.

(f), (g) The direction field for given differential equation and the curve $y = \phi(x)$ are shown in Figure B.6 in the answers of the text.

11. For this equation, the isoclines are given by $2x = c$. These are vertical lines $x = c/2$. Each element of the direction field associated with a point on $x = c/2$ has slope c. (See Figure B.7 in the answers of the text.)

13. For the equation $\partial y/\partial x = -x/y$, the isoclines are the curves $-x/y = c$. These are lines that pass through the origin and have equations of the form $y = mx$, where $m = -1/c$, $c \neq 0$. If we let $c = 0$ in $-x/y = c$, we see that the y-axis ($x = 0$) is also an isocline. Each element of the direction field associated with a point on an isocline has slope c and is, therefore, perpendicular to that isocline. Since circles have the property that at any point on the circle the tangent at that point is perpendicular to a line from that point to the center of the circle, we see that the solution curves will be circles with their centers at the origin. But since we cannot have $y = 0$ (since $-x/y$ would then have a zero in the denominator) the solutions will not be defined on the x-axis. (Note however that a related form of this differential equation is $yy' + x = 0$. This equation has implicit solutions given by the equations $y^2 + x^2 = C$. These solutions will be circles.) The graph of $\phi(x)$, the solution to the equation satisfying the initial condition $y(0) = 4$, is the upper semicircle with center at the origin and passing through the point $(0, 4)$ (see Figure B.8 in the answers of the text).

15. For the equation $dy/dx = 2x^2 - y$, the isoclines are the curves $2x^2 - y = c$, or $y = 2x^2 - c$. The curve $y = 2x^2 - c$ is a parabola which is open upward and has the vertex at $(0, -c)$. Three of them, for $c = -1$, 0, and 2 (dotted curves), as well as the solution curve satisfying the initial condition $y(0) = 0$, are depicted in Figure B.9.

17. The isoclines for the equation

$$\frac{dy}{dx} = 3 - y + \frac{1}{x}$$

are given by

$$3 - y + \frac{1}{x} = c \qquad \Leftrightarrow \qquad y = \frac{1}{x} + 3 - c,$$

which are hyperbolas having $x = 0$ as a vertical asymptote and $y = 3 - c$ as a horizontal asymptote. Each element of the direction field associated with a point on such a hyperbola has slope c. For $x > 0$ large enough: if an isocline is located *above* the line $y = 3$, then $c \leq 0$,

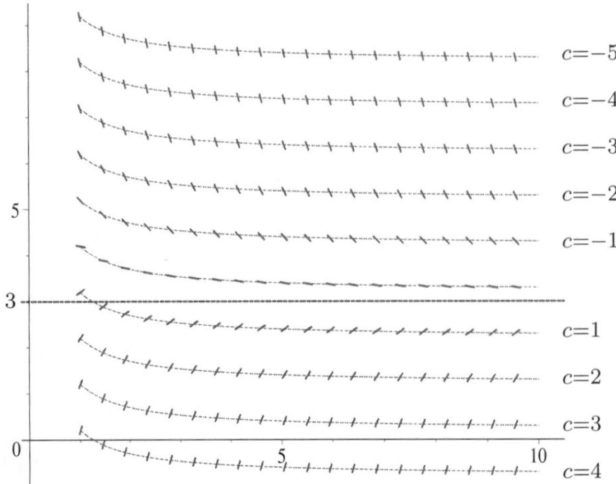

Figure 1–B: Isoclines and the direction field for Problem 17.

and so the elements of the direction field have *negative* or *zero slope*; if an isocline is located *below* the line $y = 3$, then $c > 0$, and so the elements of the direction field have *positive slope*. In other words, for $x > 0$ large enough, at any point above the line $y = 3$ a solution curve decreases passing through this point, and any solution curve increases passing through a point below $y = 3$. The direction field for this differential equation is depicted in Figure 1-B. From this picture we conclude that any solution to the differential equation $dy/dx = 3 - y + 1/x$ has the line $y = 3$ as a horizontal asymptote.

19. Integrating both sides of the equation $dy/y = -dx/x$ yields

$$\int \frac{1}{y}\,dy = -\int \frac{1}{x}\,dx \quad \Rightarrow \quad \ln|y| = -\ln|x| + C_1 \quad \Rightarrow \quad \ln|y| = \ln\frac{e^{C_1}}{|x|}$$

$$\Rightarrow \quad |y| = \frac{e^{C_1}}{|x|} \quad \Rightarrow \quad |y| = \frac{C_2}{|x|},$$

where C_1 is an arbitrary constant and so $C_2 := e^{C_1}$ is an arbitrary *positive* constant. The last equality can be written as

$$y = \pm\frac{C_2}{x} = \frac{C}{x},$$

where $C = \pm C_2$ is *any nonzero* constant. The value $C = 0$ gives $y \equiv 0$ (for $x \neq 0$), which is, clearly, also a solution to the given equation.

EXERCISES 1.4: The Approximation Method of Euler, page 28

1. In this initial value problem, $f(x, y) = x/y$, $x_0 = 0$, and $y_0 = -1$. Thus, with $h = 0.1$, the recursive formulas (2) and (3) on page 25 of the text become

$$x_{n+1} = x_n + h = x_n + 0.1\,,$$
$$y_{n+1} = y_n + hf(x_n, y_n) = y_n + 0.1 \cdot \left(\frac{x_n}{y_n}\right), \qquad n = 0, 1, \ldots .$$

We set $n = 0$ in these formulas and obtain

$$x_1 = x_0 + 0.1 = 0 + 0.1 = 0.1\,,$$
$$y_1 = y_0 + 0.1 \cdot \left(\frac{x_0}{y_0}\right) = -1 + 0.1 \cdot \left(\frac{0}{-1}\right) = -1.$$

Putting $n = 1$ in the recursive formulas yields

$$x_2 = x_1 + 0.1 = 0.1 + 0.1 = 0.2\,,$$
$$y_2 = y_1 + 0.1 \cdot \left(\frac{x_1}{y_1}\right) = -1 + 0.1 \cdot \left(\frac{0.1}{-1}\right) = -1.01\,.$$

Continuing in the same manner, we find for $n = 2$, 3, and 4:

$$x_3 = 0.2 + 0.1 = 0.3\,, \qquad y_3 = -1.01 + 0.1 \cdot \left(\frac{0.2}{-1.01}\right) = -1.02980\,;$$
$$x_4 = 0.3 + 0.1 = 0.4\,, \qquad y_4 = -1.02980 + 0.1 \cdot \left(\frac{0.3}{-1.02980}\right) = -1.05893\,;$$
$$x_5 = 0.4 + 0.1 = 0.5\,, \qquad y_5 = -1.05893 + 0.1 \cdot \left(\frac{0.4}{-1.05893}\right) = -1.09671\,,$$

where we have rounded off all answers to five decimal places.

2. In this problem, $x_0 = 0$, $y_0 = 4$, $h = 0.1$, and $f(x, y) = -x/y$. Thus, the recursive formulas given in equations (2) and (3) on page 25 of the text become

$$x_{n+1} = x_n + h = x_n + 0.1\,,$$

$$y_{n+1} = y_n + hf(x_n, y_n) = y_n + 0.1 \cdot \left(-\frac{x_n}{y_n}\right), \qquad n = 0, 1, 2, \ldots .$$

To find an approximation for the solution at the point $x_1 = x_0 + 0.1 = 0.1$, we let $n = 0$ in the last recursive formula to find

$$y_1 = y_0 + 0.1 \cdot \left(-\frac{x_0}{y_0}\right) = 4 + 0.1 \cdot (0) = 4.$$

To approximate the value of the solution at the point $x_2 = x_1 + 0.1 = 0.2$, we let $n = 1$ in the last recursive formula to obtain

$$y_2 = y_1 + 0.1 \cdot \left(-\frac{x_1}{y_1}\right) = 4 + 0.1 \cdot \left(-\frac{0.1}{4}\right) = 4 - \frac{1}{400} = 3.9975 \approx 3.998 .$$

Continuing in this way we find

$$x_3 = x_2 + 0.1 = 0.3 , \qquad y_3 = y_2 + 0.1 \cdot \left(-\frac{x_2}{y_2}\right) = 3.9975 + 0.1 \cdot \left(-\frac{0.2}{3.9975}\right) \approx 3.992 ,$$

$$x_4 = 0.4 , \qquad y_4 \approx 3.985 ,$$

$$x_5 = 0.5 , \qquad y_5 \approx 3.975 ,$$

where all of the answers have been rounded off to three decimal places.

3. Here $f(x, y) = y(2 - y)$, $x_0 = 0$, and $y_0 = 3$. We again use recursive formulas from Euler's method with $h = 0.1$. Setting $n = 0$, 1, 2, 3, and 4 and rounding off results to three decimal places, we get

$$x_1 = x_0 + 0.1 = 0.1 , \qquad y_1 = y_0 + 0.1 \cdot [y_0(2 - y_0)] = 3 + 0.1 \cdot [3(2 - 3)] = 2.700;$$

$$x_2 = 0.1 + 0.1 = 0.2 , \qquad y_2 = 2.700 + 0.1 \cdot [2.700(2 - 2.700)] = 2.511;$$

$$x_3 = 0.2 + 0.1 = 0.3 , \qquad y_3 = 2.511 + 0.1 \cdot [2.511(2 - 2.511)] \approx 2.383;$$

$$x_4 = 0.3 + 0.1 = 0.4 , \qquad y_4 = 2.383 + 0.1 \cdot [2.383(2 - 2.383)] \approx 2.292;$$

$$x_5 = 0.4 + 0.1 = 0.5 , \qquad y_5 = 2.292 + 0.1 \cdot [2.292(2 - 2.292)] \approx 2.225 .$$

5. In this problem, $f(x, y) = (y^2 + y)/x$, $x_0 = y_0 = 1$, and $h = 0.2$. The recursive formulas (2) and (3) on page 25 of the text, applied succesively with $n = 1$, 2, 3, and 4, yield

$$x_1 = x_0 + 0.2 = 1.2 , \qquad y_1 = y_0 + 0.2\left(\frac{y_0^2 + y_0}{x_0}\right) = 1 + 0.2\left(\frac{1^2 + 1}{1}\right) = 1.400;$$

$$x_2 = 1.2 + 0.2 = 1.4\,, \qquad y_2 = 1.400 + 0.2\left(\frac{1.400^2 + 1.400}{1.2}\right) \approx 1.960;$$

$$x_3 = 1.4 + 0.2 = 1.6\,, \qquad y_3 = 1.960 + 0.2\left(\frac{1.960^2 + 1.960}{1.4}\right) \approx 2.789;$$

$$x_4 = 1.6 + 0.2 = 1.8\,, \qquad y_4 = 2.789 + 0.2\left(\frac{2.789^2 + 2.789}{1.6}\right) \approx 4.110\,.$$

7. For this problem notice that the independent variable is t and the dependent variable is x. Hence, the recursive formulas given in equations (2) and (3) on page 25 of the text become

$$t_{n+1} = t_n + h \qquad \text{and} \qquad \phi(t_{n+1}) \approx x_{n+1} = x_n + hf(t_n, x_n), \qquad n = 0, 1, 2, \ldots.$$

For this problem, $f(t, x) = 1 + t\sin(tx)$, $t_0 = 0$, and $x_0 = 0$. Thus the second recursive formula above becomes

$$x_{n+1} = x_n + h\left[1 + t_n \sin(t_n x_n)\right], \qquad n = 0, 1, 2, \ldots.$$

For the case $N = 1$, we have $h = (1 - 0)/1 = 1$ which gives us

$$t_1 = 0 + 1 = 1 \qquad \text{and} \qquad \phi(1) \approx x_1 = 0 + 1 \cdot (1 + 0 \cdot \sin 0) = 1.$$

For the case $N = 2$, we have $h = 1/2 = 0.5$. Thus we have

$$t_1 = 0 + 0.5 = 0.5\,, \qquad x_1 = 0 + 0.5 \cdot (1 + 0 \cdot \sin 0) = 0.5\,,$$

and

$$t_2 = 0.5 + 0.5 = 1, \qquad \phi(1) \approx x_2 = 0.5 + 0.5 \cdot [1 + 0.5 \cdot \sin(0.25)] \approx 1.06185\,.$$

For the case $N = 4$, we have $h = 1/4 = 0.25$, and so the recursive formulas become

$$t_{n+1} = t_n + 0.25 \qquad \text{and} \qquad x_{n+1} = x_n + 0.25 \cdot [1 + t_n \sin(t_n x_n)]\,.$$

Therefore, we have

$$t_1 = 0 + 0.25 = 0.25\,, \qquad x_1 = 0 + 0.25 \cdot [1 + 0 \cdot \sin(0)] = 0.25\,.$$

Plugging these values into the recursive equations above yields

$$t_2 = 0.25 + 0.25 = 0.5 \qquad \text{and} \qquad x_2 = 0.25 + 0.25 \cdot [1 + 0.25 \cdot \sin(0.0625)] = 0.503904\,.$$

Continuing in this way gives

$$t_3 = 0.75 \qquad \text{and} \qquad x_3 = 0.503904 + 0.25 \cdot [1 + 0.5 \cdot \sin(0.251952)] = 0.785066\,,$$

$$t_4 = 1.00 \qquad \text{and} \qquad \phi(1) \approx x_4 = 1.13920\,.$$

For $N = 8$, we have $h = 1/8 = 0.125$. Thus, the recursive formulas become

$$t_{n+1} = t_n + 0.125 \qquad \text{and} \qquad x_{n+1} = x_n + 0.125 \cdot [1 + t_n \sin(t_n x_n)]\,.$$

Using these formulas and starting with $t_0 = 0$ and $x_0 = 0$, we can fill in Table 1-A. From this we see that $\phi(1) \approx x_8 = 1.19157$, which is rounded to five decimal places.

Table 1–A: Euler's method approximations for the solution of $x' = 1 + t\sin(tx)$, $x(0) = 0$, at $t = 1$ with 8 steps ($h = 1/8$).

n	t_n	x_n
1	0.125	0.125
2	0.250	0.250244
3	0.375	0.377198
4	0.500	0.508806
5	0.625	0.649535
6	0.750	0.805387
7	0.875	0.983634
8	1.000	1.191572

---

9. To approximate the solution on the whole interval $[1, 2]$ by Euler's method with the step $h = 0.1$, we first approximate the solution at the points $x_n = 1 + 0.1n$, $n = 1, \ldots, 10$. Then, on each subinterval $[x_n, x_{n+1}]$, we approximate the solution by the linear interval, connecting

(x_n, y_n) with (x_{n+1}, y_{n+1}), $n = 0, 1, \ldots, 9$. Since $f(x, y) = x^{-2} - yx^{-1} - y^2$, the recursive formulas have the form

$$x_{n+1} = x_n + 0.1\,,$$
$$y_{n+1} = y_n + 0.1\left(\frac{1}{x_n^2} - \frac{y_n}{x_n} - y_n^2\right), \qquad n = 0, 1, \ldots, 9\,,$$

$x_0 = 1$, $y_0 = -1$. Therefore,

$$x_1 = \ 1 + 0.1 = 1.1\,, \quad y_1 = -1 + 0.1\left(\frac{1}{1^2} - \frac{-1}{1} - (-1)^2\right) = -0.9\,;$$
$$x_2 = 1.1 + 0.1 = 1.2\,, \quad y_2 = -0.9 + 0.1\left(\frac{1}{1.1^2} - \frac{-0.9}{1.1} - (-0.9)^2\right) \approx -0.81653719\,;$$
$$x_3 = 1.2 + 0.1 = 1.3\,, \quad y_3 = -0.81653719 + 0.1\left(\frac{1}{1.2^2} - \frac{-0.81653719}{1.2} - (-0.81653719)^2\right) \approx -0.74572128\,;$$
$$x_4 = 1.3 + 0.1 = 1.4\,, \quad y_4 = -0.74572128 + 0.1\left(\frac{1}{1.3^2} - \frac{-0.74572128}{1.3} - (-0.74572128)^2\right) \approx -0.68479653\,;$$

etc.

The results of these computations (rounded to five decimal places) are shown in Table 1-B.

Table 1–B: Euler's method approximations for the solutions of $y' = x^{-2} - yx^{-1} - y^2$, $y(1) = -1$, on $[1, 2]$ with $h = 0.1$.

n	x_n	y_n	n	x_n	y_n
0	1.0	−1.00000	6	1.6	−0.58511
1	1.1	−0.90000	7	1.7	−0.54371
2	1.2	−0.81654	8	1.8	−0.50669
3	1.3	−0.74572	9	1.9	−0.47335
4	1.4	−0.68480	10	2.0	−0.44314
5	1.5	−0.63176			

The function $y(x) = -1/x = x^{-1}$, obviously, satisfies the initial condition, $y(1) = -1$. Further

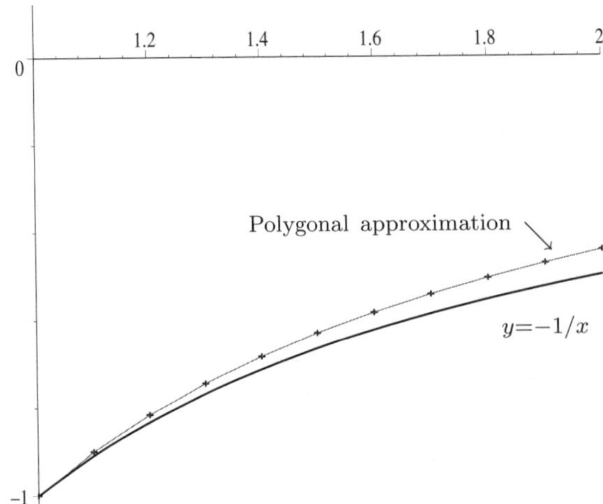

Figure 1–C: Polygonal line approximation and the actual solution for Problem 9.

we compute both sides of the given differential equation:

$$y'(x) = \left(-x^{-1}\right)' = x^{-2},$$
$$f(x, y(x)) = x^{-2} - \left(-x^{-1}\right) x^{-1} - \left(-x^{-1}\right)^2 = x^{-2} + x^{-2} - x^{-2} = x^{-2}.$$

Thus, the function $y(x) = -1/x$ is, indeed, the solution to the given initial value problem.

The graphs of the obtained polygonal line approximation and the actual solution are sketched in Figure 1-C.

11. In this problem, the independent variable is t and the dependent variable is x; $f(t, x) = 1+x^2$, $t_0 = 0$, and $x_0 = 0$.

The function $\phi(t) = \tan t$ satisfies the initial condition: $\phi(0) = \tan 0 = 0$. The differential equation is also satisfied:

$$\frac{d\phi}{dt} = \sec^2 t = 1 + \tan^2 t = 1 + \phi(t)^2.$$

Therefore, $\phi(t)$ is the solution to the given initial value problem.

For approximation of $\phi(t)$ at the point $t = 1$ with $N = 20$ steps, we take the step size $h = (1 - t_0)/20 = 0.05$. Thus, the recursive formulas for Euler's method are

$$\begin{aligned} t_{n+1} &= t_n + 0.05\,, \\ x_{n+1} &= x_n + 0.05\left(1 + x_n^2\right). \end{aligned}$$

Applying these formulas with $n = 0, 1, \ldots, 19$, we obtain

$$\begin{aligned} & x_1 = x_0 + 0.05\left(1 + x_0^2\right) = 0.05\,, \\ & x_2 = x_1 + 0.05\left(1 + x_1^2\right) = 0.05 + 0.05\left(1 + 0.05^2\right) = 0.100125\,, \\ & x_3 = x_2 + 0.05\left(1 + x_2^2\right) = 0.100125 + 0.05\left(1 + 0.100125^2\right) \approx 0.150626\,, \\ & \vdots \\ & x_{19} = x_{18} + 0.05\left(1 + x_{18}^2\right) \approx 1.328148\,, \\ \phi(1) \approx\ & x_{20} = x_{19} + 0.05\left(1 + x_{19}^2\right) = 1.328148 + 0.05\left(1 + 1.328148^2\right) \approx 1.466347\,, \end{aligned}$$

which is a good enough approximation to $\phi(1) = \tan 1 \approx 1.557408$.

13. From Problem 12, $y_n = (1 + 1/n)^n$ and so $\lim_{n\to\infty}\left[(e - y_n)/(1/n)\right]$ is a $0/0$ indeterminant. If we let $h = 1/n$ in y_n and use L'Hospital's rule, we get

$$\lim_{n\to\infty}\frac{e - y_n}{1/n} = \lim_{h\to 0}\frac{e - (1 + h)^{1/h}}{h} = \lim_{h\to 0}\frac{g(h)}{h} = \lim_{h\to 0}\frac{g'(h)}{1}\,,$$

where $g(h) = e - (1 + h)^{1/h}$. Writing $(1 + h)^{1/h}$ as $e^{\ln(1+h)/h}$ the function $g(h)$ becomes

$$g(h) = e - e^{\ln(1+h)/h}\,.$$

The first derivative is given by

$$g'(h) = 0 - \frac{d}{dh}\left[e^{\ln(1+h)/h}\right] = -e^{\ln(1+h)/h}\,\frac{d}{dh}\left[\frac{1}{h}\,\ln(1 + h)\right].$$

Substituting Maclaurin's series for $\ln(1 + h)$ we obtain

$$g'(h) = -(1 + h)^{1/h}\,\frac{d}{dh}\left[\frac{1}{h}\left(h - \frac{1}{2}\,h^2 + \frac{1}{3}\,h^3 - \frac{1}{4}\,h^4 + \cdots\right)\right]$$

$$= -(1+h)^{1/h}\frac{d}{dh}\left[1-\frac{1}{2}h+\frac{1}{3}h^2-\frac{1}{4}h^3+\cdots\right]$$
$$= -(1+h)^{1/h}\left[-\frac{1}{2}+\frac{2}{3}h-\frac{3}{4}h^2+\cdots\right].$$

Hence

$$\lim_{h\to 0} g'(h) = \lim_{h\to 0}\left\{-(1+h)^{1/h}\left[-\frac{1}{2}+\frac{2}{3}h-\frac{3}{4}h^2+\cdots\right]\right\}$$
$$= \left[-\lim_{h\to 0}(1+h)^{1/h}\right]\cdot\left[\lim_{h\to 0}\left\{-\frac{1}{2}+\frac{2}{3}h-\frac{3}{4}h^2+\cdots\right\}\right].$$

From calculus we know that $e = \lim_{h\to 0}(1+h)^{1/h}$, which gives

$$\lim_{h\to 0} g'(h) = -e\left(-\frac{1}{2}\right) = \frac{e}{2}.$$

So we have

$$\lim_{n\to\infty}\frac{e-y_n}{1/n} = \frac{e}{2}.$$

15. The independent variable in this problem is the time t and the dependent variable is the temperature $T(t)$ of a body. Thus, we will use the recursive formulas (2) and (3) on page 25 with x replaced by t and y replaced by T. In the differential equation describing the Newton's Law of Cooling, $f(t,T) = K(M(t)-T)$. With the suggested values of $K = 1\,(\text{min})^{-1}$, $M(t)\equiv 70°$, $h = 0.1$, and the initial condition $T(0) = 100°$, the initial value problem becomes

$$\frac{dT}{dt} = 70 - T, \qquad T(0) = 100,$$

and so the recursive formulas are

$$t_{n+1} = t_n + 0.1\,,$$
$$T_{n+1} = T_n + 0.1(70 - T_n).$$

For $n = 0$,

$$t_1 = t_0 + 0.1 = 0.1\,, \qquad T_1 = T_0 + 0.1(70 - T_0) = 100 + 0.1(70 - 100) = 97\,;$$

for $n = 1$,

$$t_2 = t_1 + 0.1 = 0.2\,, \qquad T_2 = T_1 + 0.1(70 - T_1) = 97 + 0.1(70 - 97) = 94.3\,;$$

for $n = 2$,

$$t_3 = t_2 + 0.1 = 0.3\,, \qquad T_3 = T_2 + 0.1(70 - T_2) = 94.3 + 0.1(70 - 94.3) = 91.87\,.$$

Table 1–C: Euler's method approximations for the solutions of $T' = K(M - T)$, $T(0) = 100$, with $K = 1$, $M = 70$, and $h = 0.1$.

n	t_n	T_n	n	t_n	T_n
0	0.0	100.00	11	1.1	79.414
1	0.1	97.000	12	1.2	78.473
2	0.2	94.300	13	1.3	77.626
3	0.3	91.870	14	1.4	76.863
4	0.4	89.683	15	1.5	76.177
5	0.5	87.715	16	1.6	75.559
6	0.6	85.943	17	1.7	75.003
7	0.7	84.349	18	1.8	74.503
8	0.8	82.914	19	1.9	74.053
9	0.9	81.623	20	2.0	73.647
10	1.0	80.460			

By continuing this way and rounding results to three decimal places, we fill in Table 1-C. From this table we conclude that

(a) the temperature of a body after 1 minute $T(1) \approx 80.460°$ and

(b) its temperature after 2 minutes $T(2) \approx 73.647°$.

16. For this problem notice that the independent variable is t and the dependent variable is T. Hence, in the recursive formulas for Euler's method, the t will take the place of the x and the

T will take the place of the y. Also we see that $h = 0.1$ and $f(t, T) = K(M^4 - T^4)$, where $K = 40^{-4}$ and $M = 70$. The recursive formulas (2) and (3) on page 25 of the text become

$$t_{n+1} = t_n + 0.1\,,$$
$$T_{n+1} = T_n + hf(t_n, T_n) = T_n + 0.1\left(40^{-4}\right)\left(70^4 - T_n^4\right), \qquad n = 0, 1, 2, \ldots .$$

From the initial condition, $T(0) = 100$, we see that $t_0 = 0$ and $T_0 = 100$. Therefore, for $n = 0$,

$$t_1 = t_0 + 0.1 = 0 + 0.1 = 0.1\,,$$
$$T_1 = T_0 + 0.1\left(40^{-4}\right)\left(70^4 - T_0^4\right) = 100 + 0.1\left(40^{-4}\right)\left(70^4 - 100^4\right) \approx 97.0316,$$

where we have rounded off to four decimal places. For $n = 1$, we have

$$t_2 = t_1 + 0.1 = 0.1 + 0.1 = 0.2\,,$$
$$T_2 = T_1 + 0.1\left(40^{-4}\right)\left(70^4 - T_1^4\right) = 97.0316 + 0.1\left(40^{-4}\right)\left(70^4 - 97.0316^4\right) \approx 94.5068\,.$$

By continuing this way, we fill in Table 1-D.

Table 1–D: Euler's method approximations for the solution of $T' = K(M^4 - T^4)$, $T(0) = 100$, with $K = 40^{-4}$, $M = 70$, and $h = 0.1$.

n	t_n	T_n	n	t_n	T_n	n	t_n	T_n
0	0	100	7	0.7	85.9402	14	1.4	79.5681
1	0.1	97.0316	8	0.8	84.7472	15	1.5	78.9403
2	0.2	94.5068	9	0.9	83.6702	16	1.6	78.3613
3	0.3	92.3286	10	1.0	82.6936	17	1.7	77.8263
4	0.4	90.4279	11	1.1	81.8049	18	1.8	77.3311
5	0.5	88.7538	12	1.2	80.9934	19	1.9	76.8721
6	0.6	87.2678	13	1.3	80.2504	20	2.0	76.4459

From this table we see that

$$T(1) = T(t_{10}) \approx T_{10} = 82.694 \qquad \text{and} \qquad T(2) = T(t_{20}) \approx T_{20} = 76.446\,.$$

CHAPTER 2: First Order Differential Equations

EXERCISES 2.2: Separable Equations, page 46

1. This equation is separable because we can separate variables by multiplying both sides by dx and dividing by $2y^3 + y + 4$.

3. This equation is separable because

$$\frac{dy}{dx} = \frac{ye^{x+y}}{x^2+2} = \left(\frac{e^x}{x^2+2}\right) ye^y = g(x)p(y).$$

5. Writing the equation in the form

$$\frac{ds}{dt} = \frac{s+1}{st} - s^2,$$

we see that the right-hand side cannot be represented in the form $g(t)p(s)$. Therefore, the equation is not separable.

7. Multiplying both sides of the equation by $y^2 dx$ and integrating yields

$$y^2 dy = (1-x^2)dx \quad \Rightarrow \quad \int y^2 dy = \int (1-x^2)dx$$
$$\Rightarrow \quad \frac{1}{3}y^3 = x - \frac{1}{3}x^3 + C_1 \quad \Rightarrow \quad y^3 = 3x - x^3 + C \quad \Rightarrow \quad y = \sqrt[3]{3x - x^3 + C}\,,$$

where $C := 3C_1$ is an arbitrary constant.

9. To separate variables, we divide the equation by y and multiply by dx. This results

$$\frac{dy}{dx} = y(2+\sin x) \quad \Rightarrow \quad \frac{dy}{y} = (2+\sin x)dx$$
$$\Rightarrow \quad \int \frac{dy}{y} = \int (2+\sin x)dx \quad \Rightarrow \quad \ln|y| = 2x - \cos x + C_1$$
$$\Rightarrow \quad |y| = e^{2x-\cos x + C_1} = e^{C_1}e^{2x-\cos x} = C_2 e^{2x-\cos x},$$

where C_1 is an arbitrary constant and, therefore, $C_2 := e^{C_1}$ is an arbitrary *positive* constant. We can rewrite the above solution in the form

$$y = \pm C_2 e^{2x-\cos x} = Ce^{2x-\cos x}, \tag{2.1}$$

with $C := C_2$ or $C = -C_2$. Thus C is an arbitrary *nonzero* constant. The value $C = 0$ in (2.1) gives $y(x) \equiv 0$, which is, clearly, is also a solution to the differential equation. Therefore, the answer to the problem is given by (2.1) with an arbitrary constant C.

11. Separating variables, we obtain

$$\frac{dy}{\sec^2 y} = \frac{dx}{1+x^2}.$$

Using the trigonometric identities $\sec y = 1/\cos y$ and $\cos^2 y = (1 + \cos 2y)/2$ and integrating, we get

$$\begin{aligned}
\frac{dy}{\sec^2 y} = \frac{dx}{1+x^2} \quad &\Rightarrow \quad \frac{(1+\cos 2y)dy}{2} = \frac{dx}{1+x^2} \\
\Rightarrow \quad & \int \frac{(1+\cos 2y)dy}{2} = \int \frac{dx}{1+x^2} \\
\Rightarrow \quad & \frac{1}{2}\left(y + \frac{1}{2}\sin 2y\right) = \arctan x + C_1 \\
\Rightarrow \quad & 2y + \sin 2y = 4\arctan x + 4C_1 \quad \Rightarrow \quad 2y + \sin 2y = 4\arctan x + C.
\end{aligned}$$

The last equation defines implicit solutions to the given differential equation.

13. Writing the given equation in the form $dx/dt = x - x^2$, we separate the variables to get

$$\frac{dx}{x - x^2} = dt.$$

Integrate (the left side is integrated by partial fractions, with $1/(x-x^2) = 1/x + 1/(1-x)$) to obtain:

$$\begin{aligned}
\ln|x| - \ln|1-x| = t + c \quad &\Rightarrow \quad \ln\left|\frac{x}{1-x}\right| = t + c \\
\Rightarrow \quad & \frac{x}{1-x} = \pm e^{t+c} = Ce^t, \quad \text{where } C = e^c \\
\Rightarrow \quad & x = Ce^t - xCe^t \quad \Rightarrow \quad x + xCe^t = Ce^t
\end{aligned}$$

$$\Rightarrow \qquad x\left(1+Ce^t\right) = Ce^t \qquad \Rightarrow \qquad x = \frac{Ce^t}{1+Ce^t}.$$

Note: When C is replaced by $-K$, this answer can also be written as $x = Ke^t/(Ke^t - 1)$. Further we observe that since we divide by $x - x^2 = x(1-x)$, then $x \equiv 0$ and $x \equiv 1$ are also solutions. Allowing K to be zero gives $x \equiv 0$, but no choice for K will give $x \equiv 1$, so we list this as a separate solution.

15. To separate variables, we move the term containin dx to the right-hand side of the equation and divide both sides of the result by y. This yields

$$y^{-1}dy = -ye^{\cos x}\sin x\,dx \qquad \Rightarrow \qquad y^{-2}dy = -e^{\cos x}\sin x\,dx.$$

Integrating the last equation, we obtain

$$\int y^{-2}dy = \int \left(-e^{\cos x}\sin x\right)dx \qquad \Rightarrow \qquad -y^{-1} + C = \int e^u du \quad (u = \cos x)$$

$$\Rightarrow \qquad -\frac{1}{y} + C = e^u = e^{\cos x} \qquad \Rightarrow \qquad y = \frac{1}{C - e^{\cos x}},$$

where C is an arbitrary constant.

17. First we find a general solution to the equation. Separating variables and integrating, we get

$$\frac{dy}{dx} = x^3(1-y) \qquad \Rightarrow \qquad \frac{dy}{1-y} = x^3dx$$

$$\Rightarrow \qquad \int \frac{dy}{1-y} = \int x^3dx \qquad \Rightarrow \qquad -\ln|1-y| + C_1 = \frac{x^4}{4}.$$

$$\Rightarrow \qquad |1-y| = \exp\left(C_1 - \frac{x^4}{4}\right) = Ce^{-x^4/4}.$$

To find C, we use the initial condition, $y(0) = 3$. Thus, substitution 3 for y and 0 for x into the last equation yields

$$|1-3| = Ce^{-0^4/4} \qquad \Rightarrow \qquad 2 = C.$$

Therefore, $|1-y| = 2e^{-x^4/4}$. Finally, since $1 - y(0) = 1 - 3 < 0$, on an interval containing $x = 0$ one has $1 - y(x) < 0$ and so $|1 - y(x)| = y(x) - 1$. The solution to the problem is then

$$y - 1 = 2e^{-x^4/4} \qquad \text{or} \qquad y = 2e^{-x^4/4} + 1.$$

19. For a general solution, separate variables and integrate:

$$\frac{dy}{d\theta} = y\sin\theta \qquad \Rightarrow \qquad \frac{dy}{y} = \sin\theta\, d\theta$$

$$\Rightarrow \qquad \int \frac{dy}{y} = \int \sin\theta\, d\theta \qquad \Rightarrow \qquad \ln|y| = -\cos\theta + C_1$$

$$\Rightarrow \qquad |y| = e^{-\cos\theta + C_1} = Ce^{-\cos\theta} \qquad \Rightarrow \qquad y = -Ce^{-\cos\theta}$$

(because at the initial point, $\theta = \pi$, $y(\pi) < 0$). We substitute now the initial condition, $y(\pi) = -3$, and obtain

$$-3 = y(\pi) = -Ce^{-\cos\pi} = -Ce \qquad \Rightarrow \qquad C = 3e^{-1}.$$

Hence, the answer is given by $y = -3e^{-1}e^{-\cos\theta} = -3e^{-1-\cos\theta}$.

21. Separate variables to obtain

$$\frac{1}{2}(y+1)^{-1/2}\, dy = \cos x\, dx.$$

Integrating, we have

$$(y+1)^{1/2} = \sin x + C.$$

Using the fact that $y(\pi) = 0$, we find

$$1 = \sin\pi + C \qquad \Rightarrow \qquad C = 1.$$

Thus

$$(y+1)^{1/2} = \sin x + 1 \qquad \Rightarrow \qquad y = (\sin x + 1)^2 - 1 = \sin^2 x + 2\sin x\,.$$

23. We have

$$\frac{dy}{dx} = 2x\cos^2 y \qquad \Rightarrow \qquad \frac{dy}{\cos^2 y} = 2x\, dx \qquad \Rightarrow \qquad \sec^2 y\, dy = 2x\, dx$$

$$\Rightarrow \qquad \int \sec^2 y\, dy = \int 2x\, dx \qquad \Rightarrow \qquad \tan y = x^2 + C.$$

Since $y = \pi/4$ when $x = 0$, we get $\tan(\pi/4) = 0^2 + C$ and so $C = 1$. The solution, therefore, is

$$\tan y = x^2 + 1 \qquad \Leftrightarrow \qquad y = \arctan\left(x^2 + 1\right).$$

25. By separating variables we obtain $(1+y)^{-1}dy = x^2\,dx$. Integrating yields

$$\ln|1+y| = \frac{x^3}{3} + C\,. \qquad (2.2)$$

Substituting $y = 3$ and $x = 0$ from the initial condition, we get $\ln 4 = 0 + C$, which implies that $C = \ln 4$. By substituting this value for C into equation (2.2) above, we have

$$\ln|1+y| = \frac{x^3}{3} + \ln 4\,.$$

Hence,

$$e^{\ln|1+y|} = e^{(x^3/3)+\ln 4} = e^{x^3/3}e^{\ln 4} = 4e^{x^3/3}$$

$$\Rightarrow \qquad 1+y = 4e^{x^3/3} \qquad \Rightarrow \qquad y = 4e^{x^3/3} - 1\,.$$

We can drop the absolute signs above because we are assuming from the initial condition that y is close to 3 and therefore $1+y$ is positive.

27. (a) The differential equation $dy/dx = e^{x^2}$ separates if we multiply by dx. We integrate the separated equation from $x = 0$ to $x = x_1$ to obtain

$$\int_0^{x_1} e^{x^2}dx = \int_{x=0}^{x=x_1} dy = y\,\Big|_{x=0}^{x=x_1} = y(x_1) - y(0).$$

If we let t be the variable of integration and replace x_1 by x and $y(0)$ by 0, then we can express the solution to the initial value problem as

$$y(x) = \int_0^x e^{t^2}dt.$$

(b) The differential equation $dy/dx = e^{x^2}y^{-2}$ separates if we multiply by y^2 and dx. We integrate the separated equation from $x = 0$ to $x = x_1$ to obtain

$$\int_0^{x_1} e^{x^2}dx = \int_0^{x_1} y^2dy = \frac{1}{3}y^3\,\Big|_{x=0}^{x=x_1} = \frac{1}{3}\left[y(x_1)^3 - y(0)^3\right].$$

If we let t be the variable of integration and replace x_1 by x and $y(0)$ by 1 in the above equation, then we can express the initial value problem as

$$\int_0^x e^{t^2}\,dt = \frac{1}{3}\left[y(x)^3 - 1\right].$$

Solving for $y(x)$ we arrive at

$$y(x) = \left[1 + 3\int_0^x e^{t^2}\,dt\right]^{1/3}. \tag{2.3}$$

(c) The differential equation $dy/dx = \sqrt{1+\sin x}(1+y^2)$ separates if we divide by $(1+y^2)$ and multiply by dx. We integrate the separated equation from $x = 0$ to $x = x_1$ and find

$$\int_0^{x_1} \sqrt{1+\sin x}\,dx = \int_{x=0}^{x=x_1} (1+y^2)^{-1}dy = \tan^{-1} y(x_1) - \tan^{-1} y(0).$$

If we let t be the variable of integration and replace x_1 by x and $y(0)$ by 1 then we can express the solution to the initial value problem by

$$y(x) = \tan\left[\int_0^x \sqrt{1+\sin t}\,dt + \frac{\pi}{4}\right].$$

(d) We will use Simpson's rule (Appendix B) to approximate the definite integral found in part (b). (Simpson's rule is implemented on the website for the text.) Simpson's rule requires an even number of intervals, but we don't know how many are required to obtain the desired three-place accuracy. Rather than make an error analysis, we will compute the approximate value of $y(0.5)$ using 2, 4, 6, ... intervals for Simpson's rule until the approximate values for $y(0.5)$ change by less than five in the fourth place.

For $n = 2$, we divide $[0, 0.5]$ into 4 equal subintervals. Thus each interval will be of length $(0.5-0)/4 = 1/8 = 0.125$. Therefore, the integral is approximated by

$$\int_0^{0.5} e^{x^2}\,dx = \frac{1}{24}\left[e^0 + 4e^{(0.125)^2} + 2e^{(0.25)^2} + 4e^{(0.325)^2} + e^{(0.5)^2}\right] \approx 0.544999003.$$

Substituting this value into equation (2.3) from part (b) yields

$$y(0.5) \approx [1 + 3(0.544999003)]^{1/3} \approx 1.38121\,.$$

Repeating these calculations for $n = 3$, 4, and 5 yields Table 2-A.

Table 2–A: Successive approximations for $y(0.5)$ using Simpson's rule.

Number of Intervals	$y(0.5)$
6	1.38120606
8	1.38120520
10	1.38120497

Since these values do not change by more than 5 in the fourth place, we can conclude that the first three places are accurate and that we have obtained an approximate solution $y(0.5) \approx 1.381$.

29. **(a)** Separating variables and integrating yields

$$\frac{dy}{y^{1/3}} = dx \qquad \Rightarrow \qquad \int \frac{dy}{y^{1/3}} = \int dx$$

$$\Rightarrow \qquad \frac{1}{2/3}\,y^{2/3} = x + C_1 \qquad \Rightarrow \qquad y = \left(\frac{2}{3}\,x + \frac{2}{3}\,C_1\right)^{3/2} = \left(\frac{2x}{3} + C\right)^{3/2}.$$

(b) Using the initial condition, $y(0) = 0$, we find that

$$0 = y(0) = \left[\frac{2(0)}{3} + C\right]^{3/2} = C^{3/2} \qquad \Rightarrow \qquad C = 0\,,$$

and so $y = (2x/3 + 0)^{3/2} = (2x/3)^{3/2}$, $x \geq 0$, is a solution to the initial value problem.

(c) The function $y(x) \equiv 0$, clearly, satisfies both, the differential equation $dy/dx = y^{1/3}$ and the initial condition $y(0) = 0$.

(d) In notation of Theorem 1 on page 12, $f(x, y) = y^{1/3}$ and so

$$\frac{\partial f}{\partial y} = \frac{d}{dy}\left(y^{1/3}\right) = \frac{1}{3}\,y^{-2/3} = \frac{1}{3y^{2/3}}\,.$$

Since $\partial f/\partial y$ is not continuous when $y=0$, there is no rectangle containing the point $(0,0)$ in which both, f and $\partial f/\partial y$, are continuous. Therefore, Theorem 1 does not apply to this initial value problem.

30. **(a)** Dividing the equation by $(y+1)^{2/3}$ and multiplying by dx separate variables. Thus we get

$$\frac{dy}{dx}=(x-3)(y+1)^{2/3} \quad \Rightarrow \quad \frac{dy}{(y+1)^{2/3}}=(x-3)dx$$
$$\Rightarrow \quad \int\frac{dy}{(y+1)^{2/3}}=\int(x-3)dx \quad \Rightarrow \quad 3(y+1)^{1/3}=\frac{x^2}{2}-3x+C_1$$
$$\Rightarrow \quad y+1=\left(\frac{x^2}{6}-x+\frac{C_1}{3}\right)^3 \quad \Rightarrow \quad y=-1+\left(\frac{x^2}{6}-x+C\right)^3. \qquad (2.4)$$

(b) Substitution $y(x)\equiv -1$ into the differential equation gives

$$\frac{d(-1)}{dx}=(x-3)[(-1)+1]^{2/3} \quad \Rightarrow \quad 0=(x-3)\cdot 0,$$

which is an identity. Therefore, $y(x)\equiv -1$ is, indeed, a solution.

(c) With any choice of constant C, $x^2/6-x+C$ is a quadratic polynomial which is not identically zero. So, in (2.4), $y=-1+(x^2/6-x+C)^3\not\equiv -1$ for all C, and the solution $y(x)\equiv -1$ was lost in separation of variables.

31. **(a)** Separating variables and integrating yields

$$\frac{dy}{y^3}=x\,dx \quad \Rightarrow \quad \int\frac{dy}{y^3}=\int x\,dx$$
$$\Rightarrow \quad \frac{1}{-2}y^{-2}=\frac{1}{2}x^2+C_1 \quad \Rightarrow \quad y^{-2}=-x^2-2C_1$$
$$\Rightarrow \quad x^2+y^{-2}=C, \qquad (2.5)$$

where $C:=-2C_1$ is an arbitrary constant.

(b) To find the solution satisfying the initial condition $y(0)=1$, we substitute in (2.5) 0 for x and 1 for y and obtain

$$0^2+1^{-2}=C \quad \Rightarrow \quad C=1 \quad \Rightarrow \quad x^2+y^{-2}=1.$$

Solving for y yields

$$y = \pm \frac{1}{\sqrt{1-x^2}}\,. \tag{2.6}$$

Since, at the initial point, $x = 0$, $y(0) = 1 > 1$, we choose the positive sign in the above expression for y. Thus, the solution is

$$y = \frac{1}{\sqrt{1-x^2}}\,.$$

Similarly we find solutions for the other two initial conditions:

$$y(0) = \frac{1}{2} \quad \Rightarrow \quad C = 4 \quad \Rightarrow \quad y = \frac{1}{\sqrt{4-x^2}}\,;$$
$$y(0) = 2 \quad \Rightarrow \quad C = \frac{1}{4} \quad \Rightarrow \quad y = \frac{1}{\sqrt{(1/4)-x^2}}\,.$$

(c) For the solution to the first initial problem in (b), $y(0) = 1$, the domain is the set of all values of x satisfying two conditions

$$\begin{cases} 1 - x^2 \geq 0 & \text{(for existence of the square root)} \\ 1 - x^2 \neq 0 & \text{(for existence of the quotient)} \end{cases} \quad \Rightarrow \quad 1 - x^2 > 0.$$

Solving for x, we get

$$x^2 < 1 \quad \Rightarrow \quad |x| < 1 \quad \text{or} \quad -1 < x < 1.$$

In the same manner, we find domains for solutions to the other two initial value problems:

$$y(0) = \frac{1}{2} \quad \Rightarrow \quad -2 < x < 2\,;$$
$$y(0) = 2 \quad \Rightarrow \quad -\frac{1}{2} < x < \frac{1}{2}\,.$$

(d) First, we find the solution to the initial value problem $y(0) = a$, $a > 0$, and its domain. Following the lines used in (b) and (c) for particular values of a, we conclude that

$$y(0) = a \quad \Rightarrow \quad 0^2 + a^{-2} = C \quad \Rightarrow \quad y = \frac{1}{\sqrt{a^{-2}-x^2}} \quad \text{and so its domain is}$$
$$a^{-2} - x^2 > 0 \quad \Rightarrow \quad x^2 < a^{-2} \quad \Rightarrow \quad -\frac{1}{a} < x < \frac{1}{a}\,.$$

As $a \to +0$, $1/a \to +\infty$, and the domain expands to the whole real line; as $a \to +\infty$, $1/a \to 0$, and the domain shrinks to $x = 0$.

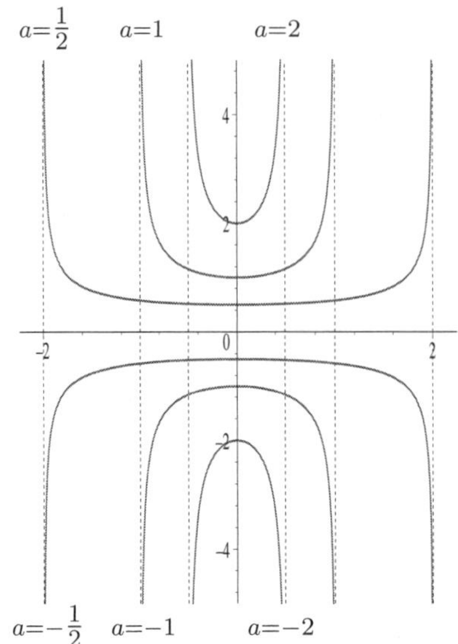

Figure 2–A: Solutions to the initial value problem $y' = xy^3$, $y(0) = a$, $a \pm 0.5$, ± 1, and ± 2.

(e) For the values $a = 1/2$, 1, and 2 the solutions are found in (b); for $a = -1$, we just have to choose the negative sign in (2.6); similarly, we reverse signs in the other two solutions in (b) to obtain the answers for $a = -1/2$ and -2. The graphs of these functions are shown in Figure 2-A.

33. Let $A(t)$ be the number of kilograms of salt in the tank at t minutes after the process begins. Then we have

$$\frac{dA(t)}{dt} = \text{rate of salt in} \; - \; \text{rate of salt out.}$$
$$\text{rate of salt in} \; = 10 \text{ L/min } \times 0.3 \text{ kg/L } = 3 \text{ kg/min.}$$

Since the tank is kept uniformly mixed, $A(t)/400$ is the mass of salt per liter that is flowing out of the tank at time t. Thus we have

$$\text{rate of salt out} = 10 \text{ L/min } \times \frac{A(t)}{400} \text{ kg/L} = \frac{A(t)}{40} \text{ kg/min.}$$

Therefore,

$$\frac{dA}{dt} = 3 - \frac{A}{40} = \frac{120 - A}{40}\,.$$

Separating this differential equation and integrating yield

$$\frac{40}{120 - A}\,dA = dt \qquad \Rightarrow \qquad -40\ln|120 - A| = t + C$$

$$\Rightarrow \qquad \ln|120 - A| = -\frac{t}{40} + C, \quad \text{where } -\frac{C}{40} \text{ is replaced by } C$$

$$\Rightarrow \qquad 120 - A = Ce^{-t/40}, \quad \text{where } C \text{ can now be positive or negative}$$

$$\Rightarrow \qquad A = 120 - Ce^{-t/40}\,.$$

There are 2 kg of salt in the tank initially, thus $A(0) = 2$. Using this initial condition, we find

$$2 = 120 - C \qquad \Rightarrow \qquad C = 118\,.$$

Substituting this value of C into the solution, we have

$$A = 120 - 118e^{-t/40}\,.$$

Thus

$$A(10) = 120 - 118e^{-10/40} \approx 28.1 \text{ kg}.$$

Note: There is a detailed discussion of mixture problems in Section 3.2.

35. In Problem 34 we saw that the differential equation $dT/dt = k(M - T)$ can be solved by separation of variables to yield

$$T = Ce^{kt} + M.$$

When the oven temperature is 120° we have $M = 120$. Also $T(0) = 40$. Thus

$$40 = C + 120 \qquad \Rightarrow \qquad C = -80.$$

Because $T(45) = 90$, we have

$$90 = -80e^{45k} + 120 \qquad \Rightarrow \qquad \frac{3}{8} = e^{45k} \qquad \Rightarrow \qquad 45k = \ln\left(\frac{3}{8}\right).$$

Thus $k = \ln(3/8)/45 \approx -0.02180$. This k is independent of M. Therefore, we have the general equation

$$T(t) = Ce^{-0.02180t} + M.$$

(a) We are given that $M = 100$. To find C we must solve the equation $T(0) = 40 = C + 100$. This gives $C = -60$. Thus the equation becomes

$$T(t) = -60e^{-0.02180t} + 100.$$

We want to solve for t when $T(t) = 90$. This gives us

$$90 = -60e^{-0.02180t} + 100 \quad \Rightarrow \quad \frac{1}{6} = e^{-0.02180t}$$
$$\Rightarrow \quad -0.0218t = \ln\left(\frac{1}{6}\right) \quad \Rightarrow \quad 0.0218t = \ln 6\,.$$

Therefore $t = \ln 6/0.0218 \approx 82.2$ min.

(b) Here $M = 140$, so we solve

$$T(0) = 40 = C + 140 \quad \Rightarrow \quad C = -100.$$

As above, solving for t in the equation

$$T(t) = -100e^{-0.02180t} + 140 = 90 \quad \Rightarrow \quad t \approx 31.8\,.$$

(c) With $M = 80$, we solve

$$40 = C + 80,$$

yielding $C = -40$. Setting

$$T(t) = -40e^{-0.02180t} + 80 = 90 \quad \Rightarrow \quad -\frac{1}{4} = e^{-0.02180t}.$$

This last equation is impossible because an exponential function is never negative. Hence it never attains desired temperature. The physical nature of this problem would lead us to expect this result. A further discussion of Newton's law of cooling is given in Section 3.3.

37. The differential equation

$$\frac{dP}{dt} = \frac{r}{100}P$$

separates if we divide by P and multiply by dt.

$$\int \frac{1}{P}\,dP = \frac{r}{100}\int dt \qquad \Rightarrow \qquad \ln P = \frac{r}{100}t + C \qquad \Rightarrow \qquad P(t) = Ke^{rt/100},$$

where K is the initial amount of money in the savings account, $K = \$1000$, and $r\%$ is the interest rate, $r = 5$. This results in

$$P(t) = 1000e^{5t/100}. \tag{2.7}$$

(a) To determine the amount of money in the account after 2 years we substitute $t = 2$ into equation (2.7), which gives

$$P(2) = 1000e^{10/100} = \$1105.17.$$

(b) To determine when the account will reach \$4000 we solve equation (2.7) for t with $P = \$4000$:

$$4000 = 1000e^{5t/100} \qquad \Rightarrow \qquad e^{5t/100} = 4 \qquad \Rightarrow \qquad t = 20\ln 4 \approx 27.73 \text{ years.}$$

(c) To determine the amount of money in the account after $3\frac{1}{2}$ years we need to determine the value of each \$1000 deposit after $3\frac{1}{2}$ years has passed. This means that the initial \$1000 is in the account for the entire $3\frac{1}{2}$ years and grows to the amount which is given by $P_0 = 1000e^{5(3.5)/100}$. For the growth of the \$1000 deposited after 12 months, we take $t = 2.5$ in equation (2.7) because that is how long this \$1000 will be in the account. This gives $P_1 = 1000e^{5(2.5)/100}$. Using the above reasoning for the remaining deposits we arrive at $P_2 = 1000e^{5(1.5)/100}$ and $P_3 = 1000e^{5(0.5)/100}$. The total amount is determined by the sum of the P_i's.

$$P = 1000\left[e^{5(3.5)/100} + e^{5(2.5)/100} + e^{5(1.5)/100} + e^{5(0.5)/100}\right] \approx \$4,427.59.$$

39. Let $s(t)$, $t > 0$, denote the distance traveled by driver A from the time $t = 0$ when he ran out of gas to time t. Then driver A's velocity $v_A(t) = ds/dt$ is a solution to the initial value problem

$$\frac{dv_A}{dt} = -kv_A^2, \qquad v_A(0) = v_B,$$

where v_B is driver B's constant velocity, and $k > 0$ is a positive constant. Separating variables we get

$$\frac{dv_A}{v_A^2} = -k\,dt \qquad \Rightarrow \qquad \int \frac{dv_A}{v_A^2} = -\int k\,dt \qquad \Rightarrow \qquad \frac{1}{v_A(t)} = kt + C\,.$$

From the initial condition we find

$$\frac{1}{v_B} = \frac{1}{v_A(0)} = k \cdot 0 + C = C \qquad \Rightarrow \qquad C = \frac{1}{v_B}\,.$$

Thus

$$v_A(t) = \frac{1}{kt + 1/v_B} = \frac{v_B}{v_B kt + 1}\,.$$

The function $s(t)$ therefore satisfies

$$\frac{ds}{dt} = \frac{v_B}{v_B kt + 1}\,, \qquad s(0) = 0.$$

Integrating we obtain

$$s(t) = \int \frac{v_B}{v_B kt + 1}\,dt = \frac{1}{k}\ln\left(v_B kt + 1\right) + C_1\,.$$

To find C_1 we use the initial condition:

$$0 = s(0) = \frac{1}{k}\ln\left(v_B k \cdot 0 + 1\right) + C_1 = C_1 \qquad \Rightarrow \qquad C_1 = 0.$$

So,

$$s(t) = \frac{1}{k}\ln\left(v_B kt + 1\right).$$

At the moment $t = t_1$ when driver A's speed was halved, i.e., $v_A(t_1) = v_A(0)/2 = v_B/2$, we have

$$\begin{aligned}
&\frac{1}{2}v_B = v_A(t_1) = \frac{v_B}{v_B kt_1 + 1} \qquad \text{and} \qquad 1 = s(t_1) = \frac{1}{k}\ln\left(v_B kt_1 + 1\right)\\
\Rightarrow\quad & v_B kt_1 + 1 = 2 \qquad \text{and so} \qquad k = \ln\left(v_B kt_1 + 1\right) = \ln 2\\
\Rightarrow\quad & s(t) = \frac{1}{\ln 2}\ln\left(v_B t \ln 2 + 1\right).
\end{aligned}$$

Since driver B was 3 miles behind driver A at time $t = 0$, and his speed remained constant, he finished the race at time $t_B = (3+2)/v_B = 5/v_B$. At this moment, driver A had already gone

$$s(t_B) = \frac{1}{\ln 2}\ln(v_B t_B \ln 2 + 1) = \frac{1}{\ln 2}\ln\left(\frac{5}{v_B} v_B \ln 2 + 1\right)$$
$$= \frac{1}{\ln 2}\ln(5\ln 2 + 1) \approx 2.1589 > 2 \text{ miles},$$

i.e., A won the race.

EXERCISES 2.3: Linear Equations, page 54

1. Writing

$$\frac{dy}{dx} - x^{-2}y = -x^{-2}\cos x\,,$$

we see that this equation has the form (4) on page 50 of the text with $P(x) = -x^{-2}$ and $Q(x) = -x^{-2}\cos x$. Therefore, it is linear.

Isolating dy/dx yields

$$\frac{dy}{dx} = \frac{y - \cos x}{x^2}.$$

Since the right-hand side cannot be represented as a product $g(x)p(y)$, the equation is not separable.

3. In this equation, the independent variable is t and the dependent variable is x. Dividing by x, we obtain

$$\frac{dx}{dt} = \frac{\sin t}{x} - t^2.$$

Therefore, it is neither linear, because of the $\sin t/x$ term, nor separable, because the right-hand side is not a product of functions of single variables x and t.

5. This is a linear equation with independent variable t and dependent variable y. This is also a separable equation because

$$\frac{dy}{dt} = \frac{y(t-1)}{t^2+1} = \left(\frac{t-1}{t^2+1}\right)y = g(t)p(y).$$

7. In this equation, $P(x) \equiv -1$ and $Q(x) = e^{3x}$. Hence the integrating factor

$$\mu(x) = \exp\left(\int P(x)dx\right) = \exp\left(\int(-1)dx\right) = e^{-x}.$$

Multiplying both sides of the equation by $\mu(x)$ and integrating, we obtain

$$e^{-x}\frac{dy}{dx} - e^{-x}y = e^{-x}e^{3x} = e^{2x} \qquad \Rightarrow \qquad \frac{d\left(e^{-x}y\right)}{dx} = e^{2x}$$

$$\Rightarrow \qquad e^{-x}y = \int e^{2x}dx = \frac{1}{2}e^{2x} + C$$

$$\Rightarrow \qquad y = \left(\frac{1}{2}e^{2x} + C\right)e^{x} = \frac{e^{3x}}{2} + Ce^{x}.$$

9. This is a linear equation with dependent variable r and independent variable θ. The method we will use to solve this equation is exactly the same as the method we use to solve an equation in the variables x and y since these variables are just dummy variables. Thus we have $P(\theta) = \tan\theta$ and $Q(\theta) = \sec\theta$ which are continuous on any interval not containing odd multiples of $\pi/2$. We proceed as usual to find the integrating factor $\mu(\theta)$. We have

$$\mu(\theta) = \exp\left(\int \tan\theta\, d\theta\right) = e^{-\ln|\cos\theta| + C} = K \cdot \frac{1}{|\cos\theta|} = K|\sec\theta|, \quad \text{where } K = e^{C}.$$

Thus we have

$$\mu(\theta) = \sec\theta,$$

where we can drop the absolute value sign by making $K = 1$ if θ is in an interval where $\sec\theta$ is positive or by making $K = -1$ if $\sec\theta$ is negative. Multiplying the equation by the integrating factor yields

$$\sec\theta\frac{dr}{d\theta} + (\sec\theta\tan\theta)r = \sec^2\theta \qquad \Rightarrow \qquad D_\theta(r\sec\theta) = \sec^2\theta\,.$$

Integrating with respect to θ yields

$$r\sec\theta = \int \sec^2\theta\, d\theta = \tan\theta + C \quad \Rightarrow \quad r = \cos\theta\tan\theta + C\cos\theta \quad \Rightarrow \quad r = \sin\theta + C\cos\theta\,.$$

Because of the continuity of $P(\theta)$ and $Q(\theta)$ this solution is valid on any open interval that has end points that are consecutive odd multiples of $\pi/2$.

11. Choosing t as the independent variable and y as the dependent variable, we put the equation put into standard form:

$$t+y+1-\frac{dy}{dt}=0 \qquad \Rightarrow \qquad \frac{dy}{dt}-y=t+1. \tag{2.8}$$

Thus $P(t)\equiv -1$ and so $\mu(t)=\exp\left[\int(-1)dt\right]=e^{-t}$. We multiply both sides of the second equation in (2.8) by $\mu(t)$ and integrate. This yields

$$\begin{aligned}
&e^{-t}\frac{dy}{dt}-e^{-t}y=(t+1)e^{-t} \qquad \Rightarrow \qquad \frac{d}{dt}\left(e^{-t}y\right)=(t+1)e^{-t}\\
\Rightarrow \qquad & e^{-t}y=\int(t+1)e^{-t}dt=-(t+1)e^{-t}+\int e^{-t}dt\\
&\qquad\qquad =-(t+1)e^{-t}-e^{-t}+C=-(t+2)e^{-t}+C\\
\Rightarrow \qquad & y=e^{t}\left(-(t+2)e^{-t}+C\right)=-t-2+Ce^{t},
\end{aligned}$$

where we have used integration by parts to find $\int(t+1)e^{-t}dt$.

13. In this problem, the independent variable is y and the dependent variable is x. So, we divide the equation by y to rewrite it in standard form.

$$y\,\frac{dx}{dy}+2x=5y^2 \qquad \Rightarrow \qquad \frac{dx}{dy}+\frac{2}{y}\,x=5y^2.$$

Therefore, $P(y)=2/y$ and the integrating factor, $\mu(y)$, is

$$\mu(y)=\exp\left(\int\frac{2}{y}\,dy\right)=\exp\left(2\ln|y|\right)=|y|^2=y^2.$$

Multiplying the equation (in standard form) by y^2 and integrating yield

$$\begin{aligned}
&y^2\,\frac{dx}{dy}+2y\,x=5y^4 \qquad \Rightarrow \qquad \frac{d}{dy}\left(y^2x\right)=5y^4\\
\Rightarrow \qquad & y^2x=\int 5y^4\,dy=y^5+C \qquad \Rightarrow \qquad x=y^{-2}\left(y^5+C\right)=y^3+Cy^{-2}.
\end{aligned}$$

15. To put this linear equation in standard form, we divide by (x^2+1) to obtain

$$\frac{dy}{dx}+\frac{x}{x^2+1}\,y=\frac{x}{x^2+1}\,. \tag{2.9}$$

Here $P(x) = x/(x^2+1)$, so

$$\int P(x)\,dx = \int \frac{x}{x^2+1}\,dx = \frac{1}{2}\ln(x^2+1).$$

Thus the integrating factor is

$$\mu(x) = e^{(1/2)\ln(x^2+1)} = e^{\ln\left[(x^2+1)^{1/2}\right]} = (x^2+1)^{1/2}.$$

Multiplying equation (2.9) by $\mu(x)$ yields

$$(x^2+1)^{1/2}\frac{dy}{dx} + \frac{x}{(x^2+1)^{1/2}}\,y = \frac{x}{(x^2+1)^{1/2}},$$

which becomes

$$\frac{d}{dx}\left[(x^2+1)^{1/2}y\right] = \frac{x}{(x^2+1)^{1/2}}.$$

Now we integrate both sides and solve for y to find

$$(x^2+1)^{1/2}y = (x^2+1)^{1/2} + C \qquad \Rightarrow \qquad y = 1 + C(x^2+1)^{-1/2}.$$

This solution is valid for all x since $P(x)$ and $Q(x)$ are continuous for all x.

17. This is a linear equation with $P(x) = -1/x$ and $Q(x) = xe^x$ which is continuous on any interval not containing 0. Therefore, the integrating factor is given by

$$\mu(x) = \exp\left[\int\left(-\frac{1}{x}\right)dx\right] = e^{-\ln x} = \frac{1}{x}, \qquad \text{for } x > 0.$$

Multiplying the equation by this integrating factor yields

$$\frac{1}{x}\frac{dy}{dx} - \frac{y}{x^2} = e^x \qquad \Rightarrow \qquad D_x\left(\frac{y}{x}\right) = e^x.$$

Integrating gives

$$\frac{y}{x} = e^x + C \qquad \Rightarrow \qquad y = xe^x + Cx.$$

Now applying the initial condition, $y(1) = e - 1$, we have

$$e - 1 = e + C \qquad \Rightarrow \qquad C = -1.$$

Thus, the solution is

$$y = xe^x - x, \quad \text{on the interval } (0, \infty).$$

Note: This interval is the largest interval containing the initial value $x = 1$ in which $P(x)$ and $Q(x)$ are continuous.

19. In this problem, t is the independent variable and x is the dependent variable. One can notice that the left-hand side is the derivative of xt^3 with respect to t. Indeed, using product rule for differentiation, we get

$$\frac{d}{dt}\left(xt^3\right) = \frac{dx}{dt}t^3 + x\,\frac{d\left(t^3\right)}{dt} = t^3\frac{dx}{dt} + 3t^2x.$$

Thus the equation becomes

$$\frac{d}{dt}\left(xt^3\right) = t \qquad \Rightarrow \qquad xt^3 = \int t\,dt = \frac{t^2}{2} + C$$

$$\Rightarrow \qquad x = t^{-3}\left(\frac{t^2}{2} + C\right) = \frac{1}{2t} + \frac{C}{t^3}.$$

(Of course, one could divide the given equation by t^3 to get standard form, conclude that $P(t) = 3/t$, find that $\mu(t) = t^3$, multiply by t^3 back, and come up with the original equation.) We now use the initial condition, $x(2) = 0$, to find C.

$$0 = x(2) = \frac{1}{2(2)} + \frac{C}{2^3} \qquad \Rightarrow \qquad \frac{1}{4} + \frac{C}{8} = 0 \qquad \Rightarrow \qquad C = -2.$$

Hence, the solution is $x = 1/(2t) - 2/(t^3)$.

21. Putting the equation in standard form yields

$$\frac{dy}{dx} + \frac{\sin x}{\cos x}y = 2x\cos x \qquad \Rightarrow \qquad \frac{dy}{dx} + (\tan x)y = 2x\cos x.$$

Therefore, $P(x) = \tan x$ and so

$$\mu(x) = \exp\left(\int \tan x\,dx\right) = \exp\left(-\ln|\cos x|\right) = |\cos x|^{-1}.$$

At the initial point, $x = \pi/4$, $\cos(\pi/4) > 0$ and, therefore, we can take $\mu(x) = (\cos x)^{-1}$. Multiplying the standard form of the given equation by $\mu(x)$ gives

$$\frac{1}{\cos x}\frac{dy}{dx} + \frac{\sin x}{\cos^2 x}\,y = 2x \qquad \Rightarrow \qquad \frac{d}{dx}\left(\frac{1}{\cos x}\,y\right) = 2x$$

$$\Rightarrow \qquad \frac{1}{\cos x}\,y = \int 2x\,dx = x^2 + C \qquad \Rightarrow \qquad y = \cos x\left(x^2 + C\right).$$

From the initial condition, we find C:

$$\frac{-15\sqrt{2}\pi^2}{32} = y\left(\frac{\pi}{4}\right) = \cos\frac{\pi}{4}\left[\left(\frac{\pi}{4}\right)^2 + C\right] \qquad \Rightarrow \qquad C = -\pi^2.$$

Hence, the solution is given by $y = \cos x\,(x^2 - \pi^2)$.

23. We proceed similarly to Example 2 on page 52 and obtain an analog of the initial value problem (13), that is,

$$\frac{dy}{dt} + 5y = 40e^{-20t}, \qquad y(0) = 10. \tag{2.10}$$

Thus $P(t) \equiv 5$ and $\mu(t) = \exp\left(\int 5dt\right) = e^{5t}$. Multiplying the differential equation in (2.10) by $\mu(t)$ and integrating, we obtain

$$e^{5t}\frac{dy}{dt} + 5e^{5t}y = 40e^{-20t}e^{5t} = 40e^{-15t}$$

$$\Rightarrow \qquad \frac{d\left(e^{5t}y\right)}{dt} = 40e^{-15t} \qquad \Rightarrow \qquad e^{5t}y = \int 40e^{-15t}\,dt = \frac{40}{-15}\,e^{-15t} + C.$$

Therefore, a general solution to the differential equation in (2.10) is

$$y = e^{-5t}\left(\frac{40}{-15}\,e^{-15t} + C\right) = Ce^{-5t} - \frac{8}{3}\,e^{-20t}.$$

Finally, we find C using the initial condition.

$$10 = y(0) = Ce^{-5\cdot 0} - \frac{8}{3}\,e^{-20\cdot 0} = C - \frac{8}{3} \qquad \Rightarrow \qquad C = 10 + \frac{8}{3} = \frac{38}{3}.$$

Hence, the mass of RA_2 for $t \geq 0$ is given by

$$y(t) = \frac{38}{3}e^{-5t} - \frac{8}{3}\,e^{-20t}.$$

25. **(a)** This is a linear problem and so an integrating factor is

$$\mu(x) = \exp\left(\int 2x\,dx\right) = \exp\left(x^2\right).$$

Multiplying the equation by this integrating factor yields

$$e^{x^2}\frac{dy}{dx} + 2xe^{x^2}y = e^{x^2} \qquad \Rightarrow \qquad D_x\left(ye^{x^2}\right) = e^{x^2}$$
$$\Rightarrow \qquad \int_2^x D_t\left(ye^{t^2}\right)dt = \int_2^x e^{t^2}dt,$$

where we have changed the dummy variable x to t and integrated with respect to t from 2 (since the initial value for x in the initial condition is 2) to x. Thus, since $y(2) = 1$,

$$ye^{x^2} - e^4 = \int_2^x e^{t^2}dt \qquad \Rightarrow \qquad y = e^{-x^2}\left(e^4 + \int_2^x e^{t^2}dt\right) = e^{4-x^2} + e^{-x^2}\int_2^x e^{t^2}dt.$$

(b) We will use Simpson's rule (page A.3 of the Appendix B) to approximate the definite integral found in part (a) with upper limit $x = 3$. Simpson's rule requires an even number of intervals, but we don't know how many are required to obtain the desired 3 place accuracy. Rather than make an error analysis, we will compute the approximate value of $y(3)$ using 4, 6, 8, 10, 12, ... intervals for Simpson's rule until the approximate values for $y(3)$ change by less than 5 in the fourth place. For $n = 2$ we divide $[2, 3]$ into 4 equal subintervals. Thus, each subinterval will be of length $(3 - 2)/4 = 1/4$. Therefore, the integral is approximated by

$$\int_2^3 e^{t^2}dt \approx \frac{1}{12}\left[e^{(2)^2} + e^{(2.25)^2} + e^{(2.5)^2} + e^{(2.75)^2} + e^{(3)^2}\right] \approx 1460.354350.$$

Dividing this by $e^{(3)^2}$ and adding $e^{4-3^2} = e^{-5}$, gives

$$y(3) \approx 0.186960.$$

Doing calculations for 6, 8, 10, and 12 intervals yields Table 2-B.

Table 2–B: Successive approximations for $y(3)$ using Simpson's rule.

Number of Intervals	$y(3)$
6	0.183905
8	0.183291
10	0.183110
12	0.183043

Since the last 3 approximate values do not change by more than 5 in the fourth place, it appears that their first three places are accurate and the approximate solution is $y(3) \approx 0.183$.

27. **(a)** The given differential equation is in standard form. Thus $P(x) = \sqrt{1+\sin^2 x}$. Since we cannot express $\int P(x)\,dx$ as an elementary function, we use fundamental theorem of calculus to conclude that, with any fixed constant a,

$$\left(\int_a^x P(t)dt\right)' = P(x),$$

that is, the above definite integral with variable upper bound is an antiderivative of $P(x)$. Since, in the formula for $\mu(x)$, one can choose any antiderivative of $P(x)$, we take the above definite integral with $a = 0$. (Such a choice of a comes from the initial point $x = 0$ and makes it easy to satisfy the initial condition.) Therefore, the integrating factor $\mu(x)$ can be chosen as

$$\mu(x) = \exp\left(\int_0^x \sqrt{1+\sin^2 t}\; dt\right).$$

Multiplying the differential equaion by $\mu(x)$ and integrating from $x = 0$ to $x = s$, we obtain

$$\frac{d[\mu(x)y]}{dx} = \mu(x)x \qquad \Rightarrow \qquad d[\mu(x)y] = \mu(x)x\,dx$$

$$\Rightarrow \quad \int_0^s d[\mu(x)y] = \int_0^s \mu(x)x\,dx \quad \Rightarrow \quad \mu(x)y(x)\Big|_{x=0}^{x=s} = \int_0^s \mu(x)x\,dx$$

$$\Rightarrow \quad \mu(s)y(s) - \mu(0)y(0) = \int_0^s \mu(x)x\,dx\,.$$

From the initial condition, $y(0) = 2$. Also, note that

$$\mu(0) = \exp\left(\int_0^0 \sqrt{1+\sin^2 t}\;dt\right) = e^0 = 1.$$

This yields $\mu(0)y(0) = 2$ and so

$$\mu(s)y(s) = \int_0^s \mu(x)x\,dx + 2\,.$$

Dividing by $\mu(s)$ and interchanging x and s give the required.

(b) The values of $\mu(x)$, $x = 0.1, 0.2, \ldots, 1.0$, approximated by using Simpson's rule, are given in Table 2-C.

Table 2–C: Approximations of $\nu(x) = \int_0^x \sqrt{1+\sin^2 t}\,dt$ and $\mu(x) = e^{\nu(x)}$ using Simpson's rule.

x	$\nu(x)$	$\mu(x)$	x	$\nu(x)$	$\mu(x)$
0.0	0.0	1.0000	0.6	0.632016	1.881401
0.1	0.100166	1.105354	0.7	0.748903	2.114679
0.2	0.201315	1.223010	0.8	0.869917	2.386713
0.3	0.304363	1.355761	0.9	0.994980	2.704670
0.4	0.410104	1.506975	1.0	1.123865	3.076723
0.5	0.519172	1.680635			

We now use these values of $\mu(x)$ to approximate $\int_0^1 \mu(s)s\,ds$ by applying Simpson's rule again. With $n = 5$ and

$$h = \frac{1-0}{2n} = 0.1$$

the Simpson's rule becomes

$$\int_0^1 \mu(s)s\,ds \approx \frac{0.1}{3}[\mu(0)(0) + 4\mu(0.1)(0.1) + 2\mu(0.2)(0.2) + 4\mu(0.3)(0.3)$$
$$+2\mu(0.4)(0.4) + 4\mu(0.5)(0.5) + 2\mu(0.6)(0.6) + 4\mu(0.7)(0.7)$$
$$+2\mu(0.8)(0.8) + 4\mu(0.9)(0.9) + \mu(1.0)(1.0)] \approx 1.064539\,.$$

Therefore,

$$y(1) \approx \frac{1}{\mu(1)}\int_0^1 \mu(s)s\,ds + \frac{2}{\mu(1)} = \frac{1}{3.076723}\cdot 1.064539 + \frac{2}{3.076723} = 0.9960\,.$$

(c) We rewrite the differential equation in the form used in Euler's method,

$$\frac{dy}{dx} = x - \sqrt{1+\sin^2 x}\,y\,, \qquad y(0) = 2,$$

and conclude that $f(x,y) = x - \sqrt{1+\sin^2 x}y$. Thus the recursive formulas (2) and (3) on page 25 of the text become

$$x_{n+1} = x_n + h,$$
$$y_{n+1} = y_n + h\left(x_n - \sqrt{1+\sin^2 x_n}\,y_n\right), \qquad n = 0, 1, \ldots\,,$$

$x_0 = 0$, $y_0 = 2$. With $h = 0.1$ we need $(1-0)/0.1$ steps to get an approximation at $x = 1$.

$$n = 0:\ \ x_1 = 0.1\,,\ \ y_1 = (2) + 0.1[(0) - \sqrt{1+\sin^2(0)}\,(2)] = 1.8000;$$
$$n = 1:\ \ x_2 = 0.2\,,\ \ y_2 = (1.8) + 0.1[(0.1) - \sqrt{1+\sin^2(0.1)}\,(1.8)] \approx 1.6291;$$
$$n = 2:\ \ x_3 = 0.3\,,\ \ y_3 = (1.6291) + 0.1[(0.2) - \sqrt{1+\sin^2(0.2)}\,(1.6291)] \approx 1.4830;$$
$$\vdots$$

Results of these computations, rounded off to four decimal places, are given in Table 2-D. Thus Euler's method with step $h = 0.1$ gives $y(1) \approx 0.9486$.

Next we take $h = 0.05$ and fill in the Table 2-E. So, with step $h = 0.05$, we have $y(1) \approx 0.9729$.

Table 2–D: Euler's method approximations for the solution of $y' + y\sqrt{1+\sin^2 x} = x$, $y(0) = 2$, at $x = 1$ with $h = 0.1$.

k	x_k	y_k	k	x_k	y_k	k	x_k	y_k
0	0.0	2.0000	4	0.4	1.3584	8	0.8	1.0304
1	0.1	1.8000	5	0.5	1.2526	9	0.9	0.9836
2	0.2	1.6291	6	0.6	1.1637	10	1.0	0.9486
3	0.3	1.4830	7	0.7	1.0900			

Table 2–E: Euler's method approximations for the solution of $y' + y\sqrt{1+\sin^2 x} = x$, $y(0) = 2$, at $x = 1$ with $h = 0.05$.

n	x_n	y_n	n	x_n	y_n	n	x_n	y_n
0	0.00	2.0000	7	0.35	1.4368	14	0.70	1.1144
1	0.05	1.9000	8	0.40	1.3784	15	0.75	1.0831
2	0.10	1.8074	9	0.45	1.3244	16	0.80	1.0551
3	0.15	1.7216	10	0.50	1.2747	17	0.85	1.0301
4	0.20	1.6420	11	0.55	1.2290	18	0.90	1.0082
5	0.25	1.5683	12	0.60	1.1872	19	0.95	0.9892
6	0.30	1.5000	13	0.65	1.1490	20	1.00	0.9729

29. In the presented form, the equation

$$\frac{dy}{dx} = \frac{1}{e^{4y} + 2x}$$

is, clearly, not linear. But, if we switch the roles of variables and consider y as the independent variable and x as the dependent variable (using the connection between derivatives of inverse functions, that is, the formula $y'(x) = 1/x'(y)$), then the equation transforms to

$$\frac{dx}{dy} = e^{4y} + 2x \qquad \Rightarrow \qquad \frac{dx}{dy} - 2x = e^{4y}.$$

This is a linear equation with $P(y) = -2$. Thus the integrating factor is

$$\mu(y) = \exp\left(\int (-2)dy\right) = e^{-2y}$$

and so

$$\frac{d}{dy}\left(e^{-2y}x\right) = e^{-2y}e^{4y} = e^{2y} \qquad \Rightarrow \qquad e^{-2y}x = \int e^{2y}dy = \frac{e^{2y}}{2} + C.$$

Solving for x yields

$$x = e^{2y}\left(\frac{e^{2y}}{2} + C\right) = \frac{e^{4y}}{2} + Ce^{2y}.$$

31. (a) On the interval $0 \le x \le 2$, we have $P(x) = 1$. Thus we are solving the equation

$$\frac{dy}{dx} + y = x, \qquad y(0) = 1.$$

The integrating factor is given by

$$\mu(x) = \exp\left(\int dx\right) = e^x.$$

Multiplying the equation by the integrating factor, we obtain

$$e^x\frac{dy}{dx} + e^x y = xe^x \qquad \Rightarrow \qquad D_x\left[e^x y\right] = xe^x \qquad \Rightarrow \qquad e^x y = \int xe^x\,dx.$$

Calculating this integral by parts and dividing by e^x yields

$$y = e^{-x}\left(xe^x - e^x + C\right) = x - 1 + Ce^{-x}.$$

(b) Using the initial condition, $y(0) = 1$, we see that

$$1 = y(0) = 0 - 1 + C = -1 + C \qquad \Rightarrow \qquad C = 2.$$

Thus the solution becomes

$$y = x - 1 + 2e^{-x}.$$

(c) In the interval $x > 2$, we have $P(x) = 3$. Therefore, the integrating factor is given by

$$\mu(x) = \exp\left(\int 3\,dx\right) = e^{3x}.$$

Multiplying the equation by this factor and solving yields

$$e^{3x}\frac{dy}{dx} + 3e^{3x}y = xe^{3x} \qquad \Rightarrow \qquad D_x\left(e^{3x}y\right) = xe^{3x} \qquad \Rightarrow \qquad e^{3x}y = \int xe^{3x}\,dx.$$

Integrating by parts and dividing by e^{3x} gives

$$y = e^{-3x}\left[\frac{1}{3}xe^{3x} - \frac{1}{9}e^{3x} + C\right] = \frac{x}{3} - \frac{1}{9} + Ce^{-3x}.$$

(d) We want the value of the initial point for the solution in part (c) to be the value of the solution found in part (b) at the point $x = 2$. This value is given by

$$y(2) = 2 - 1 + 2e^{-2} = 1 + 2e^{-2}.$$

Thus the initial point we seek is

$$y(2) = 1 + 2e^{-2}.$$

Using this initial point to find the constant C given in part (c) yields

$$1 + 2e^{-2} = y(2) = \frac{2}{3} - \frac{1}{9} + Ce^{-6} \qquad \Rightarrow \qquad C = \frac{4}{9}e^{6} + 2e^{4}.$$

Thus, the solution of the equation on the interval $x > 2$ is given by

$$y = \frac{x}{3} - \frac{1}{9} + \left[\frac{4}{9}e^{6} + 2e^{4}\right]e^{-3x}.$$

Patching these two solutions together gives us a continuous solution to the original equation on the interval $x \geq 0$:

$$y = \begin{cases} x - 1 + 2e^{-x}, & 0 \leq x \leq 2; \\ \dfrac{x}{3} - \dfrac{1}{9} + \left(\dfrac{4}{9}e^{6} + 2e^{4}\right)e^{-3x}, & 2 < x. \end{cases}$$

(e) The graph of the solution is given in Figure B.18 of the answers in the text.

33. **(a)** Writing the equation in standard form yields

$$\frac{dy}{dx} + \frac{2}{x}y = 3.$$

Therefore, $P(x) = 2/x$ and

$$\mu(x) = \exp\left(\int \frac{2}{x}\,dx\right) = \exp\left(2\ln|x|\right) = |x|^2 = x^2.$$

Hence

$$\frac{d}{dx}\left(x^2 y\right) = 3x^2 \qquad \Rightarrow \qquad x^2 y = \int 3x^2\,dx = x^3 + C \qquad \Rightarrow \qquad y = x + \frac{C}{x^2}$$

is a general solution to the given differential equation. Unless $C = 0$ and so $y = x$, the function $y = x + C/x^2$ is not defined when $x = 0$. Therefore, among all solutions, the only function defined at $x = 0$ is $\phi(x) = x$, and the initial value problem with $y(0) = y_0$ has a solution (and unique) if and only if

$$y_0 = \phi(x)\Big|_{x=0} = 0.$$

(b) Standard form of the equation $xy' - 2y = 3x$ is

$$\frac{dy}{dx} - \frac{2}{x}y = 3.$$

This gives $P(x) = -2/x$, $\mu(x) = \exp\left[\int(-2/x)dx\right] = x^{-2}$, and

$$\frac{d}{dx}\left(x^{-2}y\right) = 3x^{-2} \quad \Rightarrow \quad x^{-2}y = \int 3x^{-2}\,dx = -3x^{-1} + C \quad \Rightarrow \quad y = -3x + Cx^2.$$

Therefore, any solution is a polynomial and so is defined for all real numbers. Moreover, any solution satisfies the initial condition $y(0) = 0$ because

$$-3x + Cx^2\Big|_{x=0} = -3(0) + C(0)^2 = 0$$

and, therefore, is a solution to the initial value problem. (This also implies that the initial value problem with $y(0) = y_0 \neq 0$ has no solution.)

35. (a) This part of the problem is similar to Problem 33 in Section 2.2. So, we proceed in the same way.

Let $A(t)$ denote the mass of salt in the tank at t minutes after the process begins. Then we have

$$\begin{aligned}
&\text{rate of input } = 5 \text{ L/min } \times 0.2 \text{ kg/L } = 1 \text{ kg/min},\\
&\text{rate of exit} = 5 \text{ L/min } \times \frac{A(t)}{500} \text{ kg/L} = \frac{A(t)}{100} \text{ kg/min},\\
&\frac{dA}{dt} = 1 - \frac{A}{100} = \frac{100 - A}{100}.
\end{aligned}$$

Separating this differential equation yields $dA/(100 - A) = dt/100$. Integrating, we obtain

$$-\ln|100 - A| = \frac{t}{100} + C_1 \qquad \Rightarrow \qquad |100 - A| = e^{-t/100 - C_1} = e^{-C_1}e^{-t/100}$$

$$\Rightarrow \qquad 100 - A = Ce^{-t/100} \quad \left(C = \pm e^{-C_1}\right) \qquad \Rightarrow \qquad A = 100 - Ce^{-t/100}.$$

The initial condition, $A(0) = 5$ (initially, there were 5 kg of salt in the tank) implies that

$$5 = A(0) = 100 - C \qquad \Rightarrow \qquad C = 95.$$

Substituting this value of C into the solution, we have

$$A(t) = 100 - 95e^{-t/100}.$$

Thus the mass of salt in the tank after 10 min is

$$A(10) = 100 - 95e^{-10/100} \approx 14.04 \text{ kg},$$

which gives the concentration $14.04\,\text{kg}/500\,\text{L} \approx 0.0281\,\text{kg/L}$.

(b) After the leak develops, the system satisfies a new differential equation. While the rate of input remains the same, 1 kg/min, the rate of exit is now different. Since, every minute, 5 liters of the solution is coming in and $5 + 1 = 6$ liters are going out, the volume of the solution in the tank decreases by $6 - 5 = 1$ liter per minute. Thus, for $t \geq 10$, the volume of the solution in the tank is $500 - 1 \cdot (t - 10) = 510 - t$ liters. This gives the concentration of salt in the tank

$$\frac{A(t)}{510 - t} \text{ kg/L} \tag{2.11}$$

and

$$\text{rate of exit} = 6 \text{ L/min} \times \frac{A(t)}{510 - t} \text{ kg/L} = \frac{6A(t)}{510 - t} \text{ kg/min}.$$

Hence, the differential equation, for $t > 10$, becomes

$$\frac{dA}{dt} = 1 - \frac{6A}{510 - t} \qquad \Rightarrow \qquad \frac{dA}{dt} + \frac{6A}{510 - t} = 1$$

with the initial condition $A(10) = 14.04$ (the value found in (a)). This equation is a linear equation. We have

$$\mu(t) = \exp\left(\int \frac{6}{510 - t}\, dt\right) = \exp\left(-6 \ln|510 - t|\right) = (510 - t)^{-6}$$

$$\Rightarrow \quad \frac{d}{dt}\left[(510-t)^{-6}A\right] = 1\cdot(510-t)^{-6} = (510-t)^{-6}$$
$$\Rightarrow \quad (510-t)^{-6}A = \int (510-t)^{-6}dt = \frac{1}{5}(510-t)^{-5} + C$$
$$\Rightarrow \quad A = \frac{1}{5}(510-t) + C(510-t)^{6}.$$

Using the initial condition, $A(10) = 14.04$, we compute C.

$$14.04 = A(10) = \frac{1}{5}(510-10) + C(510-10)^6 \qquad \Rightarrow \qquad C = -\frac{85.96}{(500)^6}.$$

Therefore,

$$A(t) = \frac{1}{5}(510-t) - \frac{85.96}{(500)^6}(510-t)^6 = \frac{1}{5}(510-t) - 85.96\left(\frac{510-t}{500}\right)^6$$

and, according to (2.11), the concentration of salt is given by

$$\frac{A(t)}{510-t} = \frac{1}{5} - \frac{85.96}{510-t}\cdot\left(\frac{510-t}{500}\right)^6.$$

20 minutes after the leak develops, that is, when $t = 30$, the concentration will be

$$\frac{1}{5} - \frac{85.96}{510-30}\cdot\left(\frac{510-30}{500}\right)^6 \approx 0.0598 \text{ kg/L}.$$

37. We are solving the equation

$$\frac{dx}{dt} + 2x = 1 - \cos\left(\frac{\pi t}{12}\right), \qquad x(0) = 10.$$

This is a linear problem with dependent variable x and independent variable t so that $P(t) = 2$. Therefore, to solve this equation we first must find the integrating factor $\mu(t)$.

$$\mu(t) = \exp\left(\int 2\,dt\right) = e^{2t}.$$

Multiplying the equation by this factor yields

$$e^{2t}\frac{dx}{dt} + 2xe^{2t} = e^{2t}\left[1 - \cos\left(\frac{\pi t}{12}\right)\right] = e^{2t} - e^{2t}\cos\left(\frac{\pi t}{12}\right)$$
$$\Rightarrow \quad xe^{2t} = \int e^{2t}\,dt - \int e^{2t}\cos\left(\frac{\pi t}{12}\right)dt = \frac{1}{2}e^{2t} - \int e^{2t}\cos\left(\frac{\pi t}{12}\right)dt.$$

The last integral can be found by integrating by parts twice which leads back to an integral similar to the original. Combining these two similar integrals and simplifying, we obtain

$$\int e^{2t}\cos\left(\frac{\pi t}{12}\right)dt = \frac{e^{2t}\left[2\cos\left(\frac{\pi t}{12}\right)+\frac{\pi}{12}\sin\left(\frac{\pi t}{12}\right)\right]}{4+\left(\frac{\pi}{12}\right)^2}+C.$$

Thus we see that

$$x(t)=\frac{1}{2}-\frac{2\cos\left(\frac{\pi t}{12}\right)+\frac{\pi}{12}\sin\left(\frac{\pi t}{12}\right)}{4+\left(\frac{\pi}{12}\right)^2}+Ce^{-2t}.$$

Using the initial condition, $t=0$ and $x=10$, to solve for C, we obtain

$$C=\frac{19}{2}+\frac{2}{4+\left(\frac{\pi}{12}\right)^2}.$$

Therefore, the desired solution is

$$x(t)=\frac{1}{2}-\frac{2\cos\left(\frac{\pi t}{12}\right)+\frac{\pi}{12}\sin\left(\frac{\pi t}{12}\right)}{4+\left(\frac{\pi}{12}\right)^2}+\left[\frac{19}{2}+\frac{2}{4+\left(\frac{\pi}{12}\right)^2}\right]e^{-2t}.$$

39. Let $T_j(t)$, $j=0,1,2,\ldots$, denote the temperature in the classroom for $9+j\le t<10+j$, where $t=13$ denotes 1 : 00 P.M., $t=14$ denotes 2 : 00 P.M., etc. Then

$$T(9)=0, \tag{2.12}$$

and the continuity of the temperature implies that

$$\lim_{t\to 10+j} = T_{j+1}(10+j), \qquad j=0,1,2,\ldots. \tag{2.13}$$

According to the work of the heating unit, the temperature satisfies the equation

$$\frac{dT_j}{dt}=\begin{cases}1-T_j\,, & \text{if } j=2k\\ -T_j\,, & \text{if } j=2k+1\end{cases}, \qquad 9+j<t<10+j \quad k=0,1,\ldots.$$

The general solutions of these equations are:

for j even

$$\frac{dT_j}{dt}=1-T_j \qquad \Rightarrow \qquad \frac{dT_j}{1-T_j}=dt$$
$$\Rightarrow \qquad \ln|1-T_j|=-t+c_j \qquad \Rightarrow \qquad T_j(t)=1-C_je^{-t};$$

for j odd

$$\frac{dT_j}{dt} = -T_j \qquad \Rightarrow \qquad \frac{dT_j}{-T_j} = dt$$
$$\Rightarrow \qquad \ln|T_j| = -t + c_j \qquad \Rightarrow \qquad T_j(t) = C_j e^{-t};$$

where $C_j \neq 0$ are constants. From (2.12) we have:

$$0 = T_0(9) = \left(1 - C_0 e^{-t}\right)\Big|_{t=9} = 1 - C_0 e^{-9} \qquad \Rightarrow \qquad C_0 = e^9.$$

Also from (2.13), for even values of j (say, $j = 2k$) we get

$$\left(1 - C_{2k} e^{-t}\right)\Big|_{t=9+(2k+1)} = C_{2k+1} e^{-t}\Big|_{t=9+(2k+1)}$$
$$\Rightarrow \qquad 1 - C_{2k} e^{-(10+2k)} = C_{2k+1} e^{-(10+2k)}$$
$$\Rightarrow \qquad C_{2k+1} = e^{10+2k} - C_{2k}\,.$$

Similarly from (2.13) for odd values of j (say, $j = 2k + 1$) we get

$$C_{2k+1} e^{-t}\Big|_{t=9+(2k+2)} = \left(1 - C_{2k+2} e^{-t}\right)\Big|_{t=9+(2k+2)}$$
$$\Rightarrow \qquad C_{2k+1} e^{-(11+2k)} = 1 - C_{2k+2} e^{-(11+2k)}$$
$$\Rightarrow \qquad C_{2k+2} = e^{11+2k} - C_{2k+1}\,.$$

In general we see that for any integer j (even or odd) the following formula holds:

$$C_j = e^{9+j} - C_{j-1}.$$

Using this recurrence formula we successively compute

$$C_1 = e^{10} - C_0 = e^{10} - e^9 = e^9(e - 1)$$
$$C_2 = e^{11} - C_1 = e^{11} - e^{10} + e^9 = e^9(e^2 - e + 1)$$
$$\vdots$$
$$C_j = e^9 \sum_{k=0}^{j} (-1)^{j-k} e^k\,.$$

Therefore, the temperature at noon (when $t = 12$ and $j = 3$) is

$$T_3(12) = C_3 e^{-12} = e^{-12} e^9 \sum_{k=0}^{3} (-1)^{3-k} e^k = 1 - e^{-1} + e^{-2} - e^{-3} \approx 0.718 = 71.8^\circ \text{ F}.$$

At 5 P.M.(when $t = 17$ and $j = 8$), we find

$$\begin{aligned} T_8(17) = 1 - C_8 e^{-17} &= 1 - e^{-17} e^9 \sum_{k=0}^{8} (-1)^{8-k} e^k = \sum_{k=1}^{8} (-1)^{k+1} e^{-k} \\ &= e^{-1} \cdot \frac{1 - (-e^{-1})^8}{1 + e^{-1}} \approx 0.269 = 26.9^\circ \text{ F}. \end{aligned}$$

EXERCISES 2.4: Exact Equations, page 65

1. In this equation, $M(x, y) = x^2 y + x^4 \cos x$ and $N(x, y) = -x^3$. Taking partial derivatives, we obtain

$$\frac{\partial M}{\partial y} = \frac{\partial}{\partial y} \left(x^2 y + x^4\right) = x^2 \neq -3x^2 = \frac{\partial N}{\partial x}.$$

Therefore, according to Theorem 2 on page 61 of the text, the equation is not exact.

Rewriting the equation in the form

$$\frac{dy}{dx} = \frac{x^2 y + x^4 \cos x}{x^3} = \frac{1}{x} y + x \cos x, \tag{2.14}$$

we conclude that it is not separable because the right-hand side in (2.14) cannot be factored as $p(x)q(y)$. We also see that the equation is linear with y as the dependent variable.

3. Here $M(x, y) = y e^{xy} + 2x$, $N(x, y) = x e^{xy} - 2y$. Thus

$$\begin{aligned} \frac{\partial M}{\partial y} &= \frac{\partial}{\partial y} \left(y e^{xy} + 2x\right) = e^{xy} + y \frac{\partial}{\partial y} \left(e^{xy}\right) = e^{xy} + y e^{xy} x = e^{xy}(1 + yx), \\ \frac{\partial N}{\partial x} &= \frac{\partial}{\partial x} \left(x e^{xy} - 2y\right) = e^{xy} + x \frac{\partial}{\partial x} \left(e^{xy}\right) = e^{xy} + x e^{xy} y = e^{xy}(1 + xy), \end{aligned}$$

$\partial M/\partial y = \partial N/\partial x$, and the equation is exact.

We write the equation in the form

$$\frac{dy}{dx} = -\frac{y e^{xy} + 2x}{x e^{xy} - 2y}$$

and conclude that it is not separable because the right-hand side cannot be represented as a product of two functions of single variables x and y. Also, the right-hand side is not linear with respect to y which implies that the equation is not linear with y as the dependent variable. Similarly, choosing x as the dependent variable (taking the reciprocals of both sides) we conclude that the equation is not linear either.

5. The differential equation is not separable because $(2xy + \cos y)$ cannot be factored. This equation can be put in standard form by defining x as the dependent variable and y as the independent variable. This gives

$$\frac{dx}{dy} + \frac{2}{y}x = \frac{-\cos y}{y^2},$$

so we see that the differential equation is linear.

If we set $M(x, y) = y^2$ and $N(x, y) = 2xy + \cos y$ we are able to see that the differential equation is also exact because $M_y(x, y) = 2y = N_x(x, y)$.

7. In this problem, the variables are r and θ, $M(r, \theta) = \theta$, and $N(r, \theta) = 3r - \theta - 1$. Because

$$\frac{\partial M}{\partial \theta} = 1 \neq 3 = \frac{\partial N}{\partial r},$$

the equation is not exact. With r as the dependent variable, the equation takes the form

$$\frac{dr}{d\theta} = -\frac{3r - \theta - 1}{\theta} = -\frac{3}{\theta}r + \frac{\theta + 1}{\theta},$$

and it is linear. Since the right-hand side in the above equation cannot be factored as $p(\theta)q(r)$, the equation is not separable.

9. We have that $M(x, y) = 2xy + 3$ and $N(x, y) = x^2 - 1$. Therefore, $M_y(x, y) = 2x = N_x(x, y)$ and so the equation is exact. We will solve this equation by first integrating $M(x, y)$ with respect to x, although integration of $N(x, y)$ with respect to y is equally easy. Thus

$$F(x, y) = \int (2xy + 3)\, dx = x^2y + 3x + g(y).$$

Differentiating $F(x,y)$ with respect to y gives $F_y(x,y) = x^2 + g'(y) = N(x,y) = x^2 - 1$. From this we see that $g' = -1$. (As a partial check we note that $g'(y)$ does not involve x.) Integrating gives

$$g(y) = \int (-1)\,dy = -y.$$

Since the constant of integration will be incorporated into the parameter of the solution, it is not written here. Substituting this expression for $g(y)$ into the expression that we found for $F(x,y)$ yields

$$F(x,y) = x^2y + 3x - y.$$

Therefore, the solution of the differential equation is

$$x^2y + 3x - y = C \qquad \Rightarrow \qquad y = \frac{C - 3x}{x^2 - 1}.$$

The given equation could be solved by the method of grouping. To see this, express the differential equation in the form

$$(2xy\,dx + x^2\,dy) + (3\,dx - dy) = 0.$$

The first term of the left-hand side we recognize as the total differential of x^2y. The second term is the total differential of $(3x - y)$. Thus we again find that

$$F(x,y) = x^2y + 3x - y$$

and, again, the solution is $x^2y + 3x - y = C$.

11. Computing partial derivatives of $M(x,y) = \cos x \cos y + 2x$ and $N(x,y) = -(\sin x \sin y + 2y)$, we obtain

$$\begin{aligned} \frac{\partial M}{\partial y} &= \frac{\partial}{\partial y}(\cos x \cos y + 2x) = -\cos x \sin y\,, \\ \frac{\partial N}{\partial x} &= \frac{\partial}{\partial x}\left[-(\sin x \sin y + 2y)\right] = -\cos x \sin y\,, \\ \Rightarrow \qquad & \frac{\partial M}{\partial y} = \frac{\partial N}{\partial x}\,, \end{aligned}$$

and the equation is exact.

Integrating $M(x,y)$ with respect to x yields

$$\begin{aligned} F(x,y) = \int M(x,y)dx &= \int (\cos x \cos y + 2x)\,dx \\ &= \cos y \int \cos x\,dx + \int 2x\,dx = \sin x \cos y + x^2 + g(y). \end{aligned}$$

To find $g(y)$, we compute the partial derivative of $F(x,y)$ with respect to y and compare the result with $N(x,y)$.

$$\frac{\partial F}{\partial y} = \frac{\partial}{\partial y}\left[\sin x \cos y + x^2 + g(y)\right] = -\sin x \sin y + g'(y) = -\left(\sin x \sin y + 2y\right)$$

$$\Rightarrow \qquad g'(y) = -2y \qquad \Rightarrow \qquad g(y) = \int (-2y)dy = -y^2.$$

(We take the integration constant $C = 0$.) Therefore,

$$F(x,y) = \sin x \cos y + x^2 - y^2 = c$$

is a general solution to the given equation.

13. In this equation, the variables are y and t, $M(y,t) = t/y$, $N(y,t) = 1 + \ln y$. Since

$$\frac{\partial M}{\partial t} = \frac{\partial}{\partial t}\left(\frac{t}{y}\right) = \frac{1}{y} \qquad \text{and} \qquad \frac{\partial N}{\partial y} = \frac{\partial}{\partial y}\left(1 + \ln y\right) = \frac{1}{y},$$

the equation is exact.

Integrating $M(y,t)$ with respect to y, we get

$$F(y,t) = \int \frac{t}{y}\,dy = t\ln|y| + g(t) = t\ln y + g(t).$$

(From $N(y,t) = 1 + \ln y$ we conclude that $y > 0$.) Therefore,

$$\begin{aligned} \frac{\partial F}{\partial t} &= \frac{\partial}{\partial t}\left[t\ln y + g(t)\right] = \ln y + g'(t) = 1 + \ln y \\ \Rightarrow \quad & g'(t) = 1 \qquad \Rightarrow \qquad g(t) = t \\ \Rightarrow \quad & F(y,t) = t\ln y + t, \end{aligned}$$

and a general solution is given by $t\ln y + t = c$ (or, explicitly, $t = c/(\ln y + 1)$).

15. This differential equation is expressed in the variables r and θ. Since the variables x and y are dummy variables, this equation is solved in exactly the same way as an equation in x and y. We will look for a solution with independent variable θ and dependent variable r. We see that the differential equation is expressed in the differential form

$$M(r,\theta)\,dr + N(r,\theta)\,d\theta = 0, \quad \text{where} \quad M(r,\theta) = \cos\theta \text{ and } N(r,\theta) = -r\sin\theta + e^{\theta}.$$

This implies that

$$M_{\theta}(r,\theta) = -\sin\theta = N_r(r,\theta),$$

and so the equation is exact. Therefore, to solve the equation we need to find a function $F(r,\theta)$ that has $\cos\theta\,dr + (-r\sin\theta + e^{\theta})\,d\theta$ as its total differential. Integrating $M(r,\theta)$ with respect to r we see that

$$F(r,\theta) = \int \cos\theta\,dr = r\cos\theta + g(\theta)$$
$$\Rightarrow \qquad F_{\theta}(r,\theta) = -r\sin\theta + g'(\theta) = N(r,\theta) = -r\sin\theta + e^{\theta}.$$

Thus we have that

$$g'(\theta) = e^{\theta} \qquad \Rightarrow \qquad g(\theta) = e^{\theta},$$

where the constant of integration will be incorporated into the parameter of the solution. Substituting this expression for $g(\theta)$ into the expression we found for $F(r,\theta)$ yields

$$F(r,\theta) = r\cos\theta + e^{\theta}.$$

From this we see that the solution is given by the one parameter family $r\cos\theta + e^{\theta} = C$, or, solving for r,

$$r = \frac{C - e^{\theta}}{\cos\theta} = (C - e^{\theta})\sec\theta.$$

17. Partial derivatives of $M(x,y) = 1/y$ and $N(x,y) = -\left(3y - x/y^2\right)$ are

$$\frac{\partial M}{\partial y} = \frac{\partial}{\partial y}\left(\frac{1}{y}\right) = -\frac{1}{y^2} \quad \text{and} \quad \frac{\partial N}{\partial x} = \frac{\partial}{\partial x}\left(-3y + \frac{x}{y^2}\right) = \frac{1}{y^2}\,.$$

Since $\partial M/\partial y \neq \partial N/\partial x$, the equation is not exact.

19. Taking partial derivatives of $M(x,y)=2x+y/(1+x^2y^2)$ and $N(x,y)=-2y+x/(1+x^2y^2)$ with respect to y and x, respectively, we get

$$\begin{aligned}\frac{\partial M}{\partial y}&=\frac{\partial}{\partial y}\left(2x+\frac{y}{1+x^2y^2}\right)=\frac{(1)(1+x^2y^2)-yx^2(2y)}{(1+x^2y^2)^2}=\frac{1-x^2y^2}{(1+x^2y^2)^2}\,,\\ \frac{\partial N}{\partial x}&=\frac{\partial}{\partial x}\left(-2y+\frac{x}{1+x^2y^2}\right)=\frac{(1)(1+x^2y^2)-xy^2(2x)}{(1+x^2y^2)^2}=\frac{1-x^2y^2}{(1+x^2y^2)^2}\,.\end{aligned}$$

Therefore, the equation is exact.

$$\begin{aligned}F(x,y)&=\int\left(2x+\frac{y}{1+x^2y^2}\right)dx=x^2+\int\frac{d(xy)}{1+(xy)^2}=x^2+\arctan(xy)+g(y)\\ \frac{\partial F}{\partial y}&=\frac{\partial}{\partial y}\left[x^2+\arctan(xy)+g(y)\right]=\frac{x}{1+(xy)^2}+g'(y)=-2y+\frac{x}{1+x^2y^2}\\ \Rightarrow\quad & g'(y)=-2y \quad\Rightarrow\quad g(y)=-y^2\\ \Rightarrow\quad & F(x,y)=x^2-y^2+\arctan(xy)\end{aligned}$$

and a general solution then is given implicitly by $x^2-y^2+\arctan(xy)=c$.

21. We check the equation for exactness. We have $M(x,y)=1/x+2y^2x$, $N(x,y)=2yx^2-\cos y$,

$$\begin{aligned}\frac{\partial M}{\partial y}&=\frac{\partial}{\partial y}\left(\frac{1}{x}+2y^2x\right)=4yx,\\ \frac{\partial N}{\partial x}&=\frac{\partial}{\partial x}\left(2yx^2-\cos y\right)=4yx.\end{aligned}$$

Thus $\partial M/\partial y=\partial N/\partial x$. Integrating $M(x,y)$ with respect to x yields

$$F(x,y)=\int\left(\frac{1}{x}+2y^2x\right)dx=\ln|x|+x^2y^2+g(y).$$

Therefore,

$$\begin{aligned}\frac{\partial F}{\partial y}&=\frac{\partial}{\partial y}\left[\ln|x|+x^2y^2+g(y)\right]=2x^2y+g'(y)=N(x,y)=2yx^2-\cos y\\ \Rightarrow\quad & g'(y)=-\cos y \quad\Rightarrow\quad g(y)=\int(-\cos y)dy=-\sin y\\ \Rightarrow\quad & F(x,y)=\ln|x|+x^2y^2-\sin y,\end{aligned}$$

and a general solution to the given differential equation is

$$\ln|x|+x^2y^2-\sin y=c.$$

Substituting the initial condition, $y = \pi$ when $x = 1$, we find c.

$$\ln|1| + 1^2\pi^2 - \sin\pi = c \qquad \Rightarrow \qquad c = \pi^2.$$

Therefore, the answer is given implicitly by $\ln|x| + x^2y^2 - \sin y = \pi^2$. (We also used the fact that at the initial point, $(1, \pi)$, $x > 0$ to skip the absolute value sign in the logarithmic term.)

23. Here $M(t, y) = e^t y + te^t y$ and $N(t, y) = te^t + 2$. Thus $M_y(t, y) = e^t + te^t = N_t(t, y)$ and so the equation is exact. To find $F(t, y)$ we first integrate $N(t, y)$ with respect to y to obtain

$$F(t, y) = \int (te^t + 2)\,dy = (te^t + 2)y + h(t),$$

where we have chosen to integrate $N(t, y)$ because this integration is more easily accomplished. Thus

$$F_t(t, y) = e^t y + te^t y + h'(t) = M(t, y) = e^t y + te^t y$$
$$\Rightarrow \qquad h'(t) = 0 \qquad \Rightarrow \qquad h(t) = C.$$

We will incorporate this constant into the parameter of the solution. Combining these results gives $F(t, y) = te^t y + 2y$. Therefore, the solution is given by $te^t y + 2y = C$. Solving for y yields $y = C/(te^t + 2)$. Now we use the initial condition $y(0) = -1$ to find the solution that passes through the point $(0, -1)$. Thus

$$y(0) = \frac{C}{0+2} = -1 \qquad \Rightarrow \qquad \frac{C}{2} = -1 \qquad \Rightarrow \qquad C = -2.$$

This gives us the solution

$$y = -\frac{2}{te^t + 2}.$$

25. One can check that the equation is not exact ($\partial M/\partial y \neq \partial N/\partial x$), but it is separable because it can be written in the form

$$y^2 \sin x\,dx + \frac{1-y}{x}\,dy = 0 \qquad \Rightarrow \qquad y^2 \sin x\,dx = \frac{y-1}{x}\,dy$$
$$\Rightarrow \qquad x \sin x\,dx = \frac{y-1}{y^2}\,dy.$$

Integrating both sides yields

$$\int x\sin x\,dx = \int \frac{y-1}{y^2}\,dy \qquad \Rightarrow \qquad x(-\cos x) - \int (-\cos x)dx = \int \left(\frac{1}{y} - \frac{1}{y^2}\right) dy$$

$$\Rightarrow \qquad -x\cos x + \sin x = \ln|y| + \frac{1}{y} + C,$$

where we applied integration by parts to find $\int x\sin x\,dx$. Substitution of the initial condition, $y(\pi) = 1$, results

$$-\pi\cos\pi + \sin\pi = \ln|1| + \frac{1}{1} + C \qquad \Rightarrow \qquad C = \pi - 1.$$

So, the solution to the initial value problem is

$$-x\cos x + \sin x = \ln y + 1/y + \pi - 1\,.$$

(Since $y(\pi) = 1 > 0$, we have removed the absolute value sign in the logarithmic term.)

27. **(a)** We want to find $M(x,y)$ so that for $N(x,y) = \sec^2 y - x/y$ we have

$$M_y(x,y) = N_x(x,y) = -\frac{1}{y}\,.$$

Therefore, we must integrate this last expression with respect to y. That is,

$$M(x,y) = \int \left(-\frac{1}{y}\right) dy = -\ln|y| + f(x),$$

where $f(x)$, the "constant" of integration, is a function only of x.

(b) We want to find $M(x,y)$ so that for

$$N(x,y) = \sin x\cos y - xy - e^{-y}$$

we have

$$M_y(x,y) = N_x(x,y) = \cos x\cos y - y.$$

Therefore, we must integrate this last expression with respect to y. That is

$$\begin{aligned} M(x,y) &= \int (\cos x\cos y - y)\,dy = \cos x \int \cos y\,dy - \int y\,dy \\ &= \cos x\sin y - \frac{y^2}{2} + f(x), \end{aligned}$$

where $f(x)$, a function only of x, is the "constant" of integration.

29. **(a)** We have $M(x,y) = y^2 + 2xy$ and $N(x,y) = -x^2$. Therefore $M_y(x,y) = 2y + 2x$ and $N_x(x,y) = -2x$. Thus $M_y(x,y) \neq N_x(x,y)$, so the differential equation is not exact.

(b) If we multiply $(y^2 + 2xy)dx - x^2 dy = 0$ by y^{-2}, we obtain

$$\left(1 + \frac{2x}{y}\right) dx - \frac{x^2}{y^2}\, dy = 0.$$

In this equation we have $M(x,y) = 1 + 2xy^{-1}$ and $N(x,y) = -x^2 y^{-2}$. Therefore,

$$\frac{\partial M(x,y)}{\partial y} = -\frac{2x}{y^2} = \frac{\partial N(x,y)}{\partial x}\,.$$

So the new differential equation is exact.

(c) Following the method for solving exact equations we integrate $M(x,y)$ in part (b) with respect to x to obtain

$$F(x,y) = \int \left(1 + 2\,\frac{x}{y}\right) dx = x + \frac{x^2}{y} + g(y)\,.$$

To determine $g(y)$, take the partial derivative of both sides of the above equation with respect to y to obtain

$$\frac{\partial F}{\partial y} = -\frac{x^2}{y^2} + g'(y)\,.$$

Substituting $N(x,y)$ (given in part (b)) for $\partial F/\partial y$, we can now solve for $g'(y)$ to obtain

$$N(x,y) = -\frac{x^2}{y^2} = -\frac{x^2}{y^2} + g'(y) \qquad \Rightarrow \qquad g'(y) = 0\,.$$

The integral of $g'(y)$ will yield a constant and the choice of the constant of integration is not important so we can take $g(y) = 0$. Hence we have $F(x,y) = x + x^2/y$ and the solution to the equation is given implicitly by

$$x + \frac{x^2}{y} = C\,.$$

Solving the above equation for y, we obtain

$$y = \frac{x^2}{C - x}\,.$$

(d) By dividing both sides by y^2 we lost the solution $y \equiv 0$.

31. Following the proof of Theorem 2, we come to the expression (10) on page 63 of the text for $g'(y)$, that is

$$g'(y) = N(x, y) - \frac{\partial}{\partial y} \int_{x_0}^{x} M(s, y)\, ds \tag{2.15}$$

(where we have replaced the integration variable t by s). In other words, $g(y)$ is an antiderivative of the right-hand side in (2.15). Since an antiderivative is defined up to an additive constant and, in Theorem 2, such a constant can be chosen arbitrarily (that is, $g(y)$ can be *any* antiderivative), we choose $g(y)$ that vanishes at y_0. According to fundamental theorem of calculus, this function can be written in the form

$$\begin{aligned}
g(y) = \int_{y_0}^{y} g'(t)\, dt &= \int_{y_0}^{y} \left[N(x, t) - \frac{\partial}{\partial t} \int_{x_0}^{x} M(s, t)\, ds \right] dt \\
&= \int_{y_0}^{y} N(x, t)\, dt - \int_{y_0}^{y} \frac{\partial}{\partial t} \left[\int_{x_0}^{x} M(s, t)\, ds \right] dt \\
&= \int_{y_0}^{y} N(x, t)\, dt - \left[\int_{x_0}^{x} M(s, t)\, ds \right] \Bigg|_{t=y_0}^{t=y} \\
&= \int_{y_0}^{y} N(x, t)\, dt - \int_{x_0}^{x} M(s, y)\, ds + \int_{x_0}^{x} M(s, y_0)\, ds\,.
\end{aligned}$$

Substituting this function into the formula (9) on page 63 of the text, we conclude that

$$\begin{aligned}
F(x, y) &= \int_{x_0}^{x} M(t, y)\, dt + \left[\int_{y_0}^{y} N(x, t)\, dt - \int_{x_0}^{x} M(s, y)\, ds + \int_{x_0}^{x} M(s, y_0)\, ds \right] \\
&= \int_{y_0}^{y} N(x, t)\, dt + \int_{x_0}^{x} M(s, y_0)\, ds\,.
\end{aligned}$$

(a) In the differential form used in Example 1, $M(x, y) = 2xy^2 + 1$ and $N(x, y) = 2x^2y$.

Thus, $N(x,t)=2x^2t$ and $M(s,y_0)=2s\cdot 0^2+1=1$, and (18) yields

$$\begin{aligned} F(x,y) &= \int_0^y \left(2x^2t\right)dt+\int_0^x 1\cdot ds = x^2\int_0^y 2t\,dt+\int_0^x ds \\ &= x^2t^2\Big|_{t=0}^{t=y}+s\Big|_{s=0}^{s=x}=x^2y^2+x. \end{aligned}$$

(b) Since $M(x,y)=2xy-\sec^2 x$ and $N(x,y)=x^2+2y$, we have

$$N(x,t)=x^2+2t \quad \text{and} \quad M(s,y_0)=2s\cdot 0-\sec^2 s=-\sec^2 s,$$

$$\begin{aligned} F(x,y) &= \int_0^y \left(x^2+2t\right)dt+\int_0^x \left(-\sec^2 s\right)ds \\ &= \left(x^2t+t^2\right)\Big|_{t=0}^{t=y}-\tan s\Big|_{s=0}^{s=x}=x^2y+y^2-\tan x. \end{aligned}$$

(c) Here, $M(x,y)=1+e^xy+xe^xy$ and $N(x,y)=xe^x+2$. Therefore,

$$N(x,t)=xe^x+2 \quad \text{and} \quad M(s,y_0)=1+e^s\cdot 0+se^s\cdot 0=1,$$

$$\begin{aligned} F(x,y) &= \int_0^y \left(xe^x+2\right)dt+\int_0^x 1\cdot ds \\ &= \left(xe^x+2\right)t\Big|_{t=0}^{t=y}+s\Big|_{s=0}^{s=x}=\left(xe^x+2\right)y+x, \end{aligned}$$

which is identical to $F(x,y)$ obtained in Example 3.

32. **(a)** The slope of the orthogonal curves, say $m_\perp$, must be $-1/m$, where m is the slope of the original curves. Therefore, we have

$$m_\perp=\frac{F_y(x,y)}{F_x(x,y)} \quad \Rightarrow \quad \frac{dy}{dx}=\frac{F_y(x,y)}{F_x(x,y)} \quad \Rightarrow \quad F_y(x,y)\,dx-F_x(x,y)\,dy=0.$$

(b) Let $F(x,y)=x^2+y^2$. Then we have $F_x(x,y)=2x$ and $F_y(x,y)=2y$. Plugging these expressions into the final result of part (a) gives

$$2y\,dx-2x\,dy=0 \quad \Rightarrow \quad y\,dx-x\,dy=0.$$

To find the orthogonal trajectories, we must solve this differential equation. To this end, note that this equation is separable and thus

$$\int \frac{1}{x}\,dx = \int \frac{1}{y}\,dy \quad \Rightarrow \quad \ln|x| = \ln|y| + C$$
$$\Rightarrow \quad e^{\ln|x|-C} = e^{\ln|y|} \quad \Rightarrow \quad y = kx, \quad \text{where } k = \pm e^{-C}.$$

Therefore, the orthogonal trajectories are lines through the origin.

(c) Let $F(x,y) = xy$. Then we have $F_x(x,y) = y$ and $F_y(x,y) = x$. Plugging these expressions into the final result of part (a) gives

$$x\,dx - y\,dy = 0.$$

To find the orthogonal trajectories, we must solve this differential equation. To this end, note that this equation is separable and thus

$$\int x\,dx = \int y\,dy \quad \Rightarrow \quad \frac{x^2}{2} = \frac{y^2}{2} + C \quad \Rightarrow \quad x^2 - y^2 = k\,,$$

where $k := 2C$. Therefore, the orthogonal trajectories are hyperbolas.

33. We use notations and results of Problem 32, that is, for a family of curves given by $F(x,y) = k$, the orthogonal trajectories satisfy the differential equation

$$\frac{\partial F(x,y)}{\partial y}\,dx - \frac{\partial F(x,y)}{\partial x}\,dy = 0. \tag{2.16}$$

(a) In this problem, $F(x,y) = 2x^2 + y^2$ and the equation (2.16) becomes

$$\frac{\partial(2x^2+y^2)}{\partial y}\,dx - \frac{\partial(2x^2+y^2)}{\partial x}\,dy = 0 \quad \Rightarrow \quad 2y\,dx - 4x\,dy = 0. \tag{2.17}$$

Separating variables and integrating yield

$$2y\,dx = 4x\,dy \quad \Rightarrow \quad \frac{dx}{x} = \frac{2dy}{y} \quad \Rightarrow \quad \int \frac{dx}{x} = \int \frac{2dy}{y}$$
$$\Rightarrow \quad \ln|x| = 2\ln|y| + c_1 \quad \Rightarrow \quad e^{\ln|x|} = e^{2\ln|y|+c_1}$$
$$\Rightarrow \quad |x| = e^{c_1}|y|^2 = c_2 y^2 \quad \Rightarrow \quad x = \pm c_2 y^2 = cy^2,$$

where c as any nonzero constant.

Separating variables, we divided the equation (2.17) by xy. As a result, we lost two constant solutions $x \equiv 0$ and $y \equiv 0$ (see the discussion on pages 44–45 of Section 2.2 of the text). Thus the orthogonal trajectories for the family $2x^2 + y^2 = k$ are $x = cy^2$, $c \neq 0$, $x \equiv 0$, and $y \equiv 0$. (Note that $x \equiv 0$ can be obtained from $x = cy^2$ by taking $c = 0$ while $y \equiv 0$ cannot.)

(b) First we rewrite the equation defining the family of curves in the form $F(x, y) = k$ by dividing it by x^4. This yields $yx^{-4} = k$. We use (2.17) to set up an equation for the orthogonal trajectories:

$$\frac{\partial F}{\partial x} = -4yx^{-5}, \qquad \frac{\partial F}{\partial y} = x^{-4} \qquad \Rightarrow \qquad x^{-4}\,dx - \left(-4yx^{-5}\right) dy = 0\,.$$

Solving this separable equation yields

$$x^{-4}\,dx = -4yx^{-5}\,dy = 0 \qquad \Rightarrow \qquad x\,dx = -4y\,dy$$
$$\Rightarrow \qquad \int x\,dx = \int (-4y)dy \qquad \Rightarrow \qquad \frac{x^2}{2} = -2y^2 + c_1 \qquad \Rightarrow \qquad x^2 + 4y^2 = c.$$

Thus, the family of orthogonal trajectories is $x^2 + 4y^2 = c$.

(c) Taking logarithm of both sides of the equation, we obtain

$$\ln y = kx \qquad \Rightarrow \qquad \frac{\ln y}{x} = k,$$

and so $F(x, y) = (\ln y)/x$, $\partial F/\partial x = -(\ln y)/x^2$, $\partial F/\partial y = 1/(xy)$. The equation (2.17) becomes

$$\frac{1}{xy}\,dx - \left(-\frac{\ln y}{x^2}\right) dy = 0 \qquad \Rightarrow \qquad \frac{1}{xy}\,dx = -\frac{\ln y}{x^2}\,dy.$$

Separating variables and integrating, we obtain

$$x\,dx = -y\ln y\,dy \qquad \Rightarrow \qquad \int x\,dx = -\int y\ln y\,dy$$
$$\Rightarrow \qquad \frac{x^2}{2} = -\frac{y^2}{2}\ln y + \int \frac{y^2}{2}\cdot\frac{1}{y}\,dy = -\frac{y^2}{2}\ln y + \frac{y^2}{4} + c_1$$
$$\Rightarrow \qquad \frac{x^2}{2} + \frac{y^2}{2}\ln y - \frac{y^2}{4} = c_1 \qquad \Rightarrow \qquad 2x^2 + 2y^2\ln y - y^2 = c,$$

where $c := 4c_1$, and we have used integration by parts to find $\int y\ln y\,dy$.

(d) We divide the equation, $y^2 = kx$, by x and get $y^2/x = k$. Thus, $F(x,y) = y^2/x$ and

$$\frac{\partial F}{\partial x} = -\frac{y^2}{x^2}, \qquad \frac{\partial F}{\partial y} = \frac{2y}{x}$$

$$\Rightarrow \quad \frac{2y}{x}\,dx - \left(-\frac{y^2}{x^2}\right)dy = 0 \quad \Rightarrow \quad \frac{2y}{x}\,dx = \left(-\frac{y^2}{x^2}\right)dy$$

$$\Rightarrow \quad 2x\,dx = -y\,dy \quad \Rightarrow \quad x^2 = -\frac{y^2}{2} + c_1 \quad \Rightarrow \quad 2x^2 + y^2 = c.$$

35. Applying Leibniz's theorem, we switch the order of differentiation (with respect to y) and integration. This yields

$$g' = N(x,y) - \int_{x_0}^{x} \left(\frac{\partial}{\partial y} M(t,y)\right) dt.$$

Therefore, g' is differentiable (even continuously) with respect to x as a difference of two (continuously) differentiable functions, $N(x,y)$ and an integral with variable upper bound of a continuous function $M'_y(t,y)$. Taking partial derivatives of both sides with respect to x and using fundamental theorem of calculus, we obtain

$$\begin{aligned}\frac{\partial\,(g')}{\partial x} &= \frac{\partial}{\partial x}\left[N(x,y) - \int_{x_0}^{x}\left(\frac{\partial}{\partial y}M(t,y)\right)dt\right] \\ &= \frac{\partial}{\partial x}N(x,y) - \frac{\partial}{\partial x}\left[\int_{x_0}^{x}\left(\frac{\partial}{\partial y}M(t,y)\right)dt\right] = \frac{\partial}{\partial x}N(x,y) - \frac{\partial}{\partial y}M(x,y) = 0\end{aligned}$$

due to (5). Thus $\partial\,(g')\,/\partial x \equiv 0$ which implies that g' does not depend on x (a consequence of mean value theorem).

EXERCISES 2.5: Special Integrating Factors, page 71

1. Here $M(x,y) = 2y^3 + 2y^2$ and $N(x,y) = 3y^2x + 2xy$. Computing

$$\frac{\partial M}{\partial y} = 6y^2 + 4y \qquad \text{and} \qquad \frac{\partial N}{\partial x} = 3y^2 + 2y\,,$$

we conclude that this equation is not exact. Note that these functions, as well as M itself, depend on y only. Then, clearly, so does the expression $(\partial N/\partial x - \partial M/\partial y)/M$, and the equation has an integrating factor depending on y alone. Also, since

$$\frac{\partial M/\partial y - \partial N/\partial x}{N} = \frac{(6y^2+4y)-(3y^2+2y)}{3y^2x+2xy} = \frac{3y^2+2y}{x(3y^2+2y)} = \frac{1}{x},$$

the equation has an integrating factor depending on x.

Writing the equation in the form

$$\frac{dx}{dy} = -\frac{3y^2x+2xy}{2y^3+y^2} = -\frac{xy(3y+2)}{2y^2(y+1)} = -\frac{y(3y+2)}{2y^2(y+1)}x$$

we conclude that it is separable and linear with x as the dependent variable.

3. This equation is not separable because of the factor (y^2+2xy). It is not linear because of the factor y^2. To see if it is exact, we compute $M_y(x,y)$ and $N_x(x,y)$, and see that

$$M_y(x,y)2y+2x \neq -2x = N_x(x,y).$$

Therefore, the equation is not exact. To see if we can find an integrating factor of the form $\mu(x)$, we compute

$$\frac{\dfrac{\partial M}{\partial y}-\dfrac{\partial N}{\partial x}}{N} = \frac{2y+4x}{-x^2},$$

which is not a function of x alone. To see if we can find an integrating factor of the form $\mu(y)$, we compute

$$\frac{\dfrac{\partial N}{\partial x}-\dfrac{\partial M}{\partial y}}{M} = \frac{-4x-2y}{y^2+2xy} = \frac{-2(2x+y)}{y(y+2x)} = \frac{-2}{y}.$$

Thus the equation has an integrating factor that is a function of y alone.

5. In this problem, $M(x,y)=2y^2x-y$ and $N(x,y)=x$. Therefore,

$$\frac{\partial M}{\partial y} = 4yx-1 \quad \text{and} \quad \frac{\partial N}{\partial x} = 1 \quad \Rightarrow \quad \frac{\partial N}{\partial x}-\frac{\partial M}{\partial y} = 2-4yx\,.$$

The equation is not exact, because $\partial M/\partial y \neq \partial N/\partial x$, but it has an integrating factor depending just on y since

$$\frac{\partial N/\partial x - \partial M/\partial y}{M} = \frac{2-4yx}{2y^2x-y} = \frac{-2(2yx-1)}{y(2yx-1)} = \frac{-2}{y}.$$

Isolating dy/dx, we obtain

$$\frac{dy}{dx} = \frac{y - 2y^2 x}{x} = \frac{y}{x} - 2y^2 .$$

The right-hand side cannot be factorized as $p(x)q(y)$, and so the equation is not separable. Also, it is not linear with y as the dependent variable (because of $2y^2$ term). By taking the reciprocals we also conclude that it is not linear with the dependent variable x.

7. The equation $(3x^2 + y)\,dx + (x^2 y - x)\,dy = 0$ is not separable or linear. To see if it is exact, we compute

$$\frac{\partial M}{\partial y} = 1 \neq 2xy - 1 = \frac{\partial N}{\partial x} .$$

Thus, the equation is not exact. To see if we can find an integrating factor, we compute

$$\frac{\partial M/\partial y - \partial N/\partial x}{N} = \frac{2 - 2xy}{x^2 y - x} = \frac{-2(xy-1)}{x(xy-1)} = \frac{-2}{x} .$$

From this we see that the integrating factor will be

$$\mu(x) = \exp\left(\int \frac{-2}{x}\,dx\right) = \exp\left(-2\ln|x|\right) = x^{-2}.$$

To solve the equation, we multiply it by the integrating factor x^{-2} to obtain

$$(3 + yx^{-2})\,dx + (y - x^{-1})\,dy = 0.$$

This is now exact. Thus, we want to find $F(x, y)$. To do this, we integrate $M(x, y) = 3 + yx^{-2}$ with respect to x to get

$$F(x,y) = \int (3 + yx^{-2})\,dx = 3x - yx^{-1} + g(y)$$

$$\Rightarrow \quad F_y(x,y) = -x^{-1} + g'(y) = N(x,y) = y - x^{-1}$$

$$\Rightarrow \quad g'(y) = y \quad \Rightarrow \quad g(y) = \frac{y^2}{2} .$$

Therefore,

$$F(x,y) = 3x - yx^{-1} + \frac{y^2}{2} .$$

And so we see that an implicit solution is

$$\frac{y^2}{2} - \frac{y}{x} + 3x = C.$$

Since $\mu(x) = x^{-2}$ we must check to see if the solution $x \equiv 0$ was either gained or lost. The function $x \equiv 0$ is a solution to the original equation, but is not given by the above implicit solution for any choice of C. Hence,

$$\frac{y^2}{2} - \frac{y}{x} + 3x = C \qquad \text{and} \qquad x \equiv 0$$

are solutions.

9. We compute partial derivatives of $M(x, y) = 2y^2 + 2y + 4x^2$ and $N(x, y) = 2xy + x$.

$$\frac{\partial M}{\partial y} = \frac{\partial}{\partial y}\left(2y^2 + 2y + 4x^2\right) = 4y + 2, \qquad \frac{\partial N}{\partial x} = \frac{\partial}{\partial x}(2xy + x) = 2y + 1.$$

Although the equation is not exact ($\partial M/\partial y \neq \partial N/\partial x$), the quotient

$$\frac{\partial M/\partial y - \partial N/\partial x}{N} = \frac{(4y + 2) - (2y + 1)}{2xy + x} = \frac{2y + 1}{x(2y + 1)} = \frac{1}{x}$$

depends on x only, and so the equation has an integrating factor, which can be found by applying formula (8) on page 70 of the text. Namely,

$$\mu(x) = \exp\left(\int \frac{1}{x}\, dx\right) = \exp\left(\ln|x|\right) = |x|.$$

Note that if μ is an integrating factor, then $-\mu$ is an integrating factor as well. This observation allows us to take $\mu(x) = x$. Multiplying given differential equation by x yields an exact equation

$$\left(2y^2 + 2y + 4x^2\right) x\, dx + x^2\,(2y + 1)\, dy = 0.$$

Therefore,

$$\begin{aligned}
& F(x, y) = \int x^2(2y + 1)\, dy = x^2\left(y^2 + y\right) + h(x) \\
\Rightarrow \quad & \frac{\partial F}{\partial x} = 2x\left(y^2 + y\right) + h'(x) = \left(2y^2 + 2y + 4x^2\right) x \\
\Rightarrow \quad & h'(x) = 4x^3 \quad \Rightarrow \quad h(x) = \int 4x^3 dx = x^4 \\
\Rightarrow \quad & F(x, y) = x^2\left(y^2 + y\right) + x^4 = x^2y^2 + x^2y + x^4,
\end{aligned}$$

and $x^2y^2 + x^2y + x^4 = c$ is a general solution.

11. In this differential equation, $M(x, y) = y^2 + 2xy$, $N(x, y) = -x^2$. Therefore,

$$\frac{\partial M}{\partial y} = 2y + 2x, \qquad \frac{\partial N}{\partial x} = -2x,$$

and so $(\partial N/\partial x - \partial M/\partial y)/M = (-4x - 2y)/(y^2 + 2xy) = -2/y$ is a function of y. Then

$$\mu(y) = \exp\left[\int\left(-\frac{2}{y}\right)dy\right] = \exp\left(-2\ln|y|\right) = y^{-2}.$$

Multiplying the differential equation by $\mu(y)$ and solving the obtained exact equation, we get

$$\begin{aligned}
&y^{-2}\left(y^2 + 2xy\right)dx - y^{-2}x^2 dy = 0\\
\Rightarrow \quad & F(x, y) = \int\left(-y^{-2}x^2\right)dy = y^{-1}x^2 + h(x)\\
\Rightarrow \quad & \frac{\partial F}{\partial x} = \frac{\partial}{\partial x}\left[y^{-1}x^2 + h(x)\right] = 2y^{-1}x + h'(x) = y^{-2}\left(y^2 + 2xy\right) = 1 + 2xy^{-1}\\
\Rightarrow \quad & h'(x) = 1 \quad \Rightarrow \quad h(x) = x \quad \Rightarrow \quad F(x, y) = y^{-1}x^2 + x.
\end{aligned}$$

Since we multiplied given equation by $\mu(y) = y^{-2}$ (in fact, divided by y^2) to get an exact equation, we could lose the solution $y \equiv 0$, and this, indeed, happened: $y \equiv 0$ is, clearly, a solution to the original equation. Thus a general solution is

$$y^{-1}x^2 + x = c \qquad \text{and} \qquad y \equiv 0.$$

13. We will multiply the equation by the factor $x^n y^m$ and try to make it exact. Thus, we have

$$\left(2x^n y^{m+2} - 6x^{n+1}y^{m+1}\right)dx + \left(3x^{n+1}y^{m+1} - 4x^{n+2}y^m\right)dy = 0.$$

We want $M_y(x, y) = N_x(x, y)$. Since

$$\begin{aligned}
M_y(x, y) &= 2(m + 2)x^n y^{m+1} - 6(m + 1)x^{n+1}y^m,\\
N_x(x, y) &= 3(n + 1)x^n y^{m+1} - 4(n + 2)x^{n+1}y^m,
\end{aligned}$$

we need

$$2(m + 2) = 3(n + 1) \qquad \text{and} \qquad 6(m + 1) = 4(n + 2).$$

Solving these equations simultaneously, we obtain $n = 1$ and $m = 1$. So,

$$\mu(x, y) = xy.$$

With these choices for n and m we obtain the exact equation

$$(2xy^3 - 6x^2y^2)\,dx + (3x^2y^2 - 4x^3y)\,dy = 0.$$

Solving this equation, we have

$$\begin{aligned} F(x, y) &= \int (2xy^3 - 6x^2y^2)\,dx = x^2y^3 - 2x^3y^2 + g(y) \\ \Rightarrow \qquad F_y(x, y) &= 3x^2y^2 - 4x^3y + g'(y) = N(x, y) = 3x^2y^2 - 4x^3y. \end{aligned}$$

Therefore, $g'(y) = 0$. Since the constant of integration can be incorporated into the constant C of the solution, we can pick $g(y) \equiv 0$. Thus, we have

$$F(x, y) = x^2y^3 - 2x^3y^2$$

and the solution becomes

$$x^2y^3 - 2x^3y^2 = C.$$

Since we have multiplied the original equation by xy we could have added the extraneous solutions $y \equiv 0$ or $x \equiv 0$. But, since $y \equiv 0$ implies that $dy/dx \equiv 0$ or $x \equiv 0$ implies that $dx/dy \equiv 0$, $y \equiv 0$ and $x \equiv 0$ are solutions of the original equation as well as the transformed equation.

15. Assume that, for a differential equation

$$M(x, y)dx + N(x, y)dy = 0, \tag{2.18}$$

the expression

$$\frac{\partial N/\partial x - \partial M/\partial y}{xM - yN} = H(xy) \tag{2.19}$$

is a function of xy only. Denoting

$$\mu(z) = \exp\left(\int H(z)dz\right)$$

and multiplying (2.18) by $\mu(xy)$, we get a differential equation

$$\mu(xy)M(x,y)dx + \mu(xy)N(x,y)dy = 0. \tag{2.20}$$

Let us check it for exactness. First we note that

$$\mu'(z) = \left[\exp\left(\int H(z)dz\right)\right]' = \exp\left(\int H(z)dz\right)\left[\int H(z)dz\right]' = \mu(z)H(z).$$

Next, using this fact, we compute partial derivatives of the coefficients in (2.20).

$$\begin{aligned}
\frac{\partial}{\partial y}\{\mu(xy)M(x,y)\} &= \mu'(xy)\frac{\partial(xy)}{\partial y}M(x,y) + \mu(xy)\frac{\partial M(x,y)}{\partial y}\\
&= \mu(xy)H(xy)\,xM(x,y) + \mu(xy)\frac{\partial M(x,y)}{\partial y}\\
&= \mu(xy)\left[H(xy)\,xM(x,y) + \frac{\partial M(x,y)}{\partial y}\right],\\
\frac{\partial}{\partial x}\{\mu(xy)N(x,y)\} &= \mu'(xy)\frac{\partial(xy)}{\partial x}N(x,y) + \mu(xy)\frac{\partial N(x,y)}{\partial x}\\
&= \mu(xy)H(xy)\,yN(x,y) + \mu(xy)\frac{\partial N(x,y)}{\partial x}\\
&= \mu(xy)\left[H(xy)\,yN(x,y) + \frac{\partial N(x,y)}{\partial x}\right].
\end{aligned}$$

But (2.19) implies that

$$\frac{\partial N}{\partial x} - \frac{\partial M}{\partial y} = (xM - yN)H(xy) \quad \Leftrightarrow \quad yNH(xy) + \frac{\partial N}{\partial x} = xMH(xy) + \frac{\partial M}{\partial y},$$

and, therefore,

$$\frac{\partial[\mu(xy)M(x,y)]}{\partial y} = \frac{\partial[\mu(xy)N(x,y)]}{\partial x}.$$

This means that the equation (2.20) is exact.

17. **(a)** Expressing the family $y = x - 1 + ke^{-x}$ in the form $(y - x + 1)e^x = k$, we have (with notation of Problem 32) $F(x,y) = (y - x + 1)e^x$. We compute

$$\begin{aligned}
\frac{\partial F}{\partial x} = \frac{\partial}{\partial x}\left[(y - x + 1)e^x\right] &= \frac{\partial(y - x + 1)}{\partial x}e^x + (y - x + 1)\frac{d(e^x)}{dx}\\
&= -e^x + (y - x + 1)e^x = (y - x)e^x,
\end{aligned}$$

$$\frac{\partial F}{\partial y}=\frac{\partial}{\partial y}\left[(y-x+1)e^{x}\right]=\frac{\partial(y-x+1)}{\partial y}e^{x}=e^{x}.$$

Now we can use the result of Problem 32 to derive an equation for the orthogonal trajectories (i.e., velocity potentials) of the given family of curves:

$$\frac{\partial F}{\partial y}dx-\frac{\partial F}{\partial x}dy=0 \quad\Rightarrow\quad e^{x}\,dx-(y-x)e^{x}\,dy=0 \quad\Rightarrow\quad dx+(x-y)dy=0.$$

(b) In the differential equation $dx+(x-y)dy=0$, $M=1$ and $N=x-y$. Therefore,

$$\frac{\partial N/\partial x-\partial M/\partial y}{M}=\frac{\partial(x-y)/\partial x-\partial(1)/\partial y}{(1)}=1,$$

and an integrating factor $\mu(y)$ is given by $\mu(y)=\exp\left[\int(1)dy\right]=e^{y}$. Multiplying the equation from part (a) by $\mu(y)$ yields an exact equation, and we look for its solutions of the form $G(x,y)=c$.

$$\begin{aligned}
&e^{y}dx+(x-y)e^{y}dy=0\\
\Rightarrow\qquad & G(x,y)=\int e^{y}dx=xe^{y}+g(y)\\
\Rightarrow\qquad & \frac{\partial G}{\partial y}=xe^{y}+g'(y)=(x-y)e^{y}\qquad\Rightarrow\qquad g'(y)=-ye^{y}\\
\Rightarrow\qquad & g(y)=\int(-ye^{y})dy=-\left(ye^{y}-\int e^{y}dy\right)=-ye^{y}+e^{y}.
\end{aligned}$$

Thus, the velocity potentials are given by

$$G(x,y)=xe^{y}-ye^{y}+e^{y}=c\qquad\text{or}\qquad x=y-1+ce^{-y}.$$

EXERCISES 2.6: Substitutions and Transformations, page 78

1. We can write the equation in the form

$$\frac{dy}{dx}=(y-4x-1)^{2}=[(y-4x)-1]^{2}=G(y-4x),$$

where $G(t)=(t-1)^{2}$. Thus, it is of the form $dy/dx=G(ax+by)$.

3. In this equation, the variables are x and t. Its coefficients, $t+x+2$ and $3t-x-6$, are linear functions of x and t. Therefore, given equation is an equation with linear coefficients.

5. The given differential equation is not homogeneous due to the e^{-2x} terms. The equation $(ye^{-2x} + y^3)\,dx - e^{-2x}dy = 0$ is a Bernoulli equation because it can be written in the form $dy/dx + P(x)y = Q(x)y^n$ as follows:

$$\frac{dy}{dx} - y = e^{2x}y^3.$$

The differential equation does not have linear coefficients nor is it of the form $y' = G(ax+by)$.

7. Here, the variables are y and θ. Writing

$$\frac{dy}{d\theta} = -\frac{y^3 - \theta y^2}{2\theta^2 y} = -\frac{(y/\theta)^3 - (y/\theta)^2}{2(y/\theta)},$$

we see that the right-hand side is a function of y/θ alone. Hence, the equation is homogeneous.

9. First, we write the equation in the form

$$\frac{dy}{dx} = \frac{-3x^2 + y^2}{xy - x^3y^{-1}} = \frac{y^3 - 3x^2y}{xy^2 - x^3} = \frac{(y/x)^3 - 3(y/x)}{(y/x)^2 - 1}.$$

Therefore, it is homogeneous, and we we make a substitution $y/x = u$ or $y = xu$. Then $y' = u + xu'$, and the equation becomes

$$u + x\frac{du}{dx} = \frac{u^3 - 3u}{u^2 - 1}.$$

Separating variables and integrating yield

$$\frac{du}{dx} = \frac{u^3 - 3u}{u^2 - 1} - u = -\frac{2u}{u^2 - 1} \quad \Rightarrow \quad \frac{u^2 - 1}{u}\,du = -\frac{2}{x}\,dx$$

$$\Rightarrow \quad \int \frac{u^2 - 1}{u}\,du = -\int \frac{2}{x}\,dx \quad \Rightarrow \quad \int \left(u - \frac{1}{u}\right)du = -2\int \frac{dx}{x}$$

$$\Rightarrow \quad \frac{1}{2}u^2 - \ln|u| = -2\ln|x| + C_1 \quad \Rightarrow \quad u^2 - \ln\left(u^2\right) + \ln(x^4) = C.$$

Substituting back y/x for u and simplifying, we finally get

$$\left(\frac{y}{x}\right)^2 - \ln\left(\frac{y^2}{x^2}\right) + \ln(x^4) = C \quad \Rightarrow \quad \frac{y^2}{x^2} + \ln\left(\frac{x^6}{y^2}\right) = C,$$

which can also be written as

$$\ln\left(\frac{y^2}{x^6}\right) - \frac{y^2}{x^2} = K.$$

11. From

$$\frac{dx}{dy}=\frac{xy-y^2}{x^2}=\frac{y}{x}-\left(\frac{y}{x}\right)^2$$

we conclude that given equation is homogeneous. Let $u=y/x$. Then $y=xu$ and $y'=u+xu'$. Substitution yields

$$\begin{aligned}
&u+x\frac{du}{dx}=u-u^2 &&\Rightarrow\quad x\frac{du}{dx}=-u^2 &&\Rightarrow\quad -\frac{du}{u^2}=\frac{dx}{x}\\
\Rightarrow\quad &-\int\frac{du}{u^2}=\int\frac{dx}{x} &&\Rightarrow\quad \frac{1}{u}=\ln|x|+C\\
\Rightarrow\quad &\frac{x}{y}=\ln|x|+C &&\Rightarrow\quad y=\frac{x}{\ln|x|+C}.
\end{aligned}$$

Note that, solving this equation, we have performed two divisions: by x^2 and u^2. In doing this, we lost two solutions, $x\equiv 0$ and $u\equiv 0$. (The latter gives $y\equiv 0$.) Therefore, a general solution to the given equation is

$$y=\frac{x}{\ln|x|+C},\qquad x\equiv 0,\qquad \text{and}\qquad y\equiv 0.$$

13. Since we can express $f(t,x)$ in the form $G(x/t)$, that is, (dividing numerator and denominator by t^2)

$$\frac{x^2+t\sqrt{t^2+x^2}}{tx}=\frac{(x/t)^2+\sqrt{(x/t)^2}}{(x/t)},$$

the equation is homogeneous. Substituting $v=x/t$ and $dx/dt=v+tdv/dt$ into the equation yields

$$v+t\frac{dv}{dt}=v+\frac{\sqrt{1+v^2}}{v}\qquad\Rightarrow\qquad t\frac{dv}{dt}=\frac{\sqrt{1+v^2}}{v}.$$

This transformed equation is separable. Thus we have

$$\frac{v}{\sqrt{1+v^2}}\,dv=\frac{1}{t}\,dt\qquad\Rightarrow\qquad \sqrt{1+v^2}=\ln|t|+C,$$

where we have integrated with the integration on the left hand side being accomplished by the substitution $u=1+v^2$. Substituting x/t for v in this equation gives the solution to the original equation which is

$$\sqrt{1+\frac{x^2}{t^2}}=\ln|t|+C.$$

15. This equation is homogeneous because

$$\frac{dy}{dx} = \frac{x^2 - y^2}{3xy} = \frac{1 - (y/x)^2}{3(y/x)} .$$

Thus, we substitute $u = y/x$ ($y = xu$ and so $y' = u + xu'$) to get

$$\begin{aligned}
& u + x\frac{du}{dx} = \frac{1 - u^2}{3u} \quad \Rightarrow \quad x\frac{du}{dx} = \frac{1 - 4u^2}{3u} \quad \Rightarrow \quad \frac{3u\,du}{1 - 4u^2} = \frac{dx}{x} \\
\Rightarrow \quad & \int \frac{3u\,du}{1 - 4u^2} = \int \frac{dx}{x} \quad \Rightarrow \quad -\frac{3}{8}\ln\left|1 - 4u^2\right| = \ln|x| + C_1 \\
\Rightarrow \quad & -3\ln\left|1 - 4\left(\frac{y}{x}\right)^2\right| = 8\ln|x| + C_2 \\
\Rightarrow \quad & 3\ln(x^2) - 3\ln\left|x^2 - 4y^2\right| = 8\ln|x| + C_2 ,
\end{aligned}$$

which, after some algebra, gives $\left(x^2 - 4y^2\right)^3 x^2 = C$.

17. With the substitutions $z = x + y$ and $dz/dx = 1 + dy/dx$ or $dy/dx = dz/dx - 1$ this equation becomes the separable equation

$$\begin{aligned}
& \frac{dz}{dx} - 1 = \sqrt{z} - 1 \quad \Rightarrow \quad \frac{dz}{dx} = \sqrt{z} \\
\Rightarrow \quad & z^{-1/2}\,dz = dx \quad \Rightarrow \quad 2z^{1/2} = x + C .
\end{aligned}$$

Substituting $x + y$ for z in this solution gives the solution of the original equation

$$2\sqrt{x + y} = x + C$$

which, on solving for y, yields

$$y = \left(\frac{x}{2} + \frac{C}{2}\right)^2 - x.$$

Thus, we have

$$y = \frac{(x + C)^2}{4} - x.$$

19. The right-hand side of this equation has the form $G(x - y)$ with $G(t) = (t + 5)^2$. Thus we substitute

$$t = x - y \quad \Rightarrow \quad y = x - t \quad \Rightarrow \quad y' = 1 - t',$$

separate variables, and integrate.

$$
\begin{aligned}
& 1-\frac{dt}{dx}=(t+5)^2 \\
\Rightarrow\quad & \frac{dt}{dx}=1-(t+5)^2=(1-t-5)(1+t+5)=-(t+4)(t+6) \\
\Rightarrow\quad & \frac{dt}{(t+4)(t+6)}=-dx \quad\Rightarrow\quad \int\frac{dt}{(t+4)(t+6)}=-\int dx \\
\Rightarrow\quad & \frac{1}{2}\int\left(\frac{1}{t+4}-\frac{1}{t+6}\right)dt=-\int dx \quad\Rightarrow\quad \ln\left|\frac{t+4}{t+6}\right|=-2x+C_1 \\
\Rightarrow\quad & \ln\left|\frac{x-y+4}{x-y+6}\right|=-2x+C_1 \quad\Rightarrow\quad \frac{x-y+6}{x-y+4}=C_2e^{2x} \\
\Rightarrow\quad & 1+\frac{2}{x-y+4}=C_2e^{2x} \quad\Rightarrow\quad y=x+4+\frac{2}{Ce^{2x}+1}\,.
\end{aligned}
$$

Also, the solution

$$t+4\equiv 0 \quad\Rightarrow\quad y=x+4$$

has been lost in separation variables.

21. This is a Bernoulli equation with $n=2$. So, we make a substitution $u=y^{1-n}=y^{-1}$. We have $y=u^{-1}$, $y'=-u^{-2}u'$, and the equation becomes

$$-\frac{1}{u^2}\frac{du}{dx}+\frac{1}{ux}=\frac{x^2}{u^2} \quad\Rightarrow\quad \frac{du}{dx}-\frac{1}{x}u=-x^2.$$

The last equation is a linear equation with $P(x)=-1/x$. Following the procedure of solving linear equations, we find an integrating factor $\mu(x)=1/x$ and multiply the equation by $\mu(x)$ to get

$$
\begin{aligned}
& \frac{1}{x}\frac{du}{dx}-\frac{1}{x^2}u=-x \quad\Rightarrow\quad \frac{d}{dx}\left(\frac{1}{x}u\right)=-x \\
\Rightarrow\quad & \frac{1}{x}u=\int(-x)dx=-\frac{1}{2}x^2+C_1 \quad\Rightarrow\quad u=-\frac{1}{2}x^3+C_1x \\
\Rightarrow\quad & y=\frac{1}{-x^3/2+C_1x}=\frac{2}{Cx-x^3}\,.
\end{aligned}
$$

Also, $y\equiv 0$ is a solution which was lost when we multiplied the equation by u^2 (in terms of y, divided by y^2) to obtain a linear equation.

23. This is a Bernoulli equation with $n = 2$. Dividing it by y^2 and rewriting gives

$$y^{-2}\frac{dy}{dx} - 2x^{-1}y^{-1} = -x^2.$$

Making the substitution $v = y^{-1}$ and hence $dv/dx = -y^{-2}dy/dx$, the above equation becomes

$$\frac{dv}{dx} + 2\frac{v}{x} = x^2.$$

This is a linear equation in v and x. The integrating factor $\mu(x)$ is given by

$$\mu(x) = \exp\left(\int \frac{2}{x}\, dx\right) = \exp\left(2\ln|x|\right) = x^2.$$

Multiplying the linear equation by this integrating factor and solving, we have

$$x^2\frac{dv}{dx} + 2vx = x^4 \quad \Rightarrow \quad D_x\left(x^2 v\right) = x^4$$

$$\Rightarrow \quad x^2 v = \int x^4\, dx = \frac{x^5}{5} + C_1 \quad \Rightarrow \quad v = \frac{x^3}{5} + \frac{C_1}{x^2}.$$

Substituting y^{-1} for v in this solution gives a solution to the original equation. Therefore, we find

$$y^{-1} = \frac{x^3}{5} + \frac{C_1}{x^2} \quad \Rightarrow \quad y = \left(\frac{x^5 + 5C_1}{5x^2}\right)^{-1}.$$

Letting $C = 5C_1$ and simplifying yields

$$y = \frac{5x^2}{x^5 + C}.$$

Note: $y \equiv 0$ is also a solution to the original equation. It was lost in the first step when we divided by y^2.

25. In this Bernoulli equation, $n = 3$. Dividing the equation by x^3, we obtain

$$x^{-3}\frac{dx}{dt} + \frac{1}{t}x^{-2} = -t.$$

Now we make a substitution $u = x^{-2}$ to obtain a linear equation. Since $u' = -2x^{-3}x'$, the equation becomes

$$-\frac{1}{2}\frac{du}{dt} + \frac{1}{t}u = -t \quad \Rightarrow \quad \frac{du}{dt} - \frac{2}{t}u = 2t$$

$$\Rightarrow \quad \mu(t) = \exp\left(-\int \frac{2}{t}\,dt\right) = t^{-2}$$

$$\Rightarrow \quad \frac{d\left(t^{-2}u\right)}{dt} = \frac{2}{t} \quad \Rightarrow \quad t^{-2}u = \int \frac{2}{t}\,dt = 2\ln|t| + C$$

$$\Rightarrow \quad u = 2t^2\ln|t| + Ct^2 \quad \Rightarrow \quad x^{-2} = 2t^2\ln|t| + Ct^2\,.$$

$x \equiv 0$ is also a solution, which we lost dividing the equation by x^3.

27. This equation is a Bernoulli equation with $n = 2$, because it can be written in the form

$$\frac{dr}{d\theta} - \frac{2}{\theta}r = r^2\theta^{-2}.$$

Dividing by r^2 and making the substitution $u = r^{-1}$, we obtain a linear equation.

$$r^{-2}\frac{dr}{d\theta} - \frac{2}{\theta}r^{-1} = \theta^{-2} \quad \Rightarrow \quad -\frac{du}{d\theta} - \frac{2}{\theta}u = \theta^{-2}$$

$$\Rightarrow \quad \frac{du}{d\theta} + \frac{2}{\theta}u = -\theta^{-2} \quad \Rightarrow \quad \mu(\theta) = \exp\left(\int \frac{2}{\theta}\,d\theta\right) = \theta^2$$

$$\Rightarrow \quad \frac{d\left(\theta^2 u\right)}{d\theta} = -1 \quad \Rightarrow \quad \theta^2 u = -\theta + C \quad \Rightarrow \quad u = \frac{-\theta + C}{\theta^2}\,.$$

Making back substitution (and adding the lost solution $r \equiv 0$), we obtain a general solution

$$r = \frac{\theta^2}{C - \theta} \qquad \text{and} \qquad r \equiv 0.$$

29. Solving for h and k in the linear system

$$\begin{cases} -3h + k - 1 = 0 \\ h + k + 3 = 0 \end{cases}$$

gives $h = -1$ and $k = -2$. Thus, we make the substitutions $x = u - 1$ and $y = v - 2$, so that $dx = du$ and $dy = dv$, to obtain

$$(-3u + v)\,du + (u + v)\,dv = 0.$$

This is the same transformed equation that we encountered in Example 4 on page 77 of the text. There we found that its solution is

$$v^2 + 2uv - 3u^2 = C.$$

Substituting $x+1$ for u and $y+2$ for v gives the solution to the original equation

$$(y+2)^2+2(x+1)(y+2)-3(x+1)^2=C.$$

31. In this equation with linear coefficients, we make a substitution $x=u+h$, $y=v+k$, where h and k satisfy

$$\begin{cases} 2h-k &= 0 \\ 4h+k &= 3 \end{cases} \quad\Rightarrow\quad \begin{cases} k=2h \\ 4h+2h=3 \end{cases} \quad\Rightarrow\quad \begin{array}{l} k=1, \\ h=1/2. \end{array}$$

Thus $x=u+1/2$, $y=v+1$. As $dx=du$ and $dy=dv$, substitution yields

$$\begin{array}{llll} (2u-v)du+(4u+v)dv=0 & \Rightarrow & \dfrac{du}{dv}=-\dfrac{4u+v}{2u-v}=-\dfrac{4(u/v)+1}{2(u/v)-1} \\ \Rightarrow \quad z=\dfrac{u}{v} \quad \Rightarrow \quad u=vz & \Rightarrow & \dfrac{du}{dv}=z+v\dfrac{dz}{dv} \\ \Rightarrow \quad z+v\dfrac{dz}{dv}=-\dfrac{4z+1}{2z-1} & \Rightarrow & v\dfrac{dz}{dv}=-\dfrac{4z+1}{2z-1}-z=-\dfrac{(2z+1)(z+1)}{2z-1} \\ \Rightarrow \quad \dfrac{2z-1}{(2z+1)(z+1)}\,dz=-\dfrac{1}{v}\,dv & \Rightarrow & \displaystyle\int \frac{2z-1}{(2z+1)(z+1)}\,dz=-\int\frac{1}{v}\,dv\,. \end{array}$$

To find the integral in the left-hand side of the above equation, we use the partial fraction decomposition

$$\frac{2z-1}{(2z+1)(z+1)}=-\frac{4}{2z+1}+\frac{3}{z+1}\,.$$

Therefore, the integration yields

$$\begin{array}{ll} -2\ln|2z+1|+3\ln|z+1|=-\ln|v|+C_1 & \Rightarrow \quad |z+1|^3|v|=e^{C_1}|2z+1|^2 \\ \Rightarrow \quad \left(\dfrac{u}{v}+1\right)^3 v=C_2\left(2\dfrac{u}{v}+1\right)^2 & \Rightarrow \quad (u+v)^3=C_2(2u+v)^2 \\ \Rightarrow \quad (x-1/2+y-1)^3=C_2(2x-1+y-1)^2 & \Rightarrow \quad (2x+2y-3)^3=C(2x+y-2)^2\,. \end{array}$$

33. In Problem 1, we found that the given equation is of the form $dy/dx=G(y-4x)$ with $G(u)=(u-1)^2$. Thus we make a substitution $u=y-4x$ to get

$$\frac{dy}{dx}=(y-4x-1)^2 \quad\Rightarrow\quad 4+\frac{du}{dx}=(u-1)^2$$

$$\Rightarrow \quad \frac{du}{dx} = (u-1)^2 - 4 = (u-3)(u+1) \quad \Rightarrow \quad \int \frac{du}{(u-3)(u+1)} = \int dx\,.$$

To integrate the left-hand side, we use partial fractions:

$$\frac{1}{(u-3)(u+1)} = \frac{1}{4}\left(\frac{1}{u-3} - \frac{1}{u+1}\right).$$

Thus

$$\frac{1}{4}\left(\ln|u-3| - \ln|u+1|\right) = x + C_1 \quad \Rightarrow \quad \ln\left|\frac{u-3}{u+1}\right| = 4x + C_2$$

$$\Rightarrow \quad \frac{u-3}{u+1} = Ce^{4x} \quad \Rightarrow \quad u = \frac{Ce^{4x}+3}{1-Ce^{4x}}$$

$$\Rightarrow \quad y = 4x + \frac{Ce^{4x}+3}{1-Ce^{4x}}\,, \tag{2.21}$$

where $C \neq 0$ is an arbitrary constant. Separating variables, we lost the constant solutions $u \equiv 3$ and $u \equiv -1$, that is, $y = 4x + 3$ and $y = 4x - 1$. While $y = 4x + 3$ can be obtained from (2.21) by setting $C = 0$, the solution $y = 4x - 1$ is not included in (2.21). Therefore, a general solution to the given equation is

$$y = 4x + \frac{Ce^{4x}+3}{1-Ce^{4x}} \qquad \text{and} \qquad y = 4x - 1.$$

35. This equation has linear coefficients. Thus we make a substitution $t = u + h$ and $x = v + k$ with h and k satisfying

$$\begin{cases} h + k + 2 &= 0 \\ 3h - k - 6 &= 0 \end{cases} \quad \Rightarrow \quad \begin{array}{l} h = 1, \\ k = -3. \end{array}$$

As $dt = du$ and $dx = dv$, the substitution yields

$$(u+v)dv + (3u-v)du = 0 \quad \Rightarrow \quad \frac{du}{dv} = -\frac{u+v}{3u-v} = -\frac{(u/v)+1}{3(u/v)-1}\,.$$

With $z = u/v$, we have $u = vz$, $u' = z + vz'$, and the equation becomes

$$z + v\frac{dz}{dv} = -\frac{z+1}{3z-1} \quad \Rightarrow \quad v\frac{dz}{dv} = -\frac{3z^2+1}{3z-1}$$

$$\Rightarrow \quad \frac{3z-1}{3z^2+1}\,dz = -\frac{1}{v}\,dv \quad \Rightarrow \quad \int \frac{3z-1}{3z^2+1}\,dz = -\int \frac{1}{v}\,dv$$

$$
\begin{aligned}
\Rightarrow \quad & \int \frac{3z\,dz}{3z^2+1} - \int \frac{dz}{3z^2+1} = -\ln|v| + C_1 \\
\Rightarrow \quad & \frac{1}{2}\ln\left(3z^2+1\right) - \frac{1}{\sqrt{3}}\arctan\left(z\sqrt{3}\right) = -\ln|v| + C_1 \\
\Rightarrow \quad & \ln\left[(3z^2+1)v^2\right] - \frac{2}{\sqrt{3}}\arctan\left(z\sqrt{3}\right) = C_2.
\end{aligned}
$$

Making back substitution, after some algebra we get

$$
\ln\left[3(t-1)^2 + (x+3)^2\right] + \frac{2}{\sqrt{3}}\arctan\left[\frac{x+3}{\sqrt{3}(t-1)}\right] = C.
$$

37. In Problem 5, we have written the equation in the form

$$
\frac{dy}{dx} - y = e^{2x}y^3 \qquad \Rightarrow \qquad y^{-3}\frac{dy}{dx} - y^{-2} = e^{2x}.
$$

Making a substitution $u = y^{-2}$ (and so $u' = -2y^{-3}y'$) in this Bernoulli equation, we get

$$
\begin{aligned}
& \frac{du}{dx} + 2u = -2e^{2x} \qquad \Rightarrow \qquad \mu(x) = \exp\left(\int 2dx\right) = e^{2x} \\
\Rightarrow \quad & \frac{d\left(e^{2x}u\right)}{dx} = -2e^{2x}e^{2x} = -2e^{4x} \qquad \Rightarrow \qquad e^{2x}u = \int \left(-2e^{4x}\right)dx = -\frac{1}{2}\,e^{4x} + C \\
\Rightarrow \quad & u = -\frac{1}{2}\,e^{2x} + Ce^{-2x} \qquad \Rightarrow \qquad y^{-2} = -\frac{1}{2}\,e^{2x} + Ce^{-2x}.
\end{aligned}
$$

The constant function $y \equiv 0$ is also a solution, which we lost dividing the equation by y^3.

39. Since the equation is homogeneous, we make a substitution $u = y/\theta$. Thus we get

$$
\begin{aligned}
& \frac{dy}{d\theta} = -\frac{(y/\theta)^3 - (y/\theta)^2}{2(y/\theta)} \qquad \Rightarrow \qquad u + \theta\frac{du}{d\theta} = -\frac{u^3-u^2}{2u} = -\frac{u^2-u}{2} \\
\Rightarrow \quad & \theta\frac{du}{d\theta} = -\frac{u^2+u}{2} \qquad \Rightarrow \qquad \frac{2du}{u(u+1)} = -\frac{d\theta}{\theta} \\
\Rightarrow \quad & \int \frac{2du}{u(u+1)} = -\int \frac{d\theta}{\theta} \qquad \Rightarrow \qquad \ln\frac{u^2}{(u+1)^2} = -\ln|\theta| + C_1 \\
\Rightarrow \quad & \frac{u^2}{(u+1)^2} = \frac{C}{\theta}, \qquad C \neq 0.
\end{aligned}
$$

Back substitution $u = y/\theta$ yields

$$
\frac{y^2}{(y+\theta)^2} = \frac{C}{\theta} \qquad \Rightarrow \qquad \theta y^2 = C(y+\theta)^2, \qquad C \neq 0.
$$

When $C = 0$, the above formula gives $\theta \equiv 0$ or $y \equiv 0$, which were lost in separating variables. Also, we lost another solution, $u + 1 \equiv 0$ or $y = -\theta$. Thus, the answer is

$$\theta y^2 = C(y+\theta)^2 \quad \text{and} \quad y = -\theta,$$

where C is an arbitrary constant.

41. The right-hand side of (8) from Example 2 of the text can be written as

$$y - x - 1 + (x-y+2)^{-1} = -(x-y+2) + 1 + (x-y+2)^{-1} = G(x-y+2)$$

with $G(v) = -v + v^{-1} + 1$. With $v = x - y + 2$, we have $y' = 1 - v'$, and the equation becomes

$$\begin{aligned} 1 - \frac{dv}{dx} &= -v + v^{-1} + 1 \qquad \Rightarrow \qquad \frac{dv}{dx} = \frac{v^2-1}{v} \qquad \Rightarrow \qquad \frac{v}{v^2-1}\,dv = dx \\ \Rightarrow \qquad \ln\left|v^2-1\right| &= 2x + C_1 \qquad \Rightarrow \qquad v^2 - 1 = Ce^{2x}, \quad C \neq 0. \end{aligned}$$

Dividing by $v^2 - 1$, we lost constant solutions $v = \pm 1$, which can be obtained by taking $C = 0$ in the above formula. Therefore, a general solution to the given equation is

$$(x-y+2)^2 = Ce^{2x} + 1,$$

where C is an arbitrary constant.

43. **(a)** If $f(tx, ty) = f(x, y)$ for any t, then, substituting $t = 1/x$, we obtain

$$f(tx, ty) = f\left(\frac{1}{x}\cdot x, \frac{1}{x}\cdot y\right) = f\left(1, \frac{y}{x}\right),$$

which shows that $f(x, y)$ depends, in fact, on y/x alone.

(b) Since

$$\frac{dy}{dx} = -\frac{M(x,y)}{N(x,y)} =: f(x,y)$$

and the function $f(x, y)$ satisfies

$$f(tx,ty) = -\frac{M(tx,ty)}{N(tx,ty)} = -\frac{t^n M(x,y)}{t^n N(x,y)} = -\frac{M(x,y)}{N(x,y)} = f(x,y),$$

we apply (a) to conclude that the equation $M(x, y)dx + N(x, y)dy = 0$ is homogeneous.

45. To obtain (17), we divide given equations:

$$\frac{dy}{dx} = -\frac{4x+y}{2x-y} = \frac{4+(y/x)}{(y/x)-2}.$$

Therefore, the equation is homogeneous, and the substitution $u = y/x$ yields

$$u + x\frac{du}{dx} = \frac{4+u}{u-2} \quad \Rightarrow \quad x\frac{du}{dx} = \frac{4+u}{u-2} - u = \frac{-u^2+3u+4}{u-2}$$
$$\Rightarrow \quad \frac{u-2}{u^2-3u-4}\,du = -\frac{1}{x}\,dx \quad \Rightarrow \quad \int \frac{u-2}{u^2-3u-4}\,du = -\int \frac{1}{x}\,dx\,.$$

Using partial fractions, we get

$$\frac{u-2}{u^2-3u-4} = \frac{2}{5}\,\frac{1}{u-4} + \frac{3}{5}\,\frac{1}{u+1},$$

and so

$$\frac{2}{5}\ln|u-4| + \frac{3}{5}\ln|u+1| = -\ln|x| + C_1$$
$$\Rightarrow \quad (u-4)^2(u+1)^3x^5 = C$$
$$\Rightarrow \quad \left(\frac{y}{x}-4\right)^2\left(\frac{y}{x}+1\right)^3 x^5 = C \quad \Rightarrow \quad (y-4x)^2(y+x)^3 = C.$$

REVIEW PROBLEMS: page 81

1. Separation variables yields

$$\frac{y-1}{e^y}\,dy = e^x\,dx \quad \Rightarrow \quad (y-1)e^{-y}\,dy = e^x\,dx$$
$$\Rightarrow \quad \int (y-1)e^{-y}\,dy = \int e^x\,dx$$
$$\Rightarrow \quad -(y-1)e^{-y} + \int e^{-y}\,dy = e^x + C \quad \Rightarrow \quad -(y-1)e^{-y} - e^{-y} = e^x + C$$
$$\Rightarrow \quad e^x + ye^{-y} = -C,$$

and we can replace $-C$ by K.

3. The differential equation is an exact equation with $M = 2xy - 3x^2$ and $N = x^2 - 2y^{-3}$ because $M_y = 2x = N_x$. To solve this problem we will follow the procedure for solving exact equations given in Section 2.4. First we integrate $M(x, y)$ with respect to x to get

$$F(x,y) = \int (2xy - 3x^2)\, dx + g(y)$$
$$\Rightarrow \qquad F(x,y) = x^2y - x^3 + g(y). \tag{2.22}$$

To determine $g(y)$ take the partial derivative with respect to y of both sides and substitute $N(x, y)$ for $\partial F(x, y)/\partial y$ to obtain

$$N = x^2 - 2y^{-3} = x^2 + g'(y).$$

Solving for $g'(y)$ yields

$$g'(y) = -2y^{-3}.$$

Since the choice of the constant of integration is arbitrary we will take $g(y) = y^{-2}$. Hence, from equation (2.22) we have $F(x, y) = x^2y - x^3 + y^{-2}$ and the solution to the differential equation is given implicitly by $x^2y - x^3 + y^{-2} = C$.

5. In this problem,

$$M(x,y) = \sin(xy) + xy\cos(xy), \qquad N(x,y) = 1 + x^2\cos(xy).$$

We check the equation for exactness:

$$\frac{\partial M}{\partial y} = [x\cos(xy)] + [x\cos(xy) - xy\sin(xy)x] = 2x\cos(xy) - x^2y\sin(xy),$$
$$\frac{\partial N}{\partial x} = 0 + [2x\cos(xy) - x^2\sin(xy)y] = 2x\cos(xy) - x^2y\sin(xy).$$

Therefore, the equation is exact. So, we use the method discussed in Section 2.4 and obtain

$$F(x,y) = \int N(x,y)dy = \int \left[1 + x^2\cos(xy)\right] dy = y + x\sin(xy) + h(x)$$
$$\Rightarrow \qquad \frac{\partial F}{\partial x} = \sin(xy) + x\cos(xy)y + h'(x) = M(x,y) = \sin(xy) + xy\cos(xy)$$
$$\Rightarrow \qquad h'(x) = 0 \qquad \Rightarrow \qquad h(x) \equiv 0,$$

and a general solution is given implicitly by $y + x\sin(xy) = c$.

7. This equation is separable. Separating variables and integrating, we get

$$t^3y^2\,dt = -t^4y^{-6}\,dy \qquad \Rightarrow \qquad \frac{dt}{t} = -\frac{dy}{y^8}$$
$$\Rightarrow \qquad \ln|t| + C_1 = \frac{1}{7}y^{-7} \qquad \Rightarrow \qquad y = (7\ln|t| + C)^{-1/7}\,.$$

The function $t \equiv 0$ is also a solution. (We lost it when divided the equation by t^4.)

9. The given differential equation can be written in the form

$$\frac{dy}{dx} + \frac{1}{3x}\,y = -\frac{x}{3}\,y^{-1}\,.$$

This is a Bernoulli equation with $n = -1$, $P(x) = 1/(3x)$, and $Q(x) = -x/3$. To transform this equation into a linear equation, we first multiply by y to obtain

$$y\frac{dy}{dx} + \frac{1}{3x}\,y^2 = -\frac{1}{3}\,x.$$

Next we make the substitution $v = y^2$. Since $v' = 2yy'$, the transformed equation is

$$\frac{1}{2}\,v' + \frac{1}{3x}\,v = -\frac{1}{3}\,x,$$
$$\Rightarrow \qquad v' + \frac{2}{3x}\,v = -\frac{2}{3}\,x. \tag{2.23}$$

The above equation is linear, so we can solve it for v using the method for solving linear equations discussed in Section 2.3. Following this procedure, the integrating factor $\mu(x)$ is found to be

$$\mu(x) = \exp\left(\int \frac{2}{3x}\,dx\right) = \exp\left(\frac{2}{3}\,\ln|x|\right) = x^{2/3}.$$

Multiplying equation (2.23) by $x^{2/3}$ gives

$$x^{2/3}v' + \frac{2}{3x^{1/3}}\,v = -\frac{2}{3}\,x^{5/3} \qquad \Rightarrow \qquad \left(x^{2/3}v\right)' = -\frac{2}{3}\,x^{5/3}.$$

We now integrate both sides and solve for v to find

$$x^{2/3}v = \int \frac{-2}{3}\,x^{5/3}\,dx = \frac{-1}{4}\,x^{8/3} + C \qquad \Rightarrow \qquad v = \frac{-1}{4}\,x^2 + Cx^{-2/3}.$$

Substituting $v = y^2$ gives the solution

$$y^2 = -\frac{1}{4}\,x^2 + Cx^{-2/3} \qquad \Rightarrow \qquad (x^2 + 4y^2)x^{2/3} = 4C$$

or, cubing both sides, $(x^2 + 4y^2)^3x^2 = C_1$, where $C_1 := (4C)^3$ is an arbitrary constant.

11. The right-hand side of this equation is of the form $G(t-x)$ with $G(u)=1+\cos^2 u$. Thus we make a substitution

$$t-x=u \quad\Rightarrow\quad x=t-u \quad\Rightarrow\quad x'=1-u',$$

which yields

$$\begin{aligned} 1-\frac{du}{dt} &= 1+\cos^2 u \quad\Rightarrow\quad \frac{du}{dt}=-\cos^2 u \\ \Rightarrow\quad \sec^2 u\,du &= -dt \quad\Rightarrow\quad \int \sec^2 u\,du = -\int dt \\ \Rightarrow\quad \tan u &= -t+C \quad\Rightarrow\quad \tan(t-x)+t=C. \end{aligned}$$

13. This is a linear equation with $P(x)=-1/x$. Following the method for solving linear equations given on page 51 of the text, we find that an integrating factor $\mu(x)=1/x$, and so

$$\begin{aligned} &\frac{d[(1/x)y]}{dx} = \frac{1}{x}x^2\sin 2x = x\sin 2x \\ \Rightarrow\quad &\frac{y}{x} = \int x\sin 2x\,dx = -\frac{1}{2}x\cos 2x + \frac{1}{2}\int \cos 2x\,dx = -\frac{1}{2}x\cos 2x + \frac{1}{4}\sin 2x + C \\ \Rightarrow\quad &y = -\frac{x^2}{2}\cos 2x + \frac{x}{4}\sin 2x + Cx. \end{aligned}$$

15. The right-hand side of the differential equation $y'=2-\sqrt{2x-y+3}$ is a function of $2x-y$ and so can be solved using the method for equations of the form $y'=G(ax+by)$ on page 74 of the text. By letting $z=2x-y$ we can transform the equation into a separable one. To solve, we differentiate $z=2x-y$ with respect to x to obtain

$$\frac{dz}{dx}=2-\frac{dy}{dx} \quad\Rightarrow\quad \frac{dy}{dx}=2-\frac{dz}{dx}.$$

Substituting $z=2x-y$ and $y'=2-z'$ into the differential equation yields

$$2-\frac{dz}{dx}=2-\sqrt{z+3} \qquad\text{or}\qquad \frac{dz}{dx}=\sqrt{z+3}.$$

To solve this equation we divide by $\sqrt{z+3}$, multiply by dx, and integrate to obtain

$$\int (z+3)^{-1/2}\,dz = \int dx \quad\Rightarrow\quad 2(z+3)^{1/2}=x+C.$$

Thus we get

$$z+3=\frac{(x+C)^2}{4}.$$

Finally, replacing z by $2x-y$ yields

$$2x-y+3=\frac{(x+C)^2}{4}.$$

Solving for y, we obtain

$$y=2x+3-\frac{(x+C)^2}{4}.$$

17. This equation is a Bernoulli equation with $n=2$. So, we divide it by y^2 and substitute $u=y^{-1}$ to get

$$-\frac{du}{d\theta}+2u=1 \quad\Rightarrow\quad \frac{du}{d\theta}-2u=-1 \quad\Rightarrow\quad \mu(\theta)=\exp\left[\int(-2)d\theta\right]=e^{-2\theta}$$

$$\Rightarrow\quad \frac{d\left(e^{-2\theta}u\right)}{d\theta}=-e^{-2\theta} \quad\Rightarrow\quad e^{-2\theta}u=\int\left(-e^{-2\theta}\right)d\theta=\frac{e^{-2\theta}}{2}+C_1$$

$$\Rightarrow\quad y^{-1}=\frac{1}{2}+C_1e^{2\theta}=\frac{1+Ce^{2\theta}}{2} \quad\Rightarrow\quad y=\frac{2}{1+Ce^{2\theta}}.$$

This formula, together with $y\equiv 0$, gives a general solution to the given equation.

19. In the differential equation $M(x,y)=x^2-3y^2$ and $N(x,y)=2xy$. The differential equation is not exact because

$$\frac{\partial M}{\partial y}=-6y\neq 2x=\frac{\partial N}{\partial x}.$$

However, because $(\partial M/\partial y-\partial N/\partial x)/N=(-8y)/(2xy)=-4/x$ depends only on x, we can determine $\mu(x)$ from equation (8) on page 70 of the text. This gives

$$\mu(x)=\exp\left(\int\frac{-4}{x}\,dx\right)=x^{-4}.$$

When we multiply the differential equation by $\mu(x)=x^{-4}$ we get the exact equation

$$(x^{-2}-3x^{-4}y^2)\,dx+2x^{-3}y\,dy=0.$$

To find $F(x,y)$ we integrate $(x^{-2}-3x^{-4}y^2)$ with respect to x:

$$F(x,y)=\int\left(x^{-2}-3x^{-4}y^2\right)dx=-x^{-1}+x^{-3}y^2+g(y).$$

Next we take the partial derivative of F with respect to y and substitute $2x^{-3}y$ for $\partial F/\partial y$:

$$2x^{-3}y = 2x^{-3}y + g'(y).$$

Thus $g'(y) = 0$ and since the choice of the constant of integration is not important, we will take $g(y) \equiv 0$. Hence, we have $F(x, y) = -x^{-1} + x^{-3}y^2$ and the implicit solution to the differential equation is

$$-x^{-1} + x^{-3}y^2 = C.$$

Solving for y^2 yields $y^2 = x^2 + Cx^3$.

Finally we check to see if any solutions were lost in the process. We multiplied by the integrating factor $\mu(x) = x^{-4}$ so we check $x \equiv 0$. This is also a solution to the original equation.

21. This equation has linear coefficients. Therefore, we are looking for a substitution $x = u + h$ and $y = v + k$ with h and k satisfying

$$\begin{cases} -2h + k - 1 = 0 \\ h + k - 4 = 0 \end{cases} \quad \Rightarrow \quad \begin{aligned} h &= 1, \\ k &= 3. \end{aligned}$$

So, $x = u + 1$ $(dx = du)$ and $y = v + 3$ $(dy = dv)$, and the equation becomes

$$(-2u + v)du + (u + v)dv = 0 \quad \Rightarrow \quad \frac{dv}{du} = \frac{2u - v}{u + v} = \frac{2 - (v/u)}{1 + (v/u)}.$$

With $z = v/u$, we have $v' = z + uz'$, and so

$$\begin{aligned} & z + u\frac{dz}{du} = \frac{2 - z}{1 + z} \quad \Rightarrow \quad u\frac{dz}{du} = \frac{2 - z}{1 + z} - z = \frac{-z^2 - 2z + 2}{1 + z} \\ \Rightarrow \quad & \frac{z + 1}{z^2 + 2z - 2}\,dz = -\frac{du}{u} \quad \Rightarrow \quad \int \frac{1 + z}{z^2 + 2z - 2}\,dz = -\int \frac{du}{u} \\ \Rightarrow \quad & \frac{1}{2}\ln\left|z^2 + 2z - 2\right| = -\ln|u| + C_1 \quad \Rightarrow \quad \left(z^2 + 2z - 2\right)u^2 = C_2. \end{aligned}$$

Back substitution, $z = v/u = (y - 3)/(x - 1)$, yields

$$\begin{aligned} & v^2 + 2uv - 2u^2 = C_2 \quad \Rightarrow \quad (y - 3)^2 + 2(x - 1)(y - 3) - 2(x - 1)^2 = C_2 \\ \Rightarrow \quad & y^2 - 8y - 2x^2 - 2x + 2xy = C. \end{aligned}$$

Chapter 2

23. Given equation is homogeneous because

$$\frac{dy}{dx}=\frac{x-y}{x+y}=\frac{1-(y/x)}{1+(y/x)}\,.$$

Therefore, substituting $u=y/x$, we obtain a separable equation.

$$\begin{aligned}
&u+x\frac{du}{dx}=\frac{1-u}{1+u} &&\Rightarrow && x\frac{du}{dx}=\frac{-u^2-2u+1}{1+u}\\
\Rightarrow\quad &\frac{u+1}{u^2+2u-1}\,du=-\frac{dx}{x} &&\Rightarrow && \int\frac{1+u}{u^2+2u-1}\,du=-\int\frac{dx}{x}\\
\Rightarrow\quad &\frac{1}{2}\ln|u^2+2u-1|=-\ln|x|+C_1 &&\Rightarrow && \left(u^2+2u-1\right)x^2=C,
\end{aligned}$$

and, substituting back $u=y/x$, after some algebra we get a general solution $y^2+2xy-x^2=C$.

25. In this differential form, $M(x,y)=y(x-y-2)$ and $N(x,y)=x(y-x+4)$. Therefore,

$$\begin{aligned}
&\frac{\partial M}{\partial y}=x-2y-2, \qquad \frac{\partial N}{\partial x}=y-2x+4\\
\Rightarrow\quad &\frac{\partial N/\partial x-\partial M/\partial y}{M}=\frac{(y-2x+4)-(x-2y-2)}{y(x-y-2)}=\frac{-3(x-y-2)}{y(x-y-2)}=\frac{-3}{y}\,,
\end{aligned}$$

which is a function of y alone. Therefore, the equation has a special integrating factor $\mu(y)$. We use formula (9) on page 70 of the text to find that $\mu(y)=y^{-3}$. Multiplying the equation by $\mu(y)$ yields

$$\begin{aligned}
&y^{-2}(x-y-2)\,dx+xy^{-3}(y-x+4)\,dy=0\\
\Rightarrow\quad &F(x,y)=\int y^{-2}(x-y-2)\,dx=\frac{y^{-2}x^2}{2}-\left(y^{-1}+2y^{-2}\right)x+g(y)\\
\Rightarrow\quad &\frac{\partial F}{\partial y}=-y^{-3}x^2-\left(-y^{-2}-4y^{-3}\right)x+g'(y)=N(x,y)=xy^{-3}\left(y-x+4\right)\\
\Rightarrow\quad &g'(x)=0 \quad\Rightarrow\quad g(y)\equiv 0,
\end{aligned}$$

and so

$$F(x,y)=\frac{y^{-2}x^2}{2}-x\left(y^{-1}+2y^{-2}\right)=C_1 \qquad\Rightarrow\qquad x^2y^{-2}-2xy^{-1}-4xy^{-2}=C$$

is a general solution. In addition, $y\equiv 0$ is a solution that we lost when multiplied the equation by $\mu(y)=y^{-3}$ (i.e., divided by y^3).

27. This equation has linear coefficients. Thus we make a substitution $x = u + h$, $y = v + k$ with h and k satisfying

$$\begin{cases} 3h - k - 5 = 0 \\ h - k + 1 = 0 \end{cases} \quad \Rightarrow \quad \begin{array}{l} h = 3, \\ k = 4. \end{array}$$

With this substitution,

$$(3u - v)du + (u - v)dv = 0 \quad \Rightarrow \quad \frac{dv}{du} = -\frac{3u - v}{u - v} = -\frac{3 - (v/u)}{1 - (v/u)}$$

$$\Rightarrow \quad z = \frac{v}{u}, \quad v = uz, \quad v' = z + uz'$$

$$\Rightarrow \quad z + u\frac{dz}{du} = -\frac{3 - z}{1 - z} \quad \Rightarrow \quad u\frac{dz}{du} = -\frac{3 - z}{1 - z} - z = -\frac{z^2 - 3}{z - 1}$$

$$\Rightarrow \quad \frac{z - 1}{z^2 - 3}\,dz = -\frac{du}{u} \quad \Rightarrow \quad \int \frac{z - 1}{z^2 - 3}\,dz = -\int \frac{du}{u}.$$

We use partial fractions to find the integral in the left-hand side. Namely,

$$\frac{z - 1}{z^2 - 3} = \frac{A}{z - \sqrt{3}} + \frac{B}{z + \sqrt{3}}, \qquad A = \frac{1}{2} - \frac{1}{2\sqrt{3}}, \quad B = \frac{1}{2} + \frac{1}{2\sqrt{3}}.$$

Therefore, integration yields

$$A \ln\left|z - \sqrt{3}\right| + B \ln\left|z + \sqrt{3}\right| = -\ln|u| + C_1$$

$$\Rightarrow \quad \left(z - \sqrt{3}\right)^{1 - 1/\sqrt{3}} \left(z + \sqrt{3}\right)^{1 + 1/\sqrt{3}} u^2 = C$$

$$\Rightarrow \quad \left(v - u\sqrt{3}\right)^{1 - 1/\sqrt{3}} \left(v + u\sqrt{3}\right)^{1 + 1/\sqrt{3}} = C$$

$$\Rightarrow \quad \left(v^2 - 3u^2\right) \left(\frac{v + u\sqrt{3}}{v - u\sqrt{3}}\right)^{1/\sqrt{3}} = C$$

$$\Rightarrow \quad \left[(y - 4)^2 - 3(x - 3)^2\right] \left[\frac{(y - 4) + (x - 3)\sqrt{3}}{(y - 4) - (x - 3)\sqrt{3}}\right]^{1/\sqrt{3}} = C.$$

29. Here $M(x, y) = 4xy^3 - 9y^2 + 4xy^2$ and $N(x, y) = 3x^2y^2 - 6xy + 2x^2y$. We compute

$$\frac{\partial M}{\partial y} = 12xy^2 - 18y + 8xy, \qquad \frac{\partial N}{\partial x} = 6xy^2 - 6y + 4xy,$$

$$\frac{\partial M/\partial y - \partial N/\partial x}{N} = \frac{(12xy^2 - 18y + 8xy) - (6xy^2 - 6y + 4xy)}{3x^2y^2 - 6xy + 2x^2y} = \frac{2y(3xy - 6 + 2x)}{xy(3xy - 6 + 2x)} = \frac{2}{x},$$

which is a function of x alone. Thus, the equation has a special integrating factor

$$\mu(x) = \exp\left(\int \frac{2}{x}\, dx\right) = x^2.$$

Multiplying the equation by $\mu(x)$, we find that

$$\begin{aligned}
F(x,y) &= \int x^2\left(4xy^3 - 9y^2 + 4xy^2\right) dx = x^4y^3 - 3x^3y^2 + x^4y^2 + g(y) \\
\Rightarrow \quad & \frac{\partial F}{\partial y} = 3x^4y^2 - 6x^3y + 2x^4y + g'(y) = x^2N(x,y) = x^2\left(3x^2y^2 - 6xy + 2x^2y\right) \\
\Rightarrow \quad & g'(y) = 0 \quad \Rightarrow \quad g(y) \equiv 0 \\
\Rightarrow \quad & F(x,y) = x^4y^3 - 3x^3y^2 + x^4y^2 = C
\end{aligned}$$

is a general solution.

31. In this problem,

$$\frac{\partial M}{\partial y} = -1, \qquad \frac{\partial N}{\partial x} = 1, \qquad \text{and so} \qquad \frac{\partial M/\partial y - \partial N/\partial x}{N} = -\frac{2}{x}.$$

Therefore, the equation has a special integrating factor

$$\mu(x) = \exp\left[\int\left(\frac{-2}{x}\right) dx\right] = x^{-2}.$$

We multiply the given equation by $\mu(x)$ to get an exact equation.

$$\begin{aligned}
& \left(x - \frac{y}{x^2}\right) dx + \frac{1}{x}\, dy = 0 \\
\Rightarrow \quad & F(x,y) = \int\left(\frac{1}{x}\right) dy = \frac{y}{x} + h(x) \\
\Rightarrow \quad & \frac{\partial F}{\partial x} = -\frac{y}{x^2} + h'(x) = x - \frac{y}{x^2} \quad \Rightarrow \quad h'(x) = x \quad \Rightarrow \quad h(x) = \frac{x^2}{2},
\end{aligned}$$

and a general solution is given by

$$F(x,y) = \frac{y}{x} + \frac{x^2}{2} = C \quad \text{and} \quad x \equiv 0.$$

(The latter has been lost in multiplication by $\mu(x)$.) Substitution the initial values, $y = 3$ when $x = 1$, yields

$$\frac{3}{1} + \frac{1^2}{2} = C \quad \Rightarrow \quad C = \frac{7}{2}.$$

Hence, the answer is

$$\frac{y}{x} + \frac{x^2}{2} = \frac{7}{2} \quad \Rightarrow \quad y = -\frac{x^3}{2} + \frac{7x}{2}.$$

33. Choosing x as the dependent variable, we transform the equation to

$$\frac{dx}{dt} + x = -(t+3).$$

This equation is linear, $P(t) \equiv 1$. So, $\mu(t) = \exp\left(\int dt\right) = e^t$ and

$$\begin{aligned} &\frac{d\left(e^t x\right)}{dt} = -(t+3)e^t \\ \Rightarrow \quad & e^t x = -\int (t+3)e^t\,dt = -(t+3)e^t + \int e^t\,dt = -(t+2)e^t + C \\ \Rightarrow \quad & x = -(t+2) + Ce^{-t}. \end{aligned}$$

Using the initial condition, $x(0) = 1$, we find that

$$1 = x(0) = -(0+2) + Ce^{-0} \quad \Rightarrow \quad C = 3,$$

and so $x = -t - 2 + 3e^{-t}$.

35. For $M(x,y) = 2y^2 + 4x^2$ and $N(x,y) = -xy$, we compute

$$\frac{\partial M}{\partial y} = 4y, \qquad \frac{\partial N}{\partial x} = -y \quad \Rightarrow \quad \frac{\partial M/\partial y - \partial N/\partial x}{N} = \frac{4y - (-y)}{-xy} = \frac{-5}{x},$$

which is a function of x only. Using (8) on page 70 of the text, we find an integrating factor $\mu(x) = x^{-5}$ and multiply the equation by $\mu(x)$ to get an exact equation,

$$x^{-5}\left(2y^2 + 4x^2\right)dx - x^{-4}y\,dy = 0.$$

Hence,

$$\begin{aligned} & F(x,y) = \int \left(-x^{-4}y\right)dy = -\frac{x^{-4}y^2}{2} + h(x) \\ \Rightarrow \quad & \frac{\partial F}{\partial x} = \frac{4x^{-5}y^2}{2} + h'(x) = x^{-5}M(x,y) = 2x^{-5}y^2 + 4x^{-3} \\ \Rightarrow \quad & h'(x) = 4x^{-3} \quad \Rightarrow \quad h(x) = -2x^{-2} \end{aligned}$$

$$\Rightarrow \qquad F(x,y) = -\frac{x^{-4}y^2}{2} - 2x^{-2} = C.$$

We find C by substituting the initial condition, $y(1) = -2$:

$$-\frac{(1)^{-4}(-2)^2}{2} - 2(1)^{-2} = C \qquad \Rightarrow \qquad C = -4\,.$$

So, the solution is

$$\begin{aligned} &-\frac{x^{-4}y^2}{2} - 2x^{-2} = -4 \\ \Rightarrow \qquad & y^2 + 4x^2 = 8x^4 \\ \Rightarrow \qquad & y^2 = 8x^4 - 4x^2 = 4x^2\left(2x^2 - 1\right) \\ \Rightarrow \qquad & y = -2x\sqrt{2x^2 - 1}\,, \end{aligned}$$

where, taking the square root, we have chosen the negative sign because of the initial negative value for y.

37. In this equation with linear coefficients we make a substitution $x = u + h$, $y = v + k$ with h and k such that

$$\begin{cases} 2h - k &= 0 \\ h + k &= 3 \end{cases} \qquad \Rightarrow \qquad \begin{cases} k = 2h \\ h + (2h) = 3 \end{cases} \qquad \Rightarrow \qquad \begin{aligned} k &= 2, \\ h &= 1. \end{aligned}$$

Therefore,

$$\begin{aligned} &(2u - v)du + (u + v)dv = 0 \\ \Rightarrow \qquad & \frac{dv}{du} = \frac{v - 2u}{v + u} = \frac{(v/u) - 2}{(v/u) + 1} \\ \Rightarrow \qquad & z = v/u, \quad v = uz, \quad v' = z + uz' \\ \Rightarrow \qquad & z + u\frac{dz}{du} = \frac{z - 2}{z + 1} \qquad \Rightarrow \qquad u\frac{dz}{du} = -\frac{z^2 + 2}{z + 1} \\ \Rightarrow \qquad & \frac{z + 1}{z^2 + 2}\,dz = -\frac{du}{u}\,. \end{aligned}$$

Integration yields

$$\int \frac{z + 1}{z^2 + 2}\,dz = -\int \frac{du}{u} \qquad \Rightarrow \qquad \int \frac{z\,dz}{z^2 + 2} + \int \frac{dz}{z^2 + 2} = -\int \frac{du}{u}$$

$$\Rightarrow \quad \frac{1}{2}\ln\left(z^2+2\right)+\frac{1}{\sqrt{2}}\arctan\left(\frac{z}{\sqrt{2}}\right)=-\ln|u|+C_1$$

$$\Rightarrow \quad \ln\left[\left(z^2+2\right)u^2\right]+\sqrt{2}\arctan\left(\frac{z}{\sqrt{2}}\right)=C$$

$$\Rightarrow \quad \ln\left(v^2+2u^2\right)+\sqrt{2}\arctan\left(\frac{v}{u\sqrt{2}}\right)=C$$

$$\Rightarrow \quad \ln\left[(y-2)^2+2(x-1)^2\right]+\sqrt{2}\arctan\left[\frac{y-2}{(x-1)\sqrt{2}}\right]=C.$$

The initial condition, $y(0)=2$, gives $C=\ln 2$, and so the answer is

$$\ln\left[(y-2)^2+2(x-1)^2\right]+\sqrt{2}\arctan\left[\frac{y-2}{(x-1)\sqrt{2}}\right]=\ln 2\,.$$

39. Multiplying the equation by y, we get

$$y\frac{dy}{dx}-\frac{2}{x}y^2=\frac{1}{x}\,.$$

We substitute $u=y^2$ and obtain

$$\frac{1}{2}\frac{du}{dx}-\frac{2}{x}u=\frac{1}{x} \qquad \Rightarrow \qquad \frac{du}{dx}-\frac{4}{x}u=\frac{2}{x}\,,$$

which is linear and has an integrating factor

$$\mu(x)=\exp\left[\int\left(-\frac{4}{x}\right)dx\right]=x^{-4}.$$

Hence,

$$\frac{d\left(x^{-4}u\right)}{dx}=2x^{-5}$$

$$\Rightarrow \quad x^{-4}u=\int\left(2x^{-5}\right)dx=-\frac{x^{-4}}{2}+C$$

$$\Rightarrow \quad x^{-4}y^2=-\frac{x^{-4}}{2}+C$$

$$\Rightarrow \quad y^2=-\frac{1}{2}+Cx^4.$$

Substitution $y(1)=3$ yields

$$3^2=-\frac{1}{2}+C(1)^4 \qquad \text{or} \qquad C=\frac{19}{2}\,.$$

Therefore, the solution to the given initial value problem is

$$y^2 = -\frac{1}{2} + \frac{19x^4}{2} \qquad \text{or} \qquad y = \sqrt{\frac{19x^4 - 1}{2}}\,.$$

CHAPTER 3: Mathematical Models and Numerical Methods Involving First Order Equations

EXERCISES 3.2: Compartmental Analysis, page 98

1. Let $x(t)$ denote the mass of salt in the tank at time t with $t = 0$ denoting the moment when the process started. Thus we have $x(0) = 0.5$ kg. We use the mathematical model described by equation (1) on page 90 of the text to find $x(t)$. Since the solution is entering the tank with rate 8 L/min and contains 0.05 kg/L of salt,

$$\text{input rate} = 8\,(\text{L/min}) \cdot 0.05\,(\text{kg/L}) = 0.4\,(\text{kg/min}).$$

We can determine the concentration of salt in the tank by dividing $x(t)$ by the volume of the solution, which remains constant, 100 L, because the flow rate in is the same as the flow rate out. Therefore, the concentration of salt at time t is $x(t)/100$ kg/L and

$$\text{output rate} = \frac{x(t)}{100}\,(\text{kg/L}) \cdot 8\,(\text{L/min}) = \frac{2x(t)}{25}\,(\text{kg/min}).$$

Then the equation (1) yields

$$\frac{dx}{dt} = 0.4 - \frac{2x}{25} \qquad \Rightarrow \qquad \frac{dx}{dt} + \frac{2x}{25} = 0.4\,, \qquad x(0) = 0.5\,.$$

This equation is linear, has integrating factor $\mu(t) = \exp\left[\int (2/25)dt\right] = e^{2t/25}$, and so

$$\frac{d\left(e^{2t/25}x\right)}{dt} = 0.4e^{2t/25}$$

$$\Rightarrow \qquad e^{2t/25}x = 0.4\left(\frac{25}{2}\right)e^{2t/25} + C = 5e^{2t/25} + C \qquad \Rightarrow \qquad x = 5 + Ce^{-2t/25}.$$

Using the initial condition, we find C.

$$0.5 = x(0) = 5 + C \qquad \Rightarrow \qquad C = -4.5\,,$$

and so the mass of salt in the tank after t minutes is

$$x(t) = 5 - 4.5e^{-2t/25}.$$

If the concentration of salt in the tank is 0.02 kg/L, then the mass of salt is $0.02 \times 100 = 2$ kg, and, to find this moment, we solve

$$5 - 4.5e^{-2t/25} = 2 \quad \Rightarrow \quad e^{-2t/25} = \frac{2}{3} \quad \Rightarrow \quad t = \frac{25\ln(3/2)}{2} \approx 5.07\,(\text{min}).$$

3. Let $x(t)$ be the volume of nitric acid in the tank at time t. The tank initially held 200 L of a 0.5% nitric acid solution; therefore, $x(0) = 200 \times 0.005 = 1$. Since 6 L of 20% nitric acid solution are flowing into the tank per minute, the rate at which nitric acid is entering is $6 \times 0.2 = 1.2$ L/min. Because the rate of flow out of the tank is 8 L/min and the rate of flow in is only 6 L/min, there is a net loss in the tank of 2 L of solution every minute. Thus, at any time t, the tank will be holding $200 - 2t$ liters of solution. Combining this with the fact that the volume of nitric acid in the tank at time t is $x(t)$, we see that the concentration of nitric acid in the tank at time t is $x(t)/(200-2t)$. Here we are assuming that the tank is kept well stirred. The rate at which nitric acid flows out of the tank is, therefore, $8 \times [x(t)/(200-2t)]$ L/min. From all of these facts, we see that

$$\begin{aligned} \text{input rate} &= 1.2 \text{ L/min}, \\ \text{output rate} &= \frac{8x(t)}{200-2t} \text{ L/min}. \end{aligned}$$

We know that

$$\frac{dx}{dt} = \text{input rate} - \text{output rate}.$$

Thus we must solve the differential equation

$$\frac{dx}{dt} = 1.2 - \frac{4x(t)}{100-t}, \qquad x(0) = 1.$$

This is the linear equation

$$\frac{dx}{dt} + \frac{4}{100-t}x = 1.2, \qquad x(0) = 1.$$

An integrating factor for this equation has the form

$$\mu(t) = \exp\left(\int \frac{4}{100-t}\,dt\right) = e^{-4\ln(100-t)} = (100-t)^{-4}.$$

Multiplying the linear equation by the integrating factor yields

$$\begin{aligned}
&(100-t)^{-4}\frac{dx}{dt} + 4x(100-t)^{-5} = (1.2)(100-t)^{-4} \\
\Rightarrow \quad & D_t\left[(100-t)^{-4}x\right] = (1.2)(100-t)^{-4} \\
\Rightarrow \quad & (100-t)^{-4}x = 1.2\int (100-t)^{-4}\,dt = \frac{1.2}{3}(100-t)^{-3} + C \\
\Rightarrow \quad & x(t) = (0.4)(100-t) + C(100-t)^{4}.
\end{aligned}$$

To find the value of C, we use the initial condition $x(0) = 1$. Therefore,

$$x(0) = (0.4)(100) + C(100)^4 = 1 \qquad \Rightarrow \qquad C = \frac{-39}{100^4} = -3.9 \times 10^{-7}.$$

This means that at time t there is

$$x(t) = (0.4)(100-t) - (3.9 \times 10^{-7})(100-t)^4$$

liters of nitric acid in the tank. When the percentage of nitric acid in the tank is 10%, the concentration of nitric acid is 0.1. Thus we want to solve the equation

$$\frac{x(t)}{200-2t} = 0.1\,.$$

Therefore, we divide the solution $x(t)$ that we found above by $2(100-t)$ and solve for t. That is, we solve

$$\begin{aligned}
& (0.2) - (1.95 \times 10^{-7})(100-t)^3 = 0.1 \\
\Rightarrow \quad & t = -\left[0.1 \cdot \frac{10^7}{1.95}\right]^{1/3} + 100 \approx 19.96 \text{ (min)}.
\end{aligned}$$

5. Let $x(t)$ denote the volume of chlorine in the pool at time t. Then in the formula

$$\text{rate of change} = \text{input rate} - \text{output rate}$$

we have

$$\text{input rate} = 5\,(\text{gal/min}) \cdot \frac{0.001\%}{100\%} = 5 \cdot 10^{-5}\,(\text{gal/min}),$$
$$\text{output rate} = 5\,(\text{gal/min}) \cdot \frac{x(t)\,(\text{gal})}{10,000\,(\text{gal})} = 5 \cdot 10^{-4} x(t)\,(\text{gal/min}),$$

and the equation for $x(t)$ becomes

$$\frac{dx}{dt} = 5 \cdot 10^{-5} - 5 \cdot 10^{-4} x \qquad \Rightarrow \qquad \frac{dx}{dt} + 5 \cdot 10^{-4} x = 5 \cdot 10^{-5}.$$

This is a linear equation. Solving yields

$$x(t) = 0.1 + Ce^{5 \cdot 10^{-4} t} = 0.1 + Ce^{-0.0005t}.$$

Using the initial condition,

$$x(0) = 10,000\,(\text{gal}) \cdot \frac{0.01\%}{100\%} = 1\,(\text{gal}),$$

we find the value of C:

$$1 = 0.1 + Ce^{-0.0005 \cdot 0} \qquad \Rightarrow \qquad C = 0.9\,.$$

Therefore, $x(t) = 0.1 + 0.9e^{-0.0005t}$ and the concentration of chlorine, say, $c(t)$, in the pool at time t is

$$c(t) = \frac{x(t)\,(\text{gal})}{10,000\,(\text{gal})} \cdot 100\% = \frac{x(t)}{100}\,\% = 0.001 + 0.009e^{-0.0005t}\,\%.$$

After 1 hour (i.e., $t = 60$ min),

$$c(60) = 0.001 + 0.009e^{-0.0005 \cdot 60} = 0.001 + 0.009e^{-0.03} \approx 0.0097\,\%.$$

To answer the second question, we solve the equation

$$c(t) = 0.001 + 0.009e^{-0.0005t} = 0.002 \qquad \Rightarrow \qquad t = \frac{\ln(1/9)}{-0.0005} \approx 4394.45\,(\text{min}) \approx 73.24\,(\text{h}).$$

7. Let $x(t)$ denote the mass of salt in the first tank at time t. Assuming that the initial mass is $x(0) = x_0$, we use the mathematical model described by equation (1) on page 90 of the text to find $x(t)$. We can determine the concentration of salt in the first tank by dividing $x(t)$ by the its volume, i.e., $x(t)/60$ kg/gal. Note that the volume of brine in this tank remains constant because the flow rate in is the same as the flow rate out. Then

$$\text{output rate}_1 = (3 \text{ gal/min}) \cdot \left(\frac{x(t)}{60} \text{ kg/gal} \right) = \frac{x(t)}{20} \text{ kg/min.}$$

Since the incoming liquid is pure water, we conclude that

$$\text{input rate}_1 = 0.$$

Therefore, $x(t)$ satisfies the initial value problem

$$\frac{dx}{dt} = \text{input rate}_1 - \text{output rate}_1 = -\frac{x}{20}, \qquad x(0) = x_0 .$$

This equation is linear and separable. Solving and using the initial condition to evaluate the arbitrary constant, we find

$$x(t) = x_0 e^{-t/20} .$$

Now, let $y(t)$ denote the mass of salt in the second tank at time t. Since initially this tank contained only pure water, we have $y(0) = 0$. The function $y(t)$ can be described by the same mathematical model. We get

$$\text{input rate}_2 = \text{output rate}_1 = \frac{x(t)}{20} = \frac{x_0}{20} e^{-t/20} \text{ kg/min.}$$

Further since the volume of the second tank also remains constant, we have

$$\text{output rate}_2 = (3 \text{ gal/min}) \cdot \left(\frac{y(t)}{60} \text{ kg/gal} \right) = \frac{y(t)}{20} \text{ kg/min.}$$

Therefore, $y(t)$ satisfies the initial value problem

$$\frac{dy}{dt} = \text{input rate}_2 - \text{output rate}_2 = \frac{x_0}{20} e^{-t/20} - \frac{y(t)}{20}, \qquad y(0) = 0 .$$

or

$$\frac{dy}{dt} + \frac{y(t)}{20} = \frac{x_0}{20} e^{-t/20}, \qquad y(0) = 0 .$$

This is a linear equation in standard form. Using the method given on page 51 of the text we find the general solution to be

$$y(t) = \frac{x_0}{20} te^{-t/20} + Ce^{-t/20}.$$

The constant C can be found from the initial condition:

$$0 = y(0) = \frac{x_0}{20} \cdot 0 \cdot e^{-0/20} + Ce^{-0/20} \qquad \Rightarrow \qquad C = 0.$$

Therefore, $y(t) = (x_0/20)\, te^{-t/20}$. To investigate $y(t)$ for maximum value we calculate

$$\frac{dy}{dt} = \frac{x_0}{20} e^{-t/20} - \frac{y(t)}{20} = \frac{x_0}{20} e^{-t/20} \left(1 - \frac{t}{20}\right).$$

Thus

$$\frac{dy}{dt} = 0 \qquad \Leftrightarrow \qquad 1 - \frac{t}{20} = 0 \qquad \Leftrightarrow \qquad t = 20,$$

which is the point of global maximum (notice that $dy/dt > 0$ for $t < 20$ and $dy/dt < 0$ for $t > 20$). In other words, at this moment the water in the second tank will taste saltiest, and comparing concentrations, it will be

$$\frac{y(20)/60}{x_0/60} = \frac{y(20)}{x_0} = \frac{1}{20} \cdot 20 \cdot e^{-20/20} = e^{-1}$$

times as salty as the original brine.

9. Let $p(t)$ be the population of splake in the lake at time t. We start counting the population in 1980. Thus, we let $t = 0$ correspond to the year 1980. By the Malthusian law stated on page 93 of the text, we have

$$p(t) = p_0 e^{kt}.$$

Since $p_0 = p(0) = 1000$, we see that

$$p(t) = 1000e^{kt}.$$

To find k we use the fact that the population of splake was 3000 in 1987. Therefore,

$$p(7) = 3000 = 1000e^{k \cdot 7} \qquad \Rightarrow \qquad 3 = e^{k \cdot 7} \qquad \Rightarrow \qquad k = \frac{\ln 3}{7}.$$

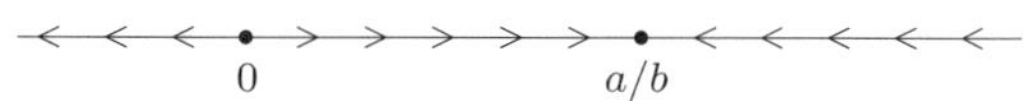

Figure 3–A: The phase line for $p' = (a - bp)p$.

Putting this value for k into the equation for $p(t)$ gives

$$p(t) = 1000e^{(t \ln 3)/7} = 1000 \cdot 3^{t/7}.$$

To estimate the population in 2010 we plug $t = 2010 - 1980 = 30$ into this formula to get

$$p(30) = 1000 \cdot 3^{30/7} \approx 110,868 \text{ splakes.}$$

11. In this problem, the dependent variable is p, the independent variable is t, and the function $f(t,p) = (a-bp)p$. Since $f(t,p) = f(p)$, i.e., does not depend on t, the equation is autonomous. To find equilibrium solutions, we solve

$$f(p) = 0 \qquad \Rightarrow \qquad (a - bp)p = 0 \qquad \Rightarrow \qquad p_1 = 0, \quad p_2 = \frac{a}{b}.$$

Thus, $p_1(t) \equiv 0$ and $p_2(t) \equiv a/b$ are equilibrium solutions. For $p_1 < p < p_2$, $f(p) > 0$, and $f(p) < 0$ when $p > p_2$. (Also, $f(p) < 0$ for $p < p_1$.) Thus the phase line for the given equation is as it is shown in Figure 3-A. From this picture, we conclude that the equilibrium $p = p_1$ is a source while $p = p_2$ is a sink. Thus, regardless of an initial point $p_0 > 0$, the solution to the corresponding initial value problem will approach $p_2 = a/b$ as $t \to \infty$.

13. With year 1980 corresponding to $t = 0$, the data given can be written as

$$\begin{aligned} t_0 &= 0, & p_0 &= p(t_0) = 1000; \\ t_a &= 1987 - 1980 = 7, & p_a &= p(t_a) = 3000; \\ t_b &= 1994 - 1980 = 14, & p_b &= p(t_b) = 5000. \end{aligned}$$

Since $t_b = 2t_a$, we can use formulas in Problem 12 to compute parameters p_1 and A in the logistic model (14) on page 94 of the text. We have:

$$p_1 = \frac{(3000)(5000) - 2(1000)(5000) + (1000)(3000)}{(3000)^2 - (1000)(5000)}(3000) = 6000;$$

$$A = \frac{1}{(6000)7} \ln \left[\frac{5000(3000 - 1000)}{1000(5000 - 3000)} \right] = \frac{\ln 5}{42000}.$$

Thus the formula (15) on page 95 of the text becomes

$$p(t) = \frac{p_0 p_1}{p_0 + (p_1 - p_0)e^{-Ap_1 t}} = \frac{(1000)(6000)}{(1000) + (6000 - 1000)e^{-(\ln 5/42000)6000t}} = \frac{6000}{1 + 5^{1-t/7}}. \tag{3.1}$$

In the year 2010, $t = 2010 - 1980 = 30$, and the estimated population of splake is

$$p(30) = \frac{6000}{1 + 5^{1-30/7}} \approx 5970.$$

Taking the limit in (3.1), as $t \to \infty$, yields

$$\lim_{t\to\infty} p(t) = \lim_{t\to\infty} \frac{6000}{1 + 5^{1-t/7}} = \frac{6000}{1 + \lim_{t\to\infty} 5^{1-t/7}} = 6000.$$

Therefore, the predicted limiting population is 6000.

15. Counting time from the year 1970, we have the following data:

$$\begin{aligned} t_0 &= 0, & p_0 &= p(t_0) = 300; \\ t_a &= 1975 - 1970 = 5, & p_a &= p(t_a) = 1200; \\ t_b &= 1980 - 1970 = 10, & p_b &= p(t_b) = 1500. \end{aligned}$$

Since $t_b = 2t_a$, we use the formulas in Problem 12 to find parameters in the logistic model.

$$p_1 = \left[\frac{(1200)(1500) - 2(300)(1500) + (300)(1200)}{(1200)^2 - (300)(1500)} \right] (1200) = \frac{16800}{11};$$

$$A = \frac{1}{(16800/11)5} \ln \left[\frac{(1500)(1200 - 300)}{(300)(1500 - 1200)} \right] = \frac{11 \ln(15)}{84000}.$$

Therefore,

$$p(t) = \frac{300(16800/11)}{300 + [(16800/11) - 300]e^{-\ln(15)t/5}} = \frac{16800}{11 + 3 \cdot 15^{1-t/5}}.$$

In the year 2010, $t = 2010 - 1970 = 40$, and so the estimated population of alligators is

$$p(40) = \frac{16800}{11 + 3 \cdot 15^{1-40/5}} = \frac{16800}{11 + 3 \cdot 15^{-7}} \approx 1527.$$

Taking the limit of $p(t)$, as $t \to \infty$, we get the predicted limiting population of

$$\lim_{t\to\infty} \frac{16800}{11 + 3 \cdot 15^{1-t/5}} = \frac{16800}{11} \approx 1527.$$

16. By definition,

$$p'(t) = \lim_{h\to 0} \frac{p(t+h)-p(t)}{h}.$$

Replacing h by $-h$ in the above equation, we obtain

$$p'(t) = \lim_{h\to 0} \frac{p(t-h)-p(t)}{-h} = \lim_{h\to 0} \frac{p(t)-p(t-h)}{h}.$$

Adding the previous two equations together yields

$$\begin{aligned} 2p'(t) &= \lim_{h\to 0} \left[\frac{p(t+h)-p(t)}{h} + \frac{p(t)-p(t-h)}{h}\right] \\ &= \lim_{h\to 0} \left[\frac{p(t+h)-p(t-h)}{h}\right]. \end{aligned}$$

Thus

$$p'(t) = \lim_{h\to 0} \left[\frac{p(t+h)-p(t-h)}{2h}\right].$$

19. This problem can be regarded as a compartmental analysis problem for the population of fish. If we let $m(t)$ denote the mass in million tons of a certain species of fish, then the mathematical model for this process is given by

$$\frac{dm}{dt} = \text{increase rate} - \text{decrease rate}.$$

The increase rate of fish is given by $2m$ million tons/yr. The decrease rate of fish is given as 15 million tons/yr. Substituting these rates into the above equation we obtain

$$\frac{dm}{dt} = 2m - 15, \qquad m(0) = 7 \text{ (million tons)}.$$

This equation is linear and separable. Using the initial condition, $m(0) = 7$ to evaluate the arbitrary constant we obtain

$$m(t) = -\frac{1}{2}e^{2t} + \frac{15}{2}.$$

Knowing this equation we can now find when all the fish will be gone. To determine when all the fish will be gone we set $m(t) = 0$ and solve for t. This gives

$$0 = -\frac{1}{2}e^{2t} + \frac{15}{2}$$

and, hence,

$$t = \frac{1}{2}\ln(15) \approx 1.354 \text{ (years)}.$$

To determine the fishing rate required to keep the fish mass constant we solve the general problem

$$\frac{dm}{dt} = 2m - r, \qquad m(0) = 7,$$

with r as the fishing rate. Thus we obtain

$$m(t) = Ke^{2t} + \frac{r}{2}.$$

The initial mass was given to be 7 million tons. Substituting this into the above equation we can find the arbitrary constant K:

$$m(0) = 7 = K + \frac{r}{2} \qquad \Rightarrow \qquad K = 7 - \frac{r}{2}.$$

Thus $m(t)$ is given by

$$m(t) = \left(7 - \frac{r}{2}\right)e^{2t} + \frac{r}{2}.$$

A fishing rate of $r = 14$ million tons/year will give a constant mass of fish by canceling out the coefficient of the e^{2t} term.

21. Let $D = D(t)$, $S(t)$, and $V(t)$ denote the diameter, surface area, and volume of the snowball at time t, respectively. From geometry, we know that $V = \pi D^3/6$ and $S = \pi D^2$. Since we are given that $V'(t)$ is proportional to $S(t)$, the equation describing the melting process is

$$\frac{dV}{dt} = kS \qquad \Rightarrow \qquad \frac{d}{dt}\left(\frac{\pi}{6}D^3\right) = k\left(\pi D^2\right)$$
$$\Rightarrow \qquad \frac{\pi}{2}D^2\frac{dD}{dt} = k\pi D^2 \qquad \Rightarrow \qquad \frac{dD}{dt} = 2k = \text{const}.$$

Solving, we get $D = 2kt + C$. Initially, $D(0) = 4$, and we also know that $D(30) = 3$. These data allow us to find k and C.

$$4 = D(0) = 2k \cdot 0 + C \qquad \Rightarrow \qquad C = 4;$$
$$3 = D(30) = 2k \cdot 30 + C = 2k \cdot 30 + 4 \qquad \Rightarrow \qquad 2k = -\frac{1}{30}.$$

Thus

$$D(t) = -\frac{t}{30} + 4.$$

The diameter $D(t)$ of the snowball will be 2 inches when

$$-\frac{t}{30} + 4 = 2 \qquad \Rightarrow \qquad t = 60\,(\text{min}) = 1\,(\text{h}),$$

and the snowball will disappear when

$$-\frac{t}{30} + 4 = 0 \qquad \Rightarrow \qquad t = 120\,(\text{min}) = 2\,(\text{h}).$$

23. If $m(t)$ (with t measured in "days") denotes the mass of a radioactive substance, the law of decay says that

$$\frac{dm}{dt} = km(t),$$

with the decay constant k depending on the substance. Solving this equation yields

$$m(t) = Ce^{kt}.$$

If the initial mass of the substance is $m(0) = m_0$, then, similarly to the equation (11) on page 93 of the text, we find that

$$m(t) = m_0 e^{kt}. \tag{3.2}$$

In this problem, $m_0 = 50$ g, and we know that $m(3) = 10$ g. These data yield

$$10 = m(3) = 50 \cdot e^{k(3)} \qquad \Rightarrow \qquad k = -\frac{\ln 5}{3},$$

and so the decay is governed by the equation

$$m(t) = 50e^{-(\ln 5)t/3} = (50)5^{-t/3}.$$

After 4 days, the remaining amount will be $m(4) = (50)5^{-4/3}$ g, which is

$$\frac{(50)5^{-4/3}}{50} \cdot 100\% = 5^{-4/3} \cdot 100\% \approx 11.7\%$$

of the original amount.

25. Let $M(t)$ denote the mass of carbon-14 present in the burnt wood of the campfire. Then since carbon-14 decays at a rate proportional to its mass, we have

$$\frac{dM}{dt} = -\alpha M,$$

where α is the proportionality constant. This equation is linear and separable. Using the initial condition, $M(0) = M_0$ we obtain

$$M(t) = M_0 e^{-\alpha t}.$$

Given the half-life of carbon-14 to be 5600 years, we solve for α since we have

$$\frac{1}{2} M_0 = M_0 e^{-\alpha(5600)} \qquad \Rightarrow \qquad \frac{1}{2} = e^{-\alpha(5600)},$$

which yields

$$\alpha = \frac{\ln(0.5)}{-5600} \approx 0.000123776\,.$$

Thus,

$$M(t) = M_0 e^{-0.000123776t}\,.$$

Now we are told that after t years 2% of the original amount of carbon-14 remains in the campfire and we are asked to determine t. Thus

$$0.02 M_0 = M_0 e^{-0.000123776t} \qquad \Rightarrow \qquad 0.02 = e^{-0.000123776t}$$
$$\Rightarrow \qquad t = \frac{\ln 0.02}{-0.000123776} \approx 31,606 \text{ (years)}.$$

27. The element Hh decays according to the general law of a radioactive decay, which is described by (3.2) (this time, with t measured in "years"). Since the initial mass of Hh is $m_0 = 1$ kg and the decay constant $k = k_{\text{Hh}} = -2/\text{yr}$, we get

$$\text{Hh}(t) = e^{k_{\text{Hh}} t} = e^{-2t}. \tag{3.3}$$

For It, the process is more complicated: it has an incoming mass from the decay of Hh and, at the same, looses its mass decaying to Bu. (This process is very similar to "brine solution" problems.) Thus we use the general idea in getting a differential equation describing this process:

$$\text{rate of change} = \text{input rate} - \text{output rate}. \tag{3.4}$$

The "input rate" is the rate of mass coming from Hh's decay, which is opposite to the rate of decay of Hh (Hh looses the mass but It gains it), i.e.,

$$\text{input rate} = -\frac{d\text{Hh}}{dt} = 2e^{-2t}, \tag{3.5}$$

where we have used (3.3). The "output rate" is the rate with which It decays, which (again, according to the general law of a radioactive decay) is proportional to its current mass. Since the decay constant for It is $k = k_{\text{It}} = -1/\text{yr}$,

$$\text{output rate} = k_{\text{It}}\text{It}(t) = -\text{It}(t). \tag{3.6}$$

Therefore, combining (3.4)–(3.6) we get the equation for It, that is,

$$\frac{d\text{It}(t)}{dt} = 2e^{-2t} - \text{It}(t) \qquad \Rightarrow \qquad \frac{d\text{It}(t)}{dt} + \text{It}(t) = 2e^{-2t}.$$

This is a linear equation with $P(t) \equiv 1$ and an integrating factor $\mu(t) = \exp\left[\int(1)dt\right] = e^t$. Multiplying the equation by $\mu(t)$ yields

$$\frac{d\left[e^t\text{It}(t)\right]}{dt} = 2e^{-t} \qquad \Rightarrow \qquad e^t\text{It}(t) = -2e^{-t} + C \qquad \Rightarrow \qquad \text{It}(t) = -2e^{-2t} + Ce^{-t}.$$

Initially, there were no It, which means that $\text{It}(0) = 0$. With this initial condition we find that

$$0 = \text{It}(0) = -2e^{-2(0)} + Ce^{-(0)} = -2 + C \qquad \Rightarrow \qquad C = 2,$$

and the mass of It remaining after t years is

$$\text{It}(t) = -2e^{-2t} + 2e^{-t} = 2\left(e^{-t} - e^{-2t}\right). \tag{3.7}$$

The element Bu only gains its mass from It, and the rate with which it does this is opposite to the rate with which It looses its mass. Hence (3.6) yields

$$\frac{d\text{Bu}(t)}{dt} = \text{It}(t) = 2\left(e^{-t} - e^{-2t}\right).$$

Integrating, we obtain

$$\mathrm{Bu}(t) = 2\int \left(e^{-t} - e^{-2t}\right) dt = -2e^{-t} + e^{-2t} + C,$$

and the initial condition $\mathrm{Bu}(0) = 0$ gives $C = 1$. Therefore,

$$\mathrm{Bu}(t) = -2e^{-t} + e^{-2t} + 1.$$

EXERCISES 3.3: Heating and Cooling of Buildings, page 107

1. Let $T(t)$ denote the temperature of coffee at time t (in minutes). According to the Newton's Law (1) on page 102 of the text,

$$\frac{dT}{dt} = K[21 - T(t)],$$

where we have taken $H(t) \equiv U(t) \equiv 0$, $M(t) \equiv 21^\circ$ C, with the initial condition $T(0) = 95^\circ$ C. Solving this initial value problem yields

$$\frac{dT}{21 - T} = K\,dt \quad \Rightarrow \quad -\ln|T - 21| = Kt + C_1 \quad \Rightarrow \quad T(t) = 21 + Ce^{-Kt};$$

$$95 = T(0) = 21 + Ce^{-K(0)} \quad \Rightarrow \quad C = 74 \quad \Rightarrow \quad T(t) = 21 + 74e^{-Kt}.$$

To find K, we use the fact that after 5 min the temperature of coffee was 80° C. Thus

$$80 = T(5) = 21 + 74e^{-K(5)} \quad \Rightarrow \quad K = \frac{\ln(74/59)}{5},$$

and so

$$T(t) = 21 + 74e^{-\ln(74/59)t/5} = 21 + 74\left(\frac{74}{59}\right)^{-t/5}.$$

Finally, we solve the equation $T(t) = 50$ to find the time appropriate for drinking coffee:

$$50 = 21 + 74\left(\frac{74}{59}\right)^{-t/5} \quad \Rightarrow \quad \left(\frac{74}{59}\right)^{-t/5} = \frac{29}{74} \quad \Rightarrow \quad t = \frac{5\ln(74/29)}{\ln(74/59)} \approx 20.7\,(\text{min}).$$

3. This problem is similar to one of cooling a building. In this problem we have no additional heating or cooling so we can say that the rate of change of the wine's temperature, $T(t)$ is given by Newton's law of cooling

$$\frac{dT}{dt} = K[M(t) - T(t)],$$

where $M(t) = 32$ is the temperature of ice. This equation is linear and is rewritten in the standard form as

$$\frac{dT}{dt} + KT(t) = 32K.$$

We find that the integrating factor is e^{Kt}. Multiplying both sides by e^{Kt} and integrating gives

$$e^{Kt}\frac{dT}{dt} + e^{Kt}KT(t) = 32Ke^{Kt} \qquad \Rightarrow \qquad e^{Kt}T(t) = \int 32Ke^{Kt}\,dt$$
$$\Rightarrow \qquad e^{Kt}T(t) = 32e^{Kt} + C \qquad \Rightarrow \qquad T(t) = 32 + Ce^{-Kt}.$$

By setting $t = 0$ and using the initial temperature 70°F, we find the constant C.

$$70 = 32 + C \qquad \Rightarrow \qquad C = 38.$$

Knowing that it takes 15 minutes for the wine to chill to 60°F, we can find the constant, K:

$$60 = 32 + 38e^{-K(15)}.$$

Solving for K yields

$$K = \frac{-1}{15}\ln\left(\frac{60-32}{38}\right) \approx 0.02035.$$

Therefore,

$$T(t) = 32 + 38e^{-0.02035t}.$$

We can now determine how long it will take for the wine to reach 56°F. Using our equation for temperature $T(t)$, we set

$$56 = 32 + 38e^{-0.02035t}$$

and, solving for t, obtain

$$t = \frac{-1}{0.02035}\ln\left(\frac{56-32}{38}\right) \approx 22.6 \text{ min.}$$

5. This problem can be treated as one similar to that of a cooling building. If we assume the air surrounding the body has not changed since the death, we can say that the rate of change of the body's temperature, $T(t)$ is given by Newton's law of cooling:

$$\frac{dT}{dt} = K[M(t) - T(t)],$$

where $M(t)$ represents the surrounding temperature which we've assumed to be a constant 16°C. This differential equation is linear and is solved using an integrating factor of e^{Kt}. Rewriting the above equation in standard form, multiplying both sides by e^{Kt} and integrating gives

$$\begin{aligned} \frac{dT}{dt} + KT(t) = K(16) \quad &\Rightarrow \quad e^{Kt}\frac{dT}{dt} + e^{Kt}KT(t) = 16Ke^{Kt} \\ \Rightarrow \quad e^{Kt}T(t) = 16e^{Kt} + C \quad &\Rightarrow \quad T(t) = 16 + Ce^{-Kt}. \end{aligned}$$

Let us take $t = 0$ as the time at which the person died. Then $T(0) = 37$°C (normal body temperature) and we get

$$37 = 16 + C \quad \Rightarrow \quad C = 21.$$

Now we know that at sometime, say X hours after death, the body temperature was measured to be 34.5°C and that at $X + 1$ hours after death the body temperature was measured to be 33.7°C. Therefore, we have

$$34.5 = 16 + 21e^{-KX} \quad \text{and} \quad 33.7 = 16 + 21e^{-K(X+1)}.$$

Solving the first equation for KX we arrive at

$$KX = -\ln\left(\frac{34.5 - 16}{21}\right) = 0.12675. \tag{3.8}$$

Substituting this value into the second equation we, can solve for K as follows:

$$\begin{aligned} &33.7 = 16 + 21e^{-0.12675-K} \\ \Rightarrow \quad &K = -\left[0.12675 + \ln\left(\frac{33.7 - 16}{21}\right)\right] = 0.04421. \end{aligned}$$

This results in an equation for the body temperature of

$$T(t) = 16 + 21e^{-0.04421t}.$$

From equation (3.8) we now find the number of hours X before 12 Noon when the person died.

$$X = \frac{0.12675}{K} = \frac{0.12675}{0.04421} \approx 2.867 \text{ (hours)}.$$

Therefore, the time of death is 2.867 hours (2 hours and 52 min) before Noon or 9 : 08 A.M.

7. The temperature function $T(t)$ changes according to Newton's law of cooling (1) on page 102 of the text. Similarly to Example 1 we conclude that, with $H(t) \equiv U(t) \equiv 0$ and the outside temperature $M(t) \equiv 35°\mathrm{C}$, a general solution formula (4) on page 102 becomes

$$T(t) = 35 + Ce^{-Kt}.$$

To find C, we use the initial condition,

$$T(0) = T(\text{at noon}) = 24°\mathrm{C},$$

and get

$$24 = T(0) = 35 + Ce^{-K(0)} \quad \Rightarrow \quad C = 24 - 35 = -11 \quad \Rightarrow \quad T(t) = 35 - 11e^{-Kt}.$$

The time constant for the building $1/K = 4\,\text{hr}$; so $K = 1/4$ and $T(t) = 35 - 11e^{-t/4}$.

At 2 : 00 P.M. $t = 2$, and $t = 6$ at 6 : 00 P.M. Substituting this values into the solution, we obtain that the temperature

$$\begin{aligned} &\text{at } 2:00\,\text{P.M. will be} \quad T(2) = 35 - 11e^{-2/4} \approx 28.3°\mathrm{C}; \\ &\text{at } 6:00\,\text{P.M. will be} \quad T(6) = 35 - 11e^{-6/4} \approx 32.5°\mathrm{C}. \end{aligned}$$

Finally, we solve the equation

$$T(t) = 35 - 11e^{-t/4} = 27$$

to find the time when the temperature inside the building reaches 27°C.

$$35 - 11e^{-t/4} = 27 \quad \Rightarrow \quad 11e^{-t/4} = 8 \quad \Rightarrow \quad t = 4\ln\left(\frac{11}{8}\right) \approx 1.27.$$

Thus, the temperature inside the building will be 27°C at 1.27 hr after noon, that is, at 1 : 16 : 12 P.M.

9. Since we are evaluating the temperature in a warehouse, we can assume that any heat generated by people or equipment in the warehouse will be negligible. Therefore, we have $H(t) = 0$.

Also, we are assuming that there is no heating or air conditioning in the warehouse. Therefore, we have that $U(t)$. We are also given that the outside temperature has a sinusoidal fluctuation. Thus, as in Example 2, page 103, we see that

$$M(t) = M_0 - B\cos\omega t\,,$$

where M_0 is the average outside temperature, B is a positive constant for the magnitude of the temperature shift from this average, and $\omega = \pi/2$ radians per hour. To find M_0 and B, we are given that at 2 : 00 A.M., $M(t)$ reaches a low of 16°C and at 2 : 00 P.M. it reaches a high of 32°C. This gives

$$M_0 = \frac{16+32}{2} = 24^\circ\text{C}.$$

By letting $t = 0$ at 2 : 00 A.M. (so that low for the outside temperature corresponds to the low for the negative cosine function), we can calculate the constant B. That is

$$16 = 24 - B\cos 0 = 24 - B \qquad \Rightarrow \qquad B = 8.$$

Therefore, we see that

$$M(t) = 24 - 8\cos\omega t,$$

where $\omega = \pi/12$. As in Example 2, using the fact that $B_0 = M_0 + H_0/K = M_0 + 0/K = M_0$, we see that

$$T(t) = 24 - 8F(t) + Ce^{-Kt}\,,$$

where

$$F(t) = \frac{\cos\omega t + (\omega/K)\sin\omega t}{1+(\omega/K)^2} = \left[1+\left(\frac{\omega}{K}\right)^2\right]^{-1/2}\cos(\omega t - \alpha).$$

In the last expression, α is chosen such that $\tan\alpha = \omega/K$. By assuming that the exponential term dies off, we obtain

$$T(t) = 24 - 8\left[1+\left(\frac{\omega}{K}\right)^2\right]^{-1/2}\cos(\omega t - \alpha).$$

This function will reach a minimum when $\cos(\omega t - \alpha) = 1$ and it will reach a maximum when $\cos(\omega t - \alpha) = -1$.

For the case when the time constant for the building is 1, we see that $1/K = 1$ which implies that $K = 1$. Therefore, the temperature will reach a maximum of K

$$T = 24 + 8\left[1 + \left(\frac{\pi}{12}\right)^2\right]^{-1/2} \approx 31.7°\text{C}.$$

It will reach a minimum of

$$T = 24 - 8\left[1 + \left(\frac{\pi}{12}\right)^2\right]^{-1/2} \approx 16.3°\text{C}.$$

For the case when the time constant of the building is 5, we have

$$\frac{1}{K} = 5 \qquad \Rightarrow \qquad K = \frac{1}{5}\,.$$

Then, the temperature will reach a maximum of

$$T = 24 + 8\left[1 + \left(\frac{5\pi}{12}\right)^2\right]^{-1/2} \approx 28.9°\text{C},$$

and a minimum of

$$T = 24 - 8\left[1 + \left(\frac{5\pi}{12}\right)^2\right]^{-1/2} \approx 19.1°\text{C}.$$

11. As in Example 3, page 105 of the text, this problem involves a thermostat to regulate the temperature in the van. Hence, we have

$$U(t) = K_U\left[T_D - T(t)\right]\,,$$

where T_D is the desired temperature 16°C and K_U is a proportionality constant. We will assume that $H(t) = 0$ and that the outside temperature $M(t)$ is a constant 35°C. The time constant for the van is $1/K = 2$ hr, hence $K = 0.5$. Since the time constant for the van with its air conditioning system is $1/K_1 = 1/3$ hr, then $K_1 = K + K_U = 3$. Therefore, $K_U = 3 - 0.5 = 2.5$. The temperature in the van is governed by the equation

$$\frac{dT}{dt} = (0.5)(35 - T) + (2.5)(16 - T) = 57.5 - 3T.$$

Solving this separable equation yields

$$T(t) = 19.17 + Ce^{-3t}.$$

When $t = 0$ we are given $T(0) = 55$. Using this information to solve for C gives $C = 35.83$. Hence, the van temperature is given by

$$T(t) = 19.17 + 35.83e^{-3t}.$$

To find out when the temperature in the van will reach 27°C, we let $T(t) = 27$ and solve for t. Thus, we see that

$$27 = 19.17 + 35.83e^{-3t} \quad \Rightarrow \quad e^{-3t} = \frac{7.83}{35.83} \approx 0.2185$$

$$\Rightarrow \quad t \approx \frac{\ln(0.2185)}{3} \approx 0.5070 \text{ (hr)} \quad \text{or} \quad 30.4 \text{ min.}$$

13. Since the time constant is 64, we have $K = 1/64$. The temperature in the tank increases at the rate of 2°F for every 1000 Btu. Furthermore, every hour of sunlight provides an input of 2000 Btu to the tank. Thus,

$$H(t) = 2 \times 2 = 4^\circ\text{F per hr.}$$

We are given that $T(0) = 110$, and that the temperature $M(t)$ outside the tank is a constant 80°F. Hence the temperature in the tank is governed by

$$\frac{dT}{dt} = \frac{1}{64}[80 - T(t)] + 4 = -\frac{1}{64}T(t) + 5.25, \qquad T(0) = 110.$$

Solving this separable equation gives

$$T(t) = 336 + Ce^{-t/64}.$$

To find C, we use the initial condition to see that

$$T(0) = 110 = 336 + C \quad \Rightarrow \quad C = -226.$$

This yields the equation

$$T(t) = 336 - 226e^{-t/64}.$$

After 12 hours of sunlight, the temperature will be

$$T(12) = 336 - 226e^{-12/64} \approx 148.6°\text{F}.$$

15. The equation $dT/dt = k\left(M^4 - T^4\right)$ is separable. Separation variables yields

$$\frac{dT}{T^4 - M^4} = -k\,dt \qquad \Rightarrow \qquad \int \frac{dT}{T^4 - M^4} = -\int k\,dt = -kt + C_1. \qquad (3.9)$$

Since $T^4 - M^4 = \left(T^2 - M^2\right)\left(T^2 + M^2\right)$, we have

$$\frac{1}{T^4 - M^4} = \frac{1}{2M^2}\frac{\left(M^2 + T^2\right) + \left(M^2 - T^2\right)}{\left(T^2 - M^2\right)\left(T^2 + M^2\right)} = \frac{1}{2M^2}\left[\frac{1}{T^2 - M^2} - \frac{1}{T^2 + M^2}\right],$$

and the integral in the left-hand side of (3.9) becomes

$$\int \frac{dT}{T^4 - M^4} = \frac{1}{2M^2}\left[\int \frac{dT}{T^2 - M^2} - \int \frac{dT}{T^2 + M^2}\right] = \frac{1}{4M^3}\left[\ln\frac{T - M}{T + M} - 2\arctan\left(\frac{T}{M}\right)\right].$$

Thus a general solution to Stefan's equation is given implicitly by

$$\frac{1}{4M^3}\left[\ln\frac{T - M}{T + M} - 2\arctan\left(\frac{T}{M}\right)\right] = -kt + C_1$$

or

$$T - M = C(T + M)\exp\left[2\arctan\left(\frac{T}{M}\right) - 4M^3kt\right].$$

When T is close to M,

$$M^4 - T^4 = (M - T)(M + T)\left(M^2 + T^2\right) \approx (M - T)(2M)\left(2M^2\right) \approx 4M^3(M - T),$$

and so

$$\frac{dT}{dt} \approx k \cdot 4M^3(M - T)4M^3 = k_1(M - T)$$

with $k_1 = 4M^3k$, which constitutes Newton's law.

EXERCISES 3.4: Newtonian Mechanics, page 115

1. This problem is a particular case of Example 1 on page 110 of the text. Therefore, we can use the general formula (6) on page 111 with $m = 5$, $b = 50$, and $v_0 = v(0) = 0$. But let us follow the general idea of Section 3.4, find an equation of the motion, and solve it.

With given data, the force due to gravity is $F_1 = mg = 5g$ and the air resistance force is $F_2 = -50v$. Therefore, the velocity $v(t)$ satisfies

$$m\frac{dv}{dt} = F_1 + F_2 = 5g - 50v \qquad \Rightarrow \qquad \frac{dv}{dt} = g - 10v, \qquad v(0) = 0.$$

Separating variables yields

$$\frac{dv}{10v - g} = -dt \qquad \Rightarrow \qquad \frac{1}{10}\ln|10v - g| = -t + C_1$$
$$\Rightarrow \qquad v(t) = \frac{g}{10} + Ce^{-10t}.$$

Substituting the initial condition, $v(0) = 0$, we get $C = -g/10$, and so

$$v(t) = \frac{g}{10}\left(1 - e^{-10t}\right).$$

Integrating this equation yields

$$x(t) = \int v(t)\,dt = \int \frac{g}{10}\left(1 - e^{-10t}\right)dt = \frac{g}{10}\left(t + \frac{1}{10}e^{-10t}\right) + C,$$

and we find C using the initial condition $x(0) = 0$:

$$0 = \frac{g}{10}\left(0 + \frac{1}{10}e^{-10(0)}\right) + C \qquad \Rightarrow \qquad C = -\frac{g}{100}$$
$$\Rightarrow \qquad x(t) = \frac{g}{10}t + \frac{g}{100}\left(e^{-10t} - 1\right) = (0.981)t + (0.0981)e^{-10t} - 0.0981\,(\text{m}).$$

When the object hits the ground, $x(t) = 1000\,\text{m}$. Thus we solve

$$(0.981)t + (0.0981)e^{-10t} - 0.0981 = 1000,$$

which gives (t is nonnegative!) $t \approx 1019.468 \approx 1019\,\text{sec}$.

3. For this problem, $m = 500$ kg, $v_0 = 0$, $g = 9.81$ m/sec^2, and $b = 50$ kg/sec. We also see that the object has 1000 m to fall before it hits the ground. Plugging these variables into equation (6) on page 111 of the text gives the equation

$$x(t) = \frac{(500)(9.81)}{50}t + \frac{500}{50}\left(0 - \frac{(500)(9.81)}{50}\right)\left(1 - e^{-50t/500}\right)$$

$$\Rightarrow \qquad x(t) = 98.1t + 981e^{-t/10} - 981.$$

To find out when the object will hit the ground, we solve $x(t) = 1000$ for t. Therefore, we have

$$1000 = 98.1t + 981e^{-t/10} - 981 \qquad \Rightarrow \qquad 98.1t + 981e^{-t/10} = 1981.$$

In this equation, if we ignore the term $981e^{-t/10}$ we will find that $t \approx 20.2$. But this means that we have ignored the term similar to $981e^{-2} \approx 132.8$ which we see is to large to ignore. Therefore, we must try to approximate t. We will use Newton's method on the equation

$$f(t) = 98.1t + 981e^{-t/10} - 1981 = 0.$$

(If we can find a root to this equation, we will have found the t we want.) Newton's method generates a sequence of approximations given by the formula

$$t_{n+1} = t_n - \frac{f(t_n)}{f'(t_n)}.$$

Since $f'(t) = 98.1 - 98.1e^{-t/10} = 98.1\left(1 - e^{-t/10}\right)$, the recursive equation above becomes

$$t_{n+1} = t_n - \frac{t_n + 10e^{-t_n/10} - (1981/98.1)}{1 - e^{-t_n/10}}. \tag{3.10}$$

To start the process, let $t_0 = 1981/98.1 \approx 20.19368$, which was the approximation we obtained when we neglected the exponential term. Then, by equation (3.10) above we have

$$t_1 = 20.19368 - \frac{20.19368 + 10e^{-2.019368} - 20.19368}{1 - e^{-2.019368}}$$
$$\Rightarrow \qquad t_1 \approx 18.663121\,.$$

To find t_2 we plug this value for t_1 into equation (3.10). This gives $t_2 \approx 18.643753$. Continuing this process, we find that $t_3 \approx 18.643749$. Since t_2 and t_3 agree to four decimal places, an approximation for the time it takes the object to strike the ground is $t \approx 18.6437$ sec.

5. We proceed similarly to the solution of Problem 1 to get

$$F_1 = 5g, \qquad F_2 = -10g$$

$$\Rightarrow \qquad 5\,\frac{dv}{dt} = F_1 + F_2 = 5g - 10v$$

$$\Rightarrow \qquad \frac{dv}{dt} = g - 2v, \qquad v(0) = 50.$$

Solving this iniial value problem yields

$$v(t) = \frac{g}{2} + Ce^{-2t};$$

$$50 = v(0) = \frac{g}{2} + Ce^{-2(0)} \qquad \Rightarrow \qquad C = \frac{100-g}{2}$$

$$\Rightarrow \qquad v(t) = \frac{g}{2} + \frac{100-g}{2}\,e^{-2t}.$$

We now integrate $v(t)$ to obtain the equation of the motion of the object:

$$x(t) = \int v(t)\,dt = \int\left(\frac{g}{2} + \frac{100-g}{2}e^{-2t}\right)dt = \frac{g}{2}\,t - \frac{100-g}{4}e^{-2t} + C,$$

where C is such that $x(0) = 0$. Computing

$$0 = x(0) = \frac{g}{2}\,(0) - \frac{100-g}{4}e^{-2(0)} + C \qquad \Rightarrow \qquad C = \frac{100-g}{4},$$

we answer the first question in this problem, that is,

$$x(t) = \frac{g}{2}\,t - \frac{100-g}{4}\,e^{-2t} + \frac{100-g}{4} \approx 4.905t + 22.5475 - 22.5475\,e^{-2t}.$$

Answering the second question, we solve the equation $x(t) = 500$ to find time t when the object passes 500 m, and so strikes the ground.

$$4.905t + 22.5475 - 22.5475\,e^{-2t} = 500 \qquad \Rightarrow \qquad t \approx 97.34\ \text{(sec)}.$$

7. Since the air resistance force has different coefficients of proportionality for closed and for opened chute, we need two differential equations describing the motion. Let $x_1(t)$, $x_1(0) = 0$, denote the distance the parachutist has fallen in t seconds, and let $v_1(t) = dx/dt$ denote her velocity. With $m = 75$, $b = b_1 = 30$ N-sec/m, and $v_0 = 0$ the initial value problem (4) on page 111 of the text becomes

$$75\,\frac{dv_1}{dt} = 75g - 30v_1 \qquad \Rightarrow \qquad \frac{dv_1}{dt} + \frac{2}{5}\,v_1 = g, \qquad v_1(0) = 0.$$

This is a linear equation. Solving yields

$$\begin{aligned}
&d\left(e^{2t/5}v_1\right) = e^{2t/5}g\,dt \qquad \Rightarrow \qquad v_1(t) = \frac{5g}{2} + C_1e^{-2t/5};\\
&0 = v_1(0) = \frac{5g}{2} + C_1e^0 = \frac{5g}{2} + C_1 \qquad \Rightarrow \qquad C_1 = -\frac{5g}{2}\\
&\Rightarrow \qquad v_1(t) = \frac{5g}{2}\left(1 - e^{-2t/5}\right)\\
&\Rightarrow \qquad x_1(t) = \int\limits_0^t v_1(s)ds = \frac{5g}{2}\left(s + \frac{5}{2}e^{-2s/5}\right)\Bigg|_{s=0}^{s=t} = \frac{5g}{2}\left(t + \frac{5}{2}e^{-2t/5} - \frac{5}{2}\right).
\end{aligned}$$

To find the time t_* when the chute opens, we solve

$$20 = v_1(t_*) \qquad \Rightarrow \qquad 20 = \frac{5g}{2}\left(1 - e^{-2t_*/5}\right) \qquad \Rightarrow \qquad t_* = -\frac{5}{2}\ln\left(1 - \frac{8}{g}\right) \approx 4.225\,(\text{sec}).$$

By this time the parachutist has fallen

$$x_1(t_*) = \frac{5g}{2}\left(t_* + \frac{5}{2}e^{-2t_*/5} - \frac{5}{2}\right) \approx \frac{5g}{2}\left(4.225 + \frac{5}{2}e^{-2\cdot 4.225/5} - \frac{5}{2}\right) \approx 53.62\,(\text{m}),$$

and so she is $2000 - 53.62 = 1946.38$ m above the ground. Setting the second equation, we for convenience reset the time t. Denoting by $x_2(t)$ the distance passed by the parachutist from the moment when the chute opens, and by $v_2(t) := x_2'(t)$ – her velocity, we have

$$75\frac{dv_2}{dt} = 75g - 90v_2, \qquad v_2(0) = v_1(t_*) = 20, \quad x_2(0) = 0.$$

Solving, we get

$$\begin{aligned}
&v_2(t) = \frac{5g}{6} + C_2e^{-6t/5};\\
&20 = v_2(0) = \frac{5g}{6} + C_2 \qquad \Rightarrow \qquad C_2 = 20 - \frac{5g}{6}\\
&\Rightarrow \qquad v_2(t) = \frac{5g}{6} + \left(20 - \frac{5g}{6}\right)e^{-6t/5}\\
&\Rightarrow \qquad x_2(t) = \int\limits_0^t v_2(s)ds = \left[\frac{5g}{6}s - \frac{5}{6}\left(20 - \frac{5g}{6}\right)e^{-6s/5}\right]\Bigg|_{s=0}^{s=t}\\
&\qquad = \frac{5g}{6}t + \frac{5}{6}\left(20 - \frac{5g}{6}\right)\left(1 - e^{-6t/5}\right).
\end{aligned}$$

With the chute open, the parachutist falls 1946.38 m. It takes t^* seconds, where t^* satisfies $x_2(t^*) = 1946.38$. Solving yields

$$\frac{5g}{6}t^* + \frac{5}{6}\left(20 - \frac{5g}{6}\right)\left(1 - e^{-6t^*/5}\right) = 1946.38 \qquad \Rightarrow \qquad t^* \approx 236.884\,(\text{sec}).$$

Therefore, the parachutist will hit the ground after $t^* + t_* \approx 241.1$ seconds.

9. This problem is similar to Example 1 on page 110 of the text with the addition of a buoyancy force of magnitude $(1/40)mg$. If we let $x(t)$ be the distance below the water at time t and $v(t)$ the velocity, then the total force acting on the object is

$$F = mg - bv - \frac{1}{40}mg.$$

We are given $m = 100$ kg, $g = 9.81$ m/sec^2, and $b = 10$ kg/sec. Applying Newton's Second Law gives

$$100\frac{dv}{dt} = (100)(9.81) - 10v - \frac{10}{4}(9.81) \qquad \Rightarrow \qquad \frac{dv}{dt} = 9.56 - (0.1)v\,.$$

Solving this equation by separation of variables, we have

$$v(t) = 95.65 + Ce^{-t/10}.$$

Since $v(0) = 0$, we find $C = -95.65$ and, hence,

$$v(t) = 95.65 - 95.65e^{-t/10}.$$

Integrating yields

$$x(t) = 95.65t + 956.5e^{-t/10} + C_1\,.$$

Using the fact that $x(0) = 0$, we find $C_1 = -956.5$. Therefore, the equation of motion of the object is

$$x(t) = 95.65t + 956.5e^{-t/10} - 956.5\,.$$

To determine when the object is traveling at the velocity of 70 m/sec, we solve $v(t) = 70$. That is,

$$70 = 95.65 - 95.65e^{-t/10} = 95.65\left(1 - e^{-t/10}\right)$$
$$\Rightarrow \qquad t = -10\ln\left(1 - \frac{70}{95.65}\right) \approx 13.2 \text{ sec.}$$

11. Let $v(t) = V[x(t)]$. Then, using the chain rule, we get

$$\frac{dv}{dt} = \frac{dV}{dx}\frac{dx}{dt} = \frac{dV}{dx}V$$

and so, for $V(x)$, the initial value problem (4) on page 111 of the text becomes

$$m\frac{dV}{dx}V = mg - bV, \qquad V(0) = V[x(0)] = v(0) = v_0.$$

This differential equation is separable. Solving yields

$$\frac{V}{g-(b/m)V}\,dV = dx \qquad \Rightarrow \qquad \frac{m}{b}\left[\frac{g}{g-(b/m)V} - 1\right]dV = dx$$

$$\Rightarrow \qquad \int \frac{m}{b}\left[\frac{g}{g-(b/m)V} - 1\right]dV = \int dx$$

$$\Rightarrow \qquad \frac{m}{b}\left[-\frac{mg}{b}\ln|g-(b/m)V| - V\right] = x + C$$

$$\Rightarrow \qquad mg\ln|mg-bV| + bV = -\frac{b^2x}{m} + C_1\,.$$

Substituting the initial condition, $V(0) = v_0$, we find that $C_1 = mg\ln|mg - bv_0| + bv_0$ and hence

$$mg\ln|mg-bV| + bV = -\frac{b^2x}{m} + mg\ln|mg-bv_0| + bv_0$$

$$\Rightarrow \qquad e^{bV}|mg-bV|^{mg} = e^{bv_0}|mg-bv_0|^{mg}e^{-b^2x/m}\,.$$

13. There are two forces acting on the shell: a constant force due to the downward pull of gravity and a force due to air resistance that acts in opposition to the motion of the shell. All of the motion occurs along a vertical axis. On this axis, we choose the origin to be the point where the shell was shot from and let $x(t)$ denote the position upward of the shell at time t. The forces acting on the object can be expressed in terms of this axis. The force due to gravity is

$$F_1 = -mg,$$

where g is the acceleration due to gravity near Earth. Note we have a minus force because our coordinate system was chosen with up as positive and gravity acts in a downward direction. The force due to air resistance is

$$F_2 = -(0.1)v^2.$$

The negative sign is present because air resistance acts in opposition to the motion of the object. Therefore the net force acting on the shell is

$$F = F_1 + F_2 = -mg - (0.1)v^2.$$

We now apply Newton's second law to obtain

$$m\,\frac{dv}{dt} = -\left[mg + (0.1)v^2\right].$$

Because the initial velocity of the shell is 500 m/sec, a model for the velocity of the rising shell is expressed as the initial-value problem

$$m\,\frac{dv}{dt} = -\left[mg + (0.1)v^2\right], \qquad v(t=0) = 500, \tag{3.11}$$

where $g = 9.81$. Separating variables, we get

$$\frac{dv}{10mg + v^2} = -\frac{dt}{10m}$$

and so

$$\int \frac{dv}{10mg + v^2} = -\int \frac{dt}{10m} \qquad \Rightarrow \qquad \frac{1}{\sqrt{10mg}}\tan^{-1}\left(\frac{v}{\sqrt{10mg}}\right) = -\frac{t}{10m} + C.$$

Setting $m = 3$, $g = 9.81$ and $v = 500$ when $t = 0$, we find

$$C = \frac{1}{\sqrt{10(3)(9.81)}}\tan^{-1}\left(\frac{500}{\sqrt{10(3)(9.81)}}\right) \approx 0.08956\,.$$

Thus the equation of velocity v as a function of time t is

$$\frac{1}{\sqrt{10mg}}\tan^{-1}\left(\frac{v}{\sqrt{10mg}}\right) = -\frac{t}{10m} + 0.08956\,.$$

From physics we know that when the shell reaches its maximum height the shell's velocity will be zero; therefore $t_{\max}$ will be

$$\begin{aligned} t_{\max} &= -10(3)\left[\frac{1}{\sqrt{10(3)(9.81)}}\tan^{-1}\left(\frac{0}{\sqrt{10(3)(9.81)}}\right) - 0.08956\right] \\ &= -(30)(-0.08956) \approx 2.69 \text{ (seconds)}. \end{aligned}$$

Using equation (3.11) and noting that $dv/dt = (dv/dx)(dx/dt) = (dv/dx)v$, we can determine the maximum height attained by the shell. With the above substitution, equation (3.11) becomes

$$mv\,\frac{dv}{dx} = -\left(mg + 0.1v^2\right), \qquad v(0) = 500.$$

Using separation of variables and integration, we get

$$\frac{v\,dv}{10mg + v^2} = -\frac{dx}{10m} \quad \Rightarrow \quad \frac{1}{2}\ln\left(10mg + v^2\right) = -\frac{x}{10m} + C \quad \Rightarrow \quad 10mg + v^2 = Ke^{-x/(5m)}.$$

Setting $v = 500$ when $x = 0$, we find

$$K = e^0\left(10(3)(9.81) + (500)^2\right) = 250294.3\,.$$

Thus the equation of velocity as a function of distance is

$$v^2 + 10mg = (250294.3)e^{-x/(5m)}\,.$$

The maximum height will occur when the shell's velocity is zero, therefore $x_{\max}$ is

$$x_{\max} = -5(3)\ln\left(\frac{0 + 10(3)(9.81)}{250294.3}\right) \approx 101.19 \text{ (meters)}.$$

15. The total torque exerted on the flywheel is the sum of the torque exerted by the motor and the retarding torque due to friction. Thus, by Newton's second law for rotation, we have

$$I\,\frac{d\omega}{dt} = T - k\omega \qquad \text{with} \qquad \omega(0) = \omega_0\,,$$

where I is the moment of inertia of the flywheel, $\omega(t)$ is the angular velocity, $d\omega/dt$ is the angular acceleration, T is the constant torque exerted by the motor, and k is a positive constant of proportionality for the torque due to friction. Solving this separable equation gives

$$\omega(t) = \frac{T}{k} + Ce^{-kt/I}\,.$$

Using the initial condition $\omega(0) = \omega_0$ we find $C = (\omega_0 - T/k)$. Hence,

$$\omega(t) = \frac{T}{k} + \left(\omega_0 - \frac{T}{k}\right)e^{-kt/I}\,.$$

17. Since the motor is turned off, its torque is $T = 0$, and the only torque acting on the flywheel is the retarding one, $-5\sqrt{\omega}$. Then Newton's second law for rotational motion becomes

$$I\frac{d\omega}{dt} = -5\sqrt{\omega} \qquad \text{with} \qquad \omega(0) = \omega_0 = 225 \text{ (rad/sec)} \qquad \text{and} \qquad I = 50 \ \left(\text{kg/m}^2\right).$$

The general solution to this separable equation is

$$\sqrt{\omega(t)} = -\frac{5}{2I}t + C = -0.05t + C.$$

Using the initial condition, we find

$$\sqrt{\omega(0)} = -0.05 \cdot 0 + C \qquad \Rightarrow \qquad C = \sqrt{\omega(0)} = \sqrt{225} = 15.$$

Thus

$$t = \frac{1}{0.05}\left[15 - \sqrt{\omega(t)}\right] = 20\left[15 - \sqrt{\omega(t)}\right].$$

At the moment $t = t_{\text{stop}}$ when the flywheel stops rotating we have $\omega\left(t_{\text{stop}}\right) = 0$ and so

$$t_{\text{stop}} = 20(15 - \sqrt{0}) = 300 \text{ (sec)}.$$

19. There are three forces acting on the object: F_1, the force due to gravity, F_2, the air resistance force, and F_3, the friction force. Using Figure 3.11 (with 30° replaced by 45°), we obtain

$$\begin{aligned} F_1 &= mg\sin 45^\circ = mg\sqrt{2}/2\,, \\ F_2 &= -3v, \\ F_3 &= -\mu N = -\mu mg\cos 45^\circ = -\mu mg\sqrt{2}/2\,, \end{aligned}$$

and so the equation describing the motion is

$$m\frac{dv}{dt} = \frac{mg\sqrt{2}}{2} - \frac{\mu mg\sqrt{2}}{2} - 3v \qquad \Rightarrow \qquad \frac{dv}{dt} = 0.475g\sqrt{2} - \frac{v}{20}$$

with the initial condition $v(0) = 0$. Solving yields

$$\begin{aligned} &v(t) = 9.5g\sqrt{2} + Ce^{-t/20}; \\ &0 = v(0) = 9.5g\sqrt{2} + C \qquad \Rightarrow \qquad C = -9.5g\sqrt{2} \end{aligned}$$

$$\Rightarrow \qquad v(t) = 9.5g\sqrt{2}\left(1 - e^{-t/20}\right).$$

Since $x(0) = 0$, integrating the above equation, we obtain

$$\begin{aligned} x(t) &= \int_0^t v(s)ds = \int_0^t 9.5g\sqrt{2}\left(1 - e^{-s/20}\right) ds = 9.5g\sqrt{2}\left(s + 20e^{-s/20}\right)\Big|_{s=0}^{s=t} \\ &= 9.5g\sqrt{2}\left(t + 20e^{-t/20} - 20\right) \approx 131.8t + 2636e^{-t/20} - 2636. \end{aligned}$$

The object reaches the end of the inclined plane when

$$x(t) = 131.8t + 2636e^{-t/20} - 2636 = 10 \qquad \Rightarrow \qquad t \approx 1.768\,(\text{sec}).$$

21. In this problem there are two forces acting on a sailboat: A constant horizontal force due to the wind and a force due to the water resistance that acts in opposition to the motion of the sailboat. All of the motion occurs along a horizontal axis. On this axis, we choose the origin to be the point where the hard blowing wind begins and $x(t)$ denotes the distance the sailboat travels in time t. The forces on the sailboat can be expressed in terms of this axis. The force due to the wind is

$$F_1 = 600 \text{ N}.$$

The force due to water resistance is

$$F_2 = -100v \text{ N}.$$

Applying Newton's second law we obtain

$$m\,\frac{dv}{dt} = 600 - 100v.$$

Since the initial velocity of the sailboat is 1 m/sec, a model for the velocity of the moving sailboat is expressed as the initial-value problem

$$m\,\frac{dv}{dt} = 600 - 100v, \qquad v(0) = 1.$$

Using separation of variables, we get, with $m = 50$ kg,

$$\frac{dv}{6 - v} = 2dt \qquad \Rightarrow \qquad -6\ln(6 - v) = 2t + C.$$

Therefore, the velocity is given by $v(t) = 6 - Ke^{-2t}$. Setting $v = 1$ when $t = 0$, we find that

$$1 = 6 - K \qquad \Rightarrow \qquad K = 5.$$

Thus the equation for velocity $v(t)$ is $v(t) = 6 - 5e^{-2t}$. The limiting velocity of the sailboat under these conditions is found by letting time approach infinity:

$$\lim_{t\to\infty} v(t) = \lim_{t\to\infty} \left(6 - 5e^{-2t}\right) = 6 \text{ (m/sec)}.$$

To determine the equation of motion we will use the equation of velocity obtained previously and substitute dx/dt for $v(t)$ to obtain

$$\frac{dx}{dt} = 6 - 5e^{-2t}, \qquad x(0) = 0.$$

Integrating this equation we obtain

$$x(t) = 6t + \frac{5}{2}\,e^{-2t} + C_1.$$

Setting $x = 0$ when $t = 0$, we find

$$0 = 0 + \frac{5}{2} + C_1 \qquad \Rightarrow \qquad C_1 = -\frac{5}{2}.$$

Thus the equation of motion for the sailboat is given by

$$x(t) = 6t + \frac{5}{2}\,e^{-2t} - \frac{5}{2}.$$

23. In this problem, there are two forces acting on a boat: the wind force F_1 and the water resistance force F_2. Since the proportionality constant in the water resistance force is different for the velocities below and above of a certain limit (5 m/sec for the boat A and 6 m/sec for the boat B), for each boat we have two differential equations. (Compare with Problem 7.) Let $x_1^{(A)}(t)$ denote the distance passed by the boat A for the time t, $v_1^{(A)}(t) := dx_1^{(A)}(t)/dt$. Then the equation describing the motion of the boat A before it reaches the velocity 5 m/sec is

$$m\,\frac{dv_1^{(A)}}{dt} = F_1 + F_2 = 650 - b_1 v_1^{(A)} \qquad \Rightarrow \qquad \frac{dv_1^{(A)}}{dt} = \frac{65}{6} - \frac{4}{3}\,v_1^{(A)}. \tag{3.12}$$

Solving this linear equation and using the initial condition, $v_1^{(A)}(0) = 2$, we get

$$v_1^{(A)}(t) = \frac{65}{8} - \frac{49}{8}\,e^{-4t/3},$$

and so

$$x_1^{(A)}(t) = \int_0^t \left(\frac{65}{8} - \frac{49}{8}\,e^{-4s/3}\right) ds = \frac{65}{8}\,t - \frac{147}{32}\left(e^{-4t/3} - 1\right).$$

The boat A will have the velocity 5 m/sec at $t = t_*$ satisfying

$$\frac{65}{8} - \frac{49}{8}\,e^{-4t_*/3} = 5 \qquad \Rightarrow \qquad t_* = -\frac{3\ln(25/49)}{4} \approx 0.5\,(\text{sec}),$$

and it will be

$$x_1^{(A)}(t_*) = \frac{65}{8}\,t_* - \frac{147}{32}\left(e^{-4t_*/3} - 1\right) \approx 1.85\,(\text{m})$$

away from the starting point or, equivalently, $500 - 1.85 = 498.15$ meters away from the finish. Similarly to (3.12), resetting the time, we obtain an equation of the motion of the boat A starting from the moment when its velocity reaches 5 m/sec. Denoting by $x_2^{(A)}(t)$ the distance passed by the boat A and by $v_2^{(A)}(t)$ its velocity, we get $x_2^{(A)}(0) = 0$, $v_2^{(A)}(0) = 5$, and

$$m\,\frac{dv_2^{(A)}}{dt} = 650 - b_2 v_2^{(A)}$$

$$\Rightarrow \qquad \frac{dv_2^{(A)}}{dt} = \frac{65}{6} - v_2^{(A)} \qquad \Rightarrow \qquad v_2^{(A)}(t) = \frac{65}{6} - \frac{35}{6}\,e^{-t}$$

$$\Rightarrow \qquad x_2^{(A)}(t) = \int_0^t \left(\frac{65}{6} - \frac{35}{6}\,e^{-s}\right) ds = \frac{65}{6}\,t + \frac{35}{6}\left(e^{-t} - 1\right).$$

Solving the equation $x_2^{(A)}(t) = 498.15$, we find the time (counting from the moment when the boat A's velocity has reached 5 m/sec) $t^* \approx 46.5$ sec, which is necessary to come to the end of the first leg. Therefore, the total time for the boat A is $t_* + t^* \approx 0.5 + 46.5 = 47$ sec.

Similarly, for the boat B, we find that

$$v_1^{(B)}(t) = \frac{65}{8} - \frac{49}{8}\,e^{-5t/3}, \quad x_1^{(B)}(t) = \frac{65}{8}\,t + \frac{147}{40}\left(e^{-5t/3} - 1\right), \quad t_* = -\frac{3\ln(17/49)}{5} \approx 0.635;$$

$$v_2^{(B)}(t) = \frac{65}{5} - \frac{35}{5}\,e^{-5t/6}, \quad x_2^{(B)}(t) = \frac{65}{5}\,t + \frac{42}{5}\left(e^{-5t/6} - 1\right), \qquad t^* \approx 38.895.$$

Thus, $t_* + t^* < 40$ sec, and so the boat B will be leading at the end of the first leg.

25. **(a)** From Newton's second law we have

$$m\frac{dv}{dt} = \frac{-GMm}{r^2}.$$

Dividing both sides by m, the mass of the rocket, and letting $g = GM/R^2$ we get

$$\frac{dv}{dt} = \frac{-gR^2}{r^2},$$

where g is the gravitational force of Earth, R is the radius of Earth and r is the distance between Earth and the projectile.

(b) Using the equation found in part (a), letting $dv/dt = (dv/dr)(dr/dt)$ and knowing that $dr/dt = v$, we get

$$v\frac{dv}{dr} = -\frac{gR^2}{r^2}.$$

(c) The differential equation found in part (b) is separable and can be written in the form

$$v\,dv = -\frac{gR^2}{r^2}\,dr.$$

If the projectile leaves Earth with a velocity of v_0 we have the initial value problem

$$v\,dv = -\frac{gR^2}{r^2}\,dr, \qquad v\Big|_{r=R} = v_0.$$

Integrating we get

$$\frac{v^2}{2} = \frac{gR^2}{r} + K,$$

where K is an arbitrary constant. We can find the constant K by using the initial value as follows:

$$K = \frac{v_0^2}{2} - \frac{gR^2}{R} = \frac{v_0^2}{2} - gR.$$

Substituting this formula for K and solving for the velocity we obtain

$$v^2 = \frac{2gR^2}{r} + v_0^2 - 2gR.$$

(d) In order for the velocity of the projectile to always remain positive, $(2gR^2/r) + v_0^2$ must be greater than $2gR$ as r approaches infinity. This means

$$\lim_{r\to\infty}\left(\frac{2gR^2}{r} + v_0^2\right) > 2gR \qquad \Rightarrow \qquad v_0^2 > 2gR.$$

Therefore, $v_0^2 - 2gR > 0$.

(e) Using the equation $v_e = \sqrt{2gR}$ for the escape velocity and converting meters to kilometers we have

$$v_e = \sqrt{2gR} = \sqrt{2 \cdot 9.81 \text{ m/sec}^2 \cdot (1 \text{ km}/1000 \text{ m})(6370 \text{ km})} \approx 11.18 \text{ km/sec}.$$

(f) Similarly to (e), we find

$$v_e = \sqrt{2(g/6)R} = \sqrt{2(9.81/6)(1/1000)(1738)} = 2.38 \text{ (km/sec)}.$$

EXERCISES 3.5: Electrical Circuits, page 122

1. In this problem, $R = 5\,\Omega$, $L = 0.05\,\text{H}$, and the voltage function is given by $E(t) = 5\cos 120t\,\text{V}$. Substituting these data into a general solution (3) to the Kirchhoff's equation (2) yields

$$\begin{aligned} I(t) &= e^{-Rt/L}\left(\int e^{Rt/L}\frac{E(t)}{L}\,dt + K\right) \\ &= e^{-5t/0.05}\left(\int e^{5t/0.05}\frac{5\cos 120t}{0.05}\,dt + K\right) = e^{-100t}\left(100\int e^{100t}\cos 120t\,dt + K\right). \end{aligned}$$

Using the integral tables, we evaluate the integral in the right-hand side and obtain

$$I(t) = e^{-100t}\left[100\,\frac{e^{100t}\left(100\cos 120t + 120\sin 120t\right)}{(100)^2 + (120)^2} + K\right] = \frac{\cos 120t + 1.2\sin 120t}{2.44} + Ke^{-100t}.$$

The initial condition, $I(0) = 1$, implies that

$$1 = I(0) = \frac{\cos(120(0)) + 1.2\sin(120(0))}{2.44} + Ke^{-100(0)} = \frac{1}{2.44} + K \quad \Rightarrow \quad K = 1 - \frac{1}{2.44} = \frac{1.44}{2.44}$$

and so

$$I(t) = \frac{1.44e^{-100t} + \cos 120t + 1.2\sin 120t}{2.44}.$$

The subsequent inductor voltage is then determined by

$$\begin{aligned} E_L(t) = L\frac{dI}{dt} &= 0.05\,\frac{d}{dt}\left(\frac{1.44e^{-100t} + \cos 120t + 1.2\sin 120t}{2.44}\right) \\ &= \frac{-7.2e^{-100t} - 6\sin 120t + 7.2\cos 120t}{2.44}. \end{aligned}$$

Chapter 3

3. In this RC circuit, $R = 100\,\Omega$, $C = 10^{-12}$ F, the initial charge of the capacitor is $Q = q(0) = 0$ coulombs, and the applied constant voltage is $V = 5$ volts. Thus we can use a general equation for the charge $q(t)$ of the capacitor derived in Example 2. Substitution of given data yields

$$q(t) = CV + [Q - CV]e^{-t/RC} = 10^{-12}(5)\left(1 - e^{-t/\left(100\cdot 10^{-12}\right)}\right) = 5 \cdot 10^{-12}\left(1 - e^{-10^{10}t}\right)$$

and so

$$E_C(t) = \frac{q(t)}{C} = 5\left(1 - e^{-10^{10}t}\right).$$

Solving the equation $E_C(t) = 3$, we get

$$5\left(1 - e^{-10^{10}t}\right) = 3 \qquad \Rightarrow \qquad e^{-10^{10}t} = 0.4 \qquad \Rightarrow \qquad t = -\frac{\ln 0.4}{10^{10}} \approx 9.2 \times 10^{-11}\ \text{(sec)}.$$

Therefore, it will take about 9.2×10^{-11} seconds for the voltage to reach 3 volts at the receiving gate.

5. Let $V(t)$ denote the voltage across an element, and let $I(t)$ be the current through this element. Then for the power, say $P = P(t)$, generated or dissipated by the element we have

$$P = I(t)V(t). \tag{3.13}$$

We use formulas given in (a), (b), and (c) on page 119–120 of the text to find P for a resistor, an inductor, and a capacitor.

(a) *Resistor.* In this case,

$$V(t) = E_R(t) = RI(t),$$

and substitution into (3.13) yields

$$P_R = I(t)\left[RI(t)\right] = I(t)^2 R.$$

(b) *Inductor.* We have

$$V(t) = E_L(t) = L\frac{dI(t)}{dt}$$

$$\Rightarrow \qquad P_L = I(t)\left[L\frac{dI(t)}{dt}\right] = \frac{L}{2}\left[2I(t)\frac{dI(t)}{dt}\right] = \frac{L}{2}\frac{d\left[I(t)^2\right]}{dt} = \frac{d\left[LI(t)^2/2\right]}{dt}.$$

(c) *Capacitor.* Here, with $q(t)$ denoting the electrical charge on the capacitor,

$$V(t)=E_C(t)=\frac{1}{C}\,q(t) \quad\Rightarrow\quad q(t)=CE_C(t) \quad\Rightarrow\quad I(t)=\frac{dq(t)}{dt}=\frac{d\,[CE_C(t)]}{dt}$$

and so

$$P_C=\frac{d\,[CE_C(t)]}{dt}\,E_C(t)=\frac{C}{2}\left[2E_C(t)\frac{dE_C(t)}{dt}\right]=\frac{C}{2}\,\frac{d\,[E_C(t)^2]}{dt}=\frac{d\,[CE_C(t)^2/2]}{dt}\,.$$

7. First, we find a formula for the current $I(t)$. Given that $R=3\,\Omega$, $L=10\,\mathrm{H}$, and the voltage function $E(t)$ is a constant, say, V, the formula (3) on page 121 (which describes currents in RL circuits) becomes

$$I(t)=e^{-3t/10}\left(\int e^{3t/10}\,\frac{V}{10}\,dt+K\right)=e^{-3t/10}\left(\frac{V}{3}\,e^{3t/10}+K\right)=\frac{V}{3}+Ke^{-3t/10}\,.$$

The initial condition, $I(0)=0$ (there were no current in the electromagnet before the voltage source was applied), yields

$$0=\frac{V}{3}+Ke^{-3(0)/10} \quad\Rightarrow\quad K=-\frac{V}{3} \quad\Rightarrow\quad I(t)=\frac{V}{3}\left(1-e^{-3t/10}\right).$$

Next, we find the limiting value I_∞ of $I(t)$, that is,

$$I_\infty=\lim_{t\to\infty}\left[\frac{V}{3}\left(1-e^{-3t/10}\right)\right]=\frac{V}{3}\,(1-0)=\frac{V}{3}\,.$$

Therefore, we are looking for the moment t when $I(t)=(0.9)I_\infty=(0.9)V/3$. Solving yields

$$\frac{0.9V}{3}=\frac{V}{3}\left(1-e^{-3t/10}\right) \quad\Rightarrow\quad e^{-3t/10}=0.1 \quad\Rightarrow\quad t=-\frac{10\ln 0.1}{3}\approx 7.68\,.$$

Thus it takes approximately 7.68 seconds for the electromagnet to reach 90% of its final value.

EXERCISES 3.6: Improved Euler's Method, page 132

1. Given the step size h and considering equally spaced points we have

$$x_{n+1}=x_n+nh, \qquad n=0,1,2,\ldots\,.$$

Euler's method is defined by equation (4) on page 125 of the text to be

$$y_{n+1} = y_n + hf(x_n, y_n), \qquad n = 0, 1, 2, \dots ,$$

where $f(x, y) = 5y$. Starting with the given value of $y_0 = 1$, we compute

$$y_1 = y_0 + h(5y_0) = 1 + 5h.$$

We can then use this value to compute y_2 to be

$$y_2 = y_1 + h(5y_1) = (1 + 5h)y_1 = (1 + 5h)^2.$$

Proceeding in this manner, we can generalize to y_n:

$$y_n = (1 + 5h)^n.$$

Referring back to our equation for x_n and using the given values of $x_0 = 0$ and $x_1 = 1$ we find

$$1 = nh \qquad \Rightarrow \qquad n = \frac{1}{h}.$$

Substituting this back into the formula for y_n we find the approximation to the initial value problem

$$y' = 5y, \qquad y(0) = 1$$

at $x = 1$ to be $(1 + 5h)^{1/h}$.

3. In this initial value problem, $f(x, y) = y$, $x_0 = 0$, and $y_0 = 1$. Formula (8) on page 127 of the text then becomes

$$y_{n+1} = y_n + \frac{h}{2}\left(y_n + y_{n+1}\right).$$

Solving this equation for y_{n+1} yields

$$\left(1 - \frac{h}{2}\right) y_{n+1} = \left(1 + \frac{h}{2}\right) y_n \qquad \Rightarrow \qquad y_{n+1} = \left(\frac{1 + h/2}{1 - h/2}\right) y_n\,, \qquad n = 0, 1, \dots . \tag{3.14}$$

If $n \geq 1$, we can use (3.14) to express y_n in terms of y_{n-1} and substitute this expression into the right-hand side of (3.14). Continuing this process, we get

$$y_{n+1} = \left(\frac{1 + h/2}{1 - h/2}\right)\left[\left(\frac{1 + h/2}{1 - h/2}\right) y_{n-1}\right] = \left(\frac{1 + h/2}{1 - h/2}\right)^2 y_{n-1} = \cdots = \left(\frac{1 + h/2}{1 - h/2}\right)^{n+1} y_0\,.$$

In order to approximate the solution $\phi(x) = e^x$ at the point $x = 1$ with N steps, we take $h = (x - x_0)/N = 1/N$, and so $N = 1/h$. Then the above formula becomes

$$y_N = \left(\frac{1+h/2}{1-h/2}\right)^N y_0 = \left(\frac{1+h/2}{1-h/2}\right)^N = \left(\frac{1+h/2}{1-h/2}\right)^{1/h}$$

and hence

$$e = \phi(1) \approx y_N = \left(\frac{1+h/2}{1-h/2}\right)^{1/h}.$$

Substituting $h = 10^{-k}$, $k = 0, 1, 2, 3$, and 4, we fill in Table 3-A.

Table 3–A: Approximations $\left(\frac{1+h/2}{1+h/2}\right)^{1/h}$ to $e \approx 2.718281828\ldots$.

h	**Approximation**	**Error**
1	3	0.281718172
10^{-1}	2.720551414	0.002269586
10^{-2}	2.718304481	0.000022653
10^{-3}	2.718282055	0.000000227
10^{-4}	2.718281831	0.000000003

These approximations are better then those in Tables 3.4 and 3.5 of the text.

5. In this problem, we have $f(x, y) = 4y$. Thus, we have

$$f(x_n, y_n) = 4y_n \quad \text{and} \quad f(x_n + h, y_n + hf(x_n, y_n)) = 4[y_n + h(4y_n)] = 4y_n + 16hy_n .$$

By equation (9) on page 128 of the text, we have

$$y_{n+1} = y_n + \frac{h}{2}(4y_n + 4y_n + 16hy_n) = \left(1 + 4h + 8h^2\right) y_n . \tag{3.15}$$

Since the initial condition $y(0) = 1/3$ implies that $x_0 = 0$ and $y_0 = 1/3$, equation (3.15) above yields

$$y_1 = \left(1 + 4h + 8h^2\right) y_0 = \frac{1}{3}\left(1 + 4h + 8h^2\right),$$

$$y_2 = \left(1+4h+8h^2\right) y_1 = \left(1+4h+8h^2\right)\left(\frac{1}{3}\right)\left(1+4h+8h^2\right) = \frac{1}{3}\left(1+4h+8h^2\right)^2,$$
$$y_3 = \left(1+4h+8h^2\right) y_2 = \left(1+4h+8h^2\right)\left(\frac{1}{3}\right)\left(1+4h+8h^2\right)^2 = \frac{1}{3}\left(1+4h+8h^2\right)^3.$$

Continuing this way we see that

$$y_n = \frac{1}{3}\left(1+4h+8h^2\right)^n. \tag{3.16}$$

(This can be proved by induction using equation (3.15) above.) We are looking for an approximation to our solution at the point $x = 1/2$. Therefore, we have

$$h = \frac{1/2 - x_0}{n} = \frac{1/2 - 0}{n} = \frac{1}{2n} \qquad \Rightarrow \qquad n = \frac{1}{2h}.$$

Substituting this value for n into equation (3.16) yields

$$y_n = \frac{1}{3}\left(1+4h+8h^2\right)^{1/(2h)}.$$

7. For this problem, $f(x,y) = x - y^2$. We need to approximate the solution on the interval $[1, 1.5]$ using a step size of $h = 0.1$. Thus the number of steps needed is $N = 5$. The inputs to the subroutine on page 129 are $x_0 = 1$, $y_0 = 0$, $c = 1.5$, and $N = 5$. For Step 3 of the subroutine we have

$$F = f(x,y) = x - y^2,$$
$$G = f\left(x+h, y+hF\right) = (x+h) - (y+hF)^2 = (x+h) - \left[y + h(x-y^2)\right]^2.$$

Starting with $x = x_0 = 1$ and $y = y_0 = 0$ we get $h = 0.1$ (as specified) and

$$F = 1 - 0^2 = 1,$$
$$G = (1+0.1) - \left[0 + 0.1(1-0^2)\right]^2 = 1.1 - (0.1)^2 = 1.09.$$

Hence in Step 4 we compute

$$x = 1 + 0.1 = 1.1,$$
$$y = 0 + 0.05(1 + 1.09) = 0.1045.$$

Thus the approximate value of the solution at 1.1 is 0.1045. Next we repeat Step 3 with $x = 1.1$ and $y = 0.1045$ to obtain

$$F = 1.1 + (0.1045)^2 \approx 1.0891,$$
$$G = (1.1 + 0.1) - \left[0.1045 + 0.1\left(1.1 - (0.1045)^2\right)\right]^2 \approx 1.1545\,.$$

Hence in Step 4 we compute

$$x = 1.1 + 0.1 = 1.2\,,$$
$$y = 0.1045 + 0.05(1.0891 + 1.1545) \approx 0.21668\,.$$

Thus the approximate value of the solution at 1.2 is 0.21668. By continuing in this way, we fill in Table 3-B. (The reader can also use the software provided free with the text.)

Table 3–B: Improved Euler's method to approximate the solution of $y' = x - y^2$, $y(1) = 0$, with $h = 0.1$.

i	x	y
0	1	0
1	1.1	0.10450
2	1.2	0.21668
3	1.3	0.33382
4	1.4	0.45300
5	1.5	0.57135

9. In this initial value problem, $f(x, y) = x + 3\cos(xy)$, $x_0 = 0$, and $y_0 = 0$. To approximate the solution on $[0, 2]$ with a step size $h = 0.2$, we need $N = 10$ steps. The functions F and G in the improved Euler's method subroutine are

$$\begin{aligned} F &= f(x, y) = x + 3\cos(xy); \\ G &= f(x + h, y + hF) = x + h + 3\cos[(x + h)(y + hF)] \\ &= x + 0.2 + 3\cos[(x + 0.2)(y + 0.2\,\{x + 3\cos(xy)\})]. \end{aligned}$$

Starting with $x = x_0 = 0$ and $y = y_0 = 0$, we compute

$$F = 0 + 3\cos(0 \cdot 0) = 3\,;$$

$$G = 0 + 0.2 + 3\cos[(0 + 0.2)(0 + 0.2\,\{0 + 3\cos(0 \cdot 0)\})] \approx 3.178426\,.$$

Using these values, we find on Step 4 that

$$x = 0 + 0.2 = 0.2\,,$$

$$y = 0 + 0.1(3 + 3.178426) \approx 0.617843\,.$$

With these new values of x and y, we repeat the Step 3 and obtain

$$F = 0.2 + 3\cos(0.2 \cdot 0.617843) \approx 3.177125\,;$$

$$G = 0.2 + 0.2 + 3\cos[(0.2 + 0.2)(0.617843 + 0.2\,\{0.2 + 3\cos(0.2 \cdot 0.617843)\})] \approx 3.030865\,.$$

Step 4 then yields an approximation of the solution at $x = 0.4$:

$$x = 0.2 + 0.2 = 0.4\,,$$

$$y = 0.617843 + 0.1(3.177125 + 3.030865) \approx 1.238642\,.$$

By continuing in this way, we obtain Table 3-C.

Table 3–C: Improved Euler's method approximations to the solution of $y' = x + 3\cos(xy)$, $y(0) = 0$, on $[0, 2]$ with $h = 0.2$.

i	x	$y \approx$	i	x	$y \approx$
0	0	0	6	1.2	1.884609
1	0.2	0.617843	7	1.4	1.724472
2	0.4	1.238642	8	1.6	1.561836
3	0.6	1.736531	9	1.8	1.417318
4	0.8	1.981106	10	2.0	1.297794
5	1.0	1.997052			

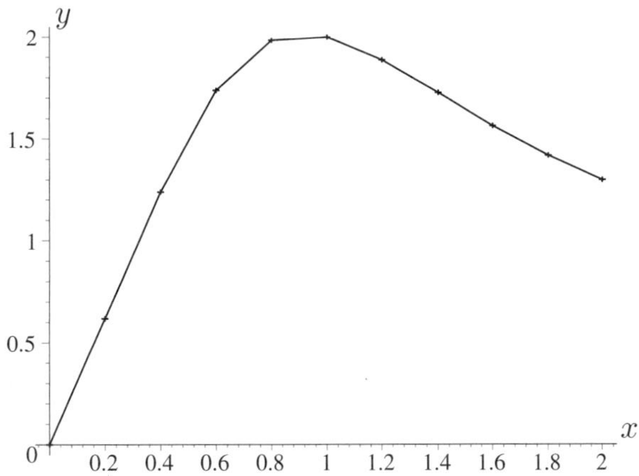

Figure 3–B: Polygonal line approximation to the solution of $y' = x + 3\cos(xy)$, $y(0) = 0$.

A polygonal line, approximating the graph of the solution to the given initial value problem, which has vertices at points (x, y) from Table 3-C, is sketched in Figure 3-B.

13. We want to approximate the solution $\phi(x)$ to $y' = 1 - y + y^3$, $y(0) = 0$, at $x = 1$. (In other words, we want to find an approximate value for $\phi(1)$.) To do this, we will use the algorithm on page 130 of the text. (We assume that the reader has a programmable calculator or microcomputer available and can transform the step-by-step outline on page 130 into an executable program. Alternatively, the reader can use the software provided free with the text.)

The inputs to the program are $x_0 = 0$, $y_0 = 0$, $c = 1$, $\varepsilon = 0.003$, and, say, $M = 100$. Notice that by Step 6 of the improved Euler's method with tolerance, the computations should terminate when two successive approximations differ by less that 0.003. The initial value for h in Step 1 of the improved Euler's method subroutine is

$$h = (1 - 0)2^{-0} = 1.$$

For the given equation, we have $f(x, y) = 1 - y + y^3$, and so the numbers F and G in Step 3 of the improved Euler's method subroutine are

$$F = f(x, y) = 1 - y + y^3,$$
$$G = f(x + h, y + hF) = 1 - (y + hF) + (y + hF)^3.$$

From Step 4 of the improved Euler's method subroutine with $x = 0$, $y = 0$, and $h = 1$, we get

$$x = x + h = 0 + 1 = 1,$$
$$y = y + \frac{h}{2}(F + G) = 0 + \frac{1}{2}\left[1 + (1 - 1 + 1^3)\right] = 1.$$

Thus,

$$\phi(1) \approx y(1; 1) = 1.$$

The algorithm (Step 1 of the improved Euler's method subroutine) next sets $h = 2^{-1} = 0.5$. The inputs to the subroutine are $x = 0$, $y = 0$, $c = 1$, and $N = 2$. For Step 3 of the subroutine we have

$$F = 1 - 0 + 0 = 1,$$
$$G = 1 - [0 + 0.5(1)] + [0 + 0.5(1)]^3 = 0.625.$$

Hence in Step 4 we compute

$$x = 0 + 0.5 = 0.5,$$
$$y = 0 + 0.25(1 + 0.625) = 0.40625.$$

Thus the approximate value of the solution at 0.5 is 0.40625. Next we repeat Step 3 with $x = 0.5$ and $y = 0.40625$ to obtain

$$F = 1 - 0.40625 + (0.40625)^3 = 0.6607971,$$
$$G = 1 - [0.40625 + 0.5(0.6607971)] + [0.40625 + 0.5(0.6607971)]^3 \approx 0.6630946.$$

In Step 4 we compute

$$x = 0.5 + 0.5 = 1,$$

Table 3–D: Improved Euler's method approximations to $\phi(1)$, where $\phi(x)$ is the solution to $y' = 1 - y + y^3$, $y(0) = 0$.

h	$y(1; h) \approx \phi(1)$
1	1.0
2^{-1}	0.7372229
2^{-2}	0.7194115
2^{-3}	0.7169839

$$y = 0.40625 + 0.25(0.6607971 + 0.6630946) \approx 0.7372229\,.$$

Thus the approximate value of the solution at $x = 1$ is 0.7372229. Further outputs of the algorithm are given in Table 3-D.

Since

$$\left|y(1; 2^{-3}) - y(1; 2^{-2})\right| = |0.7169839 - 0.7194115| < 0.003\,,$$

the algorithm stops (see Step 6 of the improved Euler's method with tolerance) and prints out that $\phi(1)$ is approximately 0.71698.

15. For this problem, $f(x, y) = (x + y + 2)^2$. We want to approximate the solution, satisfying $y(0) = -2$, on the interval $[0, 1.4]$ to find the point, with two decimal places of accuracy, where it crosses the x-axis, that is $y = 0$. Our approach is to use a step size of 0.005 and look for a change in the sign of y. This requires 280 steps. For this procedure inputs to the improved Euler's method subroutine are $x_0 = 0$, $y_0 = -2$, $c = 1.4$, and $N = 280$. We will stop the subroutine when we see a sign change in the value of y. (The subroutine is implemented on the software package provided free with the text.)

For Step 3 of the subroutine we have

$$F = f(x, y) = (x + y + 2)^2\,,$$
$$G = f(x + h, y + hF) = (x + h + y + hF + 2)^2 = [x + y + 2 + h(1 + F)]^2\,.$$

Starting with the inputs $x = x_0 = 0$, $y = y_0 = -2$, and $h = 0.005$ we obtain

$$F = (0 - 2 + 2)^2 = 0,$$
$$G = [0 - 2 + 2 + 0.005(1 + 0)]^2 = 0.000025\,.$$

Thus, in Step 4 we compute

$$x = 0 + 0.005 = 0.005\,,$$
$$y = -2 + 0.005(0 + 0.000025)(1/2) \approx -2.$$

Thus the approximate value of the solution at $x = 0.005$ is -2. We continue with Steps 3 and 4 of the improved Euler's method subroutine until we arrive at $x = 1.270$ and $y \approx -0.04658269$. The next iteration, with $x = 1.275$, yields $y \approx 0.006295411$. This tells us that $y = 0$ is occurs somewhere between $x = 1.270$ and $x = 1.275$. Therefore, rounding off to two decimal places yields $x = 1.27$.

17. In this initial value problem, $f(x, y) = -20y$, $x_0 = 0$, and $y_0 = 1$. By applying formula (4) on page 125 of the text, we can find a general formula for y_n in terms of h. Indeed,

$$y_n = y_{n-1} + h(-20y_{n-1}) = (1 - 20h)y_{n-1} = \cdots = (1 - 20h)^n y_0 = (1 - 20h)^n = [c(h)]^n\,,$$

where $c(h) = 1 - 20h$. For suggested values of h, we have

$$\begin{array}{llllll} h = 0.1 & \Rightarrow & c(0.1) = -1 & \Rightarrow & x_n = 0.1n, & y_n = (-1)^n\,, \quad n = 1, \ldots, 10; \\ h = 0.025 & \Rightarrow & c(0.025) = 0.5 & \Rightarrow & x_n = 0.025n, & y_n = (0.5)^n\,, \quad n = 1, \ldots, 40; \\ h = 0.2 & \Rightarrow & c(0.2) = -3 & \Rightarrow & x_n = 0.2n, & y_n = (-3)^n\,, \quad n = 1, \ldots, 5. \end{array}$$

These values are shown in Table 3-E.

Thus, for $h = 0.1$ we have alternating $y_n = \pm 1$; for $h = 0.2$, y_n's have an increasing magnitude and alternating sign; $h = 0.025$ is a good step size. From this example we conclude that, in Euler's method, one should be very careful in choosing a step size. Wrong choice can even lead to a diverging process.

Table 3–E: Euler's method approximations to the solution of $y' = -20y$, $y(0) = 1$, on $[0, 1]$ with $h = 0.1$, 0.2, and 0.025.

x_n	y_n $(h = 0.2)$	y_n $(h = 0.1)$	y_n $(h = 0.025)$
0.1		−1	0.062500
0.2	−3	1	0.003906
0.3		−1	0.000244
0.4	9	1	0.000015
0.5		−1	0.000001
0.6	−27	1	0.000000
0.7		−1	0.000000
0.8	81	1	0.000000
0.9		−1	0.000000
1.0	−243	1	0.000000

19. In this problem, the variables are t and p. With suggested values of parameters, the initial value problem (13) becomes

$$\frac{dp}{dt} = 3p - p^r, \qquad p(0) = 1.$$

Therefore, $f(t, p) = 3p - p^r$ and, with $h = 0.25$, functions F and G in improved Euler's method subroutine have the form

$$\begin{aligned} F &= f(t, p) = 3p - p^r; \\ G &= f(t + 0.25, p + 0.25F) = 3[p + 0.25F] - [p + 0.25F]^r \\ &= 3\left[p + 0.25\,(3p - p^r)\right] - \left[p + 0.25\,(3p - p^r)\right]^r. \end{aligned}$$

The results of computations are shown in Table 3-F.

These results indicate that the limiting populations for $r = 1.5$, $r = 2$, and $r = 3$ are $p_\infty = 9$, $p_\infty = 3$, and $p_\infty = \sqrt{3}$, respectively.

Since the right-hand side of the given logistic equation, $f(t, p) = 3p - p^r$, does not depend on t, we conclude that this equation is autonomous. Therefore, its equilibrium solutions (if any)

Table 3–F: Improved Euler's method approximations to the solution of $p' = 3p - p^r$, $p(0) = 1$, on $[0, 5]$ with $h = 0.25$ for $r = 1.5$, 2, and 3.

x_n	y_n ($r = 1.5$)	y_n ($r = 2$)	y_n ($r = 3$)
0.25	1.582860	1.531250	1.390625
0.5	2.351441	2.049597	1.553472
0.75	3.267498	2.440027	1.628847
1.0	4.253156	2.686754	1.669992
1.25	5.216751	2.829199	1.694056
1.5	6.083402	2.908038	1.708578
1.75	6.811626	2.950802	1.717479
2.0	7.392146	2.973767	1.722980
2.25	7.837090	2.986037	1.726396
2.5	8.168507	2.992574	1.728522
2.75	8.410362	2.996053	1.729847
3.0	8.584317	2.997903	1.730674
3.25	8.708165	2.998886	1.731191
3.5	8.795710	2.999408	1.731513
3.75	8.857285	2.999685	1.731715
4.0	8.900443	2.999833	1.731841
4.25	8.930619	2.999911	1.731920
4.5	8.951682	2.999953	1.731969
4.75	8.966366	2.999975	1.732000
5.0	8.976596	2.999987	1.732019

can be found by solving

$$f(p) = 3p - p^r = 0 \quad \Leftrightarrow \quad p\left(3 - p^{r-1}\right) = 0 \quad \Leftrightarrow \quad p = 0 \quad \text{or} \quad p = 3^{1/(r-1)}.$$

The condition $r > 1$ implies that $f(p) > 0$ on $\left(0, 3^{1/(r-1)}\right)$ and $f(p) < 0$ on $\left(3^{1/(r-1)}, \infty\right)$. Therefore, $p = 3^{1/(r-1)}$ is a sink and, regardless of the initial value $p(0) = p_0 > 0$, there holds

$$\lim_{t\to\infty} p(t) = 3^{1/(r-1)}.$$

21. We will use the improved Euler's method with $h = 2/3$ to approximate the solution of the problem

$$\left\{\left[75-20\cos\left(\frac{\pi t}{12}\right)\right]-T(t)\right\}+0.1+1.5[70-T(t)], \qquad T(0)=65,$$

with $K=0.2$. Since $h=2/3$, it will take 36 steps to go from $t=0$ to $t=24$. By simplifying the above expression, we obtain

$$\frac{dT}{dt}=(75K+105.1)-20K\cos\left(\frac{\pi t}{12}\right)-(K+1.5)T(t), \qquad T(0)=65.$$

(Note that here t takes the place of x and T takes the place of y.) Therefore, with $K=0.2$ the inputs to the subroutine are $t_0=0$, $T_0=65$, $c=24$, and $N=36$. For Step 3 of the subroutine we have

$$\begin{aligned} F &= f(t,T)=(75K+105.1)-20K\cos\left(\frac{\pi t}{12}\right)-(K+1.5)T, &(3.17)\\ G &= f(t+h,T+hF)\\ &= (75K+105.1)-20K\cos\left(\frac{\pi(t+h)}{12}\right)-(K+1.5)\{T+hF\}. &(3.18)\end{aligned}$$

For Step 4 in the subroutine we have

$$\begin{aligned} t&=t+h,\\ T&=T+\frac{h}{2}(F+G). \end{aligned}$$

Now, starting with $t=t_0=0$ and $T=T_0=65$, and $h=2/3$ (as specified) we have Step 3 of the subroutine to be

$$F=[75(0.2)+105.1]-20(0.2)\cos 0-[(0.2)+1.5](65)=5.6\,,$$

$$G=[75(0.2)+105.1]-20(0.2)\cos\left[\frac{\pi(0.6667)}{12}\right]-[(0.2)+1.5][65+(0.6667)(5.6)]\approx -0.6862\,.$$

Hence in Step 4 we compute

$$t=0+0.6667=0.6667$$

$$T=65+0.3333(5.6-0.6862)\approx 66.638\,.$$

Table 3–G: Improved Euler's method to approximate the temperature in a building over a 24-hour period (with $K = 0.2$).

Time	t_n	T_n
Midnight	0	65
12:40 A.M.	0.6667	66.63803
1:20 A.M.	1.3333	67.52906
2:00 A.M.	2.0000	68.07270
2:40 A.M.	2.6667	68.46956
3:20 A.M.	3.3333	68.81808
4:00 A.M.	4.0000	69.16392
8:00 A.M.	8.0000	71.48357
Noon	12.000	72.90891
4:00 P.M.	16.000	72.07140
8:00 P.M.	20.000	69.80953
Midnight	24.000	68.38519

Recalling that t_0 is midnight, we see that these results imply that at 0.6667 hours after midnight (or 12 : 40 A.M.) the temperature is approximately 66.638. Continuing with this process for $n = 1, 2, \ldots, 35$ gives us the approximate temperatures in a building with $K = 0.2$ over a 24 hr period. These results are given in Table 3-G. (This is just a partial table.)

The next step is to redo the above work with $K = 0.4$. That is, we substitute $K = 0.4$ and $h = 2/3 \approx 0.6667$ into equations (3.17) and (3.18) above. This yields

$$F = 135.1 - 8\cos\left(\frac{\pi t}{12}\right) - 1.9T,$$

$$G = 135.1 - 8\cos\left[\frac{\pi(t + 0.6667)}{12}\right] - 1.9(T + 0.6667F),$$

and

$$T = T + (0.3333)(F + G).$$

Then, using these equations, we go through the process of first finding F, then using this result to find G, and finally using both results to find T. (This process must be done for

$n = 0, 1, 2, \ldots, 35$.) Lastly, we redo this work with $K = 0.6$ and $h = 2/3$. By so doing, we obtain the results given in the table in the answers of the text. (Note that the values for T_0, T_6, T_{12}, T_{18}, T_{24}, T_{30}, and T_{36} are given in the answers.)

EXERCISES 3.7: Higher Order Numerical Methods: Taylor and Runge-Kutta, page 142

1. In this problem, $f(x,y) = \cos(x+y)$. Applying formula (4) on page 135 of the text we compute

$$\frac{\partial f(x,y)}{\partial x} = \frac{\partial}{\partial x}[\cos(x+y)] = -\sin(x+y)\frac{\partial}{\partial x}(x+y) = -\sin(x+y);$$

$$\frac{\partial f(x,y)}{\partial y} = \frac{\partial}{\partial y}[\cos(x+y)] = -\sin(x+y)\frac{\partial}{\partial y}(x+y) = -\sin(x+y);$$

$$\begin{aligned} f_2(x,y) = \frac{\partial f(x,y)}{\partial x} + \left[\frac{\partial f(x,y)}{\partial y}\right] f(x,y) &= -\sin(x+y) + [-\sin(x+y)]\cos(x+y) \\ &= -\sin(x+y)[1+\cos(x+y)], \end{aligned}$$

and so, with $p = 2$, (5) and (6) on page 135 yield

$$\begin{aligned} x_{n+1} &= x_n + h\,, \\ y_{n+1} &= y_n + h\cos(x_n+y_n) - \frac{h^2}{2}\sin(x_n+y_n)[1+\cos(x_n+y_n)]\,. \end{aligned}$$

3. Here we have $f(x,y) = x - y$ and so

$$f_2(x,y) = \frac{\partial(x-y)}{\partial x} + \frac{\partial(x-y)}{\partial y}(x-y) = 1 + (-1)(x-y) = 1 - x + y.$$

To obtain $f_3(x,y)$ and then $f_4(x,y)$, we differentiate the equation $y'' = f_2(x,y)$ twice. This yields

$$y'''(x) = [f_2(x,y)]' = (1-x+y)' = -1 + y' = -1 + x - y =: f_3(x,y);$$

$$y^{(4)}(x) = [f_3(x,y)]' = (-1+x-y)' = 1 - y' = 1 - x + y =: f_4(x,y).$$

Therefore, the recursive formulas of order 4 for the Taylor method are

$$\begin{aligned} x_{n+1} &= x_n + h, \\ y_{n+1} &= y_n + h\left(x_n - y_n\right) + \frac{h^2}{2}\left(1 - x_n + y_n\right) + \frac{h^3}{3!}\left(-1 + x_n - y_n\right) + \frac{h^4}{4!}\left(1 - x_n + y_n\right) \\ &= y_n + h\left(x_n - y_n\right) + \frac{h^2}{2}\left(1 - x_n + y_n\right) - \frac{h^3}{6}\left(1 - x_n + y_n\right) + \frac{h^4}{24}\left(1 - x_n + y_n\right) \\ &= y_n + h + \left(1 - x_n + y_n\right)\left(-h + \frac{h^2}{2} - \frac{h^3}{6} + \frac{h^4}{24}\right) \\ &= y_n + h\left(x_n - y_n\right) + \left(1 - x_n - y_n\right)\left(\frac{h^2}{2} - \frac{h^3}{6} + \frac{h^4}{24}\right). \end{aligned}$$

5. For the Taylor method of *order* 2, we need to find (see equation (4) on page 135 of the text)

$$f_2(x,y) = \frac{\partial f(x,y)}{\partial x} + \left[\frac{\partial f(x,y)}{\partial y}\right] f(x,y)$$

for $f(x,y) = x + 1 - y$. Thus, we have

$$f_2(x,y) = 1 + (-1)(x + 1 - y) = y - x.$$

Therefore, by equations (5) and (6) on page 135 of the text, we see that the recursive formulas with $h = 0.25$ become

$$\begin{aligned} x_{n+1} &= x_n + 0.25\,, \\ y_{n+1} &= y_n + 0.25\left(x_n + 1 - y_n\right) + \frac{(0.25)^2}{2}\left(y_n - x_n\right). \end{aligned}$$

By starting with $x_0 = 0$ and $y_0 = 1$ (the initial values for the problem), we find

$$y_1 = 1 + \frac{0.0625}{2} \approx 1.03125\,.$$

Plugging this value into the recursive formulas yields

$$y_2 = 1.03125 + 0.25(0.25 + 1 - 1.03125) + \left(\frac{0.0625}{2}\right)(1.03125 - 0.25) \approx 1.11035\,.$$

By continuing in this way, we can fill in the first three columns in Table 3-H.

For the Taylor method of *order* 4, we need to find f_3 and f_4. Thus, we have

$$f_3(x,y) = \frac{\partial f_2(x,y)}{\partial x} + \left[\frac{\partial f_2(x,y)}{\partial y}\right] f(x,y) = -1 + 1 \cdot (x+1-y) = x - y,$$
$$f_4(x,y) = \frac{\partial f_3(x,y)}{\partial x} + \left[\frac{\partial f_3(x,y)}{\partial y}\right] f(x,y) = 1 + (-1) \cdot (x+1-y) = y - x.$$

Hence, by equation (6) on page 135 of the text, we see that the recursive formula for y_{n+1} for the Taylor method of order 4 with $h = 0.25$ is given by

$$y_{n+1} = y_n + 0.25\,(x_n + 1 - y_n) + \frac{(0.25)^2}{2}\,(y_n - x_n) + \frac{(0.25)^3}{6}\,(x_n - y_n) + \frac{(0.25)^4}{24}\,(y_n - x_n)\,.$$

By starting with $x_0 = 0$ and $y_0 = 1$, we can fill in the fourth column of Table 3-H.

Table 3–H: Taylor approximations of order 2 and 4 for the equation $y' = x + 1 - y$.

n	x_n	y_n **(order 2)**	y_n **(order 4)**
0	0	1	1
1	0.25	1.03125	1.02881
2	0.50	1.11035	1.10654
3	0.75	1.22684	1.22238
4	1.00	1.37253	1.36789

Thus, the approximation (rounded to 4 decimal places) of the solution by the Taylor method at the point $x = 1$ is given by $\phi_2(1) = 1.3725$ if we use order 2 and by $\phi_4(1) = 1.3679$ if we use order 4. The actual solution is $y = x + e^{-x}$ and so has the value $y(1) = 1 + e^{-1} \approx 1.3678794$ at $x = 1$. Comparing these results, we see that

$$|y(1) - \phi_2(1)| = 0.00462 \qquad \text{and} \qquad |y(1) - \phi_4(1)| = 0.00002\,.$$

7. We will use the 4th order Runge-Kutta subroutine described on page 138 of the text. Since $x_0 = 0$ and $h = 0.25$, we need $N = 4$ steps to approximate the solution at $x = 1$. With $f(x,y) = 2y - 6$, we set $x = x_0 = 0$, $y = y_0 = 1$ and go to Step 3 to compute k_j's.

$$k_1 = hf(x,y) = 0.25[2(1) - 6] = -1\,;$$

$$k_2 = hf(x + h/2, y + k_1/2) = 0.25[2(1 + (-1)/2) - 6] = -1.25\,;$$
$$k_3 = hf(x + h/2, y + k_2/2) = 0.25[2(1 + (-1.25)/2) - 6] = -1.3125\,;$$
$$k_4 = hf(x + h, y + k_3) = 0.25[2(1 + (-1.3125)) - 6] = -1.65625\,.$$

Step 4 then yields

$$x = 0 + 0.25 = 0.25\,,$$
$$y = 1 + \frac{1}{6}(k_1 + 2k_2 + 2k_3 + k_4) = 1 + \frac{1}{6}(-1 - 2 \cdot 1.25 - 2 \cdot 1.3125 - 1.65625) \approx -0.29688\,.$$

Now we go back to Step 3 and recalculate k_j's for new values of x and y.

$$k_1 = 0.25[2(-0.29688) - 6] = -1.64844\,;$$
$$k_2 = 0.25[2(-0.29688 + (-1.64844)/2) - 6] = -2.06055\,;$$
$$k_3 = 0.25[2(-0.29688 + (-2.06055)/2) - 6] = -2.16358\,;$$
$$k_4 = 0.25[2(-0.29688 + (-2.16358)) - 6] = -2.73022\,;$$
$$x = 0.25 + 0.25 = 0.5\,,$$
$$y = -0.29688 + \frac{1}{6}(-1.64844 - 2 \cdot 2.06055 - 2 \cdot 2.16358 - 2.73022) \approx -2.43470\,.$$

We repeat the cycle two more times:

$$k_1 = 0.25[2(-2.43470) - 6] = -2.71735\,;$$
$$k_2 = 0.25[2(-2.43470 + (-2.71735)/2) - 6] = -3.39670\,;$$
$$k_3 = 0.25[2(-2.43470 + (-3.39670)/2) - 6] = -3.56652\,;$$
$$k_4 = 0.25[2(-2.43470 + (-3.56652)) - 6] = -4.50060\,;$$
$$x = 0.5 + 0.25 = 0.75\,,$$
$$y = -2.43470 + \frac{1}{6}(-2.71735 - 2 \cdot 3.39670 - 2 \cdot 3.56652 - 4.50060) \approx -5.95876$$

and

$$k_1 = 0.25[2(-5.95876) - 6] = -4.47938\,;$$
$$k_2 = 0.25[2(-5.95876 + (-4.47938)/2) - 6] = -5.59922\,;$$

$$k_3 = 0.25[2(-5.95876 + (-5.59922)/2) - 6] = -5.87918\,;$$

$$k_4 = 0.25[2(-5.95876 + (-5.87918)) - 6] = -7.41895\,;$$

$$x = 0.75 + 0.25 = 1.00\,,$$

$$y = -5.95876 + \frac{1}{6}(-4.47938 - 2 \cdot 5.59922 - 2 \cdot 5.87918 - 7.41895) \approx -11.7679\,.$$

Thus $\phi(1) \approx -11.7679$. The actual solution, $\phi(x) = 3 - 2e^{2x}$, evaluated at $x = 1$, gives

$$\phi(1) = 3 - 2e^{2(1)} = 3 - 2e^2 \approx -11.7781\,.$$

9. For this problem we will use the 4th order Runge-Kutta subroutine with $f(x, y) = x + 1 - y$. Using the step size of $h = 0.25$, the number of steps needed is $N = 4$ to approximate the solution at $x = 1$. For Step 3 we have

$$k_1 = hf(x, y) = 0.25(x + 1 - y),$$

$$k_2 = hf\left(x + \frac{h}{2}, y + \frac{k_1}{2}\right) = 0.25(0.875x + 1 - 0.875y),$$

$$k_3 = hf\left(x + \frac{h}{2}, y + \frac{k_2}{2}\right) = 0.25(0.890625x + 1 - 0.890625y),$$

$$k_4 = hf\left(x + h, y + k_3\right) = 0.25(0.77734375x + 1 - 0.77734375y).$$

Hence, in Step 4 we have

$$x = x + 0.25\,,$$

$$y = y + \frac{1}{6}\left(k_1 + 2k_2 + 2k_3 + k_4\right).$$

Using the initial conditions $x_0 = 0$ and $y_0 = 1$, $c = 1$, and $N = 4$ for Step 3 we obtain

$$k_1 = 0.25(0 + 1 - 1) = 0,$$

$$k_2 = 0.25(0.875(0) + 1 - 0.875(1)) = 0.03125,$$

$$k_3 = 0.25(0.890625(0) + 1 - 0.890625(1)) \approx 0.0273438,$$

$$k_4 = 0.25(0.77734375(0) + 1 - 0.77734375(1)) \approx 0.0556641.$$

Thus, Step 4 gives

$$x = 0 + 0.25 = 0.25\,,$$

$$y \approx 1 + \frac{1}{6}[0 + 2(0.03125) + 2(0.0273438) + 0.0556641] \approx 1.02881\,.$$

Thus the approximate value of the solution at 0.25 is 1.02881. By repeating Steps 3 and 4 of the algorithm we fill in the following Table 3-I.

Table 3–I: 4th order Runge-Kutta subroutine approximations for $y' = x + 1 - y$ at $x = 1$ with $h = 0.25$.

x	0	0.25	0.50	0.75	1.0
y	1	1.02881	1.10654	1.22238	1.36789

Thus, our approximation at $x = 1$ is approximately 1.36789. Comparing this with Problem 5, we see we have obtained accuracy to four decimal places as we did with the Taylor method of order four, but without having to compute any partial derivatives.

11. In this problem, $f(x, y) = 2x^{-4} - y^2$. To find the root of the solution within two decimal places of accuracy, we choose a step size $h = 0.005$ in 4th order Runge-Kutta subroutine. It will require $(2 - 1)/0.005 = 200$ steps to approximate the solution on $[1, 2]$. With the initial input $x = x_0 = 1$, $y = y_0 = -0.414$, we get

$$k_1 = hf(x, y) = 0.005[2(1)^{-4} - (-0.414)^2] = 0.009143;$$

$$k_2 = hf(x + h/2, y + k_1/2) = 0.005[2(1 + 0.005/2)^{-4} - (-0.414 + 0.009143/2)^2] = 0.009062;$$

$$k_3 = hf(x + h/2, y + k_2/2) = 0.005[2(1 + 0.005/2)^{-4} - (-0.414 + 0.009062/2)^2] = 0.009062;$$

$$k_4 = hf(x + h, y + k_3) = 0.005[2(1 + 0.005)^{-4} - (-0.414 + 0.009062)^2] = 0.008983;$$

$$\Downarrow$$

$$x = 1 + 0.005 = 1.005,$$

$$y = -0.414 + \frac{1}{6}(0.009143 + 2 \cdot 0.009062 + 2 \cdot 0.009062 + 0.008983) \approx -0.404937;$$

$$\vdots$$

On the 82nd step we get

$$x = 1.405 + 0.005 = 1.410\,,$$
$$y = -0.004425 + \frac{1}{6}\,(0.002566 + 2 \cdot 0.002548 + 2 \cdot 0.002548 + 0.002530) \approx -0.001876\,,$$

and the next step gives

$$k_1 = 0.005[2(1.410)^{-4} - (-0.001876)^2] = 0.002530\,;$$
$$k_2 = 0.005[2(1.410 + 0.005/2)^{-4} - (-0.001876 + 0.002530/2)^2] = 0.002512\,;$$
$$k_3 = 0.005[2(1.410 + 0.005/2)^{-4} - (-0.001876 + 0.002512/2)^2] = 0.002512\,;$$
$$k_4 = 0.005[2(1.410 + 0.005)^{-4} - (-0.001876 + 0.002512)^2] = 0.002494\,;$$
$$\Downarrow$$
$$x = 1.410 + 0.005 = 1.415\,,$$
$$y = -0.414 + \frac{1}{6}\,(0.002530 + 2 \cdot 0.002512 + 2 \cdot 0.002512 + 0.002494) \approx 0.000636\,.$$

Since $y(1.41) < 0$ and $y(1.415) > 0$ we conclude that the root of the solution is on the interval $(1.41, 1.415)$.

As a check, we apply the 4th order Runge-Kutta subroutine to approximate the solution to the given initial value problem on $[1, 1.5]$ with a step size $h = 0.001$, which requires $N = (1.5 - 1)/0.001 = 500$ steps. This yields $y(1.413) \approx -0.000367$, $y(1.414) \approx 0.000134$, and so, within two decimal places of accuracy, $x \approx 1.41$.

13. For this problem $f(x, y) = y^2 - 2e^x y + e^{2x} + e^x$. We want to find the vertical asymptote located in the interval $[0, 2]$ within two decimal places of accuracy using the Forth Order Runge-Kutta subroutine. One approach is to use a step size of 0.005 and look for y to approach infinity. This would require 400 steps. We will stop the subroutine when the value of y ("blows up") becomes very large. For Step 3 we have

$$k_1 = hf(x, y) = 0.005\left(y^2 - 2e^x y + e^{2x} + e^x\right),$$
$$k_2 = hf\left(x + \frac{h}{2}, y + \frac{k_1}{2}\right) = 0.005\left[\left(y + \frac{k_1}{2}\right)^2 - 2e^{(x+h/2)}\left(y + \frac{k_1}{2}\right) + e^{2(x+h/2)} + e^{(x+h/2)}\right],$$

$$k_3 = hf\left(x + \frac{h}{2}, y + \frac{k_2}{2}\right) = 0.005\left[\left(y + \frac{k_2}{2}\right)^2 - 2e^{(x+h/2)}\left(y + \frac{k_2}{2}\right) + e^{2(x+h/2)} + e^{(x+h/2)}\right],$$
$$k_4 = hf(x + h, y + k_3) = 0.005\left[(y + k_3)^2 - 2e^{(x+h)}(y + k_3) + e^{2(x+h)} + e^{(x+h)}\right].$$

Hence in Step 4 we have

$$x = x + 0.005\,,$$
$$y = y + \frac{1}{6}\,(k_1 + 2k_2 + 2k_3 + k_4)\,.$$

Using the initial conditions $x_0 = 0$, $y_0 = 3$, $c = 2$, and $N = 400$ on Step 3 we obtain

$$k_1 = 0.005\big(3^2 - 2e^0(3) + e^{2(0)} + e^0\big) = 0.025\,,$$
$$k_2 = 0.005\big[(3 + 0.0125)^2 - 2e^{(0+0.0025)}(3 + 0.0125) + e^{2(0+0.0025)} + e^{(0+0.0025)}\big] \approx 0.02522\,,$$
$$k_3 = 0.005\big[(3 + 0.01261)^2 - 2e^{(0+0.0025)}(3 + 0.01261) + e^{2(0+0.0025)} + e^{(0+0.0025)}\big] \approx 0.02522\,,$$
$$k_4 = 0.005\big[(3 + 0.02522)^2 - 2e^{(0+0.0025)}(3 + 0.02522) + e^{2(0+0.0025)} + e^{(0+0.0025)}\big] \approx 0.02543\,.$$

Thus, Step 4 yields

$$x = 0 + 0.005 = 0.005$$

and

$$y \approx 3 + \frac{1}{6}\,(0.025 + 2(0.02522) + 2(0.02522) + 0.02543) \approx 3.02522\,.$$

Thus the approximate value at $x = 0.005$ is 3.02522. By repeating Steps 3 and 4 of the subroutine we find that, at $x = 0.505$, $y = 2.0201 \cdot 10^{13}$. The next iteration gives a floating point overflow. This would lead one to think the asymptote occurs at $x = 0.51$.

As a check lets apply the 4th order Runge-Kutta subroutine with the initial conditions $x_0 = 0$, $y_0 = 3$, $c = 1$, and $N = 400$. This gives a finer step size of $h = 0.0025$. With these inputs, we find $y(0.5025) \approx 4.0402 \cdot 10^{13}$.

Repeating the subroutine one more time with a step size of 0.00125, we obtain the value $y(0.50125) \approx 8.0804 \cdot 10^{13}$. Therefore we conclude that the vertical asymptote occurs at $x = 0.50$ and not at 0.51 as was earlier thought.

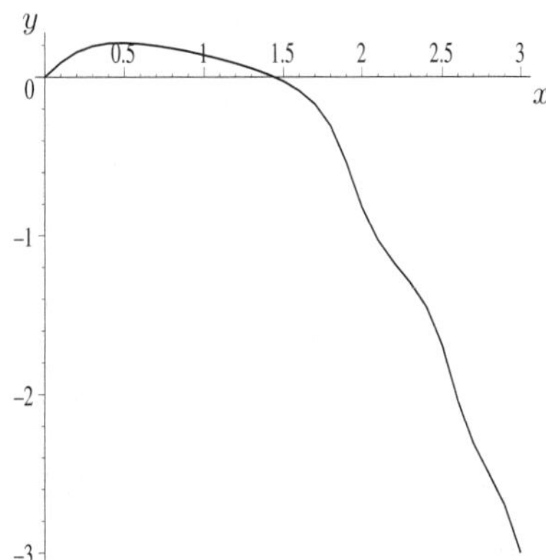

Figure 3–C: Polygonal line approximation to the solution of $y' = \cos(5y) - x$, $y(0) = 0$, on $[0, 3]$.

15. Here $f(x, y) = \cos(5y) - x$, $x_0 = 0$, and $y_0 = 0$. With a step size $h = 0.1$ we take $N = 30$ in order to approximate the solution on $[0, 3]$. We set $x = x_0 = 0$, $y = y_0 = 0$ and compute

$$k_1 = hf(x, y) = 0.1[\cos(5 \cdot 0) - 0] = 0.1\,;$$

$$k_2 = hf(x + h/2, y + k_1/2) = 0.1[\cos(5(0 + 0.1/2)) - (0 + 0.1/2)] = 0.091891\,;$$

$$k_3 = hf(x + h/2, y + k_2/2) = 0.1[\cos(5(0 + 0.091891/2)) - (0 + 0.1/2)] = 0.092373\,;$$

$$k_4 = hf(x + h, y + k_3) = 0.1[\cos(5(0 + 0.092373)) - (0 + 0.1)] = 0.079522\,;$$

$$\Downarrow$$

$$x = 0 + 0.1 = 0.1\,,$$

$$y = 0 + \frac{1}{6}(0.1 + 2 \cdot 0.091891 + 2 \cdot 0.092373 + 0.079522) \approx 0.091342\,;$$

$$\vdots$$

The results of computations are shown in Table 3-J.

Using these value, we sketch a polygonal line approximating the graph of the solution on $[0, 3]$. See Figure 3-C.

Table 3–J: 4th order Runge-Kutta approximations to the solution of $y' = \cos(5y) - x$, $y(0) = 0$, on $[0, 3]$ with $h = 0.1$.

x_n	y_n	x_n	y_n
0	0	1.5	−0.02668
0.1	0.09134	1.6	−0.85748
0.2	0.15663	1.7	−0.17029
0.3	0.19458	1.8	−0.30618
0.4	0.21165	1.9	−0.53517
0.5	0.21462	2.0	−0.81879
0.6	0.20844	2.1	−1.02887
0.7	0.19629	2.2	−1.17307
0.8	0.18006	2.3	−1.30020
0.9	0.16079	2.4	−1.45351
1.0	0.13890	2.5	−1.69491
1.1	0.11439	2.6	−2.03696
1.2	0.08686	2.7	−2.30917
1.3	0.05544	2.8	−2.50088
1.4	0.01855	2.9	−2.69767
		3.0	−2.99510

17. Taylor method of order 2 has recursive formulas given by equations (5) and (6) on page 135 of the text: that is

$$x_{j+1} = x_j + h \qquad \text{and} \qquad y_{j+1} = y_j + hf(x_j, y_j) + \frac{h^2}{2!} f_2(x_j, y_j).$$

With $f(x, y) = y$, we have

$$f_2(x, y) = y'' = \frac{\partial f(x, y)}{\partial x} + \left[\frac{\partial f(x, y)}{\partial y}\right] f(x, y) = 0 + 1 \cdot (y) = y.$$

Therefore, since $h = 1/n$, the recursive formula for y_{j+1} is given by the equation

$$y_{j+1} = y_j + \frac{1}{n} y_j + \frac{1}{2n^2} y_j = \left(1 + \frac{1}{n} + \frac{1}{2n^2}\right) y_j.$$

We are starting the process at $x_0 = 0$ and $y_0 = 1$, and we are taking steps of size $1/n$ until we reach $x = 1$. This means that we will take n steps. Thus, y_n will be an approximation for the solution to the differential equation at $x = 1$. Since the actual solution is $y = e^x$, this means that $y_n \approx e$. To find the equation we are looking for, we see that

$$\begin{aligned} y_1 &= \left(1 + \frac{1}{n} + \frac{1}{2n^2}\right) y_0 = \left(1 + \frac{1}{n} + \frac{1}{2n^2}\right), \\ y_2 &= \left(1 + \frac{1}{n} + \frac{1}{2n^2}\right) y_1 = \left(1 + \frac{1}{n} + \frac{1}{2n^2}\right)^2, \\ y_3 &= \left(1 + \frac{1}{n} + \frac{1}{2n^2}\right) y_2 = \left(1 + \frac{1}{n} + \frac{1}{2n^2}\right)^3, \\ y_4 &= \left(1 + \frac{1}{n} + \frac{1}{2n^2}\right) y_3 = \left(1 + \frac{1}{n} + \frac{1}{2n^2}\right)^4, \\ &\vdots \\ y_n &= \left(1 + \frac{1}{n} + \frac{1}{2n^2}\right) y_{n-1} = \left(1 + \frac{1}{n} + \frac{1}{2n^2}\right)^n . \end{aligned}$$

(This can be proved rigorously by mathematical induction.) As we observed above, $y_n \approx e$, and so we have

$$e \approx \left(1 + \frac{1}{n} + \frac{1}{2n^2}\right)^n .$$

19. In this initial value problem, the independent variable is u, the dependent variable is v, $u_0 = 2$, $v_0 = 0.1$, and

$$f(u, v) = u\left(\frac{u}{2} + 1\right) v^3 + \left(u + \frac{5}{2}\right) v^2 .$$

We will use the classical 4th order Runge-Kutta algorithm with tolerance given on page 139 of the text but, since the stopping criteria should be based on the relative error, we will replace the condition $|z - v| < \varepsilon$ in Step 6 by $|(z - v)/v| < \varepsilon$ (see Step 6′ on page 138).

We start with $m = 0$, $N = 2^m = 1$, and a step size $h = (3 - 2)/N = 1$. Setting $u = u_0 = 2$, $v = v_0 = 0.1$, on Step 4 we compute

$$\begin{aligned} k_1 &= hf(u, v) = (1)\left[2\left(\frac{2}{2} + 1\right)(0.1)^3 + \left(2 + \frac{5}{2}\right)(0.1)^2\right] = 0.049; \\ k_2 &= hf\left(u + h/2, v + k_1/2\right) = (1)\left[(2 + 1/2)\left(\frac{2 + 1/2}{2} + 1\right)(0.1 + 0.049/2)^3\right. \\ &\qquad \left. + \left((2 + 1/2) + \frac{5}{2}\right)(0.1 + 0.049/2)^2\right] = 0.088356 ; \end{aligned}$$

$$k_3 = hf(u+h/2, v+k_2/2) = (1)\left[(2+1/2)\left(\frac{2+1/2}{2}+1\right)(0.1+0.088356/2)^3 + \left((2+1/2)+\frac{5}{2}\right)(0.1+0.088356/2)^2\right] = 0.120795\,;$$

$$k_4 = hf(u+h, v+k_3) = (1)\left[(2+1)\left(\frac{2+1}{2}+1\right)(0.1+0.120795)^3 + \left((2+1)+\frac{5}{2}\right)(0.1+0.120795)^2\right] = 0.348857\,.$$

So,

$$u = u+h = 2+1 = 3\,,$$
$$v = v + \frac{1}{6}(0.049 + 2\cdot 0.088356 + 2\cdot 0.120795 + 0.348857) \approx 0.236027\,.$$

Because the relative error between two successive approximations, $v(3;2^0) = 0.236027$ and $v = 0.1$ is $\varepsilon = |(0.236027-0.1)/0.236027| \approx 0.576320 > 0.0001$, we go back to Step 2 and set $m = 1$, take $N = 2^m = 2$ on Step 3, compute $h = 1/N = 0.5$, and use the 4th order Runge-Kutta subroutine on page 138 of the text to find $v(3;0.5)$. This takes two steps and yields

$$k_1 = (0.5)\left[2\left(\frac{2}{2}+1\right)(0.1)^3 + \left(2+\frac{5}{2}\right)(0.1)^2\right] = 0.0245;$$

$$k_2 = (0.5)\left[(2+0.5/2)\left(\frac{2+0.5/2}{2}+1\right)(0.1+0.0245/2)^3 + \left((2+0.5/2)+\frac{5}{2}\right)(0.1+0.0245/2)^2\right] = 0.033306\,;$$

$$k_3 = (0.5)\left[(2+0.5/2)\left(\frac{2+0.5/2}{2}+1\right)(0.1+0.033306/2)^3 + \left((2+0.5/2)+\frac{5}{2}\right)(0.1+0.033306/2)^2\right] = 0.036114\,;$$

$$k_4 = (0.5)\left[(2+0.5)\left(\frac{2+0.5}{2}+1\right)(0.1+0.036114)^3 + \left((2+0.5)+\frac{5}{2}\right)(0.1+0.036114)^2\right] = 0.053410\,.$$

This gives

$$\begin{aligned} u &= 2 + 0.5 = 2.5\,, \\ v &= 0.1 + \frac{1}{6}(0.0245 + 2 \cdot 0.033306 + 2 \cdot 0.036114 + 0.053410) \approx 0.136125\,. \end{aligned}$$

We compute k_j's again and find an approximate value of $v(3)$.

$$\begin{aligned} k_1 &= (0.5)\left[2.5\left(\frac{2.5}{2}+1\right)(0.136125)^3 + \left(2.5+\frac{5}{2}\right)(0.136125)^2\right] = 0.053419; \\ k_2 &= (0.5)\left[(2.5+0.5/2)\left(\frac{2.5+0.5/2}{2}+1\right)(0.136125+0.053419/2)^3\right. \\ &\qquad \left. + \left((2.5+0.5/2)+\frac{5}{2}\right)(0.136125+0.053419/2)^2\right] = 0.083702\,; \\ k_3 &= (0.5)\left[(2.5+0.5/2)\left(\frac{2.5+0.5/2}{2}+1\right)(0.136125+0.083702/2)^3\right. \\ &\qquad \left. + \left((2.5+0.5/2)+\frac{5}{2}\right)(0.136125+0.083702/2)^2\right] = 0.101558\,; \\ k_4 &= (0.5)\left[(2.5+0.5)\left(\frac{2.5+0.5}{2}+1\right)(0.136125+0.101558)^3\right. \\ &\qquad \left. + \left((2.5+0.5)+\frac{5}{2}\right)(0.136125+0.101558)^2\right] = 0.205709\,. \end{aligned}$$

Therefore, at $u = 2.5 + 0.5 = 3.0$,

$$v = 0.136125 + \frac{1}{6}(0.053419 + 2 \cdot 0.083702 + 2 \cdot 0.101558 + 0.205709) \approx 0.241066\,.$$

This time the relative error is

$$\varepsilon = \left|\frac{v(3;2^{-1}) - v(3;2^0)}{v(3;2^{-1})}\right| = \frac{0.241066 - 0.236027}{0.241066} \approx 0.020903 > 0.0001\,.$$

Thus we set $m = 2$, $N = 2^m = 4$, $h = 1/N = 0.25$, repeat computations with this new step, and find that $v(3;2^{-2}) \approx 0.241854$ and

$$\varepsilon = \left|\frac{v(3;2^{-2}) - v(3;2^{-1})}{v(3;2^{-1})}\right| = \frac{0.241854 - 0.241066}{0.241854} \approx 0.003258 > 0.0001\,.$$

We continue increasing m and get

$$m = 3,\ h = 0.125\,,\quad v(3;2^{-3}) = 0.241924\,,\ \varepsilon = \left|\frac{0.241924 - 0.241854}{0.241924}\right| \approx 0.00029 > 10^{-4}\,;$$

$$m = 4,\ h = 0.0625\,,\ v(3;2^{-4}) = 0.241929\,,\ \varepsilon = \left|\frac{0.241929 - 0.241924}{0.241929}\right| \approx 0.00002 < 10^{-4}\,.$$

Therefore, within an accuracy of 0.0001, $v(3) \approx 0.24193$.

CHAPTER 4: Linear Second Order Equations

EXERCISES 4.1: Introduction: The Mass-Spring Oscillator, page 159

1. With $b = 0$ and $F_{\text{ext}} = 0$, equation (3) on page 155 becomes

$$my'' + ky = 0.$$

Substitution $y = \sin \omega t$, where $\omega = \sqrt{k/m}$, yields

$$\begin{aligned} m(\sin \omega t)'' + k(\sin \omega t) &= -m\omega^2 \sin \omega t + k \sin \omega t \\ &= \sin \omega t \left(-m\omega^2 + k\right) = \sin \omega t \left(-m(k/m) + k\right) = 0. \end{aligned}$$

Thus $y = \sin \omega t$ is indeed a solution.

3. Differentiating $y(t)$, we find

$$\begin{aligned} & y = 2\sin 3t + \cos 3t \\ \Rightarrow \qquad & y' = 6\cos 3t - 3\sin 3t \\ \Rightarrow \qquad & y'' = -18\sin 3t - 9\cos 3t. \end{aligned}$$

Substituting y, y', and y'' into the given equation, we get

$$\begin{aligned} 2y'' + 18y &= 2(-18\sin 3t - 9\cos 3t) + 18(2\sin 3t + \cos 3t) \\ &= [2(-18) + 18(2)]\sin 3t + [2(-9) + 18(1)]\cos 3t = 0. \end{aligned}$$

Next, we check that the initial conditions are satisfied.

$$\begin{aligned} y(0) &= (2\sin 3t + \cos 3t)\Big|_{t=0} = 2\sin 0 + \cos 0 = 1, \\ y'(0) &= (6\cos 3t - 3\sin 3t)\Big|_{t=0} = 6\cos 0 - 3\sin 0 = 6. \end{aligned}$$

Writing $y(t)$ in the form

$$y(t) = \sqrt{5}\left(\frac{2}{\sqrt{5}}\sin 3t + \frac{1}{\sqrt{5}}\cos 3t\right) = \sqrt{5}\sin(3t+\gamma),$$

where $\gamma = \arctan(1/2)$, we conclude that $|y(t)| = \sqrt{5}|\sin(3t+\gamma)|$, and so $\max|y(t)| = \sqrt{5}$ (since $\max|\sin(3t+\gamma)| = 1$).

5. We differentiate $y(t)$ twice and obtain

$$\begin{aligned} y(t) &= e^{-2t}\sin(\sqrt{2}t) \\ y'(t) &= e^{-2t}[(-2)\sin(\sqrt{2}t) + \sqrt{2}\cos(\sqrt{2}t)] \\ y''(t) &= e^{-2t}\left[(-2)^2\sin(\sqrt{2}t) + (-2)\sqrt{2}\cos(\sqrt{2}t) + (-2)\sqrt{2}\cos(\sqrt{2}t) - (\sqrt{2})^2\sin(\sqrt{2}t)\right] \\ &= e^{-2t}\left[2\sin(\sqrt{2}t) - 4\sqrt{2}\cos(\sqrt{2}t)\right]. \end{aligned}$$

Substituting these functions into the differential equation, we get

$$\begin{aligned} my'' + by' + ky &= y'' + 4y' + 6y = e^{-2t}\left[2\sin(\sqrt{2}t) - 4\sqrt{2}\cos(\sqrt{2}t)\right] \\ &\qquad + 4e^{-2t}[(-2)\sin(\sqrt{2}t) + \sqrt{2}\cos(\sqrt{2}t)] + 6e^{-2t}\sin(\sqrt{2}t) \\ &= e^{-2t}\left[(2-8+6)\sin(\sqrt{2}t) + (-4\sqrt{2}+4\sqrt{2})\cos(\sqrt{2}t)\right] = 0. \end{aligned}$$

Therefore, $y = e^{-2t}\sin(\sqrt{2}t)$ is a solution. As $t \to +\infty$, $e^{-2t} \to 0$ while $\sin(\sqrt{2}t)$ remains bounded. Therefore, $\lim_{t\to+\infty} y(t) = 0$.

7. For $y = A\cos 5t + B\sin 5t$,

$$y' = -5A\sin 5t + 5B\cos 5t, \qquad y'' = -25A\cos 5t - 25B\sin 5t.$$

Inserting y, y', and y'' into the given equation and matching coefficients yield

$$\begin{aligned} & y'' + 2y' + 4y = 3\sin 5t \\ \Rightarrow\quad & (-25A\cos 5t - 25B\sin 5t) + 2(-5A\sin 5t + 5B\cos 5t) + 4(A\cos 5t + B\sin 5t) \\ & \qquad = (-21A + 10B)\cos 5t + (-10A - 21B)\sin 5t = 3\sin 5t \\ \Rightarrow\quad & \begin{array}{l} -21A + 10B = 0, \\ -10A - 21B = 3 \end{array} \quad\Rightarrow\quad \begin{array}{l} A = -30/541, \\ B = -63/541. \end{array} \end{aligned}$$

Thus, $y = -(30/541)\cos 5t - (63/541)\sin 5t$ is a synchronous solution to $y'' + 2y' + 4y = 3\sin 5t$.

9. We differentiate $y = A\cos 2t + B\sin 2t$ twice to get

$$y' = -2A\sin 2t + 2B\cos 2t \qquad \text{and} \qquad y'' = -4A\cos 2t - 4B\sin 2t,$$

substitute y, y', and y'' into the given equation, and compare coefficients. This yields

$$\begin{aligned} y'' + 2y' + 4y &= (-4A\cos 2t - 4B\sin 2t) + 2(-2A\sin 2t + 2B\cos 2t) + 4(A\cos 2t + B\sin 2t) \\ &= 4B\cos 2t - 4A\sin 2t = 3\cos 2t + 4\sin 2t \end{aligned}$$

$$\Rightarrow \quad \begin{aligned} 4B &= 3, \\ -4A &= 4 \end{aligned} \quad \Rightarrow \quad \begin{aligned} A &= -1, \\ B &= 3/4 \end{aligned} \quad \Rightarrow \quad y = -\cos 2t + (3/4)\sin 2t.$$

EXERCISES 4.2: Homogeneous Linear Equations; The General Solution, page 167

1. The auxiliary equation for this problem is $r^2 + 5r + 6 = (r+2)(r+3) = 0$, which has the roots $r = -2$ and $r = -3$. Thus $\{e^{-2t}, e^{-3t}\}$ is a set of two linearly independent solutions for this differential equation. Therefore, a general solution is given by

$$y(t) = c_1 e^{-2t} + c_2 e^{-3t},$$

where c_1 and c_2 are arbitrary constants.

3. The auxiliary equation, $r^2 + 8r + 16 = (r+4)^2 = 0$, has a double root $r = -4$. Therefore, e^{-4t} and te^{-4t} are two linearly independent solutions for this differential equation, and a general solution is given by

$$y(t) = c_1 e^{-4t} + c_2 t e^{-4t},$$

where c_1 and c_2 are arbitrary constants.

5. The auxiliary equation for this problem is $r^2 + r - 1 = 0$. By the quadratic formula, we have

$$r = \frac{-1 \pm \sqrt{1+4}}{2} = \frac{-1 \pm \sqrt{5}}{2}.$$

Therefore, a general solution is

$$z(t) = c_1 e^{(-1-\sqrt{5})t/2} + c_2 e^{(-1+\sqrt{5})t/2}.$$

7. Solving the auxiliary equation, $2r^2 + 7r - 4 = 0$, yields $r = 1/2, -4$. Thus a general solution is given by

$$u(t) = c_1 e^{t/2} + c_2 e^{-4t},$$

where c_1 and c_2 are arbitrary constants.

9. The auxiliary equation for this problem is $r^2 - r - 11 = 0$, which has roots

$$r = \frac{1 \pm \sqrt{1 + 4 \cdot 11}}{2} = \frac{1 \pm 3\sqrt{5}}{2}.$$

Thus, a general solution to the given equation is

$$y(t) = c_1 e^{(1+3\sqrt{5})t/2} + c_2 e^{(1-3\sqrt{5})t/2}.$$

11. Solving the auxiliary equation, $4r^2 + 20r + 25 = (2r + 5)^2 = 0$, we conclude that $r = -5/2$ is its double root. Therefore, a general solution to the given differential equation is

$$w(t) = c_1 e^{-5t/2} + c_2 t e^{-5t/2}.$$

13. The auxiliary equation for this problem is $r^2 + 2r - 8 = 0$, which has roots $r = -4, 2$. Thus, a general solution is given by

$$y(t) = c_1 e^{-4t} + c_2 e^{2t},$$

where c_1, c_2 are arbitrary constants. To satisfy the initial conditions, $y(0) = 3$, $y'(0) = -12$, we find the derivative $y'(t) = -4c_1 e^{-4t} + 2c_2 e^{2t}$ and solve the system

$$\begin{aligned} y(0) &= c_1 e^{-4 \cdot 0} + c_2 e^{2 \cdot 0} = c_1 + c_2 = 3, \\ y'(0) &= -4c_1 e^{-4 \cdot 0} + 2c_2 e^{2 \cdot 0} = -4c_1 + 2c_2 = -12 \end{aligned} \quad \Rightarrow \quad \begin{aligned} c_1 &= 3, \\ c_2 &= 0. \end{aligned}$$

Therefore, the solution to the given initial value problem is

$$y(t) = (3)e^{-4t} + (0)e^{2t} = 3e^{-4t}.$$

15. The auxiliary equation for this equation is $r^2 + 2r + 1 = (r + 1)^2 = 0$. We see that $r = -1$ is a repeated root. Thus, two linearly independent solutions are $y_1(t) = e^{-t}$ and $y_2(t) = te^{-t}$. This means that a general solution is given by $y(t) = c_1 e^{-t} + c_2 t e^{-t}$.

To find the constants c_1 and c_2, we substitute the initial conditions into the general solution and its derivative, $y'(t) = -c_1e^{-t} + c_2\left(e^{-t} - te^{-t}\right)$, and obtain

$$\begin{aligned} y(0) &= 1 = c_1e^0 + c_2 \cdot 0 = c_1\,, \\ y'(0) &= -3 = -c_1e^0 + c_2\left(e^0 - 0\right) = -c_1 + c_2\,. \end{aligned}$$

So, $c_1 = 1$ and $c_2 = -2$. Therefore, the solution that satisfies the initial conditions is given by

$$y(t) = e^{-t} - 2te^{-t}.$$

17. The auxiliary equation for this problem, $r^2 - 2r - 2 = 0$, has roots $r = 1 \pm \sqrt{3}$. Thus, a general solution is given by $z(t) = c_1e^{(1+\sqrt{3})t} + c_2e^{(1-\sqrt{3})t}$. Differentiating, we find that $z'(t) = c_1(1+\sqrt{3})e^{(1+\sqrt{3})t} + c_2(1-\sqrt{3})e^{(1-\sqrt{3})t}$. Substitution of $z(t)$ and $z'(t)$ into the initial conditions yields the system

$$\begin{aligned} z(0) &= c_1 + c_2 = 0, \\ z'(0) &= c_1(1+\sqrt{3}) + c_2(1-\sqrt{3}) = \sqrt{3}(c_1 - c_2) = 3 \end{aligned} \quad \Rightarrow \quad \begin{aligned} c_1 &= \sqrt{3}/2, \\ c_2 &= -\sqrt{3}/2. \end{aligned}$$

Thus, the solution satisfying the given initial conditions is

$$z(t) = \frac{\sqrt{3}}{2}\,e^{(1+\sqrt{3})t} - \frac{\sqrt{3}}{2}\,e^{(1-\sqrt{3})t} = \frac{\sqrt{3}}{2}\left(e^{(1+\sqrt{3})t} - e^{(1-\sqrt{3})t}\right).$$

19. Here, the auxiliary equation is $r^2 - 4r - 5 = (r-5)(r+1) = 0$, which has roots $r = 5, -1$. Consequently, a general solution to the differential equation is $y(t) = c_1e^{5t} + c_2e^{-t}$, where c_1 and c_2 are arbitrary constants. To find the solution that satisfies the initial conditions, $y(-1) = 3$ and $y'(-1) = 9$, we first differentiate the solution found above, then plug in y and y' into the initial conditions. This gives

$$\begin{aligned} y(-1) &= 3 = c_1e^{-5} + c_2e \\ y'(-1) &= 9 = 5c_1e^{-5} - c_2e. \end{aligned}$$

Solving this system yields $c_1 = 2e^5$, $c_2 = e^{-1}$. Thus $y(t) = 2e^{5(t+1)} + e^{-(t+1)}$ is the desired solution.

Chapter 4

21. **(a)** With $y(t) = e^{rt}$, $y'(t) = re^{rt}$, the equation becomes

$$are^{rt} + be^{rt} = (ar + b)e^{rt} = 0.$$

Since the function e^{rt} is never zero on $(-\infty, \infty)$, to satisfy the above equation we must have

$$ar + b = 0.$$

(b) Solving the characteristic equation, $ar + b = 0$, obtained in part (a), we get $r = -b/a$. So $y(t) = e^{rt} = e^{-bt/a}$, and a general solution is given by $y = ce^{-bt/a}$, where c is an arbitrary constant.

23. We form the characteristic equation, $5r + 4 = 0$, and find its root $r = -4/5$. Therefore, $y(t) = ce^{-4t/5}$ is a general solution to the given equation.

25. The characteristic equation, $6r - 13 = 0$, has the root $r = 13/6$. Therefore, a general solution is given by $w(t) = ce^{13t/6}$.

27. Assuming that $y_1(t) = e^{-t}\cos 2t$ and $y_2(t) = e^{-t}\sin 2t$ are linearly dependent on $(0, 1)$, we conclude that, for some constant c and all $t \in (0, 1)$,

$$y_1(t) = cy_2(t) \qquad \Rightarrow \qquad e^{-t}\cos 2t = ce^{-t}\sin 2t \qquad \Rightarrow \qquad \cos 2t = c\sin 2t.$$

Choosing, say, $t = \pi/4$, we get $\cos(\pi/2) = c\sin(\pi/2)$ or $c = 0$. This implies that

$$\cos 2t \equiv 0 \cdot \sin 2t \equiv 0, \qquad t \in (0, 1),$$

which is a contradiction. Thus, $y_1(t)$ and $y_2(t)$ are linearly independent on $(0, 1)$ (and so on $(-\infty, \infty)$; see Problem 33(a) below).

29. These functions are linearly independent, because the equality $y_1(t) \equiv cy_2(t)$ would imply that, for some constant c,

$$te^{2t} \equiv ce^{2t} \qquad \Rightarrow \qquad t \equiv c$$

on $(0, 1)$.

31. Using the trigonometric identity $1 + \tan^2 t \equiv \sec^2 t$, we conclude that

$$y_1(t) = \tan^2 t - \sec^2 t \equiv -1 \qquad \Rightarrow \qquad y_2(t) \equiv 3 \equiv (-3)y_1(t),$$

and so $y_1(t)$ and $y_2(t)$ are linearly dependent on $(0, 1)$ (even on $(-\infty, \infty)$).

33. **(a)** True. Since $y_1(t)$ and $y_2(t)$ are linearly dependent on $[a, b]$, there exists a constant c such that $y_1(t) = cy_2(t)$ (or $y_2(t) = cy_1(t)$) for all t in $[a, b]$. In particular, this equality is satisfied on any smaller interval $[c, d]$, and so $y_1(t)$ and $y_2(t)$ are linearly dependent on $[c, d]$.

(b) False. As an example, consider $y_1(t) = t$ and $y_2(t) = |t|$ on $[-1, 1]$. For t in $[0, 1]$, $y_2(t) = t = y_1(t)$, and so $y_2(t) \equiv c_1 y_1(t)$ with constant $c_1 = 1$. For t in $[-1, 0]$, we have $y_2(t) = -t = -y_1(t)$, and so $y_2(t) \equiv c_2 y_1(t)$ with constant $c_2 = -1$. Therefore, these two functions are linearly dependent on $[0, 1]$ and on $[-1, 0]$. Since $c_1 \neq c_2$, there is no such a constant c that $y_1(t) \equiv cy_2(t)$ on $[-1, 1]$. So, $y_1(t)$ and $y_2(t)$ are linearly independent on $[-1, 1]$.

35. **(a)** No, because, for $t \geq 0$, $y_2(t) = |t^3| = t^3 = y_1(t)$.

(b) No, because, for $t \leq 0$, $y_2(t) = |t^3| = -t^3 = -y_1(t)$.

(c) Yes, because there is no constant c such that $y_2(t) = cy_1(t)$ is satisfied for all t (for positive t we have $c = 1$, and $c = -1$ for negative t).

(d) While $y_1'(t) = 3t^2$ on $(-\infty, \infty)$, for the derivative of $y_2(t)$ we consider three different cases: $t < 0$, $t = 0$, and $t > 0$. For $t < 0$, $y_2(t) = -t^3$, $y_2'(t) = -3t^2$, and so

$$W[y_1, y_2](t) = \begin{vmatrix} t^3 & -t^3 \\ 3t^2 & -3t^2 \end{vmatrix} = t^3(-3t^2) - 3t^2(-t^3) = 0.$$

Similarly, for $t > 0$, $y_2(t) = t^3$, $y_2'(t) = 3t^2$, and

$$W[y_1, y_2](t) = \begin{vmatrix} t^3 & t^3 \\ 3t^2 & 3t^2 \end{vmatrix} = t^3 \cdot 3t^2 - 3t^2 \cdot t^3 = 0.$$

For $t = 0$, $y_1'(0) = 3 \cdot 0^2 = 0$ and $y_2'(0) = 0$. The latter follows from the fact that one-sided derivatives of $y_2(t)$, $3t^2$ and $-3t^2$, are both zero at $t = 0$. Also, $y_1(0) = y_2(0) = 0$. Hence

$$W[y_1, y_2](0) = \begin{vmatrix} 0 & 0 \\ 0 & 0 \end{vmatrix} = 0,$$

and so $W[y_1, y_2](t) \equiv 0$ on $(-\infty, \infty)$. This result does not contradict part (b) in Problem 34 because these functions are not a pair of solutions to a homogeneous linear equation with constant coefficients.

37. If $y_1(t)$ and $y_2(t)$ are solutions to the equation $ay'' + by' + c = 0$, then, by Abel's formula, $W[y_1, y_2](t) = Ce^{-bt/a}$, where C is a constant depending on y_1 and y_2. Thus, if $C \neq 0$, then $W[y_1, y_2](t) \neq 0$ for any t in $(-\infty, \infty)$, because the exponential function, $e^{-bt/a}$, is never zero. For $C = 0$, $W[y_1, y_2](t) \equiv 0$ on $(-\infty, \infty)$.

39. **(a)** A linear combination of $y_1(t) = 1$, $y_2(t) = t$, and $y_3(t) = t^2$,

$$C_1 \cdot 1 + C_2 \cdot t + C_3 \cdot t^2 = C_1 + C_2 t + C_3 t^2,$$

is a polynomial of degree at most two and so can have at most two real roots, unless it is a zero polynomial, i.e., has all zero coefficients. Therefore, the above linear combination vanishes on $(-\infty, \infty)$ if and only if $C_1 = C_2 = C_3 = 0$, and $y_1(t)$, $y_2(t)$, and $y_3(t)$ are linearly independent on $(-\infty, \infty)$.

(b) Since

$$5y_1(t) + 3y_2(t) + 15y_3(t) = -15 + 15\sin^2 t + 15\cos^2 t = 15(-1 + \sin^2 t + \cos^2 t) \equiv 0$$

on $(-\infty, \infty)$ (the Pythagorean identity), given functions are linearly dependent.

(c) These functions are linearly independent. Indeed, since the function e^t does not vanish on $(-\infty, \infty)$,

$$C_1 y_1 + C_2 y_2 + C_3 y_3 = C_1 e^t + C_2 t e^t + C_3 t^2 e^t = \left(C_1 + C_2 t + C_3 t^2\right) e^t = 0$$

if and only if $C_1 + C_2 t + C_3 t^2 = 0$. But functions 1, t, and t^2 are linearly independent on $(-\infty, \infty)$ (see (a)) and so their linear combination is identically zero if and only if $C_1 = C_2 = C_3 = 0$.

(d) By the definition of $\cosh t$,

$$y_3(t) = \cosh t = \frac{e^t + e^{-t}}{2} = \frac{1}{2}\,e^t + \frac{1}{2}\,e^{-t} = \frac{1}{2}\,y_1(t) + \frac{1}{2}\,y_2(t)\,,$$

and given functions are linearly dependent on $(-\infty, \infty)$.

41. The auxiliary equation for this problem is $r^3 + r^2 - 6r + 4 = 0$. Factoring yields

$$\begin{aligned} r^3 + r^2 - 6r + 4 &= \left(r^3 - r^2\right) + \left(2r^2 - 2r\right) + (-4r + 4) \\ &= r^2(r-1) + 2r(r-1) - 4(r-1) = (r-1)(r^2 + 2r - 4). \end{aligned}$$

Thus the roots of the auxiliary equation are

$$r = 1 \quad \text{and} \quad r = \frac{-2 \pm \sqrt{(-2)^2 - 4(1)(-4)}}{2} = -1 \pm \sqrt{5}\,.$$

Therefore, the functions e^t, $e^{(-1-\sqrt{5})t}$, and $e^{(-1+\sqrt{5})t}$ are solutions to the given equation, and they are linearly independent on $(-\infty, \infty)$ (see Problem 40). Hence, a general solution to $y''' + y'' - 6y' + 4y = 0$ is given by

$$y(t) = c_1 e^t + c_2 e^{(-1-\sqrt{5})t} + c_3 e^{(-1+\sqrt{5})t}\,.$$

42. The auxiliary equation associated with this differential equation is $r^3 - 6r^2 - r + 6 = 0$. We see, by inspection, that $r = 1$ is a root. Dividing the cubic polynomial $r^3 - 6r^2 - r + 6$ by $r - 1$, we find that

$$r^3 - 6r^2 - r + 6 = (r-1)(r^2 - 5r - 6) = (r-1)(r+1)(r-6).$$

Hence $r = -1$, 1, 6 are the roots to the auxiliary equation, and a general solution is

$$y(t) = c_1 e^{-t} + c_2 e^t + c_3 e^{6t}.$$

43. Factoring the auxiliary polynomial yields

$$\begin{aligned} r^3 + 2r^2 - 4r - 8 &= (r^3 + 2r^2) - (4r + 8) \\ &= r^2(r+2) - 4(r+2) = (r+2)\left(r^2 - 4\right) = (r+2)(r+2)(r-2). \end{aligned}$$

Therefore, the auxiliary equation has a double root -2 and a root 2. The functions e^{-2t}, te^{-2t}, and e^{2t} form a linearly independent solution set. Therefore, a general solution in this problem is

$$z(t) = c_1 e^{-2t} + c_2 t e^{-2t} + c_3 e^{2t}.$$

45. By inspection, we see that $r = 2$ is a root of the auxiliary equation, $r^3 + 3r^2 - 4r - 12 = 0$. Dividing the polynomial $r^3 + 3r^2 - 4r - 12$ by $r - 2$ yields

$$r^3 + 3r^2 - 4r - 12 = (r-2)\left(r^2 + 5r + 6\right) = (r-2)(r+2)(r+3).$$

Hence, two other roots of the auxiliary equation are $r = -2$ and $r = -3$. The functions e^{-3t}, e^{-2t}, and e^{2t} are three linearly independent solutions to the given equation, and a general solution is given by

$$y(t) = c_1 e^{-3t} + c_2 e^{-2t} + c_3 e^{2t}.$$

47. First we find a general solution to the equation $y''' - y' = 0$. Its characteristic equation, $r^3 - r = 0$, has roots $r = 0, -1$, and 1, and so a general solution is given by

$$y(t) = c_1 e^{(0)t} + c_2 e^{(-1)t} + c_3 e^{(1)t} = c_1 + c_2 e^{-t} + c_3 e^{t}.$$

Differentiating $y(t)$ twice yields

$$y'(t) = -c_2 e^{-t} + c_3 e^{t}, \qquad y''(t) = c_2 e^{-t} + c_3 e^{t}.$$

Now we substitute y, y', and y'' into the initial conditions and find c_1, c_2, and c_3.

$$\begin{aligned} y(0) = c_1 + c_2 + c_3 &= 2, \\ y'(0) = -c_2 + c_3 &= 3, \\ y''(0) = c_2 + c_3 &= -1 \end{aligned} \qquad \Rightarrow \qquad \begin{aligned} c_1 &= 3, \\ c_2 &= -2, \\ c_3 &= 1. \end{aligned}$$

Therefore, the solution to the given initial value problem is

$$y(t) = 3 - 2e^{-t} + e^{t}.$$

49. **(a)** To find the roots of the auxiliary equation, $p(r) := 3r^3 + 18r^2 + 13r - 19 = 0$, one can use Newton's method or intermediate value theorem. We note that

$$p(-5) = -9 < 0, \qquad p(-4) = 25 > 0,$$
$$p(-2) = 3 > 0, \qquad p(-1) = -17 < 0,$$
$$p(0) = -19 < 0, \qquad p(1) = 15 > 0.$$

Therefore, the roots of $p(r)$ belong to the intervals $[-5, -4]$, $[-2, -1]$, and $[0, 1]$, and we can take $r = -5$, $r = -2$, and $r = 0$ as initial quesses. Approximation yields $r_1 \approx -4.832$, $r_2 \approx -1.869$, and $r_3 \approx 0.701$. So, a general solution is given by

$$y(t) = c_1 e^{r_1 t} + c_2 e^{r_2 t} + c_3 e^{r_3 t} = c_1 e^{-4.832t} + c_2 e^{-1.869t} + c_3 e^{0.701t}\,.$$

(b) The auxiliary equation, $r^4 - 5r^2 + 5 = 0$, is of quadratic type. The substitution $s = r^2$ yields

$$s^2 - 5s + 5 = 0 \qquad \Rightarrow \qquad s = \frac{5 \pm \sqrt{5}}{2} \qquad \Rightarrow \qquad r = \pm\sqrt{s} = \pm\sqrt{\frac{5 \pm \sqrt{5}}{2}}\,.$$

Therefore,

$$r_1 = \sqrt{\frac{5 - \sqrt{5}}{2}} \approx 1.176\,, \qquad r_2 = \sqrt{\frac{5 + \sqrt{5}}{2}} \approx 1.902\,, \quad r_3 = -r_1\,, \quad \text{and} \quad r_4 = -r_2$$

are the roots of the auxiliary equation, and a general solution to $y^{(\mathrm{iv})} - 5y'' + 5y = 0$ is given by $y(t) = c_1 e^{r_1 t} + c_2 e^{-r_1 t} + c_3 e^{r_2 t} + c_4 e^{-r_2 t}$.

(c) We can use numerical tools to find the roots of the auxiliary fifth degree polynomial equation $r^5 - 3r^4 - 5r^3 + 15r^2 + 4r - 12 = 0$. Alternatively, one can involve the rational root theorem and examine the divisors of the free coefficient, -12. These divisors are ± 1, ± 2, ± 3, ± 4, ± 6, and ± 12. By inspection, $r = \pm 1$, ± 2, and 3 satisfy the equation. Thus, a general solution is $y(t) = c_1 e^{-t} + c_2 e^{t} + c_3 e^{-2t} + c_4 e^{2t} + c_5 e^{3t}$.

EXERCISES 4.3: Auxiliary Equations with Complex Roots, page 177

1. The auxiliary equation in this problem is $r^2 + 9 = 0$, which has roots $r = \pm 3i$. We see that $\alpha = 0$ and $\beta = 3$. Thus, a general solution to the differential equation is given by

$$y(t) = c_1 e^{(0)t} \cos 3t + c_2 e^{(0)t} \sin 3t = c_1 \cos 3t + c_2 \sin 3t.$$

3. The auxiliary equation, $r^2 - 6r + 10 = 0$, has roots $r = \left(6 \pm \sqrt{6^2 - 40}\right)/2 = 3 \pm i$. So $\alpha = 3$, $\beta = 1$, and

$$z(t) = c_1 e^{3t} \cos t + c_2 e^{3t} \sin t$$

is a general solution.

5. This differential equation has the auxiliary equation $r^2 + 4r + 6 = 0$. The roots of this auxiliary equation are $r = \left(-4 \pm \sqrt{16 - 24}\right)/2 = -2 \pm \sqrt{2}\, i$. We see that $\alpha = -2$ and $\beta = \sqrt{2}$. Thus, a general solution to the differential equation is given by

$$w(t) = c_1 e^{-2t} \cos \sqrt{2}t + c_2 e^{-2t} \sin \sqrt{2}t.$$

7. The auxiliary equation for this problem is given by

$$4r^2 - 4r + 26 = 0 \qquad \Rightarrow \qquad 2r^2 - 2r + 13 = 0 \qquad \Rightarrow \qquad r = \frac{2 \pm \sqrt{4 - 104}}{4} = \frac{1}{2} \pm \frac{5}{2} i.$$

Therefore, $\alpha = 1/2$ and $\beta = 5/2$. Thus, a general solution is given by

$$y(t) = c_1 e^{t/2} \cos\left(\frac{5t}{2}\right) + c_2 e^{t/2} \sin\left(\frac{5t}{2}\right).$$

9. The associated auxiliary equation, $r^2 - 8r + 7 = 0$, has two real roots, $r = 1, 7$. Thus the answer is

$$y(t) = c_1 e^{t} + c_2 e^{7t}.$$

11. The auxiliary equation for this problem is $r^2 + 10r + 25 = (r+5)^2 = 0$. We see that $r = -5$ is a repeated root. Thus two linearly independent solutions are $z_1(t) = e^{-5t}$ and $z_2(t) = te^{-5t}$. This means that a general solution is given by

$$z(t) = c_1 e^{-5t} + c_2 t e^{-5t},$$

where c_1 and c_2 are arbitrary constants.

13. Solving the auxiliary equation yields complex roots

$$r^2 + 2r + 5 = 0 \qquad \Rightarrow \qquad r = \frac{-2 \pm \sqrt{2^2 - 4(1)(5)}}{2} = -1 \pm 2i.$$

So, $\alpha = -1$, $\beta = 2$, and a general solution is given by

$$y(t) = c_1 e^{-t} \cos 2t + c_2 e^{-t} \sin 2t.$$

15. First, we find the roots of the auxiliary equation.

$$r^2 + 10r + 41 = 0 \qquad \Rightarrow \qquad r = \frac{-10 \pm \sqrt{10^2 - 4(1)(41)}}{2} = -5 \pm 4i.$$

These are complex numbers with $\alpha = -5$ and $\beta = 4$. Hence, a general solution to the given differential equation is

$$y(t) = c_1 e^{-5t} \cos 4t + c_2 e^{-5t} \sin 4t.$$

17. The auxiliary equation in this problem, $r^2 - r + 7 = 0$, has the roots

$$r = \frac{1 \pm \sqrt{1^2 - 4(1)(7)}}{2} = \frac{1 \pm \sqrt{-27}}{2} = \frac{1}{2} \pm \frac{3\sqrt{3}}{2} i.$$

Therefore, a general solution is

$$y(t) = c_1 e^{t/2} \cos\left(\frac{3\sqrt{3}}{2} t\right) + c_2 e^{t/2} \sin\left(\frac{3\sqrt{3}}{2} t\right).$$

19. The auxiliary equation, $r^3 + r^2 + 3r - 5 = 0$, is a cubic equation. Since any cubic equation has a real root, first we examine the divisors of the free coefficient, 5, to find integer real roots (if any). By inspection, $r = 1$ satisfies the equation. Dividing $r^3 + r^2 + 3r - 5$ by $r - 1$ yields

$$r^3 + r^2 + 3r - 5 = (r - 1)(r^2 + 2r + 5).$$

Therefore, the other two roots of the auxiliary equation are the roots of the quadratic equation $r^2 + 2r + 5 = 0$, which are $r = -1 \pm 2i$. A general solution to the given equation is then given by

$$y(t) = c_1 e^{t} + c_2 e^{-t} \cos 2t + c_3 e^{-t} \sin 2t.$$

21. The auxiliary equation for this problem is $r^2 + 2r + 2 = 0$, which has the roots

$$r = \frac{-2 \pm \sqrt{4 - 8}}{2} = -1 \pm i.$$

So, a general solution is given by

$$y(t) = c_1 e^{-t} \cos t + c_2 e^{-t} \sin t\,,$$

where c_1 and c_2 are arbitrary constants. To find the solution that satisfies the initial conditions, $y(0) = 2$ and $y'(0) = 1$, we first differentiate the solution found above, then plug in given initial conditions. This yields $y'(t) = c_1 e^{-t}(-\cos t - \sin t) + c_2 e^{-t}(\cos t - \sin t)$ and

$$\begin{aligned} y(0) &= c_1 = 2, \\ y'(0) &= -c_1 + c_2 = 1\,. \end{aligned}$$

Thus $c_1 = 2$, $c_2 = 3$, and the solution is given by

$$y(t) = 2e^{-t} \cos t + 3e^{-t} \sin t\,.$$

23. The auxiliary equation for this problem is $r^2 - 4r + 2 = 0$. The roots of this equation are

$$r = \frac{4 \pm \sqrt{16-8}}{2} = 2 \pm \sqrt{2}\,,$$

which are real numbers. A general solution is given by $w(t) = c_1 e^{(2+\sqrt{2})t} + c_2 e^{(2-\sqrt{2})t}$, where c_1 and c_2 are arbitrary constants. To find the solution that satisfies the initial conditions, $w(0) = 0$ and $w'(0) = 1$, we first differentiate the solution found above, then plug in our initial conditions. This gives

$$\begin{aligned} w(0) &= c_1 + c_2 = 0, \\ w'(0) &= \left(2 + \sqrt{2}\right) c_1 + \left(2 - \sqrt{2}\right) c_2 = 1\,. \end{aligned}$$

Solving this system of equations yields $c_1 = 1/(2\sqrt{2})$ and $c_2 = -1/(2\sqrt{2})$. Thus

$$w(t) = \frac{1}{2\sqrt{2}} e^{(2+\sqrt{2})t} - \frac{1}{2\sqrt{2}} e^{(2-\sqrt{2})t} = \frac{\sqrt{2}}{4}\left(e^{(2+\sqrt{2})t} - e^{(2-\sqrt{2})t}\right)$$

is the desired solution.

25. The auxiliary equation, $r^2 - 2r + 2 = 0$, has the roots $r = 1 \pm i$. Thus, a general solution is

$$y(t) = c_1 e^t \cos t + c_2 e^t \sin t\,,$$

where c_1 and c_2 are arbitrary constants. To find the solution that satisfies the initial conditions, $y(\pi) = e^\pi$ and $y'(\pi) = 0$, we find $y'(t) = c_1 e^t(\cos t - \sin t) + c_2 e^t(\sin t + \cos t)$ and solve the system

$$\begin{aligned} e^\pi &= y(\pi) = -c_1 e^\pi, \\ 0 &= y'(\pi) = -c_1 e^\pi - c_2 e^\pi\,. \end{aligned}$$

This yields $c_1 = -1$, $c_2 = -c_1 = 1$. So, the answer is

$$y(t) = -e^t \cos t + e^t \sin t = e^t(\sin t - \cos t)\,.$$

27. To solve the auxiliary equation, $r^3 - 4r^2 + 7r - 6 = 0$, which is of the third order, we find its real root first. Examining the divisors of -6, that is, ± 1, ± 2, ± 3, and ± 6, we find that $r = 2$ satisfies the equation. Next, we divide $r^3 - 4r^2 + 7r - 6$ by $r - 2$ and obtain

$$r^3 - 4r^2 + 7r - 6 = (r-2)\left(r^2 - 2r + 3\right).$$

Therefore, the other two roots of the auxiliary equation are

$$r = \frac{2 \pm \sqrt{4 - 12}}{2} = 1 \pm \sqrt{2}i\,,$$

and a general solution to the given differential equation is given by

$$y(t) = c_1 e^{2t} + c_2 e^t \cos\sqrt{2}t + c_3 e^t \sin\sqrt{2}t\,.$$

Next, we find the derivatives,

$$\begin{aligned} y'(t) &= 2c_1 e^{2t} + c_2 e^t\left(\cos\sqrt{2}t - \sqrt{2}\sin\sqrt{2}t\right) + c_3 e^t\left(\sin\sqrt{2}t + \sqrt{2}\cos\sqrt{2}t\right), \\ y''(t) &= 4c_1 e^{2t} + c_2 e^t\left(-\cos\sqrt{2}t - 2\sqrt{2}\sin\sqrt{2}t\right) + c_3 e^t\left(-\sin\sqrt{2}t + 2\sqrt{2}\cos\sqrt{2}t\right), \end{aligned}$$

and substitute y, y', and y'' into the initial conditions. This yields

$$\begin{aligned} c_1 + c_2 &= 1, \\ 2c_1 + c_2 + \sqrt{2}c_3 &= 0, \\ 4c_1 - c_2 + 2\sqrt{2}c_3 &= 0 \end{aligned} \qquad \Rightarrow \qquad \begin{aligned} c_1 &= 1, \\ c_2 &= 0, \\ c_3 &= -\sqrt{2}\,. \end{aligned}$$

With these values of the constants c_1, c_2, and c_3, the solution becomes

$$y(t) = e^{2t} - \sqrt{2}e^t \sin \sqrt{2}t\,.$$

29. **(a)** As it was stated in Section 4.2, third order linear homogeneous differential equations with constant coefficients can be handled in the same way as second order equations. Therefore, we look for the roots of the auxiliary equation $r^3 - r^2 + r + 3 = 0$. By the rational root theorem, the only possible rational roots are $r = \pm 1$ and ± 3. By checking these values, we find that one of the roots of the auxiliary equation is $r = -1$. Factorization yields

$$r^3 - r^2 + r + 3 = (r+1)(r^2 - 2r + 3).$$

Using the quadratic formula, we find that the other two roots are

$$r = \frac{2 \pm \sqrt{4 - 12}}{2} = 1 \pm \sqrt{2}\,i.$$

A general solution is, therefore,

$$y(t) = c_1 e^{-t} + c_2 e^t \cos \sqrt{2}t + c_3 e^t \sin \sqrt{2}t\,.$$

(b) By inspection, $r = 2$ is a root of the auxiliary equation, $r^3 + 2r^2 + 5r - 26 = 0$. Since

$$r^3 + 2r^2 + 5r - 26 = (r - 2)\left(r^2 + 4r + 13\right),$$

the other two roots are the roots of $r^2 + 4r + 13 = 0$, that is, $r = -2 \pm 3i$. Therefore, a general solution to the given equation is

$$y(t) = c_1 e^{2t} + c_2 e^{-2t} \cos 3t + c_3 e^{-2t} \sin 3t\,.$$

(c) The fourth order auxiliary equation $r^4 + 13r^2 + 36 = 0$ can be reduced to a quadratic equation by making a substitution $s = r^2$. This yields

$$s^2 + 13r + 36 = 0 \qquad \Rightarrow \qquad s = \frac{-13 \pm \sqrt{169 - 144}}{2} = \frac{-13 \pm 5}{2}.$$

Thus, $s = (-13+5)/2 = -4$ or $s = (-13-5)/2 = -9$, and the solutions to the auxiliary equation are $r = \pm\sqrt{-4} = \pm 2i$ and $r = \pm\sqrt{-9} = \pm 3i$. A general solution, therefore, has the form

$$y(t) = c_1 \cos 2t + c_2 \sin 2t + c_3 \cos 3t + c_4 \sin 3t.$$

31. (a) Comparing the equation $y'' + 16y = 0$ with the mass-spring model (16) in Example 4, we conclude that the damping coefficient $b = 0$ and the stiffness constant $k = 16 > 0$. Thus, solutions should have an oscillatory behavior.

Indeed, the auxiliary equation, $r^2 + 16 = 0$, has roots $r = \pm 4i$, and a general solution is given by

$$y(t) = c_1 \cos 4t + c_2 \sin 4t.$$

Evaluating $y'(t)$ and substituting the initial conditions, we get

$$\begin{aligned} y(0) &= c_1 = 2, \\ y'(0) &= 4c_2 = 0 \end{aligned} \qquad \Rightarrow \qquad \begin{aligned} c_1 &= 2, \\ c_2 &= 0 \end{aligned} \qquad \Rightarrow \qquad y(t) = 2\cos 4t.$$

(b) Positive damping $b = 100$ and stiffness $k = 1$ imply that the displacement $y(t)$ tends to zero, as $t \to \infty$.

To confirm this prediction, we solve the given initial value problem explicitly. The roots of the associated equation are

$$r = \frac{-100 \pm \sqrt{100^2 - 4}}{2} = -50 \pm \sqrt{2499}.$$

Thus the roots $r_1 = -50 - \sqrt{2499}$ and $r_2 = -50 + \sqrt{2499}$ are both negative. A general solution is given by

$$y(t) = c_1 e^{r_1 t} + c_2 e^{r_2 t} \qquad \Rightarrow \qquad y'(t) = c_1 r_1 e^{r_1 t} + c_2 r_2 e^{r_2 t}.$$

Solving the initial value problem yields

$$\begin{aligned} y(0) &= 1 = c_1 + c_2\,, \\ y'(0) &= 0 = c_1 r_1 + c_2 r_2 \end{aligned} \quad \Rightarrow \quad \begin{aligned} c_1 &= r_2/(r_2 - r_1), \\ c_2 &= r_1/(r_1 - r_2), \end{aligned}$$

and so the desired solution is

$$y(t) = \frac{-50 + \sqrt{2499}}{2\sqrt{2499}}\, e^{(-50-\sqrt{2499})t} + \frac{50 + \sqrt{2499}}{2\sqrt{2499}}\, e^{(-50+\sqrt{2499})t}\,.$$

Since both powers in exponential functions tend to $-\infty$ as $t \to \infty$, $y(t) \to 0$.

(c) The corresponding mass-spring model has negative damping $b = -6$ and positive stiffness $k = 8$. Thus the magnitude $|y(t)|$ of the displacement $y(t)$ will increase without bound, as $t \to \infty$. Moreover, because of the positive initial displacement and initial zero velocity, the mass will move in the negative direction. Thus, our guess is that $y(t) \to -\infty$ as $t \to \infty$.

Now we find the actual solution. Since the roots of the auxiliary equation are $r = 2$ and $r = 4$, a general solution to the given equation is $y(t) = c_1 e^{2t} + c_2 e^{4t}$. Next, we find c_1 and c_2 satisfying the initial conditions.

$$\begin{aligned} y(0) &= 1 = c_1 + c_2\,, \\ y'(0) &= 0 = 2c_1 + 4c_2 \end{aligned} \quad \Rightarrow \quad \begin{aligned} c_1 &= 2, \\ c_2 &= -1. \end{aligned}$$

Thus, the desired solution is

$$y(t) = 2e^{2t} - e^{4t}\,,$$

and it approaches $-\infty$ as $t \to \infty$.

(d) In this problem, the stiffness $k = -3$ is negative. In the mass-spring model, this means that the spring forces the mass to move in the same direction as the sign of the displacement is. Initially, the displacement $y(0) = -2$ is negative, and the mass has no initial velocity. Thus the mass, when released, will move in the negative direction, and the spring will enforce this movement. So, we expect that $y(t) \to -\infty$ as $t \to \infty$.

To find the actual solution, we solve the auxiliary equation $r^2 + 2r - 3 = 0$ and obtain $r = -3, 1$. Therefore, a general solution is given by $y(t) = c_1 e^{-3t} + c_2 e^t$. We find c_1 and

c_2 from the initial conditions.

$$\begin{aligned} y(0) &= -2 = c_1 + c_2\,, \\ y'(0) &= 0 = -3c_1 + c_2 \end{aligned} \qquad \Rightarrow \qquad \begin{aligned} c_1 &= -1/2, \\ c_2 &= -3/2. \end{aligned}$$

Thus, the solution to the initial value problem is

$$y(t) = -\frac{e^{-3t}}{2} - \frac{3e^t}{2}\,,$$

and, as $t \to \infty$, it approaches $-\infty$.

(e) As in the previous problem, we have negative stiffness $k = -6$. But this time the initial displacement, $y(0) = 1$, as well as the initial velocity, $y'(0) = 1$, is positive. So, the mass will start moving in the positive direction, and will continue doing this (due to the negative stiffness) with increasing velocity. Thus our prediction is that $y(t) \to \infty$ when $t \to \infty$.

Indeed, the roots of the characteristic equation in this problem are $r = -2$ and 3, and so a general solution has the form $y(t) = c_1 e^{-2t} + c_2 e^{3t}$. To satisfy the initial conditions, we solve the system

$$\begin{aligned} y(0) &= 1 = c_1 + c_2\,, \\ y'(0) &= 1 = -2c_1 + 3c_2 \end{aligned} \qquad \Rightarrow \qquad \begin{aligned} c_1 &= 2/5, \\ c_2 &= 3/5. \end{aligned}$$

Thus, the solution to the initial value problem is

$$y(t) = \frac{2e^{-2t}}{5} + \frac{3e^{3t}}{5}\,,$$

and it approaches ∞ as $t \to \infty$.

33. From Example 3 we see that, in the study of a vibrating spring with damping, we have the initial value problem

$$my''(t) + by'(t) + ky(t) = 0; \qquad y(0) = y_0\,, \qquad y'(0) = v_0\,,$$

where m is the mass of the spring system, b is the damping constant, k is the spring constant, $y(0)$ is the initial displacement, $y'(0)$ is the initial velocity, and $y(t)$ is the displacement of the mass from the equilibrium at time t.

(a) We want to determine the equation of motion for a spring system with $m = 10$ kg, $b = 60$ kg/sec, $k = 250$ kg/sec^2, $y(0) = 0.3$ m, and $y'(0) = -0.1$ m/sec. That is, we seek the solution to the initial value problem

$$10y''(t) + 60y'(t) + 250y(t) = 0; \qquad y(0) = 0.3\,, \qquad y'(0) = -0.1\,.$$

The auxiliary equation for the above differential equation is

$$10r^2 + 60r + 250 = 0 \qquad \Rightarrow \qquad r^2 + 6r + 25 = 0,$$

which has the roots

$$r = \frac{-6 \pm \sqrt{36 - 100}}{2} = \frac{-6 \pm 8i}{2} = -3 \pm 4i.$$

Hence $\alpha = -3$ and $\beta = 4$, and the displacement $y(t)$ has the form

$$y(t) = c_1 e^{-3t} \cos 4t + c_2 e^{-3t} \sin 4t.$$

We find c_1 and c_2 by using the initial conditions. We first differentiate $y(t)$ to get

$$y'(t) = (-3c_1 + 4c_2)e^{-3t} \cos 4t + (-4c_1 - 3c_2)e^{-3t} \sin 4t.$$

Substituting y and y' into the initial conditions, we obtain the system

$$y(0) = 0.3 = c_1\,,$$
$$y'(0) = -0.1 = -3c_1 + 4c_2\,.$$

Solving, we find that $c_1 = 0.3$ and $c_2 = 0.2$. Therefore the equation of motion is given by

$$y(t) = 0.3e^{-3t} \cos 4t + 0.2e^{-3t} \sin 4t \text{ (m)}.$$

(b) From Problem 32 we know that the frequency of oscillation is given by $\beta/(2\pi)$. In part (a) we found that $\beta = 4$. Therefore the frequency of oscillation is $4/(2\pi) = 2/\pi$.

(c) We see a decrease in the frequency of oscillation. We also have the introduction of the factor e^{-3t}, which causes the solution to decay to zero. This is a result of energy loss due to the damping.

35. The equation of the motion of a swinging door is similar to that for mass-spring model (with the mass m replaced by the moment of inertia I and the displacement $y(t)$ replaced by the angle θ that the door is open). So, from the discussion following Example 3 we conclude that the door will not continually swing back and forth (that is, the solution $\theta(t)$ will not oscillate) if $b \geq \sqrt{4Ik} = 2\sqrt{Ik}$.

37. (a) The auxiliary equation for this problem is $r^4 + 2r^2 + 1 = (r^2+1)^2 = 0$. This equation has the roots $r_1 = r_2 = -i$, $r_3 = r_4 = i$. Thus, $\cos t$ and $\sin t$ are solutions and, since the roots are repeated, we get two more solutions by multiplying $\cos t$ and $\sin t$ by t, that is, $t\cos t$ and $t\sin t$ are also solutions. This gives a general solution

$$y(t) = c_1 \cos t + c_2 \sin t + c_3 t \cos t + c_4 t \sin t.$$

(b) The auxiliary equation in this problem is

$$r^4 + 4r^3 + 12r^2 + 16r + 16 = (r^2 + 2r + 4)^2 = 0.$$

The roots of the quadratic equation $r^2 + 2r + 4 = 0$ are

$$r = \frac{-2 \pm \sqrt{4-16}}{2} = -1 \pm \sqrt{3}i.$$

Hence the roots of the auxiliary equation are $r_1 = r_2 = -1-\sqrt{3}i$ and $r_3 = r_4 = -1+\sqrt{3}i$. Thus two linearly independent solutions are $e^{-t}\cos(\sqrt{3}t)$ and $e^{-t}\sin(\sqrt{3}t)$, and we get two more linearly independent by multiplying them by t. This gives a general solution of the form

$$y(t) = (c_1 + c_2 t)e^{-t}\cos(\sqrt{3}t) + (c_3 + c_4 t)e^{-t}\sin(\sqrt{3}t).$$

39. (a) Comparing given equation with the Cauchy-Euler equation (21) in general form, we conclude that $a = 3$, $b = 11$, and $c = -3$. Thus, the substitution $x = e^t$ leads to the equation (22) in Problem 38 with these values of parameters. That is,

$$a\frac{d^2y}{dt^2} + (b-a)\frac{dy}{dt} + cy = 0 \qquad \Rightarrow \qquad 3\frac{d^2y}{dt^2} + 8\frac{dy}{dt} - 3y = 0.$$

(b) The auxiliary equation to the differential equation obtained in (a) is $3r^2 + 8r - 3 = 0$, which has the roots

$$r = \frac{-8 \pm \sqrt{64 - 4(3)(-3)}}{6} = \frac{-8 \pm 10}{6} \qquad \Rightarrow \qquad r = -3, \frac{1}{3}.$$

This yields a general solution $y(t) = c_1 e^{t/3} + c_2 e^{-3t}$.

(c) Since $x = e^t$, we can express $y(t)$ as a function of x by writing

$$y = c_1 e^{t/3} + c_2 e^{-3t} = c_1 \left(e^t\right)^{1/3} + c_2 \left(e^t\right)^{-3} = c_1 x^{1/3} + c_2 x^{-3}.$$

41. This equation is a Cauchy-Euler equation. The substitution $x = e^t$ leads to the equation (22) with $a = 1$, $b = 2$, and $c = -6$. Thus we have

$$a\frac{d^2y}{dt^2} + (b - a)\frac{dy}{dt} + cy = 0 \qquad \Rightarrow \qquad \frac{d^2y}{dt^2} + \frac{dy}{dt} - 6y = 0.$$

The auxiliary equation, $r^2 + r - 6 = 0$, has the roots $r = -3$ and $r = 2$. Therefore, a general solution can be written as

$$y = c_1 e^{-3t} + c_2 e^{2t} = c_1 \left(e^t\right)^{-3} + c_2 \left(e^t\right)^2 = c_1 x^{-3} + c_2 x^2.$$

43. The substitution $x = e^t$ yields the equation

$$\frac{d^2y}{dt^2} + (9 - 1)\frac{dy}{dt} + 17y = 0 \qquad \Rightarrow \qquad \frac{d^2y}{dt^2} + 8\frac{dy}{dt} + 17y = 0.$$

Solving the characteristic equation, $r^2 + 8r + 17 = 0$, we get

$$r = \frac{-8 \pm \sqrt{64 - 68}}{2} = -4 \pm i.$$

Thus, the roots are complex with $\alpha = -4$, $\beta = 1$, and a general solution, as a function of t, is given by $y(t) = c_1 e^{-4t} \cos t + c_2 e^{-4t} \sin t$. Now we make the back substitution. Since $x = e^t$, we have $t = \ln x$ and so

$$y = \left(e^t\right)^{-4} (c_1 \cos t + c_2 \sin t) = x^{-4} \left[c_1 \cos(\ln x) + c_2 \sin(\ln x)\right].$$

EXERCISES 4.4: Nonhomogeneous Equations: The Method of Undetermined Coefficients, page 186

1. We cannot use the method of undetermined coefficients to find a particular solution because of the t^{-1} term, which is not a polynomial.

3. Rewriting the right-hand side in the form $3^t = e^{(\ln 3)t} = e^{rt}$, where $r = \ln 3$, we conclude that the method of undetermined coefficients can be applied.

5. Since $\sec\theta = 1/\cos\theta$, we cannot use the method of undetermined coefficients.

7. Given equation is not an equation with constant coefficients. Thus the method of undetermined coefficients cannot be applied.

9. The roots of the auxiliary equation, $r^2 + 3 = 0$, are $r = \pm\sqrt{3}i$. Since they are different from zero, we look for a particular solution of the form $y_p(t) \equiv A$. Substitution into the original equation yields

$$(A)'' + 3A = -9 \qquad \Rightarrow \qquad 3A = -9 \qquad \Rightarrow \qquad A = -3.$$

Thus, $y_p(t) \equiv -3$ is a particular solution to the given nonhomogeneous equation.

11. The auxiliary equation in this problem, $2r^2 + 1 = 0$, has complex roots. Therefore, e^{2t} is not a solution to the corresponding homogeneous equation, and a particular solution to the original nonhomogeneous equation has the form $z_p(t) = Ae^{2t}$. Substituting this expression into the equation, we find the constant A.

$$2\left(Ae^{2t}\right)'' + Ae^{2t} = 2\left(4Ae^{2t}\right) + Ae^{2t} = 9Ae^{2t} = 9e^{2t} \qquad \Rightarrow \qquad A = 1.$$

Hence, $z_p(t) = e^{2t}$.

12. This equation is a linear first order differential equation with constant coefficients. The corresponding homogeneous equation, $2x' + x = 0$, can be solved by the methods of Chapter 2. Alternatively, one can use the result of Problem 21 in Section 4.2. Either approach yields

$x_h(t) = Ce^{-t/2}$. So, the homogeneous equation does not have a polynomial solution (other than $x(t) \equiv 0$), and we look for a particular solution to the nonhomogeneous equation of the form $x_p(t) = A_2t^2 + A_1t + A_0$. Substitution into the original differential equation yields

$$2x_p'(t) + x_p(t) = 2\,(2A_2t + A_1) + A_2t^2 + A_1t + A_0 = A_2t^2 + (4A_2 + A_1)\,t + (2A_1 + A_0) = 3t^2.$$

By equating coefficients we obtain

$$\begin{aligned} A_2 &= 3, & & \\ 4A_2 + A_1 &= 0 \quad & \Rightarrow \quad & A_1 = -12, \\ 2A_1 + A_0 &= 0 \quad & \Rightarrow \quad & A_0 = 24. \end{aligned}$$

Therefore, a particular solution is $x_p(t) = 3t^2 - 12t + 24$.

13. The right-hand side of the original nonhomogeneous equation suggest us the form

$$y_p(t) = t^s(A\cos 3t + B\sin 3t)$$

for a particular solution. Since the roots of the auxiliary equation, $r^2 - r + 9 = 0$, are different from $3i$, neither $\cos 3t$ nor $\sin 3t$ is a solution to the corresponding homogeneous equation. Therefore, we can choose $s = 0$, and so

$$\begin{aligned} y_p(t) &= A\cos 3t + B\sin 3t, \\ y_p'(t) &= -3A\sin 3t + 3B\cos 3t, \\ y_p''(t) &= -9A\cos 3t - 9B\sin 3t. \end{aligned}$$

Substituting these expressions into the original equation and equating the corresponding coefficients, we conclude that

$$\begin{aligned} &(-9A\cos 3t - 9B\sin 3t) - (-3A\sin 3t + 3B\cos 3t) + 9\,(A\cos 3t + B\sin 3t) = 3\sin 3t \\ &\Rightarrow \qquad -3B\cos 3t + 3A\sin 3t = 3\sin 3t \qquad \Rightarrow \qquad A = 1,\ B = 0. \end{aligned}$$

Hence, the answer is $y_p(t) = \cos 3t$.

15. For this problem, the corresponding homogeneous equation is $y'' - 5y' + 6y = 0$, which has the associated auxiliary equation $r^2 - 5r + 6 = 0$. The roots of this equation are $r = 3$ and $r = 2$. Therefore, neither $y = e^x$ nor $y = xe^x$ satisfies the homogeneous equation, and in the expression $y_p(x) = x^s(Ax + B)e^x$ for a particular solution we can take $s = 0$. So

$$\begin{aligned}
& y_p(x) = (Ax + B)e^x \\
\Rightarrow \quad & y_p'(x) = (Ax + B + A)e^x \\
\Rightarrow \quad & y_p''(x) = (Ax + B + 2A)e^x \\
\Rightarrow \quad & (Ax + B + 2A)e^x - 5(Ax + B + A)e^x + 6(Ax + B)e^x = xe^x \\
\Rightarrow \quad & (2Ax - 3A + 2B)e^x = xe^x \quad \Rightarrow \quad \begin{array}{r} 2A = 1, \\ -3A + 2B = 0 \end{array} \quad \Rightarrow \quad \begin{array}{r} A = 1/2, \\ B = 3/4\,, \end{array}
\end{aligned}$$

and $y_p(x) = (x/2 + 3/4)e^x$.

16. The corresponding homogeneous equation has the auxiliary equation $r^2 - 1 = 0$, whose roots are $r = \pm 1$. Thus, in the expression $\theta_p(t) = (A_1 t + A_0)\cos t + (B_1 t + B_0)\sin t$ none of the terms is a solution to the homogeneous equation. We find

$$\begin{aligned}
& \theta_p(t) = (A_1 t + A_0)\cos t + (B_1 t + B_0)\sin t \\
\Rightarrow \quad & \theta_p'(t) = A_1 \cos t - (A_1 t + A_0)\sin t + B_1 \sin t + (B_1 t + B_0)\cos t \\
& \qquad = (B_1 t + A_1 + B_0)\cos t + (-A_1 t - A_0 + B_1)\sin t \\
\Rightarrow \quad & \theta_p''(t) = B_1 \cos t - (B_1 t + B_0 + A_1)\sin t - A_1 \sin t + (-A_1 t - A_0 + B_1)\cos t \\
& \qquad = (-A_1 t - A_0 + B_1)\cos t + (-B_1 t - B_0 - 2A_1)\sin t.
\end{aligned}$$

Substituting these expressions into the original differential equation, we get

$$\begin{aligned}
\theta_p'' - \theta_p &= (-A_1 t - A_0 + 2B_1)\cos t + (-B_1 t - B_0 - 2A_1)\sin t \\
&\qquad - (A_1 t + A_0)\cos t - (B_1 t + B_0)\sin t \\
&= -2A_1 t\cos t + (-2A_0 + 2B_1)\cos t - 2B_1 t\sin t + (-2A_1 - 2B_0)\sin t \\
&= t\sin t.
\end{aligned}$$

Equating the coefficients, we see that

$$\begin{aligned} -2A_1 &= 0 && \Rightarrow && A_1 = 0, \\ -2A_0 + 2B_1 &= 0 && \Rightarrow && B_1 = A_0\,, \\ -2B_1 &= 1 && \Rightarrow && B_1 = -\frac{1}{2} \qquad \text{and so} \quad A_0 = -\frac{1}{2}\,, \\ -2A_1 - 2B_0 &= 0 && \Rightarrow && B_0 = 0. \end{aligned}$$

Therefore, a particular solution of the nonhomogeneous equation $\theta'' - \theta = t\sin t$ is given by

$$\theta_p(t) = -\frac{t\sin t + \cos t}{2}.$$

17. The right-hand side of the original equation suggests that a particular solution should be of the form $y_p(t) = At^s e^t$. Since $r = 1$ is a double root of the corresponding auxiliary equation, $r^2 - 2r + 1 = (r-1)^2 = 0$, we take $s = 2$. Hence

$$y_p(t) = At^2e^t \quad \Rightarrow \quad y_p'(t) = A\left(t^2 + 2t\right)e^t \quad \Rightarrow \quad y_p''(t) = A\left(t^2 + 4t + 2\right)e^t\,.$$

Substituting these expressions into the original equation, we find the constant A.

$$A\left(t^2 + 4t + 2\right)e^t - 2A\left(t^2 + 2t\right)e^t + At^2e^t = 8e^t \quad \Rightarrow \quad 2Ae^t = 8e^t \quad \Rightarrow \quad A = 4.$$

Thus, $y_p(t) = 4t^2e^t$.

19. According to the right-hand side of the given equation, a particular solution has the form $y_p(t) = t^s(A_1t + A_0)e^{-3t}$. To choose s, we solve the auxiliary equation, $4r^2 + 11r - 3 = 0$, and find that $r = -3$ is its simple root. Therefore, we take $s = 1$, and so

$$y_p(t) = t\left(A_1t + A_0\right)e^{-3t} = \left(A_1t^2 + A_0t\right)e^{-3t}\,.$$

Differentiating yields

$$\begin{aligned} y_p'(t) &= \left[-3A_1t^2 + (2A_1 - 3A_0)\,t + A_0\right]e^{-3t}, \\ y_p''(t) &= \left[9A_1t^2 + (9A_0 - 12A_1)\,t + 2A_1 - 6A_0\right]e^{-3t}. \end{aligned}$$

Substituting y, y', and y'' into the original equation, after some algebra we get

$$[-26A_1 t + (8A_1 - 13A_0)]e^{-3t} = -2te^{-3t} \quad \Rightarrow \quad \begin{aligned} -26A_1 &= -2, \\ 8A_1 - 13A_0 &= 0 \end{aligned} \quad \Rightarrow \quad \begin{aligned} A_1 &= 1/13, \\ A_0 &= 8/169. \end{aligned}$$

Therefore,

$$y_p(t) = \left(\frac{t}{13} + \frac{8}{169}\right) te^{-3t}.$$

21. The nonhomogeneous term of the original equation is te^{2t}. Therefore, a particular solution has the form $x_p(t) = t^s (A_1 t + A_0) e^{2t}$. The corresponding homogeneous differential equation has the auxiliary equation $r^2 - 4r + 4 = (r-2)^2 = 0$. Since $r = 2$ is its double root, s is chosen to be 2. Thus a particular solution to the nonhomogeneous equation has the form

$$x_p(t) = t^2 (A_1 t + A_0) e^{2t} = \left(A_1 t^3 + A_0 t^2\right) e^{2t}.$$

We compute

$$\begin{aligned} x_p' &= \left(3A_1 t^2 + 2A_0 t\right) e^{2t} + 2\left(A_1 t^3 + A_0 t^2\right) e^{2t}, \\ x_p'' &= (6A_1 t + 2A_0) e^{2t} + 4\left(3A_1 t^2 + 2A_0 t\right) e^{2t} + 4\left(A_1 t^3 + A_0 t^2\right) e^{2t}. \end{aligned}$$

Substituting these expressions into the original differential equation yields

$$\begin{aligned} x_p'' - 4x_p' + 4x_p &= (6A_1 t + 2A_0) e^{2t} + 4\left(3A_1 t^2 + 2A_0 t\right) e^{2t} + 4\left(A_1 t^3 + A_0 t^2\right) e^{2t} \\ &\quad -4\left(3A_1 t^2 + 2A_0 t\right) e^{2t} - 8\left(A_1 t^3 + A_0 t^2\right) e^{2t} + 4\left(A_1 t^3 + A_0 t^2\right) e^{2t} \\ &= (6A_1 t + 2A_0) e^{2t} = te^{2t}. \end{aligned}$$

Equating coefficients yields $A_0 = 0$ and $A_1 = 1/6$. Therefore $x_p(t) = t^3 e^{2t}/6$ is a particular solution to the given nonhomogeneous equation.

23. The right-hand side of this equation suggests that $y_p(\theta) = \theta^s(A_2\theta^2 + A_1\theta + A_0)$. We choose $s = 1$ because $r = 0$ is a simple root of the auxiliary equation, $r^2 - 7r = 0$. Therefore,

$$\begin{aligned} & y_p(\theta) = \theta(A_2\theta^2 + A_1\theta + A_0) = A_2\theta^3 + A_1\theta^2 + A_0\theta \\ \Rightarrow \quad & y_p'(\theta) = 3A_2\theta^2 + 2A_1\theta + A_0 \quad \Rightarrow \quad y_p''(\theta) = 6A_2\theta + 2A_1. \end{aligned}$$

So,

$$y_p''-7y_p' = (6A_2\theta + 2A_1)-7\left(3A_2\theta^2 + 2A_1\theta + A_0\right) = -21A_2\theta^2+(6A_2-14A_1)\theta+2A_1-7A_0 = \theta^2.$$

Comparing the corresponding coefficients, we find A_2, A_1, and A_0.

$$\begin{aligned} -21A_2 &= 1, & & A_2 = -1/21,\\ 6A_2 - 14A_1 &= 0, & \Rightarrow\quad & A_1 = 3A_2/7 = -1/49,\\ 2A_1 - 7A_0 &= 0 & & A_0 = 2A_1/7 = -2/343. \end{aligned}$$

Hence

$$y_p(\theta) = -\frac{1}{21}\,\theta^3 - \frac{1}{49}\,\theta^2 - \frac{2}{343}\,\theta.$$

25. We look for a particular solution of the form $y_p(t) = t^s(A\cos 3t + B\sin 3t)e^{2t}$. Since $r = 2+3i$ is not a root of the auxiliary equation, which is $r^2 + 2r + 4 = 0$, we can take $s = 0$. Thus,

$$\begin{aligned} & y_p(t) = (A\cos 3t + B\sin 3t)e^{2t}\\ \Rightarrow\quad & y_p'(t) = [(2A + 3B)\cos 3t + (-3A + 2B)\sin 3t)]e^{2t}\\ \Rightarrow\quad & y_p''(t) = [(-5A + 12B)\cos 3t + (-12A - 5B)\sin 3t)]e^{2t}\,. \end{aligned}$$

Next, we substitute y_p, y_p', and y_p'' into the original equation and compare the corresponding coefficients.

$$y_p'' + 2y_p' + 4y_p = [(3A + 18B)\cos 3t + (-18A + 3B)\sin 3t]e^{2t} = 111e^{2t}\cos 3t$$

$$\Rightarrow\quad \begin{aligned} 3A + 18B &= 111,\\ -18A + 3B &= 0. \end{aligned}$$

This system has the solution $A = 1$, $B = 6$. So,

$$y_p(t) = (\cos 3t + 6\sin 3t)e^{2t}\,.$$

27. The right-hand side of this equation suggests that

$$y_p(t) = t^s\left(A_3t^3 + A_2t^2 + A_1t + A_0\right)\cos 3t + t^s\left(B_3t^3 + B_2t^2 + B_1t + B_0\right)\sin 3t.$$

To choose s, we find the roots of the characteristic equation, which is $r^2 + 9 = 0$. Since $r = \pm 3i$ are its simple roots, we take $s = 1$. Thus

$$y_p(t) = t\left(A_3t^3 + A_2t^2 + A_1t + A_0\right)\cos 3t + t\left(B_3t^3 + B_2t^2 + B_1t + B_0\right)\sin 3t.$$

29. The characteristic equation $r^2 - 6r + 9 = (r-3)^2 = 0$ has a double root $r = 3$. Therefore, a particular solution is of the form

$$y_p(t) = t^2\left(A_6t^6 + A_5t^5 + A_4t^4 + A_3t^3 + A_2t^2 + A_1t + A_0\right)e^{3t}.$$

31. From the form of the right-hand side, we conclude that a particular solution should be of the form

$$y_p(t) = t^s\left[\left(A_3t^3 + A_2t^2 + A_1t + A_0\right)\cos t + \left(B_3t^3 + B_2t^2 + B_1t + B_0\right)\sin t\right]e^{-t}.$$

Since $r = -1 \pm i$ are simple roots of the characteristic equation, $r^2 + 2r + 2 = 0$, we should take $s = 1$. Therefore,

$$y_p(t) = t\left[\left(A_3t^3 + A_2t^2 + A_1t + A_0\right)\cos t + \left(B_3t^3 + B_2t^2 + B_1t + B_0\right)\sin t\right]e^{-t}.$$

33. The right-hand side of the equation suggests that $y_p(t) = t^s(A\cos t + B\sin t)$. By inspection, we see that $r = i$ is not a root of the corresponding auxiliary equation, $r^3 - r^2 + 1 = 0$. Thus, with $s = 0$,

$$\begin{aligned} y_p(t) &= A\cos t + B\sin t, \\ y_p'(t) &= -A\sin t + B\cos t, \\ y_p''(t) &= -A\cos t - B\sin t, \\ y_p'''(t) &= A\sin t - B\cos t, \end{aligned}$$

and substitution into the original equation yields

$$\begin{aligned} &(A\sin t - B\cos t) - (-A\cos t - B\sin t) + (A\cos t + B\sin t) = \sin t \\ \Rightarrow\quad & (2A - B)\cos t + (A + 2B)\sin t = \sin t \\ \Rightarrow\quad & \begin{array}{l} 2A - B = 0, \\ A + 2B = 1 \end{array} \quad\Rightarrow\quad \begin{array}{l} A = 1/5, \\ B = 2/5 \end{array} \quad\Rightarrow\quad y_p(t) = \frac{1}{5}\cos t + \frac{2}{5}\sin t. \end{aligned}$$

35. We look for a particular solution of the form $y_p(t) = t^s(A_1t + A_0)e^t$, and choose $s = 1$ because the auxiliary equation, $r^3 + r^2 - 2 = (r-1)(r^2 + 2r + 2) = 0$ has $r = 1$ as a simple root. Hence,

$$\begin{aligned} y_p(t) = t(A_1t + A_0)e^t &= (A_1t^2 + A_0t)e^t \\ \Rightarrow \qquad y_p'(t) &= \left[A_1t^2 + (2A_1 + A_0)t + A_0\right] e^t \\ \Rightarrow \qquad y_p''(t) &= \left[A_1t^2 + (4A_1 + A_0)t + (2A_1 + 2A_0)\right] e^t \\ \Rightarrow \qquad y_p'''(t) &= \left[A_1t^2 + (6A_1 + A_0)t + (6A_1 + 3A_0)\right] e^t \\ \Rightarrow \qquad y''' + y'' - 2y &= \left[10A_1t + (8A_1 + 5A_0)\right] e^t = te^t\,. \end{aligned}$$

Equating the corresponding coefficients, we find that

$$\begin{array}{l} 10A_1 = 1, \\ 8A_1 + 5A_0 = 0 \end{array} \quad \Rightarrow \quad \begin{array}{l} A_1 = 1/10, \\ A_0 = -8A_1/5 = -4/25 \end{array} \quad \Rightarrow \quad y_p(t) = \left(\frac{1}{10}\,t^2 - \frac{4}{25}\,t\right)e^t.$$

EXERCISES 4.5: The Superposition Principle and Undetermined Coefficients Revisited, page 192

1. Let $g_1(t) := \sin t$ and $g_2(t) := e^{2t}$. Then $y_1(t) = \cos t$ is a solution to

$$y'' - y' + y = g_1(t)$$

and $y_2(t) = e^{2t}/3$ is a solution to

$$y'' - y' + y = g_2(t).$$

(a) The right-hand side of the given equation is $5\sin t = 5g_1(t)$. Therefore, the function $y(t) = 5y_1(t) = 5\cos t$ is a solution to $y'' - y' + y = 5\sin t$.

(b) We can express $\sin t - 3e^{2t} = g_1(t) - 3g_2(t)$. So, by the superposition principle the desired solution is $y(t) = y_1(t) - 3y_2(t) = \cos t - e^{2t}$.

(c) Since $4\sin t + 18e^{2t} = 4g_1(t) + 18g_2(t)$, the function

$$y(t) = 4y_1(t) + 18y_2(t) = 4\cos t + 6e^{2t}$$

is a solution to the given equation.

3. The corresponding homogeneous equation, $y'' - y = 0$, has the associated auxiliary equation $r^2 - 1 = (r-1)(r+1) = 0$. This gives $r = \pm 1$ as the roots of this equation, and a general solution to the homogeneous equation is $y_h(t) = c_1 e^t + c_2 e^{-t}$. Combining this solution with the particular solution, $y_p(t) = -t$, we find that a general solution is given by

$$y(t) = y_p(t) + y_h(t) = -t + c_1 e^t + c_2 e^{-t}.$$

5. The corresponding auxiliary equation, $r^2 - r - 2 = 0$, has the roots $r = -1,\ 2$. Hence, a general solution to the corresponding homogeneous equation is $\theta_h(t) = c_1 e^{2t} + c_2 e^{-t}$. By the superposition principle, a general solution to the original nonhomogeneous equation is

$$\theta(t) = \theta_p(t) + \theta_h(t) = t - 1 + c_1 e^{2t} + c_2 e^{-t}.$$

7. First, we rewrite the equation in standard form, that is,

$$y'' - 2y' + y = 2e^x.$$

The corresponding homogeneous equation, $y'' - 2y' + y = 0$, has the associated auxiliary equation $r^2 - 2r + 1 = (r-1)^2 = 0$. Thus $r = 1$ is its double root, and a general solution to the homogeneous equation is $y_h(x) = c_1 x e^x + c_2 e^x$. Combining this with the particular solution, $y_p(x) = x^2 e^x$, we find that a general solution is given by

$$y(x) = y_p(x) + y_h(x) = x^2 e^x + c_1 x e^x + c_2 e^x.$$

9. We can write the nonhomogeneous term as a difference

$$t^2 + 4t - t^2 e^t \sin t = (t^2 + 4t) - (t^2 e^t \sin t) = g_1(t) - g_2(t).$$

Both, $g_1(t)$ and $g_2(t)$, have a form suitable for the method of undetermined coefficients. Therefore, we can apply this method to find particular solutions $y_{p,1}(t)$ and $y_{p,2}(t)$ to

$$3y'' + 2y' + 8y = g_1(t) \qquad \text{and} \qquad 3y'' + 2y' + 8y = g_2(t),$$

respectively. Then, by the superposition principle, $y_p(t) = y_{p,1}(t) - y_{p,2}(t)$ is a particular solution to the given equation.

11. The answer is "no", because the method of undetermined coefficients cannot be applied to

$$y'' - 6y' - 4y = \frac{1}{t}.$$

13. In the original form, the function $\sin^2 t$ does not fit any of the cases in the method of undetermined coefficients. But it can be written as $\sin^2 t = (1 - \cos 2t)/2$, and so

$$2t + \sin^2 t + 3 = 2t + \frac{1 - \cos 2t}{2} + 3 = \left(2t + \frac{7}{2}\right) - \left(\frac{1}{2}\cos 2t\right).$$

Now, the method of undetermined coefficients can be applied to each term in the above difference to find a particular solution to the corresponding nonhomogeneous equation, and the difference of these particular solutions, by the superposition principle, is a particular solution to the original equation. Thus, the answer is "yes".

15. "No", because the given equation is not an equation with constant coefficients.

17. The auxiliary equation in this problem is $r^2 - 1 = 0$ with roots $r = \pm 1$. Hence,

$$y_h(t) = c_1 e^t + c_2 e^{-t}$$

is a general solution to the corresponding homogeneous equation. Next, we find a particular solution $y_p(t)$ to the original nonhomogeneous equation. The method of undetermined coefficients yields

$$y_p(t) = At + B \quad \Rightarrow \quad y_p'(t) \equiv A \quad \Rightarrow \quad y_p''(t) \equiv 0;$$
$$y_p'' - y_p = 0 - (At + B) = -At - B = -11t + 1 \quad \Rightarrow \quad A = 11, \ B = -1$$
$$\Rightarrow \quad y_p(t) = 11t - 1.$$

By the superposition principle, a general solution is given by

$$y(t) = y_p(t) + y_h(t) = 11t - 1 + c_1 e^t + c_2 e^{-t}.$$

19. Solving the auxiliary equation, $r^2 - 3r + 2 = 0$, we find that $r = 1, 2$. Therefore, a general solution to the homogeneous equation, $y'' - 3y' + 2y = 0$, is

$$y_h(x) = c_1 e^x + c_2 e^{2x}.$$

By the method of undetermined coefficients, a particular solution $y_p(x)$ to the original equation has the form $y_p(x) = x^s(A\cos x + B\sin x)e^x$. We choose $s = 0$ because $r = 1 + i$ is not a root of the auxiliary equation. So,

$$\begin{aligned} y_p(x) &= (A\cos x + B\sin x)e^x \\ \Rightarrow \qquad y_p'(x) &= [(A+B)\cos x + (B-A)\sin x]e^x \\ \Rightarrow \qquad y_p''(x) &= (2B\cos x - 2A\sin x)e^x . \end{aligned}$$

Substituting these expressions into the equation, we compare the corresponding coefficients and find A and B.

$$\{(2B\cos x - 2A\sin x) - 3[(A+B)\cos x + (B-A)\sin x] + 2(A\cos x + B\sin x)\}\, e^x = e^x \sin x$$

$$\Rightarrow \quad -(A+B)\cos x + (A-B)\sin x = \sin x \quad \Rightarrow \quad \begin{aligned} A+B &= 0, \\ A-B &= 1 \end{aligned} \quad \Rightarrow \quad \begin{aligned} A &= 1/2, \\ B &= -1/2. \end{aligned}$$

Therefore,

$$y_p(x) = \frac{(\cos x - \sin x)e^x}{2}$$

and

$$y(x) = \frac{(\cos x - \sin x)e^x}{2} + c_1 e^x + c_2 e^{2x}$$

is a general solution to the given nonhomogeneous equation.

21. Since the roots of the auxiliary equation, which is $r^2 + 2r + 2 = 0$, are $r = -1 \pm i$, we have a general solution to the corresponding homogeneous equation

$$y_h(\theta) = c_1 e^{-\theta}\cos\theta + c_2 e^{-\theta}\sin\theta = (c_1\cos\theta + c_2\sin\theta)\, e^{-\theta} ,$$

and look for a particular solution of the form

$$y_p(\theta) = \theta^s(A\cos\theta + B\sin\theta)e^{-\theta} \qquad \text{with} \qquad s = 1.$$

Differentiating $y_p(\theta)$, we get

$$y_p'(\theta) \;=\; (A\cos\theta + B\sin\theta)e^{-\theta} + \theta\left[(A\cos\theta + B\sin\theta)e^{-\theta}\right]' ,$$

$$\begin{aligned} y_p''(\theta) &= 2\left[(A\cos\theta + B\sin\theta)e^{-\theta}\right]' + \theta\left[(A\cos\theta + B\sin\theta)e^{-\theta}\right]'' \\ &= 2\left[(B-A)\cos\theta - (B+A)\sin\theta\right]e^{-\theta} + \theta\left[(A\cos\theta + B\sin\theta)e^{-\theta}\right]''. \end{aligned}$$

(Note that we did not evaluate the terms containing the factor θ because they give zero result when substituted into the original equation.) Therefore,

$$\begin{aligned} y_p'' + 2y_p' + 2y_p &= 2\left[(B-A)\cos\theta - (B+A)\sin\theta\right]e^{-\theta} + 2(A\cos\theta + B\sin\theta)e^{-\theta} \\ &= 2\left(B\cos\theta - A\sin\theta\right)e^{-\theta} = e^{-\theta}\cos\theta\,. \end{aligned}$$

Hence $A = 0$, $B = 1/2$, $y_p(\theta) = (1/2)\theta e^{-\theta}\sin\theta$, and a general solution is given by

$$y(\theta) = \frac{1}{2}\theta e^{-\theta}\sin\theta + (c_1\cos\theta + c_2\sin\theta)\,e^{-\theta}\,.$$

23. The corresponding homogeneous equation, $y' - y = 0$, is separable. Solving yields

$$\frac{dy}{dt} = y \quad \Rightarrow \quad \frac{dy}{y} = dt \quad \Rightarrow \quad \ln|y| = t + c \quad \Rightarrow \quad y = \pm e^c e^t = Ce^t,$$

where $C \neq 0$ is an arbitrary constant. By inspection, $y \equiv 0$ is also a solution. Therefore, $y_h(t) = Ce^t$, where C is an arbitrary constant, is a general solution to the homogeneous equation. (Alternatively, one can apply the method of solving first order linear equations in Section 2.3 or the method discussed in Problem 21, Section 4.2.) A particular solution has the form $y_p(t) = A$. Substitution into the original equation yields

$$(A)' - A = 1 \quad \Rightarrow \quad A = -1.$$

Thus $y(t) = Ce^t - 1$ is a general solution. To satisfy the initial condition, $y(0) = 0$, we find

$$0 = y(0) = Ce^0 - 1 = C - 1 \quad \Rightarrow \quad C = 1.$$

So, the answer is $y(t) = e^t - 1$.

25. The auxiliary equation, $r^2 + 1 = 0$, has roots $r = \pm i$. Therefore, a general solution to the corresponding homogeneous equation is $z_h(x) = c_1\cos x + c_2\sin x$, and a particular solution to the original equation has the form $z_p(x) = Ae^{-x}$. Substituting this function into the given equation, we find the constant A.

$$z'' + z = \left(Ae^{-x}\right)'' + Ae^{-x} = 2Ae^{-x} = 2e^{-x} \qquad \Rightarrow \qquad A = 1,$$

and a general solution to the given nonhomogeneous equation is

$$z(x) = e^{-x} + c_1 \cos x + c_2 \sin x\,.$$

Next, since $z'(x) = -e^{-x} - c_1 \sin x + c_2 \cos x$, from the initial conditions we get a system for determining constants c_1 and c_2.

$$\begin{array}{c} 0 = z(0) = 1 + c_1\,, \\ 0 = z'(0) = -1 + c_2 \end{array} \qquad \Rightarrow \qquad \begin{array}{c} c_1 = -1, \\ c_2 = 1. \end{array}$$

Hence, $z = (x) = e^{-x} - \cos x + \sin x$ is the solution to the given initial value problem.

27. The roots of the auxiliary equation, $r^2 - r - 2 = 0$, are $r = -1$ and $r = 2$. This gives a general solution to the corresponding homogeneous equation of the form $y_h(x) = c_1e^{-x} + c_2e^{2x}$. We use the superposition principle to find a particular solution to the nonhomogeneous equation.

(i) For the equation

$$y'' - y' - 2y = \cos x,$$

a particular solution has the form $y_{p,1}(x) = A\cos x + B\sin x$. Substitution into the above equation yields

$$\begin{aligned} &(-A\cos x - B\sin x) - (-A\sin x + B\cos x) - 2(A\cos x + B\sin x) \\ &\qquad = (-3A - B)\cos x + (A - 3B)\sin x = \cos x \end{aligned}$$

$$\Rightarrow \qquad \begin{array}{c} -3A - B = 1, \\ A - 3B = 0 \end{array} \qquad \Rightarrow \qquad \begin{array}{c} A = -3/10, \\ B = -1/10. \end{array}$$

So, $y_{p,1}(x) = -(3/10)\cos x - (1/10)\sin x$.

(ii) For the equation

$$y'' - y' - 2y = \sin 2x,$$

a particular solution has the form $y_{p,2}(x) = A\cos 2x + B\sin 2x$. Substitution yields

$$(-4A\cos 2x - 4B\sin 2x) - (-2A\sin 2x + 2B\cos 2x) - 2(A\cos 2x + B\sin 2x)$$
$$= (-6A - 2B)\cos 2x + (2A - 6B)\sin 2x = \sin 2x$$

$$\Rightarrow \quad \begin{array}{l} -6A - 2B = 0, \\ 2A - 6B = 1 \end{array} \quad \Rightarrow \quad \begin{array}{l} A = 1/20, \\ B = -3/20. \end{array}$$

So,

$$y_{p,2}(x) = \frac{1}{20}\cos 2x - \frac{3}{20}\sin 2x.$$

Therefore, a general solution to the original equation is

$$\begin{aligned} y(x) &= y_{p,1}(x) - y_{p,2}(x) + y_h(x) \\ &= -\frac{3}{10}\cos x - \frac{1}{10}\sin x - \frac{1}{20}\cos 2x + \frac{3}{20}\sin 2x + c_1e^{-x} + c_2e^{2x}. \end{aligned}$$

Next, we find c_1 and c_2 such that the initial conditions are satisfied.

$$\begin{array}{l} -7/20 = y(0) = -3/10 - 1/20 + c_1 + c_2\,, \\ 1/5 = y'(0) = -1/10 + 2(3/20) - c_1 + 2c_2 \end{array} \quad \Rightarrow \quad \begin{array}{l} c_1 + c_2 = 0, \\ -c_1 + 2c_2 = 0 \end{array} \quad \Rightarrow \quad \begin{array}{l} c_1 = 0, \\ c_2 = 0. \end{array}$$

With these constants, the solution becomes

$$y(x) = -\frac{3}{10}\cos x - \frac{1}{10}\sin x - \frac{1}{20}\cos 2x + \frac{3}{20}\sin 2x\,.$$

29. The roots of the auxiliary equation, $r^2 - 1 = 0$, are $r = \pm 1$. Therefore, a general solution to the corresponding homogeneous equation is

$$y_h(\theta) = c_1e^{\theta} + c_2e^{-\theta}.$$

(i) For the equation

$$y'' - y = \sin\theta,$$

a particular solution has the form $y_{p,1}(x) = A\cos\theta + B\sin\theta$. Substitution into the equation yields

$$(-A\cos\theta - B\sin\theta) - (A\cos\theta + B\sin\theta) = -2A\cos\theta - 2B\sin\theta = \sin\theta$$

$$\Rightarrow \quad \begin{aligned} -2A &= 0, \\ -2B &= 1 \end{aligned} \quad \Rightarrow \quad \begin{aligned} A &= 0, \\ B &= -1/2. \end{aligned}$$

So, $y_{p,1}(\theta) = -(1/2)\sin\theta$.

(ii) For the equation

$$y'' - y = e^{2\theta},$$

a particular solution has the form $y_{p,2}(\theta) = Ae^{2\theta}$. Substitution yields

$$\left(Ae^{2\theta}\right)'' - \left(Ae^{2\theta}\right) = 3Ae^{2\theta} = e^{2\theta} \quad \Rightarrow \quad A = 1/3,$$

and $y_{p,2}(\theta) = (1/3)e^{2\theta}$.

By the superposition principle, a particular solution to the original nonhomogeneous equation is given by

$$y_p(\theta) = y_{p,1}(\theta) - y_{p,2}(\theta) = -(1/2)\sin\theta - (1/3)e^{2\theta},$$

and a general solution is

$$y(\theta) = y_p(\theta) + y_h(\theta) = -(1/2)\sin\theta - (1/3)e^{2\theta} + c_1e^{\theta} + c_2e^{-\theta}.$$

Next, we satisfy the initial conditions.

$$\begin{aligned} 1 &= y(0) = -1/3 + c_1 + c_2, \\ -1 &= y'(0) = -1/2 - 2/3 + c_1 - c_2 \end{aligned} \quad \Rightarrow \quad \begin{aligned} c_1 + c_2 &= 4/3, \\ c_1 - c_2 &= 1/6 \end{aligned} \quad \Rightarrow \quad \begin{aligned} c_1 &= 3/4, \\ c_2 &= 7/12. \end{aligned}$$

Therefore, the solution to the given initial value problem is

$$y(\theta) = -\frac{1}{2}\sin\theta - \frac{1}{3}e^{2\theta} + \frac{3}{4}e^{\theta} + \frac{7}{12}e^{-\theta}.$$

31. For the nonhomogeneous term $\sin t + t\cos t$, a particular solution has the form

$$y_{p,1}(t) = (A_1 t + A_0)t^s \cos t + (B_1 t + B_0)t^s \sin t.$$

For $10^t = e^{t\ln 10}$, a particular solution should be of the form

$$y_{p,2}(t) = Ct^p e^{t\ln 10} = Ct^p 10^t.$$

Since the roots of the auxiliary equation, $r^2 + 1 = 0$, are $r = \pm i$, we choose $s = 1$ and $p = 0$. Thus, by the superposition principle,

$$y_p(t) = y_{p,1}(t) + y_{p,2}(t) = (A_1 t + A_0)t\cos t + (B_1 t + B_0)t\sin t + C\cdot 10^t.$$

33. The roots of the auxiliary equation, which is $r^2 - r - 2 = 0$, are $r = -1, 2$. The right-hand side of the given equation is a sum of two terms, $e^t\cos t$ and $-t^2 + t + 1$. Corresponding particular solutions have the forms

$$y_{p,1}(t) = (A\cos t + B\sin t)t^s e^t \quad \text{and} \quad y_{p,2}(t) = (C_2 t^2 + C_1 t + C_0)t^p\,,$$

and we can take $s = p = 0$ since neither $r = 1 + i$ nor $r = 0$ is a root of the auxiliary equation. By the superposition principle,

$$y_p(t) = (A\cos t + B\sin t)e^t + C_2 t^2 + C_1 t + C_0\,.$$

35. Since the roots of the auxiliary equation are

$$r = \frac{4 \pm \sqrt{16 - 20}}{2} = 2 \pm i,$$

which are different from 5 and $3i$, a particular solution has the form

$$y_p(t) = (A_1 t + A_0)\cos 3t + (B_1 t + B_0)\sin 3t + Ce^{5t}\,.$$

(The last term corresponds to e^{5t} in the right-hand side of the original equation, and the first two come from $t\sin 3t - \cos 3t$.)

37. Clearly, $r = 0$ is not a root of the auxiliary equation, $r^3 - 2r^2 - r + 2 = 0$. (One can find the roots, say, using the factorization $r^3 - 2r^2 - r + 2 = (r - 2)(r - 1)(r + 1)$, but they are not needed for the form of a particular solution: the only important thing is that they are different from zero.) Therefore, a particular solution has the form

$$y_p(t) = A_2 t^2 + A_1 t + A_0 .$$

Substitution into the original equation yields

$$\begin{aligned} y_p''' - 2y_p'' - y_p' + 2y_p &= (0) - 2(2A_2) - (2A_2 t + A_1) + 2(A_2 t^2 + A_1 t + A_0) \\ &= 2A_2 t^2 + (A_1 - 2A_2)t + (A_0 - A_1 - 4A_2) = 2t^2 + 4t - 9. \end{aligned}$$

Equating the coefficients, we obtain

$$\begin{aligned} 2A_2 &= 2, & & & A_2 &= 1, \\ 2A_1 - 2A_2 &= 4, & &\Rightarrow & A_1 &= 3, \\ 2A_0 - A_1 - 4A_2 &= -9 & & & A_0 &= -1. \end{aligned}$$

Therefore, $y_p(t) = t^2 + 3t - 1$.

39. The auxiliary equation in this problem is $r^3 + r^2 - 2 = 0$. By inspection, we see that $r = 0$ is not a root. Next, we find that $r = 1$ is a simple root because

$$\left(r^3 + r^2 - 2\right)\Big|_{r=1} = 0 \qquad \text{and} \qquad \left(r^3 + r^2 - 2\right)'\Big|_{r=1} = \left(3r^2 + 2r\right)\Big|_{r=1} \neq 0.$$

Therefore, by the superposition principle, a particular solution has the form

$$y_p(t) = t(A_1 t + A_0)e^t + B = (A_1 t^2 + A_0 t)e^t + B.$$

Differentiating, we get

$$\begin{aligned} y_p'(t) &= \left[A_1 t^2 + (A_0 + 2A_1)t + A_0\right] e^t , \\ y_p''(t) &= \left[A_1 t^2 + (A_0 + 4A_1)t + 2A_0 + 2A_1\right] e^t , \\ y_p'''(t) &= \left[A_1 t^2 + (A_0 + 6A_1)t + 3A_0 + 6A_1\right] e^t . \end{aligned}$$

We substitute y_p and its derivatives into the original equation and equate the corresponding coefficients. This yields

$$\left\{\left[A_1t^2+(A_0+6A_1)t+3A_0+6A_1\right]+\left[A_1t^2+(A_0+4A_1)t+2A_0+2A_1\right]\right.$$
$$\left.-2\left[A_1t^2+A_0t\right]\right\}e^t-2B=te^t+1$$

$$\Rightarrow \qquad \left[10A_1t+8A_1+5A_0\right]e^t-2B=te^t+1$$

$$\Rightarrow \qquad \begin{array}{l} 10A_1=1, \\ 8A_1+5A_0=0, \\ -2B=1 \end{array} \qquad \Rightarrow \qquad \begin{array}{l} A_1=1/10, \\ A_0=-4/25, \\ B=-1/2. \end{array}$$

Hence, a particular solution is

$$y_p(t)=\left(\frac{1}{10}t-\frac{4}{25}\right)te^t-\frac{1}{2}.$$

41. The characteristic equation in this problem is $r^2+2r+5=0$, which has roots $r=-1\pm 2i$. Therefore, a general solution to the corresponding homogeneous equation is given by

$$y_h(t)=(c_1\cos 2t+c_2\sin 2t)\,e^{-t}. \tag{4.1}$$

(a) For $0\le t\le 3\pi/2$, $g(t)\equiv 10$, and so the equation becomes

$$y''+2y'+5y=10.$$

Hence a particular solution has the form $y_p(t)\equiv A$. Substitution into the equation yields

$$(A)''+2(A)'+5(A)=10 \qquad \Rightarrow \qquad 5A=10 \qquad \Rightarrow \qquad A=2,$$

and so, on $[0,3\pi/2]$, a general solution to the original equation is

$$y_1(t)=(c_1\cos 2t+c_2\sin 2t)\,e^{-t}+2.$$

We find c_1 and c_2 by substituting this function into the initial conditions.

$$\begin{array}{l} 0=y_1(0)=c_1+2, \\ 0=y_1'(0)=-c_1+2c_2 \end{array} \qquad \Rightarrow \qquad \begin{array}{l} c_1=-2, \\ c_2=-1 \end{array}$$

$$\Rightarrow \qquad y_1(t)=-(2\cos 2t+\sin 2t)\,e^{-t}+2.$$

(b) For $t > 3\pi/2$, $g(t) \equiv 0$, and so the given equation becomes homogeneous. Thus, a general solution, $y_2(t)$, is given by (4.1), i.e.,

$$y_2(t) = y_h(t) = (c_1 \cos 2t + c_2 \sin 2t)\, e^{-t}.$$

(c) We want to satisfy the conditions

$$\begin{aligned} y_1(3\pi/2) &= y_2(3\pi/2), \\ y_1'(3\pi/2) &= y_2'(3\pi/2). \end{aligned}$$

Evaluating y_1, y_2, and their derivatives at $t = 3\pi/2$, we solve the system

$$\begin{aligned} 2e^{-3\pi/2} + 2 &= -c_1 e^{-3\pi/2}, \\ 0 &= (c_1 - 2c_2)e^{3\pi/2} \end{aligned} \quad \Rightarrow \quad \begin{aligned} c_1 &= -2\left(e^{3\pi/2} + 1\right), \\ c_2 &= -\left(e^{3\pi/2} + 1\right). \end{aligned}$$

43. Recall that the motion of a mass-spring system is governed by the equation

$$my'' + by' + ky = g(t),$$

where m is the mass, b is the damping coefficient, k is the spring constant, and $g(t)$ is the external force. Thus, we have an initial value problem

$$y'' + 4y' + 3y = 5\sin t, \qquad y(0) = \frac{1}{2}, \quad y'(0) = 0.$$

The roots of the auxiliary equation, $r^2 + 4r + 3 = 0$, are $r = -3, -1$, and a general solution to the corresponding homogeneous equation is

$$y_h(t) = c_1 e^{-3t} + c_2 e^{-t}.$$

We look for a particular solution to the original equation of the form $y_p(t) = A\cos t + B\sin t$. Substituting this function into the equation, we get

$$\begin{aligned} y_p'' + 4y_p' + 3y_p &= (-A\cos t - B\sin t) + 4(-A\sin t + B\cos t) + 3(A\cos t + B\sin t) \\ &= (2A + 4B)\cos t + (2B - 4A)\sin t = 5\sin t \end{aligned}$$

$$\begin{aligned} 2A + 4B &= 0, \\ 2B - 4A &= 5 \end{aligned} \quad \Rightarrow \quad \begin{aligned} A &= -1, \\ B &= 1/2. \end{aligned}$$

Thus, a general solution to the equation describing the motion is

$$y(t) = -\cos t + \frac{1}{2}\sin t + c_1 e^{-3t} + c_2 e^{-t}.$$

Differentiating, we find $y'(t) = \sin t + (1/2)\cos t - 3c_1 e^{-3t} - c_2 e^{-t}$. Initial conditions give

$$\begin{aligned} y(0) &= -1 + c_1 + c_2 = 1/2, \\ y'(0) &= 1/2 - 3c_1 - c_2 = 0 \end{aligned} \qquad \Rightarrow \qquad \begin{aligned} c_1 &= -1/2, \\ c_2 &= 2. \end{aligned}$$

Hence, the equation of motion is

$$y(t) = -\cos t + \frac{1}{2}\sin t - \frac{1}{2}e^{-3t} + 2e^{-t}.$$

45. **(a)** With $m = k = 1$ and $L = \pi$ given initial value problem becomes

$$y(t) = 0, \qquad t \le -\frac{\pi}{2V},$$

$$y'' + y' = \begin{cases} \cos Vt, & -\pi/(2V) < t < \pi/(2V), \\ 0, & t \ge \pi/(2V). \end{cases}$$

The corresponding homogeneous equation $y'' + y = 0$ is the simple harmonic equation whose general solution is

$$y_h(t) = C_1 \cos t + C_2 \sin t. \tag{4.2}$$

First, we find the solution to the given problem for $-\pi/(2V) < t < \pi/(2V)$. The nonhomogeneous term, $\cos Vt$, suggests a particular solution of the form

$$y_p(t) = A\cos Vt + B\sin Vt.$$

Substituting $y_p(t)$ into the equation yields

$$\begin{aligned} &(A\cos Vt + B\sin Vt)'' + (A\cos Vt + B\sin Vt) = \cos Vt \\ \Rightarrow \quad &\left(-V^2 A\cos Vt - V^2 B\sin Vt\right) + (A\cos Vt + B\sin Vt) = \cos Vt \\ \Rightarrow \quad &\left(1 - V^2\right) A\cos Vt + \left(1 - V^2\right) B\sin Vt = \cos Vt. \end{aligned}$$

Equating coefficients, we get

$$A = \frac{1}{1 - V^2}, \qquad B = 0,$$

Thus a general solution on $(-\pi/(2V), \pi/(2V))$ is

$$y_1(t) = y_h(t) + y_p(t) = C_1 \cos t + C_2 \sin t + \frac{1}{1-V^2} \cos Vt\,. \tag{4.3}$$

Since $y(t) \equiv 0$ for $t \le -\pi/(2V)$, the initial conditions for the above solution are

$$y_1\left(-\frac{\pi}{2V}\right) = y_1'\left(-\frac{\pi}{2V}\right) = 0.$$

From (4.3) we obtain

$$\begin{aligned} y_1\left(-\frac{\pi}{2V}\right) &= C_1 \cos\left(-\frac{\pi}{2V}\right) + C_2 \sin\left(-\frac{\pi}{2V}\right) = 0 \\ y_1'\left(-\frac{\pi}{2V}\right) &= -C_1 \sin\left(-\frac{\pi}{2V}\right) + C_2 \cos\left(-\frac{\pi}{2V}\right) + \frac{V}{1-V^2} = 0. \end{aligned}$$

Solving the system yields

$$C_1 = \frac{V}{V^2-1} \sin\frac{\pi}{2V}\,, \qquad C_2 = \frac{V}{V^2-1} \cos\frac{\pi}{2V}\,,$$

and

$$\begin{aligned} y_1(t) &= \frac{V}{V^2-1} \sin\frac{\pi}{2V} \cos t + \frac{V}{V^2-1} \cos\frac{\pi}{2V} \sin t + \frac{1}{1-V^2} \cos Vt \\ &= \frac{V}{V^2-1} \sin\left(t + \frac{\pi}{2V}\right) - \frac{1}{V^2-1} \cos Vt, \qquad -\frac{\pi}{2V} < t < \frac{\pi}{2V}\,. \end{aligned}$$

For $t > \pi/(2V)$ given equation is homogeneous, and its general solution, $y_2(t)$, is given by (4.2). That is,

$$y_2(t) = C_3 \cos t + C_4 \sin t.$$

From the initial conditions

$$\begin{aligned} y_2\left(\frac{\pi}{2V}\right) &= y_1\left(\frac{\pi}{2V}\right), \\ y_2'\left(\frac{\pi}{2V}\right) &= y_1'\left(\frac{\pi}{2V}\right), \end{aligned}$$

we conclude that

$$C_3 \cos\frac{\pi}{2V} + C_4 \sin\frac{\pi}{2V} = \frac{V}{V^2-1} \sin\frac{\pi}{V}\,,$$

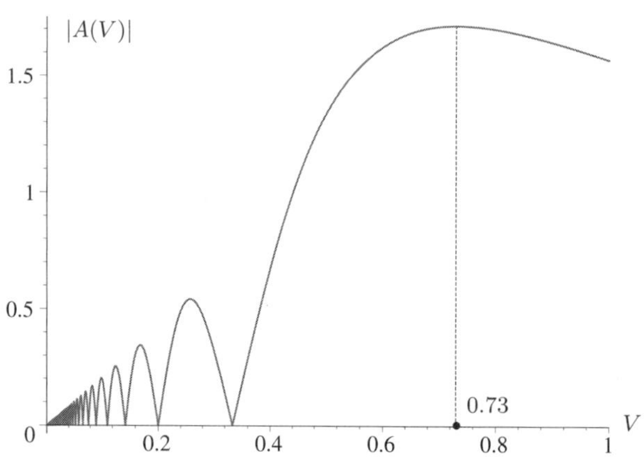

Figure 4–A: The graph of the function $|A(V)|$.

$$-C_3 \sin \frac{\pi}{2V} + C_4 \cos \frac{\pi}{2V} = \frac{V}{V^2-1} \cos \frac{\pi}{V} + \frac{V}{V^2-1} = \frac{2V}{V^2-1} \cos^2 \frac{\pi}{2V}.$$

The solution of this system is

$$C_3 = 0, \qquad C_4 = \frac{2V}{V^2-1} \cos \frac{\pi}{2V}.$$

So,

$$y_2(t) = \frac{2V}{V^2-1} \cos \frac{\pi}{2V} \sin t.$$

(b) The graph of the function

$$|A(V)| = \left| \frac{2V}{V^2-1} \cos \frac{\pi}{2V} \right|$$

is given in Figure 4-A. From this graph, we find that the most violent shaking of the vehicle (the maximum of $|A(V)|$) happens when the speed $V \approx 0.73$.

47. The auxiliary equation in this problem is $r^2+9=0$ with roots $r = \pm 3i$. So, a general solution to the corresponding homogeneous equation is

$$y_h = c_1 \cos 3t + c_2 \sin 3t.$$

The form of a particular solution, corresponding to the right-hand side, is

$$y_p(t) = A \cos 6t + B \sin 6t.$$

Substitution into the original equation yields

$$-27(A\cos 6t + B\sin 6t) = 27\cos 6t \qquad \Rightarrow \qquad A = -1,\ B = 0 \qquad \Rightarrow \qquad y_p(t) = -\cos 6t.$$

Therefore, a general solution has the form

$$y(t) = c_1\cos 3t + c_2\sin 3t - \cos 6t.$$

In (a)–(c), we have the same boundary condition at $t = 0$, that is, $y(0) = -1$. This yields

$$-1 = y(0) = c_1 - 1 \qquad \Rightarrow \qquad c_1 = 0.$$

Hence, all the solutions satisfying this condition are given by

$$y(t) = c_2\sin 3t - \cos 6t. \tag{4.4}$$

(a) The second boundary condition gives $3 = y(\pi/6) = c_2 + 1 \quad \Rightarrow \quad c_2 = 2$, and the answer is $y = 2\sin 3t - \cos 6t$.

(b) This time we have $5 = y(\pi/3) = c_2 \cdot 0 - 1 \quad \Rightarrow \quad 5 = -1$, and so there is no solution of the form (4.4) satisfying this second boundary condition.

(c) Now we have $-1 = y(\pi/3) = c_2 \cdot 0 - 1 \quad \Rightarrow \quad -1 = -1$, which is a true identity. This means that any function in (4.4) satisfies both boundary conditions.

EXERCISES 4.6: Variation of Parameters, page 197

1. The auxiliary equation in this problem is $r^2 + 4 = 0$, which has the roots $r = \pm 2i$. Therefore, $y_1(t) = \cos 2t$ and $y_2(t) = \sin 2t$ are two linearly independent solutions, and a general solution to the corresponding homogeneous equation is given by

$$y_h(t) = c_1\cos 2t + c_2\sin 2t.$$

Using the variation of parameters method, we look for a particular solution to the original nonhomogeneous equation of the form

$$y_p(t) = v_1(t)y_1(t) + v_2(t)y_2(t) = v_1(t)\cos 2t + v_2(t)\sin 2t.$$

The system (9) on page 195 in the text becomes

$$\begin{aligned} v_1'(t)\cos 2t + v_2'(t)\sin 2t &= 0 \\ -2v_1'(t)\sin 2t + 2v_2'(t)\cos 2t &= \tan 2t. \end{aligned} \tag{4.5}$$

Multiplying the first equation in (4.5) by $\sin 2t$, the second equation by $(1/2)\cos 2t$, and adding the resulting equations together, we get

$$v_2'(t) = \frac{1}{2}\sin 2t \qquad \Rightarrow \qquad v_2 = \frac{1}{2}\int \sin 2t\,dt = -\frac{1}{4}\cos 2t + c_3.$$

From the first equation in (4.5) we also obtain

$$\begin{aligned} v_1'(t) = -v_2'(t)\tan 2t = -\frac{1}{2}\frac{\sin^2 2t}{\cos 2t} &= -\frac{1}{2}\frac{1-\cos^2 2t}{\cos 2t} = \frac{1}{2}(\cos 2t - \sec 2t) \\ \Rightarrow \qquad v_1(t) = \frac{1}{2}\int(\cos 2t - \sec 2t)\,dt &= \frac{1}{4}(\sin 2t - \ln|\sec 2t + \tan 2t|) + c_4. \end{aligned}$$

We take $c_3 = c_4 = 0$ since we need just one particular solution. Thus

$$\begin{aligned} y_p(t) &= \frac{1}{4}(\sin 2t - \ln|\sec 2t + \tan 2t|)\cos 2t - \frac{1}{4}\cos 2t\sin 2t \\ &= -\frac{1}{4}\cos 2t\ln|\sec 2t + \tan 2t| \end{aligned}$$

and a general solution to the given equation is

$$y(t) = y_h(t) + y_p(t) = c_1\cos 2t + c_2\sin 2t - \frac{1}{4}\cos 2t\ln|\sec 2t + \tan 2t|.$$

2. From Example 1 on page 196 in the text, we know that functions $y_1(t) = \cos t$ and $y_2(t) = \sin t$ are two linearly independent solutions to the corresponding homogeneous equation, and so its general solution is given by

$$y_h(t) = c_1\cos t + c_2\sin t.$$

Now we apply the method of variation of parameters to find a particular solution to the original equation. By the formula (3) on page 194 in the text, $y_p(t)$ has the form

$$y_p(t) = v_1(t)y_1(t) + v_2(t)y_2(t).$$

Since

$$y_1'(t) = (\cos t)' = -\sin t, \qquad y_2'(t) = (\sin t)' = \cos t,$$

the system (9) on page 195 becomes

$$\begin{aligned} v_1'(t)\cos t + v_2'(t)\sin t &= 0, \\ -v_1'(t)\sin t + v_2'(t)\cos t &= \sec t. \end{aligned} \tag{4.6}$$

Multiplying the first equation by $\sin t$ and the second equation by $\cos t$ yields

$$\begin{aligned} v_1'(t)\sin t\cos t + v_2'(t)\sin^2 t &= 0, \\ -v_1'(t)\sin t\cos t + v_2'(t)\cos^2 t &= 1. \end{aligned}$$

Adding these equations together, we obtain

$$v_2'(t)\left(\cos^2 t + \sin^2 t\right) = 1 \qquad \text{or} \qquad v_2'(t) = 1.$$

From the first equation in (4.6), we can now find $v_1'(t)$:

$$v_1'(t) = -v_2'(t)\,\frac{\sin t}{\cos t} = -\tan t.$$

So,

$$\begin{aligned} v_1'(t) &= -\tan t, \\ v_2'(t) &= 1 \end{aligned} \qquad \Rightarrow \qquad \begin{aligned} v_1(t) &= -\int \tan t\,dt = \ln|\cos t| + c_3\,, \\ v_2(t) &= \int dt = t + c_4\,. \end{aligned}$$

Since we are looking for a particular solution, we can take $c_3 = c_4 = 0$ and get

$$y_p(t) = \cos t \ln|\cos t| + t\sin t.$$

Thus a general solution to the given equation is

$$y(t) = y_p(t) + y_h(t) = \cos t\ln|\cos t| + t\sin t + c_1\cos t + c_2\sin t.$$

3. First, we can simplify the equation by dividing both sides by 2. This yields

$$x'' - x' - 2x = e^{3t}\,.$$

This equation has associated homogeneous equation $x'' - x' - 2x = 0$. The roots of the associated auxiliary equation, $r^2 - r - 2 = 0$, are $r = 2$ and $r = -1$. Therefore, a general solution to this equation is

$$x_h(t) = c_1 e^{2t} + c_2 e^{-t}.$$

For the variation of parameters method, we let

$$x_p(t) = v_1(t)x_1(t) + v_2(t)x_2(t), \qquad \text{where} \qquad x_1(t) = e^{2t} \quad \text{and} \quad x_2(t) = e^{-t}.$$

Thus, $x_1'(t) = 2e^{2t}$ and $x_2'(t) = -e^{-t}$. This means that we have to solve the system

$$\begin{aligned} e^{2t}v_1' + e^{-t}v_2' &= 0, \\ 2e^{2t}v_1' - e^{-t}v_2' &= e^{3t}. \end{aligned}$$

Adding these two equations yields

$$3e^{2t}v_1' = e^{3t} \qquad \Rightarrow \qquad v_1' = \frac{1}{3}e^t \qquad \Rightarrow \qquad v_1(t) = \frac{1}{3}e^t.$$

Substututing v_1' into the first equation, we get

$$\frac{1}{3}e^{3t} + e^{-t}v_2' = 0 \qquad \Rightarrow \qquad v_2' = -\frac{1}{3}e^{4t} \qquad \Rightarrow \qquad v_2(t) = -\frac{1}{12}e^{4t}.$$

Therefore,

$$x_p(t) = \frac{1}{3}e^t e^{2t} - \frac{1}{12}e^{4t}e^{-t} = \frac{1}{4}e^{3t},$$

and a general solution is

$$x(t) = c_1 e^{2t} + c_2 e^{-t} + \frac{1}{4}e^{3t}.$$

5. This equation has associated homogeneous equation $y'' - 2y' + y = 0$. Its auxiliary equation, $r^2 - 2r + 1 = 0$, has a double root $r = 1$. Thus a general solution to the homogeneous equation is

$$y_h(t) = c_1 e^t + c_2 t e^t.$$

For the variation of parameters method, we let

$$y_p(t) = v_1(t)y_1(t) + v_2(t)y_2(t), \qquad \text{where} \qquad y_1(t) = e^t \quad \text{and} \quad y_2(t) = te^t.$$

Thus, $y_1'(t) = e^t$ and $y_2'(t) = te^t + e^t$. This means that we want to solve the system (see system (9) on page 195 of text)

$$\begin{aligned} e^t v_1' + te^t v_2' &= 0, \\ e^t v_1' + \left(te^t + e^t\right) v_2' &= t^{-1}e^t. \end{aligned}$$

Subtracting these two equations yields

$$e^t v_2' = t^{-1}e^t \qquad \Rightarrow \qquad v_2' = t^{-1}.$$

So

$$v_2(t) = \int t^{-1}\,dt = \ln|t| + c_3\,.$$

Also, we have from the first equation of the system

$$e^t v_1' = -te^t v_2' = -te^t t^{-1} = -e^t \qquad \Rightarrow \qquad v_1' = -1.$$

So,

$$v_1(t) = -t + c_4\,.$$

By letting c_3 and c_4 equal to zero, and plugging the expressions found above for $v_1(t)$ and $v_2(t)$ into the equation defining $y_p(t)$, we obtain a particular solution

$$y_p(t) = -te^t + te^t \ln|t|.$$

We obtain a general solution of the nonhomogeneous equation by adding this expression for $y_p(t)$ to the expression for $y_h(t)$. Thus, we obtain

$$y(t) = c_1e^t + c_2te^t - te^t + te^t \ln|t| = c_1e^t + (c_2 - 1)te^t + te^t \ln|t|.$$

If we let $C_1 = c_1$ and $C_2 = c_2 - 1$, we can express this general solution in the form

$$y(t) = C_1e^t + C_2te^t + te^t \ln|t|.$$

7. The auxiliary equation in this problem is $r^2+16=0$, which has the roots $r=\pm 4i$. Therefore, $y_1(\theta)=\cos 4\theta$ and $y_2(\theta)=\sin 4\theta$ are two linearly independent solutions, and a general solution to the corresponding homogeneous equation is given by

$$y_h(\theta)=c_1\cos 4\theta+c_2\sin 4\theta.$$

Using the variation of parameters method, we look for a particular solution to the original nonhomogeneous equation of the form

$$y_p(\theta)=v_1(\theta)y_1(\theta)+v_2(\theta)y_2(\theta)=v_1(\theta)\cos 4\theta+v_2(\theta)\sin 4\theta.$$

The system (9) on page 195 in the text becomes

$$\begin{aligned} v_1'(\theta)\cos 4\theta+v_2'(\theta)\sin 4\theta&=0,\\ -4v_1'(\theta)\sin 4\theta+4v_2'(\theta)\cos 4\theta&=\sec 4\theta. \end{aligned} \tag{4.7}$$

Multiplying the first equation in (4.7) by $\sin 4\theta$ and the second equation by $(1/4)\cos 4\theta$, and adding the resulting equations together, we get

$$v_2'(\theta)=\frac{1}{4} \qquad\Rightarrow\qquad v_2=\frac{1}{4}\theta+c_3.$$

From the first equation in (4.7) we also obtain

$$v_1'(\theta)=-\frac{1}{4}\tan 4\theta \qquad\Rightarrow\qquad v_1(\theta)=-\frac{1}{4}\int\tan 4\theta\,d\theta=\frac{1}{16}\ln|\cos 4\theta|+c_4.$$

Taking $c_3=c_4=0$, we obtain

$$\begin{aligned} y_p(\theta)&=\frac{\cos 4\theta}{16}\ln|\cos 4\theta|+\frac{1}{4}\theta\sin 4\theta\\ \Rightarrow\qquad y(\theta)&=c_1\cos 4\theta+c_2\sin 4\theta+\frac{\theta}{4}\sin 4\theta+\frac{\cos 4\theta}{16}\ln|\cos 4\theta|. \end{aligned}$$

9. In this problem, the corresponding homogeneous equation is the same as that in Problem 1. Hence $y_1(t)=\cos 2t$ and $y_2(t)=\sin 2t$ are two linearly independent solutions, and a general solution to the homogeneous equation is given by

$$y_h(t)=c_1\cos 2t+c_2\sin 2t,$$

and, in the variation of parameters method, a particular solution has the form

$$y_p(t) = v_1(t)\cos 2t + v_2(t)\sin 2t,$$

where $v_1'(t)$, $v_2'(t)$ satisfy the system

$$\begin{aligned} &v_1'(t)\cos 2t + v_2'(t)\sin 2t = 0, \\ &-2v_1'(t)\sin 2t + 2v_2'(t)\cos 2t = \csc^2 2t. \end{aligned}$$

Multiplying the first equation by $\sin 2t$ and the second equation by $(1/2)\cos 2t$, and adding the resulting equations, we get

$$v_2'(t) = \frac{1}{2}\csc^2 2t\cos 2t \qquad \Rightarrow \qquad v_2 = \frac{1}{2}\int \csc^2 2t\cos 2t\,dt = -\frac{1}{4}\csc 2t + c_3\,.$$

From the first equation in the system above we also find

$$\begin{aligned} v_1'(t) &= -v_2'(t)\tan 2t = -\frac{1}{2}\csc^2 2t\cos 2t\tan 2t = -\frac{1}{2}\csc 2t \\ \Rightarrow \qquad v_1(t) &= -\frac{1}{2}\int \csc 2t\,dt = \frac{1}{4}\ln|\csc 2t + \cot 2t| + c_4\,. \end{aligned}$$

With $c_3 = c_4 = 0$,

$$\begin{aligned} y_p(t) &= \frac{1}{4}\cos 2t\ln|\csc 2t + \cot 2t| - \frac{1}{4}\csc 2t\sin 2t = \frac{1}{4}\left(\cos 2t\ln|\csc 2t + \cot 2t| - 1\right) \\ \Rightarrow \qquad y(t) &= c_1\cos 2t + c_2\sin 2t + \frac{1}{4}\left(\cos 2t\ln|\csc 2t + \cot 2t| - 1\right). \end{aligned}$$

11. This equation is similar to that in Example 1 on page 196 in the text. Only the nonhomogeneous term is different. Thus we will follow steps in Example 1. Two independent solutions to the corresponding homogeneous equation, $y'' + y = 0$, are $y_1(t) = \cos t$ and $y_2(t) = \sin t$. A particular solution to the original equation is of the form

$$y_p(t) = v_1(t)\cos t + v_2(t)\sin t,$$

where $v_1(t)$ and $v_2(t)$ satisfy

$$\begin{aligned} &v_1'(t)\cos t + v_2'(t)\sin t = 0, \\ &-v_1'(t)\sin t + v_2'(t)\cos t = \tan^2 t. \end{aligned}$$

Multiplying the first equation by $\sin t$ and the second equation by $\cos t$, and adding them together yield

$$v_2'(t) = \tan^2 t \cos t = (\sec^2 t - 1)\cos t = \sec t - \cos t.$$

We find $v_1'(t)$ from the first equation in the system.

$$v_1'(t) = -v_2'(t)\tan t = -(\sec t - \cos t)\tan t = \sin t - \frac{\sin t}{\cos^2 t}.$$

Integrating, we get

$$v_1(t) = \int \left(\sin t - \frac{\sin t}{\cos^2 t}\right) dt = -\cos t - \sec t,$$

$$v_2(t) = \int (\sec t - \cos t)\, dt = \ln|\sec t + \tan t| - \sin t,$$

where we have taken zero integration constants. Therefore,

$$y_p(t) = -(\cos t + \sec t)\cos t + (\ln|\sec t + \tan t| - \sin t)\sin t = \sin t \ln|\sec t + \tan t| - 2,$$

and a general solution is given by

$$y(t) = c_1 \cos t + c_2 \sin t + \sin t \ln|\sec t + \tan t| - 2.$$

13. The corresponding homogeneous equation in this problem is the same as that in Problem 1 (with y replaced by v). Similarly to the solution of Problem 1, we conclude that $v_1(t) = \cos 2t$ and $v_2(t) = \sin 2t$ are two linearly independent solutions of the corresponding homogeneous equation, and a particular solution to the original equation can be found as

$$v_p(t) = u_1(t)\cos 2t + u_2(t)\sin 2t\,,$$

where $u_1(t)$ and $u_2(t)$ satisfy

$$u_1'(t)\cos 2t + u_2'(t)\sin 2t = 0,$$

$$-2u_1'(t)\sin 2t + 2u_2'(t)\cos 2t = \sec^4 2t.$$

Multiplying the first equation by $\sin 2t$ and the second equation by $(1/2)\cos 2t$, and adding the results together, we get

$$u_2'(t) = \frac{1}{2}\sec^3 2t.$$

From the first equation in the above system we also obtain

$$u_1'(t) = -u_2'(t)\tan 2t = -\frac{1}{2}\sec^4 2t \sin 2t\,.$$

Integrating yields

$$u_1(t) = -\frac{1}{2}\int \sec^4 2t \sin 2t\,dt = -\frac{1}{2}\int \cos^{-4} 2t \sin 2t\,dt = -\frac{1}{12}\sec^3 2t,$$

$$u_2(t) = \frac{1}{2}\int \sec^3 2t\,dt = \frac{1}{8}\left(\sec 2t \tan 2t + \ln|\sec 2t + \tan 2t|\right).$$

Thus,

$$\begin{aligned} v_p(t) &= -\frac{1}{12}\sec^3 2t \cos 2t + \frac{1}{8}\left(\sec 2t \tan 2t + \ln|\sec 2t + \tan 2t|\right)\sin 2t \\ &= -\frac{1}{12}\sec^2 2t + \frac{1}{8}\tan^2 2t + \frac{1}{8}\sin 2t \ln|\sec 2t + \tan 2t| \\ &= \frac{1}{24}\sec^2 2t - \frac{1}{8} + \frac{1}{8}\sin 2t \ln|\sec 2t + \tan 2t|, \end{aligned}$$

and a general solution to the given equation is

$$v(t) = c_1 \cos 2t + c_2 \sin 2t + \frac{1}{24}\sec^2 2t - \frac{1}{8} + \frac{1}{8}\sin 2t \ln|\sec 2t + \tan 2t|.$$

15. The corresponding homogeneous equation is $y'' + y = 0$. Its auxiliary equation has the roots $r = \pm i$. Hence, a general solution to the homogeneous problem is given by

$$y_h(t) = c_1 \cos t + c_2 \sin t.$$

We will find a particular solution to the original equation by first finding a particular solution for each of two problems, one with the nonhomogeneous term $g_1(t) = 3\sec t$ and the other one with the nonhomogeneous term $g_2(t) = -t^2 + 1$. Then we will use the superposition principle to obtain a particular solution for the original equation. The term $3\sec t$ is not in a form that allows us to use the method of undetermined coefficients. Therefore, we will use the method of variation of parameters. To this end, let $y_1(t) = \cos t$ and $y_2(t) = \sin t$ (linearly independent solutions to the corresponding homogeneous problem). Then a particular solution $y_{p,1}$ to $y'' + y = 3\sec t$ has the form

$$y_{p,1}(t) = v_1(t)y_1(t) + v_2(t)y_2(t) = v_1(t)\cos t + v_2(t)\sin t,$$

where $v_1(t)$ and $v_2(t)$ are determined by the system

$$v_1' \cos t + v_2' \sin t = 0,$$
$$-v_1' \sin t + v_2' \cos t = 3 \sec t.$$

Multiplying the first equation by $\cos t$ and the second equation by $\sin t$ and subtracting the results, we get

$$v_1' = -3 \sec t \sin t = -3 \tan t.$$

Hence

$$v_1(t) = -3 \int \tan t \, dt = 3 \ln |\cos t| + C_1 .$$

To find $v_2'(t)$, we multiply the first equation of the above system by $\sin t$, the second by $\cos t$, and add the results to obtain

$$v_2' = 3 \sec t \cos t = 3 \qquad \Rightarrow \qquad v_2(t) = 3t + C_2 .$$

Therefore, for this first equation (with $g_1(t) = 3 \sec t$), by letting $C_1 = C_2 = 0$, we have a particular solution given by

$$y_{p,1}(t) = 3 \cos t \ln |\cos t| + 3t \sin t.$$

The nonhomogeneous term $g_2(t) = -t^2 + 1$ is of a form that allows us to use the method of undetermined coefficients. Thus, a particular solution to this nonhomogeneous equation will have the form

$$y_{p,2}(t) = A_2 t^2 + A_1 t + A_0 \qquad \Rightarrow \qquad y_{p,2}'(t) = 2A_2 t + A_1 \qquad \Rightarrow \qquad y_{p,2}''(t) = 2A_2 .$$

Plugging these expressions into the equation $y'' + y = -t^2 + 1$ yields

$$y_{p,2}'' + y_{p,2} = 2A_2 + A_2 t^2 + A_1 t + A_0 = A_2 t^2 + A_1 t + (2A_2 + A_0) = -t^2 + 1.$$

By equating coefficients, we obtain

$$A_2 = -1, \qquad A_1 = 0, \qquad 2A_2 + A_0 = 1 \quad \Rightarrow \quad A_0 = 3.$$

Therefore, we have

$$y_{p,2}(t) = -t^2 + 3.$$

By the superposition principle, we see that a particular solution to the original problem is given by

$$y_p(t) = y_{p,1}(t) + y_{p,2}(t) = 3\cos t \ln|\cos t| + 3t\sin t - t^2 + 3.$$

Combining this solution with the general solution to the homogeneous equation yields a general solution to the original differential equation,

$$y(t) = c_1 \cos t + c_2 \sin t - t^2 + 3 + 3t\sin t + 3\cos t \ln|\cos t|.$$

17. Multiplying the given equation by 2, we get

$$y'' + 4y = 2\tan 2t - e^t.$$

The nonhomogeneous term, $2\tan 2t - e^t$, can be written as a linear combination $2g_1(t) - g_2(t)$, where $g_1(t) = \tan 2t$ and $g_2(t) = e^t$. A particular solution to the equation

$$y'' + 4y = \tan 2t$$

is found in Problem 1, that is,

$$y_{p,1}(t) = -\frac{1}{4}\cos 2t \ln|\sec 2t + \tan 2t|.$$

A particular solution to

$$y'' + 4y = e^t$$

can be found using the method of undetermined coefficients. We look for $y_{p,2}$ of the form $y_{p,2}(t) = Ae^t$. Substitution yields

$$\left(Ae^t\right)'' + 4\left(Ae^t\right) = e^t \qquad \Rightarrow \qquad 5Ae^t = e^t \qquad \Rightarrow \qquad A = \frac{1}{5},$$

and so $y_{p,2} = (1/5)e^t$. By the superposition principle, a particular solution to the original equation is

$$y_p(t) = 2y_{p,1} - y_{p,2} = -\frac{1}{2}\cos 2t \ln|\sec 2t + \tan 2t| - \frac{1}{5}e^t.$$

Adding a general solution to the homogeneous equation, we get

$$y(t) = c_1 \cos 2t + c_2 \sin 2t - \frac{1}{2} \cos 2t \ln |\sec 2t + \tan 2t| - \frac{1}{5} e^t .$$

19. A general solution of the corresponding homogeneous equation is given by

$$y_h(t) = c_1 e^{-t} + c_2 e^t .$$

We will try to find a particular solution to the original nonhomogeneous equation of the form $y_p(t) = v_1(t)y_1(t) + v_2(t)y_2(t)$, where $y_1(t) = e^{-t}$ and $y_2(t) = e^t$. We apply formulas (10) on page 195 in the text, but replace indefinite integrals by definite integrals. Note that

$$y_1(t)y_2'(t) - y_1'(t)y_2(t) = e^{-x}e^x - \left(-e^{-x}\right) e^x = 2.$$

With $g(t) = 1/t$ and integration from 1 to t, formulas (10) yield

$$v_1(t) = \int_1^t \frac{-g(x)y_2(x)}{2}\, dx = -\frac{1}{2} \int_1^t \frac{e^x}{x}\, dx ,$$

$$v_2(t) = \int_1^t \frac{g(x)y_1(x)}{2}\, dx = \frac{1}{2} \int_1^t \frac{e^{-x}}{x}\, dx .$$

(Notice that we have chosen the lower limit of integration to be equal to 1 because the initial conditions are given at 1. We could have chosen any other value for the lower limit, but the choice of 1 will make the determination of the constants c_1 and c_2 easier.) Thus

$$y_p(t) = \frac{e^t}{2} \int_1^t \frac{e^{-x}}{x}\, dx - \frac{e^{-t}}{2} \int_1^t \frac{e^x}{x}\, dx ,$$

and so a general solution to the original differential equation is

$$y(t) = c_1 e^{-t} + c_2 e^t + \frac{e^t}{2} \int_1^t \frac{e^{-x}}{x}\, dx - \frac{e^{-t}}{2} \int_1^t \frac{e^x}{x}\, dx .$$

By plugging in the first initial condition (and using the fact that the integral of a function from a to a is zero which is why we have chosen the lower limit of integration to be the initial point, $t = 1$), we find that

$$y(1) = c_1 e^{-1} + c_2 e^1 = 0.$$

Differentiating $y(t)$ yields

$$y'(t) = -c_1e^{-t} + c_2e^t + \frac{e^t}{2}\int_1^t \frac{e^{-x}}{x}\,dx + \left(\frac{e^t}{2}\right)\left(\frac{e^{-t}}{t}\right) + \frac{e^{-t}}{2}\int_1^t \frac{e^x}{x}\,dx - \left(\frac{e^{-t}}{2}\right)\left(\frac{e^t}{t}\right),$$

where we have used the product rule and the fundamental theorem of calculus to differentiate the last two terms of $y(t)$. We now plug in the second initial condition into the equation we just found for $y'(t)$ to obtain

$$y'(1) = -c_1e^{-1} + c_2e^1 + \left(\frac{-e^{-1}}{2}\right)\left(\frac{e^1}{1}\right) + \left(\frac{e^1}{2}\right)\left(\frac{e^{-1}}{1}\right) = -c_1e^{-1} + c_2e^1 - \frac{1}{2} + \frac{1}{2} = -2.$$

Solving the system

$$\begin{aligned} c_1e^{-1} + c_2e^1 &= 0, \\ -c_1e^{-1} + c_2e^1 &= -2 \end{aligned}$$

yields $c_2 = -e^{-1}$ and $c_1 = e^1$. Therefore, the solution to our problem is given by

$$y(t) = e^{1-t} - e^{t-1} + \frac{e^t}{2}\int_1^t \frac{e^{-x}}{x}\,dx - \frac{e^{-t}}{2}\int_1^t \frac{e^x}{x}\,dx\,. \tag{4.8}$$

Simpson's rule is implemented on the software package provided free with the text (see also the discussion of the solution to Problem 25 in Exercises 2.3). Simpson's rule requires an even number of intervals, but we don't know how many are required to obtain the 2-place accuracy desired. We will compute the approximate value of $y(t)$ at $t = 2$ using 2, 4, 6, ... intervals for Simpson's rule until the approximate value changes by less than five in the third place. For $n = 2$, we divide $[1, 2]$ into 4 equal subintervals. Thus each interval will be of length $(2 - 1)/4 = 1/4$. Therefore the integrals are approximated by

$$\begin{aligned} \int_1^2 \frac{e^x}{x}\,dx &\approx \frac{1}{12}\left[\frac{e^1}{1} + 4\frac{e^{1.25}}{1.25} + 2\frac{e^{1.5}}{1.5} + 4\frac{e^{1.75}}{1.75} + \frac{e^2}{2}\right] \approx 3.0592\,, \\ \int_1^2 \frac{e^{-x}}{x}\,dx &\approx \frac{1}{12}\left[\frac{e^{-1}}{1} + 4\frac{e^{-1.25}}{1.25} + 2\frac{e^{-1.5}}{1.5} + 4\frac{e^{-1.75}}{1.75} + \frac{e^{-2}}{2}\right] \approx 0.1706\,. \end{aligned}$$

Substituting these values into equation (4.8) we obtain

$$y(2) \approx e^{1-2} - e^{2-1} - \frac{e^{-2}}{2}(3.0592) + \frac{e^{2}}{2}(0.1706) = -1.9271\,.$$

Repeating these calculations for $n = 3$, 4, and 5 yields the approximations in Table 4-A.

Table 4–A: Successive approximations for $y(2)$ using Simpson's rule.

Intervals	$y(2) \approx$
6	−1.9275
8	−1.9275
10	−1.9275

Since these values do not change in the third place, we can expect that the first three places are accurate and we obtained an approximate solution of $y(2) = -1.93$.

21. A particular solution to the given equation has the form

$$y_p(t) = v_1(t)y_1(t) + v_2(t)y_2(t) = v_1(t)e^t + v_2(t)(t+1).$$

Since $y_1'(t) = e^t$, $y_2'(t) \equiv 1$, the system (9), with $a = a(t) = t$ and $g(t) = t^2$, becomes

$$\begin{aligned} v_1'(t)e^t + v_2'(t)(t+1) &= 0, \\ v_1'(t)e^t + v_2'(t) &= \frac{t^2}{t} = t. \end{aligned}$$

Subtracting the second equation from the first one, we get

$$tv_2'(t) = -t \qquad \Rightarrow \qquad v_2'(t) = -1 \qquad \Rightarrow \qquad v_2(t) = -t.$$

Substituting $v_2'(t)$ into the first equation yields

$$\begin{aligned} &v_1'(t)e^t - (t+1) = 0 \qquad \Rightarrow \qquad v_1'(t) = (t+1)e^{-t} \\ \Rightarrow \qquad &v_1(t) = \int (t+1)e^{-t}\,dt = -(t+1)e^{-t} + \int e^{-t}\,dt = -(t+2)e^{-t}. \end{aligned}$$

Thus

$$y_p(t) = -(t+2)e^{-t}e^t - t(t+1) = -t^2 - 2t - 2.$$

(Note that $-2t - 2 = -2(t+1) = -2y_2(t)$ is a solution to the corresponding homogeneous equation. Thus, $-t^2 = y_p(t) + 2y_2(t)$ is another particular solution.)

23. We are seeking for a particular solution to the given equation of the form

$$y_p(t) = v_1(t)y_1(t) + v_2(t)y_2(t) = v_1(t)(5t-1) + v_2(t)e^{-5t}.$$

Since $y_1'(t) \equiv 5$, $y_2'(t) = -5e^{-5t}$, the system (9), with $a = a(t) = t$ and $g(t) = t^2e^{-5t}$, becomes

$$\begin{aligned} v_1'(t)(5t-1) + v_2'(t)e^{-5t} &= 0, \\ 5v_1'(t) - 5v_2'(t)e^{-5t} &= \frac{t^2e^{-5t}}{t} = te^{-5t}. \end{aligned}$$

Dividing the second equation by 5 and adding to the first equation yields

$$5tv_1'(t) = \frac{1}{5}\,te^{-5t} \qquad \Rightarrow \qquad v_1'(t) = \frac{1}{25}\,e^{-5t} \qquad \Rightarrow \qquad v_1(t) = -\frac{1}{125}\,e^{-5t}.$$

Substituting $v_1'(t)$ into the first equation, we get

$$\frac{1}{25}\,e^{-5t}(5t-1) + v_2'(t)e^{-5t} = 0 \qquad \Rightarrow \qquad v_2'(t) = -\frac{5t-1}{25} \qquad \Rightarrow \qquad v_2(t) = -\frac{t^2}{10} + \frac{t}{25}.$$

Thus

$$y_p(t) = -\frac{1}{125}\,e^{-5t}(5t-1) + \left(-\frac{t^2}{10} + \frac{t}{25}\right)e^{-5t} = \left(\frac{1}{125} - \frac{t^2}{10}\right)e^{-5t}.$$

(Since $(1/125)e^{-5t} = (1/125)y_2(t)$ is a solution to the corresponding homogeneous equation, the function $-(t^2/10)e^{-5t}$ is also a particular solution.)

25. A general solution to the corresponding homogeneous equation is

$$y_h(x) = c_1y_1(x) + c_2y_2(x) = x^{-1/2}\left(c_1\cos x + c_2\sin x\right).$$

To find a particular solution to the original equation, we apply the method of variation of parameters. To form the system (9) on page 195, we need y_1' and y_2'. Applying the product rule, we get

$$y_1'(x) = -\frac{1}{2}\,x^{-3/2}\cos x - x^{-1/2}\sin x,$$

$$y_2'(x) = -\frac{1}{2}x^{-3/2}\sin x + x^{-1/2}\cos x.$$

Thus, functions $v_1(x)$ and $v_2(x)$ in a particular solution,

$$y_p(x) = v_1(x)y_1(x) + v_2(x)y_2(x),$$

satisfy the system

$$v_1'x^{-1/2}\cos x + v_2'x^{-1/2}\sin x = 0,$$
$$v_1'\left(-\frac{1}{2}x^{-3/2}\cos x - x^{-1/2}\sin x\right) + v_2'\left(-\frac{1}{2}x^{-3/2}\sin x + x^{-1/2}\cos x\right) = \frac{x^{5/2}}{x^2} = x^{1/2}.$$

From the first equation, we express $v_1' = -v_2'\tan x$ and substitute this expression into the second equation. After some algebra, the result simplifies to

$$v_2' = x\cos x \qquad \Rightarrow \qquad v_1' = -v_2'\tan x = -x\sin x.$$

Integrating, we get

$$v_1(x) = -\int x\sin x\,dx = x\cos x - \sin x + C_1,$$
$$v_2(x) = \int x\cos x\,dx = x\sin x + \cos x + C_2.$$

With $C_1 = C_2 = 0$,

$$y_p(x) = (x\cos x - \sin x)x^{-1/2}\cos x + (x\sin x + \cos x)x^{-1/2}\sin x = x^{1/2}.$$

Therefore, a general solution to the given nonhomogeneous Bessel equation is

$$y(t) = x^{1/2} + x^{-1/2}\left(c_1\cos x + c_2\sin x\right).$$

EXERCISES 4.7: Qualitative Considerations for Variable-Coefficient and Nonlinear Equations, page 208

1. Let $Y(t) := y(-t)$. Then, using the chain rule, we get

$$\frac{dY}{dt} = y'(-t)\frac{d(-t)}{dt} = -y'(-t),$$

$$\frac{d^2Y}{dt^2} = \frac{d[-y'(-t)]}{dt} = -y''(-t)\frac{d(-t)}{dt} = y''(-t).$$

Therefore, denoting $-t = s$, we obtain

$$Y''(t) + tY(t) = y''(-t) + ty(-t) = y''(s) - sy(s) = 0.$$

2. Comparing the given equation with (13) on page 202 in the text, we conclude that

$$\text{inertia } m = 1, \qquad \text{damping } b = 0, \qquad \text{stiffness "}k\text{"} = -6y.$$

For $y > 0$, the stiffness "k" is negative, and it tends to reinforce the displacement. So, we should expect that the solutions $y(t)$ grow without bound.

3. As in Problem 2, this equation describes the motion of the mass-spring system with unit mass, no damping, and stiffness "k" $= -6y$. The initial displacement $y(0) = -1$ is negative as well as the initial velocity $y'(0) = -1$. So, starting from $t = 0$, $y(t)$ will decrease for a while. This will result increasing positive stiffness, $-6y$, i.e., "the spring will become stiffer and stiffer". Eventually, the spring will become so strong that the mass will stop and then go in the positive direction. While $y(t)$ is negative, the positive stiffness will force the mass to approach zero displacement point, $y = 0$. Thereafter, with $y(t) > 0$, the stiffness becomes negative, which means that the spring itself will push the mass further away from $y = 0$ in the positive direction with force, which increases with y. Thus, the curve $y(t)$ will increase unboundedly. Figure 4.23 confirms our prediction.

5. **(a)** Comparing the equation $y'' = 2y^3$ with equation (7) in Lemma 3, we conclude that $f(y) = 2y^3$, and so

$$F(y) = \int 2y^3\,dy = \frac{1}{2}y^4 + C,$$

where C is a constant. We can choose any particular value for C, say, $C = 0$. Thus $F(y) = (1/2)y^4$. Next, with constant $K = 0$ and sign "$-$" in front of the integral, equation (11) on page 201, becomes

$$t = -\int \frac{dy}{\sqrt{2(1/2)y^4}} = -\int y^{-2}dy = y^{-1} + c,$$

or, equivalently,

$$y = \frac{1}{t - c},$$

where c is an arbitrary constant.

(b) A linear combination of $y_1(t) := 1/(t - c_1)$ and $y_2(t) := 1/(t - c_2)$,

$$C_1 y_1(t) + C_2 y_2(t) = \frac{C_1}{t - c_1} + \frac{C_2}{t - c_2} = \frac{(C_1 + C_2)t - (C_1 c_2 + C_2 c_1)}{(t - c_1)(t - c_2)},$$

is identically zero in a neighborhood of $t = 0$ if and only if $(C_1 + C_2)t - (C_1 c_2 + C_2 c_1) \equiv 0$. Thus the numerator must be the zero polynomial, i.e., C_1 and C_2 must satisfy

$$\begin{aligned} C_1 + C_2 &= 0, \\ C_1 c_2 + C_2 c_1 &= 0 \end{aligned} \quad \Rightarrow \quad \begin{aligned} C_2 &= -C_1, \\ C_1 (c_2 - c_1) &= 0. \end{aligned}$$

Since $c_1 \neq c_2$, the second equation implies that $C_1 = 0$, and then $C_2 = 0$ from the first equation. Thus, only the trivial linear combination of $y_1(t)$ and $y_2(t)$ vanishes identically around the origin, and so these functions are linearly independent.

(c) For any function of the form $y_c(t) := 1/(t - c)$, the equality

$$y_c'(t) = -\frac{1}{(t - c)^2} = -[y_c(t)]^2$$

holds for all $t \neq c$. In particular, at $t = 0$,

$$y_c'(0) = -[y_c(0)]^2.$$

(We assume that $c \neq 0$; otherwise, $t = 0$ is not in the domain.) Obviously, this equality fails for any positive initial velocity $y'(0)$, in particular, it is false for given data, $y(0) = 1$ and $y'(0) = 2$.

6. Rewriting given equation in the equivalent form $y'' = (-k/m)y$, we see that the function $f(y)$ in the energy integral lemma is $(-k/m)y$. So,

$$F(y) = \int \left(-\frac{k}{m} y \right) dy = -\frac{k}{2m} y^2 + C.$$

With $C=0$, $F(y)=-[k/(2m)]y^2$, and the energy

$$E(t)=\frac{1}{2}\left[y'(t)\right]^2-F[y(t)]=\frac{1}{2}\left[y'(t)\right]^2-\left(-\frac{k}{2m}\,y^2\right)=\frac{1}{2}\left[y'(t)\right]^2+\frac{k}{2m}\,y^2 .$$

By the energy integral lemma,

$$\frac{1}{2}\left[y'(t)\right]^2+\frac{k}{2m}\,y^2=\text{const.}$$

Multiplying both sides by $2m$, we get the stated equation.

7. **(a)** Since, for a point moving along a circle of radius ℓ, the magnitude v of its linear velocity $\vec{v}$ and the angular velocity $\omega=d\theta/dt$ are connected by $v=\omega\ell=(d\theta/dt)\ell$, and the vector $\vec{v}$ is tangent to the circle (and so, perpendicular to the radius), we have

$$\text{angular momentum}=\ell\cdot mv=\ell\cdot m\cdot\frac{d\theta}{dt}\,\ell=m\ell^2\,\frac{d\theta}{dt}\,.$$

(b) From Figure 4.18, we see that the component of the gravitational force, mg, which is perpendicular to the level arm, has the magnitude $|mg\sin\theta|$ and is directed towards decreasing θ. Thus,

$$\text{torque}=\ell\cdot(-mg\sin\theta)=-\ell mg\sin\theta.$$

(c) According to the Newton's law of rotational motion,

$$\text{torque}=\frac{d}{dt}\,(\text{angular momentum})\qquad\Rightarrow\qquad -\ell mg\sin\theta=\frac{d}{dt}\left(m\ell^2\,\frac{d\theta}{dt}\right)$$

$$\Rightarrow\qquad -\ell mg\sin\theta=m\ell^2\,\frac{d^2\theta}{dt^2}\qquad\Rightarrow\qquad \frac{d^2\theta}{dt^2}+\frac{g}{\ell}\,\sin\theta=0.$$

9. According to Problem 8, with $\ell=g$, the function $\theta(t)$ satisfies the identity

$$\frac{(\theta')^2}{2}-\cos\theta=C=\text{const.}\tag{4.9}$$

Our first purpose is to determine the constant C. Let t_{a} denote the moment when pendulum is in the apex point, i.e., $\theta(t_{\mathrm{a}})=\pi$. Since it doesn't cross the apex over, we also have $\theta'(t_{\mathrm{a}})=0$. Substituting these two values into (4.9), we obtain

$$\frac{0^2}{2}-\cos\pi=C\qquad\Rightarrow\qquad C=1.$$

Thus (4.9) becomes

$$\frac{(\theta')^2}{2} - \cos\theta = 1.$$

In particular, at the initial moment, $t = 0$,

$$\frac{[\theta'(0)]^2}{2} - \cos[\theta(0)] = 1.$$

Since $\theta(0) = 0$, we get

$$\frac{[\theta'(0)]^2}{2} - \cos 0 = 1 \quad \Rightarrow \quad [\theta'(0)]^2 = 4$$
$$\Rightarrow \quad \theta'(0) = 2 \quad \text{or} \quad \theta'(0) = -2.$$

11. The "damping coefficient" in the Rayleigh equation is $b = (y')^2 - 1$. Thus, for low velocities y', we have $b < 0$, and $b > 0$ for high velocities. Therefore, the low velocities are boosted, while high velocities are slowed, and so one should expect a limit cycle.

13. Qualitative features of solutions to Airy, Duffing, and van der Pol equations, are discussed after Example 3, in Examples 6 and 7, respectively. Comparing curves in Figure 4.26 with graphs depicted in Figures 4.13, 4.16, and 4.17, we conclude that the answers are

(a) Airy;

(b) Duffing;

(c) van der Pol.

15. **(a)** Yes, because the "stiffness" t^2 is positive and no damping.

(b) No, because of the negative "stiffness" $-t^2$.

(c) Writing $y'' + y^5 = y'' + (y^4)y$, we conclude that the mass-spring model, corresponding to this equation, has positive "stiffness" y^4 and no damping. Thus the answer is "yes".

(d) Here, the "stiffness" is y^5, which is negative for $y < 0$. So, "no".

(e) Yes, because the "stiffness" $4 + 2\cos t \geq 2 > 0$ and no damping.

(f) Since both the "damping" t and the stiffness 1 are positive, all solutions are bounded.

(g) No, because the "stiffness", -1, is negative.

17. For the radius, $r(t)$, we have the initial value problem

$$r''(t) = -GMr^{-2}, \qquad r(0) = a, \qquad r'(0) = 0.$$

Thus, in the energy integral lemma, $f(r) = -GMr^{-2}$. Since

$$\int f(r)dr = \int \left(-GMr^{-2}\right) dr = GMR^{-1} + C,$$

we can take $F(r) = GMR^{-1}$, and the energy integral lemma yields

$$\frac{1}{2}\left[r'(t)\right]^2 - \frac{GM}{r(t)} = C_1 = \text{const.}$$

To find the constant C_1, we use the initial conditions.

$$C_1 = \frac{1}{2}\left[r'(0)\right]^2 - \frac{GM}{r(0)} = \frac{1}{2}\cdot 0^2 - \frac{GM}{a} = -\frac{GM}{a}.$$

Therefore, $r(t)$ satisfies

$$\frac{1}{2}\left[r'(t)\right]^2 - \frac{GM}{r(t)} = -\frac{GM}{a} \quad\Rightarrow\quad \frac{1}{2}\left(r'\right)^2 = \frac{GM}{r} - \frac{GM}{a} \quad\Rightarrow\quad r' = -\sqrt{\frac{2GM}{a}}\sqrt{\frac{a-r}{r}}.$$

(Remember, $r(t)$ is decreasing, and so $r'(t) < 0$.) Separating variables and integrating, we get

$$\int \sqrt{\frac{r}{a-r}}\,dr = \int \left(-\sqrt{\frac{2GM}{a}}\right) dt \;\Rightarrow\; a\left(\arctan\sqrt{\frac{r}{a-r}} - \frac{\sqrt{r(a-r)}}{a}\right) = -\sqrt{\frac{2GM}{a}}\,t + C_2.$$

We apply the initial condition, $r(0) = a$, once again to find the constant C_2. But this time we have to be careful because the argument of "arctan" function becomes infinite at $r = a$. So, we take the limit of both sides rather than making simple substitution.

$$\lim_{t\to+0} a\left(\arctan\sqrt{\frac{r(t)}{a-r(t)}} - \frac{\sqrt{r(t)[a-r(t)]}}{a}\right)$$

$$= a\left(\lim_{t\to+0}\arctan\sqrt{\frac{r(t)}{a-r(t)}} - \lim_{t\to+0}\frac{\sqrt{r(t)[a-r(t)]}}{a}\right) = a\left(\frac{\pi}{2} - 0\right) = a\frac{\pi}{2},$$

and, in the right-hand side,

$$\lim_{t\to+0}\left(-\sqrt{\frac{2GM}{a}}\,t+C_2\right)=-\sqrt{\frac{2GM}{a}}\cdot 0+C_2=C_2.$$

Thus $C_2=a\pi/2$ and $r(t)$ satisfies

$$a\left(\arctan\sqrt{\frac{r(t)}{a-r(t)}}-\frac{\sqrt{r(t)[a-r(t)]}}{a}\right)=-\sqrt{\frac{2GM}{a}}\,t+\frac{a\pi}{2}\,.$$

At the moment $t=T_0$, when Earth splashes into the sun, we have $r(T_0)=0$. Substituting this condition into the last equation yields

$$\begin{aligned}
&a\left(\arctan\sqrt{\frac{0}{a-0}}-\frac{\sqrt{0(a-0)}}{a}\right)=-\sqrt{\frac{2GM}{a}}\,T_0+\frac{a\pi}{2}\\
\Rightarrow\quad & 0=-\sqrt{\frac{2GM}{a}}\,T_0+\frac{a\pi}{2}\\
\Rightarrow\quad & T_0=\frac{a\pi}{2}\sqrt{\frac{a}{2GM}}=\frac{\pi}{2\sqrt{2}}\sqrt{\frac{a^3}{GM}}\,.
\end{aligned}$$

Then the required ratio is

$$\frac{T_0}{T}=\frac{\pi}{2\sqrt{2}}\sqrt{\frac{a^3}{GM}}\Bigg/2\pi\sqrt{\frac{a^3}{GM}}=\frac{1}{4\sqrt{2}}\,.$$

EXERCISES 4.8: A Closer Look at Free Mechanical Vibrations, page 219

1. In this problem, we have undamped free vibration case governed by equation (2) on page 210 in the text. With $m=3$ and $k=48$, the equation becomes

$$3y''+48y=0 \tag{4.10}$$

with the initial conditions $y(0)=-0.5$, $y'(0)=2$.

The angular velocity of the motion is

$$\omega=\sqrt{\frac{k}{m}}=\sqrt{\frac{48}{3}}=4\,.$$

It follows that

$$\text{period} = \frac{2\pi}{\omega} = \frac{2\pi}{4} = \frac{\pi}{2},$$
$$\text{natural frequency} = \frac{\omega}{2\pi} = \frac{2}{\pi}.$$

A general solution to (4.10), given in (4) on page 211 in the text, becomes

$$y(t) = C_1 \cos \omega t + C_2 \sin \omega t = C_1 \cos 4t + C_2 \sin 4t.$$

We find C_1 and C_2 from the initial conditions.

$$\begin{aligned} y(0) &= (C_1 \cos 4t + C_2 \sin 4t)\Big|_{t=0} = C_1 = -1/2, \\ y'(0) &= (-4C_1 \sin 4t + 4C_2 \cos 4t)\Big|_{t=0} = 4C_2 = 2 \end{aligned} \qquad \Rightarrow \qquad \begin{aligned} C_1 &= -1/2, \\ C_2 &= 1/2. \end{aligned}$$

Thus, the solution to the initial value problem is

$$y(t) = -\frac{1}{2}\cos 4t + \frac{1}{2}\sin 4t = \frac{\sqrt{2}}{2}\sin\left(4t - \frac{\pi}{4}\right),$$

where we have used formulas (6) rewriting the solution in form (5), page 211 in the text. The amplitude of the motion therefore is $\sqrt{2}/2$.

Setting $y = 0$ in the above solution, we find values of t when the mass passes through the point of equilibrium.

$$\frac{\sqrt{2}}{2}\sin\left(4t - \frac{\pi}{4}\right) = 0 \qquad \Rightarrow \qquad 4t - \frac{\pi}{4} = n\pi, \quad n = 0, 1, \ldots.$$

(Time t is nonnegative.) The first moment when this happens, i.e., the smallest value of t, corresponds to $n = 0$. So,

$$4t - \frac{\pi}{4} = 0 \qquad \Rightarrow \qquad t = \frac{\pi}{16}.$$

3. The characteristic equation in this problem, $r^2 + br + 16 = 0$, has the roots

$$r = \frac{-b \pm \sqrt{b^2 - 64}}{2}. \tag{4.11}$$

Substituting given particular values of b into (4.11), we find roots of the characteristic equation and solutions to the initial value problems in each case.

$b = 0$.

$$r = \frac{\pm\sqrt{-64}}{2} = \pm 4i.$$

A general solution has the form $y = C_1 \cos 4t + C_2 \sin 4t$. Constants C_1 and C_2 can be found from the initial conditions.

$$\begin{aligned} y(0) &= (C_1 \cos 4t + C_2 \sin 4t)\,\big|_{t=0} = C_1 = 1\,, \\ y'(0) &= (-4C_1 \sin 4t + 4C_2 \cos 4t)\,\big|_{t=0} = 4C_2 = 0 \end{aligned} \qquad \Rightarrow \qquad \begin{aligned} C_1 &= 1, \\ C_2 &= 0 \end{aligned}$$

and so $y(t) = \cos 4t$.

$b = 6$.

$$r = \frac{-6 \pm \sqrt{36-64}}{2} = -3 \pm \sqrt{7}i.$$

A general solution has the form $y = (C_1 \cos\sqrt{7}t + C_2 \sin\sqrt{7}t)e^{-3t}$. For constants C_1 and C_2, we have the system

$$\begin{aligned} y(0) &= \left(C_1 \cos\sqrt{7}t + C_2 \sin\sqrt{7}t\right) e^{-3t}\,\big|_{t=0} = C_1 = 1\,, \\ y'(0) &= \left[(\sqrt{7}C_2 - 3C_1)\cos\sqrt{7}t - (\sqrt{7}C_1 + 3C_2)\sin\sqrt{7}t\right] e^{-3t}\,\big|_{t=0} = \sqrt{7}C_2 - 3C_1 = 0 \end{aligned}$$

$$\Rightarrow \qquad \begin{aligned} C_1 &= 1, \\ C_2 &= 3/\sqrt{7}\,, \end{aligned}$$

and so

$$y(t) = \left[\cos\sqrt{7}t + \frac{3}{\sqrt{7}}\sin\sqrt{7}t\right] e^{-3t} = \frac{4}{\sqrt{7}} e^{-3t} \sin\left(\sqrt{7}t + \phi\right),$$

where $\phi = \arctan(\sqrt{7}/3) \approx 0.723$.

$b = 8$.

$$r = \frac{-8 \pm \sqrt{64-64}}{2} = -4.$$

Thus, $r = -4$ is a double root of the characteristic equation. So, a general solution has the form $y = (C_1 t + C_0)e^{-4t}$. For constants C_1 and C_2, we obtain the system

$$\begin{aligned} y(0) &= (C_1 t + C_0)\, e^{-4t}\,\big|_{t=0} = C_0 = 1\,, \\ y'(0) &= (-4C_1 t - 4C_0 + C_1)\, e^{-4t}\,\big|_{t=0} = C_1 - 4C_0 = 0 \end{aligned} \qquad \Rightarrow \qquad \begin{aligned} C_0 &= 1, \\ C_1 &= 4, \end{aligned}$$

and so $y(t) = (4t + 1)e^{-4t}$.

$b = 10$.

$$r = \frac{-10 \pm \sqrt{100-64}}{2} = -5 \pm 3.$$

Thus, $r = -2,\ -8$, and a general solution is given by $y = C_1e^{-2t} + C_2e^{-8t}$. Initial conditions yield

$$\begin{aligned} y(0) &= \left(C_1e^{-2t} + C_2e^{-8t}\right)\Big|_{t=0} = C_1 + C_2 = 1\,, \\ y'(0) &= \left(-2C_1e^{-2t} - 8C_2e^{-8t}\right)\Big|_{t=0} = -2C_1 - 8C_2 = 0 \end{aligned} \quad \Rightarrow \quad \begin{aligned} C_1 &= 4/3, \\ C_2 &= -1/3, \end{aligned}$$

and, therefore, $y(t) = (4/3)e^{-2t} - (1/3)e^{-8t}$ is the solution to the initial value problem.

The graphs of the solutions are depicted in Figures B.19–B.22 in the answers in the text.

5. The auxiliary equation associated with given differential equation is $r^2 + 10r + k = 0$, and its roots are $r = -5 \pm \sqrt{25-k}$.

$k = 20$. In this case, $r = -5 \pm \sqrt{25-20} = -5 \pm \sqrt{5}$. Thus, a general solution is given by $y = C_1e^{(-5+\sqrt{5})t} + C_2e^{(-5-\sqrt{5})t}$. The initial conditions yield

$$\begin{aligned} y(0) &= \left[C_1e^{(-5+\sqrt{5})t} + C_2e^{(-5-\sqrt{5})t}\right]\Big|_{t=0} = C_1 + C_2 = 1\,, \\ y'(0) &= \left[(-5+\sqrt{5})C_1e^{(-5+\sqrt{5})t} + (-5-\sqrt{5})C_2e^{(-5-\sqrt{5})t}\right]\Big|_{t=0} \\ &= (-5+\sqrt{5})C_1 + (-5-\sqrt{5})C_2 = 0 \end{aligned}$$

$$\Rightarrow \quad \begin{aligned} C_1 &= \left(1+\sqrt{5}\right)/2, \\ C_2 &= \left(1-\sqrt{5}\right)/2, \end{aligned}$$

and, therefore, $y(t) = [\left(1+\sqrt{5}\right)/2]e^{(-5+\sqrt{5})t} + [\left(1-\sqrt{5}\right)/2]e^{(-5-\sqrt{5})t}$ is the solution to the initial value problem.

$k = 25$. Then $r = -5 \pm \sqrt{25-25} = -5$. Thus, $r = -5$ is a double root of the characteristic equation. So, a general solution has the form $y = (C_1t + C_0)e^{-5t}$. For constants C_1 and C_2, using the initial conditions, we obtain the system

$$\begin{aligned} y(0) &= \left(C_1t + C_0\right)e^{-5t}\Big|_{t=0} = C_0 = 1\,, \\ y'(0) &= \left(-5C_1t - 5C_0 + C_1\right)e^{-5t}\Big|_{t=0} = C_1 - 5C_0 = 0 \end{aligned} \quad \Rightarrow \quad \begin{aligned} C_0 &= 1, \\ C_1 &= 5, \end{aligned}$$

and so $y(t) = (5t+1)e^{-5t}$.

$k = 30$. In this case, $r = -5 \pm \sqrt{25-30} = -5 \pm \sqrt{5}i$. A general solution has the form $y = (C_1 \cos\sqrt{5}t + C_2 \sin\sqrt{5}t)e^{-5t}$. For constants C_1 and C_2, we have the system

$$\begin{aligned} y(0) &= \left(C_1 \cos\sqrt{5}t + C_2 \sin\sqrt{5}t\right) e^{-5t} \Big|_{t=0} = C_1 = 1\,, \\ y'(0) &= \left[(\sqrt{5}C_2 - 5C_1)\cos\sqrt{5}t - (\sqrt{5}C_1 + 5C_2)\sin\sqrt{5}t\right] e^{-5t} \Big|_{t=0} = \sqrt{5}C_2 - 5C_1 = 0 \end{aligned}$$

$$\Rightarrow \quad \begin{aligned} C_1 &= 1, \\ C_2 &= \sqrt{5}, \end{aligned}$$

and so

$$y(t) = \left[\cos\sqrt{5}t + \sqrt{5}\sin\sqrt{5}t\right] e^{-5t} = \sqrt{6}e^{-5t}\sin\left(\sqrt{5}t + \phi\right),$$

where $\phi = \arctan(1/\sqrt{5}) \approx 0.421$.

Graphs of the solutions for $k = 20$, 25, and 30 are shown in Figures B.23–B.25 in the answers in the text.

7. The motion of this mass-spring system is governed by equation (12) on page 213 in the text. With $m = 1/8$, $b = 2$, and $k = 16$ this equation becomes

$$\frac{1}{8}y'' + 2y' + 16y = 0, \tag{4.12}$$

and the initial conditions are $y(0) = -3/4$, $y'(0) = -2$. Since

$$b^2 - 4mk = 4 - 4(1/8)16 = -4 < 0,$$

we have a case of underdamped motion. A general solution to (4.12) is given in (16), that is, with $\alpha = -b/(2m) = -8$ and $\beta = (1/2m)\sqrt{4mk - b^2} = 8$, we have

$$y = (C_1 \cos 8t + C_2 \sin 8t)\, e^{-8t}.$$

Using the initial conditions, we find the constants C_1 and C_2.

$$\begin{aligned} y(0) &= (C_1 \cos 8t + C_2 \sin 8t)\, e^{-8t} \Big|_{t=0} = C_1 = -3/4\,, \\ y'(0) &= 8\left[(C_2 - C_1)\cos 8t - (C_2 + C_1)\sin 8t\right] e^{-8t} \Big|_{t=0} = 8\,(C_2 - C_1) = -2 \end{aligned}$$

$$\Rightarrow \quad \begin{aligned} C_1 &= -3/4, \\ C_2 &= -1, \end{aligned}$$

and so

$$y(t) = \left[-\frac{3}{4}\cos 8t - \sin 8t\right] e^{-8t} = \frac{5}{4} e^{-8t} \sin(8t + \phi),$$

where $\tan\phi = (-3/4)/(-1) = 3/4$ and $\cos\phi = -1 < 0$. Thus,

$$\phi = \pi + \arctan(3/4) \approx 3.785 .$$

The damping factor is $(5/4)e^{-8t}$, the quasiperiod is $P = 2\pi/8 = \pi/4$, and the quasifrequency is $1/P = 4/\pi$.

9. Substituting the values $m = 2$, $k = 40$, and $b = 8\sqrt{5}$ into equation (12) on page 213 in the text and using the initial conditions, we obtain the initial value problem

$$2\frac{d^2y}{dt^2} + 8\sqrt{5}\frac{dy}{dt} + 40y = 0, \qquad y(0) = 0.1 \text{ (m)}, \quad y'(0) = 2 \text{ (m/sec)}.$$

The initial conditions are positive to reflect the fact that we have taken down to be positive in our coordinate system. The auxiliary equation for this system is

$$2r^2 + 8\sqrt{5}r + 40 = 0 \qquad \text{or} \qquad r^2 + 4\sqrt{5}r + 20 = 0.$$

This equation has a double root at $r = -2\sqrt{5}$. Therefore, this system is critically damped and the equation of motion has the form

$$y(t) = (C_1 + C_2 t)\, e^{-2\sqrt{5}t} .$$

To find the constants C_1 and C_2, we use the initial conditions $y(0) = 0.1$ and $y'(0) = 2$. Thus, we have

$$\begin{aligned} &y(0) = 0.1 = C_1 , \\ &y'(0) = 2 = C_2 - 2\sqrt{5}C_1 \qquad \Rightarrow \qquad C_2 = 2 + 0.2\sqrt{5} . \end{aligned}$$

From this we obtain

$$y(t) = \left[0.1 + \left(2 + 0.2\sqrt{5}\right) t\right] e^{-2\sqrt{5}t} .$$

The maximum displacement of the mass is found by determining the first time the velocity of the mass becomes zero. Therefore, we have

$$y'(t)=0=\left(2+0.2\sqrt{5}\right)e^{-2\sqrt{5}t}-2\sqrt{5}\left[0.1+\left(2+0.2\sqrt{5}\right)t\right]e^{-2\sqrt{5}t},$$

which gives

$$t=\frac{2}{2\sqrt{5}(2+0.2\sqrt{5})}=\frac{1}{\sqrt{5}(2+0.2\sqrt{5})}.$$

Thus the maximum displacement is

$$y\left[\frac{1}{\sqrt{5}(2+0.2\sqrt{5})}\right]=\left[0.1+\left(2+0.2\sqrt{5}\right)\left(\frac{1}{\sqrt{5}(2+0.2\sqrt{5})}\right)\right]e^{-2\sqrt{5}/[\sqrt{5}(2+0.2\sqrt{5})]}\approx 0.242\,(\mathrm{m}).$$

11. The equation of the motion of this mass-spring system is

$$y''+0.2y'+100y=0,\qquad y(0)=0,\quad y'(0)=1.$$

Clearly, this is an underdamped motion because

$$b^2-4mk=(0.2)^2-4(1)(100)=-399.96<0.$$

So, we use use equation (16) on page 213 in the text for a general solution. With

$$\alpha=-\frac{b}{2m}=-\frac{0.2}{2}=-0.1\quad\text{and}\quad\beta=\frac{1}{2m}\sqrt{4mk-b^2}=\frac{1}{2}\sqrt{399.96}=\sqrt{99.99},$$

equation (16) becomes

$$y(t)=\left(C_1\cos\sqrt{99.99}t+C_2\sin\sqrt{99.99}t\right)e^{-0.1t}.$$

From the initial condiions,

$$\begin{aligned}y(0)&=\left(C_1\cos\sqrt{99.99}t+C_2\sin\sqrt{99.99}t\right)e^{-0.1t}\Big|_{t=0}=C_1=0,\\ y'(0)&=\left[\left(\sqrt{99.99}C_2-0.1C_1\right)\cos\sqrt{99.99}t-\left(0.1C_2+\sqrt{99.99}C_1\right)\sin\sqrt{99.99}t\right]e^{-0.1t}\Big|_{t=0}\\&=\sqrt{99.99}C_2-0.1C_1=1\end{aligned}$$

$$\Rightarrow\quad\begin{aligned}C_1&=0,\\ C_2&=1/\sqrt{99.99}.\end{aligned}$$

Therefore, the equation of motion is given by

$$y(t)=\frac{1}{\sqrt{99.99}}\,e^{-0.1t}\sin\sqrt{99.99}t\,.$$

The maximum displacement to the right occurs at the first point of local maximum of $y(t)$. The critical points of $y(t)$ are solutions to

$$\begin{aligned} y'(t) &= \frac{e^{-0.1t}}{\sqrt{99.99}}\left(\sqrt{99.99}\cos\sqrt{99.99}t-0.1\sin\sqrt{99.99}t\right)=0\\ \Rightarrow\quad & \sqrt{99.99}\cos\sqrt{99.99}t-0.1\sin\sqrt{99.99}t=0\\ \Rightarrow\quad & \tan\sqrt{99.99}t=10\sqrt{99.99}=\sqrt{9999}\,. \end{aligned}$$

Solving for t, we conclude that the first point of local maximum is at

$$t=(1/\sqrt{99.99})\arctan\sqrt{9999}\approx 0.156\,\text{sec}.$$

13. In Example 3, the solution was found to be

$$y(t)=\sqrt{\frac{7}{12}}\,e^{-2t}\sin\left(2\sqrt{3}t+\phi\right), \tag{4.13}$$

where $\phi=\pi+\arctan(\sqrt{3}/2)$. Therefore, we have

$$y'(t)=-\sqrt{\frac{7}{3}}\,e^{-2t}\sin\left(2\sqrt{3}t+\phi\right)+\sqrt{7}\,e^{-2t}\cos\left(2\sqrt{3}t+\phi\right).$$

Thus, to find the relative extrema for $y(t)$, we set

$$\begin{aligned} y'(t) &= -\sqrt{\frac{7}{3}}\,e^{-2t}\sin\left(2\sqrt{3}t+\phi\right)+\sqrt{7}\,e^{-2t}\cos\left(2\sqrt{3}t+\phi\right)=0\\ \Rightarrow\quad & \frac{\sin\left(2\sqrt{3}t+\phi\right)}{\cos\left(2\sqrt{3}t+\phi\right)}=\frac{\sqrt{7}}{\sqrt{7/3}}=\sqrt{3}\\ \Rightarrow\quad & \tan\left(2\sqrt{3}t+\phi\right)=\sqrt{3}\,. \end{aligned}$$

Since $\tan\theta=\sqrt{3}$ when $\theta=(\pi/3)+n\pi$, where n is an integer, we see that the relative extrema will occur at the points t_n, where

$$2\sqrt{3}t_n+\phi=\frac{\pi}{3}+n\pi \qquad\Rightarrow\qquad t_n=\frac{(\pi/3)+n\pi-\phi}{2\sqrt{3}}\,.$$

By substituting $\pi + \arctan\left(\sqrt{3}/2\right)$ for ϕ in the last equation above and by requiring that t be greater than zero, we obtain

$$t_n = \frac{(\pi/3) + (n-1)\pi - \arctan\left(\sqrt{3}/2\right)}{2\sqrt{3}}, \qquad n = 1, 2, 3, \ldots.$$

We see that the solution curve given by equation (4.13) above will touch the exponential curves $y(t) = \pm\left(\sqrt{7/12}\right)e^{-2t}$ when we have

$$\sqrt{\frac{7}{12}}\, e^{-2t} \sin\left(2\sqrt{3}t + \phi\right) = \pm\sqrt{\frac{7}{12}}\, e^{-2t},$$

where $\phi = \pi + \arctan\left(\sqrt{3}/2\right)$. This will occur when $\sin\left(2\sqrt{3}t + \phi\right) = \pm 1$. Since $\sin\theta = \pm 1$ when $\theta = (\pi/2) + m\pi$ for any integer m, we see that the times T_m, when the solution touches the exponential curves, satisfy

$$2\sqrt{3}T_m + \phi = \frac{\pi}{2} + m\pi \qquad \Rightarrow \qquad T_m = \frac{(\pi/2) + m\pi - \phi}{2\sqrt{3}},$$

where $\phi = \pi + \arctan\left(\sqrt{3}/2\right)$ and m is an integer. Again requiring that t be positive we see that $y(t)$ touches the exponential curve when

$$T_m = \frac{(\pi/2) + (m-1)\pi - \arctan\left(\sqrt{3}/2\right)}{2\sqrt{3}}, \qquad m = 1, 2, 3, \ldots.$$

From these facts it follows that, for $y(t)$ to be an extremum and, at the same time, touch the curves $y(t) = \pm\sqrt{7/12}e^{-2t}$, there must be integers m and n such that

$$\begin{aligned} \frac{(\pi/3) + n\pi - \arctan\left(\sqrt{3}/2\right)}{2\sqrt{3}} &= \frac{(\pi/2) + m\pi - \arctan\left(\sqrt{3}/2\right)}{2\sqrt{3}} \\ \Rightarrow \qquad \frac{\pi}{3} + n\pi &= \frac{\pi}{2} + m\pi \\ \Rightarrow \qquad n - m &= \frac{1}{2} - \frac{1}{3} = \frac{1}{6}. \end{aligned}$$

But, since m and n are integers, their difference is an integer and never $1/6$. Thus, the extrema of $y(t)$ do not occur on the exponential curves.

15. Since the exponential function is never zero, from the equation of motion (16) on page 213 in the text we conclude that the mass passes the equilibrium position, that is, $y(t) = 0$, if and only if

$$\sin(\omega t + \phi) = 0.$$

Therefore, the time between two successive crossings of the equilibrium position is π/ω, which is a half of the quasiperiod P. So, we can find the quasiperiod P by multiplying the time between two successive crossings of the equilibrium position by two. Whenever P is computed, we can measure the displacement $y(t)$ at any moment t (with $y(t) \neq 0$) and then at the moment $t + P$. Taking the quotient

$$\frac{y(t+P)}{y(t)} = \frac{Ae^{-(b/2m)(t+P)}\sin[\omega(t+P)+\phi]}{Ae^{-(b/2m)t}\sin(\omega t+\phi)} = e^{-(b/2m)P},$$

we can calculate the damping coefficient b as

$$b = -\frac{2m\ln[y(t+P)/y(t)]}{P}.$$

EXERCISES 4.9: A Closer Look at Forced Mechanical Vibrations, page 227

1. The frequency response curve (13) on page 223, with $m = 4$, $k = 1$, and $b = 2$, becomes

$$M(\gamma) = \frac{1}{\sqrt{(k - m\gamma^2)^2 + b^2\gamma^2}} = \frac{1}{\sqrt{(1 - 4\gamma^2)^2 + 4\gamma^2}}.$$

The graph of this function is shown in Figure B.26 in the answers in the text.

3. The auxiliary equation in this problem is $r^2 + 9 = 0$, which has roots $r = \pm 3i$. Thus, a general solution to the corresponding homogeneous equation has the form

$$y_h(t) = C_1\cos 3t + C_2\sin 3t.$$

We look for a particular solution to the original nonhomogeneous equation of the form

$$y_p(t) = t^s(A\cos 3t + B\sin 3t),$$

where we take $s = 1$ because $r = 3i$ is a simple root of the auxiliary equation. Computing the derivatives

$$y'(t) = A\cos 3t + B\sin 3t + t(-3A\sin 3t + 3B\cos 3t),$$
$$y''(t) = 6B\cos 3t - 6A\sin 3t + t(-9A\cos 3t - 9B\sin 3t),$$

and substituting $y(t)$ and $y''(t)$ into the original equation, we get

$$6B\cos 3t - 6A\sin 3t + t(-9A\cos 3t - 9B\sin 3t) + 9t(A\cos 3t + B\sin 3t) = 2\cos 3t$$

$$\Rightarrow \qquad 6B\cos 3t - 6A\sin 3t = 2\cos 3t \qquad \Rightarrow \qquad \begin{array}{l} A = 0, \\ B = 1/3. \end{array}$$

So, $y_p(t) = (1/3)t\sin 3t$, and $y(t) = C_1\cos 3t + C_2\sin 3t + (1/3)t\sin 3t$ is a general solution. To satisfy the initial conditions, we solve

$$\begin{array}{l} y(0) = C_1 = 1, \\ y'(0) = 3C_2 = 0 \end{array} \qquad \Rightarrow \qquad \begin{array}{l} C_1 = 1, \\ C_2 = 0. \end{array}$$

So, the solution to the given initial value problem is

$$y(t) = \cos 3t + \frac{1}{3}t\sin 3t\,.$$

The graph of $y(t)$ is depicted in Figure B.27 in the answers section in the text.

5. **(a)** The corresponding homogeneous equation, $my'' + ky = 0$, is the equation of a simple harmonic motion, and so its general solution is given by

$$y_h(t) = C_1\cos\omega t + C_2\sin\omega t, \qquad \omega = \sqrt{k/m}\,.$$

Since $\gamma \neq \omega$, we look for a particular solution of the form

$$\begin{aligned} & y_p(t) = A\cos\gamma t + B\sin\gamma t \\ \Rightarrow \qquad & y_p'(t) = -A\gamma\sin\gamma t + B\gamma\cos\gamma t \\ \Rightarrow \qquad & y_p''(t) = -A\gamma^2\cos\gamma t - B\gamma^2\sin\gamma t. \end{aligned}$$

Substitution into the original equation yields

$$m\left(-A\gamma^2\cos\gamma t - B\gamma^2\sin\gamma t\right) + k\left(A\cos\gamma t + B\sin\gamma t\right) = F_0\cos\gamma t$$

$$\Rightarrow \qquad A\left(-m\gamma^2 + k\right)\cos\gamma t + B\left(-m\gamma^2 + k\right)\sin\gamma t = F_0\cos\gamma t$$

$$\Rightarrow \qquad \begin{array}{l} A = F_0/\left(k - m\gamma^2\right), \\ B = 0 \end{array} \qquad \Rightarrow \qquad y_p(t) = \frac{F_0}{k - m\gamma^2}\cos\gamma t.$$

Therefore, a general solution to the original equation is

$$y(t) = C_1\cos\omega t + C_2\sin\omega t + \frac{F_0}{k - m\gamma^2}\cos\gamma t\,.$$

With the initial conditions, $y(0) = y'(0) = 0$, we get

$$\begin{array}{l} y(0) = C_1 + F_0/\left(k - m\gamma^2\right) = 0, \\ y'(0) = \omega C_2 = 0 \end{array} \qquad \Rightarrow \qquad \begin{array}{l} C_1 = -F_0/\left(k - m\gamma^2\right), \\ C_2 = 0. \end{array}$$

Therefore,

$$y(t) = -\frac{F_0}{k - m\gamma^2}\cos\omega t + \frac{F_0}{k - m\gamma^2}\cos\gamma t\,,$$

which can also be written in the form

$$y(t) = \frac{F_0}{k - m\gamma^2}\left(\cos\gamma t - \cos\omega t\right) = \frac{F_0}{m(\omega^2 - \gamma^2)}\left(\cos\gamma t - \cos\omega t\right)\,.$$

(b) Here one can apply the "difference-to-product" identity

$$\cos A - \cos B = 2\sin\left(\frac{B + A}{2}\right)\sin\left(\frac{B - A}{2}\right)$$

with $A = \gamma t$ and $B = \omega t$ to get

$$y(t) = \frac{2F_0}{m(\omega^2 - \gamma^2)}\sin\left(\frac{\omega + \gamma}{2}t\right)\sin\left(\frac{\omega - \gamma}{2}t\right).$$

(c) For $F_0 = 32$, $m = 2$, $\omega = 9$, and $\gamma = 7$, the solution in part (b) becomes

$$y(t) = \frac{2(32)}{2(9^2 - 7^2)}\sin\left(\frac{9 + 7}{2}t\right)\sin\left(\frac{9 - 7}{2}t\right) = \sin 8t\sin t\,.$$

The graph of this function is shown in Figure B.28.

7. The auxiliary equation to equation (1) on page 220 in the text, $mr^2 + br + k = 0$, has roots

$$r = \frac{-b \pm \sqrt{b^2 - 4mk}}{2m},$$

which are both real ($b^2 > 4mk$) and negative because $\sqrt{b^2 - 4mk} < b$. Let

$$r_1 := \frac{-b - \sqrt{b^2 - 4mk}}{2m},$$
$$r_2 := \frac{-b + \sqrt{b^2 - 4mk}}{2m}.$$

Then a general solution to the homogeneous equation corresponding to (1) has the form

$$y_h(t) = c_1 e^{r_1 t} + c_2 e^{r_2 t}.$$

A particular solution to (1) is still given by (7) on page 221 in the text. Thus,

$$y(t) = c_1 e^{r_1 t} + c_2 e^{r_2 t} + \frac{F_0}{\sqrt{(k - m\gamma^2)^2 + b^2\gamma^2}} \sin(\gamma t + \theta),$$

$\tan\theta = (k - m\gamma^2)/(b\gamma)$, is a general solution to the forced overdamped equation.

9. If a mass of $m = 8\,\text{kg}$ stretches the spring by $\ell = 1.96\,\text{m}$, then the spring stiffness must be

$$k = \frac{mg}{\ell} = \frac{8 \cdot 9.8}{1.96} = 40\ (\text{N/m}).$$

Substitution $m = 8$, $b = 3$, $k = 40$, and the external force $F(t) = \cos 2t$ into the equation (23) on page 226 in the text yields

$$8y'' + 3y' + 40y = \cos 2t.$$

The steady-state (a particular) solution to this equation is given in (6) and (7), page 221, that is,

$$\begin{aligned} y_p(t) &= \frac{F_0}{(k - m\gamma^2)^2 + b^2\gamma^2}\left\{\left(k - m\gamma^2\right)\cos\gamma t + b\gamma\sin\gamma t\right\} \\ &= \frac{1}{[40 - (8)(2)^2]^2 + (3)^2(2)^2}\left\{\left(40 - 8(2)^2\right)\cos 2t + (3)(2)\sin 2t\right\} \\ &= \frac{1}{100}\{8\cos 2t + 6\sin 2t\} = \frac{1}{10}\sin(2t + \theta), \end{aligned}$$

where $\theta = \arctan(8/6) \approx 0.927$.

11. First, we find the mass

$$m = \frac{8\,\text{lb}}{32\,\text{ft/sec}^2} = \frac{1}{4}\,\text{slug.}$$

Thus the equation (23), describing the motion, with $m = 1/4$, $b = 1$, $k = 10$, and the external force $F(t) = 2\cos 2t$ becomes

$$\frac{1}{4}y'' + y' + 10y = 2\cos 2t, \tag{4.14}$$

with the initial conditions are $y(0) = y'(0) = 0$. A general solution to the corresponding homogeneous equation is given in Section 4.8, formula (16). That is,

$$y_h(t) = e^{\alpha t}\left(C_1\cos\beta t + C_2\sin\beta t\right).$$

We compute

$$\alpha = -\frac{b}{2m} = -\frac{1}{2(1/4)} = -2 \quad \text{and} \quad \beta = \frac{1}{2(1/4)}\sqrt{4(1/4)(10) - 1^2} = 6.$$

So,

$$y_h(t) = e^{-2t}\left(C_1\cos 6t + C_2\sin 6t\right).$$

For a particular solution, we use formula (7), page 221 in the text.

$$\begin{aligned} y_p(t) &= \frac{F_0}{\sqrt{(k - m\gamma^2)^2 + b^2\gamma^2}}\sin(\gamma t + \theta) \\ &= \frac{2}{\sqrt{\left[10 - (1/4)(2)^2\right]^2 + (1)^2(2)^2}}\sin(2t + \theta) = \frac{2}{\sqrt{85}}\sin(2t + \theta), \end{aligned}$$

where $\theta = \arctan[(k - m\gamma^2)/(b\gamma)] = \arctan(9/2) \approx 1.352$. A general solution to (4.14) is then given by

$$y(t) = e^{-2t}\left(C_1\cos 6t + C_2\sin 6t\right) + \frac{2}{\sqrt{85}}\sin(2t + \theta).$$

From the initial conditions, we find

$$\begin{aligned} y(0) &= C_1 + (2/\sqrt{85})\sin\theta = 0, \\ y'(0) &= -2C_1 + 6C_2 + (4/\sqrt{85})\cos\theta = 0 \end{aligned}$$

$$\Rightarrow \quad \begin{aligned} C_1 &= -(2/\sqrt{85})\sin\theta = -18/85, \\ C_2 &= \left[C_1 - (2/\sqrt{85})\cos\theta\right]/3 = -22/255. \end{aligned}$$

$$\Rightarrow \qquad y(t) = e^{-2t}\left[-\frac{18}{85}\cos 6t - \frac{22}{255}\sin 6t\right] + \frac{2}{\sqrt{85}}\sin(2t+\theta)\,.$$

The resonance frequency for the system is

$$\frac{\gamma_r}{2\pi} = \frac{\sqrt{(k/m)-(b^2)/(2m^2)}}{2\pi} = \frac{\sqrt{40-8}}{2\pi} = \frac{2\sqrt{2}}{\pi}\,,$$

where we have used formula (15) on page 223 in the text for γ_r.

13. The mass attached to the spring is

$$m = \frac{32\text{ lb}}{32\text{ ft/sec}^2} = 1\text{ slug}.$$

Thus the equation governing the motion, $my'' + by' + ky = F_{\text{ext}}$, with $m = 1$, $b = 2$, $k = 5$, and $F_{\text{ext}}(t) = 3\cos 4t$ becomes

$$y'' + 2y' + 5y = 3\cos 4t.$$

This is an underdamped motion because $b^2 - 4mk = (2)^2 - 4(1)(5) = -16 < 0$. For the steady-state solution of this equation we use formula (6) on page 221 in the text. Since $F_{\text{ext}}(t) = 3\cos 4t$, we have $F_0 = 3$, and $\gamma = 4$. Substituting m, b, k, F_0, and γ into (6), we obtain

$$\begin{aligned} y_p(t) &= \frac{3}{[5-(1)(4)^2]^2 + (2)^2(4)^2}\left\{[5-(1)(4)^2]\cos 4t + (2)(4)\sin 4t\right\} \\ &= \frac{3}{185}\,(8\sin 4t - 11\cos 4t)\,. \end{aligned}$$

REVIEW PROBLEMS: page 228

1. Solving the auxiliary equation, $r^2 + 8r - 9 = 0$, we find $r_1 = -9$, $r_2 = 1$. Thus a general solution is given by

$$y(t) = c_1 e^{r_1 t} + c_2 e^{r_2 t} = c_1 e^{-9t} + c_2 e^{t}\,.$$

3. The auxiliary equation, $4r^2 - 4r + 10 = 0$, has roots $r_{1,2} = (1 \pm 3i)/2$. Therefore a general solution is

$$y(t) = \left[c_1\cos\left(\frac{3t}{2}\right) + c_2\sin\left(\frac{3t}{2}\right)\right]e^{t/2}\,.$$

5. The roots of the auxiliary equation, $6r^2 - 11r + 3 = 0$, are $r_1 = 3/2$ and $r_2 = 1/3$. Thus,

$$y(t) = c_1 e^{r_1 t} + c_2 e^{r_2 t} = c_1 e^{3t/2} + c_2 e^{t/3}$$

is a general solution.

7. Solving the auxiliary equation, $36r^2 + 24r + 5 = 0$, we find

$$r = \frac{-24 \pm \sqrt{24^2 - 4(36)(5)}}{2(36)} = -\frac{1}{3} \pm \frac{1}{6}i.$$

Thus a general solution is given by

$$y(t) = \left[c_1 \cos\left(\frac{t}{6}\right) + c_2 \sin\left(\frac{t}{6}\right)\right] e^{-t/3}.$$

9. The auxiliary equation, $16r^2 - 56r + 49 = (4r - 7)^2 = 0$, has a double root $r = 7/4$. Therefore, $e^{7t/4}$ and $te^{7t/4}$ are two linearly independent solutions, and a general solution is given by

$$y(t) = c_1 e^{7t/4} + c_2 t e^{7t/4} = (c_1 + c_2 t)\, e^{7t/4}.$$

11. This equation is a Cauchy-Euler equation. Using the approach discussed in Problem 38, Exercises 4.3, we make the substitution $t = e^s$ and obtain

$$\begin{aligned}
\frac{dx}{ds} &= \frac{dx}{dt}\frac{dt}{ds} = t\frac{dx}{dt}, \\
\frac{d^2x}{ds^2} &= \frac{d}{ds}\left(\frac{dx}{ds}\right) = \frac{dx}{ds} + t^2\frac{d^2x}{dt^2}, \\
\Rightarrow \qquad t^2\frac{d^2x}{dt^2} + 5x &= \left(\frac{d^2x}{ds^2} - \frac{dx}{ds}\right) + 5x = \frac{d^2x}{ds^2} - \frac{dx}{ds} + 5x = 0.
\end{aligned}$$

The axiliary equation to this constant coefficient linear equation is $r^2 - r + 5 = 0$, which has roots

$$r = \frac{1 \pm \sqrt{1^2 - 4(1)(5)}}{2} = \frac{1 \pm \sqrt{19}}{2}.$$

Thus,

$$y(s) = e^{s/2}\left[c_1 \cos\left(\frac{\sqrt{19}s}{2}\right) + c_2 \sin\left(\frac{\sqrt{19}s}{2}\right)\right]$$

is a general solution as a function of s. The back substitution, $s = \ln t$, yields

$$y(t) = t^{1/2}\left[c_1 \cos\left(\frac{\sqrt{19}}{2}\ln t\right) + c_2 \sin\left(\frac{\sqrt{19}}{2}\ln t\right)\right].$$

13. The roots of the auxiliary equation, $r^2 + 16 = 0$, are $r = \pm 4i$. Thus a general solution to the corresponding homogeneous equation is given by

$$y_h(t) = c_1 \cos 4t + c_2 \sin 4t\,.$$

The method of undetermined coefficients suggests the form $y_p(t) = (A_1 t + A_0)e^t$ for a particular solution to the original equation. We compute

$$y_p'(t) = (A_1 t + A_0 + A_1)e^t\,, \qquad y_p''(t) = (A_1 t + A_0 + 2A_1)e^t$$

and substitute $y_p''(t)$ and $y_p(t)$ into the given equation. This yields

$$y_p'' + 16y_p = \left[(A_1 t + A_0 + 2A_1)e^t\right] + 16\left[(A_1 t + A_0)e^t\right] = te^t$$

$$\Rightarrow \qquad (17A_1 t + 17A_0 + 2A_1)\,e^t = te^t \qquad \Rightarrow \qquad A_1 = \frac{1}{17}\,, A_0 = -\frac{2}{289}\,.$$

Therefore,

$$y_p(t) = \left(\frac{t}{17} - \frac{2}{289}\right)e^t$$

$$\Rightarrow \qquad y(t) = y_h(t) + y_p(t) = c_1 \cos 4t + c_2 \sin 4t + \left(\frac{t}{17} - \frac{2}{289}\right)e^t\,.$$

15. This is a third order homogeneous linear differential equation with constant coefficients. Its auxiliary equation is $3r^3 + 10r^2 + 9r + 2 = 0$. Factoring yields

$$3r^3 + 10r^2 + 9r + 2 = (3r^3 + 3r^2) + (7r^2 + 7r) + (2r + 2) = (3r^2 + 7r + 2)(r + 1).$$

Thus the roots of the auxiliary equation are

$$r = -1 \quad \text{and} \quad r = \frac{-7 \pm \sqrt{7^2 - 4(3)(2)}}{6} = -2,\ -\frac{1}{3}\,,$$

and a general solution is given by

$$y(t) = c_1 e^{-2t} + c_2 e^{-t} + c_3 e^{-t/3}\,.$$

17. To solve the auxiliary equation, $r^3 + 10r - 11 = 0$, we note that $r_1 = 1$ is a root. Dividing the polynomial $r^3 + 10r - 11$ by $r - 1$ we get

$$r^3 + 10r - 11 = (r - 1)(r^2 + r + 11),$$

and so the other two roots are

$$r_{2,3} = \frac{-1 \pm \sqrt{1 - 4(1)(11)}}{2} = \frac{-1}{2} \pm \frac{\sqrt{43}}{2} i.$$

A general solution is then given by

$$y(t) = c_1 e^t + e^{-t/2}\left[c_2 \cos\left(\frac{\sqrt{43}t}{2}\right) + c_3 \sin\left(\frac{\sqrt{43}t}{2}\right)\right].$$

19. By inspection, we find that $r = -3$ as a root of the auxiliary equation, $4r^3 + 8r^2 - 11r + 3 = 0$. Using, say, the long division, we get

$$4r^3 + 8r^2 - 11r + 3 = (r + 3)(4r^2 - 4r + 1) = (r + 3)(2r - 1)^2 .$$

Thus, in addition, $r = 1/2$ is a double root of the auxiliary equation. A general solution then has the form

$$y(t) = c_1 e^{-3t} + c_2 e^{t/2} + c_3 t e^{t/2} .$$

21. First, we solve the corresponding homogeneous equation,

$$y'' - 3y' + 7y = 0.$$

Since the roots of the auxiliary equation, $r^2 - 3r + 7 = 0$, are

$$r = \frac{3 \pm \sqrt{9 - 28}}{2} = \frac{3 \pm \sqrt{19}i}{2},$$

a general solution to the homogeneous equation is

$$y_h(t) = \left[c_1 \cos\left(\frac{\sqrt{19}t}{2}\right) + c_2 \sin\left(\frac{\sqrt{19}t}{2}\right)\right] e^{3t/2} .$$

We use the superposition principle to find a particular solution to the original nonhomogeneous equation.

A particular solution, $y_{p,1}(t)$ to $y'' - 3y' + 7y = 7t^2$ has the form

$$y_{p,1}(t) = A_2t^2 + A_1t + A_0 .$$

Substitution yields

$$\begin{aligned} y''_{p,1} - 3y'_{p,1} + 7y_{p,1} &= 2A_2 - 3(2A_2t + A_1) + 7(A_2t^2 + A_1t + A_0) = 7t^2 \\ \Rightarrow \qquad & (7A_2)t^2 + (7A_1 - 6A_2)t + (7A_0 - 3A_1 + 2A_2) = 7t^2 \\ \Rightarrow \qquad & \begin{array}{lcl} 7A_2 = 7, & & A_2 = 1, \\ 7A_1 - 6A_2 = 0, & \Rightarrow & A_1 = 6/7, \\ 7A_0 - 3A_1 + 2A_2 = 0 & & A_0 = 4/49, \end{array} \end{aligned}$$

and so

$$y_{p,1}(t) = t^2 + \frac{6}{7}t + \frac{4}{49} .$$

The other term in the right-hand side of the original equation is e^t. A particular solution to $y'' - 3y' + 7y = e^t$ has the form $y_{p,2}(t) = Ae^t$. Substitution yields

$$y''_{p,2} - 3y'_{p,2} + 7y_{p,2} = 5Ae^t = e^t \qquad \Rightarrow \qquad A = \frac{1}{5} \qquad \Rightarrow \qquad y_{p,2}(t) = \frac{1}{5}e^t .$$

By the superposition principle, a general solution to the original equation is

$$\begin{aligned} y(t) &= y_h(t) - y_{p,2}(t) + y_{p,1}(t) \\ &= \left[c_1 \cos\left(\frac{\sqrt{19}t}{2}\right) + c_2 \sin\left(\frac{\sqrt{19}t}{2}\right)\right] e^{3t/2} - \frac{1}{5}e^t + t^2 + \frac{6}{7}t + \frac{4}{49} . \end{aligned}$$

23. The corresponding homogeneous equation in this problem is similar to that in Problem 13. Thus, $y_1(t) = \cos 4\theta$ and $y_2(t) = \sin 4\theta$ are its two linearly independent solutions, and a general solution is given by

$$y_h(\theta) = c_1 \cos 4\theta + c_2 \sin 4\theta .$$

For a particular solution to the original equation, we use the variation of parameters method. Letting

$$y_p(\theta) = v_1(\theta) \cos 4\theta + v_2(\theta) \sin 4\theta,$$

we get the following system for v_1' and v_2' (see (9) on page 195 in the text):

$$v_1'(\theta)\cos 4\theta + v_2'(\theta)\sin 4\theta = 0$$
$$-4v_1'(\theta)\sin 4\theta + 4v_2'(\theta)\cos 4\theta = \tan 4\theta.$$

Multiplying the first equation by $\sin 4\theta$ and the second equation by $(1/4)\cos 4\theta$, and adding the resulting equations together, we get

$$v_2'(\theta) = \frac{1}{4}\sin 4\theta \qquad \Rightarrow \qquad v_2 = -\frac{1}{16}\cos 4\theta + c_3.$$

From the first equation in the above system we also obtain

$$v_1'(\theta) = -v_2'(\theta)\tan 4\theta = -\frac{1}{4}\frac{\sin^2 4\theta}{\cos 4\theta} = -\frac{1}{4}(\sec 4\theta - \cos 4\theta)$$
$$\Rightarrow \qquad v_1(\theta) = -\frac{1}{4}\int(\sec 4\theta - \cos 4\theta)\,d\theta = -\frac{1}{16}\ln|\sec 4\theta + \tan 4\theta| + \frac{1}{16}\sin 4\theta + c_4.$$

Taking $c_3 = c_4 = 0$, we obtain

$$\begin{aligned} y_p(\theta) &= \left(-\frac{1}{16}\ln|\sec 4\theta + \tan 4\theta| + \frac{1}{16}\sin 4\theta\right)\cos 4\theta + \left(-\frac{1}{16}\cos\theta\right)\sin 4\theta \\ &= -\frac{1}{16}(\cos 4\theta)\ln|\sec 4\theta + \tan 4\theta|, \end{aligned}$$

and a general solution to the original equation is

$$y(\theta) = c_1\cos 4\theta + c_2\sin 4\theta - \frac{1}{16}(\cos 4\theta)\ln|\sec 4\theta + \tan 4\theta|.$$

25. Since the auxiliary equation, $4r^2 - 12r + 9 = (2r-3)^2 = 0$, has a double root $r = 3/2$, a general solution to the corresponding homogeneous equation is

$$y_h(t) = c_1e^{3t/2} + c_2te^{3t/2}.$$

By the superposition principle, a particular solution to the original equation has the form

$$y_p(t) = Ae^{5t} + Be^{3t}.$$

Substituting this expression into the given nonhomogeneous equation, we get

$$4y_p'' - 12y_p' + 9y_p = 4\left(25Ae^{5t} + 9Be^{3t}\right) - 12\left(5Ae^{5t} + 3Be^{3t}\right) + 9\left(Ae^{5t} + Be^{3t}\right)$$

$$= \quad 49Ae^{5t} + 9Be^{3t} = e^{5t} + e^{3t} \qquad \Rightarrow \qquad A = 1/49, \ B = 1/9.$$

Therefore, $y_p(t) = (1/49)e^{5t} + (1/9)e^{3t}$ and a general solution to the original equation is

$$y(t) = c_1 e^{3t/2} + c_2 t e^{3t/2} + \frac{1}{49}e^{5t} + \frac{1}{9}e^{3t}.$$

27. This is a Cauchy-Euler equation. Thus we make the substitution $x = e^t$ and get

$$\begin{aligned} & x^2\frac{d^2y}{dx^2} + 2x\frac{dy}{dx} - 2y = 6x^{-2} + 3x \\ \Rightarrow \qquad & \left(\frac{d^2y}{dt^2} - \frac{dy}{dt}\right) + 2\frac{dy}{dt} - 2y = 6(e^t)^{-2} + 3(e^t) \\ \Rightarrow \qquad & \frac{d^2y}{dt^2} + \frac{dy}{dt} - 2y = 6e^{-2t} + 3e^t. \end{aligned} \tag{4.15}$$

The auxiliary equation, $r^2 + r - 2 = 0$, has the roots $r = -2, 1$. Therefore, a general solution to the corresponding homogeneous equation is

$$y_h(t) = c_1 e^t + c_2 e^{-2t}.$$

A particular solution to (4.15) has the form

$$y_p(t) = Ate^{-2t} + Bte^t.$$

(The factor t appeared in both terms because e^t and e^{-2t} are both solutions to the homogeneous equation.) Differentiating, we find

$$\begin{aligned} & y_p(t) = Ate^{-2t} + Bte^t \\ \Rightarrow \qquad & y_p'(t) = A(1-2t)e^{-2t} + B(t+1)e^t \\ \Rightarrow \qquad & y_p'(t) = A(4t-4)e^{-2t} + B(t+2)e^t. \end{aligned}$$

Substitution into (4.15) yields

$$-3Ae^{-2t} + 3Be^t = 6e^{-2t} + 3e^t \qquad \Rightarrow \qquad A = -2, \ B = 1.$$

Thus a general solution to (4.15) is given by

$$y(t) = y_h(t) + y_p(t) = c_1 e^t + c_2 e^{-2t} - 2te^{-2t} + te^t.$$

The back substitution $e^t = x$ (or $t = \ln x$) results

$$y(x) = c_1 x + c_2 x^{-2} - 2x^{-2}\ln x + x\ln x\,.$$

29. The roots of the auxiliary equation in this problem are

$$r = \frac{-4 \pm \sqrt{4^2 - 4(1)(7)}}{2} = -2 \pm \sqrt{3}i\,.$$

Therefore, a general solution is given by

$$y(t) = \left(c_1 \cos\sqrt{3}t + c_2 \sin\sqrt{3}t\right) e^{-2t}\,.$$

Substituting the initial conditions, we obtain

$$\begin{aligned} y(0) &= \left(c_1 \cos\sqrt{3}t + c_2 \sin\sqrt{3}t\right) e^{-2t}\,\Big|_{t=0} = c_1 = 1, \\ y'(0) &= \left[(-2c_1 + \sqrt{3}c_2)\cos\sqrt{3}t - (\sqrt{3}c_1 + 2c_2)\sin\sqrt{3}t\right] e^{-2t}\,\Big|_{t=0} = -2c_1 + \sqrt{3}c_2 = -2. \end{aligned}$$

Solving this system yields $c_1 = 1$, $c_2 = 0$. The solution to the given initial value problem is

$$y(t) = e^{-2t}\cos\sqrt{3}t\,.$$

31. We solve the corresponding homogeneous equation. Its auxiliary equation, $r^2 - 2r + 10 = 0$, has the roots $r = 1 \pm 3i$. Thus

$$y_h(t) = (c_1 \cos 3t + c_2 \sin 3t)\, e^t$$

is a general solution.

Now, we apply the method of undetermined coefficients and look for a particular solution to the original nonhomogeneous equation of the form $y_p(t) = A\cos 3t + B\sin 3t$. Differentiating $y_p(t)$ twice, we obtain $y_p'(t) = -3A\sin 3t + 3B\cos 3t$, $y_p'' = -9A\cos 3t - 9B\sin 3t$ and substitute these expressions into the original equation. Thus we get

$$(-9A\cos 3t - 9B\sin 3t) - 2(-3A\sin 3t + 3B\cos 3t) + 10(A\cos 3t + B\sin 3t)$$
$$= 6\cos 3t - \sin 3t$$

$$\Rightarrow \qquad (A-6B)\cos 3t + (6A+B)\sin 3t = 6\cos 3t - \sin 3t$$

$$\Rightarrow \qquad \begin{aligned} A-6B &= 6, \\ 6A+B &= -1 \end{aligned} \qquad \Rightarrow \qquad \begin{aligned} A &= 0, \\ B &= -1. \end{aligned}$$

So, $y_p(t) = -\sin 3t$, and $y(t) = (c_1\cos 3t + c_2\sin 3t)\,e^t - \sin 3t$ is a general solution to the given equation.

Next, we satisfy the initial conditions.

$$\begin{aligned} y(0) &= c_1 = 2, \\ y'(0) &= c_1 + 3c_2 - 3 = -8 \end{aligned} \qquad \Rightarrow \qquad \begin{aligned} c_1 &= 2, \\ c_2 &= -7/3. \end{aligned}$$

Hence, the answer is

$$y(t) = \left(2\cos 3t - \frac{7}{3}\sin 3t\right)e^t - \sin 3t.$$

33. The associated characteristic equation in this problem is $r^3 - 12r^2 + 27r + 40 = 0$, which is a third order equation. Using the rational root theorem, we look for its integer roots among the divisors of 40, which are ± 1, ± 2, ± 4, ± 8, ± 10, ± 20, and ± 40. By inspection, $r = -1$ is a root. Dividing $r^3 - 12r^2 + 27r + 40$ by $r+1$, we get

$$r^3 - 12r^2 + 27r + 40 = (r^2 - 13r + 40)(r+1),$$

and so the other two roots of the auxiliary equation are the roots of $r^2 - 13r + 40 = 0$, which are $r = 5$ and 8. Therefore, a general solution to the given equation is $y(t) = c_1e^{-t} + c_2e^{5t} + c_3e^{8t}$. We find the values of c_1, c_2, and c_3 from the initial conditions.

$$\begin{aligned} y(0) &= \left(c_1e^{-t} + c_2e^{5t} + c_3e^{8t}\right)\big|_{t=0} = c_1 + c_2 + c_3 = -3, \\ y'(0) &= \left(-c_1e^{-t} + 5c_2e^{5t} + 8c_3e^{8t}\right)\big|_{t=0} = -c_1 + 5c_2 + 8c_3 = -6, \\ y''(0) &= \left(c_1e^{-t} + 25c_2e^{5t} + 64c_3e^{8t}\right)\big|_{t=0} = c_1 + 25c_2 + 64c_3 = -12 \end{aligned} \qquad \Rightarrow \qquad \begin{aligned} c_1 &= -1, \\ c_2 &= -3, \\ c_3 &= 1. \end{aligned}$$

Therefore, $y(t) = -e^{-t} - 3e^{5t} + e^{8t}$ is the solution to the given initial value problem.

35. Since the roots of the auxiliary equation, $r^2 + 1 = 0$, are $r = \pm i$, the functions $y_1(\theta) = \cos\theta$ and $y_2(\theta) = \sin\theta$ are two linearly independent solutions to the corresponding homogeneous equation, and its general solution is given by

$$y_h(\theta) = c_1\cos\theta + c_2\sin\theta\,.$$

We apply the method of variation of parameters to find a particular solution to the original equation. We look for a particular solution of the form

$$y_p(\theta) = v_1(\theta)\cos\theta + v_2(\theta)\sin\theta,$$

where $v_1(\theta)$ and $v_2(\theta)$ satisfy the system (9), Section 4.6. That is,

$$\begin{aligned} v_1'\cos\theta + v_2'\sin\theta &= 0, \\ -v_1'\sin\theta + v_2'\cos\theta &= \sec\theta\,. \end{aligned}$$

Multiplying the first equation by $\sin\theta$, the second equation by $\cos\theta$, and adding them together yield

$$v_2'\sin^2\theta + v_2'\cos^2\theta = \sec\theta\cos\theta \qquad \Rightarrow \qquad v_2' = 1 \qquad \Rightarrow \qquad v_2(\theta) = \theta.$$

From the first equation in the above system we also get

$$v_1' = -v_2'\tan\theta = -\tan\theta \qquad \Rightarrow \qquad v_1(\theta) = -\int \tan\theta\, d\theta = \ln|\cos\theta|,$$

where we have taken the zero integration constant. So,

$$y_p(\theta) = \cos\theta\ln|\cos\theta| + \theta\sin\theta\,,$$

and

$$y(\theta) = c_1\cos\theta + c_2\sin\theta + \cos\theta\ln|\cos\theta| + \theta\sin\theta$$

is a general solution to the original equation. Differentiating we find that

$$y'(\theta) = -c_1\sin\theta + c_2\cos\theta - \sin\theta\ln|\cos\theta| + \theta\cos\theta.$$

Substitution of $y(\theta)$ and $y'(\theta)$ into the initial conditions yields

$$\begin{aligned} y(0) &= c_1 = 1, \\ y'(0) &= c_2 = 2 \end{aligned} \qquad \Rightarrow \qquad \begin{aligned} c_1 &= 1, \\ c_2 &= 2, \end{aligned}$$

and so the answer is $y(\theta) = \cos\theta + 2\sin\theta + \cos\theta\ln|\cos\theta| + \theta\sin\theta$.

Chapter 4

37. Comparing the given homogeneous equations with mass-spring oscillator equation (13) in Section 4.7,

$$[\text{inertia}]\, y'' + [\text{damping}]\, y' + [\text{stiffness}]\, y = 0,$$

we see that in equations (a) through (d) the damping coefficient is 0. So, the behavior, of solutions, as $t \to +\infty$, depends on the sign of the stiffness coefficient "k".

(a) "k"$= t^4 > 0$. This implies that all the solutions remain bounded as $t \to +\infty$.

(b) "k"$= -t^4 < 0$. The stiffness of the system is negative and increases unboundedly as $t \to +\infty$. It reinforces the displacement, $y(t)$, with magnitude increasing with time. Hence some solutions grow rapidly with time.

(c) "k"$= y^6 > 0$. Similarly to (a), we conclude that all the solutions are bounded.

(d) "k"$= y^7$. The function $f(y) = y^7$ is positive for positive y and negative if y is negative. Hence, we can expect that some of the solutions (say, ones satisfying negative initial conditions) are unbounded.

(e) "k"$= 3 + \sin t$. Since $|\sin t| \le 1$ for any t, we conclude that

$$\text{“}k\text{”} \ge 3 + (-1) = 2 > 0,$$

and all the solutions are bounded as $t \to +\infty$.

(f) Here there is positive damping "b"$= t^2$ increasing with time, which results an increasing drain of energy from the system, and positive constant stiffness $k = 1$. Thus all the solutions are bounded.

(g) Negative damping "b"$= -t^2$ increases (in absolute value) with time, which imparts energy to the system instead of draining it. Note that the stiffness $k = -1$ is also negative. Thus we should expect that some of the solutions increase unboundedly as $t \to +\infty$.

39. If a weight of $w = 32$ lb stretches the spring by $\ell = 6$ in $= 0.5$ ft, then the spring stiffness must be

$$k = \frac{w}{\ell} = \frac{32}{0.5} = 64\ (\text{lb/ft}).$$

Also, the mass m of the weight is

$$m = \frac{w}{g} = \frac{32}{32} = 1 \text{ (slug)},$$

and the damping constant $b = 2$ lb-sec/ft. The external force is given to be $F(t) = F_0 \cos \gamma t$ with $F_0 = 4$ and $\gamma = 8$.

Clearly, we have an underdamped motion because $b^2 - 4mk = 4 - 256 < 0$. So, we can use formula (6) in Section 4.9 for the steady-state solution. This yields

$$\begin{aligned} y_p(t) &= \frac{F_0}{(k - m\gamma^2)^2 + b^2\gamma^2} \left\{ (k - m\gamma^2) \cos \gamma t + b\gamma \sin \gamma t \right\} \\ &= \frac{4}{(64 - 8^2)^2 + 2^2 8^2} \left\{ (64 - 8^2) \cos 8t + (2)(8) \sin 8t \right\} = \frac{1}{4} \sin 8t \,. \end{aligned}$$

The resonant frequency for the system is $\gamma_r/(2\pi)$, where γ_r is given in (15), Section 4.9. Applying this formula, we get

$$\text{resonant frequency} = \frac{1}{2\pi} \sqrt{\frac{k}{m} - \frac{b^2}{2m^2}} = \frac{1}{2\pi} \sqrt{\frac{64}{1} - \frac{2^2}{2(1^2)}} = \frac{\sqrt{62}}{2\pi} \,.$$

CHAPTER 5: Introduction to Systems and Phase Plane Analysis

EXERCISES 5.2: Elimination Method for Systems, page 250

1. Subtracting the second equation in the system from the first one, we eliminate y and obtain

$$\begin{aligned} x' + y' &= -2y, \\ y' &= x - 2y \end{aligned} \qquad \Rightarrow \qquad x' = -x.$$

This equation is separable (also, it is linear). Separation yields

$$\frac{dx}{x} = -dt \qquad \Rightarrow \qquad \ln|x| = -t + C \qquad \Rightarrow \qquad x(t) = c_2 e^{-t}.$$

Substituting this solution into the second equation, we obtain an equation for y:

$$y' + 2y = x = c_2 e^{-t}.$$

This equation is a first order linear equation. Solving we obtain

$$\begin{aligned} &\mu(t) = \exp\left(\int (2)dt\right) = e^{2t} \\ \Rightarrow \qquad & e^{2t} y = \int \left(c_2 e^{-t}\right) e^{2t} dt = c_2 \int e^t dt = c_2 e^t + c_1 \\ \Rightarrow \qquad & y(t) = c_1 e^{-2t} + c_2 e^{-t}. \end{aligned}$$

Therefore, a general solution is

$$x(t) = c_2 e^{-t}, \qquad y(t) = c_1 e^{-2t} + c_2 e^{-t}.$$

3. We eliminate x by subtracting the second equation from the first equation. This yields

$$y' + 2y = 0 \qquad \Rightarrow \qquad \frac{dy}{y} = -2dt \qquad \Rightarrow \qquad \ln|y| = -2t + c \qquad \Rightarrow \qquad y(t) = c_2 e^{-2t}.$$

From the second equation we get

$$x' - y' = 0 \quad \Rightarrow \quad (x-y)' = 0 \quad \Rightarrow \quad x(t) - y(t) = c_1 \quad \Rightarrow \quad x(t) = c_1 + c_2 e^{-2t},$$

and a general solution is given by

$$x(t) = c_1 + c_2 e^{-2t}, \qquad y(t) = c_2 e^{-2t}.$$

5. Writing this system in operator notation yields the system

$$\begin{aligned} (D-1)[x] + D[y] &= 5, \\ D[x] + (D+1)[y] &= 1. \end{aligned} \tag{5.1}$$

We will first eliminate the function $x(t)$, although we could proceed just as easily by eliminating the function $y(t)$. Thus, we apply the operator D to the first equation and the operator $-(D-1)$ to the second equation to obtain

$$\begin{aligned} &D(D-1)[x] + D^2[y] - D[5] = 0, \\ &-(D-1)D[x] - (D-1)(D+1)[y] = -(D-1)[1] = 1. \end{aligned}$$

Adding these two equations yields

$$\begin{aligned} &\{D(D-1) - (D-1)D\}[x] + \left\{D^2 - (D^2 - 1)\right\}[y] = 1 \\ &\Rightarrow \quad 0 \cdot x + 1 \cdot y = 1 \quad \Rightarrow \quad y(t) = 1. \end{aligned}$$

To find the function $x(t)$, we will eliminate y from the system given in (5.1). Therefore, we multiply the first equation in (5.1) by $(D+1)$ and the second by $-D$ to obtain the system

$$\begin{aligned} &(D+1)(D-1)[x] + (D+1)D[y] = (D+1)[5] = 5, \\ &-D^2[x] - D(D+1)[y] = D[1] = 0. \end{aligned}$$

By adding these two equations we obtain

$$\left\{(D^2-1) - D^2\right\}[x] = 5 \quad \Rightarrow \quad -x = 5 \quad \Rightarrow \quad x(t) = -5.$$

Therefore, this system of linear differential equation is solved by the functions

$$x(t) = -5 \quad \text{and} \quad y(t) = 1.$$

7. In order to eliminate u, we multiply the first equation by $(D-1)$, the second equation – by $(D+1)$, and subtract the results.

$$(D-1)\{(D+1)[u]-(D+1)[v]\} = (D-1)[e^t] = (e^t)' - e^t = 0,$$
$$(D+1)\{(D-1)[u]+(2D+1)[v]\} = (D+1)[5] = (5)' + 5 = 5$$

$$\Rightarrow \quad \begin{array}{l} (D^2-1)[u] - (D^2-1)[v] = 0, \\ (D^2-1)[u] + \{(D+1)(2D+1)\}[v] = 5 \end{array}$$

$$\Rightarrow \quad \left\{(D+1)(2D+1) + \left(D^2-1\right)\right\}[v] = 5 \quad \Rightarrow \quad \{D(D+1)\}[v] = \frac{5}{3}. \qquad (5.2)$$

The corresponding homogeneous equation, $\{D(D+1)\}[v] = 0$, has the characteristic equation

$$r(r+1) = 0 \qquad \Rightarrow \qquad r = 0, -1,$$

and so its general solution is

$$v_h(t) = c_1 + c_2 e^{-t}.$$

Applying the method of undetermined coefficients, we look for a particular solution to (5.2) of the form $v_p(t) = ct^s$, where we choose $s = 1$ (because the homogeneous equation has constant solutions and does not have solutions of the form ct). Substitution $v = ct$ into (5.2) yields

$$\{D(D+1)\}[ct] = (D+1)[c] = c = \frac{5}{3} \qquad \Rightarrow \qquad v_p(t) = \frac{5}{3}t.$$

Therefore, a general solution to (5.2) is

$$v(t) = v_h(t) + v_p(t) = c_1 + c_2 e^{-t} + \frac{5}{3}t.$$

We now go back to the original system and subtract the second equation from the first one.

$$2u - (3D+2)[v] = e^t - 5$$
$$\Rightarrow \quad u = \left(\frac{3}{2}D + 1\right)[v] + \frac{1}{2}e^t - \frac{5}{2}$$
$$\Rightarrow \quad u = \frac{3}{2}\left(c_1 + c_2 e^{-t} + \frac{5}{3}t\right)' + \left(c_1 + c_2 e^{-t} + \frac{5}{3}t\right) + \frac{1}{2}e^t - \frac{5}{2}$$
$$\Rightarrow \quad u(t) = c_1 - \frac{1}{2}c_2 e^{-t} + \frac{1}{2}e^t + \frac{5}{3}t.$$

Thus, a general solution to the given system is

$$u(t) = c_1 - \frac{1}{2}c_2e^{-t} + \frac{1}{2}e^t + \frac{5}{3}t,$$
$$v(t) = c_1 + c_2e^{-t} + \frac{5}{3}t.$$

9. Expressed in operator notation, this system becomes

$$\begin{aligned} (D+2)[x] + D[y] &= 0, \\ (D-1)[x] + (D-1)[y] &= \sin t. \end{aligned}$$

In order to eliminate the function $y(t)$, we will apply the operator $(D-1)$ to the first equation above and the operator $-D$ to the second one. Thus, we have

$$(D-1)(D+2)[x] + (D-1)D[y] = (D-1)[0] = 0,$$
$$-D(D-1)[x] - D(D-1)[y] = -D[\sin t] = -\cos t.$$

Adding these two equations yields the differential equation involving the single function $x(t)$ given by

$$\left\{(D^2+D-2) - (D^2-D)\right\}[x] = -\cos t$$
$$\Rightarrow \qquad 2(D-1)[x] = -\cos t. \tag{5.3}$$

This is a linear first order differential equation with constant coefficients and so can be solved by the methods of Chapter 2. (See Section 2.3.) However, we will use the methods of Chapter 4. We see that the auxiliary equation associated with the corresponding homogeneous equation is given by $2(r-1) = 0$, which has the root $r = 1$. Thus, a general solution to the corresponding homogeneous equation is

$$x_h(t) = C_1e^t.$$

We will use the method of undetermined coefficients to find a particular solution to the nonhomogeneous equation. To this end, we note that a particular solution to this differential equation will have the form

$$x_p(t) = A\cos t + B\sin t \qquad \Rightarrow \qquad x_p'(t) = -A\sin t + B\cos t.$$

Substituting these expressions into the nonhomogeneous equation given in (5.3) yields

$$\begin{aligned} 2x_p' - 2x_p &= 2(-A\sin t + B\cos t) - 2(A\cos t + B\sin t) \\ &= (2B - 2A)\cos t + (-2A - 2B)\sin t = -\cos t. \end{aligned}$$

By equating coefficients we obtain

$$2B - 2A = -1 \qquad \text{and} \qquad -2A - 2B = 0.$$

By solving these two equations simultaneously for A and B, we see that

$$A = \frac{1}{4} \qquad \text{and} \qquad B = -\frac{1}{4}.$$

Thus, a particular solution to the nonhomogeneous equation given in (5.3) will be

$$x_p(t) = \frac{1}{4}\cos t - \frac{1}{4}\sin t$$

and a general solution to the nonhomogeneous equation (5.3) will be

$$x(t) = x_h(t) + x_p(t) = C_1e^t + \frac{1}{4}\cos t - \frac{1}{4}\sin t.$$

We now must find a function $y(t)$. To do this, we subtract the second of the two differential equations in the system from the first to obtain

$$3x + y = -\sin t \qquad \Rightarrow \qquad y = -3x - \sin t.$$

Therefore, we see that

$$\begin{aligned} y(t) &= -3\left[C_1e^t + \frac{1}{4}\cos t - \frac{1}{4}\sin t\right] - \sin t \\ \Rightarrow \qquad y(t) &= -3C_1e^t - \frac{3}{4}\cos t - \frac{1}{4}\sin t. \end{aligned}$$

Hence this system of differential equations has the general solution

$$x(t) = C_1e^t + \frac{1}{4}\cos t - \frac{1}{4}\sin t \qquad \text{and} \qquad y(t) = -3C_1e^t - \frac{3}{4}\cos t - \frac{1}{4}\sin t.$$

11. From the second equation, we obtain $u = -\left(D^2+2\right)[v]/2$. Substitution into the first equation eliminates u and gives

$$\begin{aligned} &\left(D^2-1\right)\left\{-\frac{1}{2}\left(D^2+2\right)[v]\right\}+5v=e^t \\ \Rightarrow \quad &\left[\left(D^2-1\right)\left(D^2+2\right)-10\right][v]=-2e^t \\ \Rightarrow \quad &\left(D^4+D^2-12\right)[v]=-2e^t. \end{aligned} \tag{5.4}$$

Solving the characteristic equation, $r^4+r^2-12=0$,

$$r^4+r^2-12=0 \quad \Rightarrow \quad \left(r^2+4\right)\left(r^2-3\right)=0 \quad \Rightarrow \quad r=\pm 2i, \pm\sqrt{3},$$

we conclude that a general solution to the corresponding homogeneous equation is

$$v_h(t)=c_1\cos 2t+c_2\sin 2t+c_3e^{\sqrt{3}t}+c_4e^{-\sqrt{3}t}.$$

A particular solution to (5.4) has the form $v_p(t)=ce^t$. Substitution yields

$$\left(D^4+D^2-12\right)\left[ce^t\right]=ce^t+ce^t-12ce^t=-10ce^t=-2e^t \quad \Rightarrow \quad c=\frac{1}{5}.$$

Therefore, $v=v_h+v_p=c_1\cos 2t+c_2\sin 2t+c_3e^{\sqrt{3}t}+c_4e^{-\sqrt{3}t}+e^t/5$ and

$$\begin{aligned} u &= -\frac{1}{2}\left(D^2+2\right)[v]=-\frac{1}{2}\left(c_1\cos 2t+c_2\sin 2t+c_3e^{\sqrt{3}t}+c_4e^{-\sqrt{3}t}+\frac{1}{5}e^t\right)'' \\ &\qquad -\left(c_1\cos 2t+c_2\sin 2t+c_3e^{\sqrt{3}t}+c_4e^{-\sqrt{3}t}+\frac{1}{5}e^t\right) \\ &= c_1\cos 2t+c_2\sin 2t-\frac{5}{2}c_3e^{\sqrt{3}t}-\frac{5}{2}c_4e^{-\sqrt{3}t}-\frac{3}{10}e^t. \end{aligned}$$

By replacing $(-5/2)c_3$ by c_3 and $(-5/2)c_4$ by c_4 we obtain the same answer as given in the text.

13. Expressing x from the second equation and substituting the result into the first equation, we obtain

$$x=y'-y \quad \Rightarrow \quad \frac{d(y'-y)}{dt}=(y'-y)-4y \quad \Rightarrow \quad y''-2y'+5y=0.$$

This homogeneous linear equation with constant coefficients has the characteristic equation $r^2 - 2r + 5 = 0$ with roots $r = 1 \pm 2i$. Thus a general solution is

$$y = c_1 e^t \cos 2t + c_2 e^t \sin 2t\,.$$

Therefore,

$$\begin{aligned} x &= \left(c_1 e^t \cos 2t + c_2 e^t \sin 2t\right)' - \left(c_1 e^t \cos 2t + c_2 e^t \sin 2t\right) \\ &= \left(c_1 e^t \cos 2t - 2c_1 e^t \sin 2t + c_2 e^t \sin 2t + 2c_2 e^t \cos 2t\right) - \left(c_1 e^t \cos 2t + c_2 e^t \sin 2t\right) \\ &= 2c_2 e^t \cos 2t - 2c_1 e^t \sin 2t. \end{aligned}$$

15. In operator form, the system becomes

$$\begin{aligned} -2z + (D-5)[w] &= 5t, \\ (D-4)[z] - 3w &= 17t. \end{aligned}$$

We multiply the first equation by 3, the second equation by $(D-5)$, and add the resulting equations.

$$\begin{aligned} &\{-6 + (D-5)(D-4)\}[z] = 3(5t) + (D-5)[17t] = -70t + 17 \\ \Rightarrow \quad &\left(D^2 - 9D + 14\right)[z] = -70t + 17. \end{aligned}$$

Solving the characteristic equation, $r^2 - 9r + 14 = 0$, we obtain $r = 2, 7$. Hence, a general solution to the corresponding homogeneous equation is $z_h(t) = c_1 e^{2t} + c_2 e^{7t}$. A particular solution has the form $z_p(t) = At + B$. Substitution yields

$$\begin{aligned} \left(D^2 - 9D + 14\right)[At + B] &= (At + B)'' - 9(At + B)' + 14(At + B) \\ &= 14At - 9A + 14B = -70t + 17 \end{aligned}$$

$$\Rightarrow \quad A = \frac{-70}{14} = -5, \quad B = \frac{17 + 9A}{14} = -2$$

$$\Rightarrow \quad z(t) = z_h(t) + z_p(t) = c_1 e^{2t} + c_2 e^{7t} - 5t - 2.$$

We use now the second equation from the original system to find w.

$$w = \frac{1}{3}\left(z' - 4z - 17t\right) = -\frac{2}{3}\, c_1 e^{2t} + c_2 e^{7t} + t + 1.$$

17. Expressed in operator notation, this system becomes

$$\begin{aligned}(D^2+5)[x]-4[y] &= 0,\\ -[x]+(D^2+2)[y] &= 0.\end{aligned}$$

In order to eliminate the function $x(t)$, we apply the operator (D^2+5) to the second equation. Thus, we have

$$\begin{aligned}\left(D^2+5\right)[x]-4[y] &= 0,\\ -\left(D^2+5\right)[x]+\left(D^2+5\right)\left(D^2+2\right)[y] &= 0.\end{aligned}$$

Adding these two equations together yields the differential equation involving the single function $y(t)$ given by

$$\left\{(D^2+5)(D^2+2)-4\right\}[y]=0 \qquad \Rightarrow \qquad \left(D^4+7D^2+6\right)[y]=0.$$

The auxiliary equation for this homogeneous equation, $r^4+7r^2+6=(r^2+1)(r^2+6)=0$, has roots $r=\pm i,\ \pm i\sqrt{6}$. Thus, a general solution is

$$y(t)=C_1\sin t+C_2\cos t+C_3\sin\sqrt{6}t+C_4\cos\sqrt{6}t.$$

We must now find a function $x(t)$ that satisfies the system of differential equations given in the problem. To do this we solve the second equation of the system of differential equations for $x(t)$ to obtain

$$x(t)=\left(D^2+2\right)[y].$$

Substituting the expression we found for $y(t)$, we see that

$$\begin{aligned}x(t) &= -C_1\sin t-C_2\cos t-6C_3\sin\sqrt{6}t-6C_4\cos\sqrt{6}t\\ &\qquad +2\left(C_1\sin t+C_2\cos t+C_3\sin\sqrt{6}t+C_4\cos\sqrt{6}t\right)\\ \Rightarrow \qquad x(t) &= C_1\sin t+C_2\cos t-4C_3\sin\sqrt{6}t-4C_4\cos\sqrt{6}t.\end{aligned}$$

Hence this system of differential equations has the general solution

$$\begin{aligned}x(t) &= C_1\sin t+C_2\cos t-4C_3\sin\sqrt{6}t-4C_4\cos\sqrt{6}t\\ y(t) &= C_1\sin t+C_2\cos t+C_3\sin\sqrt{6}t+C_4\cos\sqrt{6}t.\end{aligned}$$

19. From the first equation, we conclude that $y = x' - 4x$. Substitution into the second equation yields

$$(x' - 4x)' = -2x + (x' - 4x) \qquad \Rightarrow \qquad x'' - 5x' + 6x = 0.$$

The characteristic equation, $r^2 - 5r + 6 = 0$, has roots $r = 2, 3$, and so a general solution is

$$\begin{aligned} & x(t) = c_1 e^{2t} + c_2 e^{3t} \\ \Rightarrow \qquad & y(t) = \left(c_1 e^{2t} + c_2 e^{3t}\right)' - 4\left(c_1 e^{2t} + c_2 e^{3t}\right) = -2c_1 e^{2t} - c_2 e^{3t}. \end{aligned}$$

We find constants c_1 and c_2 from the initial condition.

$$\begin{aligned} 1 = x(0) &= c_1 e^{2(0)} + c_2 e^{3(0)} = c_1 + c_2\,, \\ 0 = y(0) &= -2c_1 e^{2(0)} - c_2 e^{3(0)} = -2c_1 - c_2 \end{aligned} \qquad \Rightarrow \qquad \begin{aligned} c_1 &= -1, \\ c_2 &= 2. \end{aligned}$$

Therefore, the answer to this problem is

$$x(t) = -e^{2t} + 2e^{3t}\,, \qquad y(t) = 2e^{2t} - 2e^{3t}\,.$$

21. To apply the elimination method, we write the system using operator notation:

$$\begin{aligned} D^2[x] - y &= 0, \\ -x + D^2[y] &= 0. \end{aligned} \tag{5.5}$$

Eliminating y by applying D^2 to the first equation and adding to the second equation gives

$$\left(D^2 D^2 - 1\right)[x] = 0,$$

which reduces to

$$\left(D^4 - 1\right)[x] = 0. \tag{5.6}$$

The corresponding auxiliary equation, $r^4 - 1 = 0$, has roots ± 1, $\pm i$. Thus, the general solution to (5.6) is given by

$$x(t) = C_1 e^t + C_2 e^{-t} + C_3 \cos t + C_4 \sin t. \tag{5.7}$$

Substituting $x(t)$ into the first equation in (5.5) yields

$$y(t) = x''(t) = C_1 e^t + C_2 e^{-t} - C_3 \cos t - C_4 \sin t. \tag{5.8}$$

We use initial conditions to determine constants C_1, C_2, C_3, and C_4. Differentiating (5.7) and (5.8), we get

$$\begin{aligned} 3 &= x(0) = C_1e^0 + C_2e^{-0} + C_3\cos 0 + C_4\sin 0 = C_1 + C_2 + C_3\,, \\ 1 &= x'(0) = C_1e^0 - C_2e^{-0} - C_3\sin 0 + C_4\cos 0 = C_1 - C_2 + C_4\,, \\ 1 &= y(0) = C_1e^0 + C_2e^{-0} - C_3\cos 0 - C_4\sin 0 = C_1 + C_2 - C_3\,, \\ -1 &= y'(0) = C_1e^0 - C_2e^{-0} + C_3\sin 0 - C_4\cos 0 = C_1 - C_2 - C_4 \end{aligned}$$

$$\Rightarrow \qquad \begin{aligned} C_1 + C_2 + C_3 &= 3, \\ C_1 - C_2 + C_4 &= 1, \\ C_1 + C_2 - C_3 &= 1, \\ C_1 - C_2 - C_4 &= -1. \end{aligned}$$

Solving we obtain $C_1 = C_2 = C_3 = C_4 = 1$. So, the desired solution is

$$\begin{aligned} x(t) &= e^t + e^{-t} + \cos t + \sin t, \\ y(t) &= e^t + e^{-t} - \cos t - \sin t. \end{aligned}$$

23. We will attempt to solve this system by first eliminating the function $y(t)$. Thus, we multiply the first equation by $(D+2)$ and the second by $-(D-1)$. Therefore, we obtain

$$\begin{aligned} (D+2)(D-1)[x] + (D+2)(D-1)D[y] &= (D+2)\left[-3e^{-2t}\right] = 6e^{-2t} - 6e^{-2t} = 0, \\ -(D-1)(D+2)[x] - (D-1)(D+2)[y] &= -(D-1)\left[3e^t\right] = -3e^t + 3e^t = 0. \end{aligned}$$

Adding these two equations yields

$$0 \cdot x + 0 \cdot y = 0,$$

which will be true for any two functions $x(t)$ and $y(t)$. (But not every pair of functions will satisfy this system of differential equations.) Thus, this is a degenerate system, and has infinitely many linearly independent solutions. To see if we can find these solutions, we will examine the system more closely. Notice that we could write this system as

$$\begin{aligned} (D-1)[x+y] &= -3e^{-2t}, \\ (D+2)[x+y] &= 3e^t. \end{aligned}$$

Therefore, let's try the substitution $z(t) = x(t) + y(t)$. We want a function $z(t)$ that satisfies the two equations

$$z'(t) - z(t) = -3e^{-2t} \qquad \text{and} \qquad z'(t) + 2z(t) = 3e^{t}, \tag{5.9}$$

simultaneously. We start by solving the first equation given in (5.9). This is a linear differential equation with constant coefficients which has the associated auxiliary equation $r - 1 = 0$. Hence, the solution to the corresponding homogeneous equation is

$$z_h(t) = Ce^{t}.$$

By the method of undetermined coefficients, we see that a particular solution will have the form

$$z_p(t) = Ae^{-2t} \qquad \Rightarrow \qquad z_p' = -2Ae^{-2t}.$$

Substituting these expressions into the first differential equation given in (5.9) yields

$$z_p'(t) - z_p(t) = -2Ae^{-2t} - Ae^{-2t} = -3Ae^{-2t} = -3e^{-2t} \qquad \Rightarrow \qquad A = 1.$$

Thus, the first equation given in (5.9) has the general solution

$$z(t) = Ce^{t} + e^{-2t}.$$

Now, substituting $z(t)$ into the second equation in (5.9) gives

$$Ce^{t} - 2e^{-2t} + 2\left(Ce^{t} + e^{-2t}\right) = 3e^{t} \qquad \Rightarrow \qquad 3Ce^{t} = 3e^{t}.$$

Hence, C must be 1. Therefore, $z(t) = e^{t} + e^{-2t}$ is the only solution that satisfies both differential equations given in (5.9) simultaneously. Thus, any two differentiable functions that satisfy the equation $x(t) + y(t) = e^{t} + e^{-2t}$ will satisfy the original system.

25. Writing the system in operator form yields

$$\begin{aligned} (D-1)[x] - 2y + z &= 0, \\ -x + D[y] - z &= 0, \\ -4x + 4y + (D-5)[z] &= 0. \end{aligned}$$

We use the second equation to express z in terms of x and y.

$$z = -x + D[y]. \tag{5.10}$$

Substituting this expression into the other two equations, we obtain

$$\begin{aligned} &(D-1)[x] - 2y + (-x + D[y]) = 0, \\ &-4x + 4y + (D-5)[-x + D[y]] = 0 \end{aligned}$$

$$\Rightarrow \qquad \begin{aligned} (D-2)[x] + (D-2)[y]) &= 0, \\ -(D-1)[x] + \left(D^2 - 5D + 4\right)[y] &= 0. \end{aligned} \tag{5.11}$$

Now we eliminate x by multiplying the first equation by $(D-1)$, the second equation – by $(D-2)$, and adding the results. This yields

$$\begin{aligned} &\left\{(D-1)(D-2) + (D-2)\left(D^2 - 5D + 4\right)\right\}[y] = 0 \\ \Rightarrow \quad &\left\{(D-2)\left(D^2 - 4D + 3\right)\right\}[y] = 0 \quad \Rightarrow \quad \{(D-2)(D-1)(D-3)\}[y] = 0. \end{aligned}$$

The roots of the characteristic equation, $(r-2)(r-1)(r-3) = 0$, are $r = 1, 2$, and 3. Thus, a general solution for y is

$$y = c_1 e^t + c_2 e^{2t} + c_3 e^{3t}.$$

With $h := x + y$, the first equation in (5.11) can be written in the form

$$(D-2)[h] = 0 \qquad \text{or} \qquad h' - 2h = 0,$$

which has a general solution $h = Ke^{2t}$. Therefore,

$$x = h - y = -c_1 e^t + (K - c_2) e^{2t} - c_3 e^{3t}.$$

To find K, we substitute the above solutions $x(t)$ and $y(t)$, with $c_1 = c_3 = 0$, into the second equation in (5.11). Thus we get

$$\begin{aligned} &-(D-1)\left[(K - c_2)e^{2t}\right] + \left(D^2 - 5D + 4\right)\left[c_2 e^{2t}\right] = 0 \\ \Rightarrow \quad &-(K - c_2)e^{2t} + (4(c_2) - 5(2c_2) + 4(c_2))\, e^{2t} = 0 \\ \Rightarrow \quad &-K - c_2 = 0 \quad \Rightarrow \quad K = -c_2. \end{aligned}$$

Hence,

$$x = -c_1 e^t - 2c_2 e^{2t} - c_3 e^{3t}.$$

Finally, we find z using (5.10).

$$z = -\left(-c_1 e^t - 2c_2 e^{2t} - c_3 e^{3t}\right) + \left(c_1 e^t + c_2 e^{2t} + c_3 e^{3t}\right)' = 2c_1 e^t + 4c_2 e^{2t} + 4c_3 e^{3t}.$$

27. We eliminate z by expressing

$$z = \frac{1}{4}\left(-x' + 4x\right) = -\frac{1}{4}(D-4)[x] \tag{5.12}$$

from the first equation and substituting (5.12) into the second and third equations. We obtain

$$\begin{aligned} &2\left\{-\frac{1}{4}(D-4)[x]\right\} + (D-4)[y] = 0, \\ &2x + 4y + D\left[-\frac{1}{4}(D-4)[x]\right] - 4\left\{-\frac{1}{4}(D-4)[x]\right\} = 0. \end{aligned}$$

After some algebra, the above system simplifies to

$$\begin{aligned} &-(D-4)[x] + 2(D-4)[y] = 0, \\ &\left(D^2 - 8D + 8\right)[x] - 16y = 0. \end{aligned}$$

We use the second equation to find that

$$y = \frac{1}{16}\left(D^2 - 8D + 8\right)[x]. \tag{5.13}$$

Then the first equation becomes

$$\begin{aligned} &-(D-4)[x] + 2(D-4)\left[\frac{1}{16}\left(D^2 - 8D + 8\right)[x]\right] = 0 \\ \Rightarrow \quad &(D-4)\left\{-1 + \frac{1}{8}\left(D^2 - 8D + 8\right)\right\}[x] = 0 \quad \Rightarrow \quad (D-4)D(D-8)[x] = 0. \end{aligned}$$

Solving the characteristic equation, we get $r = 0, 4$, and 8; so

$$x = c_1 e^{8t} + c_2 e^{4t} + c_3.$$

Substitution of this solution into (5.12) and (5.13) yield

$$z = \frac{1}{4}(-x' + 4x) = -c_1 e^{8t} + c_3 ,$$
$$y = \frac{1}{16}(x'' - 8x' + 8x) = \frac{1}{2}\left(c_1 e^{8t} - c_2 e^{4t} + c_3\right).$$

29. We begin by expressing the system in operator notation

$$(D - \lambda)[x] + y = 0,$$
$$-3x + (D - 1)[y] = 0.$$

We eliminate y by applying $(D-1)$ to the first equation and subtracting the second equation from it. This gives

$$\{(D-1)(D-\lambda) - (-3)\}[x] = 0$$
$$\Rightarrow \quad \left\{D^2 - (\lambda+1)D + (\lambda+3)\right\}[x] = 0. \tag{5.14}$$

Note that since the given system is homogeneous, $y(t)$ also satisfies this equation (compare (7) and (8) on page 247 of the text). So, we can investigate solutions $x(t)$ only. The auxiliary equation, $r^2 - (\lambda+1)r + (\lambda+3) = 0$, has roots

$$r_1 = \frac{(\lambda+1) - \sqrt{\Delta}}{2}, \qquad r_2 = \frac{(\lambda+1) + \sqrt{\Delta}}{2},$$

where the discriminant $\Delta := (\lambda+1)^2 - 4(\lambda+3)$. We consider two cases:

i) If $\lambda + 3 < 0$, i.e. $\lambda < -3$, then $\Delta > (\lambda+1)^2$ and the root

$$r_2 > \frac{(\lambda+1) + |\lambda+1|}{2} = 0.$$

Therefore, the solution $x(t) = e^{r_2 t}$ is unbounded as $t \to +\infty$.

ii) If $\lambda + 3 \geq 0$, i.e. $\lambda \geq -3$, then $\Delta \leq (\lambda+1)^2$. If $\Delta < 0$, then a fundamental solution set to (5.14) is

$$\left\{e^{(\lambda+1)t/2}\cos\left(\frac{\sqrt{-\Delta}t}{2}\right), e^{(\lambda+1)t/2}\sin\left(\frac{\sqrt{-\Delta}t}{2}\right)\right\}. \tag{5.15}$$

If $\Delta \geq 0$, then $\sqrt{\Delta} < |\lambda + 1|$ and a fundamental solution set is

$$\begin{aligned} &\{e^{r_1 t},\, e^{r_2 t}\}, \quad \text{if } \Delta > 0, \\ &\{e^{r_1 t},\, te^{r_1 t}\}, \quad \text{if } \Delta = 0, \end{aligned} \tag{5.16}$$

where both roots r_1, r_2 are non-positive if and only if $\lambda \leq -1$. For $\lambda = -1$ we have $\Delta = (-1+1)^2 - 4(-1+3) < 0$, and we have a particular case of the fundamental solution set (5.15) (without exponential term) consisting of bounded functions. Finally, if $\lambda < -1$, then $r_1 < 0$, $r_2 \leq 0$, and all the functions listed in (5.15), (5.16) are bounded.

Any solution $x(t)$ is a linear combination of fundamental solutions and, therefore, all solutions $x(t)$ are bounded if and only if $-3 \leq \lambda \leq -1$.

31. Solving this problem, we follow the arguments described in Section 5.1, page 242 of the text, i.e., $x(t)$, the mass of salt in the tank A, and $y(t)$, the mass of salt in the tank B, satisfy the system

$$\begin{aligned} \frac{dx}{dt} &= \text{input}_\text{A} - \text{output}_\text{A}\,, \\ \frac{dy}{dt} &= \text{input}_\text{B} - \text{output}_\text{B}\,, \end{aligned} \tag{5.17}$$

with initial conditions $x(0) = 0$, $y(0) = 20$. It is important to notice that the volume of each tank stays at 100 L because the net flow rate into each tank is the same as the net outflow. Next we observe that "input_A" consists of the salt coming from outside, which is

$$0.2\,\text{kg/L} \cdot 6\,\text{L/min} = 1.2\,\text{kg/min},$$

and the salt coming from the tank B, which is given by

$$\frac{y(t)}{100}\,\text{kg/L} \cdot 1\,\text{L/min} = \frac{y(t)}{100}\,\text{kg/min}.$$

Thus,

$$\text{input}_\text{A} = \left[1.2 + \frac{y(t)}{100}\right]\,\text{kg/min}.$$

"output$_A$" consists of two flows: one is going out of the system and the other one is going to the tank B. So,

$$\text{output}_A = \frac{x(t)}{100}\,\text{kg/L} \cdot (4+3)\,\text{L/min} = \frac{7x(t)}{100}\,\text{kg/min},$$

and the first equation in (5.17) becomes

$$\frac{dx}{dt} = 1.2 + \frac{y}{100} - \frac{7x}{100}\,.$$

Similarly, the second equation in (5.17) can be written as

$$\frac{dy}{dt} = \frac{3x}{100} - \frac{3y}{100}\,.$$

Rewriting this system in the operator form, we obtain

$$\begin{aligned} (D+0.07)[x] - 0.01y &= 1.2\,, \\ -0.03x + (D+0.03)[y] &= 0\,. \end{aligned} \tag{5.18}$$

Eliminating y yields

$$\{(D+0.07)(D+0.03) - (-0.01)(-0.03)\}\,[x] = (D+0.03)[1.2] = 0.036\,,$$

which simplifies to

$$\left(D^2 + 0.1D + 0.0018\right)[x] = 0.036\,. \tag{5.19}$$

The auxiliary equation, $r^2 + 0.1r + 0.0018 = 0$, has roots

$$\begin{aligned} r_1 &= -\frac{1}{20} - \sqrt{\frac{1}{400} - \frac{18}{10000}} = -\frac{1}{20} - \frac{\sqrt{7}}{100} = \frac{-5-\sqrt{7}}{100} \approx -0.0765\,, \\ r_2 &= \frac{-5+\sqrt{7}}{100} \approx -0.0235\,. \end{aligned}$$

Therefore, the general solution the corresponding homogeneous equation is

$$x_h(t) = C_1 e^{r_1 t} + C_2 e^{r_2 t}.$$

Since the nonhomogeneous term in (5.19) is a constant (0.036), we are looking for a particular solution of the form $x_p(t) = A$ =const. Substituting into (5.19) yields

$$0.0018A = 0.036 \qquad \Rightarrow \qquad A = 20,$$

and the general solution, $x(t)$, is

$$x(t) = x_h(t) + x_p(t) = C_1 e^{r_1 t} + C_2 e^{r_2 t} + 20.$$

From the first equation in (5.18) we find

$$\begin{aligned} y(t) &= 100 \cdot \{(D + 0.07)[x] - 1.2\} = 100 \frac{dx}{dt} + 7x(t) - 120 \\ &= 100 \left\{ r_1 C_1 e^{r_1 t} + r_2 C_2 e^{r_2 t} \right\} + 7 \left\{ C_1 e^{r_1 t} + C_2 e^{r_2 t} + 20 \right\} - 120 \\ &= \left(2 - \sqrt{7}\right) C_1 e^{r_1 t} + \left(2 + \sqrt{7}\right) C_2 e^{r_2 t} + 20. \end{aligned}$$

The initial conditions imply

$$\begin{aligned} 0 &= x(0) = C_1 + C_2 + 20, \\ 20 &= y(0) = (2 - \sqrt{7})\, C_1 + (2 + \sqrt{7})\, C_2 + 20 \end{aligned}$$

$$\Rightarrow \quad \begin{aligned} & C_1 + C_2 = -20, \\ & (2 - \sqrt{7})\, C_1 + (2 + \sqrt{7})\, C_2 = 0 \end{aligned}$$

$$\Rightarrow \quad C_1 = -\left(10 + \frac{20}{\sqrt{7}}\right), \qquad C_2 = -\left(10 - \frac{20}{\sqrt{7}}\right).$$

Thus the solution to the problem is

$$\begin{aligned} x(t) &= -\left(10 + \frac{20}{\sqrt{7}}\right) e^{r_1 t} - \left(10 - \frac{20}{\sqrt{7}}\right) e^{r_2 t} + 20 \text{ (kg)}, \\ y(t) &= \frac{30}{\sqrt{7}} e^{r_1 t} - \frac{30}{\sqrt{7}} e^{r_2 t} + 20 \text{ (kg)}. \end{aligned}$$

33. Since no solution flows in or out of the system from the tank B, we conclude that the solution flows from the tank B to the tank A with the same rate as it does from A to B, that is, 1 L/min. Furthermore, the solution flows in and out of the tank A with the same rate, 4 L/min, and so the volume of the solution in the tank A (as well as in the tank B) remains constant, 100 L. Thus, with $x(t)$ and $y(t)$ denoting the amount of salt in the tanks A and B, respectively, the law "rate of change = input rate – output rate" becomes

Tank A:

$$x' = \left(4\,\text{L/min} \cdot 0.2\,\text{kg/L} + 1\,\text{L/min} \cdot \frac{y}{100}\,\text{kg/L}\right) - \frac{x}{100}\,\text{kg/L} \cdot (1\,\text{L/min} + 4\,\text{L/min});$$

Tank B:

$$y' = 1\,\text{L/min} \cdot \frac{x}{100}\,\text{kg/L} - 1\,\text{L/min} \cdot \frac{y}{100}\,\text{kg/L}.$$

Hence, we obtain the system

$$\begin{aligned} x' &= 0.8 - \frac{x}{20} + \frac{y}{100}\,, \\ y' &= \frac{x}{100} - \frac{y}{100}\,. \end{aligned}$$

From the second equation, we find that $x = 100y' + y$. Substitution into the first equation yields

$$\begin{aligned} &(100y' + y)' = 0.8 - \frac{100y' + y}{20} + \frac{y}{100} \\ \Rightarrow \qquad &100y'' + 6y' + \frac{1}{25}\,y = 0.8 \qquad \Rightarrow \qquad y'' + 0.06y' + 0.0004y = 0.008\,. \quad (5.20) \end{aligned}$$

The characteristic equation $r^2 + 0.06r + 0.0004 = 0$ of the corresponding homogeneous equation has roots

$$r = \frac{-0.06 \pm \sqrt{(0.06)^2 - 4(1)(0.0004)}}{2} = \frac{-3 \pm \sqrt{5}}{100}\,,$$

and so

$$y_h(t) = c_1 e^{(-3-\sqrt{5})t/100} + c_2 e^{(-3+\sqrt{5})t/100}$$

is a general solution to the homogeneous equation. We now look for a particular solution of the form $y_p(t) = c$. Substitution into (5.20) gives

$$0.0004c = 0.008 \qquad \Rightarrow \qquad c = \frac{0.008}{0.0004} = 20.$$

Thus

$$y(t) = y_p(t) + y_h(t) = 20 + c_1 e^{(-3-\sqrt{5})t/100} + c_2 e^{(-3+\sqrt{5})t/100} \qquad (5.21)$$

is a general solution to (5.20). Then

$$\begin{aligned} x(t) = y + 100y' &= 20 + (1 - 3 - \sqrt{5})c_1 e^{(-3-\sqrt{5})t/100} + (1 - 3 + \sqrt{5})c_2 e^{(-3+\sqrt{5})t/100} \\ &= 20 - (2 + \sqrt{5})c_1 e^{(-3-\sqrt{5})t/100} + (-2 + \sqrt{5})c_2 e^{(-3+\sqrt{5})t/100}\,. \qquad (5.22) \end{aligned}$$

Next, we use the initial condition, $x(0) = 0$, $y(0) = 20$, to find values of c_1 and c_2.

$$\begin{aligned} &20 - (2+\sqrt{5})c_1 + (-2+\sqrt{5})c_2 = 0, \\ &20 + c_1 + c_2 = 20 \end{aligned} \qquad \Rightarrow \qquad \begin{aligned} c_1 &= 10/\sqrt{5}, \\ c_2 &= -10/\sqrt{5}. \end{aligned}$$

With these values, the solution given in (5.21), (5.22) becomes

$$x(t) = 20 - \left(\frac{20+10\sqrt{5}}{\sqrt{5}}\right) e^{(-3-\sqrt{5})t/100} + \left(\frac{20-10\sqrt{5}}{\sqrt{5}}\right) e^{(-3+\sqrt{5})t/100},$$

$$y(t) = 20 + \left(\frac{10}{\sqrt{5}}\right) e^{(-3-\sqrt{5})t/100} - \left(\frac{10}{\sqrt{5}}\right) e^{(-3+\sqrt{5})t/100}.$$

35. Let $x(t)$ and $y(t)$ denote the temperatures at time t in zones A and B, respectively. Therefore, the rate of change of temperature in zone A will be $x'(t)$ and in zone B will be $y'(t)$. We can apply Newton's law of cooling to help us express these rates of change in an alternate manner. Thus, we observe that the rate of change of the temperature in zone A due to the outside temperature is $k_1[100 - x(t)]$ and due to the temperature in zone B is $k_2[y(t) - x(t)]$. Since the time constant for heat transfer between zone A and the outside is 2 hrs ($= 1/k_1$), we see that $k_1 = 1/2$. Similarly, we see that $1/k_2 = 4$ which implies that $k_2 = 1/4$. Therefore, since there is no heating or cooling source in zone A, we can write the equation for the rate of change of the temperature in the attic as

$$x'(t) = \frac{1}{2}[100 - x(t)] + \frac{1}{4}[y(t) - x(t)].$$

In the same way, we see that the rate of change of the temperature in zone B due to the temperature of the attic is $k_3[x(t) - y(t)]$, where $1/k_3 = 4$; and the rate of change of the temperature in this zone due to the outside temperature is $k_4[100 - y(t)]$, where $1/k_4 = 4$. In this zone, however, we must consider the cooling due to the air conditioner. Since the heat capacity of zone B is $(1/2)°$F per thousand Btu and the air conditioner has the cooling capacity of 24 thousand Btu per hr, we see that the air conditioner removes heat from this zone at the rate of $(1/2) \times 24° = 12°$ F/hr. (Since heat is *removed* from the house, this rate will be negative.) By combining these observations, we see that the rate of change of the temperature in zone B is given by

$$y'(t) = -12 + \frac{1}{4}[x(t) - y(t)] + \frac{1}{4}[100 - y(t)].$$

By simplifying these equations, we observe that this cooling problem satisfies the system

$$\begin{aligned} 4x'(t) + 3x(t) - y(t) &= 200, \\ -x'(t) + 4y'(t) + 2y(t) &= 52. \end{aligned}$$

In operator notation, this system becomes

$$\begin{aligned} (4D+3)[x] - [y] &= 200, \\ -[x] + (4D+2)[y] &= 52. \end{aligned}$$

Since we are interested in the temperature in the attic, $x(t)$, we will eliminate the function $y(t)$ from the system above by applying $(4D+2)$ to the first equation and adding the resulting equations to obtain

$$\begin{aligned} &\{(4D+2)(4D+3) - 1\}\,[x] = (4D+2)[200] + 52 = 452 \\ \Rightarrow \qquad &\left(16D^2 + 20D + 5\right)[x] = 452. \end{aligned} \tag{5.23}$$

This last equation is a linear equation with constant coefficients whose corresponding homogeneous equation has the associated auxiliary equation $16r^2 + 20r + 5 = 0$. By the quadratic formula, the roots to this auxiliary equation are

$$r_1 = \frac{-5+\sqrt{5}}{8} \approx -0.345 \qquad \text{and} \qquad r_2 = \frac{-5-\sqrt{5}}{8} \approx -0.905\,.$$

Therefore, the homogeneous equation associated with this equation has a general solution given by

$$x_h(t) = c_1 e^{r_1 t} + c_2 e^{r_2 t},$$

where r_1 and r_2 are given above. By the method of undetermined coefficients, we observe that a particular solution to equation (5.23) will have the form

$$x_p(t) = A \qquad \Rightarrow \qquad x_p'(t) = 0 \qquad \Rightarrow \qquad x_p''(t) = 0.$$

Substituting these expressions into equation (5.23) yields

$$16x_p'' + 20x_p' + 5x_p = 5A = 452 \qquad \Rightarrow \qquad A = 90.4\,.$$

Thus, a particular solution to the differential equation given in (5.23) is $x_p(t) = 90.4$ and the general solution to this equation will be

$$x(t) = c_1e^{r_1t} + c_2e^{r_2t} + 90.4\,,$$

where $r_1 = (-5+\sqrt{5})/8$ and $r_2 = (-5-\sqrt{5})/8$. To determine the maximum temperature of the attic, we will assume that zones A and B have sufficiently cool initial temperatures. (So that, for example, c_1 and c_2 are negative.) Since r_1 and r_2 are negative, as t goes to infinity, $c_1e^{r_1t}$ and $c_2e^{r_2t}$ each go to zero. Therefore, the maximum temperature that can be attained in the attic will be

$$\lim_{t\to\infty} x(t) = 90.4^\circ\,\text{F}.$$

37. In this problem, we combine the idea exploded in interconnected tanks problems,

$$\text{rate of change} = \text{rate in} - \text{rate out}, \tag{5.24}$$

with the Newton's law of cooling

$$\frac{dT}{dt} = K(T-M). \tag{5.25}$$

Let $x(t)$ and $y(t)$ denote temperatures in rooms A and B, respectively.

Room A. It gets temperature only from the heater with a rate

$$\text{rate in} = 80,000\,\text{Btu/h}\cdot\frac{1/4^\circ}{1000\,\text{Btu}} = 20^\circ/\text{h}.$$

Temperature goes out of the room A into the room B and outside with different coefficients of proportionality in (5.25): $K_1 = 1/2$ and $K_2 = 1/4$, respectively. Therefore,

$$\begin{aligned}\text{rate out} &= \text{rate into B} + \text{rate outside}\\ &= \frac{1}{2}(x-y) + \frac{1}{4}(x-0) = \frac{3}{4}x - \frac{1}{2}y.\end{aligned}$$

Thus, (5.24) implies that

$$x' = 20 - \left(\frac{3}{4}x - \frac{1}{2}y\right) = 20 - \frac{3}{4}x + \frac{1}{2}y.$$

Room B. Similarly, we obtain

$$y' = \left[1000 \cdot \frac{2}{1000} + \frac{1}{2}(x-y)\right] - \frac{1}{5}(y-0) = 2 + \frac{1}{2}x - \frac{7}{10}y.$$

Hence, the system governing the temperature exchange is

$$\begin{aligned} x' &= 20 - (3/4)x + (1/2)y, \\ y' &= 2 + (1/2)x - (7/10)y. \end{aligned}$$

We find the critical points of this system by solving

$$\begin{aligned} 20 - (3/4)x + (1/2)y &= 0, \\ 2 + (1/2)x - (7/10)y &= 0 \end{aligned} \quad \Rightarrow \quad \begin{aligned} 3x - 2y &= 80, \\ -5x + 7y &= 20 \end{aligned} \quad \Rightarrow \quad \begin{aligned} x &= 600/11\,, \\ y &= 460/11\,. \end{aligned}$$

Therefore, $(600/11, 460/11)$ is the only critical point of the system. Analyzing the direction field, we conclude that $(600/11, 460/11)$ is an asymptotically stable node. Hence,

$$\lim_{t\to\infty} y(t) = \frac{460}{11} \approx 41.8°\text{F}.$$

(One can also find an explicit solution $y(t) = 460/11 + c_1 e^{r_1 t} + c_2 e^{r_2 t}$, where $r_1 < 0$, $r_2 < 0$, to conclude that $y(t) \to 460/11$ as $t \to \infty$.)

39. Let y be an arbitrary function differentiable as many times as necessary. Note that, for a differential operator, say, A, $A[y]$ is a function, and so we can use commutative, associative, and distributive laws operating such functions.

(a) It is straightforward that

$$(A+B)[y] := A[y] + B[y] = B[y] + A[y] =: (B+A)[y].$$

To prove commutativity of the multiplication, we will use the linearity of the differential operator D, that is, $D[\alpha x + \beta y] = \alpha D[x] + \beta D[y]$ and the fact that $D^i D^j = D^{i+j} = D^j D^i$. For the latter,

$$\left(D^i D^j\right)[y] := D^i\left[D^j[y]\right] = \left(y^{(j)}\right)^{(i)} = y^{(i+j)} = \left(y^{(i)}\right)^{(j)} = D^j\left[D^i[y]\right] =: \left(D^j D^i\right)[y].$$

Thus we have

$$\begin{aligned}
(AB)[y] &:= A\big[B[y]\big] = \left(\sum_{j=0}^{2} a_j D^j\right)\left[\left(\sum_{i=0}^{2} b_i D^i\right)[y]\right] \\
&:= \left(\sum_{j=0}^{2} a_j D^j\right)\left[\sum_{i=0}^{2} b_i D^i[y]\right] := \sum_{j=0}^{2}\left\{a_j D^j\left[\sum_{i=0}^{2} b_i D^i[y]\right]\right\} \\
&= \sum_{j=0}^{2}\sum_{i=0}^{2}\left(a_j D^j b_i D^i\right)[y] = \sum_{i=0}^{2}\sum_{j=0}^{2}\left(b_i D^i a_j D^j\right)[y] \\
&= \sum_{i=0}^{2}\left\{b_i D^i\left[\sum_{j=0}^{2} a_j D^j[y]\right]\right\} =: \left(\sum_{i=0}^{2} b_i D^i\right)\left[\sum_{j=0}^{2} a_j D^j[y]\right] \\
&=: \left(\sum_{i=0}^{2} b_i D^i\right)\left[\left(\sum_{j=0}^{2} a_j D^j\right)[y]\right] = B\big[A[y]\big] =: (BA)[y].
\end{aligned}$$

(b) We have

$$\begin{aligned}
\{(A+B)+C\}[y] &:= (A+B)[y] + C[y] := (A[y]+B[y]) + C[y] \\
&= A[y] + (B[y]+C[y]) =: A[y] + (B+C)[y] =: \{A+(B+C)\}[y]
\end{aligned}$$

and

$$\{(AB)C\}[y] := (AB)\big[C[y]\big] := A\Big[B\big[C[y]\big]\Big] =: A\big[\,(BC)[y]\,\big] =: \{A(BC)\}[y].$$

(c) Using the linearity of differential operators, we obtain

$$\begin{aligned}
\{A(B+C)\}[y] &:= A\big[(B+C)[y]\big] := A\big[B[y]+C[y]\big] \\
&= A\big[B[y]\big] + A\big[C[y]\big] =: (AB)[y] + (AC)[y] =: \{(AB)+(AC)\}[y].
\end{aligned}$$

41. As it was noticed in Example 2, we can treat a "polynomial" in D, that is, an expression of the form $p(D) = \sum_{i=0}^{n} a_i D^i$, as a regular polynomial, i.e., $p(r) = \sum_{i=0}^{n} a_i r^i$, while performing arithmetic operations. Hence, the factorization problem for $p(D)$ is equivalent to the factorization problem for $p(r)$, which is the same as finding its roots.

(a) $r = \dfrac{-3 \pm \sqrt{3^2 - 4(-4)}}{2} = \dfrac{-3 \pm 5}{2} = -4, 1 \quad \Rightarrow \quad D^2 + 3D - 4 = (D+4)(D-1).$

(b) $r = \dfrac{-1 \pm \sqrt{1^2 - 4(-6)}}{2} = \dfrac{-1 \pm 5}{2} = -3, 2 \quad \Rightarrow \quad D^2 + D - 6 = (D+3)(D-2).$

(c) $r = \dfrac{-9 \pm \sqrt{9^2 - 4(-5)2}}{4} = \dfrac{-9 \pm 11}{4} = -5, 1/2 \quad \Rightarrow \quad 2D^2 + 9D - 5 = (D+5)(2D-1).$

(d) $r = \pm\sqrt{2} \quad \Rightarrow \quad D^2 - 2 = (D + \sqrt{2})(D - \sqrt{2}).$

EXERCISES 5.3: Solving Systems and Higher–Order Equations Numerically, page 261

1. We isolate $y''(t)$ first and obtain an equivalent equation

$$y''(t) = 3y(t) - ty'(t) + t^2 .$$

Denoting $x_1 := y$, $x_2 := y'$ we conclude that

$$\begin{aligned} x_1' &= y' = x_2 , \\ x_2' &= (y')' = y'' = 3y - ty' + t^2 = 3x_1 - tx_2 + t^2 , \end{aligned}$$

with initial conditions $x_1(0) = y(0) = 3$, $x_2(0) = y'(0) = -6$. Therefore, given initial value problem is equivalent to

$$\begin{aligned} x_1' &= x_2 , \\ x_2' &= 3x_1 - tx_2 + t^2 , \\ x_1(0) &= 3, \quad x_2(0) = -6. \end{aligned}$$

3. Isolating $y^{(4)}(t)$, we get

$$y^{(4)}(t) = y^{(3)}(t) - 7y(t) + \cos t .$$

In this problem, we need four new variables – for $y(t)$, $y'(t)$, $y''(t)$, and $y^{(3)}(t)$. Thus we denote

$$x_1 = y, \qquad x_2 = y' , \qquad x_3 = y'' , \quad \text{and} \quad x_4 = y^{(3)} .$$

The initial conditions then become

$$x_1(0) = y(0) = 1,\ x_2(0) = y'(0) = 1,\ x_3(0) = y''(0) = 0,\ x_4(0) = y^{(3)}(0) = 2.$$

We have

$$x_1' = y' = x_2 ,$$

$$
\begin{aligned}
x_2' &= (y')' = y'' = x_3\,,\\
x_3' &= (y'')' = y^{(3)} = x_4\,,\\
x_4' &= \left(y^{(3)}\right)' = y^{(4)} = y^{(3)} - 7y + \cos t = x_4 - 7x_1 + \cos t\,.
\end{aligned}
$$

Hence, the required initial value problem for a system in normal form is

$$
\begin{aligned}
&x_1' = x_2\,,\\
&x_2' = x_3\,,\\
&x_3' = x_4\,,\\
&x_4' = x_4 - 7x_1 + \cos t,\\
&x_1(0) = x_2(0) = 1, \quad x_3(0) = 0, \quad x_4(0) = 2\,.
\end{aligned}
$$

5. First we express the given system as

$$
\begin{aligned}
x'' &= x' - y + 2t,\\
y'' &= x - y - 1.
\end{aligned}
$$

Setting $x_1 = x$, $x_2 = x'$, $x_3 = y$, $x_4 = y'$ we obtain

$$
\begin{aligned}
x_1' &= x' = x_2\,, & & & x_1' &= x_2\,,\\
x_2' &= x'' = x_2 - x_3 + 2t\,, & &\Rightarrow & x_2' &= x_2 - x_3 + 2t\,,\\
x_3' &= y' = x_4\,, & & & x_3' &= x_4\,,\\
x_4' &= y'' = x_1 - x_3 - 1 & & & x_4' &= x_1 - x_3 - 1
\end{aligned}
$$

with initial conditions $x_1(3) = 5$, $x_2(3) = 2$, $x_3(3) = 1$, and $x_4(3) = -1$.

7. In an equivalent form, we have a system

$$
\begin{aligned}
x''' &= y + t,\\
y'' &= \frac{2y - 2x'' + 1}{5}\,.
\end{aligned}
$$

Setting

$$
x_1 = x, \quad x_2 = x', \quad x_3 = x'', \quad x_4 = y, \quad x_5 = y',
$$

we obtain a system in normal form

$$
\begin{aligned}
x_1' &= x_2\,,\\
x_2' &= x_3\,,\\
x_3' &= x_4 + t\,,\\
x_4' &= x_5\,,\\
x_5' &= \frac{1}{5}\,(2x_4 - 2x_3 + 1)
\end{aligned}
$$

with initial conditions

$$x_1(0) = x_2(0) = x_3(0) = 4, \quad x_4(0) = x_5(0) = 1.$$

9. To see how the improved Euler's method can be extended let's recall, from Section 3.6, the improved Euler's method (pages 127–128 of the text). For the initial value problem

$$x' = f(t, x), \qquad x(t_0) = x_0\,,$$

the recursive formulas for the improved Euler's method are

$$
\begin{aligned}
t_{n+1} &= t_n + h,\\
x_{n+1} &= x_n + \frac{h}{2}\left[f(t_n, x_n) + f(t_n + h, x_n + hf(t_n, x_n))\right],
\end{aligned}
$$

where h is the step size. Now suppose we want to approximate the solution $x_1(t)$, $x_2(t)$ to the system

$$x_1' = f_1(t, x_1, x_2) \qquad \text{and} \qquad x_2' = f_2(t, x_1, x_2),$$

that satisfies the initial conditions

$$x_1(t_0) = a_1, \qquad x_2(t_0) = a_2\,.$$

Let $x_{1;n}$ and $x_{2;n}$ denote approximations to $x_1(t_n)$ and $x_2(t_n)$, respectively, where $t_n = t_0 + nh$ for $n = 0, 1, 2, \ldots$. The recursive formulas for the improved Euler's method are obtained by forming the vector analogue of the scalar formula. We obtain

$$t_{n+1} = t_n + h,$$

$$x_{1;n+1} = x_{1;n} + \frac{h}{2}\,[f_1(t_n, x_{1;n}, x_{2;n})$$
$$+f_1(t_n + h, x_{1;n} + hf_1(t_n, x_{1;n}, x_{2;n}), x_{2;n} + hf_2(t_n, x_{1;n}, x_{2;n}))],$$
$$x_{2;n+1} = x_{2;n} + \frac{h}{2}\,[f_2(t_n, x_{1;n}, x_{2;n})$$
$$+f_2(t_n + h, x_{1;n} + hf_1(t_n, x_{1;n}, x_{2;n}), x_{2;n} + hf_2(t_n, x_{1;n}, x_{2;n}))].$$

The approach can be used more generally for systems of m equations in normal form. Suppose we want to approximate the solution $x_1(t)$, $x_2(t)$, …, $x_m(t)$ to the system

$$\begin{aligned} x_1' &= f_1\left(t, x_1, x_2, \dots, x_m\right), \\ x_2' &= f_2\left(t, x_1, x_2, \dots, x_m\right), \\ &\vdots \\ x_m' &= f_m\left(t, x_1, x_2, \dots, x_m\right), \end{aligned}$$

with the initial conditions

$$x_1(t_0) = a_1\,, \quad x_2(t_0) = a_2\,, \quad \dots, \quad x_m(t_0) = a_m\,.$$

We adapt the recursive formulas above to obtain

$$\begin{aligned} t_{n+1} &= t_n + h, \qquad n = 0, 1, 2, \dots\,; \\ x_{1;n+1} &= x_{1;n} + \frac{h}{2}\,[f_1(t_n, x_{1;n}, x_{2;n}, \dots, x_{m;n}) + f_1(t_n + h, x_{1;n} + hf_1(t_n, x_{1;n}, x_{2;n}, \dots, x_{m;n}), \\ &\qquad x_{2;n} + hf_2(t_n, x_{1;n}, x_{2;n}, \dots, x_{m;n}), \dots, x_{m;n} + hf_m(t_n, x_{1;n}, x_{2;n}, \dots, x_{m;n}))]\,, \\ x_{2;n+1} &= x_{2;n} + \frac{h}{2}\,[f_2(t_n, x_{1;n}, x_{2;n}, \dots, x_{m;n}) + f_2(t_n + h, x_{1;n} + hf_1(t_n, x_{1;n}, x_{2;n}, \dots, x_{m;n}), \\ &\qquad x_{2;n} + hf_2(t_n, x_{1;n}, x_{2;n}, \dots, x_{m;n}), \dots, x_{m;n} + hf_m(t_n, x_{1;n}, x_{2;n}, \dots, x_{m;n}))]\,, \\ &\vdots \\ x_{m;n+1} &= x_{m;n} + \frac{h}{2}\,[f_m(t_n, x_{1;n}, x_{2;n}, \dots, x_{m;n}) + f_m(t_n + h, x_{1;n} + hf_1(t_n, x_{1;n}, x_{2;n}, \dots, x_{m;n}), \\ &\qquad x_{2;n} + hf_2(t_n, x_{1;n}, x_{2;n}, \dots, x_{m;n}), \dots, x_{m;n} + hf_m(t_n, x_{1;n}, x_{2;n}, \dots, x_{m;n}))]\,. \end{aligned}$$

11. See the answer in the text.

13. See the answer in the text.

15. See the answer in the text.

17. Let $x_1 := u$ and $x_2 := v$, and denote the independent variable by t (in order to be consistent with formulas in Section 5.3). In new notation, we have an initial value problem

$$\begin{aligned} x_1' &= 3x_1 - 4x_2\,, \\ x_2' &= 2x_1 - 3x_2\,, \\ x_1(0) &= x_2(0) = 1 \end{aligned}$$

for a system in normal form. Here

$$f_1(t, x_1, x_2) = 3x_1 - 4x_2\,, \qquad f_2(t, x_1, x_2) = 2x_1 - 3x_2\,.$$

Thus formulas for $k_{i,j}$'s in vectorized Runge-Kutta algorithm become

$$\begin{aligned} k_{1,1} &= h(3x_{1;n} - 4x_{2;n}), \\ k_{2,1} &= h(2x_{1;n} - 3x_{2;n}), \\ k_{1,2} &= h\left[3\left(x_{1;n} + \frac{k_{1,1}}{2}\right) - 4\left(x_{2;n} + \frac{k_{2,1}}{2}\right)\right], \\ k_{2,2} &= h\left[2\left(x_{1;n} + \frac{k_{1,1}}{2}\right) - 3\left(x_{2;n} + \frac{k_{2,1}}{2}\right)\right], \\ k_{1,3} &= h\left[3\left(x_{1;n} + \frac{k_{1,2}}{2}\right) - 4\left(x_{2;n} + \frac{k_{2,2}}{2}\right)\right], \\ k_{2,3} &= h\left[2\left(x_{1;n} + \frac{k_{1,2}}{2}\right) - 3\left(x_{2;n} + \frac{k_{2,2}}{2}\right)\right], \\ k_{1,4} &= h\left[3\left(x_{1;n} + k_{1,3}\right) - 4\left(x_{2;n} + k_{2,3}\right)\right], \\ k_{2,4} &= h\left[2\left(x_{1;n} + k_{1,3}\right) - 3\left(x_{2;n} + k_{2,3}\right)\right]. \end{aligned}$$

With the inputs $t_0 = 0$, $x_{1;0} = x_{2;0} = 1$, and step size $h = 1$ we compute

$$\begin{aligned} k_{1,1} &= h(3x_{1;0} - 4x_{2;0}) = 3(1) - 4(1) = -1, \\ k_{2,1} &= h(2x_{1;0} - 3x_{2;0}) = 2(1) - 3(1) = -1, \\ k_{1,2} &= h\left[3\left(x_{1;0} + \frac{k_{1,1}}{2}\right) - 4\left(x_{2;0} + \frac{k_{2,1}}{2}\right)\right] = 3\left(1 + \frac{-1}{2}\right) - 4\left(1 + \frac{-1}{2}\right) = -\frac{1}{2}, \end{aligned}$$

$$k_{2,2} = h\left[2\left(x_{1;0} + \frac{k_{1,1}}{2}\right) - 3\left(x_{2;0} + \frac{k_{2,1}}{2}\right)\right] = 2\left(1 + \frac{-1}{2}\right) - 3\left(1 + \frac{-1}{2}\right) = -\frac{1}{2},$$
$$k_{1,3} = h\left[3\left(x_{1;0} + \frac{k_{1,2}}{2}\right) - 4\left(x_{2;0} + \frac{k_{2,2}}{2}\right)\right] = 3\left(1 + \frac{-1/2}{2}\right) - 4\left(1 + \frac{-1/2}{2}\right) = -\frac{3}{4},$$
$$k_{2,3} = h\left[2\left(x_{1;0} + \frac{k_{1,2}}{2}\right) - 3\left(x_{2;0} + \frac{k_{2,2}}{2}\right)\right] = 2\left(1 + \frac{-1/2}{2}\right) - 3\left(1 + \frac{-1/2}{2}\right) = -\frac{3}{4},$$
$$k_{1,4} = h\left[3\left(x_{1;0} + k_{1,3}\right) - 4\left(x_{2;0} + k_{2,3}\right)\right] = 3\left(1 + \frac{-3}{4}\right) - 4\left(1 + \frac{-3}{4}\right) = -\frac{1}{4},$$
$$k_{2,4} = h\left[2\left(x_{1;0} + k_{1,3}\right) - 3\left(x_{2;0} + k_{2,3}\right)\right] = 2\left(1 + \frac{-3}{4}\right) - 3\left(1 + \frac{-3}{4}\right) = -\frac{1}{4}.$$

Using the recursive formulas, we find $t_1 = t_0 + h = 0 + 1 = 1$ and

$$x_{1;1} = x_{1;0} + \frac{1}{6}\left(k_{1,1} + 2k_{1,2} + 2k_{1,3} + k_{1,4}\right) = 1 + \frac{(-1) + 2(-1/2) + 2(-3/4) + (-1/4)}{6} = \frac{3}{8},$$
$$x_{2;1} = x_{2;0} + \frac{1}{6}\left(k_{2,1} + 2k_{2,2} + 2k_{2,3} + k_{2,4}\right) = 1 + \frac{(-1) + 2(-1/2) + 2(-3/4) + (-1/4)}{6} = \frac{3}{8}$$

as approximations to $x_1(1)$ and $x_2(1)$ with step $h = 1$.

We repeat the algorithm with $h = 2^{-m}$, $m = 1, 2, \ldots$. The results of these computations are listed in Table 5-A.

Table 5–A: Approximations of the solution to Problem 17.

m	$h = 2^{-m}$	$x_1(1;h)$	$x_2(1;h)$
0	1.0	0.375	0.375
1	0.5	0.36817	0.36817
2	0.25	0.36789	0.36789

We stopped at $m = 2$, since

$$\left|x_1(1;2^{-1}) - x_1(1;2^{-2})\right| = \left|x_2(1;2^{-1}) - x_2(1;2^{-2})\right| = 0.36817 - 0.36789 = 0.00028 < 0.001.$$

Hence $u(1) = v(1) \approx 0.36789$.

18. For starting values we take $t_0 = 0$, $x_{0,1} = 10$, and $x_{0,2} = 15$, which are determined by the initial conditions. Here $h = 0.1$, and

$$\begin{aligned} f_1(t, x_1, x_2) &= -(0.1)x_1x_2 \,, \\ f_2(t, x_1, x_2) &= -x_1 \,. \end{aligned}$$

Now, using the definitions of t_n, $x_{i;n}$, $k_{i,1}$, $k_{i,2}$, $k_{i,3}$, and $k_{i,4}$ on page 258 of the text, we have

$$\begin{aligned}
k_{1,1} &= hf_1\left(t_n, x_{1;n}, x_{2;n}\right) = -h(0.1)x_{1;n}x_{2;n} \,, \\
k_{2,1} &= hf_2\left(t_n, x_{1;n}, x_{2;n}\right) = -hx_{1;n}, \\
k_{1,2} &= hf_1\left(t_n + \frac{h}{2}, x_{1;n} + \frac{k_{1,1}}{2}, x_{2;n} + \frac{k_{2,1}}{2}\right) = -h(0.1)\left(x_{1;n} + \frac{k_{1,1}}{2}\right)\left(x_{2;n} + \frac{k_{2,1}}{2}\right), \\
k_{2,2} &= hf_2\left(t_n + \frac{h}{2}, x_{1;n} + \frac{k_{1,1}}{2}, x_{2;n} + \frac{k_{2,1}}{2}\right) = -h\left(x_{1;n} + \frac{k_{1,1}}{2}\right), \\
k_{1,3} &= hf_1\left(t_n + \frac{h}{2}, x_{1;n} + \frac{k_{1,2}}{2}, x_{2;n} + \frac{k_{2,2}}{2}\right) = -h(0.1)\left(x_{1;n} + \frac{k_{1,2}}{2}\right)\left(x_{2;n} + \frac{k_{2,2}}{2}\right), \\
k_{2,3} &= hf_2\left(t_n + \frac{h}{2}, x_{1;n} + \frac{k_{1,2}}{2}, x_{2;n} + \frac{k_{2,2}}{2}\right) = -h\left(x_{1;n} + \frac{k_{1,2}}{2}\right), \\
k_{1,4} &= hf_1\left(t_n + h, x_{1;n} + k_{1,3}, x_{2;n} + k_{2,3}\right) = -h(0.1)\left(x_{1;n} + k_{1,3}\right)\left(x_{2;n} + k_{2,3}\right), \\
k_{2,4} &= hf_2\left(t_n + h, x_{1;n} + k_{1,3}, x_{2;n} + k_{2,3}\right) = -h\left(x_{1;n} + k_{1,3}\right).
\end{aligned}$$

Using these values, we find

$$\begin{aligned}
t_{n+1} &= t_n + h = t_n + 0.1 \,, \\
x_{1;n+1} &= x_{1;n} + \frac{1}{6}\left(k_{1,1} + 2k_{1,2} + 2k_{1,3} + k_{1,4}\right), \\
x_{2;n+1} &= x_{2;n} + \frac{1}{6}\left(k_{2,1} + 2k_{2,2} + 2k_{2,3} + k_{2,4}\right).
\end{aligned}$$

In Table 5-B we give approximate values for t_n, $x_{1;n}$, and $x_{2;n}$.

From Table 5-B we see that the strength of the guerrilla troops, x_1, approaches zero, therefore with the combat effectiveness coefficients of 0.1 for guerrilla troops and 1 for conventional troops the conventional troops win.

19. See the answer in the text.

Table 5–B: Approximations of the solutions to Problem 18.

t_n	$x_{1;n} \approx$	$x_{2;n} \approx$
0	10	15
0.1	3.124	9.353
0.2	1.381	7.254
0.3	0.707	6.256
0.4	0.389	5.726
0.5	0.223	5.428

21. First, we convert given initial value problem to an initial value problem for a normal system. Let $x_1(t) = H(t)$, $x_2(t) = H'(t)$. Then $H''(t) = x_2'(t)$, $x_1(0) = H(0) = 0$, $x_2(0) = H'(0) = 0$, and we get

$$\begin{aligned} &x_1' = x_2 \,, && && x_1' = x_2 \,, \\ &60 - x_1 = (77.7)x_2' + (19.42)x_2^2 \,, && \Rightarrow && x_2' = \left[60 - x_1 - (19.42)x_2^2\right]/77.7 \,, \\ &x_1(0) = x_2(0) = 0 && && x_1(0) = x_2(0) = 0. \end{aligned}$$

Thus $f_1(t, x_1, x_2) = x_2$, $f_2(t, x_1, x_2) = \left[60 - x_1 - (19.42)x_2^2\right]/77.7$, $t_0 = 0$, $x_{1;0} = 0$, and $x_{2;0} = 0$. With $h = 0.5$, we need $(5 - 0)/0.5 = 10$ steps to approximate the solution over the interval $[0, 5]$. Taking $n = 0$ in the vectorized Runge-Kutta algorithm, we approximate the solution at $t = 0.5$.

$$\begin{aligned} k_{1,1} &= hx_{2;0} = 0.5(0) = 0, \\ k_{2,1} &= h\left[60 - x_{1;0} - (19.42)x_{2;0}^2\right]/77.7 = 0.5\left[60 - (0) - (19.42)(0)^2\right]/77.7 = 0.38610 \,, \\ k_{1,2} &= h\left(x_{2;0} + \frac{k_{2,1}}{2}\right) = 0.5\left((0) + \frac{0.38610}{2}\right) = 0.09653 \,, \\ k_{2,2} &= h\left[60 - \left(x_{1;0} + \frac{k_{1,1}}{2}\right) - (19.42)\left(x_{2;0} + \frac{k_{2,1}}{2}\right)^2\right]/77.7 = 0.38144 \,, \\ k_{1,3} &= h\left(x_{2;0} + \frac{k_{2,2}}{2}\right) = 0.5\left((0) + \frac{0.38144}{2}\right) = 0.09536 \,, \end{aligned}$$

$$k_{2,3} = h\left[60 - \left(x_{1;0} + \frac{k_{1,2}}{2}\right) - (19.42)\left(x_{2;0} + \frac{k_{2,2}}{2}\right)^2\right]/77.7 = 0.38124\,,$$

$$k_{1,4} = h\left(x_{2;0} + k_{2,3}\right) = 0.5\left((0) + 0.38124\right) = 0.19062\,,$$

$$k_{2,4} = h\left[60 - \left(x_{1;0} + k_{1,3}\right) - (19.42)\left(x_{2;0} + k_{2,3}\right)^2\right]/77.7 = 0.36732\,.$$

Using the recursive formulas, we find

$$t_1 = t_0 + h = 0 + 0.5 = 0.5$$

$$x_1(0.5) \approx x_{1;1} = x_{1;0} + \frac{1}{6}\left(k_{1,1} + 2k_{1,2} + 2k_{1,3} + k_{1,4}\right) = 0.09573\,,$$

$$x_2(0.5) \approx x_{2;1} = x_{2;0} + \frac{1}{6}\left(k_{2,1} + 2k_{2,2} + 2k_{2,3} + k_{2,4}\right) = 0.37980\,.$$

Next, we repeat the procedure with $n = 1, 2, \ldots, 9$. The results of these computations (the values of $x_{1;n}$ only) are presented in Table 5-C.

Table 5–C: Approximations of the solution to Problem 21.

n	t_n	$x_{1;n} \approx H(t_n)$	n	t_n	$x_{1;n} \approx H(t_n)$
0	0	0	6	3.0	2.75497
1	0.5	0.09573	7	3.5	3.52322
2	1.0	0.37389	8	4.0	4.31970
3	1.5	0.81045	9	4.5	5.13307
4	2.0	1.37361	10	5.0	5.95554
5	2.5	2.03111			

---

23. Let $x_1 = y$ and $x_2 = y'$ to give the initial value problem

$$x_1' = f_1(t, x_1, x_2) = x_2\,, \qquad x_1(0) = a,$$

$$x_2' = f_2(t, x_1, x_2) = -x_1\left(1 + r x_1^2\right), \qquad x_2(0) = 0.$$

Now, using the definitions of t_n, $x_{i;n}$, $k_{i,1}$, $k_{i,2}$, $k_{i,3}$, and $k_{i,4}$ on page 258 of the text, we have

$$k_{1,1} = h f_1\left(t_n, x_{1;n}, x_{2;n}\right) = h x_{2;n}\,,$$

$$k_{2,1} = hf_2(t_n, x_{1;n}, x_{2;n}) = -hx_{1;n}\left(1 + rx_{1;n}^2\right),$$

$$k_{1,2} = hf_1\left(t_n + \frac{h}{2}, x_{1;n} + \frac{k_{1,1}}{2}, x_{2;n} + \frac{k_{2,1}}{2}\right) = h\left(x_{2;n} + \frac{k_{2,1}}{2}\right),$$

$$k_{2,2} = hf_2\left(t_n + \frac{h}{2}, x_{1;n} + \frac{k_{1,1}}{2}, x_{2;n} + \frac{k_{2,1}}{2}\right) = -h\left(x_{1;n} + \frac{k_{1,1}}{2}\right)\left[1 + r\left(x_{1;n} + \frac{k_{1,1}}{2}\right)^2\right],$$

$$k_{1,3} = hf_1\left(t_n + \frac{h}{2}, x_{1;n} + \frac{k_{1,2}}{2}, x_{2;n} + \frac{k_{2,2}}{2}\right) = h\left(x_{2;n} + \frac{k_{2,2}}{2}\right),$$

$$k_{2,3} = hf_2\left(t_n + \frac{h}{2}, x_{1;n} + \frac{k_{1,2}}{2}, x_{2;n} + \frac{k_{2,2}}{2}\right) = -h\left(x_{1;n} + \frac{k_{1,2}}{2}\right)\left[1 + r\left(x_{1;n} + \frac{k_{1,2}}{2}\right)^2\right],$$

$$k_{1,4} = hf_1(t_n + h, x_{1;n} + k_{1,3}, x_{2;n} + k_{2,3}) = h(x_{2;n} + k_{2,3}),$$

$$k_{2,4} = hf_2(t_n + h, x_{1;n} + k_{1,3}, x_{2;n} + k_{2,3}) = -h(x_{1;n} + k_{1,3})\left[1 + r(x_{1;n} + k_{1,3})^2\right].$$

Using these values, we find

$$t_{n+1} = t_n + h = t_n + 0.1\,,$$

$$x_{1;n+1} = x_{1;n} + \frac{1}{6}(k_{1,1} + 2k_{1,2} + 2k_{1,3} + k_{1,4})\,,$$

$$x_{2;n+1} = x_{2;n} + \frac{1}{6}(k_{2,1} + 2k_{2,2} + 2k_{2,3} + k_{2,4})\,.$$

In Table 5-D we give the approximate period for $r = 1$ and 2 with $a = 1$, 2 and 3, from this we see that the period varies as r is varied or as a is varied.

Table 5–D: Approximate period of the solution to Problem 23.

r	$a=1$	$a=2$	$a=3$
1	4.8	3.3	2.3
2	4.0	2.4	1.7

25. With $x_1 = y$, $x_2 = y'$, and $x_3 = y''$, the initial value problem can be expressed as the system

$$\begin{aligned} x_1' &= x_2\,, & x_1(0) &= 1,\\ x_2' &= x_3\,, & x_2(0) &= 1,\\ x_3' &= t - x_3 - x_1^2\,, & x_3(0) &= 1. \end{aligned}$$

Chapter 5

Here

$$f_1(t, x_1, x_2, x_3) = x_2\,,$$
$$f_2(t, x_1, x_2, x_3) = x_3\,,$$
$$f_3(t, x_1, x_2, x_3) = t - x_3 - x_1^2\,.$$

Since we are computing the approximations for $c = 1$, the initial value for h in Step 1 of the algorithm in Appendix E of the text is $h = (1-0)2^{-0} = 1$. The equations in Step 3 are

$$k_{1,1} = hf_1\,(t, x_1, x_2, x_3) = hx_2\,,$$
$$k_{2,1} = hf_2\,(t, x_1, x_2, x_3) = hx_3\,,$$
$$k_{3,1} = hf_3\,(t, x_1, x_2, x_3) = h\left(t - x_3 - x_1^2\right),$$
$$k_{1,2} = hf_1\left(t + \frac{h}{2}, x_1 + \frac{k_{1,1}}{2}, x_2 + \frac{k_{2,1}}{2}, x_3 + \frac{k_{3,1}}{2}\right) = h\left(x_2 + \frac{k_{2,1}}{2}\right),$$
$$k_{2,2} = hf_2\left(t + \frac{h}{2}, x_1 + \frac{k_{1,1}}{2}, x_2 + \frac{k_{2,1}}{2}, x_3 + \frac{k_{3,1}}{2}\right) = h\left(x_3 + \frac{k_{3,1}}{2}\right),$$
$$k_{3,2} = hf_3\left(t + \frac{h}{2}, x_1 + \frac{k_{1,1}}{2}, x_2 + \frac{k_{2,1}}{2}, x_3 + \frac{k_{3,1}}{2}\right) = h\left[t + \frac{h}{2} - x_3 - \frac{k_{3,1}}{2} - \left(x_1 + \frac{k_{1,1}}{2}\right)^2\right],$$
$$k_{1,3} = hf_1\left(t + \frac{h}{2}, x_1 + \frac{k_{1,2}}{2}, x_2 + \frac{k_{2,2}}{2}, x_3 + \frac{k_{3,2}}{2}\right) = h\left(x_2 + \frac{k_{2,2}}{2}\right),$$
$$k_{2,3} = hf_2\left(t + \frac{h}{2}, x_1 + \frac{k_{1,2}}{2}, x_2 + \frac{k_{2,2}}{2}, x_3 + \frac{k_{3,2}}{2}\right) = h\left(x_3 + \frac{k_{3,2}}{2}\right),$$
$$k_{3,3} = hf_3\left(t + \frac{h}{2}, x_1 + \frac{k_{1,2}}{2}, x_2 + \frac{k_{2,2}}{2}, x_3 + \frac{k_{3,2}}{2}\right) = h\left[t + \frac{h}{2} - x_3 - \frac{k_{3,2}}{2} - \left(x_1 + \frac{k_{1,2}}{2}\right)^2\right],$$
$$k_{1,4} = hf_1\,(t + h, x_1 + k_{1,3}, x_2 + k_{2,3}, x_3 + k_{3,3}) = h\,(x_2 + k_{2,3})\,,$$
$$k_{2,4} = hf_2\,(t + h, x_1 + k_{1,3}, x_2 + k_{2,3}, x_3 + k_{3,3}) = h\,(x_3 + k_{3,3})\,,$$
$$k_{3,4} = hf_3\,(t + h, x_1 + k_{1,3}, x_2 + k_{2,3}, x_3 + k_{3,3}) = h\left[t + h - x_3 - k_{3,3} - (x_1 + k_{1,3})^2\right].$$

Using the starting values $t_0 = 0$, $a_1 = 1$, $a_2 = 0$, and $a_3 = 1$, we obtain the first approximations

$$x_1(1;1) = 1.29167\,,$$
$$x_2(1;1) = 0.28125\,,$$

$$x_3(1;1) = 0.03125\,.$$

Repeating the algorithm with $h = 2^{-1}$, 2^{-2}, 2^{-3} we obtain the approximations in Table 5-E.

Table 5–E: Approximations of the Solution to Problem 25.

n	h	$y(1) \approx x_1(1;2^{-n})$	$x_2(1;2^{-n})$	$x_3(1;2^{-n})$
0	1.0	1.29167	0.28125	0.03125
1	0.5	1.26039	0.34509	−0.06642
2	0.25	1.25960	0.34696	−0.06957
3	0.125	1.25958	0.34704	−0.06971

We stopped at $n = 3$ since

$$\left|\frac{x_1(1;2^{-3}) - x_1(1;2^{-2})}{x_1(1;2^{-3})}\right| = \left|\frac{1.25958 - 1.25960}{1.25958}\right| = 0.00002 < 0.01\,,$$

$$\left|\frac{x_2(1;2^{-3}) - x_2(1;2^{-2})}{x_2(1;2^{-3})}\right| = \left|\frac{0.34704 - 0.34696}{0.34704}\right| = 0.00023 < 0.01\,, \qquad \text{and}$$

$$\left|\frac{x_3(1;2^{-3}) - x_3(1;2^{-2})}{x_3(1;2^{-3})}\right| = \left|\frac{-0.06971 + 0.06957}{-0.06971}\right| = 0.00201 < 0.01\,.$$

Hence

$$y(1) \approx x_1\left(1;2^{-3}\right) = 1.25958\,,$$

with tolerance 0.01.

27. See the answer in the text.

29. See the answer in the text.

EXERCISES 5.4: Introduction to the Phase Plane, page 274

1. Substitution of $x(t) = e^{3t}$, $y(t) = e^{t}$ into the system yields

$$\frac{dx}{dt} = \frac{d}{dt}\left(e^{3t}\right) = 3e^{3t} = 3\left(e^{t}\right)^3 = 3y^3\,,$$

$$\frac{dy}{dt} = \frac{d}{dt}\left(e^t\right) = e^t = y.$$

Thus, given pair of functions is a solution. To sketch the trajectory of this solution, we express x as a function of y.

$$x = e^{3t} = \left(e^t\right)^3 = y^3 \qquad \text{for} \qquad y = e^t > 0.$$

Since $y = e^t$ is an increasing function, the flow arrows are directed away from the origin. See Figure B.29 in the answers of the text.

3. In this problem, $f(x, y) = x - y$, $g(x, y) = x^2 + y^2 - 1$. To find the critical point set, we solve the system

$$\begin{aligned} x - y &= 0, \\ x^2 + y^2 - 1 &= 0 \end{aligned} \qquad \Rightarrow \qquad \begin{aligned} x = y, \\ x^2 + y^2 = 1. \end{aligned}$$

Eliminating y yields

$$2x^2 = 1 \qquad \Rightarrow \qquad x = \pm\frac{1}{\sqrt{2}}\,.$$

Substituting x into the first equation, we find the corresponding value for y. Thus the critical points of the given system are $(1/\sqrt{2}, 1/\sqrt{2})$ and $(-1/\sqrt{2}, -1/\sqrt{2})$.

5. In this problem,

$$f(x, y) = x^2 - 2xy, \qquad g(x, y) = 3xy - y^2,$$

and so we find critical points by solving the system

$$\begin{aligned} x^2 - 2xy &= 0, \\ 3xy - y^2 &= 0 \end{aligned} \qquad \Rightarrow \qquad \begin{aligned} x(x - 2y) &= 0, \\ y(3x - y) &= 0. \end{aligned}$$

From the first equation we conclude that either $x = 0$ or $x = 2y$. Substituting these values into the second equation, we get

$$\begin{aligned} x = 0 \quad &\Rightarrow \quad y[3(0) - y] = 0 \quad \Rightarrow \quad -y^2 = 0 \quad \Rightarrow \quad y = 0; \\ x = 2y \quad &\Rightarrow \quad y[3(2y) - y] = 0 \quad \Rightarrow \quad 5y^2 = 0 \quad \Rightarrow \quad y = 0,\ x = 2(0) = 0. \end{aligned}$$

Therefore, $(0, 0)$ is the only critical point.

6. We see by Definition 1 on page 266 of the text that we must solve the system of equations given by

$$y^2 - 3y + 2 = 0,$$
$$(x-1)(y-2) = 0.$$

By factoring the first equation above, we find that this system becomes

$$(y-1)(y-2) = 0,$$
$$(x-1)(y-2) = 0.$$

Thus, we observe that if $y = 2$ and x is any constant, then the system of differential equations given in this problem will be satisfied. Therefore, one family of critical points is given by the line $y = 2$. If $y \neq 2$, then the system of equations above simplifies to $y - 1 = 0$, and $x - 1 = 0$. Hence, another critical point is the point $(1, 1)$.

7. Here $f(x, y) = y - 1$, $g(x, y) = e^{x+y}$. Thus the phase plane equation becomes

$$\frac{dy}{dx} = \frac{e^{x+y}}{y-1} = \frac{e^x e^y}{y-1}.$$

Separating variables yields

$$(y-1)e^{-y}dy = e^x dx \qquad \Rightarrow \qquad \int (y-1)e^{-y}dy = \int e^x dx$$
$$\Rightarrow \qquad -ye^{-y} + C = e^x \qquad \text{or} \qquad e^x + ye^{-y} = C.$$

9. The phase plane equation for this system is

$$\frac{dy}{dx} = \frac{g(x,y)}{f(x,y)} = \frac{e^x + y}{2y - x}.$$

We rewrite this equation in symmetric form,

$$-(e^x + y)\,dx + (2y - x)\,dy = 0,$$

and check it for exactness.

$$\frac{\partial M}{\partial y} = \frac{\partial}{\partial y}\left[-(e^x + y)\right] = -1,$$

$$\frac{\partial N}{\partial x} = \frac{\partial}{\partial x}(2y - x) = -1.$$

Therefore, the equation is exact. We have

$$F(x,y) = \int N(x,y)\,dy = \int (2y - x)\,dy = y^2 - xy + g(x);$$
$$M(x,y) = \frac{\partial}{\partial x}F(x,y) = \frac{\partial}{\partial x}\left(y^2 - xy + g(x)\right) = -y + g'(x) = -\left(e^x + y\right)$$
$$\Rightarrow \quad g'(x) = -e^x \quad \Rightarrow \quad g(x) = \int \left(-e^x\right)dx = -e^x .$$

Hence, a general solution to the phase plane equation is given implicitly by

$$F(x,y) = y^2 - xy - e^x = C \qquad \text{or} \qquad e^x + xy - y^2 = -C = c,$$

where c is an arbitrary constant.

11. In this problem, $f(x,y) = 2y$ and $g(x,y) = 2x$. Therefore, the phase plane equation for given system is

$$\frac{dy}{dx} = \frac{2x}{2y} = \frac{x}{y}.$$

Separation variables and integration yield

$$y\,dy = x\,dx \quad \Rightarrow \quad \int y\,dy = \int x\,dx$$
$$\Rightarrow \quad \frac{1}{2}y^2 = \frac{1}{2}x^2 + C \quad \Rightarrow \quad y^2 - x^2 = c.$$

Thus, the trajectories are hyperbolas if $c \neq 0$ and, for $c = 0$, the lines $y = \pm x$.

In the upper half-plane, $y > 0$, we have $x' = 2y > 0$ and, therefore, $x(t)$ increases. In the lower half-plane, $x' < 0$ and so $x(t)$ decreases. This implies that solutions flow from the left to the right in the upper half-plane and from the right to the left in the lower half-plane. See Figure B.30 in the text.

13. First, we will find the critical points of this system. Therefore, we solve the system

$$(y - x)(y - 1) = 0,$$
$$(x - y)(x - 1) = 0.$$

Notice that both of these equations will be satisfied if $y = x$. Thus, $x = C$ and $y = C$, for any fixed constant C, will be a solution to the given system of differential equations and one family of critical points is the line $y = x$. We also see that we have a critical point at the point $(1, 1)$. (This critical point is, of course, also on the line $y = x$.)

Next we will find the integral curves. Therefore, we must solve the first order differential equation given by

$$\frac{dy}{dx} = \frac{dy/dt}{dx/dt} = \frac{(x-y)(x-1)}{(y-x)(y-1)} \qquad \Rightarrow \qquad \frac{dy}{dx} = \frac{1-x}{y-1}.$$

We can solve this last differential equation by the method of separation of variables. Thus, we have

$$\begin{aligned} &\int (y-1)dy = \int (1-x)dx \\ \Rightarrow \qquad & \frac{y^2}{2} - y = x - \frac{x^2}{2} + C \\ \Rightarrow \qquad & x^2 - 2x + y^2 - 2y = 2C. \end{aligned}$$

By completing the square, we obtain

$$(x-1)^2 + (y-1)^2 = c,$$

where $c = 2C+2$. Therefore, the integral curves are concentric circles with centers at the point $(1, 1)$, including the critical point for the system of differential equations. The trajectories associated with the constants $c = 1$, 4, and 9, are sketched in Figure B.31 in the answers of the text.

Finally we will determine the flow along the trajectories. Notice that the variable t imparts a flow to the trajectories of a solution to a system of differential equations in the same manner as the parameter t imparts a direction to a curve written in parametric form. We will find this flow by determining the regions in the xy-plane where $x(t)$ is increasing (moving from left to right on each trajectory) and the regions where $x(t)$ is decreasing (moving from right to left on each trajectory). Therefore, we will use four cases to study the equation $dx/dt = (y-x)(y-1)$, the first equation in our system.

Case 1 : $y > x$ and $y < 1$. (This region is above the line $y = x$ but below the line $y = 1$.) In this case, $y - x > 0$ but $y - 1 < 0$. Thus, $dx/dt = (y - x)(y - 1) < 0$. Hence, $x(t)$ will be decreasing here. Therefore, the flow along the trajectories will be from right to left and so the movement is clockwise.

Case 2 : $y > x$ and $y > 1$. (This region is above the lines $y = x$ and $y = 1$.) In this case, we see that $y - x > 0$ and $y - 1 > 0$. Hence, $dx/dt = (y - x)(y - 1) > 0$. Thus, $x(t)$ will be increasing and the flow along the trajectories in this region will still be clockwise.

Case 3 : $y < x$ and $y < 1$. (This region is below the lines $y = x$ and $y = 1$.) In this case, $y - x < 0$ and $y - 1 < 0$. Thus, $dx/dt > 0$ and so $x(t)$ is increasing. Thus, the movement is from left to right and so the flow along the trajectories will be counterclockwise.

Case 4 : $y < x$ and $y > 1$. (This region is below the line $y = x$ but above the line $y = 1$.) In this case, $y - x < 0$ and $y - 1 > 0$. Thus, $dx/dt < 0$ and so $x(t)$ will be decreasing here. Therefore, the flow is from right to left and, thus, counterclockwise here also.

Therefore, above the line $y = x$ the flow is clockwise and below that line the flow is counterclockwise. See Figure B.31 in the answers of the text.

15. From Definition 1 on page 266 of the text, we must solve the system of equations given by

$$\begin{aligned} 2x + y + 3 &= 0, \\ -3x - 2y - 4 &= 0. \end{aligned}$$

By eliminating y in the first equation we obtain

$$x + 2 = 0$$

and by eliminating x in the first equation we obtain

$$-y + 1 = 0.$$

Thus, we observe that $x = -2$ and $y = 1$ will satisfy both equations. Therefore $(-2, 1)$ is a critical point.

From Figure B.32 in the answers of the text we see that all solutions passing near the point $(-2, 1)$ do not stay close to it therefore the critical point $(-2, 1)$ is unstable.

17. For critical points, we solve the system

$$\begin{aligned} f(x,y) &= 0, \\ g(x,y) &= 0 \end{aligned} \quad\Rightarrow\quad \begin{aligned} 2x+13y &= 0, \\ -x-2y &= 0 \end{aligned} \quad\Rightarrow\quad \begin{aligned} 2(-2y)+13y &= 0, \\ x &= 2y \end{aligned} \quad\Rightarrow\quad \begin{aligned} y&=0, \\ x&=0. \end{aligned}$$

Therefore, the system has just one critical point, $(0,0)$. The direction field is shown in Figure B.33 in the text. From this picture we conclude that $(0,0)$ is a center (stable).

19. We set $v=y'$. Then $y''=(y')'=v'$ and so given equation is equivalent to the system

$$\begin{aligned} y'&=v, \\ v'-y&=0 \end{aligned} \quad\Rightarrow\quad \begin{aligned} y'&=v, \\ v'&=y. \end{aligned}$$

In this system, $f(y,v)=v$ and $g(y,v)=y$. For critical points we solve

$$\begin{aligned} f(y,v)&=v=0, \\ g(y,v)&=y=0 \end{aligned} \quad\Rightarrow\quad \begin{aligned} y&=0, \\ v&=0 \end{aligned}$$

and conclude that, in yv-plane, the system has only one critical point, $(0,0)$. In the upper half-plane, $y'=v>0$ and, therefore, y increases and solutions flow to the right; similarly, solutions flow to the left in the lower half-plane. See Figure B.34 in the answers of the text.

The phase plane equation for the system is

$$\frac{dv}{dy}=\frac{dv/dx}{dy/dx}=\frac{y}{v} \quad\Rightarrow\quad v\,dv=y\,dy \quad\Rightarrow\quad v^2-y^2=c.$$

Thus, the integral curves are hyperbolas for $c\neq 0$ and lines $v=\pm y$ for $c=0$. On the line $v=-y$, the solutions flow into the critical point $(0,0)$, whereas solutions flow away from $(0,0)$ on $v=y$. So, $(0,0)$ is a saddle point (unstable).

21. First we convert the given equation into a system of first order equations involving the functions $y(t)$ and $v(t)$ by using the substitution

$$v(t)=y'(t) \quad\Rightarrow\quad v'(t)=y''(t).$$

Therefore, this equation becomes the system

$$\begin{aligned} y'&=v, \\ v'&=-y-y^5=-y\left(1+y^4\right). \end{aligned}$$

To find the critical points, we solve the system of equations given by $v = 0$ and $-y\left(1+y^4\right) = 0$. This system is satisfied only when $v = 0$ and $y = 0$. Thus, the only critical point is the point $(0, 0)$. To find the integral curves, we solve the first order equation given by

$$\frac{dv}{dy} = \frac{dv/dt}{dy/dt} = \frac{-y - y^5}{v}.$$

This is a separable equation and can be written as

$$\begin{aligned} v\,dv = \left(-y - y^5\right)dy \qquad &\Rightarrow \qquad \frac{v^2}{2} = -\frac{y^2}{2} - \frac{y^6}{6} + C \\ \Rightarrow \qquad 3v^2 + 3y^2 + y^6 = c \qquad &(c = 6C), \end{aligned}$$

where we have integrated to obtain the second equation above. Therefore, the integral curves for this system are given by the equations $3v^2 + 3y^2 + y^6 = c$ for each positive constant c.

To determine the flow along the trajectories, we will examine the equation $dy/dt = v$. Thus, we see that

$$\frac{dy}{dt} > 0 \quad \text{when} \quad v > 0, \quad \text{and} \quad \frac{dy}{dt} < 0 \quad \text{when} \quad v < 0.$$

Therefore, y will be increasing when $v > 0$ and decreasing when $v < 0$. Hence, above the y-axis the flow will be from left to right and below the x-axis the flow will be from right to left. Thus, the flow on these trajectories will be clockwise (Figure B.35 in the answers of the text). Thus $(0, 0)$ is a center (stable).

23. With $v = y'$, $v' = y''$, the equation transforms to the system

$$\begin{aligned} y' &= v, \qquad & \Rightarrow \qquad y' &= v, \\ v' + y - y^4 &= 0 & v' &= y^4 - y. \end{aligned} \tag{5.26}$$

Therefore, $f(y, v) = v$ and $g(y, v) = y^4 - y = y(y^3 - 1)$. We find critical points by solving

$$\begin{aligned} v &= 0, \qquad & \Rightarrow \qquad v &= 0, \\ y(y^3 - 1) &= 0 & y &= 0 \quad \text{or} \quad y = 1. \end{aligned}$$

Hence, system (5.26) has two critical points, $(0, 0)$ and $(1, 0)$.

In the upper half plane, $y' = v > 0$ and so solutions flow to the right; similarly, solutions flow to the left in the lower half-plane. See Figure B.36 in the text for the direction field. This figure indicates that $(0,0)$ is a stable critical point (center) whereas $(1,0)$ is a saddle point (unstable).

25. This system has two critical points, $(0,0)$ and $(1,0)$, which are solutions to the system

$$\begin{aligned} y &= 0, \\ -x + x^3 &= 0. \end{aligned}$$

The direction field for this system is depicted in Figure B.37. From this figure we conclude that

(a) the solution passing through the point $(0.25, 0.25)$ flows around $(0,0)$ and thus is periodic;

(b) for the solution $(x(t), y(t))$ passing through the point $(2,2)$, $y(t) \to \infty$ as $t \to \infty$, and so this solution is not periodic;

(c) the solution passing through the critical point $(1,0)$ is a constant (equilibrium) solution and so is periodic.

27. The direction field for given system is shown in Figure B.38 in the answers of the text. From the starting point, $(1,1)$, following the direction arrows the solution flows down and to the left, crosses the x-axis, has a turning point in the fourth quadrant, and then does to the left and up toward the critical point $(0,0)$. Thus we predict that, as $t \to \infty$, the solution $(x(t), y(t))$ approaches $(0,0)$.

29. **(a)** The phase plane equation for this system is

$$\frac{dy}{dx} = \frac{3y}{x} .$$

It is separable. Separating variables and integrating, we get

$$\frac{dy}{y} = \frac{3dx}{x} \qquad \Rightarrow \qquad \ln|y| = 3\ln|x| + C \qquad \Rightarrow \qquad y = cx^3 .$$

So, integral curves are cubic curves. Since in the right half-plane $x' = x > 0$, in the left half-plane $x' < 0$, the solutions flow to the right in the right half-plane and to the left in the left half-plane. Solutions starting on the y-axis stay on it ($x' = 0$); they flow up if the initial point is in the upper half-plane (because $y' = y > 0$) and flow down if the initial point in the lower half-plane. This matches the figure for unstable node.

(b) Solving the phase plane equation for this system, we get

$$\frac{dy}{dx} = \frac{-4x}{y} \qquad \Rightarrow \qquad y\,dy = -4x\,dx \qquad \Rightarrow \qquad y^2 + 4x^2 = C.$$

Thus the integral curves are ellipses. (Also, notice that the solutions flow along these ellipses in clockwise direction because x increases in the upper half-plane and decreases in the lower half-plane.) Therefore, here we have a center (stable).

(c) Solving $-5x + 2y > 0$ and $x - 4y > 0$ we find that x increases in the half-plane $y > 5x$ and decreases in the half-plane $y < 5x$, and y increases in the half-plane $y < x/4$ and decreases in the half-plane $y > x/4$. This leads to the scheme $\begin{array}{c|c} \searrow & \swarrow \\ \hline \nearrow & \nwarrow \end{array}$ for the solution's flows. Thus all solutions approach the critical point $(0, 0)$, as $t \to \infty$, which corresponds to a stable node.

(d) An analysis, similar to that in (c), shows that all the solutions flow away from $(0, 0)$. Among pictures shown in Figure 5.7, only the unstable node and the unstable spiral have this feature. Since the unstable node is the answer to (a), we have the unstable spiral in this case.

(e) The phase plane equation

$$\frac{dy}{dx} = \frac{4x - 3y}{5x - 3y},$$

has two linear solutions, $y = 2x$ and $y = 2x/3$. (One can find them by substituting $y = ax$ into the above phase plane equation and solving for a.) Solutions starting from a point on $y = 2x$ in the first quadrant, have $x' = 5x - 3(2x) = -x < 0$ and so flow toward $(0, 0)$; similarly, solutions, starting from a point on this line in the third quadrant, have $x' = -x > 0$ and, again, flow to $(0, 0)$. On the other line, $y = 2x/3$, the picture is opposite: in the first quadrant, $x' = 5x - 3(2x/3) = 3x > 0$, and $x' < 0$ in the third quadrant. Therefore, there are two lines, passing through the critical point $(0, 0)$, such that solutions to the system flow into $(0,0)$ on one of them and flow away from $(0,0)$ on the other. This is the case of a saddle (unstable) point.

(f) The only remaining picture is the asymptotically stable spiral. (One can also get a diagram $\begin{array}{c|c} \swarrow & \nwarrow \\ \hline \searrow & \nearrow \end{array}$ for solution's flows with just one matching picture in Figure 5.7.)

31. **(a)** Setting $y' = v$ and so $y'' = v'$, we transform given equation to a first order system

$$\frac{dy}{dx} = v,$$
$$\frac{dv}{dx} = f(y).$$

(b) By the chain rule,

$$\frac{dv}{dy} = \frac{dv}{dx} \cdot \frac{dx}{dy} = \frac{dv}{dx} \Big/ \frac{dy}{dx} = \frac{f(y)}{v} \qquad \Rightarrow \qquad \frac{dv}{dy} = \frac{f(y)}{v}.$$

This equation is separable. Separation variables and integration yield

$$v\,dv = f(y)\,dy \qquad \Rightarrow \qquad \int v\,dv = \int f(y)\,dy$$
$$\Rightarrow \qquad \frac{1}{2}v^2 = F(y) + K,$$

where $F(y)$ is an antiderivative of $f(y)$. Substituting back $v = y'$ gives the required.

33. Since $S(t)$ and $I(t)$ represent population and we cannot have a negative population, we are only interested in the first quadrant of the SI-plane.

(a) In order to find the trajectory corresponding to the initial conditions $I(0) = 1$ and $S(0) = 700$, we must solve the first order equation

$$\frac{dI}{dS} = \frac{dI/dt}{dS/dt} = \frac{aSI - bI}{-aSI} = -\frac{aS - b}{aS}$$
$$\Rightarrow \qquad \frac{dI}{dS} = -1 + \frac{b}{a}\frac{1}{S}. \tag{5.27}$$

By integrating both sides of equation (5.27) with respect to S, we obtain the integral curves given by

$$I(S) = -S + \frac{b}{a}\ln S + C.$$

A sketch of this curve for $a = 0.003$ and $b = 0.5$ is shown in Figure B.39 in the answers of the text.

(b) From the sketch in Figure B.39 in the answers of the text we see that the peak number of infected people is 295.

(c) The peak number of infected people occurs when $dI/dS = 0$. From equation (5.27) we have

$$\frac{dI}{dS} = 0 = -1 + \frac{b}{a}\frac{1}{S}.$$

Solving for S we obtain

$$S = \frac{b}{a} = \frac{0.5}{0.003} \approx 167 \text{ people.}$$

35. (a) We denote $v(t) = x'(t)$ to transform the equation

$$\frac{d^2x}{dt^2} = -x + \frac{1}{\lambda - x}$$

to an equivalent system of two first order differential equations, that is

$$\frac{dx}{dt} = v,$$
$$\frac{dv}{dt} = -x + \frac{1}{\lambda - x}.$$

(b) The phase plane equation in xv-plane for the system in (a) is

$$\frac{dv}{dx} = \frac{-x + 1/(\lambda - x)}{v}.$$

This equation is separable. Separating variables and integrating, we obtain

$$\begin{aligned} v\,dv &= \left(-x + \frac{1}{\lambda - x}\right) dx \quad \Rightarrow \quad \int v\,dv = \int \left(-x + \frac{1}{\lambda - x}\right) dx \\ \Rightarrow \quad \frac{1}{2}v^2 &= -\frac{1}{2}x^2 - \ln|\lambda - x| + C_1 \quad \Rightarrow \quad v^2 = C - x^2 - 2\ln|\lambda - x| \\ \Rightarrow \quad v &= \pm\sqrt{C - x^2 - 2\ln(\lambda - x)}\,. \end{aligned}$$

(The absolute value sign is not necessary because $x < \lambda$.)

(c) To find critical points for the system in (a), we solve

$$\begin{aligned} v &= 0, \\ -x + \frac{1}{\lambda - x} &= 0 \end{aligned} \quad \Rightarrow \quad \begin{aligned} v &= 0, \\ x^2 - \lambda x + 1 &= 0 \end{aligned} \quad \Rightarrow \quad \begin{aligned} v &= 0, \\ x &= \frac{\lambda \pm \sqrt{\lambda^2 - 4}}{2}. \end{aligned}$$

For $0 < \lambda < 2$, $\lambda^2 - 4 < 0$ and so both roots are complex numbers. However, for $\lambda > 2$ there are two distinct real solutions,

$$x_1 = \frac{\lambda - \sqrt{\lambda^2 - 4}}{2} \qquad \text{and} \qquad x_2 = \frac{\lambda + \sqrt{\lambda^2 - 4}}{2},$$

and the critical points are

$$\left(\frac{\lambda - \sqrt{\lambda^2 - 4}}{2}, 0 \right) \qquad \text{and} \qquad \left(\frac{\lambda + \sqrt{\lambda^2 - 4}}{2}, 0 \right).$$

(d) The phase plane diagrams for $\lambda = 1$ and $\lambda = 3$ are shown in Figures B.40 and B.41 in the answers section of the text.

(e) From Figures B.40 we conclude that, for $\lambda = 1$, all solution curves approach the vertical line $x = 1 (= \lambda)$. This means that the bar is attracted to the magnet. The case $\lambda = 3$ is more complicated. The behavior of the bar depends on the initial displacement $x(0)$ and the initial velocity $v(0) = x'(0)$. From Figure B.41 we see that (with $v(0) = 0$) if $x(0)$ is small enough, then the bar will oscillate about the position $x = x_1$; if $x(0)$ is close enough to λ, then the bar will be attracted to the magnet. It is also possible that, with an appropriate combination of $x(0)$ and $v(0)$, the bar will come to rest at the saddle point $(x_2, 0)$.

37. **(a)** Denoting $y' = v$, we have $y'' = v'$, and (with $m = \mu = k = 1$) (16) can be written as a system

$$\begin{aligned} y' &= v, \\ v' &= -y + \begin{cases} y, & \text{if } |y| < 1,\ v = 0, \\ \operatorname{sign}(y), & \text{if } |y| \geq 1,\ v = 0, \\ -\operatorname{sign}(v), & \text{if } v \neq 0 \end{cases} = \begin{cases} 0, & \text{if } |y| < 1,\ v = 0, \\ -y + \operatorname{sign}(y), & \text{if } |y| \geq 1,\ v = 0, \\ -y - \operatorname{sign}(v), & \text{if } v \neq 0. \end{cases} \end{aligned}$$

(b) The condition $v \neq 0$ corresponds to the third case in (5.28), i.e., the system has the form

$$\begin{aligned} y' &= v, \\ v' &= -y - \operatorname{sign}(v). \end{aligned}$$

The phase plane equation for this system is

$$\frac{dv}{dy} = \frac{dv/dt}{dy/dt} = \frac{-y - \operatorname{sign}(v)}{v}.$$

We consider two cases.

1) $v > 0$. In this case $\operatorname{sign}(v) = 1$ and we have

$$\begin{aligned} \frac{dv}{dy} = \frac{-y-1}{v} \quad &\Rightarrow \quad v\,dv = -(y+1)dy \\ \Rightarrow \quad &\int v\,dv = -\int (y+1)dy \\ \Rightarrow \quad &\frac{1}{2}v^2 = -\frac{1}{2}(y+1)^2 + C \quad \Rightarrow \quad v^2 + (y+1)^2 = c, \end{aligned}$$

where $c = 2C$.

2) $v < 0$. In this case $\operatorname{sign}(v) = -1$ and we have

$$\begin{aligned} \frac{dv}{dy} = \frac{-y+1}{v} \quad &\Rightarrow \quad v\,dv = -(y-1)dy \\ \Rightarrow \quad &\int v\,dv = -\int (y-1)dy \\ \Rightarrow \quad &\frac{1}{2}v^2 = -\frac{1}{2}(y-1)^2 + C \quad \Rightarrow \quad v^2 + (y-1)^2 = c. \end{aligned}$$

(c) The equation $v^2 + (y+1)^2 = c$ defines a circle in the yv-plane centered at $(-1, 0)$ and of the radius $\sqrt{c}$ if $c > 0$, and it is the empty set if $c < 0$. The condition $v > 0$ means that we have to take only the half of these circles lying in the upper half plane. Moreover, the first equation, $y' = v$, implies that trajectories flow from left to right. Similarly, in the lower half plane, $v < 0$, we have concentric semicircles $v^2 + (y-1)^2 = c$, $c \geq 0$, centered at $(1, 0)$ and flowing from right to left.

(d) For the system found in (a),

$$f(y,v) = v,$$
$$g(y,v) = \begin{cases} 0, & \text{if } |y| < 1,\ v = 0, \\ -y + \operatorname{sign}(y), & \text{if } |y| \geq 1,\ v = 0, \\ -y - \operatorname{sign}(v), & \text{if } v \neq 0. \end{cases}$$

Since $f(y,v) = 0 \ \Leftrightarrow \ v = 0$ and

$$g(y,0) = \begin{cases} 0, & \text{if } |y| < 1, \\ -y + \operatorname{sign}(y), & \text{if } |y| \geq 1, \end{cases}$$

we consider two cases. If $y < 1$, then $g(y,0) \equiv 0$. This means that any point of the interval $-1 < y < 1$ is a critical point. If $|y| \geq 1$, then $g(y,0) = -y + \operatorname{sign}(y)$ which is 0 if $y = \pm 1$. Thus the critical point set is the segment $v = 0$, $-1 \leq y \leq 1$.

(e) According to (c), the mass released at $(7.5, 0)$ goes in the lower half plane from right to left along a semicircle centered at $(1, 0)$. The radius of this semicircle is $7.5 - 1 = 6.5$, and its other end is $(1 - 6.5, 0) = (-5.5, 0)$. From this point, the mass goes from left to right in the upper half plane along the semicircle centered at $(-1, 0)$ and of the radius $-1 - (-5.5) = 4.5$, and comes to the point $(-1 + 4.5, 0) = (3.5, 0)$. Then the mass again goes from right to left in the lower half plane along the semicircle centered at $(1, 0)$ and of the radius $3.5 - 1 = 2.5$, and comes to the point $(1 - 2.5, 0) = (-1.5, 0)$. From this point, the mass goes in the upper half plane from left to right along the semicircle centered at $(-1, 0)$ and of the radius $-1 - (-1.5) = 0.5$, and comes to the point $(-1 + 0.5, 0) = (-0.5, 0)$. Here it comes to rest because $|-0.5| < 1$, and there is not a lower semicircle starting at this point. See the colored curve in Figure B.42 of the text.

EXERCISES 5.5: Coupled Mass-Spring Systems, page 284

1. For the mass m_1 there is only one force acting on it; that is the force due to the spring with constant k_1. This equals $-k_1(x - y)$. Hence, we get

$$m_1 x'' = -k_1(x - y).$$

For the mass m_2 there are two forces acting on it: the force due to the spring with constant k_2 is $-k_2y$; and the force due to the spring with constant k_1 is $k_1(y-x)$. So we get

$$m_2y'' = k_1(x-y) - k_2y.$$

So the system is

$$\begin{aligned} m_1x'' &= k_1(y-x), \\ m_2y'' &= -k_1(y-x) - k_2y, \end{aligned}$$

or, in operator form,

$$\begin{aligned} &\left(m_1D^2 + k_1\right)[x] - k_1y = 0, \\ &-k_1x + \left\{m_2D^2 + (k_1+k_2)\right\}[y] = 0. \end{aligned}$$

With $m_1 = 1$, $m_2 = 2$, $k_1 = 4$, and $k_2 = 10/3$, we get

$$\begin{aligned} &(D^2+4)[x] - 4y = 0, \\ &-4x + (2D^2 + 22/3)[y] = 0, \end{aligned} \tag{5.28}$$

with initial conditions:

$$x(0) = -1, \quad x'(0) = 0, \quad y(0) = 0, \quad y'(0) = 0.$$

Multiplying the second equation of the system given in (5.28) by 4, applying $(2D^2 + 22/3)$ to the first equation of this system, and adding the results, we get

$$\begin{aligned} &\left(D^2+4\right)\left(2D^2 + \frac{22}{3}\right)[x] - 16x = 0 \\ \Rightarrow \quad &\left(2D^4 + \frac{46}{3}D^2 + \frac{40}{3}\right)[x] = 0 \\ \Rightarrow \quad &\left(3D^4 + 23D^2 + 20\right)[x] = 0. \end{aligned}$$

The characteristic equation is

$$3r^4 + 23r^2 + 20 = 0,$$

which is a quadratic in r^2. So

$$r^2 = \frac{-23 \pm \sqrt{529 - 240}}{6} = \frac{-23 \pm 17}{6}\,.$$

Since $-20/3$ and -1 are negative, the roots of the characteristic equation are $\pm i\beta_1$ and $\pm i\beta_2$, where

$$\beta_1 = \sqrt{\frac{20}{3}}, \qquad \beta_2 = 1.$$

Hence

$$x(t) = c_1 \cos \beta_1 t + c_2 \sin \beta_1 t + c_3 \cos \beta_2 t + c_4 \sin \beta_2 t.$$

Solving the first equation of the system given in (5.28) for y, we get

$$\begin{aligned} y(t) = \frac{1}{4}\left(D^2+4\right)[x] = \frac{1}{4}\Big[&\left(-\beta_1^2+4\right) c_1 \cos \beta_1 t + \left(-\beta_1^2+4\right) c_2 \sin \beta_1 t \\ &+ \left(-\beta_2^2+4\right) c_3 \cos \beta_2 t + \left(-\beta_2^2+4\right) c_4 \sin \beta_2 t\Big]\,. \end{aligned}$$

Next we substitute into the initial conditions. Setting $x(0) = -1$, $x'(0) = 0$ yields

$$\begin{aligned} -1 &= c_1 + c_3\,, \\ 0 &= c_2\beta_1 + c_4\beta_2\,. \end{aligned}$$

From the initial conditions $y(0) = 0$, $y'(0) = 0$, we get

$$\begin{aligned} 0 &= \frac{1}{4}\left[\left(-\beta_1^2+4\right) c_1 + \left(-\beta_2^2+4\right) c_3\right], \\ 0 &= \frac{1}{4}\left[\beta_1\left(-\beta_1^2+4\right) c_2 + \beta_2\left(-\beta_2^2+4\right) c_4\right]. \end{aligned}$$

The solution to the above system is

$$c_2 = c_4 = 0, \qquad c_1 = -\frac{9}{17}, \qquad c_3 = -\frac{8}{17}\,,$$

which yields the solutions

$$\begin{aligned} x(t) &= -\frac{9}{17}\cos\sqrt{\frac{20}{3}}\,t - \frac{8}{17}\cos t\,, \\ y(t) &= \frac{6}{17}\cos\sqrt{\frac{20}{3}}\,t - \frac{6}{17}\cos t\,. \end{aligned}$$

3. We define the displacements of masses from equilibrium, x, y, and z, as in Example 2. For each mass, there are two forces acting on it due to Hook's law.

For the mass on the left,

$$F_{11} = -kx \qquad \text{and} \qquad F_{12} = k(y - x);$$

for the mass in the middle,

$$F_{21} = -k(y - x) \qquad \text{and} \qquad F_{22} = k(z - y);$$

finally, for the mass on the right,

$$F_{31} = -k(z - y) \qquad \text{and} \qquad F_{32} = -kz.$$

Applying Newton's second law for each mass, we obtain the following system

$$\begin{aligned} mx'' &= -kx + k(y - x), \\ my'' &= -k(y - x) + k(z - y), \\ mz'' &= -k(z - y) - kz, \end{aligned}$$

or, in operator form,

$$\begin{aligned} &\left(mD^2 + 2k\right)[x] - ky = 0, \\ &-kx + \left(mD^2 + 2k\right)[y] - kz = 0, \\ &-ky + \left(mD^2 + 2k\right)[z] = 0. \end{aligned}$$

From the first equation, we express

$$y = \frac{1}{k}\left(mD^2 + 2k\right)[x] \tag{5.29}$$

and substitute this expression into the other two equations to get

$$\begin{aligned} &-kx + \left(mD^2 + 2k\right)\left[\frac{1}{k}\left(mD^2 + 2k\right)[x]\right] - kz = 0, \\ &-\left(mD^2 + 2k\right)[x] + \left(mD^2 + 2k\right)[z] = 0. \end{aligned}$$

The first equation yields

$$z = -x + \left\{\frac{1}{k}\left(mD^2 + 2k\right)\right\}^2 [x] = \left\{\frac{1}{k^2}\left(mD^2 + 2k\right)^2 - 1\right\} [x], \tag{5.30}$$

and so

$$-\left(mD^2 + 2k\right)[x] + \left(mD^2 + 2k\right)\left[\left\{\frac{1}{k^2}\left(mD^2 + 2k\right)^2 - 1\right\}[x]\right]$$
$$= \left(mD^2 + 2k\right)\left\{\frac{1}{k^2}\left(mD^2 + 2k\right)^2 - 2\right\}[x] = 0.$$

The characteristic equation for this homogeneous linear equation with constant coefficients is

$$\left(mr^2 + 2k\right)\left\{\frac{1}{k^2}\left(mr^2 + 2k\right)^2 - 2\right\} = 0,$$

which splits onto two equations,

$$mr^2 + 2k = 0 \qquad \Rightarrow \qquad r = \pm i\sqrt{\frac{2k}{m}} \tag{5.31}$$

and

$$\frac{1}{k^2}\left(mr^2 + 2k\right)^2 - 2 = 0 \qquad \Rightarrow \qquad \left(mr^2 + 2k\right)^2 - 2k^2 = 0$$
$$\Rightarrow \qquad \left(mr^2 + 2k - \sqrt{2}k\right)\left(mr^2 + 2k + \sqrt{2}k\right) = 0$$
$$\Rightarrow \qquad r = \pm i\sqrt{\frac{(2-\sqrt{2})k}{m}}, \qquad r = \pm i\sqrt{\frac{(2+\sqrt{2})k}{m}}. \tag{5.32}$$

Solutions (5.31) and (5.32) give normal frequences

$$\omega_1 = \frac{1}{2\pi}\sqrt{\frac{2k}{m}}, \quad \omega_2 = \frac{1}{2\pi}\sqrt{\frac{(2-\sqrt{2})k}{m}}, \quad \omega_3 = \frac{1}{2\pi}\sqrt{\frac{(2+\sqrt{2})k}{m}}.$$

Thus, a general solution $x(t)$ has the form $x(t) = x_1(t) + x_2(t) + x_3(t)$, where functions

$$x_j(t) = c_{1j}\cos(2\pi\omega_j t) + c_{2j}\sin(2\pi\omega_j t).$$

Note that x_j's satisfy the following differential equations:

$$\left(mD^2 + 2k\right)[x_1] = 0,$$

$$
\begin{aligned}
\left(mD^2 + 2k - \sqrt{2}k\right)[x_2] &= 0, \\
\left(mD^2 + 2k + \sqrt{2}k\right)[x_3] &= 0.
\end{aligned} \tag{5.33}
$$

For normal modes, we find solutions $y_j(t)$ and $z_j(t)$, corresponding to x_j, $j = 1, 2$, and 3 by using (5.29), (5.30), and identities (5.33).

ω_1:

$$
\begin{aligned}
y_1 &= \frac{1}{k}\left(mD^2 + 2k\right)[x_1] \equiv 0, \\
z_1 &= \left\{\frac{1}{k}\left(mD^2 + 2k\right)^2 - 1\right\}[x_1] = -x_1;
\end{aligned}
$$

ω_2:

$$
\begin{aligned}
y_2 &= \frac{1}{k}\left(mD^2 + 2k\right)[x_2] = \left\{\frac{1}{k}\left(mD^2 + 2k - \sqrt{2}k\right) + \sqrt{2}\right\}[x_2] = \sqrt{2}x_2, \\
z_2 &= \left\{\frac{1}{k}\left(mD^2 + 2k\right)^2 - 1\right\}[x_2] = \left\{\left[\frac{1}{k}\left(mD^2 + 2k\right)^2 - 2\right] + 1\right\}[x_2] = x_2;
\end{aligned}
$$

ω_3:

$$
\begin{aligned}
y_3 &= \frac{1}{k}\left(mD^2 + 2k\right)[x_3] = \left\{\frac{1}{k}\left(mD^2 + 2k + \sqrt{2}k\right) - \sqrt{2}\right\}[x_3] = -\sqrt{2}x_3, \\
z_3 &= \left\{\frac{1}{k}\left(mD^2 + 2k\right)^2 - 1\right\}[x_3] = \left\{\left[\frac{1}{k}\left(mD^2 + 2k\right)^2 - 2\right] + 1\right\}[x_3] = x_3;
\end{aligned}
$$

5. This spring system is similar to the system in Example 2 on page 282 of the text, except the middle spring has been replaced by a dashpot. We proceed as in Example 1. Let x and y represent the displacement of masses m_1 and m_2 to the right of their respective equilibrium positions. The mass m_1 has a force F_1 acting on its left side due to the left spring and a force F_2 acting on its right side due to the dashpot. Applying Hooke's law, we see that

$$F_1 = -k_1 x.$$

Assuming as we did in Section 4.1 that the damping force due to the dashpot is proportional to the magnitude of the velocity, but opposite in direction, we have

$$F_2 = b\left(y' - x'\right),$$

where b is the damping constant. Notice that velocity of the arm of the dashpot is the difference between the velocities of mass m_2 and mass m_1. The mass m_2 has a force F_3 acting on its left side due to the dashpot and a force F_4 acting on its right side due to the right spring. Using similar arguments, we find

$$F_3 = -b\,(y' - x') \qquad \text{and} \qquad F_4 = -k_2 y.$$

Applying Newton's second law to each mass gives

$$\begin{aligned} m_1 x''(t) &= F_1 + F_2 = -k_1 x(t) + b\,[y'(t) - x'(t)]\,, \\ m_2 y''(t) &= F_3 + F_4 = -b\,[y'(t) - x'(t)] - k_2 y. \end{aligned}$$

Plugging in the constants $m_1 = m_2 = 1$, $k_1 = k_2 = 1$, and $b = 1$, and simplifying yields

$$\begin{aligned} x''(t) + x'(t) + x(t) - y'(t) &= 0, \\ -x'(t) + y''(t) + y'(t) + y(t) &= 0. \end{aligned} \tag{5.34}$$

The initial conditions for the system will be $y(0) = 0$ (m_2 is held in its equilibrium position), $x(0) = -2$ (m_1 is pushed to the left 2 ft), and $x'(0) = y'(0) = 0$ (the masses are simply released at time $t = 0$ with no additional velocity). In operator notation this system becomes

$$\begin{aligned} (D^2 + D + 1)\,[x] - D[y] &= 0, \\ -D[x] + y''(t) + (D^2 + D + 1)\,[y] &= 0. \end{aligned}$$

By multiplying the first equation above by D and the second by $(D^2 + D + 1)$ and adding the resulting equations, we can eliminate the function $y(t)$. Thus, we have

$$\begin{aligned} &\left\{\left(D^2 + D + 1\right)^2 - D^2\right\}[x] = 0 \\ \Rightarrow \quad &\left\{\left[\left(D^2 + D + 1\right) - D\right] \cdot \left[\left(D^2 + D + 1\right) + D\right]\right\}[x] = 0 \\ \Rightarrow \quad &\left\{\left(D^2 + 1\right)(D + 1)^2\right\}[x] = 0. \end{aligned}$$

This last equation is a fourth order linear differential equation with constant coefficients whose associated auxiliary equation has roots $r = -1, -1, i$, and $-i$. Therefore, the solution to this differential equation is

$$x(t) = c_1 e^{-t} + c_2 t e^{-t} + c_3 \cos t + c_4 \sin t$$

$$\Rightarrow \qquad x'(t) = (-c_1 + c_2)e^{-t} - c_2te^{-t} - c_3 \sin t + c_4 \cos t$$
$$\Rightarrow \qquad x''(t) = (c_1 - 2c_2)e^{-t} + c_2te^{-t} - c_3 \cos t - c_4 \sin t.$$

To find $y(t)$, note that by the first equation of the system given in (5.34), we have

$$y'(t) = x''(t) + x'(t) + x(t).$$

Substituting $x(t)$, $x'(t)$, and $x''(t)$ into this equation yields

$$\begin{aligned} y'(t) = (c_1 - 2c_2)e^{-t} + c_2te^{-t} - c_3 \cos t - c_4 \sin t \\ +(-c_1 + c_2)e^{-t} - c_2te^{-t} - c_3 \sin t + c_4 \cos t + c_1e^{-t} + c_2te^{-t} + c_3 \cos t + c_4 \sin t \\ \Rightarrow \qquad y'(t) = (c_1 - c_2)e^{-t} + c_2te^{-t} - c_3 \sin t + c_4 \cos t. \end{aligned}$$

By integrating both sides of this equation with respect to t, we obtain

$$y(t) = -(c_1 - c_2)e^{-t} - c_2te^{-t} - c_2e^{-t} + c_3 \cos t + c_4 \sin t + c_5\,,$$

where we have integrated c_2te^{-t} by parts. Simplifying yields

$$y(t) = -c_1e^{-t} - c_2te^{-t} + c_3 \cos t + c_4 \sin t + c_5\,.$$

To determine the five constants, we will use the four initial conditions and the second equation in system (5.34). (We used the first equation to determine y). Substituting into the second equation in (5.34) gives

$$\begin{aligned} &- \left[(-c_1 + c_2)e^{-t} - c_2te^{-t} - c_3 \sin t + c_4 \cos t\right] \\ &\qquad + \left[(-c_1 + 2c_2)e^{-t} - c_2te^{-t} - c_3 \cos t - c_4 \sin t\right] \\ &\qquad + \left[(c_1 - c_2)e^{-t} + c_2te^{-t} - c_3 \sin t + c_4 \cos t\right] \\ &\qquad + \left[-c_1e^{-t} - c_2te^{-t} + c_3 \cos t + c_4 \sin t + c_5\right] = 0, \end{aligned}$$

which reduces to $c_5 = 0$. Using the initial conditions and the fact that $c_5 = 0$, we see that

$$\begin{aligned} x(0) &= c_1 + c_3 = -2, & x'(0) &= (-c_1 + c_2) + c_4 = 0, \\ y(0) &= -c_1 + c_3 = 0, & y'(0) &= (c_1 - c_2) + c_4 = 0\,. \end{aligned}$$

By solving these equations simultaneously, we find

$$c_1 = -1, \quad c_2 = -1, \quad c_3 = -1, \quad \text{and} \quad c_4 = 0.$$

Therefore, the solution to this spring-mass-dashpot system is

$$x(t) = -e^{-t} - te^{-t} - \cos t, \qquad y(t) = e^{-t} + te^{-t} - \cos t.$$

7. In operator notations,

$$\begin{aligned} &\left(D^2+5\right)[x] - 2y = 0, \\ &-2x + \left(D^2+2\right)[y] = 3\sin 2t. \end{aligned}$$

Multiplying the first equation by (D^2+2) and the second equation by 2, and adding the results, we obtain

$$\begin{aligned} &\left\{\left(D^2+2\right)\left(D^2+5\right) - 4\right\}[x] = 6\sin 2t \\ \Rightarrow \qquad &\left(D^4+7D^2+6\right)[x] = 6\sin 2t \\ \Rightarrow \qquad &\left(D^2+1\right)\left(D^2+6\right)[x] = 6\sin 2t\,. \end{aligned} \tag{5.35}$$

Since the characteristic equation, $(r^2+1)(r^2+6) = 0$, has the roots $r = \pm i$ and $r = \pm i\sqrt{6}$, a general solution to the corresponding homogeneous equation is given by

$$x_h(t) = c_1\cos t + c_2\sin t + c_3\cos\sqrt{6}t + c_4\sin\sqrt{6}t\,.$$

Due to the right-hand side in (5.35), a particular solution has the form

$$x_p(t) = A\cos 2t + B\sin 2t\,.$$

In order to simplify computations, we note that both functions, $\cos 2t$ and $\sin 2t$, and so $x_p(t)$, satisfy the differential equation $(D^2+4)[x] = 0$. Thus,

$$\begin{aligned} \left(D^2+1\right)\left(D^2+6\right)[x_h] &= \left\{(D^2+4)-3\right\}\left\{(D^2+4)+2\right\}[x_h] = 2\left\{(D^2+4)-3\right\}[x_h] \\ &= -6x_h = -6A\cos 2t - 6B\sin 2t = 6\sin 2t \end{aligned}$$

$$\Rightarrow \qquad A = 0, \quad B = -1 \qquad \Rightarrow \qquad x_h(t) = -\sin 2t$$

and

$$x(t) = x_h(t) + x_p(t) = c_1 \cos t + c_2 \sin t + c_3 \cos \sqrt{6}t + c_4 \sin \sqrt{6}t - \sin 2t\,.$$

From the first equation in the original system, we have

$$\begin{aligned} y(t) &= \frac{1}{2}\left(x'' + 5x\right) \\ &= 2c_1 \cos t + 2c_2 \sin t - \frac{1}{2}\,c_3 \cos \sqrt{6}t - \frac{1}{2}\,c_4 \sin \sqrt{6}t - \frac{1}{2}\,\sin 2t\,. \end{aligned}$$

We determine constants c_1 and c_3 using the initial conditions $x(0) = 0$ and $y(0) = 1$.

$$\begin{aligned} 0 = x(0) &= c_1 + c_3\,, & & c_3 = -c_1\,, & & c_3 = -2/5, \\ 1 = y(0) &= 2c_1 - c_3/2 & \Rightarrow \quad & 2c_1 - (-c_1)/2 = 1 & \Rightarrow \quad & c_1 = 2/5. \end{aligned}$$

To find c_2 and c_4, compute $x'(t)$ and $y'(t)$, evaluate these functions at $t = 0$, and use the other two initial conditions, $x'(0) = y'(0) = 0$. This yields

$$\begin{aligned} 0 = x'(0) &= c_2 + \sqrt{6}c_4 - 2, & & c_4 = \sqrt{6}/5, \\ 0 = y'(0) &= 2c_2 - \sqrt{6}c_4/2 - 1 & \Rightarrow \quad & c_2 = 4/5. \end{aligned}$$

Therefore, the required solution is

$$\begin{aligned} x(t) &= \frac{2}{5}\,\cos t + \frac{4}{5}\,\sin t - \frac{2}{5}\,\cos \sqrt{6}t + \frac{\sqrt{6}}{5}\,\sin \sqrt{6}t - \sin 2t\,, \\ y(t) &= \frac{4}{5}\,\cos t + \frac{8}{5}\,\sin t + \frac{1}{5}\,\cos \sqrt{6}t - \frac{\sqrt{6}}{10}\,\sin \sqrt{6}t - \frac{1}{2}\,\sin 2t\,. \end{aligned}$$

9. Writing the equations of this system in operator form we obtain

$$\begin{aligned} \left\{mD^2 + \left(\frac{mg}{l} + k\right)\right\}[x_1] - kx_2 &= 0, \\ -kx_1 + \left\{mD^2 + \left(\frac{mg}{l} + k\right)\right\}[x_2] &= 0. \end{aligned}$$

Applying $\{mD^2 + (mg/l + k)\}$ to the first equation, multiplying the second equation by k, and then adding, results in

$$\left\{\left[mD^2 + \left(\frac{mg}{l} + k\right)\right]^2 - k^2\right\}[x_1] = 0.$$

This equation has the auxiliary equation

$$\left(mr^2+\frac{mg}{l}+k\right)^2-k^2=\left(mr^2+\frac{mg}{l}\right)\left(mr^2+\frac{mg}{l}+2k\right)=0$$

with roots $\pm i\sqrt{g/l}$ and $\pm i\sqrt{(g/l)+(2k/m)}$. As discussed on page 211 of the text $\sqrt{g/l}$ and $\sqrt{(g/l)+(2k/m)}$ are the normal angular frequencies. To find the normal frequencies we divide each one by 2π and obtain

$$\left(\frac{1}{2\pi}\right)\sqrt{\frac{g}{l}} \qquad \text{and} \qquad \left(\frac{1}{2\pi}\right)\sqrt{\frac{g}{l}+\frac{2k}{m}}\,.$$

EXERCISES 5.6: Electrical Circuits, page 291

1. In this problem, $R=100\,\Omega$, $L=4\,\text{H}$, $C=0.01\,\text{F}$, and $E(t)=20\,\text{V}$. Therefore, the equation (4) on page 287 of the text becomes

$$4\,\frac{d^2I}{dt^2}+100\,\frac{dI}{dt}+100I=\frac{d(20)}{dt}=0 \qquad \Rightarrow \qquad \frac{d^2I}{dt^2}+25\,\frac{dI}{dt}+25I=0.$$

The roots of the characteristic equation, $r^2+25r+25=0$, are

$$r=\frac{-25\pm\sqrt{(25)^2-4(25)(1)}}{2}=\frac{-25\pm5\sqrt{21}}{2}\,,$$

and so a general solution is

$$I(t)=c_1e^{(-25-5\sqrt{21})t/2}+c_2e^{(-25+5\sqrt{21})t/2}\,.$$

To determine constants c_1 and c_2, first we find the initial value $I'(0)$ using given $I(0)=0$ and $q(0)=4$. Substituting $t=0$ into equation (3) on page 287 of the text (with dq/dt replaced by $I(t)$), we obtain

$$\begin{aligned}
&L\,\frac{d[I(t)]}{dt}+RI(t)+\frac{1}{C}\,q(t)=E(t)\\
\Rightarrow\qquad &4I'(0)+100(0)+\frac{1}{0.01}\,(4)=20\\
\Rightarrow\qquad &I'(0)=-95.
\end{aligned}$$

Thus, $I(t)$ satisfies $I(0) = 0$, $I'(0) = -95$. Next, we compute

$$I'(t) = \frac{c_1(-25 - 5\sqrt{21})}{2} e^{(-25-5\sqrt{21})t/2} + \frac{c_2(-25 + 5\sqrt{21})}{2} e^{(-25+5\sqrt{21})t/2},$$

substitute $t = 0$ into formulas for $I(t)$ and $I'(t)$, and obtain the system

$$\begin{aligned} 0 &= I(0) = c_1 + c_2, \\ -95 &= I'(0) = c_1(-25 - 5\sqrt{21})/2 + c_2(-25 + 5\sqrt{21})/2 \end{aligned} \quad \Rightarrow \quad \begin{aligned} c_1 &= 19/\sqrt{21}, \\ c_2 &= -19/\sqrt{21}. \end{aligned}$$

So, the solution is

$$I(t) = \frac{19}{\sqrt{21}} \left(e^{(-25-5\sqrt{21})t/2} - e^{(-25+5\sqrt{21})t/2} \right).$$

3. In this problem $L = 4$, $R = 120$, $C = (2200)^{-1}$, and $E(t) = 10 \cos 20t$. Therefore, we see that $1/C = 2200$ and $E'(t) = -200 \sin 20t$. By substituting these values into equation (4) on page 287 of the text, we obtain the equation

$$4 \frac{d^2 I}{dt^2} + 120 \frac{dI}{dt} + 2200 I = -200 \sin 20t.$$

By simplifying, we have

$$\frac{d^2 I}{dt^2} + 30 \frac{dI}{dt} + 550 I = -50 \sin 20t. \tag{5.36}$$

The auxiliary equation associated with the homogeneous equation corresponding to (5.36) above is $r^2 + 30r + 550 = 0$. This equation has roots $r = -15 \pm 5\sqrt{13}i$. Therefore, the transient current, that is $I_h(t)$, is given by

$$I_h(t) = e^{-15t} \left[C_1 \cos\left(5\sqrt{13}t\right) + C_2 \sin\left(5\sqrt{13}t\right) \right].$$

By the method of undetermined coefficients, a particular solution, $I_p(t)$, of equation (5.36) will be of the form $I_p(t) = t^s[A \cos 20t + B \sin 20t]$. Since neither $y(t) = \cos 20t$ nor $y(t) = \sin 20t$ is a solution to the homogeneous equation (that is the system is not at resonance), we can let $s = 0$ in $I_p(t)$. Thus, we see that $I_p(t)$, the steady-state current, has the form

$$I_p(t) = A \cos 20t + B \sin 20t.$$

To find the steady-state current, we must, therefore, find A and B. To accomplish this, we observe that

$$I_p'(t) = -20A\sin 20t + 20B\cos 20t,$$

$$I_p''(t) = -400A\cos 20t - 400B\sin 20t.$$

Plugging these expressions into equation (5.36) yields

$$I_p''(t) + 30I_p'(t) + 550I(t) = -400A\cos 20t - 400B\sin 20t - 600A\sin 20t + 600B\cos 20t$$
$$+550A\cos 20t + 550B\sin 20t = -50\sin 20t$$

$$\Rightarrow \qquad (150A + 600B)\cos 20t + (150B - 600A)\sin 20t = -50\sin 20t.$$

By equating coefficients we obtain the system of equations

$$\begin{aligned} 15A + 60B &= 0, \\ -60A + 15B &= -5. \end{aligned}$$

By solving these equations simultaneously for A and B, we obtain $A = 4/51$ and $B = -1/51$. Thus, we have the steady-state current given by

$$I_p(t) = \frac{4}{51}\cos 20t - \frac{1}{51}\sin 20t.$$

As was observed on page 290 of the text, there is a correlation between the RLC series circuits and mechanical vibration. Therefore, we can discuss the resonance frequency of the RLC series circuit. To do so we associate the variable L with m, R with b, and $1/C$ with k. Thus, we see that the resonance frequency for an RLC series circuit is given by $\gamma_r/(2\pi)$, where

$$\gamma_r = \sqrt{\frac{1}{CL} - \frac{R^2}{2L^2}},$$

provided that $R^2 < 2L/C$. For this problem

$$R^2 = 14,400 < 2L/C = 17,600.$$

Therefore, we can find the resonance frequency of this circuit. To do so we first find

$$\gamma_r = \sqrt{\frac{1}{CL} - \frac{R^2}{2L^2}} = \sqrt{\frac{2200}{4} - \frac{14400}{32}} = 10.$$

Hence the resonance frequency of this circuit is $10/(2\pi) = 5/\pi$.

5. In this problem, $C = 0.01\,\text{F}$, $L = 4\,\text{H}$, and $R = 10\,\Omega$. Hence, the equation governing the *RLC* circuit is

$$4\frac{d^2I}{dt^2} + 10\frac{dI}{dt} + \frac{1}{0.01}I = \frac{d}{dt}\left(E_0\cos\gamma t\right) = -\frac{E_0\gamma}{4}\sin\gamma t\,.$$

The frequency response curve $M(\gamma)$ for an *RLC* curcuit is determined by

$$M(\gamma) = \frac{1}{\sqrt{[(1/C) - L\gamma^2]^2 + R^2\gamma^2}}\,,$$

which comes from the comparison Table 5.3 on page 290 of the text and equation (13) in Section 4.9. Therefore

$$M(\gamma) = \frac{1}{\sqrt{[(1/0.01) - 4\gamma^2]^2 + (10)^2\gamma^2}} = \frac{1}{\sqrt{(100 - 4\gamma^2)^2 + 100\gamma^2}}\,.$$

The graph of this function is shown in Figure B.43 in the answers of the text. $M(\gamma)$ has its maximal value at the point $\gamma_0 = \sqrt{x_0}$, where x_0 is the point where the quadratic function $(100 - 4x)^2 + 100x$ attains its minimum (the first coordinate of the vertex). We find that

$$\gamma_0 = \sqrt{\frac{175}{8}} \qquad \text{and} \qquad M(\gamma_0) = \frac{2}{25\sqrt{15}} \approx 0.02\,.$$

7. This spring system satisfies the differential equation

$$7\frac{d^2x}{dt^2} + 2\frac{dx}{dt} + 3x = 10\cos 10t.$$

Since we want to find an *RLC* series circuit analog for the spring system with $R = 10$ ohms, we must find L, $1/C$, and $E(t)$ so that the differential equation

$$L\frac{d^2q}{dt^2} + 10\frac{dq}{dt} + \frac{1}{C}q = E(t)$$

corresponds to the one above. Thus, we want $E(t) = 50\cos 10t$ volts, $L = 35$ henrys, and $C = 1/15$ farads.

11. For this electric network, there are three loops. Loop 1 is through a 10V battery, a 10Ω resistor, and a 20H inductor. Loop 2 is through a 10V battery, a 10Ω resistor, a 5Ω resistor, and a (1/30)F capacitor. Loop 3 is through a 5Ω resistor, a (1/30)F capacitor, and a 20H inductor.

Therefore, applying Kirchhoff's second law to this network yields the three equations given by

$$\begin{aligned}
\text{Loop 1}: &\quad 10I_1 + 20\frac{dI_2}{dt} = 10, \\
\text{Loop 2}: &\quad 10I_1 + 5I_3 + 30q_3 = 10, \\
\text{Loop 3}: &\quad 5I_3 + 30q_3 - 20\frac{dI_2}{dt} = 0.
\end{aligned}$$

Since the equation for Loop 2 minus the equation for Loop 1 yields the remaining equation, we will use the first and second equations above for our calculations. By examining a junction point, we see that we also have the equation $I_1 = I_2 + I_3$. Thus, we have $I_1' = I_2' + I_3'$. We begin by dividing the equation for Loop 1 by 10 and the equation for Loop 2 by 5. Differentiating the equation for Loop 2 yields the system

$$\begin{aligned}
I_1 + 2\frac{dI_2}{dt} &= 1, \\
2\frac{dI_1}{dt} + \frac{dI_3}{dt} + 6I_3 &= 0,
\end{aligned}$$

where $I_3 = q_3'$. Since $I_1 = I_2 + I_3$ and $I_1' = I_2' + I_3'$, we can rewrite the system using operator notation in the form

$$\begin{aligned}
(2D+1)[I_2] + I_3 &= 1, \\
(2D)[I_2] + (3D+6)[I_3] &= 0.
\end{aligned}$$

If we multiply the first equation above by $(3D+6)$ and then subtract the second equation, we obtain

$$\{(3D+6)(2D+1) - 2D\}[I_2] = 6 \qquad \Rightarrow \qquad \left(6D^2 + 13D + 6\right)[I_2] = 6.$$

This last differential equation is a linear equation with constant coefficients whose associated equation, $6r^2+13r+6 = 0$, has roots $-3/2$, $-2/3$. Therefore, the solution to the homogeneous equation corresponding to the equation above is given by

$$I_{2h}(t) = c_1 e^{-3t/2} + c_2 e^{-2t/3}.$$

By the method of undetermined coefficients, the form of a particular solution to the differential equation above will be $I_{2p}(t) = A$. By substituting this function into the differential equation, we see that a particular solution is given by

$$I_{2p}(t) = 1.$$

Thus, the current, I_2, will satisfy the equation

$$I_2(t) = c_1e^{-3t/2} + c_2e^{-2t/3} + 1.$$

As we noticed above, I_3 can now be found from the first equation

$$I_3(t) = -(2D+1)[I_2] + 1 = -2\left[-\frac{3}{2}c_1e^{-3t/2} - \frac{2}{3}c_2e^{-2t/3}\right] - \left[c_1e^{-3t/2} + c_2e^{-2t/3} + 1\right] + 1$$

$$\Rightarrow \qquad I_3(t) = 2c_1e^{-3t/2} + \frac{1}{3}c_2e^{-2t/3}.$$

To find I_1, we will use the equation $I_1 = I_2 + I_3$. Therefore, we have

$$I_1(t) = c_1e^{-3t/2} + c_2e^{-2t/3} + 1 + 2c_1e^{-3t/2} + \frac{1}{3}c_2e^{-2t/3}$$

$$\Rightarrow \qquad I_1(t) = 3c_1e^{-3t/2} + \frac{4}{3}c_2e^{-2t/3} + 1.$$

We will use the initial condition $I_2(0) = I_3(0) = 0$ to find the constants c_1 and c_2. Thus, we have

$$I_2(0) = c_1 + c_2 + 1 = 0 \qquad \text{and} \qquad I_3(0) = 2c_1 + \frac{1}{3}c_2 = 0.$$

Solving these two equations simultaneously yields $c_1 = 1/5$ and $c_2 = -6/5$. Therefore, the equations for the currents for this electric network are given by

$$I_1(t) = \frac{3}{5}e^{-3t/2} - \frac{8}{5}e^{-2t/3} + 1,$$
$$I_2(t) = \frac{1}{5}e^{-3t/2} - \frac{6}{5}e^{-2t/3} + 1,$$
$$I_3(t) = \frac{2}{5}e^{-3t/2} - \frac{2}{5}e^{-2t/3}.$$

13. In this problem, there are three loops. Loop 1 is through a 0.5 H inductor and a 1 Ω resistor. Loop 2 is through is through a 0.5 H inductor, a 0.5 F capacitor, and a voltage source supplying the voltage $\cos 3t$ V at time t. Loop 3 is through a 1 Ω resistor, a 0.5 F capacitor, and the voltage source. We apply Kirchhoff's voltage law, $E_L + E_R + E_C = E(t)$, to Loop 1 and Loop 2 to get two equations connecting currents in the network. (Similarly to Example 2 and Problem 11, there is no need to apply Kirchhoff's voltage law to Loop 3 because the resulting equation is just a linear combination of those for other two loops.)

Loop 1:

$$E_L + E_R = 0 \quad \Rightarrow \quad 0.5\,\frac{dI_1}{dt} + 1 \cdot I_2 = 0 \quad \Rightarrow \quad \frac{dI_1}{dt} + 2I_2 = 0. \tag{5.37}$$

Loop 2:

$$E_L + E_C = \cos 3t \quad \Rightarrow \quad 0.5\,\frac{dI_1}{dt} + \frac{q_3}{0.5} = \cos 3t \quad \Rightarrow \quad \frac{dI_1}{dt} + 4q_3 = 2\cos 3t. \tag{5.38}$$

Additionally, at joint points, by Kirchhoff's current law,

$$-I_1 + I_2 + I_3 = 0 \quad \Rightarrow \quad -I_1 + I_2 + \frac{dq_3}{dt} = 0. \tag{5.39}$$

Putting (5.37)–(5.39) together yields the following system:

$$\begin{aligned} &\frac{dI_1}{dt} + 2I_2 = 0, \\ &\frac{dI_1}{dt} + 4q_3 = 2\cos 3t, \\ &-I_1 + I_2 + \frac{dq_3}{dt} = 0 \end{aligned}$$

or, in operator form,

$$\begin{aligned} &D[I_1] + 2I_2 = 0, \\ &D[I_1] + 4q_3 = 2\cos 3t, \\ &-I_1 + I_2 + D[q_3] = 0 \end{aligned}$$

with the initial condition $I_1(0) = I_2(0) = I_3(0) = 0$ ($I_3 = dq_3/dt$).

From the first equation, $I_2 = -(1/2)D[I_1]$, which (when substituted into the third equation) leads to the system

$$\begin{aligned} &D[I_1] + 4q_3 = 2\cos 3t, \\ &-(D+2)[I_1] + 2D[q_3] = 0. \end{aligned}$$

Multiplying the first equation by D, the second equation – by 2, and subtracting the results, we eliminate q_3:

$$\left\{D^2+2(D+2)\right\}[I_1]=-6\sin 3t \qquad \Rightarrow \qquad \left(D^2+2D+4\right)[I_1]=-6\sin 3t.$$

The roots of the characteristic equation, $r^2+2r+4=0$, are $r=-1\pm\sqrt{3}i$, and so a general solution to the corresponding homogeneous equation is

$$I_{1h}=C_1e^{-t}\cos\sqrt{3}t+C_2e^{-t}\sin\sqrt{3}t.$$

A particular solution has the form $I_{1p}=A\cos 3t+B\sin 3t$. Substitution into the equation yields

$$(-5A+6B)\cos 3t+(-6A-5B)\sin 3t=-6\sin 3t$$
$$\Rightarrow \quad \begin{array}{r}-5A+6B=0,\\ -6A-5B=-6\end{array} \quad \Rightarrow \quad \begin{array}{r}A=36/61,\\ B=30/61.\end{array}$$

Therefore,

$$\begin{aligned} I_1 &= I_{1h}+I_{1p} \\ &= C_1e^{-t}\cos\sqrt{3}t+C_2e^{-t}\sin\sqrt{3}t+\frac{36}{61}\cos 3t+\frac{30}{61}\sin 3t. \end{aligned}$$

Substituting this solution into (5.37)we find that

$$\begin{aligned} I_2 &= -\frac{1}{2}\frac{dI_1}{dt} \\ &= \frac{C_1-C_2\sqrt{3}}{2}e^{-t}\cos\sqrt{3}t+\frac{C_1\sqrt{3}+C_2}{2}e^{-t}\sin\sqrt{3}t-\frac{45}{61}\cos 3t+\frac{54}{61}\sin 3t. \end{aligned}$$

The initial condition, $I_1(0)=I_2(0)=0$ yields

$$\begin{array}{l}C_1+36/61=0,\\ (C_1-C_2\sqrt{3})/2-45/61=0\end{array} \quad \Rightarrow \quad \begin{array}{l}C_1=-36/61,\\ C_2=-42\sqrt{3}/61.\end{array}$$

Thus

$$\begin{aligned} I_1 &= -\frac{36}{61}e^{-t}\cos\sqrt{3}t-\frac{42\sqrt{3}}{61}e^{-t}\sin\sqrt{3}t+\frac{36}{61}\cos 3t+\frac{30}{61}\sin 3t, \\ I_2 &= \frac{45}{61}e^{-t}\cos\sqrt{3}t-\frac{39\sqrt{3}}{61}e^{-t}\sin\sqrt{3}t-\frac{45}{61}\cos 3t+\frac{54}{61}\sin 3t, \\ I_3 &= I_1-I_2=-\frac{81}{61}e^{-t}\cos\sqrt{3}t-\frac{3\sqrt{3}}{61}e^{-t}\sin\sqrt{3}t+\frac{81}{61}\cos 3t-\frac{24}{61}\sin 3t. \end{aligned}$$

EXERCISES 5.7: Dynamical Systems, Poincarè Maps, and Chaos, page 301

1. Let $\omega = 3/2$. Using system (3) on page 294 of the text with $A = F = 1$, $\phi = 0$, and $\omega = 3/2$, we define the Poincaré map

$$x_n = \sin(3\pi n) + \frac{1}{(9/4) - (4/4)} = \sin(3\pi n) + \frac{4}{5} = \frac{4}{5},$$
$$v_n = \frac{3}{2}\cos(3\pi n) = (-1)^n \frac{3}{2},$$

for $n = 0, 1, 2, \ldots$. Calculating the first few values of (x_n, v_n), we find that they alternate between $(4/5, 3/2)$ and $(4/5, -3/2)$. Consequently, we can deduce that there is a subharmonic solution of period 4π. Let $\omega = 3/5$. Using system (3) on page 294 of the text with $A = F = 1$, $\phi = 0$, and $\omega = 3/5$, we define the Poincaré map

$$x_n = \sin\left(\frac{6\pi n}{5}\right) + \frac{1}{(9/25) - 1} = \sin\left(\frac{6\pi n}{5}\right) - 1.5625,$$
$$v_n = \frac{3}{5}\cos\left(\frac{6\pi n}{5}\right) = (0.6)\cos\left(\frac{6\pi n}{5}\right),$$

for $n = 0, 1, 2, \ldots$. Calculating the first few values of (x_n, v_n), we find that the Poincaré map cycles through the points

$$\begin{aligned}
&(-1.5625, 0.6), && n = 0, 5, 10, \ldots, \\
&(-2.1503, -0.4854), && n = 1, 6, 11, \ldots, \\
&(-0.6114, 0.1854), && n = 2, 7, 12, \ldots, \\
&(-2.5136, 0.1854), && n = 3, 8, 13, \ldots, \\
&(-0.9747, -0.4854), && n = 4, 9, 14, \ldots.
\end{aligned}$$

Consequently, we can deduce that there is a subharmonic solution of period 10π.

3. With $A = F = 1$, $\phi = 0$, $\omega = 1$, $b = -0.1$, and $\theta = 0$ (because $\tan\theta = (\omega^2 - 1)/b = 0$) the solution (5) to equation (4) becomes

$$x(t) = e^{0.05t}\sin\frac{\sqrt{3.99}}{2}t + 10\sin t.$$

Thus

$$v(t) = x'(t) = e^{0.05t}\left(0.05\sin\frac{\sqrt{3.99}}{2}t + \frac{\sqrt{3.99}}{2}\cos\frac{\sqrt{3.99}}{2}t\right) + 10\cos t$$

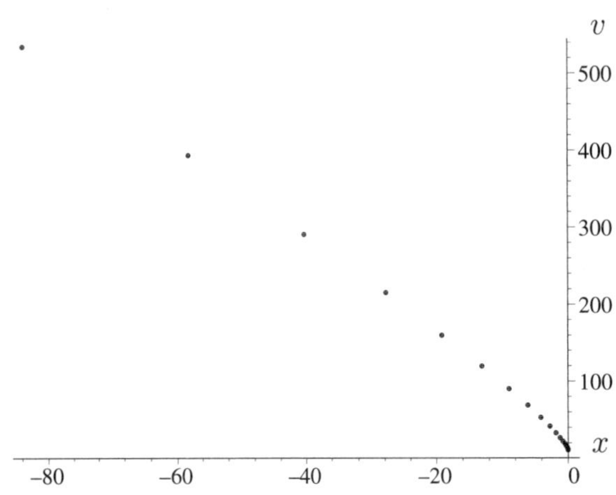

Figure 5–A: Poincaré section for Problem 3.

and, therefore,

$$x_n = x(2\pi n) \approx e^{0.1\pi n} \sin(1.997498\pi n),$$
$$v_n = v(2\pi n) \approx e^{0.1\pi n} (0.05 \sin(1.997498\pi n) + 0.998749 \cos(1.997498\pi n)) + 10.$$

The values of x_n and v_n for $n = 0, 1, \ldots, 20$ are listed in Table 5-F, and points (x_n, v_n) are shown in Figure 5-A. When $n \to \infty$, the points (x_n, v_n) become unbounded because of $e^{0.1\pi n}$ term.

5. We want to construct the Poincaré map using $t = 2\pi n$ for $x(t)$ given in equation (5) on page 295 of the text with $A = F = 1$, $\phi = 0$, $\omega = 1/3$, and $b = 0.22$. Since

$$\tan\theta = \frac{\omega^2 - 1}{b} = -4.040404\,,$$

we take $\theta = \tan^{-1}(-4.040404) = -1.328172$ and get

$$x_n = x(2\pi n) = e^{-0.22\pi n} \sin(0.629321\pi n) - (1.092050) \sin(1.328172),$$
$$v_n = x'(2\pi n) = -0.11e^{-0.22\pi n} \sin(0.629321\pi n) + (1.258642)e^{-0.22\pi n} \cos(0.629321\pi n)$$
$$+(1.092050) \cos(1.328172).$$

Table 5–F: Poincaré map for Problem 3.

n	x_n	v_n	n	x_n	v_n
0	0	10.998749	11	−2.735915	41.387469
1	−0.010761	11.366815	12	−4.085318	52.925111
2	−0.029466	11.870407	13	−6.057783	68.700143
3	−0.060511	12.559384	14	−8.929255	90.267442
4	−0.110453	13.501933	15	−13.09442	119.75193
5	−0.189009	14.791299	16	−19.11674	160.05736
6	−0.310494	16.554984	17	−27.79923	215.15152
7	−0.495883	18.967326	18	−40.28442	290.45581
8	−0.775786	22.266682	19	−58.19561	393.37721
9	−1.194692	26.778923	20	−83.83579	534.03491
10	−1.817047	32.949532			

In Table 5-G we have listed the first 21 values of the Poincaré map.

As n gets large, we see that

$$x_n \approx -(1.092050)\sin(1.328172) \approx -1.060065\,,$$

$$v_n \approx (1.092050)\cos(1.328172) \approx 0.262366\,.$$

Hence, as $n \to \infty$, the Poincaré map approaches the point $(-1.060065, 0.262366)$.

7. Let A, ϕ and A^*, ϕ^* denote the values of constants A, ϕ in solution formula (2), corresponding to initial values (x_0, v_0) and (x_0^*, v_0^*), respectively.

(i) From recursive formulas (3) we conclude that

$$x_n - F/(\omega^2 - 1) = A\sin(2\pi\omega n + \phi),$$

$$v_n/\omega = A\cos(2\pi\omega n + \phi),$$

and so $(A, 2\pi\omega n+\phi)$ are polar coordinates of the point $(v_n/\omega, x_n - F/(\omega^2-1))$ in vx-plane. Similarly, $(A^*, 2\pi\omega n+\phi^*)$ represent polar coordinates of the point $(v_n^*/\omega, x_n^* - F/(\omega^2-1))$.

Table 5–G: Poincaré map for Problem 5.

n	x_n	v_n	n	x_n	v_n
0	−1.060065	1.521008	11	−1.059944	0.261743
1	−0.599847	0.037456	12	−1.060312	0.262444
2	−1.242301	0.065170	13	−1.059997	0.262491
3	−1.103418	0.415707	14	−1.060030	0.262297
4	−0.997156	0.251142	15	−1.060096	0.262362
5	−1.074094	0.228322	16	−1.060061	0.262385
6	−1.070300	0.278664	17	−1.060058	0.262360
7	−1.052491	0.264458	18	−1.060068	0.262364
8	−1.060495	0.257447	19	−1.060065	0.262369
9	−1.061795	0.263789	20	−1.060064	0.262366
10	−1.059271	0.263037			

Therefore,

$$(v_n^*/\omega, x_n^* - F/(\omega^2 - 1)) \to (v_n/\omega, x_n - F/(\omega^2 - 1))$$

as $A^* \to A$ and $\phi^* \to \phi$ if $A \neq 0$ or as $A^* \to 0$ (regardless of ϕ^*) if $A = 0$. Note that the convergence is uniform with respect to n. (One can easily see this from the distance formula in polar coordinates.) This is equivalent to

$$\begin{aligned} x_n^* - F/(\omega^2 - 1) &\to x_n - F/(\omega^2 - 1), \\ v_n^*/\omega &\to v_n/\omega \end{aligned} \qquad \Leftrightarrow \qquad \begin{aligned} x_n^* &\to x_n\,, \\ v_n^* &\to v_n \end{aligned}$$

uniformly with respect to n.

(ii) On the other hand, A^* and ϕ^* satisfy

$$\begin{aligned} A^* \sin\phi^* + F/(\omega^2 - 1) &= x_0^*\,, \\ \omega A^* \cos\phi^* &= v_0^* \end{aligned} \qquad \Rightarrow \qquad \begin{aligned} A^* &= \sqrt{\left(x_0^* - F/(\omega^2 - 1)\right)^2 + (v_0^*/\omega)^2}\,, \\ \cos\phi^* &= v_0^*/\left(\omega A^*\right). \end{aligned}$$

Therefore, A^* is a continuous function of (x_0^*, v_0^*) and so $A^* \to A$ as $(x_0^*, v_0^*) \to (x_0, v_0)$. If (x_0, v_0) is such that $A \neq 0$, then ϕ^*, as a function of (x_0^*, v_0^*), is also continuous at (x_0, v_0) and, therefore, $\phi^* \to \phi$ as $(x_0^*, v_0^*) \to (x_0, v_0)$.

Combining (i) and (ii) we conclude that

$$(x_n^*, v_n^*) \to (x_n, v_n) \qquad \text{as} \qquad (x_0^*, v_0^*) \to (x_0, v_0)$$

uniformly with respect to n. Thus, if (x_0^*, v_0^*) is close to (x_0, v_0), (x_n^*, v_n^*) is close to (x_n, v_n) for all n.

9. (a) When $x_0 = 1/7$, the doubling modulo 1 map gives

$$x_1 = \frac{2}{7}\,(\text{mod}\,1) = \frac{2}{7}, \qquad x_2 = \frac{4}{7}\,(\text{mod}\,1) = \frac{4}{7},$$

$$x_3 = \frac{8}{7}\,(\text{mod}\,1) = \frac{1}{7}, \qquad x_4 = \frac{2}{7}\,(\text{mod}\,1) = \frac{2}{7},$$

$$x_5 = \frac{4}{7}\,(\text{mod}\,1) = \frac{4}{7}, \qquad x_6 = \frac{8}{7}\,(\text{mod}\,1) = \frac{1}{7},$$

$$x_7 = \frac{2}{7}\,(\text{mod}\,1) = \frac{2}{7}, \qquad \text{etc.}$$

This is the sequence $\left\{\frac{1}{7}, \frac{2}{7}, \frac{4}{7}, \frac{1}{7}, \ldots\right\}$. For $x_0 = \frac{k}{7}$, $k = 2, \ldots, 6$, we obtain

$$\left\{\frac{2}{7}, \frac{4}{7}, \frac{1}{7}, \frac{2}{7}, \ldots\right\}, \quad \left\{\frac{3}{7}, \frac{6}{7}, \frac{5}{7}, \frac{3}{7}, \ldots\right\},$$
$$\left\{\frac{4}{7}, \frac{1}{7}, \frac{2}{7}, \frac{4}{7}, \ldots\right\}, \quad \left\{\frac{5}{7}, \frac{3}{7}, \frac{6}{7}, \frac{5}{7}, \ldots\right\},$$
$$\left\{\frac{6}{7}, \frac{5}{7}, \frac{3}{7}, \frac{6}{7}, \ldots\right\}.$$

These sequences fall into two classes. The first has the repeating sequence $\overline{\frac{1}{7}, \frac{2}{7}, \frac{4}{7}}$ and the second has the repeating sequence $\overline{\frac{3}{7}, \frac{6}{7}, \frac{5}{7}}$.

(c) To see what happens, when $x_0 = \frac{k}{2^j}$, let's consider the special case when $x_0 = \frac{3}{2^2} = \frac{3}{4}$. Then,

$$x_1 = 2\left(\frac{3}{4}\right)(\text{mod}\,1) = \frac{3}{2}\,(\text{mod}\,1) = \frac{1}{2},$$

$$x_2 = 2\left(\frac{1}{2}\right) (\operatorname{mod} 1) = 1 \,(\operatorname{mod} 1) = 0,$$
$$x_3 = 0,$$
$$x_4 = 0,$$
etc.

Observe that

$$x_2 = 2^2\left(\frac{3}{2^2}\right) (\operatorname{mod} 1) = 3 \,(\operatorname{mod} 1) = 0.$$

In general,

$$x_j = 2^j\left(\frac{k}{2^j}\right) (\operatorname{mod} 1) = k \,(\operatorname{mod} 1) = 0.$$

Consequently, $x_n = 0$ for $n \geq j$.

11. (a) A general solution to equation (6) is given by $x(t) = x_h(t) + x_p(t)$, where

$$x_h(t) = Ae^{-0.11t} \sin\left(\sqrt{9879}t + \phi\right)$$

is the transient term (a general solution to the corresponding homogeneous equation) and

$$x_p(t) = \frac{1}{0.22} \sin t + \frac{1}{\sqrt{1 + 2(0.22)^2}} \sin\left(\sqrt{2}t + \psi\right), \quad \tan\psi = -\frac{1}{0.22\sqrt{2}},$$

is the steady-state term (a particular solution to (6)). ($x_p(t)$ can be found, say, by applying formula (7), Section 4.12, and using Superposition Principle of Section 4.7.) Differentiating $x(t)$ we get

$$v(t) = x_h'(t) + x_p'(t) = x_h'(t) + \frac{1}{0.22} \cos t + \frac{\sqrt{2}}{\sqrt{1 + 2(0.22)^2}} \cos\left(\sqrt{2}t + \psi\right).$$

The steady-state solution does not depend on initial values x_0 and v_0; these values affect only constants A and ϕ in the transient part. But, as $t \to \infty$, $x_h(t)$ and $x_h'(t)$ tend to zero and so the values of $x(t)$ and $v(t)$ approach the values of $x_p(t)$ and $x_p'(t)$, respectively. Thus the limit set of points $(x(t), v(t))$ is the same as that of $(x_p(t), x_p'(t))$ which is independent of initial values.

(b) Substitution $t = 2\pi n$ into $x_p(t)$ and $x_p'(t)$ yields

$$x_n = x(2\pi n) = x_h(2\pi n) + \frac{1}{\sqrt{1+2(0.22)^2}} \sin\left(\sqrt{2}2\pi n + \psi\right),$$
$$v_n = v(2\pi n) = x_h'(2\pi n) + \frac{1}{0.22} + \frac{\sqrt{2}}{\sqrt{1+2(0.22)^2}} \cos\left(\sqrt{2}2\pi n + \psi\right).$$

As $n \to \infty$, $x_h(2\pi n) \to 0$ and $x_h'(2\pi n) \to 0$. Therefore, for n large,

$$x_n \approx \frac{1}{\sqrt{1+2(0.22)^2}} \sin\left(\sqrt{2}2\pi n + \psi\right) = a \sin\left(2\sqrt{2}\pi n + \psi\right),$$
$$v_n \approx \frac{1}{0.22} + \frac{\sqrt{2}}{\sqrt{1+2(0.22)^2}} \cos\left(\sqrt{2}2\pi n + \psi\right) = c + \sqrt{2}a \cos\left(2\sqrt{2}\pi n + \psi\right).$$

(c) From part (b) we conclude that, for n large

$$x_n^2 \approx a^2 \sin^2\left(2\sqrt{2}\pi n + \psi\right) \quad \text{and} \quad (v_n - c)^2 \approx 2a^2 \cos^2\left(2\sqrt{2}\pi n + \psi\right).$$

Dividing the latter by 2 and summing yields

$$x_n^2 + \frac{(v_n - c)^2}{2} \approx a^2 \left[\sin^2\left(2\sqrt{2}\pi n + \psi\right) + \cos^2\left(2\sqrt{2}\pi n + \psi\right)\right] = a^2,$$

and the error (coming from the transient part) tends to zero as $n \to \infty$. Thus any limiting point of the sequence (x_n, v_n) satisfies the equation

$$x^2 + \frac{(v - c)^2}{2} = a^2,$$

which is an ellipse centered at $(0, c)$ with semiaxes a and $a\sqrt{2}$.

REVIEW PROBLEMS: page 304

1. Expressing the system in the operator notation gives

$$D[x] + \left(D^2 + 1\right)[y] = 0,$$
$$D^2[x] + D[y] = 0.$$

Eliminating x by applying D to the first equation and subtracting the second equation from it yields

$$\left\{D\left(D^2+1\right)-D\right\}[y]=0 \qquad \Rightarrow \qquad D^3[y]=0.$$

Thus on integrating 3 times we get

$$y(t)=C_3+C_2t+C_1t^2.$$

We substitute this solution into the first equation of given system to get

$$x'=-\left(y''+y\right)=-\left[(2C_1)+(C_3+C_2t+C_1t^2)\right]=-\left[(C_3+2C_1)+C_2t+C_1t^2\right].$$

Integrating we obtain

$$x(t)=-\int\left[(C_3+2C_1)+C_2t+C_1t^2\right]dt=C_4-(C_3+2C_1)t-\frac{1}{2}C_2t^2-\frac{1}{3}C_1t^3.$$

Thus the general solution of the given system is

$$\begin{aligned}x(t)&=C_4-(C_3+2C_1)t-\frac{1}{2}C_2t^2-\frac{1}{3}C_1t^3,\\ y(t)&=C_3+C_2t+C_1t^2.\end{aligned}$$

3. Writing the system in operator form yields

$$\begin{aligned}(2D-3)[x]-(D+1)[y]&=e^t,\\ (-4D+15)[x]+(3D-1)[y]&=e^{-t}.\end{aligned} \tag{5.40}$$

We eliminate y by multiplying the first equation by $(3D-1)$, the second – by $(D+1)$, and summing the results.

$$\begin{aligned}&\left\{(2D-3)(3D-1)+(-4D+15)(D+1)\right\}[x]=(3D-1)[e^t]+(D+1)[e^{-t}]\\ \Rightarrow\quad &(D^2+9)[x]=e^t.\end{aligned}$$

Since the characterictic equation, $r^2+9=0$, has roots $r=\pm 3i$, a general solution to the corresponding homogeneous equation is

$$x_h(t)=c_1\cos 3t+c_2\sin 3t.$$

We look for a particular solution of the form $x_p(t) = Ae^t$. Substituting this function into the equation, we obtain

$$Ae^t + 9Ae^t = e^t \quad \Rightarrow \quad A = \frac{1}{10} \quad \Rightarrow \quad x_p(t) = \frac{e^t}{10},$$

and so

$$x(t) = x_h(t) + x_p(t) = c_1 \cos 3t + c_2 \sin 3t + \frac{e^t}{10}.$$

To find y, we multiply the first equation in (5.40) by 3 and add to the second equation. This yields

$$2(D+3)[x] - 4y = 3e^t + e^{-t}.$$

Thus

$$\begin{aligned} y &= \frac{1}{2}(D+3)[x] - \frac{3}{4}e^t - \frac{1}{4}e^{-t} \\ &= \frac{3(c_1+c_2)}{2}\cos 3t - \frac{3(c_1-c_2)}{2}\sin 3t - \frac{11}{20}e^t - \frac{1}{4}e^{-t}. \end{aligned}$$

5. Differentiating the second equation, we obtain $y'' = z'$. We eliminate z from the first and the third equations by substituting y' for z and y'' for z' into them:

$$\begin{aligned} x' &= y' - y, \\ y'' &= y' - x \end{aligned} \quad \Rightarrow \quad \begin{aligned} x' - y' + y &= 0, \\ y'' - y' + x &= 0 \end{aligned} \tag{5.41}$$

or, in operator notation,

$$\begin{aligned} D[x] - (D-1)[y] &= 0, \\ x + (D^2 - D)[y] &= 0. \end{aligned}$$

We eliminate y by applying D to the first equation and adding the result to the second equation:

$$\left\{D^2[x] - D(D-1)[y]\right\} + \left\{x + (D^2 - D)[y]\right\} = 0 \quad \Rightarrow \quad \left(D^2+1\right)[x] = 0.$$

This equation is the simple harmonic equation, and its general solution is given by

$$x(t) = C_1 \cos t + C_2 \sin t.$$

Substituting $x(t)$ into the first equation of the system (5.41) yields

$$y' - y = -C_1 \sin t + C_2 \cos t. \tag{5.42}$$

The general solution to the corresponding homogeneous equation, $y' - y = 0$, is

$$y_h(t) = C_3 e^t .$$

We look for a particular solution to (5.42) of the form $y_p(t) = C_4 \cos t + C_5 \sin t$. Differentiating, we obtain $y_p'(t) = -C_4 \sin t + C_5 \cos t$. Thus the equation (5.42) becomes

$$\begin{aligned} -C_1 \sin t + C_2 \cos t = y_p' - y &= (-C_4 \sin t + C_5 \cos t) - (C_4 \cos t + C_5 \sin t) \\ &= (C_5 - C_4) \cos t - (C_5 + C_4) \sin t. \end{aligned}$$

Equating the coefficients yields

$$\begin{aligned} &C_5 - C_4 = C_2 \,, \\ &C_5 + C_4 = C_1 \\ &\Rightarrow \qquad \text{(by adding the equations)} \quad 2C_5 = C_1 + C_2 \qquad \Rightarrow \qquad C_5 = \frac{C_1 + C_2}{2} \,. \end{aligned} \tag{5.43}$$

From the second equation in (5.43), we find

$$C_4 = C_1 - C_5 = \frac{C_1 - C_2}{2} \,.$$

Therefore, the general solution to the equation (5.42) is

$$y(t) = y_h(t) + y_p(t) = C_3 e^t + \frac{C_1 - C_2}{2} \cos t + \frac{C_1 + C_2}{2} \sin t.$$

Finally, we find $z(t)$ from the second equation:

$$\begin{aligned} z(t) &= y'(t) = \left(C_3 e^t + \frac{C_1 - C_2}{2} \cos t + \frac{C_1 + C_2}{2} \sin t \right)' \\ &= C_3 e^t - \frac{C_1 - C_2}{2} \sin t + \frac{C_1 + C_2}{2} \cos t. \end{aligned}$$

Hence, the general solution to the given system is

$$x(t) = C_1 \cos t + C_2 \sin t,$$

$$y(t) = C_3 e^t + \frac{C_1 - C_2}{2}\cos t + \frac{C_1 + C_2}{2}\sin t,$$
$$z(t) = C_3 e^t - \frac{C_1 - C_2}{2}\sin t + \frac{C_1 + C_2}{2}\cos t.$$

To find constants C_1, C_2, and C_3, we use the initial conditions. So we get

$$0 = x(0) = C_1 \cos 0 + C_2 \sin 0 = C_1\,,$$
$$0 = y(0) = C_3 e^0 + \frac{C_1 - C_2}{2}\cos 0 + \frac{C_1 + C_2}{2}\sin 0 = C_3 + \frac{C_1 - C_2}{2}\,,$$
$$2 = z(0) = C_3 e^0 - \frac{C_1 - C_2}{2}\sin 0 + \frac{C_1 + C_2}{2}\cos 0 = C_3 + \frac{C_1 + C_2}{2}\,,$$

which simplifies to

$$C_1 = 0,$$
$$C_1 - C_2 + 2C_3 = 0,$$
$$C_1 + C_2 + 2C_3 = 4.$$

Solving we obtain $C_1 = 0$, $C_2 = 2$, $C_3 = 1$ and so

$$x(t) = 2\sin t, \qquad y(t) = e^t - \cos t + \sin t, \qquad z(t) = e^t + \cos t + \sin t.$$

7. Let $x(t)$ and $y(t)$ denote the mass of salt in tanks A and B, respectively. The only difference between this problem and the problem in Section 5.1 is that a brine solution flows in tank A instead of pure water. This change affects the input rate for tank A only, adding

$$6\,\mathrm{L/min} \times 0.2\,\mathrm{kg/L} = 1.2\,\mathrm{kg/min}$$

to the original $(y/12)\,\mathrm{kg/min}$. Thus the system (1) on page 242 becomes

$$x' = -\frac{1}{3}\,x + \frac{1}{12}\,y + 1.2\,,$$
$$y' = \frac{1}{3}\,x - \frac{1}{3}\,y.$$

Following the solution in Section 5.1, we express $x = 3y' + y$ from the second equation and substitute it into the first equation.

$$(3y' + y)' = -\frac{1}{3}\,(3y' + y) + \frac{1}{12}\,y + 1.2 \qquad \Rightarrow \qquad 3y'' + 2y' + \frac{1}{4}\,y = 1.2\,.$$

A general solution to the corresponding homogeneous equation is given in (3) on page 243 of the text:

$$y_h(t) = c_1 e^{-t/2} + c_2 e^{-t/6}.$$

A particular solution has the form $y_p(t) \equiv C$, which results

$$3(C)'' + 2(C)' + \frac{1}{4}C = 1.2 \qquad \Rightarrow \qquad C = 4.8.$$

Therefore, $y_p(t) \equiv 4.8$, and a general solution to the system is

$$\begin{aligned} y(t) &= y_h(t) + y_p(t) = c_1 e^{-t/2} + c_2 e^{-t/6} + 4.8, \\ x(t) &= 3y'(t) + y(t) = -\frac{c_1}{2}e^{-t/2} + \frac{c_2}{2}e^{-t/6} + 4.8. \end{aligned}$$

We find constants c_1 and c_2 from the initial conditions, $x(0) = 0.1$ and $y(0) = 0.3$. Substitution yields the system

$$\begin{aligned} -\frac{c_1}{2} + \frac{c_2}{2} + 4.8 &= 0.1, \\ c_1 + c_2 + 4.8 &= 0.3. \end{aligned}$$

Solving, we obtain $c_1 = 49/20$, $c_2 = -139/20$, and so

$$\begin{aligned} x(t) &= -\frac{49}{40}e^{-t/2} - \frac{139}{40}e^{-t/6} + 4.8, \\ y(t) &= \frac{49}{20}e^{-t/2} - \frac{139}{20}e^{-t/6} + 4.8. \end{aligned}$$

9. We first rewrite the given differential equation in an equivalent form as

$$y''' = \frac{1}{3}\left(5 + e^t y - 2y'\right).$$

Denoting $x_1(t) = y(t)$, $x_2(t) = y'(t)$, and $x_3(t) = y''(t)$, we conclude that

$$\begin{aligned} x_1' &= y' = x_2, \\ x_2' &= (y')' = y'' = x_3, \\ x_3' &= (y'')' = y''' = \frac{1}{3}\left(5 + e^t x_1 - 2x_2\right), \end{aligned}$$

that is,

$$x_1' = x_2\,,$$
$$x_2' = x_3\,,$$
$$x_3' = \frac{1}{3}\left(5 + e^t x_1 - 2x_2\right).$$

11. This system is equivalent to

$$x''' = t - y' - y''\,,$$
$$y''' = x' - x''\,.$$

Next, we introduce, as additional unknowns, derivatives of $x(t)$ and $y(t)$:

$$x_1(t) := x(t), \quad x_2(t) := x'(t), \quad x_3(t) := x''(t),$$
$$x_4(t) := y(t), \quad x_5(t) := y'(t), \quad x_6(t) := y''(t).$$

With new variables, the system becomes

$$x''' = (x'')' =: x_3' = t - y' - y'' =: t - x_5 - x_6\,,$$
$$y''' = (y'')' =: x_6' = x' - x'' =: x_2 - x_3\,.$$

Also, we have four new equations connecting x_j's:

$$x_1' = x' =: x_2\,,$$
$$x_2' = (x')' = x'' =: x_3\,,$$
$$x_4' = y' =: x_5\,,$$
$$x_5' = (y')' = y'' =: x_6\,.$$

Therefore, the answer is

$$x_1' = x_2\,,$$
$$x_2' = x_3\,,$$
$$x_3' = t - x_5 - x_6\,,$$

$$x_4' = x_5\,,$$
$$x_5' = x_6\,,$$
$$x_6' = x_2 - x_3\,.$$

13. With the notation used in (1) on page 264 of the text,

$$f(x,y) = 4 - 4y,$$
$$g(x,y) = -4x,$$

and the phase plane equation (see equation (2) on page 265 of the text) can be written as

$$\frac{dy}{dx} = \frac{g(x,y)}{f(x,y)} = \frac{-4x}{4-4y} = \frac{x}{y-1}\,.$$

This equation is separable. Separating variables yields

$$(y-1)\,dy = x\,dx \qquad \Rightarrow \qquad \int (y-1)\,dy = \int x\,dx \qquad \Rightarrow \qquad (y-1)^2 + C = x^2$$

or $x^2 - (y-1)^2 = C$, where C is an arbitrary constant. We find the critical points by solving the system

$$\begin{aligned} f(x,y) &= 4 - 4y = 0, \\ g(x,y) &= -4x = 0 \end{aligned} \qquad \Rightarrow \qquad \begin{aligned} y &= 1, \\ x &= 0. \end{aligned}$$

So, $(0,1)$ is the unique critical point. For $y > 1$,

$$\frac{dx}{dt} = 4(1-y) < 0,$$

which implies that trajectories flow to the left. Similarly, for $y < 1$, trajectories flow to the right. Comparing the phase plane diagram with those given on Figure 5.12 on page 270 of the text, we conclude that the critical point $(0,1)$ is a saddle (unstable) point.

15. Some integral curves and the direction field for the given system are shown in Figure 5-B. Comparing this picture with Figure 5.12 on page 270 of the text, we conclude that the origin is an asymptotically stable spiral point.

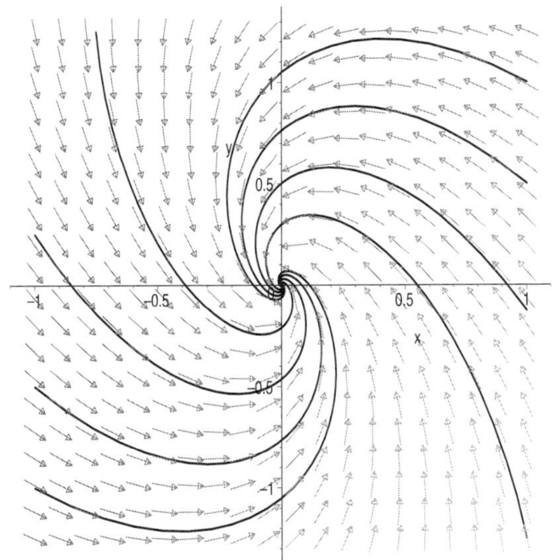

Figure 5–B: Integral curves and the direction field for Problem 15.

17. A trajectory is a path traced by an actual solution pair $(x(t), y(t))$ as t increases; thus it is a directed (oriented) curve. An integral curve is the graph of a solution to the phase plane equation; it has no direction. All trajectories lie along (parts of) integral curves. A given integral curve can be the underlying point set for several different trajectories.

19. We apply Kirchhoff's voltage law to Loops 1 and 2.

Loop 1 contains a capacitor C and a resistor R_2; note that the direction of the loop is opposite to that of I_2. Thus we have

$$\frac{q}{C} - R_2 I_2 = 0 \qquad \Rightarrow \qquad \frac{q}{C} = R_2 I_2 \,,$$

where q denotes the charge of the capacitor.

Loop 2 consists of an inductor L and two resistors R_1 and R_2; note that the loop direction is opposite to the direction of I_3. Therefore,

$$R_2 I_2 - R_1 I_3 - L I_3' = 0 \qquad \Rightarrow \qquad R_2 I_2 = R_1 I_3 + L I_3' \,.$$

For the top juncture, all the currents flow out, and the Kirchhoff's current law gives

$$-I_1 - I_2 - I_3 = 0 \qquad \Rightarrow \qquad I_1 + I_2 + I_3 = 0.$$

Therefore, the system, describing the current in RLC, is

$$\begin{aligned} \frac{q}{C} &= R_2 I_2\,, \\ R_2 I_2 &= R_1 I_3 + L I_3'\,, \\ I_1 + I_2 + I_3 &= 0. \end{aligned}$$

With given data, $R_1 = R_2 = 1\,\Omega$, $L = 1\,\text{H}$, and $C = 1\,\text{F}$, and the relation $I_1 = dq/dt$, this system becomes

$$\begin{aligned} q &= I_2\,, \\ I_2 &= I_3 + I_3'\,, \\ q' + I_2 + I_3 &= 0. \end{aligned}$$

Replacing in the last two equations I_2 by q, we get

$$\begin{aligned} I_3' + I_3 - q &= 0, \\ q' + q + I_3 &= 0. \end{aligned}$$

We eliminate q by substituting $q = I_3' + I_3$ into the second equation and obtain

$$I_3'' + 2I_3' + 2I_3 = 0.$$

The characteristic equation, $r^2 + 2r + 2 = 0$, has roots $r = -1 \pm i$ and so, a general solution to this homogeneous equation is $I_3 = e^{-t}(A\cos t + B\sin t)$. Thus

$$\begin{aligned} I_2 = q &= I_3' + I_3 \\ &= -e^{-t}(A\cos t + B\sin t) + e^{-t}(-A\sin t + B\cos t) + e^{-t}(A\cos t + B\sin t) \\ &= e^{-t}(B\cos t - A\sin t) \end{aligned}$$

and

$$\begin{aligned} I_1 = \frac{dq}{dt} &= -e^{-t}(B\cos t - A\sin t) + e^{-t}(-B\sin t - A\cos t) \\ &= e^{-t}[(A - B)\sin t - (A + B)\cos t]. \end{aligned}$$

CHAPTER 6: Theory of Higher Order Linear Differential Equations

EXERCISES 6.1: Basic Theory of Linear Differential Equations, page 324

1. Putting the equation in standard form,

$$y''' - \frac{3}{x}y' + \frac{e^x}{x}y = \frac{x^2-1}{x},$$

we find that

$$p_1(x) \equiv 0, \quad p_2(x) = -\frac{3}{x}, \quad p_3(x) = \frac{e^x}{x}, \quad \text{and} \quad q(x) = \frac{x^2-1}{x}.$$

Functions $p_2(x)$, $p_3(x)$, and $q(x)$ have only one point of discontinuity, $x = 0$, while $p_1(x)$ is continuous everywhere. Therefore, all these functions are continuous on $(-\infty, 0)$ and $(0, \infty)$. Since the initial point, $x_0 = 2$, belongs to $(-\infty, 0)$, Theorem 1 guarantees the existence of a unique solution to the given initial value problem on $(-\infty, 0)$.

3. For this problem, $p_1(x) = -1$, $p_2(x) = \sqrt{x-1}$, and $g(x) = \tan x$. Note that $p_1(x)$ is continuous everywhere, $p_2(x)$ is continuous for $x \geq 1$, and $g(x)$ is continuous everywhere except at odd multiples of $\pi/2$. Therefore, these three functions are continuous simultaneously on the intervals

$$\left[1, \frac{\pi}{2}\right), \quad \left(\frac{\pi}{2}, \frac{3\pi}{2}\right), \quad \left(\frac{3\pi}{2}, \frac{5\pi}{2}\right), \ldots .$$

Because 5, the initial point, is in the interval $(3\pi/2, 5\pi/2)$, Theorem 1 guarantees that we have a unique solution to the initial value problem on this interval.

5. Dividing the equation by $x\sqrt{x+1}$, we obtain

$$y''' - \frac{1}{x\sqrt{x+1}}y' + \frac{1}{\sqrt{x+1}}y = 0.$$

Thus $p_1(x) \equiv 0$, $p_2(x) = 1/(x\sqrt{x+1})$, $p_3(x) = 1/\sqrt{x+1}$, and $g(x) \equiv 0$. Functions $p_1(x)$ and $q(x)$ are continuous on whole real line; $p_3(x)$ is defined and continuous for $x > -1$; $p_2(x)$ is defined and continuous for $x > -1$ and $x \neq 0$. Therefore, all these function is continuous on $(-1, 0)$ and $(0, \infty)$. The initial point lies on $(0, \infty)$, and so, by Theorem 1, the given initial value problem has a unique solution on $(0, \infty)$.

7. Assume that c_1, c_2, and c_3 are constants for which

$$c_1 e^{3x} + c_2 e^{5x} + c_3 e^{-x} \equiv 0 \quad \text{on} \quad (-\infty, \infty). \tag{6.1}$$

If we show that this is possible only if $c_1 = c_2 = c_3 = 0$, then linear independence will follow. Evaluating the linear combination in (6.1) at $x = 0$, $x = \ln 2$, and $x = -\ln 2$, we find that constants c_1, c_2, and c_3 satisfy

$$\begin{aligned} &c_1 + c_2 + c_3 = 0, \\ &8c_1 + 32c_2 + \frac{1}{2}\,c_3 = 0, \\ &\frac{1}{8}\,c_1 + \frac{1}{32}\,c_2 + 2c_3 = 0. \end{aligned}$$

This system is a homogeneous system of linear equations whose determinant

$$\begin{vmatrix} 1 & 1 & 1 \\ 8 & 32 & 1/2 \\ 1/8 & 1/32 & 2 \end{vmatrix} = \begin{vmatrix} 32 & 1/2 \\ 1/32 & 2 \end{vmatrix} - \begin{vmatrix} 8 & 1/2 \\ 1/8 & 2 \end{vmatrix} + \begin{vmatrix} 8 & 32 \\ 1/8 & 1/32 \end{vmatrix} = \frac{2827}{64} \neq 0.$$

Hence it has the unique trivial solution, that is, $c_1 = c_2 = c_3 = 0$.

9. Let $y_1 = \sin^2 x$, $y_2 = \cos^2 x$, and $y_3 = 1$. We want to find c_1, c_2, and c_3, not all zero, such that

$$c_1 y_1 + c_2 y_2 + c_3 y_3 = c_1 \sin^2 x + c_2 \cos^2 x + c_3 \cdot 1 = 0,$$

for all x in the interval $(-\infty, \infty)$. Since $\sin^2 x + \cos^2 x = 1$ for all real numbers x, we can choose $c_1 = 1$, $c_2 = 1$, and $c_3 = -1$. Thus, these functions are linearly dependent.

11. Let $y_1 = x^{-1}$, $y_2 = x^{1/2}$, and $y_3 = x$. We want to find constants c_1, c_2, and c_3 such that

$$c_1 y_1 + c_2 y_2 + c_3 y_3 = c_1 x^{-1} + c_2 x^{1/2} + c_3 x = 0,$$

for all x on the interval $(0, \infty)$. This equation must hold if $x = 1$, 4, or 9 (or any other values for x in the interval $(0, \infty)$). By plugging these values for x into the equation above, we see that c_1, c_2, and c_3 must satisfy the three equations

$$\begin{aligned} c_1 + c_2 + c_3 &= 0, \\ \frac{c_1}{4} + 2c_2 + 4c_3 &= 0, \\ \frac{c_1}{9} + 3c_2 + 9c_3 &= 0. \end{aligned}$$

Solving these three equations simultaneously yields $c_1 = c_2 = c_3 = 0$. Thus, the only way for $c_1 x^{-1} + c_2 x^{1/2} + c_3 x = 0$ for all x on the interval $(0, \infty)$, is for $c_1 = c_2 = c_3 = 0$. Therefore, these three functions are linearly independent on $(0, \infty)$.

13. A linear combination, $c_1 x + c_2 x^2 + c_3 x^3 + c_4 x^4$, is a polynomial of degree at most four, and so, by the fundamental theorem of algebra, it cannot have more than four zeros unless it is the zero polynomial (that is, it has all zero coefficients). Thus, if this linear combination vanishes on *an interval*, then $c_1 = c_2 = c_3 = c_4 = 0$. Therefore, the functions x, x^2, x^3, and x^4 are linearly independent on any interval, in particular, on $(-\infty, \infty)$.

15. Since, by inspection, $r = 3$, $r = -1$, and $r = -4$ are the roots of the characteristic equation, $r^3 + 2r^2 - 11r - 12 = 0$, the functions e^{3x}, e^{-x}, and e^{-4x} form a solution set. Next, we check that these functions are linearly independent by showing that their Wronskian is never zero.

$$W\left[e^{3x}, e^{-x}, e^{-4x}\right](x) = \begin{vmatrix} e^{3x} & e^{-x} & e^{-4x} \\ 3e^{3x} & -e^{-x} & -4e^{-4x} \\ 9e^{3x} & e^{-x} & 16e^{-4x} \end{vmatrix} = e^{3x}e^{-x}e^{-4x} \begin{vmatrix} 1 & 1 & 1 \\ 3 & -1 & -4 \\ 9 & 1 & 16 \end{vmatrix} = -84e^{-2x},$$

which does not vanish. Therefore, $\{e^{3x}, e^{-x}, e^{-4x}\}$ is a fundamental solution set and, by Theorem 4, a general solution to the given differential equation is

$$y = C_1 e^{3x} + C_2 e^{-x} + C_3 e^{-4x}.$$

17. Writing the given differential equation,

$$x^3y''' - 3x^2y'' + 6xy' - 6y = 0,$$

in standard form (17), we see that its coefficients, $-3/x$, $6/x^2$, and $-6/x^3$ are continuous on the specified interval, which is $x > 0$.

Next, substituting x, x^2, and x^3 into the differential equation, we verify that these functions are indeed solutions.

$$\begin{aligned}
&x^3(x)''' - 3x^2(x)'' + 6x(x)' - 6(x) = 0 - 0 + 6x - 6x = 0,\\
&x^3(x^2)''' - 3x^2(x^2)'' + 6x(x^2)' - 6(x^2) = 0 - 6x^2 + 12x^2 - 6x^2 = 0,\\
&x^3(x^3)''' - 3x^2(x^3)'' + 6x(x^3)' - 6(x^3) = 6x^3 - 18x^3 + 18x^3 - 6x^3 = 0.
\end{aligned}$$

Evaluating the Wronskian yields

$$\begin{aligned}
W\left[x, x^2, x^3\right](x) &= \begin{vmatrix} x & x^2 & x^3 \\ 1 & 2x & 3x^2 \\ 0 & 2 & 6x \end{vmatrix} \\
&= x\begin{vmatrix} 2x & 3x^2 \\ 2 & 6x \end{vmatrix} - \begin{vmatrix} x^2 & x^3 \\ 2 & 6x \end{vmatrix} = x\left(6x^2\right) - \left(4x^3\right) = 2x^3\,.
\end{aligned}$$

Thus $W[x, x^2, x^3](x) \neq 0$ on $(0, \infty)$ and so $\{x, x^2, x^3\}$ is a fundamental solution set for the given differential equation. We involve Theorem 2 to conclude that

$$y = C_1x + C_2x^2 + C_3x^3$$

is a general solution.

19. **(a)** Since $\{e^x, e^{-x}\cos 2x, e^{-x}\sin 2x,\}$ is a fundamental solution set for the associated homogeneous differential equation and since $y_p = x^2$ is a solution to the nonhomogeneous equation, by the superposition principle, we have a general solution given by

$$y(x) = C_1e^x + C_2e^{-x}\cos 2x + C_3e^{-x}\sin 2x + x^2.$$

(b) To find the solution that satisfies the initial conditions, we must differentiate the general solution $y(x)$ twice with respect to x. Thus, we have

$$\begin{aligned} y'(x) &= C_1e^x - C_2e^{-x}\cos 2x - 2C_2e^{-x}\sin 2x - C_3e^{-x}\sin 2x + 2C_3e^{-x}\cos 2x + 2x \\ &= C_1e^x + (-C_2 + 2C_3)\,e^{-x}\cos 2x + (-2C_2 - C_3)\,e^{-x}\sin 2x + 2x\,, \\ y''(x) &= C_1e^x + (C_2 - 2C_3)\,e^{-x}\cos 2x - 2\,(-C_2 + 2C_3)\,e^{-x}\sin 2x \\ &\qquad - (-2C_2 - C_3)\,e^{-x}\sin 2x + 2\,(-2C_2 - C_3)\,e^{-x}\cos 2x + 2 \\ &= C_1e^x + (-3C_2 - 4C_3)\,e^{-x}\cos 2x + (4C_2 - 3C_3)\,e^{-x}\sin 2x + 2\,. \end{aligned}$$

Plugging the initial conditions into these formulas, yields the equations

$$\begin{aligned} y(0) &= C_1 + C_2 = -1, \\ y'(0) &= C_1 - C_2 + 2C_3 = 1, \\ y''(0) &= C_1 - 3C_2 - 4C_3 + 2 = -3. \end{aligned}$$

By solving these equations simultaneously, we obtain $C_1 = -1$, $C_2 = 0$, and $C_3 = 1$. Therefore, the solution to the initial value problem is given by

$$y(x) = -e^x + e^{-x}\sin 2x + x^2.$$

21. In the standard form, given equation becomes

$$y''' + \frac{1}{x^2}\,y' - \frac{1}{x^3}\,y = \frac{3 - \ln x}{x^3}\,.$$

Since its coefficients are continuous on $(0, \infty)$, we can apply Theorems 2 and 4 to conclude that a general solution to the corresponding homogeneous equation is

$$y_h(x) = C_1x + C_2x\ln x + C_3x(\ln x)^2$$

and a general solution to the given nonhomogeneous equation is

$$y(x) = y_p(x) + y_h(x) = \ln x + C_1x + C_2x\ln x + C_3x(\ln x)^2\,.$$

To satisfy the initial conditions, first we find

$$y'(x) = \frac{1}{x} + C_1 + C_2(\ln x + 1) + C_3\left[(\ln x)^2 + 2\ln x\right],$$
$$y''(x) = -\frac{1}{x^2} + \frac{C_2}{x} + C_3\left[\frac{2\ln x}{x} + \frac{2}{x}\right].$$

Substituting the initial conditions, $y(1) = 3$, $y'(1) = 3$, and $y''(1) = 0$, we get the system

$$\begin{aligned} 3 &= y(1) = C_1, \\ 3 &= y'(1) = 1 + C_1 + C_2, \\ 0 &= y''(1) = -1 + C_2 + 2C_3 \end{aligned} \quad \Rightarrow \quad \begin{aligned} C_1 &= 3, \\ C_1 + C_2 &= 2, \\ C_2 + 2C_3 &= 1 \end{aligned} \quad \Rightarrow \quad \begin{aligned} C_1 &= 3, \\ C_2 &= -1, \\ C_3 &= 1. \end{aligned}$$

Thus,

$$y(x) = \ln x + 3x - x\ln x + x(\ln x)^2$$

is the desired solution.

23. Substituting $y_1(x) = \sin x$ and $y_2(x) = x$ into the given differential operator yields

$$L[\sin x] = (\sin x)''' + (sinx)' + x(\sin x) = -\cos x + \cos x + x\sin x = x\sin x,$$
$$L[x] = (x)''' + (x)' + x(x) = 0 + 1 + x^2 = x^2 + 1.$$

Note that $L[y]$ is a linear operator of the form (7). So, we can use the superposition principle.

(a) Since $2x\sin x - x^2 - 1 = 2(x\sin x) - (x^2 + 1)$, by the superposition principle,

$$y(x) = 2y_1(x) - y_2(x) = 2\sin x - x$$

is a solution to $L[y] = 2x\sin x - x^2 - 1$.

(b) We can express $4x^2 + 4 - 6x\sin x = 4(x^2 + 1) - 6(x\sin x)$. Hence,

$$y(x) = 4y_2(x) - 6y_1(x) = 4x - 6\sin x$$

is a solution to $L[y] = 4x^2 + 4 - 6x\sin x$.

25. Clearly, it is sufficient to prove (9) just for two functions, y_1 and y_2. Using the linear property of differentiation, we have

$$\begin{aligned} L[y_1+y_2] &= [y_1+y_2]^{(n)} + p_1[y_1+y_2]^{(n-1)} + \cdots + p_n[y_1+y_2] \\ &= \left[y_1^{(n)} + y_2^{(n)}\right] + p_1\left[y_1^{(n-1)} + y_2^{(n-1)}\right] + \cdots + p_n[y_1+y_2] \\ &= \left[y_1^{(n)} + p_1 y_1^{(n-1)} + \cdots + p_n y_1\right] + \left[y_2^{(n)} + p_1 y_2^{(n-1)} + \cdots + p_n y_2\right] = L[y_1] + L[y_1]. \end{aligned}$$

Next, we verify (10).

$$\begin{aligned} L[cy] &= [cy]^{(n)} + p_1[cy]^{(n-1)} + \cdots + p_n[cy] = cy^{(n)} + p_1 cy^{(n-1)} + \cdots + p_n cy \\ &= c\left[y^{(n)} + p_1 y^{(n-1)} + \cdots + p_n y\right] = cL[y]. \end{aligned}$$

27. A linear combination

$$c_0 + c_1 x + c_2 x^2 + \cdots + c_n x^n$$

of the functions from the given set is a polynomial of degree at most n and so, by the fundamental theorem of algebra, it cannot have more than n zeros unless it is the zero polynomial, i.e., it has all zero coefficients. Thus, if this linear combination vanishes on a whole interval (a,b), then it follows that $c_0 = c_1 = c_2 = \ldots = c_n = 0$. Therefore, the set of functions $\{1, x, x^2, \ldots, x^n\}$ is linearly independent on any interval (a,b).

29. **(a)** Assuming that functions $f_1, f_2, \ldots, f_m$ are linearly dependent on $(-\infty,\infty)$, we can find their nontrivial linear combination vanishing identically on $(-\infty,\infty)$, i.e.,

$$c_1 f_1 + c_2 f_2 + \cdots + c_m f_m \equiv 0 \qquad \text{on} \qquad (-\infty,\infty),$$

where not all c_j's are zeros. In particular, this linear combination vanishes on $(-1,1)$, which contradicts the assumption that $f_1, f_2, \ldots, f_m$ are linearly independent on $(-1,1)$.

(b) Let

$$f_1(x) := |x-1|, \qquad f_2(x) := x - 1.$$

On $(-1, 1)$ (even on $(-\infty, 1)$) we have $f_1(x) \equiv -f_2(x)$ or, equivalently, $f_1(x)+f_2(x) \equiv 0$ and so these functions are linearly dependent on $(-1, 1)$. However, their linear combination

$$c_1 f_1(x) + c_2 f_2(x) = \begin{cases} (c_2 - c_1)(x-1), & x \le 1; \\ (c_1 + c_2)(x-1), & x > 1 \end{cases}$$

cannot vanish identically on $(-\infty, \infty)$ unless $c_1 - c_2 = 0$ and $c_1 + c_2 = 0$, which implies $c_1 = c_2 = 0$.

31. (a) Linearity of differentiation and the product rule yield

$$\begin{aligned} y'(x) &= (v(x)e^x)' = v'(x)e^x + v(x)(e^x)' = [v'(x) + v(x)]\, e^x, \\ y''(x) &= [v'(x) + v(x)]'\, e^x + [v'(x) + v(x)]\,(e^x)' = [v''(x) + 2v'(x) + v(x)]\, e^x, \\ y'''(x) &= [v''(x) + 2v'(x) + v(x)]'\, e^x + [v''(x) + 2v'(x) + v(x)]\,(e^x)' \\ &= [v'''(x) + 3v''(x) + 3v'(x) + v(x)]\, e^x. \end{aligned}$$

(b) Substituting y, y', y'', and y''' into the differential equation (32), we obtain

$$\begin{aligned} &[v''' + 3v'' + 3v' + v]\, e^x - 2\,[v'' + 2v' + v]\, e^x - 5\,[v' + v]\, e^x + 6ve^x = 0 \\ \Rightarrow \quad & [(v''' + 3v'' + 3v' + v) - 2\,(v'' + 2v' + v) - 5\,(v' + v) + 6v]\, e^x = 0 \\ \Rightarrow \quad & v''' + v'' - 6v' = 0, \end{aligned}$$

where we have used the fact that the function e^x is never zero. Let $v' =: w$. Then $v'' = w'$, $v''' = w''$, and so the above equation becomes

$$w'' + w' - 6w = 0. \tag{6.2}$$

(c) The auxiliary equation for (6.2), $r^2 + r - 6 = 0$, has the roots $r = -3$ and $r = 2$. Therefore, a general solution to this differential equation is

$$w(x) = C_1 e^{-3x} + C_2 e^{2x},$$

where C_1 and C_2 are arbitrary constants. Choosing, say, $C_1 = -3$, $C_2 = 0$ and $C_1 = 0$, $C_2 = 2$, we find two linearly independent solutions,

$$w_1(x) = -3e^{-3x} \qquad \text{and} \qquad w_2(x) = 2e^{2x}.$$

Integration yields

$$v_1(x) = \int w_1(x)\,dx = \int \left(-3e^{-3x}\right) dx = e^{-3x},$$
$$v_2(x) = \int w_2(x)\,dx = \int \left(2e^{2x}\right) dx = e^{2x},$$

where we have chosen zero integration constants.

(d) With functions $v_1(x)$ and $v_2(x)$ obtained in (c), we have

$$y_1(x) = v_1(x)e^x = e^{-3x}e^x = e^{-2x}, \quad y_2(x) = v_2(x)e^x = e^{2x}e^x = e^{3x}.$$

To show that the functions e^x, e^{-2x}, and e^{3x} are linearly independent on $(-\infty, \infty)$, we can use the approach similar to that in Problem 7. Alternatively, since these functions are solutions to the differential equation (32), one can apply Theorem 3, as we did in Problem 15. To this end,

$$W\left[e^x, e^{-2x}, e^{3x}\right](x) = \begin{vmatrix} e^x & e^{-2x} & e^{3x} \\ e^x & -2e^{-2x} & 3e^{3x} \\ e^x & 4e^{-2x} & 9e^{3x} \end{vmatrix} = e^x e^{-2x} e^{3x} \begin{vmatrix} 1 & 1 & 1 \\ 1 & -2 & 3 \\ 1 & 4 & 9 \end{vmatrix} = -30e^{2x} \neq 0$$

on $(-\infty, \infty)$ and so the functions e^x, e^{-2x}, and e^{3x} are linearly independent on $(-\infty, \infty)$.

33. Let $y(x) = v(x)e^{2x}$. Differentiating $y(x)$, we obtain

$$y'(x) = \left[v'(x) + 2v(x)\right] e^{2x},$$
$$y''(x) = \left[v''(x) + 4v'(x) + 4v(x)\right] e^{2x},$$
$$y'''(x) = \left[v'''(x) + 6v''(x) + 12v'(x) + 8v(x)\right] e^{2x}.$$

Substituting these expressions into the given differential equation yields

$$\left[(v''' + 6v'' + 12v' + 8v) - 2\left(v'' + 4v' + 4v\right) + (v' + 2v) - (2v)\right] e^{2x} = 0$$
$$\Rightarrow \quad \left[v''' + 4v'' + 5v'\right] e^{2x} = 0 \quad \Rightarrow \quad v''' + 4v'' + 5v' = 0.$$

With $w(x) := v'(x)$, the above equation becomes

$$w''(x) + 4w'(x) + 5w(x) = 0.$$

The roots of the auxiliary equation, $r^2 + 4r + 5 = 0$, for this second order equation are $r = -2 \pm i$. Therefore,

$$\{w_1(x), w_2(x)\} = \{e^{-2x}\cos x, e^{-2x}\sin x\}$$

form a fundamental solution set. Integrating, we get

$$v_1(x) = \int w_1(x) = \int e^{-2x}\cos x\,dx = \frac{e^{-2x}(\sin x - 2\cos x)}{5},$$
$$v_2(x) = \int w_2(x) = \int e^{-2x}\sin x\,dx = -\frac{e^{-2x}(2\sin x + \cos x)}{5},$$

where we have chosen integration constants to be zero. Thus, functions

$$f(x) = e^{2x},$$
$$y_1(x) = v_1(x)f(x) = \frac{e^{-2x}(\sin x - 2\cos x)}{5}e^{2x} = \frac{\sin x - 2\cos x}{5},$$
$$y_2(x) = v_2(x)f(x) = \frac{e^{-2x}(2\sin x + \cos x)}{5}e^{2x} = \frac{2\sin x + \cos x}{5}$$

are three linearly independent solutions to the given differential equation.

35. First, let us evaluate the Wronskian of the system $\{x, \sin x, \cos x\}$ to make sure that the result of Problem 34 can be applied.

$$\begin{aligned} W[x, \sin x, \cos x] &= \begin{vmatrix} x & \sin x & \cos x \\ 1 & \cos x & -\sin x \\ 0 & -\sin x & -\cos x \end{vmatrix} \\ &= x\begin{vmatrix} \cos x & -\sin x \\ -\sin x & -\cos x \end{vmatrix} - \begin{vmatrix} \sin x & \cos x \\ -\sin x & -\cos x \end{vmatrix} \\ &= x\left(-\cos^2 x - \sin^2 x\right) - (-\sin x\cos x + \sin x\cos x) = -x. \end{aligned}$$

Thus, $W[x, \sin x, \cos x] \neq 0$ on $(-\infty, 0)$ and $(0, \infty)$. Therefore, on either of these two intervals, $\{x, \sin x, \cos x\}$ is a fundamental solution set for the third order linear differential equation given in Problem 34. Expanding the determinant over its last column yields

$$\begin{aligned}
\begin{vmatrix} x & \sin x & \cos x & y \\ 1 & \cos x & -\sin x & y' \\ 0 & -\sin x & -\cos x & y'' \\ 0 & -\cos x & \sin x & y''' \end{vmatrix} &= y'''W[x, \sin x, \cos x] - y'' \begin{vmatrix} x & \sin x & \cos x \\ 1 & \cos x & -\sin x \\ 0 & -\cos x & \sin x \end{vmatrix} \\
&\quad + y' \begin{vmatrix} x & \sin x & \cos x \\ 0 & -\sin x & -\cos x \\ 0 & -\cos x & \sin x \end{vmatrix} - y \begin{vmatrix} 1 & \cos x & -\sin x \\ 0 & -\sin x & -\cos x \\ 0 & -\cos x & \sin x \end{vmatrix} \\
&= -xy''' - y'' \left[x \begin{vmatrix} \cos x & -\sin x \\ -\cos x & \sin x \end{vmatrix} - \begin{vmatrix} \sin x & \cos x \\ -\cos x & \sin x \end{vmatrix} \right] \\
&\quad + y'x \begin{vmatrix} -\sin x & -\cos x \\ -\cos x & \sin x \end{vmatrix} - y \begin{vmatrix} -\sin x & -\cos x \\ -\cos x & \sin x \end{vmatrix} \\
&= -xy''' + y'' - xy' + y = 0.
\end{aligned}$$

EXERCISES 6.2: Homogeneous Linear Equations with Constant Coefficients, page 331

1. The auxiliary equation

$$r^3 + 2r^2 - 8r = 0 \qquad \Rightarrow \qquad r\left(r^2 + 2r - 8\right) = r(r-2)(r+4) = 0$$

has the roots $r = 0$, 2, and -4. Thus a general solutions to the differential equation has the form

$$y = c_1 + c_2 e^{2x} + c_3 e^{-4x} .$$

3. The auxiliary equation for this problem is $6r^3 + 7r^2 - r - 2 = 0$. By inspection we see that $r = -1$ is a root to this equation and so we can factor it as follows

$$6r^3 + 7r^2 - r - 2 = (r+1)(6r^2 + r - 2) = (r+1)(3r+2)(2r-1) = 0.$$

Thus, we see that the roots to the auxiliary equation are $r = -1$, $-2/3$, and $1/2$. These roots are real and non-repeating. Therefore, a general solution to this problem is given by

$$z(x) = c_1 e^{-x} + c_2 e^{-2x/3} + c_3 e^{x/2} .$$

5. We can factor the auxiliary equation, $r^3 + 3r^2 + 28r + 26 = 0$, as follows:

$$\begin{aligned} r^3 + 3r^2 + 28r + 26 &= (r^3 + r^2) + (2r^2 + 2r) + (26r + 26) \\ &= r^2(r+1) + 2r(r+1) + 26(r+1) = (r+1)(r^2 + 2r + 26) = 0. \end{aligned}$$

Thus either $r + 1 = 0 \quad \Rightarrow \quad r = -1$ or $r^2 + 2r + 26 = 0 \quad \Rightarrow \quad r = -1 \pm 5i$. Therefore, a general solution is given by

$$y(x) = c_1 e^{-x} + c_2 e^{-x} \cos 5x + c_3 e^{-x} \sin 5x \,.$$

7. Factoring the characteristic polynomial yields

$$\begin{aligned} 2r^3 - r^2 - 10r - 7 &= (2r^3 + 2r^2) + (-3r^2 - 3r) + (-7r - 7) \\ &= 2r^2(r+1) - 3r(r+1) - 7(r+1) = (r+1)(2r^2 - 3r - 7). \end{aligned}$$

Thus the roots of the characteristic equation, $2r^3 - r^2 - 10r - 7 = 0$, are

$$\begin{aligned} r + 1 = 0 \quad &\Rightarrow \quad r = -1 \,, \\ 2r^2 - 3r - 7 = 0 \quad &\Rightarrow \quad r = \frac{3 \pm \sqrt{3^2 - 4(2)(-7)}}{4} = \frac{3 \pm \sqrt{65}}{4} \,, \end{aligned}$$

and a general solution is

$$y(x) = c_1 e^{-x} + c_2 e^{(3+\sqrt{65})x/4} + c_3 e^{(3-\sqrt{65})x/4} \,.$$

9. In the characteristic equation, $r^3 - 9r^2 + 27r - 27 = 0$, we recognize a complete cube, namely, $(r-3)^3 = 0$. Thus, it has just one root, $r = 3$, of multiplicity three. Therefore, a general solution to the given differential equation is given by

$$u(x) = c_1 e^{3x} + c_2 x e^{3x} + c_3 x^2 e^{3x} \,.$$

11. Since $r^4 + 4r^3 + 6r^2 + 4r + 1 = (r+1)^4$, the characteristic equation becomes $(r+1)^4 = 0$, and it has the root $r = -1$ of multiplicity four. Therefore, the functions e^{-x}, xe^{-x}, $x^2 e^{-x}$, and $x^3 e^{-x}$ form a fundamental solution set and a general solution to the given differential equation is

$$y(x) = c_1 e^{-x} + c_2 x e^{-x} + c_3 x^2 e^{-x} + c_4 x^3 e^{-x} = \left(c_1 + c_2 x + c_3 x^2 + c_4 x^3\right) e^{-x} \,.$$

13. The auxiliary equation in this problem is $r^4+4r^2+4=0$. This can be factored as $(r^2+2)^2=0$. Therefore, this equation has roots $r=\sqrt{2}i,\ -\sqrt{2}i,\ \sqrt{2}i,\ -\sqrt{2}i$, which we see are repeated and complex. Therefore, a general solution to this problem is given by

$$y(x)=c_1\cos\left(\sqrt{2}x\right)+c_2x\cos\left(\sqrt{2}x\right)+c_3\sin\left(\sqrt{2}x\right)+c_4x\sin\left(\sqrt{2}x\right).$$

15. The roots to this auxiliary equation, $(r-1)^2(r+3)(r^2+2r+5)^2=0$, are

$$r=1,\ 1,\ -3,\ -1\pm 2i,\ -1\pm 2i\,,$$

where we note that 1 and $-1\pm 2i$ are repeated roots. Therefore, a general solution to the differential equation with the given auxiliary equation is

$$y(x)=c_1e^x+c_2xe^x+c_3e^{-3x}+(c_4+c_5x)e^{-x}\cos 2x+(c_6+c_7x)e^{-x}\sin 2x\,.$$

17. From the differential operator, replacing D by r, we obtain the characteristic equation

$$(r+4)(r-3)(r+2)^3(r^2+4r+5)^2r^5=0\,,$$

whose roots

$$\begin{array}{lcl} r+4=0 & \Rightarrow & r=-4, \\ r-3=0 & \Rightarrow & r=3, \\ (r+2)^3=0 & \Rightarrow & r=-2 \text{ of multiplicity } 3, \\ (r^2+4r+5)^2=0 & \Rightarrow & r=-2\pm i \text{ of multiplicity } 2, \\ r^5=0 & \Rightarrow & r=0 \text{ of multiplicity } 5. \end{array}$$

Therefore, a general solution is given by

$$\begin{aligned} y(x) &= c_1e^{-4x}+c_2e^{3x}+\left(c_3+c_4x+c_5x^2\right)e^{-2x}+\left(c_6+c_7x\right)e^{-2x}\cos x+\left(c_8+c_9x\right)e^{-2x}\sin x \\ &\quad +c_{10}+c_{11}x+c_{12}x^2+c_{13}x^3+c_{14}x^4\,. \end{aligned}$$

19. First, we find a general solution to the given equation. Solving the auxiliary equation,

$$r^3-r^2-4r+4=(r^3-r^2)-(4r-4)=(r-1)(r^2-4)=(r-1)(r+2)(r-2)=0,$$

yields the roots $r = 1, -2$, and 2. Thus a general solution has the form

$$y(x) = c_1 e^x + c_2 e^{-2x} + c_3 e^{2x}.$$

Next, we find constants c_1, c_2, and c_3 such that the solution satisfies the initial conditions. Differentiating $y(x)$ and substituting the initial conditions, we obtain the system

$$\begin{aligned}
y(0) &= \left(c_1 e^x + c_2 e^{-2x} + c_3 e^{2x}\right)\big|_{x=0} = c_1 + c_2 + c_3 = -4, \\
y'(0) &= \left(c_1 e^x - 2c_2 e^{-2x} + 2c_3 e^{2x}\right)\big|_{x=0} = c_1 - 2c_2 + 2c_3 = -1, \\
y''(0) &= \left(c_1 e^x + 4c_2 e^{-2x} + 4c_3 e^{2x}\right)\big|_{x=0} = c_1 + 4c_2 + 4c_3 = -19.
\end{aligned}$$

Solving yields

$$c_1 = 1, \qquad c_2 = -2, \qquad c_3 = -3.$$

With these coefficients, the solution to the given initial problem is

$$y(x) = e^x - 2e^{-2x} - 3e^{2x}.$$

21. By inspection, $r = 2$ is a root of the characteristic equation, $r^3 - 4r^2 + 7r - 6 = 0$. Factoring yields

$$r^3 - 4r^2 + 7r - 6 = (r-2)(r^2 - 2r + 3) = 0.$$

Therefore, the other two roots are the roots of $r^2 - 2r + 3 = 0$, which are $r = 1 \pm \sqrt{2}i$, and so a general solution to the given differential equation is given by

$$y(x) = c_1 e^{2x} + \left(c_2 \cos\sqrt{2}x + c_3 \sin\sqrt{2}x\right) e^x.$$

Differentiating, we obtain

$$\begin{aligned}
y' &= 2c_1 e^{2x} + \left[\left(c_2 + c_3\sqrt{2}\right)\cos\sqrt{2}x + \left(c_3 - c_2\sqrt{2}\right)\sin\sqrt{2}x\right] e^x, \\
y'' &= 4c_1 e^{2x} + \left[\left(2c_3\sqrt{2} - c_2\right)\cos\sqrt{2}x - \left(2c_2\sqrt{2} + c_3\right)\sin\sqrt{2}x\right] e^x.
\end{aligned}$$

Hence, the initial conditions yield

$$\begin{aligned}
y(0) &= c_1 + c_2 = 1, & & & c_1 &= 1, \\
y'(0) &= 2c_1 + c_2 + c_3\sqrt{2} = 0, & &\Rightarrow & c_2 &= 0, \\
y''(0) &= 4c_1 - c_2 + 2c_3\sqrt{2} = 0 & & & c_3 &= -\sqrt{2}.
\end{aligned}$$

Substituting these constants into the general solution, we get the answer

$$y(x) = e^{2x} - \sqrt{2}e^{x} \sin \sqrt{2}x \,.$$

23. Rewriting the system in operator form yields

$$\begin{aligned} &(D^3 - 1)\,[x] + (D + 1)[y] = 0, \\ &(D - 1)[x] + y = 0. \end{aligned}$$

Multiplying the second equation in this sytem by $(D+1)$ and subtracting the result from the first equation, we get

$$\left\{ \left(D^3 - 1 \right) - (D + 1)(D - 1) \right\} [x] = D^2(D - 1)[x] = 0.$$

Since the roots of the characteristic equation, $r^2(r - 1) = 0$ are $r = 0$ of multiplicity two and $r = 1$, a general solution $x(t)$ is given by

$$x(t) = c_1 + c_2 t + c_3 e^t \,.$$

From the second equation in the original system, we obtain

$$y(t) = x(t) - x'(t) = \left(c_1 + c_2 t + c_3 e^t \right) - \left(c_1 + c_2 t + c_3 e^t \right)' = (c_1 - c_2) + c_2 t.$$

25. A linear combination of the given functions

$$c_0 e^{rx} + c_1 x e^{rx} + c_2 x^2 e^{rx} + \cdots + c_{m-1} x^{m-1} e^{rx} = \left(c_0 + c_1 x + c_2 x^2 + \cdots + c_m x^m \right) e^{rx} \qquad (6.3)$$

vanishes on an interval if and only if its polynomial factor, $c_0 + c_1 x + c_2 x^2 + \cdots + c_{m-1} x^{m-1}$, vanishes on this interval (the exponential factor, e^{rx}, is never zero). But, as we have proved in Problem 27, Section 6.1, the system of monomials $\{1, x, \ldots, x^n\}$ is linearly independent on any interval. Thus, the linear combination (6.3) vanishes on an inteval if and only if it has all zero coefficients, i.e., $c_0 = c_1 = \ldots = c_{m-1} = 0$. Therefore, the system $\{e^{rx}, xe^{rx}, \ldots, x^{m-1}e^{rx}\}$ is linearly independent on any interval, in particular, on $(-\infty, \infty)$.

27. Solving the auxiliary equation, $r^4 + 2r^3 - 3r^2 - r + (1/2) = 0$, using computer software yields the roots

$$r_1 = 1.119967680,\ r_2 = 0.2963247800,\ r_3 = -0.5202201098,\ r_4 = -2.896072350\,.$$

Thus, all the roots are real and distinct. A general solution to the given equation is, therefore,

$$y(x) = c_1e^{r_1x} + c_2e^{r_2x} + c_3e^{r_3x} + c_4e^{r_4x} \approx c_1e^{1.120x} + c_2e^{0.296x} + c_3e^{-0.520x} + c_4e^{-2.896x}\,.$$

29. The auxiliary equation in this problem is $r^4 + 2r^3 + 4r^2 + 3r + 2 = 0$. Let

$$g(r) = r^4 + 2r^3 + 4r^2 + 3r + 2$$

$$\Rightarrow \qquad g'(r) = 4r^3 + 6r^2 + 8r + 3.$$

Then the Newton's recursion formula (2) in Appendix A of the text becomes

$$r_{n+1} = r_n - \frac{r_n^4 + 2r_n^3 + 4r_n^2 + 3r_n + 2}{4r_n^3 + 6r_n^2 + 8r_n + 3}\,.$$

With initial guess $r_0 = 1 + i$, this formula yields

$$r_1 = (1+i) - \frac{(1+i)^4 + 2(1+i)^3 + 4(1+i)^2 + 3(1+i) + 2}{4(1+i)^3 + 6(1+i)^2 + 8(1+i) + 3} \approx 0.481715 + 0.837327i\,,$$

$$r_2 = r_1 - \frac{r_1^4 + 2r_1^3 + 4r_1^2 + 3r_1 + 2}{4r_1^3 + 6r_1^2 + 8r_1 + 3} \approx 0.052833 + 0.763496i\,,$$

$$r_3 = r_2 - \frac{r_2^4 + 2r_2^3 + 4r_2^2 + 3r_2 + 2}{4r_2^3 + 6r_2^2 + 8r_2 + 3} \approx -0.284333 + 0.789859i\,,$$

$$\vdots$$

$$r_7 = r_6 - \frac{r_6^4 + 2r_6^3 + 4r_6^2 + 3r_6 + 2}{4r_6^3 + 6r_6^2 + 8r_6 + 3} \approx -0.500000 + 0.866025i\,,$$

$$r_8 = r_7 - \frac{r_7^4 + 2r_7^3 + 4r_7^2 + 3r_7 + 2}{4r_7^3 + 6r_7^2 + 8r_7 + 3} \approx -0.500000 + 0.866025i\,.$$

Therefore, first two roots of the auxiliary equation are

$$r \approx -0.5 + 0.866i \qquad \text{and} \qquad r = \overline{-0.5 + 0.866i} = -0.5 - 0.866i\,.$$

Similarly, we find other two roots. With the initial guess $r_0 = -1-2i$, we find that

$$r_1 = (-1-2i) - \frac{(-1-2i)^4 + 2(-1-2i)^3 + 4(-1-2i)^2 + 3(-1-2i) + 2}{4(-1-2i)^3 + 6(-1-2i)^2 + 8(-1-2i) + 3} \approx -0.830703 - 1.652798i\,,$$

$$\vdots$$

$$r_6 \approx -0.499994 - 1.322875i\,,$$

$$r_7 \approx -0.500000 - 1.322876i\,,$$

$$r_8 \approx -0.500000 - 1.322876i\,.$$

Therefore, the other two roots are

$$r \approx -0.5 - 1.323i \qquad \text{and} \qquad r = \overline{-0.5 - 1.323i} = -0.5 + 1.323i\,.$$

Thus, the auxiliary equation has four complex roots, and a general solution to the given differential equation is given by

$$y(x) \approx c_1 e^{-0.5x}\cos(0.866x) + c_2 e^{-0.5x}\sin(0.866x) + c_3 e^{-0.5x}\cos(1.323x) + c_4 e^{-0.5x}\sin(1.323x)\,.$$

31. (a) If we let $y(x) = x^r$, then we see that

$$\begin{aligned} y' &= rx^{r-1}\,, \\ y'' &= r(r-1)x^{r-2} = (r^2 - r)x^{r-2}\,, \\ y''' &= r(r-1)(r-2)x^{r-3} = (r^3 - 3r^2 + 2r)x^{r-3}\,. \end{aligned} \qquad (6.4)$$

Thus, if $y = x^r$ is a solution to this third order Cauchy-Euler equation, then we must have

$$x^3(r^3 - 3r^2 + 2r)x^{r-3} + x^2(r^2 - r)x^{r-2} - 2xrx^{r-1} + 2x^r = 0$$

$$\Rightarrow \qquad (r^3 - 3r^2 + 2r)x^r + (r^2 - r)x^r - 2rx^r + 2x^r = 0$$

$$\Rightarrow \qquad (r^3 - 2r^2 - r + 2)x^r = 0. \qquad (6.5)$$

Therefore, in order for $y = x^r$ to be a solution to the equation with $x > 0$, we must have $r^3 - 2r^2 - r + 2 = 0$. Factoring this equation yields

$$r^3 - 2r^2 - r + 2 = (r^3 - 2r^2) - (r - 2) = (r-2)(r^2 - 1) = (r-2)(r+1)(r-1) = 0.$$

Equation (6.5) will equal zero and, therefore, the differential equation will be satisfied for $r = \pm 1$ and $r = 2$. Thus, three solutions to the differential equation are $y = x$, $y = x^{-1}$, and $y = x^2$. Since these functions are linearly independent, they form a fundamental solution set.

(b) Let $y(x) = x^r$. In addition to (6.4), we need the fourth derivative of $y(x)$.

$$y^{(4)} = (y''')' = r(r-1)(r-2)(r-3)x^{r-4} = (r^4 - 6r^3 + 11r^2 - 6r)x^{r-4}.$$

Thus, if $y = x^r$ is a solution to this fourth order Cauchy-Euler equation, then we must have

$$x^4(r^4 - 6r^3 + 11r^2 - 6r)x^{r-4} + 6x^3(r^3 - 3r^2 + 2r)x^{r-3}$$
$$+2x^2(r^2 - r)x^{r-2} - 4xrx^{r-1} + 4x^r = 0$$
$$\Rightarrow \quad (r^4 - 6r^3 + 11r^2 - 6r)x^r + 6(r^3 - 3r^2 + 2r)x^r + 2(r^2 - r)x^r - 4rx^r + 4x^r = 0$$
$$\Rightarrow \quad (r^4 - 5r^2 + 4)x^r = 0. \tag{6.6}$$

Therefore, in order for $y = x^r$ to be a solution to the equation with $x > 0$, we must have $r^4 - 5r^2 + 4 = 0$. Factoring this equation yields

$$r^4 - 5r^2 + 4 = (r^2 - 4)(r^2 - 1) = (r-2)(r+2)(r-1)(r+1) = 0.$$

Equation (6.6) will be satisfied if $r = \pm 1, \pm 2$. Thus, four solutions to the differential equation are $y = x$, $y = x^{-1}$, $y = x^2$, and $y = x^{-2}$. These functions are linearly independent, and so form a fundamental solution set.

(c) Substituting $y = x^r$ into this differential equation yields

$$(r^3 - 3r^2 + 2r)x^r - 2(r^2 - r)x^r + 13rx^r - 13x^r = 0$$
$$\Rightarrow \quad (r^3 - 5r^2 + 17r - 13)x^r = 0.$$

Thus, in order for $y = x^r$ to be a solution to this differential equation with $x > 0$, we must have $r^3 - 5r^2 + 17r - 13 = 0$. By inspection we find that $r = 1$ is a root to this equation. Therefore, we can factor this equation as follows

$$(r-1)(r^2 - 4r + 13) = 0.$$

We find the remaining roots by using the quadratic formula. Thus, we obtain the roots $r = 1,\ 2 \pm 3i$. From the root $r = 1$, we obtain the solution $y = x$. From the roots $r = 2 \pm 3i$, by applying the hint given in the problem, we see that a solution is given by

$$y(x) = x^{2+3i} = x^2 \{\cos(3\ln x) + i\sin(3\ln x)\}.$$

Therefore, by Lemma 2 on page 172 of the text, we find that two real-valued solutions to this differential equation are $y(x) = x^2\cos(3\ln x)$ and $y(x) = x^2\sin(3\ln x)$. Since these functions and the function $y(x) = x$ are linearly independent, we obtain the fundamental solution set

$$\left\{x, x^2\cos(3\ln x), x^2\sin(3\ln x)\right\}.$$

33. With suggested values of parameters $m_1 = m_2 = 1$, $k_1 = 3$, and $k_2 = 2$, the system (34)–(35) becomes

$$\begin{aligned} x'' + 5x - 2y &= 0, \\ y'' - 2x + 2y &= 0. \end{aligned} \tag{6.7}$$

(a) Expressing $y = (x'' + 5x)/2$ from the first equation and substituting this expression into the second equation, we obtain

$$\begin{aligned} &\frac{1}{2}(x'' + 5x)'' - 2x + (x'' + 5x) = 0 \\ \Rightarrow\quad &\left(x^{(4)} + 5x''\right) - 4x + 2(x'' + 5x) = 0 \\ \Rightarrow\quad &x^{(4)} + 7x'' + 6x = 0, \end{aligned} \tag{6.8}$$

as it is stated in (36).

(b) The characteristic equation corresponding to (6.8) is $r^4 + 7r^2 + 6 = 0$. This equation is of quadratic type. Substitution $s = r^2$ yields

$$s^2 + 7s + 6 = 0 \qquad \Rightarrow \qquad s = -1,\ -6.$$

Thus

$$r = \pm\sqrt{-1} = \pm i \qquad \text{and} \qquad r = \pm\sqrt{-6} = \pm i\sqrt{6},$$

and a general solution to (6.8) is given by

$$x(t) = c_1\cos t + c_2\sin t + c_3\cos\sqrt{6}t + c_4\sin\sqrt{6}t.$$

(c) As we have mentioned in (a), the first equation in (6.7) implies that $y = (x'' + 5x)/2$. Substituting the solution $x(t)$ yields

$$\begin{aligned} y(t) &= \frac{1}{2}\Big[\left(c_1\cos t + c_2\sin t + c_3\cos\sqrt{6}t + c_4\sin\sqrt{6}t\right)'' \\ &\qquad + 5\left(c_1\cos t + c_2\sin t + c_3\cos\sqrt{6}t + c_4\sin\sqrt{6}t\right)\Big] \\ &= \frac{1}{2}\Big[\left(-c_1\cos t - c_2\sin t - 6c_3\cos\sqrt{6}t - 6c_4\sin\sqrt{6}t\right) \\ &\qquad + 5\left(c_1\cos t + c_2\sin t + c_3\cos\sqrt{6}t + c_4\sin\sqrt{6}t\right)\Big] \\ &= 2c_1\cos t + 2c_2\sin t - \frac{c_3}{2}\cos\sqrt{6}t - \frac{c_4}{2}\sin\sqrt{6}t\,. \end{aligned}$$

(d) Initial conditions $x(0) = y(0) = 1$ and $x'(0) = y'(0) = 0$ imply the system of linear equations for c_1, c_2, c_3, and c_4. Namely,

$$\begin{aligned} x(0) &= c_1 + c_3 = 1, \\ y(0) &= 2c_1 - (c_3/2) = 1, \\ x'(0) &= c_2 + c_4\sqrt{6} = 0, \\ y'(0) &= 2c_2 - (c_4\sqrt{6}/2) = 0 \end{aligned} \quad \Rightarrow \quad \begin{aligned} c_1 &= 3/5, \\ c_3 &= 2/5, \\ c_2 &= 0, \\ c_4 &= 0. \end{aligned}$$

Thus, the solution to this initial value problem is

$$x(t) = \frac{3}{5}\cos t + \frac{2}{5}\cos\sqrt{6}t\,, \qquad y(t) = \frac{6}{5}\cos t - \frac{1}{5}\cos\sqrt{6}t\,.$$

35. Solving the characteristic equation yields

$$\begin{aligned} &EIr^4 - k = 0 \quad \Rightarrow \quad r^4 = \frac{k}{EI} \\ \Rightarrow \quad & r^2 = \sqrt{\frac{k}{EI}} \quad \text{or} \quad r^2 = -\sqrt{\frac{k}{EI}} \\ \Rightarrow \quad & r = \pm\sqrt[4]{\frac{k}{EI}} \quad \text{or} \quad r = \pm\sqrt[4]{-\frac{k}{EI}} = \pm i\sqrt[4]{\frac{k}{EI}}\,. \end{aligned}$$

The first two roots are real numbers, the other two are pure imaginary numbers. Therefore, a general solution to the vibrating beam equation is

$$y(x) = C_1 e^{\sqrt{k/(EI)}x} + C_2 e^{-\sqrt{k/(EI)}x} + C_3\sin\left(\sqrt[4]{\frac{k}{EI}}\,x\right) + C_4\cos\left(\sqrt[4]{\frac{k}{EI}}\,x\right).$$

Using the identities

$$e^{ax} = \cosh ax + \sinh ax, \qquad e^{-ax} = \cosh ax - \sinh ax,$$

we can express the solution in terms of hyperbolic and trigonometric functions as follows.

$$\begin{aligned}
y(x) &= C_1 e^{\sqrt{k/(EI)}x} + C_2 e^{-\sqrt{k/(EI)}x} + C_3 \sin\left(\sqrt[4]{\frac{k}{EI}}\,x\right) + C_4 \cos\left(\sqrt[4]{\frac{k}{EI}}\,x\right) \\
&= C_1\left[\cosh\left(\sqrt[4]{\frac{k}{EI}}\,x\right) + \sinh\left(\sqrt[4]{\frac{k}{EI}}\,x\right)\right] + C_2\left[\cosh\left(\sqrt[4]{\frac{k}{EI}}\,x\right) - \sinh\left(\sqrt[4]{\frac{k}{EI}}\,x\right)\right] \\
&\qquad + C_3 \sin\left(\sqrt[4]{\frac{k}{EI}}\,x\right) + C_4 \cos\left(\sqrt[4]{\frac{k}{EI}}\,x\right) \\
&= c_1 \cosh\left(\sqrt[4]{\frac{k}{EI}}\,x\right) + c_2 \sinh\left(\sqrt[4]{\frac{k}{EI}}\,x\right) + c_3 \sin\left(\sqrt[4]{\frac{k}{EI}}\,x\right) + c_4 \cos\left(\sqrt[4]{\frac{k}{EI}}\,x\right),
\end{aligned}$$

where $c_1 := C_1 + C_2$, $c_2 := C_1 - C_2$, $c_3 := C_3$, and $c_4 := C_4$ are arbitrary constants.

EXERCISES 6.3: Undetermined Coefficients and the Annihilator Method, page 337

1. The corresponding homogeneous equation for this problem is $y''' - 2y'' - 5y' + 6y = 0$ which has the associated auxiliary equation given by $r^3 - 2r^2 - 5r + 6 = 0$. By inspection we see that $r = 1$ is a root to this equation. Therefore, this equation can be factored as follows

$$r^3 - 2r^2 - 5r + 6 = (r-1)(r^2 - r - 6) = (r-1)(r-3)(r+2) = 0.$$

Thus, the roots to the auxiliary equation are given by $r = 1$, 3, and -2, and a general solution to the homogeneous equation is

$$y_h(x) = c_1 e^x + c_2 e^{3x} + c_3 e^{-2x}.$$

The nonhomogeneous term, $g(x) = e^x + x^2$, is the sum of an exponential term and a polynomial term. Therefore, according to Section 4.5, this equation has a particular solution of the form

$$y_p(x) = x^{s_1} C_1 e^x + x^{s_2}\left(C_2 + C_3 x + C_4 x^2\right).$$

Since e^x is a solution to the associated homogeneous equation and xe^x is not, we set $s_1 = 1$. Since none of the terms x^2, x, or 1 is a solution to the associated homogeneous equation, we set $s_2 = 0$. Thus, the form of a particular solution is

$$y_p(x) = C_1 x e^x + C_2 + C_3 x + C_4 x^2 .$$

3. The associated homogeneous equation for this equation is $y''' + 3y'' - 4y = 0$. This equation has the corresponding auxiliary equation $y^3 + 3r^2 - 4 = 0$, which, by inspection, has $r = 1$ as one of its roots. Thus, the auxiliary equation can be factored as follows

$$(r-1)(r^2 + 4r + 4) = (r-1)(r+2)^2 = 0.$$

From this we see that the roots to the auxiliary equation are $r = 1, -2, -2$. Therefore, a general solution to the homogeneous equation is

$$y_h(x) = c_1 e^x + c_2 e^{-2x} + c_3 x e^{-2x} .$$

The nonhomogeneous term is $g(x) = e^{-2x}$. Therefore, a particular solution to the original differential equation has the form $y_p(x) = x^s c_1 e^{-2x}$. Since both e^{-2x} and xe^{-2x} are solutions to the associated homogeneous equation, we set $s = 2$. (Note that this means that $r = -2$ will be a root of multiplicity three of the auxiliary equation associated with the operator equation $A[L[y]](x) = 0$, where A is an annihilator of the nonhomogeneous term $g(x) = e^{-2x}$ and L is the linear operator $L := D^3 + 3D^2 - 4$.) Thus, the form of a particular solution to this equation is

$$y_p(x) = C_1 x^2 e^{-2x} .$$

5. In the solution to Problem 1, we determined that a general solution to the homogeneous differential equation associated with this problem is

$$y_h(x) = c_1 e^x + c_2 e^{3x} + c_3 e^{-2x},$$

and that a particular solution has the form

$$y_p(x) = C_1 x e^x + C_2 + C_3 x + C_4 x^2 .$$

By differentiating $y_p(x)$, we find

$$y_p'(x) = C_1xe^x + C_1e^x + C_3 + 2C_4x$$
$$\Rightarrow \qquad y_p''(x) = C_1xe^x + 2C_1e^x + 2C_4$$
$$\Rightarrow \qquad y_p'''(x) = C_1xe^x + 3C_1e^x.$$

Substituting these expressions into the original differential equation, we obtain

$$y_p'''(x) - 2y_p''(x) - 5y_p'(x) + 6y_p(x) = C_1xe^x + 3C_1e^x - 2C_1xe^x - 4C_1e^x - 4C_4$$
$$-5C_1xe^x - 5C_1e^x - 5C_3 - 10C_4x + 6C_1xe^x + 6C_2 + 6C_3x + 6C_4x^2 = e^x + x^2$$
$$\Rightarrow \qquad -6C_1e^x + (-4C_4 - 5C_3 + 6C_2) + (-10C_4 + 6C_3)x + 6C_4x^2 = e^x + x^2\,.$$

Equating coefficients yields

$$-6C_1 = 1 \qquad \Rightarrow \quad C_1 = \frac{-1}{6}\,,$$

$$6C_4 = 1 \qquad \Rightarrow \quad C_4 = \frac{1}{6}\,,$$

$$-10C_4 + 6C_3 = 0 \qquad \Rightarrow \quad C_3 = \frac{10C_4}{6} = \frac{10}{36} = \frac{5}{18}\,,$$

$$-4C_4 - 5C_3 + 6C_2 = 0 \qquad \Rightarrow \quad C_2 = \frac{4C_4 + 5C_3}{6} = \frac{4(1/6) + 5(5/18)}{6} = \frac{37}{108}\,.$$

Thus, a general solution to the nonhomogeneous equation is given by

$$y(x) = y_h(x) + y_p(x) = c_1e^x + c_2e^{3x} + c_3e^{-2x} - \frac{1}{6}\,xe^x + \frac{1}{6}\,x^2 + \frac{5}{18}\,x + \frac{37}{108}\,.$$

7. In Problem 3, a general solution to the associated homogeneous equation was found to be

$$y_h(x) = c_1e^x + c_2e^{-2x} + c_3xe^{-2x},$$

and the form of a particular solution to the nonhomogeneous equation was

$$y_p(x) = C_1x^2e^{-2x}.$$

Differentiating $y_p(x)$ yields

$$y_p'(x) = 2C_1xe^{-2x} - 2C_1x^2e^{-2x} = 2C_1(x - x^2)e^{-2x}$$
$$\Rightarrow \quad y_p''(x) = -4C_1(x - x^2)e^{-2x} + 2C_1(1 - 2x)e^{-2x} = 2C_1(2x^2 - 4x + 1)e^{-2x}$$
$$\Rightarrow \quad y_p'''(x) = -4C_1(2x^2 - 4x + 1)e^{-2x} + 2C_1(4x - 4)e^{-2x} = 4C_1(-2x^2 + 6x - 3)e^{-2x}.$$

By substituting these expressions into the nonhomogeneous equation, we obtain

$$y_p'''(x) + 3y_p''(x) - 4y_p(x) = 4C_1(-2x^2 + 6x - 3)e^{-2x}$$
$$+6C_1(2x^2 - 4x + 1)e^{-2x} - 4C_1x^2e^{-2x} = e^{-2x}$$
$$\Rightarrow \quad -6C_1e^{-2x} = e^{-2x}.$$

By equating coefficients, we see that $C_1 = -1/6$. Thus, a general solution to the nonhomogeneous differential equation is given by

$$y(x) = y_h(x) + y_p(x) = c_1e^x + c_2e^{-2x} + c_3xe^{-2x} - \frac{1}{6}x^2e^{-2x}.$$

9. Solving the auxiliary equation, $r^3 - 3r^2 + 3r - 1 = (r - 1)^3 = 0$, we find that $r = 1$ is its root of multiplicity three. Therefore, a general solution to the associated homogeneous equation is given by

$$y_h(x) = c_1e^x + c_2xe^x + c_3x^2e^x.$$

The nonhomogeneous term, e^x, suggests a particular solution of the form $y_p(x) = Ax^se^x$, where we have to choose $s = 3$ since the root $r = 1$ of the auxiliary equation is of multiplicity three. Thus

$$y_p(x) = Ax^3e^x.$$

Differentiating $y_p(x)$ yields

$$y_p'(x) = A\left(x^3 + 3x^2\right)e^x,$$
$$y_p''(x) = A\left(x^3 + 6x^2 + 6x\right)e^x,$$
$$y_p'''(x) = A\left(x^3 + 9x^2 + 18x + 6\right)e^x.$$

By substituting these expressions into the original equation, we obtain

$$y_p''' - 3y_p'' + 3y_p' - y = e^x$$
$$\Rightarrow \quad \left[A\left(x^3+9x^2+18x+6\right)e^x\right] - 3\left[A\left(x^3+6x^2+6x\right)e^x\right]$$
$$+3\left[A\left(x^3+3x^2\right)e^x\right] - Ax^3e^x = e^x$$
$$\Rightarrow \quad 6Ae^x = e^x \quad \Rightarrow \quad A = \frac{1}{6},$$

and so $y_p(x) = x^3e^x/6$. A general solution to the given equation then has the form

$$y(x) = y_h(x) + y_p(x) = c_1e^x + c_2xe^x + c_3x^2e^x + \frac{1}{6}x^3e^x .$$

11. The operator D^5, that is, the fifth derivative operator, annihilates any polynomial of degree at most four. In particular, D^5 annihilates the polynomial $x^4 - x^2 + 11$.

13. According to (i) on page 334 of the text, the operator $[D-(-7)] = (D+7)$ annihilates the exponential function e^{-7x}.

15. The operator $(D-2)$ annihilates the function $f_1(x) := e^{2x}$ and the operator $(D-1)$ annihilates the function $f_2(x) := e^x$. Thus, the composition of these operators, namely, $(D-2)(D-1)$, annihilates both of these functions and so, by linearity, it annihilates their algebraic sum.

17. This function has the same form as the functions given in (iv) on page 334 of the text. Here we see that $\alpha = -1$, $\beta = 2$, and $m - 1 = 2$. Thus, the operator

$$\left[(D-\{-1\})^2 + 2^2\right]^3 = \left[(D+1)^2 + 4\right]^3$$

annihilates this function.

19. Given function as a sum of two functions. The first term, xe^{-2x}, is of the type (ii) on the page 334 of the text with $m = 2$ and $r = -2$; so $[D-(-2)]^2 = (D+2)^2$ annihilates this function. The second term, $xe^{-5x}\sin 3x$, is annihilated by

$$\left[(D-(-5))^2 + 3^2\right]^2 = \left[(D+5)^2 + 9\right]^2$$

according to (iv). Therefore, the composition $\left[(D+2)^2(D+5)^2 + 9\right]^2$ annihilates the function $xe^{-2x} + xe^{-5x}\sin 3x$.

21. In operator form, the given equation can be written as

$$\left(D^2 - 5D + 6\right)[u] = \cos 2x + 1.$$

The function $g(x) = \cos 2x + 1$ is a sum of two functions: $\cos 2x$ is of the type (iii) on page 334 of the text with $\beta = 2$, and so it is innihilated by $(D^2 + 4)$; 1, as a constant, is annihilated by D. Therefore, the operator $D(D^2 + 4)$ innihilates the right-hand side, $g(x)$. Applying this operator to both sides of the differential equation given in this problem yields

$$D\left(D^2 + 4\right)\left(D^2 - 5D + 6\right)[u] = D\left(D^2 + 4\right)[\cos 2x + 1] = 0$$
$$\Rightarrow \qquad D\left(D^2 + 4\right)(D - 3)(D - 2)[u] = 0.$$

This last equation has the associated auxiliary equation $r\left(r^2 + 4\right)(r - 3)(r - 2) = 0$, which has roots $r = 2,\ 3,\ 0,\ \pm 2i$. Thus, a general solution to the differential equation associated with this auxiliary equation is

$$u(x) = c_1 e^{2x} + c_2 e^{3x} + c_3 \cos 2x + c_4 \sin 2x + c_5\,.$$

The homogeneous equation, $u'' - 5u' + 6u = 0$, associated with the original problem, has as its corresponding auxiliary equation $r^2 - 5r + 6 = (r - 2)(r - 3) = 0$. Therefore, the solution to the homogeneous equation associated with the original problem is $u_h(x) = c_1 e^{2x} + c_2 e^{3x}$. Since a general solution to this original problem is given by

$$u(x) = u_h(x) + u_p(x) = c_1 e^{2x} + c_2 e^{3x} + u_p(x)$$

and since $u(x)$ must be of the form

$$u(x) = c_1 e^{2x} + c_2 e^{3x} + c_3 \cos 2x + c_4 \sin 2x + c_5\,,$$

we see that

$$u_p(x) = c_3 \cos 2x + c_4 \sin 2x + c_5\,.$$

23. The function $g(x) = e^{3x} - x^2$ is annihilated by the operator $A := D^3(D - 3)$. Applying the operator A to both sides of the differential equation given in this problem yields

$$A\left[y'' - 5y' + 6y\right] = A\left[e^{3x} - x^2\right] = 0$$

$$\Rightarrow \qquad D^3(D-3)(D^2-5D+6)[y] = D^3(D-3)^2(D-2)[y] = 0.$$

This last equation has the associated auxiliary equation

$$r^3(r-3)^2(r-2) = 0,$$

which has roots $r = 0,\ 0,\ 0,\ 3,\ 3,\ 2$. Thus, a general solution to the differential equation associated with this auxiliary equation is

$$y(x) = c_1e^{2x} + c_2e^{3x} + c_3xe^{3x} + c_4x^2 + c_5x + c_6\,.$$

The homogeneous equation, $y'' - 5y' + 6y = 0$, associated with the original problem, is the same as in Problem 21 (with u replaced by y). Therefore, the solution to the homogeneous equation associated with the original problem is $y_h(x) = c_1e^{2x} + c_2e^{3x}$. Since a general solution to this original problem is given by

$$y(x) = y_h(x) + y_p(x) = c_1e^{2x} + c_2e^{3x} + y_p(x)$$

and since $y(x)$ must be of the form

$$y(x) = c_1e^{2x} + c_2e^{3x} + c_3xe^{3x} + c_4x^2 + c_5x + c_6\,,$$

we see that

$$y_p(x) = c_3xe^{3x} + c_4x^2 + c_5x + c_6\,.$$

25. First, we rewrite the equation in operator form, that is,

$$\left(D^2 - 6D + 9\right)[y] = \sin 2x + x \qquad \Rightarrow \qquad (D-3)^2[y] = \sin 2x + x\,.$$

In this problem, the right-hand side is a sum of two functions. The first function, $\sin 2x$, is annihilated by (D^2+4), and the operator D^2 annihilates the term x. Thus $A := D^2(D^2+4)$ annihilates the function $\sin 2x + x$. Applying this operator to the original equation (in operator form) yields

$$D^2(D^2+4)(D-3)^2[y] = D^2(D^2+4)[\sin 2x + x] = 0. \tag{6.9}$$

This homogeneous equation has associated characteristic equation

$$r^2(r^2+4)(r-3)^2=0$$

with roots $\pm 2i$, and double roots $r=0$ and $r=3$. Therefore, a general solution to (6.9) is given by

$$y(x)=c_1e^{3x}+c_2xe^{3x}+c_3+c_4x+c_5\cos 2x+c_6\sin 2x\,. \tag{6.10}$$

Since the homogeneous equation, $(D-3)^2[y]=0$, which corresponds to the original equation, has a general solution $y_h(x)=c_1e^{3x}+c_2xe^{3x}$, the "tail" in (6.10) gives the form of a particular solution to the given equation.

27. Since

$$y''+2y'+2y=\left(D^2+2D+2\right)[y]=\left\{(D+1)^2+1\right\}[y],$$

the auxiliary equation in this problm is $(r+1)^2+1=0$, whose roots are $r=-1\pm i$. Therefore, a general solution to the homogeneous equation, corresponding to the original equation, is

$$y_h(x)=\left(c_1\cos x+c_2\sin x\right)e^{-x}\,.$$

Applying the operator $D^3\{(D+1)^2+1\}$ to the given equation, which annihilates its right-hand side, yields

$$D^3\left\{(D+1)^2+1\right\}\left\{(D+1)^2+1\right\}[y]=D^3\left\{(D+1)^2+1\right\}\left[e^{-x}\cos x+x^2\right]=0$$

$$\Rightarrow\qquad D^3\left[(D+1)^2+1\right]^2[y]=0. \tag{6.11}$$

The corresponding auxiliary equation, $r^3[(r+1)^2+1]^2=0$ has a root $r=0$ of multiplicity three and double roots $r=-1\pm i$. Therefore, a general solution to (6.11) is given by

$$y(x)=\left(c_1\cos x+c_2\sin x\right)e^{-x}+\left(c_3\cos x+c_4\sin x\right)xe^{-x}+c_5x^2+c_6x+c_7\,.$$

Since $y(x)=y_h(x)+y_p(x)$, we conclude that

$$y_p(x)=\left(c_3\cos x+c_4\sin x\right)xe^{-x}+c_5x^2+c_6x+c_7\,.$$

29. In operator form, the equation becomes

$$\left(D^3 - 2D^2 + D\right)[z] = D(D-1)^2[z] = x - e^x\,. \tag{6.12}$$

Solving the corresponding auxiliary equation, $r(r-1)^2 = 0$, we find that $r = 0$, 1, and 1. Thus

$$z_h(x) = C_1 + C_2 e^x + C_3 x e^x$$

is a general solution to the homogeneous equation associated with the original equation. To annihilate the right-hand side in (6.12), we apply the operator $D^2(D-1)$ to this equation. Thus we obtain

$$D^2(D-1)D(D-1)^2[z] = D^2(D-1)\left[x - e^x\right] \qquad \Rightarrow \qquad D^3(D-1)^3 = 0.$$

Solving the corresponding auxiliary equation, $r^3(r-1)^3 = 0$, we see that $r = 0$ and $r = 1$ are its roots of multiplicity three. Hence, a general solution is given by

$$z(x) = c_1 + c_2 x + c_3 x^2 + c_4 e^x + c_5 x e^x + c_6 x^2 e^x\,.$$

This general solution, when compared with $z_h(x)$, gives

$$z_p(x) = c_2 x + c_3 x^2 + c_6 x^2 e^x\,.$$

31. Writing this equation in operator form yields

$$\left(D^3 + 2D^2 - 9D - 18\right)[y] = -18x^2 - 18x + 22\,. \tag{6.13}$$

Since,

$$D^3 + 2D^2 - 9D - 18 = D^2(D+2) - 9(D+2) = (D+2)\left(D^2 - 9\right) = (D+2)(D-3)(D+3),$$

(6.13) becomes

$$(D+2)(D-3)(D+3)[y] = -18x^2 - 18x + 22\,.$$

The auxiliary equation in this problem is $(r+2)(r-3)(r+3) = 0$ with roots $r = -2$, 3, and -3. Hence, a general solution to the corresponding homogeneous equation has the form

$$y_h(x) = c_1 e^{-2x} + c_2 e^{3x} + c_3 e^{-3x}\,.$$

Since the operator D^3 annihilates the nonhomogeneous term in the original equation and $r = 0$ is not a root of the auxiliary equation, we seek for a particular solution of the form

$$y_p(x) = C_0x^2 + C_1x + C_2 .$$

Substituting y_p into the given equation (for convenience, in operator form) yileds

$$\begin{aligned}
&\left(D^3 + 2D^2 - 9D - 18\right)\left[C_0x^2 + C_1x + C_2\right] = -18x^2 - 18x + 22 \\
\Rightarrow\quad & 0 + 2\,(2C_0) - 9\,[2C_0x + C_1] - 18\left[C_0x^2 + C_1x + C_2\right] = -18x^2 - 18x + 22 \\
\Rightarrow\quad & -18C_0x^2 + (-18C_1 - 18C_0)x + (-18C_2 - 9C_1 + 4C_0) = -18x^2 - 18x + 22.
\end{aligned}$$

Equating coefficients, we obtain the system

$$\begin{aligned}
-18C_0 &= -18, & & & C_0 &= 1, \\
-18C_1 - 18C_0 &= -18, & &\Rightarrow & C_1 &= 0, \\
-18C_2 - 9C_1 + 4C_0 &= 22 & & & C_2 &= -1.
\end{aligned}$$

Thus, $y_p(x) = x^2 - 1$ and

$$y(x) = y_h(x) + y_p(x) = c_1e^{-2x} + c_2e^{3x} + c_3e^{-3x} + x^2 - 1$$

is a general solution to the original nonhomogeneous equation. Next, we satisfy the initial conditions. Differentiation yields

$$\begin{aligned}
y'(x) &= -2c_1e^{-2x} + 3c_2e^{3x} - 3c_3e^{-3x} + 2x, \\
y''(x) &= 4c_1e^{-2x} + 9c_2e^{3x} + 9c_3e^{-3x} + 2.
\end{aligned}$$

Therefore,

$$\begin{aligned}
-2 = y(0) &= c_1 + c_2 + c_3 - 1, & & & c_1 + c_2 + c_3 &= -1, \\
-8 = y'(0) &= -2c_1 + 3c_2 - 3c_3, & &\Rightarrow & -2c_1 + 3c_2 - 3c_3 &= -8, \\
-12 = y''(0) &= 4c_1 + 9c_2 + 9c_3 + 2 & & & 4c_1 + 9c_2 + 9c_3 &= -14.
\end{aligned}$$

Solving this system, we find that $c_1 = 1$, $c_2 = -2$, and $c_3 = 0$, and so

$$y(x) = e^{-2x} - 2e^{3x} + x^2 - 1$$

gives the solution to the given initial value problem.

33. Let us write given equation in operator form.

$$\left(D^3-2D^2-3D+10\right)[y]=(34x-16)e^{-2x}-10x^2+6x+34\,.$$

By inspection, $r=-2$ is a root of the characteristic equation, $r^3-2r^2-3r+10=0$. Using, say, long division we find that

$$r^3-2r^2-3r+10=(r+2)\left(r^2-4r+5\right)=(r+2)\left[(r-2)^2+1\right]$$

and so the other two roots of the auxiliary equation are $r=2\pm i$. This gives a general solution to the corresponding homogeneous equation

$$y_h(x)=c_1e^{-2x}+\left(c_2\cos x+c_3\sin x\right)e^{2x}\,.$$

According to the nonhomogeneous term, we look for a particular solution to the original equation of the form

$$y_p(x)=x\left(C_0x+C_1\right)e^{-2x}+C_2x^2+C_3x+C_4\,,$$

where the factor x in the exponential term appears due to the fact that $r=-2$ is a root of the characteristic equation. Substituting $y_p(x)$ into the given equation and simplifying yield

$$\begin{aligned}&\left(D^3-2D^2-3D+10\right)[y_p(x)]=(34x-16)e^{-2x}-10x^2+6x+34\\ \Rightarrow\qquad &\left(34C_0x+17C_1-16C_0\right)e^{-2x}+10C_2x^2+(10C_3-6C_2)x\\ &\qquad\qquad +10C_4-3C_3-4C_2=(34x-16)e^{-2x}-10x^2+6x+34.\end{aligned}$$

Equating corresponding coefficients, we obtain the system

$$\begin{aligned}34C_0&=34,\\ 17C_1-16C_0&=-16,\\ 10C_2&=-10,\\ 10C_3-6C_2&=6,\\ 10C_4-3C_3-4C_2&=34\end{aligned}\qquad\Rightarrow\qquad\begin{aligned}C_0&=1,\\ C_1&=0,\\ C_2&=-1,\\ C_3&=0,\\ C_4&=3.\end{aligned}$$

Thus, $y_p(x)=x^2e^{-2x}-x^2+3$ and

$$y(x)=y_h(x)+y_p(x)=c_1e^{-2x}+\left(c_2\cos x+c_3\sin x\right)e^{2x}+x^2e^{-2x}-x^2+3$$

is a general solution to the given nonhomogeneous equation. Next, we find constants c_1, c_2, and c_3 such that the initial conditions are satisfied. Differentiation yields

$$y'(x) = -2c_1e^{-2x} + [(2c_2 + c_3)\cos x + (2c_3 - c_2)\sin x]\, e^{2x} + (2x - 2x^2)e^{-2x} - 2x,$$
$$y''(x) = 4c_1e^{-2x} + [(3c_2 + 4c_3)\cos x + (3c_3 - 4c_2)\sin x]\, e^{2x} + (2 - 8x + 4x^2)e^{-2x} - 2.$$

Therefore,

$$\begin{array}{lcl} 3 = y(0) = c_1 + c_2 + 3, & & c_1 + c_2 = 0, \\ 0 = y'(0) = -2c_1 + 2c_2 + c_3, & \Rightarrow & -2c_1 + 2c_2 + c_3 = 0, \\ 0 = y''(0) = 4c_1 + 3c_2 + 4c_3 & & 4c_1 + 3c_2 + 4c_3 = 0. \end{array}$$

The solution of this homogeneous linear system is $c_1 = c_2 = c_3 = 0$. Hence, the answer is $y(x) = x^2e^{-2x} - x^2 + 3$.

35. If $a_0 = 0$, then equation (4) becomes

$$a_ny^{(n)} + a_{n-1}y^{(n-1)} + \cdots + a_1y' = f(x)$$

or, in operator form,

$$\begin{aligned} &\left(a_nD^n + a_{n-1}D^{n-1} + \cdots + a_1D\right)[y] = f(x) \\ \Rightarrow \qquad & D\left(a_nD^{n-1} + a_{n-1}D^{n-2} + \cdots + a_1\right)[y] = f(x). \end{aligned} \tag{6.14}$$

Since the operator D^{m+1} annihilates any polynomial $f(x) = b_mx^m + \cdots + b_0$, applying D^{m+1} to both sides in (6.14) yields

$$\begin{aligned} &D^{m+1}D\left(a_nD^{n-1} + a_{n-1}D^{n-2} + \cdots + a_1\right)[y] = D^{m+1}[f(x)] = 0 \\ \Rightarrow \qquad & D^{m+2}\left(a_nD^{n-1} + a_{n-1}D^{n-2} + \cdots + a_1\right)[y] = 0. \end{aligned} \tag{6.15}$$

The auxiliary equation, corresponding to this homogeneous equation is,

$$r^{m+2}\left(a_nr^{n-1} + a_{n-1}r^{n-2} + \cdots + a_1\right) = 0. \tag{6.16}$$

Since $a_1 \neq 0$,

$$\left.\left(a_nr^{n-1} + a_{n-1}r^{n-2} + \cdots + a_1\right)\right|_{r=0} = a_1 \neq 0,$$

which means that $r = 0$ is not a root of this polynomial. Thus, for the auxiliary equation (6.16), $r = 0$ is a root of exact multiplicity $m + 2$, and so a general solution to (6.15) is given by

$$y(x) = c_0 + c_1 x + \cdots + c_{m+1} x^{m+1} + Y(x), \tag{6.17}$$

where $Y(x)$, being associated with roots of $a_n r^{n-1} + a_{n-1} r^{n-2} + \cdots + a_1 = 0$, is a general solution to $(a_n D^{n-1} + a_{n-1} D^{n-2} + \cdots + a_1)[y] = 0$. (One can write down $Y(x)$ explicitly but there is no need in doing this.)

On the other hand, the auxiliary equation for the homogeneous equation, associated with (6.14), is $r(a_n r^{n-1} + a_{n-1} r^{n-2} + \cdots + a_1) = 0$, and $r = 0$ is its simple root. Hence, a general solution $y_h(x)$ to the homogeneous equation is given by

$$y_h(x) = c_0 + Y(x), \tag{6.18}$$

where $Y(x)$ is the same as in (6.17). Since $y(x) = y_h(x) + y_p(x)$, it follows from (6.17) and (6.18) that

$$y_p(x) = c_1 x + \cdots + c_{m+1} x^{m+1} = x\left(c_1 + \cdots + c_{m+1} x^m\right),$$

as stated.

37. Writing equation (4) in operator form yields

$$\left(a_n D^n + a_{n-1} D^{n-1} + \cdots + a_0\right)[y] = f(x). \tag{6.19}$$

The characteristic equation, corresponding to the associated homogeneous equation, is

$$a_n r^n + a_{n-1} r^{n-1} + \cdots + a_0 = 0. \tag{6.20}$$

Suppose that $r = \beta i$ is a root of (6.20) of multiplicity $s \geq 0$. ($s = 0$ means that $r = \beta i$ is *not* a root.) Then (6.20) can be factored as

$$a_n r^n + a_{n-1} r^{n-1} + \cdots + a_0 = \left(r^2 + \beta^2\right)^s \left(a_n r^{n-2s} + \cdots + a_0/\beta^{2s}\right) = 0$$

and so a general solution to the homogeneous equation is given by

$$\begin{aligned} y_h(x) = {} & (c_1 \cos\beta x + c_2 \sin\beta x) + x(c_3 \cos\beta x + c_4 \sin\beta x) \\ & + \cdots + x^{s-1}(c_{2s-1}\cos\beta x + c_{2s}\sin\beta x) + Y(x), \end{aligned} \tag{6.21}$$

where $Y(x)$ is the part of $y_h(x)$ corresponding to the roots of $a_n r^{n-2s} + \cdots + a_0/\beta^{2s} = 0$.

Since the operator $(D^2 + \beta^2)$ annihilates $f(x) = a\cos\beta x + b\sin\beta x$, applying this operator to both sides in (6.19), we obtain

$$(D^2 + \beta^2)\left(a_n D^n + a_{n-1}D^{n-1} + \cdots + a_0\right)[y] = (D^2 + \beta^2)[f(x)] = 0.$$

The corresponding auxiliary equation,

$$(r^2 + \beta^2)\left(a_n r^n + a_{n-1}r^{n-1} + \cdots + a_0\right) = 0 \quad \Rightarrow \quad \left(r^2 + \beta^2\right)^{s+1}\left(a_n r^{n-2s} + \cdots + a_0/\beta^{2s}\right) = 0$$

has $r = \beta i$ as its root of multiplicity $s + 1$. Therefore, a general solution to this equation is given by

$$\begin{aligned} y(x) &= (c_1\cos\beta x + c_2\sin\beta x) + x(c_3\cos\beta x + c_4\sin\beta x) \\ &\qquad + \cdots + x^{s-1}(c_{2s-1}\cos\beta x + c_{2s}\sin\beta x) + x^s(c_{2s+1}\cos\beta x + c_{2s+2}\sin\beta x) + Y(x). \end{aligned}$$

Since, $y(x) = y_h(x) + y_p(x)$, comparing $y(x)$ with $y_h(x)$ given in (6.21), we conclude that

$$y_p(x) = x^s(c_{2s+1}\cos\beta x + c_{2s+2}\sin\beta x).$$

All that remains is to note that, for any $m < s$, the functions $x^m\cos\beta x$ and $x^m\sin\beta x$ are presented in (6.21), meaning that they are solutions to the homogeneous equation corresponding to (6.19). Thus s is the smallest number m such that $x^m\cos\beta x$ and $x^m\sin\beta x$ are not solutions to the corresponding homogeneous equation.

39. Writing the system in operator form yields

$$\begin{aligned} (D^2 - 1)[x] + y &= 0, \\ x + (D^2 - 1)[y] &= e^{3t}. \end{aligned}$$

Subtracting the first equation from the second equation multiplied by $(D^2 - 1)$, we get

$$\begin{aligned} &\left\{(D^2 - 1)[x] + \left(D^2 - 1\right)^2[y]\right\} - \left\{(D^2 - 1)[x] + y\right\} = (D^2 - 1)\left[e^{3t}\right] - 0 = 8e^{3t} \\ \Rightarrow \quad &\left\{\left(D^2 - 1\right)^2 - 1\right\}[y] = 8e^{3t} \quad \Rightarrow \quad D^2\left(D^2 - 2\right)[y] = 8e^{3t}. \qquad (6.22) \end{aligned}$$

The auxiliary equation, $r^2(r^2-2)=0$, has roots $r=\pm\sqrt{2}$ and a double root $r=0$. Hence,

$$y_h(t)=c_1+c_2t+c_3e^{\sqrt{2}t}+c_4e^{-\sqrt{2}t}$$

is a general solution to the homogeneous equation coresponding to (6.22). A particular solution to (6.22) has the form $y_p(t)=Ae^{3t}$. Substitution yields

$$D^2\left(D^2-2\right)\left[Ae^{3x}\right]=\left(D^4-2D^2\right)\left[Ae^{3x}\right]=81Ae^{3x}-(2)9Ae^{3x}=63Ae^{3x}=8e^{3x}$$

$$\Rightarrow \qquad y_p(t)=Ae^{3x}=\frac{8e^{3x}}{63},$$

and so

$$y(t)=y_p(t)+y_h(t)=\frac{8e^{3x}}{63}+c_1+c_2t+c_3e^{\sqrt{2}t}+c_4e^{-\sqrt{2}t}$$

is a general solution to (6.22). We find $x(t)$ from the second equation in the original system.

$$\begin{aligned} x(t) &= e^{3t}+y(t)-y''(t) \\ &= e^{3t}+\left(\frac{8e^{3x}}{63}+c_1+c_2t+c_3e^{\sqrt{2}t}+c_4e^{-\sqrt{2}t}\right)-\left(\frac{72e^{3x}}{63}+2c_3e^{\sqrt{2}t}+2c_4e^{-\sqrt{2}t}\right) \\ &= -\frac{e^{3x}}{63}+c_1+c_2t-c_3e^{\sqrt{2}t}-c_4e^{-\sqrt{2}t}. \end{aligned}$$

EXERCISES 6.4: Method of Variation of Parameters, page 341

1. To apply the method of variation of parameters, first we have to find a fundamental solution set for the corresponding homogeneous equation, which is

$$y'''-3y''+4y=0.$$

Factoring the auxiliary polynomial, r^3-3r^2+4, yields

$$r^3-3r^2+4=\left(r^3+r^2\right)-\left(4r^2-4\right)=r^2(r+1)-4(r-1)(r+1)=(r+1)(r-2)^2.$$

Therefore, $r=-1$, 2, and 2 are the roots of the auxiliary equation, and $y_1=e^{-x}$, $y_2=e^{2x}$, and $y_3=xe^{2x}$ form a fundamental solution set. According to the variation of parameters method, we seek for a particular solution of the form

$$y_p(x)=v_1(x)y_1(x)+v_2(x)y_2(x)+v_3(x)y_3(x)=v_1(x)e^{-x}+v_2(x)e^{2x}+v_3(x)xe^{2x}.$$

To find functions v_j's we need four determinants, the Wronskian $W[y_1, y_2, y_3](x)$ and $W_1(x)$, $W_2(x)$, and $W_3(x)$ given in (10) on page 340 of the text. Thus we compute

$$W\left[e^{-x}, e^{2x}, xe^{2x}\right](x) = \begin{vmatrix} e^{-x} & e^{2x} & xe^{2x} \\ -e^{-x} & 2e^{2x} & (1+2x)e^{2x} \\ e^{-x} & 4e^{2x} & (4+4x)e^{2x} \end{vmatrix} = e^{-x}e^{2x}e^{2x} \begin{vmatrix} 1 & 1 & x \\ -1 & 2 & 1+2x \\ 1 & 4 & 4+4x \end{vmatrix} = 9e^{3x},$$

$$W_1(x) = (-1)^{3-1} W\left[e^{2x}, xe^{2x}\right](x) = \begin{vmatrix} e^{2x} & xe^{2x} \\ 2e^{2x} & (1+2x)e^{2x} \end{vmatrix} = e^{4x},$$

$$W_2(x) = (-1)^{3-2} W\left[e^{-x}, xe^{2x}\right](x) = -\begin{vmatrix} e^{-x} & xe^{2x} \\ -e^{-x} & (1+2x)e^{2x} \end{vmatrix} = -(1+3x)e^{x},$$

$$W_3(x) = (-1)^{3-3} W\left[e^{-x}, e^{2x}\right](x) = \begin{vmatrix} e^{-x} & e^{2x} \\ -e^{-x} & 2e^{2x} \end{vmatrix} = 3e^{x}.$$

Substituting these expressions into the formula (11) for determining v_j's, we obtain

$$v_1(x) = \int \frac{g(x)W_1(x)}{W[e^{-x}, e^{2x}, xe^{2x}]}\,dx = \int \frac{e^{2x}e^{4x}}{9e^{3x}}\,dx = \frac{1}{27}e^{3x},$$

$$v_2(x) = \int \frac{g(x)W_2(x)}{W[e^{-x}, e^{2x}, xe^{2x}]}\,dx = \int \frac{-e^{2x}(1+3x)e^{x}}{9e^{3x}}\,dx = -\frac{1}{9}\int (1+3x)\,dx = -\frac{x}{9} - \frac{x^2}{6},$$

$$v_3(x) = \int \frac{g(x)W_3(x)}{W[e^{-x}, e^{2x}, xe^{2x}]}\,dx = \int \frac{e^{2x}3e^{x}}{9e^{3x}}\,dx = \frac{x}{3},$$

where we have chosen zero integration constants. Then formula (12), page 340 of the text, gives a particular solution

$$y_p(x) = \frac{1}{27}e^{3x}e^{-x} - \left(\frac{x}{9} + \frac{x^2}{6}\right)e^{2x} + \frac{x}{3}xe^{2x} = \frac{1}{27}e^{2x} - \frac{xe^{2x}}{9} + \frac{x^2e^{2x}}{6}.$$

Note that the first two terms in $y_p(x)$ are solutions to the corresponding homogeneous equation. Thus, another (and simpler) answer is $y_p(x) = x^2e^{2x}/6$.

3. Let us find a fundamental solution set for the corresponding homogeneous equation,

$$z''' + 3z'' - 4z = 0.$$

Factoring the auxiliary polynomial, $r^3 + 3r^2 - 4$, yields

$$r^3 + 3r^2 - 4 = \left(r^3 - r^2\right) + \left(4r^2 - 4\right) = r^2(r-1) + 4(r+1)(r-1) = (r-1)(r+2)^2.$$

Therefore, $r = 1$, -2, and -2 are the roots of the auxiliary equation, and so the functions $z_1 = e^x$, $z_2 = e^{-2x}$, and $z_3 = xe^{-2x}$ form a fundamental solution set. A particular solution then has the form

$$z_p(x) = v_1(x)z_1(x) + v_2(x)z_2(x) + v_3(x)z_3(x) = v_1(x)e^x + v_2(x)e^{-2x} + v_3(x)xe^{-2x}. \quad (6.23)$$

To find functions v_j's we need four determinants, the Wronskian $W[z_1, z_2, z_3](x)$ and $W_1(x)$, $W_2(x)$, and $W_3(x)$ given in (10) on page 340 of the text. Thus we compute

$$W\left[e^x, e^{-2x}, xe^{-2x}\right](x) = \begin{vmatrix} e^x & e^{-2x} & xe^{-2x} \\ e^x & -2e^{-2x} & (1-2x)e^{-2x} \\ e^x & 4e^{-2x} & (4x-4)e^{-2x} \end{vmatrix} = e^{-3x} \begin{vmatrix} 1 & 1 & x \\ 1 & -2 & 1-2x \\ 1 & 4 & 4x-4 \end{vmatrix} = 9e^{-3x},$$

$$W_1(x) = (-1)^{3-1} W\left[e^{-2x}, xe^{-2x}\right](x) = \begin{vmatrix} e^{-2x} & xe^{-2x} \\ -2e^{-2x} & (1-2x)e^{-2x} \end{vmatrix} = e^{-4x},$$

$$W_2(x) = (-1)^{3-2} W\left[e^x, xe^{-2x}\right](x) = -\begin{vmatrix} e^x & xe^{-2x} \\ e^x & (1-2x)e^{-2x} \end{vmatrix} = (3x-1)e^{-x},$$

$$W_3(x) = (-1)^{3-3} W\left[e^x, e^{-2x}\right](x) = \begin{vmatrix} e^x & e^{-2x} \\ e^x & -2e^{-2x} \end{vmatrix} = -3e^{-x}.$$

Substituting these expressions into the formula (11) on page 340 of the text, we obtain

$$v_1(x) = \int \frac{g(x)W_1(x)}{W[e^x, e^{-2x}, xe^{-2x}]}\, dx = \int \frac{e^{2x}e^{-4x}}{9e^{-3x}}\, dx = \frac{1}{9}\, e^x,$$

$$v_2(x) = \int \frac{g(x)W_2(x)}{W[e^x, e^{-2x}, xe^{-2x}]}\, dx = \int \frac{e^{2x}(3x-1)e^{-x}}{9e^{-3x}}\, dx$$

$$= \frac{1}{9} \int (3x-1)e^{4x}\, dx = \left(\frac{x}{12} - \frac{7}{144}\right) e^{4x},$$

$$v_3(x) = \int \frac{g(x)W_3(x)}{W[e^x, e^{-2x}, xe^{-2x}]}\, dx = \int \frac{e^{2x}(-3e^{-x})}{9e^{-3x}}\, dx = -\frac{1}{12}\, e^{4x}.$$

Substituting these expressions into (6.23) yields

$$z_p(x) = \frac{1}{9}\, e^x e^x + \left(\frac{x}{12} - \frac{7}{144}\right) e^{4x} e^{-2x} - \frac{1}{12}\, e^{4x} xe^{-2x} = \frac{1}{16}\, e^{2x}.$$

5. Since the nonhomogeneous term, $g(x) = \tan x$, is not a solution to a homogeneous linear differential equation with constant coefficients, we will find a particular solution by the method of variation of parameters. To do this, we must first find a fundamental solution set for the corresponding homogeneous equation, $y''' + y' = 0$. Its auxiliary equation is $r^3 + r = 0$, which factors as $r^3 + r = r(r^2 + 1)$. Thus, the roots to this auxiliary equation are $r = 0, \pm i$. Therefore, a fundamental solution set to the homogeneous equation is $\{1, \cos x, \sin x\}$ and

$$y_p(x) = v_1(x) + v_2(x)\cos x + v_3(x)\sin x.$$

To accomplish this, we must find the four determinants $W[1, \cos x, \sin x](x)$, $W_1(x)$, $W_2(x)$, $W_3(x)$. That is, we calculate

$$W[1, \cos x, \sin x](x) = \begin{vmatrix} 1 & \cos x & \sin x \\ 0 & -\sin x & \cos x \\ 0 & -\cos x & -\sin x \end{vmatrix} = \sin^2 x + \cos^2 x = 1,$$

$$W_1(x) = (-1)^{3-1} W[\cos x, \sin x](x) = \begin{vmatrix} \cos x & \sin x \\ -\sin x & \cos x \end{vmatrix} = \left(\cos^2 x + \sin^2 x\right) = 1,$$

$$W_2(x) = (-1)^{3-2} W[1, \sin x](x) = -\begin{vmatrix} 1 & \sin x \\ 0 & \cos x \end{vmatrix} = -\cos x,$$

$$W_3(x) = (-1)^{3-3} W[1, \cos x](x) = \begin{vmatrix} 1 & \cos x \\ 0 & -\sin x \end{vmatrix} = -\sin x.$$

By using formula (11) on page 340 of the text, we can now find $v_1(x)$, $v_2(x)$, and $v_3(x)$. Since $g(x) = \tan x$, we have (assuming that all constants of integration are zero)

$$v_1(x) = \int \frac{g(x)W_1(x)}{W[1, \cos x, \sin x](x)}\, dx = \int \tan x\, dx = \ln(\sec x),$$

$$v_2(x) = \int \frac{g(x)W_2(x)}{W[1, \cos x, \sin x](x)}\, dx = \int \tan x(-\cos x)\, dx = -\int \sin x\, dx = \cos x,$$

$$v_3(x) = \int \frac{g(x)W_3(x)}{W[1, \cos x, \sin x](x)}\, dx = \int \tan x(-\sin x)\, dx = -\int \frac{\sin^2 x}{\cos x}\, dx$$
$$= -\int \frac{1 - \cos^2 x}{\cos x}\, dx = \int (\cos x - \sec x)\, dx = \sin x - \ln(\sec x + \tan x).$$

Therefore, we have

$$\begin{aligned} y_p(x) &= v_1(x) + v_2(x)\cos x + v_3(x)\sin x \\ &= \ln(\sec x) + \cos^2 x + \sin^2 x - \sin x \ln(\sec x + \tan x) \\ \Rightarrow \qquad y_p(x) &= \ln(\sec x) - \sin x \ln(\sec x + \tan x) + 1. \end{aligned}$$

Since $y \equiv 1$ is a solution to the homogeneous equation, we may choose

$$y_p(x) = \ln(\sec x) - \sin x \ln(\sec x + \tan x).$$

Note: We left the absolute value signs off $\ln(\sec x)$ and $\ln(\sec x + \tan x)$ because of the stated domain: $0 < x < \pi/2$.

7. First, we divide the differential equation by x^3 to obtain the standard form

$$y''' - 3x^{-1}y'' + 6x^{-2}y' - 6x^{-3}y = x^{-4}, \qquad x > 0,$$

from which we see that $g(x) = x^{-4}$. Given that $\{x, x^2, x^3\}$ is a fundamental solution set for the corresponding homogeneous equation, we are looking for a particular solution of the form

$$y_p(x) = v_1(x)x + v_3(x)x^2 + v_3(x)x^3. \tag{6.24}$$

Evaluating determinants $W[x, x^2, x^3](x)$, $W_1(x)$, $W_2(x)$, and $W_3(x)$ yileds

$$W[x, x^2, x^3](x) = \begin{vmatrix} x & x^2 & x^3 \\ 1 & 2x & 3x^2 \\ 0 & 2 & 6x \end{vmatrix} = x\begin{vmatrix} 2x & 3x^2 \\ 2 & 6x \end{vmatrix} - \begin{vmatrix} x^2 & x^3 \\ 2 & 6x \end{vmatrix} = 2x^3,$$

$$W_1(x) = (-1)^{3-1}W[x^2, x^3](x) = \begin{vmatrix} x^2 & x^3 \\ 2x & 3x^2 \end{vmatrix} = x^4,$$

$$W_2(x) = (-1)^{3-2}W[x, x^3](x) = -\begin{vmatrix} x & x^3 \\ 1 & 3x^2 \end{vmatrix} = -2x^3,$$

$$W_3(x) = (-1)^{3-3}W[x, x^2](x) = \begin{vmatrix} x & x^2 \\ 1 & 2x \end{vmatrix} = x^2.$$

So,

$$v_1(x) = \int \frac{g(x)W_1(x)}{W[x, x^2, x^3](x)}\,dx = \int \frac{x^{-4}x^4}{2x^3}\,dx = -\frac{1}{4x^2} + c_1\,,$$
$$v_2(x) = \int \frac{g(x)W_2(x)}{W[x, x^2, x^3](x)}\,dx = \int \frac{x^{-4}(-2x^3)}{2x^3}\,dx = \frac{1}{3x^3} + c_2\,,$$
$$v_3(x) = \int \frac{g(x)W_3(x)}{W[x, x^2, x^3](x)}\,dx = \int \frac{x^{-4}(x^2)}{2x^3}\,dx = -\frac{1}{8x^4} + c_3\,,$$

where c_1, c_2, and c_3 are constants of integration. Substitution back into (6.24) yields

$$y_p(x) = \left(-\frac{1}{4x^2} + c_1\right)x + \left(\frac{1}{3x^3} + c_2\right)x^2 + \left(-\frac{1}{8x^4} + c_3\right)x^3 = -\frac{1}{24x} + c_1x + c_2x^2 + c_3x^3\,.$$

Since $\{x, x^2, x^3\}$ is a fundamental solution set for the homogeneous equation, taking c_1, c_2, and c_3 to be arbitrary constants, we obtain a general solution to the original nonhomogeneous equation. That is,

$$y(x) = -\frac{1}{24x} + c_1x + c_2x^2 + c_3x^3\,.$$

9. To find a particular solution to the nonhomogeneous equation, we will use the method of variation of parameters. We must first calculate the four determinants $W[e^x, e^{-x}, e^{2x}](x)$, $W_1(x)$, $W_2(x)$, $W_3(x)$. Thus, we have

$$W[e^x, e^{-x}, e^{2x}](x) = \begin{vmatrix} e^x & e^{-x} & e^{2x} \\ e^x & -e^{-x} & 2e^{2x} \\ e^x & e^{-x} & 4e^{2x} \end{vmatrix} = -4e^{2x} + 2e^{2x} + e^{2x} + e^{2x} - 2e^{2x} - 4e^{2x} = -6e^{2x},$$

$$W_1(x) = \begin{vmatrix} 0 & e^{-x} & e^{2x} \\ 0 & -e^{-x} & 2e^{2x} \\ 1 & e^{-x} & 4e^{2x} \end{vmatrix} = (-1)^{3-1}\begin{vmatrix} e^{-x} & e^{2x} \\ -e^{-x} & 2e^{2x} \end{vmatrix} = 2e^x + e^x = 3e^x,$$

$$W_2(x) = \begin{vmatrix} e^x & 0 & e^{2x} \\ e^x & 0 & 2e^{2x} \\ e^x & 1 & 4e^{2x} \end{vmatrix} = (-1)^{3-2}\begin{vmatrix} e^x & e^{2x} \\ e^x & 2e^{2x} \end{vmatrix} = -\left(2e^{3x} - e^{3x}\right) = -e^{3x},$$

$$W_3(x) = \begin{vmatrix} e^x & e^{-x} & 0 \\ e^x & -e^{-x} & 0 \\ e^x & e^{-x} & 1 \end{vmatrix} = (-1)^{3-3}\begin{vmatrix} e^x & e^{-x} \\ e^x & -e^{-x} \end{vmatrix} = -1 - 1 = -2.$$

Therefore, according to formula (12) on page 340 of the text, a particular solution, $y_p(x)$, will be given by

$$y_p(x) = e^x \int \frac{3e^x g(x)}{-6e^{2x}}\,dx + e^{-x} \int \frac{-e^{3x} g(x)}{-6e^{2x}}\,dx + e^{2x} \int \frac{-2g(x)}{-6e^{2x}}\,dx$$

$$\Rightarrow \qquad y_p(x) = -\frac{1}{2}\,e^x \int e^{-x} g(x)\,dx + \frac{1}{6}\,e^{-x} \int e^x g(x)\,dx + \frac{1}{3}\,e^{2x} \int e^{-2x} g(x)\,dx.$$

11. First, we find a fundamental solution set to the corresponding homogeneous equation,

$$x^3 y''' - 3xy' + 3y = 0. \tag{6.25}$$

Here we involve the procedure of solving Cauchy-Euler equations discussed in Problem 38, Section 4.3. Thus, let $x = e^t$. Then $dx/dt = e^t = x$ and so the chain rule yields

$$\begin{aligned}
\frac{dy}{dt} &= \frac{dy}{dx}\frac{dx}{dt} = x\frac{dy}{dx}\,,\\
\frac{d^2y}{dt^2} &= \frac{d}{dt}\left(\frac{dy}{dt}\right) = \frac{d}{dx}\left(x\frac{dy}{dx}\right)\frac{dx}{dt} = \left[\frac{dy}{dx} + x\frac{d^2y}{dx^2}\right]x == x\frac{dy}{dx} + x^2\frac{d^2y}{dx^2} = \frac{dy}{dt} + x^2\frac{d^2y}{dx^2}\,,\\
\Rightarrow \qquad x^2\frac{d^2y}{dx^2} &= \frac{d^2y}{dt^2} - \frac{dy}{dt}\,,\\
\frac{d^3y}{dt^3} &= \frac{d}{dt}\left(\frac{d^2y}{dt^2}\right) = \frac{d}{dx}\left(x\frac{dy}{dx} + x^2\frac{d^2y}{dx^2}\right)\frac{dx}{dt} = \left[\frac{dy}{dx} + 3x\frac{d^2y}{dx^2} + x^2\frac{d^3y}{dx^3}\right]x\\
&= x\frac{dy}{dx} + 3x^2\frac{d^2y}{dx^2} + x^3\frac{d^3y}{dx^3} = \frac{dy}{dt} + 3\left(\frac{d^2y}{dt^2} - \frac{dy}{dt}\right) + x^3\frac{d^3y}{dx^3} = 3\frac{d^2y}{dt^2} - 2\frac{dy}{dt} + x^3\frac{d^3y}{dx^3}\\
\Rightarrow \qquad x^3\frac{d^3y}{dx^3} &= \frac{d^3y}{dt^3} - 3\frac{d^2y}{dt^2} + 2\frac{dy}{dt}\,.
\end{aligned}$$

Substituting these expressions into (6.25), we obtain

$$\left[\frac{d^3y}{dt^3} - 3\frac{d^2y}{dt^2} + 2\frac{dy}{dt}\right] - 3\left[\frac{dy}{dt}\right] + 3y = 0 \qquad \Rightarrow \qquad \frac{d^3y}{dt^3} - 3\frac{d^2y}{dt^2} - \frac{dy}{dt} + 3y = 0.$$

The auxiliary equation corresponding to this linear homogeneous equation with constant coefficients is

$$r^3 - 3r^2 - r + 3 = 0 \qquad \Rightarrow \qquad r^2(r-3) - (r-3) = 0 \qquad \Rightarrow \qquad (r-3)(r+1)(r-1) = 0,$$

whose roots are $r = 1, -1$, and 3. Therefore, the functions

$$y_1(t) = e^t\,, \qquad y_2(t) = e^{-t}\,, \quad \text{and} \quad y_3(t) = e^{3t}$$

form a fundamental solution set. Substituting back $e^t = x$ we find that

$$\begin{aligned} y_1(x) &= e^t = x\,, \\ y_2(x) &= e^{-t} = \left(e^t\right)^{-1} = x^{-1}\,, \\ y_3(x) &= e^{3t} = \left(e^t\right)^3 = x^3 \end{aligned}$$

form a fundamental solution set for the homogeneous equation (6.25). Next, we apply the variation of parameters to find a particular solution to the original equation. A particular solution has the form

$$y_p(x) = v_1(x)x + v_2(x)x^{-1} + v_3(x)x^3\,. \tag{6.26}$$

To find functions $v_1(x)$, $v_2(x)$, and $v_3(x)$ we use formula (11) on page 340 of the text. We compute

$$W[x, x^{-1}, x^3](x) = \begin{vmatrix} x & x^{-1} & x^3 \\ 1 & -x^{-2} & 3x^2 \\ 0 & 2x^{-3} & 6x \end{vmatrix} = x \begin{vmatrix} -x^{-2} & 3x^2 \\ 2x^{-3} & 6x \end{vmatrix} - \begin{vmatrix} x^{-1} & x^3 \\ 2x^{-3} & 6x \end{vmatrix} = -16\,,$$

$$W_1(x) = (-1)^{3-1} W[x^{-1}, x^3](x) = \begin{vmatrix} x^{-1} & x^3 \\ -x^{-2} & 3x^2 \end{vmatrix} = 4x\,,$$

$$W_2(x) = (-1)^{3-2} W[x, x^3](x) = -\begin{vmatrix} x & x^3 \\ 1 & 3x^2 \end{vmatrix} = -2x^3,$$

$$W_3(x) = (-1)^{3-3} W[x, x^{-1}](x) = \begin{vmatrix} x & x^{-1} \\ 1 & -x^{-2} \end{vmatrix} = -2x^{-1}.$$

Also, writing the given equation in standard form,

$$y''' - \frac{3}{x^2}\,y' + \frac{3}{x^3}\,y = x\cos x,$$

we see that the nonhomogeneous term is $g(x) = x\cos x$. Thus, by (11),

$$v_1(x) = \int \frac{x\cos x(4x)}{-16}\,dx = -\frac{1}{4}\int x^2\cos x\,dx = -\frac{1}{4}\left(x^2\sin x + 2x\cos x - 2\sin x\right) + c_1\,,$$

$$\begin{aligned}
v_2(x) &= \int \frac{x\cos x(-2x^3)}{-16}\,dx = \frac{1}{8}\int x^4\cos x\,dx \\
&= \frac{1}{8}\left(x^4\sin x + 4x^3\cos x - 12x^2\sin x - 24x\cos x + 24\sin x\right) + c_2\,, \\
v_3(x) &= \int \frac{x\cos x(-2x^{-1})}{-16}\,dx = \frac{1}{8}\int \cos x\,dx = \frac{1}{8}\sin x + c_3\,,
\end{aligned}$$

where c_1, c_2, c_3 are constants of integration, and we have used integration by parts to evaluate $v_1(x)$ and $v_2(x)$. Substituting these functions into (6.26) and simplifying yields

$$\begin{aligned}
y_p(x) &= -\frac{\left(x^2\sin x + 2x\cos x - 2\sin x\right)x}{4} + c_1x \\
&+ \frac{\left(x^4\sin x + 4x^3\cos x - 12x^2\sin x - 24x\cos x + 24\sin x\right)x^{-1}}{8} + c_2x^{-1} + \frac{x^3\sin x}{8} + c_3x^3 \\
&= c_1x + c_2x^{-1} + c_3x^3 - x\sin x - 3\cos x + 3x^{-1}\sin x\,.
\end{aligned}$$

If we allow c_1, c_2, and c_3 in the above formula to be arbitrary constants, we obtain a general solution to the original Cauchy-Euler equation. Thus, the answer is

$$y(x) = c_1x + c_2x^{-1} + c_3x^3 - x\sin x - 3\cos x + 3x^{-1}\sin x\,.$$

13. Since

$$W_k(x) = \begin{vmatrix}
y_1 & \cdots & y_{k-1} & 0 & y_{k+1} & \cdots & y_n \\
y_1' & \cdots & y_{k-1}' & 0 & y_{k+1}' & \cdots & y_n' \\
\vdots & & \vdots & \vdots & \vdots & & \vdots \\
y_1^{(n-2)} & \cdots & y_{k-1}^{(n-2)} & 0 & y_{k+1}^{(n-2)} & \cdots & y_n^{(n-2)} \\
y_1^{(n-1)} & \cdots & y_{k-1}^{(n-1)} & 1 & y_{k+1}^{(n-1)} & \cdots & y_n^{(n-1)}
\end{vmatrix},$$

the kth column of this determinant consists of all zeros except the last entry, which is 1. Therefore, expanding $W_k(x)$ by the cofactors in the kth column, we get

$$\begin{aligned}
W_k(x) &= (0)C_{1,k} + (0)C_{2,k} + \cdots + (0)C_{n-1,n} + (1)C_{n,k} \\
&= (1)(-1)^{n+k}\begin{vmatrix}
y_1 & \cdots & y_{k-1} & y_{k+1} & \cdots & y_n \\
y_1' & \cdots & y_{k-1}' & y_{k+1}' & \cdots & y_n' \\
\vdots & & \vdots & \vdots & & \vdots \\
y_1^{(n-2)} & \cdots & y_{k-1}^{(n-2)} & y_{k+1}^{(n-2)} & \cdots & y_n^{(n-2)}
\end{vmatrix}
\end{aligned}$$

$$= (-1)^{n+k} W\left[y_1, \ldots, y_{k-1}, y_{k+1}, \ldots, y_n\right](x).$$

Finally,

$$(-1)^{n+k} = (-1)^{(n-k)+(2k)} = (-1)^{n-k}.$$

REVIEW PROBLEMS: page 344

1. (a) In notation of Theorem 1, we have $p_1(x) \equiv 0$, $p_2(x) = -\ln x$, $p_3(x) = x$, $p_4(x) \equiv 2$, and $g(x) = \cos 3x$. All these functions, except $p_2(x)$, are continuous on $(-\infty, \infty)$, and $p_2(x)$ is defined and continuous on $(0, \infty)$. Thus, Theorem 1 guarantees the existence of a unique solution on $(0, \infty)$.

(b) By dividing both sides of the given differential equation by x^2-1, we rewrite the equation in standard form, that is,

$$y''' + \frac{\sin x}{x^2-1} y'' + \frac{\sqrt{x+4}}{x^2-1} y' + \frac{e^x}{x^2-1} y = \frac{x^2+3}{x^2-1}.$$

Thus we see that

$$p_1(x) = \frac{\sin x}{x^2-1}, \quad p_2(x) = \frac{\sqrt{x+4}}{x^2-1}, \quad p_3(x) = \frac{e^x}{x^2-1}, \quad \text{and} \quad g(x) = \frac{x^2+3}{x^2-1}.$$

Functions $p_1(x)$, $p_3(x)$, and $g(x)$ are defined and continuous on $(-\infty, \infty)$ except $x = \pm 1$; $p_2(x)$ is defined and continuous on $\{x \geq -4, x \neq \pm 1\}$. Thus, the common domain for $p_1(x)$, $p_2(x)$, $p_3(x)$, and $g(x)$ is $\{x \geq -4, x \neq \pm 1\}$, and, in addition, these functions are continuous there. This set consists of three intervals,

$$[-4, -1), \quad (-1, 1), \quad \text{and} \quad (1, \infty).$$

Theorem 1 guarantees the existence of a unique solution on each of these intervals.

3. A linear combination,

$$c_1 \sin x + c_2 x \sin x + c_3 x^2 \sin x + c_4 x^3 \sin x = \left(c_1 + c_2 x + c_3 x^2 + c_4 x^3\right) \sin x \tag{6.27}$$

vanishes identically on $(-\infty, \infty)$ if and only if the polynomial $c_1 + c_2 x + c_3 x^2 + c_4 x^3$ vanishes identically on $(-\infty, \infty)$. Since the number of real zeros of a polynomial does not exceed its degree, unless it's the zero polynomial, we conclude that the linear combination (6.27) vanishes identically on $(-\infty, \infty)$ if and only if $c_1 = c_2 = c_3 = c_4 = 0$. This means that the given functions are linearly independent on $(-\infty, \infty)$.

5. (a) Solving the auxiliary equation yields

$$(r+5)^2(r-2)^3(r^2+1)^2 = 0 \quad \Rightarrow \quad \begin{aligned} &(r+5)^2 = 0 \quad \text{or} \\ &(r-2)^3 = 0 \quad \text{or} \\ &(r^2+1)^2 = 0. \end{aligned}$$

Thus, the roots of the auxiliary equation are

$$\begin{aligned} r &= -5 \quad \text{of multiplicity 2,} \\ r &= 2 \quad \text{of multiplicity 3,} \\ r &= \pm i \quad \text{of multiplicity 2.} \end{aligned}$$

According to (22) on page 329 and (28) on page 330 of the text, the set of functions (assuming that x is the independent variable)

$$e^{-5x}, \; xe^{-5x}, \; e^{2x}, \; xe^{2x}, \; x^2e^{2x}, \; \cos x, \; x\cos x, \; \sin x, \; x\sin x$$

forms an independent solution set. Thus, a general solution is given by

$$c_1e^{-5x} + c_2xe^{-5x} + c_3e^{2x} + c_4xe^{2x} + c_5x^2e^{2x} + c_6\cos x + c_7x\cos x + c_8\sin x + c_9x\sin x\,.$$

(b) Solving the auxiliary equation yields

$$r^4(r-1)^2(r^2+2r+4)^2 = 0 \quad \Rightarrow \quad \begin{aligned} &r^4 = 0 \quad \text{or} \\ &(r-1)^2 = 0 \quad \text{or} \\ &(r^2+2r+4)^2 = 0. \end{aligned}$$

Thus, the roots of the auxiliary equation are

$$\begin{aligned} r &= 0 \quad \text{of multiplicity 4,} \\ r &= 1 \quad \text{of multiplicity 2,} \\ r &= -1 \pm \sqrt{3}i \quad \text{of multiplicity 2.} \end{aligned}$$

Using (22) on page 329 and (28) on page 330 of the text, we conclude that the set of functions (with x as the independent variable)

$$1\,,\ x\,,\ x^2\,,\ x^3\,,\ e^x\,,\ xe^x\,,\ e^{-x}\cos\sqrt{3}x,\ xe^{-x}\cos\sqrt{3}x,\ \sin\sqrt{3}x,\ xe^{-x}\sin\sqrt{3}x$$

forms an independent solution set. A general solution is given then by

$$\begin{aligned} &c_1 + c_2x + c_3x^2 + c_4x^3 + c_5e^x + c_6xe^x + c_7e^{-x}\cos\sqrt{3}x + c_8xe^{-x}\cos\sqrt{3}x \\ &\qquad\qquad + c_9\sin\sqrt{3}x + c_{10}xe^{-x}\sin\sqrt{3}x \\ &= c_1 + c_2x + c_3x^2 + c_4x^3 + (c_5 + c_6x)e^x + (c_7 + c_8x)e^{-x}\cos\sqrt{3}x \\ &\qquad\qquad + (c_9 + c_{10}x)e^{-x}\sin\sqrt{3}x\,. \end{aligned}$$

7. **(a)** D^3, since the third derivative of a quadratic polynomial is identically zero.

(b) The function $e^{3x}+x-1$ is the sum of e^{3x} and $x-1$. The function $x-1$ is annihilated by D^2, the second derivative operator, and, according to (i) on page 334 of the text, $(D-3)$ annihilates e^{3x}. Therefore, the composite operator

$$D^2(D-3) = (D-3)D^2$$

annihilates both functions and, hence, there sum.

(c) The function $x\sin 2x$ is of the form given in (iv) on page 334 of the text with $m=2$, $\alpha=0$, and $\beta=2$. Thus, the operator

$$\left[(D-0)^2+2^2\right]^2 = \left(D^2+4\right)^2$$

annihilates this function.

(d) We again use (iv) on page 334 of the text, this time with $m=3$, $\alpha=-2$, and $\beta=3$, to conclude that the given function is annihilated by

$$\left\{[D-(-2)]^2+3^2\right\}^3 = \left[(D+2)^2+9\right]^3.$$

(e) Representing the given function as a linear combination,

$$\left(x^2 - 2x\right) + \left(xe^{-x}\right) + (\sin 2x) - (\cos 3x),$$

we find an annihilator for each term. Thus, we have:

$$\begin{array}{lll} x^2 - 2x & \text{is annihilated by } D^3 \,, & \\ xe^{-x} & \text{is annihilated by } [D-(-1)]^2 = (D+1)^2 & (\text{by (ii)},\ \text{page } 334)\,, \\ \sin 2x & \text{is annihilated by } D^2 + 2^2 = D^2 + 4 & (\text{by (iii)},\ \text{page } 334)\,, \\ \cos 3x & \text{is annihilated by } D^2 + 3^2 = D^2 + 9 & (\text{by (iii)},\ \text{page } 334)\,. \end{array}$$

Therefore, the product $D^3(D+1)^2(D^2+4)(D^2+9)$ annihilates the given function.

9. A general solution to the corresponding homogeneous equation,

$$x^3y''' - 2x^2y'' - 5xy' + 5y = 0,$$

is given by $y_h(x) = c_1x + c_2x^5 + c_3x^{-1}$. We now apply the variation of parameters method described in Section 6.4, and seek for a particular solution to the original nonhomogeneous equation in the form

$$y_p(x) = v_1(x)x + v_2(x)x^5 + v_3(x)x^{-1}\,.$$

Since

$$\begin{array}{ll} (x)' = 1, & (x)'' = 0\,, \\ (x^5)' = 5x^4, & (x^5)'' = 20x^3\,, \\ (x^{-1})' = -x^{-2}, & (x^{-1})'' = 2x^{-3}\,, \end{array}$$

the Wronskian $W[x, x^5, x^{-1}](x)$ and determinants $W_k(x)$ given in (10) on page 340 of the text become

$$W[x, x^5, x^{-1}](x) = \begin{vmatrix} x & x^5 & x^{-1} \\ 1 & 5x^4 & -x^{-2} \\ 0 & 20x^3 & 2x^{-3} \end{vmatrix} = (x)\begin{vmatrix} 5x^4 & -x^{-2} \\ 20x^3 & 2x^{-3} \end{vmatrix} - (1)\begin{vmatrix} x^5 & x^{-1} \\ 20x^3 & 2x^{-3} \end{vmatrix}$$

$$= (x)(30x) - (-18x^2) = 48x^2\,,$$

$$W_1(x) = (-1)^{3-1}\begin{vmatrix} x^5 & x^{-1} \\ 5x^4 & -x^{-2} \end{vmatrix} = -6x^3\,,$$

$$W_2(x) = (-1)^{3-2}\begin{vmatrix} x & x^{-1} \\ 1 & -x^{-2} \end{vmatrix} = 2x^{-1},$$

$$W_3(x) = (-1)^{3-3}\begin{vmatrix} x & x^5 \\ 1 & 5x^4 \end{vmatrix} = 4x^5.$$

Now we divide both sides of the given equation by x^3 to obtain an equation in standard form, that is,

$$y''' - 2x^{-1}y'' - 5x^{-2}y' + 5x^{-3}y = x^{-5}.$$

Hence, the right-hand side, $g(x)$, in formula (1) on page 339 of the text equals to x^{-5}. Applying formula (11), page 340 of the text, yields

$$v_1(x) = \int \frac{x^{-5}(-6x^3)}{48x^2}\,dx = -\frac{1}{8}\int x^{-4}\,dx = \frac{1}{24}\,x^{-3},$$
$$v_2(x) = \int \frac{x^{-5}(2x^{-1})}{48x^2}\,dx = \frac{1}{24}\int x^{-8}\,dx = -\frac{1}{168}\,x^{-7},$$
$$v_3(x) = \int \frac{x^{-5}(4x^5)}{48x^2}\,dx = \frac{1}{12}\int x^{-2}\,dx = -\frac{1}{12}\,x^{-1}.$$

Therefore,

$$\begin{aligned} y_p(x) &= \left(\frac{1}{24}\,x^{-3}\right)x + \left(-\frac{1}{168}\,x^{-7}\right)x^5 + \left(-\frac{1}{12}\,x^{-1}\right)x^{-1} \\ &= \left(\frac{1}{24} - \frac{1}{168} - \frac{1}{12}\right)x^{-2} = -\frac{1}{21}\,x^{-2}, \end{aligned}$$

and a general solution to the given equation is given by

$$y(x) = y_h(x) + y_p(x) = c_1x + c_2x^5 + c_3x^{-1} - \frac{1}{21}\,x^{-2}.$$

CHAPTER 7: Laplace Transforms

EXERCISES 7.2: Definition of the Laplace Transform, page 359

1. For $s > 0$, using Definition 1 on page 351 and integration by parts, we compute

$$\begin{aligned}
\mathcal{L}\{t\}(s) &= \int_0^\infty e^{-st}t\,dt = \lim_{N\to\infty}\int_0^N e^{-st}t\,dt = \lim_{N\to\infty}\int_0^N t\,d\left(-\frac{e^{-st}}{s}\right) \\
&= \lim_{N\to\infty}\left[-\frac{te^{-st}}{s}\Big|_0^N + \frac{1}{s}\int_0^N e^{-st}\,dt\right] = \lim_{N\to\infty}\left[-\frac{te^{-st}}{s}\Big|_0^N - \frac{e^{-st}}{s^2}\Big|_0^N\right] \\
&= \lim_{N\to\infty}\left[-\frac{Ne^{-sN}}{s} + 0 - \frac{e^{-sN}}{s^2} + \frac{1}{s^2}\right] = \frac{1}{s^2}
\end{aligned}$$

because, for $s > 0$, $e^{-sN} \to 0$ and $Ne^{-sN} = N/e^{sN} \to 0$ as $N \to \infty$.

3. For $s > 6$, we have

$$\begin{aligned}
\mathcal{L}\{t\}(s) &= \int_0^\infty e^{-st}e^{6t}\,dt = \int_0^\infty e^{(6-s)t}\,dt = \lim_{N\to\infty}\int_0^N e^{(6-s)t}\,dt \\
&= \lim_{N\to\infty}\left[\frac{e^{(6-s)t}}{6-s}\Big|_0^N\right] = \lim_{N\to\infty}\left[\frac{e^{(6-s)N}}{6-s} - \frac{1}{6-s}\right] = 0 - \frac{1}{6-s} = \frac{1}{s-6}\,.
\end{aligned}$$

5. For $s > 0$,

$$\begin{aligned}
\mathcal{L}\{\cos 2t\}(s) &= \int_0^\infty e^{-st}\cos 2t\,dt = \lim_{N\to\infty}\int_0^N e^{-st}\cos 2t\,dt \\
&= \lim_{N\to\infty}\left[\frac{e^{-st}(-s\cos 2t + 2\sin 2t)}{s^2+4}\Big|_0^N\right] \\
&= \lim_{N\to\infty}\left[\frac{e^{-sN}(-s\cos 2N + 2\sin 2N)}{s^2+4} - \frac{-s}{s^2+4}\right] = \frac{s}{s^2+4}\,,
\end{aligned}$$

where we have used integration by parts to find an antiderivative of $e^{-st}\cos 2t$.

7. For $s > 2$,

$$\begin{aligned}
\mathcal{L}\left\{e^{2t}\cos 3t\right\}(s) &= \int_0^\infty e^{-st}e^{2t}\cos 3t\,dt = \int_0^\infty e^{(2-s)t}\cos 3t\,dt \\
&= \lim_{N\to\infty}\left[\frac{e^{(2-s)t}\left((2-s)\cos 3t + 3\sin 3t\right)}{(2-s)^2+9}\Big|_0^N\right] \\
&= \lim_{N\to\infty}\frac{e^{(2-s)N}\left[(2-s)\cos 3N + 3\sin 3N\right] - (2-s)}{(2-s)^2+9} = \frac{s-2}{(s-2)^2+9}\,.
\end{aligned}$$

9. As in Example 4 on page 353 in the text, we first break the integral into separate parts. Thus,

$$\mathcal{L}\left\{f(t)\right\}(s) = \int_0^\infty e^{-st}f(t)\,dt = \int_0^2 e^{-st}\cdot 0\,dt + \int_2^\infty te^{-st}\,dt = \int_2^\infty te^{-st}\,dt\,.$$

An antiderivative of te^{-st} was, in fact, obtained in Problem 1 using integration by parts. Thus, we have

$$\begin{aligned}
\int_2^\infty te^{-st}\,dt &= \lim_{N\to\infty}\left[\left(-\frac{te^{-st}}{s} - \frac{e^{-st}}{s^2}\right)\Big|_2^N\right] = \lim_{N\to\infty}\left[-\frac{Ne^{-sN}}{s} - \frac{e^{-sN}}{s^2} + \frac{2e^{-2s}}{s} + \frac{e^{-2s}}{s^2}\right] \\
&= \frac{2e^{-2s}}{s} + \frac{e^{-2s}}{s^2} = e^{-2s}\left(\frac{2}{s} + \frac{1}{s^2}\right) = e^{-2s}\left(\frac{2s+1}{s^2}\right).
\end{aligned}$$

11. In this problem, $f(t)$ is also a piecewise defined function. So, we split the integral and obtain

$$\begin{aligned}
\mathcal{L}\left\{f(t)\right\}(s) &= \int_0^\infty e^{-st}f(t)\,dt = \int_0^\pi e^{-st}\sin t\,dt + \int_\pi^\infty e^{-st}\cdot 0\,dt = \int_0^\pi e^{-st}\sin t\,dt \\
&= \frac{e^{-st}\left(-s\sin t - \cos t\right)}{s^2+1}\Big|_0^\pi = \frac{e^{-\pi s} - (-1)}{s^2+1} = \frac{e^{-\pi s}+1}{s^2+1}\,,
\end{aligned}$$

which is valid for all s.

13. By the linearity of the Laplace transform,

$$\mathcal{L}\left\{6e^{-3t} - t^2 + 2t - 8\right\}(s) = 6\mathcal{L}\left\{e^{-3t}\right\}(s) - \mathcal{L}\left\{t^2\right\}(s) + 2\mathcal{L}\left\{t\right\}(s) - 8\mathcal{L}\left\{1\right\}(s).$$

From Table 7.1 on page 358 in the text, we see that

$$\mathcal{L}\left\{e^{-3t}\right\}(s) = \frac{1}{s-(-3)} = \frac{1}{s+3}\,, \qquad s > -3;$$

$$\mathcal{L}\left\{t^2\right\}(s) = \frac{2!}{s^{2+1}} = \frac{2}{s^3}, \quad \mathcal{L}\{t\}(s) = \frac{1!}{s^{1+1}} = \frac{1}{s^2}, \quad \mathcal{L}\{1\}(s) = \frac{1}{s}, \qquad s > 0.$$

Thus the formula

$$\mathcal{L}\left\{6e^{-3t} - t^2 + 2t - 8\right\}(s) = 6\frac{1}{s+3} - \frac{2}{s^3} + 2\frac{1}{s^2} - 8\frac{1}{s} = \frac{6}{s+3} - \frac{2}{s^3} + \frac{2}{s^2} - \frac{8}{s},$$

is valid for s in the intersection of the sets $s > -3$ and $s > 0$, which is $s > 0$.

15. Using the linearity of Laplace transform and Table 7.1 on page 358 in the text, we get

$$\begin{aligned}\mathcal{L}\left\{t^3 - te^t + e^{4t}\cos t\right\}(s) &= \mathcal{L}\left\{t^3\right\}(s) - \mathcal{L}\left\{te^t\right\}(s) + \mathcal{L}\left\{e^{4t}\cos t\right\}(s) \\ &= \frac{3!}{s^{3+1}} - \frac{1!}{(s-1)^{1+1}} + \frac{s-4}{(s-4)^2+1^2} \\ &= \frac{6}{s^4} - \frac{1}{(s-1)^2} + \frac{s-4}{(s-4)^2+1},\end{aligned}$$

which is valid for $s > 4$.

17. Using the linearity of Laplace transform and Table 7.1 on page 358 in the text, we get

$$\begin{aligned}\mathcal{L}\left\{e^{3t}\sin 6t - t^3 + e^t\right\}(s) &= \mathcal{L}\left\{e^{3t}\sin 6t\right\}(s) - \mathcal{L}\left\{t^3\right\}(s) + \mathcal{L}\left\{e^t\right\}(s) \\ &= \frac{6}{(s-3)^2+6^2} - \frac{3!}{s^{3+1}} + \frac{1}{s-1} = \frac{6}{(s-3)^2+36} - \frac{6}{s^4} + \frac{1}{s-1},\end{aligned}$$

valid for $s > 3$.

19. For $s > 5$, we have

$$\begin{aligned}\mathcal{L}\left\{t^4e^{5t} - e^t\cos\sqrt{7}t\right\}(s) &= \mathcal{L}\left\{t^4e^{5t}\right\}(s) - \mathcal{L}\left\{e^t\cos\sqrt{7}t\right\}(s) \\ &= \frac{4!}{(s-5)^{4+1}} - \frac{s-1}{(s-1)^2+(\sqrt{7})^2} = \frac{24}{(s-5)^5} - \frac{s-1}{(s-1)^2+7}.\end{aligned}$$

21. Since the function $g_1(t) \equiv 1$ is continuous on $(-\infty, \infty)$ and $f(t) = g_1(t)$ for t in $[0, 1]$, we conclude that $f(t)$ is continuous on $[0, 1)$ and continuous from the left at $t = 1$. The function $g_2(t) \equiv (t-2)^2$ is also continuous on $(-\infty, \infty)$, and so $f(t)$ (which is the same as $g_2(t)$ on $(1, 10]$) is continuous on $(1, 10]$. Moreover,

$$\lim_{t\to 1^+} f(t) = \lim_{t\to 1^+} g_2(t) = g_2(1) = (1-2)^2 = 1 = f(1),$$

which implies that $f(t)$ is continuous from the right at $t = 1$. Thus $f(t)$ is continuous at $t = 1$ and, therefore, is continuous at any t in $[0, 10]$.

23. All the functions involved in the definition of $f(t)$, that is, $g_1(t) \equiv 1$, $g_2(t) = t - 1$, and $g_3(t) = t^2 - 4$, are continuous on $(-\infty, \infty)$. So, $f(t)$, being a restriction of these functions, on $[0, 1)$, $(1, 3)$, and $(3, 10]$, respectively, is continuous on these three intervals. At points $t = 1$ and 3, $f(t)$ is not defined and so is not continuous. But one-sided limits

$$\lim_{t\to 1^-} f(t) = \lim_{t\to 1^-} g_1(t) = g_1(1) = 1,$$
$$\lim_{t\to 1^+} f(t) = \lim_{t\to 1^+} g_2(t) = g_2(1) = 0,$$
$$\lim_{t\to 3^-} f(t) = \lim_{t\to 3^-} g_2(t) = g_2(3) = 2,$$
$$\lim_{t\to 3^+} f(t) = \lim_{t\to 3^+} g_3(t) = g_3(3) = 5,$$

exist and pairwise different. Therefore, $f(t)$ has jump discontinuities at $t = 1$ and $t = 3$, and hence piecewise continuous on $[0, 10]$.

25. Given function is a rational function and, therefore, continuous on its domain, which is all reals except zeros of the denominator. Solving $t^2 + 7t + 10 = 0$, we conclude that the points of discontinuity of $f(t)$ are $t = -2$ and $t = -5$. These points are not in $[0, 10]$. So, $f(t)$ is continuous on $[0, 10]$.

27. Since

$$\lim_{t\to 0^+} f(t) = \lim_{t\to 0^+} \frac{1}{t} = \infty,$$

$f(t)$ has infinite discontinuity at $t = 0$, and so neither continuous nor piecewise continuous $[0, 10]$.

29. **(a)** First observe that $|t^3 \sin t| \le |t^3|$ for all t. Next, three applications of L'Hospital's rule show that

$$\lim_{t\to\infty} \frac{t^3}{e^{\alpha t}} = \lim_{t\to\infty} \frac{3t^2}{\alpha e^{\alpha t}} = \lim_{t\to\infty} \frac{6t}{\alpha^2 e^{\alpha t}} = \lim_{t\to\infty} \frac{6}{\alpha^3 e^{\alpha t}} = 0$$

for all $\alpha > 0$. Thus, fixed $\alpha > 0$, for some $T = T(\alpha) > 0$, we have $|t^3| < e^{\alpha t}$ for all $t > T$, and so

$$\left|t^3 \sin t\right| \leq \left|t^3\right| < e^{\alpha t}, \qquad t > T.$$

Therefore, $t^3 \sin t$ is of exponential order α, for any $\alpha > 0$.

(b) Clearly, for any t, $|f(t)| = 100e^{49t}$, and so Definition 3 is satisfied with $M = 100$, $\alpha = 49$, and any T. Hence, $f(t)$ is of exponential order 49.

(c) Since

$$\lim_{t\to\infty} \frac{f(t)}{e^{\alpha t}} = \lim_{t\to\infty} e^{t^3-\alpha t} = \lim_{t\to\infty} e^{(t^2-\alpha)t} = \infty,$$

we see that $f(t)$ grows faster than $e^{\alpha t}$ for any α. Thus $f(t)$ is *not* of exponential order.

(d) Similarly to (a), for any $\alpha > 0$, we get

$$\lim_{t\to\infty} \frac{|t\ln t|}{e^{\alpha t}} = \lim_{t\to\infty} \frac{t\ln t}{e^{\alpha t}} = \lim_{t\to\infty} \frac{\ln t + 1}{\alpha e^{\alpha t}} = \lim_{t\to\infty} \frac{1/t}{\alpha^2 e^{\alpha t}} = 0\,,$$

and so $f(t)$ is of exponential order α for any positive α.

(e) Since,

$$f(t) = \cosh\left(t^2\right) = \frac{e^{t^2} + e^{-t^2}}{2} > \frac{1}{2}\,e^{t^2}$$

and e^{t^2} grows faster than $e^{\alpha t}$ for any fixed α (see page 357 in the text), we conclude that $\cosh\left(t^2\right)$ is *not* of exponential order.

(f) This function is bounded:

$$|f(t)| = \left|\frac{1}{t^2+1}\right| = fr1t^2 + 1 \leq \frac{1}{0+1} = 1,$$

and so Definition 3 is satisfied with $M = 1$ and $\alpha = 0$. Hence, $f(t)$ is of exponential order 0.

(g) The function $\sin\left(t^2\right)$ is bounded, namely, $|\sin\left(t^2\right)| \leq 1$. For any fixed $\beta > 0$, the limit of $t^4/e^{\beta t}$, as $t \to \infty$, is 0, which implies that $t^4 \leq e^{\beta t}$ for all $t > T = T(\beta)$. Thus,

$$\left|\sin\left(t^2\right) + t^4 e^{6t}\right| \leq 1 + e^{\beta t} e^{6t} = 2e^{\beta + 6t}\,.$$

This means that $f(t)$ is of exponential order α for any $\alpha > 6$.

(h) The function $3+\cos 4t$ is bounded because

$$|3+\cos 4t| \le 3 + |\cos 4t| \le 4.$$

Therefore, by the triangle inequality,

$$|f(t)| \ge \left|e^{t^2}\right| - |3+\cos 4t| \ge e^{t^2} - 4,$$

and, therefore, for any fixed α, $f(t)$ grows faster than $e^{\alpha t}$ (because e^{t^2} does, and the other term is bounded). So, $f(t)$ is *not* of exponential order.

(i) Clearly, for any $t > 0$,

$$\frac{t^2}{t+1} = \frac{t}{t+1}\, t < (1)t = t.$$

Therefore,

$$e^{t^2/(t+1)} < e^t,$$

and Definition 3 holds with $M = 1$, $\alpha = 1$, and $T = 0$.

(j) Since, for any x, $-1 \le \sin x \le 1$, the given function is bounded. Indeed,

$$\left|\sin\left(e^{t^2}\right) + e^{\sin t}\right| \le \left|\sin\left(e^{t^2}\right)\right| + e^{\sin t} \le 1 + e$$

Thus it is of exponential order 0.

31. **(a)**

$$\begin{aligned}\mathcal{L}\left\{e^{(a+ib)t}\right\}(s) &:= \int_0^\infty e^{-st} e^{(a+ib)t}\, dt = \int_0^\infty e^{(a+ib-s)t}\, dt = \lim_{N\to\infty} \int_0^N e^{(a+ib-s)t}\, dt \\ &= \lim_{N\to\infty} \left(\frac{e^{(a+ib-s)t}}{a+ib-s} \Bigg|_0^N \right) = \frac{1}{a+ib-s} \lim_{N\to\infty} \left(e^{(a-s+ib)N} - 1\right). \quad (7.1)\end{aligned}$$

Since

$$e^{(a-s+ib)x} = e^{(a-s)x} e^{ibx},$$

where the first factor vanishes at ∞ if $a - s < 0$ while the second factor is a bounded $\left(\left|e^{ibx}\right| \equiv 1\right)$ and periodic function, the limit in (7.1) exists if and only if $a - s < 0$. Assuming that $s > a$, we get

$$\frac{1}{a+ib-s} \lim_{N\to\infty} \left(e^{(a-s+ib)N} - 1\right) = \frac{1}{a+ib-s}(0-1) = \frac{1}{s-(a+ib)}.$$

(b) Note that $s - (a + ib) = (s - a) - ib$. Multiplying the result in (a) by the complex conjugate of the denominator, that is, $(s - a) + bi$, we get

$$\frac{1}{s-(a+ib)} = \frac{(s-a)+ib}{[(s-a)-ib]\cdot[(s-a)+ib]} = \frac{(s-a)+ib}{(s-a)^2+b^2},$$

where we used the fact that, for any complex number z, $z\bar{z} = |z|^2$.

(c) From (a) and (b) we klnow that

$$\mathcal{L}\left\{e^{(a+ib)t}\right\}(s) = \frac{(s-a)+ib}{(s-a)^2+b^2}.$$

Writing

$$\frac{(s-a)+ib}{(s-a)^2+b^2} = \frac{s-a}{(s-a)^2+b^2} + \frac{b}{(s-a)^2+b^2}\,i,$$

we see that

$$\operatorname{Re}\left[\mathcal{L}\left\{e^{(a+ib)t}\right\}(s)\right] = \operatorname{Re}\left[\frac{s-a}{(s-a)^2+b^2} + \frac{b}{(s-a)^2+b^2}\,i\right] = \frac{s-a}{(s-a)^2+b^2}, \quad (7.2)$$

$$\operatorname{Im}\left[\mathcal{L}\left\{e^{(a+ib)t}\right\}(s)\right] = \operatorname{Im}\left[\frac{s-a}{(s-a)^2+b^2} + \frac{b}{(s-a)^2+b^2}\,i\right] = \frac{b}{(s-a)^2+b^2}. \quad (7.3)$$

On the other hand, by Euler's formulas,

$$\operatorname{Re}\left[e^{-st}e^{(a+ib)t}\right] = e^{-st}\operatorname{Re}\left[e^{at}(\cos bt + i\sin bt)\right] = e^{-st}e^{at}\cos bt$$

and so

$$\begin{aligned}\operatorname{Re}\left[\mathcal{L}\left\{e^{(a+ib)t}\right\}(s)\right] &= \operatorname{Re}\left[\int_0^\infty e^{-st}e^{(a+ib)t}\,dt\right] = \operatorname{Re}\left[\int_0^\infty e^{-s}e^{(a+ib)t}\,dt\right] \\ &= \int_0^\infty \operatorname{Re}\left[e^{-s}e^{(a+ib)t}\right]dt = \int_0^\infty e^{-st}e^{at}\cos bt\,dt = \mathcal{L}\left\{e^{at}\cos bt\right\}(s),\end{aligned}$$

which together with (7.2) gives the last entry in Table 7.1. Similarly,

$$\operatorname{Im}\left[\mathcal{L}\left\{e^{(a+ib)t}\right\}(s)\right] = \mathcal{L}\left\{e^{at}\sin bt\right\}(s),$$

and so (7.3) gives the Laplace transform of $e^{at}\sin bt$.

33. Let $f(t)$ be a piecewise continuous function on $[a, b]$, and let a function $g(t)$ be continuous on $[a, b]$. At any point of continuity of $f(t)$, the function $(fg)(t)$ is continuous as the product of two continuous functions at this point. Suppose now that c is a point of discontinuity of $f(t)$. Then one-sided limits

$$\lim_{t\to c^-} f(t) = L_- \qquad \text{and} \qquad \lim_{t\to c^+} f(t) = L_+$$

exist. At the same time, continuity of $g(t)$ yields

$$\lim_{t\to c^-} g(t) = \lim_{t\to c^+} g(t) = \lim_{t\to c} g(t) = g(c).$$

Thus, the product rule implies that one-sided limits

$$\begin{aligned} \lim_{t\to c^-} (fg)(t) &= \lim_{t\to c^-} f(t) \cdot \lim_{t\to c^-} g(t) = L_- g(c) \\ \lim_{t\to c^+} (fg)(t) &= \lim_{t\to c^+} f(t) \lim_{t\to c^+} g(t) = L_+ g(c) \end{aligned}$$

exist. So, fg has a jump (even removable if $g(c) = 0$) discontinuity at $t = c$.

Therefore, the product $(fg)(t)$ is continuous at any point on $[a, b]$ except possibly a finite number of points (namely, points of discontinuity of $f(t)$).

EXERCISES 7.3: Properties of the Laplace Transform, page 365

1. Using the linearity of the Laplace transform we get

$$\mathcal{L}\left\{t^2 + e^t \sin 2t\right\}(s) = \mathcal{L}\left\{t^2\right\}(s) + \mathcal{L}\left\{e^t \sin 2t\right\}(s).$$

From Table 7.1 in Section 7.2 we know that

$$\mathcal{L}\left\{t^2\right\}(s) = \frac{2!}{s^3} = \frac{2}{s^3}, \quad \mathcal{L}\left\{e^t \sin 2t\right\}(s) = \frac{2}{(s-1)^2 + 2^2} = \frac{2}{(s-1)^2 + 4}.$$

Thus

$$\mathcal{L}\left\{t^2 + e^t \sin 2t\right\}(s) = \frac{2}{s^3} + \frac{2}{(s-1)^2 + 4}.$$

3. By the linearity of the Laplace transform,

$$\mathcal{L}\left\{e^{-t}\cos 3t + e^{6t} - 1\right\}(s) = \mathcal{L}\left\{e^{-t}\cos 3t\right\}(s) + \mathcal{L}\left\{e^{6t}\right\}(s) - \mathcal{L}\left\{1\right\}(s).$$

From Table 7.1 of the text we see that

$$\mathcal{L}\left\{e^{-t}\cos 3t\right\}(s) = \frac{s-(-1)}{[s-(-1)]^2+3^2} = \frac{s+1}{(s+1)^2+9}, \quad s > -1; \tag{7.4}$$

$$\mathcal{L}\left\{e^{6t}\right\}(s) = \frac{1}{s-6}, \quad s > 6; \tag{7.5}$$

$$\mathcal{L}\left\{1\right\}(s) = \frac{1}{s}, \quad s > 0. \tag{7.6}$$

Since (7.4), (7.5), and (7.6) all hold for $s > 6$, we see that our answer,

$$\mathcal{L}\left\{e^{-t}\cos 3t + e^{6t} - 1\right\}(s) = \frac{s+1}{(s+1)^2+9} + \frac{1}{s-6} - \frac{1}{s},$$

is valid for $s > 6$. Note that (7.4) and (7.5) could also be obtained from the Laplace transforms for $\cos 3t$ and 1, respectively, by applying the translation Theorem 3.

5. We use the linearity of the Laplace transform and Table 7.1 to get

$$\begin{aligned}\mathcal{L}\left\{2t^2e^{-t} - t + \cos 4t\right\}(s) &= 2\mathcal{L}\left\{t^2e^{-t}\right\}(s) - \mathcal{L}\left\{t\right\}(s) + \mathcal{L}\left\{\cos 4t\right\}(s) \\ &= 2\cdot\frac{2}{(s+1)^3} - \frac{1}{s^2} + \frac{s}{s^2+4^2} = \cdot\frac{4}{(s+1)^3} - \frac{1}{s^2} + \frac{s}{s^2+16},\end{aligned}$$

which is valid for $s > 0$.

7. Since $(t-1)^4 = t^4 - 4t^3 + 6t^2 - 4t + 1$, we have from the linearity of the Laplace transform that

$$\mathcal{L}\left\{(t-1)^4\right\}(s) = \mathcal{L}\left\{t^4\right\}(s) - 4\mathcal{L}\left\{t^3\right\}(s) + 6\mathcal{L}\left\{t^2\right\}(s) - 4\mathcal{L}\left\{t\right\}(s) + \mathcal{L}\left\{1\right\}(s).$$

From Table 7.1 of the text, we get that, for $s > 0$,

$$\mathcal{L}\left\{t^4\right\}(s) = \frac{4!}{s^5} = \frac{24}{s^5},$$

$$\mathcal{L}\left\{t^3\right\}(s) = \frac{3!}{s^4} = \frac{6}{s^4},$$

$$\mathcal{L}\left\{t^2\right\}(s) = \frac{2!}{s^3} = \frac{2}{s^3},$$
$$\mathcal{L}\left\{t\right\}(s) = \frac{1!}{s^2} = \frac{1}{s^2},$$
$$\mathcal{L}\left\{1\right\}(s) = \frac{1}{s}.$$

Thus

$$\mathcal{L}\left\{(t-1)^4\right\}(s) = \frac{24}{s^5} - \frac{24}{s^4} + \frac{12}{s^3} - \frac{4}{s^2} + \frac{1}{s}, \qquad s > 0.$$

9. Since

$$\mathcal{L}\left\{e^{-t}\sin 2t\right\}(s) = \frac{2}{(s+1)^2+4},$$

we use Theorem 6 to get

$$\begin{aligned}\mathcal{L}\left\{e^{-t}t\sin 2t\right\}(s) &= \mathcal{L}\left\{t\left(e^{-t}\sin 2t\right)\right\}(s) = -\left[\mathcal{L}\left\{e^{-t}\sin 2t\right\}(s)\right]' = -\left[\frac{2}{(s+1)^2+4}\right]' \\ &= -2(-1)\left[(s+1)^2+4\right]^{-2}\left[(s+1)^2+4\right]' = \frac{4(s+1)}{[(s+1)^2+4]^2}.\end{aligned}$$

11. We use the definition of $\cosh x$ and the linear property of the Laplace transform.

$$\begin{aligned}\mathcal{L}\left\{\cosh bt\right\}(s) &= \mathcal{L}\left\{\frac{e^{bt}+e^{-bt}}{2}\right\}(s) \\ &= \frac{1}{2}\left[\mathcal{L}\left\{e^{bt}\right\}(s) + \mathcal{L}\left\{e^{-bt}\right\}(s)\right] = \frac{1}{2}\left[\frac{1}{s-b} + \frac{1}{s+b}\right] = \frac{s}{s^2-b^2}.\end{aligned}$$

13. In this problem, we need the trigonometric identity $\sin^2 t = (1-\cos 2t)/2$ and the linearity of the Laplace transform.

$$\begin{aligned}\mathcal{L}\left\{\sin^2 t\right\}(s) &= \mathcal{L}\left\{\frac{1-\cos 2t}{2}\right\}(s) \\ &= \frac{1}{2}\left[\mathcal{L}\left\{1\right\}(s) - \mathcal{L}\left\{\cos 2t\right\}(s)\right] = \frac{1}{2}\left[\frac{1}{s} - \frac{s}{s^2+4}\right] = \frac{2}{s(s^2+4)}.\end{aligned}$$

15. From the trigonometric identity $\cos^2 t = (1+\cos 2t)/2$, we find that

$$\cos^3 t = \cos t\cos^2 t = \frac{1}{2}\cos t + \frac{1}{2}\cos t\cos 2t.$$

Next we write

$$\cos t \cos 2t = \frac{1}{2}\left[\cos(2t+t)+\cos(2t-t)\right] = \frac{1}{2}\cos 3t + \frac{1}{2}\cos t.$$

Thus,

$$\cos^3 t = \frac{1}{2}\cos t + \frac{1}{4}\cos 3t + \frac{1}{4}\cos t = \frac{3}{4}\cos t + \frac{1}{4}\cos 3t.$$

We now use the linearity of the Laplace transform and Table 7.1 to find that

$$\mathcal{L}\left\{\cos^3 t\right\}(s) = \frac{3}{4}\mathcal{L}\{\cos t\}(s) + \frac{1}{4}\mathcal{L}\{\cos 3t\}(s) = \frac{3}{4}\frac{s}{s^2+1} + \frac{1}{4}\frac{s}{s^2+9},$$

which holds for $s > 0$.

17. Since $\sin A \sin B = [\cos(A-B) - \cos(A+B)]/2$, we get

$$\begin{aligned}\mathcal{L}\{\sin 2t \sin 5t\}(s) &= \mathcal{L}\left\{\frac{\cos 3t - \cos 7t}{2}\right\}(s) = \frac{1}{2}\left[\mathcal{L}\{\cos 3t\}(s) - \mathcal{L}\{\cos 7t\}(s)\right] \\ &= \frac{1}{2}\left[\frac{s}{s^2+9} - \frac{s}{s^2+49}\right] = \frac{20s}{(s^2+9)(s^2+49)}.\end{aligned}$$

19. Since $\sin A \cos B = [\sin(A+B) + \sin(A-B)]/2$, we get

$$\begin{aligned}\mathcal{L}\{\cos nt \sin mt\}(s) &= \mathcal{L}\left\{\frac{\sin[(m+n)t] + \sin[(m-n)t]}{2}\right\}(s) \\ &= \frac{1}{2}\frac{m+n}{s^2+(m+n)^2} + \frac{1}{2}\frac{m-n}{s^2+(m-n)^2}.\end{aligned}$$

21. By the translation property of the Laplace transform (Theorem 3),

$$\mathcal{L}\left\{e^{at}\cos bt\right\}(s) = \mathcal{L}\{\cos bt\}(s-a) = \frac{u}{u^2+b^2}\Big|_{u=s-a} = \frac{s-a}{(s-a)^2+b^2}.$$

23. Clearly,

$$(t \sin bt)' = (t)' \sin bt + t(\sin bt)' = \sin bt + bt \cos bt.$$

Therefore, using Theorem 4 and the entry 30, that is, $\mathcal{L}\{t \sin bt\}(s) = (2bs)/[(s^2+b^2)^2]$, we obtain

$$\begin{aligned}\mathcal{L}\{\sin bt + bt\cos bt\}(s) &= \mathcal{L}\{(t\sin bt)'\}(s) = s\mathcal{L}\{t \sin bt\}(s) - (t\sin bt)\Big|_{t=0} \\ &= \frac{s(2bs)}{(s^2+b^2)^2} - 0 = \frac{2bs^2}{(s^2+b^2)^2}.\end{aligned}$$

25. **(a)** By property (6) on page 363 of the text,

$$\mathcal{L}\{t\cos bt\}(s) = -\left[\mathcal{L}\{\cos bt\}(s)\right]' = -\left[\frac{s}{s^2+b^2}\right]' = \frac{s^2-b^2}{(s^2+b^2)^2}, \qquad s>0.$$

(b) Again using the same property, we get

$$\begin{aligned}\mathcal{L}\left\{t^2\cos bt\right\}(s) &= \mathcal{L}\{t(t\cos bt)\}(s) = -\left[\mathcal{L}\{t\cos bt\}(s)\right]' \\ &= -\left[\frac{s^2-b^2}{(s^2+b^2)^2}\right]' = \frac{2s^3-6sb^2}{(s^2+b^2)^3}, \qquad s>0.\end{aligned}$$

27. First observe that since $f(t)$ is piecewise continuous on $[0,\infty)$ and $f(t)/t$ approaches a finite limit as $t\to 0^+$, we conclude that $f(t)/t$ is also piecewise continuous on $[0,\infty)$. Next, since for $t\ge 1$ we have $|f(t)/t|\le|f(t)|$, we see that $f(t)/t$ is of exponential order α since $f(t)$ is. These observations and Theorem 2 on page 357 of the text show that $\mathcal{L}\{f(t)/t\}$ exists. When the results of Problem 26 are applied to $f(t)/t$, we see that

$$\lim_{N\to\infty}\mathcal{L}\left\{\frac{f(t)}{t}\right\}(N)=0.$$

By Theorem 6, we have that

$$F(s)=\int_0^\infty e^{-st}f(t)\,dt=\int_0^\infty \frac{te^{-st}f(t)}{t}\,dt=-\frac{d}{ds}\mathcal{L}\left\{\frac{f(t)}{t}\right\}(s).$$

Thus,

$$\begin{aligned}\int_s^\infty F(u)\,du &= \int_s^\infty\left[-\frac{d}{du}\mathcal{L}\left\{\frac{f(t)}{t}\right\}(u)\right]du=\int_\infty^s\frac{d}{du}\mathcal{L}\left\{\frac{f(t)}{t}\right\}(u)\,du \\ &= \mathcal{L}\left\{\frac{f(t)}{t}\right\}(s)-\lim_{N\to\infty}\mathcal{L}\left\{\frac{f(t)}{t}\right\}(N)=\mathcal{L}\left\{\frac{f(t)}{t}\right\}(s).\end{aligned}$$

29. From the linearity properties (2) and (3) on page 354 of the text we have

$$\mathcal{L}\{g(t)\}(s)=\mathcal{L}\{y''(t)+6y'(t)+10y(t)\}(s)=\mathcal{L}\{y''(t)\}(s)+6\mathcal{L}\{y'(t)\}(s)+10\mathcal{L}\{y(t)\}(s).$$

Next, applying properties (2) and (4) on pages 361 and 362 yields

$$\mathcal{L}\{g\}(s)=\left[s^2\mathcal{L}\{y\}(s)-sy(0)-y'(0)\right]+6\left[s\mathcal{L}\{y\}(s)-y(0)\right]+10\mathcal{L}\{y\}(s).$$

Keeping in mind the fact that all initial conditions are zero the above becomes

$$G(s) = \left(s^2 + 6s + 10\right) Y(s), \qquad \text{where} \qquad Y(s) = \mathcal{L}\{y\}(s).$$

Therefore, the transfer function $H(s)$ is given by

$$H(s) = \frac{Y(s)}{G(s)} = \frac{1}{s^2 + 6s + 10}\,.$$

31. Using Definition 1 of the Laplace transform in Section 7.2, we obtain

$$\begin{aligned}
\mathcal{L}\{g(t)\}(s) &= \int_0^\infty e^{-st} g(t)\,dt = \int_0^c (0)\,dt + \int_c^\infty e^{-st} f(t-c)\,dt = \left(\, t - c \to u,\ dt \to du \,\right) \\
&= \int_0^\infty e^{-s(u+c)} f(u)\,du = e^{-cs} \int_0^\infty e^{-su} f(u)\,du = e^{-cs} \mathcal{L}\{f(t)\}(s).
\end{aligned}$$

33. The graphs of the function $f(t) = t$ and its translation $g(t)$ to the right by $c = 1$ are shown in Figure 7-A(a).

We use the result of Problem 31 to find $\mathcal{L}\{g(t)\}$.

$$\mathcal{L}\{g(t)\}(s) = e^{-(1)s} \mathcal{L}\{t\}(s) = \frac{e^{-s}}{s^2}\,.$$

35. The graphs of the function $f(t) = \sin t$ and its translation $g(t)$ to the right by $c = \pi/2$ units are shown in Figure 7-A(b).

We use the formula in Problem 31 to find $\mathcal{L}\{g(t)\}$.

$$\mathcal{L}\{g(t)\}(s) = e^{-(\pi/2)s} \mathcal{L}\{\sin t\}(s) = \frac{e^{-(\pi/2)s}}{s^2 + 1}\,.$$

37. Since $f'(t)$ is of exponential order on $[0, \infty)$, for some α, $M > 0$, and $T > 0$,

$$|f'(t)| \le M e^{\alpha t}, \qquad \text{for all} \quad t \ge T. \tag{7.7}$$

On the other hand, piecewise continuity of $f'(t)$ on $[0, \infty)$ implies that $f'(t)$ is bounded on any finite interval, in particular, on $[0, T]$. That is,

$$|f'(t)| \le C, \qquad \text{for all} \quad t \text{ in } [0, T]. \tag{7.8}$$

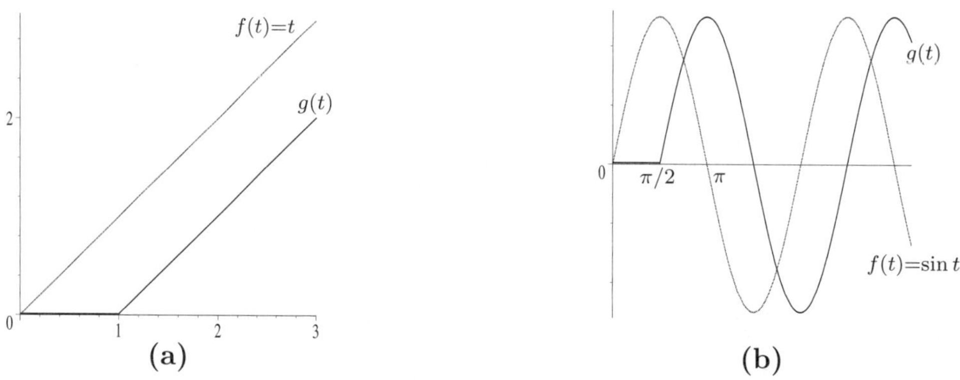

Figure 7–A: Graphs of functions in Problems 33 and 35.

From (7.7) and (7.8) it follows that, for $s > \alpha$,

$$\begin{aligned}\int_0^\infty e^{-st}|f'(t)|\,dt &= \int_0^T e^{-st}|f'(t)|\,dt + \int_T^\infty e^{-st}|f'(t)|\,dt \le C\int_0^T e^{-st}\,dt + M\int_T^\infty e^{-st}e^{\alpha t}\,dt \\ &= \left.\frac{Ce^{-st}}{-s}\right|_0^T + \lim_{N\to\infty}\left[\left.\frac{Me^{(\alpha-s)t}}{\alpha-s}\right|_T^N\right] = \frac{C\left[1-e^{-sT}\right]}{s} + \frac{Me^{(\alpha-s)T}}{s-\alpha} \longrightarrow 0\end{aligned}$$

as $s \to \infty$. Therefore, (7) yields

$$0 \le |s\mathcal{L}\{f\}(s) - f(0)| = \left|\int_0^\infty e^{-st}f'(t)\,dt\right| \le \int_0^\infty e^{-st}|f'(t)|\,dt \longrightarrow 0 \quad \text{as} \quad s \to \infty.$$

Hence, by the squeeze theorem,

$$\lim_{s\to\infty}|s\mathcal{L}\{f\}(s) - f(0)| = 0 \;\Leftrightarrow\; \lim_{s\to\infty}[s\mathcal{L}\{f\}(s) - f(0)] = 0 \;\Leftrightarrow\; \lim_{s\to\infty}s\mathcal{L}\{f\}(s) = f(0).$$

EXERCISES 7.4: Inverse Laplace Transform, page 374

1. From Table 7.1, the function $6/(s-1)^4 = (3!)/(s-1)^4$ is the Laplace transform of $e^{\alpha t}t^n$ with $\alpha = 1$ and $n = 3$. Therefore,

$$\mathcal{L}^{-1}\left\{\frac{6}{(s-1)^4}\right\}(t) = e^t t^3\,.$$

3. Writing

$$\frac{s+1}{s^2+2s+10}=\frac{s+1}{(s^2+2s+1)+9}=\frac{s+1}{(s+1)^2+3^2},$$

we see that this function is the Laplace transform of $e^{-t}\cos 3t$ (the last entry in Table 7.1 with $\alpha=-1$ and $b=3$). Hence

$$\mathcal{L}^{-1}\left\{\frac{s+1}{s^2+2s+10}\right\}(t)=e^{-t}\cos 3t\,.$$

5. We complete the square in the denominator and use the linearity of the inverse Laplace transform to get

$$\mathcal{L}^{-1}\left\{\frac{1}{s^2+4s+8}\right\}(t)=\mathcal{L}^{-1}\left\{\frac{1}{(s+2)^2+2^2}\right\}(t)=\frac{1}{2}\mathcal{L}^{-1}\left\{\frac{2}{(s+2)^2+2^2}\right\}(t)=\frac{1}{2}\,e^{-2t}\sin 2t.$$

(See the Laplace transform formula for $e^{\alpha t}\sin bt$ in Table 7.1).

7. By completing the square in the denominator, we can rewrite $(2s+16)/(s^2+4s+13)$ as

$$\frac{2s+16}{s^2+4s+4+9}=\frac{2s+16}{(s+2)^2+3^2}=\frac{2(s+2)}{(s+2)^2+3^2}+\frac{4(3)}{(s+2)^2+3^2}\,.$$

Thus, by the linearity of the inverse Laplace transform,

$$\begin{aligned}\mathcal{L}^{-1}\left\{\frac{2s+16}{s^2+4s+13}\right\}(t) &= 2\mathcal{L}^{-1}\left\{\frac{s+2}{(s+2)^2+3^2}\right\}(t)+4\mathcal{L}^{-1}\left\{\frac{3}{(s+2)^2+3^2}\right\}(t)\\ &= 2e^{-2t}\cos 3t+4e^{-2t}\sin 3t\,.\end{aligned}$$

9. We complete the square in the denominator, rewrite the given function as a sum of two entries in Table 7.1, and use the linearity of the inverse Laplace transform. This yields

$$\frac{3s-15}{2s^2-4s+10}=\frac{3}{2}\cdot\frac{s-5}{s^2-2s+5}=\frac{3}{2}\cdot\frac{(s-1)-4}{(s-1)^2+2^2}=\frac{(3/2)(s-1)}{(s-1)^2+2^2}-\frac{3(2)}{(s-1)^2+2^2}$$

$$\begin{aligned}\Rightarrow\quad \mathcal{L}^{-1}\left\{\frac{3s-15}{2s^2-4s+10}\right\} &= \frac{3}{2}\mathcal{L}^{-1}\left\{\frac{s-1}{(s-1)^2+2^2}\right\}-3\mathcal{L}^{-1}\left\{\frac{2}{(s-1)^2+2^2}\right\}\\ &= \frac{3}{2}\,e^{t}\cos 2t-3e^{t}\sin 2t.\end{aligned}$$

11. In this problem, we use the partial fractions decomposition method. Since the denominator, $(s-1)(s+2)(s+5)$, is a product of three nonrepeated linear factors, the expansion has the form

$$\begin{aligned}\frac{s^2-26s-47}{(s-1)(s+2)(s+5)} &= \frac{A}{s-1}+\frac{B}{s+2}+\frac{C}{s+5}\\ &= \frac{A(s+2)(s+5)+B(s-1)(s+5)+C(s-1)(s+2)}{(s-1)(s+2)(s+5)}.\end{aligned}$$

Therefore,

$$s^2-26s-47 = A(s+2)(s+5)+B(s-1)(s+5)+C(s-1)(s+2). \tag{7.9}$$

Evaluating both sides of (7.9) for $s=1$, $s=-2$, and $s=-5$, we find constants A, B, and C.

$$\begin{aligned}s=1: &\quad (1)^2-26(1)-47 = A(1+2)(1+5) &\Rightarrow&\quad A=-4,\\ s=-2: &\quad (-2)^2-26(-2)-47 = B(-2-1)(-2+5) &\Rightarrow&\quad B=-1,\\ s=-5: &\quad (-5)^2-26(-5)-47 = C(-5-1)(-5+2) &\Rightarrow&\quad C=6.\end{aligned}$$

Hence,

$$\frac{s^2-26s-47}{(s-1)(s+2)(s+5)} = \frac{6}{s+5}-\frac{1}{s+2}-\frac{4}{s-1}.$$

13. The denominator has a simple linear factor, s, and a double linear factor, $s+1$. Thus, we look for the decomposition of the form

$$\frac{-2s^2-3s-2}{s(s+1)^2} = \frac{A}{s}+\frac{B}{s+1}+\frac{C}{(s+1)^2} = \frac{A(s+1)^2+Bs(s+1)+Cs}{s(s+1)^2},$$

which yields

$$-2s^2-3s-2 = A(s+1)^2+Bs(s+1)+Cs. \tag{7.10}$$

Evaluating this equality for $s=0$ and $s=-1$, we find A and C, respectively.

$$\begin{aligned}s=0: &\quad -2 = A(0+1)^2 &\Rightarrow&\quad A=-2,\\ s=-1: &\quad -2(-1)^2-3(-1)-2 = C(-1) &\Rightarrow&\quad C=1.\end{aligned}$$

To find B, we compare the coefficients at s^2 in both sides of (7.10).

$$-2 = A+B \quad\Rightarrow\quad B=-2-A=0.$$

Hence,

$$\frac{-2s^2-3s-2}{s(s+1)^2}=\frac{1}{(s+1)^2}-\frac{2}{s}.$$

15. First, we complete the square in the quadratic s^2-2s+5 to make sure that this polynomial is irreducible and to find the form of the decomposition. Since

$$s^2-2s+5=(s^2-2s+1)+4=(s-1)^2+2^2,$$

we have

$$\frac{-8s-2s^2-14}{(s+1)(s^2-2s+5)}=\frac{A}{s+1}+\frac{B(s-1)+C(2)}{(s-1)^2+2^2}=\frac{A\left[(s-1)^2+4\right]+\left[B(s-1)+2C\right](s+1)}{(s+1)\left[(s-1)^2+4\right]}$$

which implies that

$$-8s-2s^2-14=A\left[(s-1)^2+4\right]+\left[B(s-1)+2C\right](s+1).$$

Taking $s=-1$, $s=1$, and $s=0$, we find A, B, and C, respectively.

$$\begin{array}{lllll} s=-1: & 8(-1)-2(-1)^2-14=A\left[(-1-1)^2+4\right] & \Rightarrow & A=-3, \\ s=1: & 8(1)-2(1)^2-14=A\left[(1-1)^2+4\right]+2C(1+1) & \Rightarrow & C=1, \\ s=0: & 8(0)-2(0)^2-14=A\left[(0-1)^2+4\right]+\left[B(0-1)+2C\right](0+1) & \Rightarrow & B=1, \end{array}$$

and so

$$\frac{-8s-2s^2-14}{(s+1)(s^2-2s+5)}=-\frac{3}{s+1}+\frac{(s-1)+2}{(s-1)^2+4}$$

17. First we need to completely factor the denominator. Since $s^2+s-6=(s-2)(s+3)$, we have

$$\frac{3s+5}{s(s^2+s-6)}=\frac{3s+5}{s(s-2)(s+3)}.$$

Since the denominator has only nonrepeated linear factors, we can write

$$\frac{3s+5}{s(s-2)(s+3)}=\frac{A}{s}+\frac{B}{s-2}+\frac{C}{s+3}$$

for some choice of A, B and C. Clearing fractions gives us

$$3s+5=A(s-2)(s+3)+Bs(s+3)+Cs(s-2).$$

With $s = 0$, this yields $5 = A(-2)(3)$ so that $A = -5/6$. With $s = 2$, we get $11 = B(2)(5)$ so that $B = 11/10$. Finally, $s = -3$ yields $-4 = C(-3)(-5)$ so that $C = -4/15$. Thus,

$$\frac{3s+5}{s(s^2+s-6)} = -\frac{5}{6s} + \frac{11}{10(s-2)} - \frac{4}{15(s+3)} .$$

19. First observe that the quadratic polynomial s^2+2s+2 is irreducible because the discriminant $2^2 - 4(1)(2) = -4$ is negative. Since the denominator has one nonrepeated linear factor and one nonrepeated quadratic factor, we can write

$$\frac{1}{(s-3)(s^2+2s+2)} = \frac{1}{(s-3)[(s+1)^2+1]} = \frac{A}{s-3} + \frac{B(s+1)+C}{(s+1)^2+1},$$

where we have chosen a form which is more convenient for taking the inverse Laplace transform. Clearing fractions gives us

$$1 = A\left[(s+1)^2+1\right] + \left[B(s+1)+C\right](s-3). \tag{7.11}$$

With $s = 3$, this yields $1 = 17A$ so that $A = 1/17$. Substituting $s = -1$, we see that $1 = A(1)+C(-4)$, or $C = (A-1)/4 = -4/17$. Finally, the coefficient $A+B$ at s^2 in the right-hand side of (7.11) must be the same as in the left-hand side, that is, 0. So $B = -A = -1/17$ and

$$\frac{1}{(s-3)(s^2+2s+2)} = \frac{1}{17}\left[\frac{1}{s-3} - \frac{s+1}{(s+1)^2+1} - \frac{4}{(s+1)^2+1}\right].$$

21. Since the denominator contains only nonrepeated linear factors, the partial fractions decomposition has the form

$$\frac{6s^2-13s+2}{s(s-1)(s-6)} = \frac{A}{s} + \frac{B}{s-1} + \frac{C}{s-6} = \frac{A(s-1)(s-6)+Bs(s-6)+Cs(s-1)}{s(s-1)(s-6)} .$$

Therefore,

$$6s^2 - 13s + 2 = A(s-1)(s-6) + Bs(s-6) + Cs(s-1).$$

Evaluating both sides of this equation for $s = 0$, $s = 1$, and $s = 6$, we find constants A, B, and C.

$$\begin{aligned} s = 0: &\quad 2 = 6A &\Rightarrow&\quad A = 1/3,\\ s = 1: &\quad -5 = -5B &\Rightarrow&\quad B = 1,\\ s = 6: &\quad 140 = 30C &\Rightarrow&\quad C = 14/3. \end{aligned}$$

Hence,

$$\frac{6s^2-13s+2}{s(s-1)(s-6)}=\frac{1/3}{s}+\frac{1}{s-1}+\frac{14/3}{s-6}$$

and the linear property of the inverse Laplace transform yields

$$\mathcal{L}^{-1}\left\{\frac{6s^2-13s+2}{s(s-1)(s-6)}\right\}=\frac{1}{3}\mathcal{L}^{-1}\left\{\frac{1}{s}\right\}+\mathcal{L}^{-1}\left\{\frac{1}{s-1}\right\}+\frac{14}{3}\mathcal{L}^{-1}\left\{\frac{1}{s-6}\right\}=\frac{1}{3}+e^t+\frac{14}{3}e^{6t}.$$

23. In this problem, the denominator of $F(s)$ has a simple linear factor, $s+1$, and a double linear factor, $s+3$. Thus, the decomposition is the form

$$\frac{5s^2+34s+53}{(s+3)^2(s+1)}=\frac{A}{(s+3)^2}+\frac{B}{s+3}+\frac{C}{s+1}=\frac{A(s+1)+B(s+1)(s+3)+C(s+3)^2}{(s+3)^2(s+1)}.$$

Therefore, we must have

$$5s^2+34s+53=A(s+1)+B(s+1)(s+3)+C(s+3)^2.$$

Substitutions $s=-3$ and $s=-1$ yield values of A and C, respectively.

$$\begin{aligned} s=-3: &\quad -4=-2A \quad \Rightarrow \quad A=2,\\ s=-1: &\quad 24=4C \quad \Rightarrow \quad C=6. \end{aligned}$$

To find B, we take, say, $s=0$ and get

$$53=A+3B+9C \qquad \Rightarrow \qquad B=\frac{53-A-9C}{3}=-1.$$

Hence,

$$\begin{aligned} \mathcal{L}^{-1}\left\{\frac{5s^2+34s+53}{(s+3)^2(s+1)}\right\}(t) &= 2\mathcal{L}^{-1}\left\{\frac{1}{(s+3)^2}\right\}(t)-\mathcal{L}^{-1}\left\{\frac{1}{s+3}\right\}(t)+6\mathcal{L}^{-1}\left\{\frac{1}{s+1}\right\}(t)\\ &= 2te^{-3t}-e^{-3t}+6e^{-t}. \end{aligned}$$

25. Observing that the quadratic $s^2+2s+5=(s+1)^2+2^2$ is irreducible, the partial fractions decomposition for $F(s)$ has the form

$$\frac{7s^2+23s+30}{(s-2)(s^2+2s+5)}=\frac{A}{s-2}+\frac{B(s+1)+C(2)}{(s+1)^2+2^2}.$$

Clearing fractions gives us

$$7s^2 + 23s + 30 = A\left[(s+1)^2 + 4\right] + \left[B(s+1) + C(2)\right](s-2).$$

With $s = 2$, this yields $104 = 13A$ so that $A = 8$; $s = -1$ gives $14 = A(4) + C(-6)$, or $C = 3$. Finally, the coefficient $A + B$ at s^2 in the right-hand side must match the one in the left-hand side, which is 7. So $B = 7 - A = -1$. Therefore,

$$\frac{7s^2 + 23s + 30}{(s-2)(s^2+2s+5)} = \frac{8}{s-2} + \frac{-(s+1) + 3(2)}{(s+1)^2 + 2^2},$$

which yields

$$\begin{aligned}\mathcal{L}^{-1}\left\{\frac{7s^2 + 23s + 30}{(s-2)(s^2+2s+5)}\right\} &= 8\mathcal{L}^{-1}\left\{\frac{1}{s-2}\right\} - \mathcal{L}^{-1}\left\{\frac{s+1}{(s+1)^2+2^2}\right\} + 3\mathcal{L}^{-1}\left\{\frac{2}{(s+1)^2+2^2}\right\}\\ &= 8e^{2t} - e^{-t}\cos 2t + 3e^{-t}\sin 2t\,.\end{aligned}$$

27. First, we find $F(s)$.

$$F(s)\left(s^2 - 4\right) = \frac{5}{s+1} \qquad \Rightarrow \qquad F(s) = \frac{5}{(s+1)(s^2-4)} = \frac{5}{(s+1)(s-2)(s+2)}\,.$$

The partial fractions expansion yields

$$\frac{5}{(s+1)(s-2)(s+2)} = \frac{A}{s+1} + \frac{B}{s-2} + \frac{C}{s+2}\,.$$

Clearing fractions gives us

$$5 = A(s-2)(s+2) + B(s+1)(s+2) + C(s+1)(s-2).$$

With $s = -1$, $s = 2$, and $s = -2$ this yields $A = -5/3$, $B = 5/12$, and $C = 5/4$. So,

$$\begin{aligned}\mathcal{L}^{-1}\{F(s)\}(t) &= -\frac{5}{3}\mathcal{L}^{-1}\left\{\frac{1}{s+1}\right\}(t) + \frac{5}{12}\mathcal{L}^{-1}\left\{\frac{1}{s-2}\right\}(t) + \frac{5}{4}\mathcal{L}^{-1}\left\{\frac{1}{s+2}\right\}(t)\\ &= -\frac{5}{3}e^{-t} + \frac{5}{12}e^{2t} + \frac{5}{4}e^{-2t}\,.\end{aligned}$$

29. Solving for $F(s)$ yields

$$F(s) = \frac{10s^2 + 12s + 14}{(s+2)(s^2 - 2s + 2)} = \frac{10s^2 + 12s + 14}{(s+2)[(s-1)^2 + 1]}\,.$$

Since, in the denominator, we have nonrepeated linear and quadratic factors, we seek for the decomposition

$$\frac{10s^2+12s+14}{(s+2)[(s-1)^2+1]}=\frac{A}{s+2}+\frac{B(s-1)+C(1)}{(s-1)^2+1}.$$

Clearing fractions, we conclude that

$$10s^2+12s+14=A[(s-1)^2+1]+[B(s-1)+C](s+2).$$

Substitution $s=-2$ into this equation yields $30=10A$ or $A=3$. With $s=1$, we get $36=A+3C$ and so $C=(36-A)/3=11$. Finally, substitution $s=0$ results $14=2A+2(C-B)$ or $B=A+C-7=7$. Now we apply the linearity of the inverse Laplace transform and obtain

$$\begin{aligned}\mathcal{L}^{-1}\{F(s)\}(t) &= 3\mathcal{L}^{-1}\left\{\frac{1}{s+2}\right\}(t)+7\mathcal{L}^{-1}\left\{\frac{s-1}{(s-1)^2+1}\right\}(t)+11\mathcal{L}^{-1}\left\{\frac{1}{(s-1)^2+1}\right\}(t)\\ &= 3e^{-2t}+7e^t\cos t+11e^t\sin t.\end{aligned}$$

31. Functions $f_1(t)$, $f_2(t)$, and $f_3(t)$ coincide for all t in $[0,\infty)$ except a finite number of points. Since the Laplace transform a function is a definite integral, it does not depend on values of the function at finite number of points. Therefore, in (a), (b), and (c) we have one and the same answer, that is

$$\mathcal{L}\{f_1(t)\}(s)=\mathcal{L}\{f_2(t)\}(s)=\mathcal{L}\{f_3(t)\}(s)=\mathcal{L}\{t\}(s)=\frac{1}{s^2}.$$

By Definition 4, the inverse Laplace transform is a continuous function on $[0,\infty)$. $f_3(t)=t$ clearly satisfies this condition while $f_1(t)$ and $f_2(t)$ have removable discontinuities at $t=2$ and $t=1,6$, respectively. Therefore,

$$\mathcal{L}^{-1}\left\{\frac{1}{s^2}\right\}(t)=f_3(t)=t.$$

33. We are looking for $\mathcal{L}^{-1}\{F(s)\}(t)=f(t)$. According to the formula given just before this problem,

$$f(t)=\frac{-1}{t}\mathcal{L}^{-1}\left\{\frac{dF}{ds}\right\}(t)$$

(take $n = 1$ in the formula). Since

$$F(s) = \ln\left(\frac{s+2}{s-5}\right) = \ln(s+2) - \ln(s-5),$$

we have

$$\begin{aligned} \frac{dF(s)}{ds} &= \frac{d}{ds}\left(\ln(s+2) - \ln(s-5)\right) = \frac{1}{s+2} - \frac{1}{s-5} \\ \Rightarrow \quad \mathcal{L}^{-1}\left\{\frac{dF}{ds}\right\}(t) &= \mathcal{L}^{-1}\left\{\frac{1}{s+2} - \frac{1}{s-5}\right\}(t) = e^{-2t} - e^{5t} \\ \Rightarrow \quad \mathcal{L}^{-1}\left\{F(s)\right\}(t) &= \frac{-1}{t}\left(e^{-2t} - e^{5t}\right) = \frac{e^{5t} - e^{-2t}}{t}. \end{aligned}$$

35. Taking the derivative of $F(s)$, we get

$$\frac{dF(s)}{ds} = \frac{d}{ds}\ln\frac{s^2+9}{s^2+1} = \frac{d}{ds}\left[\ln(s^2+9) - \ln(s^2+1)\right] = \frac{2s}{s^2+9} - \frac{2s}{s^2+1}.$$

So, using the linear property of the inverse Laplace transform, we obtain

$$\mathcal{L}^{-1}\left\{\frac{dF(s)}{ds}\right\}(t) = 2\mathcal{L}^{-1}\left\{\frac{s}{s^2+9}\right\}(t) - 2\mathcal{L}^{-1}\left\{\frac{s}{s^2+1}\right\}(t) = 2(\cos 3t - \cos t).$$

Thus

$$\mathcal{L}^{-1}\left\{F(s)\right\}(t) = \frac{-1}{t}\mathcal{L}^{-1}\left\{\frac{dF(s)}{ds}\right\}(t) = \frac{2(\cos t - \cos 3t)}{t}.$$

37. By the definition, both, $\mathcal{L}^{-1}\{F_1\}(t)$ and $\mathcal{L}^{-1}\{F_2\}(t)$, are continuous functions on $[0, \infty)$. Therefore, their sum, $\left(\mathcal{L}^{-1}\{F_1\} + \mathcal{L}^{-1}\{F_2\}\right)(t)$, is also continuous on $[0, \infty)$. Furthermore, the linearity of the Laplace transform yields

$$\mathcal{L}\left\{\left(\mathcal{L}^{-1}\{F_1\} + \mathcal{L}^{-1}\{F_2\}\right)\right\}(s) = \mathcal{L}\left\{\mathcal{L}^{-1}\{F_1\}\right\}(s) + \mathcal{L}\left\{\mathcal{L}^{-1}\{F_2\}\right\}(s) = F_1(s) + F_2(s).$$

Therefore, $\mathcal{L}^{-1}\{F_1\} + \mathcal{L}^{-1}\{F_2\}$ is a continuous function on $[0, \infty)$ whose Laplace transform is $F_1 + F_2$. By the definition of the inverse Laplace transform, this function is the inverse Laplace transform of $F_1 + F_2$, that is,

$$\mathcal{L}^{-1}\{F_1\}(t) + \mathcal{L}^{-1}\{F_2\}(t) = \mathcal{L}^{-1}\{F_1 + F_2\}(t),$$

and (3) in Theorem 7 is proved.

To show (4), we use the continuity of $\mathcal{L}^{-1}\{F\}$ to conclude that $c\mathcal{L}^{-1}\{F\}$ is a continuous function. Since the linearity of the Laplace transform yields

$$\mathcal{L}\left\{c\mathcal{L}^{-1}\{F\}\right\}(s) = c\mathcal{L}\left\{\mathcal{L}^{-1}\{F\}\right\}(s) = cF(s),$$

we have $c\mathcal{L}^{-1}\{F\}(t) = \mathcal{L}^{-1}\{cF\}(t)$.

39. In this problem, the denominator $Q(s) := s(s-1)(s+2)$ has only nonrepeated linear factors, and so the partial fractions decomposition has the form

$$F(s) := \frac{2s+1}{s(s-1)(s+2)} = \frac{A}{s} + \frac{B}{s-1} + \frac{C}{s+2}.$$

To find A, B, and C, we use the residue formula in Problem 38. This yields

$$\begin{aligned}
A &= \lim_{s\to 0} sF(s) = \lim_{s\to 0} \frac{2s+1}{(s-1)(s+2)} = \frac{2(0)+1}{(0-1)(0+2)} = -\frac{1}{2}, \\
B &= \lim_{s\to 1} (s-1)F(s) = \lim_{s\to 1} \frac{2s+1}{s(s+2)} = \frac{2(1)+1}{(1)(1+2)} = 1, \\
C &= \lim_{s\to -2} (s+2)F(s) = \lim_{s\to 2} \frac{2s+1}{s(s-1)} = \frac{2(-2)+1}{(-2)(-2-1)} = -\frac{1}{2}.
\end{aligned}$$

Therefore,

$$\frac{2s+1}{s(s-1)(s+2)} = -\frac{1/2}{s} + \frac{1}{s-1} - \frac{1/2}{s+2}.$$

41. In notation of Problem 40,

$$P(s) = 3s^2 - 16s + 5, \qquad Q(s) = (s+1)(s-3)(s-2).$$

We can apply the Heaviside's expansion formula because $Q(s)$ has only nonrepeated linear factors. We need the values of $P(s)$ and $Q'(s)$ at the points $r_1 = -1$, $r_2 = 3$, and $r_3 = 2$. Using the product rule, we find that

$$Q'(s) = (s-3)(s-2) + (s+1)(s-2) + (s+1)(s-3),$$

and so

$$Q'(-1) = (-1-3)(-1-2) = 12, \quad Q'(3) = (3+1)(3-2) = 4, \quad Q'(2) = (2+1)(2-3) = -3.$$

Also, we compute

$$P(-1) = 24, \quad P(3) = -16, \quad P(2) = -15.$$

Therefore,

$$\mathcal{L}^{-1}\left\{\frac{3s^2 - 16s + 5}{(s+1)(s-3)(s-2)}\right\}(t) = \frac{P(-1)}{Q'(-1)}\, e^{(-1)t} + \frac{P(3)}{Q'(3)}\, e^{(3)t} + \frac{P(2)}{Q'(2)}\, e^{(2)t} = 2e^{-t} - 4e^{3t} + 5e^{2t}.$$

43. Since $s^2 - 2s + 5 = (s-1)^2 + 2^2$, we see that the denominator of $F(s)$ has nonrepeated linear factor $s + 2$ and nonrepeated irreducible quadratic factor $s^2 - 2s + 5$ with $\alpha = 1$ and $\beta = 2$ (in notation of Problem 40). Thus the partial fractions decomposition has the form

$$F(s) = \frac{6s^2 + 28}{(s^2 - 2s + 5)(s+2)} = \frac{A(s-1) + 2B}{(s-1)^2 + 2^2} + \frac{C}{s+2}.$$

We find C by applying the real residue formula derived in Problem 38.

$$C = \lim_{s \to -2} \frac{(s+2)(6s^2 + 28)}{(s^2 - 2s + 5)(s+2)} = \lim_{s \to -2} \frac{6s^2 + 28}{s^2 - 2s + 5} = \frac{52}{13} = 4.$$

Next, we use the complex residue formula given in Problem 42, to find A and B. Since $\alpha = 1$ and $\beta = 2$, the formula becomes

$$2B + i2A = \lim_{s \to 1+2i} \frac{(s^2 - 2s + 5)(6s^2 + 28)}{(s^2 - 2s + 5)(s+2)} = \lim_{s \to 1+2i} \frac{6s^2 + 28}{s+2} = \frac{6(1+2i)^2 + 28}{(1+2i) + 2} = \frac{10 + 24i}{3 + 2i}.$$

Dividing we get

$$2B + i2A = \frac{(10 + 24i)(3 - 2i)}{(3 + 2i)(3 - 2i)} = \frac{78 + 52i}{13} = 6 + 4i.$$

Taking the real and imaginary parts yields

$$\begin{aligned} 2B &= 6, \\ 2A &= 4 \end{aligned} \quad \Rightarrow \quad \begin{aligned} B &= 3, \\ A &= 2. \end{aligned}$$

Therefore,

$$\frac{6s^2 + 28}{(s^2 - 2s + 5)(s+2)} = \frac{2(s-1) + 2(3)}{(s-1)^2 + 2^2} + \frac{4}{s+2}.$$

EXERCISES 7.5: Solving Initial Value Problems, page 383

1. Let $Y(s) := \mathcal{L}\{y\}(s)$. Taking the Laplace transform of both sides of the given differential equation and using its linearity, we obtain

$$\mathcal{L}\{y''\}(s) - 2\mathcal{L}\{y'\}(s) + 5Y(s) = \mathcal{L}\{0\}(s) = 0. \tag{7.12}$$

We can express $\mathcal{L}\{y''\}(s)$ and $\mathcal{L}\{y'\}(s)$ in terms of $Y(s)$ using the initial conditions and Theorem 5 in Section 7.3.

$$\begin{aligned} \mathcal{L}\{y'\}(s) &= sY(s) - y(0) = sY(s) - 2, \\ \mathcal{L}\{y''\}(s) &= s^2Y(s) - sy(0) - y'(0) = s^2Y(s) - 2s - 4. \end{aligned}$$

Substituting back into (7.12) and solving for $Y(s)$ yield

$$\begin{aligned} &\left[s^2Y(s) - 2s - 4\right] - 2\left[sY(s) - 2\right] + 5Y(s) = 0 \\ \Rightarrow \quad & Y(s)\left(s^2 - 2s + 5\right) = 2s \\ \Rightarrow \quad & Y(s) = \frac{2s}{s^2 - 2s + 5} = \frac{2s}{(s-1)^2 + 2^2} = \frac{2(s-1)}{(s-1)^2 + 2^2} + \frac{2}{(s-1)^2 + 2^2}. \end{aligned}$$

Applying now the inverse Laplace transform to both sides, we obtain

$$y(t) = 2\mathcal{L}^{-1}\left\{\frac{s-1}{(s-1)^2 + 2^2}\right\}(t) + \mathcal{L}^{-1}\left\{\frac{2}{(s-1)^2 + 2^2}\right\}(t) = 2e^t\cos 2t + e^t\sin 2t.$$

3. Let $Y(s) := \mathcal{L}\{y\}(s)$. Taking the Laplace transform of both sides of the given differential equation, $y'' + 6y' + 9y = 0$, and using the linearity of the Laplace transform, we obtain

$$\mathcal{L}\{y''\}(s) + 6\mathcal{L}\{y'\}(s) + 9Y(s) = 0.$$

We use formula (4), page 362, to express $\mathcal{L}\{y''\}(s)$ and $\mathcal{L}\{y'\}(s)$ in terms of $Y(s)$.

$$\begin{aligned} \mathcal{L}\{y'\}(s) &= sY(s) - y(0) = sY(s) + 1, \\ \mathcal{L}\{y''\}(s) &= s^2Y(s) - sy(0) - y'(0) = s^2Y(s) + s - 6. \end{aligned}$$

Therefore,

$$\left[s^2Y(s) + s - 6\right] + 6\left[sY(s) + 1\right] + 9Y(s) = 0$$

$$\Rightarrow \qquad Y(s)\left(s^2+6s+9\right)=-s$$
$$\Rightarrow \qquad Y(s)=\frac{-s}{s^2+6s+9}=\frac{-s}{(s+3)^2}=\frac{3}{(s+3)^2}-\frac{1}{s+3},$$

where the last equality comes from the partial fraction expansion of $-s/(s+3^2)$. We apply the inverse Laplace transform to both sides and use Table 7.1 to obtain

$$y(t)=3\mathcal{L}^{-1}\left\{\frac{1}{(s+3)^2}\right\}(t)-\mathcal{L}^{-1}\left\{\frac{1}{s+3}\right\}(t)=3te^{-3t}-e^{-3t}.$$

5. Let $W(s)=\mathcal{L}\{w\}(s)$. Then taking the Laplace transform of the equation and using linearity yield

$$\mathcal{L}\{w''\}(s)+W(s)=\mathcal{L}\left\{t^2+2\right\}(s)=\mathcal{L}\left\{t^2\right\}(s)+2\mathcal{L}\{1\}(s)=\frac{2}{s^3}+\frac{2}{s}.$$

Since $\mathcal{L}\{w''\}(s)=s^2W(s)-sw(0)-w'(0)=s^2W(s)-s+1$, we have

$$\left[s^2W(s)-s+1\right]+W(s)=\frac{2}{s^3}+\frac{2}{s}$$
$$\Rightarrow \qquad \left(s^2+1\right)W(s)=s-1+\frac{2(s^2+1)}{s^3} \qquad \Rightarrow \qquad W(s)=\frac{s}{s^2+1}-\frac{1}{s^2+1}+\frac{2}{s^3}.$$

Now, taking the inverse Laplace transform, we obtain

$$w=\mathcal{L}^{-1}\left\{\frac{s}{s^2+1}\right\}-\mathcal{L}^{-1}\left\{\frac{1}{s^2+1}\right\}+\mathcal{L}^{-1}\left\{\frac{2}{s^3}\right\}=\cos t-\sin t+t^2.$$

7. Let $Y(s):=\mathcal{L}\{y\}(s)$. Using the initial conditions and Theorem 5 in Section 7.3 we can express $\mathcal{L}\{y''\}(s)$ and $\mathcal{L}\{y'\}(s)$ in terms of $Y(s)$, namely,

$$\mathcal{L}\{y'\}(s)=sY(s)-y(0)=sY(s)-5,$$
$$\mathcal{L}\{y''\}(s)=s^2Y(s)-sy(0)-y'(0)=s^2Y(s)-5s+4.$$

Taking the Laplace transform of both sides of the given differential equation and using its linearity, we obtain

$$\mathcal{L}\{y''-7y'+10y\}(s)=\mathcal{L}\{9\cos t+7\sin t\}(s)$$
$$\Rightarrow \qquad \left[s^2Y(s)-5s+4\right]-7\left[sY(s)-5\right]+10Y(s)=\frac{9s}{s^2+1}+\frac{7}{s^2+1}$$

$$\Rightarrow \qquad \left(s^2-7s+10\right)Y(s)=\frac{9s+7}{s^2+1}+5s-39=\frac{5s^3-39s^2+14s-32}{s^2+1}$$

$$\Rightarrow \qquad Y(s)=\frac{9s+7}{s^2+1}+5s-39=\frac{5s^3-39s^2+14s-32}{(s^2+1)(s^2-7s+10)}=\frac{5s^3-39s^2+14s-32}{(s^2+1)(s-5)(s-2)}\,.$$

The partial fractions decomposition of $Y(s)$ has the form

$$\frac{5s^3-39s^2+14s-32}{(s^2+1)(s-5)(s-2)}=\frac{As+B}{s^2+1}+\frac{C}{s-5}+\frac{D}{s-2}\,.$$

Clearing fractions yields

$$5s^3-39s^2+14s-32=(As+B)(s-5)(s-2)+C(s^2+1)(s-2)+D(s^2+1)(s-5).$$

We substitute $s=5$ and $s=2$ to find C and D, resprectively, and then $s=0$ to find B.

$$\begin{aligned}
s=5: &\quad -312=78C & \Rightarrow &\quad C=-4,\\
s=2: &\quad -120=-15D & \Rightarrow &\quad D=8,\\
s=0: &\quad -32=10B-2C-5D & \Rightarrow &\quad B=0.
\end{aligned}$$

Equating the coefficients at s^3, we also get $A+C+D=5$, which implies that $A=1$. Thus

$$Y(s)=\frac{s}{s^2+1}-\frac{4}{s-5}+\frac{8}{s-2} \qquad \Rightarrow \qquad y(t)=\mathcal{L}^{-1}\left\{Y(s)\right\}(t)=\cos t-4e^{5t}+8e^{2t}\,.$$

9. First, note that the initial conditions are given at $t=1$. Thus, to use the method of Laplace transform, we make a shift in t and move the initial conditions to $t=0$.

$$\begin{aligned}
&z''(t)+5z'(t)-6z(t)=21e^{t-1}\\
\Rightarrow \qquad & z''(t+1)+5z'(t+1)-6z(t+1)=21e^{(t+1)-1}=21e^{t}.
\end{aligned} \tag{7.13}$$

Now, let $y(t):=z(t+1)$. Then the chain rule yields

$$\begin{aligned}
y'(t)&=z'(t+1)(t+1)'=z'(t+1),\\
y''(t)&=[y'(t)]'=z''(t+1)(t+1)'=z''(t+1),
\end{aligned}$$

and (7.13) becomes

$$y''(t)+5y'(t)-6y(t)=21e^{t} \tag{7.14}$$

with initial conditions

$$y(0) = z(0+1) = z(1) = -1, \qquad y'(0) = z'(0+1) = z'(1) = 9.$$

With $Y(s) := \mathcal{L}\{y(t)\}(s)$, we apply the Laplace transform to both sides of (7.14) and obtain

$$\mathcal{L}\{y''\}(s) + 5\mathcal{L}\{y'\}(s) - 6Y(s) = \mathcal{L}\{21e^t\}(s) = \frac{21}{s-1}. \tag{7.15}$$

By Theorem 5, Section 7.3,

$$\begin{aligned}\mathcal{L}\{y'\}(s) &= sY(s) - y(0) = sY(s) + 1, \\ \mathcal{L}\{y''\}(s) &= s^2Y(s) - sy(0) - y'(0) = s^2Y(s) + s - 9.\end{aligned}$$

Substituting these expressions back into (7.15) and solving for $Y(s)$ yield

$$\begin{aligned}&\left[s^2Y(s) + s - 9\right] + 5\left[sY(s) + 1\right] - 6Y(s) = \frac{21}{s-1} \\ \Rightarrow \quad & \left(s^2 + 5s - 6\right)Y(s) = \frac{21}{s-1} - s + 4 = \frac{-s^2+5s+17}{s-1} \\ \Rightarrow \quad & Y(s) = \frac{-s^2+5s+17}{(s-1)(s^2+5s-6)} = \frac{-s^2+5s+17}{(s-1)(s-1)(s+6)} = \frac{-s^2+5s+17}{(s-1)^2(s+6)}.\end{aligned}$$

The partial fractions decomposition for $Y(s)$ has the form

$$\frac{-s^2+5s+17}{(s-1)^2(s+6)} = \frac{A}{(s-1)^2} + \frac{B}{s-1} + \frac{C}{s+6}.$$

Clearing fractions yields

$$-s^2 + 5s + 17 = A(s+6) + B(s-1)(s+6) + C(s-1)^2.$$

Substitutions $s = 1$ and $s = -6$ give $A = 3$ and $C = -1$. Also, with $s = 0$, we have $17 = 6A - 6B + C$ or $B = 0$. Therefore,

$$Y(s) = \frac{3}{(s-1)^2} - \frac{1}{s+6} \qquad \Rightarrow \qquad y(t) = \mathcal{L}^{-1}\left\{\frac{3}{(s-1)^2} - \frac{1}{s+6}\right\}(t) = 3te^t - e^{-6t}.$$

Finally, shifting the argument back, we obtain

$$z(t) = y(t-1) = 3(t-1)e^{t-1} - e^{-6(t-1)}.$$

11. As in the previous problem (and in Example 3 in the text), we first need to shift the initial conditions to 0. If we set $v(t) = y(t+2)$, the initial value problem for $v(t)$ becomes

$$v''(t) - v(t) = (t+2) - 2 = t, \qquad v(0) = y(2) = 3, \; v'(0) = y'(2) = 0.$$

Taking the Laplace transform of both sides of this new differential equation gives us

$$\mathcal{L}\{v''\}(s) - \mathcal{L}\{v\}(s) = \mathcal{L}\{t\}(s) = \frac{1}{s^2}.$$

If we denote $V(s) := \mathcal{L}\{v\}(s)$ and express $\mathcal{L}\{v''\}(s)$ in terms of $V(s)$ using (4) in Section 4.3 (with $n = 2$), that is, $\mathcal{L}\{v''\}(s) = s^2V(s) - 3s$, we obtain

$$\begin{aligned} & \left[s^2V(s) - 3s\right] - V(s) = \frac{1}{s^2} \\ \Rightarrow \quad & V(s) = \frac{3s^3+1}{s^2(s^2-1)} = \frac{3s^3+1}{s^2(s+1)(s-1)} = -\frac{1}{s^2} + \frac{1}{s+1} + \frac{2}{s-1}. \end{aligned}$$

Hence,

$$v(t) = \mathcal{L}^{-1}\{V(s)\}(t) = \mathcal{L}^{-1}\left\{-\frac{1}{s^2} + \frac{1}{s+1} + \frac{2}{s-1}\right\}(t) = -t + e^{-t} + 2e^t.$$

Since $v(t) = y(t+2)$, we have $y(t) = v(t-2)$ and so

$$y(t) = -(t-2) + e^{-(t-2)} + 2e^{t-2} = 2 - t + e^{2-t} + 2e^{t-2}.$$

13. To shift the initial conditions to $t = 0$, we make the substitution $x(t) := y(t + \pi/2)$ in the original equation and use the fact that

$$x'(t) := y'(t+\pi/2), \qquad x''(t) := y''(t+\pi/2).$$

This yields

$$\begin{aligned} & y''(t) - y'(t) - 2y(t) = -8\cos t - 2\sin t \\ \Rightarrow \quad & -8\cos\left(t+\frac{\pi}{2}\right) - 2\sin\left(t+\frac{\pi}{2}\right) = -8\cos\left(t+\frac{\pi}{2}\right) - 2\sin\left(t+\frac{\pi}{2}\right) = 8\sin t - 2\cos t \\ \Rightarrow \quad & x''(t) - x'(t) - 2x(t) = 8\sin t - 2\cos t, \qquad x(0) = 1, \; x'(0) = 0. \end{aligned}$$

Taking the Laplace transform of both sides in this last differential equation and using the fact that, with $X(s) := \mathcal{L}\{x\}(s)$,

$$\mathcal{L}\{x'\}(s) = sX(s) - 1 \quad \text{and} \quad \mathcal{L}\{x''\}(s) = s^2X(s) - s$$

(which comes from the initial conditions and (4) in Section 7.3), we obtain

$$\begin{aligned}
&\left[s^2X(s) - s\right] - \left[sX(s) - 1\right] - 2X(s) = \mathcal{L}\{8\sin t - 2\cos t\}(s) = \frac{8}{s^2+1} - \frac{2s}{s^2+1} \\
\Rightarrow \quad & \left(s^2 - s - 2\right)X(s) = \frac{8-2s}{s^2+1} + s - 1 = \frac{s^3 - s^2 - s + 7}{s^2+1} \\
\Rightarrow \quad & X(s) = \frac{s^3 - s^2 - s + 7}{(s^2+1)(s^2-s-2)} = \frac{s^3 - s^2 - s + 7}{(s^2+1)(s-2)(s+1)}.
\end{aligned}$$

We seek for the partial fractions decomposition of $X(s)$ in the form

$$\frac{s^3 - s^2 - s + 7}{(s^2+1)(s-2)(s+1)} = \frac{As+B}{s^2+1} + \frac{C}{(s-2)} + \frac{D}{s+1}.$$

Solving yields

$$A = \frac{7}{5}, \quad B = -\frac{11}{5}, \quad C = \frac{3}{5}, \quad D = -1.$$

Therefore,

$$\begin{aligned}
& X(s) = \frac{(7/5)s}{s^2+1} + \frac{(-11/5)}{s^2+1} + \frac{(3/5)}{(s-2)} - \frac{1}{s+1} \\
\Rightarrow \quad & x(t) = \mathcal{L}^{-1}\{X(s)\}(t) = \frac{7}{5}\cos t - \frac{11}{5}\sin t + \frac{3}{5}e^{2t} - e^{-t}.
\end{aligned}$$

Finally, since $y(t) = x(t - \pi/2)$, we obtain the solution

$$\begin{aligned}
y(t) &= \frac{7}{5}\cos\left(t - \frac{\pi}{2}\right) - \frac{11}{5}\sin\left(t - \frac{\pi}{2}\right) + \frac{3}{5}e^{2(t-\pi/2)} - e^{-(t-\pi/2)} \\
&= \frac{7}{5}\sin t + \frac{11}{5}\cos t + \frac{3}{5}e^{2t-\pi} - e^{(\pi/2)-t}
\end{aligned}$$

15. Taking the Laplace transform of $y'' - 3y' + 2y = \cos t$ and applying the linearity of the Laplace transform yields

$$\mathcal{L}\{y''\}(s) - 3\mathcal{L}\{y'\}(s) + 2\mathcal{L}\{y\}(s) = \mathcal{L}\{\cos t\}(s) = \frac{s}{s^2+1}. \tag{7.16}$$

If we put $Y(s) = \mathcal{L}\{y\}(s)$ and apply the property (4), page 362 of the text, we get

$$\mathcal{L}\{y'\}(s) = sY(s), \qquad \mathcal{L}\{y''\}(s) = s^2Y(s) + 1.$$

Substitution back into (7.16) yields

$$\begin{aligned} \left[s^2Y(s)+1\right] - 3\left[sY(s)\right] + 2Y(s) &= \frac{s}{s^2+1} \\ \Rightarrow \qquad \left(s^2-3s+2\right)Y(s) &= \frac{s}{s^2+1} - 1 = \frac{-s^2+s-1}{s^2+1} \\ \Rightarrow \qquad Y(s) &= \frac{-s^2+s-1}{(s^2+1)(s^2-3s+2)} = \frac{-s^2+s-1}{(s^2+1)(s-1)(s-2)}. \end{aligned}$$

17. With $Y(s) := \mathcal{L}\{y\}(s)$, we find that

$$\mathcal{L}\{y'\}(s) = sY(s) - y(0) = sY(s) - 1, \quad \mathcal{L}\{y''\}(s) = s^2Y(s) - sy(0) - y'(0) = s^2Y(s) - s,$$

and so the Laplace transform of both sides of the original equation yields

$$\begin{aligned} \mathcal{L}\{y''+y'-y\}(s) &= \mathcal{L}\left\{t^3\right\}(s) \\ \Rightarrow \qquad \left[s^2Y(s)-s\right] + \left[sY(s)-1\right] - Y(s) &= \frac{6}{s^4} \\ \Rightarrow \qquad Y(s) = \frac{1}{s^2+s-1}\left(\frac{6}{s^4}+s+1\right) &= \frac{s^5+s^4+6}{s^4(s^2+s-1)}. \end{aligned}$$

19. Let us denote $Y(s) := \mathcal{L}\{y\}(s)$. From the initial conditions and formula (4) on page 362 of the text we get

$$\mathcal{L}\{y'\}(s) = sY(s) - y(0) = sY(s) - 1, \quad \mathcal{L}\{y''\}(s) = s^2Y(s) - sy(0) - y'(0) = s^2Y(s) - s - 1.$$

The Laplace transform, applied to both sides of the given equation, yields

$$\begin{aligned} \left[s^2Y(s)-s-1\right] + 5\left[sY(s)-1\right] - Y(s) &= \mathcal{L}\left\{e^t\right\}(s) - \mathcal{L}\{1\}(s) = \frac{1}{s-1} - \frac{1}{s} = \frac{1}{s(s-1)} \\ \Rightarrow \qquad \left(s^2+5s-1\right)Y(s) &= \frac{1}{s(s-1)} + s + 6 = \frac{s^3+5s^2-6s+1}{s(s-1)} \\ \Rightarrow \qquad Y(s) &= \frac{s^3+5s^2-6s+1}{s(s-1)(s^2+5s-1)}. \end{aligned}$$

21. Applying the Laplace transform to both sides of the given equation yields

$$\mathcal{L}\{y''\}(s) - 2\mathcal{L}\{y'\}(s) + \mathcal{L}\{t\}(s) = \mathcal{L}\{\cos t\}(s) - \mathcal{L}\{\sin t\}(s) = \frac{s-1}{s^2+1}.$$

If $\mathcal{L}\{y\}(s) =: Y(s)$, then it follows from the initial conditions and (4) on page 362 of the text that

$$\mathcal{L}\{y'\}(s) = sY(s) - 1, \quad \mathcal{L}\{y''\}(s) = s^2Y(s) - s - 3.$$

Therefore, $Y(s)$ satisfies

$$\left[s^2Y(s) - s - 3\right] - 2\left[sY(s) - 1\right] + Y(s) = \frac{s-1}{s^2+1}.$$

Solving for $Y(s)$ gives us

$$\begin{aligned} \left(s^2 - 2s + 1\right)Y(s) &= \frac{s-1}{s^2+1} + s + 1 = \frac{s^3+s^2+2s}{s^2+1} \\ \Rightarrow \qquad Y(s) &= \frac{s^3+s^2+2s}{(s^2+1)(s^2-2s+1)} = \frac{s^3+s^2+2s}{(s^2+1)(s-1)^2}. \end{aligned}$$

23. In this equation, the right-hand side is a piecewise defined function. Let us find its Laplace transform first.

$$\begin{aligned} \mathcal{L}\{g(t)\}(s) &= \int_0^\infty e^{-st}g(t)\,dt = \int_0^2 e^{-st}t\,dt + \int_2^\infty e^{-st}5\,dt \\ &= \left.\frac{te^{-st}}{-s}\right|_0^2 - \int_0^2 \frac{e^{-st}}{-s}\,dt + \lim_{N\to\infty} \left.\frac{5e^{-st}}{-s}\right|_2^N \\ &= -\left[\frac{2e^{-2s}}{s}\right] - \left[\frac{e^{-2s}}{s^2} + \frac{1}{s^2}\right] + \frac{5e^{-2s}}{s} = \frac{1+3se^{-2s}-e^{-2s}}{s^2}, \end{aligned}$$

where we used integration by parts integrating $e^{-st}t$.

Using this formula and applying the Laplace transform to the given equation yields

$$\begin{aligned} &\mathcal{L}\{y''\}(s) + 4\mathcal{L}\{y\}(s) = \mathcal{L}\{g(t)\}(s) \\ \Rightarrow \qquad & s^2\mathcal{L}\{y\}(s) + s + 4\mathcal{L}\{y\}(s) = \mathcal{L}\{g(t)\}(s) \\ \Rightarrow \qquad & \left(s^2+4\right)\mathcal{L}\{y\}(s) = \mathcal{L}\{g(t)\}(s) - s = \frac{-s^3+1+3se^{-2s}-e^{-2s}}{s^2} \end{aligned}$$

$$\Rightarrow \qquad \mathcal{L}\{y\}(s) = \frac{-s^3 + 1 + 3se^{-2s} - e^{-2s}}{s^2(s^2+4)}.$$

25. Taking the Laplace transform of $y''' - y'' + y' - y = 0$ and applying the linearity of the Laplace transform yields

$$\mathcal{L}\{y'''\}(s) - \mathcal{L}\{y''\}(s) + \mathcal{L}\{y'\}(s) - \mathcal{L}\{y\}(s) = \mathcal{L}\{0\}(s) = 0. \tag{7.17}$$

If we denote $Y(s) := \mathcal{L}\{y\}(s)$ and and apply property (4) on page 362 of the text, we get

$$\mathcal{L}\{y'\}(s) = sY(s) - 1, \quad \mathcal{L}\{y''\}(s) = s^2Y(s) - s - 1, \; LTy''' = s^3Y(s) - s^2 - s - 3.$$

Combining these equations with (7.17) gives us

$$\begin{aligned} &\left[s^3Y(s) - s^2 - s - 3\right] - \left[s^2Y(s) - s - 1\right] + [sY(s) - 1] - Y(s) = 0 \\ \Rightarrow \qquad &\left(s^3 - s^2 + s - 1\right)Y(s) = s^2 + 3 \\ \Rightarrow \qquad &Y(s) = \frac{s^2+3}{s^3 - s^2 + s - 1} = \frac{s^2+3}{(s-1)(s^2+1)}. \end{aligned}$$

Expanding $Y(s)$ by partial fractions results

$$Y(s) = \frac{2}{s-1} - \frac{s+1}{s^2+1} = \frac{2}{s-1} - \frac{s}{s^2+1} - \frac{1}{s^2+1}.$$

From Table 7.1 on page 358 of the text, we see that

$$y(t) = \mathcal{L}^{-1}\{Y(s)\}(t) = 2e^t - \cos t - \sin t.$$

27. Let $Y(s) := \mathcal{L}\{y\}(s)$. Then, by Theorem 5 in Section 7.3,

$$\begin{aligned} &\mathcal{L}\{y'\}(s) = sY(s) - y(0) = sY(s) + 4, \\ &\mathcal{L}\{y''\}(s) = s^2Y(s) - sy(0) - y'(0) = s^2Y(s) + 4s - 4, \\ &\mathcal{L}\{y'''\}(s) = s^3Y(s) - s^2y(0) - sy'(0) - y''(0) = s^3Y(s) + 4s^2 - 4s + 2. \end{aligned}$$

Using these equations and applying the Laplace transform to both sides of the given differential equation, we get

$$\left[s^3Y(s) + 4s^2 - 4s + 2\right] + 3\left[s^2Y(s) + 4s - 4\right] + 3\left[sY(s) + 4\right] + Y(s) = 0$$

$$\Rightarrow \qquad \left(s^3+3s^2+3s+1\right)Y(s)+\left(4s^2+8s+2\right)=0$$

$$\Rightarrow \qquad Y(s)=-\frac{4s^2+8s+2}{s^3+3s^2+3s+1}=-\frac{4s^2+8s+2}{(s+1)^3}.$$

Therefore, the partial fractions decomposition of $Y(s)$ has the form

$$-\frac{4s^2+8s+2}{(s+1)^3}=\frac{A}{(s+1)^3}+\frac{B}{(s+1)^2}+\frac{C}{s+1}=\frac{A+B(s+1)+C(s+1)^2}{(s+1)^3}$$

$$\Rightarrow \qquad -(4s^2+8s+2)=A+B(s+1)+C(s+1)^2.$$

Substitution $s=-1$ yields $A=2$. Equating coefficients at s^2, we get $C=-4$. At last, substituting $s=0$ we obtain

$$-2=A+B+C \qquad \Rightarrow \qquad B=-2-A-C=0.$$

Therefore,

$$Y(s)=\frac{2}{(s+1)^3}+\frac{-4}{s+1} \qquad \Rightarrow \qquad y(t)=\mathcal{L}^{-1}\{Y\}(t)=t^2e^{-t}-4e^{-t}=\left(t^2-4\right)e^{-t}.$$

29. Using the initial conditions, $y(0)=a$ and $y'(0)=b$, and formula (4) on page 362 of the text, we conclude that

$$\mathcal{L}\{y'\}(s)=sY(s)-y(0)=sY(s)-a,$$
$$\mathcal{L}\{y''\}(s)=s^2Y(s)-sy(0)-y'(0)=s^2Y(s)-as-b,$$

where $Y(s)=\mathcal{L}\{y\}(s)$. Applying the Laplace transform to the original equation yields

$$\left[s^2Y(s)-as-b\right]-4\left[sY(s)-a\right]+3Y(s)=\mathcal{L}\{0\}(s)=0$$

$$\Rightarrow \qquad \left(s^2-4s+3\right)Y(s)=as+b-4a$$

$$\Rightarrow \qquad Y(s)=\frac{as+b-4a}{s^2-4s+3}=\frac{as+b-4a}{(s-1)(s-3)}=\frac{A}{s-1}+\frac{B}{s-3}.$$

Solving for A and B, we find that $A=(3a-b)/2$, $B=(b-a)/2$. Hence

$$Y(s)=\frac{(3a-b)/2}{s-1}+\frac{(b-a)/2}{s-3}$$

$$\Rightarrow \qquad y(t)=\mathcal{L}^{-1}\{Y\}(t)=\frac{3a-b}{2}\mathcal{L}^{-1}\left\{\frac{1}{s-1}\right\}(t)+\frac{b-a}{2}\mathcal{L}^{-1}\left\{\frac{1}{s-3}\right\}(t)$$

$$=\frac{3a-b}{2}e^t+\frac{b-a}{2}e^{3t}.$$

31. Similarly to Problem 29, we have

$$\mathcal{L}\{y'\}(s) = sY(s) - y(0) = sY(s) - a, \quad \mathcal{L}\{y''\}(s) = s^2Y(s) - sy(0) - y'(0) = s^2Y(s) - as - b,$$

with $Y(s) := \mathcal{L}\{y\}(s)$. Thus the Laplace transform of both sides of the the given equation yields

$$\begin{aligned} &\mathcal{L}\{y'' + 2y' + 2y\}(s) = \mathcal{L}\{5\}(s) \\ \Rightarrow \quad & \left[s^2Y(s) - as - b\right] + 2\left[sY(s) - a\right] + 2Y(s) = \frac{5}{s} \\ \Rightarrow \quad & \left(s^2 + 2s + 2\right)Y(s) = \frac{5}{s} + as + 2a + b = \frac{as^2 + (2a+b)s + 5}{s} \\ \Rightarrow \quad & Y(s) = \frac{as^2 + (2a+b)s + 5}{s(s^2 + 2s + 2)} = \frac{as^2 + (2a+b)s + 5}{s[(s+1)^2 + 1]}. \end{aligned}$$

We seek for an expansion of $Y(s)$ of the form

$$\frac{as^2 + (2a+b)s + 5}{s[(s+1)^2 + 1]} = \frac{A}{s} + \frac{B(s+1) + C}{(s+1)^2 + 1}.$$

Clearing fractions, we obtain

$$as^2 + (2a+b)s + 5 = A\left[(s+1)^2 + 1\right] + \left[B(s+1) + C\right]s.$$

Substitutions $s = 0$ and $s = -1$ give us

$$\begin{aligned} s = 0: \quad & 5 = 2A & \Rightarrow \quad & A = 5/2, \\ s = -1: \quad & 5 - a - b = A - C & \Rightarrow \quad & C = A + a + b - 5 = a + b - 5/2. \end{aligned}$$

To find B, we can compare coefficients at s^2:

$$a = A + B \quad \Rightarrow \quad B = a - A = a - 5/2.$$

So,

$$\begin{aligned} & Y(s) = \frac{5/2}{s} + \frac{(a - 5/2)(s+1)}{(s+1)^2 + 1} + \frac{a + b - 5/2}{(s+1)^2 + 1} \\ \Rightarrow \quad & y(t) = \mathcal{L}^{-1}\{Y\}(t) = \frac{5}{2} + \left(a - \frac{5}{2}\right)e^{-t}\cos t + \left(a + b - \frac{5}{2}\right)e^{-t}\sin t. \end{aligned}$$

33. By Theorem 6 in Section 7.3,

$$\mathcal{L}\left\{t^2y'(t)\right\}(s) = (-1)^2\frac{d^2}{ds^2}\left[\mathcal{L}\left\{y'(t)\right\}(s)\right] = \frac{d^2}{ds^2}\left[\mathcal{L}\left\{y'(t)\right\}(s)\right]. \tag{7.18}$$

On the other hand, equation (4) on page 362 says that

$$\mathcal{L}\left\{y'(t)\right\}(s) = sY(s) - y(0), \qquad Y(s) := \mathcal{L}\left\{y\right\}(s).$$

Substitution back into (7.18) yields

$$\begin{aligned}\mathcal{L}\left\{t^2y'(t)\right\}(s) &= \frac{d^2}{ds^2}\left[sY(s) - y(0)\right] = \frac{d}{ds}\left\{\frac{d}{ds}\left[sY(s) - y(0)\right]\right\}\\ &= \frac{d}{ds}\left[sY'(s) + Y(s)\right] = \left(sY''(s) + Y'(s)\right) + Y'(s) = sY''(s) + 2Y'(s).\end{aligned}$$

35. Taking the Laplace transform of $y'' + 3ty' - 6y = 1$ and applying the linearity of the Laplace transform yields

$$\mathcal{L}\left\{y''\right\}(s) + 3\mathcal{L}\left\{ty'\right\}(s) - 6\mathcal{L}\left\{y\right\}(s) = \mathcal{L}\left\{1\right\}(s) = \frac{1}{s}. \tag{7.19}$$

If we put $Y(s) = \mathcal{L}\left\{y\right\}(s)$ and apply property (4) on page 362 of the text with $n = 2$, we get

$$\mathcal{L}\left\{y''\right\}(s) = s^2Y(s) - sy(0) - y'(0) = s^2Y(s). \tag{7.20}$$

Furthermore, as it was shown in Example 4, Section 4.5,

$$\mathcal{L}\left\{ty'\right\}(s) = -sY'(s) - Y(s). \tag{7.21}$$

Substitution (7.20) and (7.21) back into (7.19) yields

$$\begin{aligned} s^2Y(s) + 3\left[-sY'(s) - Y(s)\right] - 6Y(s) &= \frac{1}{s}\\ \Rightarrow \qquad -3sY'(s) + \left(s^2 - 9\right)Y(s) &= \frac{1}{s}\\ \Rightarrow \qquad Y'(s) + \left(\frac{3}{s} - \frac{s}{3}\right)Y(s) &= -\frac{1}{3s^2}.\end{aligned}$$

This is a first order linear differential equation in $Y(s)$, which can be solved by the techniques of Section 2.3. Namely, it has the integrating factor

$$\mu(s) = \exp\left[\int\left(\frac{3}{s} - \frac{s}{3}\right)ds\right] = \exp\left[3\ln s - \frac{s^2}{6}\right] = s^3e^{-s^2/6}.$$

Thus

$$\begin{aligned} Y(s) &= \frac{1}{\mu(s)} \int \mu(s) \left(-\frac{1}{3s^2}\right) ds = \frac{1}{s^3 e^{-s^2/6}} \int \frac{-s}{3} e^{-s^2/6}\, ds \\ &= \frac{1}{s^3 e^{-s^2/6}} \left(e^{-s^2/6} + C\right) = \frac{1}{s^3}\left(1 + Ce^{s^2/6}\right). \end{aligned}$$

Just as in Example 4 on page 380 of the text, C must be zero in order to ensure that $Y(s) \to 0$ as $s \to \infty$. Thus $Y(s) = 1/s^3$, and from Table 7.1 on page 358 of the text we get

$$y(t) = \mathcal{L}^{-1}\left\{\frac{1}{s^3}\right\}(t) = \frac{1}{2}\mathcal{L}^{-1}\left\{\frac{2}{s^3}\right\}(t) = \frac{t^2}{2}.$$

37. We apply the Laplace transform to the given equation and obtain

$$\mathcal{L}\{ty''\}(s) - 2\mathcal{L}\{y'\}(s) + \mathcal{L}\{ty\}(s) = 0. \tag{7.22}$$

Using Theorem 5 (Section 7.3) and the initial conditions, we express $\mathcal{L}\{y''\}(s)$ and $\mathcal{L}\{y'\}(s)$ in terms of $Y(s) := \mathcal{L}\{y\}(s)$.

$$\mathcal{L}\{y'\}(s) = sY(s) - y(0) = sY(s) - 1, \tag{7.23}$$

$$\mathcal{L}\{y''\}(s) = s^2Y(s) - sy(0) - y'(0) = s^2Y(s) - s. \tag{7.24}$$

We now involve Theorem 6 in Section 7.3 to get

$$\mathcal{L}\{ty\}(s) = -\frac{d}{ds}\left[\mathcal{L}\{y\}(s)\right] = -Y'(s). \tag{7.25}$$

Also, Theorem 6 and equation (7.24) yield

$$\mathcal{L}\{ty''\}(s) = -\frac{d}{ds}\left[\mathcal{L}\{y''\}(s)\right] = -\frac{d}{ds}\left[s^2Y(s) - s\right] = 1 - 2sY(s) - s^2Y'(s). \tag{7.26}$$

Substituting (7.23), (7.25), and (7.26) into (7.22), we obtain

$$\begin{aligned} &\left[1 - 2sY(s) - s^2Y'(s)\right] - 2\left[sY(s) - 1\right] + \left[-Y'(s)\right] = 0 \\ \Rightarrow\quad & -\left(s^2+1\right)Y'(s) - 4sY(s) + 3 = 0 \\ \Rightarrow\quad & Y'(s) + \frac{4s}{s^2+1}Y(s) = \frac{3}{s^2+1}. \end{aligned}$$

The integrating factor of this first order linear differential equation is

$$\mu(s) = \exp\left[\int \frac{4s}{s^2+1}\,ds\right] = \exp\left[2\ln\left(s^2+1\right)\right] = \left(s^2+1\right)^2.$$

Hence

$$\begin{aligned} Y(s) &= \frac{1}{\mu(s)}\int \mu(s)\left(\frac{3}{s^2+1}\right)ds = \frac{1}{(s^2+1)^2}\int 3\left(s^2+1\right)ds \\ &= \frac{1}{(s^2+1)^2}\left(s^3+3s+C\right) = \frac{(s^3+s)+(2s+C)}{(s^2+1)^2} = \frac{s}{s^2+1}+\frac{2s}{(s^2+1)^2}+\frac{C}{(s^2+1)^2}, \end{aligned}$$

where C is an arbitrary constant. Therefore,

$$y(t) = \mathcal{L}^{-1}\{Y\}(t) = \mathcal{L}^{-1}\left\{\frac{s}{s^2+1}\right\}(t) + \mathcal{L}^{-1}\left\{\frac{2s}{(s^2+1)^2}\right\}(t) + \frac{C}{2}\mathcal{L}^{-1}\left\{\frac{2}{(s^2+1)^2}\right\}(t).$$

Using formulas (24), (29) and (30) on the inside back cover of the text, we finally get

$$y(t) = \cos t + t\sin t + c(\sin t - t\cos t),$$

where $c := C/2$ is an arbitrary constant.

39. Similarly to Example 5, we have the initial value problem (18), namely,

$$Iy''(t) = -ke(t), \qquad y(0)=0, \quad y'(0)=0,$$

for the model of the mechanism. This equation leads to equation (19) for the Laplace transforms $Y(s) := \mathcal{L}\{y(t)\}(s)$ and $E(s) := \mathcal{L}\{e(t)\}(s)$:

$$s^2IY(s) = -kE(s). \tag{7.27}$$

But, this time, $e(t) = y(t) - a$ and so

$$E(s) = \mathcal{L}\{y(t)-a\}(s) = Y(s) - \frac{a}{s} \qquad \Rightarrow \qquad Y(s) = E(s) + \frac{a}{s}.$$

Substituting this relation into (7.27) yields

$$s^2IE(s) + aIs = -kE(s) \qquad \Rightarrow \qquad E(s) = -\frac{-aIs}{s^2I+k} = -\frac{as}{s^2+(k/I)}.$$

Taking the inverse Laplace transform, we obtain

$$e(t) = \mathcal{L}^{-1}\{E(s)\}(t) = -a\mathcal{L}^{-1}\left\{\frac{s}{s^2+(\sqrt{k/I})^2}\right\}(t) = -a\cos\left(\sqrt{k/I}t\right).$$

41. As in Problem 40, the differential equation modeling the automatic pilot is

$$Iy''(t) = -ke(t) - \mu e'(t)\,, \tag{7.28}$$

but now the error $e(t)$ is given by $e(t) = y(t) - at$.

Let $Y(s) := \mathcal{L}\{y(t)\}(s)$, $E(s) := \mathcal{L}\{e(t)\}(s)$. Notice that, as in Example 5 on page 382, we have $y(0) = y'(0) = 0$, and so $e(0) = 0$. Using these initial conditions and Theorem 5 in Section 7.3, we obtain

$$\mathcal{L}\{y''(t)\}(s) = s^2Y(s) \qquad \text{and} \qquad \mathcal{L}\{e'(t)\}(s) = sE(s).$$

Applying the Laplace transform to both sides of (7.28) we then conclude that

$$\begin{aligned} &I\mathcal{L}\{y''(t)\}(s) = -k\mathcal{L}\{e(t)\}(s) - \mu\mathcal{L}\{e'(t)\}(s) \\ \Rightarrow \qquad & Is^2Y(s) = -kE(s) - \mu sE(s) = -(k+\mu s)E(s). \end{aligned} \tag{7.29}$$

Since $e(t) = y(t) - at$,

$$E(s) = \mathcal{L}\{e(t)\}(s) = \mathcal{L}\{y(t) - at\}(s) = Y(s) - a\mathcal{L}\{t\}(s) = Y(s) - \frac{a}{s^2}$$

or $Y(s) = E(s) + a/s^2$. Substitution back into (7.29) yields

$$\begin{aligned} & Is^2\left(E(s) + \frac{a}{s^2}\right) = -(k+\mu s)E(s) \\ \Rightarrow \qquad & \left(Is^2 + \mu s + k\right)E(s) = -aI \\ \Rightarrow \qquad & E(s) = \frac{-aI}{Is^2 + \mu s + k} = \frac{-a}{s^2 + (\mu/I)s + (k/I)}\,. \end{aligned}$$

Completing the square in the denominator, we write $E(s)$ in the form suitable for inverse Laplace transform.

$$\begin{aligned} E(s) &= \frac{-a}{[s+\mu/(2I)]^2 + (k/I) - \mu^2/(4I^2)} \\ &= \frac{-a}{[s+\mu/(2I)]^2 + (4kI - \mu^2)/(4I^2)} = \frac{-2Ia}{\sqrt{4kI - \mu^2}} \frac{\sqrt{4kI - \mu^2}/(2I)}{[s+\mu/(2I)]^2 + (4kI - \mu^2)/(4I^2)}\,. \end{aligned}$$

Thus, using Table 7.1 on page 358 of the text, we find that

$$e(t) = \mathcal{L}^{-1}\left\{E(s)\right\}(t) = \frac{-2Ia}{\sqrt{4kI - \mu^2}}\, e^{-\mu t/(2I)} \sin\left[\frac{\sqrt{4kI - \mu^2}t}{2I}\right].$$

Compare this with Example 5 of the text and observe, how for moderate damping with $\mu < 2\sqrt{kI}$, the oscillations of Example 5 die out exponentially.

EXERCISES 7.6: Transforms of Discontinuous and Periodic Functions, page 395

1. To find the Laplace transform of $g(t) = (t-1)^2 u(t-1)$ we apply formula (5) on page 387 of the text with $a = 1$ and $f(t) = t^2$. This yields

$$\mathcal{L}\left\{(t-1)^2 u(t-1)\right\}(s) = e^{-s}\mathcal{L}\left\{t^2\right\}(s) = \frac{2e^{-s}}{s^3}.$$

The graph of $g(t) = (t-1)^2 u(t-1)$ is shown in Figure 7-B(a).

3. The graph of the function $y = t^2 u(t-2)$ is shown in Figure 7-B(b). For this function, formula (8) on page 387 is more convenient. To apply the shifting property, we observe that $g(t) = t^2$ and $a = 2$. Hence

$$g(t+a) = g(t+2) = (t+2)^2 = t^2 + 4t + 4.$$

Now the Laplace transform of $g(t+2)$ is

$$\mathcal{L}\left\{t^2 + 4t + 4\right\}(s) = \mathcal{L}\left\{t^2\right\}(s) + 4\mathcal{L}\left\{t\right\}(s) + 4\mathcal{L}\left\{1\right\}(s) = \frac{2}{s^3} + \frac{4}{s^2} + \frac{4}{s}.$$

Hence, by formula (8), we have

$$\mathcal{L}\left\{t^2 u(t-2)\right\}(s) = e^{-2s}\mathcal{L}\left\{g(t+2)\right\}(s) = e^{-2s}\left(\frac{2}{s^3} + \frac{4}{s^2} + \frac{4}{s}\right) = \frac{e^{-2s}(4s^2 + 4s + 2)}{s^3}.$$

5. The function $g(t)$ equals zero until t reaches 1, at which point $g(t)$ jumps to 2. We can express this jump by $(2-0)u(t-1)$. At $t = 2$ the function $g(t)$ jumps from the value 2 to the value 1. This can be expressed by adding the term $(1-2)u(t-2)$. Finally, the jump at $t = 3$ from 1 to 3 can be accomplished by the function $(3-1)u(t-3)$. Hence

$$g(t) = 0 + (2-0)u(t-1) + (1-2)u(t-2) + (3-1)u(t-3) = 2u(t-1) - u(t-2) + 2u(t-3)$$

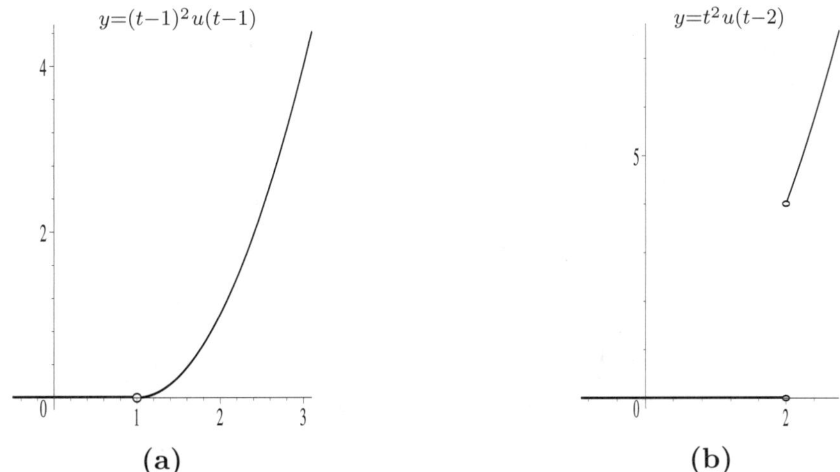

Figure 7–B: Graphs of functions in Problems 1 and 3.

and, by the linearity of the Laplace transform,

$$\begin{aligned}\mathcal{L}\{g(t)\}(s) &= 2\mathcal{L}\{u(t-1)\}(s) - \mathcal{L}\{u(t-2)\}(s) + 2\mathcal{L}\{u(t-3)\}(s) \\ &= 2\frac{e^{-s}}{s} - \frac{e^{-2s}}{s} + 2\frac{e^{-3s}}{s} \\ &= \frac{e^{-s} - e^{-2s} + 2e^{-3s}}{s}.\end{aligned}$$

7. Observe from the graph that $g(t)$ is given by

$$\begin{cases} 0, & t < 1, \\ t, & 1 < t < 2, \\ 1, & 2 < t. \end{cases}$$

The function $g(t)$ equals zero until t reaches 1, at which point $g(t)$ jumps to the function t. We can express this jump by $tu(t-1)$. At $t = 2$ the function $g(t)$ jumps from the function t to the value 1. This can be expressed by adding the term $(1-t)u(t-2)$. Hence

$$g(t) = 0 + tu(t-1) + (1-t)u(t-2) = tu(t-1) - (t-1)u(t-2).$$

Taking the Laplace transform of both sides and using formula (8) on page 387, we find that the Laplace transform of the function $g(t)$ is given by

$$\begin{aligned}
\mathcal{L}\{g(t)\}(s) &= \mathcal{L}\{tu(t-1)\}(s) - \mathcal{L}\{(t-1)u(t-2)\}(s) \\
&= e^{-s}\mathcal{L}\{(t+1)\}(s) - e^{-2s}\mathcal{L}\{(t-1)+2\}(s) \\
&= \left(e^{-s}-e^{-2s}\right)\mathcal{L}\{t+1\}(s) = \left(e^{-s}-e^{-2s}\right)\left(\frac{1}{s^2}+\frac{1}{s}\right) = \frac{(e^{-s}-e^{-2s})(s+1)}{s^2}\,.
\end{aligned}$$

9. First, we find the formula for $g(t)$ from the picture given.

$$\begin{cases} 0, & t<1, \\ t-1, & 1<t<2, \\ 3-t, & 2<t<3, \\ 0, & 3<t. \end{cases}$$

Thus, this function jumps from 0 to $t-1$ at $t=1$, from $t-1$ to $3-t$ at $t=2$, and from $3-t$ to 0 at $t=3$. Since the function $u(t-a)$ has the unit jump from 0 to 1 at $t=a$, we can express $g(t)$ as

$$\begin{aligned}
g(t) &= [(t-1)-0]u(t-1) + [(3-t)-(t-1)]u(t-2) + [0-(3-t)]u(t-3) \\
&= (t-1)u(t-1) + (4-2t)u(t-2) + (t-3)u(t-3).
\end{aligned}$$

Therefore,

$$\begin{aligned}
\mathcal{L}\{g(t)\}(s) &= \mathcal{L}\{(t-1)u(t-1)\}(s) + \mathcal{L}\{(4-2t)u(t-2)\}(s) + \mathcal{L}\{(t-3)u(t-3)\}(s) \\
&= e^{-s}\mathcal{L}\{(t+1)-1\}(s) + e^{-2s}\mathcal{L}\{4-2(t+2)\}(s) + e^{-3s}\mathcal{L}\{(t+3)-3\}(s) \\
&= e^{-s}\mathcal{L}\{t\}(s) - 2e^{-2s}\mathcal{L}\{t\}(s) + e^{-3s}\mathcal{L}\{t\}(s) = \frac{e^{-s}-2e^{-2s}+e^{-3s}}{s^2}\,.
\end{aligned}$$

11. We use formula (6) on page 387 of the text with $a=2$ and $F(s)=1/(s-1)$. Since

$$f(t) = \mathcal{L}^{-1}\{F(s)\}(t) = \mathcal{L}^{-1}\left\{\frac{1}{s-1}\right\}(t) = e^t \qquad \Rightarrow \qquad f(t-2) = e^{t-2}\,,$$

we get

$$\mathcal{L}^{-1}\left\{\frac{e^{-2s}}{s-1}\right\}(t) = f(t-2)u(t-2) = e^{t-2}u(t-2).$$

13. Using the linear property of the inverse Laplace transform, we obtain

$$\mathcal{L}^{-1}\left\{\frac{e^{-2s}-3e^{-4s}}{s+2}\right\}(t)=\mathcal{L}^{-1}\left\{\frac{e^{-2s}}{s+2}\right\}(t)-3\mathcal{L}^{-1}\left\{\frac{e^{-4s}}{s+2}\right\}(t).$$

To each term in the above equation, we can apply now formula (6), page 387 of the text with $F(s)=1/(s+2)$ and $a=2$ and $a=4$, respectively. Since

$$f(t):=\mathcal{L}^{-1}\{F(s)\}(t)=\mathcal{L}^{-1}\{1/(s+2)\}(t)=e^{-2t},$$

we get

$$\begin{aligned}\mathcal{L}^{-1}\left\{\frac{e^{-2s}}{s+2}\right\}(t)-3\mathcal{L}^{-1}\left\{\frac{e^{-4s}}{s+2}\right\}(t) &= f(t-2)u(t-2)-3f(t-4)u(t-4)\\ &= e^{-2(t-2)}u(t-2)-3e^{-2(t-4)}u(t-4).\end{aligned}$$

15. Since

$$\begin{aligned}F(s) &:= \frac{s}{s^2+4s+5}=\frac{s}{(s+2)^2+1^2}=\frac{s+2}{(s+2)^2+1^2}-2\frac{1}{(s+2)^2+1^2}\\ \Rightarrow\quad & f(t):=\mathcal{L}^{-1}\{F(s)\}(t)=e^{-2t}(\cos t-2\sin t),\end{aligned}$$

applying Theorem 8 we get

$$\mathcal{L}^{-1}\left\{\frac{se^{-3s}}{s^2+4s+5}\right\}(t)=f(t-3)u(t-3)=e^{-2(t-3)}\left[\cos(t-3)-2\sin(t-3)\right]u(t-3).$$

17. By partial fractions,

$$\frac{s-5}{(s+1)(s+2)}=-\frac{6}{s+1}+\frac{7}{s+2}$$

so that

$$\begin{aligned}\mathcal{L}^{-1}\left\{\frac{e^{-3s}(s-5)}{(s+1)(s+2)}\right\}(t) &= -6\mathcal{L}^{-1}\left\{\frac{e^{-3s}}{s+1}\right\}(t)+7\mathcal{L}^{-1}\left\{\frac{e^{-3s}}{s+2}\right\}(t)\\ &= -6\mathcal{L}^{-1}\left\{\frac{1}{s+1}\right\}(t-3)u(t-3)+7\mathcal{L}^{-1}\left\{\frac{1}{s+2}\right\}(t-3)u(t-3)\\ &= \left[-6e^{-(t-3)}+7e^{-2(t-3)}\right]u(t-3)=\left[7e^{6-2t}-6e^{3-t}\right]u(t-3).\end{aligned}$$

19. In this problem, we apply methods of Section 7.5 of solving initial value problems using the Laplace transform. Taking the Laplace transform of both sides of the given equation and using the linear property of the Laplace transform, we get

$$\mathcal{L}\left\{I''\right\}(s)+2\mathcal{L}\left\{I'\right\}(s)+2\mathcal{L}\left\{I\right\}(s)=\mathcal{L}\left\{g(t)\right\}(s). \tag{7.30}$$

Let us denote $\mathbf{I}(s):=\mathcal{L}\left\{I\right\}(s)$. By Theorem 5, Section 7.3,

$$\begin{aligned}\mathcal{L}\left\{I'\right\}(s)&=s\mathbf{I}(s)-I(0)=s\mathbf{I}(s)-10,\\ \mathcal{L}\left\{I''\right\}(s)&=s^2\mathbf{I}(s)-sI(0)-I'(0)=s^2\mathbf{I}(s)-10s.\end{aligned} \tag{7.31}$$

To find the Laplace transform of $g(t)$, we express this function using the unit step function $u(t)$. Since $g(t)$ identically equals to 20 for $0<t<3\pi$, jumps from 20 to 0 at $t=3\pi$ and then jumps from 0 to 20 at $t=4\pi$, we can write

$$g(t)=20+(0-20)u(t-3\pi)+(20-0)u(t-4\pi)=20-20u(t-3\pi)+20u(t-4\pi).$$

Therefore,

$$\begin{aligned}\mathcal{L}\left\{g(t)\right\}(s)&=\mathcal{L}\left\{20-20u(t-3\pi)+20u(t-4\pi)\right\}(s)\\ &=20\mathcal{L}\left\{1-u(t-3\pi)+u(t-4\pi)\right\}(s)=20\left(\frac{1}{s}-e^{-3\pi s}+e^{-4\pi s}\right).\end{aligned}$$

Substituting this equation and (7.31) into (7.30) yields

$$\begin{aligned}&\left[s^2\mathbf{I}(s)-10s\right]+2\left[s\mathbf{I}(s)-10\right]+2\mathbf{I}(s)=20\left(\frac{1}{s}-\frac{e^{-3\pi s}}{s}+\frac{e^{-4\pi s}}{s}\right)\\ \Rightarrow\quad&\mathbf{I}(s)=10\frac{1}{s}+20\frac{-e^{-3\pi s}+e^{-4\pi s}}{s[(s+1)^2+1]}.\end{aligned} \tag{7.32}$$

Since $\mathcal{L}^{-1}\left\{1/s\right\}(t)=1$ and

$$\begin{aligned}\mathcal{L}^{-1}\left\{\frac{1}{s[(s+1)^2+1]}\right\}(t)&=\mathcal{L}^{-1}\left\{\frac{1}{2}\left[1s-\frac{s+1}{(s+1)^2+1}-\frac{1}{(s+1)^2+1}\right]\right\}(t)\\ &=\frac{1}{2}\left[1-e^{-t}(\cos t+\sin t)\right],\end{aligned}$$

applying the inverse Laplace transform to both sides of (7.32) yields

$$I(t)=\mathcal{L}^{-1}\left\{10\frac{1}{s}+20\frac{-e^{-3\pi s}}{s[(s+1)^2+1]}+20\frac{e^{-4\pi s}}{s[(s+1)^2+1]}\right\}(t)$$

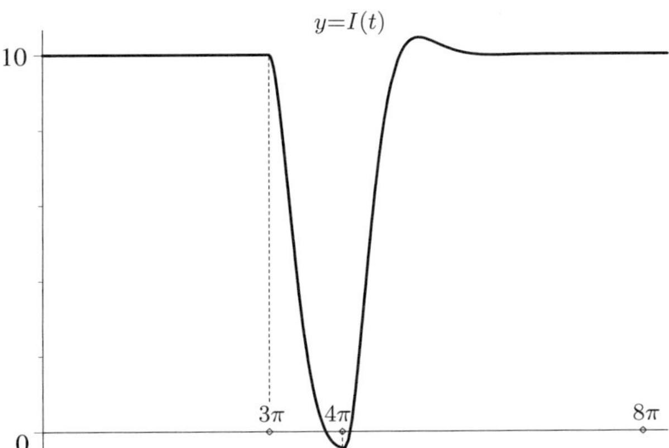

Figure 7–C: The graph of the function $y = I(t)$ in Problem 19.

$$\begin{aligned} &= 10 - 10u(t-3\pi)\left[1 - e^{-(t-3\pi)}\left(\cos(t-3\pi) + \sin(t-3\pi)\right)\right] \\ &\qquad + 10u(t-4\pi)\left[1 - e^{-(t-4\pi)}\left(\cos(t-4\pi) + \sin(t-4\pi)\right)\right] \\ &= 10 - 10u(t-3\pi)\left[1 + e^{-(t-3\pi)}\left(\cos t + \sin t\right)\right] \\ &\qquad + 10u(t-4\pi)\left[1 - e^{-(t-4\pi)}\left(\cos t + \sin t\right)\right]. \end{aligned}$$

The graph of the solution, $y = I(t)$, $0 < t < 8\pi$, is depicted in Figure 7-C.

21. In the windowed version (11) of $f(t)$, $f_T(t) = t$ and $T = 2$. Thus

$$\begin{aligned} F_T(s) &:= \int_0^\infty e^{-st} f_T(t)\,dt = \int_0^2 e^{-st} t\,dt = -\frac{te^{-st}}{s} - \frac{e^{-st}}{s^2}\bigg|_0^2 \\ &= -\frac{2e^{-2s}}{s} - \frac{e^{-2s}}{s^2} + \frac{1}{s^2} = \frac{1 - 2se^{-2s} - e^{-2s}}{s^2}. \end{aligned}$$

From Theorem 9 on page 391 of the text, we obtain

$$\mathcal{L}\{f(t)\}(s) = \frac{F_T(s)}{1 - e^{-2s}} = \frac{1 - 2se^{-2s} - e^{-2s}}{s^2(1 - e^{-2s})}.$$

The graph of the function $y = f(t)$ is given in Figure B.45 in the answers of the text.

23. We use formula (12) on page 391 of the text. With the period $T = 2$, the windowed version

$f_T(t)$ of $f(t)$ is

$$f_T(t) = \begin{cases} f(t), & 0 < t < 2, \\ 0, & \text{otherwise} \end{cases} \qquad = \qquad \begin{cases} e^{-t}, & 0 < t < 1, \\ 1, & 1 < t < 2, \\ 0, & \text{otherwise.} \end{cases}$$

Therefore,

$$\begin{aligned} F_T(s) &= \int_0^\infty e^{-st} f_T(t)\,dt = \int_0^1 e^{-st}e^{-t}\,dt + \int_1^2 e^{-st}\,dt \\ &= \left.\frac{e^{-(s+1)t}}{-(s+1)}\right|_0^1 + \left.\frac{e^{-st}}{-s}\right|_1^2 = \frac{1-e^{-(s+1)}}{s+1} + \frac{e^{-s}-e^{-2s}}{s} \end{aligned}$$

and, by (12),

$$\mathcal{L}\left\{f(t)\right\}(s) = \frac{1}{1-e^{-2s}}\left[\frac{1-e^{-(s+1)}}{s+1} + \frac{e^{-s}-e^{-2s}}{s}\right].$$

The graph of $f(t)$ is shown in Figure B.46 in the answers of the text.

25. Similarly to Example 6 on page 392 of the text, $f(t)$ is a periodic function with period $T = 2a$, whose windowed version has the form

$$f_{2a}(t) = 1 - u(t-a), \qquad 0 < t < 2a.$$

Thus, using the linearity of the Laplace transform and formula (4) on page 386 for the Laplace transform of the unit step function, we have

$$F_{2a}(s) = \mathcal{L}\left\{f_{2a}(t)\right\}(s) = \mathcal{L}\left\{1\right\}(s) - \mathcal{L}\left\{u(t-a)\right\}(s) = \frac{1}{s} - \frac{e^{-as}}{s} = \frac{1-e^{-as}}{s}.$$

Applying now Theorem 9 yields

$$\mathcal{L}\left\{f(t)\right\}(s) = \frac{1}{1-e^{-2as}}\,\frac{1-e^{-as}}{s} = \frac{1}{(1-e^{-as})(1+e^{-as})}\,\frac{1-e^{-as}}{s} = \frac{1}{s(1+e^{-as})}.$$

27. Observe that if we let

$$f_{2a}(t) = \begin{cases} f(t), & 0 < t < 2a, \\ 0, & \text{otherwise,} \end{cases}$$

denote the windowed version of $f(t)$, then from formula (12) on page 391 of the text we have

$$\mathcal{L}\{f(t)\}(s)=\frac{\mathcal{L}\{f_{2a}(t)\}(s)}{1-e^{-2as}}=\frac{\mathcal{L}\{f_{2a}(t)\}(s)}{(1-e^{-as})(1+e^{-as})}.$$

Now

$$\begin{aligned}
f_{2a}(t) &= \frac{t}{a}+\left[\left(2-\frac{t}{a}\right)-\frac{t}{a}\right]u(t-a)+\left[0-\left(2-\frac{t}{a}\right)\right]u(t-2a) \\
&= \frac{t}{a}-\frac{2(t-a)u(t-a)}{a}+\frac{(t-2a)u(t-2a)}{a}.
\end{aligned}$$

Hence,

$$\begin{aligned}
\mathcal{L}\{f_{2a}(t)\}(s) &= \frac{1}{a}\mathcal{L}\{t\}(s)-\frac{2}{a}\mathcal{L}\{(t-a)u(t-a)\}(s)+\frac{1}{a}\mathcal{L}\{(t-2a)u(t-2a)\}(s) \\
&= \frac{1}{a}\frac{1}{s^2}-\frac{2}{a}\frac{e^{-as}}{s^2}+\frac{1}{a}\frac{e^{-as}}{s^2}=\frac{1}{as^2}\left(1-2e^{-as}+e^{-2as}\right)=\frac{\left(1-e^{-as}\right)^2}{as^2}
\end{aligned}$$

and

$$\mathcal{L}\{f(t)\}(s)=\frac{\left(1-e^{-as}\right)^2/(as^2)}{(1-e^{-as})(1+e^{-as})}=\frac{1-e^{-as}}{as^2(1+e^{-as})}.$$

29. Applying the Laplace transform to both sides of the given differential equation, we obtain

$$\mathcal{L}\{y''\}(s)+\mathcal{L}\{y\}(s)=\mathcal{L}\{u(t-3)\}(s)=\frac{e^{-3s}}{s}.$$

Since

$$\mathcal{L}\{y''\}(s)=s^2\mathcal{L}\{y\}(s)-sy(0)-y'(0)=s^2\mathcal{L}\{y\}(s)-1,$$

substitution yields

$$\begin{aligned}
&\left[s^2\mathcal{L}\{y\}(s)-1\right]+\mathcal{L}\{y\}(s)=\frac{e^{-3s}}{s} \\
\Rightarrow\quad &\mathcal{L}\{y\}(s)=\frac{1}{s^2+1}+\frac{e^{-3s}}{s(s^2+1)}=\frac{1}{s^2+1}+e^{-3s}\left[\frac{1}{s}-\frac{s}{s^2+1}\right].
\end{aligned}$$

By formula (6) on page 387 of the text,

$$\mathcal{L}^{-1}\left\{e^{-3s}\left[\frac{1}{s}-\frac{s}{s^2+1}\right]\right\}(t)=\mathcal{L}^{-1}\left\{\frac{1}{s}-\frac{s}{s^2+1}\right\}(t-3)u(t-3)=[1-\cos(t-3)]u(t-3).$$

Hence

$$y(t)=\mathcal{L}^{-1}\left\{\frac{1}{s^2+1}+e^{-3s}\left[\frac{1}{s}-\frac{s}{s^2+1}\right]\right\}(t)=\sin t+[1-\cos(t-3)]u(t-3)$$

The graph of the solution is shown in Figure B.47 in the answers of the text.

31. We apply the Laplace transform to both sides of the differential equation and get

$$\mathcal{L}\left\{y''\right\}(s)+\mathcal{L}\left\{y\right\}(s)=\mathcal{L}\left\{t-(t-4)u(t-2)\right\}(s)=\frac{1}{s^2}-\mathcal{L}\left\{(t-4)u(t-2)\right\}(s). \quad (7.33)$$

Since $(t-4)u(t-2)=[(t-2)-2]u(t-2)$, we can use formula (5) from Theorem 8 to find its Laplace transform. With $f(t)=t-2$ and $a=2$, this formula yields

$$\mathcal{L}\left\{(t-4)u(t-2)\right\}(s)=e^{-2s}\mathcal{L}\left\{t-2\right\}(s)=e^{-2s}\left[\frac{1}{s^2}-\frac{2}{s}\right].$$

Also,

$$\mathcal{L}\left\{y''\right\}(s)=s^2\mathcal{L}\left\{y\right\}(s)-sy(0)-y'(0)=s^2\mathcal{L}\left\{y\right\}(s)-1.$$

Substitution back into (7.33) yields

$$\begin{aligned} \left[s^2\mathcal{L}\left\{y\right\}(s)-1\right]+\mathcal{L}\left\{y\right\}(s)&=\frac{1}{s^2}-e^{-2s}\left[\frac{1}{s^2}-\frac{2}{s}\right] \\ \Rightarrow \qquad \mathcal{L}\left\{y\right\}(s)&=\frac{1}{s^2}-e^{-2s}\frac{1-2s}{s^2(s^2+1)}=\frac{1}{s^2}-e^{-2s}\left[\frac{1}{s^2}-\frac{2}{s}+\frac{2s}{s^2+1}-\frac{1}{s^2+1}\right]. \end{aligned}$$

Applying now the inverse Laplace transform and using formula (6) on page 387 of the text, we obtain

$$\begin{aligned} y(t) &= \mathcal{L}^{-1}\left\{\frac{1}{s^2}-e^{-2s}\left[\frac{1}{s^2}-\frac{2}{s}+\frac{2s}{s^2+1}-\frac{1}{s^2+1}\right]\right\}(t) \\ &= t-\mathcal{L}^{-1}\left\{\frac{1}{s^2}-\frac{2}{s}+\frac{2s}{s^2+1}-\frac{1}{s^2+1}\right\}(t-2)u(t-2) \\ &= t-\left[(t-2)-2+2\cos(t-2)-\sin(t-2)\right]u(t-2) \\ &= t+\left[4-t+\sin(t-2)-2\cos(t-2)\right]u(t-2). \end{aligned}$$

See Figure B.48 in the answers of the text.

33. By formula (4) on page 386 of the text,

$$\mathcal{L}\left\{u(t-2\pi)-u(t-4\pi)\right\}(s)=\frac{e^{-2\pi s}}{s}-\frac{e^{-4\pi s}}{s}.$$

Thus, taking the Laplace transform of $y''+2y'+2y=u(t-2\pi)-u(t-4\pi)$ and applying the initial conditions $y(0)=y'(0)$ gives us

$$\left[s^2Y(s)-s-1\right]+2\left[sY(s)-1\right]+2Y(s)=\frac{e^{-2\pi s}-e^{-4\pi s}}{s},$$

where $Y(s)$ is the Laplace transform of $y(t)$. Solving for $Y(s)$ yields

$$\begin{aligned} Y(s) &= \frac{s+3}{s^2+2s+2} + \frac{e^{-2\pi s} - e^{-4\pi s}}{s(s^2+2s+2)} \\ &= \frac{s+1}{(s+1)^2+1^2} + \frac{2(1)}{(s+1)^2+1^2} + \frac{e^{-2\pi s}}{s[(s+1)^2+1^2]} - \frac{e^{-4\pi s}}{s[(s+1)^2+1^2]}. \end{aligned} \tag{7.34}$$

Since

$$\frac{1}{s[(s+1)^2+1^2]} = \frac{1}{2}\frac{(s^2+2s+2)-(s^2+2s)}{s[(s+1)^2+1^2]} = \frac{1}{2}\left[\frac{1}{s} - \frac{s+1}{(s+1)^2+1^2} - \frac{1}{(s+1)^2+1^2}\right],$$

we have

$$\begin{aligned} \mathcal{L}^{-1}\left\{\frac{1}{s[(s+1)^2+1^2]}\right\}(t) &= \mathcal{L}^{-1}\left\{\frac{1}{2}\left[\frac{1}{s} - \frac{s+1}{(s+1)^2+1^2} - \frac{1}{(s+1)^2+1^2}\right]\right\}(t) \\ &= \frac{1}{2}\left[1 - e^{-t}\cos t - e^{-t}\sin t\right] \end{aligned}$$

and, by formula (6) on page 387 of the text,

$$\begin{aligned} \mathcal{L}^{-1}\left\{\frac{e^{-2\pi s}}{s[(s+1)^2+1^2]}\right\}(t) &= \frac{1}{2}\left[1 - e^{-(t-2\pi)}\cos(t-2\pi) - e^{-(t-2\pi)}\sin(t-2\pi)\right]u(t-2\pi) \\ &= \frac{1}{2}\left[1 - e^{2\pi-t}(\cos t + \sin t)\right]u(t-2\pi) \\ \mathcal{L}^{-1}\left\{\frac{e^{-4\pi s}}{s[(s+1)^2+1^2]}\right\}(t) &= \frac{1}{2}\left[1 - e^{-(t-4\pi)}\cos(t-4\pi) - e^{-(t-4\pi)}\sin(t-4\pi)\right]u(t-4\pi) \\ &= \frac{1}{2}\left[1 - e^{4\pi-t}(\cos t + \sin t)\right]u(t-4\pi). \end{aligned}$$

Finally, taking the inverse Laplace transform in (7.34) yields

$$\begin{aligned} y(t) = e^{-t}\cos t + 2e^{-t}\sin t &+ \frac{1}{2}\left[1 - e^{2\pi-t}(\cos t + \sin t)\right]u(t-2\pi) \\ &- \frac{1}{2}\left[1 - e^{4\pi-t}(\cos t + \sin t)\right]u(t-4\pi). \end{aligned}$$

35. We take the Laplace transform of the both sides of the given equation and obtain

$$\mathcal{L}\{z''\}(s) + 3\mathcal{L}\{z'\}(s) + 2\mathcal{L}\{z\}(s) = \mathcal{L}\left\{e^{-3t}u(t-2)\right\}(s). \tag{7.35}$$

We use the initial conditions, $z(0) = 2$ and $z'(0) = -3$, and formula (4) from Section 7.3 to express $\mathcal{L}\{z'\}(s)$ and $\mathcal{L}\{z''\}(s)$ in terms of $Z(s) := \mathcal{L}\{z\}(s)$. That is,

$$\mathcal{L}\{z'\}(s) = sZ(s) - z(0) = sZ(s) - 2, \quad \mathcal{L}\{z''\}(s) = s^2Z(s) - sz(0) - z'(0) = s^2Z(s) - 2s + 3.$$

In the right-hand side of (7.35), we can use, say, the translation property of the Laplace transform (Theorem 3, Section 7.3) and the Laplace transform of the unit step function (formula (4), Section 7.6).

$$\mathcal{L}\left\{e^{-3t}u(t-2)\right\}(s) = \mathcal{L}\left\{u(t-2)\right\}(s+3) = \frac{e^{-2(s+3)}}{s+3}.$$

Therefore, (7.35) becomes

$$\begin{aligned}
\left[s^2Z(s) - 2s + 3\right] + 3\left[sZ(s) - 2\right] + 2Z(s) &= \frac{e^{-2(s+3)}}{s+3} \\
\Rightarrow \qquad \left(s^2 + 3s + 2\right)Z(s) &= 2s + 3 + \frac{e^{-2(s+3)}}{s+3} \\
\Rightarrow \qquad Z(s) &= \frac{2s+3}{s^2+3s+2} + e^{-2s-6}\frac{1}{(s+3)(s^2+3s+2)} \\
&= \frac{1}{s+1} + \frac{1}{s+2} + e^{-2s-6}\left[\frac{1/2}{s+3} - \frac{1}{s+2} + \frac{1/2}{s+1}\right].
\end{aligned}$$

Hence,

$$\begin{aligned}
z(t) &= \mathcal{L}^{-1}\left\{\frac{1}{s+1} + \frac{1}{s+2} + e^{-6}e^{-2s}\left[\frac{1/2}{s+3} - \frac{1}{s+2} + \frac{1/2}{s+1}\right]\right\}(t) \\
&= \mathcal{L}^{-1}\left\{\frac{1}{s+1}\right\}(t) + \mathcal{L}^{-1}\left\{\frac{1}{s+2}\right\}(t) \\
&\quad + \frac{e^{-6}}{2}\left[\mathcal{L}^{-1}\left\{\frac{1}{s+3}\right\} - 2\mathcal{L}^{-1}\left\{\frac{1}{s+2}\right\} + \mathcal{L}^{-1}\left\{\frac{1}{s+1}\right\}\right](t-2)u(t-2) \\
&= e^{-t} + e^{-2t} + \frac{e^{-6}}{2}\left[e^{-3(t-2)} - 2e^{-2(t-2)} + e^{-(t-2)}\right]u(t-2) \\
&= e^{-t} + e^{-2t} + \frac{1}{2}\left[e^{-3t} - 2e^{-2(t+1)} + e^{-(t+4)}\right]u(t-2)
\end{aligned}$$

37. Since

$$\mathcal{L}\{g(t)\}(s) = \int_0^\infty e^{-st}g(t)\,dt = \int_0^{2\pi} e^{-st}\sin t\,dt = \left.\frac{e^{-st}}{s^2+1}(-s\sin t - \cos t)\right|_0^{2\pi} = \frac{1-e^{-2\pi s}}{s^2+1},$$

applying the Laplace transform to the original equation yields

$$\begin{aligned}
&\mathcal{L}\{y''\}(s) + 4\mathcal{L}\{y\}(s) = \mathcal{L}\{g(t)\}(s) \\
\Rightarrow \quad & \left[s^2\mathcal{L}\{y\}(s) - s - 3\right] + 4\mathcal{L}\{y\}(s) = \frac{1 - e^{-2\pi s}}{s^2+1} \\
\Rightarrow \quad & \mathcal{L}\{y\}(s) = \frac{s+3}{s^2+4} + \frac{1}{(s^2+1)(s^2+4)} - \frac{e^{-2\pi s}}{(s^2+1)(s^2+4)}\,.
\end{aligned}$$

Using the partial fractions decomposition

$$\frac{1}{(s^2+1)(s^2+4)} = \frac{1}{3}\,\frac{(s^2+4)-(s^2+1)}{(s^2+1)(s^2+4)} = \frac{1}{3}\left[\frac{1}{s^2+1} - \frac{1}{6}\,\frac{2}{s^2+4}\right],$$

we conclude that

$$\mathcal{L}\{y\}(s) = \frac{s}{s^2+4} + \frac{4}{3}\,\frac{2}{s^2+4} + \frac{1}{3}\,\frac{1}{s^2+1} - e^{-2\pi s}\left[\frac{1}{3}\,\frac{1}{s^2+1} - \frac{1}{6}\,\frac{2}{s^2+4}\right]$$

and so

$$\begin{aligned}
y(t) &= \mathcal{L}^{-1}\left\{\frac{s}{s^2+4}\right\}(t) + \frac{4}{3}\mathcal{L}^{-1}\left\{\frac{2}{s^2+4}\right\}(t) + \mathcal{L}^{-1}\left\{\frac{1}{3}\,\frac{1}{s^2+1}\right\}(t) \\
&\qquad - \mathcal{L}^{-1}\left\{\frac{1}{3}\,\frac{1}{s^2+1} - \frac{1}{6}\,\frac{2}{s^2+4}\right\}(t-2\pi)u(t-2\pi) \\
&= \cos 2t + \frac{4}{3}\sin 2t + \frac{1}{3}\sin t - \left[\frac{1}{3}\sin(t-2\pi) - \frac{1}{6}\sin 2(t-2\pi)\right]u(t-2\pi) \\
&= \cos 2t + \frac{4}{3}\sin 2t + \frac{1}{3}\sin t - \left[\frac{1}{3}\sin t - \frac{1}{6}\sin 2t\right]u(t-2\pi) \\
&= \cos 2t + \frac{1}{3}\left[1 - u(t-2\pi)\right]\sin t + \frac{1}{6}\left[8 + u(t-2\pi)\right]\sin 2t\,.
\end{aligned}$$

39. We can express $g(t)$ using the unit step function as

$$g(t) = tu(t-1) + (1-t)u(t-5) = [(t-1)+1]u(t-1) - [(t-5)+4]u(t-5).$$

Thus, formula (5) on page 387 of the text yields

$$\mathcal{L}\{g(t)\}(s) = e^{-s}\mathcal{L}\{t+1\}(s) - e^{-5s}\mathcal{L}\{t+4\}(s) = e^{-s}\left(\frac{1}{s^2} + \frac{1}{s}\right) - e^{-5s}\left(\frac{1}{s^2} + \frac{4}{s}\right).$$

Let $Y(s) = \mathcal{L}\{y\}(s)$. Applying the Laplace transform to the given equation and using the initial conditions, we obtain

$$\begin{aligned}
&\mathcal{L}\{y''\}(s) + 5\mathcal{L}\{y'\}(s) + 6Y(s) = \mathcal{L}\{g(t)\}(s)\\
\Rightarrow\quad & \left[s^2Y(s) - 2\right] + 5\left[sY(s)\right] + 6Y(s) = \mathcal{L}\{g(t)\}(s)\\
\Rightarrow\quad & \left(s^2+5s+6\right)Y(s) = 2 + e^{-s}\left(\frac{1}{s^2}+\frac{1}{s}\right) - e^{-5s}\left(\frac{1}{s^2}+\frac{4}{s}\right)\\
\Rightarrow\quad & Y(s) = \frac{2}{s^2+5s+6} + e^{-s}\frac{s+1}{s^2(s^2+5s+6)} - e^{-5s}\frac{4s+1}{s^2(s^2+5s+6)}\,.
\end{aligned} \tag{7.36}$$

Using partial fractions decomposition, we can write

$$\begin{aligned}
\frac{2}{s^2+5s+6} &= \frac{2}{s+2} - \frac{2}{s+3}\,,\\
\frac{s+1}{s^2(s^2+5s+6)} &= \frac{1/36}{s} + \frac{1/6}{s^2} - \frac{1/4}{s+2} + \frac{2/9}{s+3}\,,\\
\frac{4s+1}{s^2(s^2+5s+6)} &= \frac{1/6}{s^2} + \frac{19/36}{s} - \frac{7/4}{s+2} + \frac{11/9}{s+3}\,.
\end{aligned}$$

Therefore,

$$\begin{aligned}
\mathcal{L}^{-1}\left\{\frac{2}{s^2+5s+6}\right\}(t) &= 2e^{-2t} - 2e^{-3t}\,,\\
\mathcal{L}^{-1}\left\{\frac{s+1}{s^2(s^2+5s+6)}\right\}(t) &= \frac{1}{36} + \frac{t}{6} - \frac{e^{-2t}}{4} + \frac{2e^{-3t}}{9}\,,\\
\mathcal{L}^{-1}\left\{\frac{4s+1}{s^2(s^2+5s+6)}\right\}(t) &= \frac{19}{36} + \frac{t}{6} - \frac{7e^{-2t}}{4} + \frac{11e^{-3t}}{9}\,.
\end{aligned}$$

Using these equations and taking the inverse Laplace transform in (7.36), we finally obtain

$$\begin{aligned}
y(t) = 2e^{-2t} - 2e^{-3t} &+ \left[\frac{1}{36} + \frac{t-1}{6} - \frac{e^{-2(t-1)}}{4} + \frac{2e^{-3(t-1)}}{9}\right]u(t-1)\\
&+ \left[\frac{19}{36} + \frac{t-5}{6} - \frac{7e^{-2(t-5)}}{4} + \frac{11e^{-3(t-5)}}{9}\right]u(t-5).
\end{aligned}$$

41. First observe that for $s > 0$, $T > 0$, we have $0 < e^{-Ts} < 1$ so that

$$\frac{1}{1-e^{-Ts}} = 1 + e^{-Ts} + e^{-2Ts} + e^{-3Ts} + \cdots \tag{7.37}$$

and the series converges for all $s > 0$. Thus,

$$\begin{aligned}\frac{1}{(s+\alpha)(1-e^{-Ts})} = \frac{1}{s+\alpha}\frac{1}{1-e^{-Ts}} &= \frac{1}{s+\alpha}\left(1+e^{-Ts}+e^{-2Ts}+e^{-3Ts}+\cdots\right)\\ &= \frac{1}{s+\alpha}+\frac{e^{-Ts}}{s+\alpha}+\frac{e^{-2Ts}}{s+\alpha}+\cdots,\end{aligned}$$

and so

$$\mathcal{L}^{-1}\left\{\frac{1}{(s+\alpha)(1-e^{-Ts})}\right\}(t) = \mathcal{L}^{-1}\left\{\frac{1}{s+\alpha}+\frac{e^{-Ts}}{s+\alpha}+\frac{e^{-2Ts}}{s+\alpha}+\cdots\right\}(t). \tag{7.38}$$

Taking for granted that the linearity of the inverse Laplace transform extends to the infinite sum in (7.38) and ignoring convergence questions yields

$$\begin{aligned}\mathcal{L}^{-1}\left\{\frac{1}{(s+\alpha)(1-e^{-Ts})}\right\} &= \mathcal{L}^{-1}\left\{\frac{1}{s+\alpha}\right\}+\mathcal{L}^{-1}\left\{\frac{e^{-Ts}}{s+\alpha}\right\}+\mathcal{L}^{-1}\left\{\frac{e^{-2Ts}}{s+\alpha}\right\}+\cdots\\ &= e^{-\alpha t}+e^{-\alpha(t-T)}u(t-T)+e^{-\alpha(t-2T)}u(t-2T)+\cdots\end{aligned}$$

as claimed.

43. Using the expansion (7.37) obtained in Problem 41, we can represent $\mathcal{L}\{g\}(s)$ as

$$\begin{aligned}\mathcal{L}\{g\}(s) = \frac{\beta}{s^2+\beta^2}\frac{1}{1-e^{-Ts}} &= \frac{\beta}{s^2+\beta^2}\left(1+e^{-Ts}+e^{-2Ts}+e^{-3Ts}+\cdots\right)\\ &= \frac{\beta}{s^2+\beta^2}+e^{-Ts}\frac{\beta}{s^2+\beta^2}+e^{-2Ts}\frac{\beta}{s^2+\beta^2}+\cdots.\end{aligned}$$

Since $\mathcal{L}^{-1}\{\beta/(s^2+\beta^2)\}(t) = \sin\beta t$, using the linearity of the inverse Laplace transform (extended to infinite series) and formula (6) in Theorem 8, we obtain

$$\begin{aligned}g(t) &= \mathcal{L}^{-1}\left\{\frac{\beta}{s^2+\beta^2}\right\}(t)+\mathcal{L}^{-1}\left\{\frac{\beta}{s^2+\beta^2}\right\}(t-T)u(t-T)\\ &\qquad +\mathcal{L}^{-1}\left\{\frac{\beta}{s^2+\beta^2}\right\}(t-2T)u(t-2T)+\cdots\\ &= \sin\beta t+[\sin\beta(t-T)]u(t-T)+[\sin\beta(t-2T)]u(t-2T)+\cdots\end{aligned}$$

as stated.

45. In order to apply the method of Laplace transform to given initial value problem, let us find $\mathcal{L}\{f\}(s)$ first. Since the period of $f(t)$ is $T = 1$ and $f(t) = e^t$ on $(0, 1)$, the windowed version of $f(t)$ is

$$f_1(t) = \begin{cases} e^t, & 0 < t < 1, \\ 0, & \text{otherwise}, \end{cases}$$

and so

$$F_1(s) = \int_0^\infty e^{-st} f_1(t)\,dt = \int_0^1 e^{-st} e^t\,dt = \left.\frac{e^{(1-s)t}}{1-s}\right|_0^1 = \frac{1-e^{1-s}}{s-1}.$$

Hence, Theorem 9 yields the following formula for $\mathcal{L}\{f\}(s)$:

$$\mathcal{L}\{f\}(s) = \frac{1-e^{1-s}}{(s-1)(1-e^{-s})}.$$

We can now apply the Laplace transform to the given differential equation and obtain

$$\begin{aligned}
&\mathcal{L}\{y''\}(s) + 3\mathcal{L}\{y'\}(s) + 2\mathcal{L}\{y\}(s) = \frac{1-e^{1-s}}{(s-1)(1-e^{-s})} \\
\Rightarrow\quad & \left[s^2\mathcal{L}\{y\}(s)\right] + 3\left[s\mathcal{L}\{y\}(s)\right] + 2\mathcal{L}\{y\}(s) = \frac{1-e^{1-s}}{(s-1)(1-e^{-s})} \\
\Rightarrow\quad & \mathcal{L}\{y\}(s) = \frac{1-e^{1-s}}{(s-1)(s^2+3s+2)(1-e^{-s})} = \frac{1-e^{1-s}}{(s-1)(s+1)(s+2)(1-e^{-s})} \\
\Rightarrow\quad & \mathcal{L}\{y\}(s) = \frac{e}{(s-1)(s+1)(s+2)} + \frac{1-e}{1-e^{-s}}\frac{1}{(s-1)(s+1)(s+2)}.
\end{aligned}$$

Using the partial fractions decomposition

$$\frac{1}{(s-1)(s+1)(s+2)} = \frac{1/6}{s-1} - \frac{1/2}{s+1} + \frac{1/3}{s+2}$$

we find that

$$\begin{aligned}
\mathcal{L}\{y\}(s) &= \frac{e/6}{s-1} - \frac{e/2}{s+1} + \frac{e/3}{s+2} + \frac{1-e}{6}\frac{1}{(s-1)(1-e^{-s})} \\
&\quad - \frac{1-e}{2}\frac{1}{(s+1)(1-e^{-s})} + \frac{1-e}{3}\frac{1}{(s+2)(1-e^{-s})} \\
\Rightarrow\quad y(t) &= \frac{e}{6}e^t - \frac{e}{2}e^{-t} + \frac{e}{3}e^{-2t} + \frac{1-e}{6}\mathcal{L}^{-1}\left\{\frac{1}{(s-1)(1-e^{-s})}\right\}(t) \\
&\quad - \frac{1-e}{2}\mathcal{L}^{-1}\left\{\frac{1}{(s+1)(1-e^{-s})}\right\}(t) + \frac{1-e}{3}\mathcal{L}^{-1}\left\{\frac{1}{(s+2)(1-e^{-s})}\right\}(t). \qquad (7.39)
\end{aligned}$$

To each of the three inverse Laplace transforms in the above formula we can apply results of Problem 42(a) with $T = 1$ and $\alpha = -1$, 1, and 2, respectively. Thus, for $n < t < n + 1$, we have

$$\mathcal{L}^{-1}\left\{\frac{1}{(s-1)(1-e^{-s})}\right\}(t) = e^{t}\left[\frac{e^{-(n+1)}-1}{e^{-1}-1}\right],$$
$$\mathcal{L}^{-1}\left\{\frac{1}{(s+1)(1-e^{-s})}\right\}(t) = e^{-t}\left[\frac{e^{n+1}-1}{e-1}\right],$$
$$\mathcal{L}^{-1}\left\{\frac{1}{(s+2)(1-e^{-s})}\right\}(t) = e^{-2t}\left[\frac{e^{2(n+1)}-1}{e^{2}-1}\right].$$

Finally, substitution back into (7.39) yields

$$\begin{aligned} y(t) &= \frac{e}{6}e^{t} - \frac{e}{2}e^{-t} + \frac{e}{3}e^{-2t} + \frac{1-e}{6}e^{t}\left[\frac{e^{-(n+1)}-1}{e^{-1}-1}\right] \\ &\qquad - \frac{1-e}{2}e^{-t}\left[\frac{e^{n+1}-1}{e-1}\right] + \frac{1-e}{3}e^{-2t}\left[\frac{e^{2(n+1)}-1}{e^{2}-1}\right] \\ &= \frac{e^{t-n}}{6} - \frac{e^{-t}\left(1+e-e^{n+1}\right)}{2} + \frac{e^{-2t}\left(1+e+e^{2}-e^{2n+2}\right)}{3(e+1)}. \end{aligned}$$

47. Since

$$e^{t} = \sum_{k=0}^{\infty}\frac{t^{k}}{k!}$$

and

$$\mathcal{L}\left\{t^{k}\right\}(s) = \frac{k!}{s^{k+1}},$$

using the linearity of the Laplace transform we have

$$\mathcal{L}\left\{e^{t}\right\}(s) = \mathcal{L}\left\{\sum_{k=0}^{\infty}\frac{t^{k}}{k!}\right\}(s) = \sum_{k=0}^{\infty}\frac{\mathcal{L}\left\{t^{k}\right\}(s)}{k!} = \sum_{k=0}^{\infty}\frac{k!/s^{k+1}}{k!} = \frac{1}{s}\sum_{k=0}^{\infty}\left(\frac{1}{s}\right)^{k}. \tag{7.40}$$

We can apply now the summation formula for geometric series, that is,

$$1 + x + x^{2} + \cdots = \frac{1}{1-x},$$

which is valid for $|x| < 1$. With $x = 1/s$, $s > 1$, (7.40) yields

$$\mathcal{L}\left\{e^{t}\right\}(s) = \frac{1}{s}\frac{1}{1-(1/s)} = \frac{1}{s-1}.$$

49. Recall that the Taylor's series for $\cos t$ about $t = 0$ is

$$\cos t = 1 - \frac{t^2}{2!} + \frac{t^4}{4!} - \frac{t^6}{6!} + \cdots + (-1)^n \frac{t^{2n}}{(2n)!} + \cdots$$

so that

$$\frac{1 - \cos t}{t} = \frac{t}{2!} - \frac{t^3}{4!} + \frac{t^5}{6!} + \cdots + (-1)^{n+1} \frac{t^{2n-1}}{(2n)!} + \cdots .$$

Thus

$$\begin{aligned} \mathcal{L}\left\{\frac{1 - \cos t}{t}\right\}(s) &= \frac{1}{2!}\mathcal{L}\{t\}(s) - \frac{1}{4!}\mathcal{L}\{t^3\}(s) + \cdots + \frac{(-1)^{n+1}}{(2n)!}\mathcal{L}\{t^{2n-1}\}(s) + \cdots \\ &= \frac{1}{2}\frac{1}{s^2} - \frac{1}{4}\frac{1}{s^4} + \cdots + \frac{(-1)^{n+1}}{2n}\frac{1}{s^{2n}} + \cdots \\ &= \sum_{n=1}^{\infty} \frac{(-1)^{n+1}}{2n}\frac{1}{s^{2n}} = \sum_{n=1}^{\infty} \frac{(-1)^{n+1}}{2ns^{2n}} . \end{aligned}$$

To sum this series, recall that

$$\ln(1 - x) = -\sum_{n=1}^{\infty} \frac{x^n}{n} .$$

Hence,

$$\ln\left(1 + \frac{1}{s^2}\right) = -\sum_{n=1}^{\infty} \frac{(-1)^n}{ns^{2n}} = \sum_{n=1}^{\infty} \frac{(-1)^{n+1}}{ns^{2n}} .$$

Thus, we have

$$\frac{1}{2}\ln\left(1 + \frac{1}{s^2}\right) = \sum_{n=1}^{\infty} \frac{(-1)^{n+1}}{2ns^{2n}} = \mathcal{L}\left\{\frac{1 - \cos t}{t}\right\}(s) .$$

This formula can also be obtained by using the result of Problem 27 in Section 7.3 of the text.

51. We use formula (17) on page 394 of the text.

(a) With $r = -1/2$, (17) yields

$$\mathcal{L}\left\{t^{-1/2}\right\}(s) = \frac{\Gamma[(-1/2) + 1]}{s^{(-1/2)+1}} = \frac{\Gamma(1/2)}{s^{1/2}} = \frac{\sqrt{\pi}}{\sqrt{s}} = \sqrt{\frac{\pi}{s}} .$$

(b) This time, $r = 7/2$, and (17) becomes

$$\mathcal{L}\left\{t^{7/2}\right\}(s) = \frac{\Gamma[(7/2) + 1]}{s^{(7/2)+1}} = \frac{\Gamma(9/2)}{s^{9/2}} .$$

From the recursive formula (16) we find that

$$\Gamma\left(\frac{9}{2}\right)=\Gamma\left(\frac{7}{2}+1\right)=\frac{7}{2}\Gamma\left(\frac{7}{2}\right)=\frac{7}{2}\frac{5}{2}\Gamma\left(\frac{5}{2}\right)=\frac{7}{2}\frac{5}{2}\frac{3}{2}\Gamma\left(\frac{3}{2}\right)=\frac{7}{2}\frac{5}{2}\frac{3}{2}\frac{1}{2}\Gamma\left(\frac{1}{2}\right)=\frac{105\sqrt{\pi}}{16}.$$

Therefore,

$$\mathcal{L}\left\{t^{7/2}\right\}(s)=\frac{105\sqrt{\pi}}{16s^{9/2}}.$$

53. According to the definition (11) of the function $f_T(t)$, $f_T(t-kT)=0$ if the point $t-kT$ does not belong to $(0,T)$. Therefore, fixed t, in the series (13) all the terms containing $f_T(t-kT)$ with k's such that $t-kT\le 0$ or $t-kT\ge T$ vanish. In the remaining terms, k satisfies

$$0<t-kT<T \qquad \Leftrightarrow \qquad \frac{t}{T}-1<k<\frac{t}{T}.$$

But, for any fixed t, there is at most one k satisfying this condition.

55. Recall that

$$e^x=1+x+\frac{x^2}{2!}+\cdots+\frac{x^n}{n!}+\cdots.$$

Substituting $-1/s$ for x above yields

$$e^{-1/s}=1-\frac{1}{s}+\frac{1}{2!s^2}-\frac{1}{3!s^3}+\cdots+\frac{(-1)^n}{n!s^n}+\cdots.$$

Thus, we have

$$s^{-1/2}e^{-1/s}=\frac{1}{s^{1/2}}-\frac{1}{s^{3/2}}+\frac{1}{2!s^{5/2}}+\cdots+\frac{(-1)^n}{n!s^{n+1/2}}+\cdots=\sum_{n=0}^{\infty}\frac{(-1)^n}{n!s^{n+1/2}}.$$

By Problem 52 of this section,

$$\mathcal{L}^{-1}\left\{\frac{1}{s^{n+(1/2)}}\right\}(t)=\frac{2^n t^{n-(1/2)}}{1\cdot3\cdot5\cdots(2n-1)\sqrt{\pi}},$$

so that

$$\begin{aligned}\mathcal{L}^{-1}\left\{s^{-1/2}e^{-1/s}\right\}(t) &= \mathcal{L}^{-1}\left\{\sum_{n=0}^{\infty}\frac{(-1)^n}{n!s^{n+1/2}}\right\}(t)\\ &= \sum_{n=0}^{\infty}\frac{(-1)^n}{n!}\mathcal{L}^{-1}\left\{\frac{1}{s^{n+(1/2)}}\right\}(t)=\sum_{n=0}^{\infty}\frac{(-1)^n}{n!}\frac{2^n t^{n-(1/2)}}{1\cdot3\cdot5\cdots(2n-1)\sqrt{\pi}}.\end{aligned}$$

Multiplying the nth term by $[2\cdot 4\cdots(2n)]/[2\cdot 4\cdots(2n)]$, we obtain

$$\begin{aligned}\mathcal{L}^{-1}\left\{s^{-1/2}e^{-1/s}\right\}(t) &= \sum_{n=0}^{\infty}\frac{(-1)^n(2^n)^2t^{n-(1/2)}}{(2n)!\sqrt{\pi}}=\sum_{n=0}^{\infty}\frac{(-1)^n(2^n)^2t^n}{(2n)!\sqrt{\pi t}}\\ &= \left(\frac{1}{\sqrt{\pi t}}\right)\sum_{n=0}^{\infty}\frac{(-1)^n(2\sqrt{t})^{2n}}{(2n)!}=\left(\frac{1}{\sqrt{\pi t}}\right)\cos\left(2\sqrt{t}\right).\end{aligned}$$

57. Recall that the Maclaurin expansion of $\ln(1-x)$ is

$$\ln(1-x)=-\sum_{n=1}^{\infty}\frac{x^n}{n},$$

which converges for $|x|<1$. Hence, substitution $-1/s^2$ for x yields

$$\ln\left(1+\frac{1}{s^2}\right)=-\sum_{n=1}^{\infty}\frac{(-1)^n}{ns^{2n}}=\sum_{n=1}^{\infty}\frac{(-1)^{n+1}}{ns^{2n}}.$$

Assuming that the inverse Laplace transform can be computed termwise, we obtain

$$\mathcal{L}^{-1}\left\{\ln\left(1+\frac{1}{s^2}\right)\right\}=\mathcal{L}^{-1}\left\{\sum_{n=1}^{\infty}\frac{(-1)^{n+1}}{ns^{2n}}\right\}=\sum_{n=1}^{\infty}\frac{(-1)^{n+1}}{n}\mathcal{L}^{-1}\left\{\frac{1}{s^{2n}}\right\}.$$

From Table 7.1 in Section 7.2, $\mathcal{L}\left\{t^k\right\}=k!/s^{k+1}$, $k=1,2,\ldots$. Thus $\mathcal{L}^{-1}\left\{1/s^{k+1}\right\}=t^k/k!$. With $k=2n-1$, this yields

$$\mathcal{L}^{-1}\left\{\frac{1}{s^{2n}}\right\}(t)=\frac{t^{2n-1}}{(2n-1)!},\qquad n=1,2,\ldots$$

and, therefore,

$$\mathcal{L}^{-1}\left\{\ln\left(1+\frac{1}{s^2}\right)\right\}(t)=\sum_{n=1}^{\infty}\frac{(-1)^{n+1}}{n}\frac{t^{2n-1}}{(2n-1)!}=-\frac{2}{t}\sum_{n=1}^{\infty}\frac{(-1)^n}{(2n)!}t^{2n}. \tag{7.41}$$

Since

$$\cos t=\sum_{n=0}^{\infty}\frac{(-1)^n}{(2n)!}t^{2n}=1+\sum_{n=1}^{\infty}\frac{(-1)^n}{(2n)!}t^{2n},$$

(7.41) implies that

$$\mathcal{L}^{-1}\left\{\ln\left(1+\frac{1}{s^2}\right)\right\}(t)=-\frac{2}{t}(\cos t-1)=\frac{2(1-\cos t)}{t}.$$

59. Applying the Laplace transform to both sides of the original equation and using its linearity, we obtain

$$\mathcal{L}\{y''\}(s) - \mathcal{L}\{y\}(s) = \mathcal{L}\{G_3(t-1)\}(s). \tag{7.42}$$

Initial conditions, $y(0)=0$ and $y'(0)$=2, and Theorem 5 in Section 7.3 imply that

$$\mathcal{L}\{y''\}(s) = s^2\mathcal{L}\{y\}(s) - sy(0) - y'(0) = s^2\mathcal{L}\{y\}(s) - 2.$$

In the right-hand side of (7.42), we can apply the result of Problem 58(c) with $a=3$ and $b=1$ to get

$$\mathcal{L}\{G_3(t-1)\}(s) = \frac{e^{-s}-e^{-4s}}{s}.$$

Thus (7.42) becomes

$$\begin{aligned} \left[s^2\mathcal{L}\{y\}(s) - 2\right] - \mathcal{L}\{y\}(s) &= \frac{e^{-s}-e^{-4s}}{s} \\ \Rightarrow \qquad \mathcal{L}\{y\}(s) &= \frac{2}{s^2-1} + \frac{e^{-s}-e^{-4s}}{s(s^2-1)}. \end{aligned}$$

Substituting partial fraction decompositions

$$\frac{2}{s^2-1} = \frac{1}{s-1} - \frac{1}{s+1}, \qquad \frac{1}{s(s^2-1)} = \frac{1/2}{s-1} + \frac{1/2}{s+1} - \frac{1}{s}$$

yields

$$\begin{aligned} \mathcal{L}\{y\}(s) &= \frac{1}{s-1} - \frac{1}{s+1} + \left(e^{-s}-e^{-4s}\right)\left[\frac{1/2}{s-1} + \frac{1/2}{s+1} - \frac{1}{s}\right] \\ &= \frac{1}{s-1} - \frac{1}{s+1} + e^{-s}\left[\frac{1/2}{s-1} + \frac{1/2}{s+1} - \frac{1}{s}\right] - e^{-4s}\left[\frac{1/2}{s-1} + \frac{1/2}{s+1} - \frac{1}{s}\right]. \end{aligned} \tag{7.43}$$

Since

$$\mathcal{L}^{-1}\left\{\frac{1/2}{s-1} + \frac{1/2}{s+1} - \frac{1}{s}\right\}(t) = \frac{e^t + e^{-t} - 2}{2},$$

formula (6) on page 387 of the text gives us

$$\begin{aligned} \mathcal{L}^{-1}\left\{e^{-s}\left[\frac{1/2}{s-1} + \frac{1/2}{s+1} - \frac{1}{s}\right]\right\}(t) &= \mathcal{L}^{-1}\left\{\frac{1/2}{s-1} + \frac{1/2}{s+1} - \frac{1}{s}\right\}(t-1)u(t-1) \\ &= \frac{e^{t-1} + e^{1-t} - 2}{2}u(t-1), \end{aligned}$$

$$\mathcal{L}^{-1}\left\{e^{-4s}\left[\frac{1/2}{s-1}+\frac{1/2}{s+1}-\frac{1}{s}\right]\right\}(t)=\mathcal{L}^{-1}\left\{\frac{1/2}{s-1}+\frac{1/2}{s+1}-\frac{1}{s}\right\}(t-4)u(t-4)$$
$$=\frac{e^{t-4}+e^{4-t}-2}{2}u(t-4).$$

Taking the inverse Laplace transform in (7.43) yields

$$y(t)=e^{t}-e^{-t}+\frac{e^{t-1}+e^{1-t}-2}{2}u(t-1)-\frac{e^{t-4}+e^{4-t}-2}{2}u(t-4).$$

61. In this problem, we use the method of solving "mixing problems" discussed in Section 3.2. So, let $x(t)$ denote the mass of salt in the tank at time t with $t=0$ denoting the moment when the process started. Thus, using the formula

$$\text{mass} = \text{volume} \times \text{concentration},$$

we have the initial condition

$$x(0)=500\,(\mathrm{L})\times 0.2\,(\mathrm{kg/L})=100\,(\mathrm{kg}).$$

For the rate of change of $x(t)$, that is, $x'(t)$, we use then relation

$$x'(t)=\text{input rate}-\text{output rate}. \tag{7.44}$$

While the output rate (through the exit valve C) can be computed as

$$\text{output rate}=\frac{x(t)}{500}\,(\mathrm{kg/L})\times 12\,(\mathrm{L/min})=\frac{3x(t)}{125}\,(\mathrm{kg/min})$$

for all t, the input rate has different formulas for the first 10 minute and after that. Namely,

$$0<t<10 \text{ (valve } A): \quad \text{input rate}=12\,(\mathrm{L/min})\times 0.4\,(\mathrm{kg/L})=4.8\,(\mathrm{kg/min});$$
$$10<t \text{ (valve } B): \quad \text{input rate}=12\,(\mathrm{L/min})\times 0.6\,(\mathrm{kg/L})=7.2\,(\mathrm{kg/min}).$$

In other words, the input rate is a function of t, which can be written as

$$\text{input rate}=g(t)=\begin{cases}4.8, & 0<t<10,\\ 7.2, & 10<t.\end{cases}$$

Using the unit step function, we can express $g(t) = 4.8 + 2.4u(t-10)$ (kg/min). Therefore (7.44) becomes

$$x'(t) = g(t) - \frac{3x(t)}{125} \qquad \Rightarrow \qquad x'(t) + \frac{3}{125}x(t) = 4.8 + 2.4u(t-10) \tag{7.45}$$

with the initial condition $x(0) = 100$. Taking the Laplace transform of both sides yields

$$\begin{aligned} \mathcal{L}\{x'\}(s) + \frac{3}{125}\mathcal{L}\{x\}(s) &= \mathcal{L}\{4.8 + 2.4u(t-10)\}(s) = \frac{4.8}{s} + \frac{2.4e^{-10s}}{s} \\ \Rightarrow \qquad [s\mathcal{L}\{x\}(s) - 100] + \frac{3}{125}\mathcal{L}\{x\}(s) &= \frac{4.8}{s} + \frac{2.4e^{-10s}}{s} \\ \Rightarrow \qquad \mathcal{L}\{x\}(s) &= \frac{100s + 4.8}{s[s+(3/125)]} + \frac{2.4}{s[s+(3/125)]}e^{-10s}. \end{aligned} \tag{7.46}$$

Since

$$\begin{aligned} \frac{2.4}{s[s+(3/125)]} &= 100\left(\frac{1}{s} - \frac{1}{s+(3/125)}\right), \\ \frac{100s + 4.8}{s[s+(3/125)]} &= 100\left(\frac{2}{s} - \frac{1}{s+(3/125)}\right), \end{aligned}$$

applying the inverse Laplace transform in (7.46), we get

$$x(t) = 100\left(2 - e^{-3t/125}\right) + 100\left(1 - e^{-3(t-10)/125}\right)u(t-10).$$

Finally, dividing by the volume of the solution in the tank, which constantly equals to 500 L, we conclude that

$$\text{concentration} = 0.4 - 0.2e^{-3t/125} + 0.2\left(1 - e^{-3(t-10)/125}\right)u(t-10).$$

63. In this problem, the solution still enters the tank at the rate 12 L/min, but leaves the tank at the rate only 6 L/min. Thus, every minute, the volume of the solution in the tank increases by $12 - 6 = 6$ L. Therefore, the volume, as a function of t, is given by $500 + 6t$ and so

$$\text{output rate} = \frac{x(t)}{500 + 6t}\,(\text{kg/L}) \times 6\,(\text{L/min}) = \frac{3x(t)}{250 + 3t}\,(\text{kg/min}).$$

Instead of equation (7.45) in Problem 61, we now have

$$x'(t) = g(t) - \frac{3x(t)}{250 + 3t} \qquad \Rightarrow \qquad (250 + 3t)x'(t) + 3x(t) = (250 + 3t)[48 + 24u(t-10)].$$

This equation has polynomial coefficients and can also be solved using the Laplace transform method. (See the discussion in Section 7.5, page 380, and Example 4.) But, as an intermediate step, one will obtain a first order linear differential equation for $\mathcal{L}\{x\}(s)$.

EXERCISES 7.7: Convolution, page 405

1. Let $Y(s) := \mathcal{L}\{y\}(s)$, $G(s) := \mathcal{L}\{g\}(s)$. Taking the Laplace transform of both sides of the given differential equation and using the linear property of the Laplace transform, we obtain

$$\mathcal{L}\{y''\}(s) - 2\mathcal{L}\{y'\}(s) + Y(s) = G(s).$$

The initial conditions and Theorem 5, Section 7.3, imply that

$$\begin{aligned}\mathcal{L}\{y'\}(s) &= sY(s) + 1,\\ \mathcal{L}\{y''\}(s) &= s^2Y(s) + s - 1.\end{aligned}$$

Thus, substitution yields

$$\begin{aligned}&\left[s^2Y(s) + s - 1\right] - 2\left[sY(s) + 1\right] + Y(s) = G(s)\\ \Rightarrow\quad &\left(s^2 - 2s + 1\right)Y(s) = 3 - s + G(s)\\ \Rightarrow\quad &Y(s) = \frac{3-s}{s^2-2s+1} + \frac{G(s)}{s^2-2s+1} = \frac{2}{(s-1)^2} - \frac{1}{s-1} + \frac{G(s)}{(s-1)^2}\,.\end{aligned}$$

Taking now the inverse Laplace transform, we obtain

$$y(t) = 2\mathcal{L}^{-1}\left\{\frac{1}{(s-1)^2}\right\}(t) - \mathcal{L}^{-1}\left\{\frac{1}{s-1}\right\}(t) + \mathcal{L}^{-1}\left\{\frac{G(s)}{(s-1)^2}\right\}(t)\,.$$

Using Table 7.1, we find that

$$\mathcal{L}^{-1}\left\{\frac{1}{s-1}\right\}(t) = e^t\,, \qquad \mathcal{L}^{-1}\left\{\frac{1}{(s-1)^2}\right\}(t) = te^t\,,$$

and, by the convolution theorem,

$$\mathcal{L}^{-1}\left\{\frac{G(s)}{(s-1)^2}\right\}(t) = \mathcal{L}^{-1}\left\{\frac{1}{(s-1)^2}G(s)\right\}(t) = \left(te^t\right) * g(t) = \int_0^t (t-v)e^{t-v}g(v)\,dv.$$

Thus

$$y(t) = 2te^t - e^t + \int_0^t (t-v)e^{t-v}g(v)\,dv.$$

3. Taking the Laplace transform of $y'' + 4y' + 5y = g(t)$ and applying the initial conditions $y(0) = y'(0) = 1$ gives us

$$\left[s^2Y(s) - s - 1\right] + 4\left[sY(s) - 1\right] + 5Y(s) = G(s),$$

where $Y(s) := \mathcal{L}\{y\}(s)$, $G(s) := \mathcal{L}\{g\}(s)$. Thus

$$Y(s) = \frac{s+5}{s^2+4s+5} + \frac{G(s)}{s^2+4s+5} = \frac{s+2}{(s+2)^2+1} + \frac{3}{(s+2)^2+1} + \frac{G(s)}{(s+2)^2+1}\,.$$

Taking the inverse Laplace transform of $Y(s)$ with the help of the convolution theorem yields

$$y(t) = e^{-2t}\cos t + 3e^{-2t}\sin t + \int_0^t e^{-2(t-v)}\sin(t-v)g(v)\,dv..$$

5. Since $\mathcal{L}^{-1}\{1/s\}(t) = 1$ and $\mathcal{L}^{-1}\{1/(s^2+1)\}(t) = \sin t$, writing

$$\frac{1}{s(s^2+1)} = \frac{1}{s}\cdot\frac{1}{s^2+1}$$

and using the convolution theorem, we obtain

$$\mathcal{L}^{-1}\left\{\frac{1}{s(s^2+1)}\right\}(t) = 1 * \sin t = \int_0^t \sin v\,dv = -\cos v\,\Big|_0^t = 1 - \cos t.$$

7. From Table 7.1, $\mathcal{L}^{-1}\{1/(s-a)\}(t) = e^{at}$. Therefore, using the linearity of the inverse Laplace transform and the convolution theorem, we have

$$\begin{aligned}\mathcal{L}^{-1}\left\{\frac{14}{(s+2)(s-5)}\right\}(t) &= 14\mathcal{L}^{-1}\left\{\frac{1}{s+2}\cdot\frac{1}{s-5}\right\}(t) = 14e^{-2t} * e^{5t} = 14\int_0^t e^{-2(t-v)}e^{5v}\,dv \\ &= 14e^{-2t}\int_0^t e^{7v}\,dv = 2e^{-2t}\left(e^{7t}-1\right) = 2\left(e^{5t}-e^{-2t}\right).\end{aligned}$$

9. Since $s/(s^2+1)^2 = [s/(s^2+1)] \cdot [1/(s^2+1)]$ the convolution theorem tells us that

$$\mathcal{L}^{-1}\left\{\frac{s}{(s^2+1)^2}\right\}(t) = \mathcal{L}^{-1}\left\{\frac{s}{s^2+1}\cdot\frac{s}{s^2+1}\right\}(t) = \cos t * \sin t = \int_0^t \cos(t-v)\sin v\,dv.$$

Using the identity $\sin\alpha\cos\beta = [\sin(\alpha+\beta)+\sin(\alpha-\beta)]/2$, we get

$$\begin{aligned}\mathcal{L}^{-1}\left\{\frac{s}{(s^2+1)^2}\right\}(t) &= \frac{1}{2}\int_0^t [\sin t + \sin(t-2v)]\,dv \\ &= \frac{1}{2}\left(v\sin t + \frac{\cos(t-2v)}{2}\right)\Bigg|_0^t = \frac{t\sin t}{2}.\end{aligned}$$

11. Using the hint, we can write

$$\frac{s}{(s-1)(s+2)} = \frac{1}{s+2} + \frac{1}{(s-1)(s+2)},$$

so that by the convolution theorem, Theorem 11 on page 400 of the text,

$$\begin{aligned}\mathcal{L}^{-1}\left\{\frac{s}{(s-1)(s+2)}\right\}(t) &= \mathcal{L}^{-1}\left\{\frac{1}{s+2}\right\}(t) + \mathcal{L}^{-1}\left\{\frac{1}{(s-1)(s+2)}\right\}(t) \\ &= e^{-2t} + e^t * e^{-2t} = e^{-2t} + \int_0^t e^{t-v}e^{-2v}\,dv \\ &= e^{-2t} + e^t\int_0^t e^{-3v}\,dv = e^{-2t} - \frac{e^t}{3}\left(e^{-3t}-1\right) = \frac{2e^{-2t}}{3} + \frac{e^t}{3}.\end{aligned}$$

13. Note that $f(t) = t * e^{3t}$. Hence, by (8) on page 400 of the text,

$$\mathcal{L}\{f(t)\}(s) = \mathcal{L}\{t\}(s)\mathcal{L}\left\{e^{3t}\right\}(s) = \frac{1}{s^2}\cdot\frac{1}{s-3} = \frac{1}{s^2(s-3)}.$$

15. Note that

$$\int_0^t y(v)\sin(t-v)\,dv = \sin t * y(t).$$

Let $Y(s) := \mathcal{L}\{y\}(s)$. Taking the Laplace transform of the original equation, we obtain

$$Y(s) + 3\mathcal{L}\{\sin t * y(t)\}(s) = \mathcal{L}\{t\}(s)$$

$$\Rightarrow \quad Y(s) + 3\mathcal{L}\{\sin t\}(s)Y(s) = \frac{1}{s^2} \quad \Rightarrow \quad Y(s) + \frac{3}{s^2+1}Y(s) = \frac{1}{s^2}$$

$$\Rightarrow \quad Y(s) = \frac{s^2+1}{s^2(s^2+4)} = \frac{(1/4)}{s^2} + \frac{(3/8)2}{s^2+2^2}$$

$$\Rightarrow \quad y(t) = \mathcal{L}^{-1}\left\{\frac{(1/4)}{s^2} + \frac{(3/8)2}{s^2+2^2}\right\}(t) = \frac{t}{4} + \frac{3\sin 2t}{8}.$$

17. We use the convolution Theorem 11 to find the Laplace transform of the integral term.

$$\mathcal{L}\left\{\int_0^t (t-v)y(v)\,dv\right\}(s) = \mathcal{L}\{t * y(t)\}(s) = \mathcal{L}\{t\}(s)\mathcal{L}\{y(t)\}(s) = \frac{Y(s)}{s^2},$$

where $Y(s)$ denotes the Laplace transform of $y(t)$. Thus taking the Laplace transform of both sides of the given equation yields

$$Y(s) + \frac{Y(s)}{s^2} = \frac{1}{s} \quad \Rightarrow \quad Y(s) = \frac{s}{s^2+1} \quad \Rightarrow \quad y(t) = \mathcal{L}^{-1}\left\{\frac{s}{s^2+1}\right\}(t) = \cos t.$$

19. By the convolution theorem,

$$\mathcal{L}\left\{\int_0^t (t-v)^2 y(v)\,dv\right\}(s) = \mathcal{L}\{t^2 * y(t)\}(s) = \mathcal{L}\{t^2\}(s)\mathcal{L}\{y(t)\}(s) = \frac{2Y(s)}{s^3}.$$

Hence, applying the Laplace transform to the original equation yields

$$Y(s) + \frac{2Y(s)}{s^3} = \mathcal{L}\{t^3+3\}(s) = \frac{6}{s^4} + \frac{3}{s}$$

$$\Rightarrow \quad Y(s) = \frac{s^3}{s^3+2} \cdot \frac{6+3s^3}{s^4} = \frac{3}{s}$$

$$\Rightarrow \quad y(t) = \mathcal{L}^{-1}\left\{\frac{3}{s}\right\}(t) = 3.$$

21. As in Example 3 on page 402 of the text, we first rewrite the integro-differential equation as

$$y'(t) + y(t) - y(t) * \sin t = -\sin t, \qquad y(0) = 1. \tag{7.47}$$

We now take the Laplace transform of (7.47) to obtain

$$[sY(s) - 1] + Y(s) - \frac{1}{s^2+1}Y(s) = -\frac{1}{s^2+1},$$

where $Y(s) = \mathcal{L}\{y\}(s)$. Thus,

$$\begin{aligned} Y(s) &= \frac{s^2}{s^3+s^2+s} = \frac{s}{s^2+s+1} = \frac{s}{(s+1/2)^2+3/4} \\ &= \frac{s+1/2}{(s+1/2)^2+3/4} - \frac{(1/\sqrt{3})(\sqrt{3}/2)}{(s+1/2)^2+3/4}. \end{aligned}$$

Taking the inverse Laplace transform yields

$$y(t) = e^{-t/2}\cos\left(\frac{\sqrt{3}t}{2}\right) - \frac{1}{\sqrt{3}}e^{-t/2}\sin\left(\frac{\sqrt{3}t}{2}\right).$$

23. Taking the Laplace transform of the differential equation, and assuming zero initial conditions, we obtain

$$s^2Y(s) + 9Y(s) = G(s),$$

where $Y = \mathcal{L}\{y\}$, $G = \mathcal{L}\{g\}$. Thus,

$$H(s) = \frac{Y(s)}{G(s)} = \frac{1}{s^2+9}.$$

The impulse response function is then

$$h(t) = \mathcal{L}^{-1}\{H(s)\}(t) = \mathcal{L}^{-1}\left\{\frac{1}{s^2+9}\right\}(t) = \frac{1}{3}\mathcal{L}^{-1}\left\{\frac{3}{s^2+3^2}\right\}(t) = \frac{\sin 3t}{3}.$$

To solve the initial value problem, we need the solution to the corresponding homogeneous problem. The auxiliary equation, $r^2 + 9 = 0$, has roots, $r = \pm 3i$. Thus, a general solution to the homogeneous equation is

$$y_h(t) = C_1\cos 3t + C_2\sin 3t.$$

Applying the initial conditions $y(0) = 2$ and $y'(0) = -3$, we obtain

$$\begin{aligned} 2 = y(0) = (C_1\cos 3t + C_2\sin 3t)\big|_{t=0} = C_1\,, \\ -3 = y'(0) = (-3C_1\sin 3t + 3C_2\cos 3t\big|_{t=0} = 3C_2 \end{aligned} \qquad \Rightarrow \qquad \begin{aligned} C_1 &= 2\,, \\ C_2 &= -1\,. \end{aligned}$$

So

$$y_k(t) = 2\cos 3t - \sin 3t,$$

and the formula for the solution to the original initial value problem is

$$y = (h * g)(t) + y_k(t) = \frac{1}{3}\int_0^t g(v)\sin 3(t-v)\,dv + 2\cos 3t - \sin 3t.$$

25. Taking the Laplace transform of both sides of the given equation and assuming zero initial conditions, we get

$$\mathcal{L}\{y'' - y' - 6y\}(s) = \mathcal{L}\{g(t)\}(s) \qquad \Rightarrow \qquad s^2Y(s) - sY(s) - 6Y(s) = G(s).$$

Thus,

$$H(s) = \frac{Y(s)}{G(s)} = \frac{1}{s^2 - s - 6} = \frac{1}{(s-3)(s+2)}$$

is the transfer function. The impulse response function $h(t)$ is then given by

$$h(t) = \mathcal{L}^{-1}\left\{\frac{1}{(s-3)(s+2)}\right\}(t) = e^{3t} * e^{-2t} = \int_0^t e^{3(t-v)}e^{-2v}\,dv = e^{3t}\left.\frac{e^{-5v}}{-5}\right|_0^t = \frac{e^{3t} - e^{-2t}}{5}.$$

To solve the given initial value problem, we use Theorem 12. To this end, we need the solution $y_k(t)$ to the corresponding initial value problem for the homogeneous equation. That is,

$$y'' - y' - 6y = 0, \qquad y(0) = 1, \quad y'(0) = 8$$

(see (19) in the text). Applying the Laplace transform yields

$$\begin{aligned}
&\left[s^2Y_k(s) - s - 8\right] - \left[sY_k(s) - 1\right] - 6Y_k(s) = 0\\
\Rightarrow \qquad & Y_k(s) = \frac{s+7}{s^2 - s - 6} = \frac{s+7}{(s-3)(s+2)} = \frac{2}{s-3} - \frac{1}{s+2}\\
\Rightarrow \qquad & y_k(t) = \mathcal{L}^{-1}\{Y_k(s)\}(t) = \mathcal{L}^{-1}\left\{\frac{2}{s-3} - \frac{1}{s+2}\right\}(t) = 2e^{3t} - e^{-2t}.
\end{aligned}$$

So,

$$y(t) = (h * g)(t) + y_k(t) = \frac{1}{5}\int_0^t \left[e^{3(t-v)} - e^{-2(t-v)}\right] g(v)\,dv + 2e^{3t} - e^{-2t}.$$

27. Taking the Laplace transform and assuming zero initial conditions, we find the transfer function $H(s)$.

$$s^2Y(s) - 2sY(s) + 5Y(s) = G(s) \qquad \Rightarrow \qquad H(s) = \frac{Y(s)}{G(s)} = \frac{1}{s^2 - 2s + 5}\,.$$

Therefore, the impulse response function is

$$h(t) = \mathcal{L}^{-1}\{H(s)\}(t) = \mathcal{L}^{-1}\left\{\frac{1}{(s-1)^2+2^2}\right\}(t) = \frac{1}{2}\,\mathcal{L}^{-1}\left\{\frac{2}{(s-1)^2+2^2}\right\}(t) = \frac{1}{2}\,e^t \sin 2t\,.$$

Next, we find the solution $y_k(t)$ to the corresponding initial value problem for the homogeneous equation,

$$y'' - 2y' + 5y = 0, \qquad y(0) = 0, \quad y'(0) = 2.$$

Since the associated equation, $r^2 - 2r + 5 = 0$, has roots $r = 1 \pm 2i$, a general solution to the homogeneous equations is

$$y_h(t) = e^t\left(C_1 \cos 2t + C_2 \sin 2t\right).$$

We satisfy the initial conditions by solving

$$\begin{aligned} 0 &= y(0) = C_1 \\ 2 &= y'(0) = C_1 + 2C_2 \end{aligned} \qquad \Rightarrow \qquad \begin{aligned} C_1 &= 0, \\ C_2 &= 1. \end{aligned}$$

Hence, $y_k(t) = e^t \sin 2t$ and

$$y(t) = (h * g)(t) + y_k(t) = \frac{1}{2}\int_0^t e^{t-v} \sin 2(t-v)g(v)\,dv + e^t \sin 2t$$

is the desired solution.

29. With given data, the initial value problem becomes

$$5I''(t) + 20I'(t) + \frac{1}{0.005}\,I(t) = e(t), \qquad I(0) = -1, \quad I'(0) = 8.$$

Using formula (15) on page 403 of the text, we find the transfer function

$$H(s) = \frac{1}{5s^2 + 20s + 200} = \frac{1}{5}\,\frac{1}{(s+2)^2 + 6^2}\,.$$

Therefore,

$$h(t)=\mathcal{L}^{-1}\left\{\frac{1}{5}\frac{1}{(s+2)^2+6^2}\right\}(t)=\frac{1}{30}\mathcal{L}^{-1}\left\{\frac{6}{(s+2)^2+6^2}\right\}(t)=\frac{1}{30}e^{-2t}\sin 6t.$$

Next, we consider the initial value problem

$$5I''(t)+20I'(t)+200I(t)=0, \qquad I(0)=-1, \quad I'(0)=8$$

for the corresponding homogeneous equation. Its characteristic equation, $5r^2+20r+200=0$, has roots $r=-2\pm 6i$, which yield a general solution

$$I_h(t)=e^{-2t}\left(C_1\cos 6t+C_2\sin 6t\right).$$

We find constants C_1 and C_2 so that the solution satisfies the initial conditions. Thus we have

$$\begin{aligned} -1 &= I(0)=C_1\,, \\ 8 &= I'(0)=-2C_1+6C_2 \end{aligned} \qquad \Rightarrow \qquad \begin{aligned} C_1 &= -1\,, \\ C_2 &= 1\,, \end{aligned}$$

and so $I_k(t)=e^{-2t}\left(\sin 6t-\cos 6t\right)$. Finally,

$$I(t)=h(t)*e(t)+I_k(t)=\frac{1}{30}\int_0^t e(v)e^{-2(t-v)}\sin 6(t-v)\,dv+e^{-2t}\left(\sin 6t-\cos 6t\right).$$

31. By the convolution theorem, we get

$$\mathcal{L}\left\{1*1*1\right\}(s)=\mathcal{L}\left\{1\right\}(s)\mathcal{L}\left\{1*1\right\}(s)=\mathcal{L}\left\{1\right\}(s)\mathcal{L}\left\{1\right\}(s)\mathcal{L}\left\{1\right\}(s)=\left(\frac{1}{s}\right)^3=\frac{1}{s^3}.$$

Therefore, the definition of the inverse Laplace transform yields

$$1*1*1=\mathcal{L}^{-1}\left\{\frac{1}{s^3}\right\}(t)=\frac{1}{2}\mathcal{L}^{-1}\left\{\frac{2}{s^3}\right\}(t)=\frac{1}{2}t^2.$$

33. Using the linear property of integrals, we have

$$\begin{aligned} f*(g+h) &= \int_0^t f(t-v)[g+h](v)\,dv=\int_0^t f(t-v)[g(v)+h(v)]\,dv \\ &= \int_0^t f(t-v)g(v)\,dv+\int_0^t f(t-v)h(v)\,dv=f*g+f*h. \end{aligned}$$

35. Since

$$\int_0^t f(v)\,dv = \int_0^t 1\cdot f(v)\,dv = 1 * f(t),$$

we conclude that

$$\mathcal{L}\left\{\int_0^t f(v)\,dv\right\}(s) = \mathcal{L}\{1 * f(t)\}(s) = \mathcal{L}\{1\}(s)\mathcal{L}\{f(t)\}(s) = \frac{1}{s}\,F(s).$$

Hence, by the definition of the inverse Laplace transform,

$$\int_0^t f(v)\,dv = \mathcal{L}^{-1}\left\{\frac{1}{s}\,F(s)\right\}(t).$$

(Note that the integral in the left-hand side is a continuous function.)

37. Actually, this statement holds for any continuously differentiable function $h(t)$ on $[0,\infty)$ satisfying $h(0)=0$. Indeed, first of all,

$$(h*g)(0) = \left.\int_0^t h(t-v)g(v)\,dv\right|_{t=0} = \int_0^0 h(-v)g(v)\,dv = 0$$

since the interval of integration has zero length. Next, we apply the Leibniz's rule to find the derivative of $(h*g)(t)$.

$$\begin{aligned}(h*g)'(t) &= \left(\int_0^t h(t-v)g(v)\,dv\right)' = \int_0^t \frac{\partial h(t-v)g(v)}{\partial t}\,dv + h(t-v)g(v)\Big|_{v=t} \\ &= \int_0^t h'(t-v)g(v)\,dv + h(0)g(t) = \int_0^t h'(t-v)g(v)\,dv\end{aligned}$$

since $h(0)=0$. Therefore,

$$(h*g)'(0) = \int_0^0 h'(-v)g(v)\,dv = 0,$$

again as a definite integral with equal limits of integration.

EXERCISES 7.8: Impulses and the Dirac Delta Function, page 412

1. By equation (3) on page 407 of the text,

$$\int_{-\infty}^{\infty} (t^2-1)\boldsymbol{\delta}(t)\,dt = \left(t^2-1\right)\Big|_{t=0} = -1.$$

3. By equation (3) on page 407 of the text,

$$\int_{-\infty}^{\infty} (\sin 3t)\boldsymbol{\delta}\left(t-\frac{\pi}{2}\right)dt = \sin\left(3\cdot\frac{\pi}{2}\right) = -1.$$

5. Formula (6) of the Laplace transform of the Dirac delta function yields

$$\int_{0}^{\infty} e^{-2t}\boldsymbol{\delta}(t-1)\,dt = \mathcal{L}\left\{\boldsymbol{\delta}(t-1)\right\}(2) = e^{-s}\Big|_{s=2} = e^{-2}.$$

7. Using the linearity of the Laplace transform and (6) on page 409 of the text, we get

$$\mathcal{L}\left\{\boldsymbol{\delta}(t-1)-\boldsymbol{\delta}(t-3)\right\}(s) = \mathcal{L}\left\{\boldsymbol{\delta}(t-1)\right\}(s) - \mathcal{L}\left\{\boldsymbol{\delta}(t-3)\right\}(s) = e^{-s}-e^{-3s}.$$

9. Since $\boldsymbol{\delta}(t-1)=0$ for $t<1$,

$$\mathcal{L}\left\{t\boldsymbol{\delta}(t-1)\right\}(s) := \int_{0}^{\infty} e^{-st}t\boldsymbol{\delta}(t-1)\,dt = \int_{-\infty}^{\infty} e^{-st}t\boldsymbol{\delta}(t-1)\,dt = e^{-st}t\Big|_{t=1} = e^{-s}$$

by equation (3) on page 407 of the text.

Another way to solve this problem is to use Theorem 6 inj Section 7.3. This yields

$$\mathcal{L}\left\{t\boldsymbol{\delta}(t-1)\right\}(s) = -\frac{d}{ds}\mathcal{L}\left\{\boldsymbol{\delta}(t-1)\right\}(s) = -\frac{d\left(e^{-s}\right)}{ds} = e^{-s}.$$

11. Since $\boldsymbol{\delta}(t-\pi)=0$ for $t<\pi$, we use the definition of the Laplace transform and formula (3), page 407 of the text, to conclude that

$$\mathcal{L}\left\{(\sin t)\boldsymbol{\delta}(t-\pi)\right\}(s) := \int_{0}^{\infty} e^{-st}(\sin t)\boldsymbol{\delta}(t-\pi)\,dt = \int_{-\infty}^{\infty} e^{-st}(\sin t)\boldsymbol{\delta}(t-\pi)\,dt = e^{-\pi t}\sin\pi = 0.$$

13. Let $W(s) := \mathcal{L}\{w\}(s)$. Using the initial conditions and Theorem 5 in Section 7.3, we find that

$$\mathcal{L}\{w''\}(s) = s^2W(s) - sw(0) - w'(0) = s^2W(s).$$

Thus, applying the Laplace transform to both sides of the given equation yields

$$s^2W(s) + W(s) = \mathcal{L}\{\boldsymbol{\delta}(t-\pi)\}(s) = e^{-\pi s} \qquad \Rightarrow \qquad W(s) = \frac{e^{-\pi s}}{s^2+1}.$$

Taking the inverse Laplace transform of both sides of the last equation and using Theorem 8 in Section 7.6, we get

$$w(t) = \mathcal{L}^{-1}\left\{\frac{e^{-\pi s}}{s^2+1}\right\}(t) = \mathcal{L}^{-1}\left\{\frac{1}{s^2+1}\right\}(t-\pi)u(t-\pi) = \sin(t-\pi)u(t-\pi) = -(\sin t)u(t-\pi).$$

15. Let $Y := \mathcal{L}\{y\}$. Taking the Laplace transform of $y'' + 2y' - 3y = \boldsymbol{\delta}(t-1) - \boldsymbol{\delta}(t-2)$ and applying the initial conditions $y(0) = 2$, $y'(0) = -2$, we obtain

$$\left[s^2Y(s) - 2s + 2\right] + 2\left[sY(s) - 2\right] - 3Y(s) = \mathcal{L}\{\boldsymbol{\delta}(t-1) - \boldsymbol{\delta}(t-2)\}(s) = e^{-s} - e^{-2s}$$

$$\Rightarrow \qquad Y(s) = \frac{2s+2+e^{-s}-e^{-2s}}{s^2+2s-3} = \frac{2s+2}{(s+3)(s-1)} + \frac{e^{-s}}{(s+3)(s-1)} - \frac{e^{-2s}}{(s+3)(s-1)}$$

$$= \frac{1}{s-1} + \frac{1}{s+3} + \frac{e^{-s}}{4}\left(\frac{1}{s-1} - \frac{1}{s+3}\right) - \frac{e^{-2s}}{4}\left(\frac{1}{s-1} - \frac{1}{s+3}\right),$$

so that by Theorem 8 on page 387 of the text we get

$$y(t) = e^t + e^{-3t} + \frac{1}{4}\left(e^{t-1} - e^{-3(t-1)}\right)u(t-1) - \frac{1}{4}\left(e^{t-2} - e^{-3(t-2)}\right)u(t-2).$$

17. Let $Y := \mathcal{L}\{y\}$. We use the initial conditions to find that

$$\mathcal{L}\{y''\}(s) = s^2Y(s) - sy(0) - y'(0) = s^2Y(s) - 2.$$

Thus taking the Laplace transform of both sides of the given equation and using formula (6) on page 409, we get

$$\left[s^2Y(s) - 2\right] - Y(s) = 4\mathcal{L}\{\boldsymbol{\delta}(t-2)\}(s) + \mathcal{L}\{t^2\}(s) = 4e^{-2s} + \frac{2}{s^3}$$

$$\Rightarrow \qquad Y(s) = \frac{4e^{-2s}}{s^2-1} + \frac{2(s^3+1)}{s^3(s^2-1)} = 2e^{-2s}\left(\frac{1}{s-1} - \frac{1}{s+1}\right) + \frac{2}{s-1} - \frac{2}{s^3} - \frac{2}{s}.$$

Now we can apply the inverse Laplace transform.

$$\begin{aligned} y(t) &= \mathcal{L}^{-1}\left\{2e^{-2s}\left(\frac{1}{s-1}-\frac{1}{s+1}\right)+\frac{2}{s-1}-\frac{2}{s^3}-\frac{2}{s}\right\}(t) \\ &= 2\left(\mathcal{L}^{-1}\left\{\frac{1}{s-1}\right\}-\mathcal{L}^{-1}\left\{\frac{1}{s+1}\right\}\right)(t-2)u(t-2) \\ &\qquad +2\mathcal{L}^{-1}\left\{\frac{1}{s-1}\right\}(t)-\mathcal{L}^{-1}\left\{\frac{2}{s^3}\right\}(t)-2\mathcal{L}^{-1}\left\{\frac{1}{s}\right\}(t) \\ &= 2\left(e^{t-2}-e^{2-t}\right)u(t-2)+2e^t-t^2-2. \end{aligned}$$

19. Let $W(s) := \mathcal{L}\{w\}(s)$. We apply the Laplace transform to the given equation and obtain

$$\mathcal{L}\{w''\}(s)+6\mathcal{L}\{w'\}(s)+5W(s)=\mathcal{L}\left\{e^t\boldsymbol{\delta}(t-1)\right\}(s). \tag{7.48}$$

From formula (4) on page 362 of the text we see that

$$\begin{aligned} \mathcal{L}\{w'\}(s) &= sW(s)-w(0)=sW(s), \\ \mathcal{L}\{w''\}(s) &= s^2W(s)-sw(0)-w'(0)=s^2W(s)-4. \end{aligned} \tag{7.49}$$

Also, the translation property (1), Section 7.3, of the Laplace transform yields

$$\mathcal{L}\left\{e^t\boldsymbol{\delta}(t-1)\right\}(s)=\mathcal{L}\{\boldsymbol{\delta}(t-1)\}(s-1)=e^{-(s-1)}=e^{1-s}. \tag{7.50}$$

Substituting (7.49) and (7.50) back into (7.48), we obtain

$$\begin{aligned} &\left[s^2W(s)-4\right]+6\left[sW(s)\right]+5W(s)=e^{1-s} \\ \Rightarrow\quad & W(s)=\frac{4+e^{1-s}}{s^2+6s+5}=\frac{4+e^{1-s}}{(s+1)(s+5)}=\frac{1}{s+1}-\frac{1}{s+5}+\frac{e}{4}e^{-s}\left(\frac{1}{s+1}-\frac{1}{s+5}\right). \end{aligned}$$

Finally, the inverse Laplace transform of both sides of this equation yields

$$w(t)=e^{-t}-e^{-5t}+\frac{e}{4}\left[e^{-(t-1)}-e^{-5(t-1)}\right]u(t-1).$$

21. We apply the Laplace transform to the given equation, solve the resulting equation for $\mathcal{L}\{y\}(s)$, and then use the inverse Laplace transforms. This yields

$$\mathcal{L}\{y''\}(s)+\mathcal{L}\{y\}(s)=\mathcal{L}\{\boldsymbol{\delta}(t-2\pi)\}(s)$$

$$\Rightarrow \quad \left[s^2\mathcal{L}\{y\}(s) - 1\right] + \mathcal{L}\{y\}(s) = e^{-2\pi s} \quad \Rightarrow \quad \mathcal{L}\{y\}(s) = \frac{1+e^{-2\pi s}}{s^2+1}$$

$$\Rightarrow \quad y(t) = \mathcal{L}^{-1}\left\{\frac{1}{s^2+1}\right\}(t) + \mathcal{L}^{-1}\left\{\frac{1}{s^2+1}\right\}(t-2\pi)u(t-2\pi)$$
$$= \sin t + [\sin(t-2\pi)]u(t-2\pi) = [1+u(t-2\pi)]\sin t.$$

The graph of the solution is shown in Figure B.49 in the answers of the text.

23. The solution to the initial value problem

$$y'' + y = \boldsymbol{\delta}(t-2\pi), \qquad y(0) = 0, \quad y'(0) = 1$$

is given in Problem 21, that is

$$y_1(t) = [1+u(t-2\pi)]\sin t.$$

Thus, if $y_2(t)$ is the solution to the initial value problem

$$y'' + y = -\boldsymbol{\delta}(t-\pi), \qquad y(0) = 0, \quad y'(0) = 0, \tag{7.51}$$

then, by the superposition principle (see Section 4.5), $y(t) = y_1(t) + y_2(t)$ is the desired solution. The Laplace transform of both sides in (7.51) yields

$$s^2\mathcal{L}\{y\}(s) + \mathcal{L}\{y\}(s) = -e^{-\pi s} \quad \Rightarrow \quad \mathcal{L}\{y\}(s) = -\frac{e^{-\pi s}}{s^2+1}$$

$$\Rightarrow \quad y_2(t) = -\mathcal{L}^{-1}\left\{\frac{1}{s^2+1}\right\}(t-\pi)u(t-\pi) = -[\sin(t-\pi)]u(t-\pi) = u(t-\pi)\sin t.$$

(We have used zero initial conditions to express $\mathcal{L}\{y''\}$ in terms of $\mathcal{L}\{y\}$.) Therefore, the answer is

$$y(t) = y_1(t) + y_2(t) = [1+u(t-2\pi)]\sin t + u(t-\pi)\sin t = [1+u(t-\pi)+u(t-2\pi)]\sin t.$$

The sketch of this curve is given in Figure B.50 .

25. Taking the Laplace transform of $y'' + 4y' + 8y = \boldsymbol{\delta}(t)$ with zero initial conditions yields

$$s^2Y(s) + 4sY(s) + 8Y(s) = \mathcal{L}\{\boldsymbol{\delta}(t)\}(s) = 1.$$

Solving for $Y(s)$, we obtain

$$Y(s)=\frac{1}{s^2+4s+8}=\frac{1}{(s+2)^2+4}=\frac{1}{2}\frac{2}{(s+2)^2+2^2}$$

so that

$$h(t)=\mathcal{L}^{-1}\left\{\frac{1}{2}\frac{2}{(s+2)^2+2^2}\right\}(t)=\frac{1}{2}e^{-2t}\sin 2t\,.$$

Notice that $H(s)$ for $y''+4y'+8y=g(t)$ with $y(0)=y'(0)=0$ is given by $H(s)=1/(s^2+4s+8)$, so that again

$$h(t)=\mathcal{L}^{-1}\{H(s)\}(t)=\frac{1}{2}e^{-2t}\sin 2t\,.$$

27. The Laplace transform of both sides of the given equation, with zero initial conditions and $g(t)=\delta(t)$, gives us

$$\begin{aligned}&s^2\mathcal{L}\{y\}(s)-2s\mathcal{L}\{y\}(s)+5\mathcal{L}\{y\}(s)=\mathcal{L}\{\delta(t)\}(s)\\ \Rightarrow\qquad &\mathcal{L}\{y\}(s)=\frac{1}{s^2-2s+5}=\frac{1}{(s-1)^2+2^2}\,.\end{aligned}$$

The inverse Laplace transform now yields

$$h(t)=\mathcal{L}^{-1}\left\{\frac{1}{(s-1)^2+2^2}\right\}(t)=\frac{1}{2}\mathcal{L}^{-1}\left\{\frac{2}{(s-1)^2+2^2}\right\}(t)=\frac{1}{2}e^{t}\sin 2t\,.$$

29. We solve the given initial value problem to find the displacement $x(t)$. Let $X(s):=\mathcal{L}\{x\}(s)$. Applying the Laplace transform to the differential equation yields

$$\mathcal{L}\{x''\}(s)+9X(s)=\mathcal{L}\left\{-3\delta\left(t-\frac{\pi}{2}\right)\right\}(s)=-3e^{-\pi s/2}\,.$$

Since

$$\mathcal{L}\{x''\}(s)=s^2X(s)-sx(0)-x'(0)=s^2X(s)-s,$$

the above equation becomes

$$\left[s^2X(s)-s\right]+9X(s)=-3e^{-\pi s/2}\quad\Rightarrow\quad X(s)=\frac{s-3e^{-\pi s/2}}{s^2+9}=\frac{s}{s^2+3^2}-e^{-\pi s/2}\frac{3}{s^2+3^2}\,.$$

Therefore,

$$x(t)\;=\;\mathcal{L}^{-1}\left\{\frac{s}{s^2+3^2}-e^{-\pi s/2}\frac{3}{s^2+3^2}\right\}(t)$$

$$= \cos 3t - \left[\sin 3\left(t - \frac{\pi}{2}\right)\right] u\left(t - \frac{\pi}{2}\right) = \left[1 - u\left(t - \frac{\pi}{2}\right)\right] \cos 3t\,.$$

Since, for $t > \pi/2$, $u(t - \pi/2) \equiv 1$, we conclude that

$$x(t) \equiv 0 \qquad \text{for} \quad t > \frac{\pi}{2}\,.$$

This means that the mass stops after the hit and remains in the equilibrium position thereafter.

31. By taking the Laplace transform of

$$ay'' + by' = cy = \boldsymbol{\delta}(t), \qquad y(0) = y'(0) = 0,$$

and solving for $Y := \mathcal{L}\{y\}$, we find that the transfer function is given by

$$H(s) = \frac{1}{as^2 + bs + c}\,.$$

If the roots of the polynomial $as^2 + bs + c$ are real and distinct, say r_1, r_2, then

$$H(s) = \frac{1}{(s - r_1)(s - r_2)} = \frac{1/(r_1 - r_2)}{s - r_1} - \frac{1/(r_1 - r_2)}{s - r_2}\,.$$

Thus

$$h(t) = \frac{1}{r_1 - r_2}\left(e^{r_1 t} - e^{r_2 t}\right)$$

and clearly $h(t)$ is bounded as $t \to \infty$ if and only if r_1 and r_2 are less than or equal to zero.

If the roots of $as^2 + bs + c$ are complex, then, by the quadratic formula, they are given by

$$-\frac{b}{2a} \pm \frac{\sqrt{4ac - b^2}}{2a}\,i$$

so that the real part of the roots is $-b/(2a)$. Now

$$\begin{aligned} H(s) &= \frac{1}{as^2 + bs + c} = \frac{1}{a} \cdot \frac{1}{s^2 + (b/a)s + (c/a)} = \frac{1}{a} \cdot \frac{1}{[s + b/(2a)]^2 + (4ac - b^2)/(4a^2)} \\ &= \frac{2}{\sqrt{4ac - b^2}} \cdot \frac{\sqrt{4ac - b^2}/(2a)}{[s + b/(2a)]^2 + [\sqrt{4ac - b^2}/(2a)]^2} \end{aligned}$$

so that

$$h(t) = \frac{2}{\sqrt{4ac - b^2}}\, e^{-(b/2a)t} \sin\left(\frac{\sqrt{4ac - b^2}}{2a}\, t\right),$$

and again it is clear that $h(t)$ is bounded if and only if $-b/(2a)$, the real part of the roots of $as^2 + bs + c$, is less than or equal to zero.

33. Let a function $f(t)$ be defined on $(-\infty, \infty)$ and continuous in a neighborhood of the origin, $t = 0$. Since $\boldsymbol{\delta}(t) = 0$ for any $t \neq 0$, so does the product $f(t)\boldsymbol{\delta}(t)$. Therefore,

$$\int_{-\infty}^{\infty} f(t)\boldsymbol{\delta}(t)\,dt = \int_{-\varepsilon}^{\varepsilon} f(t)\boldsymbol{\delta}(t)\,dt \qquad \text{for any } \varepsilon > 0. \tag{7.52}$$

By the mean value theorem, for any ε small enough (so that $f(t)$ is continuous on $(-\varepsilon, \varepsilon)$) there exists a point ζ_ε in $(-\varepsilon, \varepsilon)$ such that

$$\int_{-\varepsilon}^{\varepsilon} f(t)\boldsymbol{\delta}(t)\,dt = f(\zeta_\varepsilon)\int_{-\varepsilon}^{\varepsilon} \boldsymbol{\delta}(t)\,dt = f(\zeta_\varepsilon)\int_{-\infty}^{\infty} \boldsymbol{\delta}(t)\,dt = f(\zeta_\varepsilon).$$

Together with (7.52) this yields

$$\int_{-\infty}^{\infty} f(t)\boldsymbol{\delta}(t)\,dt = f(\zeta_\varepsilon), \qquad \text{for any } \varepsilon > 0.$$

Now we take limit, as $\varepsilon \to 0$, in both sides.

$$\lim_{\varepsilon \to 0}\left[\int_{-\infty}^{\infty} f(t)\boldsymbol{\delta}(t)\,dt\right] = \lim_{\varepsilon \to 0}\left[f(\zeta_\varepsilon)\right].$$

Note that the integral in the left-hand side does not depend on ε, and so the limit equals to the integral itself. In the right-hand side, since ζ_ε belongs to $(-\varepsilon, \varepsilon)$, $\zeta_\varepsilon \to 0$ as $\varepsilon \to 0$, and the continuity of $f(t)$ implies that $f(\zeta_\varepsilon)$ converges to $f(0)$, as $\varepsilon \to 0$. Combining these observations, we get the required.

35. Following the hint, we solve the initial value problem

$$EIy^{(4)}(x) = L\boldsymbol{\delta}(x - \lambda), \qquad y(0) = y'(0) = 0,\ y''(0) = A,\ y'''(0) = B.$$

Using these initial conditions and Theorem 5 in Section 7.3 with $n = 4$, we obtain

$$\mathcal{L}\left\{y^{(4)}(x)\right\}(s) = s^4\mathcal{L}\left\{y(x)\right\}(s) - sA - B,$$

and so the Laplace transform of the given equation yields

$$EI\left[s^4\mathcal{L}\{y(x)\}(s) - sA - B\right] = L\mathcal{L}\{\boldsymbol{\delta}(x-\lambda)\}(s) = Le^{-\lambda s}.$$

Therefore,

$$\begin{aligned}
\mathcal{L}\{y(x)\}(s) &= \frac{L}{EI}\frac{e^{-\lambda s}}{s^4} + \frac{A}{s^3} + \frac{B}{s^4} \\
\Rightarrow \qquad y(x) &= \mathcal{L}^{-1}\left\{\frac{L}{EI}\frac{e^{-\lambda s}}{s^4} + \frac{A}{s^3} + \frac{B}{s^4}\right\}(x) \\
&= \frac{L}{EI3!}\mathcal{L}^{-1}\left\{\frac{3!}{s^4}\right\}(x-\lambda)u(x-\lambda) + \frac{A}{2!}\mathcal{L}^{-1}\left\{\frac{2!}{s^3}\right\}(x) + \frac{B}{3!}\mathcal{L}^{-1}\left\{\frac{3!}{s^4}\right\}(x) \\
&= \frac{L}{6EI}(x-\lambda)^3u(x-\lambda) + \frac{A}{2}x^2 + \frac{B}{6}x^3. \qquad (7.53)
\end{aligned}$$

Next, we are looking for A and B such that $y''(2\lambda) = y'''(2\lambda) = 0$. Note that, for $x > \lambda$, $u(x-\lambda) \equiv 1$ and so (7.53) becomes

$$y(x) = \frac{L}{6EI}(x-\lambda)^3 + \frac{A}{2}x^2 + \frac{B}{6}x^3.$$

Differentiating we get

$$y''(x) = \frac{L}{EI}(x-\lambda) + A + Bx \qquad \text{and} \qquad y'''(x) = \frac{L}{EI} + B.$$

Hence, A and B must satisfy

$$\begin{aligned}
0 &= y''(2\lambda) = [L/(EI)](2\lambda-\lambda) + A + 2B\lambda, \\
0 &= y'''(2\lambda) = L/(EI) + B
\end{aligned} \qquad \Rightarrow \qquad \begin{aligned} A &= \lambda L/(EI), \\ B &= -L/(EI). \end{aligned}$$

Substitution back into (7.53) yields the solution

$$y(x) = \frac{L}{6EI}\left[(x-\lambda)^3u(x-\lambda) + 3\lambda x^2 - x^3\right].$$

EXERCISES 7.9: Solving Linear Systems with Laplace Transforms, page 416

1. Let $X(s) = \mathcal{L}\{x\}(s)$, $Y(s) = \mathcal{L}\{y\}(s)$. Applying the Laplace transform to both sides of the given equations yields

$$\begin{aligned}
\mathcal{L}\{x'\}(s) &= 3X(s) - 2Y(s), \\
\mathcal{L}\{y'\}(s) &= 3Y(s) - 2X(s).
\end{aligned} \qquad (7.54)$$

Since

$$\mathcal{L}\{x'\}(s) = sX(s) - x(0) = sX(s) - 1,$$
$$\mathcal{L}\{y'\}(s) = sY(s) - y(0) = sY(s) - 1,$$

the system (7.54) becomes

$$\begin{array}{l} sX(s) - 1 = 3X(s) - 2Y(s), \\ sY(s) - 1 = 3Y(s) - 2X(s) \end{array} \quad \Rightarrow \quad \begin{array}{l} (s-3)X(s) + 2Y(s) = 1, \\ 2X(s) + (s-3)Y(s) = 1. \end{array} \tag{7.55}$$

Subtracting the second equation from the first equation yields

$$(s-5)X(s) + (5-s)Y(s) = 0 \quad \Rightarrow \quad X(s) = Y(s).$$

So, from the first equation in (7.55) we get

$$(s-3)X(s) + 2X(s) = 1 \quad \Rightarrow \quad X(s) = \frac{1}{s-1} \quad \Rightarrow \quad x(t) = \mathcal{L}^{-1}\left\{\frac{1}{s-1}\right\}(t) = e^t.$$

Since $Y(s) = X(s)$, $y(t) = x(t) = e^t$.

3. Let $Z(s) = \mathcal{L}\{z\}(s)$, $W(s) = \mathcal{L}\{w\}(s)$. Using the initial conditions we conclude that

$$\mathcal{L}\{z'\}(s) = sZ(s) - z(0) = sZ(s) - 1, \quad \mathcal{L}\{w'\}(s) = sW(s) - w(0) = sW(s).$$

Using these equations and taking the Laplace transform of the equations in the given system, we obtain

$$\begin{array}{l} [sZ(s) - 1] + [sW(s)] = Z(s) - W(s), \\ sZ(s) - 1] - [sW(s)] = Z(s) - W(s) \end{array} \quad \Rightarrow \quad \begin{array}{l} (s-1)W(s) + (s+1)W(s) = 1, \\ (s-1)W(s) - (s-1)W(s) = 1. \end{array} \tag{7.56}$$

Subtracting equations yields

$$2sW(s) = 0 \quad \Rightarrow \quad W(s) = 0 \quad \Rightarrow \quad w(t) = \mathcal{L}^{-1}\{0\}(t) \equiv 0.$$

Substituting $W(s)$ into either equation in (7.56), we obtain

$$(s-1)Z(s) = 1 \quad \Rightarrow \quad Z(s) = \frac{1}{s-1} \quad \Rightarrow \quad z(t) = \mathcal{L}^{-1}\left\{\frac{1}{s-1}\right\}(t) = e^t.$$

5. Denote $X(s) = \mathcal{L}\{x\}(s)$, $Y(s) = \mathcal{L}\{y\}(s)$. The Laplace transform of the given equations yields

$$\begin{aligned}\mathcal{L}\{x'\}(s) &= Y(s) + \mathcal{L}\{\sin t\}(s),\\ \mathcal{L}\{y'\}(s) &= X(s) + 2\mathcal{L}\{\cos t\}(s),\end{aligned}$$

which becomes

$$\begin{aligned}sX(s) - 2 &= Y(s) + 1/(s^2+1),\\ sY(s) &= X(s) + 2s/(s^2+1)\end{aligned} \quad\Rightarrow\quad \begin{aligned}sX(s) - Y(s) &= (2s^2+3)/(s^2+1),\\ -X(s) + sY(s) &= 2s/(s^2+1)\end{aligned}$$

after expressing $\mathcal{L}\{x'\}$ and $\mathcal{L}\{y'\}$ in terms of $X(s)$ and $Y(s)$. Multiplying the second equation by s and adding the result to the first equation, we get

$$\left(s^2-1\right)Y(s) = \frac{4s^2+3}{s^2+1} \quad\Rightarrow\quad Y(s) = \frac{4s^2+3}{(s-1)(s+1)(s^2+1)}.$$

Since the partial fractions decomposition for $Y(s)$ is

$$\frac{4s^2+3}{(s-1)(s+1)(s^2+1)} = \frac{7/4}{s-1} - \frac{7/4}{s+1} + \frac{1/2}{s^2+1},$$

taking the inverse Laplace transform yields

$$y(t) = \mathcal{L}^{-1}\left\{\frac{7/4}{s-1} - \frac{7/4}{s+1} + \frac{1/2}{s^2+1}\right\}(t) = \frac{7}{4}e^t - \frac{7}{4}e^{-t} + \frac{1}{2}\sin t.$$

From the second equation in the original system,

$$x(t) = y' - 2\cos t = \frac{7}{4}e^t + \frac{7}{4}e^{-t} - \frac{3}{2}\cos t.$$

7. We will first write this system without using operator notation. Thus, we have

$$\begin{aligned}x' - 4x + 6y &= 9e^{-3t},\\ x - y' + y &= 5e^{-3t}.\end{aligned} \tag{7.57}$$

By taking the Laplace transform of both sides of both of these differential equations and using the linearity of the Laplace transform, we obtain

$$\begin{aligned}\mathcal{L}\{x'\}(s) - 4X(s) + 6Y(s) &= 9/(s+3),\\ X(s) - \mathcal{L}\{y'\}(s) + Y(s) &= 5/(s+3),\end{aligned} \tag{7.58}$$

where $X(s)$ and $Y(s)$ are the Laplace transforms of $x(t)$ and $y(t)$, respectively. Using the initial conditions $x(0) = -9$ and $y(0) = 4$, we can express

$$\mathcal{L}\{x'\}(s) = sX(s) - x(0) = sX(s) + 9,$$
$$\mathcal{L}\{y'\}(s) = sY(s) - y(0) = sY(s) - 4.$$

Substituting these expressions into the system given in (7.58) and simplifying yields

$$(s-4)X(s) + 6Y(s) = -9 + \frac{9}{s+3} = \frac{-9s-18}{s+3},$$
$$X(s) + (-s+1)Y(s) = -4 + \frac{5}{s+3} = \frac{-4s-7}{s+3}.$$

By multiplying the second equation above by $-(s-4)$, adding the resulting equations, and simplifying, we obtain

$$\left(s^2 - 5s + 10\right)Y(s) = \frac{(4s+7)(s-4)}{s+3} + \frac{-9s-18}{s+3} = \frac{4s^2 - 18s - 46}{s+3}$$
$$\Rightarrow \qquad Y(s) = \frac{4s^2 - 18s - 46}{(s+3)(s^2 - 5s + 10)}.$$

Note that the quadratic $s^2 - 5s + 10 = (s - 5/2)^2 + 15/4$ is irreducible. The partial fractions decomposition yields

$$\begin{aligned} Y(s) &= \frac{1}{17}\left[\frac{46s - 334}{(s-5/2)^2 + 15/4} + \frac{22}{s+3}\right] \\ &= \frac{1}{17}\left[46\left(\frac{s-5/2}{(s-5/2)^2 + 15/4}\right) - \frac{146\sqrt{15}}{5}\left(\frac{\sqrt{15}/2}{(s-5/2)^2 + 15/4}\right) + 22\,\frac{1}{s+3}\right], \end{aligned}$$

and so

$$y(t) = \mathcal{L}^{-1}\{Y(s)\}(t) = \frac{46}{17}e^{5t/2}\cos\left(\frac{\sqrt{15}t}{2}\right) - \frac{146\sqrt{15}}{85}e^{5t/2}\sin\left(\frac{\sqrt{15}t}{2}\right) + \frac{22}{17}e^{-3t}.$$

From the second equation in the system (7.57) above, we find that

$$\begin{aligned} x(t) &= 5e^{-3t} + y'(t) - y(t) = 5e^{-3t} + \frac{115}{17}e^{5t/2}\cos\left(\frac{\sqrt{15}t}{2}\right) \\ &\quad - \left(\frac{23\sqrt{15}}{17} + \frac{73\sqrt{15}}{17}\right)e^{5t/2}\sin\left(\frac{\sqrt{15}t}{2}\right) - \frac{219}{17}e^{5t/2}\cos\left(\frac{\sqrt{15}t}{2}\right) - \frac{66}{17}e^{-3t} \end{aligned}$$

$$= -\frac{150}{17} e^{5t/2} \cos\left(\frac{\sqrt{15}t}{2}\right) - \frac{334\sqrt{15}}{85} e^{5t/2} \sin\left(\frac{\sqrt{15}t}{2}\right) - \frac{3}{17} e^{-3t}.$$

9. Taking the Laplace transform of both sides of both of these differential equations yields the system

$$\mathcal{L}\{x''\}(s) + X(s) + 2\mathcal{L}\{y'\}(s) = 0,$$
$$-3\mathcal{L}\{x''\}(s) - 3X(s) + 2\mathcal{L}\{y''\}(s) + 4Y(s) = 0,$$

where $X(s) = \mathcal{L}\{x\}(s)$, $Y(s) = \mathcal{L}\{y\}(s)$. Using the initial conditions $x(0) = 2$, $x'(0) = -7$ and $y(0) = 4$, $y'(0) = -9$, we see that

$$\mathcal{L}\{x''\}(s) = s^2X(s) - sx(0) - x'(0) = s^2X(s) - 2s + 7,$$
$$\mathcal{L}\{y'\}(s) = sY(s) - y(0) = sY(s) - 4,$$
$$\mathcal{L}\{y''\}(s) = s^2Y(s) - sy(0) - y'(0) = s^2Y(s) - 4s + 9.$$

Substituting these expressions into the system given above yields

$$\left[s^2X(s) - 2s + 7\right] + X(s) + 2\left[sY(s) - 4\right] = 0,$$
$$-3\left[s^2X(s) - 2s + 7\right] - 3X(s) + 2\left[s^2Y(s) - 4s + 9\right] + 4Y(s) = 0,$$

which simplifies to

$$\begin{aligned} (s^2 + 1)\,X(s) + 2sY(s) &= 2s + 1, \\ -3\,(s^2 + 1)\,X(s) + 2\,(s^2 + 2)\,Y(s) &= 2s + 3. \end{aligned} \tag{7.59}$$

Multiplying the first equation by 3 and adding the two resulting equations eliminates the function $X(s)$. Thus, we obtain

$$\left(2s^2 + 6s + 4\right)Y(s) = 8s + 6 \quad \Rightarrow \quad Y(s) = \frac{4s + 3}{(s + 2)(s + 1)} = \frac{5}{s + 2} - \frac{1}{s + 1},$$

where we have factored the expression $2s^2 + 6s + 4$ and used the partial fractions expansion. Taking the inverse Laplace transform, we obtain

$$y(t) = \mathcal{L}^{-1}\{Y(s)\}(t) = 5\mathcal{L}^{-1}\left\{\frac{1}{s + 2}\right\}(t) - \mathcal{L}^{-1}\left\{\frac{1}{s + 1}\right\}(t) = 5e^{-2t} - e^{-t}.$$

To find the solution $x(t)$, we again examine the system given in (7.59) above. This time we will eliminate the function $Y(s)$ by multiplying the first equation by $s^2 + 2$ and the second equation by $-s$ and adding the resulting equations. Thus, we have

$$\left(s^2+3s+2\right)\left(s^2+1\right)X(s)=2s^3-s^2+s+2$$
$$\Rightarrow \qquad X(s)=\frac{2s^3-s^2+s+2}{(s+2)(s+1)(s^2+1)}\,.$$

Expressing $X(s)$ in a partial fractions expansion, we find that

$$X(s)=\frac{4}{s+2}-\frac{1}{s+1}-\frac{s}{s^2+1}$$

and so

$$x(t)=\mathcal{L}^{-1}\left\{\frac{4}{s+2}-\frac{1}{s+1}-\frac{s}{s^2+1}\right\}(t)=4e^{-2t}-e^{-t}-\cos t.$$

Hence, the solution to this initial value problem is

$$x(t)=4e^{-2t}-e^{-t}-\cos t \quad \text{and} \quad y(t)=5e^{-2t}-e^{-t}\,.$$

11. Since

$$\mathcal{L}\left\{x'\right\}(s)=sX(s)-x(0)=sX(s) \qquad \text{and}$$
$$\mathcal{L}\left\{y'\right\}(s)=sY(s)-y(0)=sY(s)\,,$$

applying the Laplace transform to the given equations yields

$$sX(s)+Y(s)=\mathcal{L}\left\{1-u(t-2)\right\}(s)=\frac{1}{s}-\frac{e^{-2s}}{s}=\frac{1-e^{-2s}}{s}\,,$$
$$X(s)+sY(s)=\mathcal{L}\left\{0\right\}(s)=0\,.$$

From the second equation, $X(s) = -sY(s)$. Substituting this into the first equation, we eliminate $X(s)$ and obtain

$$-s^2Y(s)+Y(s)=\frac{1-e^{-2s}}{s}$$
$$\Rightarrow \qquad Y(s)=\frac{1-e^{-2s}}{s(1-s^2)}=\left(1-e^{-2s}\right)\left(\frac{1}{s}-\frac{1/2}{s-1}-\frac{1/2}{s+1}\right).$$

Using now the linear property of the inverse Laplace transform and formula (6) on page 387, we get

$$y(t) \;=\; \mathcal{L}^{-1}\left\{\frac{1}{s}-\frac{1/2}{s-1}-\frac{1/2}{s+1}\right\}(t)-\mathcal{L}^{-1}\left\{\frac{1}{s}-\frac{1/2}{s-1}-\frac{1/2}{s+1}\right\}(t-2)u(t-2)$$

$$= 1 - \frac{e^t + e^{-t}}{2} - \left[1 - \frac{e^{t-2} + e^{-(t-2)}}{2}\right] u(t-2).$$

Since, from the second equation in the original system, $x = -y'$, we have

$$\begin{aligned} x(t) &= -\left\{1 - \frac{e^t + e^{-t}}{2} - \left[1 - \frac{e^{t-2} + e^{-(t-2)}}{2}\right] u(t-2)\right\} \\ &= \frac{e^t - e^{-t}}{2} - \left[\frac{e^{t-2} - e^{-(t-2)}}{2}\right] u(t-2). \end{aligned}$$

13. Since, by formula (8) on page 387 of the text,

$$\mathcal{L}\{(\sin t)u(t-\pi)\}(s) = e^{-\pi s}\mathcal{L}\{\sin(t+\pi)\}(s) = e^{-\pi s}\mathcal{L}\{-\sin t\}(s) = -\frac{e^{-\pi s}}{s^2+1},$$

applying the Laplace transform to the given system yields

$$\begin{aligned} &\mathcal{L}\{x'\}(s) - \mathcal{L}\{y'\}(s) = \mathcal{L}\{(\sin t)u(t-\pi)\}(s), \\ &\mathcal{L}\{x\}(s) + \mathcal{L}\{y'\}(s) = \mathcal{L}\{0\}(s) \\ \Rightarrow \quad &[sX(s) - 1] - [sY(s) - 1] = -\frac{e^{-\pi s}}{s^2+1}, \\ &X(s) + [sY(s) - 1] = 0, \end{aligned}$$

where we have used the initial conditions, $x(0) = 1$ and $y(0) = 1$, and Theorem 4, Section 7.3, to express $\mathcal{L}\{x'\}(s)$ and $\mathcal{L}\{y'\}(s)$ in terms of $X(s) = \mathcal{L}\{x\}(s)$ and $Y(s) = \mathcal{L}\{y\}(s)$. The above system simplifies to

$$\begin{aligned} X(s) - Y(s) &= -\frac{e^{-\pi s}}{s(s^2+1)}, \\ X(s) + sY(s) &= 1. \end{aligned}$$

From the second equation, $X(s) = 1 - sY(s)$, and with this substitution the first equation becomes

$$1 - sY(s) - Y(s) = -\frac{e^{-\pi s}}{s(s^2+1)} \quad \Rightarrow Y(s) = \left[1 + \frac{e^{-\pi s}}{s(s^2+1)}\right]\frac{1}{s+1} = \frac{1}{s+1} + \frac{e^{-\pi s}}{s(s+1)(s^2+1)}.$$

Using partial fractions we express

$$Y(s) = \frac{1}{s+1} + e^{-\pi s}\left[\frac{1}{s} - \frac{1/2}{s+1} - \frac{(1/2)s}{s^2+1} - \frac{1/2}{s^2+1}\right]$$

and so

$$\begin{aligned} y(t) &= e^{-t} + \left[1 - \frac{1}{2}e^{-(t-\pi)} - \frac{1}{2}\cos(t-\pi) - \frac{1}{2}\sin(t-\pi)\right] u(t-\pi) \\ &= e^{-t} + \left[1 - \frac{1}{2}e^{-(t-\pi)} + \frac{1}{2}\cos t + \frac{1}{2}\sin t\right] u(t-\pi). \end{aligned}$$

Finally,

$$x(t) = -y'(t) = e^{-t} - \left[\frac{1}{2}e^{-(t-\pi)} - \frac{1}{2}\sin t + \frac{1}{2}\cos t\right] u(t-\pi).$$

15. First, note that the initial conditions are given at the point $t = 1$. Thus, for the Laplace transform method, we have to shift the argument to get zero initial point. Let us denote

$$u(t) := x(t+1) \qquad \text{and} \qquad v(t) := y(t+1).$$

The chain rule yields

$$u'(t) = x'(t+1)(t+1)' = x'(t+1), \quad v'(t) = y'(t+1)(t+1)' = y'(t+1).$$

In the original system, we substitute $t+1$ for t to get

$$\begin{aligned} &x'(t+1) - 2y(t+1) = 2, \\ &x'(t+1) + x(t+1) - y'(t+1) = (t+1)^2 + 2(t+1) - 1, \end{aligned}$$

and make u and v substitution. This yields

$$\begin{aligned} &u'(t) - 2v(t) = 2, \\ &u'(t) + u(t) - v'(t) = (t+1)^2 + 2(t+1) - 1 = t^2 + 4t + 2 \end{aligned}$$

with initial conditions $u(0) = 1$, $v(0) = 0$. Taking the Laplace transform and using formula (2) on page 361 of the text, we obtain the system

$$\begin{aligned} &[sU(s) - 1] - 2V(s) = \frac{2}{s}, \\ &[sU(s) - 1] + U(s) - sV(s) = \frac{2}{s^3} + \frac{4}{s^2} + \frac{2}{s}, \end{aligned}$$

where $U(s) = \mathcal{L}\{u\}(s)$, $V(s) = \mathcal{L}\{v\}(s)$. Expressing

$$U(s) = \frac{2V(s)}{s} + \frac{2}{s^2} + \frac{1}{s}$$

from the first equation and substituting this into the second equation, we obtain

$$\left[\frac{2}{s}+2V(s)\right]+\left[\frac{2V(s)}{s}+\frac{2}{s^2}+\frac{1}{s}\right]-sV(s)=\frac{2}{s^3}+\frac{4}{s^2}+\frac{2}{s},$$

which yields

$$V(s)=\frac{1}{s^2}\qquad\Rightarrow\qquad U(s)=\frac{2}{s^3}+\frac{2}{s^2}+\frac{1}{s}.$$

Applying now inverse Laplace transforms yields

$$u(t)=t^2+2t+1=(t+1)^2,\qquad v(t)=\mathcal{L}^{-1}\left\{\frac{1}{s^2}\right\}(t)=t.$$

Finally,

$$x(t)=u(t-1)=t^2\quad\text{and}\quad y(t)=v(t-1)=t-1.$$

17. As in Problem 15, first we make a shift in t to move the initial conditions to $t=0$. Let

$$u(t):=x(t+2)\qquad\text{and}\qquad v(t):=y(t+2).$$

With t replaced by $t+2$, the original system becomes

$$\begin{aligned}x'(t+2)+x(t+2)-y'(t+2)&=2te^t,\\ x''(t+2)-x'(t+2)-2y(t+2)&=-e^t\end{aligned}$$

or

$$\begin{aligned}u'(t)+u(t)-v'(t)&=2te^t,\\ u''(t)-u'(t)-2v(t)&=-e^t,\end{aligned}\qquad\text{with}\qquad \begin{aligned}u(0)&=0,\\ u'(0)&=1,\\ v(0)&=1.\end{aligned}$$

Applying the Laplace transform to these equations and expressing $\mathcal{L}\{u''\}$, $\mathcal{L}\{u'\}$, and $\mathcal{L}\{v'\}$ in terms of $U=\mathcal{L}\{u\}$ and $V=\mathcal{L}\{v\}$ (see formula (4) on page 362 of the text, we obtain

$$\begin{aligned}[sU(s)]+U(s)-[sV(s)-1]&=2\mathcal{L}\left\{te^t\right\}(s)=\frac{2}{(s-1)^2},\\ \left[s^2U(s)-1\right]-[sU(s)]-2V(s)&=-\frac{1}{s-1}.\end{aligned}$$

We multiply the first equation by 2, the second equation by s, and subtract the resulting equations in order to eliminate $V(s)$. Thus we get

$$\left[s(s^2-s)-2(s+1)\right]U(s)=s-\frac{s}{s-1}-\frac{4}{(s-1)^2}+2$$

$$\Rightarrow \qquad \left(s^3 - s^2 - 2s - 2\right) U(s) = \frac{s^3 - s^2 - 2s - 2}{(s-1)^2} \qquad \Rightarrow \qquad U(s) = \frac{1}{(s-1)^2}\,.$$

The inverse Laplace transform then yields

$$u(t) = \mathcal{L}^{-1}\left\{\frac{1}{(s-1)^2}\right\}(t) = te^t \qquad \Rightarrow \qquad x(t) = u(t-2) = (t-2)e^{t-2}\,.$$

We find $y(t)$ from the second equation in the original system.

$$y(t) = \frac{x''(t) - x'(t) + e^{t-2}}{2} = \frac{te^{t-2} - (t-1)e^{t-2} + e^{t-2}}{2} = e^{t-2}\,.$$

19. We first take the Laplace transform of both sides of all three of these equations and use the initial conditions to obtain a system of equations for the Laplace transforms of the solution functions:

$$\begin{aligned} sX(s) + 6 &= 3X(s) + Y(s) - 2Z(s), \\ sY(s) - 2 &= -X(s) + 2Y(s) + Z(s), \\ sZ(s) + 12 &= 4X(s) + Y(s) - 3Z(s). \end{aligned}$$

Simplifying yields

$$\begin{aligned} &(s-3)X(s) - Y(s) + 2Z(s) = -6, \\ &X(s) + (s-2)Y(s) - Z(s) = 2, \\ &-4X(s) - Y(s) + (s+3)Z(s) = -12. \end{aligned} \tag{7.60}$$

To solve this system, we will use substitution to eliminate the function $Y(s)$. Therefore, we solve for $Y(s)$ in the first equation in (7.60) to obtain

$$Y(s) = (s-3)X(s) + 2Z(s) + 6.$$

Substituting this expression into the two remaining equations in (7.60) and simplifying yields

$$\begin{aligned} &(s^2 - 5s + 7)X(s) + (2s-5)Z(s) = -6s + 14, \\ &-(s+1)X(s) + (s+1)Z(s) = -6. \end{aligned} \tag{7.61}$$

Next we will eliminate the function $X(s)$ from the system given in (7.61). To do this we can either multiply the first equation by $(s+1)$ and the second by $(s^2 - 5s + 7)$ and add, or we can solve the last equation given in (7.61) for $X(s)$ to obtain

$$X(s) = Z(s) + \frac{6}{s+1}, \tag{7.62}$$

and substitute this into the first equation in (7.61). By either method we see that

$$Z(s)=\frac{-12s^2+38s-28}{(s+1)(s^2-3s+2)}=\frac{-12s^2+38s-28}{(s+1)(s-2)(s-1)}\,.$$

Now, $Z(s)$ has the partial fraction expansion

$$Z(s)=\frac{-13}{s+1}+\frac{1}{s-1}.$$

Therefore, by taking inverse Laplace transforms of both sides of this equation, we obtain

$$z(t)=\mathcal{L}^{-1}\left\{Z(s)\right\}(t)=\mathcal{L}^{-1}\left\{\frac{-13}{s+1}+\frac{1}{s-1}\right\}(t)=-13e^{-t}+e^{t}\,.$$

To find $X(s)$, we will use equation (7.62) and the expression found above for $Z(s)$. Thus, we have

$$X(s)=Z(s)+\frac{6}{s+1}=\frac{-13}{s+1}+\frac{1}{s-1}+\frac{6}{s+1}=\frac{-7}{s+1}+\frac{1}{s-1}$$

$$\Rightarrow\qquad x(t)=\mathcal{L}^{-1}\left\{X(s)\right\}(t)=\mathcal{L}^{-1}\left\{\frac{-7}{s+1}+\frac{1}{s-1}\right\}(t)=-7e^{-t}+e^{t}\,.$$

To find $y(t)$, we could substitute the expressions that we have already found for $X(s)$ and $Z(s)$ into the $Y(s)=(s-3)X(s)+2Z(s)+6$, which we found above, or we could return to the original system of differential equations and use $x(t)$ and $z(t)$ to solve for $y(t)$. For the latter method, we solve the first equation in the original system for $y(t)$ to obtain

$$\begin{aligned} y(t) &= x'(t)-3x(t)+2z(t)\\ &= 7e^{-t}+e^{t}+21e^{-t}-3e^{t}-26e^{-t}+2e^{t}=2e^{-t}\,. \end{aligned}$$

Therefore, the solution to the initial value problem is

$$x(t)=-7e^{-t}+e^{t}\,,\qquad y(t)=2e^{-t}\,,\qquad z(t)=-13e^{-t}+e^{t}\,.$$

21. We refer the reader to the discussion in Section 5.1 in obtaining the system (1) on page 242 of the text governing interconnected tanks. All the arguments provided remain in force except for the one affected by the new "valve condition", which the formula for the input rate for the tank A. In Section 5.1, just fresh water was pumped into the tank A and so there was no salt coming from outside of the system into the tank A . Now we have more complicated rule: the incoming liquid is fresh water for the first 5 min, but then it changes to a solution having a concentration 2 kg/L. This solution contributes additional

$$2\,(\text{kg/L}) \times 6\,(\text{L/min}) = 12\,(\text{kg/min})$$

to the input rate into the tank A. Thus, from the valve, we have

$$\begin{cases} 0, & t < 5, \\ 12, & t > 5 \end{cases} = 12u(t-5)\ (\text{kg/min})$$

of salt coming to the tank A. With this change, the system (1) in the text becomes

$$\begin{aligned} x' &= -x/3 + y/12 + 12u(t-5), \\ y' &= x/3 - y/3. \end{aligned} \tag{7.63}$$

Also, we have the initial conditions $x(0) = x_0 = 0$, $y(0) = y_0 = 4$. Let $X := \mathcal{L}\{x\}$ and $Y := \mathcal{L}\{y\}$. Taking the Laplace transform of both equations in the system above, we get

$$\begin{aligned} \mathcal{L}\{x'\}(s) &= -\frac{1}{3}X(s) + \frac{1}{12}Y(s) + 12\mathcal{L}\{u(t-5)\}(s), \\ \mathcal{L}\{y'\}(s) &= \frac{1}{3}X(s) - \frac{1}{3}Y(s). \end{aligned}$$

Since $\mathcal{L}\{u(t-5)\}(s) = e^{-5s}/s$ and

$$\begin{aligned} \mathcal{L}\{x'\}(s) &= sX(s) - x(0) = sX(s), \\ \mathcal{L}\{y'\}(s) &= sY(s) - y(0) = sY(s) - 4, \end{aligned}$$

we obtain

$$\begin{aligned} sX(s) &= -\frac{1}{3}X(s) + \frac{1}{12}Y(s) + \frac{12e^{-5s}}{s}, \\ sY(s) - 4 &= \frac{1}{3}X(s) - \frac{1}{3}Y(s) \end{aligned}$$

which simplifies to

$$\begin{aligned} 4(3s+1)X(s) - Y(s) &= \frac{144e^{-5s}}{s}, \\ -X(s) + (3s+1)Y(s) &= 12. \end{aligned}$$

From the second equation in this system, we have $X(s) = (3s+1)Y(s) - 12$. Substitution into the first equation yields

$$\begin{aligned} 4(3s+1)\left[(3s+1)Y(s) - 12\right] - Y(s) &= \frac{144e^{-5s}}{s} \\ \Rightarrow \qquad \left[4(3s+1)^2 - 1\right] Y(s) &= 48(3s+1) + \frac{144e^{-5s}}{s}. \end{aligned}$$

Note that

$$4(3s+1)^2 - 1 = [2(3s+1)+1]\cdot[2(3s+1)-1] = (6s+3)(6s+1) = 36\left(s+\frac{1}{2}\right)\left(s+\frac{1}{6}\right).$$

Therefore,

$$\begin{aligned} Y(s) &= \frac{4(3s+1)}{3(s+1/2)(s+1/6)} + \frac{4e^{-5s}}{s(s+1/2)(s+1/6)} \\ &= \frac{2}{(s+1/2)} + \frac{2}{(s+1/6)} + e^{-5s}\left[\frac{48}{s} + \frac{24}{s+1/2} - \frac{72}{s+1/6}\right], \end{aligned}$$

where we have applied the partial fractions decomposition. Taking the inverse Laplace transform and using Theorem 8 in Section 7.6 for the inverse Laplace transform of the term having the exponential factor, we get

$$\begin{aligned} y(t) &= 2\mathcal{L}^{-1}\left\{\frac{1}{(s+1/2)}\right\}(t) + 2\mathcal{L}^{-1}\left\{\frac{1}{(s+1/6)}\right\}(t) \\ &\quad + \left[48\mathcal{L}^{-1}\left\{\frac{1}{s}\right\} + 24\mathcal{L}^{-1}\left\{\frac{1}{s+1/2}\right\} - 72\mathcal{L}^{-1}\left\{\frac{1}{s+1/6}\right\}\right](t-5)u(t-5) \\ &= 2e^{-t/2} + 2e^{-t/6} + \left[48 + 24e^{-(t-5)/2} - 72e^{-(t-5)/6}\right]u(t-5). \end{aligned}$$

From the second equation in (7.63), after some algebra, we find $x(t)$.

$$x(t) = 3y'(t) + y = -e^{-t/2} + e^{-t/6} + \left[48 - 12e^{-(t-5)/2} - 36e^{-(t-5)/6}\right]u(t-5).$$

23. Recall that Kirchhoff's voltage law says that, in an electrical circuit consisting of an inductor of L H, a resistor of $R\,\Omega$, a capacitor of C F, and a voltage source of E V,

$$E_L + E_R + E_C = E, \tag{7.64}$$

where E_L, E_R, and E_C denote the voltage drops across the inductor, resistor, and capacitor, respectively. These voltage grops are given by

$$E_L = L\frac{dI}{dt}, \qquad E_R := RI, \qquad E_C := \frac{q}{C}, \tag{7.65}$$

where I denotes the current passing through the correspondent element.

Also, Kirchhoff's current law states that the algebraic sum of currents passing through any point in an electrical network equals to zero.

The electrical network shown in Figure 7.28 consists of three closed circuits: loop 1 through the battery, $R_1 = 2\,\Omega$ resistor, $L_1 = 0.1\,\mathrm{H}$ inductor, and $L_2 = 0.2\,\mathrm{H}$ inductor; loop 2 through the inductor L_1 and $R_2 = 1\,\Omega$ resistor; loop 3 through the battery, resistors R_1 and R_2, and inductor L_2. We apply Kirchhoff's voltage law (7.64) to two of these loops, say, the loop 1 and the loop 2, and (since the equation obtained from Kirchhoff's voltage law for the third loop is a linear combination of the other two) Kirchhoff's current law to one of the junction points, say, the upper one. Thus, choosing the clockwise direction in the loops and using formulas (7.65), we obtain

Loop 1:

$$E_{R_1} + E_{L_1} + E_{L_2} = E \qquad \Rightarrow \qquad 2I_1 + 0.1I_3' + 0.2I_1' = 6;$$

Loop 2:

$$E_{L_1} + E_{R_2} = 0 \qquad \Rightarrow \qquad 0.1I_3' - I_2 = 0$$

with the negative sign due to the counterclockwise direction of the current I_2 in this loop;

Upper junction point:

$$I_1 - I_2 - I_3 = 0.$$

Therefore, we have the following system for the currents I_1, I_2, and I_3:

$$\begin{aligned} &2I_1 + 0.1I_3' + 0.2I_1' = 6,\\ &0.1I_3' - I_2 = 0,\\ &I_1 - I_2 - I_3 = 0 \end{aligned} \tag{7.66}$$

with initial conditions $I_1(0) = I_2(0) = I_3(0) = 0$.

Let $\mathbf{I}_1(s) := \mathcal{L}\{I_1\}(s)$, $\mathbf{I}_2(s) := \mathcal{L}\{I_2\}(s)$, and $\mathbf{I}_3(s) := \mathcal{L}\{I_3\}(s)$. Using the initial conditions, we conclude that

$$\mathcal{L}\{I_1'\}(s) = s\mathbf{I}_1(s) - I_1(0) = s\mathbf{I}_1(s),$$
$$\mathcal{L}\{I_3'\}(s) = s\mathbf{I}_3(s) - I_3(0) = s\mathbf{I}_3(s).$$

Using these equations and taking the Laplace transform of the equations in (7.66), we come up with

$$\begin{aligned}
&(0.2s+2)\mathbf{I}_1(s) + 0.1s\mathbf{I}_3(s) = \frac{6}{s},\\
&0.1s\mathbf{I}_3(s) - \mathbf{I}_2(s) = 0,\\
&\mathbf{I}_1(s) - \mathbf{I}_2(s) - \mathbf{I}_3(s) = 0
\end{aligned}$$

Expressing $\mathbf{I}_2(s) = 0.1s\mathbf{I}_3(s)$ from the second equation and substituting this into the third equation, we get

$$\mathbf{I}_1(s) - 0.1s\mathbf{I}_3(s) - \mathbf{I}_3(s) = 0 \qquad \Rightarrow \qquad \mathbf{I}_1(s) = (0.1s+1)\mathbf{I}_3(s).$$

The latter, when substituted into the first equation, yields

$$\begin{aligned}
&(0.2s+2)(0.1s+1)\mathbf{I}_3(s) + 0.1s\mathbf{I}_3(s) = \frac{6}{s}\\
\Rightarrow \qquad &\left[2(0.1s+1)^2 + 0.1s\right]\mathbf{I}_3(s) = \frac{6}{s}\\
\Rightarrow \qquad &\mathbf{I}_3(s) = \frac{6}{s[2(0.1s+1)^2+0.1s]} = \frac{300}{s(s+20)(s+5)}.
\end{aligned}$$

We use the partial fractions decomposition to find that

$$\mathbf{I}_3(s) = \frac{3}{s} + \frac{1}{s+20} - \frac{4}{s+5}$$

and so

$$I_3(t) = \mathcal{L}^{-1}\left\{\frac{3}{s} + \frac{1}{s+20} - \frac{4}{s+5}\right\}(t) = 3 + e^{-20t} - 4e^{-5t}.$$

Now we can find $I_2(t)$ using the second equation in (7.66).

$$I_2(t) = 0.1I_3'(t) = 0.1\left(3 + e^{-20t} - 4e^{-5t}\right)' = -2e^{-20t} + 2e^{-5t}.$$

Finally, the third equation in (7.66) yields

$$I_1(t) = I_2(t) + I_3(t) = 3 - e^{-20t} - 2e^{-5t}.$$

REVIEW PROBLEMS: page 418

1. By the definition of Laplace transform,

$$\mathcal{L}\{f\}(s) = \int_0^\infty e^{-st} f(t)\,dt = \int_0^2 e^{-st}(3)\,dt + \int_2^\infty e^{-st}(6-t)\,dt.$$

For the first integral, we have

$$\int_0^2 e^{-st}(3)\,dt = \left.\frac{3e^{-st}}{-s}\right|_{t=0}^{t=2} = \frac{3(1-e^{-2s})}{s}.$$

The second integral is an improper integral. Using integration by parts, we obtain

$$\begin{aligned}
\int_2^\infty e^{-st}(6-t)\,dt &= \lim_{M\to\infty}\int_2^M e^{-st}(6-t)\,dt = \lim_{M\to\infty}\left[\left.(6-t)\frac{e^{-st}}{-s}\right|_{t=2}^{t=M} - \int_2^M \frac{e^{-st}}{-s}(-1)dt\right] \\
&= \lim_{M\to\infty}\left[\frac{4e^{-2s}}{s} - \frac{(6-M)e^{-sM}}{s} + \left.\frac{e^{-st}}{s^2}\right|_{t=2}^{t=M}\right] \\
&= \lim_{M\to\infty}\left[\frac{4e^{-2s}}{s} - \frac{(6-M)e^{-sM}}{s} + \frac{e^{-sM}}{s^2} - \frac{e^{-2s}}{s^2}\right] = \frac{4e^{-2s}}{s} - \frac{e^{-2s}}{s^2}.
\end{aligned}$$

Thus

$$\mathcal{L}\{f\}(s) = \frac{3(1-e^{-2s})}{s} + \frac{4e^{-2s}}{s} - \frac{e^{-2s}}{s^2} = \frac{3}{s} + e^{-2s}\left(\frac{1}{s} - \frac{1}{s^2}\right).$$

3. From Table 7.1 on page 358 of the text, using the formula for the Laplace transform of $e^{at}t^n$ with $n = 2$ and $a = -9$, we get

$$\mathcal{L}\left\{t^2 e^{-9t}\right\}(s) = \frac{2!}{[s-(-9)]^3} = \frac{2}{(s+9)^3}.$$

5. We use the linearity of the Laplace transform and Table 7.1 to obtain

$$\begin{aligned}
\mathcal{L}\left\{e^{2t} - t^3 + t^2 - \sin 5t\right\}(s) &= \mathcal{L}\left\{e^{2t}\right\}(s) - \mathcal{L}\left\{t^3\right\}(s) + \mathcal{L}\left\{t^2\right\}(s) - \mathcal{L}\{\sin 5t\}(s) \\
&= \frac{1}{s-2} - \frac{3!}{s^4} + \frac{2!}{s^3} - \frac{5}{s^2+5^2} = \frac{1}{s-2} - \frac{6}{s^4} + \frac{2}{s^3} - \frac{5}{s^2+25}.
\end{aligned}$$

7. We apply Theorem 6 in Section 7.3 and obtain

$$\mathcal{L}\{t\cos 6t\}(s) = -\frac{d}{ds}\mathcal{L}\{\cos 6t\}(s) = -\frac{d}{ds}\left[\frac{s}{s^2+6^2}\right] = -\frac{(s^2+36)-s(2s)}{(s^2+36)^2} = \frac{s^2-36}{(s^2+36)^2}.$$

9. We apply formula (8), Section 7.6, on page 387 of the text and the linear property of the Laplace transform to get

$$\begin{aligned}\mathcal{L}\{t^2u(t-4)\}(s) &= e^{-4s}\mathcal{L}\{(t+4)^2\}(s) = e^{-4s}\mathcal{L}\{t^2+8s+16\}(s)\\ &= e^{-4s}\left(\frac{2}{s^3}+\frac{8}{s^2}+\frac{16}{s}\right) = 2e^{-4s}\left(\frac{1}{s^3}+\frac{4}{s^2}+\frac{8}{s}\right).\end{aligned}$$

11. Using the linearity of the inverse Laplace transform and Table 7.1 we find

$$\mathcal{L}^{-1}\left\{\frac{7}{(s+3)^3}\right\}(t) = \frac{7}{2!}\mathcal{L}^{-1}\left\{\frac{2!}{[s-(-3)]^3}\right\}(t) = \frac{7}{2}t^2e^{-3t}.$$

13. We apply partial fractions to find the inverse Laplace transform. Since the quadratic polynomial $s^2+4s+13=(s+2)^2+3^2$ is irreducible, the partial fraction decomposition for the given function has the form

$$\frac{4s^2+13s+19}{(s-1)(s^2+4s+13)} = \frac{A}{s-1}+\frac{B(s+2)+C(3)}{(s+2)^2+3^2}.$$

Clearing fractions yields

$$4s^2+13s+19 = A[(s+2)^2+3^2]+[B(s+2)+C(3)](s-1).$$

With $s=1$, this gives $36=18A$ or $A=2$. Substituting $s=-2$, we get

$$9=9A-9C \quad\Rightarrow\quad C=A-1=1.$$

Finally, with $s=0$, we compute

$$19=13A+(2B+3C)(-1) \quad\Rightarrow\quad B=2.$$

Thus

$$\frac{4s^2+13s+19}{(s-1)(s^2+4s+13)} = \frac{2}{s-1}+\frac{2(s+2)+(1)(3)}{(s+2)^2+3^2},$$

and so

$$\begin{aligned}\mathcal{L}^{-1}\left\{\frac{4s^2+13s+19}{(s-1)(s^2+4s+13)}\right\}(t) &= 2\mathcal{L}^{-1}\left\{\frac{1}{s-1}\right\}(t)+2\mathcal{L}^{-1}\left\{\frac{s+2}{(s+2)^2+3^2}\right\}(t) \\ &\quad +\mathcal{L}^{-1}\left\{\frac{3}{(s+2)^2+3^2}\right\}(t) \\ &= 2e^t+2e^{-2t}\cos 3t+e^{-2t}\sin 3t\,.\end{aligned}$$

15. The partial fraction decomposition for the given function has the form

$$\frac{2s^2+3s-1}{(s+1)^2(s+2)}=\frac{A}{(s+1)^2}+\frac{B}{s+1}+\frac{C}{s+2}=\frac{A(s+2)+B(s+1)(s+2)+C(s+1)^2}{(s+1)^2(s+2)}\,.$$

Thus

$$2s^2+3s-1=A(s+2)+B(s+1)(s+2)+C(s+1)^2\,.$$

We evaluate both sides of this equation at $s=-2$, -1, and 0. This yields

$$\begin{aligned} s=-2: &\quad 2(-2)^2+3(-2)-1=C(-2+1)^2 &\Rightarrow&\quad C=1,\\ s=-1: &\quad 2(-1)^2+3(-1)-1=A(-1+2) &\Rightarrow&\quad A=-2,\\ s=0: &\quad -1=2A+2B+C &\Rightarrow&\quad B=(-1-2A-C)/2=1.\end{aligned}$$

Therefore,

$$\mathcal{L}^{-1}\left\{\frac{2s^2+3s-1}{(s+1)^2(s+2)}\right\}(t)=\mathcal{L}^{-1}\left\{\frac{-2}{(s+1)^2}+\frac{1}{s+1}+\frac{1}{s+2}\right\}(t)=-2te^{-t}+e^{-t}+e^{-2t}\,.$$

17. First we apply Theorem 8 in Section 7.6 to get

$$\mathcal{L}^{-1}\left\{\frac{e^{-2s}(4s+2)}{(s-1)(s+2)}\right\}(t)=\mathcal{L}^{-1}\left\{\frac{4s+2}{(s-1)(s+2)}\right\}(t-2)u(t-2). \tag{7.67}$$

Applying partial fractions yields

$$\frac{4s+2}{(s-1)(s+2)}=\frac{2}{s-1}+\frac{2}{s+2} \quad\Rightarrow\quad \mathcal{L}^{-1}\left\{\frac{4s+2}{(s-1)(s+2)}\right\}(t)=2e^t+2e^{-2t}\,.$$

Therefore, it follows from (7.67) that

$$\mathcal{L}^{-1}\left\{\frac{e^{-2s}(4s+2)}{(s-1)(s+2)}\right\}(t)=\left[2e^{t-2}+2e^{-2(t-2)}\right]u(t-2)=\left(2e^{t-2}+2e^{4-2t}\right)u(t-2).$$

19. Applying the Laplace transform to both sides of the given equation and using the linearity of the Laplace transform yields

$$\mathcal{L}\{y''-7y'+10y\}(s)=\mathcal{L}\{y''\}(s)-7\mathcal{L}\{y'\}(s)+10\mathcal{L}\{y\}(s)=0. \tag{7.68}$$

By Theorem 5 in Section 7.3,

$$\begin{aligned}\mathcal{L}\{y'\}(s)&=s\mathcal{L}\{y\}(s)-y(0)=s\mathcal{L}\{y\}(s),\\ \mathcal{L}\{y''\}(s)&=s^2\mathcal{L}\{y\}(s)-sy(0)-y'(0)=s^2\mathcal{L}\{y\}(s)+3,\end{aligned}$$

where we have used the initial conditions, $y(0)=0$ and $y'(0)=-3$. Substituting these expressions into (7.68), we get

$$\begin{aligned}&\left[s^2\mathcal{L}\{y\}(s)+3\right]-7\left[s\mathcal{L}\{y\}(s)\right]+10\mathcal{L}\{y\}(s)=0\\ \Rightarrow\quad &(s^2-7s+10)\mathcal{L}\{y\}(s)+3=0\\ \Rightarrow\quad &\mathcal{L}\{y\}(s)=\frac{-3}{s^2-7s+10}=\frac{-3}{(s-2)(s-5)}=\frac{1}{s-2}-\frac{1}{s-5}.\end{aligned}$$

Thus

$$y(t)=\mathcal{L}^{-1}\left\{\frac{1}{s-2}-\frac{1}{s-5}\right\}(t)=\mathcal{L}^{-1}\left\{\frac{1}{s-2}\right\}(t)-\mathcal{L}^{-1}\left\{\frac{1}{s-5}\right\}(t)=e^{2t}-e^{5t}.$$

21. Let $Y(s):=\mathcal{L}\{y\}(s)$. Taking the Laplace transform of the given equation and using properties of the Laplace transform, we obtain

$$\mathcal{L}\{y''+2y'+2y\}(s)=\mathcal{L}\left\{t^2+4t\right\}(s)=\frac{2}{s^3}+\frac{4}{s^2}=\frac{2+4s}{s^3}.$$

Since

$$\mathcal{L}\{y'\}(s)=sY(s)-y(0)=sY(s),\qquad \mathcal{L}\{y''\}(s)=s^2Y(s)-sy(0)-y'(0)=s^2Y(s)+1,$$

we have

$$\begin{aligned}&\left[s^2Y(s)+1\right]+2\left[sY(s)\right]+2Y(s)=\frac{2+4s}{s^3}\\ \Rightarrow\quad &(s^2+2s+2)Y(s)=\frac{2+4s}{s^3}-1=\frac{2+4s-s^3}{s^3}\end{aligned}$$

$$\Rightarrow \qquad Y(s)=\frac{2+4s-s^3}{s^3(s^2+2s+2)}=\frac{2+4s-s^3}{s^3[(s+1)^2+1^2]}\,.$$

The partial fraction decomposition for $Y(s)$ has the form

$$\frac{2+4s-s^3}{s^3[(s+1)^2+1^2]}=\frac{A}{s^3}+\frac{B}{s^2}+\frac{C}{s}+\frac{D(s+1)+E(1)}{(s+1)^2+1^2}\,.$$

Clearing fractions, we obtain

$$2+4s-s^3=A[(s+1)^2+1]+Bs[(s+1)^2+1]+Cs^2[(s+1)^2+1]+[D(s+1)+E]s^3\,.$$

Comparing coefficients at the corresponding power of s in both sides of this equation yields

$$\begin{array}{llll} s^0: & 2=2A & \Rightarrow & A=1, \\ s^1: & 4=2A+2B & \Rightarrow & B=(4-2A)/2=1, \\ s^2: & 0=A+2B+2C & \Rightarrow & C=-(A+2B)/2=-3/2, \\ s^4: & 0=C+D & \Rightarrow & D=-C=3/2, \\ s^3: & -1=B+2C+D+E & \Rightarrow & E=-1-B-2C-D=-1/2. \end{array}$$

Therefore,

$$Y(s)=\frac{1}{s^3}+\frac{1}{s^2}-\frac{3/2}{s}+\frac{(3/2)(s+1)}{(s+1)^2+1^2}-\frac{(1/2)(1)}{(s+1)^2+1^2}$$

$$\Rightarrow \qquad y(t)=\mathcal{L}^{-1}\{Y(s)\}(t)=\frac{t^2}{2}+t-\frac{3}{2}+\frac{3}{2}e^{-t}\cos t-\frac{1}{2}e^{-t}\sin t\,.$$

23. By formula (4) in Section 7.6,

$$\mathcal{L}\{u(t-1)\}(s)=\frac{e^{-s}}{s}\,.$$

Thus, applying the Laplace transform to both sides of the given equation and using the initial conditions, we get

$$\mathcal{L}\{y''+3y'+4y\}(s)=\frac{e^{-s}}{s}$$

$$\Rightarrow \qquad \left[s^2Y(s)-1\right]+3\left[sY(s)\right]+4Y(s)=\frac{e^{-s}}{s}$$

$$\Rightarrow \qquad Y(s)=\frac{1}{s^2+3s+4}+\frac{e^{-s}}{s(s^2+3s+4)}$$

$$\Rightarrow \qquad Y(s) = \frac{1}{(s+3/2)^2+(\sqrt{7}/2)^2} + e^{-s}\frac{1}{s[(s+3/2)^2+(\sqrt{7}/2)^2]},$$

where $Y(s) := \mathcal{L}\{y\}(s)$. To apply the inverse Laplace transform, we need the partial fraction decomposition of the last fraction above.

$$\frac{1}{s[(s+3/2)^2+(\sqrt{7}/2)^2]} = \frac{A}{s} + \frac{B(s+3/2)+C(\sqrt{7}/2)}{(s+3/2)^2+(\sqrt{7}/2)^2}.$$

Solving for A, B, and C yields

$$A = \frac{1}{4}, \qquad B = -\frac{1}{4}, \qquad C = -\frac{3}{4\sqrt{7}}.$$

Therefore,

$$Y(s) = \frac{1}{(s+3/2)^2+(\sqrt{7}/2)^2} + e^{-s}\left[\frac{1/4}{s} - \frac{(1/4)(s+3/2)}{(s+3/2)^2+(\sqrt{7}/2)^2} - \frac{(3/4\sqrt{7})(\sqrt{7}/2)}{(s+3/2)^2+(\sqrt{7}/2)^2}\right]$$

and the inverse Laplace transform gives

$$\begin{aligned} y(t) &= \mathcal{L}^{-1}\left\{\frac{1}{(s+3/2)^2+(\sqrt{7}/2)^2}\right\}(t) \\ &\quad + \mathcal{L}^{-1}\left\{\frac{1/4}{s} - \frac{(1/4)(s+3/2)}{(s+3/2)^2+(7/4)} - \frac{(3/4\sqrt{7})(\sqrt{7}/2)}{(s+3/2)^2+(7/4)}\right\}(t-1)u(t-1) \\ &= \frac{2}{\sqrt{7}}e^{-3t/2}\sin\left(\frac{\sqrt{7}t}{2}\right) \\ &\quad + \left[\frac{1}{4} - \frac{1}{4}e^{-3(t-1)/2}\cos\left(\frac{\sqrt{7}(t-1)}{2}\right) - \frac{3}{4\sqrt{7}}e^{-3(t-1)/2}\sin\left(\frac{\sqrt{7}(t-1)}{2}\right)\right]u(t-1). \end{aligned}$$

25. Let $Y(s) := \mathcal{L}\{y\}(s)$. Then, from the initial conditions, we have

$$\mathcal{L}\{y'\}(s) = sY(s) - y(0) = sY(s), \qquad \mathcal{L}\{y''\}(s) = s^2Y(s) - sy(0) - y'(0) = s^2Y(s).$$

Moreover, Theorem 6 in Section 7.3 yields

$$\begin{aligned} \mathcal{L}\{ty'\}(s) &= -\frac{d}{ds}\mathcal{L}\{y'\}(s) = -\frac{d}{ds}[sY(s)] = -sY'(s) - Y(s), \\ \mathcal{L}\{ty''\}(s) &= -\frac{d}{ds}\mathcal{L}\{y''\}(s) = -\frac{d}{ds}\left[s^2Y(s)\right] = -s^2Y'(s) - 2sY(s). \end{aligned}$$

Hence, applying the Laplace transform to the given equation and using the linearity of the Laplace transform, we obtain

$$\begin{aligned}
&\mathcal{L}\{ty''+2(t-1)y'-2y\}(s)=\mathcal{L}\{ty''\}(s)+2\mathcal{L}\{ty'\}(s)-2\mathcal{L}\{y'\}(s)-2\mathcal{L}\{y\}(s)=0\\
\Rightarrow\quad &\left[-s^2Y'(s)-2sY(s)\right]+2\left[-sY'(s)-Y(s)\right]-2\left[sY(s)\right]-2Y(s)=0\\
\Rightarrow\quad &-s(s+2)Y'(s)-4(s+1)Y(s)=0 \quad\Rightarrow\quad Y'(s)+\frac{4(s+1)}{s(s+2)}Y(s)=0.
\end{aligned}$$

Separating variables and integrating yields

$$\begin{aligned}
\frac{dY}{Y} &= -\frac{4(s+1)}{s(s+2)}\,ds=-2\left(\frac{1}{s}+\frac{1}{s+2}\right)ds\\
\Rightarrow\quad \ln|Y| &= -2(\ln|s|+\ln|s+2|)+C\\
\Rightarrow\quad Y(s) &= \pm\frac{e^C}{s^2(s+2)^2}=\frac{c_1}{s^2(s+2)^2},
\end{aligned}$$

where $c_1 \neq 0$ is an arbitrary constant. Allowing $c_1=0$, we also get the solution $Y(s)\equiv 0$, which was lost in separation of variables. Thus

$$Y(s)=\frac{c_1}{s^2(s+2)^2}=\frac{c_1}{4}\left[\frac{1}{s^2}-\frac{1}{s}+\frac{1}{(s+2)^2}+\frac{1}{s+2}\right]$$

and so

$$y(t)=\mathcal{L}^{-1}\{Y(s)\}(t)=\frac{c_1}{4}\left(t-1+te^{-2t}+e^{-2t}\right)=c\left(t-1+te^{-2t}+e^{-2t}\right),$$

where $c=c_1/4$ is an arbitrary constant.

27. Note that the original equation can be written in the form

$$y(t)+t*y(t)=e^{-3t}.$$

Let $Y(s):=\mathcal{L}\{y\}(s)$. Applying the Laplace transform to both sides of this equation and using Theorem 11 in Section 7.7, we obtain

$$\begin{aligned}
&\mathcal{L}\{y(t)+t*y(t)\}(s)=Y(s)+\mathcal{L}\{t\}(s)Y(s)=\mathcal{L}\left\{e^{-3t}\right\}(s)\\
\Rightarrow\quad &Y(s)+\frac{1}{s^2}Y(s)=\frac{1}{s+3} \quad\Rightarrow\quad Y(s)=\frac{s^2}{(s+3)(s^2+1)}.
\end{aligned}$$

The partial fraction decomposition for $Y(s)$ has the form

$$\frac{s^2}{(s+3)(s^2+1)} = \frac{A}{s+3} + \frac{Bs+C}{s^2+1} = \frac{A(s^2+1)+(Bs+C)(s+3)}{(s+3)(s^2+1)}.$$

Thus

$$s^2 = A(s^2+1)+(Bs+C)(s+3).$$

Evaluating both sides of this equation at $s=-3$, 0, and -2 yields

$$\begin{array}{llll} s=-3: & \Rightarrow \quad 9 = A(10) & \Rightarrow & A = 9/10, \\ s=0: & \Rightarrow \quad 0 = A+3C & \Rightarrow & C = -A/3 = -3/10, \\ s=-2: & \Rightarrow \quad 4 = 5A-2B+C & \Rightarrow & B = (5A+C-4)/2 = 1/10. \end{array}$$

Therefore,

$$\begin{aligned} Y(s) &= \frac{9/10}{s+3} + \frac{(1/10)s}{s^2+1} - \frac{3/10}{s^2+1} \\ \Rightarrow \quad y(t) &= \mathcal{L}^{-1}\{Y(s)\}(t) = \frac{9}{10}e^{-3t} + \frac{1}{10}\cos t - \frac{3}{10}\sin t\,. \end{aligned}$$

29. To find the transfer function, we use formula (15) on page 403 of the text. Comparing given equation with (14), we find that $a=1$, $b=-5$, and $c=6$. Thus (15) yields

$$H(s) = \frac{1}{as^2+bs+c} = \frac{1}{s^2-5s+6}\,.$$

The impulse response function $h(t)$ is defined as $\mathcal{L}^{-1}\{H\}(t)$. Using partial fractions, we see that

$$\begin{aligned} H(s) &= \frac{1}{s^2-5s+6} = \frac{1}{(s-3)(s-2)} = \frac{1}{s-3} - \frac{1}{s-2} \\ \Rightarrow \quad h(t) &= \mathcal{L}^{-1}\left\{\frac{1}{s-3} - \frac{1}{s-2}\right\}(t) = e^{3t} - e^{2t}\,. \end{aligned}$$

31. Let $X(s) := \mathcal{L}\{x\}(s)$, $Y(s) := \mathcal{L}\{y\}(s)$. Using the initial condition, we obtain

$$\mathcal{L}\{x'\}(s) = sX(s) - x(0) = sX(s), \qquad \mathcal{L}\{y'\}(s) = sY(s) - y(0) = sY(s).$$

Therefore, applying the Laplace transform to both sides of the equations in the given system yields

$$\begin{aligned}sX(s)+Y(s) &= \mathcal{L}\{0\}(s)=0,\\ X(s)+sY(s) &= \mathcal{L}\{1-u(t-2)\}(s)=\frac{1}{s}-\frac{e^{-2s}}{s}=\frac{1-e^{-2s}}{s}.\end{aligned}$$

Expressing $Y(s)=-sX(s)$ from the first equation and substituting this into the second equation, we eliminate $Y(s)$:

$$\begin{aligned}X(s)-s^2X(s) &= \frac{1-e^{-2s}}{s}\\ \Rightarrow \qquad X(s) &= -\frac{1-e^{-2s}}{s(s^2-1)}=-\frac{1-e^{-2s}}{s(s-1)(s+1)}.\end{aligned}$$

Since

$$-\frac{1}{s(s-1)(s+1)}=\frac{1}{s}-\frac{1/2}{s-1}-\frac{1/2}{s+1},$$

the inverse Laplace transform yields

$$\begin{aligned}x(t) &= \mathcal{L}^{-1}\left\{\left(1-e^{-2s}\right)\left(\frac{1}{s}-\frac{1/2}{s-1}-\frac{1/2}{s+1}\right)\right\}(t)\\ &= \mathcal{L}^{-1}\left\{\frac{1}{s}-\frac{1/2}{s-1}-\frac{1/2}{s+1}\right\}(t)-\mathcal{L}^{-1}\left\{\frac{1}{s}-\frac{1/2}{s-1}-\frac{1/2}{s+1}\right\}(t-2)u(t-2)\\ &= 1-\frac{e^t+e^{-t}}{2}-\left[1-\frac{e^{t-2}+e^{-(t-2)}}{2}\right]u(t-2).\end{aligned}$$

We now find $y(t)$ from the first equation in the original system.

$$y(t)=-x'(t)=\frac{e^t-e^{-t}}{2}-\frac{e^{t-2}-e^{-(t-2)}}{2}u(t-2).$$

CHAPTER 8: Series Solutions of Differential Equations

EXERCISES 8.1: Introduction: The Taylor Polynomial Approximation, page 430

1. To find Taylor approximations

$$y(0)+\frac{y'(0)}{1!}x+\frac{y''(0)}{2!}x^2+\frac{y''(0)}{3!}x^3+\cdots,$$

we need the values of $y(0)$, $y'(0)$, $y''(0)$, etc. $y(0)$ is provided by the initial condition, $y(0)=1$. Substituting $x=0$ into the given differential equation,

$$y'(x)=x^2+y(x)^2, \tag{8.1}$$

we obtain

$$y'(0)=0^2+y(0)^2=0+1^2=1.$$

Differentiating both sides of (8.1) yields

$$y''(x)=2x+2y(x)y'(x),$$

and so

$$y''(0)=2(0)+2y(0)y'(0)=0+2(1)(1)=2.$$

Hence

$$y(x)=1+\frac{1}{1!}x+\frac{2}{2!}x^2+\cdots=1+x+x^2+\cdots.$$

3. Using the initial condition, $y(0)=0$ we substitute $x=0$ and $y=0$ into the given equation and find $y'(0)$.

$$y'(0)=\sin(0)+e^0=1.$$

To determine $y''(0)$, we differentiate the given equation with respect to x and substitute $x = 0$, $y = 0$, and $y' = 1$ in the formula obtained:

$$y''(0) = (\sin y + e^x)' = (\sin y)' + (e^x)' = y' \cos y + e^x,$$

$$y''(0) = 1 \cdot \cos 0 + e^0 = 2.$$

Similarly, differentiating $y''(x)$ and substituting, we obtain

$$y''' = (y' \cos y + e^x)' = (y' \cos y)' + (e^x)' = y'' \cos y + (y')^2 (-\sin y) + e^x,$$

$$y'''(0) = y''(0) \cos 0 + (y'(0))^2 (-\sin y(0)) + e^0 = 2 \cos 0 + (1)^2(-\sin 0) + 1 = 3.$$

Thus the first three nonzero terms in the Taylor polynomial approximations to the solution of the given initial value problem are

$$\begin{aligned} y(x) &= y(0) + \frac{y'(0)}{1!}x + \frac{y''(0)}{2!}x^2 + \frac{y'''(0)}{3!}x^3 + \cdots \\ &= 0 + \frac{1}{1}x + \frac{2}{2}x^2 + \frac{3}{6}x^3 + \cdots = x + x^2 + \frac{1}{2}x^3 + \cdots . \end{aligned}$$

5. We need the values of $x(0)$, $x'(0)$, $x''(0)$, etc. The first two are given by the initial conditions:

$$x(0) = 1, \qquad x'(0) = 0.$$

Writing the given equation in the form

$$x''(t) = -tx(t) \tag{8.2}$$

we find that

$$x''(0) = -0 \cdot x(0) = -0 \cdot 1 = 0.$$

Differentiating (8.2) and substituting $t = 0$ we conclude that

$$\begin{aligned} x'''(t) &= -\left[tx'(t) + x(t)\right] &\Rightarrow\quad x'''(0) &= -\left[0 \cdot x'(0) + x(0)\right] = -1, \\ x^{(4)}(t) &= -\left[tx''(t) + 2x'(t)\right] &\Rightarrow\quad x^{(4)}(0) &= -\left[0 \cdot x''(0) + 2x'(0)\right] = 0, \\ x^{(5)}(t) &= -\left[tx'''(t) + 3x''(t)\right] &\Rightarrow\quad x^{(5)}(0) &= -\left[0 \cdot x'''(0) + 3x''(0)\right] = 0, \\ x^{(6)}(t) &= -\left[tx^{(4)}(t) + 4x'''(t)\right] &\Rightarrow\quad x^{(6)}(0) &= -\left[0 \cdot x^{(4)}(0) + 4x'''(0)\right] = 4. \end{aligned}$$

Therefore,

$$x(t) = 1 - \frac{1}{3!}t^3 + \frac{4}{6!}t^6 + \cdots = 1 - \frac{t^3}{6} + \frac{t^6}{180} + \cdots .$$

7. We use the initial conditions to find $y''(0)$. Writing the given equation in the form

$$y''(\theta) = -y(\theta)^3 + \sin\theta$$

and substituting $\theta = 0$, $y(0) = 0$ we get

$$y''(0) = -y(0)^3 + \sin 0 = 0.$$

Differentiating the given equation we obtain

$$\begin{aligned} y''' = (y'')' = -\left(y^3\right)' + (\sin\theta)' = -3y^2y' + \cos\theta \\ \Rightarrow \qquad y'''(0) = -3y(0)^2y'(0) + \cos 0 = -3(0)^2(0) + 1 = 1. \end{aligned}$$

Similarly, we get

$$\begin{aligned} y^{(4)} = (y''')' = -3y^2y'' - 6y\,(y')^2 - \sin\theta \\ \Rightarrow \qquad y^{(4)}(0) = -3y(0)^2y''(0) - 6y(0)\,(y'(0))^2 - \sin 0 = 0. \end{aligned}$$

To simplify further computations we observe that since the Taylor expansion for $y(\theta)$ has the form

$$y(\theta) = \frac{1}{3!}\,\theta^3 + \cdots,$$

then the Taylor expansion for $y(\theta)^3$ must begin with the term $(1/3!)^3\theta^9$, so that

$$\left(y(\theta)^3\right)^{(k)}\Big|_{\theta=0} = 0 \qquad \text{for} \qquad k = 0, 1, \ldots, 8\,.$$

Hence

$$\begin{aligned} y^{(5)} &= -\left(y^3\right)^{(3)} - \cos\theta \qquad \Rightarrow \qquad y^{(5)}(0) = -\left(y^3\right)^{(3)}\Big|_{\theta=0} - \cos 0 = -1, \\ y^{(6)} &= -\left(y^3\right)^{(4)} + \sin\theta \qquad \Rightarrow \qquad y^{(6)}(0) = -\left(y^3\right)^{(4)}\Big|_{\theta=0} - \sin 0 = 0, \\ y^{(7)} &= -\left(y^3\right)^{(5)} + \cos\theta \qquad \Rightarrow \qquad y^{(7)}(0) = -\left(y^3\right)^{(5)}\Big|_{\theta=0} + \cos 0 = 1. \end{aligned}$$

Thus, the first three nonzero terms of the Taylor approximations are

$$y(\theta) = \frac{1}{3!}\,\theta^3 - \frac{1}{5!}\,\theta^5 + \frac{1}{7!}\,\theta^7 + \cdots = \frac{1}{6}\,\theta^3 - \frac{1}{120}\,\theta^5 + \frac{1}{5040}\,\theta^7 + \cdots$$

9. **(a)** To construct $p_3(x)$ we need $f(1)$, $f'(1)$, $f''(1)$, and $f'''(1)$. Thus we have

$$\begin{array}{lcl} f(x) = \ln x & \Rightarrow & f(1) = \ln 1 = 0, \\ f'(x) = x^{-1} & \Rightarrow & f'(1) = (1)^{-1} = 1, \\ f''(x) = -x^{-2} & \Rightarrow & f''(1) = -(1)^{-2} = -1, \\ f'''(x) = 2x^{-3} & \Rightarrow & f'''(1) = 2(1)^{-3} = 2, \end{array}$$

and so

$$\begin{aligned} p_3(x) &= 0 + \frac{1}{1!}(x-1) + \frac{-1}{2!}(x-1)^2 + \frac{2}{3!}(x-1)^3 \\ &= x - 1 - \frac{(x-1)^2}{2} + \frac{(x-1)^3}{3}. \end{aligned}$$

(b) To apply formula (6), we first compute

$$f^{(4)}(x) = [f'''(x)]' = \left(2x^{-3}\right)' = -6x^{-4}.$$

Thus, the error formula (6) yields

$$\begin{aligned} \ln x - p_3(x) =: e_3(x) &= \frac{f^{(4)}(\xi)}{4!}(x - x_0)^4 = \frac{-6\xi^{-4}}{24}(x-1)^4 = -\frac{(x-1)^4}{4\xi^4} \\ \Rightarrow \qquad |\ln(1.5) - p_3(1.5)| &= \left| -\frac{(1.5-1)^4}{4\xi^4} \right| = \frac{(0.5)^4}{4\xi^4} \\ \Rightarrow \qquad |\ln(1.5) - p_3(1.5)| &\le \frac{(0.5)^4}{4} = \frac{1}{64} = 0.015625, \end{aligned}$$

where we have used the fact $\xi > 1$.

(c) Direct calculations yield

$$|\ln(1.5) - p_3(1.5)| \approx \left| 0.405465 - \left(0.5 - \frac{(0.5)^2}{2} + \frac{(0.5)^3}{3} \right) \right| \approx 0.011202.$$

(d) See Figure B.51 in the answers of the text.

11. First, we rewrite the given equation in the form

$$y'' = -py' - qy + g.$$

On the right-hand side of this equation, the function y' is differentiable (y'' exists) and the functions y, p, q, and g are differentiable (even twice). Thus we conclude that its left-hand side, y'', is differentiable being the product, sum, and difference of differentiable functions. Therefore, $y''' = (y'')'$ exists and is given by

$$y''' = (-py' - qy + g)' = -p'y' - py'' - q'y - qy' + g'.$$

Similarly, we conclude that the right-hand side of the equation above is a differentiable function since all the functions involved are differentiable (notice that we have just proved the differentiability of y''). Hence, y''', its left-hand side is differentiable as well, i.e., $(y''')' = y^{(4)}$ does exist.

13. With form $k = r = A = 1$ and $\omega = 10$, the Duffing's equation becomes

$$y'' + y + y^3 = \cos 10t \qquad \text{or} \qquad y'' = -y - y^3 + \cos 10t.$$

Substituting the initial conditions, $y(0) = 0$ and $y'(0) = 1$ into the latter equation yields

$$y''(0) = -y(0) - y(0)^3 + \cos(10 \cdot 0) = -0 - (0)^3 + \cos 0 = 1.$$

Differentiating the given equation, we conclude that

$$y''' = \left(-y - y^3 + \cos 10t\right)' = -y' - 3y^2y' - 10 \sin 10t,$$

which, at $t = 0$, gives

$$y'''(0) = -y'(0) - 3y(0)^2y'(0) - 10 \sin(10 \cdot 0) = -1 - 3(0)^2(1) - 10 \sin 0 = -1.$$

Thus, the Taylor polynomial approximations to the solution of the given initial value problem are

$$y(t) = y(0) + \frac{y'(0)}{1!}\,t + \frac{y''(0)}{2!}\,t^2 + \frac{y'''(0)}{3!}\,t^3 + \cdots = t + \frac{1}{2}\,t^2 - \frac{1}{6}\,t^3 + \cdots.$$

15. For the Taylor polynomial $p_2(x)$, we need $y(0)$, $y'(0)$, and $y''(0)$. We already know $y(0)$ and $y'(0)$ from the initial conditions:

$$y(0) = 1 \qquad \text{and} \qquad y'(0) = 0.$$

Expressing $y''(x)$ from the given equation yields

$$y''(x) = -\frac{2y'(x) + xy(x)}{x}. \tag{8.3}$$

The formal substitution of $x = 0$ in (8.3) gives "0/0"–indeterminate form. On the other hand, since the differentiability of a function implies its continuity, and we are given that $y(x)$ has derivatives of all orders at $x = 0$, we conclude that all the derivatives of $y(x)$ are continuous at $x = 0$. Therefore,

$$y''(0) = \lim_{x \to 0} y''(x),$$

and we can find the above limit by applying L'Hospital's rule. Namely,

$$\begin{aligned} y''(0) &= \lim_{x \to 0} \left[-\frac{2y'(x) + xy(x)}{x} \right] \\ &= -\lim_{x \to 0} \frac{[2y'(x) + xy(x)]'}{(x)'} = -\lim_{x \to 0} \left[2y''(x) + xy'(x) + y(x) \right], \end{aligned}$$

and the last limit can be found by substitution due to the continuity of $y(x)$ and its derivatives at $x = 0$. Hence,

$$y''(0) = -\left[2y''(0) + 0 \cdot y'(0) + y(0) \right] = -2y''(0) - 1.$$

Solving for $y''(0)$ yields $y''(0) = -1/3$, and so

$$p_2(x) = y(0) + \frac{y'(0)}{1!} x + \frac{y''(0)}{2!} x^2 = 1 - \frac{x^2}{6}.$$

EXERCISES 8.2: Power Series and Analytic Functions, page 438

1. Since $a_n = 2^{-n}/(n+1)$, the ratio test yields

$$\lim_{n \to \infty} \left| \frac{a_{n+1}}{a_n} \right| = \lim_{n \to \infty} \frac{2^{-(n+1)}/(n+2)}{2^{-n}/(n+1)} = \lim_{n \to \infty} \frac{2^{-1}(n+1)}{n+2} = \frac{1}{2} = L.$$

So, the radius of convergence is

$$\rho = \frac{1}{L} = 2.$$

In this power series, $x_0 = 1$. Hence, the endpoints of the interval of convergence are

$$x_1 = x_0 + \rho = 1 + 2 = 3,$$
$$x_2 = x_0 - \rho = 1 - 2 = -1.$$

At the point x_1, the series becomes

$$\sum_{n=0}^{\infty} \frac{2^{-n}}{n+1}(3-1)^n = \sum_{n=0}^{\infty} \frac{1}{n+1} = \infty$$

(harmonic series); at the point x_2 we have

$$\sum_{n=0}^{\infty} \frac{2^{-n}}{n+1}(-1-1)^n = \sum_{n=0}^{\infty} \frac{(-1)^n}{n+1} < \infty$$

by alternating series test. Therefore, the set of convergence is $[-1, 3)$.

3. We will use the ratio test given in Theorem 2 on page 432 of the text to find the radius of convergence for this power series. Since $a_n = n^2/2^n$, we see that

$$\frac{a_{n+1}}{a_n} = \frac{(n+1)^2/2^{n+1}}{n^2/2^n} = \frac{(n+1)^2}{2n^2}.$$

Therefore, we have

$$\lim_{n\to\infty}\left|\frac{a_{n+1}}{a_n}\right| = \lim_{n\to\infty}\left|\frac{(n+1)^2}{2n^2}\right| = \frac{1}{2}\lim_{n\to\infty}\frac{(n+1)^2}{n^2} = \frac{1}{2}\lim_{n\to\infty}\left(1+\frac{1}{n}\right)^2 = \frac{1}{2}.$$

Thus, the radius of convergence is $\rho = 2$. Hence, this power series converges absolutely for $|x+2| < 2$. That is, for

$$-2 < x+2 < 2 \qquad \text{or} \qquad -4 < x < 0.$$

We must now check the end points of this interval. We first check the end point -4 or $x + 2 = -2$ which yields the series

$$\sum_{n=0}^{\infty} \frac{n^2(-2)^n}{2^n} = \sum_{n=0}^{\infty}(-1)^n n^2.$$

This series diverges since the nth term, $a_n = (-1)^n n^2$, does not approach zero as n goes to infinity. (Recall that it is necessary for the nth term of a convergent series to approach zero as n goes to infinity. But this fact in itself does not prove that a series converges.) Next, we check the end point $x = 0$ or $x + 2 = 2$ which yields the series

$$\sum_{n=0}^{\infty} \frac{n^2 2^n}{2^n} = \sum_{n=0}^{\infty} n^2.$$

Again, as above, this series diverges. Therefore, this power series converges in the open interval $(-4, 0)$ and diverges outside of this interval.

5. With $a_n = 3/n^3$, the ratio test gives

$$L = \lim_{n\to\infty} \frac{3/(n+1)^3}{3/n^3} = \lim_{n\to\infty} \left(\frac{n}{n+1}\right)^3 = \left(\lim_{n\to\infty} \frac{n}{n+1}\right)^3 = 1.$$

Therefore, the radius of convergence is $\rho = 1/L = 1$. At the points $x_0 \pm \rho = 2 \pm 1$, that is, $x = 3$ and $x = 1$, we have the series

$$\sum_{n=0}^{\infty} \frac{3}{n^3} \qquad \text{and} \qquad \sum_{n=0}^{\infty} \frac{3(-1)^n}{n^3},$$

which are known to converge. Therefore, the set of convergence of the given series is the closed interval $[1, 3]$.

7. By writing

$$\sum_{k=0}^{\infty} a_{2k} x^{2k} = \sum_{k=0}^{\infty} a_{2k} \left(x^2\right)^k = \sum_{k=0}^{\infty} b_k z^k,$$

where $b_k := a_{2k}$ and $z := x^2$, we obtain a power series centered at the origin. The ratio test then yields the radius of convergence to be $1/L$, where

$$L = \lim_{k\to\infty} \left|\frac{b_{k+1}}{b_k}\right| = \lim_{k\to\infty} \left|\frac{a_{2(k+1)}}{a_{2k}}\right| = \lim_{k\to\infty} \left|\frac{a_{2k+2}}{a_{2k}}\right|.$$

So, the series $\sum_{k=0}^{\infty} b_k z^k$ converges for $|z| < 1/L$ and diverges for $|z| > 1/L$. Since $z = x^2$,

$$|z| < \frac{1}{L} \quad \Leftrightarrow \quad \left|x^2\right| < \frac{1}{L} \quad \Leftrightarrow \quad |x| < \frac{1}{\sqrt{L}}.$$

Hence, the original series converges for $|x| < 1/\sqrt{L}$ and diverges for $|x| > 1/\sqrt{L}$. By the definition, $1/\sqrt{L}$ is its radius of convergence.

The second statement can be proved in a similar way, since

$$\sum_{k=0}^{\infty} a_{2k+1} x^{2k+1} = x \sum_{k=0}^{\infty} a_{2k+1} \left(x^2\right)^k = x \sum_{k=0}^{\infty} b_k z^k ,$$

where $b_k := a_{2k+1}$ and $z := x^2$.

9. Since the addition of power series reduces to the addition of the coefficients at the corresponding powers of the variable, we make the following changes in indices of summation.

$$\begin{array}{lll} f(x): \;\; n \to k & \Rightarrow & f(x) = \sum_{k=0}^{\infty} [1/(k+1)]\, x^k , \\ g(x): \;\; n-1 \to k & \Rightarrow & g(x) = \sum_{k=0}^{\infty} 2^{-(k+1)} x^k . \end{array}$$

Therefore,

$$f(x) + g(x) = \sum_{k=0}^{\infty} \frac{1}{k+1} x^k + \sum_{k=0}^{\infty} 2^{-(k+1)} x^k = \sum_{k=0}^{\infty} \left[\frac{1}{k+1} + 2^{-k-1}\right] x^k .$$

11. We want to find the product $f(x)g(x)$ of the two series

$$f(x) = \sum_{n=0}^{\infty} \frac{x^n}{n!} = 1 + x + \frac{x^2}{2} + \frac{x^3}{6} + \frac{x^4}{24} + \cdots ,$$

and

$$g(x) = \sin x = \sum_{k=0}^{\infty} \left[\frac{(-1)^k}{(2k+1)!}\right] x^{2k+1} = x - \frac{x^3}{6} + \frac{x^5}{120} - \frac{x^7}{7!} + \cdots .$$

Therefore, we have

$$\begin{aligned} f(x)g(x) &= \left(1 + x + \frac{x^2}{2} + \frac{x^3}{6} + \frac{x^4}{24} + \cdots\right)\left(x - \frac{x^3}{6} + \frac{x^5}{120} - \frac{x^7}{7!} + \cdots\right) \\ &= x + x^2 + \left(\frac{1}{2} - \frac{1}{6}\right) x^3 + \left(\frac{1}{6} - \frac{1}{6}\right) x^4 + \left(\frac{1}{24} - \frac{1}{12} + \frac{1}{120}\right) x^5 + \cdots \\ &= x + x^2 + + \frac{1}{3} x^3 + \cdots . \end{aligned}$$

Note that since the radius of convergence for both of the given series is $\rho = \infty$, the expansion of the product $f(x)g(x)$ also converges for all values of x.

13. Using formula (6) on page 434 of the text, we obtain

$$\begin{aligned}
f(x)g(x) &= \left[\sum_{n=0}^{\infty} \frac{(-1)^n}{n!} x^n\right]\left[\sum_{n=0}^{\infty}(-1)^n x^n\right] \\
&= \left(1 - x + \frac{1}{2}x^2 - \frac{1}{6}x^3 + \cdots\right)\left(1 - x + x^2 - x^3 + \cdots\right) \\
&= (1)(1) + [(1)(-1) + (-1)(1)]\,x + \left[(1)(1) + (-1)(-1) + \left(\frac{1}{2}\right)(1)\right]x^2 + \cdots \\
&= 1 - 2x + \frac{5}{2}x^2 + \cdots
\end{aligned}$$

15. **(a)** Let $q(x) = \sum_{n=0}^{\infty} a_n x^n$. Multiplying both sides of the given equation by $\sum_{n=0}^{\infty} x^n/n!$, we obtain

$$\left(\sum_{n=0}^{\infty} a_n x^n\right)\left(\sum_{n=0}^{\infty} \frac{1}{n!} x^n\right) = \sum_{n=0}^{\infty} \frac{1}{2^n} x^n .$$

Thus, the right-hand side, $\sum_{n=0}^{\infty} x^n/2^n$, is the Cauchy product of $q(x)$ and $\sum_{n=0}^{\infty} x^n/n!$.

(b) With $c_n = 1/2^n$ and $b_n = 1/n!$, formula (6) on page 434 of the text yields:

$$\begin{aligned}
n = 0: &\quad \frac{1}{2^0} = c_0 = a_0 b_0 = a_0 \cdot \frac{1}{0!} = a_0 ; \\
n = 1: &\quad \frac{1}{2^1} = c_1 = a_0 b_1 + a_1 b_0 = a_0 \cdot \frac{1}{1!} + a_1 \cdot \frac{1}{0!} = a_0 + a_1 ; \\
n = 2: &\quad \frac{1}{2^2} = c_2 = a_0 b_2 + a_1 b_1 + a_2 b_0 = a_0 \cdot \frac{1}{2!} + a_1 \cdot \frac{1}{1!} + a_2 \cdot \frac{1}{0!} = \frac{a_0}{2} + a_1 + a_2 ; \\
n = 3: &\quad \frac{1}{2^3} = c_3 = a_0 b_3 + a_1 b_2 + a_2 b_1 + a_3 b_0 = \frac{a_0}{6} + \frac{a_1}{2} + a_2 + a_3 ;
\end{aligned}$$

etc.

(c) The system in (b) simplifies to

$$\begin{aligned}
1 &= a_0 , & & & a_0 &= 1 , \\
1/2 &= a_0 + a_1 , & & & a_1 &= 1/2 - a_0 = -1/2 , \\
1/4 &= a_0/2 + a_1 + a_2 , & &\Rightarrow & a_2 &= 1/4 - a_0/2 - a_1 = 1/4 , \\
1/8 &= a_0/6 + a_1/2 + a_2 + a_3 , & & & a_3 &= 1/8 - a_0/6 - a_1/2 - a_2 = -1/24 , \\
&\vdots & & & &\vdots
\end{aligned}$$

Thus,

$$q(x) = 1 - \frac{1}{2}x + \frac{1}{4}x^2 - \frac{1}{24}x^3 + \cdots .$$

17. Since

$$\lim_{n\to\infty}\left|\frac{a_{n+1}}{a_n}\right| = \lim_{n\to\infty}\left|\frac{(-1)^{n+1}}{(-1)^n}\right| = \lim_{n\to\infty} 1 = 1,$$

by the ratio test, we find the radius of convergence of the given series to be $\rho = 1/1 = 1 > 0$. Therefore, Theorem 4 of page 434 of the text can be applied. This yields

$$\left[(1+x)^{-1}\right]' = \sum_{n=1}^{\infty}(-1)^n n x^{n-1} \qquad \Rightarrow \qquad -(1+x)^{-2} = \sum_{n=1}^{\infty}(-1)^n n x^{n-1},$$

and the radius of convergence of this series is also $\rho = 1$.

19. Here we will assume that this series has a positive radius of convergence. Thus, since we have

$$f(x) = \sum_{n=0}^{\infty} a_n x^n = a_0 + a_1 x + a_2 x^2 + a_3 x^3 + \cdots + a_n x^n + \cdots ,$$

we can differentiate term by term to obtain

$$f'(x) = 0 + a_1 + a_2 2x + a_3 3x^2 + \cdots + a_n n x^{n-1} + \cdots = \sum_{n=1}^{\infty} a_n n x^{n-1} .$$

Note that the summation for $f(x)$ starts at zero while the summation for $f'(x)$ starts at one.

21. Using the ratio test, we find that the radius ρ of convergence of the given series is

$$\rho = \frac{1}{\lim_{n\to\infty}\left|(-1)^{n+1}/(-1)^n\right|} = \frac{1}{1} = 1 > 0.$$

Thus, by Theorem 4 on page 434 of the text,

$$\begin{aligned} g(x) &= \int_0^x f(t)\,dt = \int_0^x \left[\sum_{n=0}^{\infty}(-1)^n t^n\right] dt \\ &= \sum_{n=0}^{\infty}(-1)^n \int_0^x t^n\,dt = \sum_{n=0}^{\infty}(-1)^n \frac{1}{n+1} t^{n+1}\bigg|_0^x = \sum_{n=0}^{\infty}\frac{(-1)^n}{n+1} x^{n+1} . \end{aligned}$$

On the other hand,

$$g(x)=\int_0^x \frac{dt}{1+t}=\ln(1+t)\Big|_0^x=\ln(1+x), \quad x\in(-1,1).$$

23. Setting $k=n-1$, we have $n=k+1$. Note that $k=0$ when $n=1$. Hence, substitution into the given series yields

$$\sum_{n=1}^{\infty} na_n x^{n-1}=\sum_{k=0}^{\infty}(k+1)a_{k+1}x^k\,.$$

25. We let $n+1=k$ so that $n=k-1$; when $n=0$, then $k=1$. Thus,

$$\sum_{n=0}^{\infty} a_n x^{n+1}=\sum_{k=1}^{\infty} a_{k-1}x^k\,.$$

27. Termwise multiplication yields

$$x^2\sum_{n=0}^{\infty} n(n+1)a_n x^n=\sum_{n=0}^{\infty} n(n+1)a_n x^n x^2=\sum_{n=0}^{\infty} n(n+1)a_n x^{n+2}\,.$$

Now we can shift the summation index by letting $k=n+2$. Then we have $n=k-2$, $n+1=k-1$, $k=2$ when $n=0$, and so

$$\sum_{n=0}^{\infty} n(n+1)a_n x^{n+2}=\sum_{k=2}^{\infty}(k-2)(k-1)a_{k-2}x^k\,.$$

By replacing k by n, we obtain the desired form.

29. We need to determine the nth derivative of $f(x)$ at the point $x=\pi$. Thus, we observe that

$$\begin{aligned}
f(x)&=f^{(0)}(x)=\cos x &&\Rightarrow && f(\pi)=f^{(0)}(\pi)=\cos\pi=-1,\\
f'(x)&=-\sin x &&\Rightarrow && f'(\pi)=-\sin\pi=0,\\
f''(x)&=-\cos x &&\Rightarrow && f''(\pi)=-\cos\pi=1,\\
f'''(x)&=\sin x &&\Rightarrow && f'''(\pi)=\sin\pi=0,\\
f^{(4)}(x)&=\cos x &&\Rightarrow && f^{(4)}(\pi)=\cos\pi=-1.
\end{aligned}$$

Since $f^{(4)}(x)=\cos x=f(x)$, the four derivatives given above will be repeated indefinitely. Thus, we see that $f^{(n)}(\pi)=0$ if n is odd and $f^{(n)}(\pi)=\pm1$ if n is even (where the signs alternate starting at -1 when $n = 0$). Therefore, the Taylor series for f about the point $x_0 = \pi$ is given by

$$\begin{aligned} f(x) &= -1 + 0 + \frac{1}{2!}(x-\pi)^2 + 0 - \frac{1}{4!}(x-\pi)^4 + \cdots + \frac{(-1)^{n+1}(x-\pi)^{2n}}{(2n)!} + \cdots \\ &= \sum_{n=0}^{\infty} \frac{(-1)^{n+1}(x-\pi)^{2n}}{(2n)!}. \end{aligned}$$

31. Writing

$$f(x) = \frac{1+x}{1-x} = \frac{(1-x)+2x}{1-x} = 1 + 2x\,\frac{1}{1-x},$$

we can use the power series expansion (3) on page 433 of the text (geometric series) to obtain the desired Taylor series. Thus we have

$$f(x) = 1 + 2x\,\frac{1}{1-x} = 1 + 2x\sum_{k=0}^{\infty} x^k = 1 + \sum_{k=0}^{\infty} 2x^{k+1}.$$

Shifting the summation index, that is, letting $k+1 = n$, yields

$$f(x) = 1 + \sum_{k=0}^{\infty} 2x^{k+1} = 1 + \sum_{n=1}^{\infty} 2x^n.$$

33. Using the formula

$$c_j = \frac{f^{(j)}(x_0)}{j!}$$

for the coefficients of the Taylor series for $f(x)$ about x_0, we find

$$\begin{array}{lll} f(x_0) = x^3 + 3x - 4\,\big|_{x=1} = 0 & \Rightarrow & c_0 = 0, \\ f'(x_0) = 3x^2 + 3\,\big|_{x=1} = 6 & \Rightarrow & c_1 = 6/1! = 6, \\ f''(x_0) = 6x\,\big|_{x=1} = 6 & \Rightarrow & c_2 = 6/2! = 3, \\ f'''(x) \equiv 6 & \Rightarrow & c_3 = 6/3! = 1, \\ f^{(j)}(x) \equiv 0 & \Rightarrow & c_j = 0 \quad \text{for } j \geq 4. \end{array}$$

Therefore,

$$x^3 + 3x - 4 = 6(x-1) + 3(x-1)^2 + (x-1)^3.$$

35. **(a)** We have

$$\frac{1}{x}=\frac{1}{1+(x-1)}=\frac{1}{1-s}, \qquad \text{where} \quad s=-(x-1).$$

Since $1/(1-s)=\sum_{n=0}^{\infty} s^n$, the substitution $s=-(x-1)$ into both sides of this equality yields the expansion

$$\frac{1}{x}=\frac{1}{1-s}=\sum_{n=0}^{\infty} s^n=\sum_{n=0}^{\infty}[-(x-1)]^n=\sum_{n=0}^{\infty}(-1)^n(x-1)^n,$$

which is valid for

$$|s|=|x-1|<1 \qquad \Rightarrow \qquad 0<x<2.$$

(b) Since the above series has positive radius of convergence $\rho=1$, Theorem 4 on page 434 of the text can be applied. Hence, for $0<x<2$,

$$\begin{aligned}\ln x &= \int_1^x \frac{1}{t}\,dt=\int_1^x\left[\sum_{n=0}^{\infty}(-1)^n(t-1)^n\right]dt=\sum_{n=0}^{\infty}(-1)^n\int_1^x (t-1)^n\,dt\\ &= \sum_{n=0}^{\infty}(-1)^n\frac{1}{n+1}(t-1)^{n+1}\bigg|_1^x=\sum_{n=0}^{\infty}\frac{(-1)^n}{n+1}(x-1)^{n+1}=\sum_{k=1}^{\infty}\frac{(-1)^{k-1}}{k}(x-1)^k.\end{aligned}$$

37. For $n=0$, $f^{(0)}(0):=f(0)=0$ by the definition of $f(x)$.

To find $f'(0)$, we use the definition of the derivative.

$$f'(0)=\lim_{x\to 0}\frac{f(x)-f(0)}{x-0}=\lim_{x\to 0}\frac{e^{-1/x^2}}{x}. \tag{8.4}$$

We compute left-hand and right-hand side limits by making the substitution $t=1/x$. Note that $t\to+\infty$ when $x\to 0^+$ and $t\to-\infty$ when $x\to 0^-$. Thus we have

$$\lim_{x\to 0^\pm}\frac{e^{-1/x^2}}{x}=\lim_{t\to\pm\infty} te^{-t^2}=\lim_{t\to\pm\infty}\frac{t}{e^{t^2}}=\lim_{t\to\pm\infty}\frac{1}{2te^{t^2}}=0,$$

where we applied L'Hospital's rule to the indeterminate form ∞/∞. Therefore, the limit in (8.4) exists and equals 0. For any $x\neq 0$,

$$f'(x)=\left(e^{-1/x^2}\right)'=e^{-1/x^2}\left(-\frac{1}{x^2}\right)'=\frac{2}{x^3}e^{-1/x^2}.$$

Next, we proceed by induction. Assuming that, for some $n \geq 1$,

$$f^{(n)}(0)=0 \quad \text{and} \quad f^{(n)}(x)=p\left(\frac{1}{x}\right)e^{-1/x^2}, \quad x\neq 0,$$

where $p(t)$ is a polynomial in t, we show that

$$f^{(n+1)}(0)=0 \quad \text{and} \quad f^{(n+1)}(x)=q\left(\frac{1}{x}\right)e^{-1/x^2}, \quad x\neq 0,$$

where $q(t)$ is a polynomial in t. This will imply that $f^{(n)}(0)=0$ for all $n \geq 0$.

Indeed, the substitution $t=1/x$ in the one-sided limits yields

$$\lim_{x\to 0^{\pm}}\frac{f^{(n)}(x)-f^{(n)}(0)}{x-0}=\lim_{x\to 0^{\pm}}\frac{p(1/x)e^{-1/x^2}}{x}=\lim_{t\to\pm\infty}\frac{tp(t)}{e^{t^2}}=\lim_{t\to\pm\infty}\frac{r(t)}{e^{t^2}},$$

where $r(t)=a_0t^k+\cdots+a_k$ is a polynomial. Applying the L'Hospital's rule k times, we obtain

$$\begin{aligned}\lim_{t\to\pm\infty}\frac{r(t)}{e^{t^2}} &= \lim_{t\to\pm\infty}\frac{r'(t)}{\left(e^{t^2}\right)'}=\lim_{t\to\pm\infty}\frac{r'(t)}{2te^{t^2}}\\ &= \lim_{t\to\pm\infty}\frac{r''(t)}{(4t^2+2)e^{t^2}}=\cdots=\lim_{t\to\pm\infty}\frac{k!a_0}{(2^kt^k+\cdots)e^{t^2}}=0\,.\end{aligned}$$

Since both one-sided limits exist and are equal, the regular limit exists and equals to the same number. That is,

$$f^{(n+1)}(0)=\lim_{x\to 0}\frac{f^{(n)}(x)-f^{(n)}(0)}{x-0}=0.$$

For any $x\neq 0$,

$$\begin{aligned}f^{(n+1)}(x) &= \left[p\left(\frac{1}{x}\right)e^{-1/x^2}\right]'=\left[p'\left(\frac{1}{x}\right)\left(\frac{1}{x}\right)'\right]e^{-1/x^2}+p\left(\frac{1}{x}\right)\left[e^{-1/x^2}\left(-\frac{1}{x^2}\right)'\right]\\ &= \left[-p'\left(\frac{1}{x}\right)\frac{1}{x^2}+p\left(\frac{1}{x}\right)\frac{2}{x^3}\right]e^{-1/x^2}=q\left(\frac{1}{x}\right)e^{-1/x^2},\end{aligned}$$

where $q(t)=-p'(t)t^2+p(t)2t^3$.

EXERCISES 8.3: Power Series Solutions to Linear Differential Equations, page 449

1. Dividing the given equation by $(x+1)$ yields

$$y''-\frac{x^2}{x+1}y'+\frac{3}{x+1}y=0.$$

Thus we see that

$$p(x) = -\frac{x^2}{x+1}, \qquad q(x) = \frac{3}{x+1}.$$

These are rational functions and so they are analytic everywhere except, perhaps, at zeros of their denominators. Solving $x+1=0$, we find that $x=-1$, which is a point of infinite discontinuity for both functions. Consequently, $x=-1$ is the only singular point of the given equation.

3. Writing the equation in standard form yields

$$y'' + \frac{2}{\theta^2-2}\,y' + \frac{\sin\theta}{\theta^2-2}\,y = 0.$$

The coefficients

$$p(\theta) = \frac{2}{\theta^2-2} \qquad \text{and} \qquad q(\theta) = \frac{\sin\theta}{\theta^2-2}$$

are quotients of analytic functions, and so they are analytic everywhere except zeros $\theta = \pm\sqrt{2}$ of the denominator where they have infinite discontinuities. Hence, the given equation has two singular points, $\theta = \pm\sqrt{2}$.

5. In standard form, the equation becomes

$$x'' + \frac{t+1}{t^2-t-2}\,x' - \frac{t-2}{t^2-t-2}\,x = 0.$$

Hence

$$p(t) = \frac{t+1}{t^2-t-2} = \frac{t+1}{(t+1)(t-2)}, \qquad q(t) = -\frac{t-2}{t^2-t-2} = -\frac{t-2}{(t+1)(t-2)}.$$

The point $t=-1$ is a removable singularity for $p(t)$ since, for $t \neq -1$, we can cancel $(t+1)$-term in the numerator and denominator, and so $p(t)$ becomes analytic at $t=-1$ if we set

$$p(-1) := \lim_{t\to -1} p(t) = \lim_{t\to -1} \frac{1}{t-2} = -\frac{1}{3}.$$

At the point $t=2$, $p(t)$ has infinite discontinuity. Thus $p(t)$ is analytic everywhere except $t=2$. Similarly, $q(t)$ is analytic everywhere except $t=-1$. Therefore, the given equation has two singular points, $t=-1$ and $t=2$.

7. In standard form, this equation becomes

$$y'' + \left(\frac{\cos x}{\sin x}\right) y = 0.$$

Thus, $p(x) = 0$ and, hence, is analytic everywhere. We also see that

$$q(x) = \frac{\cos x}{\sin x} = \cot x.$$

Note that $q(x)$ is the quotient of two functions ($\cos x$ and $\sin x$) that each have a power series expansion with a positive radius of convergence about each real number x. Thus, according to page 434 of the text, we see that $q(x)$ will also have a power series expansion with a positive radius of convergence about every real number x as long as the denominator, $\sin x$, is not equal to zero. Since the cotangent function is $\pm\infty$ at integer multiples of π, we see that $q(x)$ is not defined and, therefore, not analytic at $n\pi$. Hence, the differential equation is singular only at the points $n\pi$, where n is an integer.

9. Dividing the differential equation by $\sin\theta$, we get

$$y'' - \frac{\ln\theta}{\sin\theta} y = 0.$$

Thus, $p(\theta) \equiv 0$ and $q(\theta) = -\ln\theta/\sin\theta$. The function $q(\theta)$ is not defined for $\theta \le 0$ because of the logarithmic term and has infinite discontinuities at *positive* zeros of the denominator. Namely,

$$\sin\theta = 0 \qquad \Rightarrow \qquad \theta = k\pi, \quad k = 1, 2, 3, \ldots .$$

At all other points θ, $q(\theta)$ is analytic as a quotient of two analytic functions. Hence, the singular points of the given equation are

$$\theta \le 0 \qquad \text{and} \qquad \theta = k\pi, \quad k = 1, 2, 3, \ldots .$$

11. The coefficient, $x + 2$, is a polynomial, and so it is analytic everywhere. Therefore, $x = 0$ is an ordinary point of the given equation. We seek a power series solution of the form

$$y(x) = \sum_{n=0}^{\infty} a_n x^n \qquad \Rightarrow \qquad y'(x) = \sum_{n=1}^{\infty} n a_n x^{n-1},$$

where we have applied Theorem 4 on page 434 of the text to find the power series expansion of $y'(x)$. We now substitute the power series for y and y' into the given differential equation and obtain

$$\sum_{n=1}^{\infty} n a_n x^{n-1} + (x+2) \sum_{n=0}^{\infty} a_n x^n = 0$$

$$\Rightarrow \quad \sum_{n=1}^{\infty} n a_n x^{n-1} + \sum_{n=0}^{\infty} 2 a_n x^n + \sum_{n=0}^{\infty} a_n x^{n+1} = 0. \tag{8.5}$$

To sum these series, we make shifts in indices of summation so that they sum over the same power of x. In the first sum, we set $k = n-1$ so that $n = k+1$ and k runs from 0 to ∞; in the second sum, we just replace n by k; in the third sum, we let $k = n+1$ and so $n = k-1$, and the summation starts from 1. Thus the equation (8.5) becomes

$$\sum_{k=0}^{\infty} (k+1) a_{k+1} x^k + \sum_{k=0}^{\infty} 2 a_k x^k + \sum_{k=1}^{\infty} a_{k-1} x^k = 0$$

$$\Rightarrow \quad \left[a_1 + \sum_{k=1}^{\infty} (k+1) a_{k+1} x^k \right] + \left[2a_0 + \sum_{k=1}^{\infty} 2 a_k x^k \right] + \sum_{k=1}^{\infty} a_{k-1} x^k = 0$$

$$\Rightarrow \quad (a_1 + 2a_0) + \sum_{k=1}^{\infty} \left[(k+1) a_{k+1} + 2a_k + a_{k-1} \right] x^k = 0.$$

For the power series on the left-hand side to be identically zero, we must have all zero coefficients. Hence,

$$a_1 + 2a_0 = 0 \qquad \text{and} \qquad (k+1) a_{k+1} + 2a_k + a_{k-1} = 0 \quad \text{for all} \quad k \geq 1.$$

This yields

$$\begin{aligned}
& a_1 + 2a_0 = 0 && \Rightarrow && a_1 = -2a_0\,, \\
k = 1: \ & 2a_2 + 2a_1 + a_0 = 0 && \Rightarrow && a_2 = (-2a_1 - a_0)/2 = (4a_0 - a_0)/2 = 3a_0/2\,, \\
k = 2: \ & 3a_3 + 2a_2 + a_1 = 0 && \Rightarrow && a_3 = (-2a_2 - a_1)/3 = (-3a_0 + 2a_0)/3 = -a_0/3\,, \\
& \vdots
\end{aligned}$$

Therefore,

$$y(x) = a_0 - 2a_0 x + \frac{3a_0}{2} x^2 - \frac{a_0}{3} x^3 + \cdots = a_0 \left(1 - 2x + \frac{3x^2}{2} - \frac{x^3}{3} + \cdots \right),$$

where a_0 is an arbitrary constant (which is, actually, $y(0)$).

13. This equation has no singular points since the coefficients $p(x) \equiv 0$ and $q(x) = -x^2$ are analytic everywhere. So, let

$$z(x) = \sum_{k=0}^{\infty} a_k x^k \qquad \Rightarrow \qquad z'(x) = \sum_{k=1}^{\infty} k a_k x^{k-1} \qquad \Rightarrow \qquad z''(x) = \sum_{k=2}^{\infty} k(k-1) a_k x^{k-2},$$

where we used Theorem 4 on page 434 of the text differentiating the series termwise. Substitution z and z'' into the given equation yields

$$z'' - x^2 z = \sum_{k=2}^{\infty} k(k-1) a_k x^{k-2} - x^2 \sum_{k=0}^{\infty} a_k x^k = \sum_{k=2}^{\infty} k(k-1) a_k x^{k-2} - \sum_{k=0}^{\infty} a_k x^{k+2}.$$

We now shift indices of summation so that they sum over the same power of x. For the first sum, we substitute $n = k - 2$ so that $k = n + 2$, $k - 1 = n + 1$, and the summation starts from $n = 0$. In the second summation, we let $n = k + 2$ which yields $k = n - 2$ and $n = 2$ as the starting index. Thus we obtain

$$z'' - x^2 z = \sum_{n=0}^{\infty} (n+2)(n+1) a_{n+2} x^n - \sum_{n=2}^{\infty} a_{n-2} x^n.$$

Next step in writing the right-hand side as a single power series is to start both summations at the same point. To do this we observe that

$$\begin{aligned}\sum_{n=0}^{\infty} (n+2)(n+1) a_{n+2} x^n - \sum_{n=2}^{\infty} a_{n-2} x^n &= 2a_2 + 6a_3 x + \sum_{n=2}^{\infty} (n+2)(n+1) a_{n+2} x^n - \sum_{n=2}^{\infty} a_{n-2} x^n \\ &= 2a_2 + 6a_3 x + \sum_{n=2}^{\infty} \left[(n+2)(n+1) a_{n+2} - a_{n-2}\right] x^n.\end{aligned}$$

In order for this power series to equal zero, each coefficient must be zero. Therefore, we obtain

$$2a_2 = 0, \qquad 6a_3 = 0 \qquad \text{and} \qquad (n+2)(n+1) a_{n+2} - a_{n-2} = 0, \quad n \geq 2.$$

From the first two equations we find that $a_2 = 0$ and $a_3 = 0$. Next we take $n = 2$ and $n = 3$ in the above recurrence relation and get

$$\begin{aligned} n = 2:& \quad (4)(3)a_4 - a_0 = 0 \qquad \Rightarrow \qquad a_4 = a_0/12, \\ n = 3:& \quad (5)(4)a_5 - a_1 = 0 \qquad \Rightarrow \qquad a_5 = a_1/20. \end{aligned}$$

Hence,

$$z(x)=\sum_{k=0}^{\infty}a_kx^k = a_0+a_1x+(0)x^2+(0)x^3+\frac{a_0}{12}x^4+\frac{a_1}{20}x^5+\cdots$$
$$= a_0\left(1+\frac{x^4}{12}+\cdots\right)+a_1\left(x+\frac{x^5}{20}+\cdots\right).$$

15. Zero is an ordinary point for this equation since the functions $p(x)=x-1$ and $q(x)=1$ are both analytic everywhere and, hence, at the point $x=0$. Thus, we can assume that the solution to this linear differential equation has a power series expansion with a positive radius of convergence about the point $x=0$. That is, we assume that

$$y(x)=a_0+a_1x+a_2x^2+a_3x^3+\cdots=\sum_{n=0}^{\infty}a_nx^n.$$

In order to solve the differential equation we must find the coefficients a_n. To do this, we must substitute $y(x)$ and its derivatives into the given differential equation. Hence, we must find $y'(x)$ and $y''(x)$. Since $y(x)$ has a power series expansion with a positive radius of convergence about the point $x=0$, we can find its derivative by differentiating term by term. We can similarly differentiate $y'(x)$ to find $y''(x)$. Thus, we have

$$y'(x)=0+a_1+2a_2x+3a_3x^2+\cdots=\sum_{n=1}^{\infty}na_nx^{n-1}$$
$$\Rightarrow \quad y''(x)=2a_2+6a_3x+\cdots=\sum_{n=2}^{\infty}n(n-1)a_nx^{n-2}.$$

By substituting these expressions into the differential equation, we obtain

$$y''+(x-1)y'+y=\sum_{n=2}^{\infty}n(n-1)a_nx^{n-2}+(x-1)\sum_{n=1}^{\infty}na_nx^{n-1}+\sum_{n=0}^{\infty}a_nx^n=0.$$

Simplifying yields

$$\sum_{n=2}^{\infty}n(n-1)a_nx^{n-2}+\sum_{n=1}^{\infty}na_nx^n-\sum_{n=1}^{\infty}na_nx^{n-1}+\sum_{n=0}^{\infty}a_nx^n=0. \qquad (8.6)$$

We want to be able to write the left-hand side of this equation as a single power series. This will allow us to find expressions for the coefficient of each power of x. Therefore, we first need to shift the indices in each power series above so that they sum over the same powers of x. Thus, we let $k = n - 2$ in the first summation and note that this means that $n = k + 2$ and that $k = 0$ when $n = 2$. This yields

$$\sum_{n=2}^{\infty} n(n-1)a_n x^{n-2} = \sum_{k=0}^{\infty} (k+2)(k+1)a_{k+2}x^k.$$

In the third power series, we let $k = n - 1$ which implies that $n = k + 1$ and $k = 0$ when $n = 1$. Thus, we see that

$$\sum_{n=1}^{\infty} n a_n x^{n-1} = \sum_{k=0}^{\infty} (k+1)a_{k+1}x^k.$$

For the second and last power series we need only to replace n with k. Substituting all of these expressions into their appropriate places in equation (8.6) above yields

$$\sum_{k=0}^{\infty} (k+2)(k+1)a_{k+2}x^k + \sum_{k=1}^{\infty} k a_k x^k - \sum_{k=0}^{\infty} (k+1)a_{k+1}x^k + \sum_{k=0}^{\infty} a_k x^k = 0.$$

Our next step in writing the left-hand side as a single power series is to start all of the summations at the same point. To do this we observe that

$$\sum_{k=0}^{\infty} (k+2)(k+1)a_{k+2}x^k = (2)(1)a_2x^0 + \sum_{k=1}^{\infty} (k+2)(k+1)a_{k+2}x^k,$$

$$\sum_{k=0}^{\infty} (k+1)a_{k+1}x^k = (1)a_1x^0 + \sum_{k=1}^{\infty} (k+1)a_{k+1}x^k,$$

$$\sum_{k=0}^{\infty} a_k x^k = a_0x^0 + \sum_{k=1}^{\infty} a_k x^k.$$

Thus, all of the summations now start at one. Therefore, we have

$$(2)(1)a_2x^0 + \sum_{k=1}^{\infty} (k+2)(k+1)a_{k+2}x^k + \sum_{k=1}^{\infty} k a_k x^k$$

$$-(1)a_1x^0 - \sum_{k=1}^{\infty} (k+1)a_{k+1}x^k + a_0x^0 + \sum_{k=1}^{\infty} a_k x^k = 0$$

$$\Rightarrow \qquad 2a_2 - a_1 + a_0 + \sum_{k=1}^{\infty} \left((k+2)(k+1)a_{k+2}x^k + k a_k x^k - (k+1)a_{k+1}x^k + a_k x^k\right) = 0$$

$$\Rightarrow \qquad 2a_2 - a_1 + a_0 + \sum_{k=1}^{\infty} \left((k+2)(k+1)a_{k+2} + (k+1)a_k - (k+1)a_{k+1}\right) x^k = 0.$$

In order for this power series to equal zero, each coefficient must be zero. Therefore, we obtain

$$2a_2 - a_1 + a_0 = 0 \qquad \Rightarrow \qquad a_2 = \frac{a_1 - a_0}{2},$$

and

$$(k+2)(k+1)a_{k+2} + (k+1)a_k - (k+1)a_{k+1} = 0, \qquad k \geq 1$$

$$\Rightarrow \qquad a_{k+2} = \frac{a_{k+1} - a_k}{k+2}, \qquad k \geq 1,$$

where we have canceled the factor $(k+1)$ from the recurrence relation, the last equation obtained above. *Note that in this recurrence relation we have solved for the coefficient with the largest subscript, namely* a_{k+2}. *Also, note that the first value for* k *in the recurrence relation is the same as the first value for* k *used in the summation notation.* By using the recurrence relation with $k = 1$, we find that

$$a_3 = \frac{a_2 - a_1}{3} = \frac{\frac{a_1 - a_0}{2} - a_1}{3} = \frac{-(a_1 + a_0)}{6},$$

where we have plugged in the expression for a_2 that we found above. By letting $k = 2$ in the recurrence equation, we obtain

$$a_4 = \frac{a_3 - a_2}{4} = \frac{\frac{-(a_1 + a_0)}{6} - \frac{a_1 - a_0}{2}}{4} = \frac{-2a_1 + a_0)}{12},$$

where we have plugged in the values for a_2 and a_3 found above. Continuing this process will allow us to find as many coefficients for the power series of the solution to the differential equation as we may want. Notice that the coefficients just found involve only the variables a_0 and a_1. From the recurrence equation, we see that this will be the case for all coefficients of the power series solution. Thus, a_0 and a_1 are arbitrary constants and these variables will be our arbitrary variables in the general solution. Hence, substituting the values for the coefficients that we found above into the solution

$$y(x) = \sum_{n=0}^{\infty} a_n x^n = a_0 + a_1 x + a_2 x^2 + a_3 x^3 + a_4 x^4 + \cdots,$$

yields the solution

$$\begin{aligned} y(x) &= a_0 + a_1 x + \frac{a_1 - a_0}{2} x^2 + \frac{-(a_1 + a_0)}{6} x^3 + \frac{-2a_1 + a_0}{12} x^4 + \cdots \\ &= a_0 \left(1 - \frac{x^2}{2} - \frac{x^3}{6} + \frac{x^4}{12} + \cdots \right) + a_1 \left(x + \frac{x^2}{2} - \frac{x^3}{6} - \frac{x^4}{6} + \cdots \right). \end{aligned}$$

19. Since $x = 0$ is an ordinary point for the given equation, we seek for a power series expansion of a general solution of the form

$$y(x) = \sum_{n=0}^{\infty} a_n x^n \qquad \Rightarrow \qquad y'(x) = \sum_{n=1}^{\infty} n a_n x^{n-1}.$$

Substituting $y(x)$ and $y'(x)$ into the given equation, we obtain

$$\sum_{n=1}^{\infty} n a_n x^{n-1} - 2x \sum_{n=0}^{\infty} a_n x^n = \sum_{n=1}^{\infty} n a_n x^{n-1} - \sum_{n=0}^{\infty} 2 a_n x^{n+1} = 0.$$

We shift the indices of summations so that they sum over the same powers of x. In the first sum, we let $k = n - 1$. Then $n = k + 1$ and the summation starts from $k = 0$. In the second sum, let $k = n + 1$. Then $n = k - 1$ and $k = 1$ when $n = 0$. Thus we have

$$\sum_{k=0}^{\infty} (k+1) a_{k+1} x^k - \sum_{k=1}^{\infty} 2 a_{k-1} x^k = a_1 + \sum_{k=1}^{\infty} [(k+1) a_{k+1} - 2a_{k-1}] x^k = 0.$$

In order for this power series to equal zero, each coefficient must be zero. That is,

$$\begin{aligned} &a_1 = 0, & & & a_1 &= 0, \\ &(k+1) a_{k+1} - 2a_{k-1} = 0, \quad k \ge 1 & &\Rightarrow & a_{k+1} &= 2a_{k-1}/(k+1), \quad k \ge 1. \end{aligned}$$

Since $a_1 = 0$, it follows from this recurrence relation that all odd coefficients are zeros. Indeed,

$$a_3 = \frac{2a_1}{3} = 0, \qquad a_5 = \frac{2a_3}{5} = 0, \qquad \text{etc.}$$

For even coefficients, we have

$$\begin{aligned} k = 1: \quad & a_2 = 2a_0/2, \\ k = 3: \quad & a_4 = 2a_2/4 = 2[2a_0/2]/4 = 2^2 a_0/(2 \cdot 4), \\ k = 5: \quad & a_6 = 2a_4/6 = 2[2^2 a_0/(2 \cdot 4)]/6 = 2^3 a_0/(2 \cdot 4 \cdot 6), \\ \vdots \quad & \end{aligned}$$

The pattern for the even coefficients is now apparent. Namely,

$$a_{2k} = \frac{2^k a_0}{2 \cdot 4 \cdots (2k)} = \frac{2^k a_0}{2^k (1 \cdot 2 \cdots k)} = \frac{a_0}{k!}, \qquad k = 1, 2, \ldots .$$

This formula remains correct for $k = 0$ as well with $0! := 1$. Thus

$$y(x) = \sum_{k=0}^{\infty} \frac{a_0}{k!} x^{2k} = a_0 \sum_{k=0}^{\infty} \frac{x^{2k}}{k!},$$

where a_0 is an arbitrary constant.

21. Since $x = 0$ is an ordinary point for this differential equation, we will assume that the solution has a power series expansion with a positive radius of convergence about the point $x = 0$. Thus, we have

$$y(x) = \sum_{n=0}^{\infty} a_n x^n \quad \Rightarrow \quad y'(x) = \sum_{n=1}^{\infty} n a_n x^{n-1} \quad \Rightarrow \quad y''(x) = \sum_{n=2}^{\infty} n(n-1) a_n x^{n-2}.$$

By plugging these expressions into the differential equation, we obtain

$$y'' - xy' + 4y = \sum_{n=2}^{\infty} n(n-1) a_n x^{n-2} - x \sum_{n=1}^{\infty} n a_n x^{n-1} + 4 \sum_{n=0}^{\infty} a_n x^n = 0$$

$$\Rightarrow \quad \sum_{n=2}^{\infty} n(n-1) a_n x^{n-2} - \sum_{n=1}^{\infty} n a_n x^n + \sum_{n=0}^{\infty} 4 a_n x^n = 0.$$

In order for each power series to sum over the same powers of x, we will shift the index in the first summation by letting $k = n - 2$, and we will let $k = n$ in the other two power series. Thus, we have

$$\sum_{k=0}^{\infty} (k+2)(k+1) a_{k+2} x^k - \sum_{k=1}^{\infty} k a_k x^k + \sum_{k=0}^{\infty} 4 a_k x^k = 0.$$

Next we want all of the summations to start at the same point. Therefore, we will take the first term in the first and last power series out of the summation sign. This yields

$$(2)(1) a_2 x^0 + \sum_{k=1}^{\infty} (k+2)(k+1) a_{k+2} x^k - \sum_{k=1}^{\infty} k a_k x^k + 4 a_0 x^0 + \sum_{k=1}^{\infty} 4 a_k x^k = 0$$

$$\Rightarrow \quad 2a_2 + 4a_0 + \sum_{k=1}^{\infty} (k+2)(k+1) a_{k+2} x^k - \sum_{k=1}^{\infty} k a_k x^k + \sum_{k=1}^{\infty} 4 a_k x^k = 0$$

$$\Rightarrow \qquad 2a_2 + 4a_0 + \sum_{k=1}^{\infty} \left[(k+2)(k+1)a_{k+2} + (-k+4)a_k\right] x^k = 0.$$

By setting each coefficient of the power series equal to zero, we see that

$$2a_2 + 4a_0 = 0 \qquad \Rightarrow \qquad a_2 = \frac{-4a_0}{2} = -2a_0\,,$$

$$(k+2)(k+1)a_{k+2} + (-k+4)a_k = 0 \qquad \Rightarrow \qquad a_{k+2} = \frac{(k-4)a_k}{(k+2)(k+1)}\,, \qquad k \geq 1,$$

where we have solved the recurrence equation, the last equation above, for a_{k+2}, the coefficient with the largest subscript. Thus, we have

$$k=1 \qquad \Rightarrow \qquad a_3 = \frac{-3a_1}{3\cdot 2} = \frac{-a_1}{2}\,,$$

$$k=2 \qquad \Rightarrow \qquad a_4 = \frac{-2a_2}{4\cdot 3} = \frac{(-2)(-4)a_0}{4\cdot 3\cdot 2} = \frac{a_0}{3}\,,$$

$$k=3 \qquad \Rightarrow \qquad a_5 = \frac{-a_3}{5\cdot 4} = \frac{(-3)(-1)a_1}{5\cdot 4\cdot 3\cdot 2} = \frac{a_1}{40}\,,$$

$$k=4 \qquad \Rightarrow \qquad a_6 = 0,$$

$$k=5 \qquad \Rightarrow \qquad a_7 = \frac{a_5}{7\cdot 6} = \frac{(-3)(-1)(1)a_1}{7\cdot 6\cdot 5\cdot 4\cdot 3\cdot 2} = \frac{a_1}{560}\,,$$

$$k=6 \qquad \Rightarrow \qquad a_8 = \frac{2a_6}{8\cdot 7} = 0,$$

$$k=7 \qquad \Rightarrow \qquad a_9 = \frac{3a_7}{9\cdot 8} = \frac{(-3)(-1)(1)(3)a_1}{9!}\,,$$

$$k=8 \qquad \Rightarrow \qquad a_{10} = \frac{4a_8}{10\cdot 9} = 0,$$

$$k=9 \qquad \Rightarrow \qquad a_{11} = \frac{5a_9}{11\cdot 10} = \frac{(-3)(-1)(1)(3)(5)a_1}{11!}\,.$$

Now we can see a pattern starting to develop. (*Note that it is easier to determine sucha pattern if we consider specific coefficients that have not been multiplied out.*) We first note that a_0 and a_1 can be chosen arbitrarily. Next we notice that the coefficients with even subscripts larger than 4 are zero. We also see that the general formula for a coefficient with an odd subscript is given by

$$a_{2n+1} = \frac{(-3)(-1)(1)\cdots(2n-5)a_1}{(2n+1)!}\,.$$

Notice that this formula is also valid for a_3 and a_5. Substituting these expressions for the coefficients into the solution

$$y(x)=\sum_{n=0}^{\infty}a_nx^n=a_0+a_1x+a_2x^2+a_3x^3+a_4x^4+\cdots,$$

yields

$$\begin{aligned}
y(x) &= a_0+a_1x-2a_0x^2-\frac{a_1}{2}x^3+\frac{a_0}{3}x^4+\frac{a_1}{40}x^5+\cdots \\
&\qquad +\frac{(-3)(-1)(1)\cdots(2n-5)a_1}{(2n+1)!}x^{2n+1}+\cdots \\
&= a_0\left[1-2x^2+\frac{x^4}{3}\right]+a_1\left[x-\frac{x^3}{2}+\frac{x^5}{40}+\cdots+\frac{(-3)(-1)(1)\cdots(2n-5)}{(2n+1)!}x^{2n+1}+\cdots\right] \\
&= a_0\left[1-2x^2+\frac{x^4}{3}\right]+a_1\left[x+\sum_{k=1}^{\infty}\frac{(-3)(-1)(1)\cdots(2k-5)}{(2k+1)!}x^{2k+1}\right].
\end{aligned}$$

29. Since $x=0$ is an ordinary point for this differential equation, we can assume that a solution to this problem is given by

$$y(x)=\sum_{n=0}^{\infty}a_nx^n \quad\Rightarrow\quad y'(x)=\sum_{n=1}^{\infty}na_nx^{n-1} \quad\Rightarrow\quad y''(x)=\sum_{n=2}^{\infty}n(n-1)a_nx^{n-2}.$$

By substituting the initial conditions, $y(0)=1$ and $y'(0)=-2$, into the first two equations above, we see that

$$y(0)=a_0=1, \qquad \text{and} \qquad y'(0)=a_1=-2.$$

Next we will substitute the expressions found above for $y(x)$, $y'(x)$, and $y''(x)$ into the differential equation to obtain

$$\begin{aligned}
y''+y'-xy &= \sum_{n=2}^{\infty}n(n-1)a_nx^{n-2}+\sum_{n=1}^{\infty}na_nx^{n-1}-x\sum_{n=0}^{\infty}a_nx^n=0 \\
\Rightarrow\quad & \sum_{n=2}^{\infty}n(n-1)a_nx^{n-2}+\sum_{n=1}^{\infty}na_nx^{n-1}-\sum_{n=0}^{\infty}a_nx^{n+1}=0.
\end{aligned}$$

By setting $k=n-2$ in the first power series above, $k=n-1$ in the second power series above, and $k=n+1$ in the last power series, we can shift the indices so that x is raised to the power k in each power series. Thus, we obtain

$$\sum_{k=0}^{\infty}(k+2)(k+1)a_{k+2}x^k + \sum_{k=0}^{\infty}(k+1)a_{k+1}x^k - \sum_{k=1}^{\infty} a_{k-1}x^k = 0.$$

We can start all of the summations at the same point if we remove the first term from each of the first two power series above. Therefore, we have

$$(2)(1)a_2 + \sum_{k=1}^{\infty}(k+2)(k+1)a_{k+2}x^k + (1)a_1 + \sum_{k=1}^{\infty}(k+1)a_{k+1}x^k - \sum_{k=1}^{\infty} a_{k-1}x^k = 0$$

$$\Rightarrow \qquad 2a_2 + a_1 + \sum_{k=1}^{\infty}\left[(k+2)(k+1)a_{k+2} + (k+1)a_{k+1} - a_{k-1}\right]x^k = 0.$$

By equating coefficients, we see that all of the coefficients of the terms in the power series above must be zero. Thus, we have

$$2a_2 + a_1 = 0 \qquad \Rightarrow \qquad a_2 = \frac{-a_1}{2},$$

$$(k+2)(k+1)a_{k+2} + (k+1)a_{k+1} - a_{k-1} = 0$$

$$\Rightarrow \qquad a_{k+1} = \frac{a_{k-1} - (k+1)a_{k+1}}{(k+2)(k+1)}, \qquad k \geq 1.$$

Thus, we see that

$$k = 1 \qquad \Rightarrow \qquad a_3 = \frac{a_0 - 2a_2}{3 \cdot 2} = \frac{a_0}{6} + \frac{a_1}{6}.$$

Using the fact that $a_0 = 1$ and $a_1 = -2$, which we found from the initial conditions, we calculate

$$a_2 = \frac{-(-2)}{2} = 1,$$

$$a_3 = \frac{1}{6} + \frac{-2}{6} = -\frac{1}{6}.$$

By substituting these coefficients, we obtain the cubic polynomial approximation

$$y(x) = 1 - 2x + x^2 - \frac{x^3}{6}.$$

The graphs of the linear, quadratic and cubic polynomial approximations are easily generated by using the software supplied with the text.

31. The point $x_0 = 0$ is an ordinary point for the given equation since $p(x) = 2x/(x^2+2)$ and $q(x) = 3/(x^2+2)$ are analytic at zero. Hence we can express a general solution in the form

$$y(x) = \sum_{n=0}^{\infty} a_n x^n .$$

Substituting this expansion into the given differential equation yields

$$(x^2+2)\sum_{n=2}^{\infty} n(n-1)a_n x^{n-2} + 2x\sum_{n=1}^{\infty} na_n x^{n-1} + 3\sum_{n=0}^{\infty} a_n x^n = 0$$

$$\Rightarrow \quad \sum_{n=2}^{\infty} n(n-1)a_n x^n + \sum_{n=2}^{\infty} 2n(n-1)a_n x^{n-2} + \sum_{n=1}^{\infty} 2na_n x^n + \sum_{n=0}^{\infty} 3a_n x^n = 0.$$

To sum over like powers x^k, we put $k = n-2$ into the second summation and $k = n$ into the other summations. This gives

$$\sum_{k=2}^{\infty} k(k-1)a_k x^k + \sum_{k=0}^{\infty} 2(k+2)(k+1)a_{k+2} x^k + \sum_{k=1}^{\infty} 2ka_k x^k + \sum_{k=0}^{\infty} 3a_k x^k = 0.$$

Next we separate the terms corresponding to $k = 0$ and $k = 1$ and combine the rest under one summation.

$$(4a_2 + 3a_0) + (12a_3 + 5a_1)x + \sum_{k=2}^{\infty} \left[k(k-1)a_k + 2(k+2)(k+1)a_{k+2} + 2ka_k + 3a_k\right] x^k = 0.$$

Setting the coefficients equal to zero and simplifying, we get

$$\begin{aligned} &4a_2 + 3a_0 = 0, \\ &12a_3 + 5a_1 = 0, \\ &(k^2+k+3)a_k + 2(k+2)(k+1)a_{k+2} = 0, \qquad k \ge 2 \end{aligned}$$

$$\Rightarrow \quad \begin{aligned} a_2 &= -3a_0/4\,, \\ a_3 &= -5a_1/12\,, \\ a_{k+2} &= -(k^2+k+3)a_k/[2(k+2)(k+1)], \qquad k \ge 2. \end{aligned}$$

From the initial conditions, we have

$$a_0 = y(0) = 1 \qquad \text{and} \qquad a_1 = y'(0) = 2.$$

Therefore,

$$a_2 = -3(1)/4 = -3/4\,,$$
$$a_3 = -5(2)/12 = -5/6\,,$$

and the cubic polynomial approximation for the solution is

$$y(x) = a_0 + a_1 x + x_2 x^2 + a_3 x^3 = 1 + 2x - \frac{3x^2}{4} - \frac{5x^3}{6}\,.$$

33. In Problem 7, Exercises 8.2 we showed that the radius of convergence of a power series $\sum_{n=0}^{\infty} a_{2n} x^{2n}$ is $\rho = 1/\sqrt{L}$, where

$$L = \lim_{n\to\infty} \left| \frac{a_{2(n+1)}}{a_{2n}} \right|.$$

In the series (13), $a_{2n} = (-1)^n/n!$ and so

$$L = \lim_{n\to\infty} \left| \frac{(-1)^{n+1}/(n+1)!}{(-1)^n/n!} \right| = \lim_{n\to\infty} \frac{1}{n+1} = 0.$$

Therefore, $\sqrt{L} = 0$ and $\rho = \infty$.

35. With the given values of parameters, we have an initial value problem

$$0.1q''(t) + \left(1 + \frac{t}{10}\right) q'(t) + \frac{1}{2}\, q(t) = 0, \qquad q(0) = 10, \quad q'(0) = 0.$$

Simplifying yields

$$q''(t) + (10 + t)\, q'(t) + 5q(t) = 0, \qquad q(0) = 10, \quad q'(0) = 0.$$

The point $t = 0$ is an ordinary point for this equation. Let $q(t) = \sum_{n=0}^{\infty} a_n t^n$ be the power series expansion of $q(t)$ about $t = 0$. Substituting this series into the above differential equation, we obtain

$$\sum_{n=2}^{\infty} n(n-1)a_n t^{n-2} + (10+t)\sum_{n=1}^{\infty} n a_n t^{n-1} + 5\sum_{n=0}^{\infty} a_n t^n = 0$$
$$\Rightarrow \qquad \sum_{n=2}^{\infty} n(n-1)a_n t^{n-2} + \sum_{n=1}^{\infty} 10 n a_n t^{n-1} + \sum_{n=1}^{\infty} n a_n t^n + \sum_{n=0}^{\infty} 5 a_n t^n = 0.$$

Setting $k = n - 2$ in the first summation, $k = n - 1$ in the second summation, and $k = n$ in the last two summations, we obtain

$$\sum_{k=0}^{\infty}(k+2)(k+1)a_{k+2}t^k + \sum_{k=0}^{\infty} 10(k+1)a_{k+1}t^k + \sum_{k=1}^{\infty} ka_k t^k + \sum_{k=0}^{\infty} 5a_k t^k = 0.$$

Separating the terms corresponding to $k = 0$ and combining the rest under one sum yields

$$(2a_2 + 10a_1 + 5a_0) + \sum_{k=1}^{\infty}\left[(k+2)(k+1)a_{k+2} + 10(k+1)a_{k+1} + (k+5)a_k\right]t^k = 0.$$

Setting the coefficients equal to zero, we obtain the recurrence relations

$$\begin{aligned} &2a_2 + 10a_1 + 5a_0 = 0, \\ &(k+2)(k+1)a_{k+2} + 10(k+1)a_{k+1} + (k+5)a_k = 0, \qquad k \geq 1. \end{aligned} \tag{8.7}$$

Next we use the initial conditions to find a_0 and a_1.

$$a_0 = q(0) = 10, \qquad a_1 = q'(0) = 0.$$

From the first equation in (8.7) we have

$$a_2 = \frac{-10a_1 - 5a_0}{2} = -25.$$

Taking $k = 1$ and $k = 2$ in the second equation in (8.7), we find a_3 and a_4.

$$\begin{aligned} k = 1: \quad & 6a_3 + 20a_2 + 6a_1 = 0 \quad \Rightarrow \quad && a_3 = -(20a_2 + 6a_1)/6 = 250/3, \\ k = 2: \quad & 12a_4 + 30a_3 + 7a_2 = 0 \quad \Rightarrow \quad && a_4 = -(30a_3 + 7a_2)/12 = -775/4. \end{aligned}$$

Hence

$$q(t) = 10 + (0)t - 25t^2 + \frac{250t^3}{3} - \frac{775t^4}{4} + \cdots = 10 - 25t^2 + \frac{250t^3}{3} - \frac{775t^4}{4} + \cdots.$$

EXERCISES 8.4: Equations with Analytic Coefficients, page 456

3. For this equation, $p(x) = 0$ and $q(x) = \dfrac{-3}{1+x+x^2}$. Therefore, singular points will occur when

$$1 + x + x^2 = 0 \qquad \Rightarrow \qquad x = -\frac{1}{2} \pm \frac{\sqrt{3}}{2}i.$$

Thus, $x = 1$ is an ordinary point for this equation, and we can find a power series solution with a radius of convergence of at least the minimum of the distances between 1 and points $(-1/2) \pm (\sqrt{3}/2)i$, which, in fact, are equal. Recall that the distance between two complex numbers, $z_1 = a + bi$ and $z_2 = c + di$, is given by

$$\text{dist}\,(z_1, z_2) = \sqrt{(a-c)^2 + (b-d)^2}.$$

Thus, the distance between $(1 + 0 \cdot i)$ and $(-1/2) + (\sqrt{3}/2)i$ is

$$\sqrt{\left[1 - \left(-\frac{1}{2}\right)\right]^2 + \left[0 - \frac{\sqrt{3}}{2}\right]^2} = \sqrt{\frac{9}{4} + \frac{3}{4}} = \sqrt{3}.$$

Therefore, the radius of convergence for the power series solution of this differential equation about $x = 1$ will be at least $\rho = \sqrt{3}$.

9. We see that $x = 0$ and $x = 2$ are the only singular points for this differential equation and, thus, $x = 1$ is an ordinary point. Therefore, according to Theorem 5 on page 451 of the text, there exists a power series solution of this equation about the point $x = 1$ with a radius of convergence of at least one, the distance from 1 to either 0 or 2. That is, we have a general solution for this differential equation of the form

$$y(x) = \sum_{n=0}^{\infty} a_n (x-1)^n ,$$

which is convergent for all x at least in the interval $(0, 2)$, the interval on which the inequality $|x - 1| < 1$ is satisfied. To find this solution we will proceed as in Example 3 on page 453 of the text. Thus, we make the substitution $t = x - 1$, which implies that $x = t + 1$. (Note that $dx/dt = 1$.) We then define a new function

$$\begin{aligned}
& Y(t) := y(t+1) = y(x) \\
\Rightarrow \quad & \frac{dY}{dt} = \left(\frac{dy}{dx}\right)\left(\frac{dx}{dt}\right) = \left(\frac{dy}{dx}\right) \cdot 1 = \frac{dy}{dx} \\
\Rightarrow \quad & \frac{d^2Y}{dt^2} = \frac{d}{dt}\left(\frac{dY}{dt}\right) = \frac{d}{dt}\left(\frac{dy}{dx}\right) = \left(\frac{d^2y}{dx^2}\right)\left(\frac{dx}{dt}\right) = \frac{d^2y}{dx^2}.
\end{aligned}$$

Hence, with the substitutions $t = x - 1$ and $Y(t) = y(t+1)$, we transform the differential equation, $(x^2 - 2x)\,y''(x) + 2y(x) = 0$, into the differential equation

$$\begin{aligned} & \left[(t+1)^2 - 2(t+1)\right] y''(t+1) + 2y(t+1) = 0 \\ \Rightarrow \quad & \left[(t+1)^2 - 2(t+1)\right] Y''(t) + 2Y(t) = 0 \\ \Rightarrow \quad & \left(t^2 - 1\right) Y''(t) + 2Y(t) = 0. \end{aligned} \tag{8.8}$$

To find a general solution to (8.8), we first note that zero is an ordinary point of equation (8.8). Thus, we can assume that we have a power series solution of equation (8.8) of the form

$$Y(t) = \sum_{n=0}^{\infty} a_n t^n ,$$

which converges for all t in $(-1, 1)$. (This means that $x = t + 1$ will be in the interval $(0, 2)$ as desired.) Substituting into equation (8.8) yields

$$\begin{aligned} & (t^2 - 1) \sum_{n=2}^{\infty} n(n-1)a_n t^{n-2} + 2 \sum_{n=0}^{\infty} a_n t^n = 0 \\ \Rightarrow \quad & \sum_{n=2}^{\infty} n(n-1)a_n t^n - \sum_{n=2}^{\infty} n(n-1)a_n t^{n-2} + \sum_{n=0}^{\infty} 2a_n t^n = 0. \end{aligned}$$

Making the shift in the index, $k = n - 2$, in the second power series above and replacing n with k in the other two power series allows us to take each summation over the same power of t. This gives us

$$\sum_{k=2}^{\infty} k(k-1)a_k t^k - \sum_{k=0}^{\infty} (k+2)(k+1)a_{k+2} t^k + \sum_{k=0}^{\infty} 2a_k t^k = 0.$$

In order to start all of these summations at the same point, we must take the first two terms out of the summation sign in the last two power series. Thus we have,

$$\begin{aligned} \sum_{k=2}^{\infty} k(k-1)a_k t^k - (2)(1)a_2 - (3)(2)a_3 t - \sum_{k=2}^{\infty} (k+2)(k+1)a_{k+2} t^k & \\ + 2a_0 + 2a_1 t + \sum_{k=2}^{\infty} 2a_k t^k = 0 & \end{aligned}$$

$$\Rightarrow \qquad 2a_0 - 2a_2 + (2a_1 - 6a_3)\,t + \sum_{k=2}^{\infty} \left[k(k-1)a_k - (k+2)(k+1)a_{k+2} + 2a_k\right] t^k = 0.$$

For this power series to equal zero, each coefficient must be zero. Thus, we have

$$2a_0 - 2a_2 = 0 \qquad \Rightarrow \qquad a_2 = a_0\,, \qquad\qquad 2a_1 - 6a_3 = 0 \qquad \Rightarrow \qquad a_3 = \frac{a_1}{3}\,,$$

$$k(k-1)a_k - (k+2)(k+1)a_{k+2} + 2a_k = 0, \qquad k \geq 2$$

$$\Rightarrow \qquad a_{k+2} = \frac{k(k-1)a_k + 2a_k}{(k+2)(k+1)}\,, \quad k \geq 2 \qquad \Rightarrow \qquad a_{k+2} = \frac{(k^2-k+2)a_k}{(k+2)(k+1)}\,, \quad k \geq 2.$$

Therefore, we see that

$$\begin{aligned} k = 2 \qquad &\Rightarrow \qquad a_4 = \frac{4a_2}{4 \cdot 3} = \frac{a_2}{3} = \frac{a_0}{3}\,, \\ k = 3 \qquad &\Rightarrow \qquad a_5 = \frac{8a_3}{5 \cdot 4} = \frac{2a_1}{15}\,, \quad \text{etc.} \end{aligned}$$

Plugging these values for the coefficients into the power series solution,

$$Y(t) = \sum_{n=0}^{\infty} a_n t^n = a_0 + a_1 t + a_2 t^2 + a_3 t^3 + a_4 t^4 + \cdots\,,$$

yields

$$\begin{aligned} Y(t) &= a_0 + a_1 t + a_0 t^2 + \frac{a_1 t^3}{3} + \frac{a_0 t^4}{3} + \frac{2a_1 t^5}{15} + \cdots \\ \Rightarrow \qquad Y(t) &= a_0 \left(1 + t^2 + \frac{t^4}{3} + \cdots\right) + a_1 \left(t + \frac{t^3}{3} + \frac{2t^5}{15} + \cdots\right). \end{aligned}$$

Lastly, we want to change back to the independent variable x. To do this, we recall that $Y(t) = y(t+1)$. Thus, if $t = x - 1$, then

$$Y(t) = Y(x-1) = y\left([x-1]+1\right) = y(x).$$

Thus, we replace t with $x-1$ in the solution just found, and we obtain a power series expansion for a general solution in the independent variable x. Substituting, we have

$$y(x) = a_0 \left[1 + (x-1)^2 + \frac{1}{3}(x-1)^4 + \cdots\right] + a_1 \left[(x-1) + \frac{1}{3}(x-1)^3 + \frac{2}{15}(x-1)^5 + \cdots\right].$$

17. Here $p(x) = 0$ and $q(x) = -\sin x$ both of which are analytic everywhere. Thus, $x = \pi$ is an ordinary point for this differential equation, and there are no singular points. Therefore, by Theorem 5 on page 451 of the text, we can assume that this equation has a general power series solution about the point $x = \pi$ with an infinite radius of convergence (i.e., $\rho = \infty$). That is, we assume that we have a solution to this differential equation given by

$$y(x) = \sum_{n=0}^{\infty} a_n (x-\pi)^n \qquad \left[\Rightarrow \; y'(x) = \sum_{n=1}^{\infty} n a_n (x-\pi)^{n-1} \right],$$

which converges for all x. If we apply the initial conditions, $y(\pi) = 1$ and $y'(\pi) = 0$, we see that $a_0 = 1$ and $a_1 = 0$. To find a general solution of this differential equation, we will combine the methods of Example 3 and Example 4 on pages 453–455 of the text. Thus, we will first define a new function, $Y(t)$, using the transformation $t = x - \pi$. Thus, we define

$$Y(t) := y(t+\pi) = y(x).$$

Hence, by the chain rule (using the fact that $x = t + \pi$ which implies that $dx/dt = 1$), we have $dY/dt = (dy/dx)(dx/dt) = dy/dx$, and similarly $d^2Y/dt^2 = d^2y/dx^2$. We now solve the transformed differential equation

$$\frac{d^2Y}{dt^2} - \sin(t+\pi)Y(t) = 0 \qquad \Rightarrow \qquad \frac{d^2Y}{dt^2} + (\sin t)Y(t) = 0, \tag{8.9}$$

where we have used the fact that $\sin(t+\pi) = -\sin t$. When we have found the solution $Y(t)$, we will use the fact that $y(x) = Y(x-\pi)$ to obtain the solution to the original differential equation in terms of the independent variable x. Hence, we seek a power series solution to equation (8.9) of the form

$$Y(t) = \sum_{n=0}^{\infty} a_n t^n \qquad \Rightarrow \qquad Y'(t) = \sum_{n=1}^{\infty} n a_n t^{n-1} \qquad \Rightarrow \qquad Y''(t) = \sum_{n=2}^{\infty} n(n-1) a_n t^{n-2}.$$

Since the initial conditions, $y(\pi) = 1$ and $y'(\pi) = 0$, transform into $Y(0) = 1$ and $Y'(0) = 0$, we must have

$$Y(0) = a_0 = 1 \qquad \text{and} \qquad Y'(0) = a_1 = 0.$$

Next we note that $q(t) = \sin t$ is an analytic function with a Maclaurin series given by

$$\sin t = \sum_{n=0}^{\infty} \frac{(-1)^n t^{2n+1}}{(2n+1)!} = t - \frac{t^3}{6} + \frac{t^5}{120} - \frac{t^7}{5040} + \cdots .$$

By substituting the expressions that we found for $Y(t)$, $Y''(t)$, and $\sin t$ into equation (8.9), we obtain

$$\sum_{n=2}^{\infty} n(n-1)a_n t^{n-2} + \left(t - \frac{t^3}{6} + \frac{t^5}{120} - \frac{t^7}{5040} + \cdots\right) \sum_{n=0}^{\infty} a_n t^n = 0.$$

Therefore, expanding this last equation (and explicitly showing only terms of up to order four), yields

$$\begin{aligned} &\left(2a_2 + 6a_3 t + 12a_4 t^2 + 20a_5 t^3 + 30a_6 t^4 + \cdots\right) + t\left(a_0 + a_1 t + a_2 t^2 + a_3 t^3 + \cdots\right) \\ &\qquad\qquad - \frac{t^3}{6}\left(a_0 + a_1 t + \cdots\right) + \cdots = 0 \\ \Rightarrow\quad &\left(2a_2 + 6a_3 t + 12a_4 t^2 + 20a_5 t^3 + 30a_6 t^4 + \cdots\right) + t\left(a_0 + a_1 t + a_2 t^2 + a_3 t^3 + \cdots\right) \\ &\qquad\qquad + \left(-\frac{a_0 t^3}{6} - \frac{a_1 t^4}{6} - \cdots\right) + \cdots = 0. \end{aligned}$$

By grouping these terms according to their powers of t, we obtain

$$2a_2 + (6a_3 + a_0)t + (12a_4 + a_1)t^2 + \left(20a_5 + a_2 - \frac{a_0}{6}\right)t^3 + \left(30a_6 + a_3 - \frac{a_1}{6}\right)t^4 + \cdots = 0.$$

Setting these coefficients to zero and recalling that $a_0 = 1$ and $a_1 = 0$ yields the system of equations

$$\begin{aligned} 2a_2 &= 0 && \Rightarrow && a_2 = 0, \\ 6a_3 + a_0 &= 0 && \Rightarrow && a_3 = \frac{-a_0}{6} = \frac{-1}{6}, \\ 12a_4 + a_1 &= 0 && \Rightarrow && a_4 = \frac{-a_1}{12} = 0, \\ 20a_5 + a_2 - \frac{a_0}{6} &= 0 && \Rightarrow && a_5 = \frac{\frac{a_0}{6} - a_2}{20} = \frac{\frac{1}{6}}{20} = \frac{1}{120}, \\ 30a_6 + a_3 - \frac{a_1}{6} &= 0 && \Rightarrow && a_6 = \frac{\frac{a_1}{6} - a_3}{30} = \frac{0 + \frac{1}{6}}{30} = \frac{1}{180}. \end{aligned}$$

Plugging these coefficients into the power series solution

$$Y(t) = \sum_{n=0}^{\infty} a_n t^n = a_0 + a_1 t + a_2 t^2 + \cdots,$$

yields the solution to equation (8.9):

$$Y(t) = 1 + 0 + 0 - \frac{t^3}{6} + 0 + \frac{t^5}{120} + \frac{t^6}{180} + \cdots = 1 - \frac{t^3}{6} + \frac{t^5}{120} + \frac{t^6}{180} + \cdots.$$

Lastly we want to find the solution to the original equation with the independent variable x. In order to do this, we recall that $t = x - \pi$ and $Y(x - \pi) = y(x)$. Therefore, by substituting these values into the equation above, we obtain the solution

$$y(x) = 1 - \frac{1}{6}(x - \pi)^3 + \frac{1}{120}(x - \pi)^5 + \frac{1}{180}(x - \pi)^6 + \cdots.$$

21. We assume that this differential equation has a power series solution with a positive radius of convergence about the point $x = 0$. This is reasonable because all of the coefficients and the forcing function $g(x) = \sin x$ are analytic everywhere. Thus, we assume that

$$y(x) = \sum_{n=0}^{\infty} a_n x^n \qquad \Rightarrow \qquad y'(x) = \sum_{n=1}^{\infty} n a_n x^{n-1}.$$

By substituting these expressions and the Maclaurin expansion for $\sin x$ into the differential equation, $y'(x) - xy(x) = \sin x$, we obtain

$$\sum_{n=1}^{\infty} n a_n x^{n-1} - x \sum_{n=0}^{\infty} a_n x^n = \sum_{n=0}^{\infty} (-1)^n \frac{x^{2n+1}}{(2n+1)!}.$$

In the first power series on the left, we make the shift $k = n - 1$. In the second power series on the left, we make the shift $k = n + 1$. Thus, we obtain

$$\sum_{k=0}^{\infty} (k+1) a_{k+1} x^k - \sum_{k=1}^{\infty} a_{k-1} x^k = \sum_{n=0}^{\infty} (-1)^n \frac{x^{2n+1}}{(2n+1)!}.$$

Separating out the first term of the first power series on the left yields

$$a_1 + \sum_{k=1}^{\infty} (k+1) a_{k+1} x^k - \sum_{k=1}^{\infty} a_{k-1} x^k = \sum_{n=0}^{\infty} (-1)^n \frac{x^{2n+1}}{(2n+1)!}$$

$$\Rightarrow \qquad a_1 + \sum_{k=1}^{\infty} \left[(k+1)a_{k+1} - a_{k-1}\right] x^k = \sum_{n=0}^{\infty} (-1)^n \frac{x^{2n+1}}{(2n+1)!}\,.$$

Therefore, by expanding both of the power series, we have

$$a_1 + (2a_2 - a_0)\,x + (3a_3 - a_1)\,x^2 + (4a_4 - a_2)\,x^3 + (5a_5 - a_3)\,x^4 + (6a_6 - a_4)\,x^5 + (7a_7 - a_5)\,x^6 + \cdots = x - \frac{x^3}{6} + \frac{x^5}{120} - \frac{x^7}{5040} + \cdots\,.$$

By equating the coefficients of like powers of x, we obtain

$$\begin{aligned}
&a_1 = 0, && \\
&2a_2 - a_0 = 1 && \Rightarrow \quad a_2 = \frac{a_0 + 1}{2}\,, \\
&3a_3 - a_1 = 0 && \Rightarrow \quad a_3 = \frac{a_1}{3} = 0, \\
&4a_4 - a_2 = \frac{-1}{6} && \Rightarrow \quad a_4 = \frac{a_2 - 1/6}{4} = \frac{a_0}{8} + \frac{1}{12}\,, \\
&5a_5 - a_3 = 0 && \Rightarrow \quad a_5 = \frac{a_3}{5} = 0, \\
&6a_6 - a_4 = \frac{1}{120} && \Rightarrow \quad a_6 = \frac{a_4 - 1/120}{6} = \frac{a_0}{48} + \frac{11}{720}\,.
\end{aligned}$$

Substituting these coefficients into the power series solution and noting that a_0 is an arbitrary number, yields

$$\begin{aligned}
y(x) &= \sum_{n=0}^{\infty} a_n x^n \\
&= a_0 + 0 + \left(\frac{a_0}{2} + \frac{1}{2}\right) x^2 + 0 + \left(\frac{a_0}{8} + \frac{1}{12}\right) x^4 + 0 + \left(\frac{a_0}{48} + \frac{11}{720}\right) x^6 + \cdots \\
&= a_0 \left[1 + \frac{1}{2}x^2 + \frac{1}{8}x^4 + \frac{1}{48}x^6 + \cdots\right] + \left[\frac{1}{2}x^2 + \frac{1}{12}x^4 + \frac{11}{720}x^6 + \cdots\right].
\end{aligned}$$

27. Observe that $x = 0$ is an ordinary point for this differential equation. Therefore, we can assume that this equation has a power series solution about the point $x = 0$ with a positive radius of convergence. Thus, we assume that

$$y(x)=\sum_{n=0}^{\infty}a_nx^n \qquad \Rightarrow \qquad y'(x)=\sum_{n=1}^{\infty}na_nx^{n-1} \qquad \Rightarrow \qquad y''(x)=\sum_{n=2}^{\infty}n(n-1)a_nx^{n-2}\,.$$

The Maclaurin series for $\tan x$ is

$$\tan x = x+\frac{x^3}{3}+\frac{2x^5}{15}+\cdots\,,$$

which is given in the table on the inside front cover of the text. Substituting the expressions for $y(x)$, $y'(x)$, $y''(x)$, and the Maclaurin series for the function $\tan x$ into the differential equation, $(1-x^2)y''-y'+y=\tan x$, yields

$$\begin{aligned}
&\left(1-x^2\right)\sum_{n=2}^{\infty}n(n-1)a_nx^{n-2}-\sum_{n=1}^{\infty}na_nx^{n-1}+\sum_{n=0}^{\infty}a_nx^n=x+\frac{x^3}{3}+\frac{2x^5}{15}+\cdots\\
\Rightarrow\quad &\sum_{n=2}^{\infty}n(n-1)a_nx^{n-2}-\sum_{n=2}^{\infty}n(n-1)a_nx^{n}-\sum_{n=1}^{\infty}na_nx^{n-1}+\sum_{n=0}^{\infty}a_nx^n\\
&\qquad=x+\frac{x^3}{3}+\frac{2x^5}{15}+\cdots\,.
\end{aligned}$$

By shifting the indices of the power series on the left-hand side of this equation, we obtain

$$\sum_{k=0}^{\infty}(k+2)(k+1)a_{k+2}x^k-\sum_{k=2}^{\infty}k(k-1)a_kx^k-\sum_{k=0}^{\infty}(k+1)a_{k+1}x^k+\sum_{k=0}^{\infty}a_kx^k=x+\frac{x^3}{3}+\frac{2x^5}{15}+\cdots\,.$$

Removing the first two terms from the summation notation in the first, third and fourth power series above yields

$$\begin{aligned}
&(2)(1)a_2+(3)(2)a_3x+\sum_{k=2}^{\infty}(k+2)(k+1)a_{k+2}x^k-\sum_{k=2}^{\infty}k(k-1)a_kx^k-(1)a_1-(2)a_2x\\
&\qquad-\sum_{k=2}^{\infty}(k+1)a_{k+1}x^k+a_0+a_1x+\sum_{k=2}^{\infty}a_kx^k=x+\frac{x^3}{3}+\frac{2x^5}{15}+\cdots\\
\Rightarrow\quad &(2a_2-a_1+a_0)+(6a_3-2a_2+a_1)\,x\\
&\quad+\sum_{k=2}^{\infty}\left[(k+2)(k+1)a_{k+2}-k(k-1)a_k-(k+1)a_{k+1}+a_k\right]x^k=x+\frac{x^3}{3}+\frac{2x^5}{15}+\cdots\,.
\end{aligned}$$

By equating the coefficients of the two power series, we see that

$$2a_2 - a_1 + a_0 = 0 \qquad \Rightarrow \qquad a_2 = \frac{a_1 - a_0}{2},$$

$$6a_3 - 2a_2 + a_1 = 1 \qquad \Rightarrow \qquad a_3 = \frac{2a_2 - a_1 + 1}{6} = \frac{1 - a_0}{6},$$

$$4 \cdot 3a_4 - 2 \cdot 1a_2 - 3a_3 + a_2 = 0 \qquad \Rightarrow \qquad a_4 = \frac{a_2 + 3a_3}{12} = \frac{a_1 - 2a_0 + 1}{24}.$$

Therefore, noting that a_0 and a_1 are arbitrary, we can substitute these coefficients into the power series solution $y(x) = \sum_{n=0}^{\infty} a_n x^n = a_0 + a_1 x + a_2 x^2 + a_3 x^3 + a_4 x^4 + \cdots$ to obtain

$$\begin{aligned} y(x) &= a_0 + a_1 x + \left(\frac{a_1}{2} - \frac{a_0}{2}\right) x^2 + \left(\frac{1}{6} - \frac{a_0}{6}\right) x^3 + \left(\frac{a_1}{24} - \frac{a_0}{12} + \frac{1}{24}\right) x^4 + \cdots \\ &= a_0 \left(1 - \frac{1}{2}x^2 - \frac{1}{6}x^3 - \frac{1}{12}x^4 + \cdots\right) + a_1 \left(x + \frac{1}{2}x^2 + \frac{1}{24}x^4 + \cdots\right) \\ &\qquad + \left(\frac{1}{6}x^3 + \frac{1}{24}x^4 + \cdots\right). \end{aligned}$$

EXERCISES 8.5: Cauchy-Euler (Equidimensional) Equations Revisited, page 460

5. Notice that, since $x > 0$, we can multiply this differential equation by x^2 and rewrite it to obtain

$$x^2 \frac{d^2y}{dx^2} - 5x\frac{dy}{dx} + 13y = 0.$$

We see that this is a Cauchy-Euler equation. Thus, we will assume that a solution has the form

$$y(x) = x^r \qquad \Rightarrow \qquad y'(x) = rx^{r-1} \qquad \Rightarrow \qquad y''(x) = r(r-1)x^{r-2}.$$

Substituting these expressions into the differential equation above yields

$$\begin{aligned} &r(r-1)x^r - 5rx^r + 13x^r = 0 \\ \Rightarrow \qquad &\left(r^2 - 6r + 13\right)x^r = 0 \qquad \Rightarrow \qquad r^2 - 6r + 13 = 0. \end{aligned}$$

We obtained this last equation by using the assumption that $x > 0$. (We also could arrive at this equation by using equation (4) on page 458 of the text.) Using the quadratic formula, we see that the roots to this equation are

$$r = \frac{6 \pm \sqrt{36-52}}{2} = 3 \pm 2i.$$

Therefore, using formulas (5) and (6) on page 458 of the text with complex conjugates roots (and using Euler's formula), we have two linearly independent solutions give by

$$y_1(x) = x^3 \cos(2\ln x), \qquad y_2(x) = x^3 \sin(2\ln x).$$

Hence the general solution to this equation is given by

$$y(x) = c_1 x^3 \cos(2\ln x) + c_2 x^3 \sin(2\ln x).$$

7. This equation is a third order Cauchy-Euler equation, and, thus, we will assume that a solution has the form $y(x) = x^r$. This implies that

$$y'(x) = rx^{r-1} \qquad \Rightarrow \qquad y''(x) = r(r-1)x^{r-2} \qquad \Rightarrow \qquad y'''(x) = r(r-1)(r-2)x^{r-3}.$$

By substituting these expressions into the differential equation, we obtain

$$\begin{aligned} &\left[r(r-1)(r-2) + 4r(r-1) + 10r - 10\right] x^r = 0 \\ \Rightarrow \qquad &\left[r^3 + r^2 + 8r - 10\right] x^r = 0 \qquad \Rightarrow \qquad r^3 + r^2 + 8r - 10 = 0. \end{aligned}$$

By inspection we see that $r = 1$ is a root of this last equation. Thus, one solution to this differential equation will be given by $y_1(x) = x$ and we can factor the indicial equation above as follows:

$$(r-1)(r^2 + 2r + 10) = 0.$$

Therefore, using the quadratic formula, we see that the roots to this equation are $r = 1, -1 \pm 3i$. Thus, we can find two more linearly independent solutions to this equation by using Euler's formula as was done on page 458 of the text. Thus, three linearly independent solutions to this problem are given by

$$y_1(x) = x, \qquad y_2(x) = x^{-1}\cos(3\ln x), \qquad y_3(x) = x^{-1}\sin(3\ln x).$$

Hence, the general solution to this differential equation is

$$y(x) = c_1 x + c_2 x^{-1}\cos(3\ln x) + c_3 x^{-1}\sin(3\ln x).$$

13. We first must find two linearly independent solutions to the associated homogeneous equation. Since this is a Cauchy-Euler equation, we assume that there are solutions of the form

$$y(x) = x^r \qquad \Rightarrow \qquad y'(x) = rx^{r-1} \qquad \Rightarrow \qquad y''(x) = r(r-1)x^{r-2}.$$

Substituting these expressions into the associated homogeneous equation yields

$$[r(r-1) - 2r + 2]\, x^r = 0 \qquad \Rightarrow \qquad r^2 - 3r + 2 = 0 \qquad \Rightarrow \qquad (r-1)(r-2) = 0.$$

Thus, the roots to this indicial equation are $r = 1, 2$. Therefore, a general solution to the associated homogeneous equation is

$$y_h(x) = c_1 x + c_2 x^2.$$

For the variation of parameters method, let $y_1(x) = x$ and $y_2(x) = x^2$, and then assume that a particular solution has the form

$$y_p(x) = v_1(x)y_1(x) + v_2(x)y_2(x) = v_1(x)x + v_2(x)x^2.$$

In order to find $v_1(x)$ and $v_2(x)$, we would like to use formula (10) on page 195 of the text. To use equation (10), we must first find the Wronskian of y_1 and y_2. Thus, we compute

$$W[y_1, y_2](x) = y_1(x)y_2'(x) - y_2(x)y_1'(x) = 2x^2 - x^2 = x^2.$$

Next we must write the differential equation given in this problem in standard form. When we do this, we see that $g(x) = x^{-5/2}$. Therefore, by equation (10), we have

$$v_1(x) = \int \frac{-x^{-5/2}x^2}{x^2}\, dx = \int (-x^{-5/2})dx = \frac{2}{3}\, x^{-3/2}$$

and

$$v_2(x) = \int \frac{x^{-5/2}x}{x^2}\, dx = \int x^{-7/2}dx = \frac{-2}{5}\, x^{-5/2}.$$

Thus, a particular solution is given by

$$y_p(x) = \left(\frac{2}{3}\, x^{-3/2}\right) x + \left(\frac{-2}{5}\, x^{-5/2}\right) x^2 = \frac{4}{15}\, x^{-1/2}.$$

Therefore, a general solution of the nonhomogeneous differential equation is given by

$$y(x) = y_h(x) + y_p(x) = c_1 x + c_2 x^2 + \frac{4}{15}\, x^{-1/2}.$$

19. **(a)** For this linear differential operator L, we have

$$\begin{aligned} L\left[x^r\right](x) &= x^3\left[r(r-1)(r-2)x^{r-3}\right] + x\left[rx^{r-1}\right] - x^r \\ &= r(r-1)(r-2)x^r + rx^r - x^r \\ &= \left(r^3 - 3r^2 + 3r - 1\right)x^r = (r-1)^3 x^r. \end{aligned}$$

(b) From part (a) above, we see that $r = 1$ is a root of multiplicity three of the indicial equation. Thus, we have one solution given by

$$y_1(x) = x. \tag{8.10}$$

To find two more linearly independent solutions, we use a method similar to that used in the text. By taking the partial derivative of $L\left[x^r\right](x) = (r-1)^3 x^r$ with respect to r, we have

$$\begin{aligned} &\frac{\partial}{\partial r}\left\{L\left[x^r\right](x)\right\} = \frac{\partial}{\partial r}\left\{(r-1)^3 x^r\right\} = 3(r-1)^2 x^r + (r-1)^3 x^r \ln x \\ \Rightarrow \quad &\frac{\partial^2}{\partial r^2}\left\{L\left[x^r\right](x)\right\} = \frac{\partial}{\partial r}\left\{3(r-1)^2 x^r + (r-1)^3 x^r \ln x\right\} \\ &\qquad = 6(r-1)x^r + 6(r-1)^2 x^r \ln x + (r-1)^3 x^r (\ln x)^2. \end{aligned}$$

Since $r-1$ is a factor of every term in $\partial\left\{L\left[x^r\right](x)\right\}/\partial r$ and $\partial^2\left\{L\left[x^r\right](x)\right\}/\partial r^2$ above, we see that

$$\frac{\partial}{\partial r}\left\{L\left[x^r\right](x)\right\}\Big|_{r=1} = 0, \tag{8.11}$$

and

$$\frac{\partial^2}{\partial r^2}\left\{L\left[x^r\right](x)\right\}\Big|_{r=1} = 0, \tag{8.12}$$

We can use these facts to find the two solutions that we seek. In order to find a second solution, we would like an alternative form for

$$\left.\frac{\partial\left\{L\left[x^r\right](x)\right\}}{\partial r}\right|_{r=1}.$$

Using the fact that

$$L[y](x) = x^3 y'''(x) + xy'(x) - y(x)$$

and proceeding as in equation (9) on page 458 of the text with $w(r,x)=x^r$, we have

$$\begin{aligned}\frac{\partial}{\partial r}\left\{L\left[x^r\right](x)\right\} &= \frac{\partial}{\partial r}\left\{L[w](x)\right\} = \frac{\partial}{\partial r}\left\{x^3\,\frac{\partial^3 w}{\partial x^3}+x\,\frac{\partial w}{\partial x}-w\right\}\\ &= x^3\,\frac{\partial^4 w}{\partial r\partial x^3}+x\,\frac{\partial^2 w}{\partial r\partial x}-\frac{\partial w}{\partial r} = x^3\,\frac{\partial^4 w}{\partial x^3\partial r}+x\,\frac{\partial^2 w}{\partial x\partial r}-\frac{\partial w}{\partial r}\\ &= x^3\,\frac{\partial^3}{\partial x^3}\left(\frac{\partial w}{\partial r}\right)+x\,\frac{\partial}{\partial x}\left(\frac{\partial w}{\partial r}\right)-\frac{\partial w}{\partial r} = L\left[\frac{\partial w}{\partial r}\right](x),\end{aligned}$$

where we are using the fact that mixed partials of $w(r,x)$ are equal. Therefore, combining this with equation (8.11) above yields

$$\frac{\partial}{\partial r}\left\{L\left[x^r\right](x)\right\}\Big|_{r=1}\; L\left[\frac{\partial x^r}{\partial r}\Big|_{r=1}\right] = L\left[x^r\ln x\,\big|_{r=1}\right] = L[x\ln x]=0.$$

Thus, a second linearly independent solution is given by

$$y_2(x)=x\ln x.$$

To find a third solution, we will use equation (8.12) above. Hence, we would like to find an alternative form for $\partial^2\left\{L\left[x^r\right](x)\right\}/\partial r^2$. To do this, we use the fact that

$$\frac{\partial}{\partial r}\left\{L\left[x^r\right](x)\right\} = x^3\,\frac{\partial^4 w}{\partial r\partial x^3}+x\,\frac{\partial^2 w}{\partial r\partial x}-\frac{\partial w}{\partial r},$$

which we found above and the fact that mixed partial derivatives of $w(r,x)$ are equal. Thus, we have

$$\begin{aligned}\frac{\partial^2}{\partial r^2}\left\{L\left[x^r\right](x)\right\} &= \frac{\partial}{\partial r}\left[\frac{\partial}{\partial r}\left\{L\left[x^r\right](x)\right\}\right] = \frac{\partial}{\partial r}\left\{x^3\,\frac{\partial^4 w}{\partial r\partial x^3}+x\,\frac{\partial^2 w}{\partial r\partial x}-\frac{\partial w}{\partial r}\right\}\\ &= x^3\,\frac{\partial^5 w}{\partial r^2\partial x^3}+x\,\frac{\partial^3 w}{\partial r^2\partial x}-\frac{\partial^2 w}{\partial r^2} = x^3\,\frac{\partial^5 w}{\partial x^3\partial r^2}+x\,\frac{\partial^3 w}{\partial x\partial r^2}-\frac{\partial^2 w}{\partial r^2}\\ &= x^3\,\frac{\partial^3}{\partial x^3}\left(\frac{\partial^2 w}{\partial r^2}\right)+x\,\frac{\partial}{\partial x}\left(\frac{\partial^2 w}{\partial r^2}\right)-\frac{\partial^2 w}{\partial r^2} = L\left[\frac{\partial^2 w}{\partial r^2}\right](x)=0.\end{aligned}$$

Therefore, combining this with equation (8.12) above yields

$$\frac{\partial^2}{\partial r^2}\left\{L\left[x^r\right](x)\right\}\Big|_{r=1} = L\left[\frac{\partial^2\left(x^r\right)}{\partial r^2}\Big|_{r=1}\right] = L\left[x(\ln x)^2\right]=0,$$

where we have used the fact that $\partial^2 x^r/\partial r^2 = x^r(\ln x)^2$. Thus we see that another solution is

$$y_3(x) = x(\ln x)^2,$$

which, by inspection, is linearly independent from y_1 and y_2. Thus, a general solution to the differential equation is $y(x) = C_1 x + C_2 x \ln x + C_3 x(\ln x)^2$.

EXERCISES 8.6: Method of Frobenius, page 472

5. By putting this equation in standard form, we see that

$$p(x) == -\frac{x-1}{(x^2-1)^2} = -\frac{x-1}{(x-1)^2(x+1)^2} = -\frac{1}{(x-1)(x+1)^2},$$

and

$$q(x) = \frac{3}{(x^2-1)^2} = \frac{3}{(x-1)^2(x+1)^2}.$$

Thus, $x = 1, -1$ are singular points of this equation. To check if $x = 1$ is regular, we note that

$$(x-1)p(x) = -\frac{1}{(x+1)^2} \qquad \text{and} \qquad (x-1)^2 q(x) = \frac{3}{(x+1)^2}.$$

These functions are analytic at $x = 1$. Therefore, $x = 1$ is a regular singular point for this differential equation. Next we check the singular point $x = -1$. Here

$$(x+1)p(x) = -\frac{1}{(x-1)(x+1)}$$

is not analytic at $x = -1$. Therefore, $x = -1$ is an irregular singular point for this differential equation.

13. By putting this equation in standard form, we see that

$$p(x) = \frac{x^2-4}{(x^2-x-2)^2} = \frac{(x-2)(x+2)}{(x-2)^2(x+1)^2} = \frac{x+2}{(x-2)(x+1)^2},$$

$$q(x) = \frac{-6x}{(x-2)^2(x+1)^2)}.$$

Thus, we have

$$(x-2)p(x) = \frac{x+2}{(x+1)^2} \qquad \text{and} \qquad (x-2)^2 q(x) = \frac{-6x}{(x+1)^2}.$$

Therefore, $x = 2$ is a regular singular point of this differential equation. We also observe that

$$\lim_{x\to 2}(x-2)p(x) = \lim_{x\to 2}\frac{x+2}{(x+1)^2} = \frac{4}{9} = p_0\,,$$
$$\lim_{x\to 2}(x-2)^2 q(x) = -\lim_{x\to 2}\frac{6x}{(x+1)^2} = -\frac{12}{9} = -\frac{4}{3} = q_0\,.$$

Thus, we can use equation (16) on page 463 of the text to obtain the indicial equation

$$r(r-1)+\frac{4r}{9}-\frac{4}{3}=0 \qquad \Rightarrow \qquad r^2-\frac{5r}{9}-\frac{4}{3}=0.$$

By the quadratic formula, we see that the roots to this equation and, therefore, the exponents of the singularity $x = 2$, are given by

$$r_1 = \frac{5+\sqrt{25+432}}{18} = \frac{5+\sqrt{457}}{18}\,,$$
$$r_2 = \frac{5-\sqrt{457}}{18}\,.$$

21. Here $p(x) = x^{-1}$ and $q(x) = 1$. This implies that $xp(x) = 1$ and $x^2q(x) = x^2$. Therefore, we see that $x = 0$ is a regular singular point for this differential equation, and so we can use the method of Frobenius to find a solution to this problem. (Note also that $x = 0$ is the only singular point for this equation.) Thus, we will assume that this solution has the form

$$w(r,x) = x^r\sum_{n=0}^{\infty}a_nx^n = \sum_{n=0}^{\infty}a_nx^{n+r}\,.$$

We also notice that

$$p_0 = \lim_{x\to 0}xp(x) = \lim_{x\to 0}1 = 1,$$
$$q_0 = \lim_{x\to 0}x^2q(x) = \lim_{x\to 0}x^2 = 0.$$

Hence, we see that the indicial equation is given by

$$r(r-1)+r = r^2 = 0.$$

This means that $r_1 = r_2 = 0$. Since $x = 0$ is the only singular point for this differential equation, we observe that the series solution $w(0, x)$ which we will find by the method of

Frobenius converges for all $x > 0$. To find the solution, we note that

$$\begin{aligned} w(r,x) &= \sum_{n=0}^{\infty} a_n x^{n+r} \\ \Rightarrow \qquad w'(r,x) &= \sum_{n=0}^{\infty} (n+r) a_n x^{n+r-1} \\ \Rightarrow \qquad w''(r,x) &= \sum_{n=0}^{\infty} (n+r)(n+r-1) a_n x^{n+r-2}. \end{aligned}$$

Notice that the power series for w' and w'' start at $n = 0$. Substituting these expressions into the differential equation and simplifying yields

$$\sum_{n=0}^{\infty} (n+r)(n+r-1) a_n x^{n+r} + \sum_{n=0}^{\infty} (n+r) a_n x^{n+r} + \sum_{n=0}^{\infty} a_n x^{n+r+2} = 0.$$

Next we want each power series to sum over x^{k+r}. Thus, we let $k = n$ in the first and second power series and shift the index in the last power series by letting $k = n + 2$. Therefore, we have

$$\sum_{k=0}^{\infty} (k+r)(k+r-1) a_k x^{k+r} + \sum_{k=0}^{\infty} (k+r) a_k x^{k+r} + \sum_{k=2}^{\infty} a_{k-2} x^{k+r} = 0.$$

We will separate out the first two terms from the first two power series above so that we can start all of our power series at the same place. Thus, we have

$$\begin{aligned} &(r-1) r a_0 x^r + r(1+r) a_1 x^{1+r} + \sum_{k=2}^{\infty} (k+r)(k+r-1) a_k x^{k+r} \\ &\qquad + r a_0 x^r + (1+r) a_1 x^{1+r} + \sum_{k=2}^{\infty} (k+r) a_k x^{k+r} + \sum_{k=2}^{\infty} a_{k-2} x^{k+r} = 0 \\ \Rightarrow \qquad &\left[r(r-1) + r\right] a_0 x^r + \left[r(r+1) + (r+1)\right] a_1 x^{1+r} \\ &\qquad + \sum_{k=2}^{\infty} \left[(k+r)(k+r-1) a_k + (k+r) a_k + a_{k-2}\right] x^{k+r} = 0. \end{aligned}$$

By equating coefficients and assuming that $a_0 \neq 0$, we obtain

$$\begin{aligned} &r(r-1) + r = 0 \qquad \text{(the indicial equation)}, \\ &\left[r(r+1) + (r+1)\right] a_1 = 0 \qquad \Rightarrow \qquad (r+1)^2 a_1 = 0, \end{aligned}$$

and, for $k \geq 2$, the recurrence relation

$$(k+r)(k+r-1)a_k + (k+r)a_k + a_{k-2} = 0 \qquad \Rightarrow \qquad a_k = \frac{-a_{k-2}}{(k+r)^2}, \quad k \geq 2.$$

Using the fact (which we found from the indicial equation above) that $r_1 = 0$, we observe that $a_1 = 0$. Next, using the recurrence relation (and the fact that $r_1 = 0$), we see that

$$a_k = \frac{-a_{k-2}}{k^2}, \qquad k \geq 2.$$

Hence,

$$\begin{aligned}
k = 2 \quad &\Rightarrow \quad a_2 = \frac{-a_0}{4}, \\
k = 3 \quad &\Rightarrow \quad a_3 = \frac{-a_1}{9} = 0, \\
k = 4 \quad &\Rightarrow \quad a_4 = \frac{-a_2}{16} = \frac{-\frac{-a_0}{4}}{16} = \frac{a_0}{64}, \\
k = 5 \quad &\Rightarrow \quad a_5 = \frac{-a_3}{25} = 0, \\
k = 6 \quad &\Rightarrow \quad a_6 = \frac{-a_4}{36} = \frac{-\frac{a_0}{64}}{36} = -\frac{a_0}{2304}.
\end{aligned}$$

Substituting these coefficients into the solution

$$w(0,x) = \sum_{n=0}^{\infty} a_n x^n = a_0 + a_1 x + a_2 x^2 + a_3 x^3 + a_4 x^4 + a_5 x^5 + a_6 x^6 + \cdots,$$

we obtain the series solution for $x > 0$ given by

$$w(0,x) = a_0 \left[1 - \frac{1}{4}x^2 + \frac{1}{64}x^4 - \frac{1}{2304}x^6 + \cdots\right].$$

25. For this equation, we see that $xp(x) = x/2$ and $x^2 q(x) = -(x+3)/4$. Thus, $x = 0$ is a regular singular point for this equation and we can use the method of Frobenius to find a solution. To this end, we compute

$$\lim_{x\to 0} xp(x) = \lim_{x\to 0} \frac{x}{2} = 0, \qquad \text{and} \qquad \lim_{x\to 0} x^2 q(x) = \lim_{x\to 0} \frac{-(x+3)}{4} = \frac{-3}{4}.$$

Therefore, by equation (16) on page 463 of the text, the indicial equation is

$$r(r-1)-\frac{3}{4}=0 \qquad \Rightarrow \qquad 4r^2-4r-3=0 \qquad \Rightarrow \qquad (2r+1)(2r-3)=0.$$

This indicial equation has roots $r_1 = 3/2$ and $r_2 = -1/2$. By the method of Frobenius, we can assume that a solution to this differential equation will have the form

$$w(r,x)=\sum_{n=0}^{\infty} a_n x^{n+r}$$
$$\Rightarrow \qquad w'(r,x)=\sum_{n=0}^{\infty}(n+r)a_n x^{n+r-1}$$
$$\Rightarrow \qquad w''(r,x)=\sum_{n=0}^{\infty}(n+r-1)(n+r)a_n x^{n+r-2},$$

where $r = r_1 = 3/2$. Since $x = 0$ is the only singular point for this equation, we see that the solution, $w(3/2, x)$, converges for all $x > 0$. The first step in finding this solution is to plug $w(r, x)$ and its first and second derivatives (which we have found above by term by term differentiation) into the differential equation. Thus, we obtain

$$\sum_{n=0}^{\infty} 4(n+r-1)(n+r)a_n x^{n+r}+\sum_{n=0}^{\infty} 2(n+r)a_n x^{n+r+1}-\sum_{n=0}^{\infty} a_n x^{n+r+1}-\sum_{n=0}^{\infty} 3a_n x^{n+r}=0.$$

By shifting indices, we can sum each power series over the same power of x, namely x^{k+r}. Thus, with the substitution $k = n$ in the first and last power series and the substitution $k = n + 1$ in the two remaining power series, we obtain

$$\sum_{k=0}^{\infty} 4(k+r-1)(k+r)a_k x^{k+r}+\sum_{k=1}^{\infty} 2(k+r-1)a_{k-1} x^{k+r}-\sum_{k=1}^{\infty} a_{k-1} x^{k+r}-\sum_{k=0}^{\infty} 3a_k x^{k+r}=0.$$

Next removing the first term (the $k = 0$ term) from the first and last power series above and writing the result as a single power series yields

$$4(r-1)ra_0x^r+\sum_{k=1}^{\infty} 4(k+r-1)(k+r)a_k x^{k+r}+\sum_{k=1}^{\infty} 2(k+r-1)a_{k-1} x^{k+r}$$
$$-\sum_{k=1}^{\infty} a_{k-1} x^{k+r}-3a_0x^r-\sum_{k=1}^{\infty} 3a_k x^{k+r}=0$$

$$\Rightarrow \quad [4(r-1)r-3]\,a_0x^r + \sum_{k=1}^{\infty}[4(k+r-1)(k+r)a_k + 2(k+r-1)a_{k-1} - a_{k-1} - 3a_k]\,x^{k+r} = 0.$$

By equating coefficients we see that each coefficient in the power series must be zero. Also we are assuming that $a_0 \neq 0$. Therefore, we have

$$4(r-1)r-3=0, \qquad \text{(the indicial equation)},$$

$$4(k+r-1)(k+r)a_k + 2(k+r-1)a_{k-1} - a_{k-1} - 3a_k = 0, \qquad k \geq 1.$$

Thus, the recurrence equation is given by

$$a_k = \frac{(3-2k-2r)a_{k-1}}{4(k+r-1)(k+r)-3}, \qquad k \geq 1.$$

Therefore, for $r = r_1 = 3/2$, we have

$$a_k = \frac{-2ka_{k-1}}{4(k+1/2)(k+3/2)-3}, \qquad k \geq 1 \qquad \Rightarrow \qquad a_k = \frac{-a_{k-1}}{2(k+2)}, \qquad k \geq 1.$$

Thus, we see that

$$k=1 \quad \Rightarrow \quad a_1 = \frac{-a_0}{2\cdot 3} = \frac{-a_0}{2^0\cdot 3!},$$

$$k=2 \quad \Rightarrow \quad a_2 = \frac{-a_1}{2\cdot 4} = \frac{a_0}{2\cdot 2\cdot 3\cdot 4} = \frac{a_0}{2^1\cdot 4!},$$

$$k=3 \quad \Rightarrow \quad a_3 = \frac{-a_2}{2\cdot 5} = \frac{-a_0}{2^2\cdot 5!},$$

$$k=4 \quad \Rightarrow \quad a_4 = \frac{-a_3}{2\cdot 6} = \frac{a_0}{2^3\cdot 6!}.$$

Inspection of this sequence shows that we can write the nth coefficient, a_n, for $n \geq 1$ as

$$a_n = \frac{(-1)^n a_0}{2^{n-1}(n+2)!}.$$

Substituting these coefficients into the solution given by

$$w\left(\frac{3}{2}, x\right) = \sum_{n=0}^{\infty} a_n x^{n+(3/2)},$$

yields a power series solution for $x > 0$ given by

$$w\left(\frac{3}{2}, x\right) = a_0 x^{3/2} + a_0 \sum_{n=1}^{\infty} \frac{(-1)^n x^{n+(3/2)}}{2^{n-1}(n+2)!}.$$

But since substituting $n = 0$ into the general coefficient, a_n, yields $(-1)^0 a_0/(2^{-1}2!) = a_0$, the solution that we found above can be written as

$$w\left(\frac{3}{2}, x\right) = a_0 \sum_{n=0}^{\infty} \frac{(-1)^n x^{n+(3/2)}}{2^{n-1}(n+2)!}.$$

27. In this equation, we see that $p(x) = -1/x$ and $q(x) = -1$. Thus, the only singular point is $x = 0$. Since $xp(x) = -1$ and $x^2 q(x) = -x^2$, we see that $x = 0$ is a regular singular point for this equation and so we can use the method of Frobenius to find a solution to this equation. We also note that the solution that we find by this method will converge for all $x > 0$. To find this solution we observe that

$$p_0 = \lim_{x\to 0} xp(x) = \lim_{x\to 0}(-1) = -1 \qquad \text{and} \qquad q_0 = \lim_{x\to 0} x^2 q(x) = \lim_{x\to 0}(-x^2) = 0.$$

Thus, according to equation (16) on page 463 of the text, the indicial equation for the point $x = 0$ is

$$r(r-1) - r = 0 \qquad \Rightarrow \qquad r(r-2) = 0.$$

Therefore, the roots to the indicial equation are $r_1 = 2$, $r_2 = 0$. Hence, we will use the method of Frobenius to find the solution $w(2, x)$. If we let

$$w(r, x) = \sum_{n=0}^{\infty} a_n x^{n+r},$$

then

$$w'(r, x) = \sum_{n=0}^{\infty} (n+r) a_n x^{n+r-1}, \qquad \text{and} \qquad w''(r, x) = \sum_{n=0}^{\infty} (n+r-1)(n+r) a_n x^{n+r-2}.$$

By substituting these expressions into the differential equation and simplifying, we obtain

$$\sum_{n=0}^{\infty} (n+r-1)(n+r) a_n x^{n+r-1} - \sum_{n=0}^{\infty} (n+r) a_n x^{n+r-1} - \sum_{n=0}^{\infty} a_n x^{n+r+1} = 0.$$

Next we shift the indices by letting $k = n-1$ in the first two power series above and $k = n+1$ in the last power series above. Therefore, we have

$$\sum_{k=-1}^{\infty}(k+r)(k+r+1)a_{k+1}x^{k+r} - \sum_{k=-1}^{\infty}(k+r+1)a_{k+1}x^{k+r} - \sum_{k=1}^{\infty}a_{k-1}x^{k+r} = 0.$$

We can start all three of these summations at the same term, the $k = 1$ term, if we separate out the first two terms (the $k = -1$ and $k = 0$ terms) from the first two power series. Thus, we have

$$\begin{aligned}
&(r-1)ra_0x^{r-1} + r(r+1)a_1x^r + \sum_{k=1}^{\infty}(k+r)(k+r+1)a_{k+1}x^{k+r} \\
&\qquad -ra_0x^{r-1} - (r+1)a_1x^r - \sum_{k=1}^{\infty}(k+r+1)a_{k+1}x^{k+r} - \sum_{k=1}^{\infty}a_{k-1}x^{k+r} = 0 \\
\Rightarrow\quad &[(r-1)r - r]\,a_0x^{r-1} + [r(r+1) - (r+1)]\,a_1x^r \\
&\qquad + \sum_{k=1}^{\infty}[(k+r)(k+r+1)a_{k+1} - (k+r+1)a_{k+1} - a_{k-1}]\,x^{k+r} = 0.
\end{aligned}$$

By equating coefficients and assuming that $a_0 \neq 0$, we obtain

$$\begin{aligned}
&r(r-1) - r = 0, \qquad \text{(the indicial equation)}, \\
&(r+1)(r-1)a_1 = 0, \\
&(k+r)(k+r+1)a_{k+1} - (k+r+1)a_{k+1} - a_{k-1} = 0, \qquad k \geq 1,
\end{aligned} \tag{8.13}$$

where the last equation above is the recurrence relation. Simplifying this recurrence relation yields

$$a_{k+1} = \frac{a_{k-1}}{(k+r+1)(k+r-1)}, \qquad k \geq 1. \tag{8.14}$$

Next we let $r = r_1 = 2$ in equation (8.13) and in the recurrence relation, equation (8.14), to obtain

$$\begin{aligned}
&3a_1 = 0 \qquad \Rightarrow \qquad a_1 = 0, \\
&a_{k+1} = \frac{a_{k-1}}{(k+3)(k+1)}, \qquad k \geq 1.
\end{aligned}$$

Thus, we have

$$\begin{aligned}
k = 1 \quad &\Rightarrow \quad a_2 = \frac{a_0}{4 \cdot 2}\,, \\
k = 2 \quad &\Rightarrow \quad a_3 = \frac{a_1}{5 \cdot 3} = 0\,, \\
k = 3 \quad &\Rightarrow \quad a_4 = \frac{a_2}{6 \cdot 4} = \frac{a_0}{6 \cdot 4 \cdot 4 \cdot 2} = \frac{a_0}{2^4 \cdot 3 \cdot 2 \cdot 2 \cdot 1 \cdot 1} = \frac{a_0}{2^4 \cdot 3! \cdot 2!}\,, \\
k = 4 \quad &\Rightarrow \quad a_5 = \frac{a_3}{7 \cdot 5} = 0\,, \\
k = 5 \quad &\Rightarrow \quad a_6 = \frac{a_4}{8 \cdot 6} = \frac{a_0}{8 \cdot 6 \cdot 2^4 \cdot 3! \cdot 2!} = \frac{a_0}{2^6 \cdot 4! \cdot 3!}\,.
\end{aligned}$$

By inspection we can now see that the coefficients of the power series solution $w(2, x)$ are

$$a_{2n-1} = 0$$

and

$$a_{2n} = \frac{a_0}{2^{2n} \cdot (n+1)!n!}\,,$$

for all $n \geq 1$. Thus, substituting these coefficients into the power series solution yields the solution

$$w(2, x) = a_0 \sum_{n=0}^{\infty} \frac{x^{2n+2}}{2^{2n} \cdot (n+1)!n!}\,.$$

35. In applying the method of Frobenius to this third order linear differential equation, we will seek a solution of the form

$$\begin{aligned}
w(r, x) &= \sum_{n=0}^{\infty} a_n x^{n+r} \\
\Rightarrow \quad w'(r, x) &= \sum_{n=0}^{\infty} (n+r) a_n x^{n+r-1} \\
\Rightarrow \quad w''(r, x) &= \sum_{n=0}^{\infty} (n+r-1)(n+r) a_n x^{n+r-2} \\
\Rightarrow \quad w'''(r, x) &= \sum_{n=0}^{\infty} (n+r-2)(n+r-1)(n+r) a_n x^{n+r-3}\,,
\end{aligned}$$

where we have differentiated term by term. Substituting these expressions into the differential equation and simplifying yields

$$\sum_{n=0}^{\infty} 6(n+r-2)(n+r-1)(n+r)a_n x^{n+r} + \sum_{n=0}^{\infty} 13(n+r-1)(n+r)a_n x^{n+r}$$
$$+ \sum_{n=0}^{\infty}(n+r)a_n x^{n+r} + \sum_{n=0}^{\infty}(n+r)a_n x^{n+r+1} + \sum_{n=0}^{\infty} a_n x^{n+r+1} = 0.$$

By the shift of index $k = n + 1$ in the last two power series above and the shift $k = n$ in all of the other power series, we obtain

$$\sum_{k=0}^{\infty} 6(k+r-2)(k+r-1)(k+r)a_k x^{k+r} + \sum_{k=0}^{\infty} 13(k+r-1)(k+r)a_k x^{k+r}$$
$$+ \sum_{k=0}^{\infty}(k+r)a_k x^{k+r} + \sum_{k=1}^{\infty}(k-1+r)a_{k-1} x^{k+r} + \sum_{k=1}^{\infty} a_{k-1} x^{k+r} = 0.$$

Next we remove the first term from each of the first three power series above so that all of these series start at $k = 1$. Thus, we have

$$6(r-2)(r-1)ra_0x^r + \sum_{k=1}^{\infty} 6(k+r-2)(k+r-1)(k+r)a_k x^{k+r}$$
$$+13(r-1)ra_0x^r + \sum_{k=1}^{\infty} 13(k+r-1)(k+r)a_k x^{k+r} + ra_0x^r + \sum_{k=1}^{\infty}(k+r)a_k x^{k+r}$$
$$+ \sum_{k=1}^{\infty}(k-1+r)a_{k-1} x^{k+r} + \sum_{k=1}^{\infty} a_{k-1} x^{k+r} = 0$$
$$\Rightarrow \quad [6(r-2)(r-1)r + 13(r-1)r + r]\, a_0 x^r$$
$$+ \sum_{k=1}^{\infty} [6(k+r-2)(k+r-1)(k+r)a_k + 13(k+r-1)(k+r)a_k$$
$$+(k+r)a_k + (k-1+r)a_{k-1} + a_{k-1}]\, x^{k+r} = 0. \qquad (8.15)$$

If we assume that $a_0 \neq 0$ and set the coefficient of x^r equal to zero, we find that the *indicial equation* is

$$6(r-2)(r-1)r + 13(r-1)r + r = 0 \qquad \Rightarrow \qquad r^2(6r-5) = 0.$$

Hence, the roots to the indicial equation are 0, 0, and 5/6. We will find the solution associated with the largest of these roots. That is, we will find $w(5/6, x)$. Also, from equation (8.15), we see that we have the recurrence relation

$$6(k+r-2)(k+r-1)(k+r)a_k + 13(k+r-1)(k+r)a_k$$
$$+(k+r)a_k + (k-1+r)a_{k-1} + a_{k-1} = 0, \qquad k \geq 1$$
$$\Rightarrow \qquad a_k = \frac{-a_{k-1}}{6(k+r-2)(k+r-1)+13(k+r-1)+1}, \qquad k \geq 1.$$

If we assume that $r = 5/6$, then this recurrence relation simplifies to

$$a_k = \frac{-a_{k-1}}{k(6k+5)}, \qquad k \geq 1.$$

Therefore, we have

$$\begin{aligned} k=1 \quad &\Rightarrow \quad a_1 = \frac{-a_0}{11}, \\ k=2 \quad &\Rightarrow \quad a_2 = \frac{-a_1}{34} = \frac{a_0}{374}, \\ k=3 \quad &\Rightarrow \quad a_3 = \frac{-a_2}{69} = \frac{-a_0}{25,806}. \end{aligned}$$

By substituting these coefficients into the solution $w(5/6, x) = \sum_{n=0}^{\infty} a_n x^{n+(5/6)}$, we obtain

$$w\left(\frac{5}{6}, x\right) = a_0\left(x^{5/6} - \frac{x^{11/6}}{11} + \frac{x^{17/6}}{374} - \frac{x^{23/6}}{25,806} + \cdots\right).$$

41. If we let $z = 1/x$ ($\Rightarrow dz/dx = -1/x^2$), then we can define a new function $Y(z)$ as

$$Y(z) := y\left(\frac{1}{z}\right) = y(x).$$

Thus, by the chain rule, we have

$$\frac{dy}{dx} = \frac{dY}{dx} = \left(\frac{dY}{dz}\right)\left(\frac{dz}{dx}\right) = \left(\frac{dY}{dz}\right)\left(-\frac{1}{x^2}\right) \tag{8.16}$$

$$\Rightarrow \qquad -x^2\frac{dy}{dx} = \frac{dY}{dz}. \tag{8.17}$$

Therefore, using the product rule and chain rule, we see that

$$\frac{d^2y}{dx^2} = \frac{d^2Y}{dx^2} = \frac{d}{dx}\left(\frac{dY}{dx}\right) = \frac{d}{dx}\left[\left(-\frac{1}{x^2}\right)\left(\frac{dY}{dz}\right)\right] \qquad \text{(by (8.16) above)}$$

$$= \frac{d}{dx}\left(-\frac{1}{x^2}\right) \times \left(\frac{dY}{dz}\right) + \left(-\frac{1}{x^2}\right) \times \frac{d}{dx}\left(\frac{dY}{dz}\right) \qquad \text{(by product rule)}$$

$$= \left(\frac{2}{x^3}\right) \times \left(\frac{dY}{dz}\right) + \left(-\frac{1}{x^2}\right) \times \left[\left(\frac{d^2Y}{dz^2}\right)\left(\frac{dz}{dx}\right)\right] \qquad \text{(by chain rule)}$$

$$= \left(\frac{2}{x^3}\right) \times \left(\frac{dY}{dz}\right) + \left(-\frac{1}{x^2}\right)^2 \times \left(\frac{d^2Y}{dz^2}\right) \qquad \left(\text{since } \frac{dz}{dx} = -\frac{1}{x^2}\right)$$

$$= \frac{2}{x^3}\frac{dY}{dz} + \frac{1}{x^4}\frac{d^2Y}{dz^2}.$$

Hence, we have

$$x^3\frac{d^2y}{dx^2} = 2\frac{dY}{dz} + \frac{1}{x}\frac{d^2Y}{dz^2} = 2\frac{dY}{dz} + z\frac{d^2Y}{dz^2}. \tag{8.18}$$

By using the fact that $Y(z) = y(x)$ and equations (8.17) and (8.18) above, we can now transform the original differential equation into the differential equation

$$2\frac{dY}{dz} + z\frac{d^2Y}{dz^2} + \frac{dY}{dz} - Y = 0 \qquad \Rightarrow \qquad zY'' + 3Y' - Y = 0. \tag{8.19}$$

We will now solve this transformed differential equation. To this end, we first note that

$$p(z) = \frac{3}{z} \qquad \Rightarrow \qquad zp(z) = 3,$$

and

$$q(z)\frac{-1}{z} \qquad \Rightarrow \qquad z^2g(z) = -z.$$

Therefore, $z = 0$ is a regular singular point of this equation and so infinity is a regular singular point of the original equation.

To find a power series solution for equation (8.19), we first compute

$$p_0 = \lim_{z\to 0} zp(z) = 3 \qquad \text{and} \qquad q_0 = \lim_{z\to 0} z^2q(z) = 0.$$

Thus, the indicial equation for equation (8.19) is

$$r(r-1) + 3r = 0 \qquad \Rightarrow \qquad r(r+2) = 0.$$

Hence, this indicial equation has roots $r_1 = 0$ and $r_2 = -2$. We seek a solution of the form

$$w(r, z) = \sum_{n=0}^{\infty} a_n z^{n+r}.$$

Substituting this expression into equation (8.19) above yields

$$z\sum_{n=0}^{\infty}(n+r-1)(n+r)a_nz^{n+r-2}+3\sum_{n=0}^{\infty}(n+r)a_nz^{n+r-1}-\sum_{n=0}^{\infty}a_nz^{n+r}=0.$$

By simplifying, this equation becomes

$$\sum_{n=0}^{\infty}(n+r-1)(n+r)a_nz^{n+r-1}+\sum_{n=0}^{\infty}3(n+r)a_nz^{n+r-1}-\sum_{n=0}^{\infty}a_nz^{n+r}=0.$$

Making the shift of index $k=n-1$ in the first two power series and $k=n$ in the last power series allows us to sum each power series over the same powers of z, namely z^{k+r}. Thus, we have

$$\sum_{k=-1}^{\infty}(k+r)(k+r+1)a_{k+1}z^{k+r}+\sum_{k=-1}^{\infty}3(k+r+1)a_{k+1}z^{n+r}-\sum_{k=0}^{\infty}a_kz^{k+r}=0.$$

By removing the first term from the first two power series above, we can write these three summations as a single power series. Therefore, we have

$$\begin{aligned}(r-1)ra_0z^{r-1}&+\sum_{k=0}^{\infty}(k+r)(k+r+1)a_{k+1}z^{k+r}\\&+3ra_0z^{r-1}+\sum_{k=0}^{\infty}3(k+r+1)a_{k+1}z^{n+r}-\sum_{k=0}^{\infty}a_kz^{k+r}=0\\ \Rightarrow\quad [(r-1)r+3r]\,a_0z^{r-1}&+\sum_{k=0}^{\infty}\left[(k+r)(k+r+1)a_{k+1}+3(k+r+1)a_{k+1}-a_k\right]z^{k+r}=0.\end{aligned}$$

Equating coefficients and assuming that $a_0\neq 0$ yields the indicial equation, $(r-1)r+3r=0$, and the recurrence relation

$$\begin{aligned}&(k+r)(k+r+1)a_{k+1}+3(k+r+1)a_{k+1}-a_k=0, \qquad k\geq 0\\ \Rightarrow\qquad &a_{k+1}=\frac{a_k}{(k+r+1)(k+r+3)}, \qquad k\geq 0.\end{aligned}$$

Thus, with $r=r_1=0$, we obtain the recurrence relation

$$a_{k+1}=\frac{a_k}{(k+1)(k+3)}, \qquad k\geq 3.$$

Since a_0 is an arbitrary number, we see from this recurrence equation that the next three coefficients are given by

$$\begin{aligned} k=0 \quad &\Rightarrow \quad a_1 = \frac{a_0}{3}, \\ k=1 \quad &\Rightarrow \quad a_2 = \frac{a_1}{8} = \frac{a_0}{24}, \\ k=2 \quad &\Rightarrow \quad a_3 = \frac{a_2}{15} = \frac{a_0}{360}. \end{aligned}$$

Thus, from the method of Frobenius, we obtain a power series solution for equation (8.19) given by

$$Y(z) = w(0,z) = \sum_{n=0}^{\infty} a_n z^n = a_0 \left(1 + \frac{1}{3} z + \frac{1}{24} z^2 + \frac{1}{360} z^3 + \cdots \right).$$

In order to find the solution of the original differential equation, we again make the substitution $z = 1/x$ and $Y(z) = Y(x^{-1}) = y(x)$. Therefore, in the solution found above, we replace the z's with $1/x$ to obtain the solution given by

$$y(x) = Y\left(x^{-1}\right) = a_0 \left(1 + \frac{1}{3} x^{-1} + \frac{1}{24} x^{-2} + \frac{1}{360} x^{-3} + \cdots \right).$$

EXERCISES 8.7: Finding a Second Linearly Independent Solution, page 482

3. In Problem 21 of Exercises 8.6, we found one power series solution for this differential equation about the point $x = 0$ given by

$$y_1(x) = 1 - \frac{1}{4} x^2 + \frac{1}{64} x^4 - \frac{1}{2304} x^6 + \cdots,$$

where we let $a_0 = 1$. We also found that the roots to the indicial equation are $r_1 = r_2 = 0$. Thus, to find a second linearly independent solution about the regular singular point $x = 0$, we will use part (b) of Theorem 7 on page 475 of the text. Therefore, we see that this second linearly independent solution will have the form given by

$$y_2(x) = y_1(x) \ln x + \sum_{n=1}^{\infty} b_n x^n$$

$$\Rightarrow \qquad y_2'(x) = y_1'(x) \ln x + x^{-1} y_1(x) + \sum_{n=1}^{\infty} n b_n x^{n-1}$$

$$\Rightarrow \qquad y_2''(x) = y_1''(x)\ln x + 2x^{-1}y_1'(x) - x^{-2}y_1(x) + \sum_{n=1}^{\infty} n(n-1)b_n x^{n-2}\,.$$

Substituting these expressions into the differential equation yields

$$x^2\left\{y_1''(x)\ln x + 2x^{-1}y_1'(x) - x^{-2}y_1(x) + \sum_{n=1}^{\infty} n(n-1)b_n x^{n-2}\right\}$$
$$+x\left\{y_1'(x)\ln x + x^{-1}y_1(x) + \sum_{n=1}^{\infty} nb_n x^{n-1}\right\} + x^2\left\{y_1(x)\ln x + \sum_{n=1}^{\infty} b_n x^n\right\} = 0,$$

which simplifies to

$$x^2y_1''(x)\ln x + 2xy_1'(x) - y_1(x) + \sum_{n=1}^{\infty} n(n-1)b_n x^n$$
$$+xy_1'(x)\ln x + y_1(x) + \sum_{n=1}^{\infty} nb_n x^n + x^2y_1(x)\ln x + \sum_{n=1}^{\infty} b_n x^{n+2} = 0,$$
$$\Rightarrow \qquad \left(x^2y_1''(x) + xy_1'(x) + x^2y_1(x)\right)\ln x + 2xy_1'(x)$$
$$+\sum_{n=1}^{\infty} n(n-1)b_n x^n + \sum_{n=1}^{\infty} nb_n x^n + \sum_{n=1}^{\infty} b_n x^{n+2} = 0.$$

Therefore, since $y_1(x)$ is a solution to the differential equation, the term in braces is zero and the above equation reduces to

$$2xy_1'(x) + \sum_{n=1}^{\infty} n(n-1)b_n x^n + \sum_{n=1}^{\infty} nb_n x^n + \sum_{n=1}^{\infty} b_n x^{n+2} = 0.$$

Next we make the substitution $k = n+2$ in the last power series above and the substitution $k = n$ in the other two power series so that we can sum all three of the power series over the same power of x, namely x^k. Thus, we have

$$2xy_1'(x) + \sum_{k=1}^{\infty} k(k-1)b_k x^k + \sum_{k=1}^{\infty} kb_k x^k + \sum_{k=3}^{\infty} b_{k-2} x^k = 0.$$

By separating out the first two terms in the first two summations above and simplifying, we obtain

$$2xy_1'(x) + 0 + 2b_2x^2 + \sum_{k=3}^{\infty} k(k-1)b_k x^k + b_1x + 2b_2x^2 + \sum_{k=3}^{\infty} kb_k x^k + \sum_{k=3}^{\infty} b_{k-2} x^k = 0$$

$$\Rightarrow \qquad 2xy_1'(x) + b_1x + 4b_2x^2 + \sum_{k=3}^{\infty}\left(k^2b_k + b_{k-2}\right)x^k = 0. \qquad (8.20)$$

By differentiating the series for $y_1(x)$ term by term, we obtain

$$y_1'(x) = -\frac{1}{2}x + \frac{1}{16}x^3 - \frac{1}{384}x^5 + \cdots .$$

Thus, substituting this expression for $y_1'(x)$ into equation (8.20) above and simplifying yields

$$\left\{-x^2 + \frac{1}{8}x^4 - \frac{1}{192}x^6 + \cdots\right\} + b_1x + 4b_2x^2 + \sum_{k=3}^{\infty}\left(k^2b_k + b_{k-2}\right)x^k = 0.$$

Therefore, by equating coefficients, we see that

$$\begin{aligned}
&b_1 = 0; && \\
&4b_2 - 1 = 0 &\Rightarrow\qquad & b_2 = \frac{1}{4}; \\
&9b_3 + b_1 = 0 &\Rightarrow\qquad & b_3 = 0; \\
&\frac{1}{8} + 16b_4 + b_2 = 0 &\Rightarrow\qquad & b_4 = \frac{-3}{128}; \\
&25b_5 + b_3 = 0 &\Rightarrow\qquad & b_5 = 0; \\
&\frac{-1}{192} + 36b_6 + b_4 = 0 &\Rightarrow\qquad & b_6 = \frac{11}{13,824}.
\end{aligned}$$

Substituting these coefficients into the solution

$$y_2(x) = y_1(x)\ln x + \sum_{n=1}^{\infty} b_nx^n,$$

yields

$$y_2(x) = y_1(x)\ln x + \frac{1}{4}x^2 - \frac{3}{128}x^4 + \frac{11}{13,824}x^6 + \cdots .$$

Thus, a general solution of this differential equation is given by

$$y(x) = c_1y_1(x) + c_2y_2(x),$$

where

$$\begin{aligned}
y_1(x) &= 1 - \frac{1}{4}x^2 + \frac{1}{64}x^4 - \frac{1}{2304}x^6 + \cdots, \\
y_2(x) &= y_1(x)\ln x + \frac{1}{4}x^2 - \frac{3}{128}x^4 + \frac{11}{13,824}x^6 + \cdots .
\end{aligned}$$

7. In Problem 25 of Section 8.6, we found a solution to this differential equation about the regular singular point $x = 0$ given by

$$y_1(x) = \sum_{n=0}^{\infty} \frac{(-1)^n x^{n+(3/2)}}{2^{n-1}(n+2)!} = x^{3/2} - \frac{1}{6}x^{5/2} + \frac{1}{48}x^{7/2} + \cdots ,$$

where we let $a_0 = 1$. We also found that the roots to the indicial equation for this problem are $r_1 = 3/2$ and $r_2 = -1/2$, and so $r_1 - r_2 = 2$. Thus, in order to find a second linearly independent solution about $x = 0$, we will use part (c) of Theorem 7 on page 475 of the text. Therefore, we will assume that this second solution has the form

$$y_2(x) = Cy_1(x)\ln x + \sum_{n=0}^{\infty} b_n x^{n-(1/2)}, \qquad b_0 \neq 0$$

$$\Rightarrow \quad y_2'(x) = Cy_1'(x)\ln x + C\frac{1}{x}y_1(x) + \sum_{n=0}^{\infty}\left(n - \frac{1}{2}\right) b_n x^{n-(3/2)}$$

$$\Rightarrow \quad y_2''(x) = Cy_1''(x)\ln x + 2C\frac{1}{x}y_1'(x) - C\frac{1}{x^2}y_1(x) + \sum_{n=0}^{\infty}\left(n - \frac{3}{2}\right)\left(n - \frac{1}{2}\right) b_n x^{n-(5/2)}.$$

Substituting these expressions into the differential equation yields

$$4x^2\left[Cy_1''(x)\ln x + 2C\frac{1}{x}y_1'(x) - C\frac{1}{x^2}y_1(x) + \sum_{n=0}^{\infty}\left(n - \frac{3}{2}\right)\left(n - \frac{1}{2}\right) b_n x^{n-(5/2)}\right]$$
$$+2x^2\left[Cy_1'(x)\ln x + C\frac{1}{x}y_1(x) + \sum_{n=0}^{\infty}\left(n - \frac{1}{2}\right) b_n x^{n-(3/2)}\right]$$
$$-(x+3)\left[Cy_1(x)\ln x + \sum_{n=0}^{\infty} b_n x^{n-(1/2)}\right] = 0.$$

Multiplying through, we get

$$\left[4x^2Cy_1''(x)\ln x + 8Cxy_1'(x) - 4Cy_1(x) + \sum_{n=0}^{\infty} 4\left(n - \frac{3}{2}\right)\left(n - \frac{1}{2}\right) b_n x^{n-(1/2)}\right]$$
$$+\left[2x^2Cy_1'(x)\ln x + 2Cxy_1(x) + \sum_{n=0}^{\infty} 2\left(n - \frac{1}{2}\right) b_n x^{n+(1/2)}\right]$$
$$-\left[Cxy_1(x)\ln x + \sum_{n=0}^{\infty} b_n x^{n+(1/2)} + 3Cy_1(x)\ln x + \sum_{n=0}^{\infty} 3b_n x^{n-(1/2)}\right] = 0,$$

which simplifies to

$$C\left[4x^2y_1''(x)+2x^2y_1'(x)-xy_1(x)-3y_1(x)\right]\ln x+8Cxy_1'(x)+2C(x-2)y_1(x)$$
$$+\sum_{n=0}^{\infty}(2n-3)(2n-1)\,b_nx^{n-(1/2)}+\sum_{n=0}^{\infty}(2n-1)\,b_nx^{n+(1/2)}$$
$$-\sum_{n=0}^{\infty}b_nx^{n+(1/2)}-\sum_{n=0}^{\infty}3b_nx^{n-(1/2)}=0.$$

Since $y_1(x)$ is a solution to the differential equation, the term in brackets is zero. By shifting indices so that each power series is summed over the same power of x, we have

$$8Cxy_1'(x)+2C(x-2)y_1(x)+\sum_{k=0}^{\infty}(2k-3)(2k-1)\,b_kx^{k-(1/2)}$$
$$+\sum_{k=1}^{\infty}(2k-3)\,b_{k-1}x^{k-(1/2)}-\sum_{k=1}^{\infty}b_{k-1}x^{k-(1/2)}-\sum_{k=0}^{\infty}3b_kx^{k-(1/2)}=0.$$

By writing all of these summations as a single power series (noting that the $k=0$ term of the first and last summations add to zero), we obtain

$$8Cxy_1'(x)+2C(x-2)y_1(x)+\sum_{k=0}^{\infty}(2k-3)(2k-1)\,b_kx^{k-(1/2)}$$
$$+\sum_{k=1}^{\infty}\left[(2k-3)(2k-1)\,b_k+(2k-3)\,b_{k-1}-b_{k-1}-3b_k\right]x^{k-(1/2)}=0.$$

Substituting into this equation the expressions for $y_1(x)$ and $y_1'(x)$ given by

$$y_1(x)=\sum_{n=0}^{\infty}\frac{(-1)^nx^{n+(3/2)}}{2^{n-1}(n+2)!},\qquad y_1'(x)=\sum_{n=0}^{\infty}\frac{(-1)^n[n+(3/2)]x^{n+(1/2)}}{2^{n-1}(n+2)!},$$

yields

$$\sum_{n=0}^{\infty}\frac{8C(-1)^n[n+(3/2)]x^{n+(3/2)}}{2^{n-1}(n+2)!}+\sum_{n=0}^{\infty}\frac{2C(-1)^nx^{n+(5/2)}}{2^{n-1}(n+2)!}$$
$$-\sum_{n=0}^{\infty}\frac{4C(-1)^nx^{n+(3/2)}}{2^{n-1}(n+2)!}+\sum_{k=1}^{\infty}\left[4k(k-2)b_k+2(k-2)b_{k-1}\right]x^{k-(1/2)}=0,$$

where we have simplified the expression inside the last summation. Combining the first and third power series yields

$$\sum_{n=0}^{\infty} \frac{8C(-1)^n(n+1)x^{n+(3/2)}}{2^{n-1}(n+2)!} + \sum_{n=0}^{\infty} \frac{2C(-1)^n x^{n+(5/2)}}{2^{n-1}(n+2)!} + \sum_{k=1}^{\infty} \left[4k(k-2)b_k + 2(k-2)b_{k-1}\right] x^{k-(1/2)} = 0, \quad (8.21)$$

By writing out the terms up to order $x^{7/2}$, we obtain

$$8C\left[x^{3/2} - \frac{1}{3}x^{5/2} + \frac{3}{16}x^{7/2} + \cdots\right] + 2C\left[x^{5/2} - \frac{1}{6}x^{7/2} + \cdots\right] + \left[(-4b_1 - 2b_0)x^{1/2} + (12b_3 + 2b_2)x^{5/2} + (32b_4 + 4b_3)x^{7/2} + \cdots\right] = 0.$$

Setting the coefficients equal to zero, yields

$$\begin{aligned}
-4b_1 - 2b_0 &= 0 && \Rightarrow && b_1 = -b_0/2;\\
8C &= 0 && \Rightarrow && C = 0;\\
-(8/3)C + 2C + 12b_3 + 2b_2 &= 0 && \Rightarrow && b_3 = -b_2/6;\\
(2/3)C - (1/3)C + 32b_4 + 4b_3 &= 0 && \Rightarrow && b_4 = -b_3/8 = b_2/48.
\end{aligned}$$

From this we see that b_0 and b_2 are arbitrary constants and that $C = 0$. Also, since $C = 0$, we can use the last power series in (8.21) to obtain the recurrence equation $b_k = b_{k-1}/(2k)$. Thus, every coefficient after b_4 will depend only on b_2 (not on b_0). Substituting these coefficients into the solution,

$$y_2(x) = Cy_1(x)\ln x + \sum_{n=0}^{\infty} b_n x^{n-(1/2)},$$

yields

$$y_2(x) = b_0\left[x^{-1/2} - \frac{1}{2}x^{1/2}\right] + b_2\left[x^{3/2} - \frac{1}{6}x^{5/2} + \frac{1}{48}x^{7/2} + \cdots\right]$$

The expression in the brackets following b_2 is just the series expansion for $y_1(x)$. Hence, in order to obtain a second linearly independent solution, we must choose b_0 to be nonzero. Taking $b_0 = 1$ and $b_2 = 0$ gives

$$y_2(x) = x^{-1/2} - \frac{1}{2}x^{1/2}.$$

Therefore, a general solution is

$$y(x) = c_1 y_1(x) + c_2 y_2(x),$$

where

$$y_1(x) = x^{3/2} - \frac{1}{6}x^{5/2} + \frac{1}{48}x^{7/2} + \cdots \qquad \text{and} \qquad y_2(x) = x^{-1/2} - \frac{1}{2}x^{1/2}.$$

17. In Problem 35 of Section 8.6, we assumed that there exists a series solution to this problem of the form $w(r,x) = \sum_{n=0}^{\infty} a_n x^{n+r}$. This led to the equation (cf. equation (8.15), of the solution to Problem 35, Exercises 8.6)

$$r^2(6r-5)a_0 x^r + \sum_{k=1}^{\infty} \left\{(k+r)^2[6(k+r)-5]a_k + (k+r)a_{k-1}\right\} x^{k+r} = 0. \qquad (8.22)$$

From this we found the indicial equation $r^2(6r-5) = 0$, which has roots $r = 0, 0, 5/6$. By using the root $5/6$, we found the solution $w(5/6, x)$. Hence one solution is

$$y_1(x) = x^{5/6} - \frac{x^{11/6}}{11} + \frac{x^{17/6}}{374} - \frac{x^{23/6}}{25,806} + \cdots,$$

where we have chosen $a_0 = 1$ in $w(5/6, x)$. We now seek two more linearly independent solutions to this differential equation. To find a second linearly independent solution, we will use the root $r = 0$ and set the coefficients in equation (8.22) to zero to obtain the recurrence relation

$$k^2(6k-5)a_k + k a_{k-1} = 0, \qquad k \geq 1.$$

Solving for a_k in terms of a_{k-1} gives

$$a_k = \frac{-a_{k-1}}{k(6k-5)}, \qquad k \geq 1.$$

Thus, we have

$$k = 1 \quad \Rightarrow \quad a_1 = -a_0,$$

$$k = 2 \quad \Rightarrow \quad a_2 = \frac{-a_1}{14} = \frac{a_0}{14},$$

$$
\begin{aligned}
k = 3 \quad &\Rightarrow \quad a_3 = \frac{-a_2}{39} = \frac{-a_0}{546}\,, \\
k = 4 \quad &\Rightarrow \quad a_4 = \frac{-a_3}{76} = \frac{a_0}{41,496}\,, \\
k = 5 \quad &\Rightarrow \quad a_5 = \frac{-a_4}{125} = \frac{-a_0}{5,187,000}\,.
\end{aligned}
$$

Plugging these coefficients into the solution $w(0, x)$ and setting $a_0 = 1$ yields a second linearly independent solution

$$
y_2(x) = 1 - x + \frac{1}{14}x^2 - \frac{1}{546}x^3 + \frac{1}{41,496}x^4 - \frac{1}{5,187,000}x^5 + \cdots .
$$

To find a third linearly independent solution, we will use the repeated root $r = 0$ and assume that, as in the case of second order equations with repeated roots, the solution that we seek will have the form

$$
y_3(x) = y_2(x)\ln x + \sum_{n=1}^{\infty} c_n x^n .
$$

Since the first three derivatives of $y_3(x)$ are given by

$$
\begin{aligned}
y_3'(x) &= y_2'(x)\ln x + x^{-1}y_2(x) + \sum_{n=1}^{\infty} n c_n x^{n-1}\,, \\
y_3''(x) &= y_2''(x)\ln x + 2x^{-1}y_2'(x) - x^{-2}y_2(x) + \sum_{n=1}^{\infty}(n-1)n c_n x^{n-2}\,, \\
y_3'''(x) &= y_2'''(x)\ln x + 3x^{-1}y_2''(x) - 3x^{-2}y_2'(x) + 2x^{-3}y_2(x) + \sum_{n=1}^{\infty}(n-2)(n-1)n c_n x^{n-3}\,,
\end{aligned}
$$

substituting $y_3(x)$ into the differential equation yields

$$
\begin{aligned}
&6x^3y'''(x) + 13x^2y''(x) + \left(x + x^2\right)y'(x) + xy(x) \\
&\quad = 6x^3\left[y_2'''(x)\ln x + 3x^{-1}y_2''(x) - 3x^{-2}y_2'(x) + 2x^{-3}y_2(x) + \sum_{n=1}^{\infty}(n-2)(n-1)n c_n x^{n-3}\right] \\
&\qquad + 13x^2\left[y_2''(x)\ln x + 2x^{-1}y_2'(x) - x^{-2}y_2(x) + \sum_{n=1}^{\infty}(n-1)n c_n x^{n-2}\right] \\
&\qquad + \left(x + x^2\right)\left[y_2'(x)\ln x + x^{-1}y_2(x) + \sum_{n=1}^{\infty} n c_n x^{n-1}\right] + x\left[y_2(x)\ln x + \sum_{n=1}^{\infty} c_n x^n\right] = 0.
\end{aligned}
$$

Since $y_2(x)$ is a solution to the given equation, this simplifies to

$$18x^2y_2''(x)+8xy_2'(x)+xy_2(x)+\sum_{n=1}^{\infty}6(n-2)(n-1)nc_nx^n$$
$$+\sum_{n=1}^{\infty}13(n-1)nc_nx^n+\sum_{n=1}^{\infty}nc_nx^n+\sum_{n=1}^{\infty}nc_nx^{n+1}+\sum_{n=1}^{\infty}c_nx^{n+1}=0.$$

By shifting indices and then starting all of the resulting power series at the same point, we can combine all of the summations above into a single power series. Thus, we have

$$18x^2y_2''(x)+8xy_2'(x)+xy_2(x)$$
$$+c_1x+\sum_{k=2}^{\infty}\left[6(k-2)(k-1)kc_k+13(k-1)kc_k+kc_k+kc_{k-1}\right]x^k=0. \tag{8.23}$$

By computing $y_2'(x)$ and $y_2''(x)$, we obtain

$$y_2'(x)=-1+\frac{1}{7}x-\frac{1}{182}x^2+\frac{1}{10374}x^3+\cdots,$$
$$y_2''(x)=\frac{1}{7}-\frac{1}{91}x+\frac{1}{3458}x^2+\cdots.$$

By substituting these expressions into equation (8.23), we have

$$18x^2\left(\frac{1}{7}-\frac{x}{91}+\frac{x^2}{3458}+\cdots\right)+8x\left(-1+\frac{x}{7}-\frac{x^2}{182}+\frac{x^3}{10374}+\cdots\right)$$
$$+x\left(1-x+\frac{x^2}{14}-\frac{x^3}{546}+\frac{x^4}{41,496}+\cdots\right)+c_1x+\sum_{k=2}^{\infty}\left[(6k^3-5k^2)c_k+kc_{k-1}\right]x^k=0.$$

Writing out the terms up to orderx^3 we find

$$(-7+c_1)\,x+\left(\frac{19}{7}+28c_2+2c_1\right)x^2+\left(-\frac{31}{182}+117c_3+3c_2\right)x^3+\cdots=0.$$

By equating coefficients to zero, we obtain

$$\begin{aligned}
-7+c_1&=0 &&\Rightarrow && c_1=7;\\
19/7+28c_2+2c_1&=0 &&\Rightarrow && c_2=-117/196;\\
-31/182+117c_3+3c_2&=0 &&\Rightarrow && c_3=4997/298116.
\end{aligned}$$

Therefore, plugging these coefficients into the expansion

$$y_3(x) = y_2(x)\ln x + \sum_{n=1}^{\infty} c_n x^n ,$$

yields a third linearly independent solution is given by

$$y_3(x) = y_2(x)\ln x + 7x - \frac{117}{196}x^2 + \frac{4997}{298116}x^3 + \cdots .$$

Thus, a general solution is

$$y(x) = c_1 y_1(x) + c_2 y_2(x) + c_3 y_3(x),$$

where

$$y_1(x) = x^{5/6} - \frac{x^{11/6}}{11} + \frac{x^{17/6}}{374} - \frac{x^{23/6}}{25,806} + \cdots ,$$

$$y_2(x) = 1 - x + \frac{x^2}{14} - \frac{x^3}{546} + \frac{x^4}{41,496} - \frac{x^5}{5,187,000} + \cdots ,$$

$$y_3(x) = y_2(x)\ln x + 7x - \frac{117x^2}{196} + \frac{4997x^3}{298,116} + \cdots .$$

23. We will try to find a solution of the form

$$y(x) = \sum_{n=0}^{\infty} a_n x^{n+r}$$

$$\Rightarrow \quad y'(x) = \sum_{n=0}^{\infty} (n+r) a_n x^{n+r-1}$$

$$\Rightarrow \quad y''(x) = \sum_{n=0}^{\infty} (n+r)(n+r-1) a_n x^{n+r-2} .$$

Therefore, we substitute these expressions into the differential equation to obtain

$$x^2 y'' + y' - 2y = x^2 \sum_{n=0}^{\infty} (n+r)(n+r-1) a_n x^{n+r-2} + \sum_{n=0}^{\infty} (n+r) a_n x^{n+r-1} - 2\sum_{n=0}^{\infty} a_n x^{n+r} = 0$$

$$\Rightarrow \quad \sum_{k=0}^{\infty} (k+r)(k+r-1) a_k x^{k+r} + \sum_{k=-1}^{\infty} (k+r+1) a_{k+1} x^{k+r} - \sum_{k=0}^{\infty} 2a_k x^{k+r} = 0$$

$$\Rightarrow \qquad ra_0x^{r-1}+\sum_{k=0}^{\infty}\left[(k+r)(k+r-1)a_k+(k+r+1)a_{k+1}-2a_k\right]x^{k+r}=0,$$

where we have changed all of the indices and the starting point for the second summation so that we could write these three power series as a single power series. By assuming that $a_0 \neq 0$ and $ra_0x^{r-1}=0$, we see that $r=0$. Plugging $r=0$ into the coefficients in the summation and noting that each of these coefficients must be zero yields the recurrence relation

$$k(k-1)a_k+(k+1)a_{k+1}-2a_k=0, \qquad k\geq 0$$

$$\Rightarrow \qquad a_{k+1}=(2-k)a_k, \qquad k\geq 0.$$

Thus, we see that the coefficients of the solution are given by

$$k=0 \;\Rightarrow\; a_1=2a_0\,; \quad k=1 \;\Rightarrow\; a_2=a_1=2a_0\,;$$

$$k=2 \;\Rightarrow\; a_3=0\,; \quad k=3 \;\Rightarrow\; a_4=-a_3=0\,.$$

Since each coefficient is a multiple of the previous coefficient, we see that $a_n=0$ for $n\geq 3$. If we take $a_0=1$, then one solution is

$$y_1(x)=1+2x+2x^2\,.$$

We will now use the reduction of order procedure described in Problem 31, Section 6.1, on page 326 of the text to find a second linearly independent solution. Thus we seek for a solution of the form

$$y(x)=y_1(x)v(x)$$

$$\Rightarrow \qquad y'(x)=y_1'(x)v(x)+y_1(x)v'(x)$$

$$\Rightarrow \qquad y''(x)=y_1''(x)v(x)+2y_1'(x)v'(x)+y_1(x)v''(x).$$

Substituting $y(x)$, $y'(x)$, and $y''(x)$ into the given equation yields

$$\begin{aligned} x^2y''+y'-2y &= x^2\left[y_1''v+2y_1'v'+y_1v''\right]+\left[y_1'v+y_1v'\right]-2\left[y_1v\right] \\ &= \left[x^2y_1\right]v''+\left[2x^2y_1'+y_1\right]v'+\left[x^2y_1''+y_1'-2y_1\right]v \\ &= \left[x^2y_1\right]v''+\left[2x^2y_1'+y_1\right]v'=0 \end{aligned}$$

(since y_1 is a solution, the coefficient at v equals to zero). With $w = v'$, the last equation becomes a first order separable equation which can be solved by methods of Section 2.2. Namely,

$$\begin{aligned} & \left[x^2 y_1(x)\right] w'(x) + \left[2x^2 y_1'(x) + y_1(x)\right] w(x) = 0 \\ \Rightarrow \quad & \frac{dw}{w} = -\frac{2x^2 y_1'(x) + y_1(x)}{x^2 y_1(x)}\, dx = -\left(\frac{2y'(x)}{y_1(x)} + \frac{1}{x^2}\right) dx \\ \Rightarrow \quad & \ln|w| = -\int \frac{2y'(x)dx}{y_1(x)} - \int \frac{dx}{x^2} = -2\ln|y_1(x)| + \frac{1}{x} \\ \Rightarrow \quad & w(x) = \exp\left[-2\ln|y_1(x)| + \frac{1}{x}\right] = \frac{e^{1/x}}{[y_1(x)]^2}, \end{aligned} \tag{8.24}$$

where we have taken zero integration constant and positive function w. Since

$$\begin{aligned} & [y_1(x)]^2 = 4x^4 + 8x^3 + 8x^2 + 4x + 1 \qquad \text{and} \\ & e^{1/x} = 1 + x^{-1} + \frac{x^{-2}}{2} + \frac{x^{-3}}{6} + \frac{x^{-4}}{24} + \cdots \end{aligned}$$

(we have used the Maclaurin expansion for e^z with $z = 1/x$), performing long division with descending powers of x in each polynomial, we see that

$$\frac{e^{1/x}}{[y_1(x)]^2} = \frac{1 + x^{-1} + \dfrac{x^{-2}}{2} + \dfrac{x^{-3}}{6} + \dfrac{x^{-4}}{24} + \cdots}{4x^4 + 8x^3 + 8x^2 + 4x + 1} = \frac{1}{4}x^{-4} - \frac{1}{4}x^{-5} + \frac{1}{8}x^{-6} + \cdots.$$

Therefore, (8.24) yields

$$\begin{aligned} & v'(x) = w(x) = \frac{1}{4}x^{-4} - \frac{1}{4}x^{-5} + \frac{1}{8}x^{-6} + \cdots \\ \Rightarrow \quad & v(x) = \int \left(\frac{1}{4}x^{-4} - \frac{1}{4}x^{-5} + \frac{1}{8}x^{-6} + \cdots\right) dx = -\frac{1}{12}x^{-3} + \frac{1}{16}x^{-4} - \frac{1}{40}x^{-5} + \cdots \end{aligned}$$

and so

$$\begin{aligned} y(x) &= y_1(x)v(x) = \left[1 + 2x + 2x^2\right]\left[-\frac{1}{12}x^{-3} + \frac{1}{16}x^{-4} - \frac{1}{40}x^{-5} + \cdots\right] \\ &= -\frac{1}{6}x^{-1} - \frac{1}{24}x^{-2} - \frac{1}{120}x^{-3} + \cdots. \end{aligned}$$

is a second linearly independent solution. Thus, a general solution to this differential equation is given by $y(x) = c_1 y_1(x) + c_2 y_2(x)$, where

$$y_1(x) = 1 + 2x + 2x^2 \qquad \text{and} \qquad y_2(x) = -\frac{1}{6}x^{-1} - \frac{1}{24}x^{-2} - \frac{1}{120}x^{-3} + \cdots.$$

EXERCISES 8.8: Special Functions, page 493

1. For this problem, we see that $\gamma = 1/2$, $\alpha+\beta+1/4$, and $\alpha\times\beta = 2$. First we note that γ is not an integer. Next, by solving in the last two equations above simultaneously for α and β, we see that either $\alpha = 1$ and $\beta = 1$ or $\alpha = 2$ and $\beta = 1$. Therefore, by assuming that $\alpha = 1$ and $\beta = 2$, equations (10) on page 485 and (17) on page 486 of the text yield the two solutions

$$y_1(x) = F\left(1, 2; \frac{1}{2}; x\right) \qquad \text{and} \qquad y_2(x) = x^{1/2}F\left(\frac{3}{2}, \frac{5}{2}; \frac{3}{2}; x\right).$$

Therefore, a general solution for this differential equation is given by

$$y(x) = c_1F\left(1, 2; \frac{1}{2}; x\right) + c_2x^{1/2}F\left(\frac{3}{2}, \frac{5}{2}; \frac{3}{2}; x\right).$$

Notice that

$$F(\alpha, \beta; \gamma; x) = 1 + \sum_{n=0}^{\infty}\frac{(\alpha)_n(\beta)_n}{n!(\gamma)_n}x^n = 1 + \sum_{n=0}^{\infty}\frac{(\beta)_n(\alpha)_n}{n!(\gamma)_n}x^n = F(\beta, \alpha; \gamma; x).$$

Therefore, letting $\alpha = 2$ and $\beta = 1$ yields an equivalent form of the same solution given by

$$y(x) = c_1F\left(2, 1; \frac{1}{2}; x\right) + c_2x^{1/2}F\left(\frac{5}{2}, \frac{3}{2}; \frac{3}{2}; x\right).$$

13. This equation can be written as

$$x^2y'' + xy' + \left(x^2 - \frac{1}{4}\right)y = 0.$$

Thus, $\nu^2 = 1/4$ which implies that $\nu = 1/2$. Since this is not an integer (even though 2ν is an integer), by the discussion on page 487 of the text, two linearly independent solutions to this problem are given by equations (25) and (26) also on page 487, that is

$$y_1(x) = J_{1/2}(x) = \sum_{n=0}^{\infty}\frac{(-1)^n}{n!\Gamma(3/2+n)}\left(\frac{x}{2}\right)^{2n+1/2},$$

$$y_2(x) = J_{-1/2}(x) = \sum_{n=0}^{\infty}\frac{(-1)^n}{n!\Gamma(1/2+n)}\left(\frac{x}{2}\right)^{2n-1/2}.$$

Therefore, a general solution to this differential equation is given by

$$y(x) = c_1J_{1/2}(x) + c_2J_{-1/2}(x).$$

Chapter 8

15. In this problem $\nu = 1$. Thus, one solution to this differential equation is given by

$$y_1(x) = J_1(x) = \sum_{n=0}^{\infty} \frac{(-1)^n}{n!\Gamma(2+n)} \left(\frac{x}{2}\right)^{2n+1}.$$

By the discussion on page 487 of the text, $J_{-1}(x)$ and $J_1(x)$ are linearly dependent. Thus, $J_{-1}(x)$ will not be a second linearly independent solution for this problem. But, a second linearly independent solution will be given by equation (30) on page 488 of the text with $m = 1$. That is we have

$$y_2(x) = Y_1(x) = \lim_{\nu \to 1} \frac{\cos(\nu\pi)J_\nu(x) - J_{-\nu}(x)}{\sin(\nu\pi)}.$$

Therefore, a general solution to this differential equation is given by

$$y(x) = c_1 J_1(x) + c_2 Y_1(x).$$

21. Let $y(x) = x^\nu J_\nu(x)$. Then, by equation (31) on page 488 of the text, we have

$$y'(x) = x^\nu J_{\nu-1}(x).$$

Therefore, we see that

$$\begin{aligned} y''(x) &= D_x[y'(x)] = D_x[x^\nu J_{\nu-1}(x)] = D_x\left\{x\left[x^{\nu-1}J_{\nu-1}(x)\right]\right\} \\ &= x^{\nu-1}J_{\nu-1}(x) + xD_x\left[x^{\nu-1}J_{\nu-1}(x)\right] = x^{\nu-1}J_{\nu-1}(x) + x^\nu J_{\nu-2}(x). \end{aligned}$$

Notice that in order to take the last derivative above, we have again used equation (31) on page 488 of the text. By substituting these expressions into the left-hand side of the first differential equation given in the problem, we obtain

$$\begin{aligned} xy'' + (1-2\nu)y' + xy &= x\left[x^{\nu-1}J_{\nu-1}(x) + x^\nu J_{\nu-2}(x)\right] + (1-2\nu)\left[x^\nu J_{\nu-1}(x)\right] + x\left[x^\nu J_\nu(x)\right] \\ &= x^\nu J_{\nu-1}(x) + x^{\nu+1}J_{\nu-2}(x) + x^\nu J_{\nu-1}(x) - 2\nu x^\nu J_{\nu-1}(x) + x^{\nu+1}J_\nu(x). \quad (8.25) \end{aligned}$$

Notice that by equation (33) on page 488 of the text, we have

$$J_\nu(x) = \frac{2(\nu-1)}{x} J_{\nu-1}(x) - J_{\nu-2}(x)$$

$$\Rightarrow \qquad x^{\nu+1}J_\nu(x) = 2(\nu-1)x^\nu J_{\nu-1}(x) - x^{\nu+1}J_{\nu-2}(x).$$

Replacing $x^{\nu+1}J_\nu(x)$ in equation (8.25) with the above expression and simplifying yields

$$\begin{aligned} xy'' + (1-2\nu)y' + xy &= x^\nu J_{\nu-1}(x) + x^{\nu+1}J_{\nu-2}(x) + x^\nu J_{\nu-1}(x) \\ &\quad -2\nu x^\nu J_{\nu-1}(x) + 2(\nu-1)x^\nu J_{\nu-1}(x) - x^{\nu+1}J_{\nu-2}(x) = 0. \end{aligned}$$

Therefore, $y(x) = x^\nu J_\nu(x)$ is a solution to this type of differential equation.

In order to find a solution to the differential equation $xy'' - 2y' + xy = 0$, we observe that this equation is of the same type as the equation given above with

$$1 - 2\nu = -2 \qquad \Rightarrow \qquad \nu = \frac{3}{2}.$$

Thus, a solution to this equation will be

$$y(x) = x^{3/2}J_{3/2}(x) = x^{3/2}\sum_{n=0}^{\infty}\frac{(-1)^n}{n!\Gamma(5/2+n)}\left(\frac{x}{2}\right)^{2n+3/2}.$$

29. In Legendre polynomials, n is a fixed nonnegative integer. Thus, in the first such polynomial, n equals zero. Therefore, we see that $[n/2] = [0/2] = 0$ and, by equation (43) on page 491 of the text, we have

$$P_0(x) = 2^{-0}\frac{(-1)^0 0!}{0!0!0!}\,x^0 = 1.$$

Similarly, we have

$$\begin{aligned} n=1 \quad &\Rightarrow \quad \left[\frac{1}{2}\right] = 0 \quad \Rightarrow \quad P_1(x) = 2^{-1}\frac{(-1)^0 2!}{1!0!1!}\,x^1 = x, \\ n=2 \quad &\Rightarrow \quad \left[\frac{2}{2}\right] = 1 \quad \Rightarrow \quad P_2(x) = 2^{-2}\left(\frac{(-1)^0 4!}{2!0!2!}\,x^2 + \frac{(-1)^1 2!}{1!1!0!}\,x^0\right) = \frac{3x^2-1}{2}, \\ n=3 \quad &\Rightarrow \quad \left[\frac{3}{2}\right] = 1 \quad \Rightarrow \quad P_3(x) = 2^{-3}\left(\frac{(-1)^0 6!}{3!0!3!}\,x^3 + \frac{(-1)^1 4!}{2!1!1!}\,x^1\right) = \frac{5x^3-3x}{2}, \\ n=4 \quad &\Rightarrow \quad \left[\frac{4}{2}\right] = 2 \quad \Rightarrow \quad P_4(x) = 2^{-4}\left(\frac{(-1)^0 8!}{4!0!4!}\,x^4 + \frac{(-1)^1 6!}{3!1!2!}\,x^2 + \frac{(-1)^2 4!}{2!2!0!}\,x^0\right) \\ &\qquad\qquad\qquad\qquad\qquad\qquad = \frac{35x^4 - 30x^2 + 3}{8}. \end{aligned}$$

37. Since the Taylor series expansion of an analytic function $f(t)$ about $t = 0$ is given by

$$f(t) = \sum_{n=0}^{\infty} \frac{f^{(n)}(0)}{n!}\, t^n ,$$

we see that $H(x)$ is just the nth derivative of $y(t) = e^{2tx-t^2}$ with respect to t evaluated at the point $t = 0$ (treating x as a fixed parameter). Therefore, we have

$$\begin{aligned}
y(t) &= e^{2tx-t^2} && \Rightarrow \quad H_0(x) = y(0) = e^0 = 1,\\
y'(t) &= (2x-2t)e^{2tx-t^2} && \Rightarrow \quad H_1(x) = y'(0) = 2xe^0 = 2x,\\
y''(t) &= \left[-2 + (2x-2t)^2\right] e^{2tx-t^2} && \Rightarrow \quad H_2(x) = y''(0) = \left[-2 + (2x)^2\right] e^0 = 4x^2 - 2,\\
y'''(t) &= \left[-6(2x-2t) + (2x-2t)^3\right] e^{2tx-t^2} && \Rightarrow \quad H_3(x) = y'''(0) = 8x^3 - 12x.
\end{aligned}$$

39. To find the first four Laguerre polynomials, we need to find the first four derivatives of the function $y(x) = x^n e^{-x}$. Therefore, we have

$$\begin{aligned}
y^{(0)}(x) &= x^n e^{-x},\\
y'(x) &= \left(nx^{n-1} - x^n\right) e^{-x},\\
y''(x) &= \left(n(n-1)x^{n-2} - 2nx^{n-1} + x^n\right) e^{-x},\\
y'''(x) &= \left(n(n-1)(n-2)x^{n-3} - 3n(n-1)x^{n-2} + 3nx^{n-1} - x^n\right) e^{-x}.
\end{aligned}$$

Substituting these expressions into Rodrigues's formula and plugging in the appropriate values of n yields

$$\begin{aligned}
L_0(x) &= \frac{e^x}{0!}\, x^0 e^{-x} = 1,\\
L_1(x) &= \frac{e^x}{1!}\left[1x^{1-1} - x^1\right] e^{-x} = 1 - x,\\
L_2(x) &= \frac{e^x}{2!}\left[2(2-1)x^{2-2} - 2\cdot 2x^{2-1} + x^2\right] e^{-x} = \frac{2 - 4x + x^2}{2},\\
L_3(x) &= \frac{e^x}{3!}\left[3(3-1)(3-2)x^{3-3} - 3\cdot 3(3-1)x^{3-2} + 3\cdot 3x^{3-1} - x^3\right] e^{-x}\\
&= \frac{6 - 18x + 9x^2 - x^3}{6}.
\end{aligned}$$

REVIEW PROBLEMS: page 497

1. **(a)** To construct the Taylor polynomials

$$p_n(x) = y(0) + \frac{y'(0)}{1!}x + \frac{y''(0)}{2!}x^2 + \cdots + \frac{y^{(n)}(0)}{n!}x^n$$

approximating the solution to the given initial value problem, we need $y(0)$, $y'(0)$, etc. $y(0)$ is provided by the initial condition, $y(0) = 1$. The value of $y'(0)$ can be deduced from the differential equation itself. We have

$$y'(0) = (0)y(0) - y(0)^2 = (0)(1) - (1)^2 = -1.$$

Differentiating both sides of the given equation, $y' = xy - y^2$, and substituting $x = 0$ into the resulting equation, we get

$$y'' = y + xy' - 2yy'$$
$$\Rightarrow \qquad y''(0) = y(0) + (0)y'(0) - 2y(0)y'(0) = (1) + (0)(-1) - 2(1)(-1) = 3.$$

Differentiating once more yields

$$y''' = y' + y' + xy'' - 2y'y' - 2yy''$$
$$\Rightarrow \qquad y'''(0) = (-1) + (-1) + (0)(3) - 2(-1)(-1) - 2(1)(3) = -10.$$

Thus,

$$p_3(x) = 1 + \frac{-1}{1!}x + \frac{3}{2!}x^2 + \frac{-10}{3!}x^3 = 1 - x + \frac{3x^2}{2} - \frac{5x^3}{3}.$$

(b) The values of $z(0)$ and $z'(0)$ are given. Namely, $z(0) = -1$ and $z'(0) = 1$. Substituting $x = 0$ into the given equation yields

$$z''(0) - (0)^3 z'(0) + (0)z(0)^2 = 0 \qquad \Rightarrow \qquad z''(0) = 0.$$

We now differentiate the given equation and evaluate the result at $x = 0$.

$$z''' - 3x^2 z' - x^3 z'' + z^2 + 2xzz' = 0$$

$$\Rightarrow \qquad z'''(0) = 3(0)^2 z'(0) + (0)^3 z''(0) - z(0)^2 - 2(0)z(0)z'(0) = -1.$$

One more differentiation yields

$$z^{(4)} - 6xz' - 3x^2 z'' - 3x^2 z'' - x^3 z''' + 2zz' + 2zz' + 2xz'z' + 2xzz'' = 0$$

$$\Rightarrow \qquad z^{(4)}(0) = -4z(0)z'(0) = 4.$$

Hence,

$$p_4(x) = -1 + \frac{1}{1!}x + \frac{0}{2!}x^2 + \frac{-1}{3!}x^3 + \frac{4}{4!}x^4 = -1 + x - \frac{x^3}{6} + \frac{x^4}{6}.$$

3. **(a)** Since both $p(x) = x^2$ and $q(x) = -2$ are analytic at $x = 0$, a general solution to the given equation is also analytic at this point. Thus, it has an expansion

$$y = \sum_{k=0}^{\infty} a_k x^k$$

$$\Rightarrow \qquad y' = \sum_{k=1}^{\infty} k a_k x^{k-1}$$

$$\Rightarrow \qquad y'' = \sum_{k=2}^{\infty} k(k-1) a_k x^{k-2}.$$

Substituting these expansions for y, y', and y'' into the original equation yields

$$\sum_{k=2}^{\infty} k(k-1)a_k x^{k-2} + x^2 \sum_{k=1}^{\infty} k a_k x^{k-1} - 2\sum_{k=0}^{\infty} a_k x^k = 0$$

$$\Rightarrow \qquad \sum_{k=2}^{\infty} k(k-1)a_k x^{k-2} + \sum_{k=1}^{\infty} k a_k x^{k+1} - \sum_{k=0}^{\infty} 2a_k x^k = 0.$$

We now shift the indices of summation so that all three sums contain like powers x^n. In the first sum, we let $k - 2 = n$; in the second sum, let $k + 1 = n$; and let $k = n$ in the third sum. This yields

$$\sum_{n=0}^{\infty}(n+2)(n+1)a_{n+2}x^n + \sum_{n=2}^{\infty}(n-1)a_{n-1}x^n - \sum_{n=0}^{\infty} 2a_n x^n = 0.$$

Separating the terms corresponding to $n = 0$ and $n = 1$, and combining the rest under one summation, we obtain

$$(2a_2 - 2a_0) + (6a_3 - 2a_1)x + \sum_{n=2}^{\infty}\left[(n+2)(n+1)a_{n+2} + (n-1)a_{n-1} - 2a_n\right]x^n = 0.$$

Therefore,

$$\begin{aligned}
&2a_2 - 2a_0 = 0, \\
&6a_3 - 2a_1 = 0, \\
&(n+2)(n+1)a_{n+2} + (n-1)a_{n-1} - 2a_n = 0, \quad n \geq 2.
\end{aligned}$$

This yields

$$a_2 = a_0, \qquad a_3 = \frac{a_1}{3}, \qquad \text{and} \qquad a_{n+2} = \frac{2a_n - (n-1)a_{n-1}}{(n+2)(n+1)}, \quad n \geq 2.$$

Hence,

$$\begin{aligned}
y(x) &= a_0 + a_1 x + a_2 x^2 + a_3 x^3 + \cdots = a_0 + a_1 x + a_0 x^2 + \frac{a_1}{3} x^3 + \cdots \\
&= a_0 \left(1 + x^2 + \cdots\right) + a_1 \left(x + \frac{x^3}{3} + \cdots\right).
\end{aligned}$$

5. Clearly, $x = 2$ is an ordinary point for the given equation because $p(x) = x - 2$ and $q(x) = -1$ are analytic everywhere. Thus we seek for a solution of the form

$$w(x) = \sum_{k=0}^{\infty} a_k (x-2)^k .$$

Differentiating this power series yields

$$w'(x) = \sum_{k=1}^{\infty} k a_k (x-2)^{k-1} \qquad \text{and} \qquad w''(x) = \sum_{k=2}^{\infty} k(k-1) a_k (x-2)^{k-2} .$$

Therefore,

$$\begin{aligned}
w'' + (x-2)w' - w = \sum_{k=2}^{\infty} k(k-1)a_k(x-2)^{k-2} + (x-2)\sum_{k=1}^{\infty} k a_k (x-2)^{k-1} \\
- \sum_{k=0}^{\infty} a_k (x-2)^k = 0
\end{aligned}$$

$$\Rightarrow \qquad \sum_{k=2}^{\infty} k(k-1)a_k(x-2)^{k-2} + \sum_{k=1}^{\infty} k a_k (x-2)^k - \sum_{k=0}^{\infty} a_k (x-2)^k = 0.$$

Shifting the index of summation in the first sum yields

$$\sum_{n=0}^{\infty} (n+2)(n+1)a_{n+2}(x-2)^n + \sum_{n=1}^{\infty} n a_n (x-2)^n - \sum_{n=0}^{\infty} a_n (x-2)^n = 0$$

$$\Rightarrow \quad \left[2a_2 + \sum_{n=1}^{\infty}(n+2)(n+1)a_{n+2}(x-2)^n\right] + \sum_{n=1}^{\infty} na_n(x-2)^n - \left[a_0 + \sum_{n=1}^{\infty} a_n(x-2)^n\right] = 0$$

$$\Rightarrow \quad (2a_2 - a_0) + \sum_{n=1}^{\infty}\left[(n+2)(n+1)a_{n+2} + na_n - a_n\right](x-2)^n = 0,$$

where we have separated the terms corresponding to $n = 0$ and collected the rest under one summation. In order that the above power series equals zero, it must have all zero coefficients. Thus,

$$\begin{aligned} &2a_2 - a_0 = 0, \\ &(n+2)(n+1)a_{n+2} + na_n - a_n = 0, \quad n \geq 1 \end{aligned}$$

$$\Rightarrow \quad \begin{aligned} &a_2 = a_0/2\,, \\ &a_{n+2} = (1-n)a_n/[(n+2)(n+1)]\,, \quad n \geq 1. \end{aligned}$$

For $n = 1$ and $n = 2$, the last equation gives $a_3 = 0$ and $a_4 = -a_2/12 = -a_0/24$. Therefore,

$$\begin{aligned} w(x) &= a_0 + a_1(x-2) + a_2(x-2)^2 + a_3(x-2)^3 + a_4(x-2)^4 + \cdots \\ &= a_0 + a_1(x-2) + \frac{a_0}{2}(x-2)^2 + (0)(x-2)^3 - \frac{1}{24}a_0(x-2)^4 + \cdots \\ &= a_0\left[1 + \frac{(x-2)^2}{2} - \frac{(x-2)^4}{24} + \cdots\right] + a_1(x-2). \end{aligned}$$

7. (a) The point $x = 0$ is a regular singular point for the given equation because

$$p(x) = \frac{-5x}{x^2} = -\frac{5}{x}, \qquad q(x) = \frac{9-x}{x^2},$$

and the limits

$$\begin{aligned} p_0 &= \lim_{x\to 0} xp(x) = \lim_{x\to 0}(-5) = -5, \\ q_0 &= \lim_{x\to 0} x^2 q(x) = \lim_{x\to 0}(9-x) = 9 \end{aligned}$$

exist. The indicial equation (3) on page 461 of the text becomes

$$r(r-1) + (-5)r + 9 = 0 \quad \Rightarrow \quad r^2 - 6r + 9 = 0 \quad \Rightarrow \quad (r-3)^2 = 0.$$

Hence, $r = 3$ is the exponent of the singularity $x = 0$, and a solution to the given differential equation has the form

$$y = x^3 \sum_{k=0}^{\infty} a_k x^k = \sum_{k=0}^{\infty} a_k x^{k+3} .$$

Substituting this power series into the given equation yields

$$\begin{aligned}
& x^2 \left(\sum_{k=0}^{\infty} a_k x^{k+3} \right)'' - 5x \left(\sum_{k=0}^{\infty} a_k x^{k+3} \right)' + (9 - x) \left(\sum_{k=0}^{\infty} a_k x^{k+3} \right) = 0 \\
\Rightarrow \quad & \sum_{k=0}^{\infty} (k+3)(k+2) a_k x^{k+3} - \sum_{k=0}^{\infty} 5(k+3) a_k x^{k+3} + (9 - x) \sum_{k=0}^{\infty} a_k x^{k+3} = 0 \\
\Rightarrow \quad & \sum_{k=0}^{\infty} \left[(k+3)(k+2) - 5(k+3) + 9 \right] a_k x^{k+3} - \sum_{k=0}^{\infty} a_k x^{k+4} = 0 \\
\Rightarrow \quad & \sum_{k=0}^{\infty} k^2 a_k x^{k+3} - \sum_{k=0}^{\infty} a_k x^{k+4} = 0 \\
\Rightarrow \quad & \sum_{n=1}^{\infty} n^2 a_n x^{n+3} - \sum_{n=1}^{\infty} a_{n-1} x^{n+3} = 0 \\
\Rightarrow \quad & \sum_{n=1}^{\infty} \left(n^2 a_n - a_{n-1} \right) x^{n+3} = 0 .
\end{aligned}$$

Thus,

$$n^2 a_n - a_{n-1} = 0 \qquad \text{or} \qquad a_n = \frac{a_{n-1}}{n^2} , \qquad n \geq 1.$$

This recurrence relation yields

$$\begin{aligned}
n = 1: &\quad a_1 = a_0/(1)^2 = a_0 , \\
n = 2: &\quad a_2 = a_1/(2)^2 = a_0/4 , \\
n = 3: &\quad a_3 = a_2/(3)^2 = (a_0/4)/9 = a_0/36 .
\end{aligned}$$

Therefore,

$$\begin{aligned}
y(x) &= x^3 \left(a_0 + a_1 x + a_2 x^2 + a_3 x^3 + \cdots \right) \\
&= x^3 \left(a_0 + a_0 x + \frac{a_0}{4} x^2 + \frac{a_0}{36} x^3 + \cdots \right) = a_0 \left(x^3 + x^4 + \frac{x^5}{4} + \frac{x^6}{36} + \cdots \right) .
\end{aligned}$$

CHAPTER 9: Matrix Methods for Linear Systems

EXERCISES 9.1: Introduction, page 507

3. We start by expressing right-hand sides of all equations as dot products.

$$x+y+z=[1,1,1]\cdot[x,y,z],\quad 2z-x=[-1,0,2]\cdot[x,y,z],\quad 4y=[0,4,0]\cdot[x,y,z].$$

Thus, by definition of the product of a matrix and column vector, the matrix form is given by

$$\begin{bmatrix} x \\ y \\ z \end{bmatrix}' = \begin{bmatrix} 1 & 1 & 1 \\ -1 & 0 & 2 \\ 0 & 4 & 0 \end{bmatrix} \begin{bmatrix} x \\ y \\ z \end{bmatrix}.$$

7. First we have to express the second derivative, y'', as a first derivative in order to rewrite the equation as a first order system. Denoting y' by v we get

$$\begin{aligned} y' &= v, \\ mv' + bv + ky &= 0 \end{aligned} \qquad \text{or} \qquad \begin{aligned} y' &= v, \\ v' &= -\frac{k}{m}\,y - \frac{b}{m}\,v\,. \end{aligned}$$

Expressing the right-hand side of each equation as a dot product, we obtain

$$v=[0,1]\cdot[y,v],\qquad -\frac{k}{m}\,y-\frac{b}{m}\,v=\left[-\frac{k}{m},-\frac{b}{m}\right]\cdot[y,v].$$

Thus, the matrix form of the system is

$$\begin{bmatrix} y \\ v \end{bmatrix}' = \begin{bmatrix} 0 & 1 \\ -k/m & -b/m \end{bmatrix} \begin{bmatrix} y \\ v \end{bmatrix}.$$

11. Introducing the auxiliary variables

$$x_1=x,\quad x_2=x',\quad x_3=y,\quad x_4=y'\,,$$

we can rewrite the given system in normal form:

$$\begin{aligned} x_1' &= x_2 \\ x_3' &= x_4 \\ x_2' + 3x_1 + 2x_3 &= 0 \\ x_4' - 2x_1 &= 0 \end{aligned} \qquad \text{or} \qquad \begin{aligned} x_1' &= x_2 \\ x_2' &= -3x_1 - 2x_3 \\ x_3' &= x_4 \\ x_4' &= 2x_1 \,. \end{aligned}$$

Since

$$\begin{aligned} x_2 &= [0,1,0,0] \cdot [x_1,x_2,x_3,x_4], & -3x_1 - 2x_3 &= [-3,0,-2,0] \cdot [x_1,x_2,x_3,x_4], \\ x_4 &= [0,0,0,1] \cdot [x_1,x_2,x_3,x_4], & 2x_1 &= [2,0,0,0] \cdot [x_1,x_2,x_3,x_4], \end{aligned}$$

the matrix is given by

$$\begin{bmatrix} x_1 \\ x_2 \\ x_3 \\ x_4 \end{bmatrix}' = \begin{bmatrix} 0 & 1 & 0 & 0 \\ -3 & 0 & -2 & 0 \\ 0 & 0 & 0 & 1 \\ 2 & 0 & 0 & 0 \end{bmatrix} \begin{bmatrix} x_1 \\ x_2 \\ x_3 \\ x_4 \end{bmatrix}.$$

EXERCISES 9.2: Review 1: Linear Algebraic Equations, page 512

3. By subtracting 2 times the first equation from the second, we eliminate x_1 from the latter. Similarly, x_1 is eliminated from the third equation by subtracting the first equation from it. So we get

$$\begin{aligned} x_1 + 2x_2 + x_3 &= -3, \\ -3x_3 &= 6, \\ x_2 - 3x_3 &= 6 \end{aligned} \qquad \begin{gathered} \text{or} \\ \text{(interchanging last two equations)} \end{gathered} \qquad \begin{aligned} x_1 + 2x_2 + x_3 &= -3, \\ x_2 - 3x_3 &= 6, \\ x_3 &= -2. \end{aligned}$$

The second unknown, x_2, can be eliminated from the first equation by subtracting 2 times the first one from it:

$$\begin{aligned} x_1 \qquad + 7x_3 &= -15, \\ x_2 - 3x_3 &= 6, \\ x_3 &= -2. \end{aligned}$$

Finally, we eliminate x_3 from the first two equations by adding (-7) times and 3 times, respectively, the third equation. This gives

$$\begin{aligned} x_1 &= -1, \\ x_2 &= 0, \\ x_3 &= -2. \end{aligned}$$

7. Subtracting 3 times the first equation from the second equation yields

$$\begin{aligned} -x_1 + 3x_2 &= 0, \\ 0 &= 0. \end{aligned}$$

The last equation is trivially satisfied, so we ignore it. Thus, just one equation remains:

$$-x_1 + 3x_2 = 0 \qquad \Rightarrow \qquad x_1 = 3x_2\,.$$

Choosing x_2 as a free variable, we get $x_1 = 3s$, $x_2 = s$, where s is any number.

9. We eliminate x_1 from the first equation by adding $(1-i)$ times the second equation to it:

$$\begin{aligned} [2-(1+i)(1-i)]x_2 &= 0, \\ -x_1 - (1+i)x_2 &= 0. \end{aligned}$$

Since $(1-i)(1+i) = 1^2 - i^2 = 1 - (-1) = 2$, we obtain

$$\begin{aligned} 0 &= 0, \\ -x_1 - (1+i)x_2 &= 0 \end{aligned} \qquad \Rightarrow \qquad x_2 = -\frac{1}{1+i}\,x_1 = \frac{-1+i}{2}\,x_1\,.$$

Assigning an arbitrary complex value to x_1, say $2s$, we see that the system has infinitely many solutions given by

$$x_1 = 2s, \qquad x_2 = (-1+i)s, \qquad \text{where } s \text{ is any complex number.}$$

11. It is slightly more convenient to put the last equation at the top:

$$\begin{aligned} -x_1 + x_2 + 5x_3 &= 0, \\ 2x_1 + \phantom{x_2 + 5{}} x_3 &= -1, \\ -3x_1 + x_2 + 4x_3 &= 1. \end{aligned}$$

We then eliminate x_1 from the second equation by adding 2 times the first one to it; and by subtracting 3 times the first equation from the third, we eliminate x_1 in the latter.

$$\begin{aligned} -x_1 + x_2 + \ 5x_3 &= \ \ 0, \\ -2x_2 - 11x_3 &= \ \ 1, \\ 2x_2 + 11x_3 &= -1. \end{aligned}$$

To make the computations more convenient, we multiply the first equation by 2.

$$\begin{aligned} -2x_1 + 2x_2 + 10x_3 &= \ \ 0, \\ -2x_2 - 11x_3 &= \ \ 1, \\ 2x_2 + 11x_3 &= -1. \end{aligned}$$

Now we add the second equation to each of the remaining, and obtain

$$\begin{aligned} -2x_1 \qquad\quad - x_3 &= 1, \\ -2x_2 - 11x_3 &= 1, \\ 0 &= 0 \end{aligned} \qquad \text{or} \qquad \begin{aligned} -2x_1 \qquad\quad - x_3 &= 1, \\ -2x_2 - 11x_3 &= 1. \end{aligned}$$

Choosing x_3 as free variable, i.e., $x_3 = s$, yields $x_1 = -(s+1)/2$, $x_2 = -(11s+1)/2$, $-\infty < s < \infty$.

13. The given system can be written in the equivalent form

$$\begin{aligned} (2-r)x_1 - 3x_2 &= 0, \\ x_1 - (2+r)x_2 &= 0. \end{aligned}$$

The variable x_1 can be eliminated from the first equation by subtracting $(2-r)$ times the second equation:

$$\begin{aligned} [-3 + (2-r)(2+r)]x_2 &= 0, \\ x_1 - (2+r)x_2 &= 0 \end{aligned} \qquad \text{or} \qquad \begin{aligned} (1-r^2)\,x_2 &= 0, \\ x_1 - (2+r)x_2 &= 0. \end{aligned}$$

If $1 - r^2 \neq 0$, i.e., $r \neq \pm 1$, then the first equation implies $x_2 = 0$. Substituting this into the second equation, we get x_1. Thus, the given system has a unique (zero) solution for any $r \neq \pm 1$, in particular, for $r = 2$.

If $r = 1$ or $r = -1$, then the first equation in the latter system becomes trivial $0 = 0$, and the system degenerates to

$$x_1 - (2+r)x_2 = 0 \qquad \Rightarrow \qquad x_1 = (2+r)x_2 .$$

Therefore, there are infinitely many solutions to the given system of the form

$$x_1 = (2+r)s, \qquad x_2 = s, \qquad s \in (-\infty, \infty), \quad r = \pm 1 .$$

In particular, for $r = 1$ we obtain

$$x_1 = 3s, \qquad x_2 = s, \qquad s \in (-\infty, \infty).$$

EXERCISES 9.3: Review 2: Matrices and Vectors, page 521

5. (a) $\mathbf{AB} = \begin{bmatrix} 1 & -2 \\ 2 & -3 \end{bmatrix} \begin{bmatrix} 1 & 0 \\ 1 & 1 \end{bmatrix} = \begin{bmatrix} 1-2 & 0-2 \\ 2-3 & 0-3 \end{bmatrix} = \begin{bmatrix} -1 & -2 \\ -1 & -3 \end{bmatrix}.$

(b) $\mathbf{AC} = \begin{bmatrix} 1 & -2 \\ 2 & -3 \end{bmatrix} \begin{bmatrix} -1 & 1 \\ 2 & 1 \end{bmatrix} = \begin{bmatrix} -1-4 & 1-2 \\ -2-6 & 2-3 \end{bmatrix} = \begin{bmatrix} -5 & -1 \\ -8 & -1 \end{bmatrix}.$

(c) By the Distributive Property of matrix multiplication given on page 515 of the text, we have

$$\mathbf{A}\left(\mathbf{B}+\mathbf{C}\right) = \mathbf{AB} + \mathbf{AC} = \begin{bmatrix} -1 & -2 \\ -1 & -3 \end{bmatrix} + \begin{bmatrix} -5 & -1 \\ -8 & -1 \end{bmatrix} = \begin{bmatrix} -6 & -3 \\ -9 & -4 \end{bmatrix}.$$

13. Authors note: We will use $R_i + cR_j \to R_k$ to denote the row operation "*add row i to c times row j and place the result into row k.*" We will use $cR_j \to R_k$ to denote the row operation "*multiply row j by c and place the result into row k.*"

As in Example 1 on page 517 of the text, we will perform row-reduction on the matrix $[\mathbf{A}|\mathbf{I}]$. Thus, we have

$$[\mathbf{A}|\mathbf{I}] \quad = \quad \left[\begin{array}{ccc|ccc} -2 & -1 & 1 & 1 & 0 & 0 \\ 2 & 1 & 0 & 0 & 1 & 0 \\ 3 & 1 & -1 & 0 & 0 & 1 \end{array}\right]$$

$$\begin{array}{r} R_2 + R_1 \to R_2 \\ 2R_3 + 3R_1 \to R_3 \end{array} \quad \left[\begin{array}{rrr|rrr} -2 & -1 & 1 & 1 & 0 & 0 \\ 0 & 0 & 1 & 1 & 1 & 0 \\ 0 & -1 & 1 & 3 & 0 & 2 \end{array}\right]$$

$$R_1 - R_3 \to R_1 \quad \left[\begin{array}{rrr|rrr} -2 & 0 & 0 & -2 & 0 & -2 \\ 0 & 0 & 1 & 1 & 1 & 0 \\ 0 & -1 & 1 & 3 & 0 & 2 \end{array}\right]$$

$$\begin{array}{r} -R_1/2 \to R_1 \\ R_3 \to R_2 \\ R_2 \to R_3 \end{array} \quad \left[\begin{array}{rrr|rrr} 1 & 0 & 0 & 1 & 0 & 1 \\ 0 & -1 & 1 & 3 & 0 & 2 \\ 0 & 0 & 1 & 1 & 1 & 0 \end{array}\right]$$

$$-R_2 + R_3 \to R_2 \quad \left[\begin{array}{rrr|rrr} 1 & 0 & 0 & 1 & 0 & 1 \\ 0 & 1 & 0 & -2 & 1 & -2 \\ 0 & 0 & 1 & 1 & 1 & 0 \end{array}\right].$$

Therefore, the inverse matrix is

$$\mathbf{A}^{-1} = \begin{bmatrix} 1 & 0 & 1 \\ -2 & 1 & -2 \\ 1 & 1 & 0 \end{bmatrix}.$$

To check the algebra, it's a good idea to multiply $\mathbf{A}$ by $\mathbf{A}^{-1}$ to verify that the product is the identity matrix.

19. Authors note: We will use $R_i + cR_j \to R_k$ to denote the row operation "*add row i to c times row j and place the result into row k.*" We will use $cR_j \to R_k$ to denote the row operation "*multiply row j by c and place the result into row k.*"

To find the inverse matrix $\mathbf{X}^{-1}(t)$, we will again use the method of Example 1 on page 517 of the text. Thus, we start with

$$[\mathbf{X}(t)|\mathbf{I}] = \left[\begin{array}{ccc|ccc} e^t & e^{-t} & e^{2t} & 1 & 0 & 0 \\ e^t & -e^{-t} & 2e^{2t} & 0 & 1 & 0 \\ e^t & e^{-t} & 4e^{2t} & 0 & 0 & 1 \end{array}\right]$$

$$\begin{array}{r} R_2 - R_1 \to R_2 \\ R_3 - R_1 \to R_3 \end{array} \quad \left[\begin{array}{ccc|ccc} e^t & e^{-t} & e^{2t} & 1 & 0 & 0 \\ 0 & -2e^{-t} & e^{2t} & -1 & 1 & 0 \\ 0 & 0 & 3e^{2t} & -1 & 0 & 1 \end{array}\right]$$

$$\begin{array}{r} -R_2/2 \to R_2 \\ R_3/3 \to R_3 \end{array} \quad \left[\begin{array}{ccc|ccc} e^t & e^{-t} & e^{2t} & 1 & 0 & 0 \\ 0 & e^{-t} & -e^{2t}/2 & 1/2 & -1/2 & 0 \\ 0 & 0 & e^{2t} & -1/3 & 0 & 1/3 \end{array}\right]$$

$$\begin{array}{r} R_1 - R_3 \to R_1 \\ R_2 - R_3/2 \to R_2 \end{array} \quad \left[\begin{array}{ccc|ccc} e^t & e^{-t} & 0 & 4/3 & 0 & -1/3 \\ 0 & e^{-t} & 0 & 1/3 & -1/2 & 1/6 \\ 0 & 0 & e^{2t} & -1/3 & 0 & 1/3 \end{array}\right]$$

$$R_1 - R_2 \to R_1 \quad \left[\begin{array}{ccc|ccc} e^t & 0 & 0 & 1 & 1/2 & -1/2 \\ 0 & e^{-t} & 0 & 1/3 & -1/2 & 1/6 \\ 0 & 0 & e^{2t} & -1/3 & 0 & 1/3 \end{array}\right]$$

$$\begin{array}{r} e^{-t}R_1 \to R_1 \\ e^{t}R_2 \to R_2 \\ e^{-2t}R_3 \to R_3 \end{array} \quad \left[\begin{array}{ccc|ccc} 1 & 0 & 0 & e^{-t} & e^{-t}/2 & -e^{-t}/2 \\ 0 & 1 & 0 & e^{t}/3 & -e^{t}/2 & e^{t}/6 \\ 0 & 0 & 1 & -e^{-2t}/3 & 0 & e^{-2t}/3 \end{array}\right].$$

Thus, the inverse matrix $\mathbf{X}^{-1}(t)$ is given by the matrix

$$\mathbf{X}^{-1}(t) = \begin{bmatrix} e^{-t} & e^{-t}/2 & -e^{-t}/2 \\ e^{t}/3 & -e^{t}/2 & e^{t}/6 \\ -e^{-2t}/3 & 0 & e^{-2t}/3 \end{bmatrix}.$$

23. We will calculate this determinant by first finding its cofactor expansion about row 1. Therefore, we have

$$\begin{vmatrix} 1 & 0 & 0 \\ 3 & 1 & 2 \\ 1 & 5 & -2 \end{vmatrix} = (1)\begin{vmatrix} 1 & 2 \\ 5 & -2 \end{vmatrix} - 0 + 0 = -2 - 10 = -12.$$

37. We first calculate $\mathbf{X}'(t)$ by differentiating each entry of $\mathbf{X}(t)$. Therefore, we have

$$\mathbf{X}'(t) = \begin{bmatrix} 2e^{2t} & 3e^{3t} \\ -2e^{2t} & -6e^{3t} \end{bmatrix}.$$

Thus, substituting the matrix $\mathbf{X}(t)$ into the differential equation and performing matrix multiplication yields

$$\begin{bmatrix} 2e^{2t} & 3e^{3t} \\ -2e^{2t} & -6e^{3t} \end{bmatrix} = \begin{bmatrix} 1 & -1 \\ 2 & 4 \end{bmatrix} \begin{bmatrix} e^{2t} & e^{3t} \\ -e^{2t} & -2e^{3t} \end{bmatrix} = \begin{bmatrix} e^{2t}+e^{2t} & e^{3t}+2e^{3t} \\ 2e^{2t}-4e^{2t} & 2e^{3t}-8e^{3t} \end{bmatrix}.$$

Since this equation is true, we see that $\mathbf{X}(t)$ does satisfy the given differential equation.

39. **(a)** To calculate $\int \mathbf{A}(t)\,dt$, we integrate each entry of $\mathbf{A}(t)$ to obtain

$$\int \mathbf{A}(t)\,dt = \begin{bmatrix} \int t\,dt & \int e^{\cdot} dt \\ \int 1\,dt & \int e^{\cdot} dt \end{bmatrix} = \begin{bmatrix} t^2/2 + c_1 & e^t + c_2 \\ t + c_3 & e^t + c_4 \end{bmatrix}.$$

(b) Taking the definite integral of each entry of $\mathbf{B}(t)$ yields

$$\int_0^1 \mathbf{B}(t)\,dt = \begin{bmatrix} \int_0^1 \cos t\,dt & -\int_0^1 \sin t\,dt \\ \int_0^1 \sin t\,dt & \int_0^1 \cos t\,dt \end{bmatrix} = \begin{bmatrix} \sin t\,\big|_0^1 & \cos t\,\big|_0^1 \\ -\cos t\,\big|_0^1 & \sin t\,\big|_0^1 \end{bmatrix} = \begin{bmatrix} \sin 1 & \cos 1 - 1 \\ 1 - \cos 1 & \sin 1 \end{bmatrix}.$$

(c) By the product rule on page 521 of the text, we see that

$$\frac{d}{dt}[\mathbf{A}(t)\mathbf{B}(t)] = \mathbf{A}(t)\mathbf{B}'(t) + \mathbf{A}'(t)\mathbf{B}(t).$$

Therefore, we first calculate $\mathbf{A}'(t)$ and $\mathbf{B}'(t)$ by differentiating each entry of $\mathbf{A}(t)$ and $\mathbf{B}(t)$, respectively, to obtain

$$\mathbf{A}'(t) = \begin{bmatrix} 1 & e^t \\ 0 & e^t \end{bmatrix} \quad \text{and} \quad \mathbf{B}'(t) = \begin{bmatrix} -\sin t & -\cos t \\ \cos t & -\sin t \end{bmatrix}.$$

Hence, by matrix multiplication we have

$$\begin{aligned} \frac{d}{dt}[\mathbf{A}(t)\mathbf{B}(t)] &= \mathbf{A}(t)\mathbf{B}'(t) + \mathbf{A}'(t)\mathbf{B}(t) \\ &= \begin{bmatrix} t & e^t \\ 1 & e^t \end{bmatrix} \begin{bmatrix} -\sin t & -\cos t \\ \cos t & -\sin t \end{bmatrix} + \begin{bmatrix} 1 & e^t \\ 0 & e^t \end{bmatrix} \begin{bmatrix} \cos t & -\sin t \\ \sin t & \cos t \end{bmatrix} \\ &= \begin{bmatrix} e^t \cos t - t\sin t & -t\cos t - e^t \sin t \\ e^t \cos t - \sin t & -\cos t - e^t \sin t \end{bmatrix} + \begin{bmatrix} \cos t + e^t \sin t & e^t \cos t - \sin t \\ e^t \sin t & e^t \cos t \end{bmatrix} \\ &= \begin{bmatrix} (1+e^t)\cos t + (e^t - t)\sin t & (e^t - t)\cos t - (e^t + 1)\sin t \\ e^t \cos t + (e^t - 1)\sin t & (e^t - 1)\cos t - e^t \sin t \end{bmatrix}. \end{aligned}$$

EXERCISES 9.4: Linear Systems in Normal Form, page 530

1. To write this system in matrix form, we will define the vectors $\mathbf{x}(t) = \text{col}[x(t), y(t)]$ (which means that $\mathbf{x}'(t) = \text{col}[x'(t), y'(t)]$) and $\mathbf{f}(t) = \text{col}[t^2, e^t]$, and the matrix

$$\mathbf{A}(t) = \begin{bmatrix} 3 & -1 \\ -1 & 2 \end{bmatrix}.$$

Thus, this system becomes the equation in matrix form given by

$$\begin{bmatrix} x'(t) \\ y'(t) \end{bmatrix} = \begin{bmatrix} 3 & -1 \\ -1 & 2 \end{bmatrix} \begin{bmatrix} x(t) \\ y(t) \end{bmatrix} + \begin{bmatrix} t^2 \\ e^t \end{bmatrix}.$$

We can see that this equation is equivalent to the original system by performing matrix multiplication and addition to obtain the vector equation

$$\begin{bmatrix} x'(t) \\ y'(t) \end{bmatrix} = \begin{bmatrix} 3x(t) - y(t) \\ -x(t) + 2y(t) \end{bmatrix} + \begin{bmatrix} t^2 \\ e^t \end{bmatrix} = \begin{bmatrix} 3x(t) - y(t) + t^2 \\ -x(t) + 2y(t) + e^t \end{bmatrix}.$$

Since two vectors are equal only when their corresponding components are equal, we see that this vector equation implies that

$$x'(t) = 3x(t) - y(t) + t^2\,,$$
$$y'(t) = -x(t) + 2y(t) + e^t\,,$$

which is the original system.

5. This equation can be written as a first order system in normal form by using the substitutions $x_1(t) = y(t)$ and $x_2(t) = y'(t)$. With these substitutions this differential equation becomes the system

$$x_1'(t) = 0 \cdot x_1(t) + x_2(t),$$
$$x_2'(t) = 10x_1(t) + 3x_2(t) + \sin t.$$

We can then write this system as a matrix differential equation by defining the vectors $\mathbf{x}(t) = \text{col}[x_1(t), x_2(t)]$ (which means that $\mathbf{x}'(t) = \text{col}[x_1'(t), x_2'(t)]$), $\mathbf{f}(t) = \text{col}[0, \sin t]$, and the matrix

$$\mathbf{A} = \begin{bmatrix} 0 & 1 \\ 10 & 3 \end{bmatrix}.$$

Hence, the system above in normal form becomes the differential equation given in matrix form by

$$\begin{bmatrix} x_1'(t) \\ x_2'(t) \end{bmatrix} = \begin{bmatrix} 0 & 1 \\ 10 & 3 \end{bmatrix} \begin{bmatrix} x_1(t) \\ x_2(t) \end{bmatrix} + \begin{bmatrix} 0 \\ \sin t \end{bmatrix}.$$

(As in Problem 1 above, we can see that this equation in matrix form is equivalent to the system by performing matrix multiplication and addition and then noting that corresponding components of equal vectors are equal.)

7. This equation can be written as a first order system in normal form by using the substitutions $x_1(t) = w(t)$, $x_2(t) = w'(t)$, $x_3(t) = w''(t)$, and $x_4(t) = w'''(t)$. With these substitutions this differential equation becomes the system

$$\begin{aligned} x_1'(t) &= 0 \cdot x_1(t) + x_2(t) + 0 \cdot x_3(t) + 0 \cdot x_4(t), \\ x_2'(t) &= 0 \cdot x_1(t) + 0 \cdot x_2(t) + x_3(t) + 0 \cdot x_4(t), \\ x_3'(t) &= 0 \cdot x_1(t) + 0 \cdot x_2(t) + 0 \cdot x_3(t) + x_4(t), \\ x_4'(t) &= -x_1(t) + 0 \cdot x_2(t) + 0 \cdot x_3(t) + 0 \cdot x_4(t) + t^2 . \end{aligned}$$

We can then write this system as a matrix differential equation $\mathbf{x}' = \mathbf{A}\mathbf{x}$ by defining the vectors $\mathbf{x}(t) = \text{col}[x_1(t), x_2(t), x_3(t), x_4(t)]$ (which means that $\mathbf{x}'(t) = \text{col}[x_1'(t), x_2'(t), x_3'(t), x_4'(t)]$), $\mathbf{f}(t) = \text{col}[0, 0, 0, t^2]$, and the matrix

$$\mathbf{A} = \begin{bmatrix} 0 & 1 & 0 & 0 \\ 0 & 0 & 1 & 0 \\ 0 & 0 & 0 & 1 \\ -1 & 0 & 0 & 0 \end{bmatrix}.$$

That is, the given fourth order differential equation is equivalent to the matrix system

$$\begin{bmatrix} x_1'(t) \\ x_2'(t) \\ x_3'(t) \\ x_4'(t) \end{bmatrix} = \begin{bmatrix} 0 & 1 & 0 & 0 \\ 0 & 0 & 1 & 0 \\ 0 & 0 & 0 & 1 \\ -1 & 0 & 0 & 0 \end{bmatrix} \begin{bmatrix} x_1(t) \\ x_2(t) \\ x_3(t) \\ x_4(t) \end{bmatrix} + \begin{bmatrix} 0 \\ 0 \\ 0 \\ t^2 \end{bmatrix}.$$

17. Notice that by scalar multiplication these vector functions can be written as

$$\begin{bmatrix} e^{2t} \\ 0 \\ 5e^{2t} \end{bmatrix}, \quad \begin{bmatrix} e^{2t} \\ e^{2t} \\ -e^{2t} \end{bmatrix}, \quad \begin{bmatrix} 0 \\ e^{3t} \\ 0 \end{bmatrix}.$$

Thus, as in Example 2 on page 526 of the text, we will prove that these vectors are linearly independent by showing that the only way that we can have

$$c_1 \begin{bmatrix} e^{2t} \\ 0 \\ 5e^{2t} \end{bmatrix} + c_2 \begin{bmatrix} e^{2t} \\ e^{2t} \\ -e^{2t} \end{bmatrix} + c_3 \begin{bmatrix} 0 \\ e^{3t} \\ 0 \end{bmatrix} = \mathbf{0}$$

for all t in $(-\infty, \infty)$ is for $c_1 = c_2 = c_3 = 0$. Since the equation above must be true for all t, it must be true for $t = 0$. Thus, c_1, c_2, and c_3 must satisfy

$$c_1 \begin{bmatrix} 1 \\ 0 \\ 5 \end{bmatrix} + c_2 \begin{bmatrix} 1 \\ 1 \\ -1 \end{bmatrix} + c_3 \begin{bmatrix} 0 \\ 1 \\ 0 \end{bmatrix} = \mathbf{0},$$

which is equivalent to the system

$$\begin{aligned} c_1 + c_2 &= 0, \\ c_2 + c_3 &= 0, \\ 5c_1 - c_2 &= 0. \end{aligned}$$

By solving the first and last of these equations simultaneously, we see that $c_1 = c_2 = 0$. Substituting these values into the second equation above yields $c_3 = 0$. Therefore, the original set of vectors must be linearly independent on the interval $(-\infty, \infty)$.

21. Since it is given that these vectors are solutions to the system $\mathbf{x}'(t) = \mathbf{A}\mathbf{x}(t)$, in order to determine whether they are linearly independent, we need only calculate their Wronskian. If their Wronskian is never zero, then these vectors are linearly independent and so form a fundamental solution set. If the Wronskian is identically zero, then the vectors are linearly dependent, and they do not form a fundamental solution set. Thus, we observe

$$W[\mathbf{x}_1, \mathbf{x}_2, \mathbf{x}_3](t) = \begin{vmatrix} e^{-t} & e^{t} & e^{3t} \\ 2e^{-t} & 0 & -e^{3t} \\ e^{-t} & e^{t} & 2e^{3t} \end{vmatrix}$$

$$= e^{-t}\begin{vmatrix} 0 & -e^{3t} \\ e^t & 2e^{3t} \end{vmatrix} - e^t\begin{vmatrix} 2e^{-t} & -e^{3t} \\ e^{-t} & 2e^{3t} \end{vmatrix} + e^{3t}\begin{vmatrix} 2e^{-t} & 0 \\ e^{-t} & e^t \end{vmatrix}$$

$$= e^{-t}\left(0+e^{4t}\right) - e^t\left(4e^{2t}+e^{2t}\right) + e^{3t}(2-0) = -2e^{3t} \neq 0,$$

where we have used cofactors to calculate the determinant. Therefore, this set of vectors is linearly independent and so forms a fundamental solution set for the system. Thus, a fundamental matrix is given by

$$\mathbf{X}(t) = \begin{bmatrix} e^{-t} & e^t & e^{3t} \\ 2e^{-t} & 0 & -e^{3t} \\ e^{-t} & e^t & 2e^{3t} \end{bmatrix},$$

and a general solution of the system will be

$$\mathbf{x}(t) = \mathbf{X}(t)\mathbf{c} = c_1\begin{bmatrix} e^{-t} \\ 2e^{-t} \\ e^{-t} \end{bmatrix} + c_2\begin{bmatrix} e^t \\ 0 \\ e^t \end{bmatrix} + c_3\begin{bmatrix} e^{3t} \\ -e^{3t} \\ 2e^{3t} \end{bmatrix}.$$

27. In order to show that $\mathbf{X}(t)$ is a fundamental matrix for the system, we must first show that each of its column vectors is a solution. Thus, we substitute each of the vectors

$$\mathbf{x}_1(t) = \begin{bmatrix} 6e^{-t} \\ -e^{-t} \\ -5e^{-t} \end{bmatrix}, \qquad \mathbf{x}_2(t) = \begin{bmatrix} -3e^{-2t} \\ e^{-2t} \\ e^{-2t} \end{bmatrix}, \qquad \mathbf{x}_3(t) = \begin{bmatrix} 2e^{3t} \\ e^{3t} \\ e^{3t} \end{bmatrix}$$

into the given system to obtain

$$\mathbf{A}\mathbf{x}_1(t) = \begin{bmatrix} 0 & 6 & 0 \\ 1 & 0 & 1 \\ 1 & 1 & 0 \end{bmatrix}\begin{bmatrix} 6e^{-t} \\ -e^{-t} \\ -5e^{-t} \end{bmatrix} = \begin{bmatrix} -6e^{-t} \\ e^{-t} \\ 5e^{-t} \end{bmatrix} = \mathbf{x}_1'(t),$$

$$\mathbf{A}\mathbf{x}_2(t) = \begin{bmatrix} 0 & 6 & 0 \\ 1 & 0 & 1 \\ 1 & 1 & 0 \end{bmatrix}\begin{bmatrix} -3e^{-2t} \\ e^{-2t} \\ e^{-2t} \end{bmatrix} = \begin{bmatrix} 6e^{-2t} \\ -2e^{-2t} \\ -2e^{-2t} \end{bmatrix} = \mathbf{x}_2'(t),$$

$$\mathbf{A}\mathbf{x}_3(t) = \begin{bmatrix} 0 & 6 & 0 \\ 1 & 0 & 1 \\ 1 & 1 & 0 \end{bmatrix} \begin{bmatrix} 2e^{3t} \\ e^{3t} \\ e^{3t} \end{bmatrix} = \begin{bmatrix} 6e^{3t} \\ 3e^{3t} \\ 3e^{3t} \end{bmatrix} = \mathbf{x}_3'(t).$$

Therefore, each column vector of $\mathbf{X}(t)$ is a solution to the system on $(-\infty, \infty)$.

Next we must show that these vectors are linearly independent. Since they are solutions to a differential equation in matrix form, it is enough to show that their Wronskian is never zero. Thus, we find

$$\begin{aligned} W(t) &= \begin{vmatrix} 6e^{-t} & -3e^{-2t} & 2e^{3t} \\ -e^{-t} & e^{-2t} & e^{3t} \\ -5e^{-t} & e^{-2t} & e^{3t} \end{vmatrix} \\ &= 6e^{-t} \begin{vmatrix} e^{-2t} & e^{3t} \\ e^{-2t} & e^{3t} \end{vmatrix} + 3e^{-2t} \begin{vmatrix} -e^{-t} & e^{3t} \\ -5e^{-t} & e^{3t} \end{vmatrix} + 2e^{3t} \begin{vmatrix} -e^{-t} & e^{-2t} \\ -5e^{-t} & e^{-2t} \end{vmatrix} \\ &= 6e^{-t}\left(e^{t} - e^{t}\right) + 3e^{-2t}\left(-e^{2t} + 5e^{2t}\right) + 2e^{3t}\left(-e^{-3t} + 5e^{-3t}\right) = 20 \neq 0, \end{aligned}$$

where we have used cofactors to calculate the determinant. Hence, these three vectors are linearly independent. Therefore, $\mathbf{X}(t)$ is a fundamental matrix for this system.

We will now find the inverse of the matrix $\mathbf{X}(t)$ by performing row-reduction on the matrix

$$[\mathbf{X}(t)|\mathbf{I}] \longrightarrow [\mathbf{I}|\mathbf{X}^{-1}(t)].$$

Thus, we have

$$[\mathbf{X}(t)|\mathbf{I}] = \left[\begin{array}{ccc|ccc} 6e^{-t} & -3e^{-2t} & 2e^{3t} & 1 & 0 & 0 \\ -e^{-t} & e^{-2t} & e^{3t} & 0 & 1 & 0 \\ -5e^{-t} & e^{-2t} & e^{3t} & 0 & 0 & 1 \end{array}\right]$$

$$\begin{array}{r} -R_2 \to R_1 \\ R_1 \to R_2 \end{array} \quad \left[\begin{array}{ccc|ccc} e^{-t} & -e^{-2t} & -e^{3t} & 0 & -1 & 0 \\ 6e^{-t} & -3e^{-2t} & 2e^{3t} & 1 & 0 & 0 \\ -5e^{-t} & e^{-2t} & e^{3t} & 0 & 0 & 1 \end{array}\right]$$

$$\begin{array}{r} R_2 - 6R_1 \to R_2 \\ R_3 + 5R_1 \to R_3 \end{array} \quad \left[\begin{array}{ccc|ccc} e^{-t} & -e^{-2t} & -e^{3t} & 0 & -1 & 0 \\ 0 & 3e^{-2t} & 8e^{3t} & 1 & 6 & 0 \\ 0 & -4e^{-2t} & -4e^{3t} & 0 & -5 & 1 \end{array}\right]$$

$$\begin{array}{r} -R_3/4 \to R_2 \\ R_2 \to R_3 \end{array} \left[\begin{array}{ccc|ccc} e^{-t} & -e^{-2t} & -e^{3t} & 0 & -1 & 0 \\ 0 & e^{-2t} & e^{3t} & 0 & 5/4 & -1/4 \\ 0 & 3e^{-2t} & 8e^{3t} & 1 & 6 & 0 \end{array}\right]$$

$$\begin{array}{r} R_1 + R_2 \to R_1 \\ R_3 - 3R_2 \to R_3 \end{array} \left[\begin{array}{ccc|ccc} e^{-t} & 0 & 0 & 0 & 1/4 & -1/4 \\ 0 & e^{-2t} & e^{3t} & 0 & 5/4 & -1/4 \\ 0 & 0 & 5e^{3t} & 1 & 9/4 & 3/4 \end{array}\right]$$

$$\frac{1}{5}R_3 \to R_3 \left[\begin{array}{ccc|ccc} e^{-t} & 0 & 0 & 0 & 1/4 & -1/4 \\ 0 & e^{-2t} & e^{3t} & 0 & 5/4 & -1/4 \\ 0 & 0 & e^{3t} & 1/5 & 9/20 & 3/20 \end{array}\right]$$

$$R_2 - R_3 \to R_2 \left[\begin{array}{ccc|ccc} e^{-t} & 0 & 0 & 0 & 1/4 & -1/4 \\ 0 & e^{-2t} & 0 & -1/5 & 4/5 & -2/5 \\ 0 & 0 & e^{3t} & 1/5 & 9/20 & 3/20 \end{array}\right]$$

$$\begin{array}{r} e^{t}R_1 \to R_1 \\ e^{2t}R_2 \to R_2 \\ e^{-3t}R_3 \to R_3 \end{array} \left[\begin{array}{ccc|ccc} 1 & 0 & 0 & 0 & e^{t}/4 & -e^{t}/4 \\ 0 & 1 & 0 & -e^{2t}/5 & 4e^{2t}/5 & -2e^{2t}/5 \\ 0 & 0 & 1 & e^{-3t}/5 & 9e^{-3t}/20 & 3e^{-3t}/20 \end{array}\right].$$

Therefore, we see that

$$\mathbf{X}^{-1}(t) = \begin{bmatrix} 0 & e^{t}/4 & -e^{t}/4 \\ -e^{2t}/5 & 4e^{2t}/5 & -2e^{2t}/5 \\ e^{-3t}/5 & 9e^{-3t}/20 & 3e^{-3t}/20 \end{bmatrix}.$$

We now can use Problem 26 to find the solution to this differential equation for *any* initial value. For the initial value given here we note that $t_0 = 0$. Thus, substituting $t_0 = 0$ into the matrix $\mathbf{X}^{-1}(t)$ above yields

$$\mathbf{X}^{-1}(0) = \begin{bmatrix} 0 & 1/4 & -1/4 \\ -1/5 & 4/5 & -2/5 \\ 1/5 & 9/20 & 3/20 \end{bmatrix}.$$

Hence, we see that the solution to this problem is given by

$$\mathbf{x}(t) = \mathbf{X}(t)\mathbf{X}^{-1}(0)\mathbf{x}(0)$$

$$= \begin{bmatrix} 6e^{-t} & -3e^{-2t} & 2e^{3t} \\ -e^{-t} & e^{-2t} & e^{3t} \\ -5e^{-t} & e^{-2t} & e^{3t} \end{bmatrix} \begin{bmatrix} 0 & 1/4 & -1/4 \\ -1/5 & 4/5 & -2/5 \\ 1/5 & 9/20 & 3/20 \end{bmatrix} \begin{bmatrix} -1 \\ 0 \\ 1 \end{bmatrix}$$

$$= \begin{bmatrix} 6e^{-t} & -3e^{-2t} & 2e^{3t} \\ -e^{-t} & e^{-2t} & e^{3t} \\ -5e^{-t} & e^{-2t} & e^{3t} \end{bmatrix} \begin{bmatrix} -1/4 \\ -1/5 \\ -1/20 \end{bmatrix} = \begin{bmatrix} -(3/2)e^{-t} + (3/5)e^{-2t} - (1/10)e^{3t} \\ (1/4)e^{-t} - (1/5)e^{-2t} - (1/20)e^{3t} \\ (5/4)e^{-t} - (1/5)e^{-2t} - (1/20)e^{3t} \end{bmatrix}.$$

There are two short cuts that can be taken to solve the given problem. First, since we only need $\mathbf{X}^{-1}(0)$, it suffices to compute the inverse of $\mathbf{X}(0)$, not $\mathbf{X}(t)$. Second, by producing $\mathbf{X}^{-1}(t)$ we automatically know that $\det \mathbf{X}(0) \neq 0$ and hence $\mathbf{X}(t)$ is a fundamental matrix. Thus, it was not really necessary to compute the Wronskian.

33. Let $\phi(t)$ be an arbitrary solution to the system $\mathbf{x}'(t) = \mathbf{A}(t)\mathbf{x}(t)$ on the interval I. We want to find $\mathbf{c} = \text{col}(c_1, c_2, \ldots, c_n)$ so that

$$\phi(t) = c_1\mathbf{x}_1(t) + c_2\mathbf{x}_2(t) + \cdots + c_n\mathbf{x}_n(t),$$

where $\mathbf{x}_1, \mathbf{x}_2, \ldots, \mathbf{x}_n$ are n linearly independent solutions for this system. Since

$$c_1\mathbf{x}_1(t) + c_2\mathbf{x}_2(t) + \cdots + c_n\mathbf{x}_n(t) = \mathbf{X}(t)\mathbf{c},$$

where $\mathbf{X}(t)$ is the fundamental matrix whose columns are the vectors $\mathbf{x}_1, \mathbf{x}_2, \ldots, \mathbf{x}_n$, this equation can be written as

$$\phi(t) = \mathbf{X}(t)\mathbf{c} \tag{9.1}$$

Since $\mathbf{x}_1, \mathbf{x}_2, \ldots, \mathbf{x}_n$ are linearly independent solutions of the system $\mathbf{x}'(t) = \mathbf{A}(t)\mathbf{x}(t)$, their Wronskian is never zero. Therefore, as was discussed on page 528 of the text, $\mathbf{X}(t)$ has an inverse at each point in I. Thus, at t_0, a point in I, $\mathbf{X}^{-1}(t_0)$ exists and equation (9.1) becomes

$$\phi(t_0) = \mathbf{X}(t_0)\mathbf{c} \qquad \Rightarrow \qquad \mathbf{X}^{-1}(t_0)\phi(t_0) = \mathbf{X}^{-1}(t_0)\mathbf{X}(t_0)\mathbf{c} = \mathbf{c}.$$

Hence, if we define $\mathbf{c}_0$ to be the vector $\mathbf{c}_0 = \mathbf{X}^{-1}(t_0)\phi(t_0)$, then equation (9.1) is true at the point t_0 (i. e. $\phi(t_0) = \mathbf{X}(t_0)\mathbf{X}^{-1}(t_0)\phi(t_0)$). To see that, for this definition of $\mathbf{c}_0$, equation (9.1) is true for all t in I (and so this is the vector that we seek), notice that $\phi(t)$ and $\mathbf{X}(t)\mathbf{c}_0$

are both solutions to same initial value problem (with the initial value given at the point t_0). Therefore, by the uniqueness of solutions, Theorem 2 on page 525 of the text, these solutions must be equal on I, which means that $\phi(t) = \mathbf{X}(t)\mathbf{c}_0$ for all t in I.

EXERCISES 9.5: Homogeneous Linear Systems with Constant Coefficients, page 541

5. The characteristic equation for this matrix is given by

$$\begin{aligned} |\mathbf{A} - r\mathbf{I}| &= \begin{vmatrix} 1-r & 0 & 0 \\ 0 & -r & 2 \\ 0 & 2 & -r \end{vmatrix} = (1-r)\begin{vmatrix} -r & 2 \\ 2 & -r \end{vmatrix} \\ &= (1-r)\left(r^2 - 4\right) = (1-r)(r-2)(r+2) = 0. \end{aligned}$$

Thus, the eigenvalues of this matrix are $r = 1, 2, -2$. Substituting the eigenvalue $r = 1$, into equation $(\mathbf{A} - r\mathbf{I})\mathbf{u} = \mathbf{0}$ yields

$$(\mathbf{A} - \mathbf{I})\mathbf{u} = \begin{bmatrix} 0 & 0 & 0 \\ 0 & -1 & 2 \\ 0 & 2 & -1 \end{bmatrix} \begin{bmatrix} u_1 \\ u_2 \\ u_3 \end{bmatrix} = \begin{bmatrix} 0 \\ 0 \\ 0 \end{bmatrix}, \tag{9.2}$$

which is equivalent to the system

$$\begin{aligned} -u_2 + 2u_3 &= 0, \\ 2u_2 - u_3 &= 0. \end{aligned}$$

This system reduces to the system $u_2 = 0$, $u_3 = 0$, which does not assign any value to u_1. Thus, we can let u_1 be any value, say $u_1 = s$, and $u_2 = 0$, $u_3 = 0$ and the system given by (9.2) will be satisfied. From this we see that the eigenvectors associated with the eigenvalue $r = 1$ are given by

$$\mathbf{u}_1 = \operatorname{col}(u_1, u_2, u_3) = \operatorname{col}(s, 0, 0) = s\operatorname{col}(1, 0, 0).$$

For $r = 2$ we observe that the equation $(\mathbf{A} - r\mathbf{I})\mathbf{u} = \mathbf{0}$ becomes

$$(\mathbf{A} - 2\mathbf{I})\mathbf{u} = \begin{bmatrix} -1 & 0 & 0 \\ 0 & -2 & 2 \\ 0 & 2 & -2 \end{bmatrix} \begin{bmatrix} u_1 \\ u_2 \\ u_3 \end{bmatrix} = \begin{bmatrix} 0 \\ 0 \\ 0 \end{bmatrix},$$

whose corresponding system of equations reduces to $u_1 = 0$, $u_2 = u_3$. Therefore, we can pick u_2 to be any value, say $u_2 = s$ (which means that $u_3 = s$), and we find that the eigenvectors for this matrix associated with the eigenvalue $r = 2$ are given by

$$\mathbf{u}_2 = \text{col}\,(u_1, u_2, u_3) = \text{col}(0, s, s) = s\text{col}(0, 1, 1).$$

For $r = -2$, we solve the equation

$$(\mathbf{A} + 2\mathbf{I})\mathbf{u} = \begin{bmatrix} 3 & 0 & 0 \\ 0 & 2 & 2 \\ 0 & 2 & 2 \end{bmatrix} \begin{bmatrix} u_1 \\ u_2 \\ u_3 \end{bmatrix} = \begin{bmatrix} 0 \\ 0 \\ 0 \end{bmatrix},$$

which reduces to the system $u_1 = 0$, $u_2 = -u_3$. Hence, u_3 is arbitrary, and so we will let $u_3 = s$ (which means that $u_2 = -s$). Thus, solutions to this system and, therefore, eigenvectors for this matrix associated with the eigenvalue $r = -2$ are given by the vectors

$$\mathbf{u}_3 = \text{col}\,(u_1, u_2, u_3) = \text{col}(0, -s, s) = s\text{col}(0, -1, 1).$$

13. We must first find the eigenvalues and eigenvectors associated with the given matrix $\mathbf{A}$. Thus, we note that the characteristic equation for this matrix is given by

$$|\mathbf{A} - r\mathbf{I}| = \begin{vmatrix} 1-r & 2 & 2 \\ 2 & -r & 3 \\ 2 & 3 & -r \end{vmatrix} = 0$$

$$\Rightarrow \quad (1-r)\begin{vmatrix} -r & 3 \\ 3 & -r \end{vmatrix} - 2\begin{vmatrix} 2 & 3 \\ 2 & -r \end{vmatrix} + 2\begin{vmatrix} 2 & -r \\ 2 & 3 \end{vmatrix} = 0$$

$$\Rightarrow \quad (1-r)\left(r^2 - 9\right) - 2(-2r - 6) + 2(6 + 2r) = (1-r)(r-2)(r+2) = 0$$

$$\Rightarrow \quad (r+3)[(1-r)(r-3) + 8] = 0 \quad \Rightarrow \quad (r+3)(r-5)(r+1) = 0.$$

Therefore, the eigenvalues are $r = -3, -1, 5$. To find an eigenvector associated with the eigenvalue $r = -3$, we must find a vector $\mathbf{u} = \text{col}(u_1, u_2, u_3)$ which satisfies the equation $(\mathbf{A} + 3\mathbf{I})\mathbf{u} = \mathbf{0}$. Thus, we have

$$(\mathbf{A} + 3\mathbf{I})\mathbf{u} = \begin{bmatrix} 4 & 2 & 2 \\ 2 & 3 & 3 \\ 2 & 3 & 3 \end{bmatrix} \begin{bmatrix} u_1 \\ u_2 \\ u_3 \end{bmatrix} = \begin{bmatrix} 0 \\ 0 \\ 0 \end{bmatrix} \quad \Rightarrow \quad \begin{bmatrix} 2 & 0 & 0 \\ 0 & 1 & 1 \\ 0 & 0 & 0 \end{bmatrix} \begin{bmatrix} u_1 \\ u_2 \\ u_3 \end{bmatrix} = \begin{bmatrix} 0 \\ 0 \\ 0 \end{bmatrix},$$

where we have obtained the last equation above by using elementary row operations. This equation is equivalent to the system $u_1 = 0$, $u_2 = -u_3$. Hence, if we let u_3 have the arbitrary value s_1, then we see that, for the matrix $\mathbf{A}$, the eigenvectors associated with the eigenvalue $r = -3$ are given by

$$\mathbf{u} = \text{col}\,(u_1, u_2, u_3) = \text{col}\,(0, -s_1, s_1) = s_1\text{col}(0, -1, 1).$$

Thus, if we choose $s_1 = 1$, then vector $\mathbf{u}_1 = \text{col}(0, -1, 1)$ is one eigenvector associated with this eigenvalue. For the eigenvalue $r = -1$, we must find a vector $\mathbf{u}$ which satisfies the equation $(\mathbf{A} + \mathbf{I})\mathbf{u} = \mathbf{0}$. Thus, we see that

$$(\mathbf{A} + \mathbf{I})\mathbf{u} = \begin{bmatrix} 2 & 2 & 2 \\ 2 & 1 & 3 \\ 2 & 3 & 1 \end{bmatrix} \begin{bmatrix} u_1 \\ u_2 \\ u_3 \end{bmatrix} = \begin{bmatrix} 0 \\ 0 \\ 0 \end{bmatrix} \quad \Rightarrow \quad \begin{bmatrix} 1 & 2 & 0 \\ 0 & 1 & -1 \\ 0 & 0 & 0 \end{bmatrix} \begin{bmatrix} u_1 \\ u_2 \\ u_3 \end{bmatrix} = \begin{bmatrix} 0 \\ 0 \\ 0 \end{bmatrix},$$

which is equivalent to the system $u_1 = -2u_2$, $u_3 = u_2$. Therefore, if we let $u_2 = s_2$, then we see that vectors which satisfy the equation $(\mathbf{A} + \mathbf{I})\mathbf{u} = 0$ and, hence, eigenvectors for the matrix $\mathbf{A}$ associated with the eigenvalue $r = -1$ are given by

$$\mathbf{u} = \text{col}\,(u_1, u_2, u_3) = \text{col}\,(-2s_2, s_2, s_2) = s_2\text{col}(-2, 1, 1).$$

By letting $s_2 = 1$, we find that one such vector will be the vector $\mathbf{u}_2 = \text{col}(-2, 1, 1)$. In order to find an eigenvector associated with the eigenvalue $r = 5$, we will solve the equation $(\mathbf{A} - 5\mathbf{I})\mathbf{u} = 0$. Thus, we have

$$(\mathbf{A} - 5\mathbf{I})\mathbf{u} = \begin{bmatrix} -4 & 2 & 2 \\ 2 & -5 & 3 \\ 2 & 3 & -5 \end{bmatrix} \begin{bmatrix} u_1 \\ u_2 \\ u_3 \end{bmatrix} = \begin{bmatrix} 0 \\ 0 \\ 0 \end{bmatrix} \quad \Rightarrow \quad \begin{bmatrix} 1 & 0 & -1 \\ 0 & 1 & -1 \\ 0 & 0 & 0 \end{bmatrix} \begin{bmatrix} u_1 \\ u_2 \\ u_3 \end{bmatrix} = \begin{bmatrix} 0 \\ 0 \\ 0 \end{bmatrix},$$

which is equivalent to the system $u_1 = u_3$, $u_2 = u_3$. Thus, if we let $u_3 = s_3$, then, for the matrix $\mathbf{A}$, the eigenvectors associated with the eigenvalue $r = 5$ are given by

$$\mathbf{u} = \text{col}\,(u_1, u_2, u_3) = \text{col}\,(s_3, s_3, s_3) = s_3\text{col}(1, 1, 1).$$

Hence, by letting $s_3 = 1$, we see that one such vector will be the vector $\mathbf{u}_3 = \mathrm{col}(1, 1, 1)$. Therefore, by Corollary 1 on page 538 of the text, we see that a fundamental solution set for this equation is given by

$$\left\{e^{-3t}\mathbf{u}_1\,, e^{-t}\mathbf{u}_2\,, e^{5t}\mathbf{u}_3\right\}.$$

Thus, a general solution for this system is

$$\mathbf{x}(t) = c_1e^{-3t}\mathbf{u}_1 + c_2e^{-t}\mathbf{u}_2 + c_3e^{5t}\mathbf{u}_3 = c_1e^{-3t}\begin{bmatrix} 0 \\ -1 \\ 1 \end{bmatrix} + c_2e^{-t}\begin{bmatrix} -2 \\ 1 \\ 1 \end{bmatrix} + c_3e^{5t}\begin{bmatrix} 1 \\ 1 \\ 1 \end{bmatrix}.$$

21. A fundamental matrix for this system has three columns which are linearly independent solutions. Therefore, we will first find three such solutions. To this end, we will first find the eigenvalues for the matrix $\mathbf{A}$ by solving the characteristic equation given by

$$|\mathbf{A} - r\mathbf{I}| = \begin{vmatrix} -r & 1 & 0 \\ 0 & -r & 1 \\ 8 & -14 & 7-r \end{vmatrix} = 0$$

$$\Rightarrow \qquad -r\begin{vmatrix} -r & 1 \\ -14 & 7-r \end{vmatrix} - \begin{vmatrix} 0 & 1 \\ 8 & 7-r \end{vmatrix} = 0$$

$$\Rightarrow \qquad r^3 - 7r^2 + 14r - 8 = 0 \qquad \Rightarrow \qquad (r-1)(r-2)(r-4) = 0.$$

Hence, this matrix has three distinct eigenvalues, $r = 1, 2, 4$, and, according to Theorem 6 on page 538 of the text, the eigenvectors associated with these eigenvalues will be linearly independent. Thus, these eigenvectors will be used in finding the three linearly independent solutions which we seek. To find an eigenvector, $\mathbf{u} = \mathrm{col}(u_1, u_2, u_3)$, associated with the eigenvalue $r = 1$, we will solve the equation $(\mathbf{A} - \mathbf{I})\mathbf{u} = 0$. Therefore, we have

$$(\mathbf{A} - \mathbf{I})\mathbf{u} = \begin{bmatrix} -1 & 1 & 0 \\ 0 & -1 & 1 \\ 8 & -14 & 6 \end{bmatrix}\begin{bmatrix} u_1 \\ u_2 \\ u_3 \end{bmatrix} = \begin{bmatrix} 0 \\ 0 \\ 0 \end{bmatrix} \quad \Rightarrow \quad \begin{bmatrix} -1 & 0 & 1 \\ 0 & -1 & 1 \\ 0 & 0 & 0 \end{bmatrix}\begin{bmatrix} u_1 \\ u_2 \\ u_3 \end{bmatrix} = \begin{bmatrix} 0 \\ 0 \\ 0 \end{bmatrix},$$

which is equivalent to the system $u_1 = u_3$, $u_2 = u_3$. Thus, by letting $u_3 = 1$ (which implies that $u_1 = u_2 = 1$), we find that one eigenvector associated with the eigenvalue $r = 1$ is given by the vector $\mathbf{u}_1 = \text{col}(1, 1, 1)$. To find an eigenvector associated with the eigenvalue $r = 2$, we solve the equation

$$(\mathbf{A} - 2\mathbf{I})\mathbf{u} = \begin{bmatrix} -2 & 1 & 0 \\ 0 & -2 & 1 \\ 8 & -14 & 5 \end{bmatrix} \begin{bmatrix} u_1 \\ u_2 \\ u_3 \end{bmatrix} = \begin{bmatrix} 0 \\ 0 \\ 0 \end{bmatrix} \quad \Rightarrow \quad \begin{bmatrix} 4 & 0 & -1 \\ 0 & 2 & -1 \\ 0 & 0 & 0 \end{bmatrix} \begin{bmatrix} u_1 \\ u_2 \\ u_3 \end{bmatrix} = \begin{bmatrix} 0 \\ 0 \\ 0 \end{bmatrix},$$

which is equivalent to the system $4u_1 = u_3$, $2u_2 = u_3$. Hence, letting $u_3 = 4$ implies that $u_1 = 1$ and $u_2 = 2$. Therefore, one eigenvector associated with the eigenvalue $r = 2$ is the vector $\mathbf{u}_2 = \text{col}(1, 2, 4)$. In order to find an eigenvector associated with the eigenvalue $r = 4$, we will solve the equation

$$(\mathbf{A} - 4\mathbf{I})\mathbf{u} = \begin{bmatrix} -4 & 1 & 0 \\ 0 & -4 & 1 \\ 8 & -14 & 3 \end{bmatrix} \begin{bmatrix} u_1 \\ u_2 \\ u_3 \end{bmatrix} = \begin{bmatrix} 0 \\ 0 \\ 0 \end{bmatrix} \quad \Rightarrow \quad \begin{bmatrix} 16 & 0 & -1 \\ 0 & 4 & -1 \\ 0 & 0 & 0 \end{bmatrix} \begin{bmatrix} u_1 \\ u_2 \\ u_3 \end{bmatrix} = \begin{bmatrix} 0 \\ 0 \\ 0 \end{bmatrix},$$

which is equivalent to the system $16u_1 = u_3$, $4u_2 = u_3$. Therefore, letting $u_3 = 16$ implies that $u_1 = 1$ and $u_2 = 4$. Thus, one eigenvector associated with the eigenvalue $r = 4$ is the vector $\mathbf{u}_3 = \text{col}(1, 4, 16)$. Therefore, by Theorem 5 on page 536 of the text (or Corollary 1), we see that three linearly independent solutions of this system are given by $e^t\mathbf{u}_1$, $e^{2t}\mathbf{u}_2$, and $e^{4t}\mathbf{u}_3$. Thus, a fundamental matrix for this system will be the matrix

$$\begin{bmatrix} e^t & e^{2t} & e^{4t} \\ e^t & 2e^{2t} & 4e^{4t} \\ e^t & 4e^{2t} & 16e^{4t} \end{bmatrix}.$$

33. Since the coefficient matrix for this system is a 3×3 real symmetric matrix, by the discussion on page 540 of the text, we know that we can find three linearly independent eigenvectors for this matrix. Therefore, to find the solution to this initial value problem, we must first find three such eigenvectors. To do this we first find eigenvalues for this matrix. Therefore, we solve the characteristic equation given by

$$|\mathbf{A} - r\mathbf{I}| = \begin{vmatrix} 1-r & -2 & 2 \\ -2 & 1-r & -2 \\ 2 & -2 & 1-r \end{vmatrix} = 0$$

$$\Rightarrow \quad (1-r)\begin{vmatrix} 1-r & -2 \\ -2 & 1-r \end{vmatrix} + 2\begin{vmatrix} -2 & -2 \\ 2 & 1-r \end{vmatrix} + 2\begin{vmatrix} -2 & 1-r \\ 2 & -2 \end{vmatrix} = 0$$

$$\Rightarrow \quad (1-r)\left[(1-r)^2-4\right] + 2\left[-2(1-r)+4\right] + 2\left[4-2(1-r)\right] = 0$$

$$\Rightarrow \quad (1-r)(r-3)(r+1) + 8(r+1) = -(r+1)(r-5)(r+1) = 0.$$

Thus, the eigenvalues are $r=-1$ and $r=5$, with $r=-1$ an eigenvalue of multiplicity two. In order to find an eigenvector associated with the eigenvalue $r=5$, we solve the equation

$$(\mathbf{A}-5\mathbf{I})\mathbf{u} = \begin{bmatrix} -4 & -2 & 2 \\ -2 & -4 & -2 \\ 2 & -2 & -4 \end{bmatrix}\begin{bmatrix} u_1 \\ u_2 \\ u_3 \end{bmatrix} = \begin{bmatrix} 0 \\ 0 \\ 0 \end{bmatrix} \quad \Rightarrow \quad \begin{bmatrix} 1 & 0 & -1 \\ 0 & 1 & 1 \\ 0 & 0 & 0 \end{bmatrix}\begin{bmatrix} u_1 \\ u_2 \\ u_3 \end{bmatrix} = \begin{bmatrix} 0 \\ 0 \\ 0 \end{bmatrix}.$$

This equation is equivalent to the system $u_1 = u_3$, $u_2 = -u_3$. Thus, if we let $u_3 = 1$, we see that for this coefficient matrix an eigenvector associated with the eigenvalue $r=5$ is given by the vector $\mathbf{u}_1 = \operatorname{col}(u_1, u_2, u_3) = \operatorname{col}(1, -1, 1)$. We must now find two more linearly independent eigenvectors for this coefficient matrix. By the discussion above, these eigenvectors will be associated with the eigenvalue $r=1$. Thus, we solve the equation

$$(\mathbf{A}+\mathbf{I})\mathbf{u} = \begin{bmatrix} 2 & -2 & 2 \\ -2 & 2 & -2 \\ 2 & -2 & 2 \end{bmatrix}\begin{bmatrix} u_1 \\ u_2 \\ u_3 \end{bmatrix} = \begin{bmatrix} 0 \\ 0 \\ 0 \end{bmatrix} \Rightarrow \begin{bmatrix} 1 & -1 & 1 \\ 0 & 0 & 0 \\ 0 & 0 & 0 \end{bmatrix}\begin{bmatrix} u_1 \\ u_2 \\ u_3 \end{bmatrix} = \begin{bmatrix} 0 \\ 0 \\ 0 \end{bmatrix}, \qquad (9.3)$$

which is equivalent to the equation $u_1 - u_2 + u_3 = 0$. Therefore, if we arbitrarily assign the value s to u_2 and v to u_3, we see that $u_1 = s - v$, and solutions to equation (9.3) above will be given by

$$\mathbf{u} = \begin{bmatrix} s-v \\ s \\ v \end{bmatrix} = s\begin{bmatrix} 1 \\ 1 \\ 0 \end{bmatrix} + v\begin{bmatrix} -1 \\ 0 \\ 1 \end{bmatrix}.$$

By taking $s=1$ and $v=0$, we see that one solution to equation (9.3) will be the vector $\mathbf{u}_2 = \operatorname{col}(1,1,0)$. Hence, this is one eigenvector for the coefficient matrix. Similarly, by letting $s=0$ and $v=1$, we find a second eigenvector will be the vector $\mathbf{u}_3 = \operatorname{col}(-1,0,1)$. Since the eigenvectors $\mathbf{u}_1$, $\mathbf{u}_2$, and $\mathbf{u}_3$ are linearly independent, by Theorem 5 on page 536 of the text, we see that a general solution for this system will be given by

$$\mathbf{x}(t) = c_1 e^{5t} \begin{bmatrix} 1 \\ -1 \\ 1 \end{bmatrix} + c_2 e^{-t} \begin{bmatrix} 1 \\ 1 \\ 0 \end{bmatrix} + c_3 e^{-t} \begin{bmatrix} -1 \\ 0 \\ 1 \end{bmatrix}.$$

To find a solution which satisfies the initial condition, we must solve the equation

$$\mathbf{x}(0) = c_1 \begin{bmatrix} 1 \\ -1 \\ 1 \end{bmatrix} + c_2 \begin{bmatrix} 1 \\ 1 \\ 0 \end{bmatrix} + c_3 \begin{bmatrix} -1 \\ 0 \\ 1 \end{bmatrix} \quad \Rightarrow \quad \begin{bmatrix} 1 & 1 & -1 \\ -1 & 1 & 0 \\ 1 & 0 & 1 \end{bmatrix} \begin{bmatrix} c_1 \\ c_2 \\ c_3 \end{bmatrix} = \begin{bmatrix} -2 \\ -3 \\ 2 \end{bmatrix}.$$

This equation can be solved by either using elementary row operations on the augmented matrix associated with this equation or by solving the system

$$\begin{aligned} c_1 + c_2 - c_3 &= -2, \\ -c_1 + c_2 &= -3, \\ c_1 + c_3 &= 2. \end{aligned}$$

By either method we find that $c_1 = 1$, $c_2 = -2$, and $c_3 = 1$. Therefore, the solution to this initial value problem is given by

$$\begin{aligned} \mathbf{x}(t) &= e^{5t} \begin{bmatrix} 1 \\ -1 \\ 1 \end{bmatrix} - 2e^{-t} \begin{bmatrix} 1 \\ 1 \\ 0 \end{bmatrix} + e^{-t} \begin{bmatrix} -1 \\ 0 \\ 1 \end{bmatrix} \\ &= \begin{bmatrix} e^{5t} - 2e^{-t} - e^{-t} \\ -e^{5t} - 2e^{-t} + 0 \\ e^{5t} + 0 + e^{-t} \end{bmatrix} = \begin{bmatrix} -3e^{-t} + e^{5t} \\ -2e^{-t} - e^{5t} \\ e^{-t} + e^{5t} \end{bmatrix}. \end{aligned}$$

37. **(a)** In order to find the eigenvalues for the matrix $\mathbf{A}$, we will solve the characteristic equation

$$|\mathbf{A} - r\mathbf{I}| = \begin{vmatrix} 2-r & 1 & 6 \\ 0 & 2-r & 5 \\ 0 & 0 & 2-r \end{vmatrix} = 0 \quad \Rightarrow \quad (2-r)^3 = 0.$$

Thus, $r = 2$ is an eigenvalue of multiplicity three. To find the eigenvectors for the matrix $\mathbf{A}$ associated with this eigenvalue, we solve the equation

$$(\mathbf{A} - 2\mathbf{I})\mathbf{u} = \begin{bmatrix} 0 & 1 & 6 \\ 0 & 0 & 5 \\ 0 & 0 & 0 \end{bmatrix} \begin{bmatrix} u_1 \\ u_2 \\ u_3 \end{bmatrix} = \begin{bmatrix} 0 \\ 0 \\ 0 \end{bmatrix}.$$

This equation is equivalent to the system $u_2 = 0$, $u_3 = 0$. Therefore, we can assign u_1 to be any arbitrary value, say $u_1 = s$, and we find that the vector

$$\mathbf{u} = \operatorname{col}(u_1, u_2, u_3) = \operatorname{col}(s, 0, 0) = s\operatorname{col}(1, 0, 0)$$

will solve this equation and will, thus, be an eigenvector for the matrix $\mathbf{A}$. We also notice that the vectors $\mathbf{u} = s\operatorname{col}(1, 0, 0)$ are the only vectors that will solve this equation, and, hence, they will be the only eigenvectors for the matrix $\mathbf{A}$.

(b) By taking $s = 1$, we find that, for the matrix $\mathbf{A}$, one eigenvector associated with the eigenvalue $r = 2$ will be the vector $\mathbf{u}_1 = \operatorname{col}(1, 0, 0)$. Therefore, by the way eigenvalues and eigenvectors were defined (as was discussed in the text on page 533), we see that one solution to the system $\mathbf{x}' = \mathbf{A}\mathbf{x}$ will be given by the vector

$$\mathbf{x}_1(t) = e^{2t}\mathbf{u}_1 = e^{2t} \begin{bmatrix} 1 \\ 0 \\ 0 \end{bmatrix}.$$

(c) We know that $\mathbf{u}_1 = \operatorname{col}(1, 0, 0)$ is an eigenvector for the matrix $\mathbf{A}$ associated with the eigenvalue $r = 2$. Thus, $\mathbf{u}_1$ satisfies the equation

$$(\mathbf{A} - 2\mathbf{I})\mathbf{u}_1 = \mathbf{0} \qquad \Rightarrow \qquad \mathbf{A}\mathbf{u}_1 = 2\mathbf{u}_1 . \tag{9.4}$$

We want to find a constant vector $\mathbf{u}_2 = \operatorname{col}(v_1, v_2, v_3)$ such that

$$\mathbf{x}_2(t) = te^{2t}\mathbf{u}_1 + e^{2t}\mathbf{u}_2$$

will be a second solution to the system $\mathbf{x}' = \mathbf{A}\mathbf{x}$. To do this, we will first show that $\mathbf{x}_2$ will satisfy the equation $\mathbf{x}' = \mathbf{A}\mathbf{x}$ if and only if the vector $\mathbf{u}_2$ satisfies the equation

$(\mathbf{A}-2\mathbf{I})\mathbf{u}_2 = \mathbf{u}_1$. To this end, we find that

$$\mathbf{x}_2'(t) = 2te^{2t}\mathbf{u}_1 + e^{2t}\mathbf{u}_1 + 2e^{2t}\mathbf{u}_2 = 2te^{2t}\mathbf{u}_1 + e^{2t}\left(\mathbf{u}_1 + 2\mathbf{u}_2\right),$$

where we have used the fact that $\mathbf{u}_1$ and $\mathbf{u}_2$ are constant vectors. We also have

$$\begin{aligned}
\mathbf{A}\mathbf{x}_2(t) &= \mathbf{A}\left(te^{2t}\mathbf{u}_1 + e^{2t}\mathbf{u}_2\right) \\
&= \mathbf{A}\left(te^{2t}\mathbf{u}_1\right) + \mathbf{A}\left(e^{2t}\mathbf{u}_2\right), && \text{distributive property of matrix multiplication} \\
& && \text{(page 515 of the text)} \\
&= te^{2t}\left(\mathbf{A}\mathbf{u}_1\right) + e^{2t}\left(\mathbf{A}\mathbf{u}_2\right), && \text{associative property of matrix multiplication} \\
& && \text{(page 515 of the text)} \\
&= 2te^{2t}\mathbf{u}_1 + e^{2t}\mathbf{A}\mathbf{u}_2, && \text{by equation (9.4) above.}
\end{aligned}$$

Thus, if $\mathbf{x}_2(t)$ is to be a solution to the given system we, must have

$$\begin{aligned}
& \mathbf{x}_2'(t) = \mathbf{A}\mathbf{x}_2(t) \\
\Rightarrow \quad & 2te^{2t}\mathbf{u}_1 + e^{2t}\left(\mathbf{u}_1 + 2\mathbf{u}_2\right) = 2te^{2t}\mathbf{u}_1 + e^{2t}\mathbf{A}\mathbf{u}_2 \\
\Rightarrow \quad & e^{2t}\left(\mathbf{u}_1 + 2\mathbf{u}_2\right) = e^{2t}\mathbf{A}\mathbf{u}_2 .
\end{aligned}$$

By dividing both sides of this equation by the nonzero term e^{2t}, we obtain

$$\mathbf{u}_1 + 2\mathbf{u}_2 = \mathbf{A}\mathbf{u}_2 \qquad \Rightarrow \qquad (\mathbf{A}-2\mathbf{I})\mathbf{u}_2 = \mathbf{u}_1 .$$

Since all of these steps are reversible, if a vector $\mathbf{u}_2$ satisfies this last equation, then $\mathbf{x}_2(t) = te^{2t}\mathbf{u}_1 + e^{2t}\mathbf{u}_2$ will be a solution to the system $\mathbf{x}' = \mathbf{A}\mathbf{x}$. Now we can use the formula $(\mathbf{A}-2\mathbf{I})\mathbf{u}_2 = \mathbf{u}_1$ to find the vector $\mathbf{u}_2 = \operatorname{col}(v_1, v_2, v_3)$. Hence, we solve the equation

$$(\mathbf{A}-2\mathbf{I})\mathbf{u}_2 = \begin{bmatrix} 0 & 1 & 6 \\ 0 & 0 & 5 \\ 0 & 0 & 0 \end{bmatrix}\begin{bmatrix} v_1 \\ v_2 \\ v_3 \end{bmatrix} = \begin{bmatrix} 1 \\ 0 \\ 0 \end{bmatrix}.$$

This equation is equivalent to the system $v_2+6v_3 = 1$, $5v_3 = 0$, which implies that $v_2 = 1$, $v_3 = 0$. Therefore, the vector $\mathbf{u}_2 = \operatorname{col}(0,1,0)$ will satisfy the equation $(\mathbf{A}-2\mathbf{I})\mathbf{u}_2 = \mathbf{u}_1$ and, thus,

$$\mathbf{x}_2(t) = te^{2t}\begin{bmatrix} 1 \\ 0 \\ 0 \end{bmatrix} + e^{2t}\begin{bmatrix} 0 \\ 1 \\ 0 \end{bmatrix}$$

will be a second solution to the given system. We can see by inspection $\mathbf{x}_2(t)$ and $\mathbf{x}_1(t) = e^{2t}\mathbf{u}_1$ are linearly independent.

(d) To find a third linearly independent solution to this system we will try to find a solution of the form $\mathbf{x}_3(t) = \frac{t^2}{2}e^{2t}\mathbf{u}_1 + te^{2t}\mathbf{u}_2 + e^{2t}\mathbf{u}_3$, where $\mathbf{u}_3$ is a constant vector that we must find, and $\mathbf{u}_1$ and $\mathbf{u}_2$ are the vectors that we found in parts (b) and (c), respectively. To find the vector $\mathbf{u}_3$, we will proceed as we did in part (c) above. We will first show that $\mathbf{x}_3(t)$ will be a solution to the given system if and only if the vector $\mathbf{u}_3$ satisfies the equation $(\mathbf{A} - 2\mathbf{I})\mathbf{u}_3 = \mathbf{u}_2$. To do this we observe that

$$\mathbf{x}_3'(t) = te^{2t}\mathbf{u}_1 + t^2e^{2t}\mathbf{u}_1 + e^{2t}\mathbf{u}_2 + 2te^{2t}\mathbf{u}_2 + 2e^{2t}\mathbf{u}_3 .$$

Also, using the facts that

$$(\mathbf{A} - 2\mathbf{I})\mathbf{u}_1 = \mathbf{0} \qquad \Rightarrow \qquad \mathbf{A}\mathbf{u}_1 = 2\mathbf{u}_1 \tag{9.5}$$

and

$$(\mathbf{A} - 2\mathbf{I})\mathbf{u}_2 = \mathbf{u}_1 \qquad \Rightarrow \qquad \mathbf{A}\mathbf{u}_2 = \mathbf{u}_1 + 2\mathbf{u}_2 , \tag{9.6}$$

we have

$$\begin{aligned}
\mathbf{A}\mathbf{x}_3(t) &= \mathbf{A}\left(\frac{t^2}{2}e^{2t}\mathbf{u}_1 + te^{2t}\mathbf{u}_2 + e^{2t}\mathbf{u}_3\right) \\
&= \mathbf{A}\left(\frac{t^2}{2}e^{2t}\mathbf{u}_1\right) + \mathbf{A}\left(te^{2t}\mathbf{u}_2\right) + +\mathbf{A}\left(e^{2t}\mathbf{u}_3\right), && \text{distributive property} \\
&= \frac{t^2}{2}e^{2t}\left(\mathbf{A}\mathbf{u}_1\right) + te^{2t}\left(\mathbf{A}\mathbf{u}_2\right) + e^{2t}\left(\mathbf{A}\mathbf{u}_3\right), && \text{associative property} \\
&= \frac{t^2}{2}e^{2t}\left(2\mathbf{u}_1\right) + te^{2t}\left(\mathbf{u}_1 + 2\mathbf{u}_2\right) + e^{2t}\mathbf{A}\mathbf{u}_3, && \text{equations (9.5) and (9.6)} \\
&= t^2e^{2t}\mathbf{u}_1 + te^{2t}\mathbf{u}_1 + 2te^{2t}\mathbf{u}_2 + e^{2t}\mathbf{A}\mathbf{u}_3 .
\end{aligned}$$

Therefore, for $\mathbf{x}_3(t)$ to satisfy the given system, we must have

$$\mathbf{x}_3'(t) = \mathbf{A}\mathbf{x}_3(t)$$

$$\Rightarrow \quad te^{2t}\mathbf{u}_1 + t^2e^{2t}\mathbf{u}_1 + e^{2t}\mathbf{u}_2 + 2te^{2t}\mathbf{u}_2 + 2e^{2t}\mathbf{u}_3 = t^2e^{2t}\mathbf{u}_1 + te^{2t}\mathbf{u}_1 + 2te^{2t}\mathbf{u}_2 + e^{2t}\mathbf{A}\mathbf{u}_3$$

$$\Rightarrow \quad e^{2t}\mathbf{u}_2 + 2e^{2t}\mathbf{u}_3 = e^{2t}\mathbf{A}\mathbf{u}_3$$

$$\Rightarrow \quad \mathbf{u}_2 + 2\mathbf{u}_3 = \mathbf{A}\mathbf{u}_3$$

$$\Rightarrow \quad (\mathbf{A} - 2\mathbf{I})\mathbf{u}_3 = \mathbf{u}_2 \,.$$

Again since these steps are reversible, we see that, if a vector $\mathbf{u}_3$ satisfies the equation $(\mathbf{A} - 2\mathbf{I})\mathbf{u}_3 = \mathbf{u}_2$, then the vector

$$\mathbf{x}_3(t) = \frac{t^2}{2}\,e^{2t}\mathbf{u}_1 + te^{2t}\mathbf{u}_2 + e^{2t}\mathbf{u}_3$$

will be a third linearly independent solution to the given system. Thus, we can use this equation to find the vector $\mathbf{u}_3 = \operatorname{col}(v_1, v_2, v_3)$. Hence, we solve

$$(\mathbf{A} - 2\mathbf{I})\mathbf{u}_3 = \begin{bmatrix} 0 & 1 & 6 \\ 0 & 0 & 5 \\ 0 & 0 & 0 \end{bmatrix} \begin{bmatrix} v_1 \\ v_2 \\ v_3 \end{bmatrix} = \begin{bmatrix} 0 \\ 1 \\ 0 \end{bmatrix}.$$

This equation is equivalent to the system $v_2 + 6v_3 = 0$, $5v_3 = 1$, which implies that $v_3 = 1/5$, $v_2 = -6/5$. Therefore, if we let $\mathbf{u}_3 = \operatorname{col}(0, -6/5, 1/5)$, then

$$\mathbf{x}_3(t) = \frac{t^2}{2}\,e^{2t}\begin{bmatrix} 1 \\ 0 \\ 0 \end{bmatrix} + te^{2t}\begin{bmatrix} 0 \\ 1 \\ 0 \end{bmatrix} + e^{2t}\begin{bmatrix} 0 \\ -6/5 \\ 1/5 \end{bmatrix}$$

will be a third solution to the given system and we see by inspection that this solution is linearly independent from the solutions $\mathbf{x}_1(t)$ and $\mathbf{x}_2(t)$.

(e) Notice that

$$\begin{aligned} (\mathbf{A} - 2\mathbf{I})^3\mathbf{u}_3 &= (\mathbf{A} - 2\mathbf{I})^2\left[(\mathbf{A} - 2\mathbf{I})\mathbf{u}_3\right] \\ &= (\mathbf{A} - 2\mathbf{I})^2\mathbf{u}_2 = (\mathbf{A} - 2\mathbf{I})\left[(\mathbf{A} - 2\mathbf{I})\mathbf{u}_2\right] = (\mathbf{A} - 2\mathbf{I})\mathbf{u}_1 = \mathbf{0}. \end{aligned}$$

43. According to Problem 42, we will look for solutions of the form $\mathbf{x}(t) = t^r\mathbf{u}$, where r is an eigenvalue for the coefficient matrix and $\mathbf{u}$ is an associated eigenvector. To find the eigenvalues for this matrix, we solve the equation

$$|\mathbf{A} - r\mathbf{I}| = \begin{vmatrix} 1-r & 3 \\ -1 & 5-r \end{vmatrix} = 0$$

$$\Rightarrow \qquad (1-r)(5-r)+3=0$$

$$\Rightarrow \qquad r^2-6r+8=0 \qquad \Rightarrow \qquad (r-2)(r-4)=0.$$

Therefore, the coefficient matrix has the eigenvalues $r = 2, 4$. Since these are distinct eigenvalues, Theorem 6 on page 538 of the text assures us that their associated eigenvectors will be linearly independent. To find an eigenvector $\mathbf{u} = \mathrm{col}(u_1, u_2)$ associated with the eigenvalue $r = 2$, we solve the system

$$(\mathbf{A} - 2\mathbf{I})\mathbf{u} = \begin{bmatrix} -1 & 3 \\ -1 & 3 \end{bmatrix} \begin{bmatrix} u_1 \\ u_2 \end{bmatrix} = \begin{bmatrix} 0 \\ 0 \end{bmatrix},$$

which is equivalent to the equation $-u_1 + 3u_2 = 0$. Thus, if we let $u_2 = 1$ then, in order to satisfy this equation, we must have $u_1 = 3$. Hence, we see that the vector $\mathbf{u}_1 = \mathrm{col}(3, 1)$ will be an eigenvector for the coefficient matrix of the given system associated with the eigenvalue $r = 2$. Therefore, according to Problem 42, one solution to this system will be given by

$$\mathbf{x}_1(t) = t^2\mathbf{u}_1 = t^2 \begin{bmatrix} 3 \\ 1 \end{bmatrix}.$$

To find an eigenvector associated with the eigenvalue $r = 4$, we solve the equation

$$(\mathbf{A} - 4\mathbf{I})\mathbf{u} = \begin{bmatrix} -3 & 3 \\ -1 & 1 \end{bmatrix} \begin{bmatrix} u_1 \\ u_2 \end{bmatrix} = \begin{bmatrix} 0 \\ 0 \end{bmatrix},$$

which is equivalent to the equation $u_1 = u_2$. Thus, if we let $u_2 = 1$, then we must have $u_1 = 1$ and so an eigenvector associated with the eigenvalue $r = 4$ will be given by the vector $\mathbf{u}_2 = \mathrm{col}(1, 1)$. Therefore, another solution to the given system will be

$$\mathbf{x}_2(t) = t^4\mathbf{u}_2 = t^4 \begin{bmatrix} 1 \\ 1 \end{bmatrix}.$$

Clearly the solutions $\mathbf{x}_1(t)$ and $\mathbf{x}_2(t)$ are linearly independent. So the general solution to the given system with $t > 0$ will be

$$\mathbf{x}(t) = c_1 t^2 \begin{bmatrix} 3 \\ 1 \end{bmatrix} + c_2 t^4 \begin{bmatrix} 1 \\ 1 \end{bmatrix} = c_1 \begin{bmatrix} 3t^2 \\ t^2 \end{bmatrix} + c_2 \begin{bmatrix} t^4 \\ t^4 \end{bmatrix}.$$

EXERCISES 9.6: Complex Eigenvalues, page 549

3. To find the eigenvalues for the matrix $\mathbf{A}$, we solve the characteristic equation given by

$$|\mathbf{A} - r\mathbf{I}| = \begin{vmatrix} 1-r & 2 & -1 \\ 0 & 1-r & 1 \\ 0 & -1 & 1-r \end{vmatrix} = 0$$

$$\Rightarrow \quad (1-r) \begin{vmatrix} 1-r & 1 \\ -1 & 1-r \end{vmatrix} - 0 + 0 = 0$$

$$\Rightarrow \quad (1-r)\left[(1-r)^2 + 1\right] = (1-r)\left(r^2 - 2r + 2\right) = 0.$$

By this equation and the quadratic formula, we see that the roots to the characteristic equation and, therefore, the eigenvalues for the matrix $\mathbf{A}$ are $r = 1$, and $r = 1 \pm i$. To find an eigenvector $\mathbf{u} = \text{col}(u_1, u_2, u_3)$ associated with the real eigenvalue $r = 1$, we solve the system

$$(\mathbf{A} - \mathbf{I})\mathbf{u} = \begin{bmatrix} 0 & 2 & -1 \\ 0 & 0 & 1 \\ 0 & -1 & 0 \end{bmatrix} \begin{bmatrix} u_1 \\ u_2 \\ u_3 \end{bmatrix} = \begin{bmatrix} 0 \\ 0 \\ 0 \end{bmatrix},$$

which implies that $u_2 = 0$, $u_3 = 0$. Therefore, we can set u_1 arbitrarily to any value, say $u_1 = s$. Then the vectors

$$\mathbf{u} = \text{col}(u_1, u_2, u_3) = \text{col}(s, 0, 0) = s\text{col}(1, 0, 0)$$

will satisfy the above equation and, therefore, be eigenvectors for the matrix $\mathbf{A}$. Hence, if we set $s = 1$, we see that one eigenvector associated with the eigenvalue $r = 1$ will be the vector $\mathbf{u}_1 = \text{col}(1, 0, 0)$. Therefore, one solution to the given system will be

$$\mathbf{x}_1(t) = e^t \mathbf{u}_1 = e^t \begin{bmatrix} 1 \\ 0 \\ 0 \end{bmatrix}.$$

In order to find an eigenvector $\mathbf{z} = \text{col}(z_1, z_2, z_3)$ associated with the complex eigenvalue $r = 1 + i$, we solve the equation

$$[\mathbf{A} - (1+i)\mathbf{I}]\mathbf{z} = \begin{bmatrix} -i & 2 & -1 \\ 0 & -i & 1 \\ 0 & -1 & i \end{bmatrix} \begin{bmatrix} z_1 \\ z_2 \\ z_3 \end{bmatrix} = \begin{bmatrix} 0 \\ 0 \\ 0 \end{bmatrix}.$$

This equation is equivalent to the system

$$-iz_1 + 2z_2 - z_3 = 0 \qquad \text{and} \qquad -iz_2 + z_3 = 0.$$

Thus, if we let $z_2 = s$, then we see that $z_3 = is$ and

$$-iz_1 = -2z_2 + z_3 = -2s + is \qquad \Rightarrow \qquad (i)(-iz_1) = (i)(-2s + is)$$

$$\Rightarrow \qquad z_1 = -2is - s = -s - 2is\,,$$

where we have used the fact that $i^2 = -1$. Hence, eigenvectors associated with the eigenvalue $r = 1+i$ will be $\mathbf{z} = s\text{col}(-1-2i, 1, i)$. By taking $s = 1$, we see that one eigenvector associated with this eigenvalue will be the vector

$$\mathbf{z}_1 = \begin{bmatrix} -1-2i \\ 1 \\ i \end{bmatrix} = \begin{bmatrix} -1 \\ 1 \\ 0 \end{bmatrix} + i \begin{bmatrix} -2 \\ 0 \\ 1 \end{bmatrix}.$$

Thus, by the notation on page 545 of the text, we have $\alpha = 1$, $\beta = 1$, $\mathbf{a} = \text{col}(-1, 1, 0)$, and $\mathbf{b} = \text{col}(-2, 0, 1)$. Therefore, according to formulas (6) and (7) on page 546 of the text, two more linearly independent solutions to the given system will be given by

$$\mathbf{x}_2(t) = (e^t \cos t)\mathbf{a} - (e^t \sin t)\mathbf{b} \qquad \text{and} \qquad \mathbf{x}_3(t) = (e^t \sin t)\mathbf{a} + (e^t \cos t)\mathbf{b}.$$

Hence, the general solution to the system given in this problem will be

$$\begin{aligned} \mathbf{x}(t) &= c_1\mathbf{x}_2(t) + c_2\mathbf{x}_3(t) + c_3\mathbf{x}_1(t) \\ &= c_1 e^t \cos t \begin{bmatrix} -1 \\ 1 \\ 0 \end{bmatrix} - c_1 e^t \sin t \begin{bmatrix} -2 \\ 0 \\ 1 \end{bmatrix} + c_2 e^t \sin t \begin{bmatrix} -1 \\ 1 \\ 0 \end{bmatrix} + c_2 e^t \cos t \begin{bmatrix} -2 \\ 0 \\ 1 \end{bmatrix} + c_3 e^t \begin{bmatrix} 1 \\ 0 \\ 0 \end{bmatrix}. \end{aligned}$$

7. In order to find a fundamental matrix for this system, we must first find three linearly independent solutions. Thus, we seek the eigenvalues for the matrix $\mathbf{A}$ by solving the characteristic equation given by

$$|\mathbf{A} - r\mathbf{I}| = \begin{vmatrix} -r & 0 & 1 \\ 0 & -r & -1 \\ 0 & 1 & -r \end{vmatrix} = 0$$

$$\Rightarrow \quad -r \begin{vmatrix} -r & -1 \\ 1 & -r \end{vmatrix} - 0 + 0 = 0 \quad \Rightarrow \quad -r\left(r^2 + 1\right) = 0.$$

Hence, the eigenvalues for the matrix $\mathbf{A}$ will be $r = 0$ and $r = \pm i$. To find an eigenvector $\mathbf{u} = \text{col}(u_1, u_2, u_3)$ associated with the real eigenvalue $r = 0$, we solve the equation

$$(\mathbf{A} - 0\mathbf{I})\mathbf{u} = \begin{bmatrix} 0 & 0 & 1 \\ 0 & 0 & -1 \\ 0 & 1 & 0 \end{bmatrix} \begin{bmatrix} u_1 \\ u_2 \\ u_3 \end{bmatrix} = \begin{bmatrix} 0 \\ 0 \\ 0 \end{bmatrix},$$

which is equivalent to the system $u_3 = 0$, $u_2 = 0$. Thus, if we let u_1 have the arbitrary value $u_1 = s$, then the vectors

$$\mathbf{u} = \text{col}(u_1, u_2, u_3) = \text{col}(s, 0, 0) = s\text{col}(1, 0, 0)$$

will satisfy this equation and will, therefore, be eigenvectors for the matrix $\mathbf{A}$ associated with the eigenvalue $r = 0$. Hence, by letting $s = 1$, we find that one of these eigenvectors will be the vector $\mathbf{u} = \text{col}(1, 0, 0)$. Thus, one solution to the given system will be

$$\mathbf{x}_1(t) = e^0\mathbf{u} = \begin{bmatrix} 1 \\ 0 \\ 0 \end{bmatrix}.$$

To find two more linearly independent solutions for this system, we will first look for an eigenvector associated with the complex eigenvalue $r = i$. That is, we seek a vector, say, $\mathbf{z} = \text{col}(z_1, z_2, z_3)$ which satisfies the equation

$$(\mathbf{A} - i\mathbf{I})\mathbf{z} = \begin{bmatrix} -i & 0 & 1 \\ 0 & -i & -1 \\ 0 & 1 & -i \end{bmatrix} \begin{bmatrix} z_1 \\ z_2 \\ z_3 \end{bmatrix} = \begin{bmatrix} 0 \\ 0 \\ 0 \end{bmatrix},$$

which is equivalent to the system

$$iz_1 = z_3 \qquad \text{and} \qquad iz_2 = -z_3\,.$$

Thus, if we let z_3 be any arbitrary value, say $z_3 = is$, (which means that we must have $z_1 = s$ and $z_2 = -s$), then we see that the vectors, given by

$$\mathbf{z} = \text{col}(z_1, z_2, z_3) = \text{col}(s, -s, is) = s\text{col}(1, -1, i),$$

will be eigenvectors for the matrix $\mathbf{A}$ associated with the eigenvalue $r = i$. Therefore, by letting $s = 1$, we find that one of these eigenvectors will be the vector

$$\mathbf{z} = \begin{bmatrix} 1 \\ -1 \\ i \end{bmatrix} = \begin{bmatrix} 1 \\ -1 \\ 0 \end{bmatrix} + i \begin{bmatrix} 0 \\ 0 \\ 1 \end{bmatrix}.$$

From this, by the notation given on page 546 of the text, we see that $\alpha = 0$, $\beta = 1$, $\mathbf{a} = \text{col}(1, -1, 0)$, and $\mathbf{b} = \text{col}(0, 0, 1)$. Therefore, by formulas (6) and (7) on page 546 of the text, two more linearly independent solutions for this system will be

$$\mathbf{x}_2(t) = (\cos t)\mathbf{a} - (\sin t)\mathbf{b} = \begin{bmatrix} \cos t \\ -\cos t \\ 0 \end{bmatrix} - \begin{bmatrix} 0 \\ 0 \\ \sin t \end{bmatrix} = \begin{bmatrix} \cos t \\ -\cos t \\ \sin t \end{bmatrix}$$

and

$$\mathbf{x}_3(t) = (\sin t)\mathbf{a} + (\cos t)\mathbf{b} = \begin{bmatrix} \sin t \\ -\sin t \\ 0 \end{bmatrix} + \begin{bmatrix} 0 \\ 0 \\ \cos t \end{bmatrix} = \begin{bmatrix} \sin t \\ -\sin t \\ \cos t \end{bmatrix}.$$

Finally, since a fundamental matrix for the system given in this problem must have three columns which are linearly independent solutions of the system, we see that such a fundamental matrix will be given by the matrix

$$\mathbf{X}(t) = \begin{bmatrix} 1 & \cos t & \sin t \\ 0 & -\cos t & -\sin t \\ 0 & -\sin t & \cos t \end{bmatrix}.$$

17. We will assume that $t > 0$. According to Problem 42 in Exercises 9.5, a solution to this Cauchy-Euler system will have the form $\mathbf{x}(t) = t^r\mathbf{u}$, where r is an eigenvalue for the coefficient matrix of the system and $\mathbf{u}$ is an eigenvector associated with this eigenvalue. Therefore, we first must find the eigenvalues for this matrix by solving the characteristic equation given by

$$|\mathbf{A} - r\mathbf{I}| = \begin{vmatrix} -1-r & -1 & 0 \\ 2 & -1-r & 1 \\ 0 & 1 & -1-r \end{vmatrix} = 0$$

$$\Rightarrow \quad (-1-r)\begin{vmatrix} -1-r & 1 \\ 1 & -1-r \end{vmatrix} + \begin{vmatrix} 2 & 1 \\ 0 & -1-r \end{vmatrix} = 0$$

$$\Rightarrow \quad (-1-r)\left[(-1-r)^2 - 1\right] + 2(-1-r) = -(1+r)\left(r^2 + 2r + 2\right) = 0.$$

From this equation and by using the quadratic formula, we see that the eigenvalues for this coefficient matrix will be $r = -1, -1 \pm i$. The eigenvectors associated with the real eigenvalue $r = -1$ will be the vectors $\mathbf{u} = \text{col}(u_1, u_2, u_3)$ which satisfy the equation

$$(\mathbf{A} + \mathbf{I})\mathbf{u} = \begin{bmatrix} 0 & -1 & 0 \\ 2 & 0 & 1 \\ 0 & 1 & 0 \end{bmatrix}\begin{bmatrix} u_1 \\ u_2 \\ u_3 \end{bmatrix} = \begin{bmatrix} 0 \\ 0 \\ 0 \end{bmatrix},$$

which is equivalent to the system $u_2 = 0$, $2u_1 + u_3 = 0$. Thus, by letting $u_1 = 1$ (which means that $u_3 = -2$), we see that the vector

$$\mathbf{u} = \text{col}(u_1, u_2, u_3) = \text{col}(1, 0, -2)$$

satisfies this equation and is, therefore, an eigenvector of the coefficient matrix associated with the eigenvalue $r = -1$. Hence, according to Problem 42 of Exercises 9.5, we see that a solution to this Cauchy-Euler system will be given by

$$\mathbf{x}_1(t) = t^{-1}\mathbf{u} = t^{-1}\begin{bmatrix} 1 \\ 0 \\ -2 \end{bmatrix} = \begin{bmatrix} t^{-1} \\ 0 \\ -2t^{-1} \end{bmatrix}.$$

To find the eigenvectors $\mathbf{z} = \text{col}(z_1, z_2, z_3)$ associated with the complex eigenvalue $r = -1 + i$, we solve the equation

$$(\mathbf{A} - (-1+i)\mathbf{I})\mathbf{z} = \begin{bmatrix} -i & -1 & 0 \\ 2 & -i & 1 \\ 0 & 1 & -i \end{bmatrix} \begin{bmatrix} z_1 \\ z_2 \\ z_3 \end{bmatrix} = \begin{bmatrix} 0 \\ 0 \\ 0 \end{bmatrix}$$

$$\Rightarrow \quad \begin{bmatrix} -i & -1 & 0 \\ 0 & i & 1 \\ 0 & 0 & 0 \end{bmatrix} \begin{bmatrix} z_1 \\ z_2 \\ z_3 \end{bmatrix} = \begin{bmatrix} 0 \\ 0 \\ 0 \end{bmatrix},$$

which is equivalent to the system $-iz_1 - z_2 = 0$, $iz_2 + z_3 = 0$. Thus, if we let $z_1 = 1$, we must let $z_2 = -i$ and $z_3 = -1$ in order to satisfy this system. Therefore, one eigenvector for the coefficient matrix associated with the eigenvalue $r = -1+i$ will be the vector $\mathbf{z} = \text{col}(1, -i, -1)$ and another solution to this system will be $\mathbf{x}(t) = t^{-1+i}\mathbf{z}$. We would like to find real solutions to this problem. Therefore, we note that by Euler's formula we have

$$t^{-1+i} = t^{-1}t^{i} = t^{-1}e^{i\ln t} = t^{-1}[\cos(\ln t) + i\sin(\ln t)],$$

where we have made use of our assumption that $t > 0$. Hence, the solution that we have just found becomes

$$\begin{aligned} \mathbf{x}(t) &= t^{-1+i}\mathbf{z} = t^{-1}[\cos(\ln t) + i\sin(\ln t)]\mathbf{z} \\ &= t^{-1}[\cos(\ln t) + i\sin(\ln t)] \begin{bmatrix} 1 \\ -i \\ -1 \end{bmatrix} = \begin{bmatrix} t^{-1}\cos(\ln t) \\ t^{-1}\sin(\ln t) \\ -t^{-1}\cos(\ln t) \end{bmatrix} + i \begin{bmatrix} t^{-1}\sin(\ln t) \\ -t^{-1}\cos(\ln t) \\ -t^{-1}\sin(\ln t) \end{bmatrix}. \end{aligned}$$

Thus, by Lemma 2 (adapted to systems) on page 172 of the text we see that two more linearly independent solutions to this Cauchy-Euler system will be

$$\mathbf{x}_2(t) = \begin{bmatrix} t^{-1}\cos(\ln t) \\ t^{-1}\sin(\ln t) \\ -t^{-1}\cos(\ln t) \end{bmatrix} \quad \text{and} \quad \mathbf{x}_3(t) = \begin{bmatrix} t^{-1}\sin(\ln t) \\ -t^{-1}\cos(\ln t) \\ -t^{-1}\sin(\ln t) \end{bmatrix},$$

and, hence, a general solution will be given by

$$\mathbf{x}(t) = c_1 \begin{bmatrix} t^{-1} \\ 0 \\ -2t^{-1} \end{bmatrix} + c_2 \begin{bmatrix} t^{-1}\cos(\ln t) \\ t^{-1}\sin(\ln t) \\ -t^{-1}\cos(\ln t) \end{bmatrix} + c_3 \begin{bmatrix} t^{-1}\sin(\ln t) \\ -t^{-1}\cos(\ln t) \\ -t^{-1}\sin(\ln t) \end{bmatrix}.$$

EXERCISES 9.7: Nonhomogeneous Linear Systems, page 555

3. We must first find the general solution to the corresponding homogeneous system. Therefore, we first find the eigenvalues for the coefficient matrix $\mathbf{A}$ by solving the characteristic equation given by

$$|\mathbf{A} - r\mathbf{I}| = \begin{vmatrix} 1-r & -2 & 2 \\ -2 & 1-r & 2 \\ 2 & 2 & 1-r \end{vmatrix} = 0$$

$$\Rightarrow \quad (1-r)\begin{vmatrix} 1-r & 2 \\ 2 & 1-r \end{vmatrix} + 2\begin{vmatrix} -2 & 2 \\ 2 & 1-r \end{vmatrix} + 2\begin{vmatrix} -2 & 1-r \\ 2 & 2 \end{vmatrix} = 0$$

$$\Rightarrow \quad (1-r)\left[(1-r)^2 - 4\right] + 2\left[-2(1-r) - 4\right] + 2\left[-4 - 2(1-r)\right] = 0$$

$$\Rightarrow \quad (1-r)(r^2 - 2r - 3) + 4(2r - 6) = 0$$

$$\Rightarrow \quad (1-r)(r+1)(r-3) + 8(r-3) = (r-3)(r^2-9) = (r-3)(r-3)(r+3) = 0.$$

Thus, the eigenvalues for the matrix $\mathbf{A}$ are $r = 3, -3$, where $r = 3$ is an eigenvalue of multiplicity two. Notice that, even though the matrix $\mathbf{A}$ has only two distinct eigenvalues, we are still guaranteed three linearly independent eigenvectors because $\mathbf{A}$ is a 3×3 real symmetric matrix. To find an eigenvector associated with the eigenvalue $r = -3$, we must find a vector $\mathbf{u} = \text{col}(u_1, u_2, u_3)$ which satisfies the system

$$(\mathbf{A} + 3\mathbf{I})\mathbf{u} = \begin{bmatrix} 4 & -2 & 2 \\ -2 & 4 & 2 \\ 2 & 2 & 4 \end{bmatrix} \begin{bmatrix} u_1 \\ u_2 \\ u_3 \end{bmatrix} = \begin{bmatrix} 0 \\ 0 \\ 0 \end{bmatrix} \quad \Rightarrow \quad \begin{bmatrix} 1 & 0 & 1 \\ 0 & 1 & 1 \\ 0 & 0 & 0 \end{bmatrix} \begin{bmatrix} u_1 \\ u_2 \\ u_3 \end{bmatrix} = \begin{bmatrix} 0 \\ 0 \\ 0 \end{bmatrix},$$

which is equivalent to the system $u_1 + u_3 = 0$, $u_2 + u_3 = 0$. Hence, by letting $u_3 = -1$, we must have $u_1 = u_2 = 1$, and so the vector $\mathbf{u}_1 = \text{col}(1, 1, -1)$ will then satisfy the above system.

Therefore, this vector is an eigenvector for the matrix $\mathbf{A}$ associated with the eigenvalue $r = -3$. Thus, one solution to the corresponding homogeneous system is given by

$$\mathbf{x}_1(t) = e^{-3t}\mathbf{u}_1 = e^{-3t}\begin{bmatrix} 1 \\ 1 \\ -1 \end{bmatrix}.$$

To find eigenvectors $\mathbf{u} = \mathrm{col}(u_1, u_2, u_3)$ associated with the eigenvalue $r = 3$, we solve the equation given by

$$(\mathbf{A} - 3\mathbf{I})\mathbf{u} = \begin{bmatrix} -2 & -2 & 2 \\ -2 & -2 & 2 \\ 2 & 2 & -2 \end{bmatrix}\begin{bmatrix} u_1 \\ u_2 \\ u_3 \end{bmatrix} = \begin{bmatrix} 0 \\ 0 \\ 0 \end{bmatrix},$$

which is equivalent to the equation $u_1 + u_2 - u_3 = 0$. Thus, if we let $u_3 = s$ and $u_2 = v$, then we must have $u_1 = s - v$. Hence, solutions to the above equation and, therefore, eigenvectors for $\mathbf{A}$ associated with the eigenvalue $r = 3$ will be the vectors

$$\mathbf{u} = \begin{bmatrix} s - v \\ v \\ s \end{bmatrix} = s\begin{bmatrix} 1 \\ 0 \\ 1 \end{bmatrix} + v\begin{bmatrix} -1 \\ 1 \\ 0 \end{bmatrix},$$

where s and v are arbitrary scalars. Therefore, letting $s = 1$ and $v = 0$ yields the eigenvector $\mathbf{u}_2 = \mathrm{col}(1, 0, 1)$. Similarly, by letting $s = 0$ and $v = 1$, we obtain the eigenvector $\mathbf{u}_3 = \mathrm{col}(-1, 1, 0)$, which we can see by inspection is linearly independent from $\mathbf{u}_2$. Hence, two more solutions to the corresponding homogeneous system which are linearly independent from each other and from $\mathbf{x}_1(t)$ are given by

$$\mathbf{x}_2(t) = e^{3t}\mathbf{u}_2 = e^{3t}\begin{bmatrix} 1 \\ 0 \\ 1 \end{bmatrix} \quad \text{and} \quad \mathbf{x}_3(t) = e^{3t}\mathbf{u}_3 = e^{3t}\begin{bmatrix} -1 \\ 1 \\ 0 \end{bmatrix}.$$

Thus, the general solution to the corresponding homogeneous system will be

$$\mathbf{x}_h(t) = c_1e^{-3t}\begin{bmatrix} 1 \\ 1 \\ -1 \end{bmatrix} + c_2e^{3t}\begin{bmatrix} 1 \\ 0 \\ 1 \end{bmatrix} + c_3e^{3t}\begin{bmatrix} -1 \\ 1 \\ 0 \end{bmatrix}.$$

To find a particular solution to the nonhomogeneous system, we note that

$$\mathbf{f}(t)=\begin{bmatrix}2e^t\\4e^t\\-2e^t\end{bmatrix}=e^t\begin{bmatrix}2\\4\\-2\end{bmatrix}=e^t\mathbf{g},$$

where $\mathbf{g}=\operatorname{col}(2,4,-2)$. Therefore, we will assume that a particular solution to the nonhomogeneous system will have the form $\mathbf{x}_p(t)=e^t\mathbf{a}$, where $\mathbf{a}=\operatorname{col}(a_1,a_2,a_3)$ is a constant vector which must be determined. Hence, we see that $\mathbf{x}_p'(t)=e^t\mathbf{a}$. By substituting $\mathbf{x}_p(t)$ into the given system, we obtain

$$e^t\mathbf{a}=\mathbf{A}\mathbf{x}_p(t)+\mathbf{f}(t)=\mathbf{A}e^t\mathbf{a}+e^t\mathbf{g}=e^t\mathbf{A}\mathbf{a}+e^t\mathbf{g}.$$

Therefore, we have

$$e^t\mathbf{a}=e^t\mathbf{A}\mathbf{a}+e^t\mathbf{g}\quad\Rightarrow\quad\mathbf{a}=\mathbf{A}\mathbf{a}+\mathbf{g}\quad\Rightarrow\quad(\mathbf{I}-\mathbf{A})\mathbf{a}=\mathbf{g}$$

$$\Rightarrow\quad\begin{bmatrix}0&2&-2\\2&0&-2\\-2&-2&0\end{bmatrix}\begin{bmatrix}a_1\\a_2\\a_3\end{bmatrix}=\begin{bmatrix}2\\4\\-2\end{bmatrix}.$$

The last equation above can be solved by either performing elementary row operations on the augmented matrix or by solving the system

$$\begin{aligned}2a_2-2a_3&=2,\\2a_1-2a_3&=4,\\-2a_1-2a_2&=-2.\end{aligned}$$

Either way, we obtain $a_1=1$, $a_2=0$, and $a_3=-1$. Thus, a particular solution to the nonhomogeneous system will be given by

$$\mathbf{x}_p(t)=e^t\mathbf{a}=e^t\begin{bmatrix}1\\0\\-1\end{bmatrix},$$

and so the general solution to the nonhomogeneous system will be

$$\mathbf{x}(t)=\mathbf{x}_h(t)+\mathbf{x}_p(t)=c_1e^{-3t}\begin{bmatrix}1\\1\\-1\end{bmatrix}+c_2e^{3t}\begin{bmatrix}1\\0\\1\end{bmatrix}+c_3e^{3t}\begin{bmatrix}-1\\1\\0\end{bmatrix}+e^t\begin{bmatrix}1\\0\\-1\end{bmatrix}.$$

13. We must first find a fundamental matrix for the corresponding homogeneous system $\mathbf{x}' = \mathbf{A}\mathbf{x}$. To this end, we first find the eigenvalues of the matrix $\mathbf{A}$ by solving the characteristic equation given by

$$|\mathbf{A} - r\mathbf{I}| = \begin{vmatrix} 2-r & 1 \\ -3 & -2-r \end{vmatrix} = 0 \quad \Rightarrow \quad (2-r)(-2-r)+3=0 \quad \Rightarrow \quad r^2 - 1 = 0\,.$$

Thus, the eigenvalues of the coefficient matrix $\mathbf{A}$ are $r = \pm 1$. The eigenvectors associated with the eigenvalue $r = 1$ are the vectors $\mathbf{u} = \text{col}(u_1, u_2)$ which satisfy the equation

$$(\mathbf{A} - \mathbf{I})\mathbf{u} = \begin{bmatrix} 1 & 1 \\ -3 & -3 \end{bmatrix} \begin{bmatrix} u_1 \\ u_2 \end{bmatrix} = \begin{bmatrix} 0 \\ 0 \end{bmatrix}.$$

This equation is equivalent to the equation $u_1 + u_2 = 0$. Therefore, if we let $u_1 = 1$, then we have $u_2 = -1$, so one eigenvector of the matrix $\mathbf{A}$ associated with the eigenvalue $r = 1$ is the vector $\mathbf{u}_1 = \text{col}(1, -1)$. Hence, one solution of the corresponding homogeneous system is given by

$$\mathbf{x}_1(t) = e^t \mathbf{u}_1 = e^t \begin{bmatrix} 1 \\ -1 \end{bmatrix} = \begin{bmatrix} e^t \\ -e^t \end{bmatrix}.$$

To find an eigenvector associated with the eigenvalue $r = -1$, we solve the equation

$$(\mathbf{A} + \mathbf{I})\mathbf{u} = \begin{bmatrix} 3 & 1 \\ -3 & -1 \end{bmatrix} \begin{bmatrix} u_1 \\ u_2 \end{bmatrix} = \begin{bmatrix} 0 \\ 0 \end{bmatrix},$$

which is equivalent to the equation $3u_1 + u_2 = 0$. Since $u_1 = 1$ and $u_2 = -3$ satisfy this equation, one eigenvector for the matrix $\mathbf{A}$ associated with the eigenvalue $r = -1$ is the vector $\mathbf{u}_2 = \text{col}(1, -3)$. Thus, another linearly independent solution of the corresponding homogeneous system is

$$\mathbf{x}_2(t) = e^{-t} \mathbf{u}_2 = e^{-t} \begin{bmatrix} 1 \\ -3 \end{bmatrix} = \begin{bmatrix} e^{-t} \\ -3e^{-t} \end{bmatrix}.$$

Hence, the general solution of the homogeneous system is given by

$$\mathbf{x}_h(t) = c_1 \begin{bmatrix} e^t \\ -e^t \end{bmatrix} + c_2 \begin{bmatrix} e^{-t} \\ -3e^{-t} \end{bmatrix},$$

and a fundamental matrix is

$$\mathbf{X}(t) = \begin{bmatrix} e^t & e^{-t} \\ -e^t & -3e^{-t} \end{bmatrix}.$$

To find the inverse matrix $\mathbf{X}^{-1}(t)$, we will perform row-reduction on the matrix $[\mathbf{X}(t)|\mathbf{I}]$. Thus, we have

$$[\mathbf{X}(t)|\mathbf{I}] = \left[\begin{array}{cc|cc} e^t & e^{-t} & 1 & 0 \\ -e^t & -3e^{-t} & 0 & 1 \end{array}\right] \longrightarrow \left[\begin{array}{cc|cc} e^t & e^{-t} & 1 & 0 \\ 0 & -2e^{-t} & 1 & 1 \end{array}\right]$$

$$\longrightarrow \left[\begin{array}{cc|cc} e^t & 0 & 3/2 & 1/2 \\ 0 & e^{-t} & -1/2 & -1/2 \end{array}\right] \longrightarrow \left[\begin{array}{cc|cc} 1 & 0 & (3/2)e^{-t} & (1/2)e^{-t} \\ 0 & 1 & -(1/2)e^{-t} & -(1/2)e^{-t} \end{array}\right].$$

Therefore, we see that

$$\mathbf{X}^{-1}(t) = \begin{bmatrix} (3/2)e^{-t} & (1/2)e^{-t} \\ -(1/2)e^{-t} & -(1/2)e^{-t} \end{bmatrix}.$$

Hence, we have

$$\mathbf{X}^{-1}(t)\mathbf{f}(t) = \begin{bmatrix} (3/2)e^{-t} & (1/2)e^{-t} \\ -(1/2)e^{-t} & -(1/2)e^{-t} \end{bmatrix} \begin{bmatrix} 2e^t \\ 4e^t \end{bmatrix} = \begin{bmatrix} 5 \\ -3e^{2t} \end{bmatrix},$$

and so we have

$$\int \mathbf{X}^{-1}(t)\mathbf{f}(t)\,dt = \begin{bmatrix} \int (5)dt \\ -3\int e^{2t}dt \end{bmatrix} = \begin{bmatrix} 5t \\ -(3/2)e^{2t} \end{bmatrix},$$

where we have taken the constants of integration to be zero. Thus, by equation (8) on page 553 of the text, we see that

$$\mathbf{x}_p(t) = \begin{bmatrix} e^t & e^{-t} \\ -e^t & -3e^{-t} \end{bmatrix} \begin{bmatrix} 5t \\ -(3/2)e^{2t} \end{bmatrix} = \begin{bmatrix} 5te^t - (3/2)e^t \\ -5te^t + (9/2)e^t \end{bmatrix}.$$

Therefore, by adding $\mathbf{x}_h(t)$ and $\mathbf{x}_p(t)$ we obtain

$$\mathbf{x}(t) = c_1 \begin{bmatrix} e^t \\ -e^t \end{bmatrix} + c_2 \begin{bmatrix} e^{-t} \\ -3e^{-t} \end{bmatrix} + \begin{bmatrix} 5te^t - (3/2)e^t \\ -5te^t + (9/2)e^t \end{bmatrix}.$$

We remark that this answer is the same as the answer given in the text as can be seen by replacing c_1 by $c_1 + 9/4$.

15. We must first find a fundamental matrix for the associated homogeneous system. We will do this by finding the solutions derived from the eigenvalues and the associated eigenvectors for the coefficient matrix $\mathbf{A}$. Therefore, we find these eigenvalues by solving the characteristic equation given by

$$|\mathbf{A}-r\mathbf{I}| = \begin{vmatrix} -4-r & 2 \\ 2 & -1-r \end{vmatrix} = 0$$

$$\Rightarrow \quad (-4-r)(-1-r)-4=0 \quad \Rightarrow \quad r^2+5r=0\,.$$

Thus, the eigenvalues for the matrix $\mathbf{A}$ are $r=-5,0$. An eigenvector for this matrix associated with the eigenvalue $r=0$ is the vector $\mathbf{u}=\operatorname{col}(u_1,u_2)$ which satisfies the equation

$$\mathbf{A}\mathbf{u} = \begin{bmatrix} -4 & 2 \\ 2 & -1 \end{bmatrix}\begin{bmatrix} u_1 \\ u_2 \end{bmatrix} = \begin{bmatrix} 0 \\ 0 \end{bmatrix}.$$

This equation is equivalent to the equation $2u_1=u_2$. Therefore, if we let $u_1=1$ and $u_2=2$, then the vector $\mathbf{u}_1=\operatorname{col}(1,2)$ satisfies this equation and is, therefore, an eigenvector for the matrix $\mathbf{A}$ associated with the eigenvalue $r=0$. Hence, one solution to the homogeneous system is given by

$$\mathbf{x}_1(t) = e^{(0)t}\mathbf{u}_1 = \begin{bmatrix} 1 \\ 2 \end{bmatrix}.$$

To find an eigenvector associated with the eigenvalue $r=-5$, we solve the equation

$$(\mathbf{A}+5\mathbf{I})\mathbf{u} = \begin{bmatrix} 1 & 2 \\ 2 & 4 \end{bmatrix}\begin{bmatrix} u_1 \\ u_2 \end{bmatrix} = \begin{bmatrix} 0 \\ 0 \end{bmatrix},$$

which is equivalent to the equation $u_1+2u_2=0$. Thus, by letting $u_2=1$ and $u_1=-2$, the vector $\mathbf{u}_2=\operatorname{col}(u_1,u_2)=\operatorname{col}(-2,1)$ satisfies this equation and is, therefore, an eigenvector for $\mathbf{A}$ associated with the eigenvalue $r=-5$. Hence, since the two eigenvalues of $\mathbf{A}$ are distinct, we see that another linearly independent solution to the corresponding homogeneous system is given by

$$\mathbf{x}_2(t) = e^{-5t}\mathbf{u}_2 = e^{-5t}\begin{bmatrix} -2 \\ 1 \end{bmatrix} = \begin{bmatrix} -2e^{-5t} \\ e^{-5t} \end{bmatrix}.$$

By combining these two solutions, we see that a general solution to the homogeneous system is

$$\mathbf{x}_h(t) = c_1 \begin{bmatrix} 1 \\ 2 \end{bmatrix} + c_2 \begin{bmatrix} -2e^{-5t} \\ e^{-5t} \end{bmatrix}$$

and a fundamental matrix for this system is the matrix

$$\mathbf{X}(t) = \begin{bmatrix} 1 & -2e^{-5t} \\ 2 & e^{-5t} \end{bmatrix}.$$

We will use equation (10) on page 553 of the text to find a particular solution to the nonhomogeneous system. Thus, we need to find the inverse matrix $\mathbf{X}^{-1}(t)$. This can be done, for example, by performing row-reduction on the matrix $[\mathbf{X}(t)|\mathbf{I}]$ to obtain the matrix $[\mathbf{I}|\mathbf{X}^{-1}(t)]$. In this way, we find that the required inverse matrix is given by

$$\mathbf{X}^{-1}(t) = \begin{bmatrix} 1/5 & 2/5 \\ -(2/5)e^{5t} & (1/5)e^{5t} \end{bmatrix}.$$

Therefore, we have

$$\mathbf{X}^{-1}(t)\mathbf{f}(t) = \begin{bmatrix} 1/5 & 2/5 \\ -(2/5)e^{5t} & (1/5)e^{5t} \end{bmatrix} \begin{bmatrix} t^{-1} \\ 4+2t^{-1} \end{bmatrix} = \begin{bmatrix} t^{-1}+(8/5) \\ (4/5)e^{5t} \end{bmatrix}.$$

From this we see that

$$\int \mathbf{X}^{-1}(t)\mathbf{f}(t)\,dt = \begin{bmatrix} \int [t^{-1}+(8/5)]\,dt \\ \int (4/5)e^{5t}\,dt \end{bmatrix} = \begin{bmatrix} \ln|t|+(8/5)t \\ (4/25)e^{5t} \end{bmatrix},$$

where we have taken the constants of integration to be zero. Hence, by equation (10) on page 553 of the text, we obtain

$$\begin{aligned} \mathbf{x}_p(t) &= \mathbf{X}(t)\int \mathbf{X}^{-1}(t)\mathbf{f}(t)\,dt \\ &= \begin{bmatrix} 1 & -2e^{-5t} \\ 2 & e^{-5t} \end{bmatrix} \begin{bmatrix} \ln|t|+(8/5)t \\ (4/25)e^{5t} \end{bmatrix} = \begin{bmatrix} \ln|t|+(8/5)t-(8/25) \\ 2\ln|t|+(16/5)t+(4/25) \end{bmatrix}. \end{aligned}$$

Adding $\mathbf{x}_h(t)$ and $\mathbf{x}_p(t)$ yields the general solution to the nonhomogeneous system given by

$$\mathbf{x}(t) = c_1 \begin{bmatrix} 1 \\ 2 \end{bmatrix} + c_2 \begin{bmatrix} -2e^{-5t} \\ e^{-5t} \end{bmatrix} + \begin{bmatrix} \ln|t|+(8/5)t-(8/25) \\ 2\ln|t|+(16/5)t+(4/25) \end{bmatrix}.$$

21. We will find the solution to this initial value problem by using equation (13) on page 554 of the text. Therefore, we must first find a fundamental matrix for the associated homogeneous system. This means that we must find the eigenvalues and corresponding eigenvectors for the coefficient matrix of this system by solving the characteristic equation

$$|\mathbf{A} - r\mathbf{I}| = \begin{vmatrix} -r & 2 \\ -1 & 3-r \end{vmatrix}$$

$$\Rightarrow \quad -r(3-r)+2=0 \quad \Rightarrow \quad r^2-3r+2=0 \quad \Rightarrow \quad (r-2)(r-1)=0.$$

Hence, $r = 1, 2$ are the eigenvalues for this matrix. To find an eigenvector $\mathbf{u} = \operatorname{col}(u_1, u_2)$ for this coefficient matrix associated with the eigenvalue $r = 1$, we solve the system

$$(\mathbf{A} - \mathbf{I})\mathbf{u} = \begin{bmatrix} -1 & 2 \\ -1 & 2 \end{bmatrix} \begin{bmatrix} u_1 \\ u_2 \end{bmatrix} = \begin{bmatrix} 0 \\ 0 \end{bmatrix}.$$

This system is equivalent to the equation $u_1 = 2u_2$. Thus, $u_1 = 2$ and $u_2 = 1$ is a set of values which satisfies this equation and, therefore, the vector $\mathbf{u}_1 = \operatorname{col}(2, 1)$ is an eigenvector for the coefficient matrix corresponding to the eigenvalue $r = 1$. Hence, one solution to the homogeneous system is given by

$$\mathbf{x}_1(t) = e^t\mathbf{u}_1 = e^t \begin{bmatrix} 2 \\ 1 \end{bmatrix} = \begin{bmatrix} 2e^t \\ e^t \end{bmatrix}.$$

Similarly, by solving the equation

$$(\mathbf{A} - 2\mathbf{I})\mathbf{u} = \begin{bmatrix} -2 & 2 \\ -1 & 1 \end{bmatrix} \begin{bmatrix} u_1 \\ u_2 \end{bmatrix} = \begin{bmatrix} 0 \\ 0 \end{bmatrix},$$

we find that one eigenvector for the coefficient matrix associated with the eigenvalue $r = 2$ is $\mathbf{u}_2 = \operatorname{col}(u_1, u_2) = \operatorname{col}(1, 1)$. Thus, another linearly independent solution to the associated homogeneous problem is given by

$$\mathbf{x}_2(t) = e^{2t}\mathbf{u}_2 = e^{2t} \begin{bmatrix} 1 \\ 1 \end{bmatrix} = \begin{bmatrix} e^{2t} \\ e^{2t} \end{bmatrix}.$$

By combining these two solutions, we obtain a general solution to the homogeneous system

$$\mathbf{x}_h(t) = c_1 \begin{bmatrix} 2e^t \\ e^t \end{bmatrix} + c_2 \begin{bmatrix} e^{2t} \\ e^{2t} \end{bmatrix},$$

and the fundamental matrix

$$\mathbf{X}(t) = \begin{bmatrix} 2e^t & e^{2t} \\ e^t & e^{2t} \end{bmatrix}.$$

In order to use equation (13) on page 554 of the text, we must also find the inverse of the fundamental matrix. One way of doing this is to perform row-reduction on the matrix $[\mathbf{X}(t)|\mathbf{I}]$ to obtain the matrix $[\mathbf{I}|\mathbf{X}^{-1}(t)]$. Thus, we find that

$$\mathbf{X}^{-1}(t) = \begin{bmatrix} e^{-t} & -e^{-t} \\ -e^{-2t} & 2e^{-2t} \end{bmatrix}.$$

From this we see that

$$\mathbf{X}^{-1}(s)\mathbf{f}(s) = \begin{bmatrix} e^{-s} & -e^{-s} \\ -e^{-2s} & 2e^{-2s} \end{bmatrix} \begin{bmatrix} e^s \\ -e^s \end{bmatrix} = \begin{bmatrix} 2 \\ -3e^{-s} \end{bmatrix}.$$

(a) Using the initial condition $\mathbf{x}(0) = \text{col}(5, 4)$, and $t_0 = 0$, we have

$$\mathbf{X}^{-1}(0) = \begin{bmatrix} 1 & -1 \\ -1 & 2 \end{bmatrix}.$$

Therefore

$$\int_{t_0}^{t} \mathbf{X}^{-1}(s)\mathbf{f}(s)\,ds = \int_{0}^{t} \mathbf{X}^{-1}(s)\mathbf{f}(s)\,ds = \begin{bmatrix} \int_0^t (2)ds \\ \int_0^t (-3e^{-s})\,ds \end{bmatrix} = \begin{bmatrix} 2t \\ 3e^{-t} - 3 \end{bmatrix},$$

from which it follows that

$$\mathbf{X}(t) \int_{t_0}^{t} \mathbf{X}^{-1}(s)\mathbf{f}(s)\,ds = \begin{bmatrix} 2e^t & e^{2t} \\ e^t & e^{2t} \end{bmatrix} \begin{bmatrix} 2t \\ 3e^{-t} - 3 \end{bmatrix} = \begin{bmatrix} 4te^t + 3e^t - 3e^{2t} \\ 2te^t + 3e^t - 3e^{2t} \end{bmatrix}.$$

We also find that

$$\mathbf{X}(t)\mathbf{X}^{-1}(t_0)\mathbf{x}_0 = \begin{bmatrix} 2e^t & e^{2t} \\ e^t & e^{2t} \end{bmatrix} \begin{bmatrix} 1 & -1 \\ -1 & 2 \end{bmatrix} \begin{bmatrix} 5 \\ 4 \end{bmatrix} = \begin{bmatrix} 2e^t & e^{2t} \\ e^t & e^{2t} \end{bmatrix} \begin{bmatrix} 1 \\ 3 \end{bmatrix} = \begin{bmatrix} 2e^t + 3e^{2t} \\ e^t + 3e^{2t} \end{bmatrix}.$$

Hence, by substituting these expressions into equation (13) on page 554 of the text, we obtain the solution to this initial value problem given by

$$\begin{aligned}
\mathbf{x}(t) &= \mathbf{X}(t)\mathbf{X}^{-1}(t_0)\mathbf{x}_0 + \mathbf{X}(t)\int_{t_0}^{t}\mathbf{X}^{-1}(s)\mathbf{f}(s)\,ds \\
&= \begin{bmatrix} 2e^t + 3e^{2t} \\ e^t + 3e^{2t} \end{bmatrix} + \begin{bmatrix} 4te^t + 3e^t - 3e^{2t} \\ 2te^t + 3e^t - 3e^{2t} \end{bmatrix} = \begin{bmatrix} 4te^t + 5e^t \\ 2te^t + 4e^t \end{bmatrix}.
\end{aligned}$$

(b) Using the initial condition $\mathbf{x}(1) = \text{col}(0, 1)$, and $t_0 = 1$, we have

$$\mathbf{X}^{-1}(1) = \begin{bmatrix} e^{-1} & -e^{-1} \\ -e^{-2} & 2e^{-2} \end{bmatrix}.$$

Therefore

$$\begin{aligned}
\int_{t_0}^{t}\mathbf{X}^{-1}(s)\mathbf{f}(s)\,ds &= \int_{1}^{t}\mathbf{X}^{-1}(s)\mathbf{f}(s)\,ds \\
&= \begin{bmatrix} \int_1^t (2)ds \\ \int_1^t \left(-3e^{-s}\right)ds \end{bmatrix} = \begin{bmatrix} 2t - 2 \\ 3e^{-t} - 3e^{-1} \end{bmatrix},
\end{aligned}$$

from which it follows that

$$\begin{aligned}
\mathbf{X}(t)\int_{t_0}^{t}\mathbf{X}^{-1}(s)\mathbf{f}(s)\,ds &= \begin{bmatrix} 2e^t & e^{2t} \\ e^t & e^{2t} \end{bmatrix}\begin{bmatrix} 2t - 2 \\ 3e^{-t} - 3e^{-1} \end{bmatrix} \\
&= \begin{bmatrix} 4te^t - 4e^t + 3e^t - 3e^{2t-1} \\ 2te^t - 2e^t + 3e^t - 3e^{2t-1} \end{bmatrix} = \begin{bmatrix} 4te^t - e^t - 3e^{2t-1} \\ 2te^t + e^t - 3e^{2t-1} \end{bmatrix}.
\end{aligned}$$

We also find that

$$\begin{aligned}
\mathbf{X}(t)\mathbf{X}^{-1}(t_0)\mathbf{x}_0 &= \begin{bmatrix} 2e^t & e^{2t} \\ e^t & e^{2t} \end{bmatrix}\begin{bmatrix} e^{-1} & -e^{-1} \\ -e^{-2} & 2e^{-2} \end{bmatrix}\begin{bmatrix} 0 \\ 1 \end{bmatrix} \\
&= \begin{bmatrix} 2e^t & e^{2t} \\ e^t & e^{2t} \end{bmatrix}\begin{bmatrix} -e^{-1} \\ 2e^{-2} \end{bmatrix} = \begin{bmatrix} -2e^{t-1} + 2e^{2t-2} \\ -e^{t-1} + 2e^{2t-2} \end{bmatrix}.
\end{aligned}$$

Hence, by substituting these expressions into equation (13) on page 554 of the text, we obtain the solution to this initial value problem given by

$$\begin{aligned}
\mathbf{x}(t) &= \mathbf{X}(t)\mathbf{X}^{-1}(t_0)\mathbf{x}_0 + \mathbf{X}(t)\int_{t_0}^{t} \mathbf{X}^{-1}(s)\mathbf{f}(s)\,ds \\
&= \begin{bmatrix} -2e^{t-1} + 2e^{2t-2} \\ -e^{t-1} + 2e^{2t-2} \end{bmatrix} + \begin{bmatrix} 4te^{t} - e^{t} - 3e^{2t-1} \\ 2te^{t} + e^{t} - 3e^{2t-1} \end{bmatrix} \\
&= \begin{bmatrix} -2e^{t-1} + 2e^{2t-2} + 4te^{t} - e^{t} - 3e^{2t-1} \\ -e^{t-1} + 2e^{2t-2} + 2te^{t} + e^{t} - 3e^{2t-1} \end{bmatrix}.
\end{aligned}$$

(c) Using the initial condition $\mathbf{x}(5) = \text{col}(1, 0)$, and $t_0 = 5$, we have

$$\mathbf{X}^{-1}(5) = \begin{bmatrix} e^{-5} & -e^{-5} \\ -e^{-10} & 2e^{-10} \end{bmatrix}.$$

Therefore

$$\int_{t_0}^{t} \mathbf{X}^{-1}(s)\mathbf{f}(s)\,ds = \int_{5}^{t} \mathbf{X}^{-1}(s)\mathbf{f}(s)\,ds = \begin{bmatrix} \int_5^t (2)ds \\ \int_5^t \left(-3e^{-s}\right) ds \end{bmatrix} = \begin{bmatrix} 2t - 10 \\ 3e^{-t} - 3e^{-5} \end{bmatrix},$$

from which it follows that

$$\begin{aligned}
\mathbf{X}(t)\int_{t_0}^{t} \mathbf{X}^{-1}(s)\mathbf{f}(s)\,ds &= \begin{bmatrix} 2e^{t} & e^{2t} \\ e^{t} & e^{2t} \end{bmatrix} \begin{bmatrix} 2t - 10 \\ 3e^{-t} - 3e^{-5} \end{bmatrix} \\
&= \begin{bmatrix} 4te^{t} - 20e^{t} + 3e^{t} - 3e^{2t-5} \\ 2te^{t} - 10e^{t} + 3e^{t} - 3e^{2t-5} \end{bmatrix} = \begin{bmatrix} 4te^{t} - 17e^{t} - 3e^{2t-5} \\ 2te^{t} - 7e^{t} - 3e^{2t-5} \end{bmatrix}.
\end{aligned}$$

We also find that

$$\begin{aligned}
\mathbf{X}(t)\mathbf{X}^{-1}(t_0)\mathbf{x}_0 &= \begin{bmatrix} 2e^{t} & e^{2t} \\ e^{t} & e^{2t} \end{bmatrix} \begin{bmatrix} e^{-5} & -e^{-5} \\ -e^{-10} & 2e^{-10} \end{bmatrix} \begin{bmatrix} 1 \\ 0 \end{bmatrix} \\
&= \begin{bmatrix} 2e^{t} & e^{2t} \\ e^{t} & e^{2t} \end{bmatrix} \begin{bmatrix} e^{-5} \\ -e^{-10} \end{bmatrix} = \begin{bmatrix} 2e^{t-5} - e^{2t-10} \\ e^{t-5} - e^{2t-10} \end{bmatrix}.
\end{aligned}$$

Hence, by substituting these expressions into equation (13) on page 554 of the text, we obtain the solution to this initial value problem given by

$$\begin{aligned}
\mathbf{x}(t) &= \mathbf{X}(t)\mathbf{X}^{-1}(t_0)\mathbf{x}_0 + \mathbf{X}(t)\int_{t_0}^{t} \mathbf{X}^{-1}(s)\mathbf{f}(s)\,ds \\
&= \begin{bmatrix} 2e^{t-5} - e^{2t-10} \\ e^{t-5} - e^{2t-10} \end{bmatrix} + \begin{bmatrix} 4te^{t} - 17e^{t} - 3e^{2t-5} \\ 2te^{t} - 7e^{t} - 3e^{2t-5} \end{bmatrix} \\
&= \begin{bmatrix} 2e^{t-5} - e^{2t-10} + 4te^{t} - 17e^{t} - 3e^{2t-5} \\ e^{t-5} - e^{2t-10} + 2te^{t} - 7e^{t} - 3e^{2t-5} \end{bmatrix}.
\end{aligned}$$

25. (a) We will find a fundamental solutions set for the corresponding homogeneous system by deriving solutions using the eigenvalues and associated eigenvectors for the coefficient matrix. Therefore, we first solve the characteristic equation

$$|\mathbf{A} - r\mathbf{I}| = \begin{vmatrix} -r & 1 \\ -2 & 3-r \end{vmatrix} = 0$$

$$\Rightarrow \quad -r(3-r) + 2 = 0 \quad \Rightarrow \quad r^2 - 3r + 2 = 0 \quad \Rightarrow \quad (r-2)(r-1) = 0.$$

Therefore, we see that the eigenvalues for the coefficient matrix of this problem are $r = 1, 2$. Since these eigenvalues are distinct, the associated eigenvectors will be linearly independent, and so the solutions derived from these eigenvectors will also be linearly independent. We find an eigenvector for this matrix associated with the eigenvalue $r = 1$ by solving the equation

$$(\mathbf{A} - \mathbf{I})\mathbf{u} = \begin{bmatrix} -1 & 1 \\ -2 & 2 \end{bmatrix} \begin{bmatrix} u_1 \\ u_2 \end{bmatrix} = 0.$$

Since the vector $\mathbf{u}_1 = \text{col}(u_1, u_2) = \text{col}(1, 1)$ satisfies this equation, we see that this vector is one such eigenvector and so one solution to the homogeneous problem is given by

$$\mathbf{x}_1(t) = e^{t}\mathbf{u}_1 = e^{t}\begin{bmatrix} 1 \\ 1 \end{bmatrix}.$$

To find an eigenvector associated with the eigenvalue $r = 2$, we solve the equation

$$(\mathbf{A} - 2\mathbf{I})\mathbf{u} = \begin{bmatrix} -2 & 1 \\ -2 & 1 \end{bmatrix} \begin{bmatrix} u_1 \\ u_2 \end{bmatrix} = 0.$$

The vector $\mathbf{u}_2 = \operatorname{col}(u_1, u_2) = \operatorname{col}(1, 2)$ is one vector which satisfies this equation and so it is one eigenvector of the coefficient matrix associated with the eigenvalue $r = 2$. Thus, another linearly independent solution to the corresponding homogeneous problem is given by

$$\mathbf{x}_2(t) = e^{2t}\mathbf{u}_2 = e^{2t} \begin{bmatrix} 1 \\ 2 \end{bmatrix},$$

and a fundamental solution set for this homogeneous system is the set

$$\left\{e^{t}\mathbf{u}_1\,, e^{2t}\mathbf{u}_2\right\}, \qquad \text{where} \qquad \mathbf{u}_1 = \operatorname{col}(1, 1) \quad \text{and} \quad \mathbf{u}_2 = \operatorname{col}(1, 2).$$

(b) If we assume that $\mathbf{x}_p(t) = te^{t}\mathbf{a}$ for some constant vector $\mathbf{a} = \operatorname{col}(a_1, a_2)$, then we have

$$\mathbf{x}_p'(t) = te^{t}\mathbf{a} + e^{t}\mathbf{a} = \begin{bmatrix} te^{t}a_1 \\ te^{t}a_2 \end{bmatrix} + \begin{bmatrix} e^{t}a_1 \\ e^{t}a_2 \end{bmatrix} = \begin{bmatrix} te^{t}a_1 + e^{t}a_1 \\ te^{t}a_2 + e^{t}a_2 \end{bmatrix}.$$

We also have

$$\begin{bmatrix} 0 & 1 \\ -2 & 3 \end{bmatrix} \mathbf{x}_p(t) + \mathbf{f}(t) = \begin{bmatrix} 0 & 1 \\ -2 & 3 \end{bmatrix} \begin{bmatrix} te^{t}a_1 \\ te^{t}a_2 \end{bmatrix} + \begin{bmatrix} e^{t} \\ 0 \end{bmatrix} = \begin{bmatrix} te^{t}a_2 + e^{t} \\ -2te^{t}a_1 + 3te^{t}a_2 \end{bmatrix}.$$

Thus, if $\mathbf{x}_p(t) = te^{t}\mathbf{a}$ is to satisfy this system, we must have

$$\begin{bmatrix} te^{t}a_1 + e^{t}a_1 \\ te^{t}a_2 + e^{t}a_2 \end{bmatrix} = \begin{bmatrix} te^{t}a_2 + e^{t} \\ -2te^{t}a_1 + 3te^{t}a_2 \end{bmatrix},$$

which means that

$$\begin{aligned} te^{t}a_1 + e^{t}a_1 &= te^{t}a_2 + e^{t}\,, \\ te^{t}a_2 + e^{t}a_2 &= -2te^{t}a_1 + 3te^{t}a_2\,. \end{aligned}$$

By dividing out the term e^{t} and equating coefficients, this system becomes the system

$$\begin{aligned} a_1 &= a_2\,, & a_1 &= 1, \\ a_2 &= -2a_1 + 3a_2\,, & a_2 &= 0. \end{aligned}$$

Since this set of equations implies that $1 = a_1 = a_2 = 0$, which is of course impossible, we see that this system has no solutions. Therefore, we cannot find a vector $\mathbf{a}$ for which $\mathbf{x}_p(t) = te^t\mathbf{a}$ is a particular solution to this problem.

(c) Assuming that

$$\mathbf{x}_p(t) = te^t\mathbf{a} + e^t\mathbf{b} = \begin{bmatrix} te^ta_1 \\ te^ta_2 \end{bmatrix} + \begin{bmatrix} e^tb_1 \\ e^tb_2 \end{bmatrix} = \begin{bmatrix} te^ta_1 + e^tb_1 \\ te^ta_2 + e^tb_2 \end{bmatrix},$$

where $\mathbf{a} = \text{col}(a_1, a_2)$ and $\mathbf{b} = \text{col}(b_1, b_2)$ are two constant vectors, implies that

$$\mathbf{x}_p'(t) = te^t\mathbf{a} + e^t\mathbf{a} + e^t\mathbf{b} = \begin{bmatrix} te^ta_1 + e^ta_1 + e^tb_1 \\ te^ta_2 + e^ta_2 + e^ta_2 \end{bmatrix}.$$

We also see that

$$\begin{aligned} \begin{bmatrix} 0 & 1 \\ -2 & 3 \end{bmatrix} \mathbf{x}_p(t) + \mathbf{f}(t) &= \begin{bmatrix} 0 & 1 \\ -2 & 3 \end{bmatrix} \begin{bmatrix} te^ta_1 + e^tb_1 \\ te^ta_2 + e^tb_2 \end{bmatrix} + \begin{bmatrix} e^t \\ 0 \end{bmatrix} \\ &= \begin{bmatrix} te^ta_2 + e^tb_2 + e^t \\ -2te^ta_1 - 2e^tb_1 + 3te^ta_2 + 3e^tb_2 \end{bmatrix}. \end{aligned}$$

Thus, if $\mathbf{x}_p(t)$ is to satisfy this system, we must have

$$\begin{bmatrix} te^ta_1 + e^ta_1 + e^tb_1 \\ te^ta_2 + e^ta_2 + e^tb_2 \end{bmatrix} = \begin{bmatrix} te^ta_2 + e^tb_2 + e^t \\ -2te^ta_1 - 2e^tb_1 + 3te^ta_2 + 3e^tb_2 \end{bmatrix}, \tag{9.7}$$

which implies the system of equations given by

$$\begin{aligned} te^ta_1 + e^ta_1 + e^tb_1 &= te^ta_2 + e^tb_2 + e^t, \\ te^ta_2 + e^ta_2 + e^tb_2 &= -2te^ta_1 - 2e^tb_1 + 3te^ta_2 + 3e^tb_2. \end{aligned}$$

Dividing each equation by e^t and equating the coefficients in the resulting equations yields the system

$$\begin{aligned} a_1 &= a_2, & a_1 + b_1 &= b_2 + 1, \\ a_2 &= -2a_1 + 3a_2, & a_2 + b_2 &= -2b_1 + 3b_2. \end{aligned} \tag{9.8}$$

Taking the pair of equations on the right and simplifying yields the system

$$\begin{aligned} b_1 - b_2 &= 1 - a_1, \\ 2b_1 - 2b_2 &= -a_2. \end{aligned} \tag{9.9}$$

By multiplying the first of these equations by 2, we obtain the system

$$\begin{aligned} 2b_1 - 2b_2 &= 2 - 2a_1\,, \\ 2b_1 - 2b_2 &= -a_2\,, \end{aligned}$$

which when subtracted yields $2 - 2a_1 + a_2 = 0$. Applying the first equation in (9.8) (the equation $a_1 = a_2$) to this equation yields $a_1 = a_2 = 2$. By substituting these values for a_1 and a_2 into equation (9.9) above we see that both equations reduce to the equation

$$b_2 = b_1 + 1.$$

(Note also that the remaining equation in (9.8) reduces to the first equation in that set.) Thus, b_1 is free to be any value, say $b_1 = s$, and the set of values $a_1 = a_2 = 2$, $b_1 = s$, $b_2 = s + 1$, satisfies all of the equations given in (9.8) and, hence, the system given in (9.7). Therefore, particular solutions to the nonhomogeneous equation given in this problem are

$$\mathbf{x}_p(t) = te^t \begin{bmatrix} 2 \\ 2 \end{bmatrix} + e^t \begin{bmatrix} s \\ s+1 \end{bmatrix} = te^t \begin{bmatrix} 2 \\ 2 \end{bmatrix} + e^t \begin{bmatrix} 0 \\ 1 \end{bmatrix} + se^t \begin{bmatrix} 1 \\ 1 \end{bmatrix}.$$

But, since the vector $\mathbf{u} = e^t\text{col}(1,1)$ is a solution to the corresponding homogeneous system, the last term can be incorporated into the solution $\mathbf{x}_h(t)$ and we obtain one particular solution to this problem given by

$$\mathbf{x}_p(t) = te^t \begin{bmatrix} 2 \\ 2 \end{bmatrix} + e^t \begin{bmatrix} 0 \\ 1 \end{bmatrix}.$$

(d) To find the general solution to the nonhomogeneous system given in this problem, we first form the solution to the corresponding homogeneous system using the fundamental solution set found in part (a). Thus, we have

$$\mathbf{x}_h(t) = c_1e^t \begin{bmatrix} 1 \\ 1 \end{bmatrix} + c_2e^{2t} \begin{bmatrix} 1 \\ 2 \end{bmatrix}.$$

By adding the solution found in part (c) to this solution, we obtain the general solution given by

$$\mathbf{x}(t) = c_1e^t \begin{bmatrix} 1 \\ 1 \end{bmatrix} + c_2e^{2t} \begin{bmatrix} 1 \\ 2 \end{bmatrix} + te^t \begin{bmatrix} 2 \\ 2 \end{bmatrix} + e^t \begin{bmatrix} 0 \\ 1 \end{bmatrix}.$$

EXERCISES 9.8: The Matrix Exponential Function, page 566

3. **(a)** From the characteristic equation, $|\mathbf{A}-r\mathbf{I}|=0$, we obtain

$$|\mathbf{A}-r\mathbf{I}|=\begin{vmatrix}2-r & 1 & -1\\ -3 & -1-r & 1\\ 9 & 3 & -4-r\end{vmatrix}=0$$

$$\Rightarrow \quad (2-r)\begin{vmatrix}-1-r & 1\\ 3 & -4-r\end{vmatrix}-\begin{vmatrix}-3 & 1\\ 9 & -4-r\end{vmatrix}+(-1)\begin{vmatrix}-3 & -1-r\\ 9 & 3\end{vmatrix}=0$$

$$\Rightarrow \quad (2-r)[(-1-r)(-4-r)-3]-[-3(-4-r)-9]-[-9-9(-1-r)]=0$$

$$\Rightarrow \quad r^3+3r^2+3r+1=(r+1)^3=0.$$

Therefore, for the matrix $\mathbf{A}$, $r=-1$ is an eigenvalue of multiplicity three. Thus, by the Cayley-Hamilton theorem as stated on page 561 of the text, we have

$$(\mathbf{A}+\mathbf{I})^3=\mathbf{0}$$

(so that $r=-1$ and $k=3$).

(b) In order to find $e^{\mathbf{A}t}$, we first notice (as was done in the text on page 560) that

$$\begin{aligned}e^{\mathbf{A}t}&=e^{[-\mathbf{I}+(\mathbf{A}+\mathbf{I})]t}, &&\text{commutative and associative properties of matrix addition}\\ &=e^{-\mathbf{I}t}e^{(\mathbf{A}+\mathbf{I})t}, &&\text{property (d) on page 559 of the text [since } (\mathbf{A}+\mathbf{I})\mathbf{I}=\mathbf{I}(\mathbf{A}+\mathbf{I})]\\ &=e^{-t}\mathbf{I}e^{(\mathbf{A}+\mathbf{I})t}, &&\text{property (e) on page 559 of the text}\\ &=e^{-t}e^{(\mathbf{A}+\mathbf{I})t}.\end{aligned}$$

Therefore, to find $e^{\mathbf{A}t}$ we need only to find $e^{(\mathbf{A}+\mathbf{I})t}$ then multiply the resulting expression by e^{-t}. By formula (2) on page 558 of the text and using the fact that $(\mathbf{A}+\mathbf{I})^3=\mathbf{0}$ (which implies that $(\mathbf{A}+\mathbf{I})^n=\mathbf{0}$ for $n\geq 3$), we have

$$\begin{aligned}e^{(\mathbf{A}+\mathbf{I})t}&=\mathbf{I}+(\mathbf{A}+\mathbf{I})t+(\mathbf{A}+\mathbf{I})^2\left(\frac{t^2}{2}\right)+\cdots+(\mathbf{A}+\mathbf{I})^n\left(\frac{t^n}{n!}\right)+\cdots\\ &=\mathbf{I}+(\mathbf{A}+\mathbf{I})t+(\mathbf{A}+\mathbf{I})^2\left(\frac{t^2}{2}\right). \qquad (9.10)\end{aligned}$$

Since

$$(\mathbf{A}+\mathbf{I})^2 = \begin{bmatrix} 3 & 1 & -1 \\ -3 & 0 & 1 \\ 9 & 3 & -3 \end{bmatrix} \begin{bmatrix} 3 & 1 & -1 \\ -3 & 0 & 1 \\ 9 & 3 & -3 \end{bmatrix} = \begin{bmatrix} -3 & 0 & 1 \\ 0 & 0 & 0 \\ -9 & 0 & 3 \end{bmatrix},$$

equation (9.10) becomes

$$\begin{aligned} e^{(\mathbf{A}+\mathbf{I})t} &= \begin{bmatrix} 1 & 0 & 0 \\ 0 & 1 & 0 \\ 0 & 0 & 1 \end{bmatrix} + \begin{bmatrix} 3t & t & -t \\ -3t & 0 & t \\ 9t & 3t & -3t \end{bmatrix} + \begin{bmatrix} -3(t^2/2) & 0 & t^2/2 \\ 0 & 0 & 0 \\ -9(t^2/2) & 0 & 3(t^2/2) \end{bmatrix} \\ &= \begin{bmatrix} 1+3t-3t^2/2 & t & -t+t^2/2 \\ -3t & 1 & t \\ 9t-9t^2/2 & 3t & 1-3t+3t^2/2 \end{bmatrix}. \end{aligned}$$

Hence, we have

$$e^{\mathbf{A}t} = e^{-t} \begin{bmatrix} 1+3t-3t^2/2 & t & -t+t^2/2 \\ -3t & 1 & t \\ 9t-9t^2/2 & 3t & 1-3t+3t^2/2 \end{bmatrix}.$$

9. By equation (6) on page 562 of the text, we see that $e^{\mathbf{A}t} = \mathbf{X}(t)\mathbf{X}^{-1}(0)$, where $\mathbf{X}(t)$ is a fundamental matrix for the system $\mathbf{x}' = \mathbf{A}\mathbf{x}$. We will construct this fundamental matrix from three linearly independent solutions derived from the eigenvalues and associated eigenvectors for the matrix $\mathbf{A}$. Thus, we solve the characteristic equation

$$\begin{aligned} |\mathbf{A}-r\mathbf{I}| = \begin{vmatrix} -r & 1 & 0 \\ 0 & -r & 1 \\ 1 & -1 & 1-r \end{vmatrix} = 0 \\ \Rightarrow \quad (-r)\begin{vmatrix} -r & 1 \\ -1 & 1-r \end{vmatrix} - \begin{vmatrix} 0 & 1 \\ 1 & 1-r \end{vmatrix} = 0 \\ \Rightarrow \quad -r[-r(1-r)+1]+1 = -r^3+r^2-r+1 = -(r-1)(r^2+1) = 0. \end{aligned}$$

Therefore, the eigenvalues of the matrix $\mathbf{A}$ are $r = 1$ and $r = \pm i$. To find an eigenvector

$\mathbf{u} = \text{col}(u_1, u_2, u_3)$ associated with the eigenvalue $r = 1$, we solve the system

$$(\mathbf{A} - \mathbf{I})\mathbf{u} = \mathbf{0} \quad \Rightarrow \quad \begin{bmatrix} -1 & 1 & 0 \\ 0 & -1 & 1 \\ 1 & -1 & 0 \end{bmatrix} \begin{bmatrix} u_1 \\ u_2 \\ u_3 \end{bmatrix} = \begin{bmatrix} 0 \\ 0 \\ 0 \end{bmatrix} \quad \Rightarrow \quad \begin{bmatrix} -1 & 0 & 1 \\ 0 & -1 & 1 \\ 0 & 0 & 0 \end{bmatrix} \begin{bmatrix} u_1 \\ u_2 \\ u_3 \end{bmatrix} = \begin{bmatrix} 0 \\ 0 \\ 0 \end{bmatrix}.$$

This system is equivalent to the system $u_1 = u_3$, $u_2 = u_3$. Hence, u_3 is free to be any arbitrary value, say $u_3 = 1$. Then $u_1 = u_2 = 1$, and so the vector $\mathbf{u} = \text{col}(1, 1, 1)$ is an eigenvector associated with $r = 1$. Hence, one solution to the system $\mathbf{x}' = \mathbf{A}\mathbf{x}$ is given by

$$\mathbf{x}_1(t) = e^t\mathbf{u} = e^t \begin{bmatrix} 1 \\ 1 \\ 1 \end{bmatrix} = \begin{bmatrix} e^t \\ e^t \\ e^t \end{bmatrix}.$$

Since the eigenvalue $r = i$ is complex, we want to find two more linearly independent solutions for the system $\mathbf{x}' = \mathbf{A}\mathbf{x}$ derived from the eigenvectors associated with this eigenvalue. These eigenvectors, $\mathbf{z} = \text{col}(z_1, z_2, z_3)$, must satisfy the equation

$$(\mathbf{A} - i\mathbf{I})\mathbf{z} = \begin{bmatrix} -i & 1 & 0 \\ 0 & -i & 1 \\ 1 & -1 & 1-i \end{bmatrix} \begin{bmatrix} z_1 \\ z_2 \\ z_3 \end{bmatrix} = \begin{bmatrix} 0 \\ 0 \\ 0 \end{bmatrix},$$

which is equivalent to the system $z_1 = -z_3$, $z_2 = -iz_3$. Thus, one solution to this system is $z_3 = 1$, $z_1 = -1$, and $z_2 = -i$ and so one eigenvector for $\mathbf{A}$ associated with the eigenvalue $r = i$ is given by

$$\mathbf{z} = \begin{bmatrix} z_1 \\ z_2 \\ z_3 \end{bmatrix} = \begin{bmatrix} -1 \\ -i \\ 1 \end{bmatrix} = \begin{bmatrix} -1 \\ 0 \\ 1 \end{bmatrix} + i \begin{bmatrix} 0 \\ -1 \\ 0 \end{bmatrix}.$$

By the notation on page 546 of the text, this means that $\alpha = 0$, $\beta = 1$, $\mathbf{a} = \text{col}(-1, 0, 1)$ and $\mathbf{b} = \text{col}(0, -1, 0)$. Therefore, by equations (6) and (7) on page 546 of the text we see that two more linearly independent solutions to the system $\mathbf{x}' = \mathbf{A}\mathbf{x}$ are given by

$$\mathbf{x}_2(t) = e^{(0)t}(\cos t)\mathbf{a} - e^{(0)t}(\sin t)\mathbf{b} = \begin{bmatrix} -\cos t \\ 0 \\ \cos t \end{bmatrix} - \begin{bmatrix} 0 \\ -\sin t \\ 0 \end{bmatrix} = \begin{bmatrix} -\cos t \\ \sin t \\ \cos t \end{bmatrix},$$

$$\mathbf{x}_3(t) = e^{(0)t}(\sin t)\mathbf{a} + e^{(0)t}(\cos t)\mathbf{b} = \begin{bmatrix} -\sin t \\ 0 \\ \sin t \end{bmatrix} + \begin{bmatrix} 0 \\ -\cos t \\ 0 \end{bmatrix} = \begin{bmatrix} -\sin t \\ -\cos t \\ \sin t \end{bmatrix}.$$

Thus, a fundamental matrix for this system is

$$\mathbf{X}(t) = \begin{bmatrix} e^t & -\cos t & -\sin t \\ e^t & \sin t & -\cos t \\ e^t & \cos t & \sin t \end{bmatrix} \qquad \Rightarrow \qquad \mathbf{X}(0) = \begin{bmatrix} 1 & -1 & 0 \\ 1 & 0 & -1 \\ 1 & 1 & 0 \end{bmatrix}.$$

To find the inverse of the matrix $\mathbf{X}(0)$ we can, for example, perform row-reduction on the matrix $[\mathbf{X}(0)|\mathbf{I}]$ to obtain the matrix $[\mathbf{I}|\mathbf{X}^{-1}(0)]$. Thus, we see that

$$\mathbf{X}^{-1}(0) = \begin{bmatrix} 1/2 & 0 & 1/2 \\ -1/2 & 0 & 1/2 \\ 1/2 & -1 & 1/2 \end{bmatrix}.$$

Hence, we obtain

$$\begin{aligned} e^{\mathbf{A}t} = \mathbf{X}(t)\mathbf{X}^{-1}(0) &= \begin{bmatrix} e^t & -\cos t & -\sin t \\ e^t & \sin t & -\cos t \\ e^t & \cos t & \sin t \end{bmatrix} \begin{bmatrix} 1/2 & 0 & 1/2 \\ -1/2 & 0 & 1/2 \\ 1/2 & -1 & 1/2 \end{bmatrix} \\ &= \frac{1}{2} \begin{bmatrix} e^t + \cos t - \sin t & 2\sin t & e^t - \cos t - \sin t \\ e^t - \cos t - \sin t & 2\cos t & e^t - \cos t + \sin t \\ e^t - \cos t + \sin t & -2\sin t & e^t + \cos t + \sin t \end{bmatrix}. \end{aligned}$$

11. The first step in finding $e^{\mathbf{A}t}$ using a fundamental matrix for the system $\mathbf{x}' = \mathbf{A}\mathbf{x}$ is to find the eigenvalues for the matrix $\mathbf{A}$. Thus, we solve the characteristic equation

$$|\mathbf{A} - r\mathbf{I}| = \begin{vmatrix} 5-r & -4 & 0 \\ 1 & -r & 2 \\ 0 & 2 & 5-r \end{vmatrix} = 0$$

$$\Rightarrow \qquad (5-r)\begin{vmatrix} -r & 2 \\ 2 & 5-r \end{vmatrix} + 4\begin{vmatrix} 1 & 2 \\ 0 & 5-r \end{vmatrix} = 0$$

$$\Rightarrow \qquad (5-r)[-r(5-r)-4]+4(5-r)=-r(r-5)^2=0.$$

Therefore, the eigenvalues of $\mathbf{A}$ are $r = 0, 5$, with $r = 5$ an eigenvalue of multiplicity two. Next we must find the eigenvectors and generalized eigenvectors for the matrix $\mathbf{A}$ and from these vectors derive three linearly independent solutions of the system $\mathbf{x}' = \mathbf{A}\mathbf{x}$. To find the eigenvector associated with the eigenvalue $r = 0$, we solve the equation

$$\mathbf{A}\mathbf{u} = \begin{bmatrix} 5 & -4 & 0 \\ 1 & 0 & 2 \\ 0 & 2 & 5 \end{bmatrix} \begin{bmatrix} u_1 \\ u_2 \\ u_3 \end{bmatrix} = \begin{bmatrix} 0 \\ 0 \\ 0 \end{bmatrix} \qquad \Rightarrow \qquad \begin{bmatrix} 1 & 0 & 2 \\ 0 & 2 & 5 \\ 0 & 0 & 0 \end{bmatrix} \begin{bmatrix} u_1 \\ u_2 \\ u_3 \end{bmatrix} = \begin{bmatrix} 0 \\ 0 \\ 0 \end{bmatrix}.$$

This equation is equivalent to the system $u_1 = -2u_3$, $2u_2 = -5u_3$ and one solution to this system is $u_3 = 2$, $u_1 = -4$, $u_2 = -5$. Therefore, one eigenvector of the matrix $\mathbf{A}$ associated with the eigenvalue $r = 0$ is given by the vector

$$\mathbf{u}_1 = \operatorname{col}(u_1\, u_2\, u_3) = \operatorname{col}(-4, -5, 2),$$

and so one solution to the system $\mathbf{x}' = \mathbf{A}\mathbf{x}$ is

$$\mathbf{x}_1(t) = e^0\mathbf{u}_1 = \begin{bmatrix} -4 \\ -5 \\ 2 \end{bmatrix}.$$

To find an eigenvector associated with the eigenvalue $r = 5$, we solve the equation

$$(\mathbf{A} - 5\mathbf{I})\mathbf{u} = \begin{bmatrix} 0 & -4 & 0 \\ 1 & -5 & 2 \\ 0 & 2 & 0 \end{bmatrix} \begin{bmatrix} u_1 \\ u_2 \\ u_3 \end{bmatrix} = \begin{bmatrix} 0 \\ 0 \\ 0 \end{bmatrix},$$

which is equivalent to the system $u_2 = 0$, $u_1 = -2u_3$. One solution to this system is $u_3 = 1$, $u_1 = -2$, $u_2 = 0$. Thus, one eigenvector of the matrix $\mathbf{A}$ associated with the eigenvalue $r = 5$ is the vector

$$\mathbf{u}_2 = \operatorname{col}(u_1\, u_2\, u_3) = \operatorname{col}(-2, 0, 1),$$

and so another linearly independent solution to the system $\mathbf{x}' = \mathbf{A}\mathbf{x}$ is given by

$$\mathbf{x}_2(t) = e^{5t}\mathbf{u}_2 = e^{5t} \begin{bmatrix} -2 \\ 0 \\ 1 \end{bmatrix} = \begin{bmatrix} -2e^{5t} \\ 0 \\ e^{5t} \end{bmatrix}.$$

Since $r = 5$ is an eigenvalue of multiplicity two, we can find a generalized eigenvector (with $k = 2$) associated with the eigenvalue $r = 5$ which will be linearly independent from the vector $\mathbf{u}_2$ found above. Thus, we solve the equation

$$(\mathbf{A} - 5\mathbf{I})^2\mathbf{u} = \mathbf{0}. \tag{9.11}$$

Because

$$(\mathbf{A} - 5\mathbf{I})^2 = \begin{bmatrix} 0 & -4 & 0 \\ 1 & -5 & 2 \\ 0 & 2 & 0 \end{bmatrix}\begin{bmatrix} 0 & -4 & 0 \\ 1 & -5 & 2 \\ 0 & 2 & 0 \end{bmatrix} = \begin{bmatrix} -4 & 20 & -8 \\ -5 & 25 & -10 \\ 2 & -10 & 4 \end{bmatrix},$$

we see that equation (9.11) becomes

$$\begin{bmatrix} -4 & 20 & -8 \\ -5 & 25 & -10 \\ 2 & -10 & 4 \end{bmatrix}\begin{bmatrix} u_1 \\ u_2 \\ u_3 \end{bmatrix} = \begin{bmatrix} 0 \\ 0 \\ 0 \end{bmatrix} \quad \Rightarrow \quad \begin{bmatrix} -1 & 5 & -2 \\ 0 & 0 & 0 \\ 0 & 0 & 0 \end{bmatrix}\begin{bmatrix} u_1 \\ u_2 \\ u_3 \end{bmatrix} = \begin{bmatrix} 0 \\ 0 \\ 0 \end{bmatrix}.$$

This equation is equivalent to the equation

$$-u_1 + 5u_2 - 2u_3 = 0$$

and is, therefore, satisfied if we let $u_2 = s$, $u_3 = v$, and $u_1 = 5s - 2v$ for any values of s and v. Hence, solutions to equation (9.11) are given by

$$\mathbf{u} = \begin{bmatrix} u_1 \\ u_2 \\ u_3 \end{bmatrix} = \begin{bmatrix} 5s - 2v \\ s \\ v \end{bmatrix} = s\begin{bmatrix} 5 \\ 1 \\ 0 \end{bmatrix} + v\begin{bmatrix} -2 \\ 0 \\ 1 \end{bmatrix}.$$

Notice that the vectors $v\text{col}(-2, 0, 1)$ are the eigenvectors that we found above associated with the eigenvalue $r = 5$. Since we are looking for a vector which satisfies equation (9.11) and is linearly independent from this eigenvector we will choose $s = 1$ and $v = 0$. Thus, a generalized eigenvector for the matrix $\mathbf{A}$ associated with the eigenvalue $r = 5$ and linearly independent of the eigenvector $\mathbf{u}_2$ is given by

$$\mathbf{u}_3 = \text{col}(5, 1, 0).$$

Hence, by formula (8) on page 563 of the text, we see that another linearly independent solution to the system $\mathbf{x}' = \mathbf{A}\mathbf{x}$ is given by

$$\begin{aligned}
\mathbf{x}_3(t) = e^{\mathbf{A}t}\mathbf{u}_3 &= e^{5t}\left[\mathbf{u}_3 + t(\mathbf{A} - 5\mathbf{I})\mathbf{u}_3\right] \\
&= e^{5t}\begin{bmatrix} 5 \\ 1 \\ 0 \end{bmatrix} + te^{5t}\begin{bmatrix} 0 & -4 & 0 \\ 1 & -5 & 2 \\ 0 & 2 & 0 \end{bmatrix}\begin{bmatrix} 5 \\ 1 \\ 0 \end{bmatrix} \\
&= e^{5t}\begin{bmatrix} 5 \\ 1 \\ 0 \end{bmatrix} + te^{5t}\begin{bmatrix} -4 \\ 0 \\ 2 \end{bmatrix} = \begin{bmatrix} 5e^{5t} - 4te^{5t} \\ e^{5t} \\ 2te^{5t} \end{bmatrix},
\end{aligned}$$

where we have used the fact that, by our choice of $\mathbf{u}_3$, $(\mathbf{A}-5\mathbf{I})^2\mathbf{u}_3 = \mathbf{0}$ and so $(\mathbf{A}-5\mathbf{I})^n\mathbf{u}_3 = \mathbf{0}$ for $n \geq 2$. (This is the reason why we used the generalized eigenvector to calculate $\mathbf{x}_3(t)$. The Cayley-Hamilton theorem, as given on page 561 of the text, states that $\mathbf{A}$ satisfies its characteristic equation, which in this case means that $\mathbf{A}(\mathbf{A} - 5\mathbf{I})^2 = \mathbf{0}$. However, we cannot assume from this fact that $(\mathbf{A} - 5\mathbf{I})^2 = 0$ because in matrix multiplication it is possible for two nonzero matrices to have a zero product.)

Our last step is to find a fundamental matrix for the system $\mathbf{x}' = \mathbf{A}\mathbf{x}$ using the linearly independent solutions found above and then to use this fundamental matrix to calculate $e^{\mathbf{A}t}$. Thus, from these three solutions we obtain the fundamental matrix given by

$$\mathbf{X}(t) = \begin{bmatrix} -4 & -2e^{5t} & 5e^{5t} - 4te^{5t} \\ -5 & 0 & e^{5t} \\ 2 & e^{5t} & 2te^{5t} \end{bmatrix} \qquad \Rightarrow \qquad \mathbf{X}(0) = \begin{bmatrix} -4 & -2 & 5 \\ -5 & 0 & 1 \\ 2 & 1 & 0 \end{bmatrix}.$$

We can find the inverse matrix $\mathbf{X}^{-1}(0)$ by (for example) performing row-reduction on the matrix $[\mathbf{X}(0)|\mathbf{I}]$ to obtain the matrix $[\mathbf{I}|\mathbf{X}^{-1}(0)]$. Thus, we find

$$\mathbf{X}^{-1}(0) = \frac{1}{25}\begin{bmatrix} 1 & -5 & 2 \\ -2 & 10 & 21 \\ 5 & 0 & 10 \end{bmatrix}.$$

Therefore, by formula (6) on page 562 of the text, we see that

$$e^{\mathbf{A}t} = \mathbf{X}(t)\mathbf{X}^{-1}(0) = \frac{1}{25}\begin{bmatrix} -4 & -2e^{5t} & 5e^{5t}-4te^{5t} \\ -5 & 0 & e^{5t} \\ 2 & e^{5t} & 2te^{5t} \end{bmatrix}\begin{bmatrix} 1 & -5 & 2 \\ -2 & 10 & 21 \\ 5 & 0 & 10 \end{bmatrix}$$

$$= \frac{1}{25}\begin{bmatrix} -4+29e^{5t}-20te^{5t} & 20-20e^{5t} & -8+8e^{5t}-40te^{5t} \\ -5+5e^{5t} & 25 & -10+10e^{5t} \\ 2-2e^{5t}+10te^{5t} & -10+10e^{5t} & 4+21e^{5t}+20te^{5t} \end{bmatrix}.$$

17. We first calculate the eigenvalues for the matrix **A** by solving the characteristic equation

$$|\mathbf{A}-r\mathbf{I}| = \begin{vmatrix} -r & 1 & 0 \\ 0 & -r & 1 \\ -2 & -5 & -4-r \end{vmatrix} = 0$$

$$\Rightarrow \quad (-r)\begin{vmatrix} -r & 1 \\ -5 & -4-r \end{vmatrix} - \begin{vmatrix} 0 & 1 \\ -2 & -4-r \end{vmatrix} = 0$$

$$\Rightarrow \quad -r[-r(-4-r)+5]-2 = -\left(r^3+4r^2+5r+2\right) = -(r+1)^2(r+2) = 0.$$

Thus, the eigenvalues for **A** are $r=-1,-2$, with $r=-1$ an eigenvalue of multiplicity two. To find an eigenvector $\mathbf{u} = \text{col}(u_1, u_2, u_3)$ associated with the eigenvalue $r=-1$, we solve the equation

$$(\mathbf{A}+\mathbf{I})\mathbf{u} = \begin{bmatrix} 1 & 1 & 0 \\ 0 & 1 & 1 \\ -2 & -5 & -3 \end{bmatrix}\begin{bmatrix} u_1 \\ u_2 \\ u_3 \end{bmatrix} = \begin{bmatrix} 0 \\ 0 \\ 0 \end{bmatrix},$$

which is equivalent to the system $u_1 = u_3$, $u_2 = -u_3$. Therefore, by letting $u_3 = 1$ (so that $u_1 = 1$ and $u_2 = -1$), we see that one eigenvector for the matrix **A** associated with the eigenvalue $r=-1$ is the vector

$$\mathbf{u}_1 = \text{col}(u_1, u_2, u_3) = \text{col}(1, -1, 1).$$

Hence, one solution to the system $\mathbf{x}' = \mathbf{A}\mathbf{x}$ is given by

$$\mathbf{x}_1(t) = e^{-t}\mathbf{u}_1 = e^{-t}\begin{bmatrix} 1 \\ -1 \\ 1 \end{bmatrix}.$$

Since $r = -1$ is an eigenvalue of multiplicity two, we can find a generalized eigenvector associated with this eigenvalue (with $k = 2$) which will be linearly independent from the vector $\mathbf{u}_1$. To do this, we solve the equation

$$
\begin{aligned}
&(\mathbf{A}+\mathbf{I})^2\mathbf{u} = \mathbf{0} \\
\Rightarrow \quad & \begin{bmatrix} 1 & 1 & 0 \\ 0 & 1 & 1 \\ -2 & -5 & -3 \end{bmatrix} \begin{bmatrix} 1 & 1 & 0 \\ 0 & 1 & 1 \\ -2 & -5 & -3 \end{bmatrix} \begin{bmatrix} u_1 \\ u_2 \\ u_3 \end{bmatrix} = \begin{bmatrix} 0 \\ 0 \\ 0 \end{bmatrix} \\
\Rightarrow \quad & \begin{bmatrix} 1 & 2 & 1 \\ -2 & -4 & -2 \\ 4 & 8 & 4 \end{bmatrix} \begin{bmatrix} u_1 \\ u_2 \\ u_3 \end{bmatrix} = \begin{bmatrix} 0 \\ 0 \\ 0 \end{bmatrix} \quad \Rightarrow \quad \begin{bmatrix} 1 & 2 & 1 \\ 0 & 0 & 0 \\ 0 & 0 & 0 \end{bmatrix} \begin{bmatrix} u_1 \\ u_2 \\ u_3 \end{bmatrix} = \begin{bmatrix} 0 \\ 0 \\ 0 \end{bmatrix},
\end{aligned}
$$

which is equivalent to the equation $u_1 + 2u_2 + u_3 = 0$. This equation will be satisfied if we let $u_3 = s$, $u_2 = v$, and $u_1 = -2v - s$ for any values of s and v. Thus, generalized eigenvectors associated with the eigenvalue $r = -1$ are given by

$$
\mathbf{u} = \begin{bmatrix} u_1 \\ u_2 \\ u_3 \end{bmatrix} = \begin{bmatrix} -2v - s \\ v \\ s \end{bmatrix} = s \begin{bmatrix} -1 \\ 0 \\ 1 \end{bmatrix} + v \begin{bmatrix} -2 \\ 1 \\ 0 \end{bmatrix}.
$$

Hence, by letting $s = 2$ and $v = -1$, we find one such generalized eigenvector to be the vector

$$
\mathbf{u}_2 = \operatorname{col}(0, -1, 2),
$$

which we see by inspection is linearly independent from $\mathbf{u}_1$. Therefore, by equation (8) on page 563 of the text, we obtain a second linearly independent solution of the system $\mathbf{x}' = \mathbf{A}\mathbf{x}$ given by

$$
\begin{aligned}
\mathbf{x}_2(t) &= e^{\mathbf{A}t}\mathbf{u}_2 = e^{-t}\left[\mathbf{u}_2 + t(\mathbf{A}+\mathbf{I})\mathbf{u}_2\right] \\
&= e^{-t} \begin{bmatrix} 0 \\ -1 \\ 2 \end{bmatrix} + te^{-t} \begin{bmatrix} 1 & 1 & 0 \\ 0 & 1 & 1 \\ -2 & -5 & -3 \end{bmatrix} \begin{bmatrix} 0 \\ -1 \\ 2 \end{bmatrix}
\end{aligned}
$$

$$= e^{-t}\begin{bmatrix} 0 \\ -1 \\ 2 \end{bmatrix} + te^{-t}\begin{bmatrix} -1 \\ 1 \\ -1 \end{bmatrix} = e^{-t}\begin{bmatrix} -t \\ -1+t \\ 2-t \end{bmatrix}.$$

In order to obtain a third linearly independent solution to this system, we will find an eigenvector associated with the eigenvalue $r = -2$ by solving the equation

$$(\mathbf{A} + 2\mathbf{I})\mathbf{u} = \begin{bmatrix} 2 & 1 & 0 \\ 0 & 2 & 1 \\ -2 & -5 & -2 \end{bmatrix}\begin{bmatrix} u_1 \\ u_2 \\ u_3 \end{bmatrix} = \begin{bmatrix} 0 \\ 0 \\ 0 \end{bmatrix}.$$

This equation is equivalent to the system $2u_1 + u_2 = 0$, $2u_2 + u_3 = 0$. One solution to this system is given by $u_1 = 1$, $u_2 = -2$, and $u_3 = 4$. Thus, one eigenvector associated with the eigenvalue $r = -2$ is the vector

$$\mathbf{u}_3 = \text{col}(u_1\,, u_2\,, u_3) = \text{col}(1, -2, 4),$$

and another linearly independent solution to this system is given by

$$\mathbf{x}_3(t) = e^{-2t}\mathbf{u}_3 = e^{-2t}\begin{bmatrix} 1 \\ -2 \\ 4 \end{bmatrix}.$$

Hence, by combining the three linearly independent solutions that we have just found, we see that a general solution to this system is

$$\mathbf{x}(t) = c_1e^{-t}\begin{bmatrix} 1 \\ -1 \\ 1 \end{bmatrix} + c_2e^{-t}\begin{bmatrix} -t \\ -1+t \\ 2-t \end{bmatrix} + c_3e^{-2t}\begin{bmatrix} 1 \\ -2 \\ 4 \end{bmatrix}.$$

23. In Problem 3, we found that

$$e^{\mathbf{A}t} = e^{-t}\begin{bmatrix} 1+3t-3t^2/2 & t & -t+t^2/2 \\ -3t & 1 & t \\ 9t-9t^2/2 & 3t & 1-3t+3t^2/2 \end{bmatrix}.$$

In order to use the variation of parameters formula (equation (13) on page 565 of the text), we need to find expressions for $e^{\mathbf{A}t}\mathbf{x}_0$ and $\int_0^t e^{\mathbf{A}(t-s)}\mathbf{f}(s)\,ds$, where we have used the fact that $t_0 = 0$. Thus, we first notice that

$$\int_0^t e^{\mathbf{A}(t-s)}\mathbf{f}(s)\,ds = \int_0^t e^{\mathbf{A}t-\mathbf{A}s}\mathbf{f}(s)\,ds = e^{\mathbf{A}t}\int_0^t e^{-\mathbf{A}s}\mathbf{f}(s)\,ds\,.$$

Since $\mathbf{f}(s) = \operatorname{col}(0, s, 0)$, we observe that

$$\begin{aligned} e^{-\mathbf{A}s}\mathbf{f}(s) &= e^{s}\begin{bmatrix} 1-3s-3s^2/2 & -s & s+s^2/2 \\ 3s & 1 & - \\ -9s-9s^2/2 & -3s & 1+3s+3s^2/2 \end{bmatrix}\begin{bmatrix} 0 \\ s \\ 0 \end{bmatrix} \\ &= e^{s}\begin{bmatrix} -s^2 \\ s \\ -3s^2 \end{bmatrix} = \begin{bmatrix} -s^2e^s \\ se^s \\ -3s^2e^s \end{bmatrix}. \end{aligned}$$

Therefore, we have

$$\begin{aligned} \int_0^t e^{\mathbf{A}(t-s)}\mathbf{f}(s)\,ds &= e^{\mathbf{A}t}\int_0^t e^{-\mathbf{A}s}\mathbf{f}(s)\,ds \\ &= e^{\mathbf{A}t}\begin{bmatrix} \int_0^t(-s^2e^s)ds \\ \int_0^t(se^s)ds \\ \int_0^t(-3s^2e^s)ds \end{bmatrix} \\ &= e^{\mathbf{A}t}\begin{bmatrix} 2-e^t(t^2-2t+2) \\ 1+e^t(t-1) \\ 6-3e^t(t^2-2t+2) \end{bmatrix}, \end{aligned}$$

where we have used integration by parts to evaluate the three integrals above. Next, since $\mathbf{x}_0 = \operatorname{col}(0, 3, 0)$, we see that

$$e^{\mathbf{A}t}\mathbf{x}_0 = e^{-t}\begin{bmatrix} 1+3t-3t^2/2 & t & -t+t^2/2 \\ -3t & 1 & t \\ 9t-9t^2/2 & 3t & 1-3t+3t^2/2 \end{bmatrix}\begin{bmatrix} 0 \\ 3 \\ 0 \end{bmatrix} = e^{-t}\begin{bmatrix} 3t \\ 3 \\ 9t \end{bmatrix}.$$

Finally, substituting these expressions into the variation of parameters formula (13), page 565 of the text, yields

$$\begin{aligned}
\mathbf{x}(t) &= e^{\mathbf{A}t}\mathbf{x}_0 + \int_0^t e^{\mathbf{A}(t-s)}\mathbf{f}(s)\,ds \\
&= e^{-t}\begin{bmatrix} 3t \\ 3 \\ 9t \end{bmatrix} + e^{\mathbf{A}t}\begin{bmatrix} 2-e^t(t^2-2t+2) \\ 1+e^t(t-1) \\ 6-3e^t(t^2-2t+2) \end{bmatrix},
\end{aligned}$$

where $e^{\mathbf{A}t}$ is given above.

CHAPTER 10: Partial Differential Equations

EXERCISES 10.2: Method of Separation of Variables, page 587

5. To find a general solution to this equation, we first observe that the auxiliary equation associated with the corresponding homogeneous equation is given by $r^2 - 1 = 0$. This equation has roots $r = \pm 1$. Thus, the solution to the corresponding homogeneous equation is given by

$$y_h(x) = C_1 e^x + C_2 e^{-x}.$$

By the method of undetermined coefficients, we see that the form of a particular solution to the nonhomogeneous equation is

$$y_p(x) = A + Bx,$$

where we have used the fact that neither $y = 1$ nor $y = x$ is a solution to the corresponding homogeneous equation. To find A and B, we note that

$$y_p'(x) = B \qquad \text{and} \qquad y_p''(x) = 0.$$

By substituting these expressions into the original differential equation, we obtain

$$y_p''(x) - y_p(x) = -A - Bx = 1 - 2x.$$

By equating coefficients, we see that $A = -1$ and $B = 2$. Substituting these values into the equation for $y_p(x)$ yields

$$y_p(x) = -1 + 2x.$$

Thus, we see that

$$y(x) = y_h(x) + y_p(x) = C_1 e^x + C_2 e^{-x} - 1 + 2x.$$

Next we try to find C_1 and C_2 so that the solution $y(x)$ will satisfy the boundary conditions. That is, we want to find C_1 and C_2 satisfying

$$y(0) = C_1 + C_2 - 1 = 0 \qquad \text{and} \qquad y(1) = C_1 e + C_2 e^{-1} + 1 = 1 + e.$$

From the first equation we see that $C_2 = 1 - C_1$. Substituting this expression for C_2 into the second equation and simplifying yields

$$e - e^{-1} = C_1 \left(e - e^{-1}\right).$$

Thus, $C_1 = 1$ and $C_2 = 0$. Therefore,

$$y(x) = e^x - 1 + 2x$$

is the only solution to the boundary value problem.

13. First note that the auxiliary equation for this problem is $r^2 + \lambda = 0$. To find eigenvalues which yield nontrivial solutions we will consider the three cases: $\lambda < 0$, $\lambda = 0$, and $\lambda > 0$.

Case 1, $\lambda < 0$: In this case the roots to the auxiliary equation are $r = \pm\sqrt{-\lambda}$ (where we note that $-\lambda$ is a positive number). Therefore, a general solution to the differential equation $y'' + \lambda y = 0$ is given by

$$y(x) = C_1 e^{\sqrt{-\lambda}x} + C_2 e^{-\sqrt{-\lambda}x}.$$

In order to apply the boundary conditions we need to find $y'(x)$. Thus, we have

$$y'(x) = \sqrt{-\lambda}C_1 e^{\sqrt{-\lambda}x} - \sqrt{-\lambda}C_2 e^{-\sqrt{-\lambda}x}.$$

By applying the boundary conditions we obtain

$$\begin{aligned} & y(0) - y'(0) = C_1 + C_2 - \sqrt{-\lambda}C_1 + \sqrt{-\lambda}C_2 = 0 \\ \Rightarrow \quad & \left(1 - \sqrt{-\lambda}\right) C_1 + \left(1 + \sqrt{-\lambda}\right) C_2 = 0, \end{aligned}$$

and

$$y(\pi) = C_1 e^{\sqrt{-\lambda}\pi} + C_2 e^{-\sqrt{-\lambda}\pi} = 0 \qquad \Rightarrow \qquad C_2 = -C_1 e^{2\sqrt{-\lambda}\pi}.$$

By combining these expressions, we observe that

$$\begin{aligned} &\left(1-\sqrt{-\lambda}\right)C_1 - \left(1+\sqrt{-\lambda}\right)C_1 e^{2\sqrt{-\lambda}\pi} = 0 \\ \Rightarrow \quad &C_1\left[\left(1-\sqrt{-\lambda}\right) - \left(1+\sqrt{-\lambda}\right)e^{2\sqrt{-\lambda}\pi}\right] = 0. \end{aligned} \tag{10.1}$$

This last expression will be true if $C_1 = 0$ or if

$$e^{2\sqrt{-\lambda}\pi} = \frac{1-\sqrt{-\lambda}}{1+\sqrt{-\lambda}}.$$

But since $\sqrt{-\lambda} > 0$, we see that $e^{2\sqrt{-\lambda}\pi} > 1$ while $(1-\sqrt{-\lambda})/(1+\sqrt{-\lambda}) < 1$. Therefore, the only way that equation (10.1) can be true is for $C_1 = 0$. This means that C_2 must also equal zero and so in this case we have only the trivial solution.

Case 2, $\lambda = 0$: In this case we are solving the differential equation $y'' = 0$. This equation has a general solution given by

$$y(x) = C_1 + C_2 x \qquad \Rightarrow \qquad y'(x) = C_2 .$$

By applying the boundary conditions we obtain

$$y(0) - y'(0) = C_1 - C_2 = 0 \qquad \text{and} \qquad y(\pi) = C_1 + C_2\pi = 0.$$

Solving these equations simultaneously yields $C_1 = C_2 = 0$. Thus, we again find only the trivial solution.

Case 3, $\lambda > 0$: In this case the roots to the associated auxiliary equation are $r = \pm\sqrt{\lambda}i$. Therefore, the general solution is given by

$$\begin{aligned} &y(x) = C_1\cos\left(\sqrt{\lambda}x\right) + C_2\sin\left(\sqrt{\lambda}x\right) \\ \Rightarrow \quad &y'(x) = -\sqrt{\lambda}C_1\sin\left(\sqrt{\lambda}x\right) + \sqrt{\lambda}C_2\cos\left(\sqrt{\lambda}x\right). \end{aligned}$$

By applying the boundary conditions, we obtain

$$y(0) - y'(0) = C_1 - \sqrt{\lambda}C_2 = 0 \qquad \Rightarrow \qquad C_1 = \sqrt{\lambda}C_2 ,$$

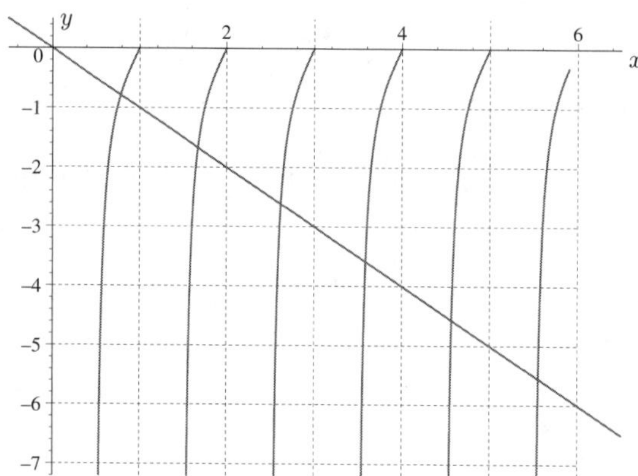

Figure 10–A: The intersection of the graphs $y = -x$ and $y = \tan(\pi x)$, $x > 0$.

and

$$y(\pi) = C_1 \cos\left(\sqrt{\lambda}\pi\right) + C_2 \sin\left(\sqrt{\lambda}\pi\right) = 0.$$

By combining these results, we obtain

$$C_2\left[\sqrt{\lambda}\cos\left(\sqrt{\lambda}\pi\right) + \sin\left(\sqrt{\lambda}\pi\right)\right] = 0$$

Therefore, in order to obtain a solution other than the trivial solution, we must solve the equation

$$\sqrt{\lambda}\cos\left(\sqrt{\lambda}\pi\right) + \sin\left(\sqrt{\lambda}\pi\right) = 0.$$

By simplifying this equation becomes

$$\tan\left(\sqrt{\lambda}\pi\right) = -\sqrt{\lambda}.$$

To see that there exist values for $\lambda > 0$ which satisfy this equation, we examine the graphs of the equations $y = -x$ and $y = \tan(\pi x)$. For any values of $x > 0$ where these two graphs intersect, we set $\lambda = x^2$. These values for λ will be the eigenvalues that we seek. From the graph in Figure 10-A, we see that there are (countably) infinitely many such eigenvalues. These values satisfy the equations

$$\tan\left(\sqrt{\lambda_n}\pi\right) + \sqrt{\lambda_n} = 0.$$

As n becomes large, we can also see from the graph that these eigenvalues approach the square of odd multiples of $1/2$. That is,

$$\lambda_n \approx \frac{(2n-1)^2}{4},$$

when n is large. Corresponding to the eigenvalue λ_n we obtain the solutions

$$y_n(x) = C_{1n}\cos\left(\sqrt{\lambda_n}x\right) + C_{2n}\sin\left(\sqrt{\lambda_n}x\right) = \sqrt{\lambda_n}C_{2n}\cos\left(\sqrt{\lambda_n}x\right) + C_{2n}\sin\left(\sqrt{\lambda_n}x\right)$$

(since $C_{1n} = \sqrt{\lambda_n}C_{2n}$). Thus

$$y_n(x) = C_n\left[\sqrt{\lambda_n}\cos\left(\sqrt{\lambda_n}x\right) + \sin\left(\sqrt{\lambda_n}x\right)\right],$$

where C_n is arbitrary.

17. We are solving the problem

$$\frac{\partial u(x,t)}{\partial t} = 3\frac{\partial^2 u(x,t)}{\partial t^2}, \qquad 0 < x < \pi, \quad t > 0,$$
$$u(0,t) = u(\pi,t) = 0, \qquad t > 0,$$
$$u(x,0) = \sin x - 7\sin 3x + \sin 5x.$$

A solution to this partial differential equation satisfying the first boundary condition is given in equation (11) on page 582 of the text. By letting $\beta = 3$ and $L = \pi$ in this equation we obtain the series

$$u(x,t) = \sum_{n=1}^{\infty} c_n e^{-3n^2 t}\sin nx\,. \tag{10.2}$$

To satisfy the initial condition, we let $t = 0$ in this equation and set the result equal to $\sin x - 7\sin 3x + \sin 5x$. This yields

$$u(x,t) = \sum_{n=1}^{\infty} c_n \sin nx = \sin x - 7\sin 3x + \sin 5x.$$

By equating the coefficients of the like terms, we see that $c_1 = 1$, $c_3 = -7$, $c_5 = 1$, and all other c_n's are zero. Plugging these values into equation (10.2) gives the solution

$$\begin{aligned} u(x,t) &= e^{-3(1)^2 t}\sin x - 7e^{-3(3)^2 t}\sin 3x + e^{-3(5)^2 t}\sin 5x \\ &= e^{-3t}\sin x - 7e^{-27t}\sin 3x + e^{-75t}\sin 5x\,. \end{aligned}$$

21. By letting $\alpha = 3$ and $L = \pi$ in formula (24) on page 585 of the text, we see that the solution we want will have the form

$$u(x,t) = \sum_{n=1}^{\infty} [a_n \cos 3nt + b_n \sin 3nt] \sin nx \,. \tag{10.3}$$

Therefore, we see that

$$\frac{\partial u}{\partial t} = \sum_{n=1}^{\infty} [-3na_n \sin 3nt + 3nb_n \cos 3nt] \sin nx \,.$$

In order for the solution to satisfy the initial conditions, we must find a_n and b_n such that

$$u(x,0) = \sum_{n=1}^{\infty} a_n \sin nx = 6 \sin 2x + 2 \sin 6x,$$

and

$$\frac{\partial u(x,0)}{\partial t} = \sum_{n=1}^{\infty} 3nb_n \sin nx = 11 \sin 9x - 14 \sin 15x.$$

From the first condition, we observe that we must have a term for $n = 2$, 6 and for these terms we want $a_2 = 6$ and $a_6 = 2$. All of the other a_n's must be zero. By comparing coefficients in the second condition, we see that we require

$$3(9)b_9 = 11 \quad \text{or} \quad b_9 = \frac{11}{27} \qquad \text{and} \qquad 3(15)b_{15} = -14 \quad \text{or} \quad b_{15} = -\frac{14}{45} \,.$$

We also see that all other values for b_n must be zero. Therefore, by substituting these values into equation (10.3) above, we obtain the solution of the vibrating string problem with $\alpha = 3$, $L = \pi$ and $f(x)$ and $g(x)$ as given. This solution is given by

$$u(x,t) = 6\cos(3\cdot 2\cdot t)\sin 2x + 2\cos(3\cdot 6\cdot t)\sin 6x + \frac{11}{27}\sin(3\cdot 9\cdot t)\sin 9x - \frac{14}{45}\sin(3\cdot 15\cdot t)\sin 15x.$$

Or by simplifying, we obtain

$$u(x,t) = 6\cos 6t \sin 2x + 2\cos 18t \sin 6x + \frac{11}{27}\sin 27t \sin 9x - \frac{14}{45}\sin 45t \sin 15x.$$

23. We know from equation (11) on page 582 of the text that a formal solution to the heat flow problem is given by

$$u(x,t) = \sum_{n=1}^{\infty} c_n e^{-2(n\pi)^2 t} \sin n\pi x \,, \tag{10.4}$$

where we have made the substitutions $\beta = 2$ and $L = 1$. For this function to be a solution to the problem it must satisfy the initial condition $u(x, 0) = f(x)$, $0 < x < 1$. Therefore, we let $t = 0$ in equation (10.4) above and set the result equal to $f(x)$ to obtain

$$u(x, 0) = \sum_{n=1}^{\infty} c_n \sin n\pi x = \sum_{n=1}^{\infty} \frac{1}{n^2} \sin n\pi x \,.$$

By equating coefficients, we see that $c_n = n^{-2}$. Substituting these values of c_n into equation (10.4) yields the solution

$$u(x, t) = \sum_{n=1}^{\infty} n^{-2} e^{-2(n\pi)^2 t} \sin n\pi x \,.$$

EXERCISES 10.3: Fourier Series, page 603

5. Note that $f(-x) = e^x \cos(-3x) = e^x \cos 3x$. Since

$$f(-x) = e^x \cos 3x \neq e^{-x} \cos 3x = f(x)$$

unless $x = 0$ we see that this function is not even. Similarly since

$$f(-x) = e^x \cos 3x \neq -e^{-x} \cos 3x = -f(x),$$

this function is also not odd.

13. For this problem $T = 1$. Thus, by Definition 1 on page 594 of the text, the Fourier series for this function will be given by

$$\frac{a_0}{2} + \sum_{n=1}^{\infty} \left(a_n \cos n\pi x + b_n \sin n\pi x \right) . \tag{10.5}$$

To compute a_0, we use equation (9) given in Definition 1 in the text noting that $\cos(0 \cdot \pi x) = 1$. Thus, we have

$$a_0 = \int_{-1}^{1} x^2 \, dx = \left. \frac{x^3}{3} \right|_{-1}^{1} = \frac{1}{3} - \frac{-1}{3} = \frac{2}{3} \,.$$

To find a_n for $n = 1, 2, 3, \ldots$, we again use equation (9) on page 594 of the text. This yields

$$a_n = \int_{-1}^{1} x^2 \cos n\pi x \, dx = 2 \int_{0}^{1} x^2 \cos n\pi x \, dx,$$

where we have used the fact that $x^2 \cos n\pi x$ is an even function. Thus, using integration by parts twice, we obtain

$$\begin{aligned}
a_n &= 2 \int_0^1 x^2 \cos n\pi x \, dx = 2 \left[x^2 \frac{\sin n\pi x}{n\pi} \bigg|_0^1 - \frac{2}{n\pi} \int_0^1 x \sin n\pi x \, dx \right] \\
&= 2 \left[\left(\frac{\sin n\pi}{n\pi} - 0 \right) - \frac{2}{n\pi} \left(-x \frac{\cos n\pi x}{n\pi} \bigg|_0^1 + \frac{1}{n\pi} \int_0^1 \cos n\pi x \, dx \right) \right] \\
&= 2 \left[0 + \frac{2}{n^2\pi^2} (\cos n\pi - 0) - \frac{2}{n^2\pi^2} \left(\frac{1}{n\pi} \sin n\pi x \bigg|_0^1 \right) \right] \\
&= \frac{4}{n^2\pi^2} (-1)^n - \frac{4}{n^3\pi^3} (\sin n\pi - 0) = \frac{4}{n^2\pi^2} (-1)^n .
\end{aligned}$$

To calculate the b_n's, note that since x^2 is even and $\sin n\pi x$ is odd, their product is odd (see Problem 7 in this section of the text). Since $x^2 \sin n\pi x$ is also continuous, by Theorem 1 on page 590 of the text, we have

$$b_n = \int_{-1}^{1} x^2 \sin n\pi x \, dx = 0 .$$

By plugging these coefficients into equation (10.5) above, we see that the Fourier series associated with x^2 is given by

$$\frac{1}{3} + \sum_{n=1}^{\infty} \frac{4}{n^2\pi^2} (-1)^n \cos n\pi x .$$

21. We use Theorem 2 on page 600 of the text. Notice that $f(x) = x^2$ and $f'(x) = 2x$ are continuous on $[-1, 1]$. Thus, the Fourier series for f converges to $f(x)$ for $-1 < x < 1$. Furthermore,

$$f\left(-1^+\right) = \lim_{x \to -1^+} x^2 = 1 \qquad \text{and} \qquad f\left(1^-\right) = \lim_{x \to 1^-} x^2 = 1.$$

Hence,

$$\frac{1}{2}\left[f\left(-1^{+}\right)+f\left(1^{-}\right)\right]=\frac{1}{2}(1+1)=1,$$

and so, by Theorem 2, the sum of the Fourier series equals 1 when $x = \pm 1$. Therefore, the Fourier series converges to

$$f(x)=x^2 \qquad \text{for} \qquad -1\le x\le 1.$$

Since the sum function must be periodic with period 2, the sum function is the 2-periodic extension of $f(x)$ which we can write as

$$g(x)=(x-2n)^2, \qquad 2n-1\le x<2n+1, \quad n=0,\pm 1,\pm 2,\ldots.$$

29. To calculate the coefficients of this expansion we use formula (20) on page 599 of the text. Thus we have

$$c_0=\frac{\int_{-1}^{1} f(x)\,dx}{\|P_0\|^2}=\frac{0}{\|P_0\|^2}=0,$$

where we have used the fact that $f(x)$ is an odd function. To find c_1 we first calculate the denominator to be

$$\|P_1\|^2=\int_{-1}^{1} P_1^2(x)\,dx=\int_{-1}^{1} x^2\,dx=\left.\frac{x^3}{3}\right|_{-1}^{1}=\frac{2}{3}.$$

Therefore, we obtain

$$c_1=\frac{3}{2}\int_{-1}^{1} f(x)P_1(x)\,dx=\frac{3}{2}\,2\int_{0}^{1} x\,dx=3\left.\frac{x^2}{2}\right|_{0}^{1}=\frac{3}{2}.$$

Notice that in order to calculate the above integral, we used the fact that the product of the two odd functions $f(x)$ and $P_1(x)$ is even. To find c_2, we first observe that, since $f(x)$ is odd and $P_2(x)$ is even, their product is odd and so we have

$$\int_{-1}^{1} f(x)P_2(x)\,dx=0.$$

Hence

$$c_2=\frac{\int_{-1}^{1} f(x)P_2(x)\,dx}{\|P_2\|^2}=\frac{0}{\|P_2\|^2}=0.$$

31. We need to show that

$$\int_{-\infty}^{\infty} H_m(x)H_n(x)e^{-x^2}\,dx = 0,$$

for $m \neq n$, where $m, n = 0, 1, 2$. Therefore, we need to calculate several integrals. Let's begin with $m = 0$, $n = 2$. Here we see that

$$\begin{aligned}\int_{-\infty}^{\infty} H_0(x)H_2(x)e^{-x^2}\,dx &= \int_{-\infty}^{\infty} \left(4x^2 - 2\right) e^{-x^2}\,dx \\ &= \lim_{N\to\infty} \int_0^N \left(4x^2 - 2\right) e^{-x^2}\,dx + \lim_{M\to\infty} \int_{-M}^0 \left(4x^2 - 2\right) e^{-x^2}\,dx\,.\end{aligned}$$

We will first calculate the indefinite integral using integration by parts with the substitution

$$\begin{aligned} u &= x, & dv &= 2xe^{-x^2}\,dx \\ du &= dx, & v &= -e^{-x^2}\,. \end{aligned}$$

That is we find

$$\begin{aligned}\int \left(4x^2 - 2\right) e^{-x^2}\,dx &= 2\int 2x^2e^{-x^2}\,dx - 2\int e^{-x^2}\,dx \\ &= 2\left[-xe^{-x^2} + \int e^{-x^2}\,dx\right] - 2\int e^{-x^2}\,dx = -2xe^{-x^2} + C.\end{aligned}$$

Substituting this result in for the integrals we are calculating and using L'Hospital's rule to find the limits, yields

$$\begin{aligned}\int_{-\infty}^{\infty} H_0(x)H_2(x)e^{-x^2}\,dx &= \lim_{N\to\infty}\left(-2xe^{-x^2}\Big|_0^N\right) + \lim_{M\to\infty}\left(-2xe^{-x^2}\Big|_{-M}^0\right) \\ &= \lim_{N\to\infty}\left(\frac{-2N}{e^{N^2}} + 0\right) + \lim_{M\to\infty}\left(0 - \frac{2M}{e^{M^2}}\right) \\ &= -\lim_{N\to\infty}\frac{2N}{e^{N^2}} - \lim_{M\to\infty}\frac{2M}{e^{M^2}} = -0 - 0 = 0.\end{aligned}$$

When $m = 0$, $n = 1$ and $m = 1$, $n = 2$, the integrals are, respectively,

$$\int_{-\infty}^{\infty} H_0(x)H_1(x)e^{-x^2}\,dx = \int_{-\infty}^{\infty} 2xe^{-x^2}\,dx$$

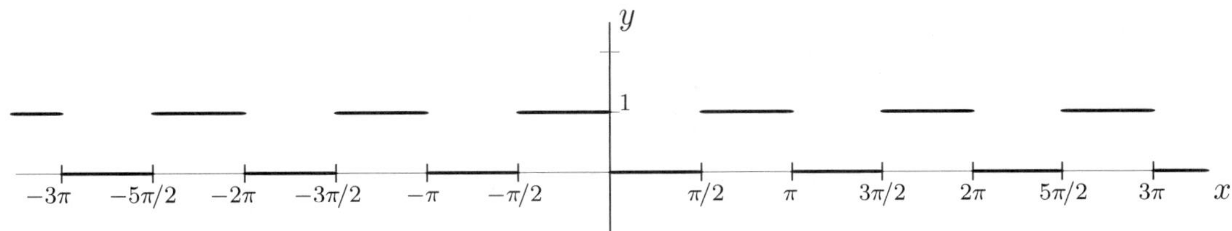

Figure 10–B: The graph of the π-periodic extension of f.

and

$$\int_{-\infty}^{\infty} H_1(x)H_2(x)e^{-x^2}\,dx = \int_{-\infty}^{\infty} 2x(4x^2-2)e^{-x^2}\,dx\,.$$

In each case the integrands are odd functions and hence their integrals over symmetric intervals of the form $(-N, N)$ are zero. Since it is easy to show that the above improper integrals are convergent, we get

$$\int_{-\infty}^{\infty} \cdots = \lim_{N\to\infty} \int_{-N}^{N} \cdots = \lim_{N\to\infty} 0 = 0.$$

Since we have shown that the 3 integrals above are all equal to zero, the first three Hermite polynomials are orthogonal.

EXERCISES 10.4: Fourier Cosine and Sine Series, page 611

3. **(a)** The π-periodic extension $\widetilde{f}(x)$ on the interval $(-\pi, \pi)$ is

$$\widetilde{f}(x) = \begin{cases} 0, & -\pi < x < -\pi/2, \\ 1, & -\pi/2 < x < 0, \\ 0, & 0 < x < \pi/2, \\ 1, & \pi/2 < x < \pi, \end{cases}$$

with $\widetilde{f}(x + 2\pi) = \widetilde{f}(x)$. The graph of this function is given in Figure 10-B.

(b) Using the formula on page 607 of the text, the odd 2π-periodic extension f_o on the

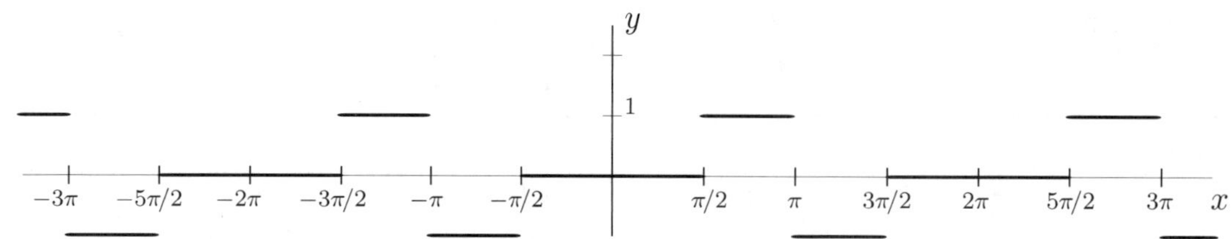

Figure 10–C: The graph of the odd 2π-periodic extension of f.

interval $(-\pi, \pi)$ is

$$f_o(x) = \begin{cases} -f(-x), & -\pi < x < 0, \\ f(x), & 0 < x < \pi \end{cases} = \begin{cases} -1, & -\pi < x < -\pi/2, \\ 0, & -\pi/2 < x < 0, \\ 0, & 0 < x < \pi/2, \\ 1, & \pi/2 < x < \pi, \end{cases}$$

with $f_o(x + 2\pi) = f_o(x)$. The graph of $f_o(x)$ is given in Figure 10-C.

(c) Using the formula on page 608 of the text, the even 2π-periodic extension f_e on the interval $(-\pi, \pi)$ is

$$f_e(x) = \begin{cases} f(-x), & -\pi < x < 0, \\ f(x), & 0 < x < \pi \end{cases} = \begin{cases} 1, & -\pi < x < -\pi/2, \\ 0, & -\pi/2 < x < 0, \\ 0, & 0 < x < \pi/2, \\ 1, & \pi/2 < x < \pi, \end{cases}$$

with $f_e(x + 2\pi) = f_e(x)$. The graph of $f_e(x)$ is given in Figure 10-D.

7. Since f is piecewise continuous on the interval $[0, \pi]$, we can use equation (6) in Definition 2 on page 609 of the text to calculate its Fourier sine series. In this problem $T = \pi$ and $f(x) = x^2$. Thus we have

$$f(x) = \sum_{n=1}^{\infty} b_n \sin nx\,, \qquad \text{with} \qquad b_n = \frac{2}{\pi}\int_0^{\pi} x^2 \sin nx\, dx\,.$$

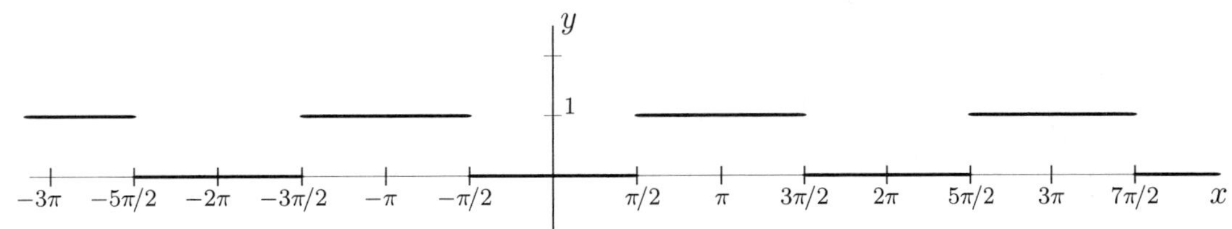

Figure 10–D: The graph of the even 2π-periodic extension of f.

To calculate the coefficients, we use integration by parts twice to obtain

$$\begin{aligned}
\frac{\pi}{2}\, b_n &= \int_0^\pi x^2 \sin nx\, dx = -x^2\, \frac{\cos nx}{n}\Big|_0^\pi + \frac{2}{n}\int_0^\pi x\cos nx\, dx \\
&= -\frac{\pi^2 \cos n\pi}{n} + 0 + \frac{2}{n}\left[x\,\frac{\sin nx}{n}\Big|_0^\pi - \frac{1}{n}\int_0^\pi \sin nx\, dx\right] \\
&= -\frac{\pi^2 \cos n\pi}{n} + \frac{2}{n}\left[0 - \frac{1}{n}\left(-\frac{\cos nx}{n}\Big|_0^\pi\right)\right] \\
&= -\frac{\pi^2 \cos n\pi}{n} + \frac{2}{n^3}\left(\cos n\pi - \cos 0\right),
\end{aligned}$$

where $n = 1, 2, 3, \ldots$. Since $\cos n\pi = 1$ if n is even and $\cos n\pi = -1$ if n is odd for all $n = 1, 2, 3, \ldots$, we see that

$$\frac{\pi}{2}\, b_n = -\frac{\pi^2(-1)^n}{n} + \frac{2[(-1)^n - 1]}{n^3}.$$

Therefore, for $n = 1, 2, 3, \ldots$, we have

$$b_n = \frac{2\pi(-1)^{n+1}}{n} + \frac{4[(-1)^n - 1]}{\pi n^3}.$$

Substituting these coefficients into the Fourier sine series for $f(x) = x^2$, yields

$$\sum_{n=1}^{\infty} \left\{ \frac{2\pi(-1)^{n+1}}{n} + \frac{4[(-1)^n - 1]}{\pi n^3} \right\} \sin nx\,.$$

Since $f(x) = x^2$ and $f\prime(x) = 2x$ are piecewise continuous on the interval $[0, \pi]$, Theorem 2 on page 600 of the text implies that this Fourier series converges pointwise to $f(x)$ on the interval $(0, \pi)$. Hence, we can write

$$f(x) = x^2 = \sum_{n=1}^{\infty} \left\{ \frac{2\pi(-1)^{n+1}}{n} + \frac{4[(-1)^n - 1]}{\pi n^3} \right\} \sin nx \,,$$

for x in the interval $(0, \pi)$. But since the odd 2π-periodic extension of $f(x)$ is discontinuous at odd multiples of π, the Gibbs' phenomenon (see Problem 39 on page 606 of the text) occurs around these points, and so the convergence of this Fourier sine series is not uniform on $(0, \pi)$.

13. Since $f(x) = e^x$ is piecewise continuous on the interval $[0, 1]$, we can use Definition 2 on page 609 of the text to find its Fourier cosine series. Therefore, we have

$$\frac{a_0}{2} + \sum_{n=1}^{\infty} a_n \cos n\pi x, \qquad \text{where} \qquad a_n = 2 \int_0^1 e^x \cos n\pi x \, dx \,.$$

Using the fact that $\cos 0 = 1$, we find the coefficient a_0 to be

$$a_0 = 2 \int_0^1 e^x \, dx = 2(e - 1).$$

We will use integration by parts twice (or the table of integrals on the inside cover of the text) to calculate the integrals in the remaining coefficients. This yields

$$\int e^x \cos n\pi x \, dx = \frac{e^x (\cos n\pi x + n\pi \sin n\pi x)}{1 + n^2\pi^2} \,,$$

where $n = 1, 2, 3, \ldots$. Thus, the remaining coefficients are given by

$$\begin{aligned} a_n = 2 \int_0^1 e^x \cos n\pi x \, dx &= \left. \frac{2e^x (\cos n\pi x + n\pi \sin n\pi x)}{1 + n^2\pi^2} \right|_0^2 \\ &= \frac{2e(\cos n\pi)}{1 + n^2\pi^2} - \frac{2e(1)}{1 + n^2\pi^2} = \frac{2\left[(-1)^n e - 1\right]}{1 + n^2\pi^2} \,, \qquad n = 1, 2, 3, \ldots \,, \end{aligned}$$

where we have used the fact that $\cos n\pi = 1$ if n is even and $\cos n\pi = -1$ if n is odd. By substituting the above coefficients into the Fourier cosine series for f given above, we obtain

$$e^x = e - 1 + 2 \sum_{n=1}^{\infty} \frac{(-1)^n e - 1}{1 + n^2\pi^2} \cos n\pi x \,,$$

for $0 < x < 1$. Note that we can say that e^x for $0 < x < 1$ equals its Fourier cosine series because this series converges uniformly. To see this, first notice that the even 2π-periodic extension of $f(x) = e^x$, $0 < x < 1$, is given by

$$f_e(x) = \begin{cases} e^{-x}, & -1 < x < 0, \\ e^x, & 0 < x < 1, \end{cases}$$

with $f_e(x+2\pi) = f_e(x)$. Since this extension is continuous on $(-\infty, \infty)$ and $f_e'(x)$ is piecewise continuous on $[-1, 1]$, Theorem 3 on page 601 of the text states that its Fourier series (which is the one we found above) converges uniformly to $f_e(x)$ on $[-1, 1]$ and so it converges uniformly to $f(x) = e^x$ on $(0, 1)$.

17. This problem is the same as the heat flow problem on page 580 of the text with $\beta = 5$, $L = \pi$ and $f(x) = 1 - \cos 2x$. Therefore, the formal solution to this problem is given in equations (11) and (12) on pages 582 and 583 of the text. Thus, the formal solution is

$$u(x,t) = \sum_{n=1}^{\infty} c_n e^{-5n^2 t} \sin nx \qquad 0 < x < \pi, \quad t > 0\,, \tag{10.6}$$

where

$$f(x) = 1 - \cos 2x = \sum_{n=1}^{\infty} c_n \sin nx\,.$$

Therefore, we must find the Fourier sine series for $1 - \cos 2x$. To do this, we can use equations (6) and (7) of Definition 2 on page 609 of the text. Hence, the coefficients are given by

$$\begin{aligned} c_n &= \frac{2}{\pi} \int_0^{\pi} (1 - \cos 2x) \sin nx \, dx \\ &= \frac{2}{\pi} \int_0^{\pi} \sin nx \, dx - \frac{2}{\pi} \int_0^{\pi} \cos 2x \sin nx \, dx\,, \qquad n = 1, 2, 3, \ldots\,. \end{aligned}$$

Calculating the first integral above yields

$$\frac{2}{\pi} \int_0^{\pi} \sin nx \, dx = -\frac{2}{n\pi} (\cos n\pi - 1) = \frac{2}{n\pi} \left[1 - (-1)^n\right],$$

where we have used the fact that $\cos n\pi = 1$ if n is even and $\cos n\pi = -1$ if n is odd. To calculate the second integral, we use the fact that $2\cos\alpha\sin\beta = \sin(\beta-\alpha)+\sin(\beta+\alpha)$, to obtain

$$\begin{aligned} -\frac{2}{\pi}\int_0^{\pi}\cos 2x\sin nx\,dx &= -\frac{1}{\pi}\left\{\int_0^{\pi}\sin[(n-2)x]\,dx+\int_0^{\pi}\sin[(n+2)x]\,dx\right\} \\ &= \frac{1}{\pi(n-2)}\{\cos[(n-2)\pi]-1\}+\frac{1}{\pi(n+2)}\{\cos[(n+2)\pi]-1\} \\ &= \frac{1}{\pi(n-2)}[(-1)^n-1]+\frac{1}{\pi(n+2)}[(-1)^n-1]\,. \end{aligned}$$

Combining these two integrals yields

$$\begin{aligned} c_n &= \frac{2}{n\pi}[1-(-1)^n]+\frac{1}{\pi(n-2)}[(-1)^n-1]+\frac{1}{\pi(n+2)}[(-1)^n-1] \\ &= \begin{cases} 0, & \text{if } n \text{ is even}, \\ 4/(n\pi)-2/[\pi(n-2)]-2/[\pi(n+2)], & \text{if } n \text{ is odd}, \end{cases} \end{aligned}$$

for $n = 1, 2, 3, \ldots$. Hence, we obtain the formal solution to this problem by substituting these coefficients into equation (10.6) above and setting $n = 2k-1$. Therefore, we have

$$u(x,t) = \frac{2}{\pi}\sum_{k=1}^{\infty}\left[\frac{2}{2k-1}-\frac{1}{2k-3}-\frac{1}{2k+1}\right]e^{-5(2k-1)^2t}\sin(2k-1)x\,.$$

EXERCISES 10.5: The Heat Equation, page 624

3. If we let $\beta = 3$, $L = \pi$, and $f(x) = x$, we see that this problem has the same form as the problem in Example 1 on page 613 of the text. Therefore, we can find the formal solution to this problem by substituting these values into equation (14) on page 615 of the text. Hence, we have

$$u(x,t) = \sum_{n=0}^{\infty} c_n\cos e^{-3n^2t}\cos nx\,, \qquad \text{where} \qquad f(x) = \sum_{n=0}^{\infty} c_n\cos nx\,. \tag{10.7}$$

Thus, we must find the Fourier cosine series coefficients for $f(x) = x$, $0 < x < \pi$. (Note that the even 2π-extension for $f(x) = x$, $0 < x < \pi$, which is given by

$$f_e(x) = \begin{cases} -x, & \text{for } -\pi < x < 0, \\ x, & \text{for } 0 < x < \pi, \end{cases}$$

with $f_e(x+2\pi) = f_e(x)$, is continuous. Also note that its derivative is piecewise continuous on $[-\pi.\pi]$. Therefore, the Fourier series for this extension converges uniformly to f_e. This means that the equality sign in the second equation given in formula (10.7) above is justified for $0 < x < \pi$.) To find the required Fourier series coefficients, we use equations (4) and (5) given in Definition 2 on page 609 of the text. Hence, we have

$$x = \frac{a_0}{2} + \sum_{n=1}^{\infty} a_n \cos nx\,,$$

(so that $c_0 = a_0/2$ and $c_n = a_n$ for $n = 1, 2, 3, \ldots$) where

$$a_0 = \frac{2}{\pi}\int_0^{\pi} x\,dx = \frac{2}{\pi}\frac{x^2}{2}\bigg|_0^{\pi} = \pi \quad \text{and} \quad a_n = \frac{2}{\pi}\int_0^{\pi} x\cos nx\,dx,$$

for $n = 1, 2, 3, \ldots$. To calculate the second integral above we use integration by parts to obtain

$$\begin{aligned} a_n &= \frac{2}{\pi}\int_0^{\pi} x\cos nx\,dx = \frac{2}{\pi}\left[\frac{x}{n}\sin nx\bigg|_0^{\pi} - \frac{1}{n}\int_0^{\pi}\sin nx\,dx\right] \\ &= \frac{2}{\pi}\left[0 - \frac{1}{n}\left(-\frac{\cos nx}{n}\bigg|_0^{\pi}\right)\right] = \frac{2}{\pi n^2}(\cos n\pi - 1) = \frac{2}{\pi n^2}\left[(-1)^n - 1\right]. \end{aligned}$$

Combining these results yields

$$a_n = \begin{cases} \pi, & \text{if } n = 0, \\ -4/(\pi n^2), & \text{if } n \text{ is odd}, \\ 0, & \text{if } n \text{ is even and } n \neq 0, \end{cases}$$

where $n = 0, 1, 2, \ldots$. The formal solution for this problem is, therefore, found by substituting these coefficients into the first equation given in formula (10.7) above. (Recall that $c_0 = a_0/2$ and $c_n = a_n$ for $n = 1, 2, 3, \ldots$.) Thus, we have

$$\begin{aligned} u(x,t) &= \frac{\pi}{2}e^{-0}\cos 0 - \sum_{k=0}^{\infty}\frac{4}{\pi(2k+1)^2}e^{-3(2k+1)^2 t}\cos(2k+1)x \\ &= \frac{\pi}{2} - \sum_{k=0}^{\infty}\frac{4}{\pi(2k+1)^2}e^{-3(2k+1)^2 t}\cos(2k+1)x \end{aligned}$$

7. This problem has nonhomogeneous boundary conditions and so has the same form as the problem in Example 2 on page 616 of the text. By comparing these two problems, we see that for this problem $\beta = 2$, $L = \pi$, $U_1 = 5$, $U_2 = 10$, and $f(x) = \sin 3x - \sin 5x$. To solve this problem, we assume that the solution consists of a steady state solution $v(x)$ and a transient solution $w(x,t)$. The steady state solution is given in equation (24) on page 617 of the text and is

$$v(x) = 5 + \frac{(10-5)x}{\pi} = 5 + \frac{5}{\pi}\,x\,.$$

The formal transient solution is given by equations (39) and (40) on page 619 of the text. By using these equations and making appropriate substitutions, we obtain

$$w(x,t) = \sum_{n=1}^{\infty} c_n e^{-2n^2 t} \sin nx\,, \tag{10.8}$$

where the coefficients (the c_n's) are given by

$$f(x) - v(x) = \sin 3x - \sin 5x - 5 - \frac{5}{\pi}\,x = \sum_{n=1}^{\infty} c_n \sin nx\,, \qquad 0 < x < \pi.$$

Therefore, we must find the Fourier sine series coefficients for the function $f(x) - v(x)$ for $0 < x < \pi$. Since the function $f(x) = \sin 3x - \sin 5x$ is already in the form of a sine series, we only need to find the Fourier sine series for $-v(x) = -5 - 5x/\pi$ and then add $\sin 3x - \sin 5x$ to this series. The resulting coefficients are the ones that we need. (Note that the Fourier sine series for $-5 - 5x/\pi$ will converge pointwise but not uniformly to $-5 - 5x/\pi$ for $0 < x < \pi$.) To find the desired Fourier series we use equations (6) and (7) in Definition 2 on page 609 of the text. Thus, with the appropriate substitutions, we have

$$-5 - \frac{5x}{\pi} = \sum_{n=1}^{\infty} b_n \sin nx\,, \qquad \text{where} \qquad b_n = \frac{2}{\pi}\int_0^{\pi} \left(-5 - \frac{5x}{\pi}\right) \sin nx\,dx\,.$$

To find the b_n's, we will use integration by parts to obtain

$$b_n = -\frac{10}{\pi}\int_0^{\pi} \sin nx\,dx - \frac{10}{\pi^2}\int_0^{\pi} x \sin nx\,dx$$

$$
\begin{aligned}
&= \frac{10}{n\pi}(\cos n\pi - 1) - \frac{10}{\pi^2}\left[-\frac{x}{n}\cos nx\Big|_0^{\pi} + \frac{1}{n}\int_0^{\pi}\cos nx\,dx\right] \\
&= \frac{10}{n\pi}(\cos n\pi - 1) - \frac{10}{\pi^2}\left[-\frac{\pi}{n}\cos n\pi + 0\right] \\
&= \frac{10}{n\pi}(2\cos n\pi - 1) = \frac{10}{n\pi}\left[2(-1)^n - 1\right], \qquad n = 1, 2, 3, \ldots .
\end{aligned}
$$

Thus, the Fourier sine series for $\sin 3x - \sin 5x - 5 - 5x/\pi$ is given by

$$
\begin{aligned}
\sin 3x - \sin 5x - 5 - \frac{5x}{\pi} &= \sin 3x - \sin 5x + \sum_{n=1}^{\infty}\frac{10}{n\pi}\left[2(-1)^n - 1\right]\sin nx \\
&= \sin 3x - \sin 5x - \frac{30}{\pi}\sin x + \frac{10}{2\pi}\sin 2x - \frac{30}{3\pi}\sin 3x + \frac{10}{4\pi}\sin 4x \\
&\qquad - \frac{30}{5\pi}\sin 5x + \sum_{n=6}^{\infty}\frac{10}{n\pi}\left[2(-1)^n - 1\right]\sin nx \\
&= -\frac{30}{\pi}\sin x + \frac{5}{\pi}\sin 2x + \left(1 - \frac{10}{\pi}\right)\sin 3x + \frac{5}{2\pi}\sin 4x \\
&\qquad - \left(1 + \frac{6}{\pi}\right)\sin 5x + \sum_{n=6}^{\infty}\frac{10}{n\pi}\left[2(-1)^n - 1\right]\sin nx .
\end{aligned}
$$

We therefore obtain the formal transient solution by taking the coefficients from this Fourier series and substituting them in for the c_n coefficients in equation (10.8) above. Thus, we find

$$
\begin{aligned}
w(x,t) = &-\frac{30}{\pi}e^{-2(1)^2t}\sin x + \frac{5}{\pi}e^{-2(2)^2t}\sin 2x + \left(1 - \frac{10}{\pi}\right)e^{-2(3)^2t}\sin 3x + \frac{5}{2\pi}e^{-2(4)^2t}\sin 4x \\
&- \left(1 + \frac{6}{\pi}\right)e^{-2(5)^2t}\sin 5x + \sum_{n=6}^{\infty}\frac{10}{n\pi}\left[2(-1)^n - 1\right]e^{-2n^2t}\sin nx ,
\end{aligned}
$$

and so the formal solution to the original problem is given by

$$
\begin{aligned}
u(x,t) &= v(x) + w(x,t) \\
&= 5 + \frac{5x}{\pi} - \frac{30}{\pi}e^{-2t}\sin x + \frac{5}{\pi}e^{-8t}\sin 2x + \left(1 - \frac{10}{\pi}\right)e^{-18t}\sin 3x + \frac{5}{2\pi}e^{-32t}\sin 4x \\
&\qquad - \left(1 + \frac{6}{\pi}\right)e^{-50t}\sin 5x + \sum_{n=6}^{\infty}\frac{10}{n\pi}\left[2(-1)^n - 1\right]e^{-2n^2t}\sin nx .
\end{aligned}
$$

9. Notice that this problem is a nonhomogeneous partial differential equation and has the same form as the problem given in Example 3 on page 618 of the text. By comparing these problems, we see that here $\beta = 1, P(x) = e^{-x}$, $L = \pi$, $U_1 = U_2 = 0$, and $f(x) = \sin 2x$. As in Example 3, we will assume that the solution is the sum of a steady state solution $v(x)$ and a transient solution $w(x, t)$. The steady state solution is the solution to the boundary value problem

$$v''(x) = -e^{-x}, \qquad 0 < x < \pi, \qquad v(0) = v(\pi) = 0.$$

Thus the steady state solution can be found either by solving this ODE or by substituting the appropriate values into equation (35) given on page 618 of the text. By either method we find

$$v(x) = \frac{e^{-\pi} - 1}{\pi} x - e^{-x} + 1.$$

The formal transient solution is then given by equations (39) and (40) on page 619 of the text. By making the appropriate substitutions into this equation, we obtain

$$w(x, t) = \sum_{n=1}^{\infty} c_n e^{-n^2 t} \sin nx\,, \tag{10.9}$$

where the c_n's are given by

$$f(x) - v(x) = \sin 2x - \frac{e^{-\pi} - 1}{\pi} x + e^{-x} - 1 = \sum_{n=1}^{\infty} c_n \sin nx\,.$$

Hence, the problem is to find the Fourier sine coefficients for $f(x) - v(x)$. The first term, $f(x) = \sin 2x$, is already in the desired form. Therefore, the Fourier sine series for $f(x) - v(x)$ is

$$\sin 2x + \sum_{n=1}^{\infty} b_n \sin nx = b_1 \sin x + (b_2 + 1) \sin 2x + \sum_{n=3}^{\infty} b_n \sin nx\,,$$

where the b_n's are the Fourier sine coefficients for $-v(x)$. This implies that if $n \neq 2$, then $c_n = b_n$ and if $n = 2$, then $c_n = b_n + 1$. The b_n coefficients are given by equation (7) on page 609 of the text. Thus, we have

$$b_n = \frac{2}{\pi} \int_0^{\pi} \left[-\frac{e^{-\pi} - 1}{\pi} x + e^{-x} - 1 \right] \sin nx\, dx$$

$$= \frac{2}{\pi}\left(-\frac{e^{-\pi}-1}{\pi}\right)\int_0^{\pi} x\sin nx\,dx + \frac{2}{\pi}\int_0^{\pi} e^{-x}\sin nx\,dx - \frac{2}{\pi}\int_0^{\pi}\sin nx\,dx\,.$$

We will calculate each integral separately. The first integral is found by using integration by parts. This yields

$$\begin{aligned}\frac{2}{\pi}\left(-\frac{e^{-\pi}-1}{\pi}\right)\int_0^{\pi} x\sin nx\,dx &= \frac{-2(e^{-\pi}-1)}{\pi^2}\left[-\frac{x}{n}\cos nx\Big|_0^{\pi} + \frac{1}{n}\int_0^{\pi}\cos nx\,dx\right]\\ &= \frac{-2(e^{-\pi}-1)}{\pi^2}\left[-\frac{\pi}{n}\cos n\pi + 0 + 0\right] = \frac{2(e^{-\pi}-1)}{n\pi}(-1)^n\,.\end{aligned}$$

To find the second integral we use the table of integrals on the inside front cover of the text (or use integration by parts twice) to obtain

$$\frac{2}{\pi}\int_0^{\pi} e^{-x}\sin nx\,dx = \frac{2}{\pi}\left[\frac{-e^{-\pi}n\cos n\pi + n}{1+n^2}\right] = \frac{2n}{(1+n^2)\pi}\left[e^{-\pi}(-1)^{n+1}+1\right].$$

The last integral is found to be

$$-\frac{2}{\pi}\int_0^{\pi}\sin nx\,dx = \frac{2}{n\pi}\left[\cos n\pi - 1\right] = \frac{2}{n\pi}\left[(-1)^n - 1\right].$$

By combining all of these results, we find that the Fourier coefficients for $-v(x)$ are given by

$$b_n = \frac{2(e^{-\pi}-1)}{n\pi}(-1)^n + \frac{2n}{(1+n^2)\pi}\left[e^{-\pi}(-1)^{n+1}+1\right] + \frac{2}{n\pi}\left[(-1)^n - 1\right].$$

Therefore, the coefficients for the formal transient solution are

$$c_n = \begin{cases} \dfrac{2(e^{-\pi}-1)}{n\pi}(-1)^n + \dfrac{2n}{(1+n^2)\pi}\left[e^{-\pi}(-1)^{n+1}+1\right] + \dfrac{2}{n\pi}\left[(-1)^n - 1\right], & \text{if } n \neq 2,\\[2ex] \dfrac{e^{-\pi}-1}{\pi} + \dfrac{4}{5\pi}\left(1-e^{-\pi}\right) + 1, & \text{if } n = 2. \end{cases}$$

Since the formal solution to the PDE given in this problem is the sum of its steady state solution and its transient solution, we find this final solution to be

$$u(x,t) = v(x) + w(x,t) = \frac{e^{-\pi}-1}{\pi}x - e^{-x} + 1 + \sum_{n=1}^{\infty} c_n e^{-n^2 t}\sin nx\,,$$

where the c_n's are given above.

11. Let $u(x,t) = X(x)T(t)$. Substituting $u(x,t) = X(x)T(t)$ into the PDE yields

$$T'(t)X(x) = 4X''(x)T(t) \qquad \Rightarrow \qquad \frac{T'(t)}{4T(t)} = \frac{X''(x)}{X(x)} = K,$$

where K is a constant. Substituting the solution $u(x,t) = X(x)T(t)$ into the boundary conditions, we obtain

$$X'(0)T(t) = 0, \qquad X(\pi)T(t) = 0, \qquad t > 0.$$

Thus, we assume that $X'(0) = 0$ and $X(\pi) = 0$ since this allows the expressions above to be true for all $t > 0$ without implying that $u(x,t) \equiv 0$. Therefore, we have the two ODE's

$$\begin{aligned} X''(x) &= KX(x), \qquad 0 < x < \pi, \\ X'(0) &= X(\pi) = 0, \end{aligned} \tag{10.10}$$

and

$$T'(t) = 4KT(t), \qquad t > 0. \tag{10.11}$$

To solve boundary value problem (10.10), we will examine three cases.

Case 1: Assume $K = 0$. Now equation (10.10) becomes $X'' = 0$. The solution is $X(x) = ax+b$, where a and b are arbitrary constants. To find these constants we use the boundary conditions in (10.10). Thus, we have

$$X'(0) = a = 0 \qquad \Rightarrow \qquad a = 0 \qquad \Rightarrow \qquad X(x) = b,$$

and so

$$X(\pi) = b = 0 \qquad \Rightarrow \qquad b = 0.$$

Therefore, in this case we have only the trivial solution.

Case 2: Assume $K > 0$. In this case the auxiliary equation for equation (10.10) is $r^2 - K = 0$. The roots to this equation are $r = \pm\sqrt{K}$. Thus, the solution is

$$X(x) = C_1 e^{\sqrt{K}x} + C_2 e^{-\sqrt{K}x},$$

where C_1 and C_2 are arbitrary constants. To find these constants we again use the boundary conditions in (10.10). We first note that

$$X'(x) = C_1\sqrt{K}e^{\sqrt{K}x} - C_2\sqrt{K}e^{-\sqrt{K}x}.$$

Therefore,

$$X'(0) = C_1\sqrt{K} - C_2\sqrt{K} = 0 \quad \Rightarrow \quad C_1 = C_2 \quad \Rightarrow \quad X(x) = C_1\left(e^{\sqrt{K}x} + e^{-\sqrt{K}x}\right).$$

The other boundary condition implies that

$$X(\pi) = C_1\left(e^{\sqrt{K}\pi} + e^{-\sqrt{K}\pi}\right) = 0 \quad \Rightarrow \quad C_1\left(e^{2\sqrt{K}\pi} + 1\right) = 0.$$

The only way that the final equation above can be zero is for C_1 to be zero. Therefore, we again obtain only the trivial solution.

Case 3: Assume $K < 0$, so $-K > 0$. Then the auxiliary equation for equation (10.10) has the roots $r = \pm\sqrt{K} = \pm i\sqrt{-K}$. Therefore, the solution is

$$\begin{aligned} &X(x) = C_1 \sin\left(\sqrt{-K}x\right) + C_2 \cos\left(\sqrt{-K}x\right) \\ \Rightarrow \quad &X'(x) = C_1\sqrt{-K}\cos\left(\sqrt{-K}x\right) - C_2\sqrt{-K}\sin\left(\sqrt{-K}x\right). \end{aligned}$$

Using the boundary condition $X'(0) = 0$, we obtain

$$0 = X'(0) = C_1\sqrt{-K}\cos 0 - C_2\sqrt{-K}\sin 0 = C_1\sqrt{-K} \quad \Rightarrow \quad C_1 = 0.$$

Hence, $X(x) = C_2\cos\left(\sqrt{-K}x\right)$. Applying the other boundary condition yields

$$\begin{aligned} &0 = X(\pi) = C_2\cos\left(\sqrt{-K}\pi\right) \\ \Rightarrow \quad &\sqrt{-K}\pi = (2n+1)\frac{\pi}{2} \quad \Rightarrow \quad K = -\frac{(2n+1)^2}{4}, \quad n = 0, 1, 2, \dots. \end{aligned}$$

Therefore, nontrivial solutions to problem (10.10) above are given by

$$X_n(x) = c_n \cos\left(\frac{2n+1}{2}x\right), \qquad n = 0, 1, 2, \dots.$$

By substituting the values of K into equation (10.11), we obtain

$$T'(t) = -(2n+1)^2 T(t), \qquad t > 0.$$

This is a separable differential equation, and we find

$$\begin{aligned} &\frac{dT}{T} = -(2n+1)^2\, dt && \Rightarrow && \int \frac{dT}{T} = -(2n+1)^2 \int dt \\ \Rightarrow \quad & \ln|T| = -(2n+1)^2 t + A && \Rightarrow && T_n(t) = b_n e^{-(2n+1)^2 t}, \qquad n = 0, 1, 2, \dots, \end{aligned}$$

(where $b_n = \pm e^A$). Hence, by the superposition principle (and since $u_n(x,t) = X_n(x)T_n(t)$), we see that the formal solution to the original PDE is

$$u(x,t) = \sum_{n=0}^{\infty} b_n e^{-(2n+1)^2 t} c_n \cos\left(\frac{2n+1}{2}x\right) = \sum_{n=0}^{\infty} a_n e^{-(2n+1)^2 t} \cos\left[\left(n+\frac{1}{2}\right)x\right], \tag{10.12}$$

where $a_n = b_n c_n$. To find the a_n's, we use the initial condition to obtain

$$u(x,0) = f(x) = \sum_{n=0}^{\infty} a_n \cos\left[\left(n+\frac{1}{2}\right)x\right]. \tag{10.13}$$

Therefore, the formal solution to this PDE is given by equation (10.12), where the a_n's are given by equation (10.13).

17. This problem is similar to the problem given in Example 4 on page 619 of the text with $\beta = 1$, $L = W = \pi$, and $f(x,y) = y$. The formal solution to this problem is given in equation (52) on page 621 of the text with its coefficients given on pages 621 and 622 in equations (54) and (55). By making appropriate substitutions in the first of these equations, we see that the formal solution to this problem is

$$u(x,y,t) = \sum_{m=0}^{\infty}\sum_{n=1}^{\infty} a_{mn} e^{-(m^2+n^2)t} \cos mx \sin ny\,. \tag{10.14}$$

We can find the coefficients, a_0n, $n = 1, 2, 3, \dots$, by using equation (54) on page 621 of the text with the appropriate substitutions. This yields

$$a_{0n} \;=\; \frac{2}{\pi^2}\int_0^{\pi}\int_0^{\pi} y \sin ny\, dx\, dy = \frac{2}{\pi^2}\int_0^{\pi} y \sin ny \left[\int_0^{\pi} dx\right] dy$$

$$= \frac{2}{\pi}\int_0^{\pi} y\sin ny\,dy \qquad \text{(use integration by parts)}$$

$$= \frac{2}{\pi}\left[-\frac{y}{n}\cos ny\Big|_0^{\pi} + \frac{1}{n}\int_0^{\pi}\cos ny\,dy\right]$$

$$= \frac{2}{\pi}\left[-\frac{\pi}{n}\cos n\pi + \left(\frac{1}{n^2}\sin ny\Big|_0^{\pi}\right)\right] = \frac{2}{\pi}\left(-\frac{\pi}{n}\cos n\pi\right) = \frac{2}{n}(-1)^{n+1}.$$

We will use equation (55) on page 622 of the text to find the other coefficients. Thus for $m \geq 1$ and $n \geq 1$, we have

$$a_{mn} = \frac{4}{\pi^2}\int_0^{\pi}\int_0^{\pi} y\cos mx\sin ny\,dx\,dy$$

$$= \frac{4}{\pi^2}\int_0^{\pi} y\sin ny\left(\int_0^{\pi}\cos mx\,dx\right)dy = \frac{4}{\pi^2}\int_0^{\pi} y\sin ny(0)\,dy = 0.$$

The formal solution to this problem is found by substituting these coefficients into equation (10.14). To do this we first note that the coefficients for any terms containing $m \neq 0$ are zero. Hence, only terms containing $m = 0$ will appears in the summation. Therefore, the formal solution is given by

$$u(x,y,t) = \sum_{n=1}^{\infty}\frac{2}{n}(-1)^{n+1}e^{-n^2t}\sin ny = 2\sum_{n=1}^{\infty}\frac{(-1)^{n+1}}{n}e^{-n^2t}\sin ny\,.$$

EXERCISES 10.6: The Wave Equation, page 636

1. This problem has the form of the problem given in equations (1)–(4) on page 625 of the text. Here, however, $\alpha = 1$, $L = 1$, $f(x) = x(1-x)$, and $g(x) = \sin 7\pi x$. This problem is consistent because

$$f(0) = 0 = f(1), \qquad \text{and} \qquad g(0) = \sin 0 = 0 = \sin 7\pi = g(1).$$

The solution to this problem was derived in Section 10.2 of the text and given again in equation (5) on page 625 of the text. Making appropriate substitutions in equation (5) yields a formal solution given by

$$u(x,t)=\sum_{n=1}^{\infty}\left[a_n\cos n\pi t+b_n\sin n\pi t\right]\sin n\pi x\,. \tag{10.15}$$

To find the a_n's we note that they are the Fourier sine coefficients for $x(1-x)$ and so are given by equation (7) on page 609 of the text. Thus, for $n=1,2,3,\ldots$, we have

$$a_n=2\int_0^1 x(1-x)\sin n\pi x\,dx=2\left[\int_0^1 x\sin n\pi x\,dx-\int_0^1 x^2\sin n\pi x\,dx\right].$$

We will use integration by parts to calculate these two integrals. This yields

$$\int_0^1 x\sin n\pi x\,dx=-\frac{1}{n\pi}\cos n\pi=-\frac{1}{n\pi}(-1)^n$$

and

$$\int_0^1 x^2\sin n\pi x\,dx=-\frac{1}{n\pi}\cos n\pi-\frac{2}{n^2\pi^2}\left(-\frac{1}{n\pi}\cos n\pi+\frac{1}{n\pi}\right)=-\frac{1}{n\pi}(-1)^n+\frac{2}{n^3\pi^3}\left[(-1)^n-1\right].$$

Therefore, for $n=1,2,3,\ldots$, we see that

$$a_n=2\left\{-\frac{1}{n\pi}(-1)^n+\frac{1}{n\pi}(-1)^n-\frac{2}{n^3\pi^3}\left[(-1)^n-1\right]\right\}=-\frac{4}{n^3\pi^3}\left[(-1)^n-1\right].$$

This can also be expressed as

$$a_n=\begin{cases}0, & \text{if } n \text{ is even,}\\ 8/(n^3\pi^3), & \text{if } n \text{ is odd.}\end{cases}$$

The b_n's were found in equation (7) on page 626. By making appropriate substitutions in this equations we have

$$\sin 7\pi x=\sum_{n=1}^{\infty}n\pi b_n\sin n\pi x.$$

From this we see that for $n=7$

$$7\pi b_7=1\qquad\Rightarrow\qquad b_7=\frac{1}{7\pi},$$

and for all other n's, $b_n = 0$. By substituting these coefficients into the formal solution given in equation (10.15) above, we obtain

$$u(x,t) = \frac{1}{7\pi}\sin 7\pi t \sin 7\pi x + \sum_{k=0}^{\infty} \frac{8}{[(2k+1)\pi]^3}\cos[(2k+1)\pi t]\sin[(2k+1)\pi x].$$

5. First we note that this problem is consistent because

$$g(0) = 0 = g(L) \qquad \text{and} \qquad f(0) = 0 = f(L).$$

The formal solution to this problem is given in equation (5) on page 625 of the text with the coefficients given in equations (6) and (7) on page 626. By equation (7), we see that

$$g(x) = 0 = \sum_{n=1}^{\infty} b_n \frac{n\pi\alpha}{L}\sin\left(\frac{n\pi x}{L}\right).$$

Thus, each term in this infinite series must be zero and so $b_n = 0$ for all n's. Therefore, the formal solution given in equation (5) on page 625 of the text becomes

$$u(x,t) = \sum_{n=1}^{\infty} a_n \cos\left(\frac{n\pi\alpha t}{L}\right)\sin\left(\frac{n\pi x}{L}\right). \tag{10.16}$$

To find the a_n's we note that by equation (6) on page 626 of the text these coefficients are the Fourier sine coefficients for $f(x)$. Therefore, by using equation (7) on page 609 of the text, for $n = 1, 2, 3, \ldots$ we have

$$\begin{aligned} a_n &= \frac{2}{L}\int_0^L f(x)\sin\left(\frac{n\pi x}{L}\right)dx = \frac{2}{L}\left[\frac{h_0}{a}\int_0^a x\sin\left(\frac{n\pi x}{L}\right)dx + h_0\int_a^L \frac{L-x}{L-a}\sin\left(\frac{n\pi x}{L}\right)dx\right] \\ &= \frac{2h_0}{L}\left[\frac{1}{a}\int_0^a x\sin\left(\frac{n\pi x}{L}\right)dx + \frac{L}{L-a}\int_a^L \sin\left(\frac{n\pi x}{L}\right)dx - \frac{1}{L-a}\int_a^L x\sin\left(\frac{n\pi x}{L}\right)dx\right]. \end{aligned}$$

By using integration by parts, we find

$$\int x\sin\left(\frac{n\pi x}{L}\right)dx = -\frac{xL}{n\pi}\cos\left(\frac{n\pi x}{L}\right) + \frac{L^2}{n^2\pi^2}\sin\left(\frac{n\pi x}{L}\right).$$

Therefore, for $n = 1, 2, 3, \ldots$, the coefficients become

$$a_n = \frac{2h_0}{L}\left\{\frac{1}{a}\left[-\frac{aL}{n\pi}\cos\left(\frac{n\pi a}{L}\right)+\frac{L^2}{n^2\pi^2}\sin\left(\frac{n\pi a}{L}\right)\right]-\frac{L^2}{n\pi(L-a)}\left[\cos n\pi-\cos\left(\frac{n\pi a}{L}\right)\right]\right.$$
$$\left.-\frac{1}{L-a}\left[-\frac{L^2}{n\pi}\cos n\pi+\frac{aL}{n\pi}\cos\left(\frac{n\pi a}{L}\right)\right]+\frac{L^2}{n^2\pi^2}\left[\sin n\pi-\sin\left(\frac{n\pi a}{L}\right)\right]\right\}.$$

After simplifying, this becomes

$$a_n = \frac{2h_0L^2}{n^2\pi^2 a(L-a)}\sin\left(\frac{n\pi a}{L}\right), \qquad n = 1, 2, 3, \ldots .$$

By substituting this result into equation (10.16) above, we obtain the formal solution to this problem given by

$$u(x,t) = \frac{2h_0L^2}{\pi^2 a(L-a)}\sum_{n=1}^{\infty}\frac{1}{n^2}\sin\left(\frac{n\pi a}{L}\right)\cos\left(\frac{n\pi\alpha t}{L}\right)\sin\left(\frac{n\pi x}{L}\right).$$

7. If we let $\alpha = 1$, $h(x,t) = tx$, $L = \pi$, $f(x) = \sin x$, and $g(x) = 5\sin 2x - 3\sin 5x$, then we see that this problem has the same form as the problem given in Example 1 on page 627 of the text. The formal solution to the problem in Example 1 is given in equation (16) on page 628 of the text. Therefore, with the appropriate substitutions, the formal solution to this problem is

$$u(x,t) = \sum_{n=1}^{\infty}\left\{a_n\cos nt + b_n\sin nt + \frac{1}{n}\int_0^t h_n(s)\sin[n(t-s)]\,ds\right\}\sin nx\,. \tag{10.17}$$

The a_n's are shown in equation (14) on page 628 of the text to satisfy

$$\sin x = \sum_{n=1}^{\infty} a_n\sin nx\,.$$

Thus, the only nonzero term in this infinite series is the term for $n = 1$. Therefore, we see that $a_1 = 1$ and $a_n = 0$ for $n \neq 1$. The b_n's are given in equation (15) on page 628 of the text and so must satisfy

$$5\sin 2x - 3\sin 5x = \sum_{n=1}^{\infty} nb_n\sin nx\,,$$

which implies that

$$2b_2 = 5 \quad\Rightarrow\quad b_2 = \frac{5}{2} \qquad\text{and}\qquad 5b_5 = -3 \quad\Rightarrow\quad b_5 = -\frac{3}{5},$$

and $b_n = 0$ for all other values of n. To calculate the integral given in the formal solution we must first find the functions $h_n(t)$. To do this, we note that in Example 1, the functions $h_n(t)$, $n = 1, 2, \ldots$, are the Fourier sine coefficients for $h(x,t) = tx$ with t fixed. These functions are given below equation (13) on page 628 of the text. (We will assume proper convergence of this series.) Thus, we have

$$\begin{aligned} h_n(t) &= \frac{2}{\pi}\int_0^{\pi} tx \sin nx\, dx = \frac{2t}{\pi}\int_0^{\pi} x \sin nx\, dx \\ &= \frac{2t}{\pi}\left[-\frac{\pi}{n}\cos n\pi + 0 + \frac{1}{n^2}\sin n\pi - \sin 0\right] = -\frac{2t}{\pi}\cos n\pi = \frac{2t}{\pi}(-1)^{n+1}, \end{aligned}$$

$n = 1, 2, 3, \ldots$, where we have used integration by parts to calculate this integral. Substituting this result into the integral in equation (10.17) above yields

$$\begin{aligned} \int_0^t h_n(s)\sin[n(t-s)]\, ds &= \int_0^t \frac{2s}{\pi}(-1)^{n+1}\sin[n(t-s)]\, ds \\ &= \frac{2(-1)^{n+1}}{n}\left[\frac{t}{n} - \frac{\sin nt}{n^2}\right] = \frac{2(-1)^{n+1}}{n^3}(nt - \sin nt), \end{aligned}$$

where $n = 1, 2, 3, \ldots$. By plugging the a_n's, the b_n's, and the result we just found into equation (10.17), we obtain the formal solution to this problem given by

$$\begin{aligned} u(x,t) &= \cos t \sin x + \frac{5}{2}\sin 2t \sin 2x - \frac{3}{5}\sin 5t \sin 5x + \sum_{n=1}^{\infty} \frac{1}{n}\left[\frac{2(-1)^{n+1}}{n^3}(nt - \sin nt)\right]\sin nx \\ &= \cos t \sin x + \frac{5}{2}\sin 2t \sin 2x - \frac{3}{5}\sin 5t \sin 5x + 2\sum_{n=1}^{\infty} \frac{(-1)^{n+1}}{n^3}\left(t - \frac{\sin nt}{n}\right)\sin nx\,. \end{aligned}$$

11. We will assume that a solution to this problem has the form $u(x,t) = X(x)T(t)$. Substituting this expression into the partial differential equations yields

$$X(x)T''(t) + X(x)T'(t) + X(x)T(t) = \alpha^2 X''(x)T(t).$$

Dividing this equation by $\alpha^2 X(x)T(t)$ yields

$$\frac{T''(t) + T'(t) + T(t)}{\alpha^2 T(t)} = \frac{X''(x)}{X(x)}\,.$$

Since these two expressions must be equal for all x in $(0, L)$ **and** all $t > 0$, they can not vary. Therefore, they must both equal a constant, say K. This gives us the two ordinary differential equations

$$\frac{T''(t) + T'(t) + T(t)}{\alpha^2 T(t)} = K \qquad \Rightarrow \qquad T''(t) + T'(t) + \left(1 - \alpha^2 K\right) T(t) = 0 \tag{10.18}$$

and

$$\frac{X''(x)}{X(x)} = K \qquad \Rightarrow \qquad X''(x) - KX(x) = 0. \tag{10.19}$$

Substituting $u(x,t) = X(x)T(t)$ into the boundary conditions, $u(0,t) = u(L,t) = 0$, $t > 0$, we obtain

$$X(0)T(t) = 0 = X(L)T(t), \qquad t > 0.$$

Since we are seeking a nontrivial solution to the partial differential equation, we do not want $T(t) \equiv 0$. Therefore, for the above equation to be zero, we must have $X(0) = X(L) = 0$. Combining this fact with equation (10.19) above yields the boundary value problem given by

$$X''(x) - KX(x) = 0, \qquad \text{with} \qquad X(0) = X(L) = 0.$$

This problem was solved in Section 10.2 of the text. There we found that for $K = -(n\pi/L)^2$, $n = 1, 2, 3, \ldots$, we obtain nonzero solutions of the form

$$X_n(x) = A_n \sin\left(\frac{n\pi x}{L}\right), \qquad n = 1, 2, 3, \ldots. \tag{10.20}$$

Plugging these values of K into equation (10.18) above yields the family of linear ordinary differential equations with constant coefficients given by

$$T''(t) + T'(t) + \left(1 + \frac{\alpha^2 n^2 \pi^2}{L^2}\right) T(t) = 0, \qquad n = 1, 2, 3, \ldots. \tag{10.21}$$

The auxiliary equations associated with these ODE's are

$$r^2 + r + \left(1 + \frac{\alpha^2 n^2 \pi^2}{L^2}\right) = 0\,.$$

By using the quadratic formula, we obtain the roots to these auxiliary equations. Thus, we have

$$r = \frac{-1 \pm \sqrt{1 - 4\left(1 + \dfrac{\alpha^2 n^2 \pi^2}{L^2}\right)}}{2} = -\frac{1}{2} \pm \frac{\sqrt{L^2 - 4L^2 - 4\alpha^2 n^2 \pi^2}}{2L}$$

$$= \quad -\frac{1}{2} \pm \frac{\sqrt{3L^2 + 4\alpha^2 n^2 \pi^2}}{2L} i\,, \qquad n = 1, 2, 3, \ldots.$$

Hence, the solutions to the linear equations given in equation (10.21) above are

$$T_n(t) = e^{-t/2}\left[B_n \cos\left(\frac{\sqrt{3L^2 + 4\alpha^2 n^2 \pi^2}}{2L} t\right) + C_n \sin\left(\frac{\sqrt{3L^2 + 4\alpha^2 n^2 \pi^2}}{2L} t\right)\right],$$

for $n = 1, 2, 3, \ldots$. By letting

$$\beta_n = \frac{\sqrt{3L^2 + 4\alpha^2 n^2 \pi^2}}{2L}, \tag{10.22}$$

for $n = 1, 2, 3, \ldots$, this family of solutions can be more easily written as

$$T_n(t) = e^{-t/2}\left[B_n \cos \beta_n t + C_n \sin \beta_n t\right].$$

Substituting the solutions we have just found and the solutions given in equation (10.20) above into $u(x,t) = X(x)T(t)$, yields solutions to the original partial differential equation given by

$$u_n(x,t) = X_n(x)T_n(t) = A_n e^{-t/2}\left[B_n \cos \beta_n t + C_n \sin \beta_n t\right] \sin\left(\frac{n\pi x}{L}\right), \qquad n = 1, 2, 3, \ldots.$$

By the superposition principle, we see that solutions to the PDE will have the form

$$u(x,t) = \sum_{n=1}^{\infty} e^{-t/2}\left[a_n \cos \beta_n t + b_n \sin \beta_n t\right] \sin\left(\frac{n\pi x}{L}\right),$$

where β_n is given in equation (10.22) above, $a_n = A_n B_n$, and $b_n = A_n C_n$. To find the coefficients a_n and b_n, we use the initial conditions $u(x,0) = f(x)$ and $\partial u(x,0)/\partial t = 0$. Therefore, since

$$\begin{aligned}\frac{\partial u(x,t)}{\partial t} = \sum_{n=1}^{\infty} \{(-1/2)\, e^{-t/2}\left[a_n \cos \beta_n t + b_n \sin \beta_n t\right] \\ + e^{-t/2}\left[-a_n \beta_n \sin \beta_n t + b_n \beta_n \cos \beta_n t\right]\} \sin\left(\frac{n\pi x}{L}\right),\end{aligned}$$

we have

$$\frac{\partial u(x,0)}{\partial t} = 0 = \sum_{n=1}^{\infty}\left\{-\frac{a_n}{2} + b_n \beta_n\right\} \sin\left(\frac{n\pi x}{L}\right).$$

Hence, each term in this infinite series must be zero which implies that

$$-\frac{a_n}{2} + b_n\beta_n = 0 \qquad \Rightarrow \qquad b_n = \frac{a_n}{2\beta_n}\,, \qquad n = 1, 2, 3, \ldots .$$

Thus, we can write

$$u(x,t) = \sum_{n=1}^{\infty} a_n e^{-t/2}\left[\cos\beta_n t + \frac{1}{2\beta_n}\sin\beta_n t\right]\sin\left(\frac{n\pi x}{L}\right), \tag{10.23}$$

where β_n is given above in equation (10.22). To find the a_n's, we use the remaining initial condition to obtain

$$u(x,0) = f(x) = \sum_{n=1}^{\infty} a_n \sin\left(\frac{n\pi x}{L}\right).$$

Therefore, the a_n's are the Fourier sine coefficients of $f(x)$ and so satisfy

$$a_n = \frac{2}{L}\int_0^L f(x)\sin\left(\frac{n\pi x}{L}\right)dx\,. \tag{10.24}$$

Combining all of these results, we see that a formal solution to the telegraph problem is given by equation (10.23) where β_n and a_n are given in equation (10.22) and (10.24), respectively.

15. This problem has the form of the problem solved in Example 2 on page 631 of the text with $f(x) = g(x) = x$. There it was found that d'Alembert's formula given in equation (32) on page 631 of the text is a solution to this problem. By making the appropriate substitutions in this equation (and noting that $f(x+\alpha t) = x+\alpha t$ and $f(x-\alpha t) = x-\alpha t$), we obtain the solution

$$\begin{aligned} u(x,t) &= \frac{1}{2}\left[(x+\alpha t)+(x-\alpha t)\right] + \frac{1}{2\alpha}\int_{x-\alpha t}^{x+\alpha t} s\,ds = x + \frac{1}{2\alpha}\left[\frac{s^2}{2}\Bigg|_{x-\alpha t}^{x+\alpha t}\right] \\ &= x + \frac{1}{4\alpha}\left[(x+\alpha t)^2 - (x-\alpha t)^2\right] = x + \frac{1}{4\alpha}\left[4\alpha t x\right] = x + tx\,. \end{aligned}$$

EXERCISES 10.7: Laplace's Equation, page 649

3. To solve this problem using separation of variables, we will assume that a solution has the form $u(x,y) = X(x)Y(y)$. Making this substitution into the partial differential equation yields

$$X''(x)Y(y) + X(x)Y''(y) = 0.$$

By dividing the above equation by $X(x)Y(y)$, we obtain

$$\frac{X''(x)}{X(x)} + \frac{Y''(y)}{Y(y)} = 0.$$

Since this equation must be true for $0 < x < \pi$ and $0 < y < \pi$, there must be a constant K such that

$$\frac{X''(x)}{X(x)} = -\frac{Y''(y)}{Y(y)} = K, \qquad 0 < x < \pi, \quad \text{and} \quad 0 < y < \pi.$$

This leads to the two ordinary differential equations given by

$$X''(x) - KX(x) = 0 \tag{10.25}$$

and

$$Y''(y) + KY(y) = 0 \tag{10.26}$$

By making the substitution $u(x, y) = X(x)Y(y)$ into the first boundary conditions, that is, $u(0, y) = u(\pi, y) = 0$, we obtain

$$X(0)Y(y) = X(\pi)Y(y) = 0.$$

Since we do not want the trivial solution which would be obtained if we let $Y(y) \equiv 0$, these boundary conditions imply that

$$X(0) = X(\pi) = 0.$$

Combining these boundary conditions with equation (10.25) above yields the boundary value problem

$$X''(x) - KX(x) = 0, \qquad \text{with} \qquad X(0) = X(\pi) = 0.$$

To solve this problem, we will consider three cases.

Case 1: $K = 0$. For this case, the differential equation becomes $X''(x) = 0$, which has solutions $X(x) = A + Bx$. By applying the first of the boundary conditions, we obtain

$$X(0) = A = 0 \qquad \Rightarrow \qquad X(x) = Bx.$$

The second boundary condition yields

$$X(\pi) = B\pi = 0 \qquad \Rightarrow \qquad B = 0.$$

Thus, in this case we obtain only the trivial solution.

Case 2: $K > 0.$ In this case, the auxiliary equation associated with this differential equation is $r^2 - K = 0$, which has the real roots $r = \pm\sqrt{K}$. Thus, solutions to this problem are given by

$$X(x) = Ae^{\sqrt{K}x} + Be^{-\sqrt{K}x}.$$

Applying the boundary conditions yields

$$X(0) = A + B = 0 \qquad \Rightarrow \qquad A = -B \qquad \Rightarrow \qquad X(x) = -Be^{\sqrt{K}x} + Be^{-\sqrt{K}x}$$

and

$$X(\pi) = -Be^{\sqrt{K}\pi} + Be^{-\sqrt{K}\pi} = 0 \qquad \Rightarrow \qquad -B\left(e^{2\sqrt{K}\pi} - 1\right) = 0.$$

This last expression is true only if $K = 0$ or if $B = 0$. Since we are assuming that $K > 0$, we must have $B = 0$ which means that $A = -B = 0$. Therefore, in this case we again find only the trivial solution.

Case 3: $K < 0.$ The auxiliary equation associated with the differential equation in this case has the complex valued roots $r = \pm\sqrt{-K}i$, (where $-K > 0$). Therefore, solutions to the ODE for this case are given by

$$X(x) = A\cos\left(\sqrt{-K}x\right) + B\sin\left(\sqrt{-K}x\right).$$

By applying the boundary conditions, we obtain

$$X(0) = A = 0 \qquad \Rightarrow \qquad X(x) = B\sin\left(\sqrt{-K}x\right)$$

and

$$X(\pi) = B\sin\left(\sqrt{-K}\pi\right) = 0 \qquad \Rightarrow \qquad \sqrt{-K} = n \qquad \Rightarrow \qquad K = -n^2, \quad n = 1, 2, 3, \ldots,$$

where we have assumed that $B \neq 0$ since this would lead to the trivial solution. Therefore, nontrivial solutions $X_n(x) = B_n \sin nx$ are obtained when $K = -n^2$, $n = 1, 2, 3 \ldots.$

To solve the differential equation given in equation (10.26) above, we use these values for K. This yields the family of linear ordinary differential equations given by

$$Y''(y) - n^2 Y(y) = 0, \qquad n = 1, 2, 3, \ldots .$$

The auxiliary equations associated with these ODE's are $r^2 - n^2 = 0$, which have the real roots $r = \pm n$, $n = 1, 2, 3, \ldots$. Hence, the solutions to this family of differential equations are given by

$$Y_n(y) = C_n e^{ny} + D_n e^{-ny}, \qquad n = 1, 2, 3, \ldots .$$

With the substitutions $K_{1n} = C_n + D_n$ and $K_{2n} = C_n - D_n$, so that

$$C_n = \frac{K_{1n} + K_{2n}}{2}, \qquad \text{and} \qquad D_n = \frac{K_{1n} - K_{2n}}{2},$$

we see that these solutions can be written as

$$\begin{aligned} Y_n(y) &= \frac{K_{1n} + K_{2n}}{2} e^{ny} + \frac{K_{1n} - K_{2n}}{2} e^{-ny} \\ &= K_{1n} \frac{e^{ny} + e^{-ny}}{2} + K_{2n} \frac{e^{ny} - e^{-ny}}{2} = K_{1n} \cosh ny + K_{2n} \sinh ny . \end{aligned}$$

This last expression can in turn be written as

$$Y_n(y) = A_n \sinh (ny + E_n),$$

where $A_n = K_{2n}^2 - K_{1n}^2$ and $E_n = \tanh^{-1}(K_{1n}/K_{2n})$. (See Problem 18.)

The last boundary condition $u(x, \pi) = X(x)Y(\pi) = 0$ implies that $Y(\pi) = 0$(since we do not want the trivial solution). Therefore, by substituting π into the solutions just found, we obtain

$$Y_n(\pi) = A_n \sinh (n\pi + E_n).$$

Since we do not want $A_n = 0$, this implies that $\sinh(n\pi + E_n) = 0$. This will be true only if $n\pi + E_n = 0$ or in other words if $E_n = -n\pi$. Substituting these expressions for E_n into the family of solutions we found for $Y(y)$, yields

$$Y_n(y) = A_n \sinh (ny - n\pi).$$

Therefore, substituting the solutions just found for $X(x)$ and $Y(y)$ into $u_n(x,y) = X_n(x)Y_n(y)$ we see that

$$u_n(x,y) = a_n \sin nx \sinh(ny - n\pi),$$

where $a_n = A_nB_n$. By the superposition principle, a formal solution to the original partial differential equation is given by

$$u(x,y) = \sum_{n=1}^{\infty} u_n(x,y) = \sum_{n=1}^{\infty} a_n \sin nx \sinh(ny - n\pi). \qquad (10.27)$$

In order to find an expression for the coefficients a_n, we will apply the remaining boundary condition, $u(x,0) = f(x)$. From this condition, we obtain

$$u(x,0) = f(x) = \sum_{n=1}^{\infty} a_n \sin nx \sinh(-n\pi),$$

which implies that $a_n \sinh(-n\pi)$ are the coefficients of the Fourier sine series of $f(x)$. Therefore, by equation (7) on page 609 of the text, we see that (with $T = \pi$)

$$a_n \sinh(-n\pi) = \frac{2}{\pi} \int_0^{\pi} f(x) \sin nx\, dx \qquad \Rightarrow \qquad a_n = \frac{2}{\pi \sinh(-n\pi)} \int_0^{\pi} f(x) \sin nx\, dx\,.$$

Thus, a formal solution to this ODE is given in equation (10.27) with the a_n's given by the equation above.

5. This problem has two nonhomogeneous boundary conditions, and, therefore, we will solve two PDE problems, one for each of these boundary conditions. These problems are

$$\frac{\partial^2 u}{\partial x^2} + \frac{\partial^2 u}{\partial y^2} = 0, \qquad 0 < x < \pi, \quad 0 < y < 1;$$
$$\frac{\partial u(0,y)}{\partial x} = \frac{\partial u(\pi,y)}{\partial x} = 0, \qquad 0 \le y \le 1,$$
$$u(x,0) = \cos x - \cos 3x, \qquad u(x,1) = 0, \qquad 0 \le x \le \pi\,,$$

and

$$\frac{\partial^2 u}{\partial x^2} + \frac{\partial^2 u}{\partial y^2} = 0, \qquad 0 < x < \pi, \quad 0 < y < 1;$$

$$\frac{\partial u(0,y)}{\partial x} = \frac{\partial u(\pi,y)}{\partial x} = 0, \qquad 0 \le y \le 1,$$
$$u(x,0) = 0, \qquad u(x,1) = \cos 2x, \qquad 0 \le x \le \pi\,.$$

If u_1 and u_2 are solutions to the first and second problems, respectively, then $u = u_1 + u_2$ will be a solution to the original problem. To see this notice that

$$\begin{aligned}
\frac{\partial^2 u}{\partial x^2} + \frac{\partial^2 u}{\partial y^2} &= \left(\frac{\partial^2 u_1}{\partial x^2} + \frac{\partial^2 u_2}{\partial x^2}\right) + \left(\frac{\partial^2 u_1}{\partial y^2} + \frac{\partial^2 u_2}{\partial y^2}\right) \\
&= \left(\frac{\partial^2 u_1}{\partial x^2} + \frac{\partial^2 u_1}{\partial y^2}\right) + \left(\frac{\partial^2 u_2}{\partial x^2} + \frac{\partial^2 u_2}{\partial y^2}\right) = 0 + 0 = 0, \\
\frac{\partial u(0,y)}{\partial x} &= \frac{\partial u_1(0,y)}{\partial x} + \frac{\partial u_2(0,y)}{\partial x} = 0 + 0 = 0, \\
\frac{\partial u(\pi,y)}{\partial x} &= \frac{\partial u_1(\pi,y)}{\partial x} + \frac{\partial u_2(\pi,y)}{\partial x} = 0 + 0 = 0, \\
u(x,0) &= u_1(x,0) + u_2(x,0) = \cos x - \cos 3x + 0 = \cos x - \cos 3x\,, \\
u(x,1) &= u_1(x,1) + u_2(x,1) = 0 + \cos 2x = \cos 2x\,.
\end{aligned}$$

This is an application of the superposition principle.

The first of these two problems has the form of the problem given in Example 1 on page 639 of the text with $a = \pi$, $b = 1$, and $f(x) = \cos x - \cos 3x$. A formal solution to this problem is given in equation (10) on page 641 of the text. Thus, by making the appropriate substitutions, we find that a formal solution to the first problem is

$$u_1(x,y) = E_0(y-1) + \sum_{n=1}^{\infty} E_n \cos nx \sinh(ny - n).$$

To find the coefficients E_n, we use the nonhomogeneous boundary condition

$$u(x,0) = \cos x - \cos 3x\,.$$

Thus, we have

$$u_1(x,0) = \cos x - \cos 3x = -E_0 + \sum_{n=1}^{\infty} E_n \cos nx \sinh(-n).$$

From this we see that for $n = 1$,

$$E_1 \sinh(-1) = 1 \qquad \Rightarrow \qquad E_1 = \frac{1}{\sinh(-1)}$$

and for $n = 3$,

$$E_3 \sinh(-3) = -1 \qquad \Rightarrow \qquad E_1 = \frac{-1}{\sinh(-3)}.$$

For all other values of n, $E_n = 0$. By substituting these values into the expression found above for u_1, we obtain the formal solution to the first of our two problems given by

$$u_1(x, y) = \frac{\cos x \sinh(y - 1)}{\sinh(-1)} - \frac{\cos 3x \sinh(3y - 3)}{\sinh(-3)}. \tag{10.28}$$

To solve the second of our problems, we note that, except for the last two boundary conditions, it is similar to the problem solved in Example 1 on page 639 of the text. As in that example, using the separation of variables technique, we find that the ODE

$$X''(x) - KX(x) = 0, \qquad X'(0) = X'(\pi) = 0,$$

has solutions $X_n(x) = a_n \cos nx$, when $K = -n^2$, $n = 1, 2, 3, \ldots$. By substituting these values for K into the ODE

$$Y''(y) + KY(y) = 0,$$

we again find that a family solutions to this differential equation is given by

$$\begin{aligned} Y_0(y) &= A_0 + B_0 y, \\ Y_n(y) &= C_n \sinh\left[n\left(y + D_n\right)\right], \qquad n = 1, 2, 3 \ldots. \end{aligned}$$

At this point, the problem we are solving differs from the example. The boundary condition $u(x, 0) = X(x)Y(0) = 0$, $0 \le x \le \pi$, implies that $Y(0) = 0$ (since we don't want the trivial solution). Therefore, applying this boundary condition to each of the solutions found above yields

$$\begin{aligned} Y_0(0) &= A_0 + 0 = 0 &&\Rightarrow \qquad A_0 = 0, \\ Y_n(0) &= C_n \sinh\left(nD_n\right) = 0 &&\Rightarrow \qquad D_n = 0, \end{aligned}$$

where we have used the fact that $\sinh x = 0$ only when $x = 0$. By substituting these results into the solutions found above, we obtain

$$Y_0(y) = B_0 y,$$
$$Y_n(y) = C_n \sinh ny, \qquad n = 1, 2, 3 \ldots .$$

Combining these solutions with the solutions $X_n(x) = a_n \cos nx$ yields

$$u_{2,0}(x, y) = X_0(x)Y_0(y) = a_0 B_0 y \cos 0 = E_0 y\,,$$
$$u_{2,n}(x, y) = X_n(x)Y_n(y) = a_n C_n \cos nx \sinh ny = E_n \cos nx \sinh ny\,,$$

where $E_0 = a_0 B_0$ and $E_n = a_n C_n$. Thus, by the superposition principle, we find that a formal solution to the second problem is given by

$$u_2(x, y) = E_0 y + \sum_{n=1}^{\infty} E_n \cos nx \sinh ny\,.$$

By applying the last boundary condition of this second problem, namely $u(x, 1) = \cos 2x$, to these solutions, we see that

$$u_2(x, 1) = E_0 + \sum_{n=1}^{\infty} E_n \cos nx \sinh n = \cos 2x\,..$$

Therefore, when $n = 2$,

$$E_2 \sinh 2 = 1 \qquad \Rightarrow \qquad E_2 = \frac{1}{\sinh 2}\,,$$

and for all other values of n, $E_n = 0$. By substituting these coefficients into the solution $u_2(x, y)$ that we found above, we obtain the formal solution to this second problem

$$u_2(x, y) = \frac{\cos 2x \sinh 2y}{\sinh 2}\,.$$

By the superposition principle (as noted at the beginning of this problem), a formal solution to the original partial differential equation is the sum of this solution and the solution given in equation (10.28). Thus, the solution that we seek is

$$u(x, y) = \frac{\cos x \sinh(y-1)}{\sinh(-1)} - \frac{\cos 3x \sinh(3y-3)}{\sinh(-3)} + \frac{\cos 2x \sinh 2y}{\sinh 2}\,.$$

11. In this problem, the technique of separation of variables, as in Example 2 on page 642 of the text, leads to the two ODE's

$$r^2R''(r) + rR'(r) - \lambda R(r) = 0 \qquad \text{and} \qquad T''(\theta) + \lambda T(\theta) = 0.$$

Again, as in Example 2, we require the solution $u(r,\theta)$ to be continuous on its domain. Therefore, $T(\theta)$ must again be periodic with period 2π. This implies that $T(-\pi) = T(\pi)$ and $T'(-\pi) = T'(\pi)$. Thus, as in Example 2, a family of solutions for the second ODE above which satisfies these periodic boundary conditions is

$$T_0(\theta) = B \qquad \text{and} \qquad T_n(\theta) = A_n \cos n\theta + B_n \sin n\theta\,, \qquad n = 1, 2, 3, \ldots.$$

In solving this problem, it was found that $\lambda = n^2$, $n = 0, 1, 2 \ldots$. Again, as in Example 2, substituting these values for λ into the first ODE above leads to the solutions

$$R_0(r) = C + D\ln r \qquad \text{and} \qquad R_n(r) = C_n r^n + D_n r^{-n}\,, \qquad n = 1, 2, 3, \ldots.$$

Here, however, we are not concerned with what happens when $r = 0$. By our assumption that $u(r,\theta) = R(r)T(\theta)$, we see that solutions of the PDE given in this problem will have the form

$$u_0(r,\theta) = B(C + D\ln r) \qquad \text{and} \qquad u_n(r,\theta) = \left(C_n r^n + D_n r^{-n}\right)\left(A_n \cos n\theta + B_n \sin n\theta\right),$$

where $n = 1, 2, 3, \ldots$. Thus, by the superposition principle, we see that a formal solution to this Dirichlet problem is given by

$$u(r,\theta) = BC + BD\ln r + \sum_{n=1}^{\infty}\left(C_n r^n + D_n r^{-n}\right)\left(A_n \cos n\theta + B_n \sin n\theta\right),$$

or

$$u(r,\theta) = a + b\ln r + \sum_{n=1}^{\infty}\left[\left(c_n r^n + e_n r^{-n}\right)\cos n\theta + \left(d_n r^n + f_n r^{-n}\right)\sin n\theta\right], \qquad (10.29)$$

where $a = BC$, $b = BD$, $c_n = C_n A_n$, $e_n = D_n A_n$, $d_n = C_n B_n$, and $f_n = D_n B_n$. To find these coefficients, we apply the boundary conditions $u(1,\theta) = \sin 4\theta - \cos\theta$, and $u(2,\theta) = \sin\theta$, $-\pi \le \theta \le \pi$. From the first boundary condition, we see that

$$u(1,\theta) = a + \sum_{n=1}^{\infty}\left[(c_n + e_n)\cos n\theta + (d_n + f_n)\sin n\theta\right] = \sin 4\theta - \cos\theta,$$

which implies that $a = 0$, $d_4 + f_4 = 1$, $c_1 + e_1 = -1$, and for all other values of n, $c_n + e_n = 0$ and $d_n + f_n = 0$. From the second boundary condition, we have

$$u(2,\theta) = a + b\ln 2 + \sum_{n=1}^{\infty} \left[\left(c_n 2^n + e_n 2^{-n}\right)\cos n\theta + \left(d_n 2^n + f_n 2^{-n}\right)\sin n\theta\right] = \sin\theta,$$

which implies that $a = 0$, $b = 0$, $2d_1 + 2^{-1}f_1 = 1$, and for all other values of n, $2^n c_1 + 2^{-n}e_1 = 0$ and $2^n d_1 + 2^{-n}f_1 = 0$. By combining these results, we obtain $a = 0$, $b = 0$, and the three systems of two equations in two unknowns given by

$$\begin{matrix} d_4 + f_4 = 1, \\ 2^4 d_4 + 2^{-4} f_4 = 0 \end{matrix} \quad \text{and} \quad \begin{matrix} c_1 + e_1 = -1, \\ 2c_1 + 2^{-1}e_1 = 0 \end{matrix} \quad \text{and} \quad \begin{matrix} d_1 + f_1 = 0, \\ 2d_1 + 2^{-1}f_1 = 1, \end{matrix}$$

(where the first equation in each system was derived from the first boundary condition and the second equation in each system was derived from the second boundary condition), and for all other values of n, $c_n = 0$, $e_n = 0$, $d_n = 0$, $f_n = 0$. Solving each system of equations simultaneously yields

$$d_4 = -\frac{1}{255}, \qquad f_4 = -\frac{256}{255}, \qquad c_1 = \frac{1}{3}, \qquad e_1 = -\frac{4}{3}, \qquad d_1 = \frac{2}{3}, \qquad f_1 = -\frac{2}{3}.$$

By substituting these values for the coefficients into equation (10.29) above, we find that a solution to this Dirichlet problem is given by

$$u(r,\theta) = \left(\frac{1}{3}r - \frac{4}{3}r^{-1}\right)\cos\theta + \left(\frac{2}{3}r - \frac{2}{3}r^{-1}\right)\sin\theta + \left(-\frac{1}{255}r^4 - \frac{256}{255}r^{-4}\right)\sin 4\theta\,.$$

15. Here, as in Example 2 on page 642 of the text, the technique of separation of variables leads to the two ODE's given by

$$r^2 R''(r) + rR'(r) - \lambda R(r) = 0 \qquad \text{and} \qquad T''(\theta) + \lambda T(\theta) = 0.$$

Since we want to avoid the trivial solution, the boundary condition $u(r,0) = R(r)T(0) = 0$ implies that $T(0) = 0$ and the boundary condition $u(r,\pi) = R(r)T(\pi) = 0$ implies that $T(\pi) = 0$. Therefore, we seek a nontrivial solution to the ODE

$$T''(\theta) + \lambda T(\theta) = 0, \qquad \text{with} \qquad T(0) = 0 \quad \text{and} \quad T(\pi) = 0. \tag{10.30}$$

To do this we will consider three cases for λ.

Case 1: $\lambda = 0$. This case leads to the differential equation $T''(\theta) = 0$, which has solutions $T(\theta) = A\theta + B$. Applying the first boundary condition yields $0 = T(0) = B$. Thus, $T(\theta) = A\theta$. The second boundary condition implies that $0 = T(\pi) = A\pi$. Hence, $A = 0$. Therefore, in this case we find only the trivial solution.

Case 2: $\lambda < 0$. In this case, the auxiliary equation associated with the linear differential equation given in equation (10.30) above is $r^2 + \lambda = 0$, which has the real roots $r = \pm\sqrt{-\lambda}$ (where $-\lambda > 0$). Thus, the solution to this differential equation has the form

$$T(\theta) = C_1 e^{\sqrt{-\lambda}\theta} + C_2 e^{-\sqrt{-\lambda}\theta}.$$

Applying the first boundary condition yields

$$0 = T(0) = C_1 + C_2 \quad \Rightarrow \quad C_1 = -C_2 \quad \Rightarrow \quad T(\theta) = -C_2 e^{\sqrt{-\lambda}\theta} + C_2 e^{-\sqrt{-\lambda}\theta}.$$

From the second boundary condition, we obtain

$$0 = T(\pi) = C_2\left(-e^{\sqrt{-\lambda}\pi} + e^{-\sqrt{-\lambda}\pi}\right) \quad \Rightarrow \quad C_2\left(e^{2\sqrt{-\lambda}\pi} - 1\right) = 0.$$

Since we are assuming that $\lambda < 0$, the only way that this last expression can be zero is for $C_2 = 0$. Thus, $C_1 = -C_2 = 0$ and we again obtain the trivial solution.

Case 3: $\lambda > 0$. In this case, the roots to the auxiliary equation associated with this differential equation are $r = \pm\sqrt{\lambda}i$. Therefore, the solution to the differential equation given in equation (10.30) is

$$T(\theta) = C_1 \sin\sqrt{\lambda}\theta + C_2 \cos\sqrt{\lambda}\theta.$$

From the boundary conditions, we see that

$$0 = T(0) = C_2 \quad \Rightarrow \quad T(\theta) = C_1 \sin\sqrt{\lambda}\theta,$$

and

$$0 = T(\pi) = C_1 \sin\sqrt{\lambda}\pi.$$

Since we do not want the trivial solution, this last boundary condition yields $\sin\sqrt{\lambda}\pi = 0$. This will be true if $\sqrt{\lambda} = n$ or, in other words, if $\lambda = n^2$, $n = 1, 2, 3, \ldots$. With these values for λ, we find nontrivial solution for the differential equation given in equation (10.30) above to be

$$T_n(\theta) = B_n \sin n\theta\,, \qquad n = 1, 2, 3, \ldots\,.$$

Substituting the values for λ that we have just found into the differential equation

$$r^2 R''(r) + rR'(r) - \lambda R(r) = 0,$$

yields the ODE

$$r^2 R''(r) + rR'(r) - n^2 R(r) = 0, \qquad n = 1, 2, 3, \ldots\,.$$

This is the same Cauchy-Euler equation that was solved in Example 2 on page 642 of the text. There it was found that the solutions have the form

$$R_n(r) = C_n r^n + D_n r^{-n}\,, \qquad n = 1, 2, 3, \ldots\,.$$

Since we require that $u(r, \theta)$ to be bounded on its domain, we see that $u(r, \theta) = R(r)T(\theta)$ must be bounded about $r = 0$. This implies that $R(\theta)$ must be bounded. Therefore, $D_n = 0$ and so the solutions to this Cauchy-Euler equation are given by

$$R_n(r) = C_n r^n\,, \qquad n = 1, 2, 3, \ldots\,.$$

Since we have assumed that $u(r, \theta) = R(r)T(\theta)$, we see that formal solutions to the original partial differential equation are

$$u_n(r, \theta) = B_n C_n r^n \sin n\theta = c_n r^n \sin n\theta\,,$$

where $c_n = B_n C_n$. Therefore, by the superposition principle, we obtain the formal solutions to this Dirichlet problem

$$u(r, \theta) = \sum_{n=1}^{\infty} c_n r^n \sin n\theta\,.$$

The final boundary condition yields

$$u(1, \theta) = \sin 3\theta = \sum_{n=1}^{\infty} c_n \sin n\theta\,.$$

This implies that $c_3 = 1$ and for all other values of n, $c_n = 0$. Substituting these values for the coefficients into the formal solution found above, yields the solution to this Dirichlet problem on the half disk

$$u(r,\theta) = r^3 \sin 3\theta\,.$$

17. As in Example 2 on page 642 of the text, we solve this problem by separation of variables. There it was found that we must solve the two ordinary differential equations

$$r^2 R''(r) + rR'(r) - \lambda R(r) = 0, \tag{10.31}$$

and

$$T''(\theta) + \lambda T(\theta) = 0 \qquad \text{with} \qquad T(\pi) = T(n\pi) \quad \text{and} \quad T'(\pi) = T'(n\pi). \tag{10.32}$$

In Example 2, we found that when $\lambda = n^2$, $n = 0, 1, 2, \ldots$, the linear differential equation given in equation (10.32) has nontrivial solutions of the form

$$T_n(\theta) = A_n \cos n\theta + B_n \sin n\theta\,, \qquad n = 0, 1, 2, \ldots\,,$$

and equation (10.31) has solutions of the form

$$R_0(r) = C + D\ln r \qquad \text{and} \qquad R_n(r) = C_n r^n + D_n r^{-n}\,, \qquad n = 1, 2, 3, \ldots\,.$$

(Note that here we are not concerned with what happens to $u(r,\theta)$ around $r = 0$.) Thus, since we are assuming that $u(r,\theta) = R(r)T(\theta)$, we see that solutions to the original partial differential equation will be given by

$$u_0(r,\theta) = A_0(C + D\ln r) = a_0 + b_0 \ln r,$$

and

$$\begin{aligned} u_n(r,\theta) &= \left(C_n r^n + D_n r^{-n}\right)\left(A_n \cos n\theta + B_n \sin n\theta\right) \\ &= \left(a_n r^n + b_n r^{-n}\right)\cos n\theta + \left(c_n r^n + d_n r^{-n}\right)\sin n\theta\,, \end{aligned}$$

where $a_0 = A_0C$, $b_0 = A_0D$, $a_n = C_nA_n$, $b_n = D_nA_n$, $c_n = C_nB_n$, and $d_n = D_nB_n$. Thus, by the superposition principle, we see that a formal solution to the partial differential equation given in this problem will have the form

$$u(r,\theta) = a_0 + b_0 \ln r + \sum_{n=1}^{\infty} \left[\left(a_n r^n + b_n r^{-n}\right) \cos n\theta + \left(c_n r^n + d_n r^{-n}\right) \sin n\theta \right]. \qquad (10.33)$$

By applying the first boundary condition, we obtain

$$u(1,\theta) = f(\theta) = a_0 + \sum_{n=1}^{\infty} \left[(a_n + b_n) \cos n\theta + (c_n + d_n) \sin n\theta \right],$$

where we have used the fact that $\ln 1 = 0$. Comparing this equation with equation (8) on page 594 of the text, we see that a_0, $(a_n + b_n)$, and $(c_n + d_n)$ are the Fourier coefficients of $f(\theta)$ (with $T = \pi$). Therefore, by equations (9) and (10) on that same page we see that

$$\begin{aligned} a_0 &= \frac{1}{2\pi} \int_{-\pi}^{\pi} f(\theta)\, d\theta\,, \\ a_n + b_n &= \frac{1}{\pi} \int_{-\pi}^{\pi} f(\theta) \cos n\theta\, d\theta\,, \\ c_n + d_n &= \frac{1}{\pi} \int_{-\pi}^{\pi} f(\theta) \sin n\theta\, d\theta\,, \qquad n = 1, 2, 3\ldots. \end{aligned} \qquad (10.34)$$

To apply the last boundary condition, we must find $\partial u/\partial r$. Hence, we find

$$\frac{\partial u(r,\theta)}{\partial r} = \frac{b_0}{r} + \sum_{n=1}^{\infty} \left[\left(a_n n r^{n-1} - b_n n r^{-n-1}\right) \cos n\theta + \left(c_n n r^{n-1} - d_n n r^{-n-1}\right) \sin n\theta \right].$$

Applying the last boundary condition yields

$$\frac{\partial u(3,\theta)}{\partial r} = g(\theta) = \frac{b_0}{3} + \sum_{n=1}^{\infty} \left[\left(a_n n 3^{n-1} - b_n n 3^{-n-1}\right) \cos n\theta + \left(c_n n 3^{n-1} - d_n n 3^{-n-1}\right) \sin n\theta \right].$$

Again by comparing this to equation (8) on page 594 of the text, we see that

$$\frac{b_0}{3}, \qquad \left(n3^{n-1}a_n - n3^{-n-1}b_n\right), \qquad \text{and} \qquad \left(n3^{n-1}c_n - n3^{-n-1}d_n\right)$$

are the Fourier coefficients of $g(\theta)$ (with $T = \pi$). Thus, by equations (9) and (10) on that same page of the text, we see that

$$\begin{aligned} b_0 &= \frac{3}{2\pi} \int_{-\pi}^{\pi} g(\theta)\, d\theta \,, \\ n3^{n-1}a_n - n3^{-n-1}b_n &= \frac{1}{\pi} \int_{-\pi}^{\pi} g(\theta) \cos n\theta \, d\theta \,, \\ n3^{n-1}c_n - n3^{-n-1}d_n &= \frac{1}{\pi} \int_{-\pi}^{\pi} g(\theta) \sin n\theta \, d\theta \,, \qquad n = 1, 2, 3 \ldots . \end{aligned} \tag{10.35}$$

Therefore, the formal solution to this partial differential equation will be given by equation (10.33) with the coefficients given by equations (10.34) and (10.35).

CHAPTER 11: Eigenvalue Problems and Sturm-Liouville Equations

EXERCISES 11.2: Eigenvalues and Eigenfunctions, page 671

1. The auxiliary equation for this problem is $r^2 + 2r + 26 = 0$, which has roots $r = -1 \pm 5i$. Hence a general solution to the differential equation $y'' + 2y' + 26y = 0$ is given by

$$y(x) = C_1 e^{-x} \cos 5x + C_2 e^{-x} \sin 5x.$$

We will now try to determine C_1 and C_2 so that the boundary conditions are satisfied. Setting $x = 0$ and $x = \pi$, we find

$$y(0) = C_1 = 1, \qquad y(\pi) = -C_1 e^{-\pi} = -e^{-\pi}.$$

Both boundary conditions yield the same result, $C_1 = 1$. Hence, there is a one parameter family of solutions,

$$y(x) = e^{-x} \cos 5x + C_2 e^{-x} \sin 5x.,$$

where C_2 is arbitrary.

13. First note that the auxiliary equation for this problem is $r^2 + \lambda = 0$. To find eigenvalues which yield nontrivial solutions we will consider the three cases $\lambda < 0$, $\lambda = 0$, and $\lambda > 0$.

<u>Case 1. $\lambda < 0$:</u> In this case the roots to the auxiliary equation are $\pm\sqrt{-\lambda}$ (where we note that $-\lambda$ is a positive number). Therefore, a general solution to the differential equation $y'' + \lambda y = 0$ is given by

$$y(x) = C_1 e^{\sqrt{-\lambda}x} + C_2 e^{-\sqrt{-\lambda}x}.$$

By applying the first boundary condition, we obtain

$$y(0) = C_1 + C_2 = 0 \qquad \Rightarrow \qquad C_2 = -C_1.$$

Thus

$$y(x) = C_1\left(e^{\sqrt{-\lambda}x} - e^{-\sqrt{-\lambda}x}\right).$$

In order to apply the second boundary conditions, we need to find $y'(x)$. Thus, we have

$$y(x) = C_1\sqrt{-\lambda}\left(e^{\sqrt{-\lambda}x} + e^{-\sqrt{-\lambda}x}\right).$$

Thus

$$y(1) = C_1\sqrt{-\lambda}\left(e^{\sqrt{-\lambda}} + e^{-\sqrt{-\lambda}}\right) = 0. \tag{11.1}$$

Since $\sqrt{-\lambda} > 0$ and $e^{\sqrt{-\lambda}} + e^{-\sqrt{-\lambda}} \neq 0$, the only way that equation (11.1) can be true is for $C_1 = 0$. So in this case we have only the trivial solution. Thus, there are no eigenvalues for $\lambda < 0$.

Case 2. $\lambda = 0$: In this case we are solving the differential equation $y'' = 0$. This equation has a general solution given by

$$y(x) = C_1 + C_2x \qquad \Rightarrow \qquad y'(x) = C_2\,.$$

By applying the boundary conditions, we obtain

$$y(0) = C_1 = 0 \qquad \text{and} \qquad y'(1) = C_1 = 0.$$

Thus $C_1 = C_2 = 0$, and zero is not an eigenvalue.

Case 3. $\lambda > 0$: In this case the roots to the associated auxiliary equation are $r = \pm\sqrt{\lambda}i$. Therefore, the general solution is given by

$$y(x) = C_1\cos\left(\sqrt{\lambda}x\right) + C_2\sin\left(\sqrt{\lambda}x\right).$$

By applying the first boundary condition, we obtain

$$y(0) = C_1 = 0 \qquad \Rightarrow \qquad y(x) = C_2\sin\left(\sqrt{\lambda}x\right).$$

In order to apply the second boundary conditions we need to find $y'(x)$. Thus, we have

$$y'(x) = C_2\sqrt{\lambda}\cos\left(\sqrt{\lambda}x\right),$$

and so

$$y'(1) = C_2\sqrt{\lambda}\cos\left(\sqrt{\lambda}\right) = 0.$$

Therefore, in order to obtain a solution other than the trivial solution, we must have

$$\cos\left(\sqrt{\lambda}\right) = 0 \qquad \Rightarrow \qquad \sqrt{\lambda} = \left(n + \frac{1}{2}\right)\pi, \qquad n = 0, 1, 2, \ldots$$

$$\Rightarrow \qquad \lambda_n = \left(n + \frac{1}{2}\right)^2 \pi^2, \qquad n = 0, 1, 2, \ldots .$$

For the eigenvalue λ_n, we have the corresponding eigenfunctions,

$$y_n(x) = C_n \sin\left[\left(n + \frac{1}{2}\right)\pi x\right], \qquad n = 0, 1, 2, \ldots ,$$

where C_n is an arbitrary nonzero constant.

19. The equation $(xy')' + \lambda x^{-1}y = 0$ can be rewritten as the Cauchy-Euler equation

$$x^2y'' + xy' + \lambda y = 0, \qquad x > 0. \tag{11.2}$$

Substituting $y = x^r$ gives $r^2 + \lambda = 0$ as the auxiliary equation for (11.2). Again we will consider the three cases $\lambda < 0$, $\lambda = 0$, and $\lambda > 0$.

Case 1. $\lambda < 0$: Let $\lambda = -\mu^2$, for $\mu > 0$. The roots of the auxiliary equation are $r = \pm\mu$ and so a general solution to (11.2) is

$$y(x) = C_1x^{\mu} + C_2x^{-\mu}.$$

We first find $y'(x)$.

$$y'(x) = C_1\mu x^{\mu-1} - C_2\mu x^{-\mu-1} = \mu\left(C_1x^{\mu-1} - C_2x^{-\mu-1}\right).$$

Substituting into the first boundary condition gives

$$y'(1) = \mu\left(C_1 - C_2\right) = 0.$$

Since $\mu > 0$,

$$C_1 - C_2 = 0 \qquad \Rightarrow \qquad C_1 = C_2 \qquad \Rightarrow \qquad y(x) = C_1\left(x^{\mu} + x^{-\mu}\right).$$

Substituting this into the second condition yields

$$y\left(e^{\pi}\right) = C_1\left(e^{\mu\pi} + e^{-\mu\pi}\right) = 0. \tag{11.3}$$

Since $e^{\mu\pi} + e^{-\mu\pi} \neq 0$ the only way that equation (11.3) can be true is for $C_1 = 0$. So in this case we have only the trivial solution. Thus, there is no eigenvalue for $\lambda < 0$.

Case 2. $\lambda = 0$: In this case we are solving the differential equation $(xy')' = 0$. This equation can be solved as follows:

$$xy' = C_1 \quad \Rightarrow \quad y' = \frac{C_1}{x} \quad \Rightarrow \quad y(x) = C_2 + C_1 \ln x\,.$$

By applying the boundary conditions, we obtain

$$y'(1) = C_1 = 0 \qquad \text{and} \qquad y\left(e^{\pi}\right) = C_2 + C_1 \ln\left(e^{\pi}\right) = C_2 + C_1\pi = 0.$$

Solving these equations simultaneously yields $C_1 = C_2 = 0$. Thus, we again find only the trivial solution. Therefore, $\lambda = 0$ is not an eigenvalue.

Case 3. $\lambda > 0$: Let $\lambda = \mu^2$, for $\mu > 0$. The roots of the auxiliary equation are $r = \pm\mu i$ and so a general solution (11.2) is

$$y(x) = C_1 \cos\left(\mu \ln x\right) + C_2 \sin\left(\mu \ln x\right).$$

We next find $y'(x)$.

$$y'(x) = -C_1\left(\frac{\mu}{x}\right)\sin\left(\mu \ln x\right) + C_2\left(\frac{\mu}{x}\right)\cos\left(\mu \ln x\right).$$

By applying the first boundary condition, we obtain

$$y'(1) = C_2\mu = 0 \quad \Rightarrow \quad C_2 = 0.$$

Applying the second boundary condition, we obtain

$$y\left(e^{\pi}\right) = C_1 \cos\left(\mu \ln(e^{\pi})\right) = C_1 \cos\left(\mu\pi\right) = 0.$$

Therefore, in order to obtain a solution other than the trivial solution, we must have

$$\cos\left(\mu\pi\right) = 0 \quad \Rightarrow \quad \mu\pi = \left(n + \frac{1}{2}\right)\pi \quad n = 0, 1, 2, \ldots$$

$$\Rightarrow \qquad \mu = n + \frac{1}{2} \qquad \Rightarrow \qquad \lambda_n = \left(n + \frac{1}{2}\right)^2, \quad n = 0, 1, 2, \ldots .$$

Corresponding to the eigenvalues, λ_n's, we have the eigenfunctions.

$$y_n(x) = C_n \cos\left[\left(n + \frac{1}{2}\right)\ln x\right], \qquad n = 0, 1, 2, \ldots ,$$

where C_n is an arbitrary nonzero constant.

25. As in Problem 13, the auxiliary equation for this problem is $r^2 + \lambda = 0$. To find eigenvalues which yield nontrivial solutions we will consider the three cases $\lambda < 0$, $\lambda = 0$, and $\lambda > 0$.

Case 1. $\lambda < 0$: The roots of the auxiliary equation are $r = \pm\sqrt{-\lambda}$ and so a general solution to the differential equation $y'' + \lambda y = 0$ is given by

$$y(x) = C_1 e^{\sqrt{-\lambda}x} + C_2 e^{-\sqrt{-\lambda}x}.$$

By applying the first boundary condition we obtain

$$y(0) = C_1 + C_2 = 0 \qquad \Rightarrow \qquad C_2 = -C_1 .$$

Thus

$$y(x) = C_1\left(e^{\sqrt{-\lambda}x} - e^{-\sqrt{-\lambda}x}\right).$$

Applying the second boundary conditions yields

$$y\left(1 + \lambda^2\right) = C_1\left(e^{\sqrt{-\lambda}(1+\lambda^2)} - e^{-\sqrt{-\lambda}(1+\lambda^2)}\right) = 0.$$

Multiplying by $e^{\sqrt{-\lambda}(1+\lambda^2)}$ yields

$$C_1\left(e^{2\sqrt{-\lambda}(1+\lambda^2)} - 1\right) = 0.$$

Now either $C_1 = 0$ or

$$e^{2\sqrt{-\lambda}(1+\lambda^2)} = 1 \qquad \Rightarrow \qquad \sqrt{-\lambda}(1 + \lambda^2) = 0 \qquad \Rightarrow \qquad \sqrt{-\lambda} = 0.$$

Since $\lambda < 0$, we must have $C_1 = 0$ and hence there are no eigenvalues for $\lambda < 0$.

Case 2. $\lambda = 0$: In this case we are solving the differential equation $y'' = 0$. This equation has a general solution given by

$$y(x) = C_1 + C_2 x.$$

By applying the boundary conditions, we obtain

$$y(0) = C_1 = 0 \qquad \text{and} \qquad y\left(1+\lambda^2\right) = C_1 + C_2\left(1+\lambda^2\right) = 0.$$

Solving these equations simultaneously yields $C_1 = C_2 = 0$. Thus, we find that is $\lambda = 0$ not an eigenvalue.

Case 3. $\lambda > 0$: The roots of the auxiliary equation are $r = \pm\sqrt{\lambda} i$ and so a general solution is

$$y(x) = C_1 \cos\left(\sqrt{\lambda} x\right) + C_2 \sin\left(\sqrt{\lambda} x\right).$$

Substituting in the first boundary condition yields

$$y(0) = C_1 \cos\left(\sqrt{\lambda}\cdot 0\right) + C_2 \sin\left(\sqrt{\lambda}\cdot 0\right) = C_1 = 0.$$

By applying the second boundary condition to $y(x) = C_2 \sin\left(\sqrt{\lambda} x\right)$, we obtain

$$y\left(1+\lambda^2\right) = C_2 \sin\left(\sqrt{\lambda}(1+\lambda^2)\right) = 0.$$

Therefore, in order to obtain a solution other than the trivial solution, we must have

$$\sin\left(\sqrt{\lambda}(1+\lambda^2)\right) = 0 \qquad \Rightarrow \qquad \sqrt{\lambda}(1+\lambda^2) = n\pi, \qquad n = 1, 2, 3, \ldots .$$

Hence choose the eigenvalues λ_n, $n = 1, 2, 3, \ldots$, such that $\sqrt{\lambda_n}(1+\lambda_n^2) = n\pi$; and the corresponding eigenfunctions are

$$y_n(x) = C_n \sin\left(\sqrt{\lambda_n} x\right), \qquad n = 1, 2, 3, \ldots ,$$

where the C_n's are arbitrary nonzero constants.

33. **(a)** We assume that $u(x,t) = X(x)T(t)$. Then

$$u_{tt} = X(x)T''(t), \qquad u_x = X'(x)T(t), \quad \text{and} \quad u_{xx} = X''(x)T(t).$$

Substituting these functions into $u_{tt} = u_{xx} + 2u_x$, we obtain

$$X(x)T''(t) = X''(x)T(t) + 2X'(x)T(t).$$

Separating variables yields

$$\frac{X''(x) + 2X'(x)}{X(x)} = -\lambda = \frac{T''(t)}{T(t)}, \tag{11.4}$$

where λ is some constant. The first equation in (11.4) gives

$$X''(x) + 2X'(x) + \lambda X(x) = 0.$$

Let's now consider the boundary conditions. From $u(0,t) = 0$ and $u(\pi,t) = 0$, $t > 0$, we conclude that

$$X(0)T(t) = 0 \qquad \text{and} \qquad X(\pi)T(t) = 0, \qquad t > 0.$$

Hence either $T(t) = 0$ for all $t > 0$, which implies $u(x,t) \equiv 0$, or

$$X(0) = X(\pi) = 0.$$

Ignoring the trivial solution $u(x,t) \equiv 0$, we obtain the boundary value problem

$$X''(x) + 2X'(x) + \lambda X(x) = 0, \qquad X(0) = X(\pi) = 0.$$

(b) The auxiliary equation for this problem, $r^2 + 2r + \lambda = 0$, has roots $r = -1 \pm \sqrt{1-\lambda}$. To find eigenvalues which yield nontrivial solutions, we will consider the three cases $1-\lambda < 0$, $1-\lambda = 0$, and $1-\lambda > 0$.

Case 1, $1-\lambda < 0$ ($\lambda > 1$): Let $\mu = \sqrt{-(1-\lambda)} = \sqrt{\lambda - 1}$. In this case the roots to the auxiliary equation are $r = -1 \pm \mu i$ (where μ is a positive number). Therefore, a general solution to the differential equation is given by

$$X(x) = C_1 e^{-x} \cos \mu x + C_2 e^{-x} \sin \mu x.$$

By applying the boundary conditions, we obtain

$$X(0) = C_1 = 0 \qquad \text{and} \qquad X(\pi) = e^{-\pi}\left(C_1 \cos \mu\pi + C_2 \sin \mu\pi\right) = 0\,.$$

Solving these equations simultaneously yields $C_1 = 0$ and $C_2 \sin \mu\pi = 0$. Therefore, in order to obtain a solution other than the trivial solution, we must have

$$\sin \mu\pi = 0 \qquad \Rightarrow \qquad \mu\pi = n\pi \qquad \Rightarrow \qquad \mu = n, \qquad n = 1, 2, 3, \ldots .$$

Since $\mu = \sqrt{\lambda - 1}$,

$$\sqrt{\lambda - 1} = n \qquad \Rightarrow \qquad \lambda = n^2 + 1, \qquad n = 1, 2, 3, \ldots .$$

Thus the eigenvalues are given by

$$\lambda_n = n^2 + 1, \qquad n = 1, 2, 3, \ldots .$$

Corresponding to the eigenvalue λ_n, we obtain the solutions

$$X_n(x) = C_n e^{-x} \sin nx, \qquad n = 1, 2, 3, \ldots ,$$

where $C_n \neq 0$ is arbitrary.

Case 2, $1 - \lambda = 0$ ($\lambda = 1$): In this case the associated auxiliary equation has double root $r = -1$. Therefore, the general solution is given by

$$X(x) = C_1 e^{-x} + C_2 x e^{-x}.$$

By applying the boundary conditions we obtain

$$X(0) = C_1 = 0 \qquad \text{and} \qquad X(\pi) = e^{-\pi}\left(C_1 + C_2\pi\right) = 0 .$$

Solving these equations simultaneously yields $C_1 = C_2 = 0$. So in this case we have only the trivial solution. Thus, $\lambda = 1$ is not an eigenvalue.

Case 3, $1 - \lambda > 0$ ($\lambda < 1$): Let $\mu = \sqrt{1 - \lambda}$. In this case the roots to the auxiliary equation are $r = -1 \pm \mu$ (where μ is a positive number). Therefore, a general solution to the differential equation is given by

$$X(x) = C_1 e^{(-1-\mu)x} + C_2 e^{(-1+\mu)x} .$$

By applying the first boundary condition we find

$$X(0) = C_1 + C_2 = 0 \qquad \Rightarrow \qquad C_2 = -C_1\,.$$

So we can express $X(x)$ as

$$X(x) = C_1\left[e^{(-1-\mu)x} - e^{(-1+\mu)x}\right].$$

Thus the second condition gives us

$$X(\pi) = C_1\left[e^{(-1-\mu)\pi} - e^{(-1+\mu)\pi}\right].$$

Since $e^{(-1-\mu)\pi} - e^{(-1+\mu)\pi} \neq 0$, $C_1 = 0$, and again in this case we have only the trivial solution. Thus, there are no eigenvalues for $\lambda < 1$.

Therefore, the eigenvalues are $\lambda_n = n^2 + 1$, $n = 1, 2, 3, \ldots$, with corresponding eigenfunctions $X_n(x) = C_n e^{-x}\sin nx$, $n = 1, 2, 3, \ldots$, where C_n is an arbitrary nonzero constant.

EXERCISES 11.3: Regular Sturm-Liouville Boundary Value Problems, page 682

3. Here $A_2 = x(1-x)$ and $A_1 = -2x$. Using formula (4) on page 673 of the text, we find

$$\begin{aligned}\mu(x) &= \frac{1}{x(1-x)}\,e^{\int[A_1(x)/A_2(x)]dx} = \frac{1}{x(1-x)}\,e^{\int[-2x/x(1-x)]dx} = \frac{1}{x(1-x)}\,e^{-2\int dx/(1-x)}\\ &= \frac{1}{x(1-x)}\,e^{2\ln(1-x)} = \frac{1}{x(1-x)}\,(1-x)^2 = \frac{1-x}{x}\,.\end{aligned}$$

Multiplying the original equation by $\mu(x) = (1-x)/x$, we get

$$\begin{aligned}&(1-x)^2 y''(x) - 2(1-x)y'(x) + \lambda\frac{1-x}{x}\,y(x) = 0\\ \Rightarrow\qquad &\left[(1-x)^2 y'(x)\right]' + \lambda\frac{1-x}{x}\,y(x) = 0.\end{aligned}$$

9. Here we consider the linear differential operator $L[y] := y'' + \lambda y$; $y(0) = -y(\pi)$, $y'(0) = -y'(\pi)$. We must show that

$$(u, L[v]) = (L[u], v),$$

where $u(x)$ and $v(x)$ are any functions in the domain of L. Now

$$(u, L[v]) = \int_0^{\pi} u(x)\left[v''(x) + \lambda v(x)\right] dx = \int_0^{\pi} u(x)v''(x)\, dx + \lambda \int_0^{\pi} u(x)v(x)\, dx$$

and

$$(L[u], v) = \int_0^{\pi} \left[u''(x) + \lambda u(x)\right] v(x)\, dx = \int_0^{\pi} u''(x)v(x)\, dx + \lambda \int_0^{\pi} u(x)v(x) dx.$$

Hence it suffices to show that $\int_0^{\pi} u(x)v''(x)\, dx = \int_0^{\pi} u''(x)v(x)\, dx$. To do this we start with $\int_0^{\pi} u''(x)v(x)\, dx$ and integrate by parts twice. Doing this we obtain

$$\int_0^{\pi} u''(x)v(x)\, dx = u'(x)v(x) \Big|_0^{\pi} - u(x)v'(x) \Big|_0^{\pi} + \int_0^{\pi} u(x)v''(x)\, dx.$$

Hence, we just need to show $u'(x)v(x) \Big|_0^{\pi} - u(x)v'(x) \Big|_0^{\pi} = 0$. Expanding gives

$$u'(x)v(x) \Big|_0^{\pi} - u(x)v'(x) \Big|_0^{\pi} = u'(\pi)v(\pi) - u'(0)v(0) - u(\pi)v'(\pi) + u(0)v'(0).$$

Since u is in the domain of L, we have $u(0) = -u(\pi)$, and $u'(0) = -u'(\pi)$. Hence,

$$u'(x)v(x) \Big|_0^{\pi} - u(x)v'(x) \Big|_0^{\pi} = u'(\pi)\left[v(\pi) + v(0)\right] - u(\pi)\left[v'(\pi) + v'(0)\right].$$

But v also lies in the domain of L and hence $v(0) = -v(\pi)$ and $v'(0) = -v'(\pi)$. This makes the expressions in the brackets zero and we have $u'(x)v(x) \Big|_0^{\pi} - u(x)v'(x) \Big|_0^{\pi} = 0$. Therefore, L is selfadjoint.

17. In Problem 13 of Section 11.2, we found the eigenvalues to be

$$\lambda_n = \left(n + \frac{1}{2}\right)^2 \pi^2, \qquad n = 0, 1, 2, \ldots$$

with the corresponding eigenfunctions

$$y_n(x) = C_n \sin\left[\left(n + \frac{1}{2}\right)\pi x\right], \qquad n = 0, 1, 2, \ldots,$$

where C_n is an arbitrary nonzero constant.

(a) We need only to choose the C_n so that

$$\int_0^1 C_n^2 \sin^2\left[\left(n+\frac{1}{2}\right)\pi x\right] dx = 1.$$

We compute

$$\begin{aligned}\int_0^1 C_n^2 \sin^2\left[\left(n+\frac{1}{2}\right)\pi x\right] dx &= \frac{1}{2}C_n^2 \int_0^1 \left(1-\cos\left[(2n+1)\pi x\right]\right) dx \\ &= \frac{1}{2}C_n^2\left(x-\frac{1}{(2n+1)\pi}\sin\left[(2n+1)\pi x\right]\right)\Bigg|_0^1 = \frac{1}{2}C_n^2 .\end{aligned}$$

Hence, we can take $C_n = \sqrt{2}$ which gives

$$\left\{\sqrt{2}\sin\left[\left(n+\frac{1}{2}\right)\pi x\right]\right\}_{n=0}^{\infty},$$

as an orthonormal system of eigenfunctions.

(b) To obtain the eigenfunction expansion for $f(x)=x$, we use formula (25) on page 679 of the text. Thus,

$$c_n = \int_0^1 x\sqrt{2}\sin\left[\left(n+\frac{1}{2}\right)\pi x\right] dx .$$

Using integration by parts with $u=\sqrt{2}x$ and $dv = \sin\left[\left(n+\frac{1}{2}\right)\pi x\right] dx$, we find

$$\begin{aligned} c_n &= \frac{-\sqrt{2}x\cos[(n+1/2)\pi x]}{(n+1/2)\pi}\Bigg|_0^1 + \int_0^1 \frac{\sqrt{2}x\cos[(n+1/2)\pi x]\,dx}{(n+1/2)\pi} \\ &= \frac{-\sqrt{2}\cos[(n+1/2)\pi]}{(n+1/2)\pi} + \frac{\sqrt{2}\sin[(n+1/2)\pi x]}{(n+1/2)^2\pi^2}\Bigg|_0^1 \\ &= 0 + \frac{\sqrt{2}\sin[(n+1/2)\pi]}{(n+1/2)^2\pi^2} = \frac{(-1)^n\sqrt{2}}{(n+1/2)^2\pi^2}.\end{aligned}$$

Therefore

$$\begin{aligned} x = \sum_{n=0}^{\infty} c_n\sqrt{2}\sin\left[\left(n+\frac{1}{2}\right)\pi x\right] &= \sum_{n=0}^{\infty}\frac{2(-1)^n}{(n+1/2)^2\pi^2}\sin\left[\left(n+\frac{1}{2}\right)\pi x\right] \\ &= \frac{8}{\pi^2}\sum_{n=0}^{\infty}\frac{(-1)^n}{(2n+1)^2}\sin\left[\left(n+\frac{1}{2}\right)\pi x\right].\end{aligned}$$

23. In Problem 19 of Section 11.2, we found the eigenvalues

$$\lambda_n = \left(n + \frac{1}{2}\right)^2, \qquad n = 0, 1, 2, \ldots ,$$

with the corresponding eigenfunctions

$$y_n(x) = C_n \cos\left[\left(n + \frac{1}{2}\right)\ln x\right], \qquad n = 0, 1, 2, \ldots ,$$

where C_n is an arbitrary nonzero constant.

(a) We need only to choose the C_n so that

$$\int_1^{e^\pi} C_n^2 \cos^2\left[\left(n + \frac{1}{2}\right)\ln x\right]\frac{1}{x}\,dx = 1.$$

To compute, we let $u = \ln x$ and so $du = dx/x$. Substituting, we find

$$\begin{aligned}
\int_1^{e^\pi} C_n^2 \cos^2\left[\left(n + \frac{1}{2}\right)\ln x\right]\frac{1}{x}\,dx &= C_n^2 \int_0^\pi \cos^2\left[\left(n + \frac{1}{2}\right)u\right] du \\
&= \frac{1}{2}C_n^2 \int_0^\pi \{1 + \cos\left[(2n+1)u\right]\}\,du \\
&= \frac{1}{2}C_n^2 \left(u + \frac{1}{2n+1}\sin\left[(2n+1)u\right]\right)\Bigg|_0^\pi = \frac{\pi}{2}C_n^2 .
\end{aligned}$$

Hence, we can take $C_n = \sqrt{2/\pi}$, which gives

$$\left\{\sqrt{\frac{2}{\pi}}\cos\left[\left(n + \frac{1}{2}\right)\ln x\right]\right\}_{n=0}^{\infty},$$

as an orthonormal system of eigenfunctions.

(b) To obtain the eigenfunction expansion for $f(x) = x$, we use formula (25) on page 679 of the text. Thus, with $w(x) = x^{-1}$, we have

$$c_n = \int_1^{e^\pi} x\sqrt{\frac{2}{\pi}}\cos\left[\left(n + \frac{1}{2}\right)\ln x\right] x^{-1}dx.$$

Let $u = \ln x$. Then $du = dx/x$, and we have

$$\begin{aligned} c_n &= \sqrt{\frac{2}{\pi}} \int_0^{\pi} e^u \cos\left[\left(n + \frac{1}{2}\right) u\right] du \\ &= \sqrt{\frac{2}{\pi}} \left. \frac{e^u \cos[(n+1/2)u] + e^u (n+1/2)\sin[(n+1/2)u]}{1+(n+1/2)^2} \right|_0^{\pi} \\ &= \sqrt{\frac{2}{\pi}} \frac{e^{\pi}(n+1/2)\sin[(n+1/2)\pi] - 1}{1+(n+1/2)^2} = \sqrt{\frac{2}{\pi}} \frac{(-1)^n e^{\pi}(n+1/2) - 1}{1+(n+1/2)^2} . \end{aligned}$$

Therefore,

$$\begin{aligned} x &= \sum_{n=0}^{\infty} c_n \sqrt{\frac{2}{\pi}} \cos\left[\left(n + \frac{1}{2}\right) \ln x\right] \\ &= \frac{2}{\pi} \sum_{n=0}^{\infty} \frac{(-1)^n e^{\pi}(n+1/2) - 1}{1+(n+1/2)^2} \cos\left[\left(n + \frac{1}{2}\right) \ln x\right] . \end{aligned}$$

EXERCISES 11.4: Nonhomogeneous Boundary Value Problems and the Fredholm Alternative, page 692

3. Here our differential operator is given by

$$L[y] = \left(1 + x^2\right) y'' + 2xy' + y.$$

Substituting into the formula (3) page 684 of the text, we obtain

$$\begin{aligned} L^+[y] &= \left[(1+x^2)y\right]'' - (2xy)' + y = \left[2xy + (1+x^2)y'\right]' - 2y - 2xy' + y \\ &= 2y + 2xy' + 2xy' + (1+x^2)y'' - 2y - 2xy' + y = (1+x^2)y'' + 2xy' + y. \end{aligned}$$

7. Here our differential operator is given by

$$L[y] = y'' - 2y' + 10y; \qquad y(0) = y(\pi) = 0.$$

Hence

$$L^+[v] = v'' + 2v' + 10v.$$

To find the $D(L^+)$, we must have

$$P(u,v)(x)\,\Big|_0^\pi = 0 \tag{11.5}$$

for all u in $D(L)$ and v in $D(L^+)$. Using formula (9) page 685 of the text for $P(u,v)$ with $A_1 = -2$ and $A_2 = 1$, we find

$$P(u,v) = -2uv - uv' + u'v.$$

Evaluating at π and 0, condition (11.5) becomes

$$-2u(\pi)v(\pi) - u(\pi)v'(\pi) + u'(\pi)v(\pi) + 2u(0)v(0) + u(0)v'(0) - u'(0)v(0) = 0.$$

Since u in $D(L)$, we know that $u(0) = u(\pi) = 0$. Thus the above equation becomes

$$u'(\pi)v(\pi) - u'(0)v(0) = 0.$$

Since $u'(\pi)$ and $u'(0)$ can take on any value, we must have $v(0) = v(\pi) = 0$ for this equation to hold for all u in $D(L)$. Hence $D(L^+)$ consists of all function v having continuous second derivatives on $[0,\pi]$ and satisfying the boundary condition

$$v(0) = v(\pi) = 0.$$

11. Here our differential operator is given by

$$L[y] = y'' + 6y' + 10y; \qquad y'(0) = y'(\pi) = 0.$$

Hence

$$L^+[v] = v'' - 6v' + 10v.$$

To find the $D(L^+)$, we must have

$$P(u,v)(x)\,\Big|_0^\pi = 0 \tag{11.6}$$

for all u in $D(L)$ and v in $D(L^+)$. Again using formula (9) page 685 of the text for $P(u,v)$ with $A_1 = 6$ and $A_2 = 1$, we find

$$P(u,v) = 6uv - uv' + u'v.$$

Evaluating at π and 0, condition (11.6) becomes

$$6u(\pi)v(\pi) - u(\pi)v'(\pi) + u'(\pi)v(\pi) - 6u(0)v(0) + u(0)v'(0) - u'(0)v(0) = 0.$$

Applying the boundary conditions $u'(0) = u'(\pi) = 0$ to the above equation yields

$$6u(\pi)v(\pi) - u(\pi)v'(\pi) - 6u(0)v(0) + u(0)v'(0) = 0$$
$$\Rightarrow \quad u(\pi)\left[6v(\pi) - v'(\pi)\right] - u(0)\left[6v(0) - v'(0)\right] = 0.$$

Since $u(\pi)$ and $u(0)$ can take on any value, we must have $6v(\pi)-v'(\pi) = 0$ and $6v(0)-v'(0) = 0$ in order for the equation to hold for all u in $D(L)$. Therefore, the adjoint boundary value problem is

$$L^+[v] = v'' - 6v' + 10v; \qquad 6v(\pi) = v'(\pi) \quad \text{and} \quad 6v(0) = v'(0).$$

17. In Problem 7 we found the adjoint boundary value problem

$$L^+[v] = v'' + 2v' + 10v; \qquad v(0) = v(\pi) = 0. \tag{11.7}$$

The auxiliary equation for (11.7) is $r^2 + 2r + 10 = 0$, which has roots $r = -1 \pm 3i$. Hence a general solution to the differential equation in (11.7) is given by

$$y(x) = C_1 e^{-x}\cos 3x + C_2 e^{-x}\sin 3x.$$

Using the boundary conditions in (11.7) to determine C_1 and C_2, we find

$$y(0) = C_1 = 0 \qquad \text{and} \qquad y(\pi) = -C_1 e^{-\pi} = 0.$$

Thus $C_1 = 0$ and C_2 is arbitrary. Therefore, every solution to the adjoint problem (11.7) has the form

$$y(x) = C_2 e^{-x}\sin 3x.$$

It follows from the Fredholm alternative that if h is continuous, then the nonhomogeneous problem has a solution if and only if

$$\int_0^\pi h(x)e^{-x}\sin 3x\,dx = 0.$$

21. In Problem 11 we found the adjoint boundary value problem

$$L^+[v] = v'' - 6v' + 10v; \qquad 6v(\pi) = v'(\pi) \quad \text{and} \quad 6v(0) = v'(0). \tag{11.8}$$

The auxiliary equation for (11.8) is $r^2 - 6r + 10 = 0$, which has roots $r = 3 \pm i$. Hence a general solution to the differential equation in (11.8) is given by

$$y(x) = C_1 e^{3x}\cos x + C_2 e^{3x}\sin x.$$

To apply the boundary conditions in (11.8), we first determine $y'(x)$.

$$y'(x) = 3C_1 e^{3x}\cos x - C_1 e^{3x}\sin x + 3C_2 e^{3x}\sin x + C_2 e^{3x}\cos x.$$

Applying the first condition, we have

$$-6C_1 e^{3\pi} = -3C_1 e^{3\pi} - C_2 e^{3\pi} \qquad \Rightarrow \qquad 3C_1 = C_2\,.$$

Applying the second condition, we have

$$6C_1 = 3C_1 + C_2 \qquad \Rightarrow \qquad 3C_1 = C_2\,.$$

Thus $C_2 = 3C_1$ where C_1 is arbitrary. Therefore, every solution to the adjoint problem (11.8) has the form

$$y(x) = C_1 e^{3x}(\cos x + 3\sin x).$$

It follows from the Fredholm alternative that if h is continuous, then the nonhomogeneous problem has a solution if and only if

$$\int_0^{\pi} h(x)e^{3x}(\cos x + 3\sin x)\,dx = 0.$$

EXERCISES 11.5: Solution by Eigenfunction Expansion, page 698

3. In Example 1 on page 696 of the text we noted that the boundary value problem

$$y'' + \lambda y = 0; \qquad y(0) = 0, \quad y(\pi) = 0,$$

has eigenvalues $\lambda_n = n^2$, $n = 1, 2, 3, \ldots$, with corresponding eigenfunctions

$$\phi_n(x) = \sin nx, \qquad n = 1, 2, 3, \ldots .$$

Here $r(x) \equiv 1$, so we need to determine coefficients γ_n such that

$$f(x) = \frac{f(x)}{r(x)} = \sum_{n=1}^{\infty} \gamma_n \sin nx = \sin 2x + \sin 8x.$$

Clearly $\gamma_2 = \gamma_8 = 1$ and the remaining γ_n's are zero. Since $\mu = 4 = \lambda_2$ and $\gamma_2 = 1 \neq 0$ there is no solution to this problem.

5. In equation (18) on page 666 of the text we noted that the boundary value problem

$$y'' + \lambda y = 0; \qquad y'(0) = 0, \quad y'(\pi) = 0,$$

has eigenvalues $\lambda_n = n^2$, $n = 0, 1, 2, \ldots$, with corresponding eigenfunctions

$$\phi_n(x) = \cos nx, \qquad n = 0, 1, 2, \ldots .$$

Here $r(x) \equiv 1$, so we need to determine coefficients γ_n such that

$$f(x) = \frac{f(x)}{r(x)} = \sum_{n=0}^{\infty} \gamma_n \cos nx = \cos 4x + \cos 7x.$$

Clearly $\gamma_4 = \gamma_7 = 1$ and the remaining γ_n's are zero. Since $\mu = 1 = \lambda_1$ and $\gamma_1 = 0$,

$$(\mu - \lambda_1)\, c_1 - \gamma_1 = 0$$

is satisfied for any value of c_1. Calculating c_4 and c_7, we get

$$c_4 = \frac{\gamma_4}{\mu - \lambda_4} = \frac{1}{1 - 16} = -\frac{1}{15}$$

and

$$c_7 = \frac{\gamma_7}{\mu - \lambda_7} = \frac{1}{1 - 49} = -\frac{1}{48}.$$

Hence a one parameter family of solutions is

$$\phi(x) = \sum_{n=0}^{\infty} c_n \phi_n(x) = c_1 \cos x - \frac{1}{15} \cos 4x - \frac{1}{48} \cos 7x\,,$$

where c_1 is arbitrary.

9. We first find the eigenvalues and corresponding eigenfunctions for this problem. Note that the auxiliary equation for this problem is $r^2 + \lambda = 0$. To find eigenvalues which yield nontrivial solutions we will consider the three cases $\lambda < 0$, $\lambda = 0$, and $\lambda > 0$.

Case 1, $\lambda < 0$: Let $\mu = \sqrt{-\lambda}$, then the roots to the auxiliary equation are $r = \pm\mu$ and a general solution to the differential equation is given by

$$y(x) = C_1 \sinh \mu x + C_2 \cosh \mu x.$$

Since

$$y'(x) = C_1 \mu \cosh \mu x + C_2 \mu \sinh \mu x,$$

by applying the boundary conditions we obtain

$$y'(0) = C_1 \mu = 0 \qquad \text{and} \qquad y(\pi) = C_1 \sinh \mu\pi + C_2 \cosh \mu\pi = 0.$$

Hence $C_1 = 0$ and $y(\pi) = C_2 \cosh \mu\pi = 0$. Therefore $C_2 = 0$ and we find only the trivial solution.

Case 2, $\lambda = 0$: In this case the differential equation becomes $y'' = 0$. This equation has a general solution given by

$$y(x) = C_1 + C_2 x.$$

Since $y'(x) = C_2$, by applying the boundary conditions we obtain

$$y'(0) = C_2 = 0 \qquad \text{and} \qquad y(\pi) = C_1 + C_2 \pi = 0.$$

Solving these equations simultaneously yields $C_1 = C_2 = 0$. Thus, we again find only the trivial solution.

Case 3, $\lambda > 0$: Let $\lambda = \mu^2$, for $\mu > 0$. The roots of the auxiliary equation are $r = \pm\mu i$ and so a general solution is

$$y(x) = C_1 \cos \mu x + C_2 \sin \mu x.$$

Since

$$y'(x) = -C_1 \mu \sin \mu x + C_2 \mu \cos \mu x,$$

using the first boundary condition we find

$$y'(0) = -C_1\mu\sin(\mu\cdot 0) + C_2\mu\cos(\mu\cdot 0) = 0 \qquad \Rightarrow \qquad C_2\mu = 0 \qquad \Rightarrow \qquad C_2 = 0.$$

Thus substituting into the second boundary condition yields

$$y(\pi) = C_1\cos\mu\pi = 0.$$

Therefore, in order to obtain a solution other than the trivial solution, we must have

$$\cos\mu\pi = 0 \qquad \Rightarrow \qquad \mu = n + \frac{1}{2}, \qquad n = 0, 1, 2, \ldots.$$

Hence choose $\lambda_n = (n + 1/2)^2$, $n = 0, 1, 2, \ldots$, and

$$y_n(x) = C_n\cos\left[\left(n + \frac{1}{2}\right)x\right],$$

where the C_n's are arbitrary nonzero constants.

Next we need to choose the C_n so that

$$\int\limits_0^\pi C_n^2\cos^2\left[\left(n + \frac{1}{2}\right)x\right]dx = 1.$$

Computing we find

$$\begin{aligned}\int\limits_0^\pi C_n^2\cos^2\left[\left(n + \frac{1}{2}\right)x\right]dx &= \frac{1}{2}C_n^2\int\limits_0^\pi \{1 + \cos[(2n+1)x]\}\,dx \\ &= \frac{1}{2}C_n^2\left\{x + \frac{1}{2n+1}\sin[(2n+1)x]\right\}\Bigg|_0^\pi = \frac{\pi}{2}C_n^2.\end{aligned}$$

An orthonormal system of eigenfunctions is given when we take $C_n = \sqrt{2/\pi}$,

$$\left\{\sqrt{\frac{2}{\pi}}\cos\left[\left(n + \frac{1}{2}\right)x\right]\right\}_{n=0}^\infty.$$

Now $f(x)$ has the eigenfunction expansion

$$f(x) = \sum_{n=0}^\infty \gamma_n\sqrt{\frac{2}{\pi}}\cos\left[\left(n + \frac{1}{2}\right)x\right],$$

where

$$\gamma_n = \sqrt{\frac{2}{\pi}} \int_0^{\pi} f(x) \cos\left[\left(n + \frac{1}{2}\right) x\right] dx.$$

Therefore, with γ_n as described above, the solution to the given boundary value problem has a formal expansion

$$\phi(x) = \sum_{n=0}^{\infty} \frac{\gamma_n}{1 - \lambda_n} \sqrt{\frac{2}{\pi}} \cos\left[\left(n + \frac{1}{2}\right) x\right] = \sum_{n=0}^{\infty} \frac{\gamma_n}{1 - (n + 1/2)^2} \sqrt{\frac{2}{\pi}} \cos\left[\left(n + \frac{1}{2}\right) x\right].$$

EXERCISES 11.6: Green's Functions, page 706

1. A general solution to the corresponding homogeneous equation, $y'' = 0$, is $y_h(x) = Ax + B$. Thus we seek for paricular solutions $z_1(x)$ and $z_2(x)$ of this form satisfying

$$\begin{aligned} z_1(0) &= 0, \\ z_2'(\pi) &= 0. \end{aligned} \tag{11.9}$$

The first equation yields

$$z_1(0) = B = 0.$$

Since A is arbitrary, we choose $A = 1$ and so $z_1(x) = x$. Next, from the second equation in (11.9) we get

$$z_2'(\pi) = A = 0.$$

Taking $B = 1$, we obtain $z_2(x) = 1$.

With $p(x) \equiv 1$, we now compute

$$C = p(x)W\left[z_1, z_2\right](x) = (1)[(x)(0) - (1)(1)] = -1.$$

Thus, the Green's function is

$$G(x, s) = \begin{cases} -z_1(s)z_2(x)/C, & 0 \le s \le x, \\ -z_1(x)z_2(s)/C, & x \le s \le \pi \end{cases} = \begin{cases} s, & 0 \le s \le x, \\ x, & x \le s \le \pi. \end{cases}$$

3. A general solution to the homogeneous problem, $y'' = 0$, is $y_h(x) = Ax + B$, so $z_1(x)$ and $z_2(x)$ must be of this form. To get $z_1(x)$ we want to choose A and B so that

$$z_1(0) = B = 0.$$

Since A is arbitrary, we can set it equal to 1 and $z_1(x) = x$. Next, to get $z_2(x)$ we need to choose A and B so that

$$z_2(\pi) + z_2'(\pi) = A\pi + B + A = 0.$$

Thus $B = -(1+\pi)A$. Taking $A = 1$, we get $z_2(x) = x - 1 - \pi$.

Now compute

$$C = p(x)W\left[z_1, z_2\right](x) = (1)[(x)(1) - (1)(x - 1 - \pi)] = 1 + \pi.$$

Thus, the Green's function is

$$G(x,s) = \begin{cases} -z_1(s)z_2(x)/C, & 0 \le s \le x, \\ -z_1(x)z_2(s)/C, & x \le s \le \pi \end{cases} = \begin{cases} \dfrac{-s(x-1-\pi)}{1+\pi}, & 0 \le s \le x, \\ \\ \dfrac{-x(s-1-\pi)}{1+\pi}, & x \le s \le \pi. \end{cases}$$

5. The corresponding homogeneous differential equation, $y'' + 4y = 0$, has the characteristic equation $r^2 + 4 = 0$, whose roots are $r = \pm 2i$. Hence, a general solution to the homogeneous problem is given by

$$y_h(x) = C_1 \cos 2x + C_2 \sin 2x.$$

A solution $z_1(x)$ must satisfy the first boundary condition, $z_1(0) = 0$. Substitution yields

$$z_1(0) = C_1 \cos(2 \cdot 0) + C_2 \sin(2 \cdot 0) = 0 \qquad \Rightarrow \qquad C_1 = 0.$$

Setting $C_2 = 1$, we get $z_1(x) = \sin 2x$. For $z_2(x)$, we have to find constants C_1 and C_2 such that the second boundary condition is satisfied. Since

$$y_h'(x) = -2C_1 \sin 2x + 2C_2 \cos 2x,$$

we have

$$z_2'(\pi) = -2C_1 \sin(2\pi) + 2C_2 \cos(2\pi) = 2C_2 = 0 \qquad \Rightarrow \qquad C_2 = 0.$$

With $C_1 = 1$, $z_2(x) = \cos 2x$.

Next we find

$$C = p(x)W\left[z_1, z_2\right](x) = (1)[(\sin 2x)(-2\sin 2x) - (\cos 2x)(2\cos 2x)] = -2.$$

Thus, the Green's function in this problem is given by

$$G(x,s) = \begin{cases} -z_1(s)z_2(x)/C, & 0 \le s \le x, \\ -z_1(x)z_2(s)/C, & x \le s \le \pi \end{cases} = \begin{cases} (\sin 2s \cos 2x)/2\,, & 0 \le s \le x, \\ (\sin 2x \cos 2s)/2\,, & x \le s \le \pi. \end{cases}$$

13. In Problem 3 we found the Green's function for this boundary value problem. When $f(x) = x$, the solution is given by equation (16) on page 702 of the text. Substituting for $f(x)$ and $G(x,s)$ yields

$$y(x) = \int_a^b G(x,s)f(s)\,ds = \int_0^\pi G(x,s)s\,ds = \int_0^x \frac{-s^2(x-1-\pi)}{1+\pi}\,ds + \int_x^\pi \frac{-xs(s-1-\pi)}{1+\pi}\,ds.$$

Computing

$$\int_0^x \frac{-s^2(x-1-\pi)}{1+\pi}\,ds = -\frac{(x-1-\pi)}{1+\pi}\left(\frac{s^3}{3}\right)\bigg|_{s=0}^{x} = -\frac{(x-1-\pi)}{1+\pi}\left(\frac{x^3}{3}\right) = -\frac{x^4}{3(1+\pi)} + \frac{x^3}{3},$$

$$\begin{aligned} \int_x^\pi \frac{-xs(s-1-\pi)}{1+\pi}\,ds &= -\frac{x}{1+\pi}\left[\frac{s^3}{3} - \frac{(1+\pi)s^2}{2}\right]\bigg|_{s=x}^{\pi} = -\frac{x}{1+\pi}\left[\frac{\pi^3}{3} - \frac{(1+\pi)\pi^2}{2}\right] \\ &\quad + \frac{x}{1+\pi}\left[\frac{x^3}{3} - \frac{(1+\pi)x^2}{2}\right] = -\frac{\pi^3 x}{3(1+\pi)} + \frac{\pi^2 x}{2} + \frac{x^4}{3(1+\pi)} - \frac{x^3}{2}, \end{aligned}$$

we finally get

$$\begin{aligned} y(x) &= \left[-\frac{x^4}{3(1+\pi)} + \frac{x^3}{3}\right] + \left[-\frac{\pi^3 x}{3(1+\pi)} + \frac{\pi^2 x}{2} + \frac{x^4}{3(1+\pi)} - \frac{x^3}{2}\right] \\ &= -\frac{x^3}{6} + \left[\frac{\pi^2}{2} - \frac{\pi^3}{3(1+\pi)}\right]x = -\frac{x^3}{6} + \frac{\pi^2(3+\pi)x}{6(1+\pi)}. \end{aligned}$$

17. A general solution to the corresponding homogeneous problem $y'' - y = 0$ is

$$y_h(x) = C_1 e^x + C_2 e^{-x}.$$

So $z_1(x)$ and $z_2(x)$ must be of this form. To get $z_1(x)$ we want to choose constants C_1 and C_2 so that

$$z_1(0) = C_1 e^0 + C_2 e^{-0} = C_1 + C_2 = 0.$$

Let $C_1 = 1$. Then $C_2 = -1$ and so $z_1(x) = e^x - e^{-x}$. Likewise, to get a $z_2(x)$, we find C_1 and C_2 so that

$$z_2(1) = C_1 e^1 + C_2 e^{-1} = 0 \qquad \Rightarrow \qquad C_2 = -C_1 e^2.$$

If we let $C_1 = 1$, then $C_2 = -e^2$. Hence $z_2(x) = e^x - e^2 e^{-x} = e^x - e^{2-x}$. We now compute

$$C = p(x)W[z_1, z_2](x) = (1)\left[\left(e^x - e^{-x}\right)\left(e^x + e^{2-x}\right) - \left(e^x + e^{-x}\right)\left(e^x - e^{2-x}\right)\right] = 2e^2 - 2.$$

Thus, the Green's function is in this problem is

$$\begin{aligned} G(x,s) &= \begin{cases} -z_1(s)z_2(x)/C, & 0 \le s \le x, \\ -z_1(x)z_2(s)/C, & x \le s \le 1 \end{cases} \\ &= \begin{cases} \left(e^s - e^{-s}\right)\left(e^x - e^{2-x}\right)/\left(2 - 2e^2\right), & 0 \le s \le x, \\ \left(e^x - e^{-x}\right)\left(e^s - e^{2-s}\right)/\left(2 - 2e^2\right), & x \le s \le 1. \end{cases} \end{aligned}$$

Here $f(x) = -x$. Using Green's function to solve the boundary value problem, we find

$$y(x) = \int_a^b G(x,s)f(s)\,ds = \int_0^x \frac{(e^s - e^{-s})(e^x - e^{2-x})(-s)}{2 - 2e^2}\,ds + \int_x^1 \frac{(e^x - e^{-x})(e^s - e^{2-s})(-s)}{2 - 2e^2}\,ds.$$

Computing integrals yields

$$\begin{aligned} \int_0^x \frac{(e^s - e^{-s})(e^x - e^{2-x})(-s)}{2 - 2e^2}\,ds &= -\frac{e^x - e^{2-x}}{2 - 2e^2}\int_0^x \left(se^s - se^{-s}\right) ds \\ &= -\frac{e^x - e^{2-x}}{2 - 2e^2}\left(se^s - e^s + se^{-s} + e^{-s}\right)\Big|_0^x \\ &= -\frac{e^x - e^{2-x}}{2 - 2e^2}\left(xe^x - e^x + xe^{-x} + e^{-x}\right), \end{aligned}$$

$$\int_x^1 \frac{(e^x-e^{-x})(e^s-e^{2-s})(-s)}{2-2e^2}\,ds = -\frac{e^x-e^{-x}}{2-2e^2}\int_x^1 \left(se^s-se^{2-s}\right)ds$$
$$= -\frac{e^x-e^{-x}}{2-2e^2}\left(se^s-e^s+se^{2-s}+e^{2-s}\right)\Big|_x^1$$
$$= -\frac{e^x-e^{-x}}{2-2e^2}\left[2e-\left(xe^x-e^x+xe^{2-x}+e^{2-x}\right)\right].$$

Thus

$$y(x) = -\frac{e^x-e^{2-x}}{2-2e^2}\left(xe^x-e^x+xe^{-x}+e^{-x}\right)-\frac{e^x-e^{-x}}{2-2e^2}\left[2e-\left(xe^x-e^x+xe^{2-x}+e^{2-x}\right)\right]$$
$$= \frac{-(e^x-e^{2-x})(xe^x-e^x+xe^{-x}+e^{-x})-(e^x-e^{-x})(2e-xe^x+e^x-xe^{2-x}-e^{2-x})}{2-2e^2}$$
$$= \frac{-2x+2xe^2-2e^{1+x}+2e^{1-x}}{2-2e^2} = -x+\frac{e^{1+x}-e^{1-x}}{e^2-1}.$$

25. Substitution $y=x^r$ into the corresponding homogeneous Cauchy-Euler equation

$$x^2y''-2xy'+2y=0,$$

we obtain the auxiliary equation

$$r(r-1)-2r+2=0 \qquad \text{or} \qquad r^2-3r+2=(r-1)(r-2)=0.$$

Hence a general solution to the corresponding homogeneous equation is

$$y_h(x)=C_1x+C_2x^2.$$

To get $z_1(x)$ we want to choose C_1 and C_2 so that

$$z_1(1)=C_1+C_2=0 \qquad \Rightarrow \qquad C_2=-C_1\,.$$

Let $C_1=1$, then $C_2=-1$ and $z_1(x)=x-x^2$. Next we find $z_2(x)$ satisfying

$$z_2(2)=2C_1+4C_2=0 \qquad \Rightarrow \qquad C_1=-2C_2\,.$$

Hence, we let $C_2=-1$, then $C_1=2$ and $z_2(x)=2x-x^2$. Now compute (see the formula for $K(x,s)$ in Problem 22)

$$C(s)=A_2(s)W\left[z_1,z_2\right](s) = \left(s^2\right)\left[(s-s^2)(2-2s)-(1-2s)(2s-s^2)\right]$$

$$= \left(s^2\right)\left(2s - 4s^2 + 2s^3 - 2s + 5s^2 - 2s^3\right) = s^4,$$

$$K(x,s) = \begin{cases} -z_1(s)z_2(x)/C(s), & 1 \le s \le x, \\ -z_1(x)z_2(s)/C(s), & x \le s \le 2 \end{cases} = \begin{cases} -\dfrac{(s-s^2)(2x-x^2)}{s^4}, & 1 \le s \le x, \\ -\dfrac{(x-x^2)(2s-s^2)}{s^4}, & x \le s \le 2. \end{cases}$$

Simplifying yields

$$K(x,s) = \begin{cases} -x(2-x)(s^{-3}-s^{-2}), & 1 \le s \le x, \\ -x(1-x)(2s^{-3}-s^{-2}), & x \le s \le 2. \end{cases}$$

Hence, a solution to the boundary value problem with $f(x) = -x$ is

$$\begin{aligned} y(x) &= \int_a^b K(x,s)f(s)\,ds = \int_1^x K(x,s)f(s)\,ds + \int_x^2 K(x,s)f(s)\,ds \\ &= \int_1^x [-x(2-x)(s^{-3}-s^{-2})](-s)\,ds + \int_x^2 [-x(1-x)(2s^{-3}-s^{-2})](-s)\,ds \\ &= \left(2x-x^2\right)\int_1^x \left(s^{-2}-s^{-1}\right)ds + \left(x-x^2\right)\int_x^2 \left(2s^{-2}-s^{-1}\right)ds \\ &= \left(2x-x^2\right)\left(-s^{-1}-\ln s\right)\Big|_1^x + \left(x-x^2\right)\left(-2s^{-1}-\ln s\right)\Big|_x^2 \\ &= x^2\ln 2 - x\ln 2 - x\ln x\,. \end{aligned}$$

29. Let $f(x) = \boldsymbol{\delta}(x-s)$. Let $H(x,s)$ be the solution to

$$\frac{\partial^4 H(x,s)}{\partial x^4} = -\boldsymbol{\delta}(x-s)$$

that satisfies the given boundary conditions, the jump condition

$$\lim_{x\to s^+}\frac{\partial^3 H(x,s)}{\partial x^3} - \lim_{x\to s^-}\frac{\partial^3 H(x,s)}{\partial x^3} = -1,$$

and H, $\partial H/\partial x$, $\partial^2 H/\partial x^2$ are continuous on the square $[0,\pi]\times[0,\pi]$. We begin by integrating to obtain

$$\frac{\partial^3 H(x,s)}{\partial x^3} = -u(x-s) + C_1\,,$$

where u is the unit step function and C_1 is a constant. (Recall in Section 7.8 we observed that $u'(t-a) = \boldsymbol{\delta}(t-a)$, at least formally.) $\partial^3 H/\partial x^3$ is not continuous along the line $x = s$, but it does satisfy the jump condition

$$\begin{aligned} \lim_{x\to s^+} \frac{\partial^3 H(x,s)}{\partial x^3} - \lim_{x\to s^-} \frac{\partial^3 H(x,s)}{\partial x^3} &= \lim_{x\to s^+} [-u(x-s)+C_1] - \lim_{x\to s^-} [-u(x-s)+C_1] \\ &= (-1+C_1) - C_1 = -1. \end{aligned}$$

We want $H(x,s)$ to satisfy the boundary condition $y'''(\pi) = 0$. So we solve

$$\frac{\partial^3 H}{\partial x^3}(\pi, s) = -u(\pi - s) + C_1 = -1 + C_1 = 0$$

to obtain $C_1 = 1$. Thus

$$\frac{\partial^3 H(x,s)}{\partial x^3} = -u(x-s) + 1\,.$$

We now integrate again with respect to x to obtain

$$\frac{\partial^2 H(x,s)}{\partial x^2} = x - u(x-s)(x-s) + C_2\,.$$

(The reader should verify this is the antiderivative for $x \neq s$ by differentiating it.) We selected this particular form of the antiderivative because we need $\partial^2 H/\partial x^2$ to be continuous on $[0,\pi] \times [0,\pi]$. (The jump of $u(x-s)$ when $x - s$ is canceled by the vanishing of this term by the factor $(x-s)$.) Since

$$\lim_{x\to s} \frac{\partial^2 H(x,s)}{\partial x^2} = s + C_2\,,$$

we can define

$$\frac{\partial^2 H}{\partial x^2}(s,s) = s + C_2\,,$$

and we now have a continuous function. Next, we want $y''(\pi) = 0$. Solving we find

$$0 = \frac{\partial^2 H}{\partial x^2}(\pi, s) = \pi - u(\pi - s)(\pi - s) + C_2 = \pi - (\pi - s) + C_2 = s + C_2\,.$$

Thus, we find that $C_2 = -s$. Now,

$$\frac{\partial^2 H(x,s)}{\partial x^2} = (x-s) - u(x-s)(x-s)\,.$$

We integrate with respect to x again to get

$$\frac{\partial H(x,s)}{\partial x} = \frac{x^2}{2} - sx - u(x-s)\frac{(x-s)^2}{2} + C_3\,,$$

which is continuous on $[0,\pi]\times[0,\pi]$. We now want the boundary condition $y'(0)=0$ satisfied. Solving, we obtain

$$0 = \frac{\partial H}{\partial x}(0,s) = -u(0-s)\frac{s^2}{2} + C_3 = C_3\,.$$

Hence,

$$\frac{\partial H(x,s)}{\partial x} = \frac{x^2}{2} - sx - u(x-s)\frac{(x-s)^2}{2}\,.$$

Integrating once more with respect to x, we have

$$H(x,s) = \frac{x^3}{6} - \frac{sx^2}{2} - u(x-s)\frac{(x-s)^3}{6} + C_4\,.$$

Now $H(x,s)$ is continuous on $[0,\pi]\times[0,\pi]$. We want $H(x,s)$ to satisfy the boundary condition $y(0)=0$. Solving, we find

$$0 = H(0,s) = -u(0-s)\frac{(0-s)^3}{6} + C_4 = C_4\,.$$

Hence,

$$H(x,s) = \frac{x^3}{6} - \frac{sx^2}{2} - u(x-s)\frac{(x-s)^3}{6}\,,$$

which we can rewrite in the form

$$H(x,s) = \begin{cases} \dfrac{s^2(s-3x)}{6}, & 0\le s\le x, \\[2ex] \dfrac{x^2(x-3s)}{6}, & x\le s\le \pi. \end{cases}$$

EXERCISES 11.7: Singular Sturm-Liouville Boundary Value Problems, page 715

1. This is a typical singular Sturm-Liouville boundary value problem. Condition (ii) of Lemma 1 on page 710 of the main text holds since

$$\lim_{x\to 0^+} p(x) = \lim_{x\to 0^+} x = 0$$

and $y(x)$, $y'(x)$ remain bounded as $x \to 0^+$. Because

$$\lim_{x \to 1^-} p(x) = p(1) = 1$$

and $y(1) = 0$, the analogue of condition (i) of Lemma 1 holds at the right endpoint. Hence L is selfadjoint.

The equation is Bessel's equation of order 2. On page 712 of the text, we observed that the solutions to this boundary value problem are given by

$$y_n(x) = c_n J_2\left(\alpha_{2n} x\right),$$

where $\sqrt{\mu_n} = \alpha_{2n}$ is the increasing sequence of real zeros of $J_2(x)$, that is, $J_2(\alpha_{2n}) = 0$.

Now to find an eigenfunction expansion for the given nonhomogeneous equation we compute the eigenfunction expansion for $f(x)/x$ (see page 694):

$$\frac{f(x)}{x} \sim \sum_{n=1}^{\infty} a_n J_2\left(\alpha_{2n} x\right),$$

where

$$a_n = \frac{\int_0^1 f(x) J_2(\alpha_{2n} x)\, dx}{\int_0^1 x J_2^2(\alpha_{2n} x)\, dx}, \qquad n = 1, 2, 3, \ldots.$$

Therefore,

$$y(x) = \sum_{n=1}^{\infty} \frac{a_n}{\mu - \alpha_{2n}^2} J_2\left(\alpha_{2n} x\right).$$

3. Again, this is a typical singular Sturm-Liouville boundary value problem. L is selfadjoint since condition (ii) of Lemma 1 on page 710 of the main text holds at the left endpoint and the analogue of condition (i) holds at the right endpoint.

This is Bessel's equation of order 0. As we observed on page 712 of the text, $J_0\left(\sqrt{\mu} x\right)$ satisfies the boundary conditions at the origin. At the right endpoint, we want $J_0'\left(\sqrt{\mu}\right) = 0$. Now it follows from equation (32) on page 488 of the text, that the zeros of J_0' and J_1 are the same. So if we let $\sqrt{\mu_n} = \alpha_{1n}$, the increasing sequence of zeros of J_1, then $J_0'(\alpha_{1n}) = 0$. Hence, the eigenfunctions are given by

$$y_n(x) = J_0\left(\alpha_{1n} x\right), \qquad n = 1, 2, 3, \ldots.$$

To find an eigenfunction expansion for the solution to the nonhomogeneous equation, we first expand $f(x)/x$ (see page 694):

$$\frac{f(x)}{x} \sim \sum_{n=1}^{\infty} b_n J_0\left(\alpha_{1n} x\right),$$

where

$$b_n = \frac{\int_0^1 f(x) J_0(\alpha_{1n} x)\, dx}{\int_0^1 x J_0^2(\alpha_{1n} x)\, dx}, \qquad n = 1, 2, 3, \ldots .$$

Therefore,

$$y(x) = \sum_{n=1}^{\infty} \frac{b_n}{\mu - \alpha_{1n}^2} J_0\left(\alpha_{1n} x\right).$$

11. **(a)** Let $\phi(x)$ be an eigenfunction for

$$\frac{d}{dx}\left[x \frac{dy}{dx}\right] - \frac{\nu^2}{x} y + \lambda x y = 0.$$

Therefore,

$$\begin{aligned} &\frac{d}{dx}\left[x\phi'(x)\right] - \frac{\nu^2}{x}\phi(x) + \lambda x \phi(x) = 0 \\ \Rightarrow \qquad &\phi'(x) + x\phi''(x) - \frac{\nu^2}{x}\phi(x) + \lambda x \phi(x) = 0. \end{aligned}$$

Multiplying both side by $\phi(x)$ and integrating both sides from 0 to 1, we obtain

$$\int_0^1 \phi(x)\phi'(x)\, dx + \int_0^1 x\phi(x)\phi''(x)\, dx - \int_0^1 \frac{\nu^2}{x}[\phi(x)]^2\, dx + \int_0^1 \lambda x[\phi(x)]^2\, dx = 0. \qquad (11.10)$$

Now integrating by parts with $u = \phi(x)\phi'(x)$ and $dv = dx$, we have

$$\begin{aligned} \int_0^1 \phi(x)\phi'(x)\, dx &= x\phi(x)\phi'(x)\Big|_0^1 - \int_0^1 x\left[\phi'(x)\phi'(x) + \phi(x)\phi''(x)\right] dx \\ &= x\phi(x)\phi'(x)\Big|_0^1 - \int_0^1 x\left[\phi'(x)\right]^2 dx - \int_0^1 x\phi(x)\phi''(x)\, dx. \end{aligned}$$

Since $\phi(1) = 0$, we have

$$x\phi(x)\phi'(x) \Big|_0^1 = 0,$$

$$\int_0^1 \phi(x)\phi'(x)\,dx = -\int_0^1 x\left[\phi'(x)\right]^2\,dx - \int_0^1 x\phi(x)\phi''(x)\,dx.$$

Thus equation (11.10) reduces to

$$-\int_0^1 x\left[\phi'(x)\right]^2\,dx - \int_0^1 x\phi(x)\phi''(x)\,dx + \int_0^1 x\phi(x)\phi''(x)\,dx$$
$$-\nu^2\int_0^1 x^{-1}[\phi(x)]^2\,dx + \lambda\int_0^1 x[\phi(x)]^2\,dx = 0$$

$$\Rightarrow \qquad -\int_0^1 x\left[\phi'(x)\right]^2\,dx - \nu^2\int_0^1 x^{-1}[\phi(x)]^2\,dx + \lambda\int_0^1 x[\phi(x)]^2\,dx = 0. \qquad (11.11)$$

(b) First note that each integrand in (11.11) is nonnegative on the interval $(0,1)$, hence each integral is nonnegative. Moreover, since $\phi(x)$ is an eigenfunction, it is a continuous function which is not the zero function. Hence, the second and third integrals are strictly positive. Thus, if $\nu > 0$, then λ must be positive in order for the left-hand side of (11.11) to sum to zero.

(c) If $\nu = 0$, then only the first and third terms remain on the left hand side of equation (11.11). Since the first integral need only be nonnegative, we only need λ to be nonnegative in order for equation (11.11) to be satisfied.

To show $\lambda = 0$ is not an eigenvalue, we solve Bessel's equation with $\nu = 0$, that is, we solve

$$xy'' + y' = 0,$$

which is the same as the Cauchy-Euler equation

$$x^2y'' + xy' = 0.$$

Solving this Cauchy-Euler equation, we find a general solution

$$y(x) = c_1 + c_2 \ln x.$$

Since $\lim_{x\to 0^+} y(x) = -\infty$ if $c_2 \neq 0$, we take $c_2 = 0$. Now $y(x) = c_1$ satisfies the boundary condition (17) in the text. The right endpoint boundary condition (18) is $y(1) = 0$. So we want $0 = y(1) = c_1$. Hence the only solution to Bessel's equation of order 0 that satisfies the boundary conditions (17) and (18) is the trivial solution. Hence $\lambda = 0$ is not an eigenvalue.

EXERCISES 11.8: Oscillation and Comparison Theory, page 725

5. To apply the Sturm fundamental theorem to

$$y'' + (1 - e^x)\, y = 0, \qquad 0 < x < \infty, \tag{11.12}$$

we must find a $q(x)$ and a function $\phi(x)$ such that $q(x) \geq 1 - e^x$, $0 < x < \infty$, and $\phi(x)$ is a solution to

$$y'' + q(x)y = 0, \qquad 0 < x < \infty. \tag{11.13}$$

Because, for $x > 0$, $1 - e^x < 0$, we choose $q(x) \equiv 0$. Hence equation (11.13) becomes $y'' = 0$. The function $\phi(x) = x + 4$ is a nontrivial solution to this differential equation. Since $\phi(x) = x + 4$ does not have a zero for $x > 0$, any nontrivial solution to (11.12) can have at most one zero in $0 < x < \infty$. To use the Sturm fundamental theorem to show that any nontrivial solution to

$$y'' + (1 - e^x)\, y = 0, \qquad -\infty < x < 0, \tag{11.14}$$

has infinitely many zeros, we must find a $q(x)$ and a function $\phi(x)$ such that $q(x) \leq 1 - e^x$, $x < 0$, and $\phi(x)$ is a solution to

$$y'' + q(x)y = 0, \qquad -\infty < x < 0.$$

Because $1 - e^{-1} \approx 0.632$, we choose $q(x) \equiv 1/4$ and only consider the interval $(-\infty, -1)$. Hence, we obtain

$$y'' + \frac{1}{4}y = 0,$$

which has nontrivial solution $\phi(x) = \sin(x/2)$. Now the function $\phi(x)$ has infinitely many zeros in $(-\infty, -1)$ and between any two consecutive zeros of $\phi(x)$ any nontrivial solution to (11.14) must have a zero; hence any nontrivial solution to (11.14) will have infinitely many zeros in $(-\infty, -1)$.

9. First express

$$y'' + x^{-2}y' + \left(4 - e^{-x}\right) y = 0,$$

in Strum-Liouville form by multiplying by the integrating factor $e^{-1/x}$:

$$e^{-1/x}y'' + e^{-1/x}x^{-2}y' + e^{-1/x}\left(4 - e^{-x}\right) y = 0 \quad \Rightarrow \quad \left(e^{-1/x}y'\right)' + e^{-1/x}\left(4 - e^{-x}\right) y = 0.$$

Now when x gets large, we have

$$\sqrt{\frac{p}{q}} \approx \sqrt{\frac{e^{-1/\text{large}}}{e^{-1/\text{large}}\left(4 - e^{-\text{large}}\right)}} \approx \sqrt{\frac{1}{(1)(4 - \text{small})}} \approx \sqrt{\frac{1}{4}} = \frac{1}{2}.$$

Hence, the distance between consecutive zeros is approximately $\pi/2$.

11. We apply Corollary 5 with $p(x) = 1 + x$, $q(x) = e^{-x}$, and $r(x) \equiv 1$ to a nontrivial solution on the interval $[0, 5]$. On this interval we have $p_M = 6$, $p_m = 1$, $q_M = 1$, $q_m = e^{-5}$, and $r_M = r_m = 1$. Therefore, for

$$\lambda > \max\left\{\frac{-q_M}{r_M}, \frac{-q_m}{r_m}, 0\right\} = 0,$$

the distance between two consecutive zeros of a nontrivial solution $\phi(x)$ to the given equation is bounded between

$$\pi\sqrt{\frac{p_m}{q_M + \lambda r_M}} = \pi\sqrt{\frac{1}{1 + \lambda}} \quad \text{and} \quad \pi\sqrt{\frac{p_M}{q_m + \lambda r_m}} = \pi\sqrt{\frac{6}{e^{-5} + \lambda}}.$$

CHAPTER 12: Stability of Autonomous Systems

EXERCISES 12.2: Linear Systems in the Plane, page 753

3. The characteristic equation for this system is $r^2 + 2r + 10 = 0$, which has roots $r = -1 \pm 3i$. Since the real part of each root is negative, the trajectories approach the origin, and the origin is an asymptotically stable spiral point.

7. The critical point is the solution to the system

$$\begin{aligned} -4x + 2y + 8 &= 0, \\ x - 2y + 1 &= 0. \end{aligned}$$

Solving this system, we obtain the critical point $(3, 2)$. Now we use the change of variables

$$x = u + 3, \qquad y = v + 2,$$

to translate the critical point $(3, 2)$ to the origin $(0, 0)$. Substituting into the system of this problem and simplifying, we obtain a system of differential equations in u and v:

$$\begin{aligned} \frac{du}{dt} &= \frac{dx}{dt} = -4(u+3) + 2(v+2) + 8 = -4u + 2v, \\ \frac{dv}{dt} &= \frac{dy}{dt} = (u+3) - 2(v+2) + 1 = u - 2v. \end{aligned}$$

The characteristic equation for this system is $r^2 + 6r + 6 = 0$, which has roots $r = -3 \pm \sqrt{3}$. Since both roots are distinct and negative, the origin is an asymptotically stable improper node of the new system. Therefore, the critical point $(3, 2)$ is an asymptotically stable improper node of the original system.

9. The critical point is the solution to the system

$$\begin{aligned} 2x + y + 9 &= 0, \\ -5x - 2y - 22 &= 0. \end{aligned}$$

Solving this system, we obtain the critical point $(-4, -1)$. Now we use the change of variables

$$x = u - 4, \qquad y = v - 1,$$

to translate the critical point $(-4, -1)$ to the origin $(0, 0)$. Substituting into the system of this problem and simplifying, we obtain a system of differential equations in u and v:

$$\frac{du}{dt} = \frac{dx}{dt} = 2(u-4) + (v-1) + 9 = 2u + v,$$
$$\frac{dv}{dt} = \frac{dy}{dt} = -5(u-4) - 2(v-1) - 22 = -5u - 2v.$$

The characteristic equation for this system is $r^2 + 1 = 0$, which has roots $r = \pm i$. Since both roots are distinct and pure imaginary, the origin is a stable center of the new system. Therefore, the critical point $(-4, -1)$ is a stable center of the original system.

15. The characteristic equation for this system is $r^2 + r - 12 = 0$, which has roots $r = -4$ and $r = 3$. Since the roots are real and have opposite signs, the origin is an unstable saddle point. To sketch the phase plane diagram, we must first determine two lines passing through the origin that correspond to the transformed axes. To find the transformed axes, we make the substitution $y = mx$ into

$$\frac{dy}{dx} = \frac{dy/dt}{dx/dt} = \frac{5x - 2y}{x + 2y}$$

to obtain

$$m = \frac{5x - 2mx}{x + 2mx}.$$

Solving for m yields

$$m(x + 2mx) = 5x - 2mx \quad \Rightarrow \quad 2m^2 + 3m - 5 = 0 \quad \Rightarrow \quad m = -\frac{5}{2} \quad \text{or} \quad m = 1.$$

So $m = -5/2$ or $m = 1$. Hence, the two axes are $y = -5x/2$ and $y = x$. On the line $y = x$ one finds

$$\frac{dx}{dt} = 3x,$$

so the trajectories move away from the origin. On the line $y = -5x/2$ one finds

$$\frac{dy}{dt} = -4y,$$

so the trajectories move towards the origin. A phase plane diagram is given in Figure B.56 in the answers of the text.

19. The characteristic equation for this system is $(r+2)(r+2)=0$ which has roots $r=-2,-2$. Since the roots are equal, real, and negative, the origin is an asymptotically stable point. To sketch the phase plane diagram, we determine the slope of the two lines passing through the origin that correspond to the transformed axes by substituting $y=mx$ into

$$\frac{dy}{dx}=\frac{dy/dt}{dx/dt}=\frac{-2y}{-2x+y}$$

to obtain

$$m=\frac{-2mx}{-2x+mx}.$$

Solving for m yields

$$m(-2x+mx)=-2mx \qquad \Rightarrow \qquad m^2=0 \qquad \Rightarrow \qquad m=0.$$

Since there is only one line ($y=0$) through the origin that is a trajectory, the origin is an improper node. A phase plane diagram is given in Figure B.58 in the answers of the text.

EXERCISES 12.3: Almost Linear Systems, page 764

5. This system is almost linear since $ad-bc=(1)(-1)-(5)(-1)\neq 0$, and the functions $F(x,y)=G(x,y)=-y^2=0$ involve only high order terms in y. Since the characteristic equation for this system is $r^2+4=0$ which has pure imaginary roots $r=\pm 2i$, the origin is either a center or a spiral point and the stability is indeterminant.

7. To see that this system is almost linear, we first express e^{x+y}, $\cos x$, and $\cos y$ using their respective Maclaurin series. Hence, the system

$$\frac{dx}{dt}=e^{x+y}-\cos x\,,$$
$$\frac{dy}{dt}=\cos y+x-1\,,$$

becomes

$$\frac{dx}{dt} = \left[1 + (x+y) + \frac{(x+y)^2}{2!} + \cdots\right] - \left[1 - \frac{x^2}{2!} + \cdots\right]$$
$$= x + y + (\text{higher orders}) = x + y + F(x,y),$$
$$\frac{dy}{dt} = \left[1 - \frac{y^2}{2!} + \cdots\right] + x - 1 = x + (\text{higher orders}) = x + G(x,y).$$

This system is almost linear since $ad - bc = (1)(0) - (1)(1) \neq 0$, and $F(x,y)$, $G(x,y)$ each only involve higher order forms in x and y. The characteristic equation for this system is $r^2 - r - 1 = 0$ which has roots $r = (1 \pm \sqrt{5})/2$. Since these roots are real and have different signs the origin is an unstable saddle point.

9. The critical points for this system are the solutions to the pair of equations

$$16 - xy = 0,$$
$$x - y^3 = 0.$$

Solving the second equation for x in terms of y and substituting this into the first equation we obtain

$$16 - y^4 = 0$$

which has solutions $y = \pm 2$. Hence the critical points are $(8,2)$ and $(-8,-2)$.

We consider the critical point $(8,2)$. Using the change of variables $x = u + 8$ and $y = v + 2$, we obtain the system

$$\frac{du}{dt} = 16 - (u+8)(v+2),$$
$$\frac{dv}{dt} = (u+8) - (v+2)^3,$$

which simplifies to the almost linear system

$$\frac{du}{dt} = -2u - 8v - uv,$$
$$\frac{dv}{dt} = u - 12v - 6v^2 - v^3.$$

The characteristic equation for this system is $r^2 + 14r + 32 = 0$, which has the distinct negative roots $r = -7 \pm \sqrt{17}$. Hence $(8,2)$ is an improper node which is asymptotically stable.

Next we consider the critical point $(-8,-2)$. Using the change of variables $x = u - 8$ and $y = v - 2$, we obtain the system

$$\frac{du}{dt} = 16 - (u-8)(v-2),$$
$$\frac{dv}{dt} = (u-8) - (v-2)^3,$$

which simplifies to the almost linear system

$$\frac{du}{dt} = 2u + 8v - uv,$$
$$\frac{dv}{dt} = u - 12v + 6v^2 - v^3.$$

The characteristic equation for this system is $r^2 + 10r - 32 = 0$, which has the distinct roots $r = -5 \pm \sqrt{57}$. Since these roots are real and have different signs, $(-8,-2)$ is an unstable saddle point.

13. The critical points for this system are the solutions to the pair of equations

$$1 - xy = 0,$$
$$x - y^3 = 0.$$

Solving the second equation for x in terms of y and substituting this into the first equation we obtain

$$1 - y^4 = 0$$

which has solutions $y = \pm 1$. Hence the critical points are $(1,1)$ and $(-1,-1)$.

We consider the critical point $(1,1)$. Using the change of variables $x = u + 1$ and $y = v + 1$, we obtain the almost linear system

$$\frac{du}{dt} = 1 - (u+1)(v+1) = -u - v - uv,$$
$$\frac{dv}{dt} = (u+1) - (v+1)^3 = u - 3v - 3v^2 - v^3.$$

The characteristic equation for this system is $r^2+4r+4 = 0$, which has the equal negative roots $r = -2$. Hence $(1,1)$ is an improper or proper node or spiral point which is asymptotically stable.

Next we consider the critical point $(-1,-1)$. Using the change of variables $x = u - 1$ and $y = v - 1$, we obtain the almost linear system

$$\frac{du}{dt} = 1 - (u-1)(v-1) = u + v - uv,$$
$$\frac{dv}{dt} = (u-1) - (v-1)^3 = u - 3v + 3v^2 - v^3.$$

The characteristic equation for this system is $r^2 + 2r - 4 = 0$, which has roots $r = -1 \pm \sqrt{5}$. Since these roots are real and have different signs, $(-1,-1)$ is an unstable saddle point. A phase plane diagram is given in Figure B.59 in the answers of the text.

21. Case 1: $h = 0$. The critical points for this system are the solutions to the pair of equations

$$x(1 - 4x - y) = 0,$$
$$y(1 - 2y - 5x) = 0.$$

To solve this system, we first let $x = 0$, then $y(1-2y) = 0$. So $y = 0$ or $y = 1/2$.

When $y = 0$, we must have $x(1-4x) = 0$. So $x = 0$ or $x = 1/4$.

And if $x \neq 0$ and $y \neq 0$, we have the system

$$1 - 4x - y = 0,$$
$$1 - 2y - 5x = 0,$$

which has the solution $x = 1/3$, $y = -1/3$. Hence the critical points are $(0,0)$, $(0,1/2)$, $(1/4,0)$, and $(1/3,-1/3)$.

At the critical point $(0,0)$, the characteristic equation is $r^2 - 2r + 1 = 0$, which has equal positive roots $r = 1$. Hence $(0,0)$ is an improper or proper node or spiral point which is unstable. From Figure B.61 in the text, we see that $(0,0)$ is an improper node.

Next we consider the critical point $(0,1/2)$. Using the change of variables $y = v + 1/2$ and $x = u$, we obtain the almost linear system

$$\frac{du}{dt} = u\left(1 - 4u - v - \frac{1}{2}\right) = \frac{1}{2}u - 4u^2 - uv,$$
$$\frac{dv}{dt} = \left(v + \frac{1}{2}\right)(1 - 2v - 1 - 5u) = -\frac{5}{2}u - v - 2v^2 - 5uv.$$

The characteristic equation for this system is $r^2 + (1/2)r - (1/2) = 0$, which has roots $r = 1/2$ and $r = -1$. Since these roots are real and have different signs, $(0, 1/2)$ is an unstable saddle point.

Now consider the critical point $(1/4, 0)$. Using the change of variables $x = u + 1/4$ and $y = v$, we obtain the almost linear system

$$\frac{du}{dt} = \left(u + \frac{1}{4}\right)(1 - 4u - 1 - v) = -u - \frac{1}{4}v - 4u^2 - uv,$$
$$\frac{dv}{dt} = v\left(1 - 2v - 5u - \frac{5}{2}\right) = -\frac{1}{4}v - 2v^2 - 5uv.$$

The characteristic equation for this system is $r^2 + (5/4)r + (1/4) = 0$, which has roots $r = -1/4$ and $r = -1$. Since these roots are distinct and negative, $(1/4, 0)$ is an improper node which is asymptotically stable.

At the critical point $(1/3, -1/3)$, we use the change of variables $x = u + 1/3$ and $y = v - 1/3$ to obtain the almost linear system

$$\frac{du}{dt} = \left(u + \frac{1}{3}\right)\left(1 - 4u - \frac{4}{3} - v + \frac{1}{3}\right) = -\frac{4}{3}u - \frac{1}{3}v - 4u^2 - uv,$$
$$\frac{dv}{dt} = \left(v - \frac{1}{3}\right)\left(1 - 2v + \frac{2}{3} - 5u - \frac{5}{3}\right) = \frac{5}{3}u + \frac{2}{3}v - 2v^2 - 5uv.$$

The characteristic equation for this system is $r^2 + (2/3)r - (1/3) = 0$ which has roots $r = 1/3$ and $r = -1$. Again since these roots are real and have different signs, $(1/3, -1/3)$ is an unstable saddle point, but not of interest since $y < 0$. Species x survives while species y dies off. A phase plane diagram is given in Figure B.61 in the answers of the text.

Case 2: $h = 1/32$. The critical points for this system are the solutions to the pair of equations

$$x(1 - 4x - y) - \frac{1}{32} = 0,$$
$$y(1 - 2y - 5x) = 0.$$

To solve this system, we first set $y = 0$ and solve $x(1 - 4x) - 1/32 = 0$, which has solutions $x = (2 \pm \sqrt{2})/16$.

If $y \neq 0$, we have $1 - 2y - 5x = 0$. So $y = (1/2) - (5/2)x$. Substituting, we obtain

$$x\left[1 - 4x - \left(\frac{1}{2} - \frac{5}{2}x\right)\right] - \frac{1}{32} = 0.$$

Simplifying, we obtain

$$-\frac{3}{2}x^2 + \frac{1}{2}x - \frac{1}{32} = 0,$$

which has the solution $x = 1/4$ or $x = 1/12$. When $x = 1/4$, we have

$$y = \frac{1}{2} - \frac{5}{2}\left(\frac{1}{4}\right) = -\frac{1}{8}.$$

And when $x = 1/12$, we have

$$y = \frac{1}{2} - \frac{5}{2}\left(\frac{1}{12}\right) = \frac{7}{24}.$$

Hence the critical points are

$$\left(\frac{2-\sqrt{2}}{16}, 0\right), \quad \left(\frac{2+\sqrt{2}}{16}, 0\right), \quad \left(\frac{1}{4}, -\frac{1}{8}\right), \quad \text{and} \quad \left(\frac{1}{12}, \frac{7}{24}\right).$$

At the critical point $\left(\frac{2-\sqrt{2}}{16}, 0\right)$, we use the change of variables $x = u + \frac{2-\sqrt{2}}{16}$ and $y = v$ to obtain the almost linear system

$$\frac{du}{dt} = \left(u + \frac{2-\sqrt{2}}{16}\right)\left(1 - 4u - \frac{2-\sqrt{2}}{4} - v\right) - \frac{1}{32} = \frac{\sqrt{2}}{2}u - \frac{2-\sqrt{2}}{16}v - 4u^2 - uv,$$

$$\frac{dv}{dt} = v\left(1 - 2v - 5u - \frac{10-5\sqrt{2}}{16}\right) = \frac{6+5\sqrt{2}}{16}v - 2v^2 - 5uv.$$

The characteristic equation for this system is

$$\left(r - \frac{\sqrt{2}}{2}\right)\left(r - \frac{6+5\sqrt{2}}{16}\right) = 0,$$

which has distinct positive roots. Hence $\left(\frac{2-\sqrt{2}}{16}, 0\right)$ is an unstable improper node.

Now consider the critical point $\left(\dfrac{2+\sqrt{2}}{16},0\right)$, where we use the change of variables $y=v$ and $x=u+\dfrac{2+\sqrt{2}}{16}$ to obtain the almost linear system

$$\frac{du}{dt}=\left(u+\frac{2+\sqrt{2}}{16}\right)\left(1-4u-\frac{2+\sqrt{2}}{4}-v\right)-\frac{1}{32}=-\frac{\sqrt{2}}{2}u-\frac{2+\sqrt{2}}{16}v-4u^2-uv,$$
$$\frac{dv}{dt}=v\left(1-2v-5u-\frac{10+5\sqrt{2}}{16}\right)=\frac{6-5\sqrt{2}}{16}v-2v^2-5uv.$$

The characteristic equation for this system is

$$\left(r+\frac{\sqrt{2}}{2}\right)\left(r-\frac{6-5\sqrt{2}}{16}\right)=0,$$

which has distinct negative roots. Hence $\left(\dfrac{2+\sqrt{2}}{16},0\right)$ is an asymptotically stable improper node.

When the critical point is $(1/12,7/24)$, the change of variables $x=u+1/12$ and $y=v+7/24$ leads to the almost linear system

$$\frac{du}{dt}=\left(u+\frac{1}{12}\right)\left(1-4u-\frac{1}{3}-v-\frac{7}{24}\right)-\frac{1}{32}=\frac{1}{24}u-\frac{1}{12}v-4u^2-uv,$$
$$\frac{dv}{dt}=\left(v+\frac{7}{24}\right)\left(1-2v-\frac{7}{12}-5u-\frac{5}{12}\right)=-\frac{35}{24}u-\frac{7}{12}v-2v^2-5uv.$$

The characteristic equation for this system is $r^2+(13/24)r-(7/48)=0$, which has roots $r=(-13\pm\sqrt{505})/48$. Since these roots have opposite signs, $(1/12,7/24)$ is an unstable saddle point.

And when the critical point is $(1/4,-1/8)$, the change of variables $x=u+1/4$ and $y=v-1/8$ leads to the almost linear system

$$\frac{du}{dt}=\left(u+\frac{1}{4}\right)\left(1-4u-1-v+\frac{1}{8}\right)-\frac{1}{32}=-\frac{7}{8}u-\frac{1}{4}v-4u^2-uv,$$
$$\frac{dv}{dt}=\left(v-\frac{1}{8}\right)\left(1-2v+\frac{1}{4}-5u-\frac{5}{4}\right)=\frac{5}{8}u+\frac{1}{4}v-2v^2-5uv.$$

The characteristic equation for this system is $r^2 + (5/8)r - (1/16) = 0$, which has roots $r = (-5 \pm \sqrt{41})/16$. Since these roots have opposite signs, $(1/4, -1/8)$ is an unstable saddle point. But since $y < 0$, this point is not of interest.

Hence, this is competitive exclusion; one species survives while the other dies off. A phase plane diagram is given in Figure B.62 in the answers of the text.

Case 3: $h = 5/32$. The critical points for this system are the solutions to the pair of equations

$$x(1 - 4x - y) - \frac{5}{32} = 0,$$
$$y(1 - 2y - 5x) = 0.$$

To solve this system, we first set $y = 0$ and solve

$$x(1 - 4x) - \frac{5}{32} = 0,$$

which has complex solutions. If $y \neq 0$, then we must have

$$1 - 2y - 5x = 0 \qquad \Rightarrow \qquad y = \frac{1}{2} - \frac{5}{2}x.$$

Substituting we obtain

$$x\left[1 - 4x - \left(\frac{1}{2} - \frac{5}{2}x\right)\right] - \frac{5}{32} = 0.$$

Simplifying, we obtain

$$-\frac{3}{2}x^2 + \frac{1}{2}x - \frac{5}{32} = 0,$$

which also has only complex solutions. Hence there are no critical points. The phase plane diagram shows that species y survives while the x dies off. A phase plane diagram is given in Figure B.63 in the answers of the text.

EXERCISES 12.4: Energy Methods, page 774

3. Here $g(x) = x^2/(x - 1) = x + 1 + 1/(x - 1)$. By integrating $g(x)$, we obtain the potential function

$$G(x) = \frac{x^2}{2} + x + \ln|x - 1| + C,$$

and so

$$E(x, v) = \frac{v^2}{2} + \frac{x^2}{2} + x + \ln|x-1| + C.$$

Since $E(0,0) = 0$ implies $C = 0$, let

$$E(x, v) = \frac{v^2}{2} + \frac{x^2}{2} + x + \ln|x-1|.$$

Now, since we are interested in E near the origin, we let $|x-1| = 1-x$ (because for x near 0, $x - 1 < 0$). Therefore,

$$E(x, v) = \frac{v^2}{2} + \frac{x^2}{2} + x + \ln(1-x).$$

9. Here we have $g(x) = 2x^2 + x - 1$ and hence the potential function

$$G(x) = \frac{2x^3}{3} + \frac{x^2}{2} - x.$$

The local maxima and minima of $G(x)$ occur when $G'(x) = g(x) = 2x^2 + x - 1 = 0$. Thus the phase plane diagram has critical points at $(-1, 0)$ and $(1/2, 0)$. Since $G(x)$ has a strict local minimum at $x = 1/2$, the critical point $(1/2, 0)$ is a center. Furthermore, since $x = -1$ is strict local maximum, the critical point $(-1, 0)$ is a saddle point. A sketch of the potential plane and phase plane diagram is given in Figure B.65 in the answers of the text.

11. Here we have $g(x) = x/(x-2) = 1 + 2/(x-2)$ so the potential function is

$$G(x) = x + 2\ln|x-2| = x + 2\ln(2-x),$$

for x near zero. Local maxima and minima of $G(x)$ occur when $G'(x) = g(x) = x/(x-2) = 0$. Thus the phase plane diagram has critical points at $(0, 0)$. Furthermore we note that $x = 2$ is not in the domain of $g(x)$ nor of $G(x)$. Now $G(x)$ has a strict local maximum at $x = 0$, hence the critical point $(0, 0)$ is a saddle point. A sketch of the potential plane and phase plane diagram for $x < 2$ is given in Figure B.66 in the answers of the text.

13. We first observe that $vh(x, v) = v^2 > 0$ for $v \neq 0$. Hence, the energy is continually decreasing along a trajectory. The level curves for the energy function

$$E(x, v) = \frac{v^2}{2} + \frac{x^2}{2} - \frac{x^4}{4}$$

are just the integral curves for Example 2(a) and are sketch in Figure 12.22 on page 770 of the text. The critical points for this damped system are the same as in the example and moreover, they are of the same type. The resulting phase plane is given in Figure B.67 in the answers of the text.

EXERCISES 12.5: Lyapunov's Direct Method, page 782

3. We compute $\dot{V}(x,y)$ with $V(x,y)=x^2+y^2$.

$$\begin{aligned}\dot{V}(x,y) &= V_x(x,y)f(x,y)+V_y(x,y)g(x,y)\\ &= 2x\left(y^2+xy^2-x^3\right)+2y\left(-xy+x^2y-y^3\right)\\ &= 4x^2y^2-2x^4-2y^4=-2\left(x^2-y^2\right)^2.\end{aligned}$$

According to Theorem 3, since $\dot{V}$ is negative semidefinite, V is positive definite function, and $(0,0)$ is an isolated critical point of the system, the origin is stable.

5. The origin is an isolated critical point for the system. Using the hint, we compute $\dot{V}(x,y)$ with $V(x,y)=x^2-y^2$. Computing, we obtain

$$\begin{aligned}\dot{V}(x,y) &= V_x(x,y)f(x,y)+V_y(x,y)g(x,y)\\ &= 2x\left(2x^3\right)-2y\left(2x^2y-y^3\right)=4x^4-4x^2y^2+2y^2=2x^4+\left(x^2-y^2\right)^2,\end{aligned}$$

which is positive definite. Now $V(0,0)=0$, and in every disk centered at the origin, V is positive at some point (namely, those points where $|x|>|y|$). Therefore, by Theorem 4, the origin is unstable.

7. We compute $\dot{V}(x,y)$ with $V(x,y)=ax^4+by^2$.

$$\begin{aligned}\dot{V}(x,y) &= V_x(x,y)f(x,y)+V_y(x,y)g(x,y)\\ &= 4ax^3\left(2y-x^3\right)+2by\left(-x^3-y^5\right)\\ &= 8ax^3y-4ax^6-2bx^3y-2by^6.\end{aligned}$$

To eliminate the x^3y term, we let $a = 1$ and $b = 4$, then

$$\dot{V}(x, y) = -4x^6 - 8y^6,$$

and we get that $\dot{V}$ is negative definite. Since V is positive definite and the origin is an isolated critical point, according to Theorem 3, the origin is asymptotically stable.

11. Here we set

$$y = \frac{dx}{dt} \qquad \Rightarrow \qquad \frac{dy}{dt} = \frac{d^2x}{dt^2}.$$

Then, we obtain the system

$$\begin{aligned} \frac{dx}{dt} &= y, \\ \frac{dy}{dt} &= -\left(1 - y^2\right) y - x. \end{aligned}$$

Clearly, the zero solution is a solution to this system. To apply Lyapunov's direct method, we try the positive definite function $V(x, y) = ax^2 + by^2$ and compute $\dot{V}$.

$$\begin{aligned} \dot{V}(x, y) &= V_x(x, y)f(x, y) + V_y(x, y)g(x, y) \\ &= 2ax\,(y) + 2by\left[-\left(1 - y^2\right) y - x\right] = 2axy - 2by^2 + 2by^4 - 2bxy. \end{aligned}$$

To eliminate the xy terms, we choose $a = b = 1$, then

$$\dot{V}(x, y) = -2y^2\left(1 - y^2\right).$$

Hence $\dot{V}$ is negative semidefinite for $|y| < 1$, so by Theorem 3, the origin is stable.

EXERCISES 12.6: Limit Cycles and Periodic Solutions, page 791

5. We compute $r\dfrac{dr}{dt}$:

$$\begin{aligned} r\frac{dr}{dt} &= x\frac{dx}{dt} + y\frac{dy}{dt} = x\left[x - y + x\left(r^3 - 4r^2 + 5r - 3\right)\right] + y\left[x + y + y\left(r^3 - 4r^2 + 5r - 3\right)\right] \\ &= x^2 - xy + x^2\left(r^3 - 4r^2 + 5r - 3\right) + xy + y^2 + y^2\left(r^3 - 4r^2 + 5r - 3\right) \\ &= r^2 + r^2\left(r^3 - 4r^2 + 5r - 3\right) = r^2\left(r^3 - 4r^2 + 5r - 2\right). \end{aligned}$$

Hence

$$\frac{dr}{dt} = r\left(r^3 - 4r^2 + 5r - 2\right) = r(r-1)^2(r-2).$$

Now $dr/dt = 0$ when $r = 0, 1, 2$. The critical point is represented by $r = 0$, and when $r = 1$ or 2, we have limit cycles of radius 1 and 2. When r lies in $(0, 1)$, we have $dr/dt < 0$, so a trajectory in this region spirals into the origin. Therefore, the origin is an asymptotically stable spiral point. Now, when r lies in $(1, 2)$, we again have $dr/dt < 0$, so a trajectory in this region spirals into the limit cycle $r = 1$. This tells us that $r = 1$ is a semistable limit cycle. Finally, when $r > 2$, $dr/dt > 0$, so a trajectory in this region spirals away from the limit cycle $r = 2$. Hence, $r = 2$ is an unstable limit cycle.

To find the direction of the trajectories, we compute $r^2\dfrac{d\theta}{dt}$.

$$\begin{aligned} r^2\frac{d\theta}{dt} &= x\frac{dy}{dt} - y\frac{dx}{dt} = x\left[x + y + y\left(r^3 - 4r^2 + 5r - 3\right)\right] - y\left[x - y + x\left(r^3 - 4r^2 + 5r - 3\right)\right] \\ &= x^2 + xy + xy\left(r^3 - 4r^2 + 5r - 3\right) - xy + y^2 - xy\left(r^3 - 4r^2 + 5r - 3\right) \\ &= x^2 + y^2 = r^2 . \end{aligned}$$

Hence $d\theta/dt = 1$, which tells us that the trajectories revolve counterclockwise about the origin. A phase plane diagram is given in Figure B.74 in the answers of the text.

11. We compute $r\,dr/dt$:

$$\begin{aligned} r\frac{dr}{dt} &= x\frac{dx}{dt} + y\frac{dy}{dt} = x\left[y + x\sin\left(\frac{1}{r}\right)\right] + y\left[-x + y\sin\left(\frac{1}{r}\right)\right] \\ &= xy + x^2\sin\left(\frac{1}{r}\right) - xy + y^2\sin\left(\frac{1}{r}\right) = r^2\sin\left(\frac{1}{r}\right). \end{aligned}$$

Hence,

$$\frac{dr}{dt} = r\sin\left(\frac{1}{r}\right),$$

and $dr/dt = 0$ when $r = 1/(n\pi)$, $n = 1, 2, \ldots$. Consequently, the origin $(r = 0)$ is not an isolated critical point. Observe that

$$\frac{dr}{dt} > 0 \qquad \text{for} \qquad \frac{1}{(2n+1)\pi} < r < \frac{1}{2n\pi},$$

$$\frac{dr}{dt} < 0 \qquad \text{for} \qquad \frac{1}{2n\pi} < r < \frac{1}{(2n-1)\pi} \, .$$

Thus, trajectories spiral into the limit cycles $r = 1/(2n\pi)$ and away from the limit cycles $r = 1/[(2n+1)\pi]$. To determine the direction of the spiral, we compute $r^2\, d\theta/dt$.

$$\begin{aligned} r^2\frac{d\theta}{dt} &= x\frac{dy}{dt} - y\frac{dx}{dt} = x\left[-x + y\sin\left(\frac{1}{r}\right)\right] - y\left[y + x\sin\left(\frac{1}{r}\right)\right] \\ &= -x^2 + xy\sin\left(\frac{1}{r}\right) - y^2 - xy\sin\left(\frac{1}{r}\right) = -r^2 \, . \end{aligned}$$

Hence $d\theta/dt = -1$, which tells us that the trajectories revolve clockwise about the origin. A phase plane diagram is given in Figure B.77 in the answers of the text.

15. We compute $f_x + g_y$ in order to apply Theorem 6. Thus

$$f_x(x,y) + g_y(x,y) = \left(-8 + 3x^2\right) + \left(-7 + 3y^2\right) = 3\left(x^2 + y^2 - 5\right),$$

which is less than 0 for the given domain. Hence, by Theorem 6, there are no nonconstant periodic solutions in the disk $x^2 + y^2 < 5$.

19. It is easily seen that $(0,0)$ is a critical point, however, it is not easily shown that it is the only critical point for this system. Using the Lyapunov function $V(x,y) = 2x^2 + y^2$, we compute $\dot{V}(x,y)$. Thus

$$\begin{aligned} \dot{V}(x,y) &= V_x(x,y)\frac{dx}{dt} + V_y(x,y)\frac{dy}{dt} \\ &= 4x\left(2x - y - 2x^3 - 3xy^2\right) + 2y\left(2x + 4y - 4y^3 - 2x^2y\right) \\ &= 8x^2 - 8x^4 - 16x^2y^2 + 8y^2 - 8y^4 = 8\left(x^2 + y^2\right) - 8\left(x^2 + y^2\right)^2 . \end{aligned}$$

Therefore, $\dot{V}(x,y) < 0$ for $x^2 + y^2 > 1$ and $\dot{V}(x,y) > 0$ for $x^2 + y^2 < 1$. Let C_1 be the curve $2x^2 + y^2 = 1/2$, which lies inside $x^2 + y^2 = 1$, and let C_2 be the curve $2x^2 + y^2 = 3$, which lies outside $x^2 + y^2 = 1$. Now $\dot{V}(x,y) > 0$ on C_1 and $\dot{V}(x,y) < 0$ on C_2. Hence, we let R be the region between the curves C_1 and C_2. Now, any trajectory that enters R is contained in R. So by Theorem 7, the system has a nonconstant periodic solution in R.

25. To apply Theorem 8, we check to see that all five conditions hold. Here we have $g(x) = x$ and $f(x) = x^2(x^2 - 1)$. Clearly, $f(x)$ is even, hence condition **(a)** holds. Now

$$F(x) = \int_0^x s^2 \left(s^2 - 1\right) ds = \frac{x^5}{5} - \frac{x^3}{3}.$$

Hence $F(x) < 0$ for $0 < x < \sqrt{5/3}$ and $F(x) > 0$ for $x > \sqrt{5/3}$. Therefore, condition **(b)** holds. Furthermore, condition **(c)** holds since $F(x) \to +\infty$ as $x \to +\infty$, monotonically for $x > \sqrt{5/3}$. As stated above, $g(x) = x$ is an odd function with $g(x) > 0$ for $x > 0$, thus condition **(d)** holds. Finally, since

$$G(x) = \int_0^x s\, ds = \frac{x^2}{2},$$

we clearly have $G(x) \to +\infty$ as $x \to +\infty$, hence condition **(e)** holds. It follows from Theorem 8, that the Lienard equation has a unique nonconstant periodic solution.

EXERCISES 12.7: Stability of Higher-Dimensional Systems, page 798

5. From the characteristic equation

$$-(r - 1)\left(r^2 + 1\right) = 0,$$

we find that the eigenvalues are $1, \pm i$. Since at least one eigenvalue, 1, has a positive real part, the zero solution is unstable.

9. The characteristic equation is

$$\left(r^2 + 1\right)\left(r^2 + 1\right) = 0,$$

which has eigenvalues $\pm i, \pm i$. Next we determine the eigenspace for the eigenvalue i. Computing we find

$$\left|\begin{array}{cccc} i & -1 & -1 & 0 \\ 1 & i & 0 & -1 \\ 0 & 0 & i & -1 \\ 0 & 0 & 1 & i \end{array}\right| \quad \Rightarrow \quad \left|\begin{array}{cccc} 1 & i & 0 & 0 \\ 0 & 0 & 1 & 0 \\ 0 & 0 & 0 & 1 \\ 0 & 0 & 0 & 0 \end{array}\right|.$$

Hence the eigenspace is degenerate and by Problem 8(c) on page 798 of the text, the zero solution is unstable. Note: it can be shown that the eigenspace for the eigenvalue $-i$ is also degenerate.

13. To find the fundamental matrix for this system we first recall the Taylor series e^x, $\sin x$, and $\cos x$. These are

$$\begin{aligned} e^x &= 1 + x + \frac{x^2}{2!} + \frac{x^3}{3!} + \cdots, \\ \sin x &= x - \frac{x^3}{3!} + \frac{x^5}{5!} - \cdots, \\ \cos x &= 1 - \frac{x^2}{2!} + \frac{x^4}{4!} - \cdots. \end{aligned}$$

Hence

$$\begin{aligned} \frac{dx_1}{dt} &= \left(1 - x_1 + \frac{x_1^2}{2!} - \cdots\right) + \left(1 - \frac{x_2^2}{2!} + \cdots\right) - 2 = -x_1 + \left(\frac{x_1^2}{2!} - \cdots\right) + \left(-\frac{x_2^2}{2!} + \cdots\right), \\ \frac{dx_2}{dt} &= -x_2 + \left(x_3 - \frac{x_3^3}{3!} + \cdots\right) = -x_2 - x_3 + \left(-\frac{x_3^3}{3!} + \cdots\right), \\ \frac{dx_3}{dt} &= 1 - \left[1 + (x_2 + x_3) + \frac{(x_2 + x_3)^2}{2!} + \cdots\right] = -x_2 - x_3 - \left[\frac{(x_2 + x_3)^2}{2!} + \cdots\right]. \end{aligned}$$

Thus,

$$\mathbf{A} = \begin{bmatrix} -1 & 0 & 0 \\ 0 & -1 & 1 \\ 0 & -1 & -1 \end{bmatrix}.$$

Calculating the eigenvalues, we have

$$|\mathbf{A} - r\mathbf{I}| = \begin{vmatrix} -1 - r & 0 & 0 \\ 0 & -1 - r & 1 \\ 0 & -1 & -1 - r \end{vmatrix} = 0.$$

Hence, the characteristic equation is $-(r+1)(r^2+2r+2) = 0$. Therefore, the eigenvalues are -1, $-1 \pm i$. Since the real part of each is negative, the zero solution is asymptotically stable.

15. Solving for the critical points, we must have

$$\begin{aligned} -x_1 + 1 &= 0, \\ -2x_1 - x_2 + 2x_3 - 4 &= 0, \\ -3x_1 - 2x_2 - x_3 + 1 &= 0. \end{aligned}$$

Solving this system, we find that the only solution is $(1, -2, 2)$. We now use the change of variables

$$x_1 = u + 1, \qquad x_2 = v - 2, \qquad x_3 = w + 2$$

to translate the critical point to the origin. Substituting, we obtain the system

$$\begin{aligned} \frac{du}{dt} &= -u, \\ \frac{dv}{dt} &= -2u - v + 2w, \\ \frac{dw}{dt} &= -3u - 2v - w. \end{aligned}$$

Here $\mathbf{A}$ is given by

$$\mathbf{A} = \begin{bmatrix} -1 & 0 & 0 \\ -2 & -1 & 2 \\ -3 & -2 & -1 \end{bmatrix}.$$

Finding the characteristic equation, we have $-(r+1)(r^2+2r+5) = 0$. Hence the eigenvalues are -1, $-1 \pm 2i$. Since each eigenvalue has a negative real part, the critical point $(1, -2, 2)$ is asymptotically stable.

CHAPTER 13: Existence and Uniqueness Theory

EXERCISES 13.1: Introduction: Successive Approximations, page 812

1. In this problem, $x_0 = 1$, $y_0 = y(x_0) = 4$, and $f(x, y) = x^2 - y$. Thus, applying formula (3) on page 807 of the text yields

$$y(x) = y_0 + \int_{x_0}^{x} f(t, y(t))\, dt = 4 + \int_{1}^{x} \left[t^2 - y(t)\right] dt = 4 + \int_{1}^{x} t^2\, dt - \int_{1}^{x} y(t)\, dt\,.$$

Since

$$\int_{1}^{x} t^2\, dt = \left.\frac{t^3}{3}\right|_1^x = \frac{x^3}{3} - \frac{1}{3},$$

the equation becomes

$$y(x) = 4 + \frac{x^3}{3} - \frac{1}{3} - \int_{1}^{x} y(t)\, dt = \frac{11}{3} + \frac{x^3}{3} - \int_{1}^{x} y(t)\, dt\,.$$

3. In the initial conditions, $x_0 = 1$ and $y_0 = -3$. Also, $f(x, y) = (y - x)^2 = y^2 - 2xy + x^2$. Therefore,

$$y(x) = y_0 + \int_{x_0}^{x} f(t, y(t))\, dt = -3 + \int_{1}^{x} \left(y^2(t) - 2ty(t) + t^2\right) dt.$$

Using the linear property of integrals, we find that

$$\begin{aligned}\int_{1}^{x} \left(y^2(t) - 2ty(t) + t^2\right) dt &= \int_{1}^{x} y^2(t)\, dt - 2\int_{1}^{x} ty(t)\, dt + \int_{1}^{x} t^2\, dt \\ &= \int_{1}^{x} \left[y^2(t) - 2ty(t)\right] dt + \frac{x^3}{3} - \frac{1}{3},\end{aligned}$$

we have

$$y(x)=\frac{x^3}{3}-\frac{10}{3}+\int_1^x y^2(t)\,dt-2\int_1^x ty(t)\,dt. \tag{13.1}$$

Note that we can rewrite the last integral using integration by parts in terms of integrals of the function $y(x)$ alone. Namely,

$$\int_1^x ty(t)\,dt = t\int_1^t y(s)\,ds\bigg|_{t=1}^{t=x} - \int_1^x\int_1^t y(s)\,ds\,dt = x\int_1^x y(s)\,ds - \int_1^x\int_1^t y(s)\,ds\,dt$$

Thus, another form of the answer (13.1) is

$$y(x)=\frac{x^3}{3}-\frac{10}{3}+\int_1^x y^2(t)\,dt + x\int_1^x y(t)\,dt - \int_1^x\int_1^t y(s)\,ds\,dt\,.$$

5. In this problem, we have

$$g(x)=\frac{1}{2}\left(x+\frac{3}{x}\right).$$

Thus the recurrence formula (7) on page 807 of the text becomes

$$x_{n+1}=g\left(x_n\right)=\frac{1}{2}\left(x_n+\frac{3}{x_n}\right), \qquad n=0,1,\ldots\,.$$

With $x_0=3$ as an initial approximation, we compute

$$x_1=\frac{1}{2}\left(x_0+\frac{3}{x_0}\right)=\frac{1}{2}\left(3+\frac{3}{3}\right)=2.0\,, \qquad x_2=\frac{1}{2}\left(x_1+\frac{3}{x_1}\right)=\frac{1}{2}\left(2+\frac{3}{2}\right)=1.75\,,$$

and so on. The results of these computations is given in Table 13-A.

Table 13–A: Approximations for a solution of $x=\frac{1}{2}\left(x+\frac{3}{x}\right)$.

$x_0=3.0$	$x_3=1.732142857$
$x_1=2.0$	$x_4=1.732050810$
$x_2=1.75$	$x_5=1.732050808$

We stopped iterating after x_5 because $x_4-x_5<10^{-8}$. Hence $x\approx 1.73205081$.

7. Since $g(x) = 1/\left(x^2+4\right)$, we have the recurrence formula

$$x_{n+1} = g\left(x_n\right) = \frac{1}{x_n^2+4}, \qquad n = 0, 1, \ldots$$

with an initial approximation $x_0 = 0.5$. Hence

$$x_1 = \frac{1}{x_0^2+4} = \frac{1}{(0.5)^2+4} = \frac{4}{17} \approx 0.2352941176,$$

$$x_2 = \frac{1}{x_1^2+4} \approx \frac{1}{(0.2352941176)^2+4} \approx 0.2465870307\,, \quad \text{etc.}$$

See Table 13-B. We stopped iterating after x_7 because the error $x_6 - x_7 < 10^{-9}$. Hence $x \approx 0.24626617$.

Table 13–B: Approximations for a solution of $x = \dfrac{1}{x^2+4}$.

$x_0 = 0.5$	$x_4 = 0.2462664586$
$x_1 = 0.2352941176$	$x_5 = 0.2462661636$
$x_2 = 0.2465870307$	$x_6 = 0.2462661724$
$x_3 = 0.2462565820$	$x_7 = 0.2462661721$

9. To start the method of successive substitutions, we observe that

$$g(x) = \left(\frac{5-x}{3}\right)^{1/4}.$$

Therefore, according to equation (7) on page 807 of the text, we can find the next approximation from the previous one by using the recurrence relation

$$x_{n+1} = g\left(x_n\right) = \left(\frac{5-x_n}{3}\right)^{1/4}.$$

We start the procedure at the point $x_0 = 1$. Thus, we obtain

$$x_1 = \left(\frac{5-x_0}{3}\right)^{1/4} = \left(\frac{5-1}{3}\right)^{1/4} = \left(\frac{4}{3}\right)^{1/4} \approx 1.074569932\,,$$

$$x_2 = \left(\frac{5 - x_1}{3}\right)^{1/4} \approx \left(\frac{5 - 1.074569932}{3}\right)^{1/4} \approx 1.069526372\,,$$
$$x_3 = \left(\frac{5 - x_2}{3}\right)^{1/4} \approx \left(\frac{5 - 1.069526372}{3}\right)^{1/4} \approx 1.069869749\,.$$

By continuing this process, we fill in Table 13-C below. Noticing that $x_7 - x_6 < 10^{-8}$, we stopped the procedure after seven steps. So, $x \approx 1.06984787$.

Table 13–C: Approximations for a solution of $x = \left(\dfrac{5 - x}{3}\right)^{1/4}$.

$x_0 = 1.0$	$x_4 = 1.069846382$
$x_1 = 1.074569932$	$x_5 = 1.069847972$
$x_2 = 1.069526372$	$x_6 = 1.069847864$
$x_3 = 1.069869749$	$x_7 = 1.069847871$

---

11. First, we derive an integral equation corresponding to the given initial value problem. We have $f(x, y) = -y$, $x_0 = 0$, $y_0 = y(0) = 2$, and so the formula (3) on page 807 of the text yields

$$y(x) = 2 + \int_0^x [-y(t)]\,dt = 2 - \int_0^x y(t)\,dt\,.$$

Thus, Picard's recurrence formula (15) becomes

$$y_{n+1}(x) = 2 - \int_0^x y_n(t)\,dt, \qquad n = 0, 1, \ldots\,.$$

Starting with $y_0(x) \equiv y_0 = 2$, we compute

$$y_1(x) = 2 - \int_0^x y_0(t)\,dt = 2 - \int_0^x 2\,dt = 2 - 2t\,\Big|_{t=0}^{t=x} = 2 - 2x\,,$$
$$y_2(x) = 2 - \int_0^x y_1(t)\,dt = 2 - \int_0^x (2 - 2t)\,dt = 2 + (t-1)^2\,\Big|_{t=0}^{t=x} = 2 - 2x + x^2\,.$$

13. In this problem, $f(x, y) = 3x^2$, $x_0 = 1$, $y_0 = y(1) = 2$, and so Picard's iterations to the solution of the given initial value problem are given by

$$y_{n+1}(x) = 2 + \int_1^x \left(3t^2\right) dt = 2 + t^3 \Big|_{t=1}^{t=x} = x^3 + 1\,.$$

Since the right-hand side does not depend on n, the sequence of iterations $y_k(x)$, $k = 1, 2, \ldots$, is a constant sequence. That is,

$$y_k(x) = x^3 + 1 \qquad \text{for any} \quad k \geq 1.$$

In particular, $y_1(x) = y_2(x) = x^3 + 1$.

(In this connection, note the following. If it happens that one of the iterations, say, $y_k(x)$, obtained via (15) matches the exact solution to the integral equation (3), then all the subsequent iterations will give the same function $y_k(x)$. In other words, the sequence of iterations will become a constant sequence starting from its kth term. In the given problem, the first application of (15) gives the *exact* solution, $x^3 + 1$, to the original initial value problem and, hence, to the corresponding integral equation (3).)

15. We first write this differential equation as an integral equation. Integrating both sides from $x_0 = 0$ to x and using the fact that $y(0) = 0$, we obtain

$$y(x) - y(0) = \int_0^x \left[y(t) - e^t\right] dt \qquad \Rightarrow \qquad y(x) = \int_0^x \left[y(t) - e^t\right] dt\,.$$

Hence, by equation (15) on page 811 of the text, the Picard iterations are given by

$$y_{n+1}(x) = \int_0^x \left[y_n(t) - e^t\right] dt\,.$$

Thus, starting with $y_0(x) \equiv y_0 = 0$, we calculate

$$y_1(x) = \int_0^x \left[y_0(t) - e^t\right] dt = -\int_0^x e^t dt = 1 - e^x\,,$$

$$y_2(x) = \int_0^x \left[y_1(t) - e^t\right] dt = \int_0^x \left(1 - 2e^t\right) dt = 1 - e^x = 2 + x - 2e^x \,.$$

17. First of all, remark that the function $f(x, y(x))$ in the integral equation (3), that is,

$$y(x) = y_0 + \int_{x_0}^x f(t, y(t))\, dt \,,$$

is a continuous function as the composition of $f(x, y)$ and $y(x)$, which are both continuous by our assumption. Next, if $y(x)$ satisfies (3), then

$$y\left(x_0\right) = y_0 + \int_{x_0}^{x_0} f(t, y(t))\, dt = y_0 \,,$$

because the integral term is zero as a definite integral of a continuous function with equal limits of integration. Therefore, $y(x)$ satisfies the initial condition in (1).

We recall that, by the fundamental theorem of calculus, if $g(x)$ is a continuous function on an interval $[a, b]$, then, for any fixed c in $[a, b]$, the function $G(x) := \int_a^x g(t)\, dt$ is an antiderivative for $g(x)$ on (a, b), i.e.,

$$G'(x) = \left(\int_a^x g(t)\, dt\right)' = g(x).$$

Thus,

$$y'(x) = \left(y_0 + \int_{x_0}^x f(t, y(t))\, dt\right)' = f(t, y(t)) \,\Big|_{t=x} = f(x, y(x)),$$

and so $y(x)$ satisfies the differential equation in (1).

19. The graphs of the functions $y = (x^2 + 1)/2$ and $y = x$ are sketched on the same coordinate axes in Figure 13-A.

By examining this figure, we see that these two graphs intersect only at $(1, 1)$. We can find this point by solving the equation

$$x = \frac{x^2 + 1}{2} \,,$$

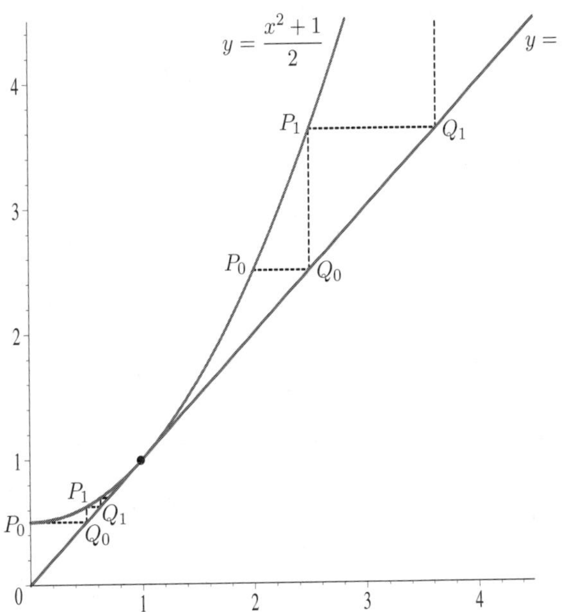

Figure 13–A: The method of successive substitution for the equation $x = \dfrac{x^2+1}{2}$.

for x. Thus, we have

$$2x = x^2 + 1 \quad \Rightarrow \quad x^2 - 2x + 1 = 0 \quad \Rightarrow \quad (x-1)^2 = 0 \quad \Rightarrow \quad x = 1.$$

Since $y = x$, the only intersection point is $(1, 1)$.

To approximate the solution to the equation $x = (x^2 + 1)/2$ using the method of successive substitutions, we use the recurrence relation

$$x_{n+1} = \frac{x_n^2 + 1}{2}.$$

Starting this method at $x_0 = 0$, we obtain the approximations given in Table 13-D. These approximations do appear to be approaching the solution $x = 1$.

However, if we start the process at the point $x = 2$, we obtain the approximations given in Table 13-E.

We observe that these approximations are getting larger and so do not seem to approach a fixed point. This also appears to be the case if we examine the pictorial representation for the

Table 13–D: Approximations for a solution of $x = \dfrac{x^2+1}{2}$ starting at $x_0 = 0$.

$x_1 = 0.5$	$x_{15} = 0.89859837$
$x_2 = 0.625$	$x_{20} = 0.91988745$
$x_3 = 0.6953125$	$x_{30} = 0.94337158$
$x_4 = 0.7417297$	$x_{40} = 0.95611749$
$x_5 = 0.7750815$	$x_{50} = 0.96414507$
$x_{10} = 0.8610982$	$x_{99} = 0.98102848$

Table 13–E: Approximations for a solution of $x = \dfrac{x^2+1}{2}$ starting at $x_0 = 2$.

$x_1 = 2.5$	$x_4 = 25.4946594$
$x_2 = 3.625$	$x_5 = 325.488829$
$x_3 = 7.0703125$	$x_6 = 52971.9891$

method of successive substitutions given in Figure 13-A. By plugging $x_0 = 0$ into the function $(x^2+1)/2$, we find P_0 to be the point $(0, 0.5)$. Then by moving parallel to the x-axis from the point P_0 to the line $y = x$, we observe that Q_0 is the point $(0.5, 0.5)$. Next, by moving parallel to the y-axis from the point Q_0 to the curve $y = (x^2+1)/2$, we find that P_1 is the point $(0.5, 0.625)$. Continuing this process moves us slowly in a step fashion to the point $(1, 1)$. However, if we start this process at $x_0 = 2$, we observe that this method moves us through larger and larger steps away from the point of intersection $(1, 1)$.

Note that for this equation, the movement of the method of successive substitutions is to the right. This is because the term $(x_n^2+1)/2$, in the recurrence relation, is increasing for $x > 0$. Thus, *the sequence of approximations* $\{x_n\}$ *is an increasing sequence.* Starting at a nonnegative point less than 1 moves us to the fixed point at $x = 1$, but starting at a point larger that 1 moves us to ever increasing values for our approximations and, therefore, away from the fixed point.

EXERCISES 13.2: Picard's Existence and Uniqueness Theorem, page 820

1. In order to determine whether this sequence of functions converges uniformly, we find $\|y_n - y\|$. Since

$$y_n(x) - y(x) = \left(1 - \frac{x}{n}\right) - 1 = -\frac{x}{n},$$

we have

$$\|y_n - y\| = \max_{x\in[-1,1]} |y_n(x) - y(x)| = \max_{x\in[-1,1]} \frac{|x|}{n} = \frac{1}{n}.$$

Thus

$$\lim_{n\to\infty} \|y_n - y\| = \lim_{n\to\infty} \frac{1}{n} = 0$$

and $\{y_n(x)\}$ converges to $y(x)$ uniformly on $[-1, 1]$.

3. In order to determine whether this sequence of functions converges uniformly, we must find

$$\lim_{n\to\infty} \|y_n - y\|.$$

Therefore, we first compute

$$\|y_n - y\| = \|y_n\| = \max_{x\in[0,1]} \left|\frac{nx}{1+n^2x^2}\right| = \max_{x\in[0,1]} \frac{nx}{1+n^2x^2},$$

where we have removed the absolute value signs because the term $(nx)/(1+n^2x^2)$ is nonnegative when $x \in [0, 1]$. We will use calculus methods to obtain this maximum value. Thus, we differentiate the function $y_n(x) = (nx)/(1+n^2x^2)$ to obtain

$$y_n'(x) = \frac{n(1-n^2x^2)}{(1+n^2x^2)^2}.$$

Setting $y_n'(x)$ equal to zero and solving yields

$$n\left(1-n^2x^2\right) = 0 \qquad \Rightarrow \qquad n^2x^2 = 1 \qquad \Rightarrow \qquad x = \pm\frac{1}{n}.$$

Since we are interested in the values of x on the interval $[0, 1]$, we will only examine the critical point $x = 1/n$. By the first derivative test, we observe that the function $y_n(x)$ has a local maximum value at the point $x = 1/n$. At this point, we have

$$y_n\left(\frac{1}{n}\right) = \frac{n\left(n^{-1}\right)}{1+n^2\left(n^{-1}\right)^2} = \frac{1}{2}.$$

Computing

$$y_n(0) = \frac{n(0)}{1+n^2(0)^2} = 0,$$
$$y_n(1) = \frac{n(1)}{1+n^2(1)^2} = \frac{n}{1+n^2} < \frac{1}{n} \le \frac{1}{2} \quad \text{for } n \ge 2,$$

we conclude that

$$\max_{x\in[0,1]} y_n(x) = \frac{1}{2}.$$

Therefore,

$$\lim_{n\to\infty} \|y_n - y\| = \lim_{n\to\infty} \frac{1}{2} = \frac{1}{2} \neq 0.$$

Thus, the given sequence of functions does *not* converge uniformly to the function $y(x) \equiv 0$ on the interval $[0, 1]$.

This sequence of functions does, however, converge pointwise to the function $y(x) \equiv 0$ on the interval $[0, 1]$. To see this, notice that for any fixed $x \in (0, 1]$ we have

$$\lim_{n\to\infty} [y_n(x) - y(x)] = \lim_{n\to\infty} \frac{nx}{1+n^2x^2} = \lim_{n\to\infty} \frac{1}{2nx} = 0,$$

where we have found this limit by using L'Hospital's rule. At the point $x = 0$, we observe that

$$\lim_{n\to\infty} [y_n(0) - y(0)] = \lim_{n\to\infty} \frac{0}{1} = 0.$$

Thus, we have pointwise convergence but *not* uniform convergence. See Figure 13-B(a) for the graphs of functions $y_1(x)$, $y_{10}(x)$, $y_{30}(x)$, and $y_{90}(x)$.

5. We know (as was stated on page 433 of the text) that for all x such that $|x| < 1$ the geometric series, $\sum_{k=0}^{\infty} x^k$, converges to the function $f(x) = 1/(1-x)$. Thus, for all $x \in [0, 1/2]$, we have

$$\frac{1}{1-x} == 1 + x + x^2 + \cdots + x^k + \cdots = \sum_{k=0}^{\infty} x^k.$$

Therefore, we see that

$$\|y_n - y\| = \max_{x\in[0,1/2]} |y_n(x) - y(x)| = \max_{x\in[0,1/2]} \left| \sum_{k=0}^{n} x^k - \sum_{k=0}^{\infty} x^k \right| = \max_{x\in[0,1/2]} \sum_{k=n+1}^{\infty} x^k = \sum_{k=n+1}^{\infty} \left(\frac{1}{2}\right)^k$$

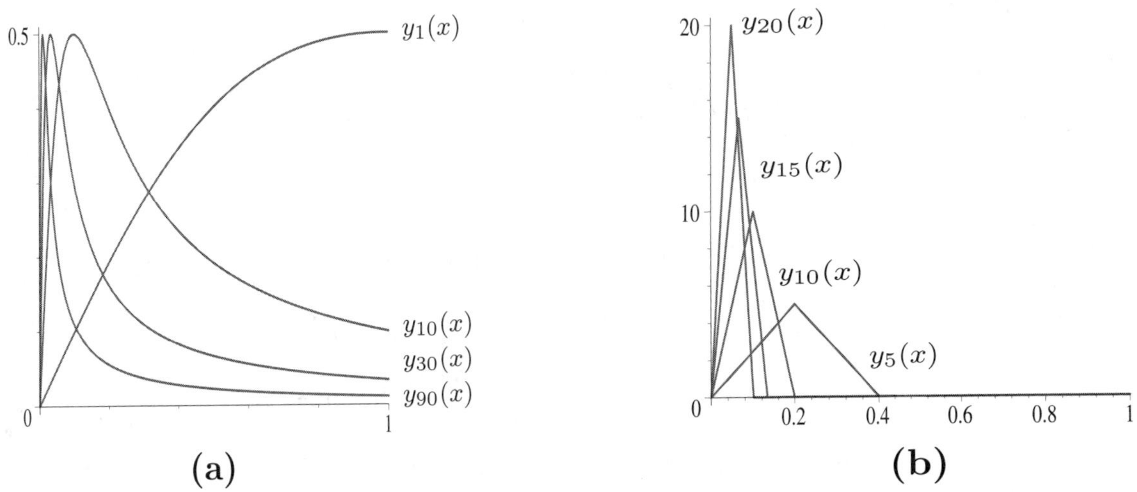

Figure 13–B: Graphs of functions in Problems 3 and 7.

and so

$$\lim_{n\to\infty}\|y_n - y\| = \lim_{n\to\infty}\left[\sum_{k=n+1}^{\infty}\left(\frac{1}{2}\right)^k\right].$$

Since $\sum_{k=n+1}^{\infty}(1/2)^k$ is the tail end of a convergent series, its limit must be zero. Hence, we have

$$\lim_{n\to\infty}\|y_n - y\| = \lim_{n\to\infty}\left[\sum_{k=n+1}^{\infty}\left(\frac{1}{2}\right)^k\right] = 0.$$

Therefore, the given sequence of functions converges uniformly to the function $y(x) = 1/(1-x)$ on the interval $[0, 1/2]$.

7. Let $x \in [0, 1]$ be fixed.

If $x = 0$, then $y_n(0) = n^2(0) = 0$ for any n and so $\lim_{n\to\infty} y_n(0) = \lim_{n\to\infty} 0 = 0$.

For $x > 0$, let $N_x := [2/x] + 1$ with $[\cdot]$ denoting the interger part of a number. Then, for $n \geq N_x$, one has

$$n \geq \left[\frac{2}{x}\right] + 1 > \frac{2}{x} \qquad \Rightarrow \qquad x > \frac{2}{n}$$

and so, in evaluating $y_n(x)$, the third line in its definition must be used. This yields $y_n(x) = 0$ for all $n \geq N_x$, which implies that $\lim_{n\to\infty} y_n(x) = \lim_{n\to\infty} 0 = 0$.

Hence, for any fixed $x \in [0,1]$, $\lim_{n\to\infty} y_n(x) = 0 = y(x)$.

On the other hand, for any n, the function $y_n(x)$ is a continuous piecewise linear function, which is increasing on $[0, 1/n]$, decreasing on $(1/n, 2/n)$, and zero on $[1/n, 1]$. Thus it attains its maximum value at $x = 1/n$, which is

$$y_n\left(\frac{1}{n}\right) = n^2\left(\frac{1}{n}\right) = n.$$

Therefore,

$$\lim_{n\to\infty} \|y_n - y\| = \lim_{n\to\infty} \|y_n\| = \lim_{n\to\infty} n = \infty,$$

and the sequence does not converge uniformly on $[0,1]$. See Figure 13-B(b) for the graphs of $y_5(x)$, $y_{10}(x)$, $y_{15}(x)$, and $y_{20}(x)$.

9. We need to find an $h > 0$ such that $h < \min(h_1, \alpha_1/M, 1/L)$. We are given that

$$R_1 = \{(x,y) : |x-1| \le 1,\ |y| \le 1\} = \{(x,y) : 0 \le x \le 2, -1 \le y \le 1\},$$

and so $h_1 = 1$ and $\alpha_1 = 1$. Thus, we must find values for M and L.

In order to find M, notice that, as was stated on page 816 of the text, we require that M satisfy the condition

$$|f(x,y)| = |y^2 - x| \le M,$$

for all (x, y) in R_1. To find this upper bound for $|f(x,y)|$, we must find the maximum and the minimum values of $f(x,y)$ on R_1. (Since $f(x,y)$ is a continuous function on the closed and bounded region R_1, it will have a maximum and a minimum there.) We will use calculus methods to find this maximum and this minimum. Since the first partial derivatives of $f(x,y)$, given by

$$f_x(x,y) = -1, \qquad \text{and} \qquad f_y(x,y) = 2y,$$

are never both zero, the maximum and minimum must occur on the boundary of R_1. Notice that R_1 is bounded on the left by the line $x = 0$, on the right by the line $x = 2$, on the top by the line $y = 1$, and on the bottom by the line $y = -1$. Therefore, we will examine the behavior of $f(x,y)$ (and, thus, of $|f(x,y)|$) on each of these lines.

Case 1: On the left side of R_1 where $x = 0$, the function $f(x, y)$ becomes the function in the single variable y, given by

$$f(0, y) = F_1(y) = y^2 - 0 = y^2, \qquad y \in [-1, 1].$$

This function has a maximum at $y = \pm 1$ and a minimum at $y = 0$. Thus, on the left side of R_1 we see that f reaches a maximum value of $f(0, \pm 1) = 1$ and a minimum value of $f(0, 0) = 0$.

Case 2: On the right side of R_1 where $x = 2$, the function $f(x, y)$ becomes the function in the single variable y, given by

$$f(2, y) = F_2(y) = y^2 - 2, \qquad y \in [-1, 1].$$

This function also has a maximum at $y = \pm 1$ and a minimum at $y = 0$. Thus, on the right side of R_1, the function $f(x, y)$ reaches a maximum value of $f(2, \pm 1) = -1$ and a minimum value of $f(2, 0) = -2$.

Case 3: On the top and bottom of R_1 where $y = \pm 1$, the function $f(x, y)$ becomes the function given by

$$f(x, \pm 1) = F_3(x) = (\pm 1)^2 - x = 1 - x, \qquad x \in [0, 2].$$

This function also has a maximum at $x = 0$ and a minimum at $x = 2$. Thus, on both the top and bottom of the region R_1, the function $f(x, y)$ reaches a maximum value of $f(0, \pm 1) = 1$ and a minimum value of $f(2, \pm 1) = -1$.

From the above cases we see that the maximum value of $f(x, y)$ is 1 and the minimum value is -2 on the boundary of R_1. Thus, we have $|f(x, y)| \leq 2$ for all (x, y) in R_1. Hence, we choose $M = 2$.

To find L, we observe that L is an upper bound for

$$\left| \frac{\partial f}{\partial y} \right| = |2y| = 2|y|,$$

on R_1. Since $y \in [-1, 1]$ in this region, we have $|y| \leq 1$. Hence, we see that

$$\left| \frac{\partial f}{\partial y} \right| = 2|y| \leq 2,$$

for all (x, y) in R_1. Therefore, we choose $L = 2$.

Now we can choose $h \geq 0$ such that

$$h < \min\left(h_1, \frac{\alpha_1}{M}, \frac{1}{L}\right) = \min\left(1, \frac{1}{2}\frac{1}{2}\right) = \frac{1}{2}.$$

Thus, Theorem 3 guarantees that the given initial value problem will have a unique solution on the interval $[1-h, 1+h]$, where $0 < h < 1/2$.

11. We are given that the recurrence relation for these approximations is $y_{n+1} = T[y_n]$. Using the definition of $T[y]$, we have

$$y_{n+1} = x^3 - x + 1 \int_0^x (u-x) y_n(u)\, du.$$

Thus, starting these approximations with $y_0(x) = x^3 - x + 1$, we obtain

$$\begin{aligned} y_1(x) &= x^3 - x + 1 + \int_0^x (u-x) y_0(u)\, du = x^3 - x + 1 + \int_0^x (u-x)\left[u^3 - u + 1\right] du \\ &= x^3 - x + 1 + \int_0^x \left(u^4 - u^2 + u - xu^3 + xu - x\right) du \\ &= x^3 - x + 1 + \left[\frac{x^5}{5} - \frac{x^3}{3} + \frac{x^2}{2} - \frac{x^5}{4} + \frac{x^3}{2} - x^2\right]. \end{aligned}$$

By simplifying, we obtain

$$y_1(x) = -\frac{1}{20}x^5 + \frac{7}{6}x^3 - \frac{1}{2}x^2 - x + 1.$$

Substituting this result into the recurrence relation yields

$$\begin{aligned} y_2(x) &= x^3 - x + 1 \int_0^x (u-x) y_1(u)\, du \\ &= x^3 - x + 1 \int_0^x (u-x)\left[-\frac{1}{20}u^5 + \frac{7}{6}u^3 - \frac{1}{2}u^2 - u + 1\right] du \end{aligned}$$

$$= x^3 - x + 1 + \left[-\frac{1}{140}x^7 + \frac{7}{30}x^5 - \frac{1}{8}x^4 - \frac{1}{3}x^3 + \frac{1}{2}x^2 + \frac{1}{120}x^7 - \frac{7}{24}x^5 + \frac{1}{6}x^4 + \frac{1}{2}x^3 - x^2 \right].$$

When simplified, this yields

$$y_2(x) = \frac{1}{840}x^7 - \frac{7}{120}x^5 + \frac{1}{24}x^4 + \frac{7}{6}x^3 - \frac{1}{2}x^2 - x + 1.$$

13. Using properties of limits and the linear property of integrals, we can rewrite the statement that

$$\lim_{n\to\infty} \int_a^b y_n(x)\,dx = \int_a^b y(x)\,dx$$

in an equivalent form

$$\lim_{n\to\infty} \left[\int_a^b y_n(x) - \int_a^b y(x)\,dx \right] = 0 \qquad \Leftrightarrow \qquad \lim_{n\to\infty} \int_a^b [y_n(x) - y(x)]\,dx = 0. \tag{13.2}$$

The sequence $\{y_n\}$ converges uniformly to y on $[a, b]$, which means, by the definitionof uniform convergence, that

$$\|y_n - y\|_{C[a,b]} := \max_{x\in[a,b]} |y_n(x) - y(x)| \to 0 \quad \text{as} \quad n \to \infty.$$

Since

$$\left| \int_a^b [y_n(x) - y(x)]\,dx \right| \le \int_a^b |y_n(x) - y(x)|\,dx \le (b-a)\,\|y_n - y\|_{C[a,b]} \to 0$$

as $n \to \infty$, we conclude that

$$\lim_{n\to\infty} \left| \int_a^b [y_n(x) - y(x)]\,dx \right| = 0,$$

and (13.2) follows. (Recall that $\lim_{n\to\infty} a_n = 0$ if and only if $\lim_{n\to\infty} |a_n| = 0$.)

15. **(a)** In the given system,

$$\begin{aligned} x'(t) &= -y^2(t), & x(0) &= 0; \\ y'(t) &= z(t), & y(0) &= 1; \\ z'(t) &= x(t)y(t), & z(0) &= 0, \end{aligned} \tag{13.3}$$

replacing t by s, integrating the differential equations from $s = 0$ to $s = t$, and using the fundamental theorem of calculus we obtain

$$\begin{aligned} \int_0^t x'(s)\,ds &= -\int_0^t y^2(s)\,ds; & & & x(t) - x(0) &= -\int_0^t y^2(s)\,ds; \\ \int_0^t y'(s)\,ds &= \int_0^t z(s)\,ds; & &\Rightarrow & y(t) - y(0) &= \int_0^t z(s)\,ds; \\ \int_0^t z'(s)\,ds &= \int_0^t x(s)y(s)\,ds & & & z(t) - z(0) &= \int_0^t x(s)y(s)\,ds. \end{aligned}$$

By the initial conditions in (13.3), $x(0) = 0$, $y(0) = z(0) = 1$. Substituting these values into the above system yields

$$\begin{aligned} x(t) &= -\int_0^t y^2(s)\,ds; \\ y(t) - 1 &= \int_0^t z(s)\,ds; \\ z(t) - 1 &= \int_0^t x(s)y(s)\,ds, \end{aligned} \tag{13.4}$$

which is equivalent to the given system of integral equations. Thus, (13.3) implies (13.4). Conversely, differentiating equations in (13.4) and using the fundamental theorem of calculus (its part regarding integrals with variable upper bound), we conclude that solutions $x(t)$, $y(t)$, and $z(t)$ to (13.4) also satisfy differential equations in (13.3). Clearly,

$$\begin{aligned} x(0) &= -\int_0^0 y^2(s)\,ds = 0; \\ y(0) - 1 &= \int_0^0 z(s)\,ds = 0; \\ z(t) - 1 &= \int_0^0 x(s)y(s)\,ds = 0, \end{aligned}$$

and the initial conditions in (13.3) are satisfied. Therefore, (13.4) implies (13.3).

(b) With starting iterations $x_0(t) \equiv x(0) = 0$, $y_0(t) \equiv y(0) = 1$, and $z_0(t) \equiv z(0) = 1$, we compute $x_1(t)$, $y_1(t)$, and $z_1(t)$.

$$x_1(t) = -\int_0^t y_0^2(s)\,ds = -\int_0^t (1)^2\,ds = -t;$$
$$y_1(t) = 1 + \int_0^t z_0(s)\,ds = 1 + \int_0^t (1)\,ds = 1 + t;$$
$$z_1(t) = 1 + \int_0^t x_0(s)y_0(s)\,ds = 1 + \int_0^t (0)\,ds = 1.$$

Applying given recurrence formulas again yields

$$x_2(t) = -\int_0^t y_1^2(s)\,ds = -\int_0^t (1+s)^2\,ds = -(1+s)^3/3\,\Big|_0^t = -t - t^2 - \frac{t^3}{3};$$
$$y_2(t) = 1 + \int_0^t z_1(s)\,ds = 1 + \int_0^t 1\,ds = 1 + t;$$
$$z_2(t) = 1 + \int_0^t x_1(s)y_1(s)\,ds = 1 - \int_0^t s(1+s)\,ds = 1 - (s^2/2 + s^3/3)\,\Big|_0^t = 1 - \frac{t^2}{2} - \frac{t^3}{3}.$$

EXERCISES 13.3: Existence of Solutions of Linear Equations, page 826

1. In this problem,

$$\mathbf{A}(t) = \begin{bmatrix} \cos t & \sqrt{t} \\ t^3 & -1 \end{bmatrix}, \qquad \mathbf{f}(t) = \begin{bmatrix} \tan t \\ e^t \end{bmatrix}.$$

In $\mathbf{A}(t)$, functions $\cos t$, t^3, and -1 are continuous on $(-\infty, \infty)$ while $\sqrt{t}$ is continuous on $[0, \infty)$. Therefore, $\mathbf{A}(t)$ is continuous on $[0, \infty)$. In $\mathbf{f}(t)$, the exponential function is continuous everywhere, but $\tan t$ has infinite discontinuities at $t = (k + 1/2)\pi$, $k = 0, \pm 1, \pm 2, \ldots$. The largest interval containing the initial point, $t = 2$, where $\tan t$ and, therefore, $\mathbf{f}(t)$, is continuous is $(\pi/2, 3\pi/2)$. Since $\mathbf{A}(t)$ is also continuous on $(\pi/2, 3\pi/2)$, by Theorem 6, given initial value problem has a unique solution on this interval.

3. By comparing this problem to the problem given in (14) on page 825 of the text, we see that in this case

$$p_1(t) = -\ln t, \qquad p_2(t) \equiv 0, \qquad p_3(t) = \tan t, \quad \text{and} \quad g(t) = e^{2t}.$$

We also observe that $t_0 = 1$. Thus, we must find an interval containing $t_0 = 1$ on which all of the functions $p_1(t)$, $p_2(t)$, $p_3(t)$, and $g(t)$ are simultaneously continuous. Therefore, we note that $p_2(t)$ and $g(t)$ are continuous everywhere; $p_1(t)$ is continuous on the interval $(0, \infty)$; and the interval which contains $t_0 = 1$ on which $p_3(t)$ is continuous is $(-\pi/2, \pi/2)$. Hence, these four functions are simultaneously continuous on the interval $(0, \pi/2)$ and this interval contains the point $t_0 = 1$. Therefore, Theorem 7 given on page 825 of the text guarantees that we will have a unique solution to this initial value problem on the whole interval $(0, \pi/2)$.

5. In this problem, we use Theorem 5. Since

$$\mathbf{f}(t, \mathbf{x}) = \begin{bmatrix} \sin x_2 \\ 3x_1 \end{bmatrix},$$

we have

$$\frac{\partial \mathbf{f}}{\partial x_1}(t, \mathbf{x}) = \begin{bmatrix} 0 \\ 3 \end{bmatrix}, \qquad \frac{\partial \mathbf{f}}{\partial x_2}(t, \mathbf{x}) = \begin{bmatrix} \cos x_2 \\ 0 \end{bmatrix}.$$

Vectors $\mathbf{f}$, $\partial \mathbf{f}/\partial x_1$, and $\partial \mathbf{f}/\partial x_2$ are continuous on

$$R = \{-\infty < t < \infty, -\infty < x_1 < \infty, -\infty < x_2 < \infty\}$$

(which is the whole space $\mathbb{R}^3$) since their components are. Moreover,

$$\left|\frac{\partial \mathbf{f}}{\partial x_1}(t, \mathbf{x})\right| = 3, \qquad \left|\frac{\partial \mathbf{f}}{\partial x_2}(t, \mathbf{x})\right| = |\cos x_2| \le 1$$

for any $(t, \mathbf{x})$, and the condition (3) in Theorem 5 is satisfied with $L = 3$. Hence, given initial value problem has a unique solution on the whole real axis $-\infty < t < \infty$.

7. The equation

$$y'''(t) - (\sin t)y'(t) + e^{-t}y(t) = 0$$

is a linear homogeneous equation and, hence, has a trivial solution, $y(t) \equiv 0$. Clearly, this solution satisfies the initial conditions, $y(0) = y'(0) = y''(0) = 0$. All that remains to note is that the coefficients, $-\sin t$ and e^{-t}, are continuous on $(-\infty, \infty)$ and so, by Theorem 7, the solution $y \equiv 0$ is unique.

EXERCISES 13.4: Continuous Dependence of Solutions, page 832

3. To apply Theorem 9, we first determine the constant L for $f(x,y)=e^{\cos y}+x^2$. To do this, we observe that

$$\frac{\partial f}{\partial y}(x,y)=-e^{\cos y}\sin y.$$

Now on any rectangle R_0, we have

$$\left|\frac{\partial f}{\partial y}(x,y)\right|=\left|-e^{\cos y}\sin y\right|=\left|e^{\cos y}\right|\,|\sin y|\le e.$$

(More detailed analysis shows that this function attains its maximum at $y^*=(\sqrt{5}-1)/2$, and this maximum equals to $1.4585\ldots$.) Thus, since $h=1$, we have by Theorem 9,

$$|\phi(x,y_0)-\phi(x,\widetilde{y}_0)|\le|y_0-\widetilde{y}_0|\,e^e\,.$$

Since we are given that $|y_0-\widetilde{y}_0|\le 10^{-2}$, we obtain the result

$$|\phi(x,y_0)-\phi(x,\widetilde{y}_0)|\le 10^{-2}e^e\approx 0.151543\,.$$

9. We can use inequality (18) in Theorem 10 to obtain the bound, but first must determine the constant L and the constant ε. Here $f(x,y)=\sin x+(1+y^2)^{-1}$ and $F(x,y)=x+1-y^2$. Now,

$$\left|\frac{\partial f}{\partial y}(x,y)\right|=\left|\frac{2y}{(1+y^2)^2}\right|$$

and

$$\left|\frac{\partial F}{\partial y}(x,y)\right|=|2y|\le 2.$$

To find an upper bound for $|\partial f/\partial y|$ on R_0, we maximize $2y/(1+y^2)^2$. Hence, we obtain

$$\left(\frac{2y}{(1+y^2)^2}\right)'=\frac{2(1+y^2)^2-2y\cdot 2(1+y^2)2y}{(1+y^2)^4}=\frac{2(1+y^2)-8y^2}{(1+y^2)^3}=\frac{2-6y^2}{(1+y^2)^3}\,.$$

Setting this equal to zero and solving for y, we obtain

$$\frac{2-6y^2}{(1+y^2)^3}=0 \quad\Rightarrow\quad 2-6y^2=0 \quad\Rightarrow\quad y=\pm\frac{1}{\sqrt{3}}\,.$$

Since $2y/(1+y^2)^2$ is odd, we need only use $y = 1/\sqrt{3}$. Thus

$$\left|\frac{\partial f}{\partial y}(x,y)\right| \le \frac{2/\sqrt{3}}{(1+1/3)^2} = \frac{3\sqrt{3}}{8},$$

and so $L = 3\sqrt{3}/8$. To obtain ε we seek an upper bound for

$$|f(x,y) - F(x,y)| = \left|\sin x + \frac{1}{1+y^2} - x - 1 + y^2\right| \le |\sin x - x| + \left|\frac{1}{1+y^2} - 1 + y^2\right|.$$

Using Taylor's theorem with remainder we have

$$\sin x = x - \frac{x^3 \cos\xi}{3!},$$

where $0 \le \xi \le x$. Thus for $-1 \le x \le 1$ we obtain

$$|\sin x - x| = \left|x - \frac{x^3\cos\xi}{3!} - x\right| = \frac{|x|^3\cos\xi}{3!} \le \frac{1}{6}.$$

Applying Taylor's theorem with remainder to $1/(1+y^2) - 1 + y^2$, we obtain

$$\begin{aligned}
g(y) &= (1+y^2)^{-1} - 1 + y^2\,,\\
g'(y) &= -2y(1+y^2)^{-2} + 2y\,,\\
g''(y) &= -2(1+y^2)^{-2} + 2(1+y^2)^{-3}(2y)^2 + 2\,,\\
g'''(y) &= 4(1+y^2)^{-3}(2y) - 6(1+y^2)^{-4}(2y)^3 + 2(1+y^2)^{-3}(8y)\,.
\end{aligned}$$

Since $g(0) = g'(0) = g''(0) = 0$, we have

$$(1+y^2)^{-1} - 1 + y^2 = \frac{g'''(\xi)}{3!},$$

where $0 \le \xi \le y$. Thus, we obtain

$$\left|(1+y^2)^{-1} - 1 + y^2\right| = \left|\frac{g'''(\xi)}{3!}\right| \le \frac{8+48+16}{6} = 12.$$

Hence

$$|f(x,y) - F(x,y)| \le \frac{1}{6} + 12 = \frac{73}{6}.$$

It now follows from inequality (18) in Theorem 10 that

$$|\phi(x) - \psi(x)| \le \frac{73}{6}\, e^{3\sqrt{3}/8} \approx 23.294541\,,$$

for x in $[-1, 1]$.